CONTEMPORARY Political Theory

New Dimensions, Basic Concepts and Major Trends

Our other books by the same author

1. Comparative Politics
2. Principles of Modern Political Science
3. International Relations and Politics
   (Diplomatic History between Two World Wars)
4. International Relations and Politics
   (Theoretical Perspective in the Post-Cold War Era)
5. Great Radical Humanist – M. N. Roy
6. The Constitution of India — A Politico – Legal Study

(Hindi Translations)

1. तुलनात्मक राजनीति
2. समकालीन राजनीतिक सिद्धान्त
3. आधुनिक राजनीति विज्ञान के सिद्धान्त
4. अन्तर्राष्ट्रीय सम्बन्ध व राजनीति (उत्तर-शीत युद्ध काल में सैद्धान्तिक परिप्रेक्ष्य)

Edited Books

1. Indian Freedom Movement and Thought (1919-29)
   by *Dr. Lal Bahadur*
2. Indian Freedom Movement and Thought (1929-47)
   by *Dr. R.C. Gupta*
3. Struggle for Pakistan (1906-47)
   by *Dr. Lal Bahadur*
4. Introduction to International Relations
   by *Pierre-Marie Martin*
5. Introduction to the Methods of Social Sciences
   by *Jean Louis Loubet del Bayle*

CONTEMPORARY Political Theory

New Dimensions, Basic Concepts and Major Trends

J.C. Johari
M.A., L.L.B., Ph.D.

STERLING

To
the living and inspiring memory
of my younger brother
Late Prof. P.C. Johari

STERLING PUBLISHERS (P) LTD.
Regd. Office: A1/256 Safdarjung Enclave,
New Delhi-110029. CIN: U22110DL1964PTC211907
Phone: +91 82877 98380
E-mail: mail@sterlingpublishers.in
www.sterlingpublishers.in

Contemporary Political Theory

ISBN 978 81 207 6992 2

First Edition: 1979
Reprint Edition: 1980, 1982, 1983, 1985
Second Revised and Enlarged Edition: 1987
Reprint Edition: 1990, 1994, 1996, 1999, 2004, 2005, 2009, 2010, 2011
Third Revised and Enlarged Edition: 2012
Reprint Edition: 2013, 2015, 2016, 2018, 2019, 2020, 2022, 2023, 2025

Printed and Published by

Sterling Publishers Pvt. Ltd.,
Plot No. 13, Ecotech-III, Greater Noida - 201306, U. P. India

Preface to the Third Edition

Political theory remained in a beleaguered state in the last century owing to the impact of many currents and cross-currents inspired by conflicting interpretations and affirmations of the Marxists and neo-Marxists of the Frankfurt School, the positivists and the logical positivists of the Vienna Circle, and the behaviouralists and the post-behaviouralists of the Chicago School. All these trends pushed classical political theory into the background so much so that a theorist like David Easton talked about its 'decline' and Peter Laslett described it as its 'demise'. The reason behind it was that all such analysts disfavoured the trend of studying political theory in terms of political philosophy and desired to refashion it in scientific terms. However, the revival of political theory in the last phase of the last century falsified all such pessimistic and rash observations. Once again, the affirmations of the normativists like John Rawls, Robert Nozick, F.A. Hayek and others received due appreciation. It was hailed as the resurgence of political theory.

Things improved of course, but the stir created by the conflicting versions of the leading social and political theorists of the twentieth century could not make the matters settled. Replacement of the capitalist society by the industrial society created fertile ground for the emergence of new themes whose study by a number of social and political theorists made the scope of political theory more diffuse and fragmented. The collapse of the socialist systems signified astonishing triumph of liberalism and yet it created the problem as to how the crises created by the new social tensions and movements be solved within the liberal-democratic framework. The post-modernists challenged the message of the Enlightenment; the feminists came forward with their demand for gender equality and justice; the multiculturalists raised their voice for the recognition of their 'identity'; the terrorists posed a serious challenge to the existence of the state that alone can ensure good life to its people. A question mark has been put on the traditional notion of sovereignty and the model of nation-state in the light of new conditions generated by the waves of globalisation. It all makes it essential to study state in different perspectives.

I have taken due note of all such momentous developments and thus sought to accommodate them in this thoroughly revised and enlarged edition. While new chapters have been added to cover the study of post-modernism, feminism, terrorism, multiculturalism and globalisation as well as to study state in different perspectives, all other chapters have been thoroughly retouched and revised with the help of latest material. I hope that it shall meet the requirements of the students offering this course at the higher academic levels or preparing for various competitive examinations. I am thankful to my publisher (Shri S.K.Ghai) who appreciated this venture of mine and managed to place this edition in the hands of the readers in a new and attractive form.

— J.C. Johari

Preface to the Second Edition

Political theory is now certainly at the crossroads. It has fallen prey to a 'bias' that has done great damage to its objective character. The obsession of the liberal theorists, particularly of the United States, to altogether refute the Marxian premises of social and political theory has added to the stock of confusion. Instead of furnishing an alternative model of political theory, it has resulted in creating a mess about the real meaning, nature and scope of this subject. The 'mad craze' for putting it into a scientific form has failed to yield the expected results. The trend of empiricism has become too heavy to be counter-balanced by the refreshing trend of normativism. As compared to their immediate predecessors, the post-behaviouralists are nothing else than the lesser sinners in vitiating the dimensions of this discipline. However, the only achievement of the works on social and political theory in the period following the Second World War should be traced in the emergence of abundant literature suggesting directions in which the new students of this subject may enter for the sake of making some fruitful exercises.

Keeping all this in view, I have added first five chapters to this edition for the benefit of the readers. One chapter on Fascism has been added towards the end so as to remove the charge of an important omission in a study of this kind. In addition to this, all chapters have been suitably revised and enlarged in the light of the contributions of some contemporary social and political theorists like Berlin's restatement of liberty, Tawney's version of equality, Rawls' reinterpretation of justice, Brinton's anatomy of revolution, etc,. In this way, I have been able to do much to the satisfaction of my esteemed friends who have been occasionally writing or speaking to me about necessary improvevments in this book. I hope that this work will win the appreciation of all those to whom it is intended.

—J.C. Johari

Preface to the First Edition

Political theory, generally identifiable with as well as distinguishable from other related themes like political thought, political philosophy, political ideology and the like, is by all means the most encompassing intellectual activity. As sugested by Andrew Hacker, it includes all like philosophy, ideology, science. However, the perplexing thing about it is that right from ancient to modern times, it has been moving back and forth on the subject of, as designated by Herbert Spencer, 'man versus the state' and thereby creating paradoxes, contradictions and controversies to the extent that today, as William C. Baum says, it has become like a storehouse of 'odd humps and bumps'. The situation has been looked at with ample apprehension so much so that while some like Alfred Cobban have expressed their concern over its 'decline' and others like T.L. Thorson have gone to the extent of wailing over its 'demise', some others like Dante Germino have sought to emphasise its 'resurgence' or 'revival'.

The subject of the nature and scope of political theory in the present times has assumed a significance of its own. In view of the pervasiveness of the contemporary crisis, the notion of 'politics' and the understanding of 'political theory' have shown due response to the problems and challenges posed by more subtle intellectual trends seemingly unrelated to the discipline of Political Science as customarily defined. The result is that contemporary political theory looks like hovering between the poles of 'post-liberalism' and 'scientific socialism' that has made its task, in the words of C.B. Macpherson, all the more 'deceptive', or as Fred D. Dalmyr says, it has put it at the 'crossroads'.

Contemporary political theory is both empirical and normative, both liberal and Marxist, both Western and non-Western, irrespective of the fact that the former dimension outweighs the latter. In other words, it is both value-laden and value-free; it is both 'utopian' and 'scientific'. Its area of concern ranges from the 'moral evaluation of political power' as commented by Allen Gewirth to a 'mad craze for scientism' as decried by David Easton.

In this humble work, an attempt has been made to keep all this in view while discussing certain important 'basic concepts' and 'major trends'. The readers may feel and complain that some important topics are missing in this volume. I hope to include such topics in the next edition in the light of critical comments coming from them. I, however, hope that they will find this study worthwhile and thereby make my labours suitably rewarded.

I shall like to record my thanks to Prof. Frank Thakurdas whose inspiring guidance has always been a source of encouragement to me. I am also beholden to my publishers who managed to bring this book out in a record time for the benefit of students offering this paper at the degree and post-graduate levels. I lack words to express my gratitude to my wife (Saroj Rani) who has been helpful to me throughout the pursuit of my advanced studies without ever grudging for the loss of material comforts of life. I shall feel obliged to those who apprise me of their critical comments for my future guidance.

—**J.C. Johari**

Contents

PART III: MAJOR TRENDS

Charts and Tabular Illustrations

Part I

NEW DIMENSIONS

Politics deserves much praise. Politics is a preoccupation of free men, and its existence is a test of freedom. The praise of the man is worth having, for it is the only praise which is free from either servility or condescension... Politics then is civilising. It rescues mankind from the morbid dilemmas in which the state is always seen as a ship threatened by a hostile environment of cruel seas, and enables us instead to see the state as a city settled on the firm and fertile ground of mother earth. It can offer us no guarantee against storms encroaching from the sea, but it can offer us something worth defending in times of emergency and amid threats of disaster.

—Bernard Crick[1]

Political speculation, I believe, is not merely an enterprise in mapping a desert, or of counting the myriad grains of sand, or of observing the changing configuration of the sand dunes but of comprehending the winds and the occasional grounds-well that shape and change it. In other words, it is an endeavour of the human mind to understand this all too human organised world and the texture of values that are embodied in it, at any moment, and the forces that shape and change it in the historical time process.

—Frank Thakurdas[2]

Nobody can complete the study of politics in a book or a series of books.... Therefore, it is not only hazardous but false to make sweeping statements about political science as a whole.

—Heinz Eulau[3]

Academics thrill at the thought of their discipline having been raked by a series of revolutions. It is the great aim of every aspiring academic to be at the forefront of the next revolution.

—Robert E. Goodin[4]

---

1. Crick: *In Defence of Politics* (London : Weidenfeld and Nicolson, 1962), p. 135.
2. Frank Thakurdas : *Essays in Political Theory* (New Delhi : Gitanjali, 1982), p. 106.
3. Eulau : "Drift of a Discipline" in *American Behavioural Scientist* (September/October, 1977), pp. 6-7.
4. Goodin (ed.): *The Oxford Handbook of Political Science* (Oxford: Oxford University press, 2009), p. 12

1

Political Theory

> Man lives in a changing society, and he is socially mobile in that society...He lives in a society where men strive deliberately to change their institutions. If he is not to feel lost in society, he needs to be able to take his bearings in it, which involves more than understanding what society is like and how it is changing. It also involves having a coherent set of values and knowing how to use them to estimate what is happening ; it involves having a practical philosophy, which cannot, in the modern world, be adequate unless it is also a social and political philosophy.
>
> **— John Plamenatz[1]**

The term 'political theory' interchangeable with other terms like 'political thought', 'political philosophy', 'political ideas', 'political analysis', 'political inquiry', 'political ideology', 'theories of the political system' etc., is that branch of political science which "attempts to arrive at generalisations, inferences, or conclusions to be drawn from the data gathered by other specialists, not only in political science, but throughout the whole range of human knowledge and experience."[2] It may rightly be regarded as the most comprehensive branch of this discipline in view of the fact that here we study the momentous theme of man in relation to his fellow beings under some form of control exercised by those in 'authority roles'. Moreover, as the dimensions of such a relationship change from time to time and, moreover, as these have different images in the minds of different students of this subject, political theory comes to have its different forms. It leads to the emergence of its different varieties ranging from purely abstract and hypothetical on the one side to perfectly causal and empirical on the other. Taking such a consideration in his view, Prof. C.W. Coker incisively sums up the meaning of political theory in these words : "When political government and its forms and activities are studied not simply as facts to be described and compared, or judged in reference to their immediate and temporary effects, but as facts to be understood and appraised in relation to the constant needs, desires and opinions of men—then we have political theory."[3]

1. Plamenatz : "The Uses of Political Theory" in *Political Studies,* Vol.8 (1960), p. 27.
2. C.C. Rodee, T.J. Anderson and C.Q. Christol : *Introduction to Political Science* (New York ; McGraW Hill. 1957), p. 11.
3. F.W. Coker : *Recent Political Thought* (New York : Appleton-Century -Crofts, 1934), p. 3. A contemporary writer on this subject like M.A. Weinstein says that political theory "can be viewed as an activity that involves posing questions, developing responses to those questions, and creating imaginative perspectives on the public life of human beings." In his view, there "is no correct definition of the scope of political theory... The great political theorists created their works in response to problems that they discovered in the realms of practical affairs or speculative thought. The best way to become a political theorist, or at least to appreciate the work of political theorists, is to become seriously concerned about a problem in public life." *Systematic Political Theory* (Columbus, Ohio : Charles E Merrill Pub., 1971), p. 1.

Meaning, Nature, Characteristics and Varieties of Political Theory

The English word 'theory' originates from a Greek word 'theoria' which suggests a well-focused mental look taken at something in a state of contemplation with an intent to grasp it. In this sense, it covers an understanding of being (ontology) as well as a causal explanation that may be in the nature of a theological, philosophical, empirical, or logical thought. If so, the term 'theory' may be studied in wider as well as narrower senses. In the former sense, it may be taken as a proposition or a set of propositions designed to explain something with reference to data or inter-relations not directly observed, or not otherwise manifest. Mere description is not theory, nor are the proposals of goals, policies, or evaluations. Only the explanations, if any, offered for descriptions or proposals may be theoretical ; the descriptions or the proposals as such do not make theory. On the other hand, theory does include 'prediction' provided it so follows from an explanation. Then, in the latter sense, it "comprises a thinker's entire teaching on a subject (his *Lehre)*, including his description of the facts, his explanations (whether religious, philosophical, or empirical), his conception of history, his value-judgements, and his proposals of goals, of policy, and of principles."[4]

In simple terms, theory "is always used to designate attempts to 'explain' a phenomenon especially when that is done in general and abstract terms."[5] But it is also usual to admit that it may be 'scientific' or 'non-scientific' according to whether or not scientific rules are followed. It is true that-scientific theorising may be differentiated from non scientific theorising, but theory in either of its forms may not be identified with 'law'. The term 'law' connotes something clear, fixed and binding, while a theory is just an explanation of some phenomenon. It may suggest the existence of a law without being itself identifiable by a law. As Norman Campbell says, it may try to explain a law of course, but if that is the intention, the theory must refer to some more general law. Exactly speaking, a law can never be deduced directly from a theory ; it can be deduced only from a more general law offered in theory.[6] Conversely, a law is not a theory, it is rather a fact, namely with which some other facts are associated either as a rule or in general. In another sense, it may refer to a legal, moral, aesthetic or procedural norm."[7]

It implies that theory covers both 'values' and 'facts' that determine its normative or speculative and causal or empirical character. It is the field where the investigations and findings of a writer or a researcher are tied together, cross-referenced, weighed, contemplated and churned so as to lay down certain conclusions in regard to the proper relationship between man and authority (power). An investigator may be mainly a political scientist, or an economist, or a psychologist, or a sociologist, or a historian, even an anthropologist ; what is essential is that his conclusions must touch the fundamental issue of man in relation to authority under which he has to

4. Arnold Brecht : "Political Theory" in David I. Sills (ed.) : *International Encyclopaedia of the Social Sciences* (New York : Macmillan and Free Press, 1969), p. 307.
5. Arnold Brecht : *Political Theory : The Foundations of the Twentieth-Century Political Thought* (Princeton : Princeton University Press, 1959), p. 14.
6. *Ibid.*, p. 15.
7. *Ibid.*, Also see Campbell : *What is Science*? (New York : Dover Publications, 1952), pp. 89-91.

survive, or his association with a community in which he desires to seek power or, his struggle for, what Hobbes calls, 'some future apparent good'. Here it should be stressed that facts—even if demonstrably incontrovertible – 'do not by themselves', point to any single, inescapable course of action. The function of the political theorist is to consider facts in all their varied ramifications and at least suggest conclusions, remedies and public policies."[8]

A student of this subject should, therefore, be concerned with both the aspects of political theory—value-laden and fact-laden. As such, political theory, for better or worse, has two distinct meanings:[9]

1. It stands for the history of political ideas. Starting with Plato, these ideas are regarded as contributions to an intellectual tradition. They are studied with due regard for the historical circumstances which produced them, and their influence on political practice is a matter of constant speculation. This understanding of political theory is the more traditional of the two and an honourable tradition of scholarship supports it.
2. The other conception of the theory is newer and, in consequence, less sure of its methods and purposes. Nevertheless, it can be said that this approach calls for the systematic study of political behaviour in the modern world.

Obviously, the field of political theory includes both the traditional and modern spheres in spite of the fact that the two may be distinguished from each other on certain valid grounds. Thus Hacker continues : "Whereas the older conception has as its subject matter the historical texts and the conditions which surrounded their writing, the more recent approach to theory sees as its subject the actual behaviour of men and institutions in our own time. Systematic theory is, then, concerned to create generalisations which describe and explain contemporary political phenomena. By and large, it places great importance on the method of collecting data, for systematic knowledge must be founded on evidence rather than intuition. On the whole, this approach to theory tries to avoid making value-judgements or enter into ethical controversies."[10]

From what we have said above about the meaning, nature, characteristics and varieties of political theory, two impressions must be formed before we go ahead with the study of this theme in other relevant directions. First, political theory, in the main, "stands for an abstract 'model' of the political order" which a professional student of this subject "is examining, a guide to the systematic collection and analysis of political data."[11] Second, it, as it is today, has become like "a blend of philosophy, scientific theory and description with far more space and emphasis given to non-scientific philosophical aspects than to strictly scientific ones."[12] Keeping all these points in view, the term 'political theory' has been defined, rather explained,

---

8. Rodee and others, *op. cit.*, p. 11.
9. Andrew Hacker : *Political Theory – Philosophy, Ideology, Science* (New York: Macmillan, 1969), p. vii.
10. *ibid.*
11. W.T. Bluhm : *Theories of the Political System : Classics of Political Thought and Modern Political Analysis* (New Delhi : Prentice-Hall of India, 1981), p. 3.
12. Brecht "Political Theory" in *International Encyclopaedia, op. cit.*, p. 310.

in these words: 'Political theory is trying to weld together the insights, data and understandings of those who study the actuality of political life into a coherent explanatory theory or the theories of political behaviour capable, even, of generating predictions. Traditionally, the classical political theorists like Plato and Hobbes, in fact, did both jobs. Ideally, political theory should probably be defined as trying to combine the empirical truths about human political reactions with the moral truths of what is politically desirable by designing institutions and constitutions which will generate the desirable by harnessing human political nature. That is clearly a massive job, perhaps never capable of more than limited achievement, but it is increasingly the goal of united and coherent political science."[13]

Essence of Politics : Expanding Horizons from 'Polis' to 'Power' and 'Activity'

As already said, political theory, is a branch of political science that is defined as 'the science of the state'.[14] It is also defined as a branch of the social sciences dealing with "the theory, organisation, government and practice of the state."[15] A French writer Paul Janet offers a succinct definition of political science by taking it as that part of social science which "treats the foundations of the state and the principles of government."[16] According to Seeley, political science investigates the phenomenon of government as political economy deals with wealth, biology with life, algebra with numbers, and geometry with space and magnitude."[17] Likewise, J. W. Garner holds: "In short, political science begins and ends with the state. In a general way,

13. David Robertson : *A Dictionary of Modern Politics* (London : EuropaPub., 1985), p.266. The word 'theory' is full of ambiguity. It is often employed as a synonym for thoughts, conjectures, or ideas. Thus, political theory is political thought or political speculation, and all three terms involve the expression of political ideas or 'philosophising about government'. R.G. McCloskey : "American Political Thought and the Study of Politics" in *American Political Science Review,* Vol. 51 (March, 1957), pp. 115-29. Sometimes, this word is used to designate a thought or an idea about how to solve a problem. Sometimes, it designates a conjecture about causal relationships or about the most effective means of promoting a given end. Statements of theory may range from a very low to a very high level of generality. In the view of T.P. Jenkin, it is an 'abstracted generalisation' and as such, it is primarily and initially a matter of mind rather than of fact, a kind of short hand that may stand in lieu of facts. *The Study of Political Theory* (Garden City : Doubleday, 1955), pp. 6-7. T.W. Hutchinson makes a distinction between pure and applied theory, both reflecting thought but while the former saying 'if p then q', the latter saying 'since p thus q'. *The Significance of Basic Postulates of Economic Theory* (London : Macmillan, 1930), p. 23. But hypothesis connotes a greater degree of doubt than theory. Karl Popper refers to theory or to quasi-theory, as an interpretation or a 'crystallisation of a point of view'. To Ernest Nagel, it "designates an explicit formulation of the determinate relations between a set of variables, in terms of which, fairly extensive class of empirically ascertainable regularities (or laws) can be explained." Whatever be the meaning of theory in a conceptual framework, as Dahl says, it is certain that political theory, in the grand manner can rarely, if ever, meet rigorous criteria of truth." See V.V. Dyke : *Political Science : A Philosophical Analysis* (Stanford : Stanford University Press, 1962), pp. 89-109.
14. R.G. Gettell: *Political Science* (Boston: Ginn and Co., 1943), p, 3.
15. Smith and Zurcher (eds): *A Dictionary of American Politics,* p. 238.
16. See J.W. Garner : *Political Science and Government* (Calcutta: World Press, 1952), p. 8
17. *Ibid.*

Some Definitional Statements

Theory: It refers to sets of systematically related generalisations, and involves viewing and thinking. It also generates insight. Loosely conceived, it comprises sets of systematically related generalisations. More specifically, it is a coherent body of generalisations and principles associated with the practice of a field of inquiry.

Method: It is the procedure or process that involves the techniques and tools utilised in inquiry for examining, testing and evaluating theory.

Methodology: It consists of methods, procedures, working concepts, rules and the like used for theory and guiding inquiry, and the search for solutions to problems of the real world. It is a particular way of testing, viewing, organising and giving shape to inquiry.

Inquiry: It involves four steps-description, classification, explanation and confirmation. The collection and description of facts are drawn from some classificatory scheme. The uniformities and differences are identified and described. Tentative hypotheses about the inter-relationships in the political process are formulated. These tentative hypotheses are verified through rigorous empirical observation. Then, the acceptable findings are set forth.

Analysis: It is the separation or breaking up of the whole into its fundamental parts and subjecting them to detailed qualitative or quantitative examination. It may involve clarification and explication.

Synthesis: It is the combining of parts into a whole, of diverse ideas and forces into a coherent or cohesive complex.

Paradigm: It is a scientific community's perspective of the world, its set of beliefs and commitments—conceptual, theoretical, methodological, instrumental. It guides scientific community's selection of problems, evaluation of data, and advocacy of theory.

Hypothesis: A generalisation is a general statement of uniformities and regularities. It is the simplest form of explanation. It may be universal or probabilistic. When it is expressed in tentative or conjectural terms, it becomes a hypothesis.

Concept: It is a mental construction, an abstract idea that refers either to a class of phenomena or to certain aspects or characteristics that a range of phenomena have in common....Concepts are abstractions from reality, designating types of movements, persons, behaviour, or other classes of phenomena.

Sources: 1. R.H. Chilcote: *Theories of Comparative Politics* (Boulder, Colarado: West-view Press, 1981), Chapter I, pp. 3-24.

2. Report of the Social Science Research Council's Committee on Historiography in the United States, cited in V.V. Dyke, *op. cit.*, p. 62.

its fundamental problems include, first, an investigation of the origin and nature of the state; second, an inquiry into the nature, history, forms of political institutions; and third, a deduction therefrom, so far as possible, of the laws of political growth and development."[18]

18. *Ibid.*, p. 9.

Political science has its original nomenclature in the word 'politics' that is derived from Greek words like 'polis', 'polity' and 'politeia'. The word 'politics' has been in currency ever since Aristotle, the universally acknowledged father of this discipline, brought out his *Politics*. It is, however, a different matter that, in recent times, it has become a fashion to redesignate it as 'political science' so as to distinguish its character from an art to that of a science. That is, while the term 'politics' refers to a particular kind of activity, called political activity, and places it into the category of an art, another term 'political science' refers to the study of state (power) in its various forms and manifestations and thereby accords to it the character of a science. Keeping it in view, Garner points out that while the meaning of politics should be restricted "to describe the activities by which officials are chosen and political policies promoted, or, in a wider sense, the sum total of the activities which have to do with the actual administration of public affairs, the term 'political science' describes the body of knowledge relating to the phenomenon of the state."[19]

However, what is striking about the study of political theory in contemporary times is that matters relating to the traditional meaning of politics and its technical distinction with political science have become outdated. A good number of writers taking inspiration from the contributions of Hobbes and Max Weber (like Charles Merriam, David Easton, Harold Lasswell, R.A. Dahl, Carl J. Friedrich, Reinhold Niebuhr, M.A. Kaplan, H.J. Morgenthau, G.E.G. Catlin, Bertrand Russell, F.M. Walkins, Bertrand de Jouvenel, Michael Curtis, Jean Blondel, GA. Almond, David Apter, Myron Weiner, etc.) treat 'power' as the fundamental concept of this discipline.[20] This has been done so as to widen the field of the study and, more than that, so as to raise it to the level of a 'science' that may enable us to understand and explain 'political reality' in empirical terms. It is owing to this that, as we shall see in due course, the empirical or causal aspect of political theory has overshadowed its speculative or normative aspect, and that has been described by some leading writers as 'decline', nay 'demise', of political theory in recent times.

The earlier writers brought out the distinction between'state' and 'government' by throwing light on the point that while the former should be regarded as a collectivity for the sake of promoting some common purposes, the latter its instrument to implement the will of the community.[21] The recent writers go ahead in this direction by pointing out the distinction between 'government' and 'politics'. The former "concerns the institutional framework of rule in a state, that is to say,

19. *Ibid.*, pp. 2-3. At another place, he repeats that the term 'political science' "has come to be more generally employed by the best writers and thinkers to describe the mass of knowledge, derived from the systematic study of the state, while the meaning of the term 'politics' is confined to that of the business or activity which has to do with the actual conduct of affairs of state." *Ibid.*, pp. 4-5.
20. For this purpose, we may refer to the representative view of Bertrand de Jouvenel who says: "There is no natural affinity between the word 'politics' and the word 'meat', but they come together as soon as it is proposed that the government should do something about meat. We call 'political' the pressures exerted upon the public authorities to bring about this or that decision desired by this or that private interest. We also call'political'the stand taken on the matter by the parties, with a view to attaining or retaining popularity and power." *Sovereignty : An Inquiry into the Political Good* (Chicago: University of Chicago Press, 1957), p. 15.
21. Garner, *op.cit.*, pp. 48-49.

Field of Political Theory—Traditional and Modern

Statement of Pennock[1]

1. Ethical, dealing with what 'ought' to be, and employing the rationalistic, deductive method;
2. Speculative, consisting of 'imaginative construction of ideal or utopian states';
3. Sociological, studying the state as a form of social organisation in relation to society as a whole and using empirical method;
4. Legal or juristic, dealing with the nature of law, sovereignty, and constitutions; and
5. Scientific, seeking to extract generalisations, trends and laws from data gathered by observation, measurement and analysis.

Statement of Brecht[2]

1. Non-scientific types of explanations, especially those of a religious and philosophical character;
2. Non-scientific value judgements especially moral ones;
3. Proposals offered for the selection of political goals and political actions; and
4. Mere description of phenomena as seen by political philosophers of the past.

Statement of S.S. Wolin[3]

Politics includes:

(*i*) a form of acitivity centring around the quest for competitive advantage between groups, individuals or societies;

(*ii*) a form of activity conditioned by the fact that it occurs within a situation of change and relative scarcity;

(*iii*) a from of activity in which the pursuit of advantage produces consequences of such magnitude that they affect, in a significant way, the whole society or a substantial part of it.

1. J.Ronald Pennock: "Political Theory" in E.C. Smth and A.J. Zurcher (ed.s): *A Dictionary of American Politics* (New York: Barnes and Noble Ins., 1944), pp. 238-39.
2. Brecht in *International Encyclopaedia,* p. 310.
3. S.S. Wolin: *Politics and Vision* (Boston, 1960), pp. 10-11.

the structure and procedure of the legislative body (in Britain, Parliament), of the executive administrative bodies (roughly, the cabinet, other holders of ministerial staff, and the civil service) and of the analogous institutions in local government., *e.g.*, in voting, in forming and running political parties, or in exerting influence in other ways on those responsible for the conduct of government. I shall be using the term politics more widely so as to cover 'government' as well. For the purpose, I include under 'government', the institutions for interpreting and enforcing the law in addition to those for making and applying it."[22]

As such, political theory is concerned not only with the study of 'state' and 'government' as conceived till the first half of the twentieth century), it is also (as now understood) the study of 'power'. It covers all those activities that have their bearing on or connection with the 'struggle for power'. Obviously, the new meaning of political theory covers within its fold all activities that, in the words of Easton, are

22. D.D. Raphael: *Problems of Political Philosophy* (Delhi : Macmillan, 1976), p. 27.

related to the 'authoritative allocation of values' which are binding in a society, or, which, in the words of Lasswell and Dahl, are related to the exercise of 'influence' in the process, and situation of making and implementing decisions. Keeping the whole picture in view, B. de Jouvenel defines the 'essense of politics' in these words : "Politics may be taken to denote the tussle which precedes the decision, and 'policy', the course adopted."[23]

If politics is a struggle for power, it may be traced everywhere in a situation of conflicting wills, or it may occur whenever a project requires the support of other wills to the extent to which its author sets out to rally those wills. "It is a significant fact that the word 'campaign' covers strivings for very different objects, while the conditions necessary to the attainment of all of them are similar, whether it is a man aiming at a public office or admission to a club, or a social climber seeking an entry into someone's salon, or an industrialist trying to put a new product in the market, not one of them, different though these ends are, can achieve his own, except by disarming hostility, rallying popularity, winning support, conciliating wills."[24]

If politics deals with power and struggle for its sake in any form, whether peaceful or violent, it has these implications :[25]

1. In an apolitical sense, power involves human beings and presupposes the existence of two or more persons. It is not the name of a thing but it is a concept describing a relationship between two or more persons. As it is not a substantive thing but a *relational concept,* it may take many forms, of which brute force is only one. It may take the form of superior knowledge, wealth, reputation and the like. Moreover, it depends upon the acceptance of something as power and it is the acceptance of that something which makes it power, not the claim of possession of power as a substantive thing.
2. Power manifests itself only in action. It is concerned with the wills and interests of particular individuals and with the inevitable conflict between these individual interests and wills. Politics is successful when it succeeds in reconciling them, when it succeeds in formulating policies that are mutually acceptable. The end of politics is policy— the integration of conflicting interests in terms of certain interests and values which are held in common.
3. Although politics comes into being as a result of the conflict of wills and interests, it presupposes the existence of certain interests and values in common, for without this basis for reconciliation, there could be no politics. Politics has sometimes been defined as the technique of compromise. Persons are willing to make compromises only because they value certain things more than they do the things which they are compromising. When a society no longer values common interests above personal interests, it disintegrates, compromise is no longer possible, and politics ceases. And war, international or civil, generally signals the breakdown of politics, and the end of compromise.

Politics involves everything like activity of the individuals and their groups for the reconciliation of conflicting interests without undermining, nay destroying, a

23. Bertrand de Jouvenel, *op. cit.*, p. 16.
24. *Ibid.*, p. 17.
25. J.H. Hallowell : *Main Currents in Modern Political Thought* (New York : Holt, Rinehart and Winston, 1950), pp. 2-6.

sense of security and participation among members of the community. In a sense, politics implies some kind of democracy. "It emerges when the rulers are willing to consult other people."[26]

The latest development in this direction is to define politics as the study of 'political activity' in the same way as the economists define economics as the study of man's economic activities.[27] This way is so comprehensive that it embraces all what we have said above. Moreover, as man is a social being and as his every activity forms part of his social activity, politics automatically becomes a branch of social sciences. By saying so, we offer a working concept of politics signifying that it "is the way in which we understand and order our social affairs especially in relation to the allocation of scarce resources, the principles underlying this, and the means by which some people or groups acquire and maintain a greater control over the situation than others. This means that politics is above all a social activity concerned with people's social and material relationships, varied in expression in different spatial areas and continually changing through time—a dynamic social activity."[28]

Following important points must, however, be borne in mind while defining political activity : [29]

1. Not every activity of man is 'political'. It may be'political', 'semi-political', 'para-political' and 'non-political'. The implication is that political activity takes place within a certain defined arena of social affairs and that wider social and economic considerations can be ignored. The question of racial prejudice is'political', the activities and concerns of sport and the arts are not, and the two should not intrude on one another.
2. Political activity takes place only between bodies, in some sense publicly recognised as having an accepted right to behave in this way, and according to certain common recognised and enforceable rules. Bodies without this kind of legitimacy or which act outside the rules as defined by the same public authorities are deemed to be acting outside the 'arena' of politics.
3. The 'arena' of political activity may vary from time to time and from place to place. It may be restricted in a backward country, it may be much restricted in a country under some form of totalitarian system of government. Different from this, it may be quite brisk in an 'open' and advanced country.

---

26. A.H. Doctor : *Issues in Political Theory* (New Delhi : Sterling, 1985), p. 2. One may, however, disagree with this observation of Doctor that "in an authoritarian or dictatorial regime, where the dictator hardly consults others, there is no politics." *Ibid.*
27. "Activity is political when it relates to a public issue, and it relates to a public issue when two conditions are met. In the first place, it must relate to the decision-making of a group, *i.e.*, it must concern group policy, group organisation, or group leadership, or it must concern the regulation of group inter-relationships. In the second place, it must come within the realm of the controversial." V.V. Dyke, *op. cit.*, p. 133.
28. Geoffery Ponton and Peter Gill : *Introduction to Politics* (Oxford : Martin Robertson, 1982), p. 6. "Political activity may be understood as relating to the management of man's collective life whose outward manifestation is the state. Those who are engaged in this activity are concerned with seeking power with a view to manage and arrange things according to their point of view. In this sense, the activity itself assumes the character of a particular kind of skill, with which many are not endowed with, because the 'art' of management of human affairs is not given to everyone." Frank Thakurdas, *Essays in Political Theory*, p. 1.
29. Ponton and Gill, *op. cit.*, pp. 6-9.

Catlin's Barest Outlines of a Conceptual System of Politics

1. Political theory deals with 'political man'. He is the kind of man who, hypothetically, is primarily preoccupied with control, for whatever reasons. The 'political act' is that of control of man, and every day we can find its numerous instances in domestic, civil, ecclestiastical and industrial affairs alike.
2. Politics, like Gaul, is divided into three parts: the art of practice, the philosophy, and the science. The last two comprise the theory.
3. It would be idle to pretend that the whole field of politics is quantitative. Some areas cannot be usefully dealt with in this way.
4. It must clearly understood that prediction in political science does not involve any political philosophy of determinism, cycles, crystal-gazing, or the like. We only say that granted the character of human nature, if there are similar recurrent conditions, then results no less alike or similar will result.
5. The immense force of the desire to acquire power over means is, a commonplace observation, although some people seek power to escape from obstacles rather than to overcome them. In the social relations of men with men, this desire is fundamental; it is the preferred hypothesis in the explanation of the behaviour of majority men in politics.
6. Power is synonymous with domination. Power is the potentiality of control; and control may be just as certain and predictable when it issues from a routine and habitual cooperation as when it is dominative. There are circumstances where it may be more stable than domination or the 'over-under' relationship with its tensions.
7. It lies in the dialectic of power that, in many cases, in order to guarantee freedom in particulars, it can be exercised only through co-operative association with others. Such a power generally recognised is authority. The association, by its nature, restricts the absolute and general freedom of its members, making their actions assured, and also some particular freedoms. The rest remain, and these are recognised as liberties.
8. Those freedoms, which logically or empirically, are held to be essential to the functioning of healthy and sane men, constitute the basis of Natural Law.
9. The relation, polar but not contradictory, between men's demands for freedoms and their demand for authority to guarantee these freedoms is crucial to political science, and is comparable to the relation in economics between demand and supply. Men always want the goods of social authority; but they are also reluctant to pay the costs in terms of the restrictions on freedom.
10. The political market presupposes political liberalism. While it remains free, we must expect not doctrinaire rigidity but fluctuations in the demands for particular goods, authorities and agencies. Where there is a demand, there must be support and the unit of support is the crucial item in political calculation.
11. The producers of political goods are alternately and reciprocally dependent upon the consumers and their demand. Nevertheless, the interests of the producers, whether called government, executive, management or hierarchy, are not, from the nature of the case, identical with that of the consumer populace or electorate. In order to produce what will be demanded in the long range, it may be necessary to forfeit a measure of support in the short range. To do this, as little as possible, is part of the tactics of politics. The producer as citizen may also be a consumer, but he is primarily a part of the system of rule; the consumer may, by his demand, shape and even dictate production, but he is primarily a plain consumer.

12. It is the wish of every consumer to obtain, as much as possible, in the way of political goods and securities without paying the costs. But goods and costs are unavoidably linked. The optimist, sometimes called the idealist, overlooks this link; the pessimist denies that the costs will be paid. The issue of pessimism is slow market and political stagnation.
13. The consumer market is limited by factual considerations, such as those of strategy over which, in particular cases, the consumer can have no control just as economic activity is conditioned by the distribution of raw materials. Democracy, as a system, represents, broadly, a free or consumer's market. Dictatorship provides a closed, monopolistic or producers' market with high cost. When allowance is made for minority demands and diversity in the markets, a pluralistic society emerges.
14. The sense of community, valuing the goods of community, prejudices men in favour of accepting a market compromise favourable to production but where cooperation can exclude dominative techniques.
15. Conflict in society, resulting from the pursuit of power, is an eternal factor in politics. Nevertheless, an emotional (or calculated or both) sense of community can so far register disapproval of conflict that men become disposed to subordinate obstinate interests to rational compromise. On the other hand, the urgency of need inclines to resort to dominative and violent measures.
16. To the extent to which, in a technical age, the production of effective political goods itself becomes technical, the professional politician (with his demands) is likely to replace the amateur. This is not necessarily to the disadvantage of the consumer, provided he can keep the producers (through elections) sensitive to the fluctuations of support. Under despotism, these fluctuations are ignored until a revolutionary danger point is reached.
17. Whether political parties or machines should be regarded as major producers depends upon how they are functioning in the particular conditions. All political agencies should be regarded functionally, and not statically, in the social structure.
18. Most men are not hungry for grand power or to be producers, because they think they have enough of what they want. The demands of most men are small, routine, and disinterested. Their interest in power is not absent but moves in a narrower and more domestic or business circles. They fear attention and their interest and freedom is rather in avoiding the burden of responsibility. But where new expectations are frustrated, the mass also becomes ambitious for more and even ready to pay high costs.
19. Men's demands, fundamentally shaped by their nature, can be changed by their education or by the cruder mass media influence.
20. Political science reduces the confused to the intelligible in means, as philosophy should do with a view to rational action.

Source: Catlin: *Political and Sociological Theory and Its Applications,* Ch. V.

Thus, Ponton and Gill conclude : "Fundamentally politics is about the arrangement for ordering our social affairs and the degree of control individuals and groups have over this ordering. Essential to this situation is that all participants should have some influence and that the relationships between individuals and groups should, to some degree be flexible and susceptible to change. People who can do nothing to influence their situation cannot act politically, while social relationships which are rigidly governed and controlled by custom, law or technical rules also have a low political content."[30]

To sum up, politics can be defined as (1) an activity occurring within and among groups, (2) something which operates on the basis of desires that are to some extent shared, (3) an essential feature of the activity being a struggle of actors, (4) to achieve their desires, (5) questions of group policy, group organisation, group leadership, or the regulation of inter-group relations, (6) against the opposition of others with conflicting desires. More briefly, politics may be defined as a struggle among actors pursuing conflicting desires on public issues.[31] Thus, politics exists only when ends and means are controversial.[32] So Quincy Wright defines politics as the art of influencing, manipulating, or controlling (groups) "so as to advance the purposes of some against the opposition of others."[33] It implies that most commonly the activity must confront opposition if it is to be classified as political. This is suggested by the notion that politics should stop at the water's edge, which means that disagreement, should stop there and that a united front should be presented to the foreign adversary."[34]

Political Theory Distinguished from Political Thought, Political Philosophy, Political Ideology, Political Inquiry and Political Analysis

The speculations and explanations about 'political reality' have certain recognisable forms bearing the designations of 'political theory', 'political thought', 'political ideology', 'political inquiry', 'political philosophy,' 'political analysis', etc. Eminent text-book writers and commentators have taken these designations as interchangeable.[35]

---

30. *Ibid.*, p.79.
31. V.V. Dyke, *op. cit.*, p. 134.
32. Wright: "Political Science and World Stabilisation" in *American Political Science Review*, Vol. 44 (March, 1950), pp. 1-13.
33. *Ibid.* Also see Wright : *A Study of International Relations* (New York: Appleton-Century Crofts, 1955), pp. 130-35.
34. V.V. Dyke, *op. cit.*, p. 133.
35. For instance, while G.H. Sabine puts the study of great thinkers from the Greeks to the Fascists in his book *A History of Political Theory,* C.L. Wayper covers only the most important ones (excluding Aristotle) in his concise work titled *Political Thought.* R.W. Carlyle and A.J Carlyle cover the study of political thought of the middle ages (in 6 volumes) titled as *A History of Medieval Political Theory in the West,* but W.A. Dunning covers the long history of the development of political ideas (in 4 volumes) known as *A History of Political Theories.* Likewise, we may take note of the fact that while T.I. Cook titles his book as *History of Political Philosophy.* the book of C.C. Maxey on the same theme is titled *Political Philosophies.* E. Barker discusses the political ideas of Plato, including his predecssors and contemporaries, in his *Greek Political Theory* and also discusses the political ideas of the two great Greek giants in another book called *The Political Thought of Plato and Aristotle,* C.A. Vaughan deals with the study of Hobbes, Locke and Rousseau (in 2 volumes) in his books each titled as *Studies in the History of Political Philosophy.* The title of Frohock' s book is *Nature of Political Inquiry* ; R.A. Dahl has his *Modern Political Analysis,* while a collection of articles on contemporary political theories, approaches, methods and methodologies edited by J.C. Charlesworth is *Contemporary Political Analysis.* A peculiar example can be seen in the contribution of Arnold Brecht who titles his book as *Political Theory : The Foundations of Twentieth Century Political Thought.* Andrew Hacker cautiously includes the study of great political thinkers from Plato to Mill in his *Political Theory : Philosophy, Ideology, Science.* It is with a view to extricate himself from such a dilemma that W.T. Bluhm designates his study as *Theories of the Political System.*

Obviously, it creates a problem whether a student of this subject should take all these designations as inter-changeable terms, or he should try to distinguish political theory with each of them. In this section an attempt has been made to bring out the main points of distinction with the view to enable a student to be aware of all this, while, at the same time, maintaining his impression that all these terms are easily interchangeable.

Political Thought and Political Theory: It is widely believed that political thought is the study of the political speculations of a whole community, over a certain period. By the whole community we mean its articulate section consisting of the leaders, statesmen, commentators, writers, poets, publicists, social reformers, litterateurs and the like who react to the events of the time in their own ways. So is the factor of age. The time span may not be specified or categorised in a rigid way, though one may earmark some loose contours in which certain events of great public importance have taken place. Thus, we have the Greek and Roman political thoughts of the ancient period followed by the thought of about one thousand years later (5th to 15th century) known as the Middle Ages. It is also possible that the time span may be short as we see in the case of England in the seventeenth century, or of France and America in the eighteenth century.

What should be noted in this connection is that we may put milestones on the occurrence of significant changes in the policies, programmes, activities, plans, organisations, constitutions, etc. that evoke different responses of the articulate sections of the community. In this sense, political thought is taken as 'time bound'. It is due to this that political thought "has no fixed form. In other words, it expresses itself in various ways, to include speeches of the statesmen, the political commentaries of the publicists, the scholarly articles written by academicians, a poem composed by a poet who may catch the anguish of a people at any one particular moment of time and the letters of protest or affirmation written by whoever reacts to all the government decisions and policies."[36]

Political theory is different from political thought if we keep these points in consideration. First, it is the speculation of a particular thinker or writer who expresses his views on its three fundamental themes—state, government and power. His explanation is based on some hypothesis which may range from speculative to empirical directions. In this way, theory offers a model of explanation of political reality as understood and described by a writer. Naturally, one may come across the great variety in the field of political theory ranging from one extreme of idealism as contained in the *Republic* of Plato, *Social Contract* of Rousseau and *Political Obligation* of Green to the point of realism as contained in the *Prince* of Machiavelli, *Leviathan* of Hobbes and *Communist Manifesto* of Marx and Engels. Second, political theory finds its basis in a discipline or approach as philosophical, historical, economic, psychological, sociological, theological, anthropological and the like. It creates the problem of approaches in the field of political theory. For instance, while St. Thomas expresses his view on political themes from a theological angle of vision, William

36. Frank Thakurdas, *op. cit.*, p. 4. Also see J.A. Gould and V.V. Thursby (ed.s): *Contemporary Political Thought: Issues in Scope, Value and Direction* (New York : Holt, Rinehart and Winston, 1969), pp. 1-6.

McDougall does it from a psychological standpoint. The variety of approach leads to a variety of explanations. Last, political theory may be speculative or causal, it may be noted that a writer may assume the role of a critic, a reformer, or both. For instance, Burke is a critic, of change, Bentham is an advocate of reforms. The greatness of Marx is that he is a vehement critic of the existing bourgeois system and an apostle of the revolution that would bring about socialism.

The distinction between political theory and political thought, as made out above, is rather of a technical nature that may perhaps be beyond the comprehension of an average student of this subject. However, we may depend upon this admirable elaboration of Prof. E. Barker: "There is such a thing as political thought which is distinct from and greater than political theory. Political theory is the speculation of particular thinkers, which may be remote from the actual facts of the time. Political thought is the immanent philosophy of a whole age which determines its action and shapes its life. The one is explicit, self-conscious and (may be) detached; the other is implicit, unconscious and immersed in the stream of vital action."[37]

Political Philosophy and Political Theory: In a general sense, philosophy is the 'science of wisdom'. To Plato and Aristotle, it is the 'search for truth'. Obviously, the field of philosophy is so vast that it tries to explain not *something* but *everything*—the universe, the macrocosmos and the microcosmos. It examines not only what *is* but also what *ought to be,* or ought to be done, or to be approved. It is not limited to the physical world but entitled and even supposed to meditate also about metaphysical questions. Nor is it limited by the rules of pre-established scientific procedure, or by the requirements of exact proof, but it is entitled and even supposed to engage in speculation beyond the reach of observational tests."[38] Hallowell says that philosophy "is the search for meaning, it seeks to synthesise our knowledge in terms of some rational meaningful pattern."[39]

The real aim of philosophy is not to increase our knowledge as much as to deepen our understanding. When it is applied to the study of political phenomena, it becomes political philosophy. It is true that philosophy has four principal branches—metaphysics (knowledge of ultimate reality), epistemology (science of knowledge), logic, and ethics. Political philosophy is concerned with all these branches, though its connection with metaphysics (as in the case of Hegel and Feuerbach) and with ethics (as in the case of Plato and Aristotle) is very intimate. As Hallowell continues:

37. Barker: "Medieval Political Thought" in F.J.C. Hearnshaw (ed.): *The Social and Political Ideas of Some Great Medieval Thinkers,* p. 10. A thought is an intellectual exercise of a general order encompassing desire, speculation, comment, criticism and explanation. A theory is, more than anything else, a 'logical file of knowledge' with explanatory purpose. While such knowledge may lead to other variants of thought, its immediate concern is restricted to verifiability. See S.K. Chaube: "Politics Among the Social Sciences: A Historical Overview" in S. Kaviraj, P. Chatterjee and others: *The State of Political Theory: Some Marxist Essays* (Calcutta: Research India Publications, 1978), p. 66. Also see Nicholas Georgescu-Roegen: *Analytical Economics; Issues and Problems* (Cambridge, Mass: Harvard Univ. Press, 1977), pp. 12-14.
38. Brecht: *Political Theory,* pp. 15-16.
39. Hallowell, *op. cit.,* p. 7.

"It is one of the principal tasks of political philosophy to bring men's political beliefs to self-consciousness and to subject them to the scrutiny of reason."[40]

The difference between political philosophy and political theory may be stressed on this point that while a philosopher may be a theorist, a theorist may not necessarily be a philosopher.[41] For instance, eminent American writers like Charles Merriam and Harold Lasswell are leading analysts and theorists, but they are not great philosophers like Hobbes and Locke. It is true that both political theorists and political philosophers deal with significant themes of politics like nature and purpose of political authority, liberty, equality, rights, justice, political obligation and resistance etc., the difference between the two hinges on the point that a philosopher is concerned with the *how* and *why of* things so as to offer a rational explanation that, in his view, seems to be the best of all. Different from this, the field of a political theorist is wider. He may be a philosopher like Plato or Hegel, but he may be much more competent in explaining the nature and dimensions of 'political reality' like Laski and Lasswell. As such, the scope of political theory is wider than that of political philosophy. Besides, political philosophy is invariably abstract, while political theory may be both abstract or speculative and concrete or empirical. It is well pointed out: "Political philosophy, thus, broadens and at the same time narrows the field of political theory by continuing to eliminate much from contemporary political theory."[42]

If so, political philosophy "is not so much concerned with political institutions as it is with the ideas and aspirations that are embodied in these institutions. It looks

---

40. *Ibid.,* pp. 8-9. Philosophy is conceived of as a conversation or dialogue about the reality in which man participates. It is best portrayed as the love *(philia),* rather than possession of wisdom *(sophid);* it involves the whole person including the passionate side of man (his erotic constitution), rather than being solely an affair of the intellect; and the effect of its consistent pursuit is to open the psyche to new dimensions of reality and new priorities for life and action... Although theory needs to be distinguished from philosophy, it should not be *separated.* A philosophy gives rise to and nourishes theory. Theory (or the disinterested observation and explanation of a given segment of reality) derives its nourishment from philosophy (or the attempt to see reality, in so far as man can, as a meaningful whole). While theory can be analytically distinguished from philosophy, it is disastrous to separate these two activities. Thus, one can have theories of social change, types of regime, the circulation of elites, voting behaviour and political development, for example, but if they are separated from the concerns that have perenially occupied political philosophy, their meaning will appear distorted or proved barren and irreleveant. The intellectuality of theory must be leavened with the poetic vision of philosophy." Dante Germino: *Modern Western Political Thought: Machiavelli to Marx* (Chicago: Rand McNally, 1972), p 389.
41. As Frank Thakurdas says, it "will be incorrect to describe David Easton as a political philosopher, outstanding theorist he is of course." *Op. cit.,* p. 9.
42. See F.G. Wilson : *The Elements of Modern Politics* (New York, 1933), p. 5. As Arnold Brecht says: "A theory tries to explain 'something'; a philosophy in one use of the term, 'everything'. Philosophical explanations are theories, too, but in their most characteristic efforts, non-scientific ones. They begin where science in the narrow sense of the term leaves off...Yet the prevailing use of the term leaves the philosopher free to follow intuition and to speculate about things and inter-relations not accessible to science, at least if that is done with full regard to the results of scientific work." Brecht in *International Encyclopaedia,* p. 309.

behind the surface of political events and institutions in an effort to discover the underlying motives, beliefs and aspirations that brought those events and institutions about. It looks behind the superficial struggle for power in an effort to determine why this struggle is taking place and where it is leading. It is not so much interested in how things occur as it is in what occurs and why. It is less interested in the efficiency of political techniques and institutions than it is in their legitimacy."[43] Despite these points of differences, it should be remembered that an intimate relationship between the two makes political science value-laden and, for that reason, refreshing. Though the empiricists may follow a different line, a normativist like Friedrich may go to the extent of saying that "one cannot be usefully pursued without the other."[44]

Political Ideology and Political Theory: Ideology means a set of ideas in the nature of a belief or a conviction for the application or implementation of which people fight and go to the extent of making any sacrifices. For this reason, ideology is also known by the name of 'political religion'. It embraces the whole system of ideas by which people allow themselves to be governed. They may struggle for the sake of a particular pattern of ideas. Thus, ideology is regarded as an action-oriented belief system. It may also assume the form of a final or perfect model of political community that has to be established at any cost. Obviously, an ideology inheres the characteristic of dogmatism. It is rigid so much so that its adherents do not want to change the line of their commitments. It may also be called by the name of 'political doctrine' to which the leaders and their followers are fully committed. It demands complete intellectual acceptance and emotional allegiance from those who choose to follow its any variety (like Fascism and Communism). Obviously, it "generates a kind of fanaticism and blind faith for which any sacrifice on the part of the individual is not too great."[45]

An ideology may, and also may not, be akin to a philosophy. It may receive sustenance from a kind of blind philosophy. Philosophy is a very wide term that seeks to offer rational explanation about the ultimate goodness of a particular object or system. Ideology is like a closed-door affair. The ideological premises of a system may be subjected to a philosophical system by its adherents as we may see in the case of Marxism, or it may be bereft of any logical explanation as we may see in the

43. Hallowell, *op cit.*, p. 9. In this connection, Hacker makes a good point : "The theorist whose pursuit is political science is interested in describing and explaining the realities of political behaviour. He attempts to draw up generalised propositions about actual relations between states and citizens and about the role of power in society. Theory is an essay in political science if it seems to be the author's intention to offer generalised descriptions or explanations of the behaviour of men and political institutions. The theorist whose interest in writing political philosophy, on the other hand, is concerned with prescribing the goals which citizens, states and societies ought to pursue, his aim is to generalise about right conduct in the political life and about the legitimate use of power.... The theorist may be regarded as engaging in political philosophy as his aim is to suggest rule of political behaviour which states and citizens ought to follow." *Op. cit.* pp. 1-2.
44. Carl J. Friedrich: "Political Philosophy and the Science of Politics" in Ronald Young (ed.); *Approaches to the Study of Politics* (Evanston, Illinois: Northwestern University Press, 1958), p. 188. For an interesting study see Leo Strauss: "What is Political Philosophy?" in *Journal of Politics*, Vol. XIX, No. 3 (August, 1957), pp. 343-68.
45. Frank Thakurdas, *op. cit.*, p. 11.

case of Fascism. For instance, the principle of racial superiority or of hero-worship as espoused by the Fascists has no logical foundation. Likewise, the inexorable laws of social development as laid down by the dialectics of Marxism may be scientifically tenable only to its adherents. "A set of value-judgements, which have not been subjected to rational scrutiny by the tests of consistency and accordance may be called ideological."[46]

Political ideology may be taken as a part of political theory. Thus, we study different ideologies (nationalism, fascism, communism, even liberalism) in the field of political theory. It is clear that the scope of political theory is wider than that of ideology. A political thinker may not be an ideologue, but an ideologue is certainly a political theorist. It is also possible that a thinker may be both as we find in the peculiar case of Karl Marx. Marx not only studied the development of a society like a dialectical theoretician, he also suggested the picture of an ideal society signifying emancipation of man from all sorts of coercion and exploitation. In his *Theses on Feuerbach,* he wrote that "the philosophers have so far interpreted the world, the problem is how to change it." Another great thing about Marx is that he sought to establish unity between thought and action and in that way aligned political theory with political activity.

It is, however, a different matter that a commentator on political theory may go to the extent of identifying a political theorist with a political ideologue on the plea that every great theorist has certain biases, prejudices, convictions, choices and commitments of his own and he endeavours to understand and explain political reality in the light of these 'beliefs'. Thus, Plato and Aristotle showed their 'preference' for the excellence of an aristocratic system ; Hobbes and Locke imparted philosophical justification to the rising 'bourgeois' system ; Bentham and Mill defended the role of the rising middle class in the liberal political systems of the nineteenth century. Politics is a social process characterised by activity involving rivalry and cooperation in the exercise of power, and culminating in the making of decisions for a group. The object of political theorists "is to understand politics in the most comprehensive fashion possible, but with the greatest possible parsimony of explanatory terms. They want to discover the general order and pattern of political facts, to explain these adequately and to construct rules of political action based on this analysis."[47]

46. Raphael, *op.cit.,* p. 19. "Ideologies are, in fact, usually fragmentary, unsophisticated, and sometimes composed of parts that do not fit together. But no matter how internally consistent or inconsistent, they serve as frames of reference which guide citizens and rulers in the making of public policy." See Bluhm, *op. cit.,* pp. 2-3.

47. Bluhm, *op. cit,* p. 5. Prof. Hacker is of the view that all political theory is political ideology for the reason that the line of difference between the two cannot be drawn. A political theorist may either be a Utopian like Plato or a realist like Machiavelli or both like Aristotle. The merit of the ideologues is that they 'are more down to earth', though the chief criticism against such persons is that their feet 'are too firmly planted in their own soil'. Every theorist has some vested interest. "Devoid of such an interest, his vision of reality and his image of good life will not be clouded, nor will his theory be especially pleading. The intention of ideology is to justify a particular system of power in society. The ideologue is an interested party ; his interest may be to defend things as they are or to criticise the *status quo* in the hope that a new distribution of power will come into being. In the latter case, the writer has a vested interest in the future : he will be speaking in the name of revolution or reform and he has a stake in the political arrangements which may emerge in the time to come. *Op. cit.,* pp. 4-5:

While closing a discussion in this important direction, it should be reiterated that though it is worthwhile to remove any kind of semantic confusion in regard to the meaning and scope of various important terms like political theory, political philosophy, political thought, political ideology and the like, the fact of their very close and intimate relatedness cannot be lost sight of. Thus, Hacker confidently affirms : "All political theorists are inevitable ideologues, because, like other men, they are creatures of emotion and interest. A theory in ideal terms is dispassionate and disinterested. As science, it will describe political reality without trying to pass judgement on what is being depicted either implicitly or explicitly. As philosophy, it will prescribe rules of conduct "which will secure the good life for all society and not simply for certain individuals or classes. The theorist in theory will not himself have a personal interest in the political arrangements of any one country, or class, or party...Much of what passes for political philosophy then is ideology. Rather than disinterested prescription, we have rationalisation Much of what passes for political science is no less ideological."[48]

Political Inquiry and Political Theory: Sometimes, a line of distinction is drawn between political inquiry and political theory despite the fact that a clear-cut boundary line between the two may hardly be drawn. A definition of political inquiry has two ingredients. First, political investigations may be distinguished by a certain approach or a set of techniques assumed by the investigator. In this case, it is the method which sets off political analysis from all other kinds of investigations. Second, the distinctiveness of political inquiry may turn on the subject which is being investigated. A line of difference between classical and modern political inquiries may be drawn at this stage. Classical inquiry never assumes a sharp separation between analysis as such and the object of investigation. But the scientific climate in modern political inquiry radically separates techniques from the subject, to the point where the ideal scientific observer is without any subjective location. However, both share the same positive framework. But while the relationship of method and substance varies, the separation is never collapsed. "In any inquiry, someone is inquiring and something is being inquired about. To deny this is to deny the investigatory process itself."[49]

The question of political inquiry is fundamentally a question of political theory. When we investigate something, we normally try to explain it, which means that we encase it within one theory or another. Even the identification of facts entails some form of theoretical reference. But all theories are not as tightly woven as established scientific ones. Political theory is the scheme which ascribes meanings to the political universe, and as the idealised form of political reality expresses, with exactness, those empirical regularities which yield the uniformity of experience. The analyst cannot separate himself from this general experience in an institutional framework. The constant theme in political inquiry is the prescriptive behaviour found in all political action.[50]

---

48. *Ibid.*
49. F.M. Frohock : *The Nature of Political Inquiry* (Homewood, Illinois: The Dorsey Press, 1967), p. 3.
50. *Ibid.*, p. 13.

If so, following important elements of political inquiry may be enumerated:[51]

1. Tacit dimension of theory, an examination of philosophical frameworks and methodological possibilities afforded by one epistemology or another, discussion of instrumental function of theories in terms of net physical and positivist foundations for political inquiry.
2. Examination of the patterns of explanation constituting method and methodology, including functional and causal analysis, establishment of the criteria for a properly functioning system demonstrating necessity of values in functional explanations.
3. Examination of the role of science in all physical and social phenomena and theoretical approaches appropriate to each kind of data, and reply to the issue whether political inquiry can be a science or not.
4. Scrutinisation of the question of values in political investigation, discussion of insight schism, deletion of value-free political science in the context of distinction between factual and value-judgements, defence of a qualified emotism as a basis for reconsiderations in political inquiry.
5. Discussion of the cognitive or intuitive foundation of all inquiry, identification of a common theme in political inquiry as an object of study—prescriptive behaviour or the imposition of norms by actors on one another.

Political theory is an objective description of politics. Normative as well as historical theories have now been subordinated to causal theory which, in turn, is taken as ethically neutral.[52] While the classical tradition of Plato and Aristotle incorporates the normative dimension of politics, contemporary political inquiry is directed towards describing and explaining the ongoing political system. Some modern theorists (like Easton) argue for a general theory of politics to guide and order this kind of research. Others remain content with special theories. But in all cases theory is taken to mean the neutral explanatory framework for political events.

Political Analysis and Political Theory: Theory and analysis may be distinguished. So is the case with political theory and political analysis in spite of the fact that both are concerned with certain fundamental issues, most important of which maybe thus enumerated:[53]

1. What is the role of power and influence in political systems?
2. What do political systems have in common and in what ways do they differ from one another?
3. What conditions induce stability, change or revolution in different political systems? What is required if peace is to be maintained and violence avoided?

---

51. *Ibid.,* p. 11.
52. According to Frohock, theories may be of two kinds—descriptive and instrumental. The former, and the older, amounts to the assertion that theories are factual statements about the worlds which are either true or false. The latter says that theories do not make true claims about the world but are frameworks which make the world meaningful. It is like a map. It is not a descriptive picture of the world but a tool to help us get where we are going. In so far as the theory does that, it is a good or true theory. *Ibid.,* p. 9.
53. See R.A. Dahl: *Modern Political Analysis* (Englewood Cliffs, New Jersey : Prentice-Hall, 1977), pp. 23-24.

4. How do men behave in politics? What are the distinguishing features of *homo politicus*?
5. What sort of political system is the best? How can we evaluate different political systems?
6. How can we act wisely in the midst of the great uncertainty that appears to be characteristic of political life?

A political theorist deals with these questions and tries to offer plausible answers to them. So does a political analyst. However, the difference between the two may be traced in the point that while a theorist goes deeper and deeper before offering his description, the analyst just makes a description of things as they are visible to him. That is, while a theorist makes use of his insight and speculative power, the analyst works like a mechanic. It may be seen in the fact that a large number of books written by contemporary American political analysts lack the depth of political theory. It is for this reason that while a theorist may or may not prefer the normative approach, but an analyst deliberately sticks to the course of empirical investigation of things. As we shall see, in the period following the Second World War, the fad of political analysis has given a setback to the normative tradition that has been mistakenly designated as the 'decline', nay demise, of political theory.

Importance of the Classics of Political Theory

According to *Oxford English Dictionary,* a classic is a work that is a 'class' by itself, or it is a work of the first rank and of acknowledged excellence. Plato's *Republic,* Aristotle's *Politics,* Machiavelli's *Prince,* Hobbes's *Leviathan,* Locke's *Second Treatise of Civil Government,* Rousseau's *Social Contract,* Hegel's *Philosophy of History* and *Philosophy of Right,* Mill's *Essay on Liberty* and *Considerations on Representative Government,* Green's *Lectures on the Principles of Political Obligation,* Montesquieu's *Spirit of the Laws,* and Marx's *Capital* may be referred to at this stage in particular. In other words, we may say that any work of lasting significance may be ranked in the category of a 'classic'. Such a work must be 'notable for its depth and penetration of insight, conceptual luminosity, freshness of vision, and quality of thought.'[54]

A pertinent question arises as to why we should study these classics of political theory. To answer this question, Dante Germino has given these cogent reasons :[55]

1. It is difficult to imagine a single key concept of political science that does not have its roots in one of the classics of political philosophy The very word 'politics' comes to us from the Greeks ; the symbol 'state' was articulated as a result of the attempt in early modern times to free the governmental power structure from feudal and ecclesiastical control ; and such terms as power, sovereignty, consent, representation, tyranny, democracy, and the public interest have a precise pre-history in the Western intellectual tradition. Thus, the classics of Western political thought have uses for every political scientist, regardless of his field of specialisation. For example, the specialist in public administration can ill-afford to

54. Dante Germino : "The Contemporary Relevance of the Classics of Political Philosophy" in Greenstein and Polsby (ed s) : *Political Science: Scope and Theory* (California : Addison-Wesley, 1975), Vol I, p. 237.
55. *Ibid.*, pp. 230-33.

ignore Rousseau's 'general will' in grappling with the concept of public interest; a student of comparative government who wishes to construct a new typology of governments will want to refer explicitly to the earlier formulations of Aristotle and Montesquieu ; scholars of international politics will wish to be familiar with the teachings on war and peace of St. Augustine, Machiavelli, Hobbes, Grotius, Kant and Hegel ; and those who teach and write about American politics can scarcely be unaware of the influence of Locke and Calvinist tradition on the early American political thought. Nor would it do for students of political behaviour to ignore hypotheses about patterns of political and social change and the conditions of political rule found in Aristotle, Machiavelli, Harrington, Rousseau, Marx and other authors of the past.

2. The study of the classics helps to convince us that politics *per se* is an activity or a process far more extensive than an ordinary way of conceiving it suggests. Certainly some of the preoccupations of the authors of the classics of political philosophy will now seem laboured, strange and foreign to our conventional understanding of competitive electoral politics. And yet, it may be contended that the idea of politics suggested in the 'great conversations', that is, the history of political philosophy, is an *expansion from* rather than an *opposition to* the conventional view of politics accepted today. Thus, for example, Plato turned to philosophical reflection about politics in an attempt to understand better the breakdown of constitutional order in fifth century B.C. Athens; Augustine did so to make sense of the fall of Rome to Alaric the Goth; Machiavelli, in response to the political decadence in the midst of economic and artistic greatness in the fifteenth and sixteenth century Italy; Hobbes, because of the English civil war of the 1640s; and Hegel, after the turmoil of the French revolution and in the wake of the Napoleonic conquests.

3. Political reality is a vast canvas before which we stand and which, with the help of political scientists, we wish to understand more carefully. Political society, in an extended sense, is the dimension of total reality which concerns itself with continuing attempts to order man's life with his fellows in the light of his imperfect but noetically differentiated understanding of the structure of existence. Therefore, political activity, in the larger sense, must be seen as the process of participation by mankind in the drama of humanity. In the more extended but nevertheless concrete and empirical "conception implicit in the work of great political philosophers, politics is the participation of man with his fellows in a greater order of things and the history of philosophy is the continuing story of man's important yet impressive attempts to articulate and symbolise this expression.

On this point an Indian writer makes a fine comment : "If we look at those texts closely, we find that there were also the classical theorists' questions, the ones that they considered important : problems of 'seeing' society. That is why, they are the classics after all. They have a strange way of coming back to relevance. Despite the obituaries that the behaviouralists wrote for them throughout the fifties and sixties, they are not quite obsolete. After the outbreak of the behavioural revolution, political scientists started looking at them rather patronizingly, the way a man would look in museums at his somewhat ridiculous predecessors. They were 'philosophers' ; we are 'scientists'. As it turned out, the advantages were not all on our side. No one would, of course, defend them wholly. Just as no one would claim that the behavioural revolution has been entirely futile, though its critics would claim that it has been, in the main, negatively useful. What political scientists have done over the last twenty years, clearly outlines how not to study politics. The classics, by contrast, clearly thought of the central questions of political processes—relations between economic and political power structures, the role of prejudice, of ideology, problems of establishing causality, totalisation, temporality and their implications. They thought, in other words, of politics in the larger sense, not of its infinitesimal particles after grinding into a fine dust of strictly political events. Behavioural concerns sometimes look trivial in comparison."[56]

In brief, classics of political theory place before us a description or explanation of'political reality' as conceived by the great authors. We may agree with some or disagree with some others, this is a different matter. It is certain that in the field of social sciences, unanimity of approach or similarity of description is impossible. Since politics is a social science, it is futile to expect that all great books speak the same thing about the phenomena of state, government and power. Another important thing to be noted at this stage is that there is no hiatus between what is given in the classics and what is being given to us by contemporary writers. A sort of bridge-building exercise can be done so as to establish a plausible relationship between the voice of the old and the voice of the new. The central concepts of theories contained in the classics "find restatement in the theories of the modern students of politics. Modern scholarship, in fact, contains few fundamental assumptions about the nature of political reality and about what the vital political questions are which are not expressed in one or other of the great books. The new behavioural approaches, despite their great originality, build on the past, some on the naturalism of Machiavelli or Hobbes, others on the *Politics* of Aristotle (Books IV-VI), still others on the teleo-naturalism of J.S. Mill. And besides them we find noumenalist theories in profusion which also draw freely from the classical fountainhead— neo-Platonist, neo-Augustinian, and neo-Thomist theories."[57] The 'classics'of political philosophy, in short, "are thought to contain truths and insights which are of permanent relevance for anyone who thinks philosophically about man and society."[58]

Uses of Political Theory

Political theory, whether ethical, philosophical, historical metaphysical, or scientific, (in other words whether normative. empirical, or trans-empirical) has its own relevance. It is because of the fact that political theory, apart from having its different types, has its uses in which lies an answer to this question as to why anyone should theorise about politics. William Glazer enumerates the following points in this regard :[59]

56. S. Kaviraj : "How Not to Study Method : A Critical Note on Positivist Teaching of Methodology" in Kaviraj and others : *The State of Political Theory*, pp. 30-31.
57. Bluhm, *op. cit*, p. 15.
58. Norman P. Barry : *An Introduction to Modern Political Theory* (London : Macmillan, 1981), pp. 3-4.
59. William A Glazer: "The Types and Uses of Political Theory" in Gould and Thursby, *op. cit.*, pp. 70-88.

1. The study of past political theories and the creation of new theories can be valuable both in constructing scientific laws and in proposing public policy. The need is that the political theorists should clarify what they are trying to do, and then to employ the methods necessary for fulfilling their objectives. An historian of political thought who contributes to something new in this area has produced a great achievement. But the historians of political ideas should broaden their role to become historians of political institutions too. The task of making methodologically valid and useful analyses of political institutions may be left to the historians of political institutions. Such research can be used in contemporary political policy-making and in contemporary political science in many of the same ways as can the findings made by historians of political ideas. Ethical or empirical theories that are logically valid may then be used as modern ethical guides or as scientific models."[60]
2. A theorist may take benefit from the sociology of knowledge technique.[61] That is, he may survey the entire socio-political history of a period, summarise all of that period's political ideas and state broad correlations between the two. There are two ways in which this technique in intellectual history can furnish valuable assistance to the political scientist when he constructs laws about the relationships between the content of thought and socio-political phenomena. First, it can suggest hypotheses which the political scientist can verify in the current world. Second, it can furnish data which supports or casts doubt upon the scientific laws that the political scientist independently derives from analysis of the current world.[62]
3. Some historians of political philosophy attempt to make causal inferences relating certain socio-political phenomena with certain ideas. The scholar may cite the ideas either as the causes or as the effects of the socio-political phenomena. He may designate one particular cause as exclusive, he may cite one particular cause as primary, or he may demonstrate the operation of many equally important causes. Such causal imputations go a step beyond the sociology of knowledge, which merely establishes correlations between the occurrence of specific content of ideas and socio-political phenomena. Some intellectual historians identify a single universal causal law recurring throughout history and in some way relating all political ideas to all socio-political phenomena. It is true that no one can prove that all events are reducible to any one exclusive or primary cause. But such writers can make certain valuable contributions to political science. First, like the sociology-of-knowledge school, they can furnish much evidence

---

60. *Ibid.*, p. 73.
61. Sociology of knowledge' is the attempt to explain the social origins of beliefs that people hold. It is also used by some Marxists to mean that all knowledge in social sciences is *relative* to the particular class position of those who profess it, so that there cannot be *objective* knowledge of society. Norman P. Barry, *op. cit.*, p. xvi.
62. Glazer, *op. cit.*, p. 75.

about correlations between ideas and socio-political phenomena. Second, they can suggest causal hypotheses which political scientists can test[63]

4. A historian of political philosophy can profitably select and adapt certain past ideas; and then he can analyse precisely how much normative ideas might prescribe what should and should not be done at present. Thus, certain enduringly valid ethical norms from the past—after any necessary revision—would help modern men evaluate and solve their practical problems. In this area the historian of political theory would be helping the political policy-maker rather than helping the political scientist. Some intellectual historians have actually attempted to show how the ideas of past writers contain suggestive implications for the present. For example, Richard Crossman demonstrates how Plato's political philosophy constitutes a standard for criticising and solving the problems of modern democracy, and then he shows how certain fundamental weakness in Plato's elitist philosophy make it an inappropriate substitute for modern democracy. Russell Kirk traces the history of the conservative idea on England and America since Burke and he concludes that it can still serve these two countries better than liberalism or socialism. Some writers like G.D.H. Cole, Sidney Hook, Rudolf Schlesinger and Henry Bamford Parkes have examined how the political philosophy of Karl Marx can and cannot help understand, evaluate and solve contemporary social, economic and political problems. Some other writers like J H. Hallowell, Benedetto Croce, Carl J. Friedrich and David Spitz have treated other past philosophers or past currents of thought in a similar fashion whether by using these past ideas as models for contemporary reform, or by using certain past arguments as 'straw men' for defending contemporary values and institutions, or by using these theories as 'straw men' for defending a scholar's own norms.[64]
5. So the scholars of political theory do original normative theorising themselves. They do not apply the arguments of the past writers to current events but originate their own recommendations for public policy. The best of them—Reinhold Niebuhr, for example—combine clear ethical or theological premises, logic and knowledge of the practical world, in order to produce a political philosophy which is insightful, internally consistent, and realistic. A scholar who aspires to such work needs a thorough grounding in contemporary ethics and theology, logical habit of thinking, and knowledge of the real world. Since scholars are professional thinkers, they should be expected to conform to such rigorous standards in their policy recommendations.[65]
6. Political theory can be useful as a source of conceptual frameworks, operational concepts, and logical relationships for the use of political scientists. Realisation that theoretical insights are indispensable to reliable understanding of the empirical world has become a commonplace principle of the modern philosophy of science—in both the natural sciences and the social sciences. To create new analytical methods and testable hypotheses is the work of the imagination, and

63. *Ibid.*, pp. 78-79.
64. *Ibid.*, *p.* 80.
65. *Ibid.*, pp. 81-82.

this accomplishment could be the theory-minded scholar's greatest contribution to the progress of political science. Where political theorists have contributed something, it is the formulation of the frames of reference (or conceptual frameworks) within which schools of political scientists have worked. A frame of reference is an overall viewpoint which determines how the political scientist selects and thus specifies research techniques, and how he will perceive his data, and which suggests many hypotheses to him. A frame of reference constitutes the fundamental habits of thinking which the scientist carries into research. Some frames of reference that guide contemporary political scientists were either created or perfected by political theorists. For example, Bentley's picture of politics as a competition among pressure groups has been widely adopted by scientists seeking regularities in electoral behaviour, in legislative voting, in administrative behaviour and the like.[66]

7. The political theorist can also furnish concepts for a scientific analysis. Every scientist requires clear and precisely defined concepts according to which the data can be quantified and arranged in an intelligent and manageable fashion. There are many questions that must be satisfactorily answered before concepts can be scientifically useful and the political theorist—who is a specialist in imaginative construction—could make a great contribution in solving them. For instance, we may refer to terms like 'political party', 'pressure group', 'political behaviour of a non-political group', role of 'power' or 'influence' in the decision-making process etc. Many other concepts can be exhaustively classified and clarified and made scientifically operational in political science.[67]
8. The political theorist may also help the political scientist by suggesting how valid relationships may be stated when describing data. For example, from the recent literature in logic and in the philosophy of science, and also from his original theorising, the political theorist may inform a political scientist about the nature of causality, probability and predictability. He may also prescribe as to what should be the quantity and type of facts that must be found before a law concerning certain political phenomena might be stated at a particular degree of probability. Besides setting forth such abstract logical relationships, the political theorist may also collaborate directly with a political scientist by showing how particular generalisations about certain designated political data might satisfy logical requirements and thereby become scientific laws.[68]
9. Besides clarifying existing logical relationships and constructing new statements for the use of political scientists, a political theorist should also help to construct a new language, if needed, for describing political relationships. The political theorists should help the political scientists, think through the question of how (if at all) such special languages may fruitfully be employed in political science. They should also collaborate with the mathematicians and logicians in adapting

66. *Ibid.*, p. 82.
67. *Ibid.*, p. 83.
68. *Ibid.*, pp. 84-85.

any existing models, and in inventing new models that may be needed for analysing and generalising about politics.[69]

10. Not only can the political theorist construct new concepts and methodologies for use by the political scientists, but he can also perfect existing models by making constructive criticisms of past research. Here, the political theorist would be seeking to improve the efficiency of techniques and the clarity with which research findings are expressed. He might also be able to establish the degree to which the research data support research findings and therefore the degree to which these findings may be considered to be scientific laws. Empirical proof depends upon success in prediction. But the political theorist can judge the form in which findings are presented. It is necessary that the political theorist must be acquainted with the literature of political science and must work closely with the political scientist in order to understand the latter's general analytical problems and the particular empirical situation to be investigated. In many cases the role of a political theorist and a political scientist may be combined in the same person.[70]

In short, political theory can be of great use to a political scientist if this salient point is borne in mind that in his formulations, theory and facts should supplement each other. As he says: "If the study of theory and the study of facts do not fertilise each other, both will be barren.... Theorising without relevance to fact is a dilettantish rather than a useful contribution; and fact-finding without theory produces a jumble that is either wholly useless or is used to justify defective empirical or ethical propositions....Political theory must be combined with policy-making and political science."[71]

Many new dimensions to the study of political science have been added in recent times as a result of which different kinds of theories and sub-theories have come into being and more than that the word 'theory' itself has become interchangeable with other words like hypothesis, paradigm, model and the like. These have also been labelled as 'grand', 'medium' and 'narrow' gauge theories, conceptual frameworks, taxonomies, typologies, approaches and the like. But a defender of the new dimensions of political theory may contend that all these current political theories "are useful in the interpretation of ordinary political life because they provide alternative perspectives through which to view the political world. The individual can enhance his understanding of the political situations that he reads about and the political activities in which he engages by adopting different viewpoints. By adopting different perspectives the individual clarifies, generalises and revitalises his predicament. All of these uses of political theory are important to the attainment of good life."[72]

69. *Ibid.*, pp. 84-85.
70. *Ibid.*, p. 85.
71. *Ibid.*, *p.* 86.
72. M.A. Weinstein : *Systematic Political Theory* (Columbus. Chio : Charles Merrill Pub., 1971), p. 128.

Hacker's Formulations on How to Understand and Appreciate Political Theory

1. *Capital and Carbuncles:* It should be seen as to how a particular writer comes to produce a particular book in a particular way at a particular time. It may be Machiavelli's spleen in the form of a 'bad-tempered explosion', or Marx's carbuncles, or Rousseau's bladder. The validity of a theory ought to stand or fall on the merits of the written text itself. A literary work can be good, true or beautiful even if its author is a rouge, a knave or even an anonymous scribe whose name and character are no longer known to us.
2. *Lost Laundry Lists:* Only some important works must be studied and the rest discarded. The student must be discriminating and he must always ask whether minor writings or anything of the sort is of any importance to a writer's theoretical arguments. Those who search after lost laundry lists have ceased to concern themselves with the study of politics.
3. *Pursuits of Pedigree:* One should not go deep into the influencing factors or establishing similarities between great theorists. Ideas never emerge in a vacuum, it is true. On the other hand, an intelligent theorist is quite capable of coming to conclusions about political reality without the help of influencing predecessors. At all events the tracing of pedigrees is bound to be speculative, and it contributes very little to our knowledge of politics.
4. *Nothing New under the Sun:* There is nothing absolutely original in the field of politics as in the case of other social sciences. What makes a theorist great is the way of his treatment and description. For instance, the importance of Marx is that he took the thoughts of others and integrated them in a new and persuasive way. Shakespeare did not invent the words of the English language, but he was able to combine them in a way that no one before him had done.
5. *Meaningful Representations:* The significance of political theory lies in the mind of the reader rather than in the actual motives of its author. The search for hidden motives (as in the case of Machiavelli and Hobbes) has very little relevance to the study of political theory.
6. *Representative Reflections:* Indeed, a book on political theory represents the thoughts of its author and perhaps those of some kindred intellectuals who like to think in theoretical terms. In any historical period, the vast majority of people do not think much at all, and such sentiments as arise in their minds, are represented, not by learned texts but by the popular press and political oratory. In the final analysis, one of the claims to greatness of the historical writings is that they are representative of their time, they are not bound by the immediate needs of the period, and they dwell on the enduring questions of politics. Much the same error is made if it is assumed that a book on theory gives an accurate depiction of contemporaneous institutions and behaviour. Works like Walter Bagehot's *English Constitution* and A. de Tocqueville's *American Democracy,* etc. are like convenient caricatures rather than objective analyses of certain political institutions at a particular time. The student of politics is, therefore, obliged to know a good deal about social and political history, but he must not suppose that he can acquire this knowledge from the texts on political theory.
7. *Influential Intellects:* Action precedes theory in most of the cases. As such, works written by men of action have an importance of their own in this connection. Hence, one should study the works of Locke, Rousseau, Montesquieu, Robbespierre,

Madison and Jackson. The writings of Marx, Engels and Lenin have a like relevance. There have been hundreds of significant events in politics which were inspired by no theory at all. The danger in attempting to show the influence of theory on practice is that the process actually works the other way round. The politician occasionally uses the words and phrases of a theorist to justify his actions. But when he does this, he does not draw on a theory as a theory. On the contrary, he selects those portions which suit his purposes and then simplifies and circulates them for popular consumption. It is the politician, then, who gives a public representation to the intellectual. The student of politics does well not to concern himself with the supposed influence of the books he reads. These writings have importance because they are a means to understanding political reality, and they would have this importance even if they were never introduced into the practical arena. The historical texts have their greatest value in that the theories they offer transcend the times and the personalities which produced them. In this sense, they are timeless and, in an important respect, anonymous.

Source: Hacker: *Political Theory,* pp. 13-19.

Concluding Observations

Following important impressions may be gathered from what we have said in the preceding sections :

1. Like other sciences, the science of politics has witnessed marvellous development. Alexander Hamilton in Ninth Paper of the *Federalist* says well that the 'efficacy of various principles is now well understood, which were either not known at all, or imperfectly known to the ancients.'[73] If so, the meaning and nature of the word 'political' have also changed to a surprising extent. The theory of politics is not merely concerned with the themes of state and government ; it has become wide enough to deal with everything that is related to 'power', 'influence' and 'political activity'. That is, it is concerned with everything that forms part of a man's 'political activity' ; its main purpose is to comprehend and explain 'political reality'. It shows that the frontiers of political theory have expanded so as to include within themselves three central processes—"the selection of society's preferences, the enforcement of the choices that revealed them, and, finally, the production of goals and outputs that embody the choices. The art of politics is the actual selection, enforcement and production."[74]
2. The development of political theory has created a problem in its own way. It is running in various directions some of which have just an incidental connection with the basic theme of politics. It leads to the problem as to what political theory now really includes. Sometimes, it appears that political theory in recent times has lost its autonomous character ; it has become a handmaid of some other discipline like sociology or psychology. The normative side of political theory has been discarded and a mad craze for scientism has imparted a new

73. Cited, in Bernard Crick : *In Defence of Politics* (London : Weidenfeld and Nicolson, 1962), p. 144.
74. W.H. Riker and P.C. Ordeshook : *An Introduction to Positive Political Theory* (Englewood Cliffs, New Jersey : Prentice-Hall, 1973), p. 2.

complexion to it so much so that it has been dubbed by some critics as the decline, nay demise, of political theory. Theories ranging from metaphysical idealism and scientific socialism to nihilism and existentialism constitute the stock of the puzzle : whether political theory exists. But a keen and conscientious student of political theory takes it all in a different way. To him the expanding frontiers of political theory are engaging and interesting. It should be taken as the surprising enrichment of political theory.[75]

3. Political theory in recent times looks like hovering somewhere between the poles of philosophy and science. It is neither pure philosophy, nor is it pure science in spite of the fact that it is an important branch of the discipline of political science. As we shall see in the following chapters, it is losing its connection more and more with the discipline of philosophy and drawing closer and closer to that of a science. The saner and wiser course is that a political theorist should play the role of a philosopher as well as of a scientist so as to keep this study enriched with the fruits of the innate wisdom of man as well as to bring it out of the intricacies of metaphysics. It is well counselled : "Every political theorist worthy of the name plays a double role....He is part scientist and part philosopher and he will divide his time between the two pursuits according to his own temperament and interests ...What is important to bear in mind is that no theorist can make a lasting contribution to human knowledge unless he works in the realms of both the science and the philosophy. The scientific part of a theory can only achieve coherence and significance if the writer has a preconceived idea of the goals of political life."[76]
4. Perhaps the most important problem besetting contemporary political theory is not the question of whether theory ought to be firmly wedded to the method and outlook of the natural sciences, but rather what version of science it will choose : the rigorous fact-minded, anti-conceptual view which believes that cumulative knowledge is the result of patient and dogged application of scientific methods or the view of science as an imaginative undertaking, with its full share of speculation, playfulness, proclivity to error, and its ability to imagine worlds as yet undreamed of— an ability which would maintain the critical, projective quality that has enabled past theories to speak meaningfully to the quandaries of political existence."[77]
5. Political theory has its own relevance in modern times in spite of the fact that it is involved in a serious quest of identity. The Marxists treat liberal political theory as *status quoist,* the liberal theorist belonging to the behavioural and post-behavioural schools strive to offer an alternative to the political theory of a pernicious 'ideology'. Much literature has come out of a debate on such points. The classics of political theory have not become a dead weight; still the new theorists strive to draw inspiration from them in their own right. Instead of taking sides in an ideological debate, a student of political theory should

75. For a very interesting study in this direction, see Isaiah Berlin : "Does Political Theory Still Exist ?" in Gould and Thursby, *op. cit.,* pp. 328-57.
76. Hacker, *op. cit.* p. 2.
77. S.S. Wolin in *International Encyclopaedia, op. cit.,* p. 329.

Political Theory Today

Political theory is an interdisciplinary endeavour whose centre of gravity lies at the humanities end of the happily still undisciplined discipline of political science. Its traditions, approaches and styles vary, but the field is united by a commitment to theorise, critique, and diagnose the norms, practices and organisation of political action in the past and present, in our own places and elsewhere.

—J.S. Dryzek, B. Honing and A. Phillips

"Overview of Political Theory" in R.E. Goodin (ed.): *The Oxford Handbook of Political Science* (Oxford: Oxford University Press, 2009), p.62.

Political theory confronts a number of problems and challenges as it enters the twenty-first century. Threatened in the mid-twentieth century by positivism, which suggested that the entire tradition of normative political thought is meaningless, political theory revived after the 1960s. However, it has subsequently become diffuse and fragmented.

—Andrew Heywood

Political Theory: An Introduction (New York: Palgrave, Macmillan, 2005) p.14.

The intellectual landscape in political philosophy today is quite different from what it was twenty or even ten years ago. The arguments being advanced are often genuinely original, not only in developing new variations on old themes but also in the development of new perspectives. One result of these developments is that the traditional categories within which political theories are discussed and evaluated are increasingly inadequate.

—Will Kymlicka

Contemporary Political Philosophy: An Introduction (Oxford: Oxford University Press, 2005), p.1.

appreciate the new definition that it is a study of man's 'political activity'. And as Crick says, a political activity "is a kind of a moral activity; it is free activity, and it is inventive, flexible, enjoyable and human; it can create some sense of community and yet it is not, for instance, a slave to nationalism; it does not claim to settle every problem or to make every sad heart glad, but it can help some way in nearly everything and, where it is strong it can prevent the vast cruelties and deceits of ideological rule.'[78]

In short, political theory is the study *of polis* (state), government, power, influence and activity. It is a way of comprehending, describing, and explaining political reality. To some extent, it has the capacity to make predictions about things to come. However, as theorising is a very difficult task, political theory is the contribution of the very few. Moreover, as every genius has his own frame of mind, political theory is bound to be 'committed' in that way. The element of human subjectivity has its inevitable place in it. It is well observed : "Political theory requires a political conscience. It is no enterprise of those who are unable to care deeply about the world in which they live. To be sure, the play of conscience is prone to distort perception and to influence theory with ideology. The price, however, is well worth paying. For without the stir of emotion, it is important to come to grips with the significant questions of an age."[79]

78. Bernard Crick, *op. cit.*, p. 136.
79. Andrew Hacker, *op. cit.*, p. 19.

2

Forms, Traditions and Problems of Political Theory

> There can be no such thing as 'pure' prescription or objective political philosophy. A philosopher is obliged to demonstrate that he understands what may reasonably be expected of men and societies in their pursuit of political goals. It is left to each reader to ask where the scientific part of a theory stops and the philosophy begins. It is his responsibility as well to ascertain how far and at what junctions one influences the other.
>
> **—Andrew Hacker[1]**

Political theory is as old as the Indians, the Chinese, the Hebrews, the Egyptians, the Greeks, and the Romans, though it is a different matter that the Greeks deserve the credit of being its originators owing to their special contributions. What is, however, noticeable in this direction is that the forms and traditions of political theory have varied from time to time at the hands of leading thinkers, theorists and analysts. Broadly, there are two forms of political theory—classical and modern—each having its distinctive features. While the former is mainly of a *normative* character and, for that reason, a political theorist looks like a *political philosopher,* the latter is predominantly *empirical* with the result that a theorist of this subject looks like a *political scientist.* But we cannot draw a Chinese wall between the two traditions. The peculiar features of both overlap and it would be a mistake to say that the discipline has never had a clear conception of its content.[2] One more point that should be noted at this stage is that the subject of political theory has been a matter of diverse interpretations with the result that it looks like terribly caught up in a welter of controversies. It informs some to come forward with an alternative position claiming that it "is a waste of time to attempt an explicit definition of politics."[3] Such a view is also untenable in view of the fact that diverse interpretations of political theories have their own share in the enrichment of this subject.[4]

---

1. Hacker: *Political Theory* (New York: Macmillan, 1969), p. 3.
2. Albert Somit and Joseph Tanenhaus: *The Development of American Political Science: From Burgess to Behaviouralism* (Boston: Allyn and Beacon, 1967), p. 24. In 1896 More Stephens reported that he had not been able to find anyone, after teaching this subject for two years, who could tell him precisely what political science was. *Ibid.*
3. A.C. Isaak: *Scope and Methods of Political Science* (Homewood, Illinois: The Dorsey Press, 1969), p. 9.
4. See Elizabeth James: *Political Theory* (Chicago: Rand McNally, 1976), p. 4.

Classical Political Theory: Alignment of Politics with Ethics and Philosophy and Search for a Perfect Political Order

In general terms, political theory is categorised into 'classical' and 'modern' forms. While the former is speculative and for this reason abstract, the latter is empirical and for that reason 'scientific'. Simply stated, the former refers to the diverse thought systems developed in the ancient age from sixth century B.C. to the decline of the Roman empire in the fifth century A D. Obviously, it covers the political ideas of a very large number of Greek and Roman thinkers from Solon and Pericles to Cicero and St. Augustine. Naturally, it includes the study of many schools of thought like those of the Sophists, the Sceptics, the Epicureans, the Cynics and the Cyrenaics. However, as Plato and Aristotle are the two great giants of the ancient age, classical political theory, in a restricted sense, means a study of these two Greek thinkers. Moreover, as Plato is the teacher of Aristotle and as the dialogues of Plato provide a starting point to the thought of Aristotle in most of the cases, classical political theory, in the most restricted sense, may be said to have its particular manifestation in the works of Plato.[5]

Some important features of the classical political theory, as given by Sibley, are as under:[6]

1. ***Personality and State :*** The basic framework of classical political theory is the conception of the 'soul' in its relation to 'society' and 'state'. The soul is the essence of the principle of life in a man and a man is a full man only in an organised—and, when complete, in a rationally organised —society. Men are not men except in society and therefore the individual 'soul' can achieve its *telos* or end only through sharing in the life of the group. Only in this sense, is the individual subservient to the state or 'absorbed' by the state or rather organised groups. And it should be remembered that in both Plato and Aristotle the political 'Good of State' is strictly subordinate to the ultimate moral 'Good' in which both States and souls participate and for which they are in constant search. In short, the purpose of the state is the production of best possible human beings.
2. ***Three Factors in Politics:*** Plato speaks about the tripartite conception of the soul. Reason, courage and appetite are the three elements of human personality, though the first one is the most important. The rational element enables man to know the distinction between good and bad. Since the ruler of the state (philosopher-king) alone can comprehend the Idea of the Good, his authority is absolute over the well-organised society. Both the state and the soul are such wholes when rationally organised and both, in turn, find their overriding end in the Idea of the Good or Righteousness. Political science is, therefore, both scientific and normative. It is scientific in the sense that it systematically studies 'facts' and the 'laws' behind them, and it is normative because here a goal (good life) is set before the state and the individual.

---

5. Mulford Q. Sibley: "The Place of Classical Political Theory in the Study of Politics: The Legitimate Spell of Plato" in Ronald Young (ed): *Approaches to the Study of Politics* (Evanston, Illinois: Northwestern University Press, 1958), p. 125.
6. *Ibid.*, pp. 128-33.

3. ***Three-Factor Analysis of Organisation:*** It can be applied to all organised purposeful human activity. Every organisation is 'political' in the sense that it must formulate, implement, and evaluate policies for itself. It is also political in the sense of being built around a single purpose—common good. Plato and Aristotle are conscious of politics as the integrating factor of civilised life. Thus, the three-factor analysis implies, first, a factor of rationality that is behind the organisation of any society or community. Second, every organisation embodies within itself an element of 'spirit'. It smacks of the capacity for righteous indignation at injustice of any kind. Last, there is the factor of *sophrosyne* or 'reasonable limits' that keeps all the elements of human personality in a harmonious situation.
4. ***Disintegration in Organisation:*** No political order is stable for all times to come. One system disintegrates and another one comes up. This may be called the law of political degeneracy. Monarchy is replaced by aristocracy and aristocracy by democracy. Aristotle is very clear on this point in his theory of the cycle of change. To him change from one system to another is a matter of inevitability. It amounts to a revolution. Both Plato and Aristotle give certain 'ideal' types of different forms of political systems, though both disfavour the course of a revolution. A solution to this difficulty is found in the search for a best possible state that may be a 'sophocracy', to Plato, and a 'polity', to his student (Aristotle).
5. ***Ideas and Understanding of Politics:*** The theme of classical political theory is contained in search for a perfect political order. It makes it 'utopian', no matter the picture offered by the writers is a grand one. Here, a goal is set before the existing imperfect political systems. It is true that what Plato presents in the *Republic* is modified in the *Laws* (where supremacy of a super-man is replaced by the supremacy of the laws) and that Aristotle takes inspiration from the second best state of his teacher, and yet it may be pointed out that even the best state of Aristotle called 'polity' (being a mixture of the oligarchical and democratic elements signifying power in the hands of the middle class) is a Utopia though of a lesser degree as compared to the ideal state of Plato set in the *Republic*.

The tradition of classical political theory has its strong adherents in a very large number of thinkers belonging to modern age. Thus, we may see reflections of the ideas of Plato and Aristotle in the works of Rousseau, Kant, Hegel, Green, Bosanquet, Laski, Oakeshott, Leo Strauss, etc. Wolin studies the case of classical political theory in a wider perspective and sums up its main features as under:[7]

1. Political theory is the practice of systematic inquiry whose aim is to acquire reliable knowledge about matters concerning the political province. Knowledge is valued as the supreme means of improving the quality of human life in the political association. As a political pursuit, it seeks to establish a rational basis for belief; as a politically inspired pursuit, it seeks to establish a rational basis for action.
2. It identifies the political with the common involvements which men share by virtue of their membership of the same *polis* (state). The Romans of the republican

---

7. S.S. Wolin: "Political Theory: Trends and Goals" in David I. Sills (ed.): *International Encyclopaedia of the Social Sciences* (New York: Macmillan and Free Press, 1968), pp. 319-21.

period called their political order a *'res publica'* (literally a public thing); the same idea was reflected in the sixteenth century English usage of commonwealth. Theory is not restricted to the problems of securing and extending the common benefits of political life; it is shaped by the sobering recognition that these are common predicaments and a common fate issuing from politics and that the ordinary evils besetting human existence tend to be magnified by politics because where power is concentrated, the possibilities of injustice and violence, whether intended or inadvertent, are enhanced.

3. It deals with political wholes, or it must be as comprehensive and inclusive as the political conviction itself. A moral concern with the quality of political life provides the impetus for developing analytical methods and concepts.
4. Theory is preoccupied with analysing the sources of conflict and trying to enunciate the principles of justice which might guide the political association in discharging its distributive function of assigning material and non-material goods in the context of competing claims. The attempt to explain disorder leads classical theory to develop that basic political vocabulary of diagnosis: instability, anarchy, anomie, and revolution.
5. From the beginning it has insisted upon the significance of comparative studies for supplying a more comprehensive form of explanation and a wider range of alternatives. In order to cope with the many and diverse phenomena introduced by comparative studies, classical theory develops a diversification of political forms (e.g., monarchy, aristocracy, democracy, their variants and their perversions) and a set of concepts which enable a theorist to place comparable phenomena side by side. Concepts such as law, citizenship, participation, and justice are used to order the relevant phenomena, thus preparing the way for an explanation which would account for differences and similarities.
6. The theoretical imagination of the classical writers looks challenged more by the diversity of political phenomena disclosed by comparison than by the regularities. This response is rooted in a moral outlook which conceives of a constitution as a manifestation of the particular culture. Each constitution represents distinct beliefs about the ordering of society, the treatment of individuals and classes, the possession and distribution of power, the qualifications for participating in political deliberations, and the promotion of certain collective values. Theory undertakes to appraise the various constitutional forms, to determine the form most suitable for a particular set of circumstances and, above all, to decide whether it is the only absolutely best form.
7. Search for an absolutely best form of state reveals, as perhaps nothing else does, the intellectual boldness and radicalism of classical theorising. The creation of an ideal state is the best way of teaching the fundamental elements of theorising; the reduction of the world to manageable proportions and its simultaneous reassembling in a new way so that others may see concentrated relationships of the whole. Far from being an ideal pastime, the projection of an ideal state provides an invaluable means of practising theory and of acquiring experience in its handling. Moreover, classical theorising hopes to effect an alliance between thought and action, which would lead to the world becoming the embodiment

of a theory. This is exactly opposite to what is the main motive of theorising inspired by modern science, which is to make theory into a miniature of the world.

No doubt, speculations of Plato and Aristotle about the phenomenon of state are so deep as well as so vast that they perhaps touch every possible area of political inquiry. That is, the works of these two great political thinkers have a significance of their own. Sibley earmarks these important points in this direction:[8]

1. ***First Systematic Political Discussion*** : Politics involves the formulation, speculation and execution of 'public policy' and the distribution of power in a human society. A full comprehension of the political phenomena embraces an understanding of the way in which men in all ages and cultures actually formulate and implement public policy as well as of the goals which they achieve, thoughts they are achieving, or thoughts that they ought to achieve. Such speculations were made by the Jews and the Egyptians in remote past, but Plato is the first thinker to make political questions the centre of his attention and to ask certain epistemological, metaphysical, and ethical questions that must arise in any political inquiry.
2. ***Illumination of Greek Politics*** : The works of Plato and Aristotle cast light on the theory and practice of politics in Greece of the fourth century B.C. If the Greek city-states are significant examples of the ways in which men have been organised politically, then the classical political theorists certainly give us important clues as to their development and functioning. These are not dead but have remained very much alive.
3. ***Scientific Method*** : Plato and Aristotle are the earliest thinkers to lay down the very notion of 'scientific' method in politics. They are the great pioneers in suggesting that the apparently multifarious phenomena of political life may be tied together by underlying patterns of principles and that men can, through rationality and observation, know these patterns despite the fact that we may disagree with the notion that these patterns have a metaphysical reality.
4. ***Shaping of Institutions and Ideas*** : The ideas of Plato and Aristotle have had an enormous effect on the way in which institutions have actually developed and even on the manner in which people have thought about politics. In its broadest sense, understanding politics means not only the comprehension, through whatever tools are available, of the actual way in which men have conducted themselves politically but also an understanding of how they explained reality and what they thought of as desirable goals. For instance, during the Middle Ages when ecclesiastical political theory wrestled with the problem of reconciling the primitive Christian hostility to the state with the apparent permanence of the state as an institution, Plato, to some extent, became a tool with which writers sought to uphold the idea that, while private property would be defended as an institution justified by natural law, communism was an ideal. Gratian, the great codifier of canon law, supports the ideal of communism by reference not only to the practice of the primitive Church at Jerusalem but also on the authority

8. Sibley, *op. cit.*, pp. 128-33.

of Plato. The prohibition of clerical marriage after Pope Gregory VII is largely from motives which animated Plato in the construction of his ruling class. The medieval notion of the universals owes much to the *Timaeus* of Plato.

5. ***Influence of Political Ideas*** : The picture of an ideal state as given in the *Republic* has its reflection in the *Utopia* of More, the *Oceana* of Harrington and the *Social Contract* of Rousseau. The idealist trend set by Plato and Aristotle has its clear reflection in the ideas of Kant, Fichte and Hegel of Germany and Green, Bradley, Bosanquet and Nettleship of Britain. That is, the Platonic line may be seen coming down to the writings of Leo Strauss. Likewise, Aristotle's empirical politics has its impact on a very large number of contemporary social theorists like R.M. Maclver and S.M. Lipset.

On the basis of all these arguments, Sibley comes to assert that the value of classical political theory "is twofold. It is, first, a phase of the history of ideas and institutions and, therefore, important in an *historical* sense. Secondly, it constitutes a set of principles of possible system of hypotheses about politics conceived as a universal aspect and experience of life—and is, consequently, significant *analytically*."[9]

Classical political theory is criticised for being abstract, deductive, hypothetical and thus 'unscientific'. The main argument of the critics is that it is heavily value-laden or goal-oriented and, as such, its formulations cannot be put to an empirical investigation. Hence, in modern times, political theory should be recast in a way that it assumes the character of a scientific discipline. As we shall see in the following sections, modern political theory is in a quest of this kind. The view of the modern theorists is that science provides us with causal laws or mechanisms which operate in a particular field; it also tells us which variables or conditions we must manipulate in order to achieve results that we desire. Prediction is also necessary that implies the 'desirability of control'.[10] A leading exponent of the modern, rather contemporary, political theory like G.A. Almond lays strong emphasis on the need for "an explanatory, predictive and manipulative political theory that can be used to solve the problem of violence and coercion in human affairs."[11]

Despite such criticisms, the value of classical political theory has not been totally discarded. A minority of new theorists like Michael Oakeshott, Isaiah Berlin, John Plamenatz, Leo Strauss and Dante Germino have been at the forefront of the crusade to save the classical tradition from total eclipse. In defence of the classical tradition, Germino contends: "The philosophical political scientist is on a safer ground *qua* philosopher if he speaks 'against what he concludes to be abuses of power that threaten the unity of mankind (as in condemning an unjust war, or the prosecution of political dissenters, or the injustices of the racial discrimination) than he is in *advocating* specific reforms or policies which lie at the area of decision by the practical

9. Sibley, *op. cit.*, p. 33.
10. See M.J. Falco: *Truth and Meaning in Political Science* (Columbus, Ohio: Charles Merril Pub'. 1973), p. 55. About the real nature of scientific theories J. Habermas says: "Scientific theories are validated in the context of successful instrumental action, whether in experiments or in technological applications." *Knowledge and Human Interests* (Boston: Beacon Press 1971), Part II.
11. See Almond: "Political Theory and Political Science" in I. de Sola Pool (ed.): *Contemporary Political Science* (New York: McGraw Hill, 1967), pp.7 and 10.

reason and where no obvious and fundamental violation of the right by nature or by right philosophically understood (Hegel) has occurred."[12]

Modern Political Theory : Dominance of Empiricism – In Quest of a Science of Politics

A fundamental change occurred in the social and economic spheres after 1500 A.D. that had its natural effect on the political conditions of the European countries. The inventions of science created industrial revolution. A new class (bourgeois class) emerged that procreated another new class (middle class) to maintain itself in the political sphere. This new class desired to have a share in political power. Thus, a new movement started that saw its culmination in the triumph of the representative system of government. The system of absolute monarchy was replaced by the system of liberal democracy. The social and political theorists justified the case of constitutionalism and liberalism. The defenders of the new economic order justified the case of 'capitalism', while its critics threw more and more light on its discredited character and, instead, advocated a new system of socialism. A French theorist named August Comte gave the new line of 'positivism' and advised social and political theorists to study politics in positive (scientific) terms. The net result of all this was that the 'utopias' were replaced by a hard-headed analysis of "the failings of the current world."[13]

The new trend is said to have begun with Thomas Hobbes who studied politics in terms of 'power' and a ceaseless struggle for it in which a man remains involved till the last moment of his life.[14] This line was faithfully accepted by Max Weber of Germany and through him it came over to the United States where Charles Merriam became its ardent advocate. Easton, Apter, Almond, Dahl and Lasswell subscribe to this line and so they all may be termed 'modernists'. In the period following the Second World War, this line became so powerful that a very large number of American theorists made it a sort of their commitment to study politics as something emanating from the behaviour of human beings as members of a political community. As a result, behaviouralism became a dominant trend of modern political theory. It all looked like a powerful assault on the traditional political theory that was described by some as the decline, even demise, of political theory. In other words, the emergence of a strong positivist and scientific line among the empirical political scientists after the Second World War was, therefore, only the least of a long line of events which "profoundly undermined the strength of political theory and the self-assurance of those who practised it."[15]

---

12. Dante Germino; "The Contemporary Relevance of the Classics of Political Philosophy" in F. Greenstein and N. Polsby (ed. s): *Political Science: Scope and Theory* (California: Addison-Wesley, 1975), Vol. I, p. 255.
13. Jean Blondel: *The Discipline of Politics* (London: Butterworths, 1981), p. 139.
14. This point should, however, be studied with a caution that the political theory of Hobbes "was hardly empirical by contemporary standards, yet it remains the first systematic effort to assimilate political to scientific and mathematical reasoning. At the same time the Hobbesian political order was in no sense a replication of what the political world was like, but rather a projection of what it must or should be." Wolin, *op. cit.*, p. 326.
15. Blondel, *op. cit.*, p. 140.

It may, therefore, be easily suggested that the features of modern political theory are emphasis on empiricism, dissatisfaction with the Utopias, search for making politics a science, alternative vision of society on causal lines, and a critical examination of the underlying premises of political and social sciences. From all this, it is increasingly evident that "in order to gain a critical understanding of the social and political disciplines, we must face not only epistemological but metaphysical issues."[16]

The main features of modern, rather contemporary, political theory may be thus enumerated:[17]

1. To a very large extent, the relationship of political science with ethics and philosophy has been severed. Although there are some signs of attempts being made to utilise contemporary philosophical techniques of language analysis and its variants, most theorists proceed on the assumption that the adoption of scientific methods obviates the need for elaborate philosophical techniques. The new trend is to align the study of politics with other social sciences like economics, sociology, psychology and social anthropology so that the laws of this discipline may be subjected to an empirical verification.
2. The contemporary conventions reject so-called grand or comprehensive theories and prefer to pursue tenable hypotheses. Analysis has tended to replace theory as the preferred expression. This change is accompanied by a determination to utilise whatever methods appear to have scientific authority—survey data, sociological and psychological findings, decision-making, bargaining, communication theories, etc. Those of an empirical and quantitative persuasion frequently express the hope that by patient and systematic investigation, it will be possible to establish tested propositions of ever-increasing generality and that gradually, an inter-connected and logically consistent series of propositions will culminate in a general theory of universal validity.
3. Theorising tends to be sustained by the belief that the political world exhibits sufficiently recurrent regularities and repetition of causal consequences to allow for the testing of generalisations. Theory thus becomes the search for what is repetitious, ubiquitous and uniform.
4. Traditional theory had been powerfully influenced by the hope of providing knowledge for action; its language, concepts and various values were primarily those of the actors. Contemporary theory with its emphasis upon objectivity, scientific detachment, and testable hypotheses tends to be governed by the values of inquiry rather than of potential action.[18] This appears most strikingly in systems theory where conceptions such as equilibrium, homeostatis, feedback, inputs and outputs are, whatever their value for research, wholly irrelevent to action. For the present, at least, theory appears to have surrendered the critical function which has been one of its dominant characteristics since Plato.

---

16. R.J. Bernstein: *The Restructuring of Social and Political Theory* (Oxford: Basil Blackwell, 1976), p. 117.
17. Wolin, *op. cit.*, pp. 327-29.
18. As Robert A. Dahl says: "Whether the proposition is true or false depends upon the degree to which the proposition and the real world correspond." *Modern Political Analysis* (Englewood Cliffs. New Jersey : Prentice-Hall, 1976), p. 8.

5. It is fair to say that most scientifically-minded theorists today are bored by the fact-value controversy and are trying to negotiate an armistice along the lines of the division of political theory into 'empirical' and 'normative' theories. The former would represent theorising based upon scientific methods of collecting and classifying data and of testing hypotheses by statistical or mathematical methods. Its goal would be the empirically verified hypothesis. To normative theory would be assigned an ill-assorted collection of activities whose common element would be a lack of scientific method. It would include all questions regarding value, all historcal studies, and all conceptual inquiries.[19]

One important point about contemporary political theory, that should be taken note of at this stage, is that it has the phases of empiricism and neo-empiricism. While the empiricists are staunch 'modernists' who stick exclusively to the side of 'facts' in the study of politics and thereby endeavour to impart politics the character of a 'science', the neo-empiricists are those who, after feeling disillusioned with a purely causal theory of politics, prefer to accord some place to the role of values, goals and norms in the study of politics. And yet the neo-empiricists cannot be taken as 'traditionalists' who contributed to the stock of an ethicised or philosophised study of politics. In other words, while the traditionalists are non-positivists, the neo-empiricists are neo-positivists. It all may be traced in the latest trend of post-behaviouralism when a leading exponent of this kind of political theory like David Easton advises us to think over the reaffirmation of norms and values in the study of politics.[20]

In modern, including contemporary, political theory, empiricism overshadows normativism though without discarding it in entirety. It is due to this that the combination of normative and empirical analysis "is at the heart of the discipline of politics. This is why, there is not just a case but a basic need for a general political theory which is concerned, as in the past, with the analysis of values and with the determination of the conditions under which these values can be translated into broad institutional arrangements. But this is also why more perhaps than before,

---

19. See Easton : *A Framework for Political Analysis* (Englewood Cliffs, New Jersey : Prentice-Hall, 1965), p 15. It is the task of theory to detect in the unique facts of experience that which is uniform, similar and typical. See H.J. Morgenthau : "The Nature and Limits of Theory in International Relations" in W.T.R. Fox (ed.) : *Theoretical Aspects of International Relations* (University of Notre Dame Press, 1959), pp. 15-28.

20. Even a little earlier, Easton says : "What is true of research in general is no less true of systematic theory. Without attempting to argue here what I have sought to demonstrate elsewhere, it can be said that the kind of variables which a theorist considers for his theory, the type of data he selects to test it, even the kinds of relations he sees among his variables, normally show a significant relation to his moral premises. In systematic theory, as in purely factual research, we may banish all references to values, but this does not in itself prove that our ultimate preferences may not have exercised an unobtrusive influence on our observation and reasoning." *Political System* (New York : Alfred A Knopf, 1959), p. 277. Hence, we may endorse this view of W.H. Riker and P.C. Ordeshook that it "is the stuff of politics to prescribe norms. To deny that the political analyst can do so is to misrepresent a logician's dilemma. Political inquiry is an instrument to make sense of the political world, and one way of doing this is to tie together the cognitive and evaluative approaches to politics." *An Introduction to Positive Political Theory* (Englewood Cliffs, New Jersey : Prentice-Hall, 1973), p. 204.

much of this desire for 'morality', for 'improvements' comes to find its way into detailed study of political life."[21]

Modern, including contemporary, political theory may be criticised for being too empirical and, for that reason, immune from the freshness of normativism in spite of the fact that the neo-empiricists have veered round to the idea of the reaffirmation of norms and values in the study of politics. But the admirers of the traditional or classical political theory rightly contend that a value-free political theory is like a valueless political theory. The brute empiricism of the 'modernists' has culminated in, what Easton himself feels, 'a mad craze for scientism'. Its most scathing denunciation is contained in these words of Leo Strauss : "One may say that the new political science fiddles while Rome burns. It is excused by two facts : it does not know that it fiddles, and it does not know that Rome burns."[22]

Political Theory and Political Reality : Juxtaposition of Ideas and Action

The question of facts and values in political theory has its natural interconnectedness with the problem of 'reality' involving the elements of 'proof and 'truth' in the comprehension and description of politics. Facts pertain to the world of reality ; even values have a concern with facts in their own right and, by virtue of that, assume a place of their own in the realm of political reality. The normativists and the empiricists may be distinguished on this point. But now the widely appreciated view is that neither pure normativism nor pure empiricism is desired. A happy reconciliation of the two is the most desirable thing in order to make political theory alive as well as refreshing. As Moon says: "If political theory is to provide objective knowledge, then it must be value-free ; but if it is to have a central role in political action, then it must be committed to certain values and standards, and it must provide a grounding or justification for them."[23]

A pertinent question at this stage arises as to what 'political reality' is. It finds its place in the question of proper relationship between liberty of the individual and the authority under which he has to live ; it also involves the train of his activities having direct or indirect connection with the fundamental question of his existence as a member of an organised community. Thus, political reality of a country may be traced in the sphere of the political activities of its people. An English scholar, Prof. Michael Oakeshoot, thus defines the term 'political activity' : "It is an activity in which human beings are related to one another as members of a *civil association, think* and *speak* about the arrangement and conditions of their association from the point of view of their desirability; make *proposals about change* in these arrangements and conditions; try to *persuade* others of the desirability of the proposed changes and *act* in such a manner as to *promote* the change."[24]

---

21. Blondel, *op. eit..* p. 296.
22. Leo Strauss : "Epilogue" in H.J. Storing (ed.) : *Essays on the Scientific Study of Politics* (New York : Holt, Rinehart and Winston, 1962), p. 327.
23. Donald Moon : "The Logic of Political Inquiry : A Synthesis of Opposed Perspectives" in Greenstein and Polsby, *op. cit.*, Vol. I, pp. 131 ff.
24. Cited in Frank Thakurdas : *Essays in Political Theory,* p. 33.

Prominent Themes in Classical and Modern Political Theory

1. Classical

(i) Concept of Rationalism and Rational Man

(*a*) If man is a rational creature and he can know truth, he has a responsibility to live up to the standard revealed in truth.

(*b*) Consequently Western political theory has a gravity and a seriousness to it that resembles seventeenth century American Puritans' sermons. The prose is often turgid, the arguments are straightforward with a premium placed on clarity and logical development.

(*c*) There is in the rationalist tradition a suggestion of democracy. If true knowledge is available to the public, why should not the public participate in the making of policy? It would certainly be a serious contradiction in rationalism to argue for public virtue and personal rule. The idea was not fully developed until at last the seventeenth century, but it served as a counterweight to role by whims and caprice. Aristotle was firmly committed to the view of a collective wisdom.

(ii) Law of Nature

(*a*) There is a structured reality embedded in the very nature of things which man has the capacity to discover by reason.

(b) Each being has a natural purpose, or end, or goal.

(c) There is an order of inclinations in each being which 'pushes' it towards its end.

(d) Goodness is the fufilment and the completion of this end.

(e) Man, thus, can know not only what he is, he can also know what he has to do.

(f) This knowledge is general and man can understand that there are certain fundamental principles of justice and morality which govern all human conduct.

(iii) Conception of an Organic Community and Common Good

(a) Nourished by reason, man can realise his purpose only as a member of some association of human beings.

(b) The society is like an organism and the individual is its integral part. Man is like a part in relation to the whole.

(c) Individual good is a part of and, therefore, subordinate to the good of all or common good.

(iv) Concept of a Utopian Future

(a) Each character of quality tends towards something to be reached in future. Entities have a nature to fulfil and they are fulfilled during the course of growth and maturation, easing at a given point.

(b) It shows that in Western political theory, past and present are future.

2. Modern

(i) Atomistic Individualism

In fact, the bulk of modern political theory is a debate over the meaning and consequences of individualism which, in its severest form, becomes of an atomistic type. In early modern period (16th to 18th centuries) it was seen as a necessary pre-requisite to the liberation of man from tyranny, monarchical government, and non-representative government.It would be no exaggeration to say that such important ooncepts as natural rights, social contract, government by consent and the right to revolution all depended on this very concept. Put simply, it established the matter of priority: Who is ultimately supreme, a man and his conscience or the state? The answer was in favour of man who came first (than the state) and was endowed with certain inalienable rights given by the Creator.

(ii) Machine View of the State

State, by virtue of being based on a social contract, is an artifact an artificial contrivance devised by man to do only what he wills to do. The state has the status of a tool or a machine. It is useful to the man who is its master. Such a concept directly flies in the face of the idea of common good and organic community. Genuine entity is the individual and that government is the best which governs the least. Modern democracy, rise of Protestantism, and the development of capitalism are all associated with the emancipation of the individual.

(iii) Conservatism

Men are naturally unequal and society requires 'orders' and 'classes' for the good of all. Man is a creature of appetite and will and is governed more by emotion than by reason. Actually society is governed by a Divine being and so it is incredibly mysterious and complex. In understanding the evolution of society, there is presumption in favour of that which has survived. Change takes place but only that which is necessary for the orderly continuation of a given society, should be allowed. If and when changes are proposed, the burden of proof is on urging the change to prove that the change is, indeed, necessary.

(iv) Ideology (Marxism, Fascism, Nationalism)

It refers to a set of generalisations which rationalise or justify a given political system. Fascism is an ideology of the right, Marxism is of the left. The ideology of nationalism is a product of the French revolution of 1789. It is a by-product of individualism, popular sovereignty and secularisation.

3. **Empirical-Scientific**
   (*a*) Explanation of political behaviour must be in quite empirical terms.
   (*b*) Fact-value dichotomy must be accepted.
   (*c*) Political theories must lead set standards, point out the problems to be considered, in short, to act as a conscience for a wayward discipline.
   (*d*) Political theory is meaningful to the point or degree it is verifiable.
   (*e*) The concern should be not with who rules, should rule and why, but on who does rule and how.
   (*f*) We should study concepts like power, elite, class, function, freedom, alienation, anomie, party, group, leader etc. for the relevance of these concepts to science is dependent on empirical indicators which relate the phenomenon in question and the concept being used.
   (*g*) A good political theory should order, explain and predict political phenomena.

Source: W.C. Baum: "Political Theory" in S.L. Wasby: *Political Science*, Ch.9.

In theoretical terms, political reality finds its place in the phenomena of state, goverment and power. In practical terms, it may be seen in the activities of the members of an organised community relating to their role as participants in the sharing and exercising of power. If so, politics becomes an activity occurring within and amongst groups. It operates on the basis of desires that are to some extent shared, an essential feature of the activity being a struggle of actors to achieve their desires on questions of group policy, group organisation, group leadership, or the regulation of inter-group relationships against the opposition of others with conflicting desires. Briefly speaking, "political reality may be seen in the struggle among actors pursuing conflicting desires on a public issue."[25]

The problem of understanding and describing reality in the field of politics is that it has different forms having their different appeals to different kinds of people. It is due to this that while some theorists treat something as a. part of political reality, others repudiate it. So we may take note of the distinction between Hegel and Marx, for instance. If the idealists like Kant and Green say something, it is disfavoured by the pragmatists like Mead, James and John Dewey. Keeping it in view, we may throw light on three varieties of political reality :

1. ***Objective Reality*** : It is what a natural scientist calls reality by all means. The laws of physics and chemistry are based on objective reality created by the world of nature. In the sphere of philosophy, it is known by the name of 'ontology'. It deals with 'being' as 'being'. It examines not particular things but being as distinct from not being, including the difference between propositions such as 'something *is*' and '*what it is*'. In its broadest sense, it refers by no means only to the metaphysical aspects of being but also to the mere clarification of the meaning of a proposition that asserts the being of something and to observable data about being and the modes of being.[26] It is, however, a different matter that some social thinkers have depended heavily on the *Metaphysics* of Aristotle, and thereby studied the element of 'being' in a wider way so as to include within its fold things like 'ideas' and 'essences' of things, men, angels, even God.[27]
2. ***Subjective or Metaphysical Reality:*** Reality is not only what is visible to the naked eye. It has its subjective existence as well. It is not within the reach of a photographer, but it is contained in the mind of an artist. It is something invisible to the eye, but comprehensible to the mind. This may be called metaphysical reality. As Hegel says : 'What is real is rational, what is rational is real.' William James, Henry Bergson, G.H. Mead, Edmund Husserl and Alfred Schutz are its advocates. It may not be acceptable to the natural scientists who stick to the requirements of observation, measurement and quantification of a given phenomenon. But it is a reality by all means to those who distinguish between the *essence* and the *existence* and lay more emphasis on the former in comparison to the latter. It is a mystical reality that is *subjectively* experienced by human beings.[28]

---

25. V.V. Dyke: *Political Science : A Philosophical Analysis* (Stanford : Stanford University Press, 1982), p.134.
26. Brecht : *Political Theory,* p. 53.
27. *Ibid.*
28. *Ibid.* "Mysticism contends that the supreme course of truth (in this case real knowledge) is supersensory and superlogical intuition or revelation. There are many varieties of mysticism. Some allege that Plato was a mystic in the final analysis, because the Philosopher-King understood or comprehended real knowledge by some form of intuition or revelation. Mysticism and radical rationalism share one important characteristic in that they tend to be private or personal. Despite their differences, rationalism and empiricism are public. They claim that their knowledge is communicable." See Baum, *op. cit.,* p. 286.

3. ***Ideal Types*** : A particular type of concept which combines the features of arbitrariness and relatedness to the real world is the 'ideal type', a logical construct, the purpose of which is to identify clearly by simplifying significant aspects of an event or institution. The ideal type, although never found in reality, being ideal precisely in the sense that it is an abstraction, accentuation, and extension of relations found in social life.[29] It provides us with a useful base-line against which we may judge and explain certain phenomena. Sometimes, the ideal type is referred to us as an extreme or polar type, particularly when used in pairs as opposites.[30]

Political theory, whether classical or modern, may be close to political reality in any of the three forms given above. Its closeness to objective reality may be easily traced in the writings of Machiavelli, Hobbes, Locke, Bentham, Montesquieu and Marx. Then, its closeness to subjective reality may be seen in the writings of Plato, Aristotle, St. Augustine, St. Thomas, Rousseau, Kant and Hegel. Finally, its closeness to both may be noted in the works of Max Weber and Charles Merriam. A student of this subject is, however, faced with the difficulty of great diversity that prevents him from having a uniform and clear-cut impression of the theories he has to deal with.

Wolin sums up the whole situation in these words : "A theory is preceded by and is a working out of a decision to study political life in one way rather than another. Whether it is the classical way of dialectical inquiry, the Machiavellian way of juxtaposing contemporary and ancient practices, the Hobbesian procedure of developing axioms about human nature, or the Marxist search for the dynamics of historical development, every theory represents a commitment to a particular way of viewing political realities, a particular method of inquiry, a particular language or way of talking about political subjects, and a particular distribution of emphasis indicative of what the theorist deems important. The paradox that is involved in this enterprise—and it is a paradox common to all forms of theorising, not just to political theorising—is that while aiming at a complete understanding of the subject matter of politics, it is deliberately selective, that is, it omits some matters and exaggerates others. By a complete understanding of politics is meant the ancient and persistent attempt to grasp the political society in the round, so to speak, and to explain its workings as a unified whole. To achieve this, the theorist is compelled to select what is significant and relevant and, above all, to reduce the world to intellectually manageable proportions."[31]

---

29. Don Montindale : "Sociological Theory and Ideal Type" in L. Gross (ed.) : *Symposium on Sociological Theory* (New York : Harper and Row, 1959), p. 77.
30. Wasby, *op. cit.*, pp.64-65. Ideal types may be quite abstractions and, for that reason, far away from the world of reality. But in essence they may be very close to reality as we may notice in the case of Weber's ideal types about bureaucracy. In appreciation of this, David Beetham says : "Of all the features which Weber regarded as definitive of the modern state and its politics, his account of bureaucracy is the most familiar." *Max Weber and the Theory of Modern Politics* (London : George Allen and Unwin, 1974), p. 63.
31. Wolin : "Political Theory : Trends and Goals", *op. cit.*, p. 322.

Issue of Values and Facts : Normative, Empirical and Trans-Empirical Theory

We have already seen that in social sciences, the term 'theory' has its own meaning and scope. However, considering what many distinguished writers in the field of politics have contributed to the understanding and explanation of political reality, three implications may be said to arise therefrom—conceptual frameworks understood as a set of *questions* capable of guiding research, conceptual frameworks defined more ambitiously as a system of working *hypotheses* whose main function is also to orient research, and even more ambitious set of interrelated *propositions* which purport to explain a range of behaviour, to account for part or even for the whole of the field. Such propositions can either be deduced from the kind of conceptual framework or derived from the kind of research to which any adequate framework leads. Thus viewed, theory not only refers to these three implications, but it also offers an answer to the problems or issues raised by the first and second implications.[32]

Since the term 'theory' covers the areas of values or norms or goals as well as facts, it is said to have two broad varieties—normative and empirical. While normativism is the hallmark of the former, empiricism is of the latter, though, the two may be seen to be reconciled to some extent in the third variety of trans-empiricism. Let us briefly study them in the following order :

Normative Theory : Also known by the name of speculative, metaphysical, and value-laden theory, it takes the study of politics very close to the world of ethics and philosophy. The reason is that here a student rambles in the realm of imagination so as to discover an ideal solution to the problem before him. For instance, Plato's dream of a perfect state under the rule of a philosopher-king or Kant's scheme of a federation of the world (European states), or Gandhi's goal of a *Ram Raj* (Rule of Perfect Justice) belongs to this category. Here the place of 'values' and 'goals' is predominant and, for this reason, Kenneth Thompson designates it as the study of politics in terms of 'ethical desiderata'. Here moral issues are persistently raised with the conviction that people are essentially good and they seek to do the right thing in their individual and collective capacities. It is for this reason that they cannot follow their interest without claiming to do so in obedience to some general scheme of values.[33]

A normative theorist is primarily concerned with things as they *ought to be*. That is, he is not concerned with the actual form of things. In a way, he assumes the role of a reformer and suggests the path which might help mankind to overcome obstacles that hinder the community of people from achieving a condition of peace, goodwill

32. Stanley Hoffmann : *Contemporary Theory in International Relations* (Englewood Cliffs, New Jersey : Prentice-Hall, 1964), p. 8.
33. See Quincy Wright : "Development of a General Theory of International Relations" in H.V. Harrison (ed.) : *The Role of Theory in International Relations* (New York : D. Von Nostrand, 1964), p. 38. As Plato says : "In the world of knowledge, the last thing to be perceived and only with great difficulty is the essential Form of Goodness. Once it is perceived, the conclusion must follow that, for all things, this is the cause of whatever is right and good ; in the visible world it gives birth to light, while it is itself sovereign in the intelligible world and the parent of intelligence and truth. Without having had a vision of this Form no one can act with wisdom, either in his own life, or in matters of state." *Republic* (Eng. translation by Francis Cornford) (New York : Oxford Univ. Press, 1945), p. 220.

and harmony. He dwells on the significance of values (like liberty, equality, rights, justice, co-operation, peace, non-exploitation) for the members of an organised body. The names of Rousseau, Kant, Bentham, Green, Mill, Barker and Laski immediately engage our attention at this stage. We may say that even Marxian approach assumes a normative character when the 'father of scientific socialism' hopes for total emancipation of man in the final stage of social development (communism)—an era in which 'glorious human values' shall prevail. Thus, in a general way, this approach suggests the mode by which an imperfect social or political order "could be made perfect. The thinker is expressing himself in the *imperative mood* and is primarily concerned with political values which ought to be implemented in order to achieve a great degree of harmony and stability and unity in our common political life."[34]

Normative theory is prescriptive, because it lays down certain standards of evaluation whereby we may judge the imperfectness of a particular system and also suggest measures for its improvement. Alfred Cobban is, therefore, right when he says that the function of normative theory is to provide us with a criteria of judgement.[35] Another exponent of this view, John Plamenatz contends that the aim of this kind of theory is to create commitment to certain values. Moreover, values may be hierarchised in the sense that some may be said to be heavier as compared to others. It is also possible that a normative theorist may try to establish a reconciliation between two sets of values. For instance, while Plato and Aristotle defend liberty for the aristocratic class, Tawney and Laski try to harmonise liberty with equality so as to build up a new democratic order. Thus, this kind of theory "tries to produce a hierarchy of principles or scale of values and also tries to explain how men should use them to make their choices."[36]

The normative political theory is generally criticised for being *a priori,* deductive, speculative, hypothetical, abstract, imaginative, and utopian. It is based on certain ideal assumptions and it seeks solution of the existing problems within a perfect or ideal framework. Thus, it is away from the world of reality. Its premises cannot be put to an empirical investigation and, for that reason, it cannot be termed 'scientific'. It remains involved in the debate over 'should' and 'should not' without taking into consideration the real world of politics as understood and described by Machiavelli and Hobbes. Much setback has been given to this kind of theory by the marvellous developments of science in modern times and, as a result of that, empirical political theory has overshadowed it, though it is a matter of satisfaction that even now the normative theorists "are not extinct. They are, in fact, very much alive—and vocal."[37]

However, the merit of normative theory is that it is quite refreshing. It is goal-oriented ; it aligns politics with the case of, what Aristotle said, 'good life'. A great advocate of this kind of theory in present times like Prof. Leo Strauss says : "All political action aims at either preservation or change. When desiring to preserve, we wish to prevent a change to the worse ; when desiring to change, we wish to

34. Frank Thakurdas, *op. cit.*, pp. 6-7.
35. Alfred Cobban : "Ethics and the Decline of Political Theory" in Gould and Thursby (ed s): *Contemporary Political Thought* (New York: Holt, Rinehart and Winston. 1969), pp. 289-303.
36. See John Plamenatz : "The Use of Political Theory" in Anthony Quinton (ed.) : *Political Philosophy* (London : Oxford University Press, 1967), pp. 19-31.
37. Wasby, *op. cit.*, p. 36.

bring about something better. All political action is, then, guided by some thought of better or worse. But thought of better or worse implies the thought of the good. The awareness of the good, which guides all our actions, has the character of opinion : it is no longer questioned, but, on the reflection, it proves to be questionable. The very fact that we can question it, directs us towards such a thought of the good as is no longer questionable towards a thought which is no longer opinion but knowledge. All political action has then in itself a directedness towards knowledge of the good : of the good life, or the good society. For the good society is the complete political good."[38]

Empirical Theory : Here the writer is concerned with facts or actualities. The facts can be subjected to scrutiny and so the theory can be called 'scientific' Obviously, empirical theory is known as causal theory. Here, politics is studied in terms of 'interest' for whose sake people fight by any possible means—peaceful or violent, evolutionary or revolutionary, constitutional or unconstitutional. Evidence for this is sought in the facts of human behaviour that shape events and that eventually find their place in the accounts of history. As such, the writer seeks to understand and explain political reality as it is and offers solution to the prevailing problems in political terms. The names of Aristotle (relating to his theories on revolution and classification of states), Machiavelli, Hobbes, Locke, Montesquieu and Marx may engage our immediate attention at this stage. It shows that an empirical theorist is a 'fact grubber' and, for that reason, empirical theory should also be treated as an analytical description of reality.[39]

In other words, we may say that while normative theory is concerned with the *subjective* aspect of human behaviour, the empirical theory concerns itself with the *objective* behaviour of man finding its manifestation in the struggle for power for the sake of protecting and promoting his interest. That power corrupts man, and that power alone can be a check to power, are empirical rules. Montesquieu, therefore, suggests that liberty of the individual can be secured by implementing the principle of 'separation of powers'. If 'exploitation' is a curse, it can be removed in a socialist order that abolishes the capitalist system. The behaviour of a man as a voter, or a legislator, or an administrator, or a judge may be studied and all material relating to it may be quantified and on that basis we may lay down some general principles that may be valid in similar situations elsewhere. If so, empirical theory is fact-laden; it discards the place of values in the study of politics ; it also treats all values as of equal weight and significance.

Empirical theory has the merit of taking the study of politics to the world of reality. Instead of delving deep into the world of utopia, it seeks to examine politics in a way verifiable by facts. It is fact-laden. Its best example may be seen in the writings of a German sociologist Max Weber who advises us to accept 'dichotomy' of facts and values but stick exclusively to the realm of the former. Obviously, a critic of this approach like Leo Strauss holds: "By teaching, in effect, the equality of literally all desires, it teaches, in effect, that there is nothing that a man ought to

38. Leo Strauss : "What is Political Philosophy?" in Gould and Thursby (eds) : *Contemporary Political Thought*, p. 47.
39. Wasby, *op. cit.*, p. 38.

be ashamed of; by destroying the possibility of self-contempt, it destroys, with the best of intentions, the possibility of self-respect. By teaching the equality of values, by denying that there are things which are intrinsically high and others which are intrinsically low as well as by denying that there is an essential difference between men and brutes, it unwittingly contributes to the victory of the gutter."[40]

Trans-Empirical Theory: The Weberian line has been followed by a good number of social theorists. In particular, we may refer to the leading lights of the 'Chicago School' like Charles Merriam and David Easton. However, a new idea has also developed that seeks to soften the dichotomy of facts and values and desires a harmonious construction between the worlds of 'values' and 'facts'. The names of John Dewey and Felix Kaufmann may be referred to at this stage. A fact is a fact whether it is analytical or rational. An empiricist wants to discover 'truth' that itself is a matter of value-judgement. For instance, a liberal finds no truth in the Marxian charge of 'exploitation' in a capitalist system, but a Marxist takes it as an irrefutable fact and hopes for its full elimination in the final stage of socialism. Thus, Dahl correctly advises that political appraisal being a constant inter-weaving of fact-finding and evaluation, it will be of no help to us to set our factual knowledge off to one side, neatly sealed up in an aspectic container, and values off to the other side where they have no bearing on reality.'[41]

Contemporary empiricists like Easton and Dahl prefer the line of trans-empiricism. They not only criticise the .pure empirical approach as'hyperfactual', but they also desire to integrate values with facts in a study of politics to some possible extent. The burden of their argument is that any scientific judgement is ultimately a moral judgement. Some followers of this line like Jacques Maritain (known as Neo-Thomists) and Ernest Mach (known as Logical Positivists) do not like to discard value judgements thoroughly, though they do insist that theory must have the character of a "science'. Every social theorist must take it for granted that some place must be given to the role of values. Though ardent empirical theorists of modern times like James Bryce insists on 'facts, facts, facts', they make every possible and practicable effort to save their preferred system (democracy). For that reason, it may be said that they smuggle into their theories their own values which are usually those of an unavow-ed commitment to a particular version of liberal democracy. This may be termed 'democratism.'[42]

---

40. Strauss : "An Epilogue", *op. cit.*, p. 326. For like criticism see Eric Vogelin : *The New Science of Politics* (Chicago : Chicago University Press, 1952). Empiricism involves logical positivism that becomes like a phenomenalistic thesis on the ground that any transcendent reality must be rejected as a prior condition to the discarding of metaphysics. What is missing in such an inquiry, as Frohock says, "is a feel for the relational patterns of human life. The cutting edge of the verification thesis, strictly defined, becomes paradoxical again in the self-other relationships... Positivism is not the whole story of empiricism. As a special and extreme case, it denotes some of the problems awaiting extravagant claims made from modest promises. But a more general problem plagues empiricism which is that knowledge derived from experience is relative to experience, and hence not of universal validity." *The Nature of Political Inquiry* (Homewood, Illinois : The Dorsey Press, 1967), pp. 27-28.
41. R.A. Dahl : *Modern Political Analysis* (Englewood Cliffs, New Jersey Prentice-Hall, 1964), p. 104.
42. An Indian writer on this theme confidently affirms that politics 'implies some kind of democracy.' A.H. Doctor : *Issues in Political Theory* (New Delhi : Sterling Pub., 19 84), p. 2.

The main charges made by the trans-empiricists against the empiricists, as pointed out by Dahl, are : (*i*) the empiricists offer no criteria of relevance ; (*ii*) in striving for neutrality and objectivity, the empiricists have adopted a new and complicated form of jargon ; *(iii)* in their attempt to eschew values, the empiricists reject all grounds for evaluation and treat all values as equal; and (*iv*) above all, while professing neutrality, their commitment to the liberal-democratic system is so obvious.[43] In this way, trans-empiricism seeks to highlight what is already, otherwise what ought to have been, implicit in empirical theories on politics. Bluhm suggests well: "The expression 'causal theory' is also usually taken to mean only theory which can be tested in some empirical fashion. Yet many of the great theories contain causal notions, both about the empirical order and about the rational order, which cannot be so tested, or which at least at present, *seem* not to be testable by scientific means, for example, the Thomistic theory concerning the way in which the Natural Law is made known to men. But this is no reason to deny the causal character of the idea in classifying it for analysis."[44]

Adherence to the side of normativism or empiricism alone leads to the formulation of, what may be termed, 'partial theories'. What is really desirable is that there should be a convergence of the two so that political reality may be understood and explained in concrete or practicable terms and that the system of values may be integrated with the study of facts. The fact-value dichotomy should be discarded. Instead the view should be that both approaches (normative and empirical) may be useful in daily life, even if they do not think that both have an equal place within political science.[45] Moreover, it should not be taken for granted that with the growth of science, empirical political theory has totally eclipsed the normative political theory, though it has been able to give a great setback to the latter. The scientific findings did not by themselves bring about the downfall of normative political philosophy; they merely helped to put in proper perspective an approach which had earlier begun to lose intellectual stature as a result of other shifts in political outlook."[46]

It may also be added in this connection that while trans-empiricists agree with the proposal of integrating values with facts, or they try to discover value-system in the empirical findings of the great empiricists, they do not at all like to return to the classical tradition in which values and goals have a predominant place of their own. Their only argument is to highlight the deficiency of the pure empirical approach by which the theorists, what Easton calls, in their 'mad craze for scientism', very much restrict the scope of political inquiry. The brute or hard-nosed empiricism "constricted and crippled theory philosophically and methodically. The fact-value distinction has encouraged an undesirable foreshortening of vision and moral sensibility."[47] This

43. Dahl, *op. cit.*
44. Bluhm, *Theories of the Political System.*, p. 7.
45. Wasby, *op. cit.*, p. 36.
46. *Ibid.*
47. Dwight Waldo : "Political Science : Tradition, Discipline, Profession, Science, Enterprise" in Fred Greenstein and N.W. Polsby (ed.s) : *Political Science : Scope and Theory* (California : Addison-Wesley, 1975) Vol. I, p. 114.

point of view has found itself accommodated in the post-behavioural tradition of political theory.[48]

Different Traditions and the Problem of Interpretation in Political Theory

The most interesting as well as the most perplexing thing about political theory relates to the problem of its critical interpretation. We have abundant literature on this subject from Plato and Aristotle in ancient to Laski and Lasswell in present times. But the problem stands out as to how we should categorise the ideas of the stalwarts of political theory. Commentaries on the political ideas of these great thinkers are varying in the nature ot their description and treatment that look like hovering between the poles of full appreciation on the one side and that of uncompromising attack on the other, though some taking a balanced or middle-of-the-road view of things. At the same time, we are struck with the fact of continuous flow of the tradition of political theory running in diverse directions. It is well visualised: "Philosophical tradition about politics from Plato to Oakeshott has come down to us like a continuous flowing stream, now thin and limped, now turgid and muddy, absorbing as it has moved down the centuries, diverse streams, some clear, others confusing, like a whirlpool yet moving all the time."[49]

The first and foremost problem in this regard is how to lay down a universally valid criterion for the sake of a critical comprehension and interpretation of political theory. Western political theory has different traditions each having its strong and weak sides, the most important of which are:

1. ***Rational-Natural:*** According to this tradition, society and state can be understood only when they are related to an absolute standard, which exists in nature and which is, therefore, outside human control, but which nevertheless can be known by the people through the use of their reason. It also implies that society must imitate the pattern offered and apprehended by nature. If we want to know whether laws and institutions are good, we have only to ask if they are close copies of the existing standards. The names of Plato, Aristotle, Rousseau, Hegel and Green may be included in this category. If Plato says that 'the state is an individual writ large', Hegel says that the 'state is the externalisation of man's freedom'. It constitutes an organic view of state whereby individual is treated as an integral part of the social whole. Its practical manifestation can be seen in the philosophy of Fascism (Nazism) where individual interest is wholly subordinated to the interest of the state. A critic of political theory is, therefore, faced with the dilemma of lauding or denouncing the organic view of social and political whole. To some it looks like encouraging 'both the best and the social of me' and, at the same time, treating 'man as nothing more than a conduit pipe of the divine energy as a passive creature for whom things must be done, not as a being who finds fulfilment in positive activity.'[50] That is, while an idealist like Rousseau may say that it is impossible for a sovereign to maim or injure his subjects, a

48. Thomas Spragens, Jr. : *The Dilemmas of Contemporary Political Theory : Towards a Post-Behovioural Science of Politics* (New York : Dunellen, 1973), p. 1.
49. Frank Thakurdas, *op. cit.*, p. 86.
50. C.L. Wayper : *Political Thought*, (London : The English University Press,. 1964), p. 248.

liberal like Hobhouse may say that the cause of the German bombardment on England during the First World War may be traced in Hegel's theory of god-state.

2. ***Will and Artifice:*** According to this tradition, it is not the faculty of reason but will in man that is required to produce the state and, as such, human will has freedom to produce the state. Its concrete form may be seen in the mechanistic theory of state according to which state is like a machine or an artificial contrivance that may be made and remade as per the will of its members. It is like a house that can be demolished and then rebuilt according to the choice of its owners. Thus, political institutions or forms and structures of government are like artificial contrivances and the people have a valid right to switch over from one form to another according to their will. Thus, Hobbes and Locke justified people's uprisings of the seventeenth century England and thereby refuted the dogma of the divine origin of political authority. This was the idea of the French revolutionaries who destroyed the monarchical system and instead sought to establish a new kind of political order ensuring the boons of liberty, equality and fraternity. It became the basis of the individualist theory of state that was so powerfully advocated by Mill and Spencer in the nineteenth century. In due course, it became the basis of liberal-democratic theory. Like organic theory, the mechanistic theory has its advocates in a very large number of liberal thinkers from Hobbes, Locke and Green to Hayek, Rawls and Nozick. It has its equally strong critics ranging from Burke to Mussolini. In spite of the fact that such a political theory inspires people to revolt whenever their transient will so informs, its greatest merit lies in its safeguarding the liberty of the individual.[51]
3. ***Historical Coherence:*** According to it, both the above traditions are defective. Since natural laws have to be changed to suit civil society, it maintains that rational-natural theory is neither natural nor non-natural. And since man's will is always limited by the will of others and by what has been willed previously, the tradition of will and artifice attributes too much importance to both. Thus, the best way is to combine reason with will. It emphasises the importance of institutional growth and denies that absolute standards exist. Goodness and justice, it avers, consist of the coherence of the past with the whole, and if we want to know what is goodness, we must seek conformity not with will and desire of society at any given moment but with the standard of coherence in that society as it has developed historically over the years. The state, according to this tradition, is not a copy of the natural world. But to some extent it can be seen as natural, because it is the result of an historical evolution that can be thought of as a part of nature.[52]
4. ***Marxist*** **:** It is different from all the traditions discussed above. Here politics has its foundations in economics. The prevailing economic structure determines the nature and composition of social and political structures and, as such, a change in the basic structure causes a corresponding change in all superstructures. On the basis of this fundamental assumption, the Marxists say that as state has

51. *Ibid.* p. *xi.*
52. *Ibid.*

come into existence due to the emergence of class war, it will inevitably go with the elimination of class contradictions. State is an instrument of exploitation and oppression by one class over another. There was no state in the primitive communistic society, and so there would be no state in the final stage of social development. It came into existence in the slave society to protect the interest of the people of the free class; it continued in the feudal society to protect the interests of the landlords and feudal chiefs; it continues to exist in the present capitalist society so as to protect the interest of the bourgeois class. It will continue for some time in the socialist society so as to protect the interest of the working class against any counter-revolutionary measure and then it will eventually wither away. As Lenin says: "The state will be able to wither away completely when society adopts the rule: 'From each according to his ability, to each according to his needs', i.e., when people have become so accustomed to observing the fundamental rules of social intercourse and when their labour has become so productive that they will voluntarily work according to their ability."[53] In fine, Marxism "has demonstrated that state is not something introduced into society from the outside, but is a product of society's internal development."[54]

Problem of Critical Appraisal in Political Theory

Apart from briefly discussing different traditions of political theory, we may now enumerate certain important points that constitute the dilemma of critical interpretation and evaluation in political theory. These are:

In the first place, there is the problem relating to disagreement over first principles. Political thinkers have sought to understand and explain political reality as a result of which we find different observations, explanations, even predictions, in some cases. For instance, Plato and Aristotle treat state as a moral association having its end in the attainment of 'good life'; the state is identified with the 'march of God on earth' by Hegel. Extreme individualists like Spencer and Donisthorpe push the state to the wall after denouncing it as a 'necessary evil'. The anarchists like Bakunin and Kropotkin frankly dub state as an 'unnecessary evil' and on that count suggest its total abolition so as to usher in a new order ensuring complete freedom of man. The Marxists arrive at the same conclusion with a different logic according to which the state is to wither away in the final stage of social development when society is free from any sort of exploitation. The utilitarians like Jeremy Bentham and James Stuart Mill discover the source of political obligation in the principle of 'utility', but the Fabian socialists like Bernard Shaw and Sidney Webb treat state as an agency of public welfare. While the classical liberals like John Stuart Mill and Adam Smith advocate the principle of minimum possible state activity, the neo-liberals like Keynes and Laski prefer extension of state activity for the sake of public welfare. It all shows that there is nothing like unanimity of views on the nature and end of the state. Moreover, the diversity of views is so astonishing that it becomes a matter of problem for a student to grasp this subject with a sense of easy confidence. However,

53. V.I. Lenin: "The State and Revolution" in his *Collected Works,* Vol. 25, p. 474.
54. V.G. Afanasyev: *Marxist Philosophy* (Moscow: Progress Publishers, 1980), p. 281.

Wayper well advises that a student of this subject should not feel discouraged with the mark of disagreement in the views of great political theorists and if he does so, he is like an alchemist "vainly searching for the elixir that would turn everything into gold."[55]

Then, there is the argument of consistency. It is desired that the ideas of a social and political theorist must be thoroughly consistent so that he may be easily and safely put into a particular rubric of school like that of an individualist, a socialist, an anarchist, or a communist and the like. If this is not there, we criticise a particular thinker for being inconsistent and his political theory is accused of being full of contradictions. For instance, Hobbes and Locke are admired for being thoroughly consistent in their treatment of the nature and end of political authority, but different is the case with Rousseau who is lauded as a liberal by Wright and denounced as a totalitarian by Barker.[56]

When the element of consistency is lacking, the critic raises his accusing finger. We find that what Plato says in the *Republic,* he says something different in his *Politicus, (Statesman)* and still something more different in the *Laws.* Ever since some early writings of Marx saw the light of the day, it is said that the 'old Marx' is different from the 'young Marx'. Such a criticism is strongly levelled against Laski who is said to shift his position from one of a pluralist to that of a Marxist and then to that of a Fabian socialist. He is also accused of dwindling between the negative and positive views of liberty at different stages. Mill's courageous, though fruitless, attempt at defining the areas that belong to Caesar and those which do not, has been a warning to others of the impossibility of such a theoretical undertaking. The current debate of the 'open' versus 'closed' society stems from this baffling problem, although the current literature on the subject has hardly contributed towards a clearer understanding of this dilemma, except in the most general terms."[57]

Political science is a social science and, as such, it deals with the behaviour of man as a social and political creature. Once again, we are struck with this fact that wide divergence in respect of understanding human nature leads to wide divergences in the field of epistemology. Whether man is intrinsically good or bad and, as such, what is the *raison d' etre* of his political obligation. This is a basic question which has been answered by different theorists in different ways. Great Christian political thinkers like St. Augustine and St. Thomas find the cause of the creation of political authority in the 'fall of man', but idealists like Rousseau and Hegel find it in man's real or pure will. To Machiavelli and Hobbes, man is essentially selfish and wicked and, for this reason, state is needed to keep him under control, but to Gandhi, man is essentially good and noble and, for this reason, political authority may not be needed in the ideal condition of life, what he calls 'Ram Raj'. All anti-statists (like extreme individualists, anarchists and Marxists) hope for the advent of an ideal

55. Wayper, *op. cit.,* p. vii.

56. Rousseau's political theory is, indeed, a classic model which has encouraged this sort of debate, for his ambiguity lends itself conveniently to either description—'a thorough-going individualist' or a thorough going collectivist (a'Janus-like figure' in Barker's telling metaphor)—depending upon the cogency of the crime's case. Do we accept, in this context, Vaughan or Cobban as our critical guide? See Frank Thakurdas, *op. cit.,* p. 97.

57. *Ibid.,*p. 96.

order in which there is no state, no government, no law, no authority and the like and then all public affairs are to be managed by the free and voluntary associations (soviets or communes) of the people. In this way, the source of political obligation should be traced in the world of psychology—pessimistic and cynical (Machiavelli), macabre (Hobbes), and moral (Gandhi).

Another problem relating to the critical appraisal of political theory finds its source in the fact/value dichotomy. Thinkers belonging to the classical (normative) tradition adopt a value-based outlook, and thereby endeavour to lay down certain norms or ideals which should be pursued by a civilised man living in a civilised community. A move in this direction inevitably culminates in search for a utopia or a perfect order marked by the existence of justice and freedom. So we may find models of such a grand dream in Plato's ideal state, Rousseau's community, Kant's association of European states, Hegel's nation-state, and Green's federation of the world. Opposed to it, is the empirical tradition where political theory is based exclusively on facts. For instance, Aristotle's theory of revolution, Machiavelli's aphorisms on statecraft, Hobbes's design of commonwealth, Locke's thesis of constitutional government, Montesquieu's doctrine of separation of powers and Easton's analysis of political system are the leading examples where political theory has its distinctly empirical dimensions.

The latest trend in this direction (as adopted by the behaviouralists) is to discard the place of norms and values as far as possible and to make fact-based political theory so as to give it the character of a science. Positivists like Comte, logical positivists like Mach, and neo-positivists like Lasswell adhere to such a line. The post-behavioural trend has once again sought to establish a logical connection between facts and values, though with the predominant position of the former. Hence the important point of debate in modern political theory is whether it should be normative or empirical or both and, as such, whether its students should appreciate the classical (normative) tradition, or condemn it for being totally *a priori* or speculative and then jump to laud empirical theory with a full-throated voice.[58]

One more problem in this direction relates to the use of words and phrases by some leading thinkers, theorists and analysts of political theory. We find that same terms have different implications at the hands of different political thinkers, theorists and analysts. For instance, what Plato means by the term 'justice' is different from what is taken by Kant and Dicey. Machiavelli uses the word 'virtue' in different senses at different places so as to include within it the quality of bravery, soldiery, chivalry, hardihood, industriousness, patriotic conviction and any other thing that goes to contribute its part in the making of a strong state. Bentham makes use of the word 'utility' in a comprehensive sense so as to include within it anything like

58. As W.C. Baum says; "What distinguishes contemporary from earlier political theory is a reluctance on the part of most contemporary political scientists to work in what they deem to be the non-scientific areas, *i.e.*, prescription and evaluation. This is largely due to the acceptance of the fact-value dichotomy by most scientists. Accordingly, only facts and concepts are deemed relevant to the primary aim of science: explanation and phenomena. Traditional philosophy also had a deep interest in ethical and normative judgements. So, too, did political theory until very recently." See Wasby, *op. cit.*, p. 279.

pleasure, benefit, advantage, usefulness, etc. The word 'freedom' as used by Hegel and Green has a purely metaphysical connotation that is different from one taken by Mill, Laski, Barker, Berlin and Hayek. Hegel talks of 'dialectics' in a metaphysical sense, but Marx does the same in materialistic terms. While Easton defines politics as 'authoritative allocation of values', his approach is not at all normative that identifies 'values' with high principles; by the term 'value' he means something having a binding character on account of being a command of the proper authority.

In spite of the efforts of the logical positivists, political theory continues to suffer from semantic confusion at many crucial points.[59] The same problem stands out as to which meaning should be accepted and appreciated, or refuted and denounced. As Barry says: "The problem is further compounded in political philosophy by the fact that many of the key words are often given 'persuasive definitions' by social theorists, that is, definitions designed to provoke some favourable or unfavourable response from the reader. In the history of political thought, the concept of state has been a frequent victim of this approach, being defined in highly favourable and highly derogatory terms."[60] However, in order to get out of this dilemma, Karl Popper advises that important objections to linguistic philosophy lie in *theories,* which, true or false, are important, and not the *meanings* of the words. Nevertheless, we shall maintain that the clarification of concepts is important in political analysis. It may not be the case that political arguments turn upon the use of words, but it is certainly true that conceptual clarification is required even to know what the arguments are about."[61]

The study of political theory with a biographical approach presents its own set of difficulties. Here, the works of a theorist are evaluated in reference to the events of his life and thereby some categorical evaluations are made that may not find coherence with the purpose which an interpreter should have in his mind. For instance, it is said that Plato and Aristotle justified the excellence of aristocratic system on account of their own association with such a class of the Greek society. Such a standpoint may be relevant to some extent, but if it is given too much emphasis, then our whole effort may be frustrated. Also, Rousseau's theory of ideal state cannot be interpreted and evaluated in the light of his early life as a vagabond.[62] Such a standpoint must be adopted and utilised with a sense of restraint as Peter Laslett has done in the case of John Locke.[63] The denunciation of the capitalist system

59. According to Norman P. Barry, it was a reaction to the Logical Positivists' highly restrictive account of meaning that inspired the school of 'ordinary language' philosophy. Meaningfulness is, in this school's view, to be found in the *use* to which words are put. Since common usage itself is the benchmark of meaningfulness, there is much greater variety of meaningful statements than appears to be the case with Logical Positivism, and the meaning of words such as law and state can be found only by locating the particular uses such words have in the languages of law and politics. *An Introduction to Modern Political Theory* (London: Macmillan, 1981), p. 9.
60. *Ibid.*
61. Karl Popper: *Unended Quest* (London: Fontana and Collins, 1976), pp. 22-24.
62. See Judith N. Shklar: *Men and Citizens* (Cambridge Univ. Press, 1969).
63. Laslett (ed.): *John Locke's Two Treatises of Civil Government* (New York: New American Library, 1965).

at the hands of Marx is often attributed to the experiences of his personal life, but such an argument does not at all apply to the case of Fredrick Engels. We may, therefore, come to this conclusion that biographical approach should be taken as nothing beyond a necessary insight into a particular aspect of the work of a theorist.[64]

Allied with it is the problem of linking the motives of a particular thinker to the effects of his works. It is contended by others who hold the view that the intent of a theorist is irrelevant in the search for meaning. These motives and intents may be conditioned by any reason whatsoever. For instance, Rousseau being a lover of freedom, presents the model of a kind of political community in which the individual, who is a free-born person, remains free even after becoming a citizen. The social contract just converts 'a limited and stupid animal' into 'an intelligent citizen'. Since Hegel had to run away from the city of Jena in the event of French invasion, as a result of which he lost his job and library there, he developed a sort of obsession to see a powerful German state that would destroy the French power and thereby wreak vengeance of her humiliation. Karl Popper, who had suffered at the hands of Nazi fascists, developed a sort of mission "to label and then condemn any political philosophy supportive of a closed (totalitarian) system."[65]

Above all, there is the problem of 'bias' or personal point of view of a particular social and political thinker, theorist, or analyst, who seeks to understand and explain political reality in his own chosen way and may also go to the extent of making certain strong justifications or predictions in that very regard. Both Plato and Aristotle hailed from the class of free and rich people and, for that reason, they justified the excellence of the aristocratic form of government. The classical liberals of the nineteenth century like Adam Smith and John Stuart Mill sought to justify the *laissez faire* system in the interest of the rising capitalist class. Burke attacked the political philosophy of the French revolution so as to offset its impact upon the people of England having a conservative bent of mind. Hugh Cecil and Michael Oakeshott are the latest representatives of the conservative tradition that defends and exalts the *status quo* and thereby benefits the privileged class of the English society.

A very large number of American social theorists and analysts like Joseph Schumpeter, Eric Fromm, Talcott Parsons, John Rawls and Robert Nozick refine the premises of positive liberalism so as to defend the liberal-democratic system with the sneaking motive of denouncing totalitarian systems of the world. Opposed to it, we find that Marx and his followers have their vested interest in denouncing the *status quo* as based on 'exploitation' and thereby desire a new social order free from class contradictions in the transitional stage and from 'power' in the last stages of social development. It shows that unbiased political theory is an impossibility. Obviously, a student of this subject is puzzled with the fact that thinkers "have condemned or stand condemned in each other's eyes. And this mutual condemnation has spared not even the middle-of-the-road theorist. The world is either black or white, for there can be no diluted grey in so severe a world."[66]

64. Elizabeth James, *op. cit.,p.* 30.
65. *Ibid.,* p. 71.

No doubt, the study of political theory is ridden with the problem of its proper interpretation and critical evaluation. But the question also stands out as to what is the way out, or what is really needed in this direction. Two important points may be made at this stage. First, none of the traditions, as discussed above, is either good or bad in an absolute sense; each has its own merits and demerits. The wise course is to have a peaceful coexistence of all so that the students may themselves understand and critically evaluate different political trends or traditions as per their best judgement. Second, the fact of diversity or divergence should not be taken as the cause of apprehension or discouragement. We may discard the view of Leslie Stephen that 'happy is the society which has no political philosophy, for it is generally the offspring of a recent or the symptom of an approaching revolution.' Instead, we may endorse this view of Wayper that political theory (thought) "is the distilled wisdom of the ages which one only has to imbibe sufficiently to be translated into a rosier world where men stumble not and hangovers are unknown."[67]

Professionalisation of the Discipline: Emergence of Different Study Groups

Changing social and economic conditions have their definite impact on the political institutions and processes of the country. Social theorists study new phenomena or revisit old conceptions so as to understand and explain political reality in a better way. In the twentieth century, the trends of urbanisation, industrialisation and democratisation along with the occurrence of the two Great Wars and emergence of totalitarianism in the form of Fascism and Communism, provided abundant material for the study of politics. It inspired a very large number of social and political theorists and analysts to study as to how a liberal democratic order could be saved from such onslaughts and how normativism could be reconciled with the premises of empiricism. Some such theorists or analysts formed an alliance of their own that came to be known as their 'school' signifying their adherence to a specific set of notions or the modes of investigation and analysis.

Chicago School: In the United States, the leading role was played by Prof. Charles Merriam of the Chicago University who in his *New Aspects of Politics* (1925) studied politics in terms of 'power'. He advised his colleagues and students to formulate theories on the basis of 'facts'. Thus, thoroughly empirical techniques were adopted by the researchers to 'scientise' the subject of politics. The writers utilised the cross-disciplinary or interdisciplinary approach that broadened the scope of the discipline by cultivating many hitherto untouched areas. H.F. Gosnell in his *Getting Out of Vote* (1924) studied the behaviour of the voters and interest groups. Leonard White's *The Prestige Value of Public Employment* (1929) was based on survey research. Harold. D.

66. Frank Thakurdas, *op. cit.*, p. 99. At another place, Thakurdas warns against the tendency of reposing full faith in the criticism of any scholar, however great he may be, like Karl Popper—a distinguished philosopher in his own right. The reader "should not allow himself to be carried away by the sheer weight of authority, since the world of political speculation is still an open one in which the reader has to find his own bearings." Refer to his paper titled "The Problem of Approaches and Interpretation of Political Theory" in J.S. Bains and R.B. Jain (eds.): *Political Science in Transition* (New Delhi: Gitanjali, 1981), p. 17.

67. Wayper, *op. cit.*, p. viii.

Lasswell produced *Propaganda Techniques in the World War* (1927) and *Psychopathology and Politics* (1930) in which he introduced the themes of political communication, propaganda and public relations. Quincy Wright's *The Study of War* (1942) involved testing of sociological and psychological hypotheses by quantitative methods.

Obviously, in the inter-war period a new trend emerged as a result of the pioneering efforts of Merriam and his colleagues and students at the Chicago University. The post-1945 period "turned out to be a laboratory and an important training experience for many of the scholars who would seed the behavioural revolution."[68] The trend became so popular that Lasswell and R.A. Dahl followed it at the Yale University and G.E.G. Catlin did it at the Cornell University. Besides, a good number of European scholars, who had shifted to the United States after 1920, brought with them the messages of psychologist Sigmund Freud and sociologist Max Weber. After 1950 this new trend became so powerful that it "represented a new approach, and a challenge, a new orientation and a reform movement."[69]

Frankfurt School: The Institute of Social Science Research established at Frankfurt, known as the Frankfurt School, came into being in 1923 with the support of some native businessmen. However, it came into limelight when Max Horkheimer, the author of *Critical Theory,* took over its directorship in 1930 after replacing Carl Grunsberg of Vienna, the author of the *Archive for the History of Socialism and Workers' Movement.* Theodor W.Adorno, Herbert Marcuse, Leo Lowenthal, Eric Fromm, Friedrich Pollock, Franz Neumann, Otto Kirchheimer and Henry K. Grossman were its leading lights. Others like Jurgen Habermas, Claus Offe, Klaus Eder and Albrecht Wellmer joined later and so they are known as the members of the second generation. Since the Institute was financed by the German businessmen and most of the leading figures of this Institute were the Jews, they suffered torture at the hands of the Nazi dictator (Hitler). So the centre was shifted to New York in 1936. However, after the Second Great War, some of them came back to Germany and restarted their work.

Certain unexpected and turbulent developments took place in the period following the World War II like collapse of mass left-wing parties in Germany into reformist or Moscow-dominated movements, the degeneration of the Russian socialist revolution into Stalinism, and the rise and fall of Fascism in Italy and Germany. It inspired these intellectuals to revisit or reinterpret the basic premises of Marxism with a thoroughly critical standpoint. They adhered to the Marxian tradition in criticising the capitalist system; at the same time, they found fault with the application of Marxism in Russia by Stalin, what they derisively termed 'Soviet socialism', and thereby they created the 'third way' or an alternative path that was preferred by the 'new left' in the 1960s and 1970s. Hence, the Frankfurt School "can be associated directly with an anti-Bolshevik radicalism and an open-ended or critical Marxism."[70]

---

68 R.E. Goodin and Hans-Dieter Klingemann (eds.): *A New Handbook of Political Science* (Oxford: Oxford University Press, 1996), p. 68.

69. E.M. Kirkpatrick: "The Impact of Behavioural Approach on Traditional Political Science" in Austin Ranney (ed.): *Essays on the Behavioural Study of Politics*, p. 11.

70. Tom Bottomore (ed.): *A Dictionary of Marxist Thought* (World View, Maya Blackwell, 1991), p. 208.

Irrespective of the sharp differences in the views and the reiterations of the advocates of the Frankfurt School, some common strands of their thought may be thus enumerated:

1. The Frankfurtians elaborate a critical theory of society in a way that looks like a peculiar mixture of the ideas of Kant, Hegel, Marx, Weber and Freud. One may note their concern with the conditions of possibility of reason and knowledge (Kant), to a a reflection on the emergence of spirit (Hegel), and then to a focus on historical forms like capitalism (Marx). Their main endeavour is to make a critical study of the social conditions that create asymmetric power-relations or unequal forms of domination. The roots of authoritarianism or domination have their place in the psychological and sociological spheres.
2. Since the leading figures of this School were Germans, they confined their attention to the social and political ideas of the great German thinkers like Hegel and Marx. Hence, one may find here a kind of synthesis of idealism (metaphysics) and materialism. Each of them maintains that all knowledge "is historically conditioned; they contended that truth claims can be rationally adjudicated, independent of political, social or class interests."[71]
3. Particularly the Frankfurtians of the second generation like Habermas (and also Marcuse) widened their attention so as to borrow something from the Anglo-American thought such as linguistic philosophy and other philosophies of science, and thereby they adopted an interdisciplinary approach so as to find out an answer to this question as to why a socialist revolution, as predicted by Marx, could not occur in the Western countries and as to how the Soviet leaders could manage to distort the basic premises of Marxism. They may be labelled as 'neo-Marxists' in view of the fact that they found fault with the Marxian formulations of course, but they also obdurately sought to revisit, reinvigorate and develop them. "Hence, political sociology, cultural criticism, psychoanalysis and other disciplines found a place in the framework of critical theory. By raising issues concerning the division of labour, bureaucracy, patterns of culture, family structure as well as the central question of ownership and control, the Frankfurt school decisively broadened the terms of reference of critique and helped to transform the notion of the political."[72]
4. The Frankfurtians attack the capitalist system in which even culture becomes an 'industry'. The increasing interlocking of economy and polity ensures the subordination of local initiative to bureaucratic domination. Thus, critical theory "is addressed to the examination of the interplay between structure and social practices, the mediation of the objective and subjective and through particular social phenomena."[73]
5. In the Marxian fashion, the critical theorists, particularly Adorno, Marcuse and Habermas hold that the power of 'liberation' entails the process of self-emancipation and self-creation. In this way, they look like making an attempt to

---

71. *Ibid.*, pp. 208-09.
72. *Ibid.*, p. 209.
73. *Ibid.*, p. 210.

link socialism to the liberty of the individual so as to realise the ideal of a 'good society'. As Bottomore says: "Although the critical theorists did not produce a sustained political theory, they stood in the tradition of those who maintain the unity of socialism and liberty and who argue that the aims of a rational society must be prefigured in and be consistent with the means used to attain that society."[74]

Horkheimer's work (*Critical Theory*) became so popular that the theories of the Frankfurt School came to be generally placed in this category. It makes it liable for attack on two grounds. First, political theory has been under critical examination from the times of Plato and Aristotle to those of Laski, Lasswell and Lyotard. As such, the contributions of the Frankfurtians cannot be singled out for being 'critical'. Second, their formulations do not form a unity, it does not mean same thing to all its all adherents. The critical observations and explanations of the eminent figures of this School look like intriguing interpretations and re-interpretations of Marxism in the light of turbulent developments after the World Wars I and II. Hence, Bottomore comments that the label 'critical theory' "is a misleading one, for the work of the Institute members did not always form a series of tightly woven complementary projects."[75]

However, the contributions of the critical theorists may be appreciated for attacking the capitalist system in a Marxian fashion as well as trying to reform it by alleviating its inherent evils so as to usher in the 'era of man's emancipation' as conceived by the anarchists like Bakunin and Kropotkin. They are known for being the pioneers of 'new leftism' by attacking the structures of the capitalist society, developed into an industrial, rather post-industrial society. At the same time, they are known for being the vanguards of post-modernism by reproaching the 'totalising idea of Enlightenment'. Strangely enough, they think of an ideal situation or a 'good society' in which the basic premises of socialism have their harmonisation with the ideal of a society of self-liberated individuals. Critical theory becomes utopian at the hands of some of its advocates like Marcuse and Habermas. "In a utopian vein, Marcuse anticipated a society in which labour would finally destroy the power of the death instinct."[76] In the view of Habermas, 'communicative action' would establish a 'public sphere' or a 'civil society' and thereby solve the problems of the crises of legitimacy, rationality and motivation. It is a matter of pity that he could see no solution to these staggered crises apart from recourse to a new set of norms that would involve the communicative competence."[77]

Vienna Circle: Complete victory of empiricism may be seen in the trend of positivism having its arch-priest in August Comte of France. Positivism contends that only phenomena which are, in principle, capable of being observed, are of any significance for social sciences. Facts are separable from values or metaphysical notions. In a scientific work, ethical and metaphysical terms must be eliminated; the designation of any synthetic sentence that is not ultimately verifiable through

74. *Ibid.*
75. *Ibid.*, p. 208.
76. David McLellan: *Marxism after Marx* (London: Macmillan, 1979), p. 270.
77. *Ibid.*, p. 274.

perceptions is unscientific, and hence meaningless. The line of Comte was followed by many others who made some modifications in it. As a physicist, Ernst Mach of Austria, in his *Essays on the Philosophy of Marxism*, sought to establish the unity of all sciences through radical elimination of metaphysics in a scientific work. In other words, he "attempted to construct a view of the world which consisted entirely of sensations; what we call objects (including the self) were merely groupings of sensations classified in the most economical and coherent manner."[78]

Modifications made by Mach in the trend of positivism became so popular that his followers came to be known as belonging to the 'Vienna Circle' founded in 1929. Positivism assumed the new name of logical positivism. It included a galaxy of natural and social scientists like Hans Hahn (a mathematician), Rudolph Carnap (a philosopher) and Otto Neurath (an economist). Some others joined the circle a little later like Hans Kelsen (a jurist) and Josef Schumpeter (an economist). Like the leading figures of the Frankfurt School, the zealous members of the Vienna Circle pushed the trend of positivism in different directions as a result of which it lost its original sense. While the Frankfurtians created a lot of confusion by their attempts to reinterpret or reinvigorate Marxism, the leading lights of the Vienna Circle also did considerable harm to the general understanding of scientific method and scientific value relativism.[79]

Concluding Observations

Following important impressions may be gathered from what we have discussed in the preceding sections:

1. Great social and political thinkers and theorists from Plato and Aristotle in the ancient to Laski and Lasswell in the modern times have tried to understand and explain 'political reality' in their own ways. They have expounded different views as per their judgements arrived at either by way of a philosophical discourse or by means of an empirical investigation of any kind. Thus, political theory has two main traditions—classical and modern. While the former is heavily deductive and normative, the latter is heavily inductive and empirical.[80] That is, while in the former tradition the thinkers and theorists, on the basis of their presuppositions are engaged in the pursuit of some ideals, goals and norms so as to have anything like a'good rule', a 'good life', or a 'perpetual peace', in the latter tradition we find theorists engaged in making formulations based

78. *Ibid.*, p. 105.
79. Arnold Brecht: *Political Theory* (Princeton: Princeton University Press, 1959), p. 182.
80. Deduction is the form of reasoning in which the conclusion of an argument necessarily follows from the premises. The validity of a deductive argument is established if it is impossible to assert the premises and deny the conclusion without self-contradiction. But induction is the method of reasoning by which general statements are derived from the observation of particular facts. Therefore, inductive arguments are always *probabilistic,* in contrast to deductive arguments. Induction was thought to characterise physical science in that laws were established by the constant confirmation of observed regularities. However, since no amount of observations can establish a general law (the most firmly established regularity may be refuted in the future), the generalities established by science seemed to rest on insecure, if not irrational, foundations. Popper argued that while theories cannot be logically established by repeated confirmations, they may be falsified." Norman P. Barry, *op. cit.*, pp. xiv-xv.

on collected facts and, therefore, verifiable by the methods of observation and quantification. However, the two traditions are not antithetical to each other. One supplements the other if we want to have a complete political theory. It is rightly visualised: "No single perspective holds any monopoly on wisdom; the quality of insight of the observer and his intellectual power outweighs the merits of a particular social theory or methodology. If this is heresy for modern social science, it is orthodoxy in the long history of social thought, for any other conclusion would observe the timeless importance of Thucydides, Machiavelli, Marx and Burke."[81]

2. Empiricism is good and empirical political theory has a place of its own. However, empiricism should not be carried to the extent of making classical tradition thoroughly discredited. Brute or crude empiricism of the modern, rather contemporary, political theory has done more of a harm than good to classical political theory. The neo-empiricists have realised the mistake of the empiricists and thus thought it better to emphasise reaffirmation of the norms and values in political theory to the possible extent. Not all important questions of a political inquiry can be answered by the tradition of empiricism. Laying emphasis on the inherent value of the philosophical political theory and thereby hitting at the zealousness of empirical political theory in the direction of making a new science of politics, Berlin says: "When we ask why a man should obey, we are asking for the explanation of what is normative in such notions as authority, sovereignty, liberty, and the justification of their validity in political arguments. These are words in the name of which orders are issued, men are coerced, wars are fought, new societies are created and old ones destroyed, expressions which play as great a part as any in our lives today. What makes such questions *prima facie* philosophical is the fact that no wide agreement exists on the meaning of some of the concepts involved...So long as conflicting replies to such questions continue to be given by different schools and thinkers, the prospects of establishing a science in this field, whether empirical or formal, seem remote."[82]
3. The real significance of the classical tradition cannot be dismissed. Scientific theory does not mean anything like a theory of physics or biology based strictly on 'facts'. It has its integral connection with the elements of 'ought' and 'nought'. A political theory of lasting value must, therefore, have certain philosophical orientations so that it may appeal to the heads as well as to the hearts of the people. "Thus if theories in the social sciences are put forward without any explicit philosophical underpinnings, they may lose their noetic character and uncritically support particular interests whether of a nation, regime, religion, party, or socio-economic class. Strictly speaking, the alternative to a philosophical political science is one that is parochial. One of the principal criticisms of the recent 'behavioural' social sciences has been that it has often implicitly and uncritically endorsed the policies and practices of the established order instead of performing Socratic function of 'speaking truth to power'.[83]

81. K.W. Thompson: "The Empirical, Normative and Theoretical Foundations of International Relations" in *The Review of Politics*, Vol. 29, 1967, pp. 147-59.
82. Barry, *op. cit.*, p. 7.
83. Dante Germino: "The Contemporary Relevance of the Classics of Political Theory" in Greenstein and Polsby, *op. cit.*, pp. 251-52.

Reasons and Gains of Divergent Interpretations

1. Political theory is not a theory in the strict sense of the word as it is used in science. Like scientific theory, political theory *describes* and *analyses* what is and tries to *predict* what *will* be, but in political theory there is no mathematically precise model the merits of which can be proved or disproved in carefully observed experiments. Political theory goes further than scientific theory. It has critical and constructive functions beyond the descriptive and predictive aspects of scientific theory. That is, political theory is value-based activity and, therefore, one in which it is helpful to have many viewpoints.
2. All the description, prediction, criticism and construction in political theory is stated in the imprecise language of the author's life time. Further, the author's thoughts are coloured by the elements of his personality and culture. While imprecision of language and the impact of culture and personality might be viewed as liabilities in scientific theory, in political philosophy they serve as triggers for interpretation and contribute to the development of new, creative political speculation.
3. Like great works of art, great political theory reflects the complexity of human consciousness. Political theories take on different meanings when viewed from different angles.Their richness is disclosed more fully when filtered through other consciousness and examined in the light of various approaches conceived by other minds.
4. Some of the functions of a good interpreter may be seen by looking at the word *interpretation.* It comes from a Latin word meaning broker or negotiator. In political theory the interpreter mediates between the theorist and the reader.
5. Interpretation can be a vehicle for gaining greater insight into the theory and practice of politics. But the interpreter, like all human beings, has 'interests' that will affect his interpretation of theory today just as comparable factors affected earlier philosophers' attempts to deal with the theoretical issues.
6. The goal of political theory is not 'correct' meaning but understanding of probable meanings which can educate us about politics. The process can provide new adventures into creative political thinking. As readers attempt to interpret great thought, they also engage in criticism of it and develop their own theories of politics. The problems of each age challenge great thought but also allow it to provide fresh insights in new settings. Thus, a good interpreter uses prior thought as a vehicle for creative development and carries on the discourse, that is, political theory.
7. Interpretation rests on recognition that no interpreter, professional or non-professional, is instantaneously and simultaneously an expert in the whole body of a theorist's writings; in manuscript analysis; in translation; in the author's mental and physical life, and in the social, cultural and economic history of the author's era and that of the previous eras. A positive assessment of the contributions of interpretation rests on the realisation that such 'facts' do not have the same significance for various scholars in the discipline. The relevance of 'facts' varies with scholars' ideas about meaning, and their judgements about the best approaches for studying political theory.
8. A great number of scholars with a wide variety of skills, approaches and outlooks, produce a discipline that polices itself. It provides criticism of critics. An interpretation may present new views, attack or defend existing views, or choose among competing views. This policing function in the discipline helps to account for the variety of interpretation available for readers. The existence of these alternate approaches, each with its own limitations, is part of the discipline's pursuit of the 'whole story' which is the understanding of politics.
9. Sometimes, an individual interpretation over-reaches the limits of its analytical tools and thus creates some of the disadvantages. However, even when an interpretation over-reaches itself, it can make a contribution as long as the discipline of political

theory polices itself to provide the constant intricate shifting and catching of the balance necessary for intellectual health.

10. Without realisation that each of us is a theorist, political thought will appear to be a dead, past-oriented subject matter. The field will appear irrelevant and will be pushed aside as a scholastic exercise to support the 'publish or perish' ordeal of college professors. With the realisation that we all are political theorists, even if not professional publishers of our findings, we can be future-oriented, self-aware receivers, reviewers, and evaluators of political thoughts. In this way, individuals can arouse their own creative as well as critical faculties and add to their enjoyment of political thought and politics. The stimulation from theorist to reader which produces worthwhile interpretation keeps the discipline of political theory vital and current.

Elizabeth James: *Political Theory*, pp. 2-3, 4-5, 80-81, 85.

4. In the case of 'political theories', the title 'classical' is especially appropriate, because here the premises, in question, are inherited, unchanged in all essentials since the Greek writers of the classical period. The greater part of 'classical political philosophy' is really concerned with recommending and providing worthless logical grounds for the adoption and perpetuation of axioms and definitions involving political words like 'state', 'law' and 'rights'. And the practical results of adopting the recommended redefinitions are often important, though the redefinitions themselves are no more puzzling than are alterations in the rules of bridge or football. Hence, there "is the temptation to say that classical political philosophers were occupied with logic chopping, often with a view to underwriting more or less *disreputable* politics, and with nothing else."[84]
5. In political theory as an academic discipline, the reader is struck by the astonishing as well as frightening variety of interpretative books and papers written about the works of great political thinkers and theorists. Such endeavours include radically different and often conflicting views about the meaning and significance of the literature on political theory. Such a study of political theory can, however, help us to identify our own emotionally-supported ideological commitment and to develop a more rational consideration of our political values.[85]

On the whole, various forms and traditions of political theory and the ever-increasing stock of their divergent critical interpretations and evaluations have a significance of their own. lt can produce "better understanding of the prevailing ideology of the society, of contemporary political conventions, of the social environment, and of the individual's place within the cultural framework. The individual can also learn how to critically evaluate an argument about political thought and how to grasp what is implied in various interpretations. Through the development of critical thinking, students can improve their insights into politics and into themselves as political thinkers and actors. They can use a critical approach to gain insight into alternative possible political futures produced by theorists and politicians."[86]

84. T.D. Weldon: *The Vocabulary of Politics* (Penguin Books, 1955), pp. 41-42.
85. D.D. Raphael: *Problems of Political Philosophy*, p. 18.
86. Elizabeth James, *op. cit.*, p. 84.

3

State of the Discipline

> It is universally acknowledged that there is a great uniformity among the actions of men, in all nations and ages, and that human nature remains still the same in its principles and operations. The same motives always produce the same actions. The same events always follow from the same causes. Ambition, avarice, self-love, vanity, friendship, generosity, public spirit: these passions, mixed in various degrees, and distributed through society have been from the beginning of the world, and still are, the source of all the actions and enterprises which have ever been observed among mankind.
>
> **—David Hume[1]**

Marvellous developments have taken place in the field of political theory in the present times, particularly after the Second World War. The additions of many new things have been lauded as 'new horizons' or the 'expanding frontiers of political science' (Frank Thakurdas) which in a surprising way has also been misconstrued as the decline, nay demise, of political theory (Peter Laslett). The starting point to be noted at this stage is that political theory has been overshadowed by 'political analysis' at the hands of certain leading American political scientists. 'State' and 'government' are no longer the fundamental themes of political science; this place has been given to the concept of 'power' (Weber, Easton and Almond) and that has also been synonymised with 'influence' (Lasswell and Dahl). Such a study is under the powerful impact of sociology and psychology; it informs a student of this subject to study and explain 'political reality' in terms of man as an 'actor' in the organised life of his community. As a result, political theory has come to find its "starting point in the fact that members of the human species live together."[2] Obviously, its scope has become wide so as to include the organisational structure, the processes of decision-making and action, the politics of control, the policies and actions, and the human environment of legal government."[3]

Birth of New Political Science: Increasing Trend Towards Empirical Political Theory

The credit for making significant developments in the domain of political science goes to leading English and American writers of the twentieth century. In 1908, Graham Wallas published his *Human Nature in Politics* in which he laid stress on the socio-

---

1. Hume: *Enquiries Concerning the Human Understanding and the Principles of Morals,* edited by L.A. Selby-Bigge (Oxford, 1927), II Ed.,p. 83.
2. R.A Dahl: *Modern Political Analysis* (Englewood Cliffs, New Jersey: Prentice-Hall, 1976), p. 100.
3. C.S. Hyneman: *The Study of Politics: The Present State of American Political Science* (Urbana: University of Illinois Press, 1959).

psychological foundations of political behaviour. He rabidly attacked the tradition of rationalism in politics coming down since the times of Plato and Aristotle through Rousseau, Kant, Hegel and Green and instead laid emphasis on the role of irrational forces in the sphere of human behaviour. A realistic study of politics must be based on the role of habits, sentiments, instincts, emotions and the like which certainly influence and mould political attitudes of human beings.[4] Lord James Bryce endorsed the point of Wallas that the curiously unsatisfactory condition of political science of the time was owing to the persistence of an outdated, mistaken psychology. He also emphasised that the study of politics must be based on 'facts'.[5] Finally, we may refer to the name of G.E.G. Catlin who desired integration of politics with the study of other social sciences and thereby pioneered the course of interdisciplinary studies.[6]

However, such a change is specially noticeable in the United States where an increasingly large number of political scientists took much inspiration from the progress made in many other fields of intellectual inquiry like biology and anthropology, for the reason that these had given a powerful stimulus to the ways of, what is popularly called, 'scientific method'. The brunt of their argument was that man being the object of study in other social sciences too, political scientists could gain a great deal by using the methods of research cultivated by them, particularly in the fields of psychology, sociology, social anthropology and psychiatry. The establishment of the American Political Science Association in 1903 came as a bold proof of this new tendency on the part of the American political scientists concerned with the organisation, collection and classification of facts having an essential place in the study of politics.[7]

This trend became dominant in the issues of the *American Political Science Review* started in 1906. The new generation of political scientists drew inspiration from the exhortation of Lord James Bryce (in his presidential address delivered at the

---

4. See M.J. Wiener: *Between Two Worlds: The Political Thought of Graham Wallas* (Oxford: Clarendon Press., 1971).
5. Graham Wallas: *Human Nature in Politics* (London: Constable, 1948). As Wallas says: 'In politics, as in footfall, the tactics which prevail are not those which the makers of the rule intended, but those by which the players find that they can win, and men feel vaguely that the expedients by which their party is most likely to win may turn out not to be those by which a state is being governed." *Ibid.*, p. 4.
6. See G.E.G. Catlin: *The Science and Method of Politics* (London: Kegan Paul, 1927); and his *A Study of the Principles of Politics* (New York: Macmillan, 1930).
7. With the establishment of American Political Science Association in 1903 and thereafter, political theory, potentially, came to have a new master. Now the crucial question became: what the newly founded political science profession should assign to political theory. Until recently, little concern was given to this question and political theory remained much as it had been before—an area wherein study and investigation were largely confined to explaining and assessing the great masters of yesteryear: Plato, Aristotle, Rousseau, J.S. Mill and the like. Then shortly, after World War II, serious stock-taking was applied to political theory. Many of the young leaders in political science, intent upon developing an empirical science, raised the question: Is political theory, as it now stands, relevant to political science? Easton 'set off a wave of action and reaction which has resulted in a bifurcation of the discipline.' Eugene Meehan: *Contemporary Political Thought* (Homewood, Illinois: Dorsey Press, 1967), p. 1.

congress of the American Political Science Association in 1908) that they should be concerned with, 'facts, facts, facts'.[8] Among other leading figures, Arthur Bentley, Charles A. Beard and A.L. Lowell became highly critical of the 'speculative theorists' and 'utopia-makers' and instead, they insisted on the greater use of statistical techniques for ensuring complete objectivity. These writers could demonstrate that political science should change in a direction where there were decreasing references to the speculative entities like 'natural law' and 'natural rights'. In the same vein, they expressed their increasing hesitation to ascribe political events to providential causes. They rejected all divine and racial theories of institutions and instead went in for a 'persistent attempt to get more precise notions about causations in politics'[9]

However, the most important name in this connection is that of Charles Merriam of the Chicago University. Though a traditionalist, he preferred the line of empirical political theory as is evident from the study of his *Primary Elections* published in 1908. Subsequently, he took more and more inspiration from Max Weber of Germany and Lord Bryce of England. After 1920, he frankly jumped into the new field and thereby earned for himself the credit of being the arch-priest of what afterwards came to be known as the 'behavioural tradition' in political science. He now urged that an increasing attention should be given to the methods and findings of sociology, social psychology, geography, ethnology, biology and statistics. In this way, he took upon himself the responsibility of propagating the interdisciplinary and scientific character of political science.

Merriam, therefore, deserves the credit for being the pioneer of the new study of politics. He emphasised that 'power' was the main theme of the study of this subject and that a student should make full use of all the advances made by human intelligence in the field of social and natural sciences.[10] In 1925 he delivered the presidential address at the conference of the American Political Science Association, in the course of which he emphasised that the great need of the hour was the development of a scientific technique and methodology for political science. He laid special stress on the urgent need for the minute, thorough, patient and intensive study of the details of political phenomena in a way so as to have empirical political theory for the benefit of the coming generations.[11] Then, in his *New Aspects of Politics* (published in 1925) he explicated and advocated most of the characteristic goals, methods, procedures and stressed upon the importance of quantifying data and findings. He very hopefully visualised the emergence of a higher type of political and social science through which human behaviour may be more finely adjusted and its deeper values more perfectly unfolded.[12]

8. See *American Political Science Review,* Vol. 3, No. 3 (February, 1909).
9. Cited in Louis Wirth "The Social Science" in Merle Curtis (ed.): *American Scholarship in the Twentieth Century* (Cambridge: Massachusetts, 1953), p. 49.
10. See Charles Merriam: "The Present State of the Study of Politics" in *American Political Science Review,* Vol. 15, No. 1, 1921, pp. 173-85.
11. *Ibid.*
12. Bernard Crick: *The American Science of Politics: Its Origin and Conditions* (London: Routledge and Kegan Paul, 1959), p. 145.

Like Merriam, Harold Gosnell saw the possibilities of statistical and behavioural analysis in the use of voting data. A student of Merriam, Harold Lasswell brought out his *Psychopathology and Politics* (1930), in which he integrated the study of politics with the premises of Freudian psychology, as a distinct improvement upon Lippmann's *Preface to Politics.*[13] As a result of such efforts, a new type of political theory came up at the hands of the political scientists of the Chicago University (known as the 'Chicago School'), who made a clear break with the study of philosophical, historical and institutional approaches and instead laid all emphasis on the observable behaviour of man as a political creature. They concentrated more and more on group interaction wherein 'behaviouralism' found its natural start. "The pursuit of such behavioural concepts at Chicago became contagious and eventually went far beyond the political science arena to permeate the fields of educational testing, urban sociology, and statistical measurement."[14]

By 1930 the 'Chicago School' could carve out a place for itself in the domain of empirical political theory. In due course, apart from Merriam, Gosnell and Lasswell, others like David Easton, Stuart Rice and V.O. Key, Jr. came forward with their writings. It demonstrated that the teachers of the Chicago University "had made the first dent in the armoury of traditional political science. In the main, these political scientists, in breaking away from the traditional approach, sought to rest their generalisation about men and politics on an extensive empirical evidence, eschewing any ideological or valuational presuppositions. The application of statistics to the available data was a necessary ingredient of this whole drive towards empirical research. The erstwhile constitutional/institutional formalistic studies began to fade into the background, as the stream swelled into a torrent of what came to be christened as the behaviouralistic approach and its close ally (Political Sociology), both of which received a tremendous fillip from the school of 'logical positivism' with its emphasis on fact-value dichotomy."[15]

Some of the formative influences of the 'Chicago School' of behaviouralism may be summed up as under:[16]

1. It shifted emphasis from political ideals and institutions to the examination of individual and group conduct.
2. It favoured a natural science paradigm over a normative one (how people act, as opposed to how they should act.)
3. It preferred explanations of behaviour derived from theories of learning and motivation rather than from models of institutional power.
4. It subdivided behavioural political science into new lines of inquiry: the distribution and individual attitudes, beliefs, opinions, and preferences; and models of social learning.

---

13. *Ibid.*, p. 109.
14 David Apter: *Introduction to Political Analysis* (Englewood Cliffs, New Jersey: Prentice-Hall, 1977), p. 220.
15. Frank Thakurdas, *Essays in Political Theory,* p. 69.
16. David Apter, *op. cit.*, p. 220.

Certainly, this appeared as a new development in political theory. "In contrast to the *a priori* and deductive methods of politics prior to 1850, and to the historical and comparative method which was dominant in' the later half of the nineteenth century, the modern method shows a distinct tendency towards observation, survey and measurement."[17]

From Empiricism to Neo-Empiricisim: Reconstruction of Political Theory after World War II

Political theory underwent an important change in the period following the Second World War. It is evident from the fact that many American political scientists moved out of their ivory towers and stood face to face with the realities of social, economic and political life. Three important reasons may be assigned to it. First, the character of the governments in East European countries changed from the feudalism of a landed aristocracy to that of a peculiar kind and in other West European countries from the individualism of the *laissez faire* model to that of democratic socialism embodied in the concept of a welfare state. Second, the United States emerged as a superpower that took to the commitment of saving 'democracy' from slipping into the throes of totalitarianism. Above all, the emergence of the Soviet Union as another superpower stood as a powerful as well as a formidable challenge. It appeared in the form of a great struggle between Marxism of the USSR and the liberalism of the USA. As a result of this, the political scientists of the United States engaged themselves in a serious endeavour to put forward a political theory which would present a viable and successful alternative to the political theory of Marxism-Leninism.

It may be worthwhile to note at this stage that the new American political scientists definitely took inspiration from a great number of European sociologists and psychologists like A. de Tocqueville, Robert Michels, G. Mosca, W. Pareto, James Bryce, Max Weber, M. Ostrogorski, Graham Wallas, Sigmund Freud, Talcott Parsons, Barrington Moore, etc. However, their distinctive contribution is that they adopted a new approach, a new orientation, a new method, a new methodology or anything of the sort just to meet the challenge of the times. For this sake, an interdisciplinary focus came quite handy. Their contributions revealed that in their view, political science "is now less parochial than before the War, but this exercise in togetherness has demonstrated all too clearly that there is little difference between the social science disciplines, save only as they are shaped by their intellectual history, the vested interests of the departments and of book publishers, and the budgets of academic deans."[18]

The line of the Chicago School witnessed its more and more adherents, though with certain modifications, in terms of strategies and paradigms, in leading study centres of the United States that now came up at the Michigan, the Princeton and the Stanford Universities. It showed that what the leading lights of the Chicago University had done in the 1920s and 1930s was taken over in the period after the World War II by other institutions known as Social Science Research Committees on

17. R.G. Gettell: *History of American Political Thought,* (New York : Appleton-Century-Crofts, 1928), p. 611.
18. Ronald Young: "Comment on Prof. Deutsch's Paper", in *A Design for Political Science : Scope, Objectives and Methods,* edited by James C. Charlesworth (Philadelphia, 1966), p. 193.

Political Behaviour and Comparative Politics. Among other such institutions, we may refer to the Survey Research Centre at Michigan under the charge of E. Pendleton Herring and Angus Campbell banking on the cooperation of V.O. Key, Jr., David B. Truman and S.J. Eldersveld. Centres for advanced studies in behavioural sciences were opened at some other places like the Stanford and the Princeton Universities. The most important event in this direction is the establishment of the Inter-University Consortium for Political Research set up in 1962 under the charge of Warren Miller. In a very short time, it had its affiliated wings in many leading colleges of the United States; it became the major depository of data from many research projects in the field of politics and the single-most important institutional vehicle for the study of political behaviour.

The story of the development of political theory after 1945 till this time may, however, be put into two phases. While in the first phase running upto 1970, the trend of behaviouralism dominated in which political theory discarded the traditional way of aligning politics with norms, values and goals, the second phase starts from 1970 in which leading political scientists realised the inadequacy of purely empirical political theory and veered round to the idea of the reaffirmation of norms and values to the possible extent. These two phases may be termed as empirical and trans-empirical or neo-empirical. It may, however, be repeated at this stage that the difference between the empiricists and trans-empiricists or neo-empiricists is not as deep and sharp as it seems to be. The leaders of the movement of neo-empiricism in politics do not indulge in the total repudiation of the traditional school—as an unfit garment—but only seek to understand the limitations that flow from its necessarily subjective, normative and prescriptive mode of theorising and analysis, hence experience the difficulty of formulating a method of analysis of approach, of universal acceptance. However, in order to get round its obvious subjectivity, of all speculation about politics, its empirical investigations "confined itself to the formal legal and institutional aspects of governmental systems; restricting its inquiry (and its attention) to the readily observable aspects of the political reality *viz.*, the institutional/legal."[19]

The main features of this kind of political theory as developed by the leading American writers in the period following the World War II, are:[20]

19. Frank Thakurdas, *op. cit.*, p. 70.
20. *Ibid* , pp. 70—72. However, in the hope of avoiding controversy over intangible matters, behaviouralists "took as their proper concern the realm of investigations into concrete actuality which they chose to call 'science'. See Ricci : *The Tragedy of Political Science,* p. 137. Lasswell and Kaplan hold that the basic concepts and hypotheses of political science should contain no elaboration of political doctrine, or what the state and society ought to be." *Power, and Society : A Framework for Political Inquiry* (London : Lowe and Brydone. 1952), p. xi. D.B. Truman also concludes that behaviouralism specifically informs that an inquiry into how many *ought* to act is not a concern of research in political behaviour." 'The Implications of Political Behaviour Research" in *Items* (December, 1951), pp 37-38. For a critical study of behaviouralism also see Marvin Surkin : "Sense and Nonsense in Politics" in Surkin and Wolfe (eds.) : *An End to Political Science,* (New York : Basic Books, 1970), pp. 13-33 and J.S. Gunnell : *Philosophy, Science and Political Inquiry,* (Morristown, New Jersey : General Learning Press, 1975).

1. The empirically inclined political scientist of the traditional school started or worked on the assumption that all forms of politics emerge from and are concentrated on the fact of the government—the total legal structure in and through which is manifested sovereignty of the state.
2. The politics of any state is the politics of its legal entity (government). And it can best be understood by a study of its structure, mode of its formation and operation. This assumption not only entailed a descriptive analysis but also demanded an investigation of the historical development of each institution of the government, including its process of evolution, causes of its change in powers or structures and the like. This style of political empiricism was regarded less as an ally but more an enemy of the purely speculative, especially *a priori,* mode of politics.
3. By following an interdisciplinary approach the new writers broke through the traditional boundaries. They attempted to discover merely some of the glaring deficiencies of the old style with a view not to search for a substitute or to supplant it but merely to supplement the political knowledge already acquired and definitely to search for a higher order of generalisations regarding the multifarious forms of man's political behaviour. It is characterised as being interdisciplinary, hence the stress on practice/experience.
4. Here we find a search for the probabilistic laws of human behaviour with reference to individuals or groups in various social contexts. It specifies as the unit of political/ empirical analysis, behaviour of persons or social groups instead of events, structures, institutions and ideologies.
5. It has a marked prediction for quantification whose need is promoted by the extensive data collection (of behaviour) and the demands of scientific method—*i.e.* the value of developing more precise techniques for observing, classifying and measuring data with a view to exclude non-verifiable evidence whatever be its form.

It is obvious that political theory has its peculiar meaning at the hands of the behaviouralists. To them, speculative theory is fruitless. Since traditional political theory is by and large speculative, it should be discarded as far as possible. Instead, only that part of political theory should be accepted that is in consonance with the requirements of a scientific theory. Thus, in order to distinguish their political theory from the theory of the traditionalists, they adopt a different style. They prefer to write traditional political theory with capital initial letters as 'Political Theory'. It signifies a speculative manner of studying things of a political nature applicable to constitutional law, local government, voting system, legislative functioning, international relations and a host of other subjects bearing on the same themes. They prefer to use small letters as in 'political theory' so as to cover a wide variety or political theories like the democratic theory, the empirical theory, the systems theory, etc., the distinctive feature of all being concerned with explanation to the exclusion of philosophy and ideology.[21]

21. David M. Ricci, *op. cit.,* p. 147.

Articles of Faith of Behaviouralism

1. **Testability:** It is a crucial requirement of scientific propositions. In the language of science, definitions must be operational. No matter how concrete or abstract conceptually, they must be relevant empirically.[1] Such an inquiry should proceed from carefully developed theoretical formations which yield operationalisable hypotheses and which can be tested against empirical data.[2] Ideally, adherents of the new approach would frame political statements in such a way that these propositions could be denied or confirmed, and thereby add to the general stock of political knowledge.
2. **Falsifiability:** Falsification tests can at least remove a great many mistaken beliefs from the accepted stock of political knowledge. The methods of science do not so much function to create knowledge as to reduce ignorance.[3] Deutsch is in agreement with this view and he holds that a political scientist pursues what he calls 'implication analysis'.[4]
3. **Testability:** The behaviouralists constantly remind themselves that all which they hold true may at times be proved false. They must always remain open-minded and ready to believe in the new. Scepticism has its own place in the field of behaviouralism.
4. **Methodology:** In fact, what the behaviouralists deserved to be called scientific for was not because of their accomplishments, whatever they might have been, but because their work was modelled after the methodological assumptions of the natural sciences.[5] In this sense, political scientists were seen as potential noviates for a larger vocation if only they would adopt appropriate habits.[6]
5. **Scientific Community:** Only right or scientific method must be adopted because it, if properly used, can at least reduce the margin of possible error inevitably attaching to all beliefs and thus expand the scope of acceptable knowledge. In its view, science is commendable for providing a systematically articulated and comprehensive body of maximally reliable knowledge claims. Without reliability, agrument and deliberation cannot proceed and rationality itself is abandoned.[7]

Thus, the behaviouralists "envisioned themselves as spokesmen for a very broad and deep conviction that the political science discipline should (i) abandon certain traditional kinds of research, (ii) execute a more modern sort of inquiry instead, and (iii) teach new truths based on the findings of those new inquiries.[8]

1. Heinz Eualu: *Behavioural Persuasion in Politics*, p. 6.
2. Somit and Tanenhaus: *The Development of American Political Science from Burgess to Behaviouralism* (Boston: Allyn and Bacon, 1967), p. 176.
3 Eulau's comment of Prof. Karl Deutsch's paper in J.C. Charlesworth (ed.): *A Design for Political Science: Scope, Objectives and Methods* (Philadelphia: The American Academy of Political and Social Science, 1966), p. 182.
4. K. Deutsch: "Recent Trends in Research Methods", *ibid.*, p. 169.
5. Easton: "Current Meaning of Behaviouralism" in Charlesworth (ed.): *Contemporary Political Analysis*, p. 9.
6. D.M. Ricci: *The Tragedy of PoliticalScience: Politics, Scholarship and Democracy* (New Haven, Conn: Yale University Press, 1984), p. 139.
7. Greggor, *op. cit.*, pp. 21-23.
8. Ricci, *op. cit.*, p. 144.

Traditional, Behavioural and Post-Behavioural Political Theory

	Traditional	*Behavioural*	*Post-Behavioural*
1.	Interrelates fact and value: speculative	Separates fact from value	Fact and value tied to action and relevancy
2.	Prescriptive and normative.	Non-prescriptive, objective and empirical	Humanistically and problem-oriented: normative
3.	Qualitative	Quantitative	Qualitative and quantitative
4.	Concerned with irregularities and regularities	Concerned with uniformities and regularities	Concerned with irre-gularities and regularities
5.	Configurative and non-comparative; focuses on individual countries	Comparative; focuses on several countries	Comparative : focuses on several countries
6.	Ethnocentric: focuses especially on Western European democracies	Ethnocentric, especially concerned with Anglo-American	Especially third world oriented model
7.	Descriptive, parochial and static	Abstract, ideologically conservative and static	Theoretical, and radical, change-oriented
8.	Focuses on formal (constitutional and governmental) structure	Focuses on formal and informal (group) structures and functions	Focuses on class and group relations and conflict
9.	Historical or ahistorical	Ahistorical	Holistic

Source: R.H. Chilcote: *Theories of Comparative Politics* (Boulder, Colorado: Westview Press, 1981), p. 57.

In other words, according to the behaviouralists, political theory is an activity that means explaining what *is* rather than what *ought* to be.[22] Theorising about politics "is not to be confused with metaphysical speculation in terms of abstractions hopelessly removed from empirical observation and control."[23] A subscriber to such a trend like Harry Eckstein says that all types of political inquiry involve the construction of theory, implicit or explicit, and the title of 'political theory' has been unjustifiably appropriated by the historians of political thought."[24] As an admirer of the new meaning of theory, D.B. Truman says : "In noting a revived interest in theory, I prefer to the creation, development, or application of theory and to theorising, or the readiness to draw inferences for a set of data to the class of events to which they belong."[25]

22. Neil MacDonald and James Rosenau : "Political Theory as Academic Field and Intellectual Activity" in Marian D. Irish (ed,): *Political Science: Advance of the Discipline* (Englewood Cliffs, New Jersey: Prentice-Hall, 1968), p. 27.
23. Lasswell and Kaplan : *Power and Society*, p. x.
24. Eckstein cited in John Plamenatz : "The Use of Political Theory" in Anthony Quinton (ed.) : *Political Philosophy* (New York : Oxford University Press, 1967), pp. 18-19
25. D.B. Truman: "Disillusionment and Regeneration: The Quest for a Discipline" in *American Political Science Review* (December, 1955), p. 870.

Behavioural political theory came up like a revolution and then got down in the face of a counter-revolution known by the name of 'neo-behaviouralism' but more popularly known as 'post-behaviouralism'. During the phase of twenty years (1950-70), it was never quite clear as to what kind of science the behaviouralists wished to pursue, or how thoroughly the same scholars were wedded to each of its tenets. In fact, the members of the discipline spoke vaguely about where political scientists should stand in relation to the formal models of science then available. And thus the discipline's writings sometimes equated the behavioural approach with no more than the 'scientific method'.[26] According to E.M. Kirkpatrick, behaviouralism assumed that the concepts and the theories of social sciences "can and ought to be made identical with those of the natural sciences."[27]

What, however, unpopularised behaviouralism was its obsession in the form of a 'mad craze for scientism'. It sought to do the impossible and so it was its love's labour lost. A critic like Bernard Susser despaired achieving a theoretical description and concluded that behaviouralism, for all practical intents and purposes, was "nothing more than the application of precise scientific methods to the study of politics."[28] A.S Goldberg asserted that 'the exact nature of the system of scientific thought is a matter of some controversy, and it is felt that a discussion of these controversies could prove more confusing than beneficial.'[29]

It may, however, be added at this stage that if behaviouralism had any definite character, it does not appear in the contradictory accounts of the points of fact and theory involved in the post-war switch to a new form of science. Yet there was a certain behavioural understanding of how to proceed professionally in support of a free society, and it can be seen by reconstructing what happened in the discipline of political science after World War II. In that analysis, it "becomes clear that behaviouralism strongly resembled Popperism in many respects. The congruence between the two goes far to explain why the behavioural approach was originally attractive for combining science with socially useful research and why its usefulness was consequently challenged, when the mid-century liberal matrix became less persuasive and Popperism as an over-all scheme for social inquiry began to fall from grace during the late 1960s."[30]

A new development in the form of a 'counter-culture' took place when the new caucus of dissenters turned away from pure behaviouralism to the side of post-behaviouralism. It is true that one may seek in vain within the caucus writings to find out a set of common principles that can be said to characterise the new

26. D.M. Ricci, *op. cit.*, p. 135.
27. Kirkpatrick: "The Impact of the Behavioural Approach on Traditional Political Science" in Howard Ball and Thomas Lanth (ed.s): *Changing Perspectives in Contemporary Political Analysis* (Englewood Cliffs, New Jersey: Prentice-Hall, 1971), p. 79.
28. Susser : "The Behavioural Ideology : A Review and a Retrospect" in *Political Studies* (September, 1974), p. 272.
29. Goldberg: "Political Science as a Science" in Ball and Lanth, *op. cit.*, p. 47. Also see Leiserson: "The Behavioural Approach" in Robert Connery (ed.) : *Teaching Political Science* (Durham : Duke University Press, 1965), pp. 61-62 and Greggor : *An Introduction to Metapolitics* (New York: Free Press, 1971), pp. 19-20.
30. Ricci, *op. cit.*, p. 136.

approach to political inquiry.[31] In fact, there is no satisfactory way of summarising in their totality the beliefs that the caucus members entertained concerning what should be done either in the American society as a whole or within political science as a learned discipline. "This is so because the caucus was less a circle of scholars constituting a unified school of thought than it was a floating faction riding the currents of discontent inside and outside of political science whose ranks over the years included petitioners as diverse as Daniel Moynihan, David Easton, Leo Strauss, Alan Wolf, Philip Green, Henry S. Kariel, Theodre Lowi, Michael Walzer, Morris Janowitz, H. Mark Roelofs, Charles McCoy and Howard Zinn."[32]

Thus, post-behaviouralism appeared on the scene of political science as a phenomenon indicating a shared determination to leave something definite behind rather than a common notion of the direction in which the discipline should move forward. The new trend of commitment signified that scholarly research should be relevant to specific social issues. But which issues would they be and who would define their significant features? It was also true that many practitioners feeling worried over various issues were willing to call for research leading to amelioratory action. But which action would they recommend from among the very large spectrum of nostrums available? To such questions post-behaviouralism offers only eclectic responses.

No doubt, political theory has seen great strides from its traditional to behavioural and thereon to post-behavioural phases. What is striking in this very connection is that in recent times the phase of traditionalism has lost its weight considerably. But political theory has certainly developed at the hands of its empirical and neo-empirical theorists. Viewed critically, two points may be stressed at this stage. First, the new enterprise "is unmindful of the chief difficulty confronting social sciences in general—the large number of variable factors, which make control and findings difficult, but also unlike the natural sciences, there is no agreement yet between either methods to be adopted or procedures to be followed, which has resulted in a large variety of empirical research studies, whose techniques vary considerably allowing for considerable differences."[33] Second, "unfortunately there is no commonly accepted explication of the structure of scientific theories, and, even more significantly, it is not clear how theories can be tested and rejected."[34]

Kuhn's Paradigms : Process of the Advancement of Political Theory

When the behavioural political theory was in its heyday, Thomas Kuhn presented his thesis of the development of political theory through the process of paradigms. In his study on the structure of scientific revolution, he argues that new paradigms are accepted through a process that differs significantly from the techniques of first falsifying beliefs and then replacing them with propositions deemed tentatively and temporarily true. According to his assumptions, a scientific debate on patent

31. *Ibid,*. p. 189.
32. *Ibid.*
33. Frank Thakurdas, *op. cit.,* p. 72.
34. J. Donald Moon : "The Logic of Political Inquiry : A Synthesis of Opposed Perspectives" in Greenstein and Polsby : (eds.) *Political Science : Scope and Theory* (California : Addison-Wesley, 1975), Vol. I, p. 207.

anomalies starts with a suspicion that the old paradigm is still partly right. And when a new paradigm is proposed, it is so crudely formulated that it is not, and cannot be entirely persuasive. After all, if the new paradigm is accepted, it will later be refined and improved during a period of normal science. But at the moment of its inception, it is not so thoroughly elaborated as to be clearly and objectively true.[35]

Kuhn's affirmations are based on the assumption that confrontation and shifting emphasis of different approaches as well as the revolutionary replacement of one approach by another make clear the struggle of social science to see a 'paradigm'. Such a notion of 'paradigm' relates to research firmly based upon one or more past scientific achievements that a particular scientific community acknowledges for a time as supplying the foundation for its further practice.[36] These achievements become paradigmatic or examples of actual scientific practice. These examples include law, theory, application, and instrumentation together and provide models from which spring particular coherent traditions of scientific research. Thus, the paradigms shape and condition one's orientations. The paradigm to which one subscribes, however, guides research by direct modelling and abstracted rules.[37]

Moreover, according to Kuhn, paradigms establish the limit of what is possible, the boundaries of acceptable inquiry. A successful paradigm then enables a scientific community to maintain criteria for the selection of problems to be used for finding solutions. Scientists working with a successful paradigm, however, might be unable to perceive possibilities beyond their own assumptions. The consequence of their parochialism may be a failure to keep adherents from shifting their attention to competing modes of scientific activity. In order to make his point clear, Kuhn suggests a number of phases through which science tends to pass. These are:[38]

1. There is the pre-paradigmatic phase in which no single theoretical approach or school predominates in the scientific community, although a number of such approaches or schools are in competition with each other.
2. There is another paradigmatic phase in which the scientific community adheres to a dominant paradigm.
3. Then there is the crisis phase. The dominant paradigm is subject to challenge and revision, and new paradigms may evolve and the old one's may be revived, giving rise to debate and competition among a variety of perspectives.

---

35. Thomas Kuhn : *The Structure of Scientific Revolution* (Chicago : Chicago University Press, 1962), p. 7.
36. *Ibid.*, p. 10. In this regard, Frohock says : "Instead of unbiased sceptics, we get a picture of partitions defending the established order. However, we must not take the established order as only a hindrance to research. It is also a necessity. Kuhn defines this order as a paradigm, meaning the agreement on theory, problems and techniques which characterise normal science. Without a paradigm, scientific research could not take place as a collective enterprise, for science needs an organising principle. A paradigm fulfils the requirements at all levels, from the simple task of defining facts to the broader view of establishing criteria for recognising problems and research approaches. The paradigm is the commonality underlying a scientific community." *The Nature of Political Inquiry* (Homewood, Illinois: The Dorsey Press, 1967), p. 104.
37. R.H. Chilcote : *Theories of Comparative Politics : The Search for a Paradigm* (Boulder, Colorado : Westview Press, 1981), p. 59.
38. *Ibid.*

4. There is the phase of scientific revolution which occurs when the scientific community shifts to significantly different paradigms. A paradigm is thus a scientific community's perspective of the world, its set of beliefs and commitments—theoretical, conceptual, methodological, etc.

To take a specific example, we may say that the Copernican cosmology appeared on the scientific scene, not graced with the Newtonian laws of motion and at a time when the Ptolemaic cosmology was considered weak but entirely invalid as a guide to cosmic events. The Copernican cosmology was nevertheless accepted with all its imperfections. With such shifts of allegiance in mind, Kuhn generalised that every scientific revolution succeeds by joining a little falsification of the old paradigm with a little verification of the new. Paradigm change thus depends on a blurred combination of negative and positive impulses that does not resemble the methodological stereotype of falsification by direct comparison with nature.[39]

It may be admitted at this stage that Kuhn tried to make a correction in the erratic line of behavioural political theory. He noted that there were a good number of complaints to the effect that political science in the behavioural era was more of a 'closed' than an 'open' community and more likely to generate useless rather than useful knowledge exercising social issues of great urgency. In this sense, professional unease paralleled the 'counter-culture' notion that substantive rationality was somehow lacking all over America, that absolute values were denigrated and an intolerable situation was tolerated both in the fashioning of pubic policy and in the work carried on by university scholars. Eventually, Kuhn decided that advancing in this realm may be described in a theory based on the concepts of paradigms, normal science, anomalies and scientific revolutions.

In defence of Kuhn's thesis it may be stated that the concept of paradigms is certainly useful inasmuch as it explains the manner of growth of a discipline. Then, at any given time, it provides the structure within which researchers can work and feel that they are making progress. Indeed, the notion of falsification as a hallmark of scientific progress is flatly contradicted by the fact that every old paradigm holds sway even though known anomalies, while being disregarded, give the lie to at least a part of it. Kuhn calls it 'gestalt switch', *i.e.,* transmission from one set of perception to another. The world may be the same after the paradigm change as before, but the scientists who accept the new paradigm will perceive and judge that world differently. It is as though the old paradigm teaches half a glass of water is half full, while the new paradigm suggests that the glass is half empty. It infers that the theory of paradigm may be handled differently by different kinds of researchers. Hirschman, therefore, feels that "the search for paradigm, if successful, would actually constitute a hindrance to understanding."[40]

---

39. D.M. Ricci, *op. cit.,* pp. 193-94.

40. A.O. Hirchman: 'The Search for Paradigms as a Hindrance to Understanding" in *World Politics* (April, 1970), pp. 329-43. As Prof. Sudipta Kaviraj says that paradigms "change and thereby they give rise to problems of incommensurability and difficulties of translation. Concepts do not mean the same thing in different paradigmatic or theoretical contexts. Owing to this, it is difficult to mould the history of social science in Kuhn's format." Refer to his paper "Are there Paradigms in Political Theory?" in J.S. Bains and R.B. Jain (ed. s) : *Political Science in Transition* (New Delhi : Gitanjali, 1981), pp 48-62.

Decline of Political Theory: Arguments of Easton and Cobban

The debate on this important issue finds its first expression in the paper of David Easton whose argument is contained in his indictment of contemporary political theory (including thought) for living on centuries-old ideas and, more than that, for failing to develop new political syntheses.[41] His argument is based on some points, the first and foremost of which is the absence of a congenial climate. Political ideas emerge and flourish in the soil of social conflict and change. The socio-political upheavals of ancient Greece produced great thinkers like Plato and Aristotle. So the social and religious conflicts of the Middle Ages produced great thinkers ranging from St. Augustine and St. Thomas Aquinas who defended the supreme position of the Church on the one hand, to Marsiglio of Padua and William of Occam, who did the same for the independent position of the State on the other. To carry this argument further, we may say that the struggle between an obdurate monarchy on the one side, and an equally adamant parliament on the other, in seventeenth century England released much philosophical food for the thoughts of Hobbes and Locke.

Likewise, the American and French revolutions in the latter half of the eighteenth century produced a very large number of social theorists like Burke, Paine and Voltaire. The absolute ways of the French monarchy impelled Rousseau and Montesquieu to find out the rules of legitimate political obligation. As no such social and political and economic upheavals are now in existence, political theory is witnessing its impoverishment. As he says: "Contemporary political thought lives parasitically on ideas a century old and, what is more discouraging, we see little prospect of the development of new political syntheses. It is said that the social sciences await a new Aristotle or a new Newton. For political theory, if present prospects are any indication of the actual turn of future events, this wait will be in vain, for we are not preparing the soil out of which revolutionary creative thinking can arise."[42]

Another reason for the decline of political theory should be traced in taking the subject very close to the discipline of history with a view to lay down certain inexorable laws of social development as we may find in the great books written by G H. Sabine, R.W. Carlyle, A.J. Carlyle, W.A. Dunning, H.C. McIlwain, C.K. Allen and A.D. Lindsay.[43] These writers have studied political theory and its development in the context of the history of the Western (European) countries. A deep study of their works "reveals that they have been motivated less by an interest in analysing and formulating new value theory than in retailing information about the meaning, internal consistency, and historical development of contemporary and past political

41. See David Easton : "The Decline of Modern Political Theory" in *Journal of Politics*, Vol. XIII, No. 1 (February, 1951), pp. 36-58 reproduced in Gould and Thursby, *Contemporary Political Thought*, pp.307-327.
42. *Ibid*, p. 308. According to Prof, M M. Sankdher, "The twentieth century is barren. No creative thinking, no cross-fertilisation of ideas, no political synthesis has taken place. Poverty of thought and impoverishment of political speculation is conspicuous." See his paper "Creative Potential in Political Theory" in J.S. Bains and R.B. Jain (ed.s), *op. cit.*, p. 30.
43. See Sabine : *A History of Political Theory* ; Carlyle and Carlyle : *A History of Medieval Political Theory in the West* (6 Volumes) ; Allen : *A History of Political Theory in the Sixteenth Century* : Dunning: *A History of Political Theories* (3 Volumes); McIlwain : *Growth of Political Thought in the West;* and A.D. Lindsay: *The Modern Democratic State.*

values."[44] This kind of analysis has played a major part in destroying a species of mental activity that has prevailed in literate civilisations and which emerges out of universal human needs.[45] Then it "has unwittingly helped to divert the attention and energies of political theorists from the task of building systematic theory about political behaviour and the operation of political institutions."[46]

Easton is not satisfied with the contributions of those who subscribe to the way of historical analysis. He calls some theorists (like Carlyle and McIlwain) as 'institutionalists' who usually treat the history of ideas as the study of epiphenomena, as mere froth on the ocean, as it were, that has little effect on the waves. For them, political theory involves a discussion of the kind of ideas that have emerged to help rationalise political interests and institutional development. More than that, they seem to be in agreement with the prevailing indictment that such ideas are just 'myths' and therefore incapable of determining political activity.[47] Same is the case with others (like Dunning and Allen), whom he calls 'interactionists', who insist that ideas do play a vital part in political life interacting with institutions as a significant variable in the whole process of social change. For them, the task of political theory is to unveil the actual role of ideas at each historical juncture.[48] Finally, others (like Sabine and Dunning), whom he calls 'materialists', approach political theory with the objective of uncovering the historical and cultural conditions that gave rise to the prevailing political conceptions of an age.[49] The common point about all is that they are historicists in their fundamental orientation. "In the interstices of their works, lurks the prevailing conceptions of social science, that all a social scientist can legitimately say about moral categories is that they are a product of the historical situation."[50]

What Easton really wants to convey is that the tendency of historicism suffers from want of dynamism. Instead of discovering the new set of values congenial to the changed conditions of human life, the theorists try to assess the utility of the present notions in the light of age-old values, some of which have certainly lost their relevance and, for that reason, cannot be taken as a determinant of political activity. As he continues: "The history of political values has led theorists to concentrate on the relation of values to the milieu in which they appear rather than on the task of attempting to create new conceptions of values commensurate with men's needs. Political theorists have been devoting themselves to what is essentially an empirical rather than a value problem, at least in terms of the traditional disjunction between facts and values. In doing so, they have assimilated value theory into empirical or causal social science and have thereby given up theory's traditional task of reformulating the content of values."[51]

44. Easton in Gould and Thursby, *op. cit.*. p, 311.
45. *Ibid.,* p. 308.
46. *Ibid.,* p. 309.
47. *Ibid.,* p. 312.
48. *Ibid.*
49. *Ibid.*
50. *Ibid.,p.* 313.
51. *Ibid.,* p. 312.

Easton is generally known as an advocate of empirical political theory. And yet this impression should not be formed that he accords no place to values in the field of political inquiry. What he really attacks is the excessive emphasis on the role of values in the field of political investigations, for it has an adverse effect on the prosecution of empirical investigations. It was, and is still, felt that the adoption of a value frame of reference "would either distract the empirical worker from his main interest in observing human behaviour, or distort his results, since the wish easily becomes father to the thought."[52] However, such a statement should be read with this affirmation that "whatever effort is exerted, values cannot be shed in the way a person removes his coat. They are an integral part of personality and as we are human, we can assume that our mental sets and preferences will be with us."[53] A way out of this problem of political theory should be discovered in formulating a new kind of theory what Easton calls 'creative theory'. It is that kind of theory which is, by and large, empirical but at the same time sustained by certain moral considerations having relevance to the determination of political activity. Neither a purely normative nor an absolutely empirical but a new kind of theory should come up having a judicious blending of the two. "This is the function of sensitively responding to the urgent problems of society and to the emerging social needs so that it becomes possible to articulate a sophisticated system of values that will help both the citizen and the statesman to define their situation. Such a definition requires the conjunction of three elements : a statement of the actual situation, a statement of goals, both long-run and proximate, and a statement of the means to achieve these goals."[54]

This may be called 'bridge-building' exercise. It would establish a link between the needs of the society and the scientific knowlege of the social sciences. It would help both the statesmen and the citizens to define their situation thereby serving to clarify for them the grounds of political action. If the discipline of political science is to be saved from decline and instead, if it is to be reinvigorated, it is needed that it should be recast in a new conceptual framework what Easton calls 'broad-gauge theory'. Both the traditionalists (by and large normativists) and the modernists (by and large empiricists) have committed the common mistake of setting the cart to draw the horse. The decline of political theory is due to barren normativism as well as due to crude empiricism. "Contemporary knowledge in political science can be criticised not because it fails to measure up to the rigorous canons of unadulterated science but because it does not use the more modest methods and techniques that are at present available in the social sciences as a whole and that have proved exceedingly fruitful in research."[55]

On the whole, Easton throws light on certain factors playing their part in the decline of political theory and then suggests a conceptual framework in which political theory is, by and large, empirical with the incidental touch of a value frame of reference necessary for social requirements as well as congruent to the

52. *Ibid.*, p. 316.
53. *Ibid.*
54. *Ibid.*, pp. 318-19.
55. *Ibid.*, p. 326.

causal study of politics. Only this can make political theory 'creative' and assign to it the character of a 'broad-gauge' formulation. As he concludes: "The burden of my argument is, then, that in addition to its task of helping to analyse and formulate new political values, political theory ought to devote itself to the equally vital job of conceptualising the basic areas for empirical research in political science. It ought to undertake this in two concurrent and parallel ways: first, by synthesising and codifying the limited generalisations we have in the various fields of political science and by so formulating the resulting theory that it lends itself to verification and invalidation and, second, by attempting the more massive task of elaborating a usable conceptual framework for the whole body of political science. In this way, it would be possible for political theory to assimilate itself to the main current of empirical research in political science, and thereby to revivify itself after the unrewarding historical study to which it has been devoted in the last fifty years."[56]

After Easton we come to Cobban who joins this debate with this own set of arguments.[57] To him, contemporary political theory is no longer a 'progressive science' in view of the fact that it has failed to revise itself in the light of new conditions. It looks like a worn-out coin that requires its recoining. Thus, the decline of political theory may be traced in its failure to be revised or renovated in the light of the post-war conditions of the present age. As he says: "The conditions of social life alter, sometimes more slowly and sometimes more rapidly, in the last few centuries at an increasingly dizzy pace, and as they alter, the words we use and the ideas they convey, lose old meanings and acquire new ones. For this reason, a continual restatement of political principles is both necessary and inevitable—as long as, that is, the tradition of political thinking, which is one of the peculiar characteristics of Western civilisation, remains alive."[58]

The first argument raised by Cobban is that political theory is a product of active political life. Obviously, here he follows the line of Easton. It was the active political life of the ancient Greeks that led to the emergence of political theory in so developed a form. "One does not expect to find it flourishing among Australian aboriginal tribes, in the Russia of Ivan or Peter, the Paraguay of the Jesuits, or the empire of the Caesars."[59] To take an example, we may say that what is now known as the Greek political theory was a product of Athens where the people had an active life and not that of Sparta, Macedonia or Syracuse where the people lived meekly under a despotic rule. Political theory developed during the days of struggle between the Church and the State in the later part of the Middle Ages. It had the same development in the seventeenth and eighteenth centuries when people took an active part in struggling against monarchical absolutism. Surprisingly, the advent of the popular system of democracy has made the life of people 'dull' in its own way, despite the fact that one may take note of a very active political life in this system. A proof of this may be traced in the fact that now there is no contemporary Burke

56. *Ibid.*, pp. 326-27.
57. See Alfred Cobban: "The Decline of Political Theory" in *Political Science Quarterly*, Vol. LXVIII, No. 3 (September, 1953), pp. 321-37 reproduced in Gould and Thursby, *op. cit.*, pp. 289-303.
58. *Ibid.*, p. 290.
59. *Ibid.*, p. 293.

or Bentham implying that there "are no intellectual giants in the field of political theory today."[60]

It follows from above that the success of democratic system should be held responsible for the decline of political theory in its own way. People look like satisfied with the aims of their life and, for that reason, active political life has come to an end. Whatever political activity we may take note of in a democratic system is an indication of search for power by any means whatsoever and not an endeavour in the direction of finding out a better alternative to it. As Cobban says: "The dominant political idea in the modern world is democracy. Most of the contradictions of contemporary politics find their place under the democratic umbrella, but broad as that is, they jostle one another, and moreover the umbrella seems to be leaking badly. And where are the political theorists of democracy today? Instead of a rational theory, it has become a sort of incantation. It is the 'open sesame' of political treasure hunters everywhere. The world is full of would-be Aladdins chanting 'democracy'. The masses, at least in those countries which have no experience of democracy, are waiting in a state of mystic faith for the revelation that the word is to produce... Meanwhile, democracy, for lack of thought, has ceased to be a living political idea. It has become a shibboleth, and not even serviceable as such.... It has largely become a meaningless formula. Politicians, like the princess in the fairy tale condemned to the oracular utterance of frogs, seem scarcely able to open their mouths without some platitude flopping out, wet and flabby and slightly repulsive, but is this political theory? If it is, no wonder that practical men prefer to ignore it."[61]

Another factor that has played its part in the decline of political theory in the modern age is the obsession of some great writers and theorists to align it exclusively with the concept of 'power' as given by Machiavelli of Italy and Hobbes of England and revisited by Max Weber of Germany. For this Cobban refers to the contributions of Ferro, Bertrand de Jouvenel, Bertrand Russell, E.H. Carr, Reinhold Niebuhr, Harold Lasswell and H.J. Morgenthau in particular. What attracts all these great figures about political life is the state as power. "They envisage power as a kind of electric force, now diffused and now concentrated, which not merely runs through society but is its very essence....The wretched individual atoms of which society. is composed are massed together, hurled violently about, disintegrated by power which they did not create and cannot control."[62]

The case of values in the study of politics is sacrificed at the altar of the power theory of politics having its first vulgar manifestation in the works of Machiavelli

---

60. *Ibid.*
61. *Ibid.*, pp. 293-94.
62. *Ibid.*, p. 294. To substantiate his argument Cobban cites the words of Bertrand Russell who said that "the laws of social dynamism are only capable of being stated in terms of power." Then, he quotes these words of Niebuhr: "It may be possible, though it is never easy, to establish just relations between individuals within a group by moral and rational suasion and accommodation. In inter-group relations this is practically an impossibility. The relations between groups must, therefore, always be predominantly political rather than ethical, that is, they will be determined by the proportion of power which each group possesses at least as much as by any rational and moral appraisal of the comparative needs and claims of each group." *Moral Man and Immoral Society* (New York: Charles Scibner's Sons, 1933), pp. 22-23.

and witnessing its reiteration in the recent writings of Morgenthau, Niebuhr and O.Y. Gasset. In other words, one more reason for the decline of political theory may be traced in the affirmation of cynical pessimism that discards the place of morals in any discussion of politics and, more curiously, comes to hold that somehow good would come out of the evil. The politician of today is no longer an advocate of the primacy of values over action in the field of social dynamics and power politics. If political theory remained so popular in the past, the reason was that it lived like a branch of morals or ethics. In contrast to it, modern political theory has largely ceased to be discussed in terms of what ought to be; and the reason, I believe, is that it has fallen under the influence of two modes of thought which had a fatal effect on its ethical content. These, and they have come to dominate the modern mind, are history and science."[63]

Like Easton, Cobban attacks the tendency of historicism for this purpose. The historian sees all ideas and ways of behaviour as historically conditioned and transient. The historical approach to the study of politics should be regarded as the reiteration of power theory of politics in view of the fact that a man of history is mainly concerned with the role of power in the determination of political events. Obviously, this tendency militates against the way of laying stress on the role of morals in the field of politics. As he continues: "By itself, in political theory, history can produce only the crudest Machiavellianism. If all historians are not little Machiavellis, it is only because they take their political ideals from some other source and carry them into history. It is sufficient to say that at least there is a tendency among modern historians to regard the passing of ethical judgement as an illegitimate process against which historical discipline should be a safeguard...History acquires more positive, and more dangerous, implications when it is made into a philosophy of history."[64]

Another reason for the decline of political theory should be traced in making the study of politics a matter of mere academic study. Cobban's argument is that in the past, political theory was essentially practical. The political theorist, in his own way, was a party man, and party men themselves used not to be afraid to season their practice with the salt of theory. In the past the study of political theory was the work of men intensely concerned with practical issues. Now, instead, it "has become an academic discipline, written in various esoteric jargons almost as though for the purpose of preventing it from being understood by those who, if they did understand it, might try to put it into practice.... Political theory, in this way, has become disengaged on principle, as it has seldom, if ever been, in the past. The academic political theorist of today may study the great political thinkers of the past, but in the name of academic impartiality he must carefully abstain from doing the kind of thing they did."[65]

Finally, Cobban points out that, in contemporary political theory, a sense of direction is lacking. There is no feeling of purpose. Hegelian politics is already dead,

63. Cobban, *op. cit.,* p. 299.

64. *Ibid.,* p. 300.

65. *Ibid.,* p. 298. In his defence he quotes these words of A.N. Whitehead: "They canalise thought and observation within the predetermined limits, based upon inadequate metaphysical assumptions dogmatically assumed." *Adventures of Ideas* (London, 1933), p. 151.

Marxist politics is increasingly revealed as a dialectical apologia for the pursuit of power for its own sake. Mad craze for empiricism has created a wide chasm between facts and values. The result is that in the absence of a rational theory to justify its sense of political obligation and the rightful purpose of political activity in a governed community, it has fallen victim to an irrational theory of power politics. Thus, he concludes: "After a generation's experience of drifting directionless on a stormy sea, the need of recovering a sense of direction and, therefore, control is beginning to be felt. And if political theory revives, if the idea of purpose is reintroduced into political thinking, we may take up again the tradition of Western political thought and in doing so, resume that continuous transformation of morals into politics which still remains politics and in which, according to Croce, lies the real ethical progress of mankind."[66]

Resurgence of Political Theory : Arguments of Berlin, Blondel and Strauss

To say that political theory has declined, nay demised, is to make a misstatement for two reasons. First, such a statement refers to a part of political theory based on the classical tradition, it does not at all apply to the modern or contemporary political theory that is heavily empirical, even trans-empirical. Second, it ignores the aspect of the great development of political theory in the period following World War II that is lauded as the marvellous rejuvenation or 'resurgence' of political theory. Here is a rejoinder to the contention of the decline of political theory. If Easton and Cobban are on one side, as seen in the preceding section, Berlin, Blondel and Strauss are on the other side of the controversy, who with equal force contend that political theory is neither dying nor dead, it very much exists.[67] We may briefly discuss the views of these great writers as under:

What Easton and Cobban have said about the decline of political theory in the early 1950s finds its forceful rebuttal at the hands of Prof. Isaiah Berlin.[68] First, he takes up the main points on which the contention of the decline of political theory depends. These are:[69]

66. Cobban, *op. cit.*, p. 303.
67. These two important terms 'decline' and 'resurgence' of political theory have a particular appellation. While the former signifies rejection of the classical (speculative or metaphysical) theory, the latter signifies remarkable growth of empirical political theory in the period following the Second World War. "In the broadest sense, what happened was a logical reflection of the point of view summed up in the initial dichotomy between facts and values. It was not that philosophical matters were deemed unimportant in principle but that there seemed no way of dealing with them significantly. In terms popular at the time, scholars increasingly accepted the proposition that a difference in kind separates facts from values and that the latter should be discarded. This resulted in the decline of political theory. See Ricci, *op. cit*, p. 145. In opposition to this, an admirer of the empirical tradition like G.A. Almond says that it represents a genuinely important step in the direction of science. "It is a step comparable to the one taken in the Enlightenment (eighteenth century) political theory over the earlier classical formulations." Refer to his paper "Political Theory and Political Science" in *American Political Science Review* (December, 1966), p. 875.
68. Berlin: "Does Political Theory Still Exist?" in Peter Laslett and W.G. Runciman (eds.) : *Philosophy, Politics and Society* (Oxford : Basil Blackwell, 1962), II Series, pp. 1-33, reproduced in Gould and Thursby, *op. cit* pp. 328-57.
69. *Ibid.*, pp. 331-32.

1. The principal symptom which seems to support this belief is that no commanding work on political philosophy has appeared in the present century. By a commanding work in the field of general ideas is meant, at the very least, one that has in a large area converted paradoxes into platitudes or *vice versa.*
2. The conceptual propositions of political theory, whether empirical or metaphysical or logical, are no longer accepted because they have (with the world of which they were a part) withered away, or because they have been discredited or refuted.
3. Many new disciplines have come up to perform the work originally undertaken by the older study. These disciplines may have their own limitations but they exist, they function, and have either inherited or usurped the functions of their predecessors. There is no room left for the ancestors from whom they sprang. This is the fate that overtook astrology, alchemy, phrenology (positivists, both old and new, would include theology and metaphysics). The postulates on which these disciplines were based were either destroyed by argument or collapsed for other reasons; consequently, they are today regarded merely as instances of systematic delusion.
4. Among the topics that remain obstinately philosophical and have, despite repeated efforts, failed to transform themselves into sciences, are some that in their very essence involve value-judgements. The mere fact that value-judgements are relevant to an intellectual pursuit is clearly not sufficient to disqualify it from being recognised as a science.

Berlin refutes all such points in order to prove that the discipline of political theory still exists. His first important contention is that politics exists in a society where ends collide. The end of politics may be possible in the future society of Marx, but it is not at all possible in a liberal order and, as such, political theory can never see its end. "It follows that the only society in which political philosophy in its traditional sense, that is, an inquiry concerned not solely with the elucidation of concepts, but with the critical examination of presuppositions and assumptions, and the questioning of the order of priorities and ultimate ends, is possible, is a society in which there is no total acceptance of any single kind. There may be a variety of reasons for this: no single end has been accepted by a sufficient number of persons because no one end can be regarded as ultimate, since there can be, in principle, no guarantee that other values may not at some time engage men's reason or their passions; because no unique, final end can be found—inasmuch as men can pursue many distinct ends, none of them means to, or parts of, one another: and so on. Some among these ends may be public or political; nor is there any reason to suppose that all of these must, even in principle, be compatible with one another. Unless political philosophy is confined to the analysis of conflicts or expressions, it can be pursued consistently only in a pluralist, or potentially pluralist, society"[70]

The hard-nosed empiricists have done a great disservice to the study of politics not only by discarding the place of values and thereby contributing to the decline of classical political theory, but their more serious fault is that they have tried to

70. *Ibid.*, p. 336.

understand and explain political reality in a wrong way. All issues having their relationship with politics can neither be studied empirically, nor deduced formally. Those who confine themselves to observation of human behaviour and empirical hypotheses about it (as historians, psychologists, sociologists), however profound and original they may be, are not, as such, political theorists, even though they may have much to say on what is crucial in the field of political philosophy. In a way it implies that the responsibilty for causing decline of political theory should be laid on rank empiricists who have displaced the classical tradition. On this basis, Berlin goes to the length of commenting: "That is why, we do not consider such dedicated empiricists as the students, say of the formation and behaviour of parties, or elites or classes, or of the methods and consequences of various types of democratic procedure, to be political philosophers or social theorists in the larger sense."[71]

Ever since civilisation started, man has tried to establish some form of authority and accept it. Political theory has arisen from an inquiry of this crucial issue of political obligation. Thus, as authority has been in every age, so has been political theory. It implies that so long as man lives under some authority, ends shall collide and possible solutions for them be conceived and implemented. So political theory shall continue to exist as a result of the inquisitive and rational inquiry of man. "So long as rational curiosity exists—a desire for justification and explanation in terms of motives and reasons, and not only of causes or functional correlations or statistical probabilities—political theory will not wholly perish from the earth, however many of its rivals, such as sociology, philosophical analysis, social psychology, political science, economics, jurisprudence, semantics may claim to have dispelled its imaginary realm."[72]

Berlin does admit that some portions of political theory may lose their relevance or significance for being outdated or outmoded, but it does not mean that the subject as a whole goes out of existence. For instance, when the theological and metaphysical models of the Middle Ages were swept away by the science of the seventeenth and eighteenth centuries, they disappeared largely because they could not compete in describing, predicting, controlling the contents of the external world without new disciplines. "Great scientists like Galileo and Newton with their power of reason and experiment sentenced for ever the idle chatter of the *ignoramus,* the dark muttering of the metaphysician, the thunder of the preacher, the hysterical shrieks of the obscurantists. But new political theories came up so as to expand the horizons of this discipline. Thus, Berlin asserts: "To suppose, then, that there have been, or could be, ages without political philosophy, is like supposing that as there are ages of faith, so there are or could be ages of total disbelief. This is an absurd notion."[73]

Like Berlin, Blondel examines this question and concludes in like manner.[74] To him, the term 'decline of political theory' means: (i) scientific professionalism and positivist assertiveness have taken over the study of politics; (ii) in this climate old

71. *Ibid.*, p. 352.
72. *Ibid.*, p.356.
73. *Ibid.*, p. 343.
74. See Jean Blondel: *The Discipline of Politics* (London : Butterworths, 1981), Chapter 6 titled 'Whither Political Theory'.

ways of reflecting on politics are viewed as no longer relevant on the grounds that old methods of investigation were usually too simple and that the problems used to be badly pursued; (iii) moral considerations were often discussed in the midst of the analysis of facts. This appeared as a breakthrough. To many new political scientists, this passing away of political theory is, by and large, real progress. But, for the traditionalists, a vacuum was kept in the centre of the discipline because the really important problems were now being ignored. "Political scientists had ceased to be interested in the broad questions relating to the organisation of society to fundamental moral standpoints, or they arrogantly—and impossibly—tried to fill the vacuum by scientific analysis of behaviour as if what 'ought to be' could be deduced from an examination of what could be done."[75]

The significance of Blondel's argument is that he, first of all, defends the classical tradition, then, eulogises the nature of modern empirical political theory, and, finally, contends that the empirical tradition can be of invaluable use in resurging the classical tradition and thereby doing a great service to the growth of political theory in contemporary times. While defending the classical tradition, he dwells upon the views of eminent figures like Sabine,[76] Oakeshott[77] and Strauss[78] so as to insist that the "close reading and the constant rethinking of the great classics creates an attitude of mind which will lead to, what might be called, the 'correct' approach to man and his destiny.[79] But as a critical admirer of the classical tradition, he also throws light on its weaker side. As he says: "In this approach, the role of political theory and political philosophy is negative; it almost amounts to making sure that politics keeps to its relatively low state and does not go above its station."[80]

75. *Ibid.*, pp. 134-35.
76. As Sabine says: "Political theory is quite simply man's attempts to consciously understand and solve the problems of group life and organisation, and if it is the disciplined investigation of political problems, it seems difficult to claim seriously that political theory was dead in the 1950s and early 1960s." *A History of Political Theory,* revised by Thorson (New York : Holt Saunders, 1973), p. 3.
77. As a critic of positivism, Oakeshott endeavours to reduce the belief in the over-all value of political science and to diminish the role of scientific analysis, both for human knowledge and human happiness. The purpose of political philosophy is to consider the place of political activity in the map of our total experience; it is not to provide an end for mankind to seek. The ideologues, not the political philosophers, attempt to provide this end—and they lead mankind to 'bogus eternity'. See his 'Introduction' to the *Leviathan* of Hobbes (Oxford: Basil Blackwell, 1946), p. lxv.
78. Leo Strauss says that political philosophy is central and the study of politics can only be truly great if it has once more the characteristics which it had with Aristotle. He is convinced that "the crime of our times comes from the 'positivist' approach which views human being as an engineer would view material for building bridges." Refer to his "Epilogue" in H.J. Storing, *(ed.): Essays on the Scientific Study of Politics.*, p. 310.
79. Blondel, *op. cit.*, p. 143.
80. *Ibid.*, p. 142. In criticism of Oakeshott, Blondel says that while he helped to maintain the tradition of or case for political theory, he did so in such a sceptical manner that it clearly did not contritute to the continuation of the tradition of political theory, rather he did contribute to the continued reputation of the 'museum' of the political theory of the past. *Ibid.*, p. 142. Then, while dealing with the charge of Leo Strauss that new political theorists neither know that they are fiddling nor do they know that Rome is burning, he says that Strauss himself did not know how to handle the great Roman fire. *Ibid.*, p. 150.

Blondel contends that empiricism has a significant place of its own in the realm of political theory. Here he dwells on the views of some other recent writers like Brian Barry and John Rawls who are of the view that political principles are inextricably linked with the state of society in its most basic structure, because until some minimum amount of order and material welfare has been secured, there are technical difficulties but not philosophically interesting problems. Giving a new interpretation to the contribution of John Rawls to the theory of justice, he says that it stands out as the best example of the resurgence of the classical tradition strengthened with the weight of empiricism. As he continues: "The publication of Rawls' *A Theory of Justice* showed that there was no ground in principle for such a pessimism; his work is a morale-booster for the classical theorists...Thus, the enormous contribution of Rawls is that he provides the long-awaited evidence that political theory is not dead and can stand on its own without having to demean itself in trying to pose itself in opposition to the new developments in political science. It also shows that the role of political theory is essentially alongside scientific inquiries from which political theory can, indeed, greatly benefit."[81]

Above all, empirical political theory is not the enemy of its normative counterpart; it may well supplement as well as strengthen the value-based or goal-oriented study of politics. A good number of exercises done with such a consideration have enriched the stock of political science by contributing to, what may be called, second-order or middle-range theories.[82] The correct view, as Blondel forcefully asserts, should be that political theory far from being killed by empirical analysis can thrive better in those fields in which empirical work has also been most successful; empiricists identified the difficulties and the paradoxes which political theorists came to find increasingly intriguing. Political theory, conceived as an analysis, and based on or triggered by empirical findings, leads, therefore, to significant results and can find a new *raison d'être*."[83]

On the basis of such strong affirmations, Blondel concludes: "Political theory does exist. It seems to know a little better in the 1980s where it is going and how it should proceed. Not that political theory is a critique or empirical political analysis has ceased to exist; what might be described as its civilised and skeptical form still interests thinkers whose main ambition is to continue the tradition of historians of political thought, a tradition which has its importance. 'Critical' political theory is also

81. *Ibid.*, pp. 156-57.
82. For this purpose, see R. Nozick : *Anarchy, State and Utopia* (New York; Basic Books, 1970). This writer presents in Chapter 3, the thesis of a 'minimal state' that gives full protection to our rights. Also see M.J. Taylor : *Anarchy of Co-operation* (London : Wiley, 1978). It is based on a combination of classical and modern empirical approaches with slant in favour of normative analysis. The author uses empirical findings instead of insisting on a lofty purity or somewhat bitter denunciation of those who search for facts. John Plamenatz : *Democracy and Illusion* (London: Longman, 1973). It attempts to extricate some broad conclusions in the midst of the major opposition between the pro-Western and anti-Western supporters of democracy. His conclusion is that the result is not quite the Tower of Babel that it seems to be. P. Birbaum, J. Lively and G. Parry (eds.) : *Democracy, Consensus and Social Contract* (London : Sage Pub., 1978). It demonstrates that empirical analysis and reflections of a logical and moral character can and must exist.
83. Blondel, *op. cit.*, p. 158.

alive, but it is in the constant danger of becoming an ideology highly charged with emotion but covered with strong layer of abstract vocabulary, and it is even more in danger of concentrating on the past and present while leaving the delineation of the promised land for future generations. It is often content with apocalyptic and convoluted descriptions of the current land; by doing so, and on the basis of its own action-oriented theory, it ensures that the promised land is truly remote. For it is by talking to man about ideals that one can make these ideals come near."[84]

But the most outstanding of all is Prof. Leo Strauss of Chicago University who affirms that though political philosophy may be in a state of decay and perhaps putrefaction, it "has not vanished altogether."[85] The distinctive thing about him is that he identifies theory with philosophy in the fashion of great classicists and, more than that, he presents himself as a speculative political philosopher after forcefully discarding the lines of positivism, historicism, and crude empiricism. His way of interpretations of the political philosophy of great thinkers like Plato, Machiavelli and Hobbes leaves this impression that he himself is a political philosopher and not a mere historian of political philosophy. So penetrating are his comments and so deep is his vision of the political ideas of the .great social and political thinkers that he is regarded as the lone crusader in the cause of normative political theory in recent times. It is well remarked: "Seldom, if ever before, has one man been respected for such cogent and illuminating interpretations of so many of the great political philosophers."[86]

Strauss prefers the term 'political philosophy' to 'political theory' for the simple reason that it certainly suggests the unbreakable connection of politics with norms, goals, ideals and value-judgements. To him, political philosophy is a distinctive kind of political thought; it is an attempt truly to know both the nature of political things and the right, or the good, political order. If so, then political philosophy is the conscious, coherent and relentless effort to replace opinions about the political fundamentals by knowledge regarding them. A student of political science is not merely concerned with the study of man in relation to authority or his role in struggle for power, he is also a seeker of the knowledge of the right or good political order. As he says: "All political action has then in itself a directedness towards knowledge of the good; of the good life, or of good society. For the society is the complete political good."[87]

Strauss gives three important reasons to emphasise the eternal significance of normative political theory, what he calls by the name of political philosophy:

1. Political life is characterised by the struggle for power between groups of men who defend their claims to rule in terms of what is good or bad for the whole community. Philosophy is the highest activity of man, it is the attempt to replace

84. *Ibid.*, p.159.
85. Leo Strauss: "What is Political Philosophy?" in *Journal of Politics*, Vol XIX, No. 3 (1957), pp. 343-68 reproduced in Gould and Thursby, *op. cit.* pp. 46-69.
86. E.P. Miller: "Leo Strauss: The Recovery of Political Philosophy" in Anthony de Crespigny and Kenneth Minnogue (eds.): *Contemporary Political Philosophers* (New York: Dodd Mead & Co., 1975), p. 67.
87. Strauss: *What is Political Philosophy!*, p. 47. Further, political philosophy "is concerned with the best of just order of society which is by nature best or just everywhere or always." *Ibid.*

opinions about all things by the knowledge of all things. It is impossible to think about the fundamental and comprehensive problems of philosophy without being inclined towards a desirable, perhaps ideal, solution. The significance of the classics of political philosophy is that they have touched this important issue in relation to the 'soul' of man so as to find out a perfect solution to the problem standing before them. As he says: " The classics understood the nature of man by reference to the proper ordering of the soul...The best regime is the rule of wisdom, either by wise men directly or by the rule of wise laws that are administered by reasonable men. The classics taught that man cannot live well or reach the perfection of his nature except by living with others and cultivating justice, the social virtue *par excellence*."[88]

2. What has really given a rude setback to such a glorious tradition of political philosophy is, according to Strauss, the modern trend of historicism and positivism. Political philosophy is a futile enterprise according to positivism, because it proceeds on the erroneous assumption that the knowledge of values is useless. So is the case with historicism of some like Hegel, Nietzsche and Heidegger. While theoretical historicism identifies the task of science as the contemplation of historical process—a process that has developed rationally and is completed in all essential respects, radical historicism agrees with Hegel that man must be understood in the light of history, but it denies that the historical process is fundamentally progressive or rational. Though historicism and positivism are distinguishable from each other, the common thing about them is that they are serious antagonists of political philosophy.[89] But the crucial point to be considered is whether we can ignore the permanent characteristics of humanity such as the distinction between the noble and the base.
3. It is said that the growth of liberal democracy has created conditions for the decline of political theory by offering standard solutions to complex human problems. Strauss refutes this point on the ground that specifically liberal democracy can be defended on the classical principle that the rule of wise laws administered by prudent men is superior to such form of absolute rule as can be expected in practice. Moreover, philosophy has a better chance to survive under liberal democracy than under the modern forms of tyranny. He identifies the primary internal danger to liberal democracy as its steady decline into permissive

---

88 Miller, *op. cit.*, p. 75.

89. As he says, after having reached its full growth, historicism is distinguished from positivism by these characteristics: (1) It abandons the distinction between facts and values, because every understanding, however theoretical, implies specific evaluations. (2) It denies the authoritative character of modern science, which appears as only one among the many forms of man's intellectual orientations in the world. (3) It refuses to regard the historical process as fundamentally progressive, or, more generally stated, as reasonable. (4) It denies the relevance of the evolutionist thesis by contending that the evolution of man out of non-man cannot make intelligible man's humanity. Historicism rejects the question of good society because of the essentially historical character of society and of human thought: there is no essential necessity for raising the question of good society; this question is not in principle coeval with man; its very possibility is the outcome of a mysterious dispensation of fate." Gould and Thursby, *op. cit.*, p. 57.

egalitarianism. He points out that the founders of liberal democracy had believed that the success of their project would require the people and their leaders to respect human excellence and also to possess a measure of virtue and self-restraint. Yet under positivist and historicist influence, contemporary liberalism has abandoned its absolutist basis and is trying to become entirely relativistic. The abandonment of all standards of excellence has led to a degraded and permissive form of liberal democracy, or to, what is often called, 'mass democracy'. Positivist political science reflects and, at the same time, strengthens the most dangerous proclivities of contemporary democracy. As he says: "By teaching in effect the equality of literally all desires, it teaches in effect that there is nothing of which a man ought to be ashamed; by destroying the possibility of self-contempt, it destroys with the best of intentions the possibility of self-respect."[90]

Thus, Strauss comes to hold that evaluation is indispensable to an adequate understanding of social and political things. Education towards virtue is indispensable to liberal democracy at its highest.[91]

What should be the proper decision of this, rather futile, debate? Two points may be put in this regard. First, the creation of the debate on the present state of political theory emanates from the contributions of those recent theorists who have studied politics in terms of human behaviour, or who have made elaborate models of political system by sticking to the course of empirical inquiry, or who have attempted to quantify basic concepts such as power and the like. Such theorists, rather analysts, have gloomily felt that the discipline of politics has lost its soul. Such a melancholy feeling has been described as the decline, nay demise, of political theory.[92] Second, this term 'decline' refers to the case of classical political theory and that too in a wrong way as we have already seen. The empirical tradition has supplemented as well as strengthened the normative tradition of the classical theory in its own right. It has assumed a dominant position that cannot be reversed now to the satisfaction of the traditionalists. Thus, we may come to this definite conclusion that political theory, even in its classical form, has neither demised nor so declined, nor is it ever possible in times to come. The new generation of political theorists must take it happily that "an agonising reappraisal of political theory now leads to this end that scientism is here to stay and that accommodation (with goals, norms and values) is the best and, perhaps, the only sensible line of conduct."[93]

We may agree with the view of Karl Popper, or not, that it "is theories, whether true or false, that are important and not the meaning of words."[94] But we may by all means endorse the view that just as the development of general theory of politics involves a critical appraisal of the practice of politics and an effort to recover an

---

90. Strauss: *Liberalism – Ancient and Modern*, p. 222.
91. Strauss: *What is Political Philosophy*, p. 38.
92. See Peter Laslett (ed.): *Introduction to Philosophy, Politics and Society* (New York : Macmillian, 1956): R.A. Dahl "Political Theory: Truth and Consequences" in *World Politics*, Vol, XI, October, 1958, pp. 89-102; and Neil Riemer : *The Revival of Democratic Theory* (New York : Appleton-Century-Crofts, 1961).
93. Blondel, *op. cit.*, p. 136.
94. Popper: *Unended Quest* (London: Fontana/Collins, 1976) pp. 22-24.

understanding of the political reality that might inform the practice, so does an inquiry that the activities of a political scientist involve a critical examination of the intellectual activity in an attempt to discern what makes it succeed or fail in its purposes. If a prevailing theory of politics proves on examination to fall short of the claims asserted on its behalf, it is incumbent on the critic to suggest ways in which the theoretical effort might be made more effective. Currently, the more promising shift "appears to be towards a process of recovering knowledge we once possessed and apparently misplaced."[95] In short, there has developed out of the revolution in philosophy, a broadly philosophical subject called political theory which is analytical theory in style and concerned with methodology, clarification of concepts and, in contrast with logical positivists, the logic of political appraisal. But in the recent past some writings (as Rawls and Nozick) "have breathed a new life into the discipline so that to say that political philosophy is dead, as was once said so confidently, would be a gross exaggeration."[96]

Political Theory in the Twenty-first Century

"Political theory was in a beleaguered state throughout much of the twentieth century."[97] The reason was that the behaviouralist tradition vigorously adopted by the American theorists and analysts had created a stir. Normativism was overshadowed by empiricism due to the 'mad craze for scientism', as commented by David Easton, of the behaviouralists wedded to logical positivism originally advanced by the leading lights of the Vienna Circle. In 1951 Easton wrote a paper titled 'The Decline of Political Theory' implying withering away of the phase of normative political theory. In 1956 Peter Laslett in the 'Introduction' to his *Philosophy, Politics and Society* declared its 'death'. Such impressions were quite rash and so their shine declined after a couple of decades.

However, normative political theory saw its resurgence after 1970 when works of Rawls, Nozick, Hayek, Macpherson and David Held appeared. The behavioural tradition withnessed its replacement by the post-behavioural tradition that was like a return to the past as well as a call for the future. The revived or resurged political theory in the 1970s and thereafter did not discard empiricism altogether, rather it placed it under the cover of normativism. As a result of this, facts were subordinated to values. Classical theories were revisited in the light of new developments as a result of which new themes have come into currency. Thus, significant changes have appeared in the domain of political theory in the present century which may be noted as under:

1. Now political theory has become increasingly diffuse and fragmented. Its reason lies in the fact that politics or political science is no longer confined to the study of state, government and formal power. It covers all avenues of power and struggle for its sake in a very comprehensive sense in the Foucaultian fashion

95. W.C. Harward : *The Recovery of Political Theory : Limits and Possibilities* (Baton Rouge and London: Louisiana State University Press, 1984), p. 7.
96. N.P. Barry : *An Introduction to Modern Political Theory* (London : Macmillan, 1981), p. 5.
97. Andrew Heywood: *Political Theory: An Introduction* (New York: Palgrave Macmillan, 2005), p. 11.

and thereby it assigns a para-political character to many aspects of man's life. It is due to this that many themes have found their place in the domain of political theory like civic republicanism, multiculturalism, environmentalism, feminism, etc. Old definitions of politics have been overshadowed by the new ones, the example of which may be seen in the assertion of David Held: "Accordingly, politics is about power; about the forces which influence and reflect its distribution and use; and about the 'transformative capacity' of social agents, agencies and institutions: it is about Government or governments alone."[98]

2. Modern political theory had its foundations in the impact of Enlightement that "sought to release humankind from its bondage to superstition and ignorance by unleashing an age of reason."[99] Thus, Comte's positivism came to dominate the scene. It had its culmination at the hands of Marx who rejected the metaphysics of Hegel by discovering the inexorable laws of social development and on that basis he made certain predictions. It was really an innovation in the domain of social sciences. The American behaviouralists obdurately worked for presenting an alternative political theory by discarding the premises of Marxism and instead revitalising the liberal tradition with the 'grand failure', as called by Zbigniew Brzezinski, of the 'great socialist power'. Thus, in the last phase of the twentieth century, emerged a new trend called post-modernism or post-structuralism, also known as anti-foundationalism. Advocated by the French theorists like Lyotard, Baudrillard and Foucault, it rejected the idea that there "is a moral or rational high point from which all values and claims to knowledge can be judged."[100]
3. Liberalism is a very old idea, a philosophy, a trend, an attitude, a principle, even a way of life. It had its doom in the middle or dark ages when the church made man a creature of his destiny written by the finger of God. However, it had its resurgence in the modern age as a result of the achievements of science and rise of the trend of secularism which reinforced the tradition of humanism. Philosophers like Locke, Rousseau, Montesquieu, Bentham, Mill and Green laid stress on the liberty of the individual that could be possible only in a limited and responsible state. The trend of democratisation developed with an unprecedented vigour so much so that the twentieth century came to be lauded as the 'age of democracy'. Fascism and Communism also emerged after the First World War that posed a potential challenge to the trend of liberalism. Being resilient, liberalism underwent a transformation. The classical or negative liberalism was replaced by the modern or positive liberalism. It justified the case of the extension of the scope of state activity for the sake of social welfare, though at the cost of individual liberty as little as possible. The model of a welfare state as established in Britain after the Second World War became more and more popular. However, it lost its shine after a couple of decades owing to some inherent fallacies injected into it by the premises of democratic socialism. Thus, arose the idea of the curtailment of the welfare state, also known as rolling back of the state. Positive or modern liberalism of the twentieth century, that replaced

98. David Held: *Political Theory and the Modern State* (Cambridge: Polity Press, 1995), p. 247.
99. Heywood, *op. cit.*, p. 13.
100. *Ibid.*

classical or negative liberalism of the nineteenth century, has now been replaced by neo-liberalism or new right, also called neo-conservatism.

4. Surprisingly, with the collapse of the socialist system in the countries of Eastern Europe, liberal-democratic system found its entry there and thereby it produced a new phenomenon what is called, 'post-communism'. Fascism and Communism lost their place because of their notoriety. However, liberalism is now riddled with the problem of its specific contours. In the present age of globalisation and liberalisation, the new problems of multiculturalism, racialism, ethnic nationalism, cultural pluralism and civic republicanism have arisen and the dominat issue of the day is how to solve them within a liberal framework. A cynic may say that now 'liberalism is on the retreat'. But the Rawlsian view is apt that liberalism is political, not metaphysical. Now the real fight is not between liberalism and authoritarianism (whether fascism or communism), it is within itself and it may certainly have a satisfactory solution by revisiting its established premises. It is well observed: "In the rapidly changing circumstances of the contemporary world, the need to go beyond the assumptions of liberalism has become an urgent task."[101]
5. In spite of the fact that now liberalism is ridden with fights within itself, the outstanding fact is that, as Fukuyama says, it has won the game. In the political sphere, liberalism implies a democratic system that alone can ensure the boons of liberty, equality, justice and welfare. Such a system makes the government limited and accountable. The philosophers may have divergent views about the functions and role of the state, but all are unanimous on the point that a limited and accountable government has no substitute or alternative. The issue of 'good governance' has now come to be associated with it. It has its abiding impact. The concept of rights has come to be associated with the concept of duties and obligations. It seeks to redefine the relationship between the individual and the state. The common theme of all liberal philosophers "is the centrality of liberal democracy to contemporary political philosophy."[102]
6. The behaviouralist tradition came with the wind, it went away with the whirlwind. However, it left behind a healthy and positive feature in the form of multidisciplinary focus or interdisciplinary approach. More and more theorists and analysts studied political issues with the help of material or data available in the domains of economics, sociology, psychology, mathematics, statistics, anthropology, biology and mechanical engineering. As a result of this, new approaches, strategies, methods, and methodologies came into vogue. It makes contemporary political theory very interesting as well as confusing. It has certainly led to the enrichment of the discipline; at the same time, it has created a problem for a student of this subject as to how such a multifarious knowledge be utilised for properly understanding and explaining political reality. As Will Kymlicka says: "Indeed, confronted with a growing diversity of approaches, each with its

101. Richard Bellamy: "Liberalism" in Roger Eatwell and Anthony Wright (eds.): *Contemporary Political Ideologies* (Delhi: Rawat Publications, 2003), p. 46.
102. Kymlicka: *Contemporary Political Philosophy* (Oxford: Oxford University Press, 2005), p. x.

own vocabulary and preoccupations, it may seem that contemporary political philosophy is simply a disconnected series of discrete arguments or debates, each developing according to its own inner logic, unrelated to the rest of the field. The dizzying array of new theories in the last decade only increases this sense of fragmentation and dislocation."[103]

The present position is that political theory has divergent directions which make it both very rich and fascinating as well as contradictory and confusing. "There are many who think that the discipline of political science has, over the past half century, taken wrong turns and gone up blind alleys, that too many eggs have been put in far too few methodological baskets. There are many who think that the disciplinary control exercised over the profession by certain sects has been far too tight."[104] At the same time, it should also be taken into account: "Diversity is a healthy attribute of a gene-pool but only if the carriers of these diverse genes actually interbreed."[105]

Concluding Observations

Following critical impressions may be gathered from what we have seen in the preceding sections:

1. Though as an invention of the Greeks political theory has been developing since ancient times, it has seen its marvellous development in the period following the two World Wars. The noticeable point is that the empirical side has now heavily overshadowed its normative counterpart, though it would be incorrect to say that the normative aspect has been thoroughly discarded. Rejection of the normative side is the hallmark of the empirical tradition in the behavioural phase; to realise the inadequacy of the empirical tradition and supplement it with the touch of normativism is the voice of neo-empiricism that has witnessed itself in the post-behavioural phase. Besides, the process of correction and self-correction has been the underlying feature of the development of political theory. Keeping this in view, it is rightly said: "Political theory is a never-ending conversation among theorists. And while the greatest of the debates are never resolved, the criticism which the writers make of each other are always the most vivid and illuminating. Politics is, after all, the most democratic of sciences. The final judgement concerning political reality and the good life are the responsibility of all who undertake the study of theory."[106]
2. It is certainly wrong to talk about the decline, nay demise, of the political theory in the present age of democracy, socialism, or ideology. To apply such allegation even to the case of philosophical or speculative political theory is not justified. Each theory presupposes a notion of what is required for the theory to be accepted as true. The function of theory is not to amass new facts but to disclose hitherto unsuspected relationships between them. This disclosure is achieved by looking at the facts differently in diverse theoretical perspectives. It is impossible

103. *Ibid.*, pp. ix-x.
104. R.E. Goodin: *The Oxford Handbook of Political Science* (Oxford: Oxford University Press, 2009), p. 9.
105. *Ibid.*, p. 32.
106. Hacker, *op. cit.*, p. *x*.

to recall that as long as one of the major functions of a theory is to account for events or impressions about what appears as 'reality' to a theorist and as long as the world is changing, the diversity of meanings and impressions is inevitable. It might be argued, therefore, that political theory has not declined and, "that far from being a deficiency, it" is one of the achievements of the language of Western political theory that it has been sufficiently elastic and adaptable to be used for a wide variety of circumstances."[107]

3. It follows from the above that political theory has seen its marvellous development, may be rejuvenation or resurgence, in recent times. "It is now a strange paradox that political theory should seem to lead so shadowy an existence at a time when, for the first time in history, literally, the whole of mankind is violently divided by issues, the reality of which is, and has always been, the sole *raison d'etre* of this branch of study. But this, we may be sure, is not the end of the story. Neo-Marxism, neo-Thomism, nationalism, historicism, anti-essentialist existentialism, liberalism and socialism, transposition of doctrines and natural right and natural law into empirical terms: discoveries made by skilful application of models derived from economic and related techniques to political behaviour, and the collisions, combinations and consequences in action of these ideas indicate not the death of a great tradition but, if anything, new and unpredictable developments."[108]

Thus, we may conclude our study with these fine words: "The central problems of politics are timeless; the aims and purposes of political theory are forever in need of discussion. The study of political theory will be sustained in our day only if students bring to it commitments which are both personal and intense. The goal of theory is to enhance the understanding. And great knowledge arises out of those insights which only the engaged minds, the quickened insight, are able to create."[109]

107. S,S. Wolin: "Political Theory: Trends and Goals" in David I Sills (ed). *International Encyclopaedia of the Social Sciences* (New York : Macmillan and Free Press. 1968), p. 324.

108. Berlin, *op. cit.*, p. 257.

109. Hacker, *op. cit.*, p. 20.

4

Approaches and Methods

> By far the most important trend in contemporary political studies is the widespread determination to reduce politics to non-political terms. Even the scholar whose genius it is to discover politics at work in the most out-of-the-way places (churches, universities, business firms, even literary coteries), when it comes to politics itself, baulks at the thought of discussing it in its own terms. It would seem that politics is psychology, or it is sociology, that it is moral philosophy or theology— that it is almost anything but politics.
>
> **—Norman Jacobson**[1]

Politics has been studied from ancient times to the present. The contributions of the Greeks to the study of 'polis', 'polity' and 'politeia' constitute the foundations of our subject. Much development in the form of superstructures has taken place over the last two millenniums. From Plato and Aristotle in the remote past to Laski and Lasswell in the present, we have a very large number of great thinkers, theorists and analysts who have made an attempt to understand and explain political reality in their own ways, with their own approaches, and with the use of their own tools and techniques. Obviously, it has led to the diversity of approaches and methods that looks baffling to a student of this subject in present times. Thus, we may take note of the fact that while some (like Plato and Aristotle) have found their base in ethics and philosophy, others (like St. Augustine and St. Thomas) have found the same in Christian theology. Or, if Seeley and Maine have studied political phenomena from a historical standpoint, others like Maclver and Easton have found their source of inspiration in the field of sociology. Likewise, we may take note of the fact that while Hegel finds his source of investigation in metaphysics, Marx treats economics as the base for the same purpose. According to Bentham and Austin, politics should be studied with the approach of jurisprudence, while it is psychology to Wallas and Ginsberg. In this chapter an attempt has been made to discuss different approaches, methods and methodologies for the study of politics in view of their significance as well as in the light of the heat generated by the partisans of each approach battling to prove the supreme virtue of their own way.[2]

Meaning and Nature of Approaches and Methods: Similarity and Distinction with Certain Related Themes

In simple terms, an approach may be defined as a way of looking at and then explaining a particular phenomenon. The perspective may be broad enough to cover

1. Jacobson: "The Unity of Political Theory, Science, Morals and Politics" in Ronald Young (ed.) : *Approaches to the Study of Politics* (Evanston, Illinois : Northwestern University Press, 1958), p. 116.
2. Stephen L. Wasby : *Political Science—The Discipline and Its Dimensions : An Introduction* (Calcutta : Scientific Book Agency, 1970), p. 35.

a vast area like world as a whole in the study of politics, or it may be very small embracing just an aspect of local, regional, national, and international politics. Besides, it also covers within its fold every other thing related to the collection and selection of evidence followed by an investigation and analysis of a particular hypothesis for an academic purpose. Thus, an approach "consists of a criteria of selection—criteria employed in selecting the problems or questions to consider and in selecting the data to bring to bear ; it consists of standards governing the inclusion and exclusion of questions and data."[3]

It is for this reason that approaches to the study of politics are so many. As the criteria for selecting the problems and data or issues seeking answers to some questions are determined by the standpoint that a scholar adopts or makes use of, so there may be several approaches. However, when a scholar seeks to channelise his efforts into a presentable form, the same approach leads to the utilisation of a particular method. In this way, approaches and methods become closely interrelated themes ; the latter becomes an integral part of the former. Thus, Van Dyke observes: "In brief, approaches consist of criteria for selecting problems and relevant data, whereas methods are procedures for getting and utilising data."[4]

However, with a view to bring about a subtle distinction between an approach and a method, we may say that the latter is commonly used either to denote epistemological assumptions on which the search for knowledge is based, or the operation and activities that occur in the acquisition and treatment of data. It is because of the use of varying methods generally borrowed from other social and natural sciences that modern political science looks like moving closer to the domains of other disciplines such as economics, psychology, sociology, biology and anthropology. It is all done to fit better the specific problems of data collection and interpretation faced in political studies. As a result of this, political science "seems to some like history or sociology or economics applied to political data."[5]

Sometimes, the word 'methodology' is used. It means the study of method, though some writers mistakenly use it as a supposedly learned synonym for the word 'method' itself. Scientists, including social scientists, often use this term to mean the study of particular methods of research that are appropriate for particular kinds of investigation. The philosophers use the term in a broader sense so as to mean the study of methods of inquiry that are common to all the sciences. This is regarded as a philosophical problem because the idea that the main scientific method of reasoning was induction could be justified. Obviously, the term 'methodology' is too narrow to cover the philosophical questions having their natural connection with

---

3. V.V. Dyke : *Political Science : A Philosophical Analysis* (Stanford : Stanford University Press, 1962), p. 114.

4. *Ibid.* In the words of A.C. Isaak: "An approach, in political inquiry, is a general strategy for studying political phenomena. Approaches are formulated and used for a number of reasons. They can function at both heuristic and explanatory levels. That is, an approach might provide the framework for, or even take the form of, a model or conceptual scheme, or it might serve as the impetus for the development of theory of politics." *Scope and Methods of Political Science*, p. 157.

5. Wasby, *op. cit.*, p. 7.

man as a part of his community the various facets of which constitute the subject matter of 'social sciences'.[6]

While the term 'approach' may be, though rashly or mistakenly, identified with another term like 'method' or 'technique', it is certainly different from 'theory'. An approach looks closely related to a theory in view of the fact that its very character determines the way of generalisation, explanation, prediction and prescription—all of which are the main functions of a theory. But a line of difference between the two may also be drawn. The term 'theory' is so vague that its real meaning becomes indeterminable in some critical situations. It may be identified with anything like idea, thought, trend, tendency, conjecture, principle, doctrine, hypothesis, speculation, explanation, even interpetation of some kind.[7] Different is the case with approach that may be defined as the creator of or a precursor to a theory. An approach is transformed into a theory if and when its functions extend beyond the selection of problems and data about the subject under study.

An eminent American writer defines all these related themes in the following manner :[8]

1. **Theory:** It is a generalised statement summarising actions, supposed or real, of a particular set of variables.
2. **Methods:** These are the ways of organising theories for their application to data. Sometimes, these are called conceptual schemes.
3. **Techniques:** These link methods to the relevant data; they also represent various modes of observation and recording empirical information.
4. **Models:** These are simplified ways of describing relationship.
5. **Paradigm:** It is a framework of ideas that establishes the general context of analysis.
6. **Strategies:** These are the particular ways to apply one or any combination of the above to a research problem.
7. **Research Design:** It converts strategy into an operational plan for field work or an experiment.

In brief, an approach is a way whereby a student manages to understand and explain the 'reality' of his concern and, for that, wins the credit of formulating a particular theory that may be abstract or concrete, utopian or realistic, normative or empirical, or a combination of both. When applied to political science, it refers to the way a particular thinker or a theorist has the understanding of 'political reality' and then offers something in his aspiration to be "a guide of the statesmen and of the citizens."[9]

6. D.D. Raphael : *Problems of Political Philosophy* (London : Macmillan, 1976), p. 25. So conceived, a method may also be called a 'technique'. The difference, if any, between the two is that the latter "may be more susceptible to routine or mechanical application and more highly specialised, depending less (once they are mastered) on imaginative intelligence." See Van Dyke, *op. cit*, p. 114.
7. See M.H. Marx: "The General Nature of Theory Construction" in his *Psychological Theory* (New York, 1951), p. 6.
8. David Apter : *Introduction to Political Analysis* (New Delhi: Prentice-Hall of India, 1978), pp. 31-32.
9. W.T. Bluhm : *Theories of the Political Systems* (New Delhi: Prentice-Hall of India, 1981), p. 3.

Major Traditional Approaches and Methods

Approaches and methods to the study of politics are many and most of them seem to overlap each other in varying measures. However, the distinguishing feature of the traditional approaches and methods should be traced in their heavily speculative and prescriptive nature. In contrast to it, the hallmark of the modern approaches is to give to the study of politics the character of a science as far as possible. Thus, leaving aside the behavioural and other empirical approaches like the systems approach with its offshoots in the form of structural-functional and input-output approaches, simulation approach, decision-making approach, communications approach, etc., all other approaches may be treated as 'traditional' in terms of their non-scientific nature and non-revolutionary expression. Mention, in this regard, may be made of the philosophical, historical, institutional, and legal approaches that may be briefly discussed as under:

Philosophical Approach: The oldest approach to the study of politics is philosophical. It is also known by the names of speculative, ethical and metaphysical approaches. Here the study of state, government, power and man as a political being is inextricably linked with the pursuit of certain goals, morals, truths, or high principles supposedly underlying all knowledge and reality. A study of politics from this approach assumes a speculative character, because the very word 'philosophical' "refers to thoughts about thoughts; a philosophical analysis is an effort to clarify thought about the nature of the subject and about ends and means in studying it. Put more generally, a person who adopts a philosophical approach to a subject aims to enhance linguistic clarity and reduce linguistic confusion; he assumes that the language used in description reflects the conceptions of reality, and he wants to make conceptions of reality as clear, consistent, coherent, and helpful as possible. He seeks to influence and guide thinking and the expression of thought so as to maximise the prospect that the selected aspect of reality (politics) will be made intelligible."[10]

It is for this reason that the theorists subscribing to this approach move closer to the world of ethics and look like counselling the rulers as well as the members of an organised community to pursue certain higher ends understandable by our rational faculty. Obviously, the great works of Plato, More, Bacon, Harrington, Rousseau, Kant, Hegel, Green, Bosanquet, Nettleship, Lindsay, Hobhouse, Oakeshott, Leo Strauss, John Rawls and Robert Nozick take the study of politics to a very high level of abstraction and they also try to mix up the system of values with certain high norms of an ideal social and political order. Of course, normativism dominates, but empiricism (as contained in the works of Aristotle, Machiavelli, Bodin, Hobbes, Locke, Montesquieu, Marx, etc.) looks like integrating the study of politics either with ethics, or with history, or with psychology, or with, law, in an effort to present the model of a best-ordered political community.

The study of politics with the use of such an approach converts it into 'political philosophy'. Here an endeavour is made to comprehend reality hidden behind the apparent reality. The objective reality is a concern of the science, the subjective reality is the concern of philosophy. Naturally, political philosophy is deeper than

10. V.V. Dyke, *op. cit.*, p. 129.

pure science. "The goal of the general is victory, whereas the goal of the statesman is the common good. What victory means is not essentially controversial, but the meaning of the common good is essentially controversial. The ambiguity of the political goal is due to its comprehensive character. Thus, the temptation arises to deny, or to evade, the comprehensive character of politics and to treat politics as one compartment among many. This temptation must be resisted if we are to face our situation as human beings *i.e.*, the whole situation."[11]

The philosophical (ethical or metaphysical) approach is criticised for being speculative and abstract. It is said that it takes us far away from the world of reality. At the hands of Rousseau and Hegel, it culminates in the exaltation of the state to mystical heights. Instead of seeing things as they are, it seeks to examine things in their abstract nature and purpose. The result is that politics becomes incomprehensible to a man of average understanding who may probably find comfort in the study of politics from a historicist or a positivist approach. However, a great admirer of this approach like Leo Strauss contends: "Men are constantly attracted and deluded by two opposite charms: the charm of competence which is engendered by mathematics, and the charm of humble awe, which is engendered by meditation of the human soul and its experiences. Philosophy is characterised by the gentle, if firm, refusal to succumb to either charm. It is the highest form of the mating of courage and moderation. In spite of its highness or mobility, it could appear as Sisyphian or ugly, when one contrasts its achievement with its goal. Yet it is necessarily accompanied, sustained and elevated by *eros*. It is graced by nature's grace."[12]

The philosophical approach to the study of politics may, however, be appreciated from another angle of vision. It is correct to say that every philosopher tries to seek answers to the questions that arise before him. The conditions of ancient Greece informed Plato and Aristotle to find out philosophical solutions to their contemporary social and political problems. Likewise, the struggle between an obdurate monarchy and the rising middle class of England inspired Hobbes and Locke to find out the legitimate basis of political obligation. In other words, it is correct to say that Machiavelli wrote for a specific 'prince' who could restore the grandeur of the great Roman state, Hobbes discovered a 'leviathan' who could maintain law and order in his country, and Locke imparted a philosophical justification to the supremacy of 'parliament' in England. But the real merit of all these philosophical discourses is that the solutions offered by them may be applied to a similar situation wherever it comes up. "Our distance in time from these philosophers may make us see their work only as philosophy and not as a partisan argument."[13]

Historical Approach: The distinguishing feature of this approach is to throw light on the past or on a selected period of time as well as on a sequence of selected events within a particular phase so as to find out "an explanation of what institutions are, and are tending to be, more in knowledge of what they have been and how they came to be, what they are than in the analysis of them as they stand."[14] It may also

11. Leo Strauss: "What is Political Philosophy?" in Gould and Thursby (eds.) *Contemporary Political Thought* (New York: Holt, Rinehart and Winston, 1969), p. 49.
12. *Ibid.*, p. 69.
13. Wasby, *op. cit.*, p. 39.
14. Sir Fredrick Pollock : *An Introduction to the History of the Science of Politics* (London: Macmillan, 1923), p. 126.

be added that here a scholar treats history as a genetic process—as the study of how man got to be, what man once was, and now is."[15] A study of politics with such an approach also informs him to look into the role of individual motives, actions, accomplishments, failures and contingencies in historical continuity and change.[16]

The historical approach stands on the assumption that the stock of political theory comes out of socio-economic crises as well as the reactions they leave on the minds of the great thinkers. It implies that in order to understand political theory, it is equally necessary to understand clearly the time, place and circumstances in which it was evolved. It is not at all required that a political theorist may actually take part in the creation of events or in the solution of problems. However, what is necessary is that he must be affected by it and he may try to affect it in any way. Sabine thus affirms that political theories "are secreted in the interstices of political and social crisis. They are produced not indeed by the crisis as such, but by the reactions on minds that have the sensitivity and the intellectual penetration to be aware of crisis. Hence, there is in every political theory a reference to a pretty specific situation, which needs to be grasped in order to understand what the philosopher is thinking about."[17]

It may, however, be added at this stage that the historical approach to burning political questions varies in certain ways depending upon the range of choice that a scholar adopts for his purpose. If Machiavelli could make a perceptible use of history for exalting the achievements of the Romans and thereby exhorting his rulers to restore the glory of the great Roman empire, Burke and Oakeshott adhere to the historical approach so as to provide a philosophical justification for their conservative impressions. Burke forcefully criticised the philosophy of the French revolution of 1789 and instead eulogised the British political institutions for their stability, the reason for which he could trace in their prescriptive character. Likewise, Oakeshott says: "What we are learning to understand is a political tradition, a concrete manner of behaviour. And for this reason it is proper that, at the academic level, the study of politics should be an historical study."[18]

The historical approach suffers from certain weaknesses. For instance, as James Bryce says, it is often loaded with superficial resemblances. As such, historical parallels may sometimes be illuminating, but they are also misleading in most of the cases.[19] Likewise, Prof. Ernest Barker holds: "There are many lines—some that suddenly stop, some that turn back, some that cross one another; and one may think rather of the maze of tracks on a wide common than of any broad king's highway."[20] Holding a less favourable view of this approach, Sidgwick maintains that the primary aim

15. Louis Gottschalk: "A Professor of History in a Quandary" in *The American Political Science Review,* Vol. 59 (January, 1964), p. 279.
16. *Ibid.*
17. Sabine: "What is Political Theory?" in Gould and Thursby, *op. cit.,* p. 10.
18. Michael Oakeshott: "Political Education" in Peter Laslett (ed.): *Philosophy, Politics and Society* (New York : Macmillan, 1956), p. 12.
19. Lord James Bryce: *Modern Democracies* (London : Macmillan, 1921), Vol. I, p. 16.
20. Barker : *Political Thought in England* (London: Oxford University Press, 1951), p. 166.

of political science is to determine what *ought to be* so far as the constitution and action of government are concerned and this end cannot be discovered by a historical study of the forms and functions of government. In very clear terms he observes: "I do not think that the historical method is one to be primarily used in attempting to find reasoned solutions to the problems of practical politics."[21]

However, the real significance of the historical approach cannot be denied. It has its importance in studying the relevance of the origin and growth of political institutions. Works on political theory like those of G.H. Sabine. R.G. Gettell, C.H. Mcllwain, R.W. Carlyle, A.J. Carlyle, G.E.G. Catlin, W.A. Dunning, T.I. Cook and C.E. Vaughan, for this reason, have an importance of their own. Such an approach has its own usefulness in understanding the meaning of great social and political theorists from Plato and Aristotle in the ancient to Leo Strauss and Lasswell in the present times. If political theory has a universal and respectable character, its reason should be traced in the affirmation that it is rooted in historical traditions. Studying the growth and survival of political theory in recent times, Watkins confidently opens his paper with these words: "Whether we like it or not, the existence of political theory is a fact. Ever since the beginnings of history, and perhaps even from the days of prehistory, men have been speculating about the nature and justification of political authority. A large mass of written documents survive to record a substantial part of this speculation."[22]

Legal Approach: Here the study of politics is linked with the study of legal or juridical processes and institutions created by the state for maintaining a political organisation. The themes of law and justice are treated not as mere affairs of jurisprudence, rather political theorists look at the state as the maintainer of an effective and equitable system of law and order. Matters relating to the organisation, jurisdiction and independence of judicial institutions, therefore, become an essential concern of a political theorist. Analytical jurists from Cicero in the ancient to Dicey in the present times have regarded state as primarily a corporation or a juridical person and, in this way, viewed politics as a science of legal norms having nothing in common with the science of the state as a social organism. Thus, this approach treats the state primarily as an organisation for the creation and enforcement of law. That is, it describes the constitution and activities of the state in terms of their legal or juristic nature. It "treats organised society, not as a social or a political phenomenon but as a purely juridical regime, an *ensemble* of public law, rights and obligations, founded on a system of pure logic and reason."[23]

In this connection, we may refer to the works of Jean Bodin of the early modern period who propounded the doctrine of sovereignty and of others like Grotius and

21. Henry Sidgwick : *The Development of European Polity,* p. 5.
22. Fredrick M. Watkins : "Political Theory as a Datum of Political Science" in Ronald Young, *op. cit.,* p. 148. Even a critic of this approch like Sidgwick at one place says that by means of it "we can ascertain the laws of political evolution and thus forecast, though dimly, the future." *Elements of Politics,* pp. 7-14. According to EM. Sait, the historical approach "is indispensable. It affords the only means of appreciating the true nature of institutions and the peculiar way in which they have been fashioned." *Political Institutions: A Preface* (New York : Appleton-Century, 1938), p. 529.
23. See J.W. Garner: *Political Science and Government* (Calcutta : World Press, 1952), p. 22.

Hobbes who clarified its premises. In the system of Hobbes the sovereign of the state is the highest lawmaker and his command is law that must be obeyed either to avoid punishment following its infraction, or to keep the dreadful state of nature away. The works of Bentham, Austin, Savigny, Sir Henry Maine and A.V. Dicey may be referred to in this connection. The result is that the study of politics is integrally bound up with the legal processes of the country and the existence of a harmonious state of liberty and equality is earmarked by the glorious name of the 'rule of law'.

Applied to national and international politics, the legal approach stands on the assumption that law prescribes action to be taken in a given situation and also forbids the same in some other situations; it even fixes the limits of permissible action. It also emphasises the fact that where the citizens are law-abiding, the knowledge of law provides a very important basis for predictions relating to political behaviour of the people. A distinguished student of this approach like Jellinek advises us to treat organised society not as a mere social or political phenomenon but as an ensemble of public law, rights and obligations founded on a system of pure logic or reason. It implies that the state as an organism of growth and development cannot be understood without a consideration of those forces and factors that constitute the domain of law and justice. As Leband states, "it is that of the analysis of public law relations, the establishment of juristic nature of the state, the discovery of general superior juridical principles and the deduction therefrom of conclusions."[24]

It may, however, be pointed out that this approach has a very narrow perspective. Law embraces only one aspect of a people's life and, as such, it cannot cover the entire behaviour of the political man. As the idealists can be criticised for treating state as nothing else but a moral entity, so the analytical jurists commit the mistake of reducing every aspect of a political system to a juridical entity. As Garner says: "The state as an organism of growth and development, however, cannot be understood without a consideration of those extra-legal and extra-social forces which lie at the back of the constitution and which are responsible for many of its actions and reciprocal reactions. Any view which, therefore, conceives the state merely as a public corporation, is as narrow and fruitless as the Hegelian doctrine which goes to the opposite extreme and considers it merely as moral entity."[25] Likewise, Van Dyke says: "Determination of the content of law through legislative power is a political act, ordinarily to be explained on the basis of something other than a legal approach."[26]

Institutional Approach: Here a student of politics lays stress on the formal structures of a political organisation like legislature, executive and judiciary. This trend may be discovered in a very large number of political thinkers and theorists from Aristotle and Polybius in the ancient to Laski and Finer in the present times. However, the peculiar thing about modern writers is that they also include party system as the 'fourth estate' in the structures of a political system. More important thing in this direction is this that a large number of writers like Bentley, Truman, Key, Jr., Latham, Beer, Eckstein, etc., go a step further by including numerous interest groups that constitute the infrastructure of a political system. Since the emphasis is

24. *Ibid.*
25. *Ibid.*
26. V.V. Dyke, *op. cit.*, p. 140

on the superstructure and infrastructure of a political system, this approach is also known by the name of 'structural approach'.

We may trace this approach in the writings of a very large number of theorists like Walter Bagehot, F.A. Ogg, W.B. Munro, James Bryce, Herman Finer, H.J. Laski, Harold Zink, C.F. Strong, R G. Neumann, Maurice Duverger, Giovanni Sartori, etc. The striking feature of these works is that the study of politics has covered the formal as well as informal institutional structures of a political system. Moreover, in order to substantiate their conclusions, a comparative study of the major governmental systems of certain advanced countries has also been made. The new trend in this direction is to throw light on the political systems of the Afro-Asian and Latin-American countries (also known by the name of the developing countries of the Third World) where writers like G A. Almond and J.C. Coleman find abundant raw material for the study of politics.

Like other approaches, this approach is also criticised for being too narrow. It ignores the role of the individuals who constitute and operate the formal as well as informal structures and sub-structures of a political system. Another difficulty is that the meaning and range of an institutional system varies with the view of a scholar. Those who have conceived governmental institutions, offices and agencies have been inclined to teach and write about government, accordingly; organisation charts being suggestive of much of what they have done. Under this conception, the study of politics becomes, at the extreme, the study of one narrow, specific fact about another.[27] It is also criticised as "a routine description and pedestrian analysis of formal political structures and processes based on the more readily accessible official sources and records."[28]

However, this approach has come to have an importance of its own in an indirect way. It has found its assimilation into the behavioural approach. The structural-functionalists have made an improvement upon it by laying focus on the role of political parties and pressure groups as agencies of interest aggregation and interest articulation respectively. Thus, the study of political processes has been supplemented with the study of political institutions. New terms have been coined or old terms have been given a new version so as to describe political reality in a scientific way as far as possible. The state has its equivalent in a political system; the organs of a government (like legislature, executive and judiciary) have been given the name of formal structures of a political system, while political parties, pressure groups, channels of communication, leadership, elites, factions, etc., have been put into the category of informal or infrastructure of a political system. Moreover, the role of these infrastructural agencies in the decision-making process of formal institutions of a government and the continuation of this chain due to the role of the feedback mechanism has led new theorists to formulate input-output approach. Viewed thus, we may come to point out that the structural-functional and input-output approaches of a political system (as devised by Easton and Almond) are an extension of, or an improvement upon, the institutional approach discussed above.[29]

27. *Ibid*, p 136.
28. Albert Somit and Joseph Tanenhaus: *The Development of American Political Science: From Burgess to Behaviouralism* (Boston, 1967), p. 70.
29. Wasby, *op. cit.*, p. 43.

Modern Approaches and Methods

From the above, it is evident that the study of politics, in the context of philosophical-ethical, institutional-structural, historical and legal-juridical approaches cannot assign to it the character of, what behaviouralists call, a 'pure science'. Their contention is that normativism should be replaced by empiricism to the best possible extent. It may, however, be reiterated, at this stage that modern approaches have their roots in the traditional approaches. The distinction between the two is that while the former are mainly value-laden, the latter are fact-laden. In other words, it implies that while normativism dominates the former, empiricism dominates the latter. It may also be said in this connection that what really characterises modern approaches is their 'scientific' nature and 'revolutionary' expression. These are marked by empirical investigation of the relevant data and have arisen from the realisation that "a search for fuller integration was not thought of or even hinted at by the political scientists belonging to the old order and, for this reason, the positivism of this science was not dreamt as posing a challenge to the already age-worn methods of study and approach."[30]

Sociological Approach: Ever since Comte of France and Spencer of England made their contributions to the discipline of sociology, political theorists have realised the relevance of a sociological approach to the study of politics. In contemporary times it has witnessed remarkable development in the United States where R.M. MacIver, David Easton and G.A. Almond have taken into their recognition this essential point that ample data is available in the realm of sociology with the help of which empirical rules of political behaviour can be laid down. A leading German sociologist (Max Weber) has treated sociology as the basis of politics and Easton has managed to develop certain theories of the political system on the basis of the Weberian formulations as reinterpreted and redevised by Talcott Parsons and Robert Merton. As a result of this, a new discipline, known by the name of 'political sociology', has come up.

This approach emphasises that social context is necessary for the understanding and explanation of political behaviour of the members of a community. It is the social whole in which we may find individuals having their status and playing their role that is determined by certain traits and that are transmitted from one generation to another with necessary modifications. It is called 'political socialisation'. Its objective manifestation is the 'political culture' of the people that shows their commitments to and convictions in certain political values as those of liberty, equality, rights, justice, democracy, rule of law and the like. The political system of every country is influenced by the political culture of its people. For instance, a bloody revolution aiming at the total change of social and political institutions is not possible in a country like England because of the conservative nature of the people. Democracy has been a failure in most of the Asian and African countries for the reason its values do not find coherence with the tenets of the political culture of the people.[31]

30. Frank Thakurdas: "The Expanding Frontiers of Political Sceince" in the *Indian Journal of Political Science,* Vol. XXXIV, No. 4, 1973, p. 420.
31. Ely Chinoy says that 'political culture refers to the totality of what is learned by individuals as members of a society ; it is a way of life, a mode of thinking, acting and feeling.,' *Sociological Perspective* (Garden City : Doubleday, 1954) pp. 10-11.

It is, therefore, obvious that this approach considers the state primarily as a social organism, whose component parts are individuals and seeks to deduce its qualities and attributes from the qualities and attributes of the men composing it.[32] "Society should be treated as the basis of political as of all other sciences ; it is a network of numerous associations and groups which play their own part in the operation of the politics of a country. Factors like kinship, racialism, tribalism, religion, caste, linguistic affinity and the like form part of the study of sociology, but their role in the political process of a country cannot be ignored in an empirical study of a political system. The law of the state is binding either because of the force of some 'myth' working in the background or because of the fear of punishment entailing from its infraction. The structuralists, therefore, advise us to study the social system of a people before understanding and explaining the political reality of a country.

What is striking in this connection is that some writers have laid stress on the value of sociology in the study of politics and also gone to the extent of developing their theories with the help of some aspect of the sociological make-up of a country. Thus, sociological approach has come to have its many varieties so much so that some writers prefer to use a new term 'sociological approaches'. It is also insisted by the structuralists that a political system may be made successful by correcting or renovating a particular aspect of the sociological make-up of a people. For instance, the American military commanders imposed a new constitution on Japan in 1947 (called 'Peace Constitution') and during the period of their stay they foisted a new type of political culture whereby people strengthened their conviction in the liberal-democratic order. It inflicted a serious setback on the traditional force of Japanese militarism.

The sociological approach is appreciated for being comprehensive. Since it studies society in all its aspects and then seeks to link politics with those sociological forces, it cannot be criticised for being narrow like other approaches discussed above. The only fear is that by laying so much emphasis on the role and usefulness of sociology, it goes to the extent of playing with the autonomy of the discipline of political science. It may be feared that such a study may convert politics into a handmaid of sociology. The problem of the relative autonomy of the discipline is, therefore, raised. The new advocates of this approach dismiss such apprehensions and instead contend that the theories of great sociologists (like Emile Durkheim, Malinowski, Shils, Eisenstadt, Parsons and Merton) provide useful tools and materials with the help of which we may take the study of politics to the level of a 'science'. If the purpose of politics is to deal with 'conflicts', as J.D.B. Miller says, sociology helps us to know the causes of such tensions and their possible solutions.[33]

Psychological Approach: Political science has moved very close to the discipline of psychology in modern times at the hands of Graham Wallas, Charles Merriam, Harold Lasswell, Robert Dahl, Eric Fromm, etc. In early modern times, Machiavelli and Hobbes had stressed the point of security of life and material possessions as a motivating force and held that the desire for it was inseparable from the desire for power. Recently a good number of political theorists have borrowed material from the

32. Garner, *op. clt.*, p. 20.

33. See David Apter: *An Introduction to Political Analysis* (Englewood Cliffs, New Jersey: Prentice-Hall, 1977), p. 380.

writings of eminent psychologists like Freud, Jung, Eyesenck and McDougall so as to lay down certain valid rules of political behaviour. A study of politics is, therefore, made by these writers in a way so as to deal with the role of emotions, habits, sentiments, instincts, ego, etc., that constitute essential elements of human personality.

The writers subscribing to this approach try to study and explain social and political institutions and phenomena through psychological laws. To them politics, whether national or international, is structured. If one knows as to how it is structured, then it is possible to locate gaps in one's knowledge or missing pieces. For this sake, they take the help of Freud who developed a set of rules describing the structure of personality. By doing so he located the boundaries of knowledge in such a way as to project new knowledge; something must be going on just beyond what we know. Structuralism frames this potentiality in terms *of functions.* While Freud gave the names *ego, id* and *super-ego* to psychological functions, political functionalists have used other names instead like information, communication and aggregation.[34]

The tools of psychoanalysis can be made use of in the study of politics. Thus, Lasswell has sought to apply Freudian psychology to the study of political behaviour.[35] According to him, the psychoanalysis of political leaders reveals significant knowledge about politics. It tells us as to why some leaders are conservatives and others are radicals, or why some politicians are agitators and others like to be administrators. The significance of political opinions is not to be grasped apart from the private motives which they symbolise. Since political movements derive their vitality from the displacement of private effects upon public objects and since primitive psychological structures, in more or less disguised form, control individual thought and effort, we can discover significant knowledge about political beliefs and behaviour through the use of psychoanalysis.[36] As this fact becomes increasingly accepted, the social psychiatrists will replace the social philosopher and the politics of the future will be more 'preventive' in character.[37]

Ever since Merriam advised us to treat politics in quite empirical terms, the study of politics has largely been a study of 'power' what Laswell calls 'influence'.[38] To him, politics is the study of the influence and the influential. However, what is so striking about him is that he very confidently asserts that in future, political problems will be solved less and less by discussion and more and more by psychoanalytical therapy. As he says: "Discussion frequently complicates social difficulties, for the discussion by far-flung interests arouses a psychology of conflict which produces destructive, fictitious, and irrelevant values. The problem of politics is less to make conflict than to prevent them; less to serve as a safety-valve for social protest than to apply social energy to the abolition of recurrent sources of strain in society. This redefinition of the problem of politics may be called the idea of preventive politics."[39]

34. *Ibid.*, p. 379.
35. For a deeper study see Karen Horney : *The Neurotic Personality of Our Time* (New York, 1937); Eric Fromm: *Escape from Freedom* (New York, 1945); and J.C. Flugel: *Man, Morals and Society* (London, 1945).
36. Lasswell: *Psychopathology and Politics* (Chicago: Chicago University Press, 1930) p. 125.
37. J.H. Hallowell: *Main Currents in Modern Political Thought* (New York: Holt, Rinehart and Winston, 1950), p. 532.
38. See Lasswell and Kaplan : *Power and Society* (New Haven: Yale University Press, 1950).
39. Laswell: *Psychopathology and Politics,* pp. 196-97.

By way of criticism, it may be said that this approach is partially correct. It is right in enabling us to study politics with the help of psychological tools, but it cannot be treated as a comprehensive approach in view of the fact that it does not take into account some other essential elements covered by the approaches discussed above. That is, the role of sociological, legal, and economic factors cannot be ignored entirely in an empirical study of politics. It may also be said that this approach seeks to accommodate normativism in empirical political theory in its own way by throwing light on the role of 'belief system' in the operation of the political system of a country. As Apter says: "In political science terms, the structuralist is interested in belief systems not simply as a distribution of public opinions, but as a way of ordering the world according to the principles of equity, or moral right and wrong. One aspect of structuralism is that it restores the normative, or moral side of reciprocity and obligation. In this it resembles political philosophy."[40]

Economic Approach: Matters relating to the production and distribution of goods have an economic character. But as their regulation is done by the state, they are very much involved in the process of politics. The prominent schools of liberalism, socialism and communism emerge because of the divergent interpretations of the role of state in regulating economic matters. Eminent political theorists like Mill, Marx, Mitchell, Schumpeter, Friedman and a host of others have written volumes having a relevance of their own in the domain of political economy. However, in this regard the most outstanding name is that of Karl Marx who has built his political theory on the basis of the criticism of the prevailing capitalist system. It is contained in his well-known assumption: "The mode of production of the material means of existence conditions the whole process of social, political and intellectual life."[41] So says Engels: "The ultimate causes of all social changes and political revolutions are to be sought not in the minds of men, but in changes in the mode of production and exchange; they are to be sought not in philosophy but in the economics of the period concerned."[42]

Economic affairs are inextricably involved in the political process when we find that the public issues in connection with which political actors pursue conflicting desires, are parts of their economic activity. Thus, those adopting an economic approach to politics feel particularly inclined to raise questions about interrelationships of the economic and the political life of human beings. "Out of all the varied activities of the government, they will be inclined to examine particularly those pertaining to economic relationships, *e.g.*, monetary and tax policies, legislation concerning relationships between management and labour, relative roles of governmental personnel and private persons in making crucial decisions. Further, out of the various factors that motivate the behaviour of persons and groups and that provide a basis for explaining and predicting that behaviour, those taking an economic approach will be inclined to examine the desire for wealth—for control over the production and distribution of the comforts and luxuries of life."[43]

40. Apter, *op. cit.*, p. 380.
41. See Alexander Gray: *The Socialist Tradition* (New York: Longmans, 1946), p. 303.
42. *Ibid.* p. 304.
43. V.V. Dyke, *op. cit.*, pp. 123-24.

Thinkers like Machiavelli and Hobbes treat man as a selfish creature. Economists interpret the same thing in terms of man's *interests.* Man has certain interests and he wants to protect as well as promote them. For this he forms groups and associations. The result is that every society has a number of conflicting interests and the people form associations for the sake of their protection and promotion. It creates stuff for the study of organised groups in a political community. Obviously, the interest or interest-group conception of politics is closely associated with an economic approach. "Those who take an economic approach are likely to seek to relate economic interests to all major public policies and events, wondering, for example, whether the American armament programme may not be designed as much to keep the economy operating at a high level as to promote security and peace. And they are likely to take the view that coherence within political parties and struggle among them reflect common and conflicting economic concerns. An economic approach frequently takes on a psychological colour, for it is frequently based on an assumption about human motivation : that people commonly act in such a way as to promote their own economic gain."[44]

The contribution of economics to the study of politics in recent times may be seen in the field of systems theory. By and large, economic inputs lead to political outputs. Groups and organisations of people make demands, for example, for the enhancement of their salaries and allowances, or for checking inflationary trends, or for nationalising a particular industry and the like. Sometimes the pressure is so strong that the government has to take decisions on such vital economic matters. Democracy is adorned as a system based on the will of the people. In realistic terms, it is run by the power of money. Elections are conducted with the help of economic resources. The result is that politics is influenced by the power of money. The Marxists understand political reality in terms of class war in which economics plays the decisive role. In their view, real democracy cannot be established unless the system of capitalism is abolished and all private property is converted into public property by the ruthless action of the dictatorship of the proletariat.

Although economic problem-solving is still dominated by piecemeal and incrementalist schemes, econometric techniques have long been used to determine linear cause and effect relationships. However, these techniques tend to be restricted to mechanistic systems which do not account for the processes of change and lose touch with such reality. In recent years, computer simulation has begun to supplant many of the econometric techniques. Game theory has generated mathematical explanations of strategies, especially for marketing and advertising in business firms. It has had an impact on economics, and it has been widely used in political science analyses of international confrontations and electoral strategies. In fact, game theory has been used extensively by political scientists in the testing and implementation of rational choice theory, which assumes that the structural constraints of society do not necessarily determine the actions of individuals and that individuals tend to choose actions that bring them the best results. Cooperative and competitive relations in one's bargaining with best allies and opponents are emphasised by the

44. *Ibid.*, p. 124.

political scientist "in a fashion modelled after the economist's attention to exchange, expecially through competitive market systems."[45]

Behavioural Approach: Modern empirical approaches have found their best manifestation in the trend of behaviouralism where a host of leading American writers have laid emphasis on the collection and examination of 'facts' relating to the actual or observable behaviour of man as a social and political being.[46] This approach has emerged on the scene in the midst of a large amount of turmoil and controversy within the profession widely lauded by its protagonists as a 'revolution' in the realm of political science.[47] E. Kirkpatrick, the then Executive Director of the American Political Science Association, explained its meaning thus: "Between World War II and the midfifties the term 'political behaviour' represents both an approach and a challenge, an orientation and a reform movement, a type of research and a rallying cry, a 'hurrah' term and a 'boo' term. Debate about the behavioural techniques and methods was often accompanied by vituperations, discussions were more often aimed at vanquishing adversaries than at clarifying issues."[48]

The credit for popularising the behavioural approach, or approaches, is ascribed to the Ford Foundation of the United States. With a view to make social sciences useful to the task of human welfare, it set up a committee that recommended the use of interdisciplinary focus to understand and explain political reality. It suggested five important 'programme areas'—establishing peace, strengthening economy, stabilising democracy, providing education in a democratic order, and understanding properly human behaviour and relations. It attracted wide attention in the period following World War II, since it emphasised the need for a scientific approach to the study of human behaviour. A new trend was thus set in, whose ardent advocates rejected the study of formal political institutions or structures as the basic unit of research and instead, advised us to study the behaviour of the individuals in political situations. As a result, this new approach is concerned with acts, attitudes, preferences and expectations of men in political contexts.[49]

45. Chilcote : *Theories of Comparative Politics* (Boulder, Colorado : Westview Press, 1981), p. 57.
46. Behaviouralism must be distinguished from behaviourism. "Behaviourism is a psychological doctrine which holds that the only basis for the study of human behaviour is *observable* behaviour. Therefore, all statements about mental phenomena, such as motives and intentions, are irrelevant, because they depend upon introspective knowledge which cannot be verified by experimental methods. But behaviouralism is a form of social explanation in which *observed* behaviour is stressed rather than simple description of institutions. In behavioural political science formal political institutions are dissolved into 'systems' and 'processes'. It is distinct from *behaviourism* in that it is not psychological theory about individual behaviour but involves sociological statements about collectivities." Norman P. Barry: *An Introduction to Modern Political Theory* (London: Macmillan, 1981), p. xiii.
47. Benjamin E. Lippincott: "Political Theory in the United States" in *Contemporary Political Science* (Paris: UNESCO Pub., 1950), p, 219.
48. Kirkpatrick: "The Impact of Behavioural Approach on Traditional Political Science" in Austin Ranney (ed.): *Essays on the Behavioural Study of Politics* (Urbana; University of Illinois Press, 1962), p. 11.
49. A staff paper, as approved by the trustees of the Ford Foundation, made it clear that human behaviour included overt acts as well as subjective behaviour such as attitudes, beliefs, expectations and motivations relating to economic, social, political, educational or personal problems. See Doctor, *op. cit.*, p. 18,

Tenets or Basic Goals of Behavioural Approach

Statement of Eulau, Eldersweld and Janowitz (a)

1. It specifies as the unit or object of both theoretical and empirical analysis the behaviour of persons and social groups rather than events, structures, institutions, or ideologies.
2. It seeks to place theory and research in a frame of reference common to that of social psychology, sociology and cultural anthropology.
3. It stresses the mutual interdependence of theory and research. Theoretical questions need to be stated in operational terms for purposes of empirical research. And, in turn, empirical findings should have a bearing on the development of political theory.
4. It tries to develop rigorous research design and to apply precise methods of analysis to political behaviour problems.

Statement of Easton (b)

1. That regularities exist which are discoverable and which can be expressed in generalisations.
2. Such generalisations must be testable with reference to behaviour.
3. Means for acquiring and interpreting data connot be taken for granted. They are problematic and need to be examined self-consciously.
4. Measurement and quantification are necessary, but only where such measurement makes sense in terms of other purposes.
5. Ethical evaluation and empirical explanation should be kept apart.
6. Research ought to be systematic. Research untutored by theory may prove trivial, and theory unsupported by data futile.
7. The understanding and explanation of political behaviour should precede application of this knowledge.
8. Material from the various social sciences should be integrated.

Statement of Sorauf (c)

1. The behaviouralists wanted political scientists to explore new kinds of data; they would bring to the study of politics a new concern for the individual and group behaviour that goes on within political institutions.
2. The behaviouralists advocated new methods for studying political phenomena; they would undertake survey research, statistical analysis, and various types of disciplined field work.
3. The behaviouralists wanted political scientists to use new concepts like role, group, elite, influence, system, subsystem, precision, etc. borrowed from different natural and social sciences.
4. The behaviouralists advocated work on generalistations that would explain relationships among political phenomena so as to have the further development of political science. Thus, they brought hypothesis and theoretical proposition back into even narrowly circumstanced research.

Statement of Frank Thakurdas (d)

1. The first fundamental shift in focus is from the concept of the state towards smaller units like interest groups or electorate, political parties, factions, elites etc. which are more easily comprehensible and play a vital role in the actual political process.

2. Behavioural studies have been adopting two separate units—(i) the units of power—the ability of the individuals or groups to affect the behaviour of other individuals or groups, and (ii) the units of decision-making with reference to the choice as a matter of policy among alternative courses of action.
3. Since the process of politics is extensive and complex, it extends the scope of its empirical inquiry to the activities outside the area of government but within the conspectus of society.
4. Its development analysis model aims at the creation of clear and precise conceptual models that would enable them to explain the varieties of existence of reality.
5. It recognises the necessity of an interdependence between theory and research.

(a) Heinz Eulau, Samuel J. Eldersveld and Morris Janowitz: (ed.s): *Political Behaviour: A Reader in Theory and Research* (New York: Free Press of Glencoe, 1956), pp. 3-4.
(b) David Easton: "Introduction: The Current Meaning of Behaviouralism" in J.C. Charlesworth (ed.). *Contemporary Political Analysis* (New York: Free Press of Glencoe, 1967), pp. 11-31.
(c) Frank J. Sorauf: *Perspective on Political Science*, pp. 15-16.
(d) Thakurdas: *Essays in Political Theory*, pp. 44-45.

The 'newness' of the behavioural approach may be said to lie in its four broad goals that may be put as under:[50]

1. The behaviouralists, first of all, want to explore a new kind of data that has not been attended hitherto. They want to study politics by focusing attention on the individual and group behaviour and also what goes on in the political process and within political institutions.
2. They advocate a new method. They insist upon survey research and the application of statistics to the data observed and other field work exercises.
3. They invent many interpretative categories largely borrowed from the social sciences, particularly sociology, and even to a certain extent from natural sciences. These concepts like elite, role, influence, decision-making, policy-making, systems, sub-systems, structures and functioning of structures, political culture etc. have all passed into very wide currency in the political literature of our times. These concepts are the essence of contemporary empirical political theory and are related to the type of question which the theorist has in mind.
4. Neo-empiricists are concerned with drawing generalisations from the data collected and also constructing models through which interpretation of the political process could be made with scientific accuracy. All this was done with a view to establish a science of politics; to infuse a new spirit in the study of the subject and to make the approach as realistic (scientific) and precise as possible so that it could be almost parallel to the natural sciences.

It is true that as a result of the utilisation of the behavioural approach, the scope of political science has widened and the nature of this discipline has improved in

50. Heinz Eulau, S.J. Eldersveld and M. Janowitz (ed. s): *Political Behaviour. A Reader in Theory and Research*, (New York: Free Press, 1956), pp. 3-4.

understanding and explaining political reality.[51] However, it may be criticised on these grounds:

1. It is based upon a false theory of knowledge. It takes facts alone as real. On the contrary, universal norms are as real as facts and facts can have meaning only in connection with the universal values.[52]
2. It is based on a false conception of scientific method. Even after collecting facts and doing their measurement and quantification, the writer cannot free himself from the limitations of subjectivity or his own sense of value-judgements while making some observations on their basis. Thus, fixity and finiteness of a natural science cannot be infused in the discipline of a social science.[53]
3. It circumscribes the scope of political science by advising us to study only those aspects of political life that are amenable to measurement and quantification. In this way, the significance of speculative political theory is sacrificed at the altar of 'a dry, barren and mad craze of scientism'.[54]
4. It lacks orientation regarding all political matters. It has no protection whatsoever except by recourse to commonsense against losing itself in the study of irrelevances.[55]
5. It makes political science a handmaid of sociology by laying down that all political activities and institutions reflect the nature of society and are determined and patterned to a large extent by divisions within society.[56]
6. It is unmindful of the chief difficulty confronting social sciences in general – the large number of variable factors, which make control and finding difficult, but also unlike the natural sciences, there is no agreement yet between either methods to be adopted or procedures to be followed, which has resulted in a large variety of empirical research studies, whose techniques vary considerably allowing for considerable differences.[57]
7. Above all, normativism cannot be discarded from the study of politics in entirety. Facts make sense only when there is an ideological conceptual framework. Mere facts without such a framework would become incoherent data. The very

---

51. Frank Thakurdas: *Essays in Political Theory,* pp. 8-9.
52. Lippincott, *op. cit.,* p. 219.
53. H.J. Morgenthau; *The Decline of Democratic Politics* (Chicago: Chicago University Press, 1962), pp. 26-27.
54. G. Sartori: "From the Sociology of Politics to Political Sociology" in S.M. Lipset (ed.): *Politics and the Social Science* (New York: Oxford University Press, 1969),
55. See Leo Strauss: "Epilogue" in H.J. Storing: *Essays on the Scientific Study of Politics,* (New York: Holt, Rinehart and Winston, 1969). p. 310. A subscriber to the normative political theory says: "Behavioural study suffers from two limitations – the impossiblity of ever being able to produce generalisation of a high order, *i.e.,* proximate to the precision of the natural sciences on the one hand and not being able to explain the higher ends of Liberty, Equality, Justice and Rights that inhere in the political systems of the world, of the East and of the West, commonly referred to as ideologies or doctrines, the inner core of political belief, which is, as it were, the controlling and guiding spirit of any political system." Frank Thakurdas, *op. cit.,* p. 43.
56. *Ibid.*
57. See A.H. Doctor, *op. cit.,* p. 19.

collection of data itself requires a value framework. In other words, without a value framework, it is impossible to ferret, search out and collect facts.[58]

No doubt, the behavioural approach has its own strong and weak points. It has widened the horizons of the study of politics by taking resort to the interdisciplinary focus. At the same time, it has done a sort of disservice to the subject of political science by sticking to the side of facts and thereby discarding the place of norms, goals and values. A balanced evaluation of this approach is contained in these words: "Whether they (behaviouralists) succeeded or failed in clarifying or understanding is a matter of individual judgement, but it could be said in fairness with the new perspectives that some of the interpretative categories and empirical studies have thrown a flood of light on many problems and processes of politics which the older theories were either not able to explain or explained inadequately. In this respect, their work has been illuminating even if their final objective of providing an overall theoretical edifice of universal validity has not been achieved, or if at all is highly controversial."[59]

Neo-Institutional Approach: "Neo-Institutionalism combines older institutionalist concerns with developmentalism."[60] State is no longer a police institution, it is concerned with the welfare and development of the people. So, it is a social welfare and a democractic organisation. Dahl, Rokkan, Dogan, Benedix, Inkeles and Apter are its main advocates who lay stress on their concern with 'transitions' to democracy. They touch many new issues such as termination of authoritarianism and its replacement by a liberal-democratic order, link between industrial capitalism and parliamentary democracy, and the nature of a pluralist society. The operation of party system and voting behaviour of the people are other areas of their concern. They think about the prospects and possibilities of 'consociationalism' with its emphasis on how to establish viable democratic institutions in the face of deep-seated social cleavages.

Neo-institutionalism is less constitutional than its older form. It is more prone to economic analysis in so far as it deals with fiscal and monetary policy, banks,

---

58. See R.A. Dahl: "The Behavioural Approach in Political Science: Epitaph for a Monument to a Successful Protest' in *American Political Science Review* (December, 1961), pp. 763-72. In terms of ideological content, behavioural theory had very little to say that was new. It represented a stage in which democratic theory had lost its innocence. It incorporated within the general democratic theoretical framework, a strong dose of the elitist cynicism about the basic possibility of a democratic government. See T.B. Bottomore: *Elites and Society* (Harmondsworth: Penguin, 1966.) In not much time it could be noticed that the behavioural political theory was only superficially analytic, achieving none of the rigour and the relentless demystifying energy that go with logical positivism of a superior variety." See Sudipta Kaviraj "How Not to Study Method: A Critical Note on Positivist Teaching of Methodology" in Kaviraj, Partha Chatterjee, S.K. Chaube and S.D. Gupta: *The State of Political Theory: Some Marxist Essays* (Catcutta: Research India Publications, 1978), pp. 10-13.
59. Frank Thakurdas, *op. cit.*, p, 9. This contention of the behaviouralists is without any sense that political science before 1950 had no clear intellectual identity, though this much of their contention may be accepted that it "was a heterogenous, plural, and diverse discipline with little agreement about its central goods." F.J. Souraf, *Perspectives on Political Science* (Columbus, Charles E. Merrill Pub., 1965), p. 15.
60. David Apter: "Comparative Politics: Old and New" in R.E. Goodin and Hans-Dieter Klingemann (eds.): *A New Handbook of Political Science* (Oxford: Oxford University Press, 1996), p. 386.

markets and globalisation. It is also concerned with locating changes in the legislative and administrative processes, shifts in long established party politics, working of coalitions, etc. as these impinge on the state. Like its old form, it is concerned with the state as an instrumentality in its own right, with its own tendencies and needs, and as a configuring power, how it determines the nature of civil society. "In general, one can say that new institutionalism is more connected to social and political theory and less to political philosophy, than its predecessor, and also more engaged in political economy."[61]

Marxist Approach: In this direction, the Marxist approach has a place of its own that may be regarded as basically different from both traditional and modern approaches in several important respects, though we may also discover certain points of resembance with both. The astonishing feature of this approach is that here the 'state', being the central theme of political science, is conceived as an inevitable consequence of class contradictions. As such, the system of Marxian dialectics culminates in the justification of a stateless condition of social life that would come into being as the final stage of social development. Moreover, economics dominates the scene so much so that all other disciplines like history, sociology, psychology and ethics become its offshoots. Politics is integrally connected with the basic economic structure finding its manifestation in the forces and relations of production. Thus, it is stressed that in the real world "economic and political forces and factors are constantly interacting and are extremely hard to disentangle one from the other."[62]

The significance of the Marxist approach is traceable in the fact that its utilisation calls for a deeper scrutiny of the meaning and nature of politics. Instead of keeping the focus of study confined to the formal structures and sub-structures of a political system, it lays emphasis on going to the roots. Thus, it holds that the economic system determines the class structure and as there is a change in the means of production, so there is a corresponding change in the relations of the free men and the slaves, the feudal lords and the serfs, the capitalists and the workers—the dominant and the dominated classes. Struggle for power constituting the bedrock of politics should, therefore, be studied in the context of the conflict between two antagonistic classes. This state of contradictions can end only in the establishment of a socialist society. Obviously, this approach not only lays stress on the fact of social contraditions, but it also finds out the way of their reconciliation. In this way, it assumes a deterministic character.

If so, the Marxist approach becomes like an ideology. It stands on a particular set of propositions that are not open to question and that call for a concerted action for the sake of their realisation and implementation so as to change the world and not merely interpret it. It not only exposes the inherent weaknesses and defects of the existing capitalist system, it also informs the exploited and the oppressed class of the workers, peasants and toilers to unite so as to break the chains of slavery and win the whole world. Thus, it treats state as an instrument of exploitation and

61. *Ibid.*, p. 389.
62. S. Strange: "The Study of Trans-National Relations" in *International Affairs* (London), July, 1952, No 3, 337.

oppression by one class over another and lays down that class character of the state cannot come to an end until the classless society is culminated in the stateless condition of life signifying complete emancipation of man. As Marx in his *German Ideology* says: "... in a communist society, where nobody has one exclusive sphere of activity, but where each can become accomplished in any branch he wishes, society regulates the general production and thus makes it possible for me to do one thing today and another thing tomorrow, to hunt in the morning, fish in the afternoon, rear cattle in the evening, criticise after dinner, just as I have a mind, without ever becoming a hunter, a fisherman, a shepherd, or a critic."[63]

As given by Marx and his collaborator (Engels) and developed by Lenin, this approach claims itself to be both scientific and progressive. It rejects the present system as oppressive, exploitative and inequitable and instead, desires a new set up in which exploitation and oppression are replaced by the glorious virtues of harmony and cooperation. Politics is treated as a manifestation of class antagonisms and its end is conceived in the culmination of social development when the phase of class identification and resolution of conflicts would unleash glorious human values. Thus, this approach, that has been empirical so far, assumes a normative character in the end. In short, the whole approach looks like a theory which *qua* theory provides a broad-based vision of society in all stages of development; at its base lies the fundamental importance of production, and from there the economic substructure of society and the crucial role of the class."[64]

We may easily take note of the fact that the Marxist approach is basically different from the approach of the neo-empiricists known by the name of 'behaviouralists'. While the latter treats politics just as a study of power in the present capitalist system without accepting the fact of class contradictions, the former treats politics as a struggle between the dominant and dominated classes. Thus, while the latter approach defends and justifies the present system as good, the former approach rejects the present as unjust and instead, desires a new system free from exploitation and oppression of one class by another. Obviously, while the latter approach seeks to defend the *status quo,* the former approach desires a change. In his *Theses on Feuerbach,* Marx has written that the job of a philosopher is not only to interpret the world, it is to tell as how 'to change it'. For this reason, writers subscribing to the Marxist approach discredit the behavioural approach as a false conception of social and political reality, designed to perpetrate the bourgeois system of exploitation. In this way, this approach has the ability to explain the hard reality of social and political life; it helps to understand the real, though hidden, forces which continue to produce severe consequences such as poverty, unemployment and war, both in highly developed and developing countries.[65]

An English writer has made these critical points against the Marxist approach to the study of politics:[66]

63. See L.S. Feuer (ed.): *Marx and Engels* (London: Fontana, 1969), p. 295.
64. Tony Throndike: "The Revolutionary Approach: The Marxist Perspective" in Trevor Taylor (ed.): *Approaches and Theory in International Relations* (London: Longman, 1978), pp. 61-62.
65. *The Fundamentals of Marxist-Leninist Philosophy* (Moscow: Progress Publishers, 1974) XVII.
66. Field: *Political Theory* (London: Methuen, 1965), pp. 258-61.

1. It pays very little and superficial attention to psychological analysis. This, sometimes, seems to be claimed as a virtue, and it is argued that the so-called 'objective' factors are of more importance than what is going on in individual human minds. But, in fact, institutions and the like are just as much psychological facts as are impulses and desires. They are really, if fully analysed, just sets of acquired habits, and habits have no existence outside human beings.
2. The economic structure of any society is not something fixed and unalterable, nor is it something that we simply have to accept as a given fact. Except in entirely custom-ridden societies, it is something which is fluid and changeable into a protean variety of forms. And this change and variety itself needs an explanation which cannot always be found in the nature of the economic structure itself. The political structure may, and often does, influence the development of the economic system, and we cannot set any *a priori* limits to the extent to which it can do that. It is true that there are always strong influences at work favouring the maintenance of any existing system, economic or otherwise.
3. Further Marxist deductions are equally lacking in cogency. They seem to consist of taking certain influences or tendencies which are observable at certain limits and showing what would happen if they were developed to their logical extremes and no counter-influences arose to check or modify them. It is only one among many influences and the extent of it varies enormously from country to country and from time to time.
4. The prophecy that the division into two classes will become harder and sharper and that the differences in wealth and status will continually increase has been falsified by events. The fundamental fact is that as long as the supply of good things in the world is limited, there will always be the possibility of a conflict over the division of wealth available at any given time. When people are thinking of increasing their share of the available wealth, the conflict can just as well be horizontal as vertical, between different industries as much as between different ranks in the same industry. The view relating to the eventual disappearance of the state is doubtful and not taken very seriously nowadays. It has, in effect, been abandoned even by the Marxists themselves, though they still seem to pay lip-service to it as a kind of millenial aspiration.

The paramount weakness of the Marxist approach may be traced in its rigid and deterministic character. By treating economic factors as 'decisive', it discards the place of other factors of non-economic character (like religion, morality, emotions, patriotism, etc.) whose role in the politics of a country has its own significance that should not altogether be lost sight of, by a student of empirical political theory. Moreover, its deterministic character renders to it the character of an ideology that blinds its subscriber to comprehend social and political reality in a detached manner. However, the merit of this approach lies in the fact that it seeks to study and explain political reality in realistic terms, though in its own way. It exposes the hollowness of the present bourgeois system that perpetrates social and economic evils for its vested interest. We may take note of the fact that "many of the predictions that Marx, Engels and Lenin made have come true compelling us to study the framework of analysis which Marx has left behind."[67]

67. Frank Thakurdas, *op. cit.*, p. 47.

Some Other Modern Approaches and Theories

In the later part of the twentieth century, some new approaches and theories came into currency which may be included in the category of mainstream empirical formulations. Their foundations are quite old that may be traced in the assumptions of Machiavelli, Hobbes, Montesquieu, Bentham and Marx, but the superstructures have a modern look reinforced by the trend of behaviouralism and interdisciplinary focus. Once again, it appears that such theorists have sought to push traditional approaches and theories aside in certain factual contexts or perspectives with the help or use of 'discourses' about preference or choice of the analytical frameworks or designs.

Rational Choice Approach: Known by various names as public choice theory, social choice theory, game theory, formal political theory, spatial model political behavioural theory, institutional public choice theory and preferential behaviour theory, this theory (popularly known as rational choice theory) has come to have a significant place in political science since the 1950s at the hands of economists like Buchanan and Downs and political scientists like Olson and Riker. Having its source in the conceptions of economics and mathematics, it provides insights into the actions of the traders, consumers, voters, lobbyists, bureaucrats, players and politicians. A mathematician may solve the puzzles of individual behaviour of the players involved in a game,[68] or the dilemma of two prisoners[69] may make us conclude that rationally self-interested behaviour can be generally less beneficial than cooperation.[70]

Faint reflections of this approach may be traced in the assumptions of Hobbes and Bentham who consider individuals as utterly selfish creatures, always seeking fulfilment of ends that would give them anything like felicity or happiness. However, associated in particular with the Virginia School of the United States, it became very popular in the economic sphere. It draws heavily upon the examples of economic theory in building models based on procedural rules usually about the rationally

68. Game theory deals with rationalist choice where there is strategic interdependence. As a sub-field of rational choice theory it had its development when the economists asked whether any satisfactory or broadly democratic way could be found out for segregating the preference of individual citizens to arrive at the social ranking of the alternatives.

69. The 'prisoners' dilemma' is the study of two prisoners, each being interrogated separately for an alleged crime. The interrogator tells each prisoner that if one of them confesses and the other one does not, the one who confesses will be acquitted and the one who keeps silent will get a long term of imprisonment. If both confess, both will get somewhat reduced prison terms. If neither confesses, both will receive short prison terms based on lack of evidence. What is the solution to the dilemma of the prisoners? Both prisoners will confess, and thus each will serve a longer sentence than if they had cooperated and kept silent. Why did cooperation fail to occur? Each prisoner is faced with a one-time choice. Neither prisoner knows how the other will respond; the cost of not confessing if the other confesses is extraordinarly high. So both will confess, leading to a less than optimal outcome. But if the game is repeated, the possibility of reciprocity makes it rational to cooperate. Had the two prisoners cooperated with each other by remaining silent, then the outcomes would have been much better for both. It was actually in the self-interest of each to cooperate. Karen Mingst: *Essentials of International Relations* (New York: W.W. Norton and Company, 1999), pp. 68-69.

70. Andrew Heywood: *Political Theory: An Introduction* (New York: Palgrave Macmillan, 2005), p. 246.

self-interested behaviour of the individuals. James Buchanan, in his *Fiscal Theory and Political Economy* (1960), applies it to the economic sphere for the sake of defending free market and arguing in favour of a minimal state in spite of his admission that many interest groups manage to reap benefits at the expense of the interest of the community as a whole. Anthony Downs in his *An Economic Theory of Democracy* (1957) develops a theory of democracy based on the assumptions of economics. It presupposes a policy space in which voters, candidates and political actors of all sorts can measure where they stand in relation to other political actors in competition with each other. The case of party politics naturally figures in, because the role of political parties is very crucial in determining the behaviour of the individuals.[71]

Mancur Olson is a political scientist whose work *The Logic of Collective Action* (1968) analyses the behaviour of many interest groups. Individuals form and join interest groups to secure public goods. As the indiviuals become free riders by reaping the benefits of group action without incurring the cost of membership, there is no guarantee that the existence of a common interest will lead to the formation of an organisation to advance or defend that interest. He questions pluralist assumptions about the distribution of group power and suggests that strong networks of interest groups can threaten a nation's performance. W.H. Riker applies it to the study of political coalitions and finds the source of the merit of democratic system here. In his *Liberalism against Populism* he says: "Democracy is the implementation of the popular will represented by a social preference ranking. "Like others, he defends the case of a minimal state and cautions that the innovations of the democratic governments to repair market failures often creates more problems than it solves."[72]

Rational choice as a positive approach to political explanations is based on the following assumptions:

1. There are important forms of political behaviour that are the results of the choices made with a view to the efficient achievements of given ends.
2. Individuals are essentially self-interested, but the concept of self-interest is potentially extremely elastic.
3. All individuals have the rational capacity, time and emotional detachment necessary to choose the best course of action, no matter how complex be the choice.
4. Its object is strategy equilibrium.

This theory or approach may be criticised for laying too much stress on the rationality of the individual. A political psychologist like Graham Wallas may argue that most of the actions of man are irrational, than being rational. It is a fact that human beings are psychologically complex. They frequently act irrationally; they operate within many systems which cannot be easily comprehended fully when seen from a rational choice perspective.[73] In proceeding from an abstract model of the individual, it "pays insufficient attention to social and historical factors, failing to recognise, among other things, that human self-interestedness may be socially conditioned, and not innate."[74]

71. *Ibid.*, p. 247.
72. Hugh Ward: "Rational Choice Theory" in David Marsh and Gerry Stoker (eds.): *Theory and Methods in Political Science* (London: Macmillan, 1995) p. 79.
73. *Ibid.*, p. 92.
74. Heywood, *op. cit.*, p. 247.

Discourse Theory: The concept of discourse includes all types of social and political processes, institutions and organisations within its frame of reference. Hence, discourse theory draws inspiration from interpretative sciences such as hermeneutics, phenomenology, structuralism and deconstructivism. For instance, Michael Foucault in his *The Archeology of Knowledge* (1972) endeavours to use discursive formations which refer to regular set of ideas and concepts and which claim to produce knowledge about the world. In his historical accounts of scientific discourses, he endeavours to sketch out their underlying discursive regularities and connects their production and transformation to the broader social and political processes of which they are a part. In his case, discourses are a form of power in that they set up antagonisms and structure relations between people who are defined as subjects and objects, as insiders and outsiders.[75] Ernst Laclau and Chantal Mouffe have developed a concept of discourse that is concerned specifically with the analysis of political processes.[76] They have attempted to deepen the Marxist category of ideology by utilising the insights of 'post-modernist' philosophy and theory.[77]

This theory constitutes a relatively new approach to political analysis, although it has its strong roots in the past theoretical traditions and perspectives. Drawing on and extending the approaches of the Marxist theorists like Gramsci of Italy and Althusser of France, and while taking on broad issues and assumptions put forward by the political modernist theorists, it "examines the logics and structures of discursive articulation."[78]

The term 'discourse' as used here implies "human interaction, especially communication, that may disclose or illustrate power-relationships.[79] Thus, discourse theory analyses all the practices and meanings shaping a particular community of social actors. It assumes that all objects and actions are meaningful and that their meaning is the product of historically-specific systems of rulers. "Discourse analysis refers to the analysis of linguistic and non-linguistic material as texts that enable subjects to experience the world of objects, words and practices."[80] The overall aim of social and political analysis from a discursive perspective is to describe, understand, interpret, and evaluate carefully constructed objects of investigation. Hence, instead of applying theory mechanically to empirical objects, or testing theories against

75. *Ibid.*, p. 128.
76. Laclau occupies a peculiar place in that while "his debt to post-structuralism has undermined many of the characteristic themes of Marxist thinking, for example, his emphasis on the role of discourses and historical contingency leaves little room for Marxist social analysis with its basic materialism - nonetheless, he leaves us with the deconstruction of institutions as discourse." R.A.W. Rhodes: "Old Institutionalisms" in R.E. Goodin: (ed.): *The Oxford Handbook of Political Science* (Oxford: Oxford University Press, 2009), p. 151.
77. The label of 'post-modernism' includes a wide array of theorists like Foucault, Derrida, Lyotard, Baudrillard and Rorty who indulged in discourses and questioned the foundations and the essentialist assumptions of their respective traditions and disciplines. A critic may, however, say that unfortunately in many ways the notion of post-modernism is something of a misnomer." *Ibid.*, p. 16.
78. David Howarth: "Discourse Theory" in Marsh and Stoker, *op. cit.*, p. 132.
79. Andrew Heywood: *Politics* (Houndmills, Basingstroke: Palgrave Foundations, 2005), p. 17.
80. Howarth, *op. cit.*, p. 10.

empirical reality, discourse theories argue for the articulation and modification of concepts and logics in each particular research context."[81]

Contextual Approach: In a certain sense, this approach may be taken as an extension or elaboration of the discourse theory.[82] Adopted by many theorists and analysts like Butler, Stokes, Marsh, Ward, Miller and Sanders, it contends that the individuals must be correctly assigned to the context of time, place and environment. Despite certain difficulties, contextual models are important, because there is a clear evidence that the same persons behave differently at different times and in different places and circumstances. Political behaviour is very much a matter of individual response to an environment that includes family, friends, neighbours, workplace associates, state of the economy and the like.

It may be pointed out here that a completely comprehensive account of all contexts is neither desirable nor possible. Contextual accounts typically work by helping the analyst to get a grip on some puzzling phenomenon. To understand how social power is exercised, one needs to understand both technology of ideas or strategy. To understand why certain social forms are widely acceptable in one time and place but not another, one may need to understand differing social ontologies.[83]

As contextual analysis does not require a complete and comprehensive account of all contexts to be used as correctives for the purpose of the analysts, it differs fundamentally from the search for general laws. The analysts may prefer commonsense division of the contextual areas as under:[84]

1. **Philosophy:** As so many disputes and confusions in political science actually pivot on epistemology, ontology, logic and general conceptions of argument, so philosophy demands its place at the contextual table.
2. **Psychology:** Political analysts may employ conceptions of political psychology to make serious reflections on relations between individual psychological processes and the collective phenomena.
3. **Ideas:** Political analysts may attribute importance to ideas about liberty, equality, justice, democracy and social order. Contextual analysis helps them see how to take ideas into account as contexts for the understanding of political processes, evidence available for empirical examination of the political processes, and influences on or components of the processes themselves.
4. **Culture:** Culturally embedded ideas, relations and practices profoundly affect the operation of superficially similar political processes. Even within the same politics, analysts sometimes object that linguistic, ethnic, religious, and regional cultures differ so dramatic ally that all efforts to direct general political principles in those polities must fail.

---

81. R.A.W. Rhodes: "Old Institutionalisms" in R.E. Goodin (ed.): *The Oxford Handbook of Political Science*, (Oxford: Oxford University Press, 2009), p. 150.
82. "At the heart of the approach is an analogy with language. Just as we understand the meaning of a word from its context, so we understand a political institution as sedimented beliefs within a particular discourse." Rhodes, *op. cit.*, pp. 150-51.
83. *Ibid.* p. 452.
84. *Ibid.*, pp. 453-55.

5. **History:** In all three types of contextual effects on analysts' understanding of political processes, on the evidence available for empirical examination of political processes, and on the processes themselves, history figures significantly. The knowledge of historical context provides a means of producing more systematic knowledge of the political processes.
6. **Place:** In some definitions, history as location in space and time exhausts the influence of place. Yet geographically attuned political analysis detect effects of adjacency, distance, environment, and climate that easily escape historians who deal with the same time and places.
7. **Population:** The demographic tools can advance political analysis. The discipline of demography does, indeed, offer a number of formal techniques such as life tables and migrant stream analyses that bear directly on political processes and suggest valuable analogies for political analysis.
8. **Technology:** In contemporary political analysis, technology often appears as a black box, a demonic force, or an exogeneous variable that somehow affects politics, but does not belong to politics as such.

Such a view is hard to sustain, however, when the subject is war or economic imperialism. In fact, technologies of communication, production, distribution, organisation and of rule pervade political processes, and receive insufficient attention for their specific properties.

Like the two approaches or theories discussed above, this theory may be subjected to attack. A pertinent question arises as to how a researcher or a theorist may cover all possible or available contexts in the presentation of his analysis or in the formulation of his theories. He has to adopt the strategy of 'pick and choose'. That is, he may take some and ignore some other contexts as a result of which his conclusions may not be thoroughly empirical.

Empirical approaches or theories dominated the scene in the period following the Second World War in the form of behavioural, positivist and neo-positivist trends. The trend of empiricism, however, saw its decline after 1970 when the trend of normativism had its resurgence. What was lauded by the empiricists in the recent past was denounced by the normativists in the last phase of the twentieth century as is evident from Ada Finifter's *Political Science: State of the Discipline* (1983) and David Ricci's *The Tragedy of Political Science* (1984). "Among contemporary political scientists, there is prevailing, perhaps, predominant view of the history of the discipline that we are now in a post-positivist, post-scientific, post-behavioural stage."[85]

Concluding Observations

A detailed study of the major traditional and modern approaches, as contained in the preceding sections, leaves following important impressions:

1. While several approaches to the study of politics may be broadly grouped into two categories—traditional and modern—a sort of overlapping cannot be lost sight of. It is a different matter that we treat the former as loaded with normativism and

85. R.E. Goodin and Hans-Dieter Klingemann (eds.) *A New Handbook of Political Science* (Oxford: Oxford University Press, 1996), p. 81.

the latter with empiricism. The fact stands out that empiricism is available in the traditional approaches of great political theorists from Aristotle and Polybius in the ancient to A. de Tocqueville and James Bryce in the modern ages. Similarly, normativism has not been discarded by the most prominent figures subscribing to modern approaches. Even Marxism has a normative orientation in the end when it conceives of an era of emancipated humanity wedded to the observance of glorious human values. Thus, it may be asserted that the label of traditionalism is neither a criticism nor a refutation of the patent fact that norms still play an important role in modern political studies, although no longer monopolising the avenues of approach.[86] It also follows that several approaches to the study of politics should not be treated as mutually exclusive. Most of them are interrelated in some respects. It is correct to say that different categories "do not meet the requirements of logic. They are employed, nevertheless, in the belief that they reject usage and in the belief that it is more significant to comment on usage than to devise an entirely logical classification scheme."[87]

2. Every approach, or method, or methodology has its own use and value. Even the rationalistic, deductive, *a priori* method provides hypotheses and frames of reference which can readily be discarded if and when scientific method proves them wrong. The historical and philosophical methods have their advocates even now. The legalistic-juristic approach to the state, closely linked with political theory, is still vital. The empirical and scientific methods have helped to replace dogma with fact, despite the lack of sufficiently precise standards of measurement.[88]
3. It is good that the study of politics, as desired by the behaviouralists and the Marxists, should be made on scientific lines as far as possible. But it should also be remembered that scientific method has its own limitations. It cannot be applied to political science in a way it is done in the field of natural sciences. "The material with which the political scientist has to deal is very different from that which the investigator in the physical sciences is concerned, being of such a character as not to permit the use of artificial contrivances or apparatus for increasing or guiding his power of observation or for registering results. Not only must the investigator work without the assistance of mechanical aids, but he is also handicapped by the fact that the phenomena with which political science deals do not follow one another according to invariable laws of sequence, but rather at indeterminate intervals, constituting, as G.C. Lewis says, an interminable and perpetually varying series."[89]
4. On the whole, traditional and modern approaches have a relevance of their own in the study of political phenomena. The purpose is to understand and explain political reality and, as such, it should not be tried to be achieve it in a way that the conclusions become thoroughly abstract or too mechanistic not at all applicable to the life of a living and dynamic people. It is permissible to doubt

86. A.R. Ball : *Modern Politics and Government* (London: Macmillan, 1976), II ed., p.10.
87. Van Dyke, *op. cit.*, p.115.
88. Rodee, Christol and Anderson : *Introduction to Political Science*, p. 9.
89. Garner, *op. cit.*, pp. 15-16.

the all-embracing sufficiency of a single approach which is presumed to solve all the myriad questions presented by the state and its politics. Many 'moderns' who smile tolerantly at the idealism of the Greek, Stoic, and medieval Catholic philosophers and as such 'naive' notions as those of 'natural law' and 'natural rights' ('excogitated ideas', impossible to substantiate or prove) are themselves easily hypnotised by a new 'scientific explanation, especially if replete with tables of statistics. It is well to remind ourselves that man is a complex as well as a perverse creature and that we are still far from having all the answers which will explain even the political phases of his behaviour, let alone the whole man. The mythical 'economic man' of the classical economists and the equally imaginary reasonable and 'prudent man' of the lawyers are not more ridiculous than many current assumptions about 'political man'. Man is, indeed, as Aristotle declared, a 'political animal' but he is no more monopolised by the 'power' urge, as many infer from recent politico-psychological studies, than he is by acquisitiveness, greed or Marxist class consciousness."[90]

A student of this subject should, therefore, be guided by two important considerations. First, the way of eclecticism is desirable. That is, he may borrow from different approaches and mix them up in his study of politics in view of the fact that no approach can serve his purpose in an exclusive manner. Second, the object of a researcher should be to give due importance to both facts and values so as to develop theories applicable to all questions concerning the explanation, and also prediction, to the possible extent, of events having their connection with the political reality of a place. This should be done with a sense of humility and this is sure to lead to the growth and development of this discipline. As Rodee, Christol and Anderson observe: "The readiness of political science to learn all it can from other branches of human knowledge—without claiming, as do some of its sister sciences, to have arrived at final, definitive principles—is evidence of its vitality and continuing growth."[91] We may conclude our study with this impression that there are certain characteristics (like making assumptions for shaping analysis and research of a political scientist, or making use of nomological relationships) which all approaches have in common. The whole idea "is one of cutting into politics at a number of points in order to examine different slices of political life. Thus, on the face of it, no approach is right or wrong, but some may be more useful than others. Because we do not have a finely honed knife available, there is some overlap between the approaches. But there are differences to be drawn which are meaningful for the political scientist."[92]

90. Rodee, Christol and Anderson, *op. cit.*, p. 9.
91. *Ibid.*
92. A.C. Isaak, *op. cit.*, p. 159.

5

Science and Political Theory

> The 'fact' is the first thing. Make sure of it. Get it perfectly clear. Polish it till it shines and sparkles like a gem. Then connect it with other facts. Examine it in its relation to them, for in that lies its worth and its significance. To counsel it to stick to facts is not to dissuade you from philosophical generalisations, but only to remind you – though indeed you as trained students do not need to be reminded – that the generalisations must spring out of the facts, and without the facts, are worthless.
>
> **—Lord James Bryce[1]**

From the days of Aristotle, universally recognised as the 'Father of Politics' or 'First Political Scientist', this subject has been regarded as the 'master science'. But the point of debate is whether it may be ranked as a 'science'. Views in this regard range from those of Pollock[2] and Bryce on the one hand, to those of Amos, Comte and Ford on the other.[3] Thus, while the former contend that political science may be treated as the 'science' of state (or of government, or of power), the latter scoff at all such claims. It naturally leads to a debatable issue relating to the existence of any thing like 'scientific' political theory, as so strongly advocated by a good number of writers belonging to the schools of behaviourism and 'behaviouralism'[4]. In this chapter an attempt has been made to discuss the

1. Cited in David Easton : *The Political System: An Inquiry into the State of Political Science* (Calcutta : Scientific Book Agency, 1971), p. 64.
2. For instance, Sir Fredrick Pollock says that there "is a political science in the same sense that there is a science of morals" *An Intrroduction to the History of the Science of Politics* (London : Macmillan, 1923), p.2.
3. For instance, Amos asserts that politics "floats in the public mind either as a mere field for ingenious chicane or as a boundless waste for the evolution of scholastic fantasy." *The Science of Politics,* pp. 2-16. August Comte denies the claim of politics to be ranked as a science, because there is no consensus of opinion among experts as to its methods, principles and conclusions ; it lacks continuity ; and it also lacks the elements which constitute the basis of precision. *Positive Philosophy* (Translated from French into English by Martineau), Vol. II. Ch.3. Prof. Henry J. Ford says that the idea of determining state policy upon 'scientific principles' has no place in practical politics. *Proceedings of the American Political Science Association,* 1905, Vol II, p. 198. Also see J.W. Garner: *Political Science and Government* (Calcutta: World Press, 1952), p. 11.
4. 'Behaviourism', in the field of psychology is regarded like a natural science that takes the whole field of human adjustments as its own. Historically considered, it "is only the current phase of a persistent aspiration to know the springs and motives of men in order to be able to predict to control their behaviour as the physicists know the physical world and can predict and control natural events." See H.M. Kallen :"Behaviourism in Seligman (ed.) : *Encyclopaedia of the Social Science* (New York : Macmillan 1964), Volume 1-2, 4th Ptg., pp, 495-96. According to J.B. Watson, a behaviourist drops from the scientific vocabulary all subjective terms such as sensation, perception, image, desire, purpose and even thinking and emotion as they are subjectively defined. *Behaviourism* (New York, 1924), p. 6. It is intrinsically interested in 'what the whole animal will do from morning to night and from night to morning.' *Ibid.*, p. 11.

meaning of 'science' and 'scientific method' and its application to the study of social sciences with particular emphasis on the study of political phenomena so as to have a scientific political theory. Moreover, as science deals with facts and as place of'value' cannot be entirely discarded in the study of social sciences, an attempt has also been made to discuss the case relating to 'facts' and 'values' and the issue of dichotomy between the two culminating in, what is now called, 'scientific value relativism'. Such a study is certainly informed by this essential point that "until political science begins constructing sound scientific theories, it will be considered an immature discipline".[5]

Scientific Method : Meaning and Assumptions

The present age is an age of science and technology[6]. It is universally believed that science has enabled man to grow as a human being by liberating him from the shackles of superstition and prejudice. It has enabled man to view his problems objectively and look for their solutions fruitfully in keeping with his capacity and dignity as a rational and a moral being. Without it, man would have remained a mere lump of protoplasm. Credit goes to science because of which man has been able to understand this universe as well as his own self in relation to his Creator. Thus, while physics is a result of man's understanding of the universe, metaphysics is a result of his understanding of the self in relation to his Creator. Obviously, if knowledge is a liberating force, it is especially true of what is called, 'scientific knowledge'. Thus, while some distinguished figures like Galileo, Copernicus, Kepler and Newton have their names in the field of natural sciences, others like Bacon, Locke, Hume, Hegel, Spencer, Comte and Marx deserve the same place in the field of social sciences.

In other words, it means that 'scientific method' is an invention of the modern age. In order to obtain the kind of impartial, well-founded and systematic knowledge at which the sciences aim, certain modes of investigation are followed. These are

Again, "Don't you get the idea, please, that the inside of our body is any different or any more mysterious than the outside of our body." *Ibid.*, p. 12. A deeper study of behaviourism shows that, in its extreme from, it rejects any operation with concepts such as consciousness, soul, mind, purpose, and introspection. It substitutes the careful observation of bodily phenomena, in particular, responses of the human body to stimuli, including both external responses (doings) and internal ones (visceral, muscular, glandular etc.) but only those of a physical character. The object of the behavioural research in the social sciences is what men really do when they are faced with situations rather than with their alleged opinions or feelings. However, behaviourism, as such, may not be included in the scientific method, for behaviouralist taboos are not mandatory within scientific method. Arnold Brecht : *Political Theory : The Foundations of Twentieth Century Political Thought* (Princeton : Princeton University Prees, 1959 p. 36.

5. Alan C. Issak : *Scope and Method of Political Science : An Introduction to the Methodology of Political Inquiry* (Homewood, Illinois : The Dorsey Press, 1969), p. 69.
6. Science may be characterised as a search for rationality rooted in facts,". But science and technology are not the same thing, though it is true that the latter is the applied form of the former. Science is primarily a quest for knowledge. The relation between science and technology is what we find in theory and its application. The theories of science, when put to empirical use, give rise to technology. See A.B. Shah : *Scientific Method* (Bombay : Allied Publishers, 1964), pp. and 41.

known by the name of 'scientific methods'. In a wide sense, any mode of investigation by which the sciences have been built up and are being developed is entitled to be called a scientific method. Broadly speaking, these methods are of two distinct kinds:[7]

1. There are the *technical* or *technological* methods of manipulating and measuring the phenomenon under investigation and the conditions under which it can be observed fruitfully. Probably, it is these technical methods of manipulation and measurement that are most readily recalled by the expression 'scientific method'. These technical methods are mostly different in different sciences, and few men of science ever master the technical methods of more than one science or one group of connected sciences.
2. There are the *logical* methods of reasoning according to the nature of the data obtained. These logical methods are intimately connected with the technical methods. In a very real sense, the technical methods, although they are extremely important or even indispensable in many scientific investigations, are mainly auxiliary to the logical methods of science.

What it means is that "in pure sciences, the technical methods of science are not usually an end in themselves. They are aids either to observation or to inference. Sometimes, they render possible the observation and measurement of certain phenomena which either could not be observed and measured at all, or could not be observed so well and measured so accurately. At other times, the technical methods enable the investigator to determine the conditions and circumstances of the occurrence of the phenomena which he is investigating so that he can reason about them in a definite and reliable manner instead of merely speculating about them vaguely."[8]

To be very clear about the meaning of 'science', we may put it at the very outset that it neither desires absolute perfection nor complete unity, since it is not possible. It also does not require a fixed or absolute subject matter.[9] Its chief assumptions are:

(i) The phenomena occur in patterns and it is the task of science to ascertain what these patterns are.

(ii) The scientist assumes that the observable world is the real world for him.

(iii) If something is to be subjected to scientific study, it must be subject to the study in the same way by more than one person.

(iv) It must be inter-subjectively communicable. The ways of detecting and of measuring the phenomena must be 'public', so that different individuals can investigate independently and possibly arrive at the same conclusions.

(v) Above all, the same object can be received through the senses in like ways by more than one person. Obviously, there may be many ways and so we may come across many 'scientific methods'.[10]

---

7. A.Wolf: *Essentials of Scientific Method* (London : George Allen and Unwin, n.y.) Ed. II, p. 15.
8. *Ibid.*
9. S.L. Wasby: *Political Science: The Discipline and Its Dimensions: An Introduction* (Calcutta : Scientific Book Agency, 1970), p. 18.
10. F S.C. Northrop uses the term 'scientific method' for each individual step (observation, description, forming a hypothesis, etc.) and holds that there "is no one scientific method." *The Logic of the Sciences and the Humanities* (New York, 1947), p. 107,

However, with a view to give a precise definition of the term 'scientific method', we may say that it "can be more accurately looked at as a general way of doing things, the specifics of which vary in practice from situation to situation. It is an outlook, a means of study which involves precisions, rigour and a systematic way of proceeding. It involves a heightened consciousness of what one is doing in one's work."[11]

It follows from the above that scientific method can be used in different senses. In its broadest meaning, it sets off any method that is considered 'scientific' from any other that is considered 'non-scientific' without indicating what makes it such. When used in this way, it designates a problem as to what is 'scientific' rather than an answer to it. In its more specific sense, however, it refers to a definite type of method concentrating on following the 'scientific actions', 'scientific operations', or steps of 'scientific procedures':[12]

1. **Observation** of what can be observed, and tentative acceptance or non-acceptance of the observation as sufficiently exact.
2. **Description** of what has been observed, and tentative acceptance or non-acceptance of the description as correct or adequate.
3. **Measurement** of what can be measured; this being merely a particular type of observation and description, but one sufficiently distinct and important to merit separate listing.
4. **Acceptance** or non-acceptance (tentative) as *facts* or *reality* of the results of observation, description and measurement.
5. **Inductive generalisation** (tentative) of accepted individual facts offered as a factual hypothesis.
6. **Explanation** (tentative) of accepted individual facts or of inductively reached factual generalisations, especially causal relations offered as a 'theoretical hypothesis'.
7. **Logical deductive reasoning** from inductively reached factual generalisations or hypothetical explanations so as to make explicit what is implied in them regarding previously accepted facts, factual generalisations and hypothetical explanations.
8. **Testing** by further observations, reports and measurements as properly made and of their results as facts, or tentative expectations as warranted.
9. **Correcting** the tentative acceptance of observation etc., and of their results of inductive generalisations and hypothetical explanations whenever they are incompatible with other accepted observations, generalisations or explanations, or correcting the previously accepted contributions.
10. **Predicting** events or conditions to be expected as a consequence of past, present or future events or conditions, or of any possible constellation of such, in order either (i) to test factual or theoretical hypothesis, this being identical with logical deductive reasoning and testing, and (ii) to supply a scientific contribution to the practical process of choosing between several possible alternatives of action.

---

11. Wasby, *op. cit.*, pp. 18-19.
12. Arnold Brecht, *op. cit.*, pp. 28-29.

11. **Non-acceptance** (elimination from acceptable propositions) of all statements not obtained or confirmed described here, especially of *a priori* propositions, except when immanent in 'scientific method' or offered merely as 'tentative assumptions' or 'working hypothesis'.

The notion of a 'scientific purpose' has these connotations :

1. It calls for an effort to develop generalisations about political behaviour, i.e., to advance hypotheses about relationships, to discover uniformities or regularities or laws, and to suggest theories; the higher the level of generalisation, the better.
2. It denotes an insistence that the generalisations be verified or verifiable. Normative propositions are avoided; the object is description, including explanation and descriptive statements about normative attitudes. If prescriptive statements are made, their normative component falls outside the realm of science.
3. The requirement that the generalisations be verified or verifiable calls for empiricism—for reliance on observation and refusal to rely on alleged *a priori* truths. It also calls for precision in the definition of concepts, clarity in the formulation of hypotheses and, in effect, restraint about calling generalisation anything other than a hypothesis until it has been demonstrated to be true.
4. In addition to generality and verifiability, the notion of a scientific purpose connotes a system; that is, the object is to develop a set of verified generalisations that fit together in a coherent system—a coherent interlocking network—giving a comprehensive description and explanation of the realm of behaviour in question.[13]

In short, the scientific attitude "consists of a syndrome of belief, method, and value. The *belief* is that there is an underlying continuity between man's natural and human environments to which he can gradually penetrate through his creative powers of imagination ...logical reasoning and observation .... The *method* requires that ordering concepts and propositions, procedures of selecting and analysing evidence, and modes of interpretation be public, communicable, and ultimately connectible with the experience of others. The *values* lie in the enjoyment of the common motivation and heritage known to men who seek the truth."[14] Likewise, Easton says: "In political research scientific method has, therefore, been conceived as involving, on the one hand, the accumulation of new information about the political system, and on the other the acceptance of these facts for the purpose of showing at once how they can be used to revamp some part of the political structure. If some judgement must be passed, it would seem that those interested in the immediate application of their knowledge are predominant today in political research."[15]

13. V.V. Dyke: *Political Science : A Philosophical Analysis*, p. 159.
14. Avery Leiserson : "The Behavioural Approach" in *Teaching Political Science: A Challenge to Higher Education*, edited by R.H. Connery (Durham, N.C., 1965), p. 52.
15. Easton, *op. cit.*, p. 79.

Components of Scientific Method: The Case of Natural Versus Social Sciences

We have already seen that scientific method aims at the elimination of *a priori* reasoning;[16] it stands for workable hypotheses that have a causal nature.[17] It deals with the phenomenal world or objective reality that may be observed, quantified and measured. However, such a view is applicable only to the world of natural sciences. In the sphere of social sciences, scientific method does take into consideration the case of noumenal or subjective reality'[18] that may have its externalised form in the explanation of a metaphysicist like Hegel. A social scientist may agree with the 'positivism' of Comte, or 'economic determinism' of Marx; he may also appreciate the 'ideal types' of Weber[19] or the 'constructive types' of Becker.[20] Such a point of variability may convince a student of social sciences with this argument of the critics that scientific method, as followed in the natural sciences, cannot be applied to the study of social and political phenomena. Before touching this delicate issue, we may first look into the components of scientific method as discussed by Brecht:[21]

16. It points to notions, propositions or postulates that are considered true or necessary irrespective of experience or anterior to it, *i.e.*, not derived from experience and yet considered valid. See Brecht, *op. cit.*, p. 99.
17. Assumptions and working hypotheses are tentative propositions that have not yet been, and may never become, definitely accepted, but are employed as useful tools in the course of a scientific inquiry. The assumption or working hypothesis may concern: (1) a fact or event, past, present, or future—the latter, for instance, when we assume the death of a ruler, a change in election figures, a poor harvest, or the outbreak of a war; (2) the goal, as when we assume that a certain goal like preserving peace, ought to be achieved on the ground that our country's government has decided to pursue it, or on any other ground; or (3) a law of causal relationship or other regularity, as when we assume that an increase in density of population will increase per capita public expenditures, or that the use of atomic bombs by one party in a war will cause their use by the other. The term 'assumption' is more often used for facts and goals, the term 'working hypothesis' for causal inter-relations, but there is no definite regularity in the limitation of either term to the one or the other category. In a narrower sense, however, the term 'working hypothesis' is reserved for causal theories provisionally adopted on the ground of their presumptive correctness or plausibility. We may call them 'working hypotheses of higher order. *Ibid*, p. 107.
18. As Immanuel Kant, the father of German Idealism, says,: "Natural science will never disclose to us the inner nature of things, i. *e.* that which is not phenomenon but might serve as the ultimate explanatory ground of the phenomena, nor does it need that knowledge for its purpose of physical explanation. Yes, even if natural science should be offered such explanation from some other quarter, it should reject it and not include it into the process of its own explanations, but should base these at all times exclusively on that which is an object of the senses pertaining to experience and can be brought into connection with our actual perceptions according to rules of experience. *Prolegomena to Ethics* edited by Cassirer and translated from German into English by Carl J. Friedrich, p. 101.
19. The term 'ideal types', as used by Max Weber, is "here meant to designate not some *moral* ideal but the perfectly representative construction of the type in question, though in this combination of qualities and atttitudes, it may exist only in our own minds." See Brecht, *op. cit.*, pp. 110-11.
20. Howard Becker's 'constructive types' are essentially identical with Weber's 'ideal types', although he puts greater emphasis on the requirement that the construct must be 'objectively probable', not merely possible. *Through Values to Social Interpretation* (Durham, N.C., 1950), pp. 93ff.
21. See Brecht, *op. cit.*, pp. 27-116.

1. **Role of an Investigator:** In order to engage in a scientific work at all, as distinct from other activities, the investigator must always begin by forming in his own mind some tentative *ideas* about (i) the objective of his inquiry i.e., the question for which the answer is sought, (ii) the relevance of this question for human knowledge in general, as distinct from a merely private interest of the investigator, and (iii) the relevance of the scientific actions the investigator is about to take for his purpose of finding the answer. Scientific method must not be understood as a merely mechanical procedure of indiscriminately gathering data and of processing them in line with prescribed steps, leaving every progress to assiduity and little if anything to genius. Rather the opposite is true. Even the mere selection of a problem, i.e., of a question for a worthwhile inquiry, is as a rule no mechanical act but an act of the creative mind and, in the most important cases, one of genius. It offers no substitute for the creative mind; nor does it tell a person how to be creative. Data and hypotheses are selected according to their preferential relevance for the solution of a problem that is under actual or potential inquiry.[22]
2. **Observation:** An empirical observation may be limited to a single situation or be repeated in essentially similar situations. It may be 'extrospective' focusing on the outside or 'introspective' focusing on the inner self. Strictly speaking, it is always an observation by a particular person, though other persons may, or may not, make similar observations. The one and the same thing may cause parallel impressions in different persons what Hocking names 'consubjectivity' and Brecht calls 'intersubjectivity'. In permitting a scientist to accept it as scientific method, it makes the first and greatest concession to commonsense. But every empirical observation is always subject to a challenge about its exactness. It may, or may not, be *accepted* by a scientist as exact. In every case, acceptance is tentative that may be withdrawn on better grounds at any time. As Democritus said, scientific method follows commonsense in this respect.[23]
3. **Description:** The best way, we can do apparently, is to analyse the meaning of the words actually used in a report by reference to whatever other data are available to clarify their meaning. The scientist who studies another person's report on an observation may, or may not, accept it as correct and adequate. Carefully planned questionnaires and interviews play a major role in directing mass observations. But these are exposed to the particular source of error in that most respondents are motivated by a tendency towards reporting 'respectable' views or facts than they actually are or were, or atleast they try to give their statements a respectable slant or explanation. A more ambitious scheme, called 'latent structure analysis', has been devised in order to find out, by a battery of indirect questions, some underlying structure of thinking and feeling that dominates all the answers, or many of them, of the individual respondent.[24]
4. **Measurement and Quantification:** In social sciences the possibilities of measurement have remained and will continue to remain limited due to the

22. *Ibid.*, pp. 30-32.
23. *Ibid.*, pp. 32-38.
24. *Ibid,*, pp. 38-42.

great number of variables, all of which cannot be included in the scientific analysis and in so far as they can, are not at all measurable. A potential factor of 'disturbance' must, therefore, generally be taken into account. The collection of facts and their classification has been called the 'natural history stage' of scientific inquiry. Classification plays an important role in the directed mass observation, general census, sampling through questionnaires, interviews and the like. When qualitative factors are involved, classification can serve the purpose of measurement to some extent. First, the various categories may be so devised as to constitute a scale of measurement, with the order of the categories providing a social order of ranking, as in the rating of examinations. Second, the number of observations listed in each category may yield useful figures either absolute or relative. A special construction is that of the 'ideal types' as called by Weber where the observational material is classified according to its greater proximity to one of the types than to the others. Another device is the use of 'indicators' *i.e.*, of easily observable single data indicative of a broader attribute, as the institution of *habeas corpus* or its equivalent is indicative of a system of government. In order that observations can be properly listed in classifications, all categories must be clear, unambiguous as to their meaning and mutually exclusive. Where 'preferences' play a role, classification may follow a 'utility index', despite the fact that preferences of one differ from the preferences of others. Finally, we may refer to the role of a quantitative content analyst who subjects the contents of newspapers, public speeches, state documents, radio announcements, private letters, or other means of communication to a painstaking scrutiny regarding the frequency with which certain subjects have been mentioned or key words have been used or have been referred to in a favourable context, or with a different meaning, or in coordination with other terms.[25]

5. **Acceptance of Facts, Truth or Reality:** A proposition is true when it corresponds to reality. It leads to 'warranted assertibility' (Dewey) or 'empirical validity' (Kaufman). Scientific method is concerned only with truth that is empirically ascertainable. But an acceptance of propositions about alleged facts as being true, or corresponding to reality, is only tentative. Psychologically speaking, belief or faith plays a powerful role in science also; it often determines the acceptance by the scientist of reports on empirical observations. Reality may be objectively visible or subjectively experienced. The former is physical, the latter metaphysical. Scientific method is concerned with the former alone. Hence, it may be called 'ontology' or something that deals with 'being' as being.[26]
6. **Logical Reasoning:** It is accepted as a full proof by scientific method when, and only when, it is strictly analytic. It is analytic when it adds nothing to the meaning of a given term or proposition,but merely makes explicit what is implied in that meaning. When a proposition adds something to the meaning of a given term or proposition, it is not analytic but synthetic. It then cannot be arrived at by deductive reasoning from the given term or proposition. Whether a proposition is meant to be analytic or synthetic cannot always be seen at once; it depends

25. *Ibid.*, pp. 43-47.
26. *Ibid.*, pp. 48-54.

upon the meaning of the terms used. Clarity and unambiguity of all terms used are the first requirements of a logical reasoning. Most words are ambiguous; they cover a great variety of facts or values, or both. This is specially so in the political field where terms like freedom, equality and justice carry different meanings to different persons. But a political scientist would wish to have a few basic concepts that are both clear and useful or serviceable as building stones within a logically developed theory. To be useful, they must be 'realistic' in the sense that they themselves or their analytical derivations, correspond to carefully observed facts. However, the better way is that of inductive reasoning. Here the investigator dees not begin with some *a priori,* or religious convictions, instead he proceeds with the help of facts. In scientific method deductive as well as inductive reasoning count, though the latter has greater relevance.[27]

7. **Excursus on Acceptance of Propositions:** From the standpoint of a logician, it is possible to divide all synthetic propositions into two classes—'accepted' and 'non-accepted'—and then define scientific method as that method by which propositions are allocated to the one or to the other class according to the presupposed rules of procedure. Felix Kaufman calls it a 'scientific situation' which he defines as the totality of synthetic propositions adopted at a particular time. He anticipates the objection that it is arbitrary to draw a sharp line of demarcation between accepted and unaccepted propositions but answers that this objection may be met by pointing out that the procedure of scientific control presupposes such a strict division. Science, seen as a dynamic concern of humanity, moves on irrespective of what the majority of scientists at any given time are ready to accept. The body of science is living, not petrified. It includes all tentative acceptances, or refusals to accept, that are legitimately offered by any scientist.[28]
8. **Causality:** *Cause and effect* is the conventional name for the interrelation between two successive events where the occurrence of the earlier is regarded as a condition for that of the latter. It was a decisive factor in Kant's argument that causal determinism in the realm of appearances (phenomena) might be coexistent with 'freedom' in the realm of the things in themselves. In this connection, it should be borne in mind that we cannot label separate clusters of minute events the 'cause' or the 'effect', except for our convenience in the pursuit of some inquiry or the like. The human will is not so free that it is immune to outside influences. Motivations can be 'manipulated' to a great extent. The doctrine of 'teleology' or 'entelechy'[29] is not fully correct that tells us about the residence of a goal, or end, or purpose within a thing itself. Either there is incorporation

27. *Ibid.*, pp. 55-68.
28. *Ibid,* pp. 69-72.
29. Teleology "is a doctrine that explains the nature of things in terms of the ends or purposes they are designed to bring about. In ideological ethics, moral action is evaluated in accordance with how far it brings about a desirable state of affairs. Norman P. Barry, *op.cit.,* p. xvi. Explanation is sometimes called teleological, meaning that it rests on reference to purposes. It takes the form ot an argument or assertion that all changes or growth are to be explained in terms of purposes fixed by nature, by morality or by God. A predetermined destiny thus controls and, in a sense, causes the events of the present." V.V. Dyke, *op. cit.,* p. 33.

of goals or purposes in non-conscious entities like seeds and organs, and this presupposes some kind of divine Creator; or things behave as they do merely as a result of chance and survival, and then the existence of a Creator is not presupposed, although it is not excluded either. Scientific method provides no answer to the question which alternative is correct.[30]

9. **Testing and Correcting:** Careful tests or experimentations constitute an essential element in scientific method on two grounds. They fortify the operating scientist's own acceptance of observations and conclusion; and they increase the inter-subjective (interpersonal) transmissibility of scientifically acquired knowledge. The ideal test is the pure-type experiment in which two situations essentially alike in every respect but one are brought about and their outcome is watched in expectation that it will reveal the influence of the one different element. In the field of social sciences the case is quite different. Here even when external conditions can be arranged in line with strict postulates, many variables enter the experiment because of the human factor involved, for no two human beings are entirely alike. Veracity of a hypothesis can be established with the help of testing or correction. For instance, the entire history of government and institutions supplies an almost inexhaustible source of tested hypotheses. Comparative government, including government administration, is still the most important substitute for laboratory tests in political science today. Theory *qua* theory profits from practical experiments even when they have been based on imperfect deductive reasoning, though the price may be too heavy.[31]
10. **Prediction:** Considering that in the social sciences human behaviour plays a decisive role and that the assumption of a certain amount of human freedom obstructs all our efforts to formulate strict laws wherever human behaviour in the future is a factor, it might seem that predictions in this field can have no practical value. But this would be a fallacious conclusion. It is true that exact predictions are not, as a rule, possible because of the great number of variables that have to be taken into account. Wherever a large number of people are involved, however, predictions based on probability of human behaviour can often be made with great accuracy. Just as in economics we can to some extent (and only to some extent) assume that the guiding motivation of the average businessman is that he prefers gain to loss, so in political science we can assume, for example, that it is the desire of the average representative in a legislature that he be re-elected. There are many other situations in the political field where behaviour of the people can be predicted to some extent on a similar basis.[32]

Thus, Brecht comes to hold that all scientists, both in the natural and in the social sciences, agree that contributions made according to the above principles are contributions to science. "Objections are raised solely against claims that it alone is scientific and that results reached through other methods, unless checked in line with scientific method, apart from being non-scientific in terms of scientific method, are

30. Brecht, *op. cit.*, pp. 73-93.
31. *Ibid.*, pp. 93-96.
32. *Ibid.*, pp. 96-98.

non-scientific also in every other sense, so as not to add to science in any reasonable sense of the term. These objections are tantamount to denying that the elements of scientific method are necessary elements of every scientific procedure... Scientific method does not insist that a scientist must accept as unchallengeable either the exactness of the observations or the validity of the conclusions, beyond the purely logical implications of meaning. Such an acceptance is ultimately left to the judgement of the receiver of the communication. What is intersubjectively transmitted *qua* knowledge is the evidence, not the conclusions therefrom. Scientific method, quite consistently, is zealous to exclude evidence that cannot be transmitted."[33]

In short, as an attitude, scientific method consists of the persistent search for truth. "To what extent it is so? Why is it so?—that is, what general conditions or considerations determine it to be so ? And this can be seen in reflection of the demand for the best available evidence, the determination of which we call logic... In essence, scientific method is simply the pursuit of truth as determined by logical considerations."[34] According to Charles S. Hyneman, a political scientist 'pursues scientific study (1) if he has as his object of inquiry a matter that can be illuminated by empirical evidence, (2) if he accords to empirical evidence highest probative force, (3) if in search for analysis and evaluation of evidence he approaches the highest standards other social scientists have proved to be attainable, and (4) if he reports his procedures and his findings in a way that affords other students ample opportunity to judge whether his evidence supports his findings."[35]

Empiricism and Scientific Method in Political Theory

Empiricism seeks to deal with a thing as it is and, therefore, finds its justification or validation in practical or realistic terms. It lays all emphasis on the elements of observation, verification and experimentation and, as such, it also takes into account the possibility of revision and modification in the light of new observations, perceptions, experiments, or interpretations. To our purpose, the noticeable thing is that an empirical analysis, though most evident in the field of natural sciences, is also present in the world of social (particularly behavioural) sciences. The reason is that like natural scientists (as Newton and Einstein), social scientists (including political theorists) try to discover and describe, explain and predict statistical, probabilistic, functional and even causal relationships among events, things and persons. It makes political science an art as well a science. "To the extent that many aspects of political analysis are most easily acquired by practice and training under the supervision of a person already skilled in this area, it is an art. Whenever students of politics scrupulously test their generalisations and theories against the data of experience by means of meticulous observation, classification and measurement, the empirical political analysis is scientific in its approach. To the extent that this approach actually yields tested propositions of considerable generality, political analysis can be regarded as scientific in its results."[36]

33. *Ibid.*, pp. 113-14.
34. Cohen and Nagel : *An Introduction to Logic and Scientific Method,* p. 192.
35. Hyneman: *The Study of Politics* (Urbana: University of Illinois Press, 1956), p. 76.
36 R.A. Dahl: *Modern Political Analysis,* pp. 20-21.

Scientific Method

It is the way in which one can test opinions, impressions or guesses by examining the available evidence both for and against them. It is simply the pursuit of truth which is determined by logical considerations. It is the most assured technique for controlling a host of things and establishing belief.

Essentials

1. It aims at discovering facts. It can be done with the help of a hypothesis that may be regarded as a suggestion of possible conditions between an imagined and an actual fact. A scientific inquiry has to determine which of the possible explanations is in best conformity with the facts.
2. It is based on systematic doubt. When new and more probable facts are found, the earlier ones are given up.
3. It aims at establishing a systematic interlinking of facts. It is responsible for high probabilities of their propositions.
4. It is self-corrective in nature. The process of inquiry goes on and the doubtful matters are detected and deleted.
5. Scientific theories are abstract in nature.
6. Scientific explanations rest on certain principles which seek to explain events of particular types.

Scope

1. Human society is progressing through prediction of human behaviour and in most of the cases predictions prove to be true. The variations, if any, become a matter of degree. There is nothing to prevent broad generalisations.
2. In social sciences the personal prejudices of an observer of human behaviour can be minimised with the help of some standard techniques developed for that purpose.
3. In social sciences, difficulties in observation and experiment may be reduced to a considerable extent by making the inquiry confined to a particular class whose behaviour is taken up for study. If the analysis is carried on for the same situations, circumstances, environment, institutions, etc. it can be broadly realistic and successful.
4. The existence of a complex phenomenon does not eliminate the possibility of using scientific method altogether. For instance, it can be used successfully in the study of physics irrespective of the fact that here a student is sometimes confronted with complex situations.
5. It can be used in the study of social phenomena and in predicting human behaviour to the possible extent, because exactness and uniformity of a natural science cannot be there in social sciences.

Limitations

1. It involves abstractions.
2. A scientific explanation is never complete. At every stage there are some basic principles which remain unexplained in social sciences.
3. Its conclusions are never final; they are only relative to observed phenomena, facts discovered and reasoning developed.
4. Sciences have a limited scope. Each science is concerned with a particular area and is based on certain assumptions.
5. Superstitions and cherished beliefs are hostile to the use of this method.

6. Formal procedures are fruitless. Definitions and formal distinctions are not often used properly; and statistical informations may be irrelevant and inconclusive.
7. Scientific judgement is difficult and sometimes impossible when situations demand immediate action.
8. In a society where there is no desire for truth or freedom for the expression of intellectual doubt, its growth is surely hampered.
9. The time required for reflection and material for experiments are often lacking for the proper development of this method.
10. Scientific researches in social field are often in the hands of those who cannot always oppose established opinions or taboos.
11. No scientific method can guarantee certainty of achieving the goal and can prevent human life from being an adventure.

Difficulties

1. Human behaviour is so complete, subtle and varied due to which it is very difficult to categorise it.
2. When human behaviour is studied and analysed by other human beings, the personal characteristics of such human beings, come into the picture and distort the analytical facts.
3. Different aspects of human behaviour are psychological in nature and, as such, are incapable of measurement.
4. Human behaviour is not uniform and predictable. All people do not behave in the same way in similar circumstances.
5. The choice or decision involving human beings, which is essential for observing human behaviour for the use of the method of experiment, becomes difficult. Thus, reliable scientific data cannot always be collected.

Source: B.N. Ghosh: *Scientific Method and Social Research* (New Delhi: Sterling Pub., 1985), III Ed., pp. 34-39.

Empiricism has its brilliant manifestation, first of all, in the works of Aristotle. He begins his analysis of politics with an empirical investigation rather than with the help of deductive logic, though he never discards the original rationalistic vision. He uses it to establish a more realistic ethical foundation for the state. The ethical goodness and practical wisdom must go together. What starts people along the line of 'goodness' is not some abstract standard to be realised in a contemplative vision, but rather the concrete choices they make every day. "Good and bad choices may be of two kinds—moral and practical. A good practical choice may be a bad moral one. But to prefer the moral to the practical is foolish just as to prefer the practical to the moral is corrupt. Wisdom consists of striking a good balance and so becoming both practical and virtuous."[37]

Empiricism and normativism find a peculiar confluence in the works of Aristotle, though one may say that his theories relating to the classification of states in their true and perverted forms and then his study of the revolutions (including their causes, general as well as particular, degrees, and the methods of their control and prevention) find a significant place in the domain of empirical political science. In the modern age, we may, first of all, look to Francis Bacon who advises us to set

37. See F.M. Cornford: *Before and After Socrates* (Cambridge: Cambridge University Press, 1972), p. 88.

aside all preconceived notions or prejudices and also resist the temptation to jump to hypothesis at the slightest provocation. Instead, one should concentrate on facts to observe them, classify them and abstract, step by step, the principles governing them. The most general principles should also be the last to be reached, for otherwise what one would get is an 'anticipation of nature' instead of an 'interpretation of nature'. Condemning the knowledge of the Middle Ages as 'degenerate learning' or 'indeed cobwebs of learning', he describes it as 'admirable for the fineness of threat and wars, but of no substance or profit.'[38]

Then comes the case of John Locke who launches a vigorous attack on the rationalist belief in the existence of innate ideas—a belief common to philosophy since the time of Plato. The human mind at birth is like a *tabula rasa* or a white sheet of paper on which nothing is written. Says he: "Whence has it all the materials of reason and knowledge? To this I answer in one word, from experience: in that all our knowledge is found, and from that it ultimately derives itself, our observation, employed either about external sensible objects, or about the internal operations of our minds perceived and reflected on by ourselves, is that which supplies our understandings with all the materials of thinking. These two are the fountains of knowledge from whence all the ideas we have, or can naturally have, do spring."[39]

It follows that from *experience* alone mind derives its content. The source of our ideas are sensation and reflection.[40] These senses are projected by the mind so as to clothe appropriate bodies in external nature. In this way, the bodies are perceived as with the qualities which, in fact, are purely the offsprings of the mind. "Thus, nature gets credit which should in truth be reserved for ourselves: the rose for its scent: the nightingale for its song: and the sun for its radiance."[41] In appreciation of Locke's empiricism, it is observed that his view that experience, in the sense of perception, is the source of all knowledge, was a new and revolutionary doctrine. New, because it denied a philosophical tradition established by Plato and perpetuated throughout the Middle Ages, and revolutionary because it exalted individual experience as the *ultimate* source of all knowledge."[42]

Empiricism witnessed its reiteration in the works of David Hume; it also saw its modification at his hands and became 'skepticism'. That is, by adhering strictly to the empirical theory of knowledge formulated by Locke, Hume demonstrated that this theory leads, of necessity, to a new direction where the philosopher may feel 'doubts' about his own findings based on observation and experience. All that anyone can say by relying upon empirical observation alone is that one event precedes another, or that one event follows another. The moment we label one of the events as 'cause' and the other as 'effect', we are indulging in a metaphysical speculation for which there is no adequate empirical evidence. In a way, it may be said that Hume diluted the empirical method as suggested by Locke. He showed that a method that could be used to destroy the traditional theological conceptions

38. D.E. Apter : *Introduction to Political Analysis,* p. 112.
39. Cited in L. McDonald: *Western Political Theory: The Modern Age* (New York, 1962), p. 11.
40. Locke: *Essay Concerning Human Understanding,* Book II, Ch. 1, Sec. 2
41. A.N. Whitehead: *Science and the Modern World* (New York: Macmillan, 1925). pp. 79-80.
42 Hallowell, *op. cit.,* p. 100.

could be used with equal efficacy to destroy the 'rational' and 'natural' concepts which the eighteenth century had sought to substitute for them."[43]

Some attention should be paid to the 'Logic of the Moral Sciences'of John Stuart Mill. He is also an empiricist, because he believes that all experience may be reduced to sensations, which, when combined by the laws of association, constitute our knowledge and our only knowledge of the world about us. He denies that we know anything *a priori;* all knowledge consists ultimately of inductions from experience. Reality is reduced by him to nothing more than the possibilities of sensation. In fact, according to him, not only is the external reality resolved into these possibilities, but so is the sentient subject. "What is really incomprehensible, he says, is that a thing which has ceased to exist, should, nevertheless, be able to be in some manner present: that "a series of feelings of which the greater part lies in the past or the future could be incorporated, so to speak, in a present situation, accompanied by the belief in its reality."[44]

Empiricism is dominated by rationalism at the hands of Immanuel Kant who divides the world of things into two—as they appear to us to be (phenomenal) and as they are really in themselves (noumenal). We gain knowledge about this in three ways—through the senses, through the intellect, and through the moral will. The knowledge which we gain through the senses and the intellect is the knowledge of the world of the things as they appear to us to be. It can never be knowledge of the world of things as they really are for the reason that in seeking knowledge through the senses and the intellect we necessarily impose upon the things themselves forms of intuition (space and time) and categories 'such as quality, quantity, substance, and causality' which exist not in the things themselves but in our own minds. Nature can only answer the questions which we put to it and its answers must conform to the way in which we frame the questions. There is one way and one way only that we can have contact with the world as it really is and this is through our moral will.'[45]

In a way, Kant brings science and ethics closer by telling us that while the former deals with the phenomenal world, noumenal world is the concern of the latter. However, as an idealist he attributes ultimate reality to the noumenal world, and yet he denies that it can ever be known through the senses and the intellect. Thus, he saves morality (including religion) from the criticism of Hume by denying that it has any sensory or intellectual reality. Reason is employed by Kant in a way that it can entertain conceptions about God without proving the existence of God in empirical terms. It can be done by means of faith that he calls 'practical reason'. On the whole, Kant's *a priori* principles of pure reason are essentially of a negative character. They tell us what pure reason cannot do. "Reason may speculate freely, and may do so also to good practical purposes, but it cannot lead to any definite statement about things beyond the possibilities of sensual experiences."[46]

Finally, we may refer to John Dewey at whose hands empiricism is clothed with the philosophy of pragmatism. Under the influence of the evolutionary thought of Darwin, he seeks to erect a philosophy, if not a religion, upon the foundations of

43. *Ibid.*, p. 127.
44. Guido de Ruggiero: *Modern Philosophy* (New York: Macmillan, 1921), English translation by A.H. Hannay and R G. Collingwood, pp. 235-36.
45. Hallowell, *op. cit.*, p. 241.
46. Brecht, *op. cit.*, p. 105.

biological evolution and the methods of natural sciences. He discards the conception of truth for a different conception he calls 'warranted assertibility' and for the traditional search for truth he would substitute 'inquiry' by the methods and with the concept of natural science. Truth is what individuals, who carry on such an inquiry, agree upon. Thinking is more important than thought, the search for truth more important than its discovery. The search for first causes and ultimate goals is abandoned. Truth 'evolves'—it is a product of the evolutionary process and the process is the only lasting truth. To understand the process is the task of philosophy as the handmaiden of science. With the great advances made by the natural sciences in their control of 'nature', Dewey foresees man finally coming into his own as the master of his destiny. The reason for the failure of classical liberalism was "to recognise what the true and final source of change has been, and now is, the corporate intelligence embodied in science."[47]

Empiricism has its own place in the world of scientific method and, as modern political theory is more of an empirical nature, it has its place of dominance therein. It is rightly pointed out that modern political theory "has two heads—although it appears that political scientists will give more food and support to the scientific head than it will to the other.'[48] And yet it may be added at this stage that empiricism has its own limitations which cannot be lost sight of. For pure empiricism, in the sense of a refusal to go beyond experience, can only be a sterile approach. Facts may be the same in a given situation, but they have varying degrees of appeal and attraction for men belonging to different professions. Each has a framework of his own in terms of which he interprets his facts and then derives conclusions out of them. It is for this reason that even the pattern of empirical political theory is received critically at the hands of its students.

Positivism and Neo-Positivism:Scientific Trends in Philosophy, Law, History and Politics

Natural sciences made marvellous achievements in the modern age. They stimulated inventions, improved methods of economic production, and added greatly to the stature of man as a civilised creature. It had its impact on the study of social sciences. People started losing faith in the theological and metaphysical premises of the Middle Ages and instead taking to the ways of science so as to understand reality in empirical terms endowed with the qualities of technical efficiency and mechanical certainty.[49] That is, in a hope to achieve for the study of human phenomena the same calculable certainty that characterised the natural sciences, the enlightened students of social phenomena accepted with eagerness the new way, the scientific way, known as 'positivism'.[50]

47. Dewey: "Authority and Social Change" in *Authority and the Individual* (Cambridge: Harvard University Press, 1937), p. 188.
48. W.C. Baum in Wasby, *op. cit.*, p. 300.
49. A theory according to the established positivist conception is a systematically related set of statements including some law-like generalisations that is empirically testable. R S Rudner: *Philosophy of Social Sciences* (Englewood Cliffs, New Jersey: Prentice-Hall, 1966). p. 10. It is also said that the strongest law-like generalisations are those which are deterministic, irreversible, sequential, necessary and sufficient. See H.L. Zetterberg: *On Theory and Verification in Sociology* (Totoma: New Jersey: Badminster, 1965).
50. J.H. Hallowell: *Main Currents in Modern Political Thought* (New York: Holt, Rinehart and Winston, 1950), p. 289.

It shows that positivism forms part of the well-known scientific method. It stands for the rejection of all speculative, hypothetical, abstract, theological and metaphysical premises and instead for the acceptance of the premises that may be subjected to the rules of an empirical inquiry. Thus, it "is an attempt to transfer to the study of the social and human phenomena the methods and concepts of the natural sciences in the belief that human phenomena, like, physical phenomena, obey certain laws of nature which can be inductively discovered by the empirical examination of successive events. These laws do not transcend experience, according to the positivist, but are found immanently in the things themselves, and behind them in the compulsion of nature which, independent of the individual will or reason, determines the course of human events."[51]

Such a trend had its abiding impact on the study of social sciences. Hallowell continues: "With the rise of positivism in the nineteenth century, the only task left to social science and jurisprudence is the description of events and the induction from these events of general laws of causality—the evaluation of goodness or badness, justice or injustice, of particular events being regarded not only as irrelevant but as being incompatible with scientific methods and 'ideals'. In an effort to confine himself to the 'pure' description of empirically observable 'facts', the positivist substitutes the inductive reasoning of the physical scientist for the 'right reason' of the seventeenth century philosopher. In a word, positivism is an attempt to substitute an immanent conception of order for the earlier transcendental conception; an attempt to substitute the physical laws of nature for the natural law of reason. Positivism is "an outgrowth of the natural sciences, but it is not, indeed, synonymous with them. As an intellectual perspective, it is more commonly found among social scientists than among natural scientists."[52]

In other words, positivism "is a philosophical tendency oriented around natural sciences and striving for a unified view of the world of phenomena, both physical and human, through the appplication of the methods and the extension of the results whereby the natural sciences have attained their unrivalled position in the modern world. It represents the complete victory of empiricism and calls 'positive' the facts and things of immediate perception as well as the relations and uniformities which thought may discover without transcending experience. It regards every inquiry as metaphysical which claims to go beyond the sphere of the empirical and seeks either hidden essences behind phenomenal appearances or ultimate, efficient and final causes behind things as well as any attempt to attribute reality to species, ideas, concepts, or the mind's logical 'intentions' in general."[53]

51. *Ibid.*, pp. 289-90.
52. *Ibid.*, p. 290. According to Norman P. Barry, positivism "has two meanings. First, a positivist believes in the clear separation of fact and value and argues that theoretical and descriptive accounts of man and society can be made which do not involve evaluative judgements. For example, in jurisprudence a positive lawyer maintains that law must be separated from morals so that a rule is assessed for legal validity not by reference to its content but to certain objective, non-moral criteria. In the second and more extreme sense, it is the theory that only phenomena which are in principle capable of being observed are of any significance for social science. *An Introduction to Modern Political Theory* (London: Macmillan, 1981), p. xvi
53. Guido de Ruggiero: "Positivism" in Seligman (ed.): *Encyclopaedia of the Social Sciences* (New York: Macmillan, 1964), Vol. VI, p. 260.

Rationalism, Positivism and Metaphysics

Rationalism: An action is rational to the extent that it is correctly designed to maximise goal achievement. Given more than one goal (the usual human situation), an action is rational to the extent that it is correctly designed to maximise *net* goal achievement.[1] Since rationality can be judged from differing vantage points, the word should be qualified so as to indicate the standard employed.

A decision may be *objectively* rational if, in fact, it is the correct behaviour for maximising given values in a given situation.

It is *subjectively* rational if it maximises attainment relative to the actual knowledge of the subject.

It is *consciously* rational to the degree that the adjustment of means to ends is a conscious process.

It is *deliberately* rational to the degree that the adjustment of means to ends has been deliberately brought about.

A decision is *organisationally* rational if it is oriented to the organisation's goals.

It is *personally* rational if it is oriented to the individual goals.[2]

In sum, "scholarship is significant when it contributes to the political rationality of a political decision."[3]

'Liberal rationalism' embraces both *explanation* and *evaluation*. Its explanatory concern is with accounting for that order of events which we call a 'social order'; and this includes economic, legal and political phenomena. Its interest in evaluation consists largely in sharing how, from the standpoint of a particular individualistic conception of liberty, existing social orders may be improved. However, liberal rationalists maintain that these two aspects are separate and that their contributions to the scientific study of society are valuable in their own right irrespective of the individualistic bias of their evaluative and prescriptive writing.[4]

'Radical rationalism' is a term sometimes used to describe the belief that there is a supra-sensible world which is more than the world of sense. This unchangeable world of ideas constitutes reality and differs sharply from the changeable world of 'sense data' or empiricism. Plato is an example of radical rationalism. His famous student, Aristotle, took a more moderate road on this issue by emphasising the role played by 'sense data' in the process of knowledge. Hence, Aristotle is sometimes referred to as a realist or moderate rationalist. Rationalism of any kind represents a strong challenge to the modern and contemporary political theorists who primarily rely on empiricism as the vivid theory of knowledge.[5]

Rationalism, whether classical or not, assumes *a priori* knowledge, which may be taken to mean substantive or mechanistic framework which is independent of experience.[6]

Positivism: It is a philosophy of natural phenomena, or more directly a philosophy which excludes everything that is not knowable in the sense in which knowable things can be expressed clearly in the language. What is accepted in positivism are commonsense explanations of how natural things relate to one another. As one might expect, this locates positivism squarely within any empiricist epistemology. The empiricist position on knowledge is that all knowledge derives from experience and also that the human mind cannot encounter universals independent of experience.[7]

But the fundamental thesis of logical positivism is that the meaning of a statement is tied to its mode of verification, and further that statements which cannot be verified are meaningless. In similar fashion, scientific knowledge is the body of statements verified in accordance with the accepted standards of the scientific community.[8]

Metaphysics: It is concerned with the external or essential nature of reality which leads to such matters as the fundamental causes and processes in things. It goes considerably beyond the relationship of things apparent to the eye. It is being or existence in the complete sense that is discussed. Accordingly, rationalism is entitled in metaphysics, although all rationalists need not embrace metaphysics. Rationalism is the thesis that human mind can apprehend universals independent of phenomena, and hence a form of knowledge or set of categories exist which are prior to experience.[9]

1. R.A. Dahl and C.E. Lindblom: *Politics, Economics and Welfare* (New York: Harper, 1953), p. 38.
2. H.A. Simon: *Administrative Behaviour* (New York: Macmillan, 1957), pp. 67, 75-77, 102.
3. V.V. Dyke: *Political Science: A Philosophical Analysis*, p. 5.
4. N.P. Barry: *An Introduction to Modern Political Theory* (London: Macmillan, 1981), p. 11.
5. See Baum, *op. cit.*, p. 284.
6. F.M. Frohock: *Nature of Political Inquiry* (Homewood, Illinois: The Dorsey Press, 1967), pp. 41-42.
7. *Ibid.*, p. 17.
8. *Ibid.*, p. 19.
9. *Ibid.*, p. 17.

The credit for starting the trend of positivism goes to August Comte of France who laid down the law of three stages of the history of human thought.[54] In the first (theological) stage man attempted to explain everything in terms of supernatural causes, progressing from animism to polytheism and thereon to monotheism. It was replaced by the second metaphysical stage that characterised the substitution of abstractions with a personal God or gods. Nature was substituted for God and the great thinkers and statesmen used political fictions like 'social contract', 'natural rights' and 'sovereignty of the people'. If theology dominated the ancient, metaphysics dominated the Middle Ages. The modern age represents the stage of positivism. It is an age of science in which man discards all theological and metaphysical assumptions and confines himself to the empirical observation of successive events from which he induces natural laws. Thus, he rejects the first and second stages of the progress of human civilisation and accepts the last one for the sake of its being in tune with the scientific spirit. As he says: "The first stage is the necessary point of departure of the human understanding, the third is the fixed and definite state. The second is merely a state of transition."[55]

The line of Comte was followed, though with some modifications, by French sociologists like Emile Durkheim, L. Levy-Bruhl and C. Bougle. However, it had a marked change at the hands of Rudolf Carnap and Otto Neurath who contributed to the trend of 'neo-positivism' also known as 'logical positivism'. As a matter of fact,

54. Comte introduced the term 'positivism' in social sciences. He used it to distinguish the 'scientific approach' in the modern (positive) era from theological and metaphysical speculations of the ancient and medieval eras respectively. See Brecht. *op. cit.*, p. 170.
55. Lancaster: *Masters of Political Thought*, Vol. Ill, p. 77.

it arose in the wake of the efforts made by Ernst Mach of Austria who wanted to establish the unity of all sciences through the radical elimination of metaphysics in every scientific work and through common recognition that all scientific authority must ultimately be based on perception. The neo-positivism has these important features:

(i) insistence on strictly 'physicalist' or behaviourist methods, which imply the rejection of any merely introspective source of psychology,

(ii) elimination of metaphysical terms not only in the final stages of scientific work but in any type of sentences, and hence especially also in preparatory steps, where they are merely used as inspiration for the formulation of problems, as working hypotheses, or as avowed assumptions, and

(iii) designation of any synthetic sentence which is not ultimately verifiable through perceptions as not only 'non-scientific' but 'meaningless'.[56]

The line of Mach became so popular that its adherents came to be known as belonging to the'Vienna Circle' founded in 1929.[57] It included a galaxy of natural and social scientists like Hans Hahn (mathematics), Otto Neurath (economics), Phillip Franck (physics) and Rudolf Carnap, Herbert Feigl, Friedrich Waismann and Moritz Schlick (philosophy). A number of other scholars were subsequently associated with the Vienna Circle like Hans Reichbenbach (philosophy), Ludwig Wittgenstein, Kurt Godel, Karl Menger and Richard von Mises (mathematics), E. Schroedinger (physics), Josef Schumpeter (economics) and Hans Kelsen (law). Some leading American intellectuals like Ernest Nagel and Charles W. Morris also established contact with this circle. However, the noticeable point at this stage is that with the association of a very large number of intellectuals with this Vienna Circle, the line of positivism was pushed in different directions as a result of which it lost its original sense. It discredited the very name of positivism and did considerable harm to the general understanding of scientific method and scientific value relativism.[58]

Positivism in the legal sphere originates with Jean Bodin of France. It saw its radical manifestation in the works of Thomas Hobbes and then its reiteration at the hands of William Blackstone, Jeremy Bentham and John Austin of England. It shows that 'legal positivism' is prior to Comte's philosophical and sociological positivism. It denies the existence of any 'higher' or supernatural law and instead lays all emphasis on the sanctity and imperative character of the law of the sovereign state. As a legal entity, state is sovereign and the law of the state is binding on all. Anything lacking the force of law (like custom or practice) has no binding character. In other words, there can be nothing like Natural Law (as believed by the Roman lawyers) or Divine Law (as believed by the people during the Middle Ages) for the reason that such 'laws' lack the fact of 'scientific verifiability'[59]

---

56. Brecht, *op. cit.*, pp. 174-75:
57. See A.J. Ayer. "The Vienna Circle" in Gilbert Riple (ed.): *The Revolution in Philosophy* (London, 1957), pp. 70 ff.
58. Brecht. *op. cit.*, p. 182.
59. *Ibid.*, p. IS5.

Positivism saw its emergence in the field of history where it came to be known as 'historical positivism' or 'historicism'[60] Credit for this should go to Friedrich Karl von Savigny of Germany and Sir Henry Maine of England. However, its best manifestation is contained in the philosophy of Hegel where ideas of particularity and universality of history and of absolute laws are welded within the doctrine that some sort of objective or absolute reason (God, or World Spirit, or Absolute Mind) reveals itself in the events of history though differently at different places and times in the case of different nations. It is associated with the idea that all human knowledge "is historically conditioned and that human beings could not entirely disentangle themselves from the singular social conditions under which their minds have been shaped."[61]

When we take up the case of positivism in political theory, we are struck with the fact that here its meaning has a rather different connotation. Political theory looks like caught between the two implications of positivism—one used in the fields of philosophy and sociology and the other in that of law and justice—though it may be found that here political theory comes very close to jurisprudence by virtue of laying all emphasis on the fact of 'legal' sovereignty. It is on account of the fact that in political as well as in legal philosophy positivism designates the idea that only those norms are juridically valid which have been established or recognised by the government of a sovereign state in the form prescribed by the written as well as unwritten or conventional rules of the fundamental law of the land (constitution). Obviously, it amounted to the revision of the classical liberal political theory in some important directions. Instead of taking man's rights and liberty as 'absolute' affairs, the new liberals preferred to justify these in empirical terms. For instance, they discarded the view of taking justice in abstract or hypothetical terms and linked it with the role of the state according to a well-established system of law. Under the influence of positivism, "it all came to mean that man could not be compelled to do anything except by a law enacted in accordance with the prescribed procedure (any prescribed procedure) with sufficient force behind it to compel obedience."[62]

It may be pointed out that though positivism resembles a scientific method, it is not identical with it in all respects. We may come to the point where scientific method cannot cover all that is possible in a study on positivistic lines. Comte committed a mistake by absolutising progress and science. A positivist cannot thoroughly ignore the aspect of speculative and ethical considerations in studying the reality of social development. The scientific method cannot even state as to what the moral goals should be. So Brecht says: "As regards progress, scientific method cannot even say what in the human situation as a whole *is* progress. It can, of course, say what is technological progress, progress in the knowledge of facts and the causal relations

60. Historicism is the doctrine, mainly but by no means exclusively, associated with Marxism, that the study of history reveals trends or patterns similar to a law, from which it is possible to predict *future* economic and social structures and historical events. Historical 'laws' are of a quasi-empirical kind in that they are based on supposedly observable regularities and are therefore different from the laws of conventional economics which are a historical deduction from axioms of human nature." Norman P. Barry, *op cit.*, pp. xiv-xv.
61. Brecht, *op. cit.*, 186.
62. Hallowell, *op. cit.*, p. 325.

within the universe and within the human society, progress in medicine , in material social welfare and the like. But it cannot advise us as to what progress means with regard to the human situation in its totality whenever an advance in one sphere is attained at the price of some impairment in another. At that point, ultimate value-judgements are required, and to supply them, scientific method is unable."[63]

Then, positivism ignores the patent fact of variability in human behaviour—a fact due to which scientific method, as we have already pointed out, cannot be applied to the social sciences in a way it can be done in the field of natural sciences. John Stuart Mill had a better understanding of social reality when he said: "All phenomena of society are phenomena of human nature, generated by the action of outward circumstances upon masses of human beings; and if, therefore, the phenomena of the human thought, feeling, and action are subject to fixed laws, phenomena of society cannot but conform to fixed laws, the consequence of the preceding. There is, indeed, no hope that these laws, though our knowledge of them were as certain and as complete as it is in astronomy, would enable us to predict the history of society like that of celestial appearances, for thousands of years to come. But the difference of certainty is not in the laws themselves, it is in the data to which these laws are to be applied."[64]

Positivism in social sciences may not be likened with positivism in natural sciences in a study of scientific method. Strictly applied to the field of natural sciences, the scientific method minimises the role of man as an originator of theories. As a genius, man can be an inventor or a discoverer. But he cannot be the originator of the theories, for he is not the creator of the object of his study. Different is the case with social sciences which deal with man and man-made institutions and, for that reason, here a genius is credited with being the founder or originator of theories. Due to this we still remember the names of a very large number of social and political thinkers and still find relevance in their theories. It is well commented that "in science the importance of the 'author' or originator is at a minimum, it never being justifiable in scientific institutions to set up an individual or body who will either be the originator of pronouncements or who will decide finally on the truth of pronouncements made. The procedural rules of science lay it down, roughly speaking, that hypothesis must be decided on by looking at the evidence, not by appealing to a man. There are also, and can be, no rules to decide who will be the originators of scientific theories."[65]

Above all, by eliminating the 'rational' from the 'real', positivism commits the wrong of eliminating, at the same time, any possibility of adequately explaining, at least in rational terms, the reality it seeks to describe. Morris R. Cohen argues that positivism "begins with a great show of respect for 'fact' as the rock of intellectual salvation. On it we are to escape from the winds of dialectical illusion. But as science critically analyses the 'facts', more of them are seen to be the products of old prejudices or survivals of obsolete metaphysics...the 'facts' of science are admittedly checked

63. Brecht, *op. cit.*, p. 171.

64. J.S. Mill: *A System of Logic* (New York, 1890), 8 Ed., pp. 607-8.

65. S.I. Benn and R.S. Peters: *Social Principles and the Democratic State* (London: George Allen and Unwin, 1975), p. 22.

Science, Scientific Method and Scientism

Contemporary political science is not 'mere' empiricism.... Generalisations from a sample of observations is one way of creating theory, but deductions from axioms and propositions is another. Both co-exist in contemporary political science. If modern political theory is empirical, it is only in the sense of seeking for enough quantitative and descriptive precision to permit ultimate verification or disproof by means of observation.

—Ithiel de Sola Pool

Contemporary Political Science: Towards Empirical Theory (New York: McGraw Hill, 1967), pp. viii-x.

Science, meaning knowledge, is a field of study that aims to develop reliable explanations of phenomena through repeatable experiments, observations and deductions. The scientific method by which hypotheses are tested (proved true) by testing them against the available evidence is, therefore, seen as a means of disclosing value-free and objective truth. Scientism is the belief that the scientific method is the only source of reliable knowledge, and so should be applied to fields such as philosophy, history and politics, as well as the natural sciences.

—Andrew Heywood

Politics (Houndmills, Basingstroke: Palgrave Foundations, 2005), p. 16

Scientific mood or posture can be distinguished on the basis of two basic features- first, the scientific temperament is alleged to be unbiased at the concrete level; second, the conclusions of science are supposed to be capable of verification by any observer who follows the same techniques. But while scientists may only aspire to Brecht's neat outline, the idea conveyed by a scientific method is crucial; some agreed upon procedure must standardise scientific inquiry.

—F.M. Frohock

The Nature of Political Inquiry (Homewood, Illinois: The Dorsey Press, 1967), pp. 110-11.

and controlled by theoretic considerations, for they are characterised by rational or mathematical relations. Hence, the empiricism which has an anti-intellectual animus consistently turns from the rational scientific elaboration of specific facts to a mystical pure experience in which all clear distinctions are eliminated as the conceptual fictions of the mind. Thus does the worship of fact become the apotheosis of an abstraction devoid of all the concrete characteristics of facts."[66]

66. Cohen: *Reason and Nature: An Essay on the Meaning of the Scientific Method* (New York, 1931), pp 36-37. Positivists see no way of establishing what ought to be by observing what is. They see no way of verifying normative statements by empirical methods. They see no logical way of proceeding from the realm of fact to the realm of value. From their point of view, values or conceptions of the desirable stem, ultimately at least, from will and emotion, and are thus volitional rather than being dictated by empiricism or logic. Thus, ultimate values must be regarded as self-justifying ; they are simply postulated. See Hans Reichenbach : *The Rise of Scientific Philosophy* (Berkeley and Los Angeles : University of California Press, 1951), pp. 291-302. The implication of this position is that political inquiry of a positivist sort provides no basis for choice among ultimate values. If liberals, fascists, communists, and others choose different sets of ultimate values, the positivist can react emotionally along with others, but he cannot demonstrate that one set is to be preferred over the others except perhaps in terms of a still more ultimate set of values which, in turn, is simply postulated. V.V. Dyke, *op. cit.*, p. 10.

Marxism and the Case of Scientific Political Theory

Positivism, as we have seen in the preceding section, is appreciated for introducing 'science' into the field of political theory. If so, then Marxism has a place of its own in this important direction. It is said that Marxist philosophy is a powerful theoretical instrument for cognising and transforming the world, but is only is applied creatively and with strict consideration of the concrete historical conditions in which its laws and principles operate. It cultivates a broad, correct world outlook in man and trains him to discern the importance of seemingly insignificant things. It stimulates the thought, makes it more flexible and incisive and hostile to stagnation and routine, and imbues man with the valuable sense of the new.[67] It tells us that philosophical knowledge is not a fruit of idle reflections of dilettantes, but a form of social consciousness which reflects the advances of scientific and social progress, the ideals and world outlook of different classes, social contradictions and conflicts in the given country and in the given epoch. That is why, Marx called philosophy the 'intellectual quintessence' of its time and the 'living soul of culture'.[68]

According to Marxism, the fundamental question of philosophy is the antithesis of idealism (primacy of the ideas) and materialism (primacy of the matter). It is the nature of this connection (of the relation of consciousness to being or of the spiritual to the material) that constitutes the fundamental question of philosophy. It treats the world as cognisable and, for that reason, man's reason can penetrate the secrets of nature and thereby ascertain the laws of its development. Idealism denies the objective existence of the world by regarding it as a product of consciousness alone, it attributes all social contradictions and sufferings, all the vices of capitalism to the delusions of the people and their moral failings. Thus, like religion, it diverts the working people from fighting against the forces of imperialism. Opposed to this, Marxism is based on dialectical materialism. Drawing on scientific achievements and society's practical experience at different stages of history, it maintains that the world is an endless process of movement, regeneration, the demise of the old and the birth of the new."[69]

Obviously, dialectical materialism is a science which on the basis of a materialist solution of the fundamental questions of philosophy discloses the more general, dialectical laws of the development of the material world and the ways for its cognition and revolutionary transformation. Its net conclusion is that the very development of the proletarian movement confronts science with the immensely important task of evolving a revolutionary theory and forging an ideological weapon for the proletariat in its struggle against capitalism and for socialism. And science in the person of its brilliant proponents like Marx and Engels "fulfilled the pressing demand of history;

67. V.G. Afanasyev: *Marxist Philosophy* (Moscow: Progress Publishers, 1978), p. 11.
68. Marx and Engels: *Collected Works* (Moscow: Progress Publishers, 1965), Vol. I, p. 195.
69. Afanasyev, *op. cit.*, p. 19. As Engels says: "For it (dialectical philosophy) nothing is absolute.... It reveals the transitory character of everything and in everything ; nothing can endure before it except the uninterrupted process of becoming and passing away, of endless ascendancy from the lower to the higher." Refer to his paper titled "Ludwig Feuerbach and the End of Classical German Philosophy" in Marx-Engels: *Selected Works* (published in 3 volumes by the Progress Publishers of Moscow, 1976), Vol III, p. 339.

they created Marxism whose component part and theoretical foundation is Marxist philosophy—dialectical and historical materialism."[70]

The novel feature of Marxism at this stage may be seen in this affirmation that philosophy is the root and science is like its branches. It follows that a scientific political theory must be based on the philosophy of dialectical materialism. It is for this reason that Marxism establishes the unity of theory and practice. Political theory must be of a revolutionary nature. It is possible when a theoretician makes a correct study of the laws of social development and then leaves a correct guide to his followers like Lenin of Russia. Lenin's interpretations, therefore, constitute an integral part of Marxism and may be designated as 'scientific socialism' that, as a science in its own right, has its own laws and categories, reflecting the basic aspects of the revolutionary transformation of the capitalist into a communist society. Among these laws there is that of the socialist revolution and establishment of the dictatorship of the proletariat in the transitional period from capitalism to socialism. These laws are neither general-sociological nor economic by nature, but precisely socio-political ones, expressing the essence of scientific socialism in the most graphic way. "They are general laws, since they operate in all countries where society's life is being reconstructed along the communist lines and since they deal with society as a whole, and not just with one of its spheres."[71]

According to Marxism-Leninism, a scientific political theory is one that can be used for understanding as well as changing the social system. Since Marx, Engels and Lenin could do so, only Marxism-Leninism can be designated as the model of a scientific political theory. If Marx argued that 'the philosophers have so far interpreted the world, the problem is how to change it', so Lenin contended that, 'without a revolutionary theory, there cannot be a revolutionary movement.'[72] He knew better than anyone else the immense importance of theory. As far back as 1902, he said that 'only a party guided by an advanced theory can act as a vanguard in the fight.'[73] Paraphrasing the meaning of Lenin, Stalin once said: "The endeavour of practical persons to have no truck with theories runs counter to the whole spirit of Leninism and is a great danger to our cause. Of course, theory out of touch with revolutionary practice is like a mill that runs without any grist, just as practice gropes in the dark unless revolutionary theory throws light on the path. But theory becomes the greatest force in the working class movement when it is inseparably linked

70. Afanasyev, *op. cit.*, p. 26. While defending the case of the scientific character of the theory of historical materialism, Marx and Engels confidently assert that its premises "are men, not in any fantastic isolation or fixity, but in their actual, empirically perceptible process of development under definite conditions.... Where speculation ends, where real life starts, there consequently begins real, positive science, the expounding of the practical process of development of men. Empty phrases about consciousness end, and real knowledge has to take their place. When the reality is described, a self-sufficient philosophy loses its medium of existence. At best, its place can only be taken by a summing-up of the most general results, abstractions which are derived from the observation of the historical development of men. These abstractions in themselves, divorced from real history, have no value whatsoever." *German Ideology*, p. 43.
71. *A Dictionary of Scientific Communism* (Moscow: Progress Publishers, 1980), p. 212.
72. V.I. Lenin: *Collected Works*, Vol. 5, p. 133.
73. *Ibid.*, p. 136.

with revolutionary practice; for it, and it alone, can give the movement confidence, guidance, an understanding of the inner links between events."[74]

The critics of Marxism-Leninism do not accept such a contention and they disagree with the whole idea of putting it into the rank of a scientific political theory. The brunt of their argument is that it is all like a 'propagandist ideology' that cannot be identified with a scientific theory. Brecht points out three reasons which demonstrate that Marxism does not stand the test of a modern scientific theory:[75]

1. Marx and Engels claimed that they could predict the general course of human history with certainty, at least in the long run. This claim is scientifically untenable because of the many variables involved. It is possible, to some extent, to predict what will happen if a number of conditions are fulfilled, among which there may be the assumption that in other respects everything remains as it now is. Such predictions are of the essence of genuine science. It is also often possible to state in advance that predicted developments, should they come true, will entail specific human tendencies in response such as the tendency of capitalistic entrepreneurs in a crisis to look for new areas of favourable investments, and of workers and tenants to revolt if exploited. It is unscientific, however, to ignore the possibility that conditions may develop differently and that human responses may take a different course.
2. Marx and Engels projected experiences of the past onto the future as a scientifically untenable assumption that in human and social affairs, just as in inanimate nature, what happened in the past will always and necessarily happen essentially in the same way in the future, irrespective of changes in circumstances, improvement in scientific analysis, better awareness of implied risks, alteration of ethical standards, and new governmental methods. In pointing to past experiences, they signalled many serious warnings to our own and to future generations; but again they failed to take full account of the variables, in particular, the unpredictable potentialities of human ingenuity, determination and organisation. They pretended to have offered scientific certainty where the utmost they could have done was to point to probabilities or risks. Their reliance on the past experiences was the more tenuous, because it was chiefly based on only three case histories—slave economy, feudal economy, and early capitalism.
3. In denouncing the value-judgements of their contemporaries and of former generations Marx and Engels freely expressed value-judgements of their own, both negative and positive. Their polemic emphasis that the prevailing ideas of justice and morals in each epoch depended on economic factors, in particular on methods of production and class interests, and were nothing but 'superstructures' erected on material interests, was relativistic in character, of course; but the relativity asserted therein did not imply for them that science was unable to ascertain the validity of ultimate value-judgements. On the contrary, while teaching in the first place that history would inevitably move to the final stage of socialism anyway, whether or not that was the fairer system, Marx and Engels were far from treating this course of events as a merely factual process

74. Cited in Brecht, *op. cit.*, p. 18.
75. *Ibid.*, pp. 187-88.

devoid of value; it meant to them the establishment of true justice. They did not try to classify their own value-judgements as a mere 'super-structure' based on personal economic preferences, or otherwise as merely subjective and relative in the transpositive, or trans-traditional, sphere of value-judgements, their ideas were rather absolutistic in character.

On the basis of these three strong points, Brecht comes to assert that "for all their incidental application of empirical-research and relativistic references, Marx and Engels did not obey the rules of scientific method, as now understood."[76]

In opposition to all this, while justifying the case of Marxism as a scientific political theory, George Lukacs says: 'The framework is complete. As a requirement and approach to the general study of society, as an interpretation of society, in its globality, in its totality, in view of its structural and cultural, *i.e.,* historical transformation – in these respects, Marxism is really complete. But it is complete as a method, *i,e.,* as a mode of analysis and as the criterion for establishing the theoretical hierarchy of the constitutive factors of society. Completeness of method, however, does not necessarily imply that one can find in Marx everything in all its specific contents. Instead, these can come to light only through long, patient research conducted on the basis of the Marxist method, which brings out the global, historical sense of social evolution... What the positivists do not understand is precisely this: facts must be interpreted, thus transcended; the process of abstraction is fundamental for the construction of a general theory. And without a general theory, facts are and remain meaningless."[77]

Scientific Political Theory

The term 'scientific' must be understood in a particular sense when it is prefixed to 'political theory'. The wrong view is that scientific political theory is concerned with the *means* only, for the deliberation of the *ends* (goals, norms, values, etc.) must be left to the spheres of ethics, theology and philosophy. Such an antithesis is incorrect,

76. *Ibid., p.* 188. An Indian critic of Marxism-Leninism rejects the case of putting it into the category of 'scientific theory' for these reasons. First, all predictions of this school have gone wrong. Communist revolutions have occurred in industrially backward countries. Second, the growth of industrialisation in non-communist countries has not led to increasing pauperisation of the masses. On the contrary, it has tended to reduce economic inequalities and make the worker a self-respecting and respectable member of the society. Third, the dictatorship of the proletariat has, in practice, been the dictatorship of a very small coterie of the Communist Party having the power of life and death over its subjects and using it in an arbitrary and inhuman manner. Last there is no sign of this dictatorship loosening its hold even after three generations' time in Soviet Russia, or of the state showing signs of withering away even though there are no vestiges of capitalism left there. Yet, like astrology, Marxism has got away with its failures because the testability criterion is not applicable to it. For each failure, it has an *ad hoc* explanation, such as 'betrayal by the social democrats', 'immaturity of the proletariat', 'leftwing sectarianism', and the like. All these are generally *post facto* discoveries. The theory remains as sterile as before, but the jargon is enriched and the faithful are happy until a confession by a Khrushchev or an aggression by a Mao shocks them out of their state of benumbed intoxication. A.B. Shah, *op. cit.,* pp. 88-89.
77. Cited in Partha Chatterjee: "On the Scientific Study of Politics: A Review of the Positivist Method" in Sudipta Kaviraj and others (eds.: *The State of Political Theory* (Calcutta: Research India Publications, 1978), p. 64.

for scientific political theory can also deal with the ends in various significant ways. For instance, it can examine:

(a) the meanings of goals or values, and all the implications of that meaning;
(b) the possibility or impossibility of reaching the goals or values;
(c) the cost of pursuing and reaching such goals or values, especially the price to be paid through the sacrifice of other goals or values and through other undesired side effects;
(d) all the other consequences and the risks involved; and
(e) implications, consequences and risks of the alternative goals (goal values) so as to make an informed choice possible.

"To engage in these various types of legitimate explanation of goals is the proper task of scientific political theory."[78] If so, a political scientist pursues a scientific study, if he

1. has as his subject of inquiry a matter that can be illuminated by empirical evidence;
2. accords to empirical evidence highest probative force;
3. if in search for analysis and evaluation of evidence, approaches the highest standards other social scientists have proved to be attainable; and
4. reports his procedure and his findings in a way that affords other students ample opportunities to judge whether his evidence supports his findings.[79]

In other words, scientific political theory aims at a scientific explanation of the political phenomena in relation to its origin, nature and end. The standard account of a scientific explanation is known as the 'covering law' model requiring generalisations and explication of the nature of these laws.[80] To explain as to why something occurred is to show why, given the conditions, it had to occur or to show that nothing else could have occurred under such and such conditions. If so, the laws which "figure in explanations, then, must be unrestricted universals, and they must support counterfactual and subjective conditionals. These requirements arise from the need to make sense of our intuitive idea that laws must apply to all possible cases and not simply reflect an accidental concomitance of events. If an explanation shows that an event in question had to occur, that it could not have been otherwise, then the generalisation on which the explanation is based must not simply be a summation of some set of particular instances or express the coincidence

78. Brecht in *International Encyclopaedia, op. cit.*, p. 313.
79. Charles S. Hyneman: *The Study of Politics*, p. 76. "I venture to define science as a series of interconnected concepts and conceptual schemes arising from experiment and observation and fruitful of further experiments and observations. The test of a scientific theory is its ability to suggest, stimulate, and direct experiment....A scientific theory is a policy—an economical and fruitful guide to action by scientific investigators." J.H. Conant: *Modern Science and Modern Man* (New York : Columbia University Press, 1952), pp. 54 and 57, If so, the scientific method "consists in the persistent search for truth as determined by logical considerations." See Cohen and Nagel: *An Introduction to Logic and Scientific Method*, p. 192.
80. J. Donald Moon: "The Logic of Political Inquiry: A Synthesis of Opposed Perspectives" in Greenstein ard Polsby, *op. cit.*, p. 135.

that the empirically and logically possible combination of factors which would falsify the generalisations does not happen to occur."[81]

With this standpoint, Moon comes to lay down these characteristics of a scientific political theory:[82]

1. It designates a set of basic ideas about a subject—a fundamental conceptualisation of a field or a set of phenomena. It is a very wide term and it may include anything like paradigm, research programme, conceptual framework, cyberneticisation, systematic analysis, rational choice, individual behaviour, etc.
2. Any set of loosely articulated reasons for expecting a particular outcome (that may be vague) and for that reason theory becomes like a conjecture or a hypothesis and so lacks a genuinely explanatory form.
3. It may be a well-developed systematically related sets of propositions as kinetic theory of gases.

For this reason, scientific theories "represent a range of diverse phenomena and regularities as the manifestations of small number of theoretical entities and their interrelationships and they do so in terms of a conceptual structure with 'heuristic power' which provides a basis for the further articulation and the development of theories of even greater scope. This systematically progressive nature of science is one of its greatest attractions. But some have argued that the methods of science are unable to account for the kinds of the phenomena which the social and political scientist seeks to understand."[83]

It shall be pertinent at this stage to point out that philosophical political theory can be distinguished from a scientific political theory. An account of how things have come to be as they are, is a causal explanation of the type sought in scientific theory. A philosophical theory attempts to supply justifying reasons for accepting a belief (in the instance, the belief that we ought to obey the laws), not explanatory causes of the belief or its objects."[84] However, it should also be noted in this connection that a purely scientific political theory, like a theory in the fields of physics and chemistry, is neither possible nor desirable. The element of subjectivity of the author as well as the norms of a civilised life are the necessary limitations within which a social and political theorist has to operate. So Raphael continues: "The point is that the

81. *Ibid.*, p. 135. "Explanation by a reference to a law is ordinarily incomplete in the sense that we are likely to want to know...Why the law holds. For this purpose, we seek a theory. Having explained the want of reference to a law, we seek to explain the law by reference to a theory." Dyke. *op. cit.*, p. 41.
82. Moon, *op, cit.*, p. 141.
83. *Ibid.*, p. 154. Quentin Gibson offers a basic definition of the term 'theory' when he describes it as "sets or systems of statements logically interconnected in various complex ways." *The Logic of Social Enquiry* (London: Routledge and Kegan Paul, 1960), p. 113. Such a definition, however, is well applicable' to the case of 'scientific' political theory. Nelson, Dentler and Smith comment that a scientific theory ' is a deductive network of generalisations from which explanations or predictions of certain types of known events may be derived." *Politics and Social Life* (Boston: Houghton and Mifflin Co., 1963), p. 69. In the view of Carl G. Hempel, any scientific theory "may be conceived of as consisting of an uninterrupted, deductively developed system and an interpretation which confers empirical import upon the terms and sentences of the latter." *Fundamentals of Concept Formation in Empirical Science* (Chicago: University of Chicago Press, 1952), p. 34.
84. D.D. Raphael: *Problems of Political Philosophy* (London: Macmillian 1976), pp. 89-90.

philosophical discussion of values is a discussion by means of rational argument of the same kind and is used in the philosophy of knowledge and in scientific theory. It is normative, in that it seems to justify (to give reasons for) the acceptance or rejection of doctrines, but so are the philosophy of knowledge and scientific theory in aiming to justify (to give reasons for) the acceptance or rejection of beliefs about matters of fact."[85]

And yet scientific political theory and a philosophical theory of politics resemble each other in some respects. Science cannot accept a thing that fails to stand to reason and scrutiny. So is the case with philosophy. Anything that stands on the premises of dogma or blind faith becomes an ideology. Scientific political theory may, for this reason, be very close to philosophical political theory but not to an ideological political theory. The case of Hobbes is an instance of this kind. His philosophical interpretation is so sound that at his hands political theory is said to have a scientific character. As Raphael further says: "The reasoning process in the philosophy of knowledge or in scientific theory does exactly the same thing and is normative in the same sense. Neither is ideological. A set of value-judgements which have not been subjected to rational scrutiny by the tests of consistency and accordance may be called ideological."[86] The fundamental continuities between political theory and political philosophy "suggest that the pursuit of either subject in isolation from the other is impossible."[87]

What strikingly distinguishes a scientific from a non-scientific theory is its form, the hypothetic-deductive form, rather than its truth. Of course, no scientific theory can survive for long unless it explains in a fairly satisfactory manner the observed facts in its domain.[88] It may be quite true about natural sciences. One may ask as to what about psychoanalysis? Prof. A.B. Shah is of the view that here a generally acceptable scientific theory is yet to emerge. Much work has been done in this important field and its therapeutic methods "seem to work in too large a number of cases to justify brushing aside as mumbo-jumbo. And, still what is offered as its theory is more a set of brilliant insights than a proper theory that can be subjected to any rigorous test. At the same time, there is nothing in the motivation and the methods of inquiry adopted by psychoanalysis which may prevent its development into a theory that meets the conditions for being considered scientific."[89]

Then, what about the theory of politics? Like psychoanalysis, it is also making strides in the same direction. It may not reach the stage of a 'pure science' like physics, but it may certainly reach what is possible in the field of social sciences. As Prof. Shah optimistically visualises: "This is not to suggest that politics cannot be an advanced science in the sense of a deductively formulated theory. It may not reach the degree of precision and accuracy that is characteristic of a natural science. However, it may very well be able to unify and explain its facts and sometimes even predict unknown ones. If it has not done this, it is primarily because very little inductive work has preceded the attempts at formulating political theory. Marx undertook to show how such a formulation could be accomplished, and he very

85. *Ibid.*, pp. 18-19.
86. *Ibid.*, p. 19
87. Moon, *op. cit.*, p. 213.
88. Shah, *op. cit.*, p. 81.
89. *Ibid.*

nearly succeeded. But he was too much of a system-builder and an Old Testament prophet to leave the social scientist in him free to pursue his insights."[90]

Dichotomy of Fact and Value: Place of Scientific Value Relativism

Whether political science should be treated as a 'science' or not requires, first of all, an examination of the distinction between 'facts' and 'values' and then the relatedness between the two on the basis of which alone a political theory of lasting benefit to civilised human society can be formulated. Such an examination "is particularly necessary because of the centrality of values in politics and because of the frequent confusion between statements of facts and statements of values by those who write about politics."[91] In other words, this problem hinges on the point that facts alone can make a science and, as such, a student of politics is not at all concerned with the discussion of values that are of a hypothetical and empirically non-verifiable kind. Value-laden political theory (as given by Plato, Aristotle, Rousseau, Green, Gandhi, etc.) cannot be termed 'scientific', whereas fact-laden theories (as presented by Weber, Easton and Lasswell) deserve to be treated as scientific for the reason of being based on facts. "Those who argue that these types of statements are different and should be kept separate say that the former are scientific, the latter unscientific. Science, it is claimed, is value-free. Metaphysicians may deal with values, but scientists may not, unless they treat the values as facts. However, to treat values as facts is not to suggest that no difference exists between factual statements and statements of preferences."[92]

A fact refers to *something that actually happened.*[93] For instance, it is a fact that Socrates was put to death by the Athenian democrats in ancient times, or an English king (Charles I) was executed in 1649, or the American leaders declared their independence in 1776, or there occurred a great revolution in France in 1789, or the Bolsheviks under Lenin assumed power in Russia in 1917, or Italy became a Fascist state under Mussolini in 1922, or the British left India in 1947, or China became a communist state in 1949, or containment of communism was the hallmark of American foreign policy, etc. Such instances can be multiplied to any possible extent. The notable point at this stage is that a fact is a reality and, for that reason, it can be subjected to empirical scrutiny. Its existence cannot be denied, because it refers

90. *Ibid.*, p. 63. However, as a stern critic of Marxism like Arthur Koestler and Karl Popper, Shah says: "Actually, the social theory of Marx and Engels on scrutiny turns out to be a closed system, to which the criteria of testability is not applicable at all. A large number of major predictions made by Marxism have proved miserably wrong." *Ibid*, p. 87.
91. S.L. Wasby, *op. cit., p.* 26.
92. *Ibid.*, pp. 26-27.
93. A number of definitions of the word 'fact' have been advanced which may help to bring out its real meaning. According to W.G. Goode and P.K. Hatt, it is 'an empirically verifiable observation'. *Methods in Social Research* (New York: McGraw-Hill, 1952), p. 8. F.G. Wilson says that facts "are situations or circumstances concerning which there does not seem to be valid room for disagreement." *The Elements of Modern Politics* (New York: McGraw-Hill, 1956). p. 2. Easton defines it as 'a particular ordering of reality in terms of a theoretical interest'. *The Political System* (New York: Alfred A. Knopf, 1953), p. 53. The word 'fact' may, then, designate anything from the most minute detail to the most general truth. In the subject of political science, a fact becomes significant only when it relates to the question under consideration. Thus, its significance may vary considerably according to the degree of interest of the political scientist. See V.V. Dyke, *op. cit.*, pp. 58-59.

to 'is' and not to anything like 'ought' or 'nought' smacking of some preferential orientation. To say that man is essentially selfish and wicked is a fact and, for this reason, the theories of Machiavelli and Hobbes are empirical. Likewise, to say that man desires 'power' and struggles for its sake is a fact and, for this reason, the theories of Morgenthau and Lasswell have an empirical character.[94]

A fact is an objective reality, though it may also be pointed out here that the appreciation of facts varies from man to man owing to his nature and temperament, even vested interest.[95] For instance, Marx could, emphasise the fact of 'exploitation' as an essential characteristic of the capitalist system. It is accepted by all Marxists, though it is flatly contradicted by those who find fault with the social and economic theories of the father of 'scientific socialism'. As such, bias or prejudice has its essential place in the mind of a theorist who tries to understand and evaluate reality in the light of his own set of 'preferences'. Thus, we may come to the point that facts are observable, but their proof by observation "depends on more than observation, description and measurement. It depends on (1) acceptance of the observation as sufficiently exact to support the report made on it, (2) acceptance of the report as sufficiently correct and adequate; and (3) acceptance of the apparently observed facts as actual facts."[96]

It follows from the above that values cannot be treated as facts, for they are related to the 'ought' and 'nought' of things. For instance, a statement that 'all people should take part in the management of public affairs so as to make their democratic system successful' is a matter of value-judgement. Likewise, it is a matter of value-judgement that 'all are equal in the eye of nature or God'. (Here the word 'are' is to be taken as 'should be'.) A moralist may say that a man should always be guided by the idea of'good life', a metaphysicist may say that 'a man should inform his activity by the principle of self-imposed categorical imperative of duty.' Obviously, "a value is a preference, positive or negative."[97]

---

94. According to Norman P. Barry, "normative statements set standards and prescribe forms of conduct; they do not describe facts or events. While they are frequently used in connection with moral standards, this is not always the case. Legal rules are technically normative in that they make certain forms of conduct obligatory, but they are not necessarily moral. Normative statements typically involve the use of words such as 'ought', 'should' and 'must'. But empiricism is the epistemological doctrine that the only foundation for knowledge apart from mathematical and logical relationships is experience. It is contrasted with the various forms of *idealism,* all of which maintain that the mind is already equipped with the conceptual apparatus which enables us to understand the external world. In the social sciences empiricists reject *a priori* reasoning about man and society in favour of factual and statistical enquiries." *op. cit.,* pp.. xiv-xv.
95. As Thomas Hobbes says: "Good and bad terms are ever being used with relation to the person that uses them. There being nothing simply and absolutely so; nor any common rule of Good or Evil, to be taken from the objects themselves but from the person of the man who uses the terms." *Leviathan* (London: Oxford University Press, 1909), p. 41.
96. Brecht, *op. cit.,* p. 49.
97. Dwight Waldo: "Values in Political Science Curriculum" in Ronald J. Young (ed.): *Approaches to the Study of Politics* (Evanston, Illinois: Northwestern University Press, 1958), p. 98. He refers to the operational definition of values as given by J.G. Miller: "The total of the strains within the individual resulting from his genetic input and variations in the input from his environment is often referred to as his values. The relative urgency of reducing these individual strains determines his hierarchy of values." *Ibid.*

Scientific Theory

Meaning

A scientific theory is a hypothesis that relates one class of facts to another in the form of what may be called a causal relationship. It should satisfy two basic conditions :

1. All true statements about observed facts can be deduced as logical consequences of the hypothesis, and
2. Predictions or postdictions can be made of observable phenomena that were not known before.

Stages of development

1. Breaking up the problem into its component parts,
2. Collecting, by observation and experimentation, all the available relevant facts and classifying them according to some common properties,
3. Proposing a hypothesis that would explain all the observed facts and resolve the problem situation,
4. It the hypothesis permits it, the working out of its logical implications for making predictions of phenomena not known so far, and
5. Testing of these predictions against observation.

Characteristics

1. It has the premiss-conclusion form. This is precisely what is meant by saying that it is rational in form. Scientific truth is public truth. Unlike the vision of the artist or the mystic, it has nothing esoteric or essentially personal about it.
2. Science is concerned with the happenings in this world, not in some hypothetical world beyond the ken of human observation. In this sense, the content of scientific truth is empirical. It does not mean that there is no speculation in sciences. But scientific truth, however speculative some parts of it may appear, has to satisfy one ineluctable criterion : it must make contact with physical reality at some crucial point of experience. In this respect, scientific truth differs from transcendental truth which by its very nature cannot stand this test.
3. The empirical character of scientific truth is closely related to its secular import. The notion of the ultimate good of man and its independence from the affairs of this world discounts the importance of his secular pursuits. It also leads to a neglect of the need to test theory against fact, action against ideal, and the ideal against the actual.
4. By relating ethics to a secular ideal and by further indicating a method of realising it, scientific truth gives morality a locus standi in earthly life.

Structure

1. For a theory to be scientific, it should be capable of explaining observed facts as its logically necessary consequences. This is the minimum condition that any 'explanation' in natural science must fulfil.
2. A further condition to be satisfied by a scientific theory is that it should be compatible with other theories. It should be free from hypothesis *ad hoc*. That is, it should not go on piling up one hypothesis on another to explain each newly discovered fact that cannot be shown to follow from the original hypothesis.
3. Another criterion is testability. A hypothesis which does not meet this condition would at best be non-scientific. This explains why metaphysical or aesthetic theories, howsoever subtle or reasonable, cannot be accorded the status of scientific theory even if they are based on concepts by intellection. Thus, 'God', 'soul' and

'electron' are all concepts by intellection. Yet 'electron' is a scientific concept and the theory in which it occurs is scientific, because it meets the testability criterion.

4. But what makes a theory scientific is its logical structure and its relation to empirical facts irrespective of whether or not it is formulated in mathematical language.
5. Scientific knowledge is rational in structure, empirical in content, and secular in character. The fact that it is empirical in content makes its truth probable instead of certain, as is the case with the 'truths' revealed by intuition or by pure reason. Logical validity and empirical truth are mutually independent properties of propositions.
6. The ultimate authority for any theory of science is facts. It is liable to modification, rejection, or incorporation into a more comprehensive theory in the light of fresh evidence. Scientific truth is thus tentative and scientific method self-correcting in character.

Presuppositions of Scientific Theory

1. **Simplicity:** It does not imply that the laws of nature are such as can be grasped by anyone without adequate preparation. It means that the working of nature can be understood by human reason and so the laws can be laid down in the form of rational theories. Understood in this sense, simplicity provides the raison d' etre of science and also a criterion of choice between two theories that are otherwise equally eligible for acceptance.
2. **Uniformity:** It has two implications. First, nature is regulated by universal laws. For instance, the law of gravitation or of the propagation of electro-magnetic waves is the same at all places. Second, the passage of time though by itself important - to us personally in a number of ways - may be disregarded in formulating certain fundamental laws. For example, the equation connecting the mass and energy of a material particle, though discovered in 1905, is still assumed to be valid. Such an assumption leads to the principle of causality. It means that every event has an antecedent and that the structural relationship that the events of a given type have with their antecedents is more or less permanent.

Thus, scientific theory is a generic form covering a number of scientific theories each of which satisfies a certain criterion to the lesser or greater extent. These theories are not always mutually related; that is, they do not always together constitute a unified doctrine. . . . Hence, it is to be expected that scientific theories which are attempts at a rational formulation of the workings of such processes would not together form a single organic whole whose parts must be inseparably related to one another.

Source : A.B. Shah : *Scientific Method.*

A value is an ought-form premise in contrast to an is-form statement.[98] A study of values in all possible forms is called 'axiology' wherein focus on epistemological and metaphysical (not operational) aspects of values is characteristically noticeable. But values are taken and stressed not in an absolute but in a relational manner and there the personal point of view gets the opportunity to creep in. Keeping it in view, Moon says: "In short, when we make judgements on value or worth, we are not saying something about ourselves. The terms which we use to make value-judgements, according to this analysis, do not designate any property of the objects

98. A.H. Doctor: *Issues in Political Theory* (New Delhi: Sterling, 1985), p. 26.

of which they are predicated; rather they are actually relational concepts: they expose a relationship, between the speaker and the objects of which he is speaking. Nothing has value in itself, but only for some particular person, and a value-judgement merely reports or expresses the stance or attitude which the speaker takes to some object."[99]

A great advocate of this point of view like Frohock says that the role of values in political investigations has been shown to be multiple in these respects:[100]

1. Values enter the cultural framework within which all political analysis takes place. This is the long-range bias of any intellectual undertaking. Further, the cultural framework is a necessary condition for social analysis and, therefore, cannot be placed in abeyance.
2. Values (as judgements made by actors) are factual objects of inquiry. This particular function of values is of more import in political than in social analysis, inasmuch as the political investigator focuses on that apparatus which is prescriptive for society generally.
3. Values are a part of political inquiry in the recommendations that the political analysts can make in policy-making areas.

The dichotomy of facts and values cannot be denied. And yet it may be affirmed, at the same time, that in social sciences this should not be taken in the way it is done in the field of natural sciences. A physicist like Newton may give his law of gravitation on the basis of facts without delving into the question of values at all, but a social theorist like Marx has a wider mission. He should not only throw focus on the existing reality, he should also say something about its good and bad aspects and then suggest some measures to deal with the bad side of the matter in question. It leads to, what is now known, 'scientific value relativism'. That is, facts and values should not be studied in an 'absolute' sense, rather they should be studied in relative terms. As Brecht says: "Compactly formulated, Scientific Value Relativism (or Alternativism) holds that: (1) The question whether something is 'valuable' can be answered *scientifically* only in relation to (a) some good or purpose for the pursuit of which it is or is not useful (valuable), or (b) the ideas held by some person or group of persons regarding what is or is not valuable; and that consequently, (2) it is impossible to establish scientifically what goals or purposes are valuable *irrespective* of (a) the value they have in the pursuit of other goals or purposes, or (b) of someone's ideas about ulterior or ultimate goals or purposes.[101]

The important features of scientific value relativism may be summed up as under:

1. Anything like the ultimate, highest, or absolute values or standards of values are chosen by mind or will, or possibly grasped by faith, intuition or instinct, but

99. J. Donald Moon: "Values and Political Theory: A Modest Defence of Qualified Cognitivism" in *Journal of Politics,* Vol. 39, No. 4 (November, 1977), p. 877 W.R. Mead offers a rejoinder to what Moon says. In his view, value cognitivism "is used to indicate the position of those who go further than maintaining the objective status, the truth or falsity of values and assert that value-judgement can be *demonstrated* or *proved* to be true or false. Correspondingly, non-value cognitivism then logically suggests that the truth or falsity of values is beyond proof or demonstration." Refer to his paper titled "A Call for Conceptual Clarification in Value Theory: A Response to Prof. Moon", *ibid.,* p. 905.

100. Frohock, *op. cit.,* pp. 184-85.

101. Brecht, *op. cit.,* pp. 117-18.

they are not proved by science excepting however that science can help a great deal in clarifying the meaning of ideas about such values and the consequences and risks entailed in their pursuit. In other words, science can approach values only indirectly, not directly.

2. It follows that here a student is faced with certain alternatives out of which he has to choose some and discard others. If so, scientific value relativism should better be designated as scientific value alternativism.
3. There is no logical way by which a student of social sciences may establish as to what ought to be from what actually is. As suggested by Georg Simmel, it becomes like an original datum beyond which we may ask no logical question. Thus, in its own right, it amounts to the doctrine of ends what John Stuart Mill calls teleology.
4. Values can be hierarchicalised keeping in view the factors of duration, degree of satisfaction, and comparative benefits over losses. This is the argument of Schiller who holds that values which have a longer life or whose weight increases with the passage of time (as friendship) are higher than those being of a shorter duration.
5. The best use of science in this direction is that it informs us about the factor of 'costs' in the maintenance and achievement of values. With the help of such a calculation, we may make an order of values and then strive for their realisation. Thus, science can help us in the selection of values as well as the means for their realisation.

Now we may come to have a balanced view of the proper relationship between facts and values in the sphere of political theory. It is based on the recognition that values and facts both affect the the study of politics in their own right. In spite of the fact that we may never completely succeed, our concern"is to attempt to keep values to one side, rather than to eliminate them completely. The researcher must be aware of the various values held by those he is studying, and the possible impact of those values on their behaviour. Thus, what we are interested in is not value rejection but value neutralisation, a sensitivity to, rather than ignoring of values."[102] Again: "The fact-value distinction is a scientific canon; the purpose of the value-free stance is to safeguard political science from ideological infiltration. If this scientific canon should, however, be transmuted into a personal ideology by the scientist, in which the individual completely surrenders any judgement over the uses to which he and his skills or information are put or in which he does not speak out in defence of his values, then he definitely may find himself morally implicated in the uses to which the material is put."[103]

102. Wasby, *op. cit.*, p. 28.

103. *Ibid.*, p. 31. To strengthen his impression, Wasby cites the view of David Butler: "Although the aim of every academic writer on politics should *be* a detached search for truth, *objectivity is only a goal that can be striven for, it is not one that can be achieved." The Study of Political Behaviour* (London, 1958), p. 25. Prof. M.Q Sibley makes a very fine point that 'value' and 'fact' are first cousins. "In selecting and organising facts, a value system is involved, and that facts, in turn, affect the way we see our value schemes." Refer to his paper "The Place of Classical Political Theory in the Study of Politics: The Legitimate Spell of Plato" in Ronald Young (ed.): *Approaches to the Study of Politics* (Evanston, Illinois: Northwestern University Press, 1958), p. 138.

Concluding Observations

In the preceding sections, we have studied the case of science and its role in the advancement of political theory. We have seen that science "is a method for acquiring knowledge and not knowledge itself. Those who employ the method and abide by its rules are players of the game whatever their field."[104] As such, a scientific method "is a persistent critique of arguments in the light of tried canons of judging the reliability of the procedures by which evidential datas are obtained, and for assessing the probative force of the evidence on which conclusions are based."[105] But the question arises whether scientific method can be applied successfully to the understanding and explanation or description of the political phenomena. Following points may be considered in this direction:

1. Scientific method cannot be applied to the study of social (including political) phenomena in the same way as it can be done in the field of natural phenomena. It works well only when it is applied to things that have a tangible existence. The consequences are severe for political values which are the very stuff of traditional political theory. As they entail loosely defined concepts (such as justice, liberty, freedom, equality, etc.), they are deemed to remain in the non-scientific realm. It follows that political studies, no matter how carefully pursued in a scientific way, may help us to achieve the ends people cherish, but they cannot prove which ends we should espouse. Men of different backgrounds and faiths will always entertain conflicting opinions about such matters and political theory will, therefore, always be plagued by its origins, that is, by the sociology of knowledge.[106] Weldon makes a good point: "The central doctrine taken for granted by all political theorists is that words have meaning in the same sense as that in which children have parents...,whereas in fact, words have no meanings in the required sense at all, they might have uses."[107]
2. The tendency of scientism leads to historicism that carries with it a set of its own follies. Human behaviour cannot be subjected to certain rigid and unalterable rules of growth and development. Social sciences must be flexible enough to redefine themselves with the discovery of new things. The method of trial and error should be followed. We may take note of the fact that political theorists have appreciated the course of correcting themselves as well as others. For instance, Plato changed his own ideas of the *Republic* when he wrote the *Laws;* Aristotle corrected some of the ideas of Plato (relating to communism) in his *Politics.* Hobbes improved upon the idea of sovereignty given by Bodin; Marx followed the dialectics of

104. James Rosenau: *The Dramas of Politics: An Introduction to the Joys of Inquiry* (Boston: Little Brown, 1973), p. 121. The word'science'is now used in an honorofic sense. "Just as a nation in the contemporary world is judged good if it is democratic, a political scientist's status is raised if he is scientific. Therefore, nations call themselves democratic and political scientists call their work scientific with a public relations pay-off in mind." A C. Isaak: *Scope and Methods of Political Science,* p. 23.
105. Ernest Nagel: *The Structure of Science* (New York: Harcourt Brace and World, 1961), p. 13.
106. D.M. Ricci: *The Tragedy of Political Science: Politics, Scholarship and Democracy* (New Haven: Yale University Press, 1984), p. 145.
107. T.D. Weldon: *The Vocabulary of Politics* (Baltimore: Penguin, 1953), pp. 18-19.

Political Science as a Science	
Negative View	*Positive View*
1. Lack of precise and standard definitions of terms 2. Complexity of political phenomena due to variation in the nature and habits of the people 3. Diversity of 'environment' in which political developments take place. 4. Problem of experimentation to arrive at valid conclusions.	1. Marvellous developments of political theory based on facts and verifiable data. 2. Status of an inexact science like meteorology. 3. To a certain extent possibility of making predictions on the basis of social experimentation.

Hegel but formulated different laws of social development. Popper, therefore, holds that the tendency to subject the course of human or social development to certain inexorable laws or historicism "has a most dangerous form which can prove lasting devotion to fixed ethical principles even while denying that they can be found in the annals of ordinary philosophy."[108] Leo Strauss also holds that historicism in the intellectual history has gone hand in hand with the tendency to highlight various mistakes made by some prominent thinkers living in more primitive and superstitious times. In his view, many great books of western civilisation became empty of enduring faith and as a result of the time-bound error, a void has come to occur. He goes on to say that even great figures like Plato and Marx committed scientific blunders and that every ten-year-old child knows how to avoid the error of inference from facts to values.[109]

3. The meaning of science should also be understood in the light of this affirmation that it is both a myth and a reality. This in itself is neither here nor there, inasmuch as most things in the world are. But the peculiar myth of science is that it dispenses with all other myths. Conceptual discussions of science, sooner or later, settle on the topic loosely called 'scientific method'. We need not believe that in the actual practice of science any formalised procedure is rigidly followed.[110] P.W. Bridgman claims that a scientist has no method other than doing the damnedest.[111] Even in Kuhn's model we find that instead of unbiased sceptics, we get a picture of the partisans defending the established order. We

108. Karl Popper: *The Poverty of Historicism* (New York: Harper and Row, 1961).

109. Leo Strauss: "Political Philosophy and the Crisis of Our Time" in G.J. Graham and G.W. Carey (ed.s): *The Post-Behavioural Era: Perspectives on Political Science* (New York: McKay, 1972), p. 227.

110. "Descriptions of the 'scientific method' are patently misleading, for the implication is that there is only one. In fact, there are many. The processes by which important scientific advances have been made are scarcely reducible either to method or to rule. Those who strive to master one or another method that is ostensibly scientific in the hope that it will guide them to scientific achievement are likely to be disappointed." V.V. Dyke, *op. cit.*, p. 186.

111. Cited in M A. Kaplan: *The Conduct of Inquiry* (San Francisco: Chandler Pub., 1964), p 27.

also find that disagreement ensues between the supporters of the old and the new principles that culminates in the acceptance of the new paradigm and establishment of the normal research. It implies that partnership is a necessary condition for creativity, even though it is in purpose antagonistic to it."[112]

4. The use of scientific method in the study of political science may hardly go beyond the domain of logical empiricism. It signifies a tie between the meaning and verification of a statement; something that cannot be verified is treated as meaningless or irrelevant. Notwithstanding frequent references to terms like 'scientific method', 'scientific rules' and 'scientific credo' in the prestigious theoretical literature of political science, the students of this discipline seldom interpret the meaning of science beyond formal and empty statements relating to 'generalisations' and propositions' or the like. Thus, Gunnell challenges the advocates of behaviouralism who believe that within the philosophy of science there is a consensus favouring a positivist conception of scientific inquiry.[113] Thorson joins the anti-positivist revolt with a detailed examination of the links between science and social science, essentially revealing the misconceptions that pervade the literature on political science.[114] Morgenthau frankly admits: "The social sciences can, at best, do what is their regular task, that is, present a series of hypothetical possibilities, each of which may occur under certain conditions—and which of them will actually occur is anybody's guess."[115]

5. Science is based on facts. But the difficulty is that in the sphere of social sciences we deal with human behaviour. Same facts have different appeal to different types of people. For instance, same facts would have different attractions to a poet, a painter, a physicist and the like. This is so because each has a framework of his own in terms of which he interprets his facts and, indeed, sees them through his own selective diffraction grating and recombines them so as to build up a pattern characteristic of his way of looking at them. One could go further and assert that there are no 'pure' facts as such, since any fact before it can become a subject of discourse, has to be formulated in a language and thus brought under a definite conceptual system. Most men living in a given culture, share a common set of concepts and hence look at a given set of facts in more or less the same way. The very high degree of agreement on the conceptual system ensures continuity and communicability of man's moral creation. However, it is fortunate that this agreement is not perfect, for otherwise it would have left no scope for development.[116]

---

112. F.M. Frohock, *op. cit.*, pp. 105-6.
113. See J.G. Gunnell: "Deduction, Explanation and Social Scientific Inquiry" in *American Political Science Review*, Vol. LXI1I, No 4, pp. 1233-46.
114. For a criticism of the assumption that political science is like a science see T.L. Thorson: *Biopolitics* (New York : Holt, Rinehart and Winston, 1970).
115. Morgenthau: *Scientific Man Versus Power Politics* (Chicago: Chicago Univ. Press. 1946), p. 130.
116. A.B. Shah, *op. cit.*, pp. 39-40. "It is an utterly superficial view... that the truth is to be found by studying the facts. It is idle to collect facts unless there is a problem upon which they are supposed to bear." Cohen and Nagel: *An Introduction to Logic and Scientific Method*, pp. 199 and 392. Also see Gunnar Myrdal : *Value in Social Theory* (London: Routledge and Kegan Paul, 1958), pp. 51-52.

6. Science and scientific method can flourish only in a society which encourages free and critical inquiry. An inquiry is free if it is unrestrained by any initial adherence to dogmas or orthodoxy in pursuing its course in its search for the sake of truth; and it is critical if there is a genuine willingness to subject its conclusion to the test of evidence and logic. Such willingness, in turn, involves the surrender of all claims to private and mysterious access to truth and the recognition and acceptance of all men as rational beings, as partners in a cooperative search for truth. It also involves the acceptance of a certain ideal of intellectual integrity, a determination to play the game, to give up one's hypotheses, beliefs, one's most cherished convictions if the verdict of evidence goes against them, and not to try to cling to them at all costs by buttressing them with a plethora of subsidiary and *ad hoc* hypotheses. Thus, in the final analysis, the acceptance of scientific method is rooted in a moral choice."[117]
7. Above all, the term 'science' should be taken in a particular sense and the utility of the 'scientific' method' should be evaluated in a different way. The former should be used just to mean 'a connected body of knowledge or the knowledge of the system of relations based upon observation and, as Lord Kelvin said, preferably upon qualitative measurement.' Moreover, it is here thought of as 'yielding through its studies empirically testable laws or conclusions about constants which give to man, or to the professors of these matters some hope of powers of prediction and control.'[118] Thus, R.B. Braithwaite in his *Scientific Explanation* holds that scientific theory, in the strictest sense, "is a set of propositions from which further propositions of increasing specificity are derived according to logical principles."[119] For this reason, a scientific theory becomes like a 'concatenated theory' consisting of general statements held together by some other factor such as relevance to a common class of phenomena. Social science theories, at present, come under this category, not that of deductive theories.[120] Though many hold the belief that politics can be reduced to a science, both in understanding and in action, it is not a product of scientific reasoning,[121] but is simply ideology using pseudo-science to justify the application of technological thought to society.[122]

In short, political science cannot take the shape of a natural science like physics even in which something is left out.[123] And yet it cannot be lost sight of that it

117. M.P. Rege: "Foreword", in A.B. Shah, *op. cit.*, p. xv.

118. G.E.G.Catlin: *Systematic Politics* (University of Toronto Press, 1962), pp. 5-6.

119. H.V. Wiserman: *Politics – The Master Science* (London: Routledge and Kegan Paul, 1969), p. 40.

120. *Ibid.*, pp. 54-55 .

121. *Ibid.*, p. 63. To strengthen his point, Wiserman refers to the view of Conant given by him in his *Science and Common Sense* where he says: "I believe that almost all modern historians of the natural sciences would agree that there is no such thing as the 'scientific method'. Others have suggested that there is no one single fixed 'scientific method'; it varies according to the problem being investigated and is itself constantly changing. This is, of course, a form of study involving codified processes of comparison, classification, generalisation, hypothesis and theory which is the very essence of scientific procedure. *Ibid.*, p. 36.

122 For a frank criticism of the proposal of taking politics as a science, see H.S Kariel: *The Promise of Politics* (Englewood Cliffs, New Jersey: Prentice-Hall, 1966).

123. A. James Gregor : *An Introduction to Metapolitics* (New York: Free Press, 1971), p. 27.

has developed a scientific character ever since Hobbes produced his *Leviathan*. Since then, it is widely accepted that science "is the only method available for responsibly assigning maximally reliable truth status to statements."[124] The use of scientific method in the study of politics is made with the assumption that the element of probability cannot be ruled out. Keeping this in view, Moon well observes: "Political science differs from the activities of professional fact-compilers by its systematic character and by its concern for the explanation of political phenomena. We do not simply assemble information: we seek coherent accounts of political life. Perhaps the most popular methodological position in political science is one that might broadly be called 'naturalist' or scientific method, for it seeks to structure political science in terms of the methodological principles of the natural sciences. Adherents of this model deny the existence of any fundamental methodological difference between the natural and social sciences. For both natural and social, the goals of the scientific enterprise are the explanation and prediction of natural or social phenomena. In both areas of inquiry, moreover, scientific explanation consists in showing that the particular event or state of affairs to be explained could be expected, given certain initial conditions and the general laws or regularities in the field."[125] In a word, once again, it must be emphasised that scientific method is not a philosopher's stone capable of providing ready answers to every question."[126]

---

124. "Thus to chastise political science for something which is true even of physics is perhaps unfair." Issak, *op cit.*, p. 48. Russell Kirk says: "Human beings are the least controllable, verifiable, law-obeying and predictable of subjects." Refer to his paper "Is Social Science Scientific?" in N.W. Polsby, R.A. Dentler and P.A. Smith (ed.s): *Politics and Social Life* (Boston: Houghton Mifflin Co., 1963) p. 63.
125. Moon, *op. cit.*, pp. 131-32. We may appreciate this statement of M.A. Weinstein: "No significant political theorist begins his work with a blank slate for a mind. Originality in political theory is the result of extensive and deep knowledge of the traditions of political theorising." *Systematic Political Theory* (Columbus, Ohio: Charles Merrill Pub., 1971), p. 127.
126. Isaak, *op. cit.*, p. 55.

Part II

BASIC CONCEPTS

It is the functions of the political theorist to see, sooner than others, and to analyse, more profoundly than others, the immediate and the potential problems of the political life of society; to supply the practical politician, well in advance with alternative courses of action, the foreseeable consequences of which have been fully thought through; and to supply him not only with brilliant asides, but with a solid block of knowledge on which to build.

—Arnold Brecht[1]

Contemporary political science is not 'mere' empiricism....Generalisation from a sample of observations is one way of creating theory, but deduction from axioms and propositions is another. Both co-exist in contemporary political science. If modern political theory is empirical, it is so only in the sense of seeking for enough quantitative and descriptive precision to permit ultimate verification or disproof by means of observation.

—Ithiel de Sola Pool[2]

Theorising about values, though a speculative activity, is not independent of reality. The idealisations of philosophy have a habit of becoming the currency of the marketplace. Conversely, ideas grow out of experience; and when they are developed into a coherent whole—which is what a philosophy is supposed to be—they serve as signpost to further experience.

—Leslie Lipson[3]

1. Brecht: *Political Theory: The Foundations of Twentieth Century Political Thought* (Princeton: Princeton Univ Press, 1959), p. 20.
2. Sola Pool: *Contemporary Political Science: Towards Empirical Theory* (New York: McGraw Hill, 1967), pp. viii-x.
3. Lipson: *The Great Issues of Politics: An Introduction to Political Science* (Englewood Cliffs, New Jersey: Prentice-Hall, 1960), pp. 19-20.

6
Law

> Law is independent of, anterior to, above and more comprehensive than the State. There are positive and negative limits of a jural sort to the State's competence: things a 'legal sovereign' must or must not do, are judged by the standard of the laws. If the State, through either its statute-making bodies or its constitution-making organs, violates any of the rules of social solidarity, it acts unlawfully. The force of government is legitimate not in itself but only when employed to sustain law—that is, to guarantee co-operation towards social solidarity.
>
> **-F.W. Coker**[1]

A study of the basic concepts of political theory should begin with a discussion of the idea of law in view of the fact that the state—the fundamental subject of politics—is, in a most widely understood sense, a legal association or'a juridically organised nation.' The state is distinguished from society, nation, country and the like by virtue of its being the exclusive possessor of a 'coercive power'—a power that issues in the form of law. Naturally, the state is like a nation organised for action according to certain specific and well-set rules. In other words, it "exists for law: it exists in and through law: we may even see that it exists as a law, if by law we mean not only a sum of legal rules, but also, and in addition, an operative system of effective rules which are actually valid and regularly enforced. The essence of the State is a living body of effective rules; and in that sense, the State is law."[2] We, thus, enter into the realm of 'Law and the State'—a subject having three main currents: first, of Individualism holding that an individual has a definite sphere of private life free from the legal intervention of the state; second, of Pluralism advocating that within any normal community there are important and enduring social groups which are at par with the state in their social and moral values—a fact that does not entitle the state to coerce these voluntary organisations indiscriminately or purposelessly in the name of its supreme legal authority; last, of Internationalism signifying that the authority of the state is, in fact, and by right, limited by its own law so that municipal law and international law have a harmonious blending.

Law: Meaning and Sources

The difficulty of offering a precise definition of the term 'law' arises from its use in a variety of senses. For instance, in the realm of physics, it denotes the sequence of cause and effect. The laws of motion and gravitation may be referred to in this connection. There are social laws or customary laws which guide the behaviour of men in their collective life. The observance of a festival in a certain order or the performance of a marriage ceremony in a particular manner may be cited as instances

1. Coker: *Recent Political Thought* (New York; Appleton-Century, 1934), p. 535.
2. E.Barker: *Principles of Social and Political Theory* (London: Oxford Univ. Press, 1951), p. 89.

in this regard. Allied with this is the case of moral laws which relate to questions of intrinsic right and wrong, good and bad. That is, their necessary relationship is with issues of motive and conscience. Speaking truth and helping the poor are the examples belonging to this category. In the field of political theory, however, we are concerned with laws that regulate man's behaviour as a member of an organised society and which, for the most part, "deal with external conduct and are enforced by a system of compulsions."[3]

Etymologically, the word 'law' comes from the old Teutonic root 'lag' which means to lay, to place, to set, or to fix something in an even manner. Law is, for this reason, something positive or 'imposed'; it is something laid down or set. Thus, *The Oxford English Dictionary* defines it as 'a rule of conduct imposed by an authority'. In a deeper sense, the word 'law' originates from the Latin word *jus* that is essentially connected with another Latin word *jungere* implying primarily a bond or tie. If so, the term law denotes 'primarily a joining or fitting that readily glides into the sense of binding or obliging.'[4] We may also say that it conveys the idea of 'a valid custom to which any citizen can appeal, and which is recognised and can be enforced by a human authority.'[5]

Despite this etymological origin of the word, the fact of the variety of its senses stands out due to its different uses by persons belonging to different schools ranging from the Positivists who treat it as 'the command of the sovereign' to the Marxists who regard it as 'an expression of society's general interests and needs emerging from a given material means of production'. The variety is also affected by the differences in approaches ranging from the historical jurists who find sanction of law in the established habits and customs of the people to the sociologists who discover the same in the needs and interests of the community it serves. Keeping all this in view, law as distinguished from theory, is described as:[6]

3. E. Asirvatham: *Political Theory* (Lucknow: Upper India Pub., 1961), p. 381. It is said that the term 'Law' is one of the most ambiguous and fluid terms known to man. There is little agreement as to its meaning, and it may be that there is no final answer. A basic difficulty is that it means so many different things to so many different persons at so many different times and places. Inspite of all these problems, the central idea in law is that of *control*. In a democratic society, it is a technique with a purpose —it is the sum of the social influences regularly recognised and applied by the state in the administration of justice. Rodee, Christol and Anderson: *Introduction to Political Science* (New York: McGraw Hill, 1957), p. 80. Dean Pound considers law to be social control through the systematic application of force of politically organised society. Dean E.H. Levi defines law as a set of principles dealing with justice and a set of normative rules regulating human behaviour. *Ibid.* "The legal system of a modern state is characterised not just by duty-imposing laws but by what are called power-conferring rules." See H.A.L. Hart: *The Concept of Law* (Oxford: Clarendon Press, 1961), pp. 27-33.
4. Barker, *op. cit.*, p. 94.
5. *Ibid.*
6. Benn and Peters: *Social Principles and the Democratic State* (London: George Allen and Unwin, 1975), p. 57. A line of distinction may be drawn between a theory and a law. The former provides a higher level explanation than the latter, because it construes phenomena as manifestation of entities that lie behind or beneath them, as it were. "These entities are assumed to be governed by characteristic theoretical laws, or theoretical principles by means of which the theory then explains empirical uniformities." Carl G. Hempel: *Aspects of Scientific Explanation* (New York: Free Press, 1965), p. 343.

Law

Law is reason, not passion. It is equally the sum of all spiritual limits, under which man's actions must proceed. The great spiritual limitation upon man is reason. It is the duty of man to bring his passions under the control and the limitation of reason.

—**Aristotle**

Politics, 1280 a.

The constitution represents a protective super-structure designed to regulate the continuous process of developing an existing body of law and to prevent any confusion of the powers of government in enforcing the rules on which the spontaneous order of society rests.

—**F.A. von Hayek**

The Constitution of Liberty, Vol. III, pp. 122-23.

Law is found in all modern societies, and is actually regarded as the bedrock of civilised existence. Law commands citizens telling them what they must do; it lays down prohibitions indicating what citizens cannot do; and it allocates entitlements defining what the citizens have the right to do.

—**Andrew Heywood**

Political Theory: An Introduction, p. 152.

1. the normal expression of conventional morality, or of that part of it which the State should enforce; or
2. a system of rules by which the interests of a dominant class are safeguarded; or
3. a system of rules held to be binding or obligatory; or
4. a system of rules aimed at realising justice; or
5. a system of rules discoverable by reason; or
6. a command of the sovereign; or
7. what judges decide in the courts; or
8. a system of rules backed by coercive sanctions.

It is, however, a different matter that, in the most widely understood sense, the term 'law' has an imperative connotation: it signifies 'a body of rules enforced by the courts.'[7]

The cause of an embarrassing variety in the senses of law, in the sphere of social sciences, finds its place in the world of its sources that may be enumerated as under:

1. **Custom:** In every community the earliest form of law is traceable in the well-established practices of the people. These practices, once started, gradually but imperceptibly developed because of the utility that inhered in them. In due course, a practice became a usage which after sufficient standing hardened into a custom. History shows that primitive communities attached great significance to the observance of their customs. Even now custom seems to play an important part where the life of people is quite simple. The law of today is very much based

7. A.L. Lowell: *The Government of England,* Vol. II, p. 473. He further says: "The essential point is that what the courts recognise and enforce is law and what they refuse to recognise is not law." *Ibid.*

on the customs of the people inasmuch as it is, for the most part, a translation of an age-old established practice rendered into specific written terms by the State.

2. **Religion:** Allied to the source of custom is that of religion. It finds its sanction in the religious scriptures of the people. Since times immemorial people have reposed their faith in the power of some supernatural agencies and tried to lay down rules for the regulation of their behaviour so as to be respectful to their deities. The result is that words contained in the holy books and their interpretations made by the priests and the divines constitute, what is known, the religious law of the people. In course of time, most of the principles of religious law have been translated by the State in terms of specific rules. Thus, we may take note of the personal laws of the Hindus, Muslims, Christians and the like.
3. **Adjudication:** As the process of social organisation became more and more complex in response to the growth of civilisation, the force of custom declined. Disputes among the people on the meaning or nature of a custom were referred to the 'wisest men of the community' who delivered their verdicts to settle the points in question. The decisions formed precedents for future guidance even if they were handed down by tradition and only subsequently put in writing as the interpreter and enforcer of the customs of the people. As judges became the 'wisest men of the community', their decisions came to have a special sanctity and as these were given in writing, they constituted, what came to be known, the case-law.
4. **Equity:** One more important source of law is contained in equity—an informal method of making new law or altering an old one depending on intrinsic fairness or equality of treatment. In simple words, it means equality or natural justice in cases where the existing law does not apply properly and judgement has to be given according to commonsense or fairness. Obviously, as a source of law, equity arises from the fact that as time passes and new conditions of life develop, positive law becomes unsuitable or inadequate to the new situation. To make it suitable either the old law should be changed or adapted by some informal method. Thus, equity enters to fill the void. In the absence of a positive law, judges decide the cases on general principles of fairness, reasonableness, commonsense and natural justice. The principles of equity thus supplement the premises of law when they are put into specific terms by the State.
5. **Legislation:** However, the most prolific source of law is legislation. It means placing of a specific rule on the statute book of the land. It reflects the will of the State as declared by its law-making organs. Whether it is in the form of a royal decree, or an ordinance promulgated by the head of the state, or assented to by him after being passed by the legislature, it has the validity of the law of the land and is to be implemented by the executive and enforced by the judicial departments of the state. The noticeable point at this stage is that with the pace of political development, legislation has become the most important source that has outplaced the significance of other traditional sources like custom and religion. Due to the codification of law, uncertainties and ambiguities which used to get easily accommodated in the spheres of religious and customary law have been sufficiently narrowed down.

6. **Standard Works:** The source of law may also be traced in the scientific commentaries in which leading thinkers, jurists and statesmen express their views on important points of law and which, when recognised, are treated as binding by virtue of being the decisions of the 'wisest men of the community'. Not only this, the opinions of these great men are accepted by the courts and also incorporated into the law of the land. The works of Edward Coke, Hale, Littleton and Blackstone in England and of Kent and Story in the United States may be referred to in this conection. The importance of these standard works lies in the fact that they compile, compare and logically arrange legal principles, customs and decisions of the 'wisest men of the community' and then lay down important principles for the guidance of the people in future possible cases.

The whole process of the development of law in the light of the role of various sources is thus summed up by Woodrow Wilson: "Custom is the earliest fountain of law, but religion is a contemporary, and equally prolific, and in the same stages of national development an almost identical source. Adjudication comes almost as authority itself and from a very antique time goes hand in hand with equity. Only legislation, the conscious and deliberate organisation of law, and scientific discussion, the reasoned development of its principles, await an advanced stage of its growth in the body-politic to assert their influence in law-making."[8]

Since law has arisen from different sources, its meaning has acquired a range of embarrassing multiplicity denoting 'rules' and 'systems of roles' ranging from the 'laws of football' to 'Talmudic law.'[9] It, therefore, depends upon the approach of a person to stipulate a definition of his own, and so conscientiously limit the discussion to the rules which fit it exactly. Naturally, such a view would be inapplicable to other rules called 'laws' and, for this reason, be an object of attack from the side of others holding different notions. In order to avoid this confusion or, as we may say, to solve this predicament, we should study the nature of law in the light of varying theories—natural, analytical, historical, philosophical, sociological, comparative and Marxist—that would enable us to know the diverse meanings of this term, all of them hinging on the ingredient that law, in ordinary usage, denotes, 'a set of rules."[10]

Natural Theory: Law as a Dictate of Right Reason of Universal and Eternal Application

This theory considers law as eternal, universal, constant and immutable, discoverable by the rational faculty of man. Being universal, it has the merit of prevailing everywhere; being eternal, it has its validity at all times; being constant, it is the same at all places and under all circumstances; and being immutable it cannot be changed by any power on earth. Nature is the author of this law and, as such, it is based on right reason. It has two aspects—positive and negative. Positively, it is in the nature of a call and a command to one's duty: negatively, it is a warning against the performance of some deceitful or evil act. If so, the natural law is the higher law and the civil law must conform to it in order to be valid.

8. See Asirvatham, *op, cit.*, p. 385.
9. Benn and Peters, *op. cit.*, p. 73 n.
10. *Ibid.*

This idea originally found its manifestation in Plato's theory of justice as contained in his *Republic* whereby the 'Father of Philosophy' sought to establish a harmonious order of society. However, he gave it a metaphysical complexion by insisting on the strict observance of the principle of social righteousness. It, therefore, found a clear affirmation in the ideas of the Stoics who decried the system of slavery as based on the principle of natural inequality of mankind and instead insisted on a new order informed by the rational, eternal, universal and unchangeable law, which they termed as the law of nature. Cicero borrowed it from them. He added" "There is, in fact, a true law, namely right reason, which in accordance with nature, applies to all men and is unchangeable and eternal. By its commands this law summons men to the performance of their duties, by its prohibitions it restricts them from doing wrong. Its commands and prohibitions always influence good men but are without effect upon the bad. To invalidate this law by human legislation is never morally right, nor is it permissible ever to restrict its operation, and to annul it is wholly impossible."[11]

This idea prevailed throughout the medieval period with the formal distinction that with the advent of Christianity, the law of nature *(jus naturale)* became the law of God (*jus divina*) as contained in the Bible. That is, the precepts of a rational, universal, eternal and immutable law were given a Biblical tapestry. It is, for this reason, that though St. Thomas Aquinas presented a fourfold classification of law (Eternal, Natural, Divine, Human), what he meant by eternal, natural and divine laws was the same what the Roman lawyers meant by their *jus naturale.* It is evident from his affirmation: "The very idea of the government of things in God, the Ruler of the Universe, has the nature of law. And since the divine reason's conception of things is not subject to time but is eternal, therefore, it is that kind of law that must be eternal."[12]

The meaning of the law of nature is thus well presented by two eminent writers on the subject of medieval political theory: "Justice is a principle of nature, a principle which lies behind all the order of the world, the expression of a universal principle behind all law. . . . There is a law which is the same as true reason accordant with nature, a law which is constant and eternal, which calls and commands to duty, which warns and terrifies men from the practice of deceit. This law is not one thing at Rome, another at Athens, but is eternal and immutable, the expression of the command and sovereignty of God. . . The people or the prince may make laws, but they have not the true character of *jus* unless they are derived from the ultimate law. The original source and the foundation of *jus* must be studied in that supreme law which came into being ages before any State existed."[13]

The idea of natural law continued to prevail even in the modern age. Social contractualists like Spinoza, Hobbes and Locke referred to it. What is, however, noticeable at this stage is that now natural law "was understood as quasi-geometrical or deductive system, resting on self-evident axioms about man's nature and place

11. Cited in G. H. Sabine: *A History of Political Theory* (New York: Harper, 1948), p. 164.
12. St. Thomas : *Summa Theologica.*1-11, q. 91; a 1.
13. See R.W. Carlyle and A.J. Carlyle: *A History of Medieval Political Theory in the West.* Vol. 1. pp. 5-6.

in the universe, and prescribing general rules for the dealings of man with man. Resting on the nature of man, it was held to be universal, valid without respect to time and place; and because it was said to be the law of reason, it was thought to provide irrefutable justification for any act or judgement that accorded with it. The legislator's duty was to enact natural law; the subject's to obey because (or to the extent that) it was so enacted."[14] In this way, the law of nature "was thought to be a system in which the reason moved progressively from higher order to lower order general rules, and thence to particular prescriptions."[15]

The idea of natural law witnessed its rejection in the nineteenth century when the exponents of the utilitarian and analytical schools insisted on the study of law in positive terms. Jeremy Bentham described the dogma of natural law and rights as mere 'rhetorical nonsense upon stilts', while John Austin defined law as 'the command of the sovereign'. The generation of the eighteenth century liberals realised that "the more general the rule, the vaguer it will be, and greater the possibility of disagreement when it is applied to a particular case."[16] The theory of natural law, they came to the conclusion, "sought an ultimate standard by which to test the justice of positive legal rules and decisions, a law behind the law; but in adopting geometry as its model, it misconceived the logical structure of systems where decisions are taken according to rules and confused the conclusion of a chain of reasoning with a decision taken after weighing evidence and argument."[17]

In the face of attack on the traditional theory of natural law, some jurists in the nineteenth century sought to update it by laying down, what came to be known, the 'doctrine of natural law with a variable content'. Instead of thinking of natural law as a body of theorems eliminating decisions, they defined it as a body of flexible general rules discoverable by rational reflection on man's nature, within which decisions are taken, and which operate variously under different conditions."[18] It may be visualised in the jurisprudence of Stammler who viewed society as constantly in a process of development towards a goal conceivable by human reason. In a bid to understand the flexibility of application of what human reason informs, he held that the actual content of right law varied infinitely. In his *Theory of Justice,* he said that the principal task of a jurist "is to find the criterion for 'right' law—or a methodical and well-founded judgement concerning the presence or absence of the equality of justice in a legal content."[19]

14. Benn and Peters, *op. cit.,* p. 63.
15. *Ibid.,* p. 64.
16. *Ibid.*
17. *Ibid.,* pp. 65-66.
18. *Ibid.,* p. 65.
19. See Coker, *op. cit.,* p. 528. As N. P. Barry says: 'The difficulty with the natural law theories of the absolutist kind is that of securing agreement on the ends which men ought to pursue. Natural lawyers often write as if their prescriptions were as necessary as the laws that govern the physical world but clearly that is not so. Natural law relates to human conduct and has, therefore, quite a different logic from scientific law; it is normative law; it is normative not predictive or discipline, and is, therefore, concerned with demonstrating those rules of *behaviour* which ought to be followed. But men's needs and desires change and actions which were regarded as universal by one generation may not be acceptable to another." *Introduction to Modern Political Theory* (London: Macmillan, 1981), p. 25.

Even this revised version of the theory of natural law failed to meet the fundamental deficiency. The problem remained that reason being abstract would inform different things to different persons under different circumstances. As such, there could be nothing like universal and eternal law. For instance, if the law of nature informed that all debts should be paid, it said nothing about how soon or in what form it ought to be done. Feeling thus, the community of the Positivists, in particular, came to hold: "We shall make no progress by alleging that somewhere, somehow, there is one right answer to the problem, established as part of the universal order independent of anyone's existence. Anyone adopting that view will be inclined to assume that the one right attitude is his own (for it would be odd to adopt a moral position without believing it to be the true one), and may be reluctant to accept any reconciliation that requires him to yield any ground at all."[20]

Analytical Theory: Law as the Command of the Sovereign

The significance of the natural theory of law has been overshadowed by the affirmations of the leading lights of the analytical school like Bodin, Hobbes, Bentham and Austin. Sharply contradistinguished from the theory of natural law, it uses the word 'law' in a positive sense *i.e.* it maintains that the laws with which the jurists or political scientists have to deal are the commands of a determinate political authority.[21] Also known by the name of the doctrine of 'legal positivism', it designates that only those norms "are juridically valid which have been established or recognised by the government of a sovereign state in the forms prescribed by its written or unwritten constitution. No Divine Law and no Natural Law is juridically valid, according to legal positivism, unless so recognised by the state or its government."[22]

In this category the name of a French thinker Jean Bodin occupies the first and foremost place. He very carefully ruled out the consideration of theological and metaphysical elements by explicitly pointing out that when he spoke of 'supreme' power *(legibus solutus)*, he meant by it something unrestrained by civil law. He contended that sovereignty alone was the supreme legislative authority whose foremost function was to give laws to citizens generally and individually, and it must be added, not necessarily with the consent of superiors, equals or inferiors. Thus, the 'Father' of the doctrine of sovereignty held that in every independent community governed by law, there "must be some authority, whether residing in one person or several, whereby the laws themselves are established and from which they proceed. And this power, being the source of law, must itself be above the law."[23]

However, this theory finds its eloquent manifestation in the works of Thomas Hobbes of England. He lays down that sovereign alone can make laws while he

20. Benn and Peters, *op. cit.*, p. 69. These writers hold: "If natural law theory does seek to establish necessary and sufficient conditions for obedience, it must fail, either because its *detailed* criteria cannot be applied universally without outraging our sense of what is fitting, or because they are too *general* to be a useful test." *Ibid.*
21. Coker, *op. cit.*, p. 523.
22. Arnold Brecht: *Political Theory: Foundations of Twentieth Century Political Thought* (Princeton: Princeton Univ., Press, 1965), pp. 182-83.
23. Fredrick Pollock: *An Introduction to the History of the Science of Politics*, (London: Macmillan, 1923), p. 47.

himself is above it. Obviously, nothing but the command of the sovereign can have the force of law. Law is the word of him who by right had command over others. As he says: "Civil law is, to every subject, those rules which the commonwealth has commanded him by word, writing or other sufficient sign of the will, to make use of for the distinction of right and wrong; that is to say, of what is contrary, and what is not contrary, to the rule."[24] According to his classic affirmation: "Covenants without the sword are but words, and of no strength to secure a man at all."[25]

The same idea finds its utilitarian affirmation in the works of Jeremy Bentham —'the reformer of the science of law'. According to him, law is the medium through which reconciliation of private and public interests can be maintained. How to reconcile the two is the problem of a legislator. The rights or obligations of man have to be balanced with punishments through law in such a way that in effect it leads to the greatest happiness of the greatest number. In his *Introduction to the Principles of Morals and Legislation,* he goes to the extent of holding that "rights so called are the creatures of law". It is the government that creates the 'obligations' and also the conditions whereby they can be realised by the individuals. It alone can place restrictions on the liberties of the people, or punish those who violate its laws.[26]

However, the best exposition of this theory is contained in the jurisprudence of John Austin who, in very clear terms, lays down that laws, properly so called, are a species of commands. He says that a command is "as a signification of desire... distinguished from other significations of desire by this peculiarity that the party to whom it is directed is liable to evil from the other, in case he comply not with the desire."[27] Furthermore, a signification of desire implies a determinate person or body of persons having the desire, while the definition of command implies that these persons have the ability to inflict the sanction on the disobedient, this being what is meant in saying that laws are addressed by 'superiors' to 'inferiors'.[28]

Though the positive theory of law is regarded as the most convincing of all theories on this subject, it suffers from two main weaknesses. In the first place, it lays too much reliance on positivism—that is, law is something put in very set or positive terms by the state whose violation is visited with punishment—and thereby ignores the force of laws or rules emanating from religion or custom or backed by the force of public opinion in view of their not being backed by the authority of 'a determinate human superior' or sovereign. Naturally, it makes their view rigid and introduces an element of conservatism in their juristic conclusion on the subject of law and the state. Then, the emphasis of the Positivists on the force of command confuses the distinction between law, as expected to be observed by the people, and order that may even provoke the people to destroy the political system. Laski is of the view that to think of laws as simply a command is even for the jurist "to strain definition to the verge of decency."[29]

24. Hobbes: *Leviathan,* Chapter 17.
25. *Ibid.*
26. Frank Thakurdas: *The English Utilitarians and the Idealists* (Delhi: Vishal, 1977), p.79.
27. H.A.L. Hart (ed.): *Austin's Province of Jurisprudence Determined* (London, 1954), p. 14.
28. *Ibid.*, p. 24,
29. Laski: *A Grammar of Politics* (London: George Allen and Unwin, 1951), p. 51.

Historical Theory: Law as a Result of Social Development

Different from the two standpoints, as seen in the preceding sections, is the historical theory that treats law as a result of the silent forces at work in society. In other words, law is neither authored by nature (or God), nor is it a deliberate creation of the state. In the correct sense, it is the result of the inevitable but imperceptible social development. If so, it is independent of, and anterior to, the state. As such, the function of the state is not to create law but merely to recognise and enforce it. Thus, an exponent of this theory like Gustav von Hugo rejected the traditional (natural) theory of law and in its place put a conception of laws determined by characteristics and experiences of a particular people.[30]

Mention may be made of Savigny, in this direction, who took law as 'the organ of folk-right' that moved and grew like every other expression of the life of the people; that was formed by custom and popular feeling, through the operation of silent forces and not by the arbitrary will of a legislator. Subscribing to the same view, Sir Henry Maine wrote his *Ancient Law* in which he sought to prove how modern law originated and developed from the ancient Roman habits, practices and institutions. For the same purpose, F.W. Maitland studied the history of the Middle Ages. Drawing inspiration from such sources, Bryce came to hold: "Law cannot be always and everywhere the creation of the State, because instances can be adduced where law existed in a community before there was any State."[31] Likewise, Sir Fredrick Pollock observes that law existed before the state and it had "any adequate means of compelling its observations and indeed before there was any regular process of enforcement at all."[32]

In other words, this theory holds that the law of the state is found in the process of historical evolution of a people. As such, the sanction behind law is the pressure of the will of the community. The laws of a state have their origin neither in a universal and unchanging reason, nor in the conscience of the people, nor in the 'commands of the sovereign', but in a national will or mind that reveals itself in the orderly practices of a community. Judges, informed by legal history, find out that law and make their decision accordingly. The courts play the chief part in building up the essential features of national law. Enacted law should be an informal embodiment of historical law. A legislative body, which confines itself to its proper field, merely decides what customary rules of conduct need formal definition in order to secure their better observance. Its task is to clarify the existing law or indicate certain particular applications and sanctions for social rules already in force.

The historical theory of law is partly correct and partly incorrect. Its merit lies in analysing the role of historical forces that play their part in the sphere of legal obligation. It also contributes to the understanding of the nature of law by emphasising that legal systems change and they should undergo modifications in order to meet new conditions. It, however, errs in ignoring or reducing the element of command to the point of a mere metaphor. We may not be entirely oblivious to the fact of imperativeness behind the premises of law. It may also be said that historical theory

30 See Coker, *op. cit.*, p. 523.

31. James Bryce: *Studies in History and Jurisprudence* (Oxford, 1951), Vol II, p. 249.

32. Fredrick Pollock: *First Book of Jurisprudence,* p.24.

assumes a conservative character because of its reverence for the past and its distrust for deliberate efforts directed at reform of the law and legal systems. It is hardly disputable that the analytical view, as compared to the affirmations of the historical school, is simple and straightforward.

Sociological Theory: Sanction of Law in the Canons of Relevance or Expediency

The sociological theory of law, in a sense, should be treated as an extension of the historical theory on this subject inasmuch as it argues that law is the product of social forces and, for this reason, must be studied in the light of social needs. It denies that law is made by an organised body of men, or that it is just the command of a determinate sovereign, rather it should be judged by its results than by certain abstract standards as we find in the case of natural theory on this subject. Thus, the state does not create law, it only imputes legal value to a rule or practice that grows out of social needs. If so, law has a pre-political character; its authority is superior to that of the state itself in this respect. In other words, law finds its sanction in the social needs as well as in the interests it serves.

The names of Duguit in France, Krabbe in Holland, Roscoe Pound and Justice Holmes in the United States and Laski in England are associated with this theory. To Duguit, law simply denotes the rules of conduct actually controlling men who live in society. Its obligations arise not from having commanded, expressly or by implication, by any organised authority but solely and directly from the necessities of social life. Likewise, Krabbe holds that the obligations of the people are based on the fact that men live in society and they must so live in order to survive, and that life in society requires a certain manner of conduct. Law is the totality of the rules, general or particular, written or unwritten, which spring from men's feelings or 'sense of right.' Thus, this theory of law accepts "no authority as valid except that of law;.... the sovereign disappears, as a source of law, from both legal and political theory."[33]

This theory has its advocates in the United States in Pound and Holmes. In discussing the broad social aspects of law, Dean Roscoe Pound regards law as an instrument for the furtherance of human welfare. The source of legal obligation, therefore, lies in man's awareness of the benefits that accrue to him by obeying the rules of social behaviour. Likewise, Justice Holmes suggests that we should consider not only what the laws are as they appear in the constitutions, statutes, and judicial decisions but also what effects they have produced in the past, how they operate today, and how they may be improved by deliberate human effort in time to come. Echoing such a reminder, Laski says: "We have to search for the mechanisms of our law in life as it actually is, rather than fit the life we live to *a priori* rules of rigid legal system."[34]

Simply stated, this theory insists that the essence of law is not logic but experience. The advocates of this theory describe the positivist conception of law as a pernicious

33. See Coker, *op. cit.*, p. 536.

34. Laski: *The Foundations of Sovereignty and Other Essays* (London: George Allen and Unwin, 1922), p. 261.

truth, a truism, or a barren and futile doctrine, since there are definite agencies in society which issue commands or make decisions normally obeyed by the bulk of the community. They argue that '"the convictions, beliefs, desires and prejudices of various people, in and out of office, enter into the determination of the rules laid down by political organs. Statutes reflect the ideas and wishes of the legislators or of persons whom the legislators like, respect, or fear."[35] The necessity of laws arises from the paramount consideration of guaranteeing security to the norms of social behaviour. Thus, they argue that the interrelations among individuals and groups in society are such that an organisation of unification and co-ordination "is necessary in order to fulfil adequately its essential functions, (which) must be comprehensive and compulsive in membership and be equipped with a power to issue commands that may be executed through the organised force of the community in the form, for example, of constraint directed against the body of an individual or distraint of his property; and this organisation must normally, within any given community, have a monopoly of that sort of power."[36]

This theory has the merit of emphasising the role of social needs in the sphere of legal obligation. It cannot be denied that law exists to serve social purposes and people obey it because of their 'sense of right'. However, the weakness of this theory lies in its ignoring what the advocates of imperative theory so strongly affirm. We cannot lose sight of the role of force that lies behind law and which is a result of the will of the sovereign authority. To say that law is prior or anterior to the state is to misunderstand the significance of the analytical theory. It is true that a sovereign pays respect to the fact of social purpose, it is equally true that he launches the campaign of social reform and, for this purpose, makes laws that ban obsolete conventions, or place severe restrictions on the bad practices of the people. Thus, we may not detach law from the fact of the existence of a coercive power vested in the state that refutes the idea of law being prior, or anterior, to the existence of political authority.

Marxian Theory: Law as an Instrument of Class Exploitation and Oppression

Fundamentally different from certain theories on the nature of law and legal obligation, as discussed in the preceding sections, is the doctrine of Marxism that first integrates law with the state and then integrates both with the economic and social structure of a community. According to Marx, the economic structure constitutes the real basis upon which the political and juridical superstructures are built. Since legal relationships are rooted in the material conditions of life, laws merely express the will and interests of the dominant class. Thus, the statutes of the state are the forms wherein the dominant class in a given society imposes obligations on all the other classes to conduct themselves in a manner advantageous and pleasing to itself. As Marx says: "Law is an expression of society's general interests and needs, as they emerge from a given material means of production."[37]

Owing to this, the legal system of a 'socialist' country is at fundamental variance with that of a liberal-democratic country. We may refer to the case of the former

35. Coker, *op. cit.*, p. 540.
36. *Ibid.*, pp. 540-41.
37. See A. Y. Vyshinsky: *The Law of the Soviet State* (New York: Macmillan, 1948), p. 37.

Soviet Union where, according to Lenin, law was considered as the expression of what was expedient for the construction of socialism and to fight for it. According to a leading Soviet jurist, A.Y. Vyshinsky, a court of whatever sort was an organ of the class dominant in a given state depending on and guiding its interests.[38] If so, law has a special and peculiar sense in a socialist country like China. It becomes an instrument of exploitation and oppression by one class over another. If the bourgeois class used it like this in the pre-revolutionary phase, the proletariat will do the same in the revolutionary phase of social development.[39] Hence, there is nothing like constitutional law distinguished from ordinary law, or a public law distinguished from private law in such a country. Julian Towster affirmed that after the victory of socialism there could be no juxtaposition of public and private rights and interests in the Soviet society. The interests of the state, society and personality were synthesised in a new unity. Hence, all branches of law were a part and parcel of the same uniform law—Soviet law.[40]

In other words, Marx's theory of law is a corollary to his general view of the state. If the political power is merely the 'organised power of one class for oppressing another',[41] law becomes an instrument for the same purpose. Influenced by the philosophy of Marxism, Laski holds that if the will of the State, for all practical purposes, implies the decision of the government, and the government means the power with the dominant class of the society, naturally the supreme coercive power of the state must be so used as to subserve the interest of the class in power. Law is, therefore, used as an instrument that determines class relations of the society. As such, in a bourgeois society, the ultimate purpose of law "is always concerned with conferring legal right upon some method of distributing what is produced by the economic process. Behind the title implicit in any given system, the State puts all the force at its command. It makes the barren title of law actual by satisfying its demands."[42]

In this regard, we may depend upon the statement of a communist writer who says: "Law is the totality of *obligatory* standards and rules of behaviour of people in society. These rules are expressed in corresponding laws which are safeguarded by the state and its numerous instruments of compulsion and education. Law, like politics, arose with classes and the state. It is the will of the ruling class expressed in legal forms and it defends the political and economic interests of the ruling class. The history of antagonistic class society has known slave, feudal and capitalist law, each of which served the exploiters in their struggle against the exploited. Only

38. *Ibid.*, p. 500. The law of the Soviet state stood in sharp contrast to the theories of law acceptable to the liberal-democratic countries which, according to Russian jurists, were artificial, unscientific, perverse and false. In the words of A.Y. Vyshinsky, all liberal theories of state disguised the class-exploiting character of the bourgeois law. "By phrases about the 'general welfare' and 'social' and 'popular' interests, they strive to conceal the fact that bourgeois law, that subtle and poisoned instrument which defends the interests of the exploiters, is oppressive and hostile to the people." *Ibid.*, p. 6.
39. Karpinsky: *The Social and State Structure of the USSR*, p. 194.
40. Towster: *Political Power in the USSR*, p. 116.
41. Marx and Engels; *Communist Manifesto*, p. 72.
42 Laski: *The State in Theory and Practice* (London: George Allen and Unwin, 1960), p. 199.

socialist law expresses the interests of the working people and is the true law of the people....Socialist law and the legal ideas underlying it radically differ from the law and legal ideas of antagonistic class societies. They express the interests of the entire people, protect and help to consolidate the economic basis of socialism, socialist property, and teach the people to observe the law and conscientiously do their duty. The socialist system is incompatible with lawlessness and contempt for the interests of the individual, and therefore the Socialist state and the Communist Party constantly reinforce socialist law and order and brook no attempts to violate it."[43]

The merit of this theory lies in its integration of the principle of legal obligation with the general character of the society. It is this theory alone that puts emphasis on the economic structure of the society that has its decisive impact on the organisation and working of political and legal institutions. However, it suffers from certain grave weaknesses. For instance, its denunciation of the state, and of law as its corollary, in the name of being an instrument of exploitation and oppression by one class over another may not convince the advocates of a liberal-democratic order. It may also be said that the Marxian theory ruthlessly rejects the case of the rule of law that is considered as the hallmark of a democratic order. The view of Marx, as advocated by the communist leaders and implemented in a 'socialist' country like the former USSR, may prevail only in a totalitarian system. Moreover, what applies to Marx's theory of state as a whole may be invoked here too that he "did not work out a satisfactory theory of power in a capitalist society."[44]

Problem of Legal Obligation: Kelsen's Theory of Pure Law

Various theories on the subject of the nature of law, as briefly discussed in the preceding sections, have their own points of strength and weakness.[45] A pertinent question at this stage arises as to which of them should be regarded as the most convincing theory of legal obligation. A possible answer to such a question lies in linking the essential element of the analytical theory with others on this subject so that a synthesised picture may emerge with the essential merits of all. Coercion plays a really important part. For this reason, a convincing theory of legal obligation must take it as a self-evident truth. However, mere coercion is not enough. We should also look into the factor of the acquiescence of the people that issues forth in the form of their usages, customs, habits and the like. It is owing to this that people accept law and regulate their behaviour accordingly, or they rise in revolt to violate a 'black law' and pay even with their lives to defend and preserve their well-established traditions.

43 V. G. Afanasyev: *Marxist Philosophy* (Moscow: Progress Publishers, 1978), pp. 372-73.

44. Alan Swingewood: *Marx and Modern Political Theory* (London: Macmillan, 1975), p 139.

45. Besides major theories on the subject as discussed here, there are two more theories. The name of Joseph Kohler is associated with the Philosophical School who desires to make the study of law in actual as well as metaphysical terms. To him the idea of law is necessarily concerned with the norm of justice. As such, a jurist is as much concerned with the ideal as with the actual content of law. Law is, therefore, an idea, and the purpose of a juristic philosopher is to think in terms of building an ideal system. The name of Paul Vinogrodoff is associated with the Comparative School on this subject. To him generalisations can be obtained by examining and comparing various legal systems and practices of the past as well as of the present. This theory also seeks help from other social sciences to enrich the scope of its subject.

In this direction, we may refer to the 'pure theory of law' as enunciated by Hans Kelsen that, in a sense, seeks to offer an improvement upon the 'command theory' of Austin by avoiding its severe difficulties. The most outstanding feature of this theory is that the proposition of 'a determinate human superior' of Austin is replaced by a 'norm'. A legal system is a normative hierarchy in which the creation of one norm—the lower one—is determined by another—the higher—the creation of which is determined by a still higher 'norm' and this *regressus* is terminated by the highest, the basic norm which, being the supreme reason of validity of the whole legal order, constitutes its unity.[46] The basic norm is nothing but the fundamental rule according to which "the various norms of the order are to be created."[47]

In other words, Kelsen lays down the doctrine of a legal postulate. His main reliance is on the element of a 'norm' that may be anything from the will of the Parliament (as in England) to that of the whim of the Court (as in the United States) in view of the fact that the 'basic norm' must be valid inasmuch as without this presupposition no human act could be interpreted as a legal, especially a norm-creating act.[48] The normative interpretation of Kelsen assumes a thoroughly empirical character when he says: "The basic norm of a national legal order is not the arbitrary product of juristic imagination. Its content is determined by facts....Legal norms are considered to be valid only if they belong to an order which is by and large efficacious....The validity of a legal order is thus dependent upon agreement with reality, upon its efficacy."[49]

Viewed from a critical standpoint, it may be said that Kelsen's theory of pure law is not free from defect inasmuch as it lays too much reliance on some 'norm'. The confusion, therefore, continues to persist and one may quarrel on the real meaning of this 'legal postulate'. Moreover, it may also be doubted whether law can be raised to the level of a science by means of empiricism as suggested by him. Law and its obligation cannot be studied in terms of natural sciences. However, the meaning of the term 'norm' may be extended so as to mean several things like 'social needs and purposes', 'age-old established customs and practices of the community', 'imperative will of the sovereign' and the like. As we shall see in the following sections, the theory of legal obligation includes within itself the case of moral obligation as well. Hence, a proper theory of legal obligation must not depend exclusively upon the factor of 'the command of the sovereign', nor should it ignore this most important factor in its entirety. The plausible course is to suggest that though both (legal and moral) spheres are different, elements of bindingness are common. Thus, to speak in a legal context that a law is binding "is to say that it satisfies the criteria of validity of a given legal system."[50]

46. See Kelsen: *General Theory of Law and State,* p. 124.
47. Benn and Peters, *op. cit.,* p. 78.
48. *Ibid.*
49. *Ibid.,* pp. 78-79.
50. *Ibid.* p. 87. As Barker says: "But when once it is made, by whatever bodies, and when in addition it is steadily imposed by the recognition and enforcement of the courts, law possesses the attribute of validity and produces an effect of obligation. *Valet* – its injunction avails and prevails; oblige – it binds men to an engagement of performing what is enjoined." *Principles of Social and Political Theory,* p. 97.

Specific Kinds of Law

Law has been classified into various forms according to the basis taken by a juristic thinker on this subject. For instance, on the basis of the relations which it seeks to adjust between the people and their organised communities, it has been described as of two varieties—national and international. Then, on the basis of the manner of its formulation and the sanctity behind it, law is divided into two more varieties—constitutional and ordinary. Then, keeping in view the nature of the wrong committed by a person and the availability of the remedy to undo its evil effect, law is further divided into two varieties—civil and criminal. One may also keep in consideration the idea of the creator of the law and the nature of its premises and then come to divide it into two categories—natural and positive.

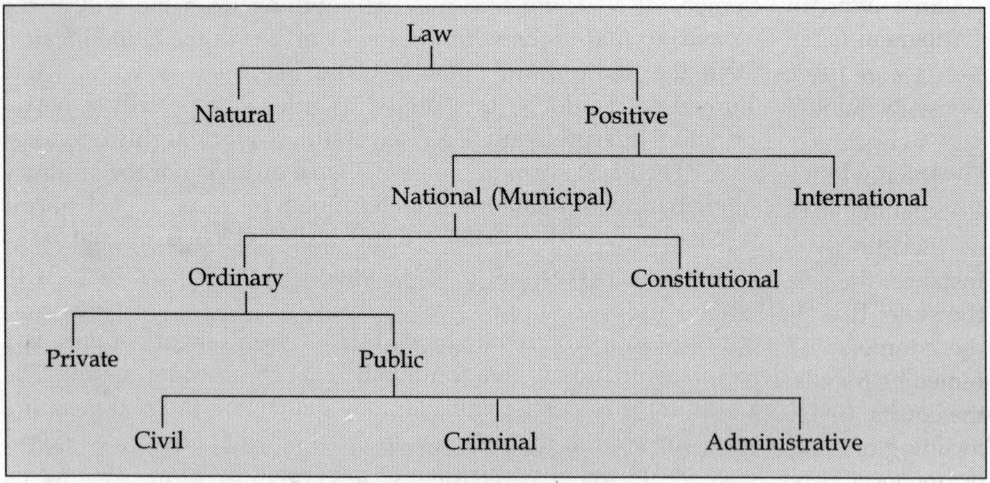

A neat and watertight classification may hardly be presented on this subject, though we may point out the essential varieties of law in the following manner :

1. **Natural Law and Positive Law:** While the former is abstract on account of being authored by nature or some supernatural agency, the latter is concrete for the reason of being a creation of man. As such, while the dictates of natural law are understandable by the rational faculty of man as 'written into the heart of man by the finger of God', the positive law can be easily understood as it is written and has its place in the statute book. It is called positive, for its terms are quite specific. Moreover, while the former has its sanction in respect for or fear of some metaphysical power, the latter is enforced by the sovereign authority. For this reason too, it is called determinate or positive.
2. **National Law and International Law:** A law formulated by the sovereign authority and applicable to the people living within its territorial jurisdiction is called national (or municipal) law. It determines the private and public relations of the people living in a state. Different from this, international law regulates the conduct of states in their intercourse with each other. Both are man-made laws. However, the essential point of difference between the two lies in that while the former has the force of a sovereign authority on its back, the latter derives its sanction from the good sense of the civilised nations of the world.

3. **Constitutional Law and Ordinary Law:** While both are laws of the state, they differ from each other in respect of the sanctity attached to them. While the former has a higher status on account of being a part of the constitution of the land, the latter occupies a lower place and has to keep itself in consonance with the former. The former may be partly written by some constitutional convention and partly unwritten on account of being in the form of well-established practices, the latter is a creation of the legislative organ or of some other authority having delegated powers. It is a different matter that in a country like United Kingdom there is no difference between the two, because there is an unwritten constitution.
4. **Civil Law and Criminal Law:** While the former deals with a civil wrong committed by a person going to harm the interests of another like non-payment of dues or violation of the terms of a contract, the latter relates to the criminal acts of a person like theft, robbery and murder. In both cases, the procedure is different.
5. **Private Law and Public Law:** According to Holland, while the former is concerned with the relations between individuals, the latter involves the state. Public law is concerned with the organisation of the state, the limits on the functions of the government and the relations between the state and its citizens. Private law regulates relations between individuals only.

Besides these major varieties, we may also speak about other forms of law. For instance, there is administrative law that determines the relations of the officials to the state. It is that part of public law which fixes the organisation and determines the competence of the administrative authorities and indicates to the person the remedies for the violation of his rights. Then, there is the case-law or law made by the courts. In certain situations, the court gives its own view to clarify or explain the meaning of a legal provision. Out of such interpretations, made whether consciously or unconsciously, a new kind of law comes into existence known as case-law. It has its place in the decisions of the courts. Sometimes, the weight of a local usage is too strong to be accepted by the court, sometimes the court is guided by the canon of equity or natural justice. Thus comes into existence, what is known, 'common law' in England.

Law and Scientific Value Relativism: Empirical Determination or Legal Positivism

If the term 'law' denotes a 'set of rules' laid down by nature, or 'written into the hearts of men by the finger of God', or evolved out of the age-old established practices of the people, or formulated by some 'determinate human superior', a question arises as to how it can be reconciled with the doctrine of scientific value relativism that seeks to determine the relativity between realisable value-judgements and the ultimate standards guiding them whose validity is not scientifically verifiable.[51] An answer to such a question lies in this affirmation that law has a value of its own which is both absolute (that is, determined by mind or will or possibly grasped by faith, intuition or instinct) and qualified (that is, specific and circumscribed by qualifying provisions), it is the latter and not the former that may be put to empirical

51. Arnold Brecht, *op cit,*, p. 118.

tests and, therefore, be taken closer to the doctrine of scientific value relativism. Obviously, not a law as authored by nature or some supernatural agency like God embodying 'ultimate' or 'highest' value but positive law as formulated by the state involving qualified value can be subjected to empirical investigations. Scientific value relativism, in this context, "designates the theory that only those norms are juridically valid which have been established or recognised by the government of a sovereign state in the forms prescribed by its written or unwritten constitution. No Divine Law and no Natural Law is juridically valid, according to legal positivism, unless so recognised by the state or its government."[52]

If so, relationship of scientific value relativism can be established with legal positivism inasmuch as it is concerned exclusively with a set of specific rules formulated by a determinate authority. The terms of such a law are quite specific and the obedience to them is binding. The value of such a law is, therefore, qualified as well as determinate. As such, the validity of such a law at a given time and place can be determined in the context of the legal system of a country and the philosophy working behind it. For this reason, we find that while in a liberal-democratic country, positive law regulates the behaviour of the people without suppressing their essential freedoms as a matter of deliberate policy, in a communist country, the law of the state does it in the name of bringing about a particular social, economic and political order conducive to the existence of true socialism. The fact, however, remains that whether it is a liberal-democratic or a communist system, it is the positive law that can be taken in conjunction with the doctrine of scientific value relativism.

There may, however, arise a case when the relationship between the concept of positive law and the doctrine of scientific value relativism may not be established. Mention, in this direction, may be made of the utilitarian theory of jurisprudence of Jeremy Bentham who connects the case of the validity of the law of the state with the consideration of the greatest happiness of the greatest number. The formula of Bentham, one may rightly say, is too abstract to be put to a scientific investigation. It is, however, a different matter to say that, as Bentham denounces the law of nature as 'mere rhetorical nonsense upon stilts', his formula of general utility is not an abstract proposition and the benefits and harms of a particular law may, therefore, be put to an empirical investigation.

The subject of law, despite its having a normative character, can, in this way, be made a matter of scientific investigation so far as its value to the people or its validity in a given time and place are concerned. It may be visualised in the following important directions:

1. As we have already seen, law is broadly of two categories— natural (or divine) and man-made (or positive)—and it is the latter that has its relationship with the doctrine of scientific value relativism. Instances can be gathered and data collected to show that a particular law was accepted or opposed by the people for such and such reasons. A scientific analysis of the situation may thus enable a student of jurisprudence to say that the validity of a certain law comes from such a source or not. If examined in a particular context, we may come to the

52. *Ibid.*, p. 183.

point that Bentham was not a utopian thinker when he connected the idea of legal obligation with the norm of general utility.

2. It is on the application of a scientific standard that we may make divisions and subdivisions of law into national and international law, or civil and criminal law, or ordinary and constitutional law, and the like.
3. The problem of legal obligation can be studied in empirical terms. Why do people obey law? Conversely, why do they oppose it? These are the questions that may be answered by a student indulging in normative as well as empirical exercises. For instance, while having a normative approach, one may say that people obey law, whether natural or positive, on account of their 'faith'; a man of empirical orientation may find the element of 'faith' too abstract to be put to some scientific investigation, but he may definitely collect enough evidence to prove that the facts of legal obligation lie in the good sense, habits, instincts as well as fear-psychosis of the people.

A peculiar impression in this regard, however, is that while the doctrine of scientific value relativism finds the source of the validity of law in some concrete measure and it rejects the 'ultimate' or 'highest' standards of value, the same conclusion curiously assumes the character of an absolute value in the realm of positive political theory. For instance, the very affirmation that only the command of a sovereign authority makes a law is absolutist in character. Political and legal positivism, on the one hand, and scientific value relativism, on the other, therefore, develop a point of fundamental distinction in the sense that while the former tends to identify the sanction of scientifically determined value with a standard of highest value, the latter denies verifiability of 'absolute' value by any empirical standard.[53]

Law and Liberty: Problem of Proper Reconciliation

The question relating to the proper relationship between law and liberty has engaged the attention of eminent thinkers.[54] However, the views on this subject may be divided into three categories. While the Anarchists and the Syndicalists have gone to the extent of undermining the state with its legal and judicial system as blocks into the way of the liberty of the individuals, others like the Socialists and the Idealists have gone to the opposite extreme of emphasising the fact of organic relationship between liberty of the individual and the law of the state. In between the two, there are the Individualists who denounce law as antithetical to the essential liberties of the individual and yet concede that state being 'a necessary evil', law should be so framed as to regulate the most essential spheres of human life and leave the rest undisturbed so that people may exercise their free initiative.

In the first place, we take up the notion of the rank anti-authoritarians. Mention may be made of the leading Anarchists like Proudhon, Bakunin, and Kropotkin who denounce the state as an instrument of violence and desire a classless and stateless society in which there is neither state, nor government, nor law, nor anything of the

53. Brecht, *op. cit.*, pp. 184-85.
54. For a detailed treatment of the subject of liberty in the context of its real meaning see Chapter 8.

Law and Liberty

The liberty which a citizen enjoys is to be measured, not by the nature of government machinery he lives under, whether representative or other, but by the relative paucity of the restraints it imposes on him.

—**Herbert Spencer.**
Man Versus State, p. 54.

Civil law is to every subject those rules which the commonwealth has commanded him by word, writing, or other sufficient sign of the will, to make use of, for the distinction of right and wrong; that is to say, of what is contrary, and what is not contrary to the rule.

—**Thomas Hobbes.**
Leviathan, Ch. 17.

Civil disobedience is an overt and public act; it aims to break a law in order 'to make a point' rather than in an attempt to get away with it.

—**Andrew Heywood**
Political Theory: An Introduction, p. 180.

sort that undermines the enjoyment of real liberty. Law implies restraints. As restraint of any kind undermines liberty, there should be no law at all. The Anarchists claim that only in a society without authority of any kind, individual "would be able to develop his full nature and to realise all that he has it in him to be. This complete development of individuality would be rendered possible by the entire absence of external restraints: the individual would, in fact, for the first time, be really free."[55] Influenced by the philosophy of Proudhon, the Syndicalists hold that the workers as producers should exercise control not only in the economic but also in the political sphere, or, to put it more accurately, the political sphere with its organ of state should cease to exist as such, and that its functions should be taken over by the bodies of producers organised on a vocational basis.[56]

A somewhat modified view in this respect is furnished by the Individualists who treat law as antithetical to the liberty of the individual and yet find it essential for the maintenance of peace and order in the state. The names of John Stuart Mill, Adam Smith and David Ricardo may be mentioned in this connection who desire minimum possible restraints on the life of an individual. Mill says: "Mankind are greater gainers by suffering each other to live as seems good to themselves, than by compelling each to live as seems good to the rest."[57] The case of Herbert Spencer is an exception in this direction who carries the philosophy of Individualism to the extreme by adding that law is a 'sin' and that the legislators are 'sinners'.[58] The statute book, he laments, is a record of 'unhappy guesses'.[59]

On the other side, there is the view of the Socialists who hold that law and liberty are complementary. There can be no liberty without law. If liberty lies in restraints, it is law that lays down conditions in which people may do and enjoy what is so

55. C.E.M. Joad: *Modern Political Theory* (London: Oxford Univ. Press, 1946), pp. 101-102.
56. *Ibid.,* p. 64.
57. *Ibid.,* p. 28.
58. J W. Garner: *Political Science and Government* (Calcutta: World Press, 1952), p. 158.
59. *Ibid.*

worthy in their collective existence. Liberty, as conceived by the Anarchists and the Syndicalists is a misnomer, it is nothing else than 'license' or man's freedom to do what he wills. In a real sense, liberty has its social connotation and, as such, it lives within restraints imposed by some authority for the interest of all. Naturally, the law of the state is the protector of the liberty of the individuals. Locke, therefore, said: "Where there is no law, there is no freedom." In this connection, we may appreciate the view of Laski who says that law comes very close to the world of liberty that demands the observance of 'common rules' which bind the conduct of men in their civilised collective life.[60] It is the rules of convenience framed in the interest of all that constitute "the conditions of freedom. They define its limits and possibilities. Instead, the restraints they impose are, in fact, the basis of liberty. No restraint, no liberty."[61]

An extreme position, in this regard, has been taken by the Idealists who admire law as the essential condition for the maintenance and enjoyment of real liberty. Rousseau says: "Obedience to a law which we prescribe to ourselves is liberty." Kant and Hegel advise us to obey law as it denotes the externalisation of our freedom. Green says that man is free when he obeys the law of which he himself is the author and which he obeys from the impulse of his self-perfection. He goes to the extent of adding that there should be a strong legal and judicial system to correct the erratic behaviour of an individual so that he can be 'forced to be free' when he acts otherwise. Likewise, D.G. Ritchie says: "Liberty in the sense of positive opportunity for self-development is the creation of law and not something that could exist apart from the action of the State."[62]

It follows that liberty in order to be real has got to be limited and this is possible only when the concepts of law and liberty are properly integrated. Peaceful and progressive social existence demands certain checks on the reckless behaviour of the individuals. Hence, one has to pay the price for enjoying his freedom and it lies in obedience to law. So long as an individual feels that law is an external compulsion devised for the benefit of a particular section of the community, he is bound to nurse certain grievances and it is the accumulation of such discontent that results in the violation of law and its concomitant disturbance in the liberty of his fellow beings. The legal machinery is, therefore, the best safeguard to preserve the system of rights that ensure liberty of the individuals. Naturally, a paradoxical situation arises that law is needed as a constraint to constrain the distraction of liberty. This is also known by the name of 'rule of law.'[63]

60. See Harold J. Laski: *A Grammar of Politics* (London: George Allen and Unwin, 1951), Chapter 4.
61. See Frank Thakurdas: *Recent English Political Theory* (Calcutta: Minerva, 1972), p. 335.
62. Ritchie: *Natural Rights* (London: George Allen and Unwin, 1903) pp. 139-140.
63. See Benn and Peters, *op. cit.*, p. 213. The aim of the rule of law doctrine is that citizens should know how laws will affect them. Laws should be perfectly *general* in form so that no individual or group is specifically picked out for preferential treatment; they should treat people equally: they should not be retrospective in application; and all laws should bind everyone, including governments. The last point links the rule of law to the idea of *constitutionalism* and may be exemplified by the systems of government that have a rigorous separation of powers, written constitutions and other devices to limit the actions of officials by general rules. It should be clear that the doctrine in principle is in conflict with the notion of sovereignty as traditionally understood since in a sovereign system, although the unlimited power of Parliament is authorised by the rule of the recognition, the legislative body is permitted to do things which are in conflict with the rule of law." Barry, *op. cit.*, p. 43.

How the law and liberty should be properly reconciled is, for this reason, an important question of political theory. It is the law that destroys the liberty of the people as we find in a totalitarian system, it defends and preserves the liberty of the individuals in a liberal-democratic order. The problem of legal obligation, therefore, finds its proper solution in the affirmation that the state based on the general will should devise its legal machinery in a way so that obedience to law is sincerely associated with the consent of the people. In this way, legal and political obligations have their genuine reconciliation. We know that people rise in revolt and disturbances of a very serious nature follow if they refuse to obey a law which they denounce as a 'black' or 'draconian measure'. We may appreciate the view: "So long as the actions of the State are in the interest of the common good, the disobedient individual can be forced to be free, for even when he is being compelled, he is constrained in his own true interest."[64]

Law and Morality: A Delicate Problem of Proper Relationship

The matter relating to the proper relationship between law and morality is a very delicate one. It is owing to this that law and morality differ from each other in their content, sanction and definiteness. While law (positive law) is concerned with the outward acts of man, the morality is with his inner motives. In other words, while law is concerned with the regulation of the objective behaviour of man, morality has its connection with the subjective aspect of the same. As such, while the purpose of law is to restrain a man from doing a crime like theft or burglary, the purpose of morality is to save him from committing a sin like speaking untruth or practising ingratitude. Moreover, the two differ in respect of their application. While law is universal in character and, as such, it is applicable to a large number of people in a uniform measure, morality has its application to individual cases and, as such, it differs from man to man and from group to group. Thus, law is quite specific and its terms are very clear, whereas morality is rather ambiguous and uncertain. Above all, while the former is mandatory as it is backed by the authority of the sovereign, the latter has an optional character having its source of sanction in the good sense or conscience of the people.

Despite these important points of difference, law and morality are related to each other. However, while dealing with this relationship, we must differentiate natural law from positive law in view of the fact that while the former is quite identifiable with morality, the latter is and is also not. Both morality and natural law are unwritten; they have their source in the rational nature of man and, by virtue of this fundamental trait, they are of universal application. The two, for this reason, are interchangeable. In ancient Greece, Socrates insisted that the individual should accept only those rules which he himself could justify. Likewise, Protagoras suggested that whatever their civic allegiances, all individuals were bound by a common bond by virtue of being reasonable creatures. In other words, it was believed that all men shared a certain common 'nature' whatever conventions they happened to live under. The Stoics, in a similar vein, argued that all men were equal in the eye of the law of nature. Thus came into being a sort of moral code having a set of unwritten rules to be regarded as universally applicable and rationally acceptable to the individual.

64. Asirvatham, *op. cit.*, p. 192.

In this way, natural law and morality became one and they exerted a simplifying and humanising influence on the Roman *jus gentium* (law common to all nations)—a practical system of law developed to regulate dealings with those foreign peoples with whom Rome was brought into contact through her commercial and military expansions. These precepts received a religious sanction with the advent of Christianity. Later with the development of theology, the system of natural law "came to be regarded by St. Thomas Aquinas as a selection from God's rules which could be rationally discerned and which did not need to be supernaturally) revealed. It was appealed to by the more philosophically minded of the clergy to humanise, and others to condemn current laws and customs."[65] Thus, the law of nature "provided a system of universal principles binding on kings and subjects alike to which appeal could be made on calling in question the justice of laws."[66]

The situation is, however, different when we take up the issue of relationship between morality and positive law. We have seen that with the coming of 'new knowledge', people gradually adopted a 'scientific' outlook and, as such, they lost their faith in the existence of a universal law that was at one with the precepts of morality. Now arose the difficulty of reconciling the implications of unwritten morality with the dictates of a written law. The liberal thinkers took it into view that the two were different inasmuch as the sphere of one could never be coincidental with the sphere of the other. What they aimed at justifying was that morality was always an individual affair and, in relation to the whole, it presented a situation of which the political fact was never more than an aspect. Mention in this connection must be made of the Idealists, like Kant and Green, who laid stress on the doctrine of state's function to hinder the hindrances to good life. In practical terms it implied that law had nothing to do with the regulation of the 'inner life' of an individual. Green insisted that the function of government "is to maintain conditions of life in which morality shall be possible, and morality consists in the disinterested performance of self-imposed duties."[67]

We may say that while the theory of natural law has become outdated, the Idealistic view is too abstract to present a realistic form of the relationship between law and morality. As a matter of fact, the two are related to each other in certain respects, and not in certain others. The two are related in the sense that law seeks to enforce what is desired by a norm of morality. For instance, morality requires that one should not practise unfair means in one's public life and in order to make it mandatory law prohibits fraud and cheating. In this way, a precept of morality is enforced by a coercive legal authority. The two are also related in the sense that law cannot undermine or violate a well-established norm of morality. Laski has made a point that the English Parliament, despite being a sovereign authority, can not make a law that all blue-eyed babies be exposed to the sun or thrown into the seas. In his words, it "becomes clear that if the state is to be a moral entity, it must be built on the organised acquiescence of its members."[68]

---

65. See Benn and Peters, *op. cit.*, p. 27.
66. *Ibid.*, p. 28.
67. See E. Barker: *Political Thought in England* (London: Oxford Unversity Press, 1951), p. 37.
68. See H.J. Laski: *A Grammar of Politics*, (London: George Allen and Unwin, 1977), p. 62.

Law and Morality

The relationship between law and morality is one of the thorniest problems in political theory.

—Andrew Heywood,
Political Theory: An Introduction, p. 156.

Morality consists in a life according to reason: the words of reason are the moral code. The law which is one with reason must, therefore, also be one with the moral code.

—Ernest Barker,
The Political Thought of Plato and Aristotle, p. 321.

To maintain that we must deliberately plan modern society, because it has become so complex is, therefore, paradoxical, and the result of complete misunderstanding of these circumstances. The fact is, rather that we can preserve an order of such complexity not by the method of directing the members, but only indirectly by enforcing and improving the rules conducive to the formation of a spontaneous order.

—F.A. von Hayek,
Law, Legislation and Liberty, Vol. I. pp. 50-51.

It, however, does not imply that law is subordinate to morality in each and every situation. Though most of the norms of traditional morality have been translated into terms of law and it is true that law cannot, and also should not, invade the sphere of morality, there may arise situations calling for urgent social reform along new lines. If the state undertakes to bring about a new social order, it may well make laws to break or revise the norms of morality as Kemal Ataturk did in Turkey by modernising the Islam, Nehru did in India to reform Hindu personal law, or communist leaders like Lenin did in Russia and Mao in China to usher in a new system. Such a case, however, needs proper restatement. It does not leave an impression of the law being above the canons of morality; it simply means that the former has gone ahead of the latter. In due course, people develop new outlooks about a radical legislation and then law and morality become coincidental with each other.

In brief, we may say that it is always good that law and morality live like coincidental affairs in view of the fact that people rise in revolt against a law that goes to undermine or invade the sphere of their morality. However, if the time calls for change, the machinery of law should also be redevised so as to fulfil the main task of a political organisation—civilising man. Law cannot cover total sphere of morality in view of the fact that "to turn all moral obligations into legal obligations would be to destroy morality."[69] If there is an urgent need to bring about a new order not in consonance with the established norm of morality, proper climate should be made, or people be trained to think along the lines of reform so that, sooner or later, the principle of legal obligation is joined in harmony with the premises of the ethical system of the society. As Barker says: "In order that law may be valid, it is enough that it should satisfy the canons of declaration, recognition and enforcement by a constituted authority acting on behalf of the community. In order that it may have

69. R.M. Maclver: *The Modern State* (London; Oxford University Press, 1962), p. 157.

value, over and above validity, law must also satisfy—*as much as it can, and so far as its strength avails*—the canon of conformity to the demands of moral conscience as expressed in the general notion of justice."[70]

Critical Appreciation

The subject of law, as discussed under different heads and in varying perspectives, may be subjected to certain lines of criticism.

1. In spite of having an importance of its own in the realm of political theory, the subject under our study is beset with the problem of a precise definition of the term 'law'. The controversy over the relationship between the two arises principally from different senses in which the term 'law' is used. According to Coker, "No word in social theory is used with a greater variety of meanings. Some writers apply the term to rules of social conduct which everywhere men of normal intelligence and disposition understand and ordinarily obey independently of any pressure from the organs of political government. Others—notably certain anthropologists describing primitive societies—apply the term to any uniformity of social behaviour. Still others consider that laws are the rules that have the stamp of some moral approval—a sense of right of the community, or of the majority of the right-minded part of the community; or laws are, for each individual, the dictates of his own conscience. Others, again, call laws the customs that have certain social consequences or tendencies—the 'behaviour patterns' that tend towards 'social solidarity', or that make possible the line of civilisation. With others, laws are the rules that are backed by the comprehensive and compulsive social institutions we call the State."[71]
2. Another perplexing problem in the study of law is created by the idea of the law of nature. Not only the word 'law' but its variety called 'law of nature'has been a source of great confusion ever since its inception in the days of ancient Greeks and Romans. What it really connotes remained a subject of verbal understating till the close of the Middle Ages despite the fact that it exerted a lot of influence on legal and political thinking of the times. One may say that its general contours could be deciphered inasmuch as they related to the dictates of reason, or he may come to face hazards when he finds its use at the hands of modern thinkers like Hobbes and Locke in sharply different senses. Thus, the elements of confusion and inconsistency persist. In order to get out of the predicament, a student of politics or jurisprudence identifies the law of nature with the code of morality and in that case it fails to be included in the category of law. And in case the doctrine of natural law "looks beyond the particular judgement to an independently existing moral order, it is either

70. E. Barker: *Principles of Social and Political Theory,* p. 117. Nevertheless, Prof. Salmond has given abundant proof that justice is the ultimate guide by which law is judged and that law is the basic technique by which justice may be achieved. In this sense, justice is a guide to the moral, fundamental, civilised expectations of man. The purpose of an ideal system of law is, or ought to be, justice. Justice means the existence of ideal relations among men and between men and state. *Jurisprudence* (London, 1947), X Ed., p. 41.
71. Coker, *op. cit.,* p. 541.

barren, declaring the existence of unknowable, and therefore useless standards, or it leads to a rigid dogmatism which, so far from settling arguments, can only embitter them."[72]

3. Though law is a very important institution whereby the state regulates the behaviour of its citizens, it would, however, be too much to say that law is everything in the life of man. Modern pluralists are, therefore, justified in asserting that the state has a sphere of its own and, as such, it should not encroach upon the spheres of other groups and associations that play an important part of their own in regulating and shaping the behaviour of human beings. It is, for this reason, that the view of analytical jurists, despite having a merit of its own (in linking up the fact of legal obligation with the coercive authority of the sovereign) is unacceptable to those who do not agree with this assumption that a rule is not 'law' unless enacted by a legislative body, a court, or some constitution-making body. The critics "either apply the term to some earlier stage of the rule or else withhold the term until they see how effectively, with what consequences, or with what correspondence to their own or some other judgements of right, the rule is executed. All the jurists appear to agree essentially in their ideas as to the relations between any of the various social imperatives, on the one hand, and organised political authority, on the other hand."[73]
4. A difficulty also arises when we deal with the subject of law's relationship with morality. Law is a normative term inasmuch as it seeks to prescribe rules for the good behaviour of human beings. In a sense, it has an empirical character also when we find that the premises of 'positive law' can be subjected to scientific investigation in respect of their validity. The relationship between the two, however, remains a matter of debate in view of the fact that while morality remains a normative affair through and through, the subject of law dwindles between the poles of normativism and empiricism in spite of the fact that we confine its meaning to the sphere of positivism. It is well commented : "Words like 'right', 'duty', or 'binding' occur in both moral and legal contexts. It is tempting to think that just as a man either is, or is not, bound by a rule. But to be bound by a rope is a matter of fact; to be bound by a law is not, at any rate, a fact of the same sort, if it is a fact at all. For to say, in a legal context, that a law is binding is to say that it satisfies the criteria of validity of a given legal system. But to use the same words in moral context is to recommend that people obey it, and to suggest that there are other than purely legal reasons for doing so. The legal obligation is not the same as the moral obligation, neither is it a reflection of it. One of the weaknesses of natural law theory is that it tends to blur this distinction."[74]

72. Benn and Peters, *op. cit.*, p. 69. Barker correctly holds the view that with the strong emphasis on the ideas of the law of nature coupled with this affirmation that positive law must conform to it had a problem of its own type. As he says: "Law became 'two and two', one against another; there was a natural law and a positive law, and the two might fail to meet." *Op. cit*, pp. 99-100.
73. Coker, *op. cit.*, p. 541.
74. Benn and Peters, *op. cit.*, p. 87.

We may conclude our study with this salient fact that the sovereignty of the state is most obviously manifested in the laws which it promulgates, administers and enforces. In a general sense, one may talk about natural law, divine law, moral law and the like, but in the special sense of political theory, law connotes the rules issued by the state to regulate the relationship of man with his fellow-beings. It is, indeed, the hallmark, the very essence, of the state. Hobbes affirms well that of the rights of the sovereign, which are also his duties, the most important is the making of laws. His right is to be the sole legislative authority; nothing is law but which the sovereign law expressly commanded, and the authority of law derives from the will of the sovereign. His duty is to make equitable and necessary laws.[75] Oakeshott paraphrases the meaning of Hobbes in these words: "A law is a command, the expression of will. Its mood is imperative; its essence is authority."[76]

75., Hobbes: *Leviathan,* Ch. XXVI.

76. Michael Oakeshott: "Introduction" to *Leviathan* (Oxford; Basil Blackwell, 1946), p. xl.

7
Rights

> Any system of rights, therefore, has three essential aspects from which it must be regarded. There is the interest of the individual always, at least ultimately, finally isolated from his fellow men. There is the interest of various groups in and through which his personality finds channels of expression. There is the interest of the community which is the total result of the whole pressure of social forces.
>
> **—Harold J. Laski[1]**

If the purpose of normative political theory is to prescribe conduct according to rules, a pertinent question arises as to how these roles are made and enforced. A discussion of this problem involves the issue of proper relationship between the individual who has to pattern his life according to the rules and the state that has to ensure due enforcement of the rules. The concept of rights, thus, finds its broad manifestation in the liberties of the individual on the one hand, and in the scope of state activity, on the other. Since the aim of liberal political theory is to discover what contributes to the happiness of man as well as to the development of his personality, rights occupy a significance of their own in view of the fact that such a subject necessarily involves, within its fold a discussion of individual liberty *vis-a-vis* state authority. Laski, therefore, well observes that "without rights there cannot be liberty"[2] and that "every State is known by the rights it maintains."[3]

Rights: Real Meaning and Nature

Simply stated, a right is a claim of an individual recognised by the society and the state. Obviously, a proper definition of the term 'right' has three ingredients. First, it is a claim of the individual. However, not every claim can become a right. It is required that the claim should be like a disinterested desire, or something which is capable of universal application. The guiding factor is that what an individual wills should be of common interest. That is, in asserting a claim one should feel like rendering a public service. In other words, the motivating force should be a rational consideration and not a personal caprice of the individual. Paraphrasing the idea of T.H. Green, Barker says that the will that issues in the form of a claim to something "not only wills the good of itself, it wills the goodness of itself in relation to others; it wills the goodness of the society which is constituted by such relations."[4]

1. Laski: *A Grammar of Politics* (London: George Allen and Unwin, 1951), p. 141.
2. *Ibid.*, p. 142.
3. *Ibid.*, p. 89.
4. E. Barker: *Political Thought in England* (London: Geoffrey Cumberledge, Oxford University Press, 1951), p. 25.

Second, the claim of the individual should receive recognition by the community. Since individual's claim is backed by a disinterested desire, it involves the good of all and, as such, it receives social recognition. For instance, an individual's claim that none should take his life receives social recognition as every individual wills in the same direction. The recognition of a claim of this type ultimately leads to the creation of right to life. Likewise, an individual's will that none should take away his property creates in him a sense that he should not take away the property of others. When this claim gets social recognition, it becomes right to property. "Claims thus recognised are translated into rights, and it is such recognition that constitutes them as rights. Thus, if we care to make the distinction, we may say that rights have a double aspect. On the one hand, a right is a claim of an individual, arising from the nature of self-consciousness, for permission to will his own ideal objects; on the other hand, it is the recognition of that claim by society and, therein and thereby, the addition of a new power to pursue these objects."[5]

Finally, we come to the point of political recognition. Rights are just like moral declarations unless they are protected by the state. Individuals are guided by their real wills when they think in terms of patterning their conduct according to the rules of 'common behaviour'. However, in actual practice, they are motivated, in most of the cases, by their selfish wills. The result is the violation of the system of rights. Naturally, there must be some coercive force to ensure the exercise of these rights. The state translates the socially recognised claims or moral rights into terms of law and thereby accords them legal recognition. The state, therefore, acts like a coercive agency to prevent the operation of the selfish wills of the individuals. Rights, therefore, have a threefold character. They are ethical when we deal with the claims of the individuals based on their real wills and therefore recognised by the community. They are legal when translated into law by the state. In the sphere of politics, we are concerned with 'moral rights' which would be legally enforceable if law were what it ought to be.

A proper definition of the term 'right' should, therefore, involve all the three ingredients. However, the most important ingredient, in the realm of political theory, is the fact of political recognition that connects the element of disinterested claims of the individuals with the sovereign authority of the state. The version of Gilchrist is, for this reason, partly correct when he says: "Rights arise, therefore, from individuals as members of society, and from the recognition that, for society, there is ultimate good which may be reached by the development of the powers inherent in every individual."[6] We may, however, appreciate the view of Laski: "Rights, in fact, are those conditions of social life without which no man can seek, in general, to be himself at his best. For since the State exists to make possible that achievement, it is only by maintaining rights that its end may be secured."[7]

However, one point relating to the development of the concept of rights in recent times is that the 'claim aspect' has overshadowed the 'duty aspect' of this important term. It may be seen in the marked tendendy to inflate the notion of rights. Now

---

5. *Ibid.*
6. R.N. Gilchrist: *Principles of Political Science,* p. 135.
7. Laski, *op. cit,* p. 91.

the rights are not merely asserted defensively against state action, they are rather interpreted as legitimate claims on government to satisfy human needs. Thus, the distinction between rights as 'liberties' and rights as 'claims' has become a matter of its own importance to social and political theory.[8] Such an assertion has put a premium on the ideal relationship between rights and duties in view of the fact that 'claim rights' entitle their holder to limit the liberty of another person. In the case of certain rights, the argument that duties and rights are logically linked seems to be watertight, but there are uses of the word 'duty' which do not imply correlative rights.[9] Sometimes, this is put in a form of distinction between 'special' and 'general' rights. The former, which arise out of specific undertakings and agreements between individuals, presuppose the existence of general rights, because one needs a special right or claim to justify a limitation on another's freedom, and in the absence of such a right everyone has the general right not to be coerced.[10]

Viewed in a detailed perspective, the meaning of right is necessarily connected with its nature that is contained in the following important points:

1. Rights are implicit in the conscience of man and the community ceaselessly presses for their legal recognition so that the morally recognised claims of the individuals have their proper protection. As such, a state is set between the rights that have been recognised by the community and rights that demand proper protection. In this way, rights have a moral character. They are rights which the individual deems significant; they are essential for self-realisation and the society accords its tacit approval to them. In other words, they are the rights which a society properly organised on the basis of goodwill should recognise.
2. Rights are organically bound up with duties. As a matter of fact, they are like a coin having rights on the one side and duties on the other. Since rights prescribe the rules of behaviour, in doing so they are said to impose duties or obligations. According to Radin, the two terms "are as identical in what they seek to describe as the active and passive forms of indicating an act." The correlation between the two is a logical and not a moral or legal affair inasmuch as a rule giving rise to a right does not give rise to a duty as a separate and different entity. "Rights and duties are different names for the same normative relation, according to the point of view from which it is regarded. . . . The enjoyment of rights. . . . is conditional on the performance of duties; no one can reasonably expect that his interests will be safeguarded by the social order unless he recognises and respects corresponding obligations towards others."[11]
3. In a sense, rights have a pre-political character. They may be independent of state but not of society. Social recognition comes first. If studied in historical terms, we may say that selfless claims of the individuals became well-established

8. See D D. Raphael: *Political Theory and the Rights of Man* (London: Macmillan, 1967), pp. 56-57 and J. Feinberg : *Social Philosophy* (Englewood Cliffs, New Jersey: Prentice-Hall, 1973), Ch. 4.
9. N.P. Barry: *An Introduction to Modern Political Theory* (London : Macmillan, 1981), pp. 186-87.
10. H.A.L. Hart; "Are There Any Natural Rights?" in A. Quinton (ed.): *Political Philosophy* (London: Oxford University Press, 1967), pp. 60-64.
11. Benn and Peters: *Social Principles and the Democratic State* (London: George Allen and Unwin, 1975), p. 89.

usages and customs,—which were translated by the state in terms of law in due course. Thus, rights have a pre-political character. In another sense, they may be described as prior to the state. It may be traced in the fact that "recognised or not, they are that from which the validity of state action is derived and that at some given period and place, they are demanded by the character of its civilisation."[12]

4. Rights have a natural and social-utilitarian character. They are natural not in the sense of prevailing in the state of nature (as described by Locke) as in view of the character of a civilisation, the facts of social existence demand their recognition.[13] Moreover, their social-utilitarian character is traceable in the fact that they are of value both to the individual and to the society. The utility of a right is a matter of value to each member of the state. Besides, they "are useful to the end the State seeks to serve."[14]
5. Rights are not mere abstract entities. They need their exercise. Thus, the issue of rights and duties figures in. A man is expected to exercise his right in a way that he does not harm the right of another. The exercise of a right, naturally, calls for the observance of a duty and makes it correlated with the functions of a man. A man possesses rights so that he may seek the best possible development of his personality and, at the same time, contribute to the social end. Functions thus become implicit in rights. As Laski says: "I have to do something that is worth doing in order to enjoy that which the experience of history has proved to be worth enjoying. I may pay my debt to the State by being a bricklayer, or an artist, or a mathematician. Whatever form my payment takes, it is essential that I should realise that the rights I have are given to me, because I am performing some given duties."[15]
6. Rights are also connected with the functions of the state. In theory, rights of the individuals and functions of the state may be separate; in practice, they are not. The two are so closely related that Barker regards them "indistinguishable' like the obverse and reverse sides of a coin. As he says: "On the one hand, the functions of government are a condition of the rights of persons because they are necessary to the enjoyment of those rights and because they exist in order to secure them. On the other hand, the rights of persons are a condition of the functions of government, because they are the source and cause of the existence and action of government. . . . We may accordingly say that government is service on behalf of rights, and not a power outside their range."[16]
7. The subject of rights is necessarily related with other important themes like liberty, law, justice and sovereignty. As we shall see in the following chapters, liberties of the individuals are like an extension of their rights in the sphere of their social existence. Rights and laws become like a closely related phenomenon in the sense that while the former is subjective, the latter constitutes objective

12. Laski, *op. cit.*, p. 91.
13. *Ibid.*
14. *Ibid.*, p. 92
15. *Ibid.*, p. 94.
16 E. Barker: *Principles of Social and Political Theory* (London: Oxford Univ. Press, 1967), p. 226.

side of the same thing. What law does is the translation of a right in specific terms as sanctioned by the sovereign authority. Likewise, rights and justice become one and the same thing if viewed in a particular sense. To declare and enforce law is the same thing as to recognise rights and guarantee them in a proper manner that brings about the situation of justice. The state is expected to translate rights into legal terms and then ensure their due protection so that justice prevails. In this way, "all authority; and all the functions of government, including the functions of immediate sovereignty, are services owed to rights."[17]

In fine, rights are claims based on the disinterested or selfless desires of the individuals so that they first receive their moral recognition by the society and then legal recognition by the state in view of their essential usefulness both to the individual and the community as well as their urgency at a particular period in history that reveals a record of man's social progress. Laski says that non-recognition of a right under the conditions specified above, would lead to disastrous results and that a historical process is a record of man's moral progress looking at which we can safely guide our future.[18]

Natural Theory: 'A Rhetorical Nonsense upon Stilts'

From time to time various explanations regarding the origin and nature of rights have been adduced that have led to the emergence of different theories in this direction. The earliest explanation in this regard is known by the name of the natural theory of rights. It holds that rights being rationally deducible from man's nature have their universal application irrespective of the difference of place, time and environment. The nature is the author of certain rights that have a universal, rational, eternal and immutable character. Going back to the days of the ancient Greeks, it holds that rights belong to man by nature. They inhere in him. They "are as much a part of man's nature as, say, the colour of his skin. They do not require any elaborate explanation or justification. They are self-evident truths."[19]

The origin of the natural theory of rights goes back to ancient Greece when the Stoics preached the doctrine of natural equality of mankind. In the Roman age, Polybius and Cicero drew inspiration from the creed of Stoicism and held that civil law should conform to the dictates of the law of nature that was universal, eternal, rational and immutable. During the Middle Ages, it was given a Biblical complexion so that the law of nature became the law of God whereby, instead of nature, God became the author of man's rights. However, the exposition of this idea took a very prominent shape in the seventeenth century when social contractualists like Spinoza,

---

17. *Ibid.*, p. 228. Thus, the state has every right to punish and crush anti-social and antinational elements. As Justice Story of the American Supreme Court in the case of *Gitlow v People of New York* (1925) observed: "That a state, in the exercise of its police power, may punish those who abuse this freedom by utterances inimical to the public welfare, tending to corrupt public morals, incite to crime, or disturb the public peace is not open to question. . . . And for yet more imperative reasons, a state may punish utterances endangering the foundations of organised government and threatening its overthrow by unlawful means."
18. Frank Thakurdas: *Recent English Political Theory* (Calcutta: Minerva, 1972), p. 310.
19. E. Asirvatham: *Political Theory* (Lucknow: Upper India Pub., 1967), p. 160.

Hobbes and Locke accepted this version so as to establish a proper relationship between the liberty of the individual and the authority of the state.

The social contractualists treated the dogma of natural rights as a favourite theme. They contemplated the existence of rights in a hypothetical 'state of nature' and termed them 'natural rights'. They sought to establish that the individuals had certain rights even before the state came into being as a result of some social compact. Thus, essential rights of the individual have a pre-political character, while Hobbes treated them 'pre-social' as well. Besides, he identified his theory of rights with his well-known doctrine of power. He insisted that every man had the right of 'self-preservation' that could not be taken away even by the sovereign, rather the individuals were justified in violating the terms of the compact in case the government were determined to take away the life of its subjects.[20]

The most outstanding place, in this direction, is occupied by John Locke who includes three rights (relating to life, liberty, and property) in his catalogue of natural rights. To him, the main function of the state is to protect these natural rights of the individuals inasmuch as the need for entering into a social compact is motivated by a due protection of the rights authored by nature. The individuals have every right to resist, even overthrow, the government in case the rulers violate the sanctity of the natural rights. These rights cannot be surrendered to any alien authority (even to state or government) and if ever an agreement to this effect is made under duress or through some miscalculation, the very agreement becomes void. In this way, the rights are an integral part of human personality and if the government ever seeks to encroach upon them, it will entitle the people to rise in revolt for the sake of preserving their natural rights.[21]

The trend continued in the eighteenth century and some of the important political documents found their basis in the theory of natural rights. For instance, the Constitution of Virginia declared: "That all men are by nature equally free and independent, and have certain inherent rights, of which, when they enter into a state of society, they cannot by any compact deprive or divest their posterity, namely, the enjoyment of life and liberty, with the means of acquiring and possessing property, and pursuing, and obtaining happiness and safety." The American Declaration of Independence of 1776 reiterated that 'all men are endowed by their Creator with certain unalienable rights.' Likewise, the French Declaration of the Rights of Man and Citizen of 1791 took it as self-evident truth that 'men are born free and live free and equal in their rights'. To refer to the latest instance, we may invoke the Universal Declaration of Human Rights of 1948 which says: "All human beings are born free and equal in dignity and rights."

However, to make this point clearer, it may be added that in the seventeenth and eighteenth centuries, inalienable rights would have been appropriately described as moral rather than institutional or legal; politically basic rather than derived; natural rather than fortuitous, conventional or supernatural, and self-evident rather than inferred. To assert an inalienable right is to assert a right that has these features:

20. See Hobbes: *Leviathan,* Chapters 14 and 15.
21. See Locke: *Second Treatise of Civil Government.* Chapters 7 and 9.

1. Inalienable rights are moral rights rather than institutional or legal. Regardless of how we wish to interpret the relations between morality and institutions, legal or otherwise, it is essential to interpret them in such a way as to admit the possibility of institutions requiring or permitting what is morally wrong. To admit this is not to deny a general obligation to submit to the control of institutions, even those which are manifestly unjust. It is to recognise, however, that such things as legal statutes, decrees and decisions may permit acts which ought to be forbidden and require acts which are morally evil and intolerable.
2. Inalienable rights are politically basic, because the protection of moral interests, persons and estates is the condition of an individual's moral consent to government. The assertion of any right to an object is incompatible with moral consent to refusals of that object. Part of the evidence that one knows how to use these assertions correctly is furnished by specific kinds of attitudes and acts which occur when rights are asserted.
3. Inalienable rights are natural rather than fortuitous, conventional, or supernatural. To say this is to emphasise that these rights are the rights of each and every man, irrespective of the characteristics which enable us to distinguish one man from another and one group of men from other groups. There are two very different reasons for using the term 'natural' in this way: (1) There are certain properties common to all men. (2) The word 'natural' may be used as a moral idea to express a moral commitment based in part on scientific studies about differences among men.
4. Inalienable rights are self-evident in the sense that if one man has a right to the protection of his interest, then all have it.[22]

In short, the whole idea of natural rights is based on the assumption that irrespective of his merit as an individual in his personal or moral capacity, man is at least equal to all others in human worth. Even convicted criminals, who have violated the rights of others and therefore do not score highly in moral grading, still have the right not to be treated in cruel or inhuman ways by the jail staff. The point in saying that certain natural rights are inalienable is that if a person voluntarily gives them up, he in a sense resigns from the moral community and puts the determination of his future into the hands of somebody else. To argue that natural rights are inalienable is to argue that certain contracts (as a contract between a master and a slave) do not take away the right of a person who may, for various reasons, wish to abandon his control over his own future, but this does not mean that he has extinguished a right in the way that one might waive the right to be repaid a loan given to a friend.[23]

The idea of the theory of natural rights that man's nature abstracted from the environment could yield a body of rights had been a subject of attack in the nineteenth and twentieth centuries. In the first place, it is said that since there "can be no right without a rule, to abstract man from society is to abstract him from the context of rules and, therfore, to make a distinction of rights irrelevant. Since rights imply duties, they imply someone in social relationship with their subject

22. S.M. Brown: "Inalienable Rights" in A. de Crespigny and A. Wertheimer (eds.): *Contemporary Political Theory* (London: Nelson, 1970), pp. 245-61.
23. Barry, *op. cit.*, p. 192.

upon whom the duties can rest. Robinson Crusoe had no rights until he met Man Friday.'[24] Second, this theory takes it for granted that rights are created by nature and, as such, they may be pre-social as well (as we find in the case of Hobbes). It is quite untenable in view of the fact that there can be no right without first acquiring social recognition. As we have already seen, every right must be justified in terms of some end which the rest of the community does, in fact, consider good and which could not be achieved without the recognition of that right.[25] Moreover, to have any hope of securing positive recognition of a right, it must be defensible in terms of moral standards acceptable, at least, to an influential part of the society.[26]

Then, it is almost an impossible job to prepare a catalogue of the natural rights after adding a precise definition of the term 'natural' that may mean anything from the whole universe to the real happiness of man. Taking that the terms 'natural' and 'nature' are indefinite and used rather loosely, we are not surprised to find that among the supporters of this theory, there "is an ambiguity as to what these rights are. There is no official, or complete, or generally agreed upon list of natural rights."[27] Moreover, the so-called natural rights conflict with each other. For instance, an absolute right to liberty, as justified by this theory, is bound to clash with the idea of absolute equality. Above all, this theory takes the wrong view of state and of other political institutions as being artificial. The state is a natural growth not a make. "It is not a secondary product, much less an intruder and a usurper."[28]

It is in the light of these inherent weaknesses of this theory that Jeremy Bentham denounced natural rights as 'rhetorical nonsense upon stilts'. The nineteenth century witnessed a vehement attack on the theory of natural rights first by the Utilitarians like Bentham and Mill and then by the Idealists like Green and Bosanquet. It may, however, be added that this theory has a value of its own if the meaning of natural rights is revised. Instead of treating rights as ordained by nature or by the Creator in some hypothetical or prehistoric past, we should interpret them as ideal or moral rights which we ought to have in the future and in the light of which we can criticise existing conditions.[29] As Laski says, we "do not mean by rights the grant to some historic conditions possessed in the childhood of race, but lost in the process of time,"[30] and they "are not natural in the sense that a permanent and unchanging catalogue of them can be compiled, rather they are natural in the sense that under the limitations of a civilised life, facts demand their recognition."[31]

24. Benn and Peters, *op. cit.*, pp. 96-97.
25. T.H. Green: *Lectures on the Principles of Political Obligation,* Sec. 144.
26. Bosanquet: *The Philosophical Theory of State,* Chapter VIII, Sec. 6.
27. Asirvatham, *op. cit.*, p. 163.
28. *Ibid*
29. *Ibid.*, p. 165. Laski rejects the case of natural rights interpreted as 'the reflection of a natural order which lies behind the shifting appearance of contemporary society'. His argument is that such a concept is static and is belied by the rapidity and frequency of change which is characteristic of modern society under the influence of sense. There is no fixed and unchanging picture of perfection to which the world may constantly look up for inspiration. 'For there is no such *finis ultimus,* utmost aim, or *summum bonum,* greatest good, as is spoken of in the books of old moral philosophers. Nor can a man anymore live, whose desires are at an end, than he, whose senses and imaginations are at stand.' *A Grammar of Politics,* pp. 89-90.
30. *Ibid.*, p. 89.
31. *Ibid.*, p. 91.

Legal Theory: Account of Rights in Terms of the Power of the State

According to this theory, rights are neither absolute nor ordained by nature or by the Creator, they are the creations of the law of the state. As such, the state is the only source of rights. It provides the machinery to guarantee the enjoyment of rights, and that rights are dynamic inasmuch as they change with the law of the land. Obviously, such an affirmation regards rights as the creation of the political community. It may be traced in the view of Hobbes who equates rights with powers. Though the individuals have right to life in the 'state of nature', they enter into the social compact with this conviction that the state would ensure their better protection. Thus, whatever the sovereign accords to the subject constitutes their rights.[32]

The positive theory of rights, as it is also called, finds its clear exposition in the works of Jeremy Bentham who decries natural rights as 'rhetorical nonsense' and insists that rights are the creature of law and of organised society; at the same time, they arise out of and correspond to the principle of utility.[33] However, the account of rights in terms of the power of the state witnesses its best representation in the writings of Austin who says that every right, whether divine, legal, or moral "rests on a relative duty; that is to say, a duty lying on a party or parties other than the party or parties in whom the right resides. And, manifestly, that relative duty would not be a duty substantially, if the law which affects to impose it were not sustained by might."[34]

The legal theory of rights implying 'there is no right where there is no power to secure the object of right' and the power arising from the 'exercise of a coercive sanction to enforce the correlative duty'[35] suffers from certain weaknesses. First, it is wrong to believe that law can make everything right. Prof. Hocking, for this reason, asks whether a law of the state can make corruption a right? We have already seen that social recognition is as much necessary as the legal recognition of the state. Second, to say that the state is the sole creator of rights is to make it absolute and thereby deprive the people of the power of resistance. Last, this theory discards ethical consideration in entirety. It "does not enable us to decide whether rights that are recognised are the rights that ought to be recognised. It does not help us to make the State what it should be. Therefore, it seems clear that we need an external standard for judging the State, and that standard is supplied by the law of personality."[36]

The legal theory of rights is, however, partly correct in asserting that rights are no rights until they are secured by the state. Mere social recognition is not enough. Thus, even an idealist like Green realised that 'rights demand the State'. Thinkers like Machiavelli and Hobbes were not thoroughly wrong when they treated man as essentially wicked and selfish. Thus, there is every possibility that man would act according to his selfish will and thereby harm the moral rights of the people.

32. See Warrender: *The Political Philosophy of Hobbes,* Chapter, VIII.
33. Frank Thakurdas: *The English Utilitarians and the Idealists* (Delhi: Vishal Pub., 1977), p. 60.
34. Austin: *The Province of Jurisprudence Determined,* edited by H.A.L. Hart, p. 285 n.
35. Benn and Peters, *op. cit.,* p. 91.
36. Asirvatham, *op. cit.,* p. 167.

As such, there should be a coercive authority to give protection to the moral rights. Law, therefore, serves the desired purpose. An idealist like Bosanquet could, for this reason, well realise that a right "has both a legal and a moral reference. It is a claim which can be enforced at law, which no moral imperative can be; but it is also recognised to be a claim which ought to be capable of enforcement at law, and thus it has a moral aspect."[37]

Idealistic Theory: Emphasis on External Conditions as Essential to Man's Moral Development

Different from the natural theory of rights (which takes rights as the creation of nature) and the legal theory on the same subject (which treats rights as the creation of the will of the state), the idealistic or personality theory defines a right as that 'which is really necessary to the maintenance of material conditions essential to the existence and perfection of human personality. As Krausse says, rights constitute the organic whole of the outward conditions necessary to the rational life. In simple words, it means "that without rights no man can become the best self that he is capable of becoming. The supreme right of every man is the right of personality. By this, we mean that it is the right and duty of every human being to freely develop his potentiality. Every other right is derived from this one fundamental right. Even such important rights as the right to life, the right to liberty, the right to property, etc., are not absolute rights. They are conditional or presumptive. They are relative to the right of personality."[38]

Rights which exist in the social consciousness but not manifested in the law of the community and so struggling for legal expression may be regarded as ideal or moral rights. "They are rights which the individual deems significant; they are essential to self-realisation and society accords its tacit approval to them. They are rights which a society, properly organised on the basis of goodwill, should recognise, if it seeks to be true to its own basic principle. An ideal society, in this sense, may be described as one whose legal system and morality are in the closest possible harmony."[39] In Hegel's highly philosophical language, a right is an externalised expression of man's internal will for freedom. As he says: "The will is free, so that freedom is both the substance of right and its goal, while the system of right is the realm of freedom made actual, the world of mind brought forth out of itself like a second nature."[40] Likewise, William Wallace says: "They (legal and moral rights) are two partial aspects of a single fact, that fact being the fact of human society: of which they respectively present the statistical and the dynamical element, the element of order and the element of progress. . . . Law is but the deposit, the fixed result, of the operation of that instinct which, while still heaving shapelessly, is called morality. In the actual world, they are never wholly separate; one without the other is dangerous to the community."[41]

---

37. Bosanquet, *op. cit.*, p. 187.
38. Asirvatham, *op. cit.*, p. 173.
39. See G.N. Sarma: *Political Thought of Harold J. Laski* (New Delhi: Sterling, 1984), p. 96.
40. Knox (ed.): *Hegel's Philosophy of Right*, p. 20.
41. Wallace: *Lectures and Essays*, p. 259.

In other words, a right is a claim based on the rational will of man and, for this reason, it is first recognised by the society and then translated into law by the state. Its best presentation is contained in the political philosophy of Green who, as we have already seen, begins with this assumption that human consciousness thinks of the goodness of the 'self as well as of other human beings and thus the recognition of a claim as conducive to the common interest brings about a system of rights. The idealistic interpretation of Green is thus summed up by Barker: "Human consciousness postulates liberty: liberty involves rights: rights demand the State."[42] It may be seen in the affirmation of Bosanquet that a right is both a legal and a moral reference. "It is a claim which can be enforced at law, which no moral imperative can be; but it is also recognised to be a claim which ought to be capable of enforcement at law, and thus it has a moral aspect. . . . A typical right unites the two sides."[43]

We may refer to the ideas of Bosanquet for the purpose of explaining the meaning of this theory in further detail. To him, rights are the conditions for the realisation of the end of the state, claims recognised by the state, i.e., by society acting as ultimate authority for the maintenance of conditions favourable to the best life.[44] The system of rights maintained by the state may be considered from two points of view: (i) that of the whole community, and (ii) that of the individuals who compose it. Viewing from the first point, we can assess the value of any social order *qua* order which enables life to be lived, and determine if limited common good is to be realised. From the second point of view, these rights are the external incidents so far as maintained by law, the authoritative gesture as it were of a person's position in the world of his community.[45]

Thus, this theory looks at rights from a highly moral point of view. Rights are rooted in the mind of man; they are powers granted to him by the community in order that he with others may realise a common good of which his good is an intrinsic part. A right must establish two things—the individual claiming it must be able to convince society that in doing so he is not interfering with the like claims of his fellow beings, and that he must be able to convince society that his claim is absolutely necessary for his self-development. Thus, a right "is a freedom of action possessed by a man by virtue of his occupying a certain place and fulfilling a certain function in a social order."[46]

Like other theories on the subject of rights, this theory also suffers from certain weaknesses. First, the idealistic interpretation is too abstract to be easily understood by an average man and, moreover, difficulty may arise when we begin to reduce the conception of moral recognition into practical terms. It may be asked that the idea of moral development being too abstract, how the state can judge conditions conducive to the best possible development of the personality of its subjects. Since the very idea of personality is a subjective affair, no generally acceptable list of rights can be drawn on the basis of this theory. Moreover, this theory seems to sacrifice

42. Barker: *Political Thought in England*, p. 23.
43. Bernard Bosanquet: *Philosophical Theory of State*, p. 188.
44. See Frank Thakurdas: *The English Utilitarians and the Idealists*, p. 441.
45. *Ibid.*, pp. 441-42.
46. N. Wilde: *The Ethical Basis of the State*, p. 12.

social goods for the sake of individual good. It is based on the assumption of the infallibility of the state that, in practical terms, means justification of totalitarianism. However, the merit of this theory lies on the theoretical plane where we find that it "furnishes a safe test to rights which can be applied at all times, and herein it is superior to the legal, historical and social welfare theories. The one absolute right of all human beings is the right of personality."[47]

Historical Theory: Creation of Rights by Prescription

This theory assumes that rights are the creation of time. That is, they are based on long established usages and customs. For instance, the right of way on a public road or land becomes a right by way of prescription. The essential sanction behind a right is, for this reason, a tradition or custom ripened on account of its long observance. Sociologists like MacIver have dwelt on the significance of the role of custom in creating rights of the people. To them, law of today is nothing but the crystallisation of age-old customs into the form of legal sanctions that the state enforces with coercive power at its command. Thus, we find that the rights which people 'think they ought to have are just those rights which they have been accustomed to have, or which they have a tradition of once having possessed. Custom is primitive law.'[48]

An emphatic assertion of this theory may be traced in Burke's doctrine of prescriptive institutions. To him, political institutions form a vast and complicated system of prescriptive rights and customary observances, that these practices grow out of the past and adapt themselves with the present without any break in the continuity, and that the tradition of the constitution and of the society at large ought to be the objects of reverence similar to religion, because it forms the repository of a collective wisdom and intelligence of a particular civilisation. With this view, he criticised French Revolution as being an injudicious exercise in the direction of a struggle for liberty, equality and fraternity, and lauded the Glorious Revolution of 1688 as a reassertion of the centuries-old rights of the Englishmen. Thus, he warned: "To destroy any power, growing wild from the rank productive force of the human mind, is almost tantamount in the moral world to the destruction of the apparently active properties of body in the material world."[49]

This theory is partly correct and partly incorrect. It cannot be accepted that all rights are a result of the well-established customs. Had this been so, till today slavery would have been in existence as a matter of right by virtue of being based on a long established tradition. However, one feature of this theory cannot be dismissed: that the passage of time does result in the creation of rights. A practice once started becomes a usage if it is repeated without any break or obstruction; it hardens into a custom over a long period of time and then people begin to take it as a matter of right. It is, for this reason, a plausible statement: "History cannot be ignored, but history cannot be relied on alone."[50]

---

47. Asirvatham, *op. cit.*, pp. 175-76.
48. D.G. Ritchie: *Natural Rights*, p. 82.
49. Edmund Burke: *Reflections on the Revolution in France*, p. 58.
50. W.E. Hocking: *Law and Rights*, p. 7.

Social Welfare Theory: Emphasis on Rights as Conditions of Social Expediency

Finally, we come to the social welfare or social expediency theory of rights that seems to be the most plausible of all theories on this subject. It implies that rights are the creation of society inasmuch as they are based on the consideration of common welfare.

Rights make what is conducive to the greatest good of the greatest number; they are the conditions of social good. Thus, claims not in conformity with the general welfare would not be recognised by the society and thus fail from being rights. It has its best manifestation in the works of Bentham who developed the principle of utility so as to show that the system of rights is beneficial both to the individual and the society. Rights are of utility both to the individual and the society inasmuch as the principle of utility is that which "approves or disapproves of any action according to its tendencies to promote or oppose the happiness of the party whose interest is in question whether of a private individual or of a government."[51]

Among other leading exponents of this theory, we may refer to Laski who, while following the tradition of English liberalism, integrates his theory of rights with what was once suggested by the exponents of the utilitarian school. Though in a much modified form, he puts the principle of utility so as to mean that nothing but social welfare is the test of rights. As he says: "We are making the test of rights utility; and that, it is clear, involves the question of those to whom the rights are to be useful. There is only one possible answer. In any State the demands of each citizen for the fulfilment of his best self must be taken as of equal worth; and the utility of a right is, therefore, its value to all the members of the State."[52]

As we have seen in the case of other theories on the subject of rights, this theory also has certain weaknesses. First, it dwells on the maxim of 'social welfare'—a term that may hardly be put to a precise definition. It is highly ambiguous, or, if put into practice it may mean different things to different persons. One may say that the yardstick of 'greatest good of the greatest number' may mean something to the liberals, something else to the socialists, and something fundamentally different from both to the communists. Then, if carried to extreme, the point of individual welfare may be lost, as it seeks to sacrifice individual good at the altar of social welfare. Thus, a critic like N. Wilde is of the view that if rights are created by the consideration of social expediency (that is, by the society) the individual is without an appeal and helplessly dependent upon its arbitrary will.[53] However, the essential merit of this theory lies in its linking up the idealistic version of rights to its utilitarian counterpart and thereby making it a commendable affair so far as the liberal political theory is concerned. As such, rights are not only related to the essential consideration of social welfare, they are also given a dynamic character.

51. See Frank Thakurdas, *op. cit.*, p. 69.
52. Laski, *op. cit.*, p. 92. The important point is that the welfare theories of rights wish to capture the special obligatoriness of the concept of a right so that coercion is legitimate for meeting claims to well being " Barry, *op. cit.*, p. 197. Also see R. Peffer: "A Defense of Rights to Well-Being" in *Philosophy and Public Affairs*, 1978, Vol. 8, pp. 74-75.
53. Wilde, *op. cit.*, p. 124.

Specific Kinds of Rights

Rights are of different kinds. However, a taxonomic illustration of rights in a neat and watertight form is not possible inasmuch as some of the specific rights overlap their categories. We may also find a lot of differences in the opinions of leading writers on this subject. For instance, Barker groups them into three main heads relating to Fraternity, Equality and Liberty and divides the last one into two categories—political and economic. He banks upon the view of a leading French jurist Leon Duguit in putting rights to public assistance, education and public employment under the head of 'fraternity'; he includes rights to be treated equally in the eye of law and matters relating to justice, taxation and admissibility to honours and offices of public employment under the second head of 'Equality' and, finally, lists well-known political and economic freedoms under the last head of 'Liberty.'[54]

Different from this, Laski puts them into two broad categories – general and particular.[55] We may say that what he calls by the name of 'particular rights' may be identified with what are known as 'fundamental rights'. In order to discuss the specific kinds of rights in a simplified and intelligible form, we may, however, deal with them in the following manner:

1. **Moral Rights:** These rights are the claims based on the conscience of the community. In other words, these are the claims recognised by the conscience of the community. For instance, a teacher has a moral right to be respected by his students. The noticeable point, in this direction, is that these rights have the support of the good sense of the society. There is no coercive power to enforce them. Thus, we cannot move the courts for seeking an enforcement of our moral rights. The moral rights are like pious precepts whose enforcement depends upon the good sense of the community. When moral rights are translated into legal terms, they become legal rights, since coercive power of the state remains at their back. Violation of law is visited with punishment.
2. **Civil Rights:** These rights relate to the person and property of the individuals. They are called 'civil' (or social) rights as they relate to the essential conditions of a civilised life. This broad category includes a number of rights like those relating to life, personal liberty, thought and expression, property, religion and the like. Of all the civil rights, right to life is most important, since enjoyment of all the other rights depends upon it. It implies that no person can take the life of another. Not only this, a person has the right to save his life even by killing another in case his opponent has the intention to kill him. It is called right to 'self-defence'. So significant is right to life that suicide is a crime and a person trying to commit it is held liable for punishment. Thus, a person accused of committing murder gets the punishment of death. This right, however, is not absolute and the state may restrict it during the times of crisis by ordering conscriptions in the name of 'national interest'. Allied to this is the right to personal liberty inasmuch as mere life, without right to exercise one's faculties and to determine the general conditions of life, would be valueless. This right includes abolition of slavery, free movement and freedom from arbitrary arrest

54. Barker: *Principles of Social and Political Theory*, pp. 228-35.
55. Laski, *op. cit.*, Chapters 3, 4, and 5.

RIGHTS

(relating to)

- **Liberty**
  - **Civil**
    Rights to:
    (i) Personal freedom
    (ii) Personal security
    (iii) Personal property
    (iv) Religion
    (v) Speech and expression
    (vi) Formation of unions
    (vii) Movement throughout the country
  - **Political**
    Rights to:
    (i) vote
    (ii) Contest elections
    (iii) Form parties
    (iv) Hold public meetings
    (v) Criticise and change the government by peaceful means
  - **Economic**
    Rights to:
    (i) Work
    (ii) Rest and leisure
    (iii) Form trade unions
    (iv) Carry on some profession or trade
    (v) Avail social insurance
    (vi) Bargain freely for adequate remuneration
    (vii) Enjoy status of partners in control of industry
- **Equality**
  Right to be treated equally and on equal footing with others in matters of:
  (i) Legal protection
  (ii) Corrective justice
  (iii) Taxation
  (iv) Admissibility to honours and offices of public employment
- **Fraternity**
  Rights to:
  (i) Education
  (ii) Public Assistance
  (iii) Public Employment

> **Marshall's Tripartite Conception of Rights**
>
> Citizenship is essentially a matter of ensuring that everyone is treated as a full and equal member of the society. And the way to ensure this sense of membership is through according people an increasing number of citizenship rights—civil, political and social.
> **Civil Rights** (secured by the people in the eighteenth century) are essential for the liberty of the individual. This category includes rights as those of speech, assembly, movement, conscience, private property, equality before law etc. The enjoyment of such rights requires a civil society.
> **Political Rights** (secured by the people in the nineteenth century) enable the people to take part in the affairs of the state. This category includes rights to vote, to contest elections, to hold public office, and to support or oppose the political order. It requires a democratic system.
> **Social Rights** (secured by the people in the twentieth century) are like a charge on the role of the state. This category includes rights to basic economic welfare, provision of social security, and creation of conditions which enable the people to lead 'good life'. It requires a social welfare state.
>
> T.H. Marshall: "Citizenship and Social Class" in his (ed.): *Sociology at the Crossroads* (London: Heinemann, 1963), p. 70.

and detention. Then, comes right to think and express. An individual should have freedom to think and express his ideas by tongue or print. Naturally, this right includes freedom of publications, broadcasting and telecasting. Right to property also falls within this category. It means right to hold, transfer or dispose off property by a person. In the sphere of law and justice, it includes equality before law and its equal protection. Finally, it covers religious freedom. A person should have the right to profess and practise any religion as per his conscience.

3. **Political Rights:** These rights relate to a man's participation in the affairs of the state. As such, this category includes the most important right to vote. In a democratic state, all adult citizens must have franchise whereby they may choose their rulers. It also includes the right to contest elections that take place from time to time whereby the people register their confidence in their chosen representatives. Then, comes the right to hold public offices. All able and qualified citizens irrespective of any difference on the grounds of religion, race, caste, creed, etc. should have the right to hold a public office. It also includes the right to address, whether individually or collectively, petitions to the government embodying their grievances. Finally, people should have the right to appreciate or denounce the actions of their government so that they may renew their confidence in their rulers, or change them in case they forfeit their trust or goodwill.
4. **Economic Rights:** These rights relate to man's vocation, his engagement in a gainful employment so as to solve the problem of food, clothing and shelter. Every person should have the right to work so that he may earn his livelihood. Apart from this, he should have the right to rest and leisure. It also includes the right to form trade unions so as to protect and promote their specific interest. Workers should have the right to bargain freely for remunerative work. This category also includes the right of the workers to enjoy the status of free partners

in the general control and running of industry. The subject of economic rights is, however, a matter of controversy. Thus, while the liberals regard it as man's right to own and manage the means of production, distribution and exchange with certain restrictions so as to subserve the social good, the men of socialist disposition lay stress on the overriding interests of the society and, for that reason, advocate more and more stringent restrictions on the ownership and control of the means of production, distribution and exchange so that private property is not allowed to have the character of an agency of exploitation and oppression. However, the communists go a step ahead. Their catalogue of economic rights includes rights relating to work, rest and leisure, social security in the event of physical disablement and the like. As a socialist, Laski includes in it workers' right to control industry.

5. **Human Rights:** A modified version of, what was once called, 'natural rights' coupled with certain civil rights has assumed a significance of its own ever since the formulation of the Universal Declaration of Human Rights by the Human Rights Commission and their adoption by the General Assembly of the United Nations in 1948. The Preamble offers it as a declaration of "a common standard of achievement for all peoples and all nations", to the end that every individual and every organ of society "shall strive by teaching and education to promote respect for these rights and freedoms and by progressive measures, national and international, to secure their universal and effective recognition and observance, both among the peoples of member-states themselves and among the peoples of territories under their jurisdiction." The Declaration is quite comprehensive and, as already said, it incorporates a host of other rights that have their necessary connection with moral or natural and civil rights as pointed out above. For instance, Art. I says that all human beings are born free and equal in dignity and rights. They are endowed with reason and conscience and should act towards one another in a spirit of brotherhood. Art. 25 speaks of the right to security in the event of unemployment, sickness, disability, old age, widowhood or other lack of livelihood in circumstances beyond one's control. An examination of the list of rights in this category shows that these "are obviously prescriptive statements which command wide support among member-nations (or their governments), and which they were prepared to subscribe to, not as formulae by which their policies were to be determined, but as general aims, and common standards of achievements."[56]

Though we may prepare a long catalogue of rights, whether moral, civil, political, economic or human, it remains a matter of controversy as to which of them should be included in the category of 'fundamental rights'. The reason for this should be traced in different approaches and commitments of the thinkers. For instance, while the men of liberal disposition lay emphasis on political rights as those relating to the freedom of thought and expression, the Marxists do the same in regard to economic rights like those of work and social security. Hence, we can take note of the fact that while the Constitution of India attaches top importance to the rights to equality and freedom, the Chinese Constitution does the same for right to work. With a view

56. Benn and Peters, *op. cit.* p. 101.

to write something on the subject of 'fundamental rights' without entering into the domain of controversy between Liberal and Marxist schools, we may dwell on the interpretation of Laski who has offered a list of 'particular rights'.[57]

Laski on Particular Rights

As a man of socialist disposition and then under the influence of Marxism, Laski lays emphasis, first of all, on the availability of those rights whereby the minimum possible needs of the people may be satisfied. "Differentiation arises only when the elementary needs of each individual have been satisfied."[58] The problem of particular rights, however, remains. To him, these rights pertain to the civil, political and economic spheres and they may be enumerated as under:

1. Every citizen should have the right to work. It means right to be occupied in producing a share of the goods and commodities that are essential for the society.
2. Every citizen should have the right to adequate wages. It means that all those who work must be given sufficient wages to maintain themselves.
3. Every citizen should have the right to reasonable hours of work. It means that he should be asked to put in that amount of work which does not exhaust him completely and thereby make him unfit to discharge his duties as an active member of the community.
4. Every citizen should have the right to education. It means that he should be given that minimum of education which is essential for the performance of his duties.
5. Every citizen should have the right to share in the political power. It means that he should have the right to vote, to be elected, and also the right to remove corrupt government and run administrative machinery properly.
6. Every citizen should have the right to form associations and organise public meetings and be provided with judicial safeguards so that justice may be secured without fear or favour.
7. Every citizen should have the right to property limited only to the extent that is necessary for the growth of his personality and does not prove detrimental to the interests of the society.
8. Every citizen should have a right to industrial self-government. It means that he, as an industrial unit, must somehow be given the power to share in the making of those decisions which affect him as a producer, if he is to be in a position to maximise his freedom.
9. Every citizen should have the right to speech and expression. It means that he should have the right to ventilate his grievances and organise public opinion in that matter.
10. Every citizen should have the right to equality before law so that he may get justice without discrimination. It must not be harder upon the poor than upon the rich.

---

57. See Laski, *op. cit,*. Chapter 3. Also see his *Liberty in the Modern State* (London: George Allen and Unwin, 1930.)
58. Laski: *A Grammar of Politics,* p. 95.

Rights and Obligations

In Swaraj based on *Ahimsa* people need not know their rights, but it is necessary for them to know their duties. There is no duty that does not create a corresponding right, and those only are true rights which flow from a due performance of one's duties. Hence, rights of citizenship accrue only to those who serve the state to which they belong. And they alone can do justice to the rights that accrue to them.

—M.K. Gandhi,
Harijan, 25 March, 1939, p. 64.

From the ancient world to the present day, all forms of citizenship have had certain common attributes. Citizenship has meant a certain reciprocity of rights against, and duties towards, the community.

—David Held,
Political Theory and the Modern State, p. 199.

When we speak of freedom as something to be so highly prized, we mean a positive power or capacity of doing or enjoying something and that too something that we do or enjoy in common with others.

—T.H. Green,
"Liberal Legislation and the Freedom of Contract" in Allen Bullock and M.Shock (ed.s): ***The Liberal Tradition from Locke to Keynes***, p. 181.

While one may have his own reservations in regard to the appreciation of the catalogue of particular rights as offered by Laski, it cannot be lost sight of that concepts like those of 'human', 'natural', or 'fundamental' rights, however, are more puzzling, because they are not clearly related to rules. Statements of the rights of this type are statements of moral principles of a very high order of generality. No particular course of action ever follows as a necessary consequence of such a principle. Nevertheless, they draw attention to important interests which are shared by most men, like the interest in living and in being let alone, in security of person and property. "To recognise these interests as 'natural rights' is to lay down that they can rightly be impaired only for very special reasons, that the onus of proof rests heavily on whoever would set them aside."[59]

Rights and Obligations

Simply stated, a right is a power or a privilege or an entitlement to act or to be treated in a particular way. But as man lives in society and all members of the society have their rights, each right has a corresponding duty or obligation. If I have a right to live, it becomes my duty to let others live. If I want that nobody should take away my property, I am also bound to honour such a right of others. The exercise of a particular right requires a duty to act in a particular way so that the whole system of rights safely prevails. So Heywood says: "In a sense, rights and obligations are the reverse sides of the same coin... However, if citizens are bearers of rights alone and all obligations fall upon the state, orderly and civilised life would be impossible: individuals who possess rights but acknowledge no obligations would be lawless and unrestrained. Citizenship, therefore, entails a blend of rights and obligations; the duty of the citizen to acknowledge the authority of the sate and obey its laws."[60]

59. Benn and Peters, *op. cit.*, p. 104.
60. Andrew Heywood: *Political Theory: An Introduction*, p. 197.

Not only this, since people are expected to lead a 'good life', it also becomes essential that rights should be exercised in a proper way so as to make the performance of corresponding duty equally well. It implies that proper exercise of rights leads to proper discharge of corresponding duty. Problems arise when the balance between the two is broken down or disturbed. In the present age of globalisation its meaning should be expanded to cover the world as a whole. As Mahatma Gandhi says: "I learnt from my illiterate but wise mother that all rights to be deserved and protected come from duty well done. Thus, the very right to life accrues to us only when we do the duty of citizenship of the world. From this one fundamental statement, perhaps, it is easy enough to define duties of men and women and correlate every right to some corresponding duty to be first performed. Every other right can be shown to be a usurpation badly worth fighting for."

Realisation of Rights: Provision of Special Safeguards

Mere conferment of rights on the citizen is not sufficient. What, in addition, is required is that there should be proper safeguards for their realisation. They may be enumerated as under:

1. The most important rights of the citizens should be provided in the basic law of the land so that they may know and exercise their, what are called, 'fundamental rights'. As already pointed out, it is a rather controversial subject as to what rights should be included in this category. For instance, while a liberal-democratic order attaches primary significance to socio-political rights like those relating to freedom of thought and expression and no arrest without sufficient cause coupled with the citizen's right to move the courts for seeking their adequate protection, a communist order does the same for economic rights. However, while taking a synthesised view, we may say that essential freedoms like those relating to the person and goods of the citizens along with provisions for social security should be included in this category. By including such rights in the category of fundamental rights, the state accords them constitutional protection and empowers the courts to issue prerogative writs for their enforcement.
2. Another safeguard is the rule of law. It has two important characteristics. First, it ensures equality before law and its equal protection to all. As such, every citizen is under the same legal obligation regardless of differences in the matter of religion, caste, creed, wealth, race, sex and the like. Second, it ensures personal liberty so that no person can be arrested without cause and that he cannot be punished either in body or in goods unless the case is decided against him by a court of competent jurisdiction by means of a fair and free trial.
3. There should be free and honest press so that people have a straightforward dissemination of news. In case the facts are not presented in their true aspect, or they are deliberately perverted, the judgement of the people is bound to be wrong. A free press is also required to safeguard the rights of the people. Newspapers are the best means to check political despotism. People may write in the columns of leading papers about the serious lapses on the part of their rulers. They may create healthy public opinion in defence of their rights and thereby compel their rulers to do or not to do something. As Laski says, a people without reliable news is, sooner or later, a people without the basis of freedom.

4. The state should observe the principle of decentralisation of powers. That is, the organs which exercise power must not be concentrated at a single point in the body politic. Local government must be empowered to deal with local matters, though under the control and supervision of the provincial or central government. Likewise, matters of regional interest should be entrusted to the regional or provincial government. It would certainly prevent the abuse of authority, and naturally result in the protection of the rights of the citizens.
5. It is also necessary that government organs are surrounded by consultative agencies. Since society has a plural character, it has varied interests that demand their adequate representation at the time of decision-making. Every association or group is made to protect and promote the specific interests of its members. The departments of the government should, therefore, consult the concerned organizations before coming to a decision as it would help not only in understanding the problem from the side of those going to be affected but also involve their due participation and thereby lessen the prospects of general dissatisfaction. Persons concerned would, in this way, feel that their rights are secure, and that they may safeguard them through their organisations.
6. Allied to this is the requirement that a state should not extend its area of activity into the legitimate domains of voluntary groups. For instance, religion is a private affair. As such, state should refrain from interfering in the jurisdiction of religious organisations. Likewise, it has no right to intervene in the field of social organisations that work for the betterment of the people. State intervention in the area of voluntary associations would automatically lead to the violation of the rights of the people, unless it is done to safeguard the overriding interest of the nation as a whole.
7. The most important safeguard, however, is eternal vigilance. The people must be vigilant to fight for their liberty. They should have the capacity to understand the nature and genesis of the problem posing threat to the security of their rights, and then they should have the will to fight for the defence of their rights. It is because of this that the people of England and France rose in revolt against royal despotism and forced their rulers to recognise in principle the supremacy of law.

In the end, it needs to be emphasised that rights are not safeguarded merely by their incorporation into the pages of the fundamental law of the land, or by the availability of provisions relating to the decentralisation of authority, or guarantee of the rule of law. What is really important is that the maintenance of rights is much more a question of habit and tradition than the formality of written enactment. The value of written provisions is simply this that while attacking the government in the name of its arbitrary action, the people may invoke the letter or spirit of the constitution. However, what can break or defeat the purpose of an arbitrary government is the will of the citizens determined to safeguard their rights. It is, therefore, rightly said: "It is the proud spirit of citizens, less than the letter of the law, that is their most real safeguard."[61]

61. Laski. *A Grammar of Politics*, p. 104.

Critical Appreciation

As a matter of fact, the idea of rights forms an intergal part of the case of active and enlightened citizenship. Historical evidence shows that as the idea of active citizenship has grown with the passage of time, so has been the development of the idea of rights. It also shows that the acquisition of rights is a definite result of long and persistent struggles by men 'having hearts pregnant with celestial fire' against the obstinate and powerful monarchies. It is in the course of such struggles that great thinkers have coined terms like 'natural rights' and 'fundamental rights'. We have already referred to the Glorious Revolution of England of 1688, the American War of Independence of 1776 and the Great Revolution of France of 1789 which brought about the era of modern democratic system in which people came to have their rights in the real sense of the term. The idea of the 'people' underwent change so much so that what once covered a very small section of the 'free men' has now become a large community consisting of 'every Tom, Dick and Harry'. It shows that the possession of rights "has been regarded as an essential characteristic of citizenship in all ages and climes."[62]

From whatever standpoint we may look at the matter, it is bound to be clear to us that in a free and open society maximum possible opportunity should be given to everyone irrespective of any discrimination on some artificial ground so that he may seek the best possible development of his personality. In essence, rights are essentials of a good and happy social life. And as state protects our rights, it is impossible to think of a system of rights in a society without state.[63]

Viewed thus, the provision, protection and enforcement of the system of rights furnishes the criteria by which we may evaluate the worth and legitimacy of a political system. Laski well advises that our method of judging the character of the political authority "lies, above all, in the contribution that it makes to the substance of man's happiness. The State, therefore, is not at least for political philosophy simply a sovereign organisation with the power to get its will obeyed. It cannot, save in narrowly legal sense, demand allegiance from its subjects save in terms of what the allegiance is to serve."[64]

62. G.N. Singh: *Fundamentals of Political Science and Organisation* (Allahabad: Kitab Mahal, 1966), p. 117.
63. Whether the system of rights can be maintained in a stateless society is not only doubtful, it is utopian too. It is well asserted." "But if the coercionless cooperative society fails to materialise and the legal system which could, in principle, embody positive expressions of human rights is abolished, there is little prospect that the individual will be protected against the invasions of the state. That Marx himself would be horrified by the behaviour of Communist regimes is no doubt true, but the abolition of these systems of law which can effectively protect individual rights finds ample justification in Marxism." Barry, *op cit.*, p. 196.
64. Laski, *op. cit.*, p. 89.

8

Liberty

> I am still doubtful how far liberty is to be valued for itself and how far I am really counting...on the good effects of variety and experiment to which Mill so often appeals. For liberty itself is what I value; it must have this high merit equally in the bad action and the good, and I cannot feel sure that in case where I knew I was doing wrong, it was at least one good element in the situation that no one tried to stop me.
>
> **—J.D. Mabbot**[1]

A discussion of the idea of liberty in its various aspects looks like an extension of what we have said in the preceding chapter in view of the fact that the momentous subject of rights is integrally connected with the concept of freedom. It is the provision of rights with their due enforcement by the state that ensures freedom to a citizen and thereby enables him to seek the best possible development of his personality. The purpose of the state is not confined merely to the maintenance of law and order, or protection of the weak against the strong, it is also concerned with the creation and preservation of that atmosphere in which an individual has every opportunity to sharpen his constructive initiative. The subject of rights, naturally, ushers in the form of one of the essential ingredients of a liberal political order attaching significance to the continuous initiative of man. In other words, it is the elaborate provision of rights that prevents the frustration of the creative impulse resulting in the destruction of the special character of man. It is, therefore, obvious: "Without rights there cannot be liberty, because without rights, men are the subjects of law unrelated to the needs of personality."[2]

Liberty: Real Meaning and Nature

Though the term 'liberty' comes from the Latin word *liber* meaning 'free', it has not meant the same thing for all thinkers in the realm of western political philosophy. "The word 'free' is one which is often used, especially by politicians, but it is not always clear what is meant."[3] Thus, we may find a wide margin of difference between the views of eminent political scientists ranging from that of Mill who treats liberty as something absolutely immune from restraints at least in the 'self-regarding sphere' of human activity[4] to that of Laski who takes it as "the eager maintenance of that atmosphere in which men have the opportunity to be their best selves."[5] It is owing to this diversity that the negative and positive dimensions of liberty have

1. Mabbott: *The State and the Citizen* (London: Hutchinson Univ., 1948), p. 62.
2. Laski: *A Grammar of Politics* (London: George Allen and Unwin, 1951), p. 142.
3. Benn and Peters: *Social Principles and the Democratic State* (London: George Allen and Unwin, 1975), p. 196.
4. J S. Mill.: *On Liberty* (London: Everyman, 1984), pp. 67-68.
5. Laski, *op.cit.*, p. 142.

been differently treated, particularly by the thinkers of the English liberal school. At the same time, on account of the burden of serious limitations like happiness and goodness, nature and reality, the meaning of this term has become "so porous that there is little interpretation that it seems able to resist."[6]

It follows that, like other important themes of normative political theory, the idea of liberty also cannot be defined in quite precise terms. What really besets is how to reconcile the idea of liberty with the provision of restraints. In others words, if liberty is to be differentiated from licence, or man's right to do what he wills, the issue of restraints is bound to figure in. At the same time, what engages our attention is that if restraints can preserve liberty, they can destroy it also. Hence, the question arises: what should be done to reconcile the two in a harmonious manner and thereby offer a plausible definition of the term 'liberty'? Two important points, however, have come to our knowledge so far – (i) the real meaning of liberty changes from age to age, and (ii) liberty lives within restraints and that a proper definition of the term "should be made in a way it incorporates both in view of the fact that liberty of each individual is necessarily relative to that of others."[7]

Liberty means the absence of constraints and not the absence of restraints and limitations. It does embrace the area of man's choice and, at the same time, calls for the proper justification of the limits or restrictions on such an area.[8] The case of 'unfreedom' smacks of a situation in which the conditions of choice have been so manipulated by external factors that the choice becomes limited solely to those to be determined by the coercer.[9] The important problem about freedom as the absence of restraints is that it accommodates a potentiality for the satisfaction of man's desires or options as permitted by the reasonable law of the state. As Berlin says: "Liberty is increased when sovereignty is put into right hands."[10]

If so, we may come to distinguish between 'feeling free' and 'being free': A man may feel free even when he gets himself locked up in a room as per his own choice, though he may not feel so in case he is inadvertently locked up in a room by another person. In the latter situation, the unfortunate person is certainly unfree, although this is not the result of anyone's deliberate contrivance.[11] What is to be seen in a situation like this is that one should feel free to use one's options without impediments. This point should be further examined in the context of being free to do something and being able to do something. For instance, a man may feel free to help the poor, but be may not be able to do so because of his financial conditions. The society and the state are, therefore, expected to create conditions for man so that he may feel like being free to do so and also able to do so. The social and political advancement of a community must be evaluated with this standpoint. However, the condition of 'being able to be free' does not imply that a man may do something wrong so as

6. Isaiah Berlin: "Two Concepts of Liberty" in Preston King (ed.): *The Study of Politics* (London: Frank Cass, 1977), p. 122.
7. E. Barker: *Principles of Social and Political Theory* (London: Oxford Univ Press, 1951), p. 145.
8. See Maurice Cranston: *Freedom: A New Analysis* (London: Longman, 1953), Ch. 1.
9. Barry, *op cit.*, p. 162.
10. Berlin: *Four Essays on Liberty* (London: Oxford University Press, 1969), pp. 162-66.
11. W. Parent: "Some Recent Works on the Concept of Liberty" in *American Philosophical Quarterly*, Vol 11 (1974), p. 151.

to convert his freedom into a state of unfreedom. Barry makes an interesting point in this direction when he says: "The old lag may deliberately commit a crime in order to recapture the security of prison life, but it would be absurd to describe his resulting condition as one of liberty"[12]

As such, the negative concept of liberty, as contained in the works of some liberal thinkers like John Stuart Mill, is not acceptable to the modern age. Mill in his well-known essay on liberty says: "The sole end for which mankind are warranted, individually or collectively, in interfering with the liberty of action of any of their number, is self-protection. That the only purpose for which power can be rightfully exercised over any member of a civilised community, against his will, is to prevent harm to others. His own good, either physical or moral, is not a sufficient warrant. . . . Over himself, his own body and mind, the individual is sovereign."[13] What this English liberal thinker of the nineteenth century is trying to say is that there can be no interference in the liberty of a man unless he becomes a nuisance to the liberty of another. That is, a man's sphere of activity can be divided into 'self-regarding' and 'others-regarding' compartments, and state interference is justified only in the latter sphere in case his action amounts to an intervention into the domain of freedom of his fellow-beings. Such a negative notion of liberty is well-contained in the statement of Mill when he says: "All restraint *qua* restraint, is an evil. . . . leaving people to themselves is always better *ceateris paribus,* than controlling them."[14]

In not much time, Mill's theory of liberty, along with the theory of individualism that was based upon it, became a discredited affair as the trend of English liberalism irresistibly moved towards socialism. It was found that he "was the prophet of an empty liberty and an abstract individual. He had no clear philosophy of rights, through which alone the conception of liberty attains a concrete meaning; he had no clear idea of that social whole in whose realisation the false antithesis of 'state' and 'individual' disappears."[15] It was realised that the idea of liberty should not ignore the social aspect of man's life. Thus, liberalism took a new turn in the direction of

---

12. Barry, *op cit.*, p. 160. "Any theory of liberty must take account of the range of alternatives that are open to the individual, so that wider the range, the more free an individual is." *Ibid.*, p. 163.
13. Mill, *op. cit.*, pp. 72-73.
14. *Ibid.*, pp. 150-51. 'The negative view of liberty flourished at a time when the individuals were struggling to be free from unnecessary restraints of arbitrary government and when individual choice determined the allocation of resources. Its main political axiom was that everyone knows his own interest best and that the state should not decide his ends and purposes. So Mill came out with his idea of hands off for the state in the strictly self-regarding sphere. He ruled out the case of 'paternalism'. And yet Barry feels that Mill leaves a very big room for state intervention in the domain of individual liberty by sanctioning restraints in the name of preventing an individual from being a nuisance to the liberty of his fellow beings. The qualifying clause of Mill is capable of any libertarian interpretation. "Since all but the most trivial acts affect somebody in some way, then could this not allow the law to protect the public freedom from certain immoral acts which although they do not cause injury in a direct sense, nevertheless cause offence? The use of the words which are deliberately designed to incite people to commit acts of violence would clearly be prohibited by most interpretations of the harm principle." *Op. cit.*, pp. 172-74.
15. Ernest Barker: *Political Thought in England* (London: Home Univ. Lib., 1951), p. 4.

realising man's organic relationship with society and a conscientious student of this philosophy in the early phase of the twentieth century could confidently assert that the argument of the separability of man's action into two watertight compartments was thoroughly untenable inasmuch as there "is no side of a man's life which is unimportant to society, for whatever he is, does, or thinks may affect his own well-being, which is and ought to be a matter of common concern, and may also directly or indirectly affect the thought, action and character of those with whom he comes into contact."[16]

Among the recent exponents of the case of 'negative liberty', we may refer to F.A. Hayek. To him the positive idea of liberty which is supposed to be more easily linked with equality is not really a concept of liberty at all, but something else masquerading as liberty. The individual has some assured private sphere, that there is some set of circumstances in his environment with which others cannot interfere.[17] The element of 'choice' is decisive. The range of physical possibilities from which a person can choose, at a given moment, has no direct relevance to freedom. The rock climber on a difficult pitch who sees only one way to save his life is unquestionably free, though we could say that he has hardly any choice.[18] "A man is free when he is not subjected to coercion by the arbitrary will of another person. Coecrion occurs when an agent's actions are made to serve the will of another, not for his own but for other's purposes. Coercion implies *action* in the sense that a person who is coerced chooses to be what he does. It occurs only when one person threatens with the intention of thereby getting the other to act in conformity with his will."[19] It follows that, according to Hayek, freedom implies the availability and capacity to exercise meaningful and effective choices. Mere economic factor should not be taken into account. For instance, the courtier living in the lap of luxury but at the beck and call of his prince may be much less free than a poor peasant or artisan, less able to live his own life, and to choose his own opportunities for usefulness. Political and institutional power, economic wealth and the growth of understanding through education and experience are positive sources of freedom and that the absence of these is as much an impediment to freedom as is direct coercion.[20]

The meaning of liberty finds its positive affirmation in the thought of T.H Green who describes it as a power to do or enjoy something that is worth doing or enjoying in common with others. The well-known Oxford Idealist insists that the one thing the state must do is to liberate its energies by removing the obstacles to their action. "Liberty can only be liberty for this goodwill; it can only be liberty for the pursuit of objects which such a will presents to itself. It is, therefore, no negative absence of restraints any more than beauty is the absence of ugliness. Inhering as it does in the good will and in that will only, it is not a power of pursuing any and every object, but a power of pursuing those objects which the good will presents to

16. L.T. Hobhouse: *Liberalism* (New York: Oxford Univ. Press, 1964), p. 65.
17. Hayek: *The Constitution of Liberty* (London: Routledge and Kegan Paul, 1960), p. 13.
18. *Ibid.*, pp. 12ff.
19. Crespigny: "Hayek: Freedom for Progress" in Crespigny and Minnogue (ed.s): *Contemporary Political Philosophers* (New York: Dodd Mead & Co., 1975), p. 50.
20. Hayek, *op cit.*, p. 94.

Liberty

'Licence' means the abuse of freedom; it is the point at which freedom becomes 'excessive'. Whereas liberty is usually thought to be wholesome, desirable and morally enlightening, licence is oppressive, objectionable and morally corrupt.

—**Andrew Heywood**

Political Theory: An Introduction, pp. 254-55.

Freedom must be given a concrete content; it only exists in everyday life as freedoms. An assessment of freedom must be made on the basis of liberties that are tangible, and capable of being used here and now within the realm of both state and civil society.

—**David Held**

Political Theory and the Modern State, p. 170.

Liberty is obedience to a law one prescribes to oneself.

—**Jean Jacques Rousseau**

Social Contract.

itself. In a word, it has two qualities. It is positive—a freedom to do something, not a freedom from having something done to one. It is determinate—a freedom to do something of a definite character, something which possesses the quality of being worth doing, and not any and everything."[21]

As a result of this, the meaning of liberty has come to involve within itself both the individual and social sides of man's existence. Moreover, as the social life requires a network of regulations, the idea of liberty has also been bound up with the necessity of due restraints. Liberty has, therefore, come to have a derivative value arising ultimately from the supreme value of the moral personality acting and developing its capacities as such. If so, the liberty which the state upholds, and makes a principle of its action, must be a liberty relative to, and therefore regulated by, the nature of such a personality. It is not "the indefinite liberty of an undefined 'individual'; it is the definite liberty of a defined personality, seeking to realise specific capacities."[22]

The case of 'positive liberty' finds its powerful defence in the statement of Leo Strauss: "There is no relation of man to man in which man is absolutely free to act as he pleases, or as it suits him. And all men are somehow aware of this fact. Every ideology is an attempt to justify before one's self or others such course of action as is somehow felt to be in need of justification, that is, as is not obviously right. . . . By virtue of his rationality man has a latitude of alternatives such as no other earthly being has. The sense of the latitude of this freedom is accompanied by a sense that the full and unrestrained exercise of that freedom is not right. Man's freedom is accompanied by a sacred awe, by a kind of divination that not everything is permitted. We may call this awe-inspired fear man's 'natural conscience'. Restraint is, therefore, as natural or as primeval as freedom."[23]

21. Barker: *Political Thought in England,* p. 24.
22. Barker: *Principles of Social and Political Theory,* p. 145.
23. Leo Strauss: *Natural Right and History,* pp. 129-30.

The real meaning of liberty is, therefore, integrally bound up with the availability of opportunities whereby an individual can seek the best possible development of his personality. Keeping this in view, a well-known English political scientist says: "The minds of citizens must be active minds. They must be given the habit of thought. They must be given the avenues through which thought can act. They must be accustomed to the exercise of will and conscience, if they are to be alert to the duties implied in their function as citizens. Liberty consists in nothing so much as the encouragement of the will based on the instructed conscience of humble men. . . . Freedoms are, therefore, opportunities which history has shown to be essential to the development of personality. And freedoms are inseparable from rights because, otherwise, their realisation is hedged about with an uncertainty which destroys their quality."[24]

The real meaning of liberty, moreover, not only requires a proper understanding of what it really carries forth, it also necessitates the enumeration of certain provisions for its achievement. Laski deals with this question and he enumerates three important guarantees for this purpose. They are:[25]

1. Liberty can never exist in the presence of special privileges. Unless one enjoys the same access to power as others, he lives in an atmosphere of contingent frustration. It does not matter that he shall probably not desire to take full advantage of that access. Its denial will mean that he accepts an allotted station as a permanent condition of his life; and that, in its turn, is fatal to the spontaneity that is the essence of freedoms.
2. There can be no liberty when the rights of some depend upon the pleasures of others. The common rules must bind those who exercise power as well as those who are the subject of power. No groups of men must be in a position to encroach upon one's enjoyment of the rights which attach to him as a citizen.
3. The incidence of the State action should be unbiased. Though in any society the varied personalities of which it is composed, the weight of the different interests involved, the degrees of efforts men will make, the amount of knowledge they will possess, are certain to bend its authority in the support of some special interest. The most we can do for the maintenance of freedom is to seek the system which will minimise the bias involved.

Negative and Positive Concepts: Absence of Restraints Versus Burden of Constraints

If studied in elaborate terms, the real meaning of liberty is involved in the dilemma of its negative and positive dimensions. The point of difficulty is that while we apparently reject the individualistic version of Mill and appreciate the idealistic interpretation of Green, the problem at hand remains unsolved. The delicate question of the proper relationship between liberty, on the one hand, and authority, on the other, is such that a serious student of this subject feels bound to hover between two opposite poles (as we find in the case of Laski), or he tries to steer himself out by

24. Laski: *A Grammar of Politics*, pp. 143-44.
25. *Ibid.*, pp. 149-51.

presenting his ideas in a theoretically correct form (as we find in the case of Berlin), unless he takes to a purely idealistic course (as we find in the case of Bosanquet), or he makes a deliberate attempt to offer a plausible rejoinder to the doctrine of socialism (as we find in the case of Friedman).[26]

The negative dimension of liberty is contained in an affirmation of the 'absence of restraints'. In purely idealistic terms, it means to hinder the hindrances to good life. As such, the version of Prof. Bernard Bosanquet pertains to the realm of negative freedom when he says that liberty is an essential condition of life whereby man can seek the best possible development of his 'self'. When is a man free? In order to answer this complex question, he distinguishes between one's 'actual self' and the 'higher self' that guides and directs a rational purpose. "If so, in moral terms, it is not doing what we please that constitutes our freedom, but doing as we *ought*. We are free in so far as we are self-determined only as we are determined by this law of a larger and rational purpose."[27] Thus, liberty, according to this neo-Hegelian of the Oxford school of idealism, is "a state of mind in which the impulse towards self-satisfaction sets itself upon an object which represents the nature of self as a whole, as free from contradictions of partial self—the tendency to narrower tracks of indulgence when entangled in which it feels itself oppressed and constrained by foreign influence, but when the mind wills the whole, it feels free."[28]

Such a philosophical interpretation of freedom has a strictly negative character, no matter Bosanquet takes it as 'a condition of mind' instead of an 'absence of physical restraint'. Curiously, a man of socialist orientation like Laski could not save himself from the impact of the negative dimension of liberty that made him a protagonist of both dimensions of this momentous subject. This is evident from the fact that while in 1919 he treated liberty as a set of restraints that circumscribe the authority of the state,[29] he showed a shift some five years later when he introduced the element of 'moral development' of the personality of the individual in the real meaning of liberty.[30] Again, in 1929, he (in his Preface to the second edition of his *A Grammar of Politics)* realised his 'mistake' and confessed that the old view of liberty as an absence of restraint could alone safeguard the personality of the citizen.[31] It had its culmination in the Clover lectures delivered by him at the Brown University in 1929 when he said: "I mean by liberty the absence of restraint upon the existence of those social conditions which, in modern civilisation, are the necessary guarantees of individual happiness."[32]

---

26. Since the notion of 'positive liberty' appreciates the system of 'reasonable restraints', it becomes an anathema to those who harbour certain lurking apprehensions about the increasing encroachments upon the liberty of the individual in the name of anything like'public welfare'or'class interest'. "The route to totalitarianism is plainly laid out when the higher purposes of the individual are made equivalent to those of collectivities such as classes, nation and races." Barry, *op. cit.*, p. 167.
27. Frank Thakurdas: "Two Interpretations of Liberty: A Study in Contrast" in *Indian Journal of Political Studies*, Jodhpur, Vol. 1, No. 2, 1977, p. 136.
28. Bosanquet: *The Philosophical Theory of State* (London: Macmillan, 1920), p. 132.
29. Laski: *Authority in the Modern State* (New Haven: Yale Univ. Press, 1919), p. 326.
30. Laski: *A Grammar of Politics*, p. 144.
31. *Ibid.*, p. 7.
32. Laski: *Liberty in the Modern State* (London: George Allen and Unwin, 1961), p. 42.

Libertarianism

Libertarian political thought is characterised by the strict priority given to liberty (understood in negative sense) over other values, such as tradition and equality. Libertarians thus seek to maximise the realm of individual freedom and minimise the scope of public authority, typically seeing the state as the principal threat to liberty.

—**Andrew Heywood**

Political Theory: An Introduction, p. 337.

Libertarianism shares with liberal equality a commitment to the principle of respect for people's choices, but rejects the principle of rectifying unequal circumstances.

—**Will Kymlicka**

Contemporary Political Philosophy, p. 154.

Effective limitation of power is the most important problem of social order. Government is indispensable for the formation of such an order only to protect all against coercion and violence, it becomes also the chief threat to individual freedom.

—**F.A. von Hayek**

Law, Legislation and Liberty, Vol. III, p. 128.

As a matter of fact, the real meaning of liberty involves its negative as well as positive sides.[33] As such, we may neither thoroughly reject the individualistic interpretation of Mill who desires no state intervention in the 'self-regarding' sphere of man's conduct and modifies his view subsequently when he desires more and more state regulation of public economy, including nationalisation of very important industries, in the social interest, nor can we unreservedly appreciate the idealistic version of Green who takes liberty to the final extreme of 'making a man free' at the hands of a paternalistic government. In other words, neither a mere emphasis on the 'absence of restraints' nor a powerful defence of the 'imposition of constraints by the state' is required. What is really desired is a happy synthesis of both dimensions so that the liberty of the individual and the authority of the state witness a harmonious reconciliation. In this way, an important task of political theory is, in fact, "to decide between the claims of liberty and authority, and to fix their proper frontiers."[34] What should be borne in mind is, as Oakeshott says, that the genuine freedom with which we should be concerned "is not a dream or abstraction but something concrete which is embodied in the laws and customs and enjoyed in actual way of living; and inquiry about it is not merely the definition of a word but the detection of the secret of this enjoyment, also the recognition of what is inimical to it."[35]

Keeping all this in view, Laski thus offers a definition of his own. According to him, liberty "may be defined as the affirmation by an individual or group of his or

33. As Oppenheim says: "There is no such thing as freedom in general; every organised society consists of an intricate network of specific relations of both freedom and unfreedom. If freedom becomes a label for anybody's moral or political ends, then everybody's value commitment to freedom will be vacuous." Refer to his paper "Freedom" in David I. Sills (ed.): *International Encyclopaedia of the Social Sciences* (New York: Macmillan and Free Press, 1968), Vol. 5, pp. 557-58.
34. Benn and Peters, *op. cit.*, p. 212.
35. W.H. Greenleaf: *Oakeshott's Philosophical Politics* (London: Longmans, 1966), p. 85.

its own essence. It seems to require the presence of three factors. It seeks, in the first place, a certain harmonious balance of personality; it requires, on the negative side, the absence of restraint upon the exercise of that affirmation; and it demands, on the positive, the organisation of opportunities for the exercise of continuous initiative. The problem of liberty has always been the prevention of those restraints, upon the one hand, that men at any given period are not prepared to tolerate and, upon the other, the organisation of those opportunities the denial of which results in the sense of frustration which, when widely felt, leads to imminent or actual disorder."[36]

Berlin's Rejoinder: Refutation of the Case of Negative Versus Positive Liberty

Now we may take note of the new interpretation of liberty at the hands of Prof. Isaiah Berlin. The striking feature of his thesis is the refutation of the line of distinction between the negative and positive aspects of liberty. The way he defines the term 'liberty' is not at all surprising when he identifies it with the'free choice'of an individual. What is really striking in this regard is that he takes the two sides of liberty as integrated in a way that they are virtually indistinguishable and, therefore, inseparable in their practical dimensions. Liberty presupposes the need of an area for free choice, the dimunition of which is incompatible with the existence of anything that can properly be called political (or social) liberty. That is, liberty is the 'absence of obstacles to the fulfilment of a man's desires'.[37]

In order to make this point more explicit, Berlin says: "The sense of freedom in which I use this term, entails not simply the absence of obstacles to possible choices and activities—absence of obstructions on roads along which a man can decide to walk. Such freedom ultimately depends not on whether I wish to walk at all, or how far, but on how many doors are open, how open they are, upon their relative importance in my life, even though it may be impossible literally to measure this in any quantitative fashion. The extent of my social or political freedom consists in the absence of obstacles not merely to my actual, but to my potential choices—to my acting in this or that way if I chooss to do so. Similarly, absence of such freedom is due to the closing of such doors or failure to open them, as a result, intended or unintended, of alterable human practices, of the operation of human agencies: although only if such acts are deliberately intended (or, perhaps, are accompanied by awareness that they may block paths) will they be liable to be called oppression. Unless this is conceded, the Stoic conception of liberty ('true freedom'—the state of the morally autonomous slave), which is compatible with a very high degree of political despotism will merely confuse the issue."[38]

36. Laski: "Liberty" in Seligman (ed.): *Encyclopaedia of the Social Sciences* (.New York: Macmillan, 1967), Vol. IX, p. 144. We may, however, appreciate the view of Sir J.F. Stephen that fire and liberty could not be good or bad according to time, place and circumstances. Certain kinds of immortal acts are so degrading that society must express its disgust and abhorrence of them by punishing the perpetrators irrespective of the fact that the acts in question rest on consent and harm no one. See Chapter IV of *Liberty, Equality and Fraternity*, edited by J. Whyte (London: Cambridge University Press, 1967).
37. Berlin: *Four Essays on Liberty*, p. xxxviii.
38. *Ibid.*, pp. xxxix-xl.

It is true that liberty involves free choice, but one should not take a fatalistic or deterministic view of things, though the case of self-determinism may be thought in a particular situation. Fatalism implies that human decisions are mere byproducts, epiphenomena, incapable of influencing events which take their inscrutable course independently of human wishes. In Berlin's view, most of the people cling to self-determinism which implies that men's characters and personality structures and the emotions, attitudes, choices, decisions, and acts that flow from them do indeed play a full part in what occurs, but are themselves the results of causes, psychical and physical, social and individual, which in turn are effects of other causes and so on in an unbreakable sequence. Self-determinism may be identified with 'weak determinism' in which, since its original formulation by the Stoic sage Chyrissipus, many thinkers have come to rest, was described by Kant as a 'miserable subterfuge'; William James called it 'soft determinism' and perhaps too harshly dubbed it as 'a quagmire of evasion'.[39]

Berlin further observes: "If I judge that a man's conduct was, in fact, determined, that he could not have behaved (felt, thought, desired, chosen), otherwise I should regard this kind of praise or blame as inappropriate to his case. If determinism is true, the concept of merit or desert, as these are usually understood, has no application. If all things and events and persons are determined, then praise and blame do, indeed, become purely pedagogical devices—history and minatory; or else they are quasi-descriptive— they grade in terms of distance from some ideal. They comment on the quality of men, what men are and can be and do, and may themselves alter it and, indeed, be used as deliberate means towards it, as when we reward or punish an animal: save that in the case of men we assume the possibility of communication with them, which we cannot do in the case of animals. That is the heart of 'soft determinism'—the so-called Hobbes-Hume-Schlick doctrine. If, however, the notions of desert, merit, responsibility etc. rested on the notion of choices not themselves fully caused, they would, on this view, turn out to be irrational or incoherent; and would be abandoned by rational men."[40]

The fact of determinism, whether self-determinism or fatalism, impedes the case of free choice of a man. It is also possible that some factors like ignorance, insensitiveness, haste, lack of imagination darken our sense of judgement or blind us to the true facts. It is also true that because of such factors our judgements are often shallow, dogmatic, complacent, irresponsible, unjust, barbarous. A patient of kleptomania or dipsomania may also feel incapable of exercising his freedom of choice. Since these characteristics vary from man to man in respect of their effects, such notions as justice, equity, desert, fairness would certainly have to be re-examined if they are to be kept alive at all and not relegated to the role of discarded fragments—fancies rendered harmless by the march of reason, myths potent in our irrational youth exploded, or at any rate rendered innocuous, by the progress of scientific knowledge. If determinism is valid, this is a price that we must pay. Whether or not we are ready to do so, let this prospect at least be faced."[41]

39. *Ibid.*, pp. xiii-xiv.
40. *Ibid.*, p. xv.
41. *Ibid.*, p. xxii. Berlin prefers to appreciate these words of Prof. E.H. Carr: "The fact is that all human actions are both free and determined according to the point of view from which one considers them." *What is History* (London, 1964), p. 95.

As already pointed out, Berlin's main argument is that we may not distinguish between the negative and positive aspects of liberty in a way as we do in the case of others like J.S. Mill, T.H. Green, H.J. Laski, Eric Fromm and Bernard Crick. Freedom is the spontaneous and rational activity of the total integrated personality of man that expresses itself in the form of action. As he continues: "The freedom of which I speak is opportunity for action, rather than action itself. If, although I enjoy the right to walk through the open doors, I prefer not to do so, but to sit still and vegetate, I am not thereby rendered less free. Freedom is the opportunity to act, not action itself, not necessarily the dynamic realisation of it."[42]

That the two aspects of liberty cannot be distinguished from each other in their particular application is evident from the following arguments of Berlin:

1. There is some area of a man's life that must be free from restraint of any kind so that he may wish to determine the course of his action without any direction from others, no matter how benevolent. The conduct of man derives irreplacable value from the sole fact that it is his own and not imposed upon him by others. As he says: "But I am not, and cannot expect to be, wholly self-sufficient or socially omnipotent. I cannot remove all the obstacles in my path that stem from the conduct of my fellows. I can try to ignore them, treat them as illusory, or 'intermingle' them and attribute them to my own inner principles, conscience, moral sense; or try to dissolve my sense of personal identity in a common enterprise, as an element in a larger self-directed whole. Nevertheless, despite such heroic efforts to transcend or dissolve the conflicts and resistance of others, if I do not wish to be deceived, I shall recognise the fact that total harmony with others is incompatible with self-identity, that if I am not to be dependent on others in every respect, I shall need some area within which I am not, and can count on not being freely interfered with by them."[43]
2. Liberty is not a dualistic but a monistic creed. Any curb on liberty affects its both sides—negative and positive. The positivists appreciate the system of restraints on man's freedom in general interest, but the fact is that they talk of restraints on freedom and not on freedom itself. They forget that the imposition of restraints in the name of any myth like public interests affects freedom as a whole, whether it is its positive side or negative side. For instance, curtailment of the freedom of the rich to give certain benefits to the poor would be like freedom for the wolves meaning death to the freedom of the sheep. The evils of unrestricted *laissez faire* and of the social and legal systems that permitted and encouraged it led to brutal violations of 'negative liberty,—of basic human rights (always a negative notion: a wall against oppressors), including that of free expression or association without which there may exist justice and fraternity and even happiness of a kind, but not democracy. . . . . Legal liberties are compatible with extremes of exploitation, brutality and injustice. The case for intervention by the state or other effective agencies to secure conditions for both positive, and at least a minimum degree of negative liberty for individuals is overwhelmingly strong.[44]

42. Berlin, *op. cit.*, p. xlii.
43. *Ibid.*, pp. xlii-xliv.
44. *Ibid.*, pp. xlv-xlvi.

3. The two aspects of liberty may be theoretically distinguishable, but both are ends in themselves. The two may clash irreconciliably. But the question arises whether democracy should be promoted at the expense of individual freedom, or equality at the cost of individual freedom, or mercy at the expense of justice. The simple point is that where ultimate values are irreconciliable, clear-cut solutions cannot, in principle, be found. We are living in an age of expanding economic productivity. If a situation is permitted or promoted in which entire groups and nations are progressively shut off from benefits which have been allowed to accumulate too exclusively in the hands of groups and nations, the restrictions will certainly curb both sides of human freedom. In other words, it implies that the activities of state in the name of public welfare services have adversely affected the area of man's freedom. "This has been done by social and economic policies that were sometimes openly discriminatory, at other times camouflaged, by the rigging of educational policies and the means of influencing opinion, by legislation in the sphere of morals, and similar measures, which have blocked and diminished human freedom at times as effectively as the more overt and brutal methods of direct oppression— slavery and imprisonment—against which the original defenders of liberty lifted their voices."[45]
4. The mistake of a person holding the positivist view of liberty is that he prescribes a code of uniform restrictions on the enjoyment of liberty, but he forgets that some values may conflict intrinsically. The very notion that a pattern must in principle be discoverable in which they are all rendered harmonious is founded on a false *a priori* view of what the world is like. If I am right in this, and the human condition is such that men cannot always avoid choices, they cannot avoid them not merely for the obvious reasons which philosophers have seldom ignored, namely, that there are many possible courses of action and forms of life worth living, and therefore to choose between them is part of being rational or capable of moral judgement; they cannot avoid choice for one central reason, namely, that ends collide; that one cannot have everything. . . . . There is a minimum level of opportunity for choice—not of rational or virtuous choice alone—below which human activity ceases to be free in any meaningful sense. It is true that the cry for individual liberty has often disguised desire for privilege, or for power to oppress and exploit, and simply fear of social change. Nevertheless, the modern horror of uniformity, conformism, and mechanisation of life is not groundless."[46]
5. It is important to discriminate between liberty and the conditions of its exercise. If a man is too poor, or too ignorant, or too feeble to make use of his legal rights, the liberty that these rights confer upon him is nothing to him, but it is not thereby annihilated. The obligation to promote education, health, justice, to raise standards of living, to provide opportunity for the growth of the arts and the sciences, to prevent reactionary political or social or legal policies or arbitrary inequalities is not made less stringent because it is not necessarily directed to the promotion of liberty itself, but to conditions in which alone its possession is of value, or to values which may be independent of it. "And still liberty is

45. *Ibid.*, pp. xlvii-xlviii.
46. *Ibid.*, pp. li-lii.

one thing, and the conditions for it are another. . . . Useless freedoms should be made usable, but they are not identical with the conditions indispensable for their utility. This is not merely a pedantic distinction, for if it is ignored, the meaning and value of freedom of choice is apt to be downgraded. In their zeal to create social and economic conditions in which alone freedom is of genuine value, men tend to forget freedom itself, and if it is remembered, it is liable to be pushed aside and to make room for those other values with which the reformers or reactionaries have become preoccupied."[47]

Despite this all, it may be commented that though Berlin advances the argument that the two aspects of liberty cannot be so distinguished in practical terms, one may differ from him and come to hold that his ultimate preference is for the defence of the negative view of liberty. Hence, he obviously belongs to the category of Mill and Hayek. It is evident from his emphatic affirmation: "The fundamental sense of freedom is freedom from chains, from imprisonment, by others.The rest is extension of this sense, or else metaphor. To strive to be free is to seek to remove obstacles, to struggle for personal freedom is to seek to curbing interference, exploitation, enslavement by men whose ends are theirs, not one's own. Freedom, at least in its political sense, is coterminous with the absence of bullying or domination. . . . One freedom may absorb another; one freedom may obstruct or fail to create conditions which make other freedoms, or a larger degree of freedom, or freedom for more persons, possible; positive and negative freedom may collide; the freedom of the individual or the group may not be fully compatible with a full degree of participation in a common life, with its demands for cooperation, solidarity, fraternity.. . . Individual freedom may or may not clash with democratic organisation and the positive liberty of self-realisation with the negative liberty of non-interference. Emphasis on negative liberty, as a rule, leaves more paths for individuals or groups to pursue; positive liberty, as a rule, opens fewer paths, but with better reasons or greater resources for moving along them; the two may or may not clash. . . . Those who are obsessed by the truth that negative freedom is worth little without sufficient conditions for the active exercise, or without the satisfaction of other human aspirations, are liable to minimise its importance, to deny it the very title of freedom, to transfer it to something that they regard as more precious, and finally to forget that without human life, both social and individual, withers away."[48]

We may come across a situation of confusion when we find Berlin behaving like a positivist when he denies the case of absoluteness of liberty in any respect and, at the same time, he expresses his frank disapproval of the thesis of positive liberty as so powerfully defended by Green.[49] That is, at one place, he asserts that what he says should not be taken to mean that freedom in any of its meanings is either inviolable or sufficient, in some absolute senses. It is not inviolable, because

47. *Ibid.*, pp. liii-liv.
48. *Ibid.*, pp. xlvi-xlix.
49. As Green says in his monograph titled "The Liberal Legislation and the Freedom of Contract": "The mere removal of compulsion, the mere enabling of a man to do as he likes,' is in itself no contribution to true freedom. . . the ideal of true freedom is the maximum of power for all members of human society alike to make the best of themselves." See Green: *Works*, Vol. Ill, pp. 371-72.

abnormal conditions may occur in which even the sacred frontiers of which Constant speaks, e.g., those violated by retrospective laws, punishment of the innocent, judicial murder, information laid against parents by children, the bearing of false witness may have to be disregarded if some sufficiently terrible alternative is to be averted."[50] But he accuses Green of creating a confusion between 'true freedom' and the 'best of themselves'. It looks like a metaphysical doctrine of the two selves—the individual streams versus the social river in which they should be merged, a dualistic fallacy used too often to support a variety of despotism."[51] Similar confusion may be noted in Berlin's rejection of the purely negative view of liberty as given by Bentham that 'every law is an infraction of liberty'[52] and his own interpretation that 'every law seems to me to curtail some liberty, although it may be a means to increasing another'.[53] In a word, the whole affirmation of Berlin looks like a reinterpretation of the thesis of a great liberal thinker of the seventeenth century England like John Locke that liberty "is the power a man has to do or forbear doing any particular action according. . . . as he himself wills it"[54] and that 'the end of law is not to abolish or restrain but to preserve and enlarge freedom'.[55]

Specific Kinds of Liberty

Simply stated, liberty implies "a state of freedom especially opposed to political subjection, imprisonment or slavery."[56] However, in a wider sense, it is a multiple concept that may be understood if we look at its specific varieties. These are:

1. **Natural Liberty:** It implies complete freedom for a man to do what he wills. It is another name for the liberty of the woods that is also known by the name of 'licence'. It existed in the state of nature as suggested by Hobbes. Naturally, it was terminated when civil society came into existence. It may be easily understood that this kind of liberty is no liberty at all inasmuch as it is a euphemism for the

---

50. Berlin, *op. cit.*, p. lx.
51. *Ibid.*, p. xlix, n 1.
52. The keynote of the whole case of negative freedom is that it cannot be curtailed by state action, because it would create a condition in which everyone would come to interfere in the affairs of every other man leading to social chaos. Thus, this concept "implies that there ought to be a certain minimum or limited area of personal freedom which is inviolable, that is, in which others cannot interfere." A. H. Doctor: *Issues in Political Theory* (New Delhi: Sterling, 1985), p. 131.
53. See David Nicholls: "Positive Liberty—1880-1914" in *The American Political Science Review* (March, 1962); A.S. Kaufmann: "Berlin on Negative Freedom" in *Mind* (April, 1962); Marshall Cohen: "Berlin and the Liberal Tradition" in *Philosophical Quarterly* (1957), pp. 215-28. This is in clear refutation of the view of G.C. McCallum, Jr, that all liberty is at once negative and positive, or better sttill neither. It has triadic relationship. See his 'Negative and Positive Liberty" in *Philosophical Review*, Vol. 76, No. 3 (1967), pp. 312-34 reproduced in A. de Crespigny and A Wertheimer (eds.): *Contemporary Political Theory* (London: Nelson, 1970), pp. 107-26. Instead Berlin asserts that this seems like an error. "A man struggling against his chains or a people against enslavement need not consciously aim at any definite further state. A man need not know how he will use his freedom; he just wants to remove the yoke. So do classes and nations. *Op. cit*, p. xliii n. 1.
54. Locke: *Essay Concerning Human Understanding*, Book II, Chapter XXI, Sec. 15.
55. Locke: *Second Treatise of Civil Government*, Sec. 57.
56. *Encyclopaedia Britannica*, Vol. 13, 1967 ptg., p. 1029.

freedom of the forest. It is not applicable to the life of man as a social being. What we call liberty pertains to the realm of man's social existence. Thus, Rousseau who started with the assumption that 'man is born free, he is everywhere in chains' came to stress the point that 'what man loses by the social contract is his natural liberty and an unlimited right to everything he tries to get and succeeds in getting; what he gains is civil liberty and the proprietorship of all he possesses.'[57]

2. **Social Liberty:** What we really mean by the term liberty lies in its social variety that has its wider ramifications in personal, political, economic, domestic, national and international spheres. It relates to man's freedom in his life as a member of the social organisation. As such, it refers to a man's right to do what he wills in compliance with the restraints imposed on him in the general interest. Thus, man's freedom in the spheres of professing any religion or expressing his ideas and the like fall in this category. One may also include equality before law and security of possessions in this category. In other words, civil or social liberty consists in the rights and privileges that the society recognises and the state protects in the spheres of private and public life of an individual. Thus, social liberty liberates a man from the fear of arbitrary aggression or 'coercion'.[58] Social liberty has the following sub-categories:

(a) **Personal Liberty:** As already said, personal liberty is an important variety of social liberty.[59] It refers to the opportunity to exercise freedom of choice in those areas of a man's life where the results of his efforts mainly affect him in that isolation by which, at least, he is always surrounded. "Private liberty", says Laski, "is that aspect of which the substance is mainly personal to a man's self. It is the opportunity to be fully himself in the private relations of life. It is the chance practically to avail himself of the safeguards evolved for the maintenance of those relations."[60] According to Blackstone, this type of liberty consists in three directions: (i) personal security not only of health and life but also of reputation, (ii) personal freedom especially of movement; and (iii) personal property or the free use, enjoyment and disposal of all acquisitions. Ernest Barker (who identifies personal liberty with civil liberty) says that such liberty "consists in three somewhat differently expressed articles (i) physical freedom from injury or threat to the life, health and movement of the body, (ii) intellectual freedom for the expression of thought and belief; and (iii) practical freedom for the play of will and the exercise of choice in the general field of contractual action and relations with other persons."[61]

---

57. Rousseau: Social *Contract,* Book I, Chapter VIII.
58. Hobhouse, *op. cit,* p. 17.
59. One may hardly agree with this observation of E. Asirvatham: "Yet there is a sense in which natural liberty can be interpreted sensibly. It stands for those areas of life where a man does not want to be interfered with so long as he does not interfere with others. The freedom of motion and locomotion is a case in point." *Political Theory* (Lucknow: Upper India, 1961), p. 186.
60. Laski: *A Grammar of Politics,* p. 146.
61. Barker: *Principles of Social and Political Theory,* pp. 146-47.

(b) **Political Liberty:** It refers to the power of the people to be active in the affairs of the state. Thus, it is integrally connected with the life of man as a citizen. "It means that I can let my mind play freely about the substance of public business. I must be able without hindrance to add my special experience to the general sum of experience. I must find no barriers that are not general barriers in the way of access to positions of authority. I must be able to announce my opinions and to concert with others in the announcement of opinion."[62] It requires two things—political education and free supply of news.[63] Simply stated, political liberty consists in provisions for universal adult franchise, free and fair elections, and freedom for the avenues that make a healthy public opinion. Blackstone was partly correct when he identified this type of liberty only with man's power to curb government. As a matter of fact, it consists in curbing as well as constituting and controlling the government."[64]

(c) **Economic Liberty:** It belongs to the individual in the capacity of a producer or a worker, whether manual or mental, engaged in some gainful occupation or service. It means "security and the opportunity to find reasonable significance in the earning of one's daily bread". The individual should be free from the constant fear of unemployment and insufficiency which, perhaps more than any other inadequacies, sap the whole strength of personality. In a wider perspective, it covers two important spheres: (i) The industrial government is subject to the system of rights which obtain for men as citizens (ii) The industrial direction must be of a character that makes it the rule of law made by cooperation and not by compulsion. Thus, economic liberty implies democracy in industry.[65] The subject of economic liberty is, however, a matter of some controversy. Thus, while the men of socialist orientation have defined it as man's role as a producer of goods subject to the control and regulation of the state, others subscribing to the school of liberalism have interpreted it as relating to the freedom of contract, association, production and distribution of goods.[66]

(d) **Domestic Liberty:** It is by and large a sociological concept that takes the discussion of liberty to the sphere of man's family life. It implies that of all associations within the state, the miniature community of the family is the most universal and of the strongest independent vitality. There was a time when the authoritarian state was reflected in the authoritarian family. Thus, with the advent of democracy, liberty pervaded the sphere of family life as well. Here it consists in (i) rendering the wife a fully responsible individual capable of holding property, suing and being sued, conducting business on her own account, and enjoying full personal protection against her husband, (ii) in establishing marriage as far as the law is concerned on

62. Laski, *op. cit*, pp. 146-47.
63. *Ibid.*, p. 147.
64. Barker, *op. cit.*, p. 174.
65. Laski, *op. cit.*, p. 148.
66. Hobhouse, *op. cit.*, p. 23.

a purely contractual basis, and leaving the sacramental aspect of marriage to the ordinances of the religion professed by the parties, and (iii) in securing the physical, mental and moral care of the children, partly by imposing definite responsibilities on the parents and punishing them for neglect, partly by elaborating a public system of education and hygiene.[67]

(e) **National Liberty:** It is synonymous with national independence. As such, it implies that no nation should be under the subjection of another. For instance, the Americans gained national liberty in 1776 and the Indians in 1947. Thus, national movements or wars of independence can be identified as struggles for the attainment of national liberty. For this reason, love for national liberty is identified with patriotism. Historical evidence shows that love for one's country is deepseated in human heart as a result of which millions of people lay down their lives for the sake of the honour and security of their motherland.

(f) **International Liberty:** The ideal of liberty covers the world as a whole. Thus, in the international sphere, it implies renunciation of war, limitation on the production of armaments, abandonment of the use of force, and pacific settlement of disputes. It also desires adequate curbs on the strength of military force so that it may not crush the liberties of the local people (as happens in a country under a military dictatorship) or of the people of a different country as German troops did in Austria, the Russian troops did the same in Hungary and Czechoslovakia and the American forces did in Vietnam. The ideal of international liberty is based on this pious conviction that "in proportion as the world becomes free, the use of force becomes meaningless and that there is no purpose in aggression if it is not to issue in one form or another of national subjection.[68]

3. **Moral Liberty:** This type of freedom is contained in the idealistic interpretations of thinkers form Plato and Aristotle in ancient to Rousseau, Kant, Hegel, Green and Bosanquet in modern times. In this context, it is suggested that though a person may have all the kinds of freedom, as given above, he lacks the essential quality of a human being in case he does not have moral freedom. This type of freedom lies in man's capacity to act as per his rational self. Every individual has a personality of his own and, unless he seeks the best possible development of his personality and, at the same time, he desires the same thing for others and more than this he pays sincere respect for the real worth and dignity of his fellow-beings, he is morally not free. Kant calls it the fulfilment of the will to 'categorical self-imposed imperative of duty' and 'the autonomy of the rational will'. To Hegel, such freedom has its objective realisation in the state. Thus, the idea of moral freedom implies that the individual should, what Bradley says, recognise and, fulfil the obligations of his station and its duties. Moral liberty is, thus, necessarily connected with man's self-realisation that "has a meaning only in the context of the common good, and the latter, in turn, is founded on human

67. *Ibid.*, p. 25.
68. *Ibid.*, p. 27.

personality, and, as such, includes the good of each member and postulates free scope for the development of his personality."[69]

4. **Purposive Liberty:** Everyone loves liberty, but the value of this boon differs from person to person. For instance, religious liberty is regarded more valuable than traffic liberty as it serves more important interests of most of the believers. It implies that the amount of freedom contained in a particular form of liberty depends on how important that liberty is to the people, given their interests and purposes. "Freedom is important to us, because we are purposive beings. But then there must be distinctions in the significance of different kinds of freedom based on the distinction in the significance of different purposes."[70] However, such a definition of liberty "requires some standard for assessing the importance of liberty in order to measure the amount of freedom it contains."[71]

Liberal Versus Marxist Notions of Liberty: Controversy on the Nature and Scope of Liberty

What we have said in the preceding sections largely pertains to the sphere of liberal political theory. It shall, therefore, be in the natural fitness of things if we throw some light on the liberal *vis-a vis* Marxist interpretations regarding the meaning and nature of liberty hinging mainly on the nature and scope of economic liberty along with the institutions and arrangements that preserve and protect the enjoyment of freedom in its varied ramifications. The important point to be noted here is that there is hardly any difference between the two so far as the real meaning and nature of liberty are concerned in view of the fact that a controversy of this type is the result not so much of Marx's criticism of the bourgeois economic system as that of the great changes that overtook Russia in the period following the First World War. It is on account of the proletarian or socialist movement and economic dislocations after the First Great War that liberty "has been increasingly defined in terms of economic opportunity and security. In Anglo-American countries liberty has often been identified with constitutional government, political democracy and the orderly administration of common law system."[72]

The real meaning of liberty constitutes, what Hobhouse says, the 'heart of liberalism'. But what type of liberty? As we shall see in the chapter on Liberalism, it should be reiterated that this highly fluid philosophy or doctrine has witnessed a marked change in the direction of socialism in the present times as a result of which the idea of individual liberty has been integrated with the good of the society. As such, an emphasis on man's search for the best possible development of his personality has been bound up with the needs and interests of the society. In this revised form, the rule of liberty "is just the application of rational method. It is the opening of the door to the appeal of reason, of imagination, of social feeling; and except through the response to this appeal there is no assured progress of society."[73]

69. Frank Thakurdas: *Recent English Political Theory* (Calcutta: Minerva, 1972), p. 27.
70. Charles Taylor: *Philosophy and Human Science: Philosophical Papers,* (Cambridge: Cambridge University Press, 1985), Vol. II, p. 219.
71. Will Kymlicka: *Contemporary Political Philosophy: An Introduction* (Oxford: Oxford University Press, 2005), p. 145.
72. *Encyclopaedia Britannica,* Vol. 13, 1967 Ptg., p. 1030.
73. Hobhouse: *Liberalism,* p. 66.

It is on account of this change in the nature of liberalism that the concept of liberty has witnessed a simultaneous change particularly in the economic sphere The uppermost consideration in the minds of recent liberal thinkers is the case of economic freedom that would ensure to the workers a just reward for their labour, it would banish destructive cut-throat competition, abolish blind alley jobs and remove such artificial regulations of manufacture and trade which result in the demoralisalion of the workers. Moreover, it is economic freedom that helps creation of a harmonious industrial system in which everyone would produce only that which he is best capable of, and the society would have need for what he produces. The burden of insistence is that unless this freedom "is achieved, it cannot be said that we have solved the problem of liberty in its fullness."[74]

Not merely different from, rather basically opposed to it, is the Marxian contention. To Marx, there can be no real freedom unless the system of capitalism is replaced by the socialist system. The bourgeois order with its system of private property and wage slavery unleashes the whole era of unfreedom. It throws men at the mercy of the blind forces of the market-producers at all levels in society. Thus, liberty is crucified 'upon a cross of gold'.[75] The profound moral validity of Marx's condemnation of capitalism as a system of unfreedom and the universal moral element in his concept of freedom is thus acknowledged by James Maritain: "Marx had a profound intuition, an intuition which is to my eyes the great lightning flash of truth which traverses all his work of the condition of heteronomy and loss of freedom produced in the capitalist world by wage slavery, and of dehumanisation which the possessing classes and the proletariat alike are thereby simultaneously stricken."[76]

An important point that follows from what we have said above is that Marx not merely takes liberty as synonymous with the end of exploitation of man, he also integrates it with the glorious human values possible only in the stateless era of social development. In this direction, Marx reaches very close to Rousseau's concept of moral freedom despite the fact that he is the most uncompromising critic of this precursor of the theory of modern political idealism.[77] For Marx, the abolition of capitalism or the establishment of socialism does not by itself usher in the 'truly human society', it only makes it possible. "What is more, material fulfilment is for him only the condition, the necessary basis, and not the sum, of man's spiritual, that is, truly human development. The vision which underlies his whole work from the early 1840's to the end is the vision of human emancipation. His was a powerful plea to replace the pitiable, fragmentary and self-alienated existence which is man's lot in a class-divided and exploitative society with a truly rich human life, his was an assertion of life abundant against mere existence."[78]

74. Asirvatham, *op, cit.*, p. 189.
75. Caudwell: *The Concept of Freedom* (London, 1965), p. 75.
76. Cited in Harry Slochower: *No Voice is Wholly Lost* (London. 1946), pp. 220-21.
77. As Marx says: "Every emancipation is a *restoration* of the human world and of human relationship to *man himself.*" See De Caute (ed.): *The Essential Writings of Marx* (London: Panther, 1967), pp. 187-88.
78. Randhir Singh: *Reason, Revolution and Political Theory* (New Delhi: People's Pub. House, 1976), p.271 n. 28.

Kinds of Liberty

Natural	Social/Civil	Moral
Freedom to do what one wills; hence total absence of restraints	Man's right to do or enjoy something that is worth doing or enjoying in his collective life; hence hedging of due restraints	Man's capacity to act as per his rational self so as to have the best possible development of his personality

Social/Civil:

Personal	Political	Economic	Domestic	National	International
(i) Freedom of choice in strictly private matters	(i) Freedom to take part in the affairs of the state	(i) Freedom to have some gainful employment	(i) A responsible and respectable position of the wife and children	(i) Freedom from colonial subjection or achievement of independence	(i) Renunciation of war
(ii) Security of health, person and honour	(ii) Freedom to exercise franchise	(ii) Freedom from want	(ii) Freedom of entering into matrimonial alliances	(ii) Exercise of patriotism	(ii) Abandonment of the use of force
(iii) Freedom of thought expression and faith	(iii) Free supply of news	(iii) Right to produce and distribute goods	(iii) Responsibility of the parents to seek mental and moral development of family members		(iii) Pacific settlement of disputes among nations
(iv) Freedom of movement	(iv) Right to fight free and fair elections	(iv) Workers' right to participate in the management of industry			(iv) Limitation on the production of armaments
(v) Possession and use of private property	(v) Supporting or opposing governmental policies and actions by peaceful means	(v) Establishment of industrial democracy			

It is obvious that what Marx has said in regard to the real meaning and nature of liberty cannot be acceptable to the 'bourgeois' thinkers and writers. Such a rejoinder may be seen in the writings of Milton Friedman who has endeavoured to present a 'classic defence of free-market liberalism.'[79] Though he has apparently portrayed the model of a welfare state, as a matter of fact, his work is a clear attack on the premises of Marxism in which liberty is thoroughly sacrificed at the altar of a coercive social and political order. His deepest concern is with 'socialism' that he undertakes to prove as 'quite inconsistent' with 'political freedom' in two respects: (i) that competitive capitalism, which is, of coure, negated by socialism, is unnecessary (although not a sufficient) condition of political freedom; and (ii) that a socialist society is so constructed that it cannot guarantee political freedom.[80] As he says: "The market removes the organisation of economic activity from the control of political authority. It thus reduces the concentration of power which enables economic strength to be a check to political power rather than a reinforcement."[81]

In spite of the fact that liberal and Marxist interpretations on the real meaning and nature of liberty differ in kind, it cannot be lost sight of that both strongly advocate the idea of liberty. The difference between the two schools is due to the extension of the meaning of liberty with development of social process that has had its impact not merely on the areas of action other than political or economic but also to agents other than the individuals. Essentially speaking, there is truth in both the interpretations inasmuch as both adhere to the values of an 'inward mind'. The point of dispute is the obtaining economic system that has made the enjoyment of liberty possible to some and impossible, or less possible, to many. How should this be corrected? It constitutes the basis of the divergence of views. However, it cannot be denied that liberty "has grown from its original root to a great and branching tree, and some of its branches chafe and jar against others."[82]

Defence of Particular Freedoms: Essential Safeguards Against the Abuse of Power

If liberty, in the words of Lord Acton, implies the assurance that every man shall be protected in doing, what he believes, his duty against the influence of authority and majority custom and opinion, it is necessary to look into the special safeguards whereby the abuse of power may be effectively restricted. Thus enters the matter relating to the defence of 'particular' freedoms that may mean anything like freedom of mind to a liberal and right to work and leisure to a Marxist thinker. We may also label such freedoms as 'fundamental' keeping in view the fact that these "provide safeguards against the abuse of power in *other ways;* that where they are denied, those in authority need not justify either the objects or their methods."[83] We may mention some of the very important freedoms in this section in the following order:

79. Macpherson: *Democratic Theory.*, p. 143.
80. *Ibid.*, p. 147.
81. Milton Friedman: *Capitalism and Freedom* (Chicago, 1962), p. 15.
82. Ernest Barker: *Reflections on Government* (London: Oxford Univ. Press, 1958), p. 2.
83. Benn and Peters, *op. cit.*, p. 225.

1. **Freedom of Mind:** First of all, there is the case of intellectual freedom that includes right to speak, print, or seek in concert with others its translation into an event. There should be complete freedom of speech and opinion in matters of religion and social affairs. For this, it is needed that there should be no censorship on the publication of the news, or that no man should be punished or harassed for expressing his dissent. The means of mass communication should be free so that people may not be misled by the trend of Goebbelism. Methods of surgery or electric shock for the sake of brainwashing the opponents and the dissidents are politically unwise and ethically unsound. Allied to this is the freedom of discussion that enables the people to understand the views of others and form their own views after making a critical evaluation of different trends. In brief, the freedom of mind is based on the assumption that the men "who cease to think, cease also to be in any genuine sense citizens. . . . freedom of speech, in fact, ... is at once the catharsis, discontent and the condition of necessary reform. A government can always learn more from the criticism of its opponents than from the eulogy of its supporters. To stifle that criticism is, at least, ultimately, to prepare its own destruction."[84]
2. **Freedom of Assembly and Association:** This type of freedom is necesssary if criticism is to be heard and results produced. The people should be free to assemble and express their pent-up feelings. They should also have the freedom to make associations to fight for the protection and promotion of their specific interests. It is warranted by the fact that in the modern world the individual cannot impress his views save by acting with his fellows. Though certain restrictions can be placed on this freedom so as to forestall the dangers of disturbance of peace, it is required that no such attempt should be made so as to make the activities of the opponents hard to discover. The state may ban associations or right to assemble for the traitors or the preachers of violence in the name of its 'self-protection', but it should be in obvious danger before it is given leave to act. Laski rightly says that to prohibit a meeting on the ground that the peace may be disturbed is, in fact, to enthrone intimidation in the seat of power.[85]
3. **Freedom of the Press:** In a democratic system the instruction of public opinion by a free and full supply of news is an urgent necessity. The people who are expected to judge every issue on its merit are unfree if they have to judge not between rival theories of what an agreed set of fact means by competing distortion but what is at the outset an unedifying and invented mythology. Whether this distortion or suppression or censorship is state-controlled or by special interests operating within a democratic system, tends to make prisoners of men who believe themselves to be free. The press has been described as the 'fourth estate' of the realm in view of its importance in relation to the existence and operation of other principal organs of a political organisation . So strong is the emphasis of Laski on the freedom of the press that he disapproves of any censorship even during the times of war on the ground that an executive that

84. Laski: *A Grammar of Politics*, p. 121.
85. *Ibid.*, p. 122.

has a free hand "will commit all the natural follies of dictatorship. It will assume the semi-divine character of its acts. It will deprive the people of information upon which it can be judged."[86]

4. **Freedom to Work and Get Adequate Payments:** Economic freedom precedes its political counterpart in the degree of importance. As everyone is involved in solving the problem of bread and butter, he needs work. Not only that, work must be of such a type that brings him adequate return in the form of remunerations. Thus, enter a host of rights like those relating to work, rest and leisure, adequate wages and workers' control of industry. A. complex problem, in this direction, finds place in workers' freedom to go on a strike for seeking fulfilment of their demands. A proper answer to such a complex question lies in the affirmation that the right to strike for a genuine cause is a necessary part of economic freedom. However, this freedom should not be made use of at the cost of public convenience. If the workers are to be saved from industrial servitude or exploitation and oppression of an industrial autocracy, it is required that we "effect institutions upon which the workers are represented for the governance of industry, and compel reference to them for the settlement of industrial methods."[87]
5. **Freedom to Choose and Control Governors:** Above all, the people should have freedom to choose and control their rulers. For this it is required that free and fair elections are held periodically on the basis of universal adult suffrage. Political education should also be imparted so that average voters may understand the general problems of politics and their proper role in consonance with the norms of their instructed judgements. Effective citizenship demands that people not only freely choose their rulers, they also exercise control over their working. In case the behaviour of their rulers violates the norms of mandate given to them, they should have the freedom to censure the conduct of the rulers and also change them in order to confirm that sovereignty is vested in the masses, not in the government. Laski rightly affirms that liberty is never real unless the government "can be called to account; and it should always be called to account when it invades rights."[88]

It, however, remains to be added that the defence of these freedoms, called 'particular' or 'fundamental', should be made in the name of 'public interest'. One may say that anything like general or public good is a quite ambiguous term. It cannot, however, be totally lost sight of that, at least in the realm of normative political theory, one may lay down the frontiers of what falls within the ambit of'public advantage'.

Libertarianism: Empirical Determination of Liberty and Scientific Value Relativism

The term 'libertarianism' carries different connotations in the realm of social sciences. For instance, in ethics, it is a doctrine which refers to the maintenance of the freedom of the will as opposed to anything like necessitarianism or determinism. However,

86. *Ibid.*, p. 126.
87. *Ibid., p.* 113.
88. *Ibid*, p. 146.

in the realm of politics, its meaning varies from one of the extreme libertarians who hold that the individual is free to choose this or that action indifferently to that of the moderate ones who maintain that acquired tendencies, environment and the like exercise control in a greater or lesser degree that prevent a man from doing everything in a purely arbitrary manner. We may, therefore, classify the libertarians between unenlightened and enlightened groups with this proviso that while both try to measure everything by the yardstick of liberty, saner are the latter who ardently oppose steps intruding on liberty, while the former, along with unenlightened equalitarians, welcome them as just. For our purpose, a libertarian is one who is enlightened and who, for this reason, definitely thinks as to what he really means by the term liberty.

The principle of libertarianism, correctly stated, thus enjoins that "many an individual, because in a certain case he definitely desires liberty, thinks he desires it in all cases, whereas better thinking would convince him that actually he would wish to restrict liberty in many situations which he has not yet thoroughly considered. By articulate thinking the majority-worshipper may modify his ideas on what he really worships. Not only may the group worshipper who disparages another group may be corrected in his factual convictions, but also his thinking about the separation of groups, if any, may be made more articulate and considerate in regard to the means to be employed and the consequences of the application of the various means"[89] Reduced to simple terms, it means that while the ideal of liberty is loved by all, its practice differs from man to man, place to place, and time to time. Thus, the notion of absolute liberty is a contradiction in terms. Liberty lies within restraints and the burden of restraints cannot be applied in a uniform manner.

A pertinent question that arises at this stage is that while liberty is an ideal of an inward mind and, as such, is an important subject of normative political theory, how it can be reconciled with the implications of scientific value relativism—a concept according to which absolute or highest values are chosen by mind or will, or grasped by faith, intuition or instinct which cannot be proved by science even if it can help a great deal in clarifying the meaning of the ideas about such values, or the consequences and risks entailed in their pursuits. In other words, the question is whether liberty being largely of a normative character can be determined, tested or measured in empirical terms. An answer to such a question lies partly in negative and partly in positive terms. That is, liberty cannot be put to empirical tests, if we confine our attention to its purely abstract or philosophical interpretations as given to us by idealist thinkers like Kant and Bosanquet. Howover, an empirical determination or evaluation of the idea of liberty can be made if we take into consideration its realistic interpretations as made by Barker and Laski.

We thus come to the point that scientific method can contribute a great deal to the proper explanation of the meaning of real liberty in the context of consequences that follow in the event of its over-grant or denial to the people. It may be visualised in these important directions:

1. The application of scientific method can clarify the differences in the meaning of the question whether human beings are free to think as they like. One may

89. Arnold Brecht: *Political Theory: Foundations of Twentieth Century Political Thought* (Princeton: Princeton Univ. Press, 1959), p. 412.

doubt whether the metaphysical interpretation of T.H. Green was right when he said that 'human consciousness postulates freedom'. But none can contradict the same thing, if it is put in a scientific form whereby it may be proved that an individual has a thinking capacity and it is because of this that a person like Netwton could think over and discover the law of gravitation. "If freedom of thought", says Brecht, "were a sheer illusion and all our thinking necessary there could be no science, since any question, whether relevant or irrelevant, and any answer, whether true or false, would be equally necessary, and it would also be necessary that we consider true what is false whenever we think so, and false what is true."[90]

2. An application of scientific method can supply an adequate description and analysis of all data concerning freedom to act. If so, a student of scientific method can make numerous categories and sub-categories of freedom in social, economic and political spheres, including freedom from something and freedom for something along with freedom to follow reason or passion. In this way, science can point out that each type of freedom may be either merely negative or positive, either passive or active, and that some types are compatible with equality while others are not, as, e.g., economic freedom is incompatible with economic equality. "Science can also examine whether there can be true freedom to be right unless there is the freedom to err, and so forth."[91]
3. An application of scientific method can lead to the establishment of a number of important substantive points. For instance, it can be stated unconditionally that the presumptive human ability, within limits set by nature, to think and act in accordance with reason is valuable in an objective sense because it enables humanity to reach certain stages of life and knowledge not attainable without that freedom. It can also be stated unconditionally that no human being is entirely free to do what he likes, because everyone is subject at least to the constraints imposed by nature. Finally, every one considers freedom to do what he really and ultimately considers a positive value.[92]
4. A student of science can gather ample data regarding the results of either excessive grant or denial of freedom. Thus, he can establish that the denial of freedom is bound, for psychological reasons, to stir up very deep feelings of resentment, feelings that may even lead to the outbreak of a revolution if not assuaged in good time. He can also prove that while the people could make so much progress in the event of freedom, so much decline took place in the event of its denial. Thus, a student of empirical politics may well point out the dangers or disasters that occur in the event of the suppression of freedom. In this way, he "may compare the possible achievements and the setbacks that threaten under various forms of freedom or its absence."[93]
5. Not only this, by an application of scientific method we may churn historical evidence to prove that so much of liberty should or should not be provided, or

90. *Ibid.*, p. 316.
91. *Ibid.*,
92. *Ibid.*, p. 317.
93. *Ibid.*

that so much restraint is or is not needed. We may also lay down that under such and such conditions the enjoyment of liberty, and that much of liberty, is valid. In other words, science can determine the limits "beyond which suppression of freedom is impossible, as is the suppression of the freedom to think and to believe as long as persons are fully conscious, that is, neither asleep nor doped: and it can reveal the interconnection between morals and freedom on the ground that a universal feeling seems to forbid us to blame someone for failing to do what he was not free to do."[94]

An empirically tenable character of liberty, thus, can be traced in leading historical events. For instance, the people of England rose in revolt against the Stuart monarch Charles I and put him to the gallows in 1649 for the sake of establishing the supremacy of *lex* (law) over *rex* (king). Likewise, the people of America took to the course of unilateral declaration of independence in 1776 and thereby terminated the era of British colonial hegemony. The people of France did the same in 1789 to achieve 'liberty' along with 'equality' and 'fraternity'. Not only this, even the statements of eminent political thinkers can be put to empirical tests. For instance, who can refute the judicious explanation of Mill that the doctrine of liberty cannot be applicable to those who suffer from the deficiencies of mind, body and character. As such, not a democratic but a despotic government is the legitimate form of political system for the barbarians and very backward peoples. According to him, liberty as a principle "has no application to any state or things anterior to time when mankind has become capable of being improved by force and equal discussion."[95] Likewise, we may refer to Montesquieu's idea of liberty contained in his explanation of the doctrine of separation of powers as borrowed from Locke. Abundant historical evidence available to us demonstrates the truth of this statement of Montesquieu that when the legislative, executive and judicial powers are united in the same hands, there is the end of liberty.[96]

What science, however, cannot verify relates to that aspect of liberty which lies in purely philosophical or normative directions. Thus, while we may empirically test or determine the risks or consequences of the denial of liberty, or we may authoritatively speak about the advantages that emanate from the grant of liberty, we cannot generalise a conclusion that the freedom of every individual is an absolute value and, moreover, this is the case with all people and under all circumstances. A student of scientific method is bound to admit that sometimes one person's or group's lack of freedom may be more valuable for reaching another person's or group's aims than would be full freedom for both. It is only from religious or ethical standpoints that we may speak of equal liberty for all irrespective of all sorts of differences which science does recognise. In clear contrast to moral or theological convictions, an empirical examination of liberty leads to this definite conclusion that a person's freedom is rarely valuable for all others, unless it is limited by some principle of regard for others, whether this limitation is effected by self-restraint or by constraint imposed from outside. Thus, every scientist "is free to engage in research under the

94. *Ibid.*, pp. 317-18.
95. Mill: *Utilitarianism, Liberty and Representative Government,* p. 73.
96. See Montesquieu: *Spirit of the Laws,* Book XI, Chapter VI.

'avowed assumption' that in the particular case under his investigation freedom is desirable, or is actually being desired, and then concentrate on the methods by which it can be secured, broadened in substance, spread further, and best be defended, defended also from the consequences of its abuse."[97]

Liberty and Authority: Problem of Proper Reconciliation

Whether liberty and authority are exclusive of, or complementary to, each other, is a very delicate question that has engaged the attention of many an eminent thinker and writer on this subject. Two contradictory opinions have come to us in this regard. While the schools of classical individualism and anarchism have treated the two as opposed to each other, the liberal and socialist views are different is that they regard the *laissez faire* or non-rule approach as thoroughly mistaken. The former view is based on two assumptions—(i) liberty and authority do not go together, and if they go together, it is not applicable to every individual at all places and under all circumstances; (ii) liberty implies the absence of restraint and, as such, every restraint *qua* restraint is an evil. Aristotle was guided by the first assumption when he said that liberty could be enjoyed only by the free people who had leisure time to take part in the deliberative and judicial affairs of the state. The second assumption can be traced in the explanations of the individualists and anarchists, even Marxists, who dub liberty of the individual and authority of the state as antithetical terms.

The reason for taking authority of the state as inimical to the liberty of the individual lies in treating the state as evil, or an instrument of exploitation and oppression by one class over another. Thus, the individualists, mainly of the nineteenth century like John Stuart Mill and Herbert Spencer made an indictment of the state as a necessary evil and desired minimum possible state activity so as to ensure maximum possible individual liberty. It witnessed its elaborate manifestation in the economic sphere where classical economists like David Ricardo, Alfred Marshall and Adam Smith defended the doctrine of the *laissez faire* in the name of non-interference in the initiative of the individual. Even in the present century, the defenders of the bourgeois political order regard with grave distaste any restraint imposed by the state in the name of public welfare. Restraints imposed by the state undermine the scope of individual liberty that issues forth in the form of enterprise and co-operation. Thus, Friedman says: "As in the simple model, so in the complex enterprise and money-exchange economy, co-operation is strictly individual and voluntary, provided: (a) enterprises are private, so that the ultimate contracting parties are individuals, and (b) individuals are effectively free to enter or not to enter into any particular exchange, so that every transaction is strictly voluntary."[98]

The anarchists go ahead in the direction of political extremism. They advocate the idea of a stateless society in which there is all liberty and no authority. To them, even a state with limited interference into the liberty of the individual is an anathema. Real liberty is possible when the state goes. Thus, anarchism offers an absolute cult of the free individual. The peculiar thing about the philosophy of anarchism as developed by Proudhon, Bakunin and Kropotkin is that it wants no

97. Brecht, *op. cit.*, p. 319.
98. Friedman, *op. cit.*, p. 14.

Liberty and Authority

At best the Anarchists are seen as an absurd romantic breed, who cannot come to terms with the realities of a highly industrialised, bureaucratic and modernised world. But can anarchism be so easily dismissed, especially in an age which has become increasingly sceptical about the efficiency and the benefits of the state's action and where there is a need for radical solutions to urban ecological problems? For all its weaknesses, failures and naivety, anarchism might still have something to offer.

—Jeremy Jennings

"Anarchism" in Roger Eatwell and Anthony Wright (eds.): ***Contemporary Political Ideologies*** (Delhi: Rawat Publication, 1999), p. 148.

Of course, force is certainly not the normal or the only means of the state-nobody save that-but force is a means specific to the state. . . . the state is a relation of men dominationg men (and, generally, men dominating women) a relation supported by means of legitimate (i.e. considered to be legitimate) violence.

—Max Weber

H.H. Gerth and C.W. Mills (eds.): *From Max Weber* (Oxford: Oxford University Press, 1972), p. 78.

Power brings about compliance through coercion or violence. Authority, on the other hand, is based upon a 'perceived right to rule' and brings about compliance through a moral obligation on the part of the ruled to obey.

—Andrew Heywood,

Political Theory: An Introduction, p. 130.

form of authority at all—whether political, economic or religious—and thus desires to save man from the yokes of the state, capitalist and God in his capacities respectively as a citizen, a producer, and a man.[99] In this way, anarchism desires to confer all forms of emancipation (liberty) on the individual by saving him from the subjection to all kinds of authority.[100]

If the anarchists, like the individualists, regard political authority as antithetical to individual liberty in the name of the state being an evil, they also denigrate the state, like the Marxists, as an instrument of exploitation and oppression by one class over the other. According to them, the state deprives the class of the 'have-nots' to enjoy liberty in the midst of numerous restraints imposed by it to protect and promote the interests of the class of the 'haves'. This point is shared by the Marxists who, in the same vein, denounce the state and desire its abolition after the transitional stage is over when there will be neither any class nor any authority and that will mean the inauguration of the era of real freedom. In this way, liberty and authority are not complementary to one another as the former has to be enjoyed by all in the real sense of the term after the 'withering away of the state' when men "have grown accustomed to observing the elementary conditions of social existence without force and without subjection."[101]

99. C.E.M. Joad: *Modern Political Theory* (London: Oxford Univ. Press, 1946), p. 102.

100. *Ibid.*

101. See V.I. Lenin; *State and Revolution,* Chapter 4.

On the other side is the view that liberty and authority are complementary to each other. Experience clearly shows that there can be no liberty in the absence of authority. Liberty lies within restraints and restraints can be imposed only by some authority. The only liberty possible for a civilised man is a defined and a limited affair; to leave each man to do what he pleases means anarchy and return to the 'state of nature' as described by Hobbes in his *Leviathan.* It is a different thing that people struggle against and defy some form of authority in order to save their liberty, but they re-establish it as they can't do without it. Thus, the modern age witnessed the substitution of the authority of an infallible Pope with the unlimited sway of a national monarch. The execution of Charles I in 1649 did not mean an end of authority in England, rather it meant the replacement of the authority of an autocratic king with that of a people's leader called Lord Protector.

Thus, we find that far from being opposed to each other, liberty and authority complement each other. Hobbes differentiated between liberty and licence on the ground that while the former was possible under the authority of a sovereign, the latter existed in an era of non-rule. Locke discovered that where there was no authority (law), there was no liberty. Hocking goes so far as to say that the greater the liberty a person desires, the greater is the authority to which he should submit himself. For this, he has coined the argument of specialisation. Specialisation means authority that keeps a man of inferior mind under the subjection of a superior mind. In other words, the man who is a specialist in his field is our authority. In this way, freedom lies in one's concentration on the things that he can do best. "One has to buy one's freedom at a price and that price is submission to authority in those spheres in which one does not aspire to become a specialist. Specialisation, therefore, calls for the delegation of freedom."[102]

It, however, does not mean that the existence and enjoyment of liberty can be reconciled with any amount of authority. In other words, if liberty has its own limitations on account of not being an absolute phenomenon, authority must also be limited. That is, only limited liberty and limited authority can go together. There is no liberty in an era of statelessness (called 'state of nature' by Hobbes) as there is no restraint on the arbitrary actions of the individual; likewise, there is extinction of liberty under a totalitarian system where an individual finds himself enchained at every inch of his life. Laski could well understand this fact and while he identified liberty with the possession and enjoyment of rights, he also suggested that only provisions of rights can ensure adequate restrictions on the powers of the state.[103]

As a matter of fact, liberty by its very nature involves restraints, because the freedom of one does not mean the right to destroy the freedom of others. In other words, since the freedom of one always involves the like freedom of others, rules and regulations are necessary to ensure the conditions of minimum freedom common to all. The uniformities that the rules impose ensure liberty and they are less terrifying than the uncertainties the individuals would experience in their absence. Historic experience has evolved for us rules of convenience, as Laski says, which promote right living, to compel obedience to them is a justifiable limitation of freedom. Thus,

102. Asirvatham: *Political Theory,* pp. 190-91.

103. Laski: *Authority in the Modern State,* p. 326.

the 'rules of convenience' imposed by some authority make conditions of freedom. These define its limits and possibilities. Indeed, the restraints they impose are the basis of liberty. 'No restraint, on liberty.'[104]

Two points should, therefore, be borne in mind in this connection. First, there can be no liberty in the absence of authority. That is, state intervention is necessary in the sphere of individual liberty in order to keep it within reasonable limits and, as such, there can be no area totally free from the control of authority what Mill termed as 'self-regarding'. Thus, one of his strong critics, roundly declares: "There are acts of wickedness so gross and outrageous that, self-protection apart, they must be prevented as far as possible at any cost to the offender, and punished, if they occur, with exemplary severity."[105]

Second, the authority of the state should not be absolute so as to menace, even destroy, every iota of liberty as happens under a Fascist or a Communist system. The restraints imposed by the authority must be adequate, reasonable and legitimate. That is, they should satisfy these criteria: (1) in the case of a particular application of restraint, that the act, in question, infringes no rule; (2) in the case of a general application of restraint, by a rule, (a) that the object of the rule is bad; (b) that while the object of the rule is good, the means proposed cannot reasonably be expected to attain it; and (c) that though the object is good, and the proposed means would secure it, it is not of sufficient importance to warrant the degree of restraint proposed.[106]

Critical Appreciation

From what we have said above, following important impressions may be gathered if we desire to have a critical examination of the term 'liberty' in its different manifestations:

1. The real problem with the word 'liberty' is that it "means too little, because it means too much."[107] In other words, liberty is the most used as well as the most abused term. Philosophers have explained its meaning in so many ways that it becomes difficult, even impossible, to offer a standard definition of such a momentous subject of political theory. It is owing to this that what Rousseau means by his affirmation 'man is born free' is different from what Mill says that 'over himself, his own body and mind, the individual is sovereign'. Kant's conception of freedom as 'right to will a self-imposed categorical imperative of duty' is at variance with that of Laski who treats it as 'eager maintenance of that atmosphere in which a man may find the best possible development of his personality.' Besides, if liberty, for the sake of convenience, be taken as the 'absence of restraint', the trouble with this interpretation of the term as a political idea is that it "excludes nothing". Any condition can be described as the absence of its opposite. If health is 'freedom from disease', and education 'freedom from ignorance', there is no conceivable object of social organisation and action that cannot be called 'freedom'.[108]

104. Frank Thakurdas: *Recent English Political Theory*, p. 335.
105. Fitzjames Stephen; *Liberty, Equality, Fraternity*, p. 163.
106. Benn and Peters, *op. cit.*, p. 224.
107. *Ibid.*, p. 197.
108. *Ibid.*, p. 212.

2. Not merely in the world of theory is the determination of the real meaning of liberty a complex problem, it has its formidable dimensions in the world of practice as well. The state of confusion continues to persist despite the fact that some workable definitions of the term have been coined (as we have already seen) keeping in view its negative and positive aspects as done by Mill and Green or its extractive and developmental dimensions as traceable in the explanation of Isaiah Berlin. The problem still remains and a contemporary student of political theory is bound to feel amply handicapped by the cobweb of negativism versus positivism in case he struggles with the problem of solving the dilemma of the two concepts of liberty. It is due to this that a versatile writer like Laski had to dwindle between the two poles and what he could offer by aligning the real meaning of liberty sometimes with a particular 'atmosphere' conducive to the best possible development of human personality, sometimes by equating it with a system of rights putting adequate restraints on the scope of state authority, sometimes grounding it in the 'common good', and sometimes making its ramifications wide enough so as to place severe limitations on the system of capitalist economy (to some extent on the lines of Marxian socialism), has added to the stock of already existing confusion.
3. Above all, the idea of liberty is such that it has been the source of debate among the political philosophers and statesmen; it has also been a powerful cause of struggle between one individual and another, one group and anothere and the like. The real meaning of the ingredients, that are said to make up the generally understood meaning of this term, is also said to have changed from age to age, place to place, and people to people. It has left its bright as well as dark impressions on the pages of history. The most perplexing problem lies in the world of economics where liberty for the rich or the 'haves' and for the poor or the 'have-nots' makes itself not only a subject of elaborate discussion but also raises the problem of saving the world from portents of destruction in the event of a war between the two antagonistic social, economic and political systems—both desiring 'democracy' (ensuring liberty) to the mankind in their own ways.

In the end, it may be reiterated that liberty is one of the important political themes, but its implications largely pertain to a philosophical discussion in the realm of normative political theory. Besides, it should also be borne in mind that a proper discussion of liberty should not be treated like an isolated phenomenon; it is integrally connected with the study of other related themes like those of equality and justice. A proper understanding of a term like liberty with regard to its real meaning along with its varying manifestations is, therefore, possible only when it is studied in relation to other sister themes. Thus, freedom "if it is to remain significant", demands that we "must be prepared to see it rub shoulders with other ideals.'[109] Such an attempt has been made in the following chapters so as to show that liberty along with other related themes is an idea of our 'inward mind' and that "the collaboration of the free State, based on civil and political liberty, with the free play of voluntary cooperation, acting in the area of society, is the sum and substance of modern liberty."[110]

109. *Ibid.*, p. 215.

110. Barker: *Reflections on Government* p. 25.

9

Equality

> As a matter of the interpretation of experience, there is something peculiar to human beings and common to human beings without distinction of class, race or sex, which lies far deeper than all differences between them. Call it what we may, soul, reason, the abysmal capacity for suffering, or just human nature, it is something generic, of which there may be many specific, as well as quantitative differences, but which underlies and embraces them all. If this common nature is what the doctrine of equal rights postulates, it has no reason to fear the test of our ordinary experience of life, or of our study of history and anthropology.
>
> **—L.T. Hobhouse[1]**

Like liberty, equality is an equally important theme of normative political theory. Moreover, like liberty, it is also a subject that cannot be studied in isolation from other related themes. As a matter of fact, the subject of equality consitutes a concomitant of the principle of liberty, on the one hand, and of justice, on the other. It is due to this that great thinkers as well as revolutionaries have treated it is an integral part of their movement for liberty and social transformation. Thus, the 'representative thinker' of the social contract school held that the Law of Nature 'teaches all mankind who will but consult it, that being all equal and independent, no one ought to harm another in his life, health, liberty or possessions.'[2] The Founding Fathers of the American revolution adopted the Declaration of Independence in 1776 that *inter alia,* said ". . . . all men are created equal, that they are endowed by their Creator with certain unalienable rights." Likewise, the National Assembly of France adopted the Declaration of the Rights of Man and Citizen in 1789 which *inter alia,* reiterated that "all human beings are born free and equal in dignity and rights."[3]

Equality: Real Meaning and Nature

So close is the involvement of the concept of equality with the themes of rights, liberty, fraternity, property and justice that it has become a 'multidimensional concept' so much so that "of all the basic concepts of social, moral and political philosophy, none is more intriguing and none is more baffling than it."[4] Realising this difficulty, an eminent English political scientist like Laski has confessed that no

1. Hobhouse: *The Elements of Social Justice* (London: George Allen and Unwin, 1922), p. 95.
2. John Locke: *Second Treatise of Civil Government,* Ch. II, 18-19.
3. See S.I. Benn and R.S. Peters: *Social Principles and the Democratic State* (London: George Allen and Unwin, 1975), p. 107.
4. Frank Thakurdas: "In Defence of Social Equality", being the Presidential Address delivered at the XXXV session of the annual conference of the Indian Political Science Association held at Triputi in Jan. 1976, reprodued in *The Indian Journal of Political Science,* Vol. XXXVII, No. 1, 1976, p. 1.

idea is more difficult to be defined in the whole realm of political science than the concept of equality. Among other leading writers, we may refer to the observation of Ernest Barker who, while realising the same difficulty, states: "Equality is a Protean notion: it changes its shape and assumes new forms with a ready facility."[5] It is, therefore, said that the term 'equality' possesses more than one meaning, and that the controversies surrounding it arise partly, at least, because the same term is employed with different connotations. Thus, it may either purport to state a fact, or convey the expression of an ethical judgement. On the one hand, it may affirm that men are, on the whole, very similar in their natural endowments of character and intelligence. On the other hand, it may assert that while they differ profoundly as individuals in capacity and character, they are equally entitled as human beings to consideration and respect, and that the well-being of society is likely to be increased if it so plans its organization that, whether their powers are great or small, all its members may be equally enabled to make the best of such powers as they possess."[6]

It, however, does not imply that the idea of equality lacks a plausible definition. In spite of the fact, that it is a multidimensional concept absorbing implications of certain related themes like those of liberty and justice, it has been defined in the light of *equal conditions guaranteed to each for making the best of himself.* Accordingly, it "means that whatever conditions are guaranteed to me, in the form of rights, shall also, and in the same measure, be guaranteed to others, and that whatever rights are given to others shall also be given to me."[7] In the context of social sciences, the concept of equality refers sometimes to certain *properties* which men are held to have in common but more often to certain *treatment* which men either receive or ought to receive. According to *Oxford English Dictionary,* it implies (i) the condition of having equal dignity, rank or privileges with others, (ii) the condition of being equal in power, ability, achievement, or excellence, (iii) fairness, impartiality, due proportion, proportionateness. It is generally defined in the sense of 'equality of opportunity' which simply is not a matter of legal equality. Its existence depends not merely on the absence of disabilities, but on the presence of abilities. It obtains in so far as, and only in so far as each member of a community, whatever his birth or occupation, or social position, possesses in fact and not merely in form, equal chances of using to the full his natural endowments of physique, of character, and of intelligence."[8]

In a strict sense, equality does not mean identical treatment inasmuch as there can be no similarity of treatment so long as men are different in want, capacity and need. For instance, the purpose of society would be frustrated at the outset if the

5. Barker: *Principles of Social and Political Theory* (London Oxford Univ. Press, 1967), p. 151.
6. Tawney: *Equality* (London: George Allen and Unwin, 1938), p. 22.
7. Barker, *op. cit.,* p. 151.
8. R.H. Tawney: *op. cit.,* pp. 103-4. It may, however, be added now that those who take a negative or aristocratic view of equality desire to justify the meaning of equality of opportunity in the context of the principle of merit or desert. Thus, one writer says: 'Equality of opportunity will inevitably result in inequality of conditions, since some men are more able, more energetic and more fortunate than others." F.E. Oppenheim: "The Concept of Equality" in David I. Sills (ed.): *International Encyclopaedia of the Social Sciences* (New York: Macmillan and Free Press, 1968), Vol 5, p. 110.

nature of the job of a mathematician is given an identical treatment with that of the nature of the work of a bricklayer. Similarly, equalitly does not mean an identity of reward, as Laski says, for efforts so long as the difference in reward does not enable a man, by its magnitude, to invade the rights of others. "Undoubtedly, it implies fundamentally a certain levelling process. It means that no man shall be so placed in society that he can overreach his neighbour to the extent which constitutes a denial of the latter's citizenship."[9]

Broadly speaking, equality implies a coherence of ideas that cover spheres ranging from man's search for the development of his personality to a sort of social order in which the strong and the weak not only live together, rather both have and exercise the right of due hearing. Thus, Laski elaborates: "It means that my realisation of my best self must involve as its logical result the realisation by others of their best selves. It means such an ordering of social forces as will balance a share in the toil of living with a share in its gain also. It means that my share in that gain must be adequate for the purpose of citizenship. It implies that even if my voice be weighed as less weighty than that of another, it must yet receive consideration in the decisions that are made. The meaning, ultimately, of equality surely lies in the fact that the very differences in the nature of men require mechanism for the expression of their wills that give to each its due hearing."[10]

Viewed thus, the idea of equality has two sides—positive and negative—that may be discussed as under:

1. In a positive sense, equality means the provision of adequate opportunities for all. However, the term 'adequate opportunities' is not a synonym of the term 'equal opportunities'. Since men differ in their needs and capacities and also in their efforts, they need different opportunities for their individual self-development. The native endowments are by no means equal. Children who are brought up in an atmosphere where things of mind are accounted highly are bound to start the race of life with advantages no legislation can secure.[11] It is also needed that such forces, if any, should be liquidated so that success or failure must be made to depend on the capacity and character of the persons concerned, not on the accidents of birth or wealth. Thus, equality of opportunity is achieved only when there "is an *appropriate* opportunity for each; what is to be equalised is not the opportunity to enter professions or to be successful in business but the opportunity to lead a good life, or to fulfil one's personality."[12]
2. In a negative sense, equality means the absence of undue privileges. That is, there should be no artificial grounds of discrimination like those of religion, caste, colour, wealth, sex, etc., so that no talent should suffer from frustration for want of encouragement. It means that one can move forward to any public office by his ability which he is prepared to choose. There should be no

9. Laski: *A Grammar of Politics* (London: George Allen and Unwin, 1951), p. 153. Cicero's fine words may be cited here: "For no one thing is as like, as equal, to another one as we human beings are like and equal to one another."
10. *Ibid.*
11. *Ibid.*, p.154.
12. Benn and Peters, *op. cit.* p. 119.

arrangement whereby the authority of few is qualitatively more than that of the many. So also, no office that carries with it power can ever be rightly regarded as an incorporal hereditament, for that is to associate important functions with qualities other than fitness for their performance.[13] It, however, does not mean that there should be no discrimination on any material ground whatsoever. For instance, a discrimination on the ground of sex can, and must, be made in recruitment of police and military posts. Thus, a provision regarding eligibility of women for such posts, or special preference for the men of chivalrous races in such selections should not be construed as a violation of the principle of equality. What is required is that the principle of equality should be linked to the principle of efficiency and public benefit.

The concept of the equality of opportunity should, however, be understood in a particular sense. We treat people equally in the way that we would not (normally) treat men and dogs equally.[14] Yet, at the same time, we do not treat them as equals which clearly they are not. Anti-egalitarians often argue that the imposition of socialist egalitarian measures undermines this dignity and self-respect in that the paternalism, that often accompanies such measures, negates the idea of man as a rational chooser. It is well counselled that there "is no need to speculate further on this theme to realise that there is something deeply unsatisfactory at the heart of the doctrine of equality of opportunity. It would be unwise to push the doctrine beyond justifying the removal of the most obvious type of arbitrary discrimination based on race, religion and sex. Since most of the egalitarian ideals can be pursued in ways that do not require the precarious distinction between nature and convention."[15]

When we speak of equal opportunities for all, what we really have in mind is appropriate opportunity for all. The really important demand of the champions of equality of opportunity is that certain extraneous factors like wealth or birth or class should not determine or limit one's opportunities. As an operative principle, it means that each man should have equal rights and opportunities to develop his own talents, or to lead a good life and develop his personality.[16] J. Rees says that natural inequalities of physical strength, beauty and so on are acceptable; social inequalities, because they are a product of pure convention, seem to turn upon the assumption that conventional inequalities are *alterable,* while natural ones are not, and it is that which seems to live behind the contemporary doctrine of the equality of opportunity."[17]

---

13. Laski, *op. cit.*, pp.153-54.
14. J. Wilson: *Equality* (London: Hutchinson, 1966), p. 103.
15. N.P. Barry, *An Introduction to Modern Political Theory* (London: Macmillan, 1981), p. 147.
16. A.H. Doctor: *Issues in Political Theory* (New Delhi: Sterling, 1985), pp. 15-16.
17. But J.H. Schaar rejects the whole case of the equality of opportunity on these grounds: First, the idea is rather misleading, for the fact always is that not all the talents can be developed equally in any given society. Out of the great variety of human resources available to it, a given society will admire and reward some abilities more than others. Second, the equal opportunity policy will increase inequalities among men. Third, the more closely a society approaches meritocracy, the wider grows the gap in ability and achievement between the highest and the lowest social orders. See his paper "Equality of Opportunity and Beyond" in *Equality,* Vol. IX, 1967 reproduced in Crespigny and Wertheimer (eds): *Contemporary Political Theory,* pp. 136-38.

Equality and Egalitarianism

Equality must not be merely apparent, must not apply merely to the sphere of state, but must also be real, must also be extended to social and economic spheres.

—**Fredrick Engels**

Anti-Duhring (Moscow: Foreign Publishing House, 1959), pp. 146-47.

Egalitarianism is a crucial principle of modern political struggles and social movements for social change. To ignore equality is to ignore an important moral component of organised social movements for the reform of modern conditions.

—**Bryan S. Turner**

Equality (London: Tavistock Publications, 1986), p. 15.

An egalitarian might hold that whatever political arrangements are most likely to achieve a fair distribution of good quality lives or opportunities for good quality lives to people should be instituted and upheld.

—**Richard J. Arneson**

"Justice after Rawls" in R.E. Goodin (ed.): *The Oxford Handbook of Political Science* (Oxford: Oxford University Press, 2009), p. 123.

Like all great political abstractions, the notion of equality bears rich association with the complexities of human life.

—**Crane Brinton**

"Equality" in E.R.A. Seligman (ed.): *Encyclopaedia of the Social Sciences* (New York: Macmillan, 1967), Volumes Vand VI, p. 574.

Turner on Four Types of Equality

1. *Ontological Equality* implying fundamental equality of all persons.
2. *Equality of opportunity* implying achievement of desirable ends.
3. *Equality of condition* implying making of conditions of life equal for relevant social groups.
4. *Equality of outcome* implying equality of results.

Bryan S. Turner: *Equality*, p. 34

At this stage we may have a peep into the concept of reverse discrimination or compensatory justice in favour of some oppressed communities in the name of undoing centuries-old injustice done to them or, in positive terms, to raise them to the level of others. The foundation of the egalitarian rejection of the achievements of equality by income transfers is really a metaphysical view of man and his society. The social philosophy that lies behind the policy of affirmative action is somewhat confused and may have objected to it and without dissenting from the general egalitarian sentiment, or from the idea that social philosophy ought to take account of the injustices inflicted on the black people and the women in the United States in the past. The policy involves injustice at least in the procedural sense (and quite possibly in the substantive sense), since granting privileges to individuals because of their race or sex is as discriminatory and unjust as denying them opportunity and jobs for the same reasons.[18]

18. Barry, *op. cit.*, p. 155. Equality of opportunity was nowhere near fully realised, because certain factors such as parental hostility to education and the desire and perhaps need to earn high wages early in life, deterred to working class children from taking advantage of those opportunities which natural intelligence entitled them. *Ibid.*, p. 147. Also see C.A.R. Crossland: *The Conservative Enemy* (London: Cape, 1962), pp. 169-74.

In short, the idea of equality implies that all human beings should be treated equally in respect of certain fundamental traits common to all like human nature, human worth and dignity, human personality and the like. In this direction, we may appreciate the maxim of Immanuel Kant, the Father of Modern Idealism, who said: "Treat humanity, whether in your own or in that of any other, in every case as an end, never solely as a means." Thus, the principle of equality comes to stand on the rational principle of the equality of consideration. "What we really demand, when we say that all men are equal, is that none shall be held to have a claim to better treatment than another, in advance of good grounds being produced."[19]

Egalitarianism: Justification of Equality in the Midst of Inequality

An understanding of the meaning of egalitarianism is necessary in order to grasp the correct nature of the ideal of equality. Here it means that equality is no substitute for uniformity. After all, equality is a matter of derivative value; it is derived from the supreme value of the development of personality—in each alike and equally but in each along its own different line and of its own separate notion. That is, the principle of equality needs to be adjusted to the values of man's functional capacity. "When the primary needs of all men are met, the differences they enounter must be differences their function requires: requirement involving always the context of social benefit."[20] That is, what is derived by a man must not divert, or defeat, the source from which it comes in view of the fact that any equality that "spelled uniformity would necessarily divert and defeat the spontaneous development of all the varieties of human personality."[21] Again: "Equality in all its forms, must always be subject and instrumental to the free development of capacity; but if it be pressed to the length of uniformity, and if uniformity be made to thwart the free development of capacity, the subject becomes the master, and the world is turned topsy-turvy."[22]

In other words, the idea of equality is more of a prescriptive than of a descriptive nature. Hence, the simple aphorism that 'all men are equal' simply means that they should be treated alike in respect of certain fundamental traits common to all like their dignity and worth as human beings and not that they all possess attributes or capacities in an equal measure. In the world of medical sciences all patients cannot be treated with the same medicine; likewise, in the world of jurisprudence, theft and murder cannot be treated as identical crimes deserving equal punishment. Therefore, it is hardly desirable that all men should be treated equally in all respects. Thus understood, the principle of equality "does not prescribe positively that all human beings be treated alike; it is a presumption against treating them differently, in any respect, until grounds for distinction have been shown. It does not assume, therefore, a quality which all men have to the same degree, which is the ground of the presumption, for to say that there is a presumption means that no grounds need be shown."[23]

19. Benn and Peters, *op. cit.*, p. 110.
20. Laski, *op. cit.*, p. 159.
21. Barker, *op. cit.*, p. 155.
22. *Ibid.*, p. 157.
23. Benn and Peters, *op. cit.*, p. 111.

In this direction, we may refer especially to the work of Hugo Bedau who reminds us that to think as an egalitarian "is to consider the degree and range of all inequalities among men and to explore ways to remove or at least diminish them."[24] He lays down seven propositions to explain his thesis in the following manner:[25]

1. There is the principle of *radical egalitarianism* which seeks to abolish differences on the plea that all social inequalities, which are unnecessary and unjustifiable, ought to be eliminated.
2. There is the principle of *metaphysical egalitarianism* which treats all persons as equal—now and for ever, in intrinsic value, inherent worth, essential nature.
3. There is the principle of *ethical egalitarianism* which holds natural inequality as the law of nature and also based on recognisable and accepted human differences.
4. There is the principle of *social egalitarianism.* It suggests that social equalities need no special justification whereas social inequalities always do.
5. There is the principle *pragmatic egalitarianism* which informs that all persons are to be treated alike except where circumstances require different treatment.
6. There is the principle of *scientific egalitarianism* which informs that though some social inequalities are necessary, and even if equal conditions are granted, the fact of inherent equalities sooner or later will break through.
7. There is the principle of *diehard egalitarianism* which is based on the assumption that in view of the complexity of every social organization, some forms of social inequalities are definitely justifiable.

Bedau thus confidently concludes: "These principles remain as the quadrants of social justice, equalitarian instruments for social criticism and reform. Instead of radical egalitarianism what we are left with is universal principle that all social inequalities not necessary or justifiable should be eliminated."[26]

In short, equality is an empty idea if it is studied in a purely abstract or isolated sense. It has content when it is particularised. That is, it should be studied in the context of actual things. In this sense, it implies that *equals should be treated equally, and unequals unequally,* and the respect in which they are considered unequal must be relevant to the differences in treatment that are under specific consideration. If there is a norm that equal pay should be given for equal work, it is also needed that work done should be equally well. Thus, a conscientious follower of the English liberal thought like Prof. Isaiah Berlin feels that though the ideal limit or idealised model at the heart of the egalitarian thought is a society in which not only will every one be treated alike, but in which natural differences will have been ironed out, but that when the pursuit of equality comes into conflict with other human aims, it is only the most fanatical egalitarian who will demand that such conflicts invariably be decided in favour of equality alone with relative disregard for other values concerned.[27]

---

24. Bedau: *Egalitarianism and the Idea of Equality* in *Nomos*, IX, pp. 13-26, cited in Frank Thakurdas, *op. cit.*, p. 14.
25. *Ibid.*, pp. 14-16.
26. *Ibid.*, p. 17.
27. Cited in Benn and Peters, *op. cit.*, p. 378 n. 8.

Specific Kinds of Equality

Since equality is a 'multidimensional concept', it has different kinds ranging from its natural or moral variety, that is purely an ideal, to its social or economic counterpart that is purely a realistic affair. We may briefly mention specific kinds of equality in the following manner:

1. **Natural Equality:** It implies that nature has made all men equal. In ancient times the Stoics of Greece and Roman thinkers like Cicero and Polybius contradicted the principle of natural inequality as advocated by Plato and Aristotle by insisting that all men were equal according to the law of nature. It was reiterated by the Schoolmen of the Church who advocated the principle of the'Fatherhood of God and brotherhood of man'. In the modern age, it was Rousseau who imparted a secular version to the Biblical injunction. In his *Second Discourse on the Origin of Inequality* he regretted that the moral innocence of man was perverted by the civilising process. Later on, Marx also attached importance to it and he desired that every man should be treated equally as a human creature. However, being an uncompromising critic of the capitalist system, he hoped that such a sublime pattern of life dedicated to glorious values of human existence would be possible only in the final stage of socialism. It may, however, be added that the concept of natural or moral equality is just like an ideal to say that all earth is surface.[28]
2. **Social Equality:** While natural or moral equality is just an idea, civil or social equality is an actuality. What we really mean by the term equality is its existence in the sphere of man's social existence. Moreover, though there are some other kinds of equality as well, as we shall see in the following sections, they are, virtually the offshoots of social equality. Here equality implies that the rights of all should be equal; that all should be treated equally in the eyes of the law. In other words, the respect shown to one man should be determined by his qualities and not by the grace of some traditional or ancestral privileges. There should be no discrimination on some artificial ground. As Laski says: "There is an aspect in which the things without which life is meaningless must be accessible to all without distinction in degree or kind. . . . We can never, therefore, as a matter of principle justify the existence of differences until the point is reached when the primary claims of men win a full response. I have no right to cake if my neighbour, because of that right, is compelled to go without bread. Any social organization from which the basis is absent by denying equality denies all that gives meaning to the personality of men."[29]
3. **Political Equality:** It means access of everyone to the avenues of power. All citizens irrespective of their artificial differences should have an equal voice in the management of public affairs or in the holding of public offices. Thus, every adult citizen should have the right to vote, to be elected, to hold a public office, to appreciate or criticise some act of commission or omission of his government and the like. As such, there is no justification for the retention of the special rights of the nobility or a hereditary upper chamber like the English House of Lords.

28. See A. Appadorai: *The Substance of Politics*, p. 81.
29. Laski, *op. cit.*, pp. 158-59.

Carl J. Friedrich makes a very penetrating observation that "political equality is increased by the degree to which democratic legitimacy is embodied in the political order." He further says that while this "may embody the normative essence, there is another dimension which has to be kept in mind, namely, the opportunity of participating in the exercisable powers. Without this, opportunity in democratic polity is bound to throw up what is now set up as a principle of the self-generating political equality increasing rapid circulation of the elite. Everything in the way of increased participation, which recalls political equality, will be constrained by the well functioning of the political order."[30]

4. **Economic Equality:** The case of political equality is integrally bound up with the case of economic equality. It, in simple terms, implies equality in the realm of economic power. There should be no concentration of economic power in the hands of a few people. Distribution of national wealth should be such that no section of the people becomes over-affluent so as to misuse its economic power, or any section starves on account of not reaching even upto the margin of sufficiency. Thus, we enter into the realm of 'equality of proportions'. The principle of equality requires that there should be a specific civic minimum in the realm of economic benefits accruing to all, otherwise a "state divided into a small number of rich and a large number of poor will always develop a government manipulated by the rich to protect the amenities represented by their property. It, therefore, follows that inequalities of any social system are justified only as it can be demonstrated that the level of service they procure are obviously higher because of their existence. . . . The differences in the social or economic position of men can only be admitted after a minimum basis of civilisation is attained by the community as a whole. That minimum basis must admit of my realising the implications of personality. Above that level, the advantages of the situation I occupy must be advantages necessary to the performance of a social function."[31]

5. **Legal Equality:** Here equality means that all people are alike in the eyes of the law and that they are entitled to its equal protection. It "is in the spirit of modern law to hold certain fundamentals of rights and duties equally applicable to all human beings.[32] Thus, the principle of equality implies equal protection of life and limb for everyone under the law, and equal penalties on everyone violating them. In a strictly technical sense, the principle of equality before law is integrally bound up with the maxim of equal protection of law to all denying discrimination on any artificial ground whatsoever. Besides, the factor of equal protection under equal circumstances is also bound up with the same.[33] In simple

30. Friedrich: *A Discourse on the Origin of Political Equality* in *Nomos,* IX, p. 222.
31. Laski, *op. cit.,* pp. 157-58. The idea of economic equality is taken in a comprehensive sense. It involves a large measure of economic equality not necessarily in the sense of an identical level of pecuniary incomes, but of equality of environment, of access to education and the means of civilization, of security and independence, and of the social consideration which equality in those matters usually carries with it." Tawney, *op. cit.,* p. 17. Also see Andre Beteille: *The Idea of Natural Inequality and Other Essays* (London: Oxford University Press, 1983).
32. Hobhouse, *op. cit* , p. 104.

terms, it means that the prerogatives of the monarch cannot be made equal to the privileges of a parliamentarian, or that the rights of a manager serving some public undertaking cannot be made equal to those of a judge. Viewed in a wider perspective, it also means justice at a low cost at the earliest practicable time so that everyone irrespective of his social or economic status may get it according to the established procedure of the land. In short, legal equality stands on the maxim: "Equals in law should be treated equally by the law." What the celebrated English jurist says about the features of the 'Rule of Law' in his country may be referred to here: "With us every official from the Prime Minister to a constable or a collector of taxes is under the same responsibility for every act done without legal justification as any other citizen."[34]

6. **Material or Distributive Equality:** Also known as the 'equality of outcome', it implies that "all runners finish the race in line together, regardless of their starting point and the speed at which they run."[35] It goes much beyond what Rousseau says that 'no citizen should be rich enough to buy another, and none so poor as to be forced to sell himself.' It negates the principle of the equality of opportunities which allows room for the display of one's merit. Rather it places the deserving and the undeserving on the same pedestal by arguing that all citizens should have equal share in the equality of resources as well as in their outcomes. The equality of opportunities results in the inequality of the outcomes. The diehard Maoists (Red Guards) created an upheaval in China by demanding abolition of wage differentiation and they banned competitive sports like football during that days of, what they called, 'great proletarian cultural revolution'. A liberal like David Miller puts that "a society of social equals is a community in which people's dealing with and emotional attachments to others are not inhibited by the barriers of class."[36] Even a new English Fabian like Crosland argues that the goal of social justice is to weaken the existing deep-seated stratification, with its concomitant feelings of envy and inferiority, and its barriers to uninhibited minglings between the classes."[37]
7. **Equality of Resources:** Some recent writers like Rawls, Roemer and Dworkin

---

33. Refer to the judgement of the Supreme Court of India in *Chiranjitlal Chaudhary v. The Union of India,* AIR 1951, SC 1. The acceptance of the notion of 'equality before law' has played a very important part in bringing liberty and equality nearer each other. The leading statesmen and the social thinkers of the nineteenth century were disposed to think that since men are naturally unequal, the admission of a general equality of legal status would be the end of civilization. But the modern statesmen of almost all democratic countries do not agree with such a view. Thanks to the struggle of the past, they "have inherited a tradition of legal equality, and fortified by that tradition, they see that the fact that men are naturally unequal is not relevant to the question whether they should or should not be treated as equal before the law." Tawney, *op. cit.,* p. 30.
34. A.V. Dicey: *The Law of the Constitution,* pp. 202-03.
35. Andrew Heywood: *Political Theory: An Introduction,* p. 291.
36. David Miller: "Equality and Market Socialism" in Pranab Bardhan and John Roemer (eds.): *Market Socialism: The Current Debate* (Oxford: Oxford University Press, 1993), p. 302.
37. C.A.R. Crosland: *The Future of Socialism* (London: Cape, 1964), p. 77.

Equality

Natural	Social	Political	Economic	Legal	International
(all are born equal, hence no discrimination on any ground whatsoever)	(equality of rights and opportunities subject to genuine grounds of discrimination)	(equality of share for all in the management of public affairs) 1. Universal adult suffrage 2. Open recruitment to public offices 3. Free and fair periodic elections 4. Free press and mass media agencies 5. No retention of speical rights of any section of the community	(non-concentration of national wealth in fewer hands, equality of proportions) 1. Guarantee of a specific civic minimum 2. Provision of special safeguards to protect the interests of weaker sections of the community 3. Placing of private sector under social control	(fundamental rights and duties applicable to all in an equal measure) 1. Equality before law 2. Equal protection of law to all 3. Equality at equal levels 4. Availability of justice at a low cost and without undue delay	(no discrimination among states on the basis of demographic, geographical, economic or military potential) 1. Equal treatment to all nations 2. Distribution of scientific and technological achievements among all nations 3. Eradication of gigantic evils like slavery and racial segregation 4. Renunciation of the use of force 5. Pacific settlement of international disputes by free and frank discussions.

argue that all persons should have resources so that they may enter into a competition based on the rules of fairness and thereby may pursue the ideal of good life by sharing rewards and offices of the state as per their choices. Rawls says that affirmative action of the state would minimise economic inequality so that everyone may have a share of the basic or primary social goods. Dworkin puts the same idea in a different way by arguing that the state should compensate the naturally disadvantaged persons by introducing the schemes of subsidies, insurance and graduated taxation. Only then the situation of imbalance between the naturally advantaged and disadvantaged persons would be removed or rectified. It constitutes the case of 'luck egalitarianism' which "is said to be too unforgiving to individuals who make bad choices. Its critics accuse it of exaggerating the significance of choice and of giving undue weight to the distribution-of-resources aspect of social justices."[38]

8. **International Equality:** It means the extension of the principle of equality to the international sphere. All nations of the world should be treated equally irrespective of their demographic, geographical, economic or military compositions. That is, the principle of internationalism requires that all nations of the world should be treated on identical terms whether they are big or small in terms of their size, location, natural resources, wealth, military potential and the like. However, viewed in a wider perspective, it also implies that international disputes should be settled through pacific means in which every nation has a right to discuss matters in a free and frank manner and that the use of force, or a threat of this type, is ruled out from consideration. If the meaning of this perspective is carried further, it implies outlawry of war. In ethical terms, it implies that a power-drunk nation going to war in order to settle its terms with a relatively weaker state without first exhausting the avenues of peaceful settlement deserves condemnation at the bar of human conscience. In economic terms, it demands that the benefits of scientific and technological achievements should be shared by all. In terms of humanism, it implies that traditional evils like those of slavery, forced labour, primitive backwardness and the like should be eradicated. The problem here "is rather the discovery of principles which, when applied, will enable the backward races to draw from life such means of happiness as they desire."[39]

Idea of Equality: Liberal Versus Marxist Views

As we have seen in the case of liberty so here, the idea of equality carries different implications to the men of liberal and Marxist views. What we have seen in the preceding sections pertains to the realm of liberal political theory. However, with a view to recapitulate what we have already said on the subject as well as in order to make its meaning more specific, we may add that the idea of equality, according to liberal notion, is: "Equals should be treated equally, unequals unequally and the respect in which they are considered unequal must be relevant to the differences

38. R.J. Arneson: "Justice aflter Rawls" in R.E. Goodin (ed.): *The Oxford Handbook of Politial Science* (Oxford: Oxford University Press, 2009), p. 121.
39. Laski, *op. cit.*, p. 168.

in treatment that we propose."[40] It is, however, a different matter that with the assimilation of socialist content in the philosophy of liberalism, the real meaning of equality has been integrated with the consideration of social good as a result of which the concept of social equality has become all pervasive. Keeping it in view, Rawls suggests two essential points inherent in the notion of equality: "First, each person is to have an equal right to the extensive basic liberty compatible with similar liberty for others. Second, social and economic inequalities are to be arranged so that they are both (a) reasonably expected to be to everyone's advantage, and (b) attached to position and offices equally open to all."[41]

The liberal doctrine of equality, strictly speaking, stands on the premise of the 'equality of adequate opportunities' available to everyman in what Macpherson calls, a market society now turned into a 'quasi-market society'. That is, let all people have liberty to compete with each other in the midst of equal opportunities with the result that those who can make best use of their chances may go ahead of others. Inequality in the midst of equal opportunities is thus a valid affair. In a very perceptive expression, J.H. Schaar thus explains the meaning of, what is called, egalitarianism: "The doctrine of equality of opportunity is the product of a competitive and fragmented society, a society in which individualism, in Tocqueville's sense of the word, is the reigning ethical principle. It is a precise symbolic expression of the liberal-bourgeois model society, for it extends the market place mentality to all the spheres of life. It views the whole of human relations as a contest in which each man competes with his fellows for scarce goods; a contest resting upon the attractive conviction that all should be allowed to improve their conditions as far as their abilities permit. . . . Thus, it is the perfect embodiment of the liberal conception of reform; the fundamental character of the social economic system is altered in substance."[42]

Basically opposed to it is the Marxist notion of equality. If examined closely, the concept of equality, according to Marxist notion, has only two aspects—economic in the socialist and humanistic in the communist phases of social development. That is, what we call equality has mainly an economic aspect so long as we live in a classful or a classless society; it shall have a humanistic form when the era of final stage of socialism (called communism) ushers in with the 'withering away of the state'. There can be no equality so long as there are class contradictions. Unless capitalism is thoroughly liquidated in the period of transition by the dictatorship of the proletariat, there can be nothing like real equality. The existence of equality is naturally bound up with the true application of the rule: 'He who shall work, shall eat.' It shows that "Marx's sovereign concept, as we all know, was of economic equality; his life and writings are a glorious epitaph on that; for after all, it is economic injustice and economic exploitation that have characterised the whole course of human history."[43]

Since economics plays a decisive part in the determination of the relations of

40. Benn and Peters, *op. cit.*, p. 114.
41. John Rawls: *A Theory of Justice* (London: Oxford Univ. Press, 1972), p. 61.
42. Schaar: *Equality of Opportunity and Beyond* in *Nomos*, IX, p. 237.
43. Frank Thakurdas, *op. cit.*, p. 5.

production, naturally it is the propertied class that possesses and controls the levers of power. All benefits of liberty and equality are shared by the class of the 'haves', while the class of the 'have-nots' suffers from the pangs of slavery of servitude. How can a poor worker make use of equal opportunities in competition with the sons of the rich? How can a worker successfully compete when his rival is a member of the capitalist class? The provision of equal opportunity is thus a hoax whatever rational justification may be behind it. Lenin's analysis, thus, stands on this assumption that "no democratic order is possible within the framework of capitalism, for the capitalist class is far too strong and uses the political power symbolised in the State for the preservation of its own interests, and to fasten the bonds of enslavement on the workers and peasants."[44]

Equality thus comes to prevail when classless society is established after the successful results of the revolution. All kinds of equality—social, economic, legal and political—merge so as to prove that what we know by the name of equality is possible only after the liquidation of class antagonisms. All persons engaged in work, whether mental or physical, belong to the class of the toilers and intelligentsia that shows the existence of a new kind of collective life. "The organic unification in one classless collective of all workers means an end to dividing society will be a society of peaceful creative labour, equality and the happiness of all people. This will be a society where, for the first time in history, the personality of each worker will attain a full, general and perfect development."[45]

The Marxist interpretation of a classless society under the dictatorship of proletariat certainly presents a good model of the reconciliation of liberty and equality, at least on a theoretical plane. It may be accepted that Marxism "is the only internally coherent egalitarian philosophy."[46] We may appreciate this statement in the light of a very pertinent question wherein lies the real sense of the principle of equality of opportunity. The principle, as such, is not bad or useless, it is so until we offer a real solution to this problem as 'opportunity to do what'? If it means opportunity to compete in a hierarchical system, then it is not substantially an egalitarian principle. However, its genuinely egalitarian implication would be 'equal opportunity to live a worthwhile life'.[47] Only then we may come to appreciate the meaning of this statement: "Any definition of liberty is humbug that does not mean this: liberty to do what one wants. The people want to be happy and not to be starved or despised or deprived of the decencies of life. They want to be secure and friendly with their fellows, and not conscripted to slaughter and be slaughtered. They want to marry and beget children and help not oppress each other. . . . Who, then is free in a bourgeois society, for not a few but millions are forced by circumstances to be unemployed, and miserable, and despised, and unable to enjoy the decencies of life."[48]

As already pointed out, the Marxist notion of equality assumes a humanistic

44. *Ibid.*, p. 12.
45. Victor Afanasyev: "Basis and Superstructure of Society" in *USSR- Soviet Life Today,* Sept. 1963, p. 39.
46. Joseph and Sumption, *op. cit.,* p. 8.
47. Richard Norman, *op. cit.,* p. 103.
48. C. Caudwell: *Studies in a Dying Culture* (London: Bodley Head, 1938), p. 225.

form in the final stage of social development. That is, the existence of equality will merge with the prevalence of 'glorious human values' when the state withers away and people come to lead a life of perfect co-operation. It is in such an ideal state that Rousseau's concept of moral equality shall prevail. Though a critic of Rousseau's abstract man, Marx appreciates the doctrine of moral equality in that ideal stage of human existence when the notion of abstract man entitled to moral equality will have a concrete form. As he says: "Human emancipation will only be complete when the real, individual man has absorbed into himself the abstract citizen; when as an individual man, in his everyday life, in his relationships, he has become a *species being;* and when he has recognised and organised his powers *(forces propers)* as social *powers* so that he no longer separates this social power from himself as a *political* power."[49]

On the whole, it implies that equality "is the existence of identical conditions and opportunities for the free development of the individual and the fulfilment of the requirements of all members of society, the equal position of people in society being understood differently in different historical epochs."[50] The meaning of equality varies from one social epoch to another. At the time when feudalism was being replaced by capitalism, equality as understood by the then revolutionary bourgeois class meant the abolition of the privileges of the nobility and the equality of all citizens before law, the concept of legal equality, progressive in its time, conceals the existence of a growing economic and social inequality. So Lenin says that "under the guise of equality of the individuals in general, bourgeois democracy proclaims the formal or legal equality of the property owner and the proletariat, the exploiter and the exploited, thereby grossly deceiving the oppressed classes."[51]

In this way, legal equality cannot be fully exercised unless it is based on the actual social equality of the people. Socio-political, racial and national discrimination, inequality between men and women etc. all show that capitalism has failed to provide even formal and legal equality. It is typical of modern bourgeois sociology and policy to present social inequality as a permanent category and to reject the possibility of building a society on the basis of social equality. Scientific communism calls for a concrete historical, not abstract, approach to this problem, for equality has never existed in general outside a given socio-economic and political structure of society. Since the social status of the individual in the class society is determined by his affiliation to a certain class, according to the Marxist-Leninist view, equality does not simply mean the liquidation of certain legal privileges of particular classes, but also the abolition of those classes, the complete elimination of all social and class distinctions, the creation of a classless, socially homogeneous, communist society. As Lenin says: "Equality is an empty phrase if it does not imply the abolition of classes. We want to abolish classes, and in this sense we are for equality. But the claim that we want all men to be alike is just nonsense . . . ."[52]

49. Marx: "On Rousseau" in D. Caute (ed.): *Essential Writings of Marx* (London: Panther, 1567), p. 188.
50. *A Dictionary of Scientific Communism* (Moscow: Progress Publishers 1980), p. 85.
51. Lenin: *Collected Works,* Vol. 31, p. 145.
52. *Ibid.,* Vol. 29, p. 358.

Egalitarianism and Scientific Value Relativism: Empirical Determination of Equality

Equality is mainly a normative concept implying that though all persons should have 'equal opportunities', yet 'all wills are not to be weighed equally'.[53] As such, the principle of egalitarianism, as we have seen in the preceding sections, is not only an ideal; but it is to be understood in a certain context. Moreover, the norm of equality does admit scope for differentiation on certain legitimate grounds. As such, any idea of equality giving no room for the prevalence of discriminations shall amount to its contradiction. "A positive egalitarianism, demanding similar treatment of all, irrespective of any difference, would clearly lead to absurdities. To sweep away all distinctions would be to commit injustices as inexcusable as any under attack. Moral progress is made as much by making new and justifiable distinctions as by eliminating established but irrelevant inequalities."[54]

The pertinent question that arises at this stage is: how the idea of equality being a non-scientific phenomenon can be studied in empirical terms, or how can a purely normative term be scientifically determined. In other words, it is generally understood that an ethical or a political ideal implying that, inspite of all artificial differences all human beings should be treated as 'essentially equal', is necessarily beyond the scope of inter-subjective verifiability. A proper answer to such a query is that the concept of equality or the principle of egalitarianism should be understood in a different light. If so, we shall arrive at a different conclusion and thereby find ourselves poles apart from one like Leonard Nelson who, in explicit words, recognised that a merely logical proof of ethical norms was impossible.[55] Perhaps, Herbert Spiegelberg made a better assessment in his paper titled 'A Defence of Human Equality' when he visualised that sometimes the eighteenth century argument that all men ought to be treated equally on the ground that they were born equal "is still heard today in the somewhat more precise form that equal treatment is evidently required on the ground that all men are by birth in the same plight, because they had no influence on whether they were born at all, into what conditions they were born, and from whom they descended."[56]

Such a way of arguing, as Brecht says, "supplies a forceful emotional appeal, but no scientific proof that only equal treatment of all human beings is just unless we have previously accepted a major premise to the effect that all those who are born into the same plight ought to be treated equally."[57]As such, the principle of equality can be adjudged, tested, evaluated, even determined in certain empirical terms where possible and not in all cases inasmuch as even the scope of scientific enquiry is not unlimited. Thus, science "may not prove, although religion may teach and ethical volition may accept that on this ground all men are essentially equal. The absolute value of this one feature cannot be ascertained by scientific method,

53. Laski, *op. cit.*, p. 164.
54. Benn and Peters, *op. cit.*, p. 133.
55. See Arnold Brecht: *Political Theory: The Foundations of Twentieth Century Political Thought* (Princeton : Princeton Univ. Press, 1959), p. 309.
56. *Ibid.*
57. *Ibid.*

and if asserted on the basis of intuition, or any other source, its validity cannot be inter-subjectively verified."[58] As such, the ideal of equality may be subjected to empirical determination in these respects:

1. It may be verified that all men not only distinguish between good and evil but also are subject to some inner urge towards the ideal: only equal cases ought to be treated equally. Science can continue to explore the interconnections or the lack of interconnections between physical and mental or moral traits and to refute unscientific contentions as to racial differences in this respect. Further, science can do psychological and phenomenological research on the manner in which men become aware of equalities and inequalities, real or imaginary, for instance in the relations between in-group or out-group individuals. As such, it can distinguish various mutually incompatible yardsticks of equal treatment like those of needs or abilities and point to the impossibility of establishing full equality.[59]
2. It follows that the principle of natural equality in some and of natural inequality in some other respects is accepted by science. If so, the ideal of equality is necessarily accompanied by a set of distinctions that should be valid or legitimate. The real meaning of the principle of egalitarianism that only equals can be treated equally or that all men cannot be treated identically regardless of consequences is a scientifically tenable proposition. The only requirement is that the ground of discrimination should be legitimate. However, these grounds can be empirically tested and evaluated. Thus, it shall be a scientifically valid statement to offer that while a distinction on the basis of colour or creed in respect of the requirement to public services shall be scientifically wrong, a discrimination on the basis of sex in the recruitment to defence personnel might be scientifically valid.
3. It can be verified scientifically that while the prevalence of equality leads to political stability, its absence results in mass discontent. By all means, science "can predict the consequences and risks entailed by flagrant discriminations, from feelings hurt to violent uprisings."[60] Thus, Aristotle was perfectly right in holding that the cause of sedition lay in inequality.[61]

We are thus driven to this conclusion that the ideal of equality has both normative and empirical dimensions and, as such, it can be determined by religious, ethical or non-scientific measures in some cases and by empirical or scientific yardsticks in others.

Equality and Liberty: Problem of Reconciliation

Now we turn to another complex subject of the relationship between equality and liberty with special reference to the political aspect of the latter and economic aspect of the former. The difficulty, in this direction, arises from the fact that, historically speaking, the glorification of liberty precedes that of equality and until recent times many thinkers can be seen assigning a higher and superior position to the former.

58. *Ibid.*, p. 311.
59. *Ibid.*, pp. 311-12.
60. *Ibid.*, p. 312.
61. Aristotle: *Politics*, Book V.

For instance, ancient Greek and Roman ideals of liberty were not coupled with the notion of equality, as not all men were free in the slave societies. Though the Stoics preached the principle of natural equality, it received limited response. Moreover, when thinkers like Polybius and Cicero of the Roman period repeated the Stoic doctrine, they did so just to make their political philosophy in consonance with the changing conditions of the empire. The whim of difference between a Greek and a barbarian and subsequently between a Roman and a non-Roman continued until Christianity became the official religion that preached the doctrine of the 'Fatherhood of God and brotherhood of man'.

Liberty, therefore, remained the privilege of the aristocratic section of the society. Under feudalism the rights of the serfs were not equal to those of the landlords and nobles. It continued even in the modern period. A representative thinker of the social contract school like John Locke did not include equality in the list of his three natural rights (relating to life, liberty, and property). For the first time, the idea of equality got itself aligned with that of liberty in the Declaration of Independence adopted by the American Founding Fathers in 1776 which *inter alia* said that "all men are created equal. . . . "A little later, it had an equally strong affirmation in the French Declaration of 1789 that *inter alia* said that "all human beings are born free and equal in dignity and rights."

However, nothing tangible could take place in the direction of reconciling the true meaning of equality with that of liberty as there continued a lot of suspicion and resistance not merely in theory but also in practice at the hands of the rich and aristocratic classes of the society. Thus, men like. Lord Acton in England and Alexis de Tocqueville in France insisted that equality and liberty were antithetical terms as a result of which the passion for one made vain the hope for another. They, in very clear terms, argued that the desire to have equality destroyed the possibility of having liberty.[62] Such persons defend the cause of liberty for the privileged section of the society that naturally came to have its place in the representative political systems of the present times—an age which "is fast becoming a graveyard of those persons who sought to turn their backs on this hard won gain of centuries of human endeavour"[63]

In the early years of the twentieth century, an English poet Matthew Arnold spoke strongly on the incompatibility of the attitude of equality with the spirit of humanity and sense of dignity of man as man, which are the marks of a true civilised society. As he argued: "On the one side, in fact, inequality harms by pampering; on the other, by vulgarising and depressing. A system founded on it is against nature

62. State's role in curbing economic freedom so as to bring equality looks like "an exploration of the trades off between liberty, equality and prosperity." S. Brittan: *Capitalism and the Permissive Society* (London: Macmillan, 1973), p. 128. The classical liberals maintain that a movement towards equality would count as unjustified, since it might entail paying the same income to.individuals who make widely differing contributions to the output of an economy. So Hayek says: "Our objection is against all attempts to impress upon society a deliberately chosen pattern of distribution, whether it be an order of equality, or of inequality." *The Constitution of Liberty,* p. 87. Robert Nozick epitomises it in the principle 'from each as they choose, to each as they are chosen'. *Anarchy, State and Utopia,* p. 160.

63. Frank Thakurdas, *op. cit.*, p. 160.

Equality and Social Stratification

Equality is not the enemy of human diversity, nor is its goal to make everyone alike.

—Andrew Heywood

Political Theory: An Introduction, p. 285.

Perhaps equality requires certain vulgarity in opposition to elitist principles of hierarchical prestige, privilege and power.

—Bryan S. Turner

Equality, p. 130.

To focus solely on post factum redistribution is to make the great error of reformers and philanthropists.... to nibble at the consequences of unjust power, instead of redressing the injustice itself.

—John Stuart Mill

Principles of Political Economy in his *Collected Works*, Vol. III, p. 953.

and, in the long run, breaks down."[64] It implies that equality not only results in pampering one class; it also results in depressing another. Representing the same point, an English Tory statesman Lord Birkenhead declared that the idea that 'all men are equal' is 'a poisonous doctrine', and he wrung his hands at the thought of the 'glittering prizes' of life being diminished in value. Likewise, Garvin, with his eyes on the dangers of the moment created by people's movement for liberty and equality displaying the temptations to which his fellow countrymen were most prone to succumb, warned us against the spirit that seeks the dead level and ignores the inequality of human endowments. Sir Ernest Benn writes that economic equality is 'a scientific impossibility', because as Prof. Pareto has proved, "if the logarithms of income size be charted on a horizontal scale, and the logarithms of the number of persons having an income of a particular size or over be charted on a vertical scale, then the resulting observational points will be approximately along a straight line."[65]

There is no dearth of such statements if one tries to collect and put them together. A great industrialist of England like Sir Herbert Austin and a distinguished minister of religion like Dean Inge harp on the same theme. While the former implores us "to cease teaching that all men are equal and entitled to an equal share of the common wealth and enrich the men who make sacrifices justifying enrichment and leave the others in their contentment rather than try to mould material that was intended to withstand the fires of refinement", the latter complains that the government "is taking the pick of the working classes and educating them at the expense of the tax payers to enable them to take the bread out of the mouths of the sons of the professional men." This deplorable procedure, he argues, cannot fail to be injurious to the nation as a whole, since it injures the upper middle classes who are 'the cream of the community'.[66]

---

64. Arnold: "Lecture on Equality" in *Mixed Essays* (1903), pp. 48-97 cited in Tawney, *op. cit.*, p. 1.
65. *Ibid.*, p. 19.
66. *Ibid*, pp. 19-20.

It is quite obvious that such a view is based on the defence of the existing system of inequalities as procreated by the capitalist system. So the purpose of the defendants is first to admit the fact of social inequality and then to conceal it behind the mask of a verbal justification. The argument takes a clever turn when it is emphasised that the critics of the capitalist system must also realise that capitalism is maintained not only by the capitalists but by those who, like some of themselves, would be capitalists if they could, and that the injustices survive not merely because the rich exploit the poor but because in their hearts too many of the poor admire the rich. They know and complain that they are tyrannised over by the the power of money. "But they do not yet see that what makes money the tyrant of society is largely their own reverence for it. They do not sufficiently realise that, if they were as determined to maintain their dignity as they are, quite rightly, to maintain their wages, they would produce a world in which their material miseries would become less unmanageable, since they would be no longer under a kind of nervous tutelage on the part of the minority, and the determination of their economic destinies would rest in their own hands."[67]

That liberty and equality are antithetical terms is strongly asserted even in present times the examples of which may be seen in affirmations of some liberal thinkers. Here the burden of argument is either to stick to the principle of desert or to denounce the increasing area of state activity in the name of general welfare that automatically amounts to the curtailment of individual liberty for the sake of creating the conditions of social equality. It is, for example, asserted: "That the pursuit of equality has in practice led to inequality and tyranny. . . . is not mere accident. It is the direct result of conditions which are inherent in the very concept of equality. Egalitarians rely for the achievement of their objects on the coercive power of the state, as they are bound to do by the nature of the human material with which they deal. A society in which the choices fundamental to human existence are determined by coercion is not a free society. It follows irresistibly that egalitarians must choose between liberty and equality."[68]

Similar line of thought may be seen in the statement of F. A. Hayek who holds: "From the fact that people are very different it follows that if we treat them equally, the result must be inequality in their actual position, and that the only way to place them in an equal position would be to treat them differently... . The equality before the law, which freedom requires, leads to material inequality. The desire of making people more alike in their condition cannot be accepted in a free society as a justification for further and discriminatory coercion."[69]

The essence of all such affirmations is that equality does not mean uniformity; it may mean equal well-being or equality of satisfaction that is thus bound to prove an authoritarian deal. The differences of temperament will have a similar effect. Persons endowed with an energetic disposition, or with an equable temperament, stand to get more out of life than their more sluggish or morose fellows. In short,

---

67. *Ibid.*, pp. 14-15.
68. K.Joseph and J. Sumption: *Equality* (London: John Murray, 1979), p. 47.
69. F.A. Hayek: *The Constitution of Liberty* (London: Routledge; and Kegan Paul, 1960), p. 87.

human capacities for happiness are so multi-form that "equality in this area can be reached only by massive external intervention in people's lives."[70]

A definite change took place in the nature of liberal political philosophy in this regard in the twentieth century. Thus, a great liberal like L.T. Hobhouse said that liberty without equality is 'a high sounding phrase with squalid results'. Likewise, R.H. Tawney strongly observed that 'a large measure of equality, so far from being inimical to liberty, is essential to it.'[71] Pollard opined that there was only one solution to the problem of liberty: it lay in equality. In other words, it means that if liberty is to realise its end, it is necessary that it must be accompanied by equality: liberty without equality degenerates into license. So fine is the observation of Barker: "It remains to add that equality is not an isolated principle. It stands by the principle of liberty and fraternity. It has to be reconciled with both and, in particular, with the principle of liberty."[72]

What is really important in this regard is that while the ideals of equality and liberty are complementary to each other, the latter carries more weight in the actual affairs of life. Liberty has, of course, been an older idea in terms of historical advancement of human civilisation and the cause of equality, if exclusively pressed, inculcates feelings of jealousy among the people, still it cannot be forgotten that both are integrally connected with the same ideal—development of human personality. That the two are contributory is thus put by a conscientious writer: "Liberty and equality are not in conflict, nor even separate, but are different facets of the same ideal. . . indeed, since they are identical, there can be no problem of law or to what extent, they are or can be related, this is surely the nearest, if not the most satisfactory, solution ever devised for a perennial problem in political philosophy."[73]

The problem of bringing about a proper reconciliation between the ideals of liberty and equality assumes a serious form when it is examined in the sphere of economics. Here the subject of equality happens to entangle itself with the subject of property in view of the fact that the Marxist and the liberal-socialist thinkers alike desire equitable distribution of property in order to ensure real equality that may not disable a man from making use of equal opportunities granted to him. "Political equality, therefore, is never real unless it is accompanied by virtual economic equality. . . . By virtual equality in economic power is meant more than approximate equality of wealth. It means that the authority which exerts that power must be subject to the rules of democratic government. It means the abrogation of unfettered and irresponsible will in the industrial world. It involves building decisions on principles which can be explained, and the relation of those principles to the service any given industry is seeking to render."[74]

70. Richard Norman: "Does Equality Destroy Liberty?" in Keith Graham (ed.): *Contemporary Political Philosophy* (London: Cambridge University Press, 1982), p. 85.
71. While lamenting over the 'religion of inequality', Tawney says that "the people accepted the *mana* (a mysterious wisdom) and *karakia* (a magical influence) of social and economic inequality in the same way that primitive people accepted the ritual of tribal society. There is no rational justification for social inequality; its survival is a matter of prejudice." *Op. cit.*, p. 13.
72. Barker, *op. cit.*, p. 159.
73. H.A. Deane: *The Political Ideas of Harold J. Laski* (Columbia: Columbia Univ. Press, 1954), p. 46.
74. Laski, *op. cit.*, pp. 162-63.

Negative and Positive Views on the Relationship Between Liberty and Equality

Negative View

All men are not equal, nor can they ever be. The argument of natural inequality of mankind still stands valid in the light of the 'rule of the privilege'. The number of persons competent to share in political, social, economic and political affairs is limited. Government is an expert undertaking that requires a highly specialised technical competence and consequently demands of its practitioners more than ordinary qualities of character of mind. Let the deserving get more than those who deserve less or none at all.

1. Aristocracy and priesthood, a governing class and a teaching class; these two sometimes separate, and endeavouring to harmonise themselves, sometimes conjoining as one, and the King a Pontiff King; there did no society exist without these two vital elements, there will none exist.[1]
2. The parliamentary principle of decision by majority, by denying the authority of the person and placing in its stead the number of crowd in question, sins against the aristocratic basic idea of nature.[2]
3. Society is always a dynamic unity of two component factors: minorities and masses. The minorities are individuals or groups of individuals which are specially qualified. The mass is the assemblage of persons not specially qualified.[3]

Positive View

It is not in their skill, intelligence, strength or virtue that men are equal, but merely in their being men; it is their common humanity that constitutes their equality. On this interpretation we should not seek for some special characteristics in respect of which men are equal, but merely remind ourselves that they are all men, because:

(i) *Argument of Common Humanity:* That all men are human is, if a tautology, a useful one, serving as a reminder that those who belong automatically to the species, *homo sapiens,* and can speak a language, use tools, live in societies, can interbreed despite racial differences etc. are also alike in certain other respects more likely to be forgotten. The Nazis' anthropologists who tried to construct theories of Aryanism were paying, in very poor coin, the homage of irrationality to reason.

(ii) *Argument of Moral Capacities:* 'Treat every man as an end in himself and never as a means only', (Kant). In such a picture of the 'kingdom of ends', the idea of *respect* which is owed to each man as a rational moral agent and since men are equally such agents—is owed equally to all, unlike admiration and similar attitudes, which are commanded unequally by men in proportion to their unequal possessions of different kinds of natural excellence. Each man is to be, as it were, free from certain conspicuous structures of inequality in which we find him.

(iii) *Argument of Equality under Unequal Circumstances:* The notion of inequality is invoked not only in connections where all men are claimed in some sense to be equal, but in connections where they are agreed to be unequal (e.g., in situations of *need* and *merit* and the question arises of the distribution of or access to, certain goods to which their inequalities are relevant. Where everything about a person is controllable, equality of opportunity and absolute equality seem to coincide. It is all the more obvious that we should not throw one set of claims out of the window, but should rather seek in each situation the best way of eating and having as much cake as possible. It is an uncomfortable situation but the discomfort is just that of genuine political thought.[4]

1. Thomas Carlyle cited in *Round Table* (June, 1954), p. 235.
2. Hitler: *Mein Kampf* (New York: Reynal and Hitchcock, 1939), p. 103.
3. O.Y. Gasset: *The Revolt of the Masses* (New York: W.W. Norton, 1932), p. 9.
4. Bernard Williams: "The Idea of Equality" in Peter Laslett and G. Runciman (eds.): *Philosophy, Politics, and Society* (Oxford: Basil Blackwell, 1962), pp. 110-31.

The implementation of the principle of equality thus requires an end of the *laissez faire* system based on the economics of free competition. It demands active interference of the state in the realm of economics. There can be no political equality in the real sense of the term unless there is redistribution of national wealth, for it is the possession of property along with rights to its use and enjoyment by the people that brings about a state of inequality and thereby enables only the wealthy and privileged class to make use of liberty. Thus, Rousseau—the great idealist thinker and the 'poet of politics'—first treated property as the originator of social inequality and thereby the killer of the condition of idyllic happiness and primitive simplicity (in his *Second Discourse)* and thereafter came to lay down the doctrine of liberty (in his *Social Contract)* that 'man is born free'. How such a reconciliation of liberty and equality can be acceptable to the men of the privileged class constitutes the main crux of the problem. It is owing to this that the doctrine of liberty is said to work disastrously when applied to the field of economics.[75]

If the idea of equality is presented in a reasonable way, then it may well be harmonised with the idea of liberty. When the revolutionaries of France raised the slogan of 'Liberty, Equality, Fraternity' and they demanded the synthesisation of the two great boons of liberty and equality, they did not mean that "all men are equally intelligent or equally virtuous, any more than that they are equally tall or equally fat, but that the unity of their national life should no longer be torn to pieces by obsolete property rights and meaningless juristic distinctions."[76] It has its satirical expression in these words of Montesquieu: "The creatures in question are black from head to feet, and their noses are so flat that it is almost impossible to pity them. It is not to be supposed that God, an all-wise Being, can have lodged a soul—still less a good soul—in a body completely black."[77]

It is a different thing that harmonisation of the two terms— liberty and equality—has not yet taken place to the desired extent due to the prevalence of non-egalitarian forces coming down from times immemorial and that they will continue to elude us for many more years to come, but it is equally true that this should be the goal before us so that we may go on making more and more progress in that direction. As Tawney hopefully counsels: "The important thing, however, is not that it should be completely attained, but that it should be sincerely sought. What matters to the health of society is the objective towards which its face is set, and to suggest that it is immaterial in which direction it moves, the goal must always elude it, is not

75. C.E.M. Joad: *Introduction to Modern Political Theory:* (Oxford: Clarendon Press, 1946), p. 30.
76. Tawney, *op. cit.*, p. 24.
77. *Ibid.*, p. 28.

scientific, but irrational. It is like using the impossibility of absolute cleanliness as a pretext for rolling in a manure heap, or denying the importance of honesty, because no one can be wholly honest. It may well be the case that capricious inequalities are in some measure inevitable in the sense that, like crime and disease, they are a malady which the most rigorous precautions cannot wholly overcome. But even when crime is known as crime, and disease as disease, the ravages of both are circumscribed by the mere fact that they are recognised for what they are, and described by their proper names, not by flattering euphemisms. And a society which is convinced that inequality is an evil need not be alarmed, because the evil is one which cannot wholly be subdued. In recognising the poison, it will have armed itself with an antidote. It will have deprived inequality of its sting by stripping it of its esteem."[78]

We thus arrive at this conclusion that if the aim of normative political theory is to seek and analyse the avenues relating to the development of human personality, it is required that the ideals of equality and liberty should have a simultaneous flow despite the fact that in terms of historical evolution the latter is older than, and no matter now outshone by, the former. Both are necessarily connected with the supreme worth and dignity of human personality and the spontaneous development of its capacities. As a matter of fact, the traditional lovers of the doctrine of freedom without equality have made the ideal of liberty weaker by obdurately trying to swim across the current. The modern age is not prepared to tolerate that the boons of liberty and with it of equality remain confined to the world of the'peers'; rather it wants to emphasise: "There must, indeed, be equality of opportunity before all capacity can be free to develop; but the major and ultimate aim is the liberation of capacity."[79]

Critical Appreciation

What we have said in the preceding sections leads to certain definite impressions. First, equality implies equal opportunities for all without artificial or unwarranted discriminations. Second, if there are certain lines of distinction, they should be legitimate. Third, equality has both normative and empirical dimensions. Though mainly a normative concept, it can be measured in empirical terms in certain respects. Fourth, the ideal of equality is not antithetical but complementary to the ideal of liberty. Above all, there can be no liberty in the absence of economic equality. It may, however, be added that the concept of equality is still a victim of certain misconnotations. It not only makes the issue of its reconciliation with liberty a very complex affair but also creates the problem of its proper understanding. Two important points may be made in this connection:

1. Though the history of the development of the ideal of equality is quite old and by now every believer in the system of democracy has come to believe that it is one of the two pillars of popular government (the other being liberty), he is not prepared to define or explain its real meaning in the direction of bringing about its plausible reconciliation with the ideal of liberty. Nothing but the consideration of vested interests stands in the background. The shrewd attempts of several

78. *Ibid.*, pp. 37-38.
79. Barker, *op.cit.*, p. 160.

Some Important Statements

The freedom of the pike is death to the winnows.

—R.H. Tawney

Liberty is obedience to a law one prescribes to oneself.

—J.J. Rousseau

Libertarian political thought is characterised by the strict priority given to liberty (understood in negative sense) over other values, such as authority, tradition and equality.

—Andrew Heywood

Libertarianism shares with liberal equality a commitment to the principle of respect for people's choices, but rejects the principle of rectifying unequal circumstances.

—Will Kymlicka

liberal thinkers in the direction of first, though willy-nilly, accepting the case for the reconciliation of equality with liberty and then endeavouring to solve the problem in their own dexterous way not only smacks of intellectual dishonesty on their part, but also shows their vested interest in maintaining the *status quo* to any possible extent so that their vested interests do not suffer in a thorough-going manner. The result is that till now a universally acceptable definition of the term 'equality' remains the need of the hour.[80]

2. The problem has been made more complex by the Marxists who find no equality until the classless society is established. One may wonder how there can be equality in the midst of no liberty during the era of the 'dictatorship of the proletariat'. Though we may fully appreciate the view of Marx and Lenin that unless all have economic freedom, there is neither liberty nor equality, we may also ask as to what sort of liberty there remains when the political system establishes a ruthlessly regimented order. Would it not be correct to say that there is hardly any fundamental difference between liberal-democratic and communist orders in this respect in view of the fact that while the former ensures liberty at the expense of equality, the latter brings about equality at the expense of liberty.[81]

80. John Rawls says that "meritocracy follows the principle of careers open to talents and uses equality of opportunity as a way of releasing men's energies in the pursuit of economic prosperity and political domination." *A Theory of Justice,* p. 107. Also see John Stanley: "Equality of Opportunity as Philosophy and Ideology" in *Political Theory,* London, Vol. V, No. 1 (February, 1977). Ralph Dahrendorf cites the words of Immanuel Kant that "inequality is a source of much that is evil, but also of everything that is good." And then affirms that social inequality "exists at all, however, is an impetus towards liberty, because it guarantees the historical quality of societies. The perfectly egalitarian society is not only unrealistic, it is also a terrible idea." Refer to his paper "On the Origin of Social Inequality" in Peter Laslett and G. Runciman (ed. s): *Philosophy, Politics, Society* (Oxford: Basil Balackwell, 1962), pp. 108-9.

81. It appears that there is an initial presumption in favour of the equality of treatment just as there is an initial presumption in favour of liberty in the basic sense of non-interference. Both interference and discrimination have to justify themselves. See A.C. Graham: "Liberty and Equality" in *Mind,* Vol. 74 (1965), pp. 59-65. The presumption of equality is but one side of a coin, the other being the presumption that unequals should be treated unequally. In some cases, inequality is so obvious that we jump immediately to the other side of the proposition. J.R. Pennock; *Democratic Political Theory* (Princeton: Princeton University Press, 1979), p. 146.

In a word, we are still in search of finding a proper and universally acceptable version of the real meaning of equality and its proper reconciliation with liberty. What we have with us is just a workable arrangement more or less of a normative character. Differences in the social, political and economic philosophies of the people shall continue so long as there is liberty of thought and expression and with it differences in the real meaning of equality shall continue so as to defy the problem of any standard solution to the problem of giving a rigid or precise connotation to this great value of human life. At the same time, the tendency of taming the brute shall continue so that authority being a political trust remains a representative and, for this reason, a responsible affair. It has by now been well-established that inequality is an artifical contrivance that ought to be eradicated. If liberty and equality are to survive in a harmonious manner, economic liberty and political authority should be redevised in a way that there is equalisation of power and wealth, having its healthy and constructive effects on the moral and intellectual capacities of the human beings. The goal should be achieved without sacrificing the individual or his personality. As Russell says: "The greatest political evil is not inequality of wealth as the Bolshevik theorists insist, but inequality of power."[82]

82. Bertrand Russell: *Roads to Freedom* (London: George Allen and Unwin. 1919), p. 111.

10

Property

> No man is fully free unless possessing some rights of property in something, since property is the means whereby he develops his personality by impressing upon his external surroundings without dependence on the will of others. No degree of security, no rational scale however generous, no organised hostelry with furniture and services all provided, no uniform clothing however lavish or becoming is a substitute for property. Property is in itself good and a legitimate aspiration for human striving.
>
> **—Quinton Hogg[1]**

A system of property in the sense of a set of norms allocating control over the physical resources at its disposal is considered essential for any community according to the traditional liberal democratic theory; no matter one of its main weaknesses is traceable in its retention of the concept of man as an infinite appropriator—a concept of man clearly inextricable from a concept of property.[2] The relevant question that, however, arises at this stage is that if justice is the rendering to each man which is his own, or if the determination of mine and thine is the principal object of a civil society, the political scientist must elucidate certain principles of its proper ownership and enjoyment. That is: What reasons can a man give for calling a thing his own? How are we to distinguish valid claims of ownership from those which are unjust? A history of the answers to these questions is the history of the theory of property.[3]

Property: Real Meaning and Nature

It is rather a tedious job to offer a precise definition of the term property in view of the fact that its real meaning and nature vary with the developments in the spheres of science and technology as well as with the views of men in regard to their social and economic philosophy. As a. result, the term would have one meaning in the primitive society with a simple agricultural economy and quite another in a highly developed technological society ever finding new and developed methods of controlling resources and using the end products for the community proposed in a hundred ways. It is only in a loose manner that property is defined as 'a bundle of rights' which the owner possesses and enjoys as a matter of his claim to the exclusion of others, though subject to the laws of social behaviour.

Hence, property may be defined as the *control of man over things or an appropriation of certain objects recognised by the society*. It does not mean mere possession that confers

1. See Quinton Hogg: *Case for Conservatism* (London, 1947), Ch. 18.
2. C.B. Macpherson: *Democratic Theory: Essays in Retrieval* (Oxford: Clarendon Press, 1975), p. 120.
3. K.K. Matthew: "The Right to Property" in *Journal of Constitutional and Parliamentary Studies*, New Delhi, Vol. V, No. 1, 1976, p. 5.

upon the man only a delegated right. What is basic in this direction is that it calls for exclusive and permanent control of man over things whether material in the form of house, land, cattle and the like or non-material like goodwill. The most, essential element of the right to property is the right of excluding others permanently from interference with a particular control over some material or non-material object. In the modern age, consideration for the welfare of the community has become another essential point. It shows that property has come to have an important social aspect and, as such, its right has become a relative affair. As such, now property implies a form of regulated control that cannot be claimed by an individual against the well-being of society.[4]

A proper definition of the term 'property' should, therefore, be offered keeping in view its two essential ingredients: individual's right in exclusion to that of others, and (ii) use and enjoyment of this right subject to the norms of social welfare. Thus, by property, we mean generally "an exclusive right to control an economic good. It implies the exclusive right of a political unit—city, state, nation, etc.—to control an economic good. Property is not a thing, but the rights which extend over a thing. In short, property is the right and not the object over which the right extends. The essence of property is in the relations among men arising out of their relations to things."[5] It is also said that whatever technical definition of property we may prefer, we must recognise that property right is a relation not between an owner and a thing, but between the owner and other individuals in reference to things. A right is always against one or more individuals. This becomes unmistakably clear, as Justice Matthew says, if we take specifically modern forms of property such as franchises, patents or goodwills etc., which constitute such a large part of the capital assets of our industrial and commercial enterprises.[6]

From what we have said, we may derive certain important points regarding the nature of the right to and institution of property. They are:

1. Property is a private affair. Here it implies a right of the person to exclude others from its control or engagement. Property is the claim which the individual can count on having enforced it in his favour by the society or the state, by some convention of law. It refers to the case of individual proprietorship where exclusive rights of control vest in persons. On this pattern, the owner of an object is entitled, to the exclusion of other private persons, to decide what shall be done with it, except where he is limited by law, or by some voluntary agreement.
2. Property is a public affair as well. Now we enter into the domain of 'public property' or property under a 'corporate person'. Thus, property belonging to a municipality, local or state government, or some corporation and the like falls in this category. For instance, roads, bridges, parks, hospitals, temples, railway lines, etc., are property of the public. One may say that while persons exercise control over public property, they are not individuals; they are 'corporate persons' who change from time to time and are also held accountable for their acts of commission or omission.

4. E. Asirvatham: *Political Theory* (Lucknow: Upper India, 1967), VII Ed., p. 214.
5. Ely: *The Fundamentals in the Existing Socio-Economic Order Treated from the Standpoint of Distribution,* Vol. I, Book I, Chapter III, cited in Matthew, *op. cit.*, p. 2.
6. *Ibid.*, pp. 2-3.

3. Property has both the individual and the social sides. In the former aspect, it relates to the exclusive possession of an individual over some objects, whether material or immaterial, whereby he may make use of his right in exclusion to the claim of others, though subject to the norms of social behaviour; in the latter case, it relates to the authority of the state that may impose reasonable restrictions in the name of general good. Take, for instance, the power of the state to levy tax on private property, or implement the rule of estate duty, or go to the extent of nationalisation. The important point to be taken note of at this stage is that, in modern times, both the individual and social aspects of property have become integrally connected so much so that the traditional concept has undergone a basic change in this regard.

In fine, the term 'property', according to the Supreme Court of India, "must be understood in a corporeal sense as having reference to all those specific things that are susceptible to appropriate appropriation and enjoyment as well as in its juridical or legal sense of a bundle of rights which the owner can exercise under the municipal law with respect to the use and enjoyment of those things to term exclusion of others."[7] In another leading case, the Supreme Court observed that the property "means the highest right a man can have to anything, being that right which one has to lands or tenements, goods or chattels which does not depend on another's courtesy. It includes ownership, estates and interests in corporeal things and also rights such as trade marks, copyrights, patents and even rights *in personam* capable of transfer or transmission such as debts; and signifies a beneficial right to or a thing considered as having a money value, especially with reference to transfer succession and to their capacity of being injured."[8] In a word, property stands for a miscellany of equities that persons hold in the Commonwealth.[9]

Forms of Property: Private, Quasi-Public and Public

A peculiar feature of the institution of property in the modern age is that though a product of the capitalist society, it has assumed different forms in view of the fact that the position of ownership has changed from that of a master to that of an agent. With the rise of modern corporations and the predominance of corporate property system and, more particularly with the increasing scope of state activity in social and economic spheres, the concept of ownership has now not remained what it once was. In certain cases, the owner has control over his property, whether limited by the law of the land, it is his private property. However, in certain other cases, he simply holds a piece of paper representing a set of rights and expectations in respect of an enterprise, while over the physical property he has little control. In the field of corporate enterprise, the normal owner—the shareholder—is becoming more and more powerless. He turns into a mere recipient of dividends, barely distinguishable from the bondholder.[10] There are also some forms of property like annuities which

7. *Subodh Gopal v. The State of West Bengal,* 1954, SCR 587.
8. *R.C. Cooper* v. *The Union of India,* 1970, 1 SCC 248, SCR 531.
9. See Hamilton and Till: "Property" in Seligman (ed.): *Encyclopaedia of the Social Sciences,* 1933 Ed., p. 528.
10. See Matthew, *op. cit.,* p. 11.

consist wholly in titles to income and which entail rights of control only over the things that income will purchase year by year except in so far as they might be sold for cash in the open market.[11]

The emergence of the welfare state has created new forms of property. Today the government is not merely an administrative agency, it is the regulator, dispenser of benefits, and a mass employer. It renders great services to the people in the form of social security, pensions to political sufferers, subsidies to the disabled and the destitutes, etc. Besides, thousands of people are employed in public corporations. The government issues licenses to the private entrepreneurs to run some industry and it may withhold its permission also. The government also holds hundreds of acres of land for mining and other purposes. These resources are available for utilisation by private individuals by way of some lease or licenses or letters of intent. The result is that property has taken a new form that may, for the sake of convenience, be described as quasi-private or quasi-public, though the latter appellation would be more appropriate in the nature of things, because several arrangements made by the government in the name of rendering social services mean growth in official largesse which, in turn, means dependence upon the political organisation. As such today more and more of our wealth takes the form of right or status than of tangible goods.[12]

Finally, there is the state property that may also be described as public or common property. Here property refers to a right of a corporate entity—central, provincial or local government, or some subordinate agency so authorised by the state. The important thing to be noted in this context is that property of this kind is not subject to the exclusive control of any individual, nor its dividends go to him, rather it remain under the ownership of some corporate entity that guarantees to the individuals that its use will be made for the common good and in that case they will become its beneficiary. As such, the case of public property has also undergone a change due to the pressures of a democratic system. As such, state property is no longer the patrimony of the rulers who may dispense it as per their will by alienating its part in some dowry or donation, it is the property of the community and, for this reason, it should be made use of in the common interest.

We may, therefore, suggest three broad forms of property— private, quasi-public and public. It may. however, be emphasised that due to change in the character of the society, the concept of property has also changed so much so that what we generally call private property is no longer 'private' as it was in the previous centuries. The most remarkable change in the character of private property is that it is now being seen as a right to a revenue or an income, rather than as rights in specific material things.[13] The state has gained the power of imposing restrictions on the use of private property. It is called the doctrine of eminent domain. Not only this, the state may go to the extent of acquiring private property in the name of

11. S.I. Benn and R.S. Peters: *Social Principles and the Democratic State* (London: George Allen and Unwin, 1975), p. 157.
12. Matthew, *op. cit.*, p. 12.
13. Macpherson, *op. cit.*, p. 131.

'public purpose', though by the authority of law and on the payment of a 'paltry' compensation to the owner so that there is no 'fraud on the constitution'.[14]

We no longer live in an age in which the concept of property implies an exclusive and inalienable right of an individual over some material objects. Gone are the days when human beings in the form of slaves were bought and sold, even butchered, at the hands of freemen; also gone are the days when the owners had absolute right over their possessions and a thinker like Locke could have been highly indignant had he ever been presented with a Compulsory Purchase Order in England. As Macpherson says: "We have moved from a market society to a quasi-market society. In all capitalist countries, the society as a whole, or the most influential sections of it, operating through the instrumentality of the welfare state and the welfare state—in any case, the regulatory state—is doing more and more of the work of allocation. Property as exclusive, alienable, 'absolute', individual or corporate rights in things, therefore, becomes less necessary."[15]

Liberal View: Justification of the Private Property System

The most perplexing thing in the discussion of various theories on the subject of property is its ambiguous nature arising out of the involvement of a multitude of rights that have nothing in common except that they are exercised by persons and enforced by the state. More important than this is the fact that right to property and its protection "vary indefinitely in economic character, in social effect, and in moral justification. They may be conditional like the grant of patent rights, or absolute like the ownership of ground rents, terminable like copyright, or permanent like a freehold, as comprehensive as sovereign, or as restricted as an easement, as intimate and personal as the ownership of clothes and books, or as remote and intangible as shares in a gold mine or rubber plantation."[16] For this reason, the subject of property has been treated differently by persons subscribing to different schools or viewpoints as a result of which enormous literature has appeared ranging from one of rank idealisation to the vehement denunciation of the system of property.

First of all, we take up the case of liberal view coming to us from ancient to modern times hinging on the justification, even glorification, of the institution of private property. In ancient Greece, Plato, in his *Republic,* justified the system of private property for the members of the economic class only, but he changed his mind in his *Laws* when he suggested that property should be divided amongst the people in almost equal proportions. Aristotle in his *Politics* defended the system of property as essential for the full use of human faculties and as making for a more efficient use of resources. He also argued that the equality of property was necessary to preserve the community and to prevent seditions (revolutions) that could destroy

14. It is owing to this that even modern liberal thinkers have accepted that right to property should no longer be treated as 'fundamental'. The UNESCO Committee of Experts reporting on Human Rights in 1949 limited the 'fundamental rights of property' to 'what is necessary for a man's personal use and the use of his family; no other form of property is in itself a fundamental right. See Benn and Peters, *op. cit.,* p. 155.
15. Macpherson. *op. cit.* p. 134.
16. See R.H. Tawney: *The Acquisitive Society,* Ch. 5.

a state. In the Roman period, Cicero defended the ownership of property as an institution of nature and he also pleaded that, as far as possible, private property should be distributed among the people in equal shares. The trend continued in the medieval times. St. Augustine described the system of property both as a punishment and as a partial remedy for the 'original sin'. St Thomas held it in accord with the law of nature.

The justification of the system of private property, however, witnessed its powerful defence in the modern age. In Italy, Machiavelli said that the love for property was so deep in the heart of man that while he could forget the fact of his patricide, he could never be oblivious to the loss of his patrimony. In France, Jean Bodin labelled the opponents of the private property system as foolhardy dreamers. Hobbes held protection of private property as one of the essential functions of the sovereign. However, the name of Locke is more important who said that the sole end for which mankind entered into the social compact was the preservation of their property. David Hume held that whatever is produced or improved by a man's art or industry ought forever be secured to him in order to give encouragement to such useful habits and accomplishments. In Germany, Kant sought to justify the abstract idea of the system of property on the grounds of occupation and compact. Another leading idealist, Hegel, said that property was the realisation of the idea of liberty.

The justification of the private property system found a very concrete form in the works of modern English liberals. Bentham, who scorned the idea of natural rights as developed by his predecessors like Locke, did borrow this much from him that the security or enjoyment of the fruits of one's labour was the result of property and without it utility could not be maximised. He even said that law and property were born together and must die together. Blackstone ruled that 'nothing so generally engages the affection of mankind as that sole and despotic dominion which one claims and exercises over the external things of the world in total exclusion of the right of any other individuals in the universe.'[17]

For this purpose, we may especially refer to the works of Mill and Green—the representative thinkers of English liberalism in the nineteenth century. As an ardent champion of the school of individualism, John Stuart Mill said: "The institution of property, when limited to its essential elements, consists in the recognition, in each person, of a right to the exclusive disposal of what he or she has produced by their own exertions, or received either by gift or by fair agreement, without force or fraud, from those who produced it. The foundation of the whole is the right of producers to what they themselves have produced."[18] Likewise, while giving an idealistic tinge to the issue of property system, Thomas Hill Green observed : "The rationale of property, in short, requires that everyone who will conform to the positive condition of possessing it, *viz.*, labour, and the negative condition, *viz.*, respect for it as possessed by others, should, so far as social arrangements can make him to be a possessor of property himself, and of such property as will at least enable him to develop a sense of responsibility, as distinct from mere property in the immediate necessaries of life."[19]

17. Blackstone: *Commentaries on the Laws of England,* Book I, Chapter 1.
18. Mill: *Principles of Political Economy,* Book II, Ch. 2, Sec. 1.
19. Green: *Lectures on the Principles of Political Obligation,* Sec. 221.

Obviously, the liberal view in regard to property became a potential justification for the system of capitalism in economics and individualism in politics in view of the fact that it "provided a justification of precisely the kind of property that was required by a full capitalist market society. A man's own labour, as well as capital and land, was made so much a private exclusive property as to be alienable, i.e., marketable. The concept of property as nothing but an exclusive, alienable, individual right not only in material things but even in one's own productive capacities was thus a creation of capitalist society. It was only needed, and only brought forth, when the formal equality of the market superseded the formal inequality of pre-capitalist society."[20]

It is owing to this that liberalism in the period before the First World War became a refined nomenclature for the system of capitalism. It desired what was congenial to the interest of the capitalist class. It may be visualised in the affirmation of a great English writer who said: "Individualism, as ordinarily understood, not only takes the policeman and the law court for granted. It also takes the right of property for granted. But what is meant by the right of property? In ordinary use, the phrase means just that system to which long usage has accustomed us. This is a system under which a man is free to acquire by any method of production or exchange within the limits of the law whatever he can of land, consumable goods, or capital; to dispose of it at his own will and pleasure for his own purposes, to destroy it if he likes, to give it away or sell it as it suits him, and at death to bequeath it to whosoever he will. The state, it is admitted, can take a part of man's property by taxation. For the state it is a necessity, and men must pay a price for security, but in all taxation the state in this way, is taking something from a man which is 'his', and in so doing is justified only by necessity. It has no right to deprive the individual of anything that is his in order to promote objects of its own which are not necessary to the common order. To do so is to infringe individual rights and force a man to contribute to objects which he may view with indifference or even with dislike. 'Socialistic' taxation is an infringement of individual freedom, the freedom to hold one's own and do as one will with one's own. Such seems to be the ordinary view."[21]

Among the contemporary liberal thinkers, Robert Nozick goes much ahead of Locke in defending the private property system. The point to be noted here is that he not only regards right to property as a natural right, he sacrifices the state at its altar. Even the ultra-minimal state endowed with the mandate of a night watchman is replaced by a state-like entity what he calls the 'dominant protective agency'. He argues that the modern democratic state is a natural extension of the minimal state without any blatant violation of anybody's rights. The state is like a corporation. Though each shareholder has control over the functioning of the corporation (which includes his own rights as a shareholder), he has neither time nor inclination to exercise such control. Each shareholder delegates his powers to the 'proxies' who act like his representatives. The best system is one which establishes ownership of the people, by the people, and for the people in respect of their possessions or 'holdings'.

---

20. Macpherson, *op. cit.*, p. 130.
21. L.T. Hobhouse: *Liberalism* (New York: Oxford Univ. Press, 1964), pp. 51-52.

He says it 'demoktesis', a system of each person's having an equal say (within some specified limits) in the lives of all others is the best and fairest imaginable.[22]

Socialistic View: Appreciation of Private Property System Subject to the Norm of Social Good

A major change took place after the First World War when the champions of the liberal school started thinking in terms of changing the notion of private property so as to make it in accord with the requirements of the new age. Modern democracy by the same process that led to the increasing modification of individual rights by social duties towards neighbours and community, everywhere led to tamper the freedom of property with the store of responsibilities attached to it. It engaged the attention of some conscientious thinkers who sought to justify the state's right of taxation, its police power and the power of expropriation subject to fair compensation. It also covered a host of interferences by the state touching the freedom of the use of property through the growing number of social obligations attached by law to the use of industrial property or contracts of employment.

Such an important change witnessed its first brilliant manifestation in the thought of John Stuart Mill who in the revised edition of his principal work on classical economics advanced the theory of special taxation on 'unearned increments' and 'socially created values'. If there was an income which constantly tended to increase without any exertion or sacrifice on the part of the owners, it would be no violation of liberty of the individual in case the state appropriated or specially taxed the enhanced portion of his income. Mill held that it would not be like taking anything from anybody, rather be like applying an accession of wealth created by the circumstances to the benefits to society instead of allowing it to become an unearned appendage to the riches of a particular individual or class.[23] Likewise, in another work written towards the end of his life in 1872, he said: "The social problem of the future was considered to be how to unite the greatest individual liberty of action with a common ownership in the raw materials of the globe, and an equal participation of all in the benefits of combined labour."[24]

In this way, Mill precursed the thought of the English Fabians. The leading lights of the Fabian society (established in 1884) took inspiration from the collectivistic affirmations of Mill and thus thought in terms of reformulating the doctrine of English liberalism in the direction of democratic socialism. Thus emerged a 'flexible school of socialist thought' that, adapting itself to the changed conditions, "regarded the transition from capitalism to socialism as a gradual process, looked forward to the socialisation of industry by the peaceful economic and political agencies already at hand, saw in the middle class a group that could be utilised in developing the technique of administration on behalf of the new social order, and felt that an important step in the attainment of socialism was the arousing of the social conscience of the community in favour of the socialist ideal."[25]

22. Nozick: *Anarchy, State and Utopia* (Oxford: Basil Blackwell, 1974), p. 290.
23. Mill: *Principles of Political Economy*, VII Ed. 1864, pp. 573-603.
24. Mill: *Autobiography*, p. 232.
25. H.W. Laidler: *Social and Economic Movements* (London: Routledge and Kegan Paul, 1960), p. 184.

A new view in regard to the system of property thus came into limelight with the publication of the *Fabian Essays* in 1889. Leading thinkers of this school like Sidney Webb, G.B. Shaw and William Clarke argued:[26]

1. That with private property as the necessary instrument of production, individual liberty as understood by the eighteenth century reformers must be more and more restricted, *i.e.*, in our existing economic conditions, individualism is impossible and absurd.
2. That even hostile or indifferent politicians have been compelled to recognise this.
3. That unrestrained capitalism tends as surely to cruelty and oppression as did feudalism or chattel slavery.
4. That the remedy has been, as a matter of fact, of a socialistic character, involving collective checking of individual greed and pairing of slices of the profits of capital in the interests of the working community.

In a very confident tone, the authors of the *Fabian Essays* contended that these four propositions could scarcely be contested. Such a view, thus, imbibed both a critique of the capitalist system and an emphasis on linking the institution of property to the overall interest of the community. It found its brilliant manifestation in the works of Prof. Harold J. Laski who integrated the system of property with the functions that a man performs and thus by and large disapproved of the system of full inheritance. He also laid down the principle of 'civic minimum' so that each individual could have some amount of property so as to enrich his personality. Above all, he warned that greater disparities of wealth were incompatible with the system of democracy and in case the wide gulf was not bridged up, revolution would supervene to alter the balance.[27]

In may be conceded that while the socialistic view is different from the liberal view in regard to the system of property, as seen in the preceding section, it would not be incorrect to say that it, to a very great extent, is like an extension of or an improvement upon its former self. It is owing to this reason that the socialistic line is regarded as the revised form of liberalism in the light of new aspirations and requirements of the age. It may be visualised in the development of liberalism in the twentieth century when leading liberal lights of this school like L.T. Hobhouse and J.A. Hobson argued in favour of the intervention of the state in the field of socially created values and urged that the individual was not the only unit of economic production; that the community itself was a producer of values and that the State, which is the organ of the community, could claim a special right to impose special taxation on such values. The old individualistic view of the state thus "seems to be definitely shed by modern Liberalism."[28]

Marxian View: Stern Indictment of Private Property System

Basically different from the liberal and socialistic views, as given above, is the Marxian view. It attacks the institution of private property as the source of exploitation and

26. *Ibid.*, p. 200.
27. See Laski: *A Grammar of Politics*, p. 177.
28. E. Barker: *Political Thought in England, 1848 to 1914* (London: Geoffrey Cumberledge, Oxford Univ. Press 1951), p. 189.

oppression. The roots of social and economic inequality are contained in the system of private property. The institution of property is necessarily connected with the system of production. According to Marx, all social change is determined chiefly by the economic class struggles that have pervaded history since the break-up of the tribal community organisation. The history of humanity, for this reason, is largely the history of class conflict. Every system of production gives rise to two principal, naturally hostile classes—the exploiters and the exploited, the owners and the toilers—the character of the contending classes being determined by the particular character of the prevailing modes of production and exchange of commodities.[29]

If private property is a source of exploitation and oppression, it would go after the successful results of the revolution. Instead of private property system, there would be collective property system under which all property would belong to the society and be protected by the state. In the era of the 'dictatorship of the proletariat', all property shall belong to the society and the rule of 'he who shall work, shall eat' shall prevail. It, however, does not imply that there shall be no room for private property system at all after the establishment of 'socialist' system in the country. What it really means is that property as the source of exploitation and oppression shall go. Moreover, private property system shall be allowed to prevail in a basically new form: it shall be linked up with man's right to work. That is, if a man earns something by his work, it shall become his personal property.[30] It is for this reason that the Stalin Constitution of 1936 had incorporated right to property in the category of 'fundamental rights' of the citizens of the Soviet Union.

Personal property exists in a form in which the citizens of a socialist society appropriate consumer goods and other benefits used to satisfy their individual needs. Here may be included essential objects as required to satisfy everyday needs of the people like household utensils, some transport facility, housing accommodation, individual savings, some kinds of tools or cattle, small piece of land, etc. It cannot be called private property, because it does not entitle the owner to use his property in a way so as to exploit others; its scale is very much limited and it is meant to satisfy a person's needs; it is, above all, not the main source from which its owner obtains material benefits. As real income of the people grows, the size of the personal property also develops. And yet it cannot embrace the entire range of material and intellectual benefits that satisfy individual needs; part of them are met out of social consumption funds. Personal property is safeguarded by socialist society and its protection is guaranteed by the law of the state.

The Marxist writers admit that the issue of private property has always evoked an acute ideological struggle. In the last century the apologists of the bourgeois system accused Marx and his followers of abolishing all private property as such. Thus, Marx countered such allegations by holding: "We by no means intend to

29. See Coker: *Recent Political Thought* (New York: Appleton-Century, 1934), p. 48.
30. It may be said here that Marx's linking up of private property with man's right to work has a special connotation which is at fundamental variance with the approach of liberal thinkers like Montesquieu who said that a man 'is poor not because he possesses nothing but because he is out of work", or of Justice Douglas of the United States who said: "Man has as much right to work as he has to live, to be free, to own property. . . . To work means to eat. It also means to live." See Matthew, *op. cit.*, p. 18.

abolish this personal appropriation of the products of labour, an appropriation that is made for the maintenance and reproduction of human life, and that leaves no surplus wherewith to command the labour of others. All that we want to do away with is the miserable character of this appropriation."[31] Any assertion to the effect that people's welfare has improved and that private property under socialism leads to the restoration of capitalism have nothing to do with Marxism, but reflect petty-bourgeois strivings for egalitarianism. Personal property cannot be converted into private property under socialism or bring back capitalism, because the main means of production cannot become its object. Works, factories, land, mineral wealth, etc. are not to be bought and sold. "Besides, a socialist society makes it sure that personal property does not turn into a source of unearned income. Persons guilty of using it to derive profit are regarded as law-breakers."[32]

Two important points should, however, be borne in mind in this connection. First, under the communist system, right to property, as in the case of every other right, is integrally bound up with a corresponding duty. It may also be said that the weight of 'duty' is such that it pervades the enjoyment of a 'right'. As such, a fundamental right to property is accompanied, rather subordinated, by the corresponding fundamental duty whereby every citizen is obliged to safeguard and fortify the socialist property. Second, the rule of 'he who shall work, shall eat' shall be replaced by the rule 'from each according to his ability, to each according to his need' in the final stage of socialism called 'communism'. There shall be restoration of primitive communism in the final stage of socialism when nothing like private and everything like public property system shall prevail.

In short, the Marxian view of property is based on his labour theory of value whereby he seeks to prove that since labour is the only means of production, the value of a commodity should be determined by the amount of labour spent over its production. Allied to this is the theory of surplus value whereby Marx desires that labour being the sole factor of production, all dividends should go to it. Marx contends that in each factory of enterprise, the wages paid to the workers "are not equivalent of the full value they produce but only equal to about half of this value, even less. The rest of the value produced by the worker during his working day is taken outright by his employer."[33] The accumulation of surplus profits thus unleashes the situation of increasing misery and degradation of the working class with the result that the poor, hungry and exploited millions of the working class are forced to change the existing order by means of a revolution. "The interregnum is burst asunder. The knell of capitalist private property sounds. The expropriators are expropriated."[34]

Gandhian View: Trusteeship System Sustained by Moral Regeneration

Gandhism is neither capitalism nor socialism. It is not even a mixture of the two. Both systems, as developed in the West, have their inherent limitations. As such, a third

31. Marx-Engels: *Collected Works,* Vol. 6, p. 499.
32. *A Dictionary of Scientific Communism* (Moscow: Progress Publishers, 1980), p. 178.
33. Emile Burns: *What is Marxism?*, p. 21.
34. Carew Hunt: *The Theory and Practice of Communism,* p. 89.

method should prevail. It is the system of trusteeship which desires that property should be under the control of a private person, but he should regard himself as its protector not its master. It is based on the ideal of non-possession (*aparigraha*) as given in the *Isopanishada*. It also conforms to the idea of the *Bhagwata* which holds that we have a claim only to so much as would satisfy our hunger, otherwise desiring more than that is like theft deserving punishment. While acknowledging his debt to the *Bhagwad Gita*, Gandhiji once said: "I understand the Gita teaching of non-possession to mean that he who desires salvation should act like a trustee who, though having control over great possessions, regards not an iota of them as his own."[35]

This theory of trusteeship has some important implications. First, it applies with to accumulated wealth and earnings beyond one's needs. It desires that any superfluous wealth should be held in trust. It also implies an ideal of economic equality in the ideal state. Second, it implies the case of equality of rights, not of rewards. More talented people have a right to keep greater amount of wealth. Gandhiji does not like to cramp the intellectual attainments of the people and allows them to make full use of their talent in the interest of the community. Third, it discards the case of nationalisation or abolition of private property. Instead, it desires a change of heart or mentality. The property-owners should not consider themselves as the absolute lords of what they possess; instead they should regard themselves as the custodians of social wealth or trustees utilising their property for the good of the whole community. Fourth, Gandhiji is not in favour of the modern capitalist system, because he rejects the law of inheritance. The choice of a trustee or his successor should be subject to the final approval of the community. The misue of trust property may be set right by the action of the state. The state may make a law for the regulation of private property system, or it may confiscate it with minimum use of violence.

The salient implications of Gandhian concept of trusteeship may be put as under;

1. Trusteeship provides a means for transferring the present capitalist order of society into an egalitarian one.
2. It does not recognise any right of private ownership of property except inasmuch as it may be permitted by the society.
3. It does not exclude legislative regulation of the ownership and use of wealth.
4. Thus, under state regulated trusteeship, an individual would not be free to hold or use his wealth for his own satisfaction or in disregard of the interest of society.
5. Just as it is proposed to fix a decent minimum living wage, even so a limit should be fixed for the maximum income that could be allowed to any person in society. The difference between such minimum and maximum incomes should be reasonable and equitable and variable from time to time so much so that the tendency would be towards obliteration of the difference.

35. Gandhi: *The Story of My Experiments with Truth*, pp. 221-22. Gandhiji is much influenced with the teaching of Christ who said: "Persons, then being God's one real concern and their welfare being the end for which everything can become human property exists and is held in trust from God, all life becomes a proving of loyalty and love to him through loyal love to one's brother man."

6. Under the Gandhian economic order, the character of production would be determined by social necessity and not by personal whim or greed.

A critic may say that Gandhi's theory of trusteeship is quite utopian. Man's love for wealth is so ingrained that, in Machiavelli's words, he may forget as to who had killed his father but not as to who usurped his property. It may be taken as an idealistic defence of the private property system. A democratic socialist would scoff at such an idea and he would, like Laski, frankly advocate the way of state control over public property, while a communist would discard it as a tenet of utopian socialism. Even Jawaharlal Nehru could raise this question: "Is it reasonable to believe in the theory of trusteeship to give unchecked power and wealth to an individual and to expect him to use it entirely for the public good? Are the best of us so perfect as to use it entirely for the public good? Are the best of us so perfect as to be entrusted in this way? Even Plato's philosopher-kings would hardly have borne this burden worthily. And is it good for others to have even these benevolent supermen over them?"[36]

Property as Power: Case of Economic Inequality and the 'Odious Phenomenon of Two Nations'

What has, however, dragged the economic institution of property into the realm of political theory is its character as power that enables a man to have a share in the decision-making process or, what Easton calls, the 'authoritative allocation of values'. In this direction, a new orientation has taken place that informs us to treat property as a right to a kind of society or a set of power-relations which will enable the individual to live a fully human life.[37] It is said that with the developments in the spheres of science and technology, the importance to each individual of the access to the means of labour "will clearly diminish if and in so far as the amount of current human labour required to produce an acceptable flow of the means of life for all diminishes. The property that would then be most important to the individual would no longer be the right of access to the means of labour; it would be instead, the right to a share in the control of the massed productive resources. That right would presumably have to be exercised politically. Political power then becomes the most important kind of property. Property, as an individual right, becomes essentially the individual's share in political power."[38]

The discovery of the idea of treating property as the source of political power should be attributed to Karl Marx who said: "Within the capitalist system. . . all means for the development of production transform themselves into the means of domination over, and exploitation of, the producers; they mutilate the labourer into a fragment of a man, degrade him to the level of an appendage of a machine, destroy every remnant of charm in his work and turn it into a hated toil; they estrange from him the intellectual potentialities of labour process in the same proportion as science is incorporated in it as an independent power; they distort the conditions under which he works, subject him during the labour process to a despotism the more hateful

36. Nehru: *An Autobiography,* p. 528.
37. Macpherson, *op. cit.,* p. 136.
38. *Ibid.,* pp. 136 37.

for its meanness. They transform his life-time into working time, and drag his wife and children beneath the wheels of the Juggernaut of capital. But all methods for the production of surplus value are at the same time methods of accumulation; and every extension of accumulation becomes again the means for the development of those methods. It follows, therefore, that in proportion as capital accumulates, the lot of the labourer, be his payment high or low, must grow worse."[39]

The character of property as sovereign power compelling services and obedience may be obscured in a commercial economy by the fiction of the so-called labour contract as a free bargain and by the frequency with which service is rendered indirectly through a money payment. The case is, however, different in the realm of Anglo-Saxon jurisprudence wher, in law, control of property means control of matter and it becomes control over human beings as well. As a result, dominion over things is also *imperium* over human beings.[40]

That property in modern conditions has become a means of control over the life and labour of other people, strictly speaking of the propertied class over the propertyless, is thus understood by Marx: "The capitalist is not a capitalist because he directs (the work), but he becomes an industrial commander because he is a capitalist. Industrial command becomes an attribute of capital as under feudalism, the power of command was in war as in law, an attribute of the ownership of land.[41]

Though one may find several faults with the contention of Marx, it is hardly disputable that the system of private property as justified, even glorified, by the liberal thinkers seeks to make room for undesirable economic inequalities allied to which is the feeling of economic injustice. It is grounded in the belief that gross inequalities in the realm of economic possession make for social differences that divide the community into classes with little mutual sympathy and almost no sense of solidarity as a result of which the society becomes like an 'odious phenomenon of two nations' or, in the words of Plato 'a city of the swine divided against itself.' What is still worse is that property titles, unlike those of desert or need, are transmissible by inheritance so that families become congealed, as it were, in their class habits and attitudes. And even if a case might be made out of the founder of a large fortune, his heirs succeed to his advantages through no merits of their own. Inheritance apart, since the owner of a fortune is able to give his children advantages in education, and to use his influence to start them off well in life, the initial inequality is perpetuated by inequality of opportunity, while positions of leadership and influence become the prerogative of a limited number of families forming a wealthy elite."[42]

Property and capitalism, in this way, become interchangeable terms. An idealisation of property becomes a solid justification for the system of capitalism; likewise, an attack on the institution of private property becomes a potential criticism of the same system. Prof. Harold J. Laski, for this reason, treated the subject of property in the context of the capitalist system and thus desired the end of the obtaining system of economic injustice in these words; "Men may begin to acquire

39. Marx: *Capital,* Vol. I, pp. 660-61.
40. Matthew, *op. cit.,* p. 3.
41. Marx: *Capital,* Vol. I, p. 297.
42. Benn and Peters, *op. cit.,* p. 167.

Property and Social Obligations

He that gathered a hundred bushels of acorns or apples had thereby a property in them, they were his goods as soon as he gathered. He was only to look that he used them before they spoiled, else he took more than his share and robbed others. And indeed it was a foolish thing and dishonest to hoard up more than he could make use of. If he gave away a part to anyone else, so that it perished not uselessly in his possession, these he also made use of.

—John Locke

Second Treatise of Civil Government, Ch. 5.

Supposing I have come by a fair amount of wealth either by way of legacy, or by means of trade and industry, I must know that all that wealth does not belong to me. What belongs to me is the right to an honourable livelihood, no better than that enjoyed by millions of others. The rest of my wealth belongs to the community and must be used for the welfare of the community.

—M.K. Gandhi,

Harijan, 3 June, 1939, p. 145.

Property is an established and enforceable claim to an object or possession, it is a 'right' not a 'thing'. The ownership of property is, therefore, reflected in the existence of rights and powers over an object and also the acceptance of duties and liabilities in relation to it. From this point of view, property may confer the ability to use and dispose of an object, but it may also involve the responsibility to conserve or repair it.

—Andrew Heywood,

Political Theory: An Introduction, p. 317.

property to safeguard their lives from want, but they continue to acquire it because of the distinction which comes from its possession. It satisfies their vanity and their lust for power: it enables them to attune the will of society to their own . . . . It remains historically obvious that a community divided into rich and poor is, when the latter are numerous, built upon foundations of sand. . . . Yet the State remains divided into rich and poor; and men, after a period, refuse to suffer quietly. Then revolution supervenes to alter the balance in the State."[43]

Critical Appreciation

The subject of property, private property in the strict sense of the term, has been a matter of justification as well as indictment from ancient to modern times. The protagonists of the institution of property have used very colourful phrases to commend that it gives a man a sense of security and opens avenues for the enrichment of his personality. It is said that the fate of a propertyless man is no better than that of a slave. A man of property is said to be one who has a stake in the life of his state and, as such, he is not likely to be swept off by every new-fangled doctrine leading to a violent insurrection. In ancient times Aristotle admired the system of property in the name of its power by which a man could be liberal and hospitable. Individualists like Mill and Ricardo held the view that property was the best incentive whereby a man could produce more wealth. John Locke appreciated property as being a result of man's labour and upheld it as a matter of natural right. It is the

43. Laski: *A Grammar of Politics,* pp. 175-77.

institution of property that helps man to make great achievements in the fields of production, arts, science, etc. Viewing the issue from an idealistic point of view, Hegel and Green held it necessary for the free play of a capacity which can be exerted for the common benefit: it is "means of realising a will, which in possibility is a will directed to the social good."[44]

The institution of property is also justified in several other ways. It is said that, in modern times, it has certainly meant colossal production, increased prosperity and comfort, maximum utilisation of natural resources and marvellous growth of material civilisation. If so, the pervailing situation of economic inequality is a natural affair that should not be interfered with by the state in the name of bringing about social justice. Thus, Burke in one of his fiery orations said: "The power of perpetuating our property in our families is one of the most valuable and interesting circumstances belonging to it, and that which tends most to the perpetuation of society itself. It makes our weakness subservient to our virtue, it grafts benevolence even upon avarice. The possessors of family wealth, and of the distinction which attends hereditary possession, are the natural securities for this transmission."[45] Burke not merely advances a powerful defence of the system of private property, he also issues a word of warning that in case whoever deprives men of their consolation (in regard to possession of property) deadens their industry and strikes at the root of all conservation."[46]

On the contrary, the institution of property has been denounced in no less strong terms. In ancient Greece, the Stoics laid emphasis on the pattern of austere living and denounced property for being a source of evil existence. Among the champions of the idealist tradition, Plato understood the evil effects of the charm of property and in his *Republic* he laid down the doctrine of communism in property whereby be sought to save his Guardians and Auxiliary Guardians from the possession of any property as it was a potential source of material temptations. Among the followers of the idealist tradition, however, it is Rousseau who made a scathing attack on the institution of property in his *Second Discourse* in the name of its being the originator of social and economic inequality that deprived man of the life of 'idyllic happiness and primitive simplicity'.

The subject of private property was vehemently attacked by the anarchists in the nineteenth century. Proudhon called property as 'theft of labour'. Though Marx disagreed with Proudhon on many points, he did agree with him in denouncing the institution of private property in the name of its being a source of exploitation and oppression. The socialists have their own reservations. To them, despite marking colossal achievements in the material field, property has entailed moral and spiritual degradation. "Values have been vulgarised to a large extent, and there is widespread tendency to worship power and wealth. Modern society is so organised as to whet the desire for personal gain. It teaches a man to compete with his fellow-men and scramble for power and wealth rather than to co-operate with him in achieving common ends. It makes effective citizenship for the masses practically impossible of

---

44. Barker, *op. cit.*, p. 42.
45. Burke: *Reflections on the Revolution in France*, p. 49.
46. *Ibid.*, p. 241.

attainment. Even in the material world, the opportunities for development are not so great as they have been in the recent past. We have almost reached the saturation point."[47]

An attack on the institution of property is also made from the standpoint of the role of money in the politics of a country, Thus, we come to deal with the politics of tainted gold. It is said that power is shared and exercised only by the men of 'black money' with the result that democracy degenerates itself into plutocracy. Keeping in view the all-sided evil effects of property on the politics of the country, Laski strongly asserts that wealthy men "produce goods and services, not for use, but to acquire property from their production. They produce not to satisfy usual demands, but demands which can be made to pay. They will ruin natural resources. They will adulterate commodities. They will float dishonest enterprises. They will corrupt legislatures. They will pervert the sources of knowledge. They will artificially combine to increase the cost of their commodities to the public. They will exploit, sometimes with hideous cruelty, the backward races of mankind. They infect with their poison those who work for the wages they offer. They induce sabotage in its varied forms. They compel strikes which result in serious damage to the community. And it is the grim irony of the system that the vaster part of those engaged in its promotion have little or no hope of enduring gain from the process they support. They may destroy the quality of political life. They may possess themselves, as in America, of the educational instruments of the community. They may even pervert religious institutions to the protection of their ideas. They do not, nevertheless, secure a well-ordered State."[48]

In spite of the fact that the private property system has its own essential points of strength and weakness, two important points should not be ignored while presenting a balanced view in regard to the worth of the obtaining system. First, as already discussed, property means a 'bundle of rights' and that even private property system has its varied forms. It is, therefore, necessary that while attacking the system of property, we should keep the scope of observation confined to a particular variety instead of making an attack on the system as a whole. Neither an idealisation of property in the name of its being a 'foundation of civilisation' nor its indictment in the name of being 'theft of labour' is justified. As a matter of fact, both are meaningless according to Tawney who says: "Arguments which support or demolish certain kinds of property may have no application to others; considerations which are conclusive in one stage of economic organisation may be almost irrelevant in the next. The course of wisdom is neither to attack private property in general nor to defend it in general...for things are not similar in quality, merely because they are identical in name. It is to discriminate between the various concrete embodiments of what, in itself, is after all, little more than an abstraction."[49]

Second, the institution of property, even in the form of private property, is not without some advantage. A critic of Marx like B. de Jouvenel could, therefore, say that it was the private property of Engels that enabled Marx to work on his *Das*

47. Asirvatham, *op. cit.*, p. 222.
48. Laski, *op. cit.*, pp. 175-76.
49. R.H. Tawney: *The Acquisitive Society* (1921), Ch. 5.

Kapital.[50] Though one may not agree with the observation of Lord Acton that 'a people averse to the institution of private property is without the first element of freedom', one may not quarrel with this practical truth that different categories of the property system "would then take their place in their own right alongside skill, function, need, etc., as criteria to be applied in determining what a person's income ought to be."[51]

As such, the case of economic inequality *vis-a-vis* the issue of economic injustice resulting in the creation of an ominous 'phenomenon of two nations' should be studied in the light of varying capacities of the individuals to preserve and multiply their property and also in the context of this equitable principle that the accumulation and possession of wealth, on the one hand, and the realisation and discharge of public responsibilities, on the other, should go hand in hand. That is, the idea of property should be integrated with the idea of public functions and responsibilities of the man. "If a Ford or a Rockefeller is able to use his wealth in the production of greater wealth in the service of mankind, we would let him have it. If, on the other hand, he uses it for utterly selfish ends or abuses it in other ways, we would by means of law or public opinion or by both make it impossible for him to hold it."[52]

If so, a socialist argument that inherited property enables some men to enjoy income without contributing anything to the common fund would be quite beside the point for it demands that one criterion shall be justified in terms of another, instead of by its own beneficial results. A wholesale nationalisation of private property would entail social and economic disaster and as happened in Russia during the phase of War Communism under Lenin and the blunder could be rectified by the inauguration of the New Economic Policy in 1921. The Gandhian doctrine of trusteeship (that the owner of a property should consider himself merely as a custodian of the property ordained by the will of God), is too high an ideal to be realised by the community of imperfect human beings. Likewise, any revolutionary settlement in the distribution of property in the name of unleashing an era of economic justice (as accompanied by the German inflation of the early 1920's) "is more likely than anything else to disrupt a nation's solidarity, set class against class, and endanger all its settled institutions and traditional standards."[53]

50. See Benn and Peters, *op. cit.*, p. 168.
51. Lord Acton: *The History of Freedom* (London, 1907), p. 297.
52. Asirvatham, *op. cit.*, p. 224.
53. Benn and Peters, *op. cit.*, p. 172.

11

Justice

> There is no better test of excellence of a government than the efficiency of its judicial system, for nothing more nearly touches the welfare and security of the average citizen than his sense that he can rely on the certain and prompt administration of justice. Law is respected and supported when it is treated as the shield of innocence and the impartial guardian of every private civil right...if the law be dishonestly administered, the salt has lost its flavour, if it be weakly or fitfully coerced, the guarantees of order fail...if the lamp of justice goes out in darkness, how great is the darkness.
>
> **—James Bryce[1]**

A study of the idea of justice not followed by a chapter on law but after the discussion of the concepts of rights, liberty, equality and property is informed by a certain pertinent reason. If political theory is studied in purely normative terms, one comes to this important conclusion that what really connects the themes of law, rights, liberty and equality (including fraternity or cooperation), is the element of justice. In every organised community the ideals of law, rights, liberty and equality have their values and there must be something to bring them together so that we may understand the concept of a well-ordered community. As we shall see, justice "is the reconciler and synthesiser of political values; it is their union in an adjusted and integrated whole; it is in Aristotle's words, 'what answers to the whole of goodness. . . being the exercise, of goodness as a whole. . . towards one's neighbour".[2] Curiously, the subject of justice has a significance of its own in the realm of political theory in view of the fact that among the proper ends of state and government, it has been given a high rank at all times. "Two axioms have been generally accepted without question: first, that government's own actions ought to be just; second, that governmental institutions, such as law courts, ought to ensure the preservation of justice."[3]

Justice: Real Meaning and Nature

As we have seen in the case of other concepts of political theory, particularly those having a normative character, so here we are confronted with the problem of offering a precise definition of the term 'justice' on account of three major difficulties. First, the term 'justice' is assigned different meanings by different people at different times and different places. Not only this, its implications vary from man to man on account

---

1. James Bryce: *Modern Democracies* (London: Macmillan, 1921), Vol II, p. 421.
2. Ernest Barker: *Principles of Social and Political Theory* (London: Oxford Univ. Press, 1967), p. 102.
3. Arnold Brecht: *Political Theory: Foundations of Twentieth Century Political Thought* (Princeton: Princeton Univ. Press, 1965), p. 136.

of their varying interpretations. Second, the idea of justice is a dynamic affair. As such, its implications change with the passage of time. Thus, what was justice in the past may be injustice in the present and *vice versa;* it is also possible that the justice of today becomes the injustice of tomorrow and *vice versa.* A further difficulty arises in reconciling the abstract notions of justice with its practical manifestations. For instance, one may talk of the divine justice or moral justice, but it will not be conformable to any set of empirical standards and, for this reason, not capable of practical application. Due to this, we may appreciate the view of Potter that "most men think that they understand the meaning of justice, but, in fact, their notions prove to be vague."[4]

The concept of justice has some important implications. First, it requires a just state of affairs. That is, it is impossible to assess the justice of actions without a prior identification of just state of affairs.[5] Second, it is aligned with the conditions of morality. For instance, a fair race is one in which a person who wins morally deserves to win but one in which there is no cheating, nobody jumps the gun or has an unfair advantage through the use of bad things like drugs.[6] Third, it carries the sense of proper distribution of favours and losses. It means that it is primarily concerned with the way rewards and punishments are distributed to individuals in a rule-governed practice and its intimate connection with fairness indicates that if a ruler were to boil his subjects in oil, jumping in afterwards himself, it would amount to an act of injustice though there would be no inequality of treatment[7]. Fourth, it normally prevails in a congenial atmosphere that is provided by a democratic set up, but it may also survive in a non-democratic set up as an exception. "Fair rules may be impartially enforced in regimes which allow little political participation and majority rule democracies may generate arbitrary treatment of individuals and minorities."[8]

While dealing with the problem of offering a precise definition of the term 'justice', we should, however, keep this paramount fact in our mind that "not only do different individuals hold various ideas about the ideal state of affairs they would consider really just ; every individual is capable of several such ideas. Our ideas and feelings of justice may be twofold or threefold, or even morefold, in accordance with different systems of values to which we respond positively at different times, or even simultaneously. Justice, in the light of personal ideas is, or at least may be, a barrel with several bottoms."[9] In order to solve this predicament, Brecht divides justice into two broad categories :[10]

1. **Traditional Justice:** It accepts the fundamental institutions which constitute the basis of our daily life, takes them for granted, does not question them. Insofar as these institutions have been established by the positive law, written constitution,

4. Harold Potter: *The Quest of Justice* (London: Sweet and Maxwell. 1951), p. 3.
5. David Miller: *Social Justice* (Oxford: Clarendon Press, 1976), pp. 17-18.
6. Brian Barry: *Political Argument* (London: Routledge and Kegan Paul, 1965), p. 103.
7. W.K. Frankena: "The Concept of Social Justice" in R. Brandt (ed.): *Social Justice* (Englewood Cliffs, New Jersey: Prentice-Hall, 1962), p. 17.
8. N.P. Barry: *An Introduction to Modern Political Theory* (London: Macmillan, 1981), p. 116.
9. Brecht, *op. cit.,* pp. 147-48.
10. *Ibid.,* p. 148.

legislation, judicial precedents, and the like, the traditional idea of justice is positivistic.

2. **Trans-traditional Justice:** It detaches itself from the existing institutions, either in whole or in part, and criticises them according to principles which are taken from a trans-traditional scheme of evaluation. This, again, may be done in dependence on group ideas that are accepted and carried on by the individual in some condition of submission, as, for example, ideas of a party or revolutionary junta, or merely in deference to the opinions of a strong personality, a friend, the husband, or wife, or the priest.

Though there are these two 'distinct levels in our ideas of justice', the problem of having a precise definition of the term remains inasmuch as an individual "may penetrate to a third level, in more courageous hours, where he discovers what he 'really' thinks and where he may be critical also of the trans-traditional ideas of his friends. Within a single day he may move through all three levels, in his business hours living and feeling with the traditional sense of justice, in the evening joining with his friends in their criticism, and at night isolating himself from his friends. It may even be possible for the individual to shift at will from one level to the other."[11]

However, for the sake of "an intelligible study of the concept of justice, we may keep our attention confined to the case of 'two distinct levels' what Brecht calls 'traditional' and 'trans-traditional' which are simply other names for the objective and subjective aspects of the same. What he means by the former is nothing else than the 'external' or 'positive' meaning of justice in view of the fact that such an idea of objective justice, in the strict sense of the term, is relative to the existing institutions."[12] Contradistinguished from this, the latter may be identified with a subjective aspect of the same inasmach as it is concerned with the variety of conditions of state of affairs which people "regard as standard goals in their ideas of justice either for the distant future or for the present moment."[13] A few ideal types or characteristic patterns of this variety of justice may be enumerated as under:[14]

1. **The Equalitarian:** He places equality at the highest place in matters of justice and derives from this ultimate ideal his standards about it. Though a certain segment of equality is contained in every idea of justice, the equalitarian wants more. He wants the whole thing.
2. **The Libertarian:** He tends to measure everything by the yardstick of liberty. He will ardently oppose as unjust steps intruding on liberty which the equalitarian would welcome as just, and *vice versa*.
3. **The Revelationist:** His highest aim is the execution of God's will. Whether the divine will is individualistic, or national, or universal, in its purpose, it is in principle quite irrelevant to him. Hence, we may also call him trans-personalist.
4. **The Conservative:** He respects, even worships, the temple of traditional institutions and wants them to remain unchanged. Justice, as it has been, ought to continue to prevail.

11. *Ibid.*
12. *Ibid.*, p. 150.
13. *Ibid.*, p. 151.
14. *Ibid.*, pp. 151-55.

5. **The Authoritarian:** He regards leadership as the principle of highest value. To follow leadership is just, to counteract it is unjust.
6. **The Majority Worshipper:** He holds that whatever the majority decides is the highest value to be accepted by everyone. To follow the majority will is just, to oppose its execution is unjust.
7. **The Hedonist:** He looks for individual happiness for the greatest good of the greatest number.
8. **The Group Worshipper:** He wants the subordination of the desires of an individual to the interest of the group.
9. **The Harmoniser:** He thinks of harmony as an ultimate value. Justice lives in a state of non-disturbance as much as possible.
10. **The Pyramid-Builder:** He would like to associate the implications of justice with the spiritual part of his country's culture or civilisation, or with the evolution of the folklore spirit, or some specific achievements of his race.
11. **The Man of Duty:** He looks at life as a chain of duties rather than of rights or a struggle for survival and happiness. He derives rights from his duties or functions, not from selfish wants; man should be given at least as much freedom as he needs to fulfil his moral duties.
12. **The Peace-and-Order Fanatic:** He places the consideration of peace and order at the top regardless of what they preserve. He may not be a conservative, nor may consider the present state of affairs to be harmonious; he may be in favour of thorough reforms, but he wishes them to be brought about in an orderly way.

This writer further adds that many more items "might be added to this list. However, in every case, the trans-traditional ideas on what is just and unjust vary according to the subjective scheme of values. *One who changes from one conviction to the other will thenceforth have a different idea of justice.*"[15]

In brief, a precise definition of the term justice is beset with the problem of its normative as well as empirical connotations. While in the normative sense, it implies the 'idea of joining or fitting, the idea of a bond or a tie',[16] in an empirical context, it has its relation with the concept of positive law with the result that law and justice become sister-concepts. It is owing to this affirmation that the fundamental purpose of law is said to be the quest for justice which is to be administered without passion as when it (passion) "comes at the door, justice flies out of window."[17] If justice is viewed in this sense, it implies "the fulfilment of the legitimate expectations of individual under the existing laws and ensuring him the benefits promised therein and to afford him protection against any violation of his rights or against any encroachment on his rights."[18]

15. *Ibid.*, p. 155.
16. Barker, *op. cit.*, p. 102.
17. C.K. Allen: *Aspects of Justice* (London: Stevens and Sons, 1955), p. 34.
18. Bakhshish Singh: *The Supreme Court as an Instrument of Social Justice* (New Delhi: Sterling, 1976), p. 33.

Philosophical Theory: Justice as the Principle of Right Order

What we have said in the preceding section leaves this strong impression that the term 'justice' has different connotations in different contexts. It is owing to this that various theories have been propounded to highlight the meaning and significance of justice in diverse spheres. First of all, we take up the philosophical interpretation finding its place in the ancient scriptures as well as in the affirmations of the men of ideas. For instance, justice in India has been identified with the *Dharma* having its English equivalent in the idea of 'righteousness'. As such, it not merely implies what is covered under the word 'religion', it also implies all what comes within the fold of a righteous way of life. Dr. U.C. Sarkar refers to four senses in which the term 'Dharma' may be used: (1) It means religion in the category of theology. (2) It means virtue as opposed to vice in the category of ethics. (3) It means law in the category of jurisprudence. (4) It means duty in the category of actions.[19] According to Hindu jurisprudence, *Dharmanyaya,* meaning equity and justice, is given precedence over *Dharma* meaning law, whenever there is any conflict between the two. It prevails; generally speaking, there is no seperation between law and religion as both are treated interchangeably.[20]

The best example of a philosophical interpretation of this term in the history of Western political thought is, however, available in Plato's theory of justice as contained in his *Republic.* Here justice has a purely philosophical connotation implying a life of people conforming to the rule of functional specialisation. The original principle underlying it is that one man should practise one thing only and the thing to which his nature is best adapted. Plato stresses the point that each individual should be put to the use for which nature "intended him, one to one work, and then everyman would do his own business, and the one and not many."[21] Justice, thus, becomes another name for the principle of 'proper stations'. It signifies "doing your own work and not meddling with what belongs to others."[22]

From the above, it may be inferred that justice, as conceived by Plato, has both individual and social aspects. While it asks the individual to take only that office to which his nature is best suited, it is also required that the society must assign that office to him that is in conformity with his natural aptitude. The highest good of both the individual and the society is conserved if we take it for granted that there is nothing better for a man than to do a work that he is best fitted to do, there is equally nothing better for the society than to see that each should be filling the station to which he is best entitled by virtue of the special element of his personality. It follows that, as in the state, which is the analogue and the product of man's mind, there are three elements, so in the mind of each man there are parallel to them, and the source of their existence, three elements of reason, spirit and appetite. And as the justice of the state means that each of the three elements retains its place, so the justice of the individual means that reason, spirit and appetite all keep their proper bounds.[23]

19. Sarkar: *Epochs in Hindu Legal History* (Hoshiarpur, 1948), p. 19.
20. See Bakhshish Singh, *op. cit.,* p. 31.
21. *Republic,* IV, 423.
22. R.L. Nettleship: *Lectures on the Republic of Plato,* p. 152.
23. E. Barker: *Greek Political Theory: Plato and His Predecessors,* pp. 205-06.

The philosophical interpretation of justice takes an empirical direction at the hands of Aristotle who says: "Injustice arises when equals are treated unequally, and also when unequals are treated equally."[24] As we shall see in the following sections, the idea of Aristotle came to lay down the foundation of, what is now called, the doctrine of distributive justice. The essential implication of Aristotle's explanation is that justice is either 'distributive' or 'corrective', the former requiring equal distribution among the equals, the latter applying wherein remedy for a wrong is provided. It may also be pointed out that after the death of Aristotle, the philosophical conception of justice was mixed up with the natural idea of justice developed first by the Stoics and then followed by the Roman lawyers. Subsequently, it assumed a religious complexion when Christianity became the official religion of the great Roman empire.

Natural Theory: Justice as an Ultimate End

The natural theory of justice should be understood as an extension of the philosophical theory on this subject in that, first enunciated by the Stoics and then borrowed from them by the Roman lawyers, it treated justice as an ideal of absolute value whereby the right order could be established.[25] What the Stoics meant by nature was that the ruling principle in the universe was 'reason'. Their idea of living 'in agreement with nature' was, therefore, fundamentally a canon of living according to the norm which man ought to realise.[26] We may even say that nature, according to them, "was man's art: it was man's conception, achieved in the course of a conscious effort to fit himself into the Universe, of an ideal by which he could judge the mere given facts of his life in the past, and by which he could shape his life for the future into its rational, God-intended, 'natural' form."[27]

This idea was borrowed by the Roman lawyers who took justice as an ultimate end. The distinctive contribution of the Roman lawyers, however, lies in their integration of the idea of 'natural justice' with the positive law of the State with the result that *jus civile* (civil law) and *just gentium* (law of nations), as they called it, were insisted upon to be in conformity with the law of nature. According to the Digest, "Justice is a fixed and binding disposition to give to every man his right. The precepts of the law are as follows: to live honourably, to injure no one, to give to every man his own. Jurisprudence is a knowledge of things, human and divine, the science of the just and unjust."

24. See P.B. Mukharji: *Three Elemental Problems of the Indian Constitution* (Delhi: National, 1972), p. 4.
25. If the idea of natural justice implies 'an organised principle of universe', it dates back to the Vedic period in India when our sages used the word 'Rta' It signifies a principle that regulated earthly life and was of universal application. According to Dr. Radha Binod Pal, "it is conceived as the organised principle of the Universe and is indeed, the *lex aeterna* (Eternal Law) of the later Roman thought. As the ordering principle of earthly life, it is imbued with human purposes and is for human benefit and exemplified in. . .the institutions of family and in man's sense of responsibility for his sins." See B.N. Bannerji: *Natural and Social Justice* (Calcutta: Eastern Law House, 1960), p. 4.
26. See E.R. Bevan: *Stoics and Sceptics*, p. 61.
27. Barker: *Principles of Social and Political Theory*, p. 107.

Some Important Statements

The term justice is currently used in two senses: as representing, on the one hand, the faithful realisation of an existing law as against any arbitrary infraction of it, and as representing, on the other, the ideal element in all law-the 'ideas which the law tends to subserve. It is only in the second sense that the term can have a separate substantial meaning.

—**Georges Gurvitch**

"Justice" in E.R.A. Seligman (ed.): ***Encyclopaedia of the Social Sciences*** (New York: Macmillan, 1967), Volumes VII and VIII, p. 509.

Justice may be defined substantively some distributive principle prescribing the dispersion of rights and benefits over a society in order to maximise the advantages of all.

—**Bryan S. Turner**

Equality (London: Tavistock Publications, 1986), p. 43.

In everyday language, in fact, justice is used so imprecisely that it is taken to mean 'fairness', 'rightness', or simply that which is morally correct. Without doubt, justice is a moral or normative concept: that which is 'just' is certainly morally 'good', and to call something 'unjust' is to condemn it as morally 'bad'. But justice does not simply mean 'moral'. Rather, it denotes a particular kind of moral judgement, in particular one about the distribution of rewards and punishments.

—**Andrew Heywood**

Political Theory: An Introduction (Houndmills, Basingstroke: Palgrave Macmillan, 2005), p. 173.

The idea of natural justice was mixed up with the myth of divine sanction with the advent of Christianity. What the Stoics and the Romans meant by 'nature' became 'God' to the Church Fathers. The result was that religious canons became handy instruments to distinguish between the just and the unjust. St. Augustine linked up the idea of justice with the precepts of the Christian religion. St. Thomas ruled that in case the civil law was contrary to natural law, it was not binding on the 'conscience of the ruled'. In this way, theological basis "provided absolute ideal of justice at the beginning of society. It was also the starting point of the intuitive and inspirational ideal of justice. Later on, the scholastic philosophy and its non-scholastic development were responsible for the growth of absolute and universal elements in justice."[28] In other words, it signified that nature "is not, in this context, a source of justice which is distinct from religion and from ethics: it is rather a combination and fusion of religion and ethics."[29]

The philosophical or metaphysical concept of justice received a setback in the modern period with the growth of 'new learning'. It, however, could not be outplaced in its entirety. Curiously, Grotius, who is known as the Father of International Law, advocated the supremacy of the Law of Nature. More astonishing than this is the conversion of the idea of natural justice into 'transcendental idealism' as conceived by Immanuel Kant, 'the Father of Modern Idealism'. So much so that in the eighteenth century, the idea of natural law was regarded as a key to unlock all the evils of the

28. Mukharji, *op. cit.*, pp. 6-7.
29. Barker, *op. cit.*, p. 109.

world. A look at the great revolutions of America (1776) and France (1789) shows that the natural rights based on the principles of natural justice were regarded fundamental as endowed by the 'Creator' of the human race.[30]

The idea of natural justice, though quite abstract on account of its philosophical or metaphysical connotations, has been a source of inspiration to the men of liberal jurisprudence. The learned judges have, therefore, paid it due respect. For instance, Justice Hegde of the Indian Supreme Court in the *Karaipak's Case* of 1969 observed: "The aim of the rules of natural justice is to secure justice, or to put it negatively, to prevent miscarriage of justice." The question, however, remains as to what are the implications of this idea? In this respect, we may appreciate the view of Justice Mukharji who highlighted its ninefold elements: fair hearing of a case while adhering to the maxims of neutrality and impartiality of a judge, extension of opportunity, giving of notice, insurance against surprise, facilities for adequate legal representation, tested evidence as right of cross-examination, provision to produce evidence, delivery of reasoned decisions, and balancing verifiable human factors by providing for appeals, revisions and the like.[31]

The philosophical as well as natural theories of justice may, likewise, be accused of being too abstract to be easily grafted into the premises of positive jurisprudence. While understanding such a difficulty, Paton feels that much confusion "would have been avoided, if the term 'law' had been confined to positive law and another term for the natural law which essentially lays down general principles rather than detailed rules. The principle of natural justice is a phrase which expresses better the medieval notion."[32] It, however, does not mean that the idea of natural justice has become thoroughly outdated. It still constitutes the sheet-anchor of the philosophy of liberal jurisprudence though the inherent fallacies of its doctrine may not be ignored in entirety. We may agree with this view that the idea of natural law is nothing but a set of the norms of natural justice— fairplay, equity, and righteousness—in its practical manifestation. The law courts "cannot introduce the principles of natural justice in disregard to positive law, yet if it is possible within the limits of law, to apply law in a way so as to avoid injustice and to apply these principles in field to which no statutory law is found applicable."[33]

Legal Theory: Justice as the Enforcement of the Law of the State

When we pass from an abstract to a concrete plane of jurisprudence, we find that justice lies in the enforcement of the positive law. Moreover, as it is done by the judicial or quasi-judicial bodies, it implies what is given by the courts in the form of interpretations of the statutes or verdicts delivered after hearing the parties involved in a dispute. The idea of justice, for this reason, draws very close to the world of law and both seem interchangeable. Such a view is subscribed mainly by the advocates of the analytical school like John Austin and Dicey who, taking inspiration from Hobbes and Bentham, insist that law has to function as an instrument of justice, on

30. Bakhshish Singh, *op. cit.*, p. [illegible]
31. P.B. Mukharji: *New Jurisprudence* (Calcutta: Eastern Law House, 1970). p. 27.
32. Paton: *Jurisprudence* (London: Oxford Univ. Press), p. 100.
33. Bakhshish Singh, *op. cit.*, pp. 39-40.

the one hand, and as an instrument to suppress mischief, on the other. If so, justice "is the immediate purpose of law, and law without an element of justice will become an instrument of oppression."[34]

It, however, does not mean that judicial bodies pay no respect to the abstract principles of natural justice. They do it in order to ensure that the laws of the state are enforced for the good of the community. Thus, English courts took slavery as an institution contrary to natural law and refused to enforce the judgement of a foreign court in which the celebrated principle of natural justice was violated. And yet the courts may come to say that the laws of the state may override a principle of natural justice under certain exceptional circumstances. For instance, the services of an employee can be terminated without assigning 'specific reasons' during the times of national crisis 'in the interest of the state'.

The idea of justice, in this sense, requires a happy synthesis of the principles of natural justice with the premises of positive law. Viewed thus, justice requires that (1) the accused should know the nature of the charges levelled against him, (2) he should be given a reasonable opportunity to state his case either himself or through his attorney, (3) the tribunal or the court trying the case should be fair and impartial, and (4) the proceedings of the trial should be conducted in a free and fair manner. In other words, it implies that a court of competent jurisdiction should deliver its 'just decision' fulfilling three conclusions:[35]

1. It presupposes rules.
2. Differences in treatment must be justified by reference to relevant differences of attribute or condition, i.e., differences recognised by the rules. Other distinctions would be legitimate only if by making them the rules were amended universally, *i.e.,* there can be no particular exceptions, only an elaboration of criteria, creating new distinctions to be applied generally.
3. Differences in treatment must be, in a loose sense, proportionate. That is, given the grounds of distinction, we may still challenge the degree of discrimination.

One may easily trace the merit of this theory to its being very clear and precise. Justice, like law of the state, becomes a positivistic affair. We may say that what the people, in general, mean by justice belongs to this variety. Thus, disputes are taken to a court of competent jurisdiction, The hearing in the court is open, free and fair. Finally, the interpretation of the learned judge is considered as being an embodiment of justice. It may, however, be added by way of a critical appreciation that the theory of positive justice is not free from certain inherent weaknesses. For instance, it lays too much emphasis on the sanctity of a verdict given by a court. It certainly ignores the role of social, economic and political forces that remain at work in every society and an understanding of which may convince a critical observer that in the administration of public justice the hand of non-judicial elements cannot be lost sight of. The result is that what is meant by justice, as Justice Delvin says, varies with the 'length of judge's foot'. Moreover, as we shall see later on, this theory cannot be acceptable to the Marxists who advocate the doctrine of 'class justice'.[36]

34. *Ibid.,* p. 1.
35. S.I. Benn and R.S. Peters: *Social Principles and the Democratic State* (London: George Allen & Unwin, 1975), p. 128.
36. See Mukharji, *op. cit.,* p. 3.

Marxist Theory: Class Concept of Justice

Viewed from an ideological stand-point, the idea of justice may be divided into two categories—Liberal and Marxist. What we have seen in the preceding sections pertains to the former category. It takes justice in terms of law as pronounced by the state through its accredited government, including the organs of legislature, executive and judiciary. However, justice is not mere performance according to law; it has an overriding effect too in case the administration of law leads to manifest injustice either due to violation of the principles of the natural justice or due to the exercise of unfettered conscience of the persons administering justice. Mention, in particular, may be made of Dean Roscoe Pound who emphasises that justice and its administration must always be according to the law of the state as proclaimed by the state. He goes to the extent of criticising that there could be anything like justice outside this law, for the danger in that event "would be justice according to the uncontrolled passion, prejudice and instinct of the person administering justice and, therefore, running the risk of being whimsical and unpredictable."[37]

We may also include sociological interpretation of a man like Justice Holmes of the United States in the same category. He asserts that justice is not merely technically confined to the proclaimed law, it must also reflect the unproclaimed custom and conscience of the society in which justice is administered. Morality, religion and custom, in practice. are powerful aids of this ideology. It is said that when justice disagrees with law, it is the law which comes into disrepute in course of time and it "leads to what is called the lawless laws for the correction of which reforms, agitations and revolutions are sought according to the degree of dissociation between law and justice."[38]

The essential point to be taken note of, in this context, is that people subscribing to the liberal view seek to bring about a harmonious synthesis between the abstract precepts of natural justice and the concrete premises of positive law. They recognise that in case there is a conflict between the two, the matter, in question, should be decided in a way so that the interest of the community is subserved. In this way, the meaning of justice should be revised so as to meet the changing requirements of a civilised social life. As Lord Hailsham (Lord Chancellor of the United Kingdom) once observed: "The principles of justice do not change, but their application in terms of law must alter with changes in circumstances. This presupposes a race of lawyers, a breed of judges, not aloof from society of theirs, but alive to its realities. It implies a system of law, durable but constantly under revision. But law remains an instrument, not an end in itself. Law is the means to achieve justice, it can never remain still. It must never be allowed to go out of touch."[39]

Fundamentally different from this is the Marxist view of justice that integrates the idea of justice with the doctrine of class war. If state is an instrument of exploitation and oppression by one class over another, naturally the systems of law and justice are originally bound up with it. According to this view, the laws are needed by the

37. *Ibid.*, pp. 2-3.
38. *Ibid.*, p. 3.
39. Quoted in *The Indian Express* (New Delhi) Jan. 7, 1971.

bourgeois class to keep itself in power by hook or by crook. Naturally, after the successful revolution, the entire system is changed. In the era of the dictatorship of the proletariat, laws are needed to affect the transformation of the bourgeois society into a socialist order. Since all power is with the 'vanguard of the working class'—Communist Party—the courts have to toe the line of the party in power in order to accelerate the implementation of the programme of socialism. Thus, the policy and programme coupled with the application of the principles of justice, correctly speaking, social justice, are to be determined by the higher echelons of the party and the courts are required "to act with the zeal of ideological adherence in order to achieve that object."[40]

It is owing to this ideological standpoint pervading the entire political system that a leading Soviet jurist remarked that a court of whatever sort "is an organ of the class dominant in a given state defending and guarding its interest. The bourgeois court is one of the key weapons for repressing the toilers and resisting encroachments upon the system of capitalist relations."[41] Another leading Soviet writer affirmed that "in the land of the dictatorship of the proletariat, the courts are needed first to fight the enemies of the Soviet government and, secondly, to fight for the consolidation of the new Soviet system, to firmly anchor the new socialist discipline among the working people."[42]

The main characteristics of the Marxist view of justice may be enumerated as under.[43]

1. A sharp distinction is drawn between the ownership of the means of production which is wholly under the State and ownership of consumer goods which is open to individuals;
2. In the sphere of production, all economic business relationships are essentially transactions between State organs, either subsidised organs, or autonomous bodies known as State trusts;
3. Relationship between State and individul, e.g., between State trusts and its employees;
4. Recognition of private right over consumer goods to a restricted extent, resale being subject to strict scrutiny;
5. Regulation of relations and disputes between various parties being entrusted to tribunals, which are impartial and independent;
6. Strict enforcement of legislation.

In short, the judiciary in a communist country is 'committed' to implement the ideology of scientific socialism as expounded by Marx and developed by Lenin. It is due to this that the sociology of the judges and their background and training, somehow or other, are supposed to give support to their prejudices acquired in the society in which they are trained and brought up leading to the failure of justice. Justice rendered by human agencies may suffer from these inherent defects in the

40. Bakshish Singh, *op. cit.*, p. 72.
41. A. Vyshinsky: *The Law of the Soviet State*, p. 500.
42. Karpinsky: *The Social and State Structure of the USSR*, p. 194.
43. N.B. Bannerji, *op. cit.*, pp. 26-27.

nature of human mind, human intellect and human scholarships but those inherent defects are to be seen in every system of justice so long as individual agencies have to administer justice. "The concealed implications of this theory is a kind of collective justice said to be administered by the impersonality of the State or the Government which also can be open to the very same charge of prejudice or bias."[44]

In brief, while the liberal interpretation of justice is quite flexible that places judiciary in a 'free' position, the Marxist notion desires its 'committed' form. The result is that while the former is too flexible and, for this reason, amenable to diverse, even conflicting, interpretations, in various important directions, the latter is inherent with very rigid postures. Obviously, while the former is necessarily connected with the premises of, what is popularly known as the rule of law, the latter constitutes a flagrant negation of the same. Highlighting this essential point of distinction between liberal and totalitarian (including Fascist and Communist) varieties, an eminent writer says: "In modern democratic society, the judge must steer his way between the Scylla of subservience to government and the Charybdis of remoteness from constantly changing social pressures and economic needs . . . the administration of law under these systems becomes a predominantly political function and an instrument of government policy . . . . The independence of the judiciary from both the executive and the legislature remains a cornerstone of democratic government."[45]

Social Justice: Predominance of the Interest of the Community

What is known by the name of justice in common parlance relates to the settlement of disputes through judicial bodies. It is in this respect that the term 'justice' has a positive character and by virtue of which law of the state and justice of the courts become very close affairs. However, this sort of justice has three broad dimensions—social, economic and political. With the penetration of democracy into social and economic spheres, the meaning of justice has expanded itself so as to cover all walks of human life. A new awareness has developed that informs that the rights of an individual should be reasonably restricted in the wider interests of the community so that the ends of social justice are properly achieved. In other words, it is widely recognised that the well-being of society depends on the co-ordination and reconciliation between the rights of the individul and interests of the community. Not only this, if there is a conflict between the two, the latter should prevail over the former.

Thus, figures in the issue of justice in social, economic and political directions. Social justice relates to the 'balance between an individual's rights and social control

44. Mukharji, *op. cit.*, pp. 3-4.
45. W. Friedman: *Law in Changing Society* (Middlesex: Penguin Books, 1964), pp. 65-66. However. the Marxist view of social justice is said to have its own pitfalls. It is from Marxism of course, that the most extreme views on social justice emanate. The theory of justice that applies to a socialist society in which bourgeois ownership and exploitation has been abolished, holds that a distribution is just when each receives that which is in accord with his labour contribution to the social product. Nevertheless, some inequality will persist, since people's labour contributions will vary according to their talents, and many of the objectionable features of a money economy will remain. This last point means that man's 'essence' cannot be captured under socialism." N.P. Barry, *op. cit.*, pp. 126-27.

ensuring the fulfilment of the legitimate expectations of the individual under the existing laws and to assure him benefits thereunder and protection in case of any violation or encroachment on his rights, consistent with the unity of nation and needs of the society."[46] Undoubtedly, the idea of social justice requires the sacrifice of certain rights of an individual at the altar of the general interest. However, viewed in a wider perspective, the idea of social justice not only aims at the proper reconciliation of the interest of an individual with the overall interest of the community or prevalence of the latter over the former in the event of any conflict, it also constitutes "an essential part of the great complex of social change, for which something may have to be sacrificed for greater good."[47]

It is evident that the concept of social justice is a very wide term that covers within its fold everything pertaining to the norm of 'general interest' ranging from the protection of the interests of the minorities to the eradication of poverty and illiteracy. It not merely relates to the observance of the principle of equality before law and independence of judiciary as we find in the developed countries of the West, it also relates to the eradication of gigantic social evils like those of pauperism, disease, unemployment and starvation which have their stigmatic expression on the face of the developing countries of the East. Moreover, all this also relates to the liquidation of the vested interests that obstruct the achievement of common good and have their interest in the maintenance of the *status quo* to their own advantage. As such, in the backward countries of the world, the idea of social justice enjoins upon the state to make concerted efforts for the improvement of the lot of the downtrodden and weaker sections of the community. Its area widens itself so as to cover the economic domain of a people's life for the obvious reason that it demands non-exploitation of the working class. Viewed in another perspective, it also demands harmony and co-operation between labour and capital, a substantial minimum wage to the capacity of each industry and other incidental benefits that improve the standard of living of the people.

The affirmation of the idea of social justice is very well contained in the interpretation of Dean Roscoe Pound who presents a sixfold illustration of social interests and lays down eight jural postulates to ensure social justice. Thus, the ideal of social justice envisages to promote the welfare of the people by securing and developing a just social order. As such, law becomes "a social science and lawyers must regard themselves as social scientists."[48] The premises of the rule of law are, for this reason, broadened. Apart from ensuring equality and liberty to the people, it "enjoins to bring about a social order in which justice—social, economic and political—shall inform the institutions of national life."[49]

---

46. Bakhshish Singh, *op. cit.*, p. 73.
47. Boalding: "Social Justice in Social Dynamics" in Richard Brandt (ed.): *Social Justice* (New York: Prentice-Hall, 1965), p. 92.
48. Lord Hailsham, *op. cit.*
49. Chief Justice K. Subba Rao of the Indian Supreme Court in *Golak Nath V. The State of Punjab*, AIR 1967, SC 1643.

But the concept of social justice has different implications at the hands of negative liberals who take it as antithetical to the principle of equality of opportunites.[50] Its best affirmation can be seen in the views of F. A. Hayek who holds: "For in such a system in which each is allowed to use his knowledge for his own purposes, the concept of social justice is empty and meaningless, because in it nobody's will can determine the relative incomes of the different people, or prevent that they be partly dependent on accident. Social justice can be given a meaning only in a directed or 'command' economy (such as an army) in which the individuals are ordered what to do and any particular conception of social justice could be realised only in such a centrally directed system."[51] The idea of the equality of opportunity cuts across the principle of justice despite the fact that it looks quite attractive. But once it "is extended beyond the facilities which for other reasons have to be provided by government, it becomes a wholly illusory ideal and any attempt concretely to realise it is apt to produce a nightmare."[52]

The whole concept of social interest, as presented by the collectivists is so distorted in the view of Hayek that much of what is today done in the name of social justice "is not only unjust but also highly unsocial in the true sense of the word; it amounts simply to the protection of entrenched interests."[53] This line of argument obviously attacks the whole thesis of socialism that stresses the principle of supremacy of social interest over individual interest. So the argument runs that what we call 'socialism' is based throughout on the atrocious idea that political power ought to determine the material position of different individuals and groups—an idea defended by the false assertion that this must always be so and socialism merely wishes to transfer this power from the privileged to the most numerous class."[54] The worst danger entailing from the whole case of social justice is that its obstinate pursuance eventuates in totalitarianism, since it requires an ever-increasing use of coercion at the hands of the state in social and economic life of the people.[55] All non-market criteria of income such as those based on need are necessarily subjective and can work only in a regimented, oppressive and illiberal society.[56]

50. The idea of social justice clashes with the idea of equality in respect of equal opportunities in the view of the negative liberals. For instance, A.M. MacLead says that the word 'opportunity' must necessarily mean opportunity to do something, or become something, or obtain something, else the phrase "equality of opportunity' is empty without such specification. Refer to his "Equality of Opportunity: Some Ambiguities in the Ideal" in Dorsey Gary (ed.): *Equality and Freedom: International and Comparative Jurisprudence* (New York: Dobbs Ferry, 1966), Vol. 3. So says Scott Gordon : "In a world where people differ in their natural endowments or their preferences, or both, equality of opportunity will lead to inequality of resulting states (such as income); while if we insist on producing... equality of resulting status, we will prevent the working of opportunity." *Op. cit.*, p. 111. Perhaps, summing up the whole case in a roundabout manner, J.L. Lucas has gone so far as to argue that the concept of equality "is so muddy and treacherous that it should be eliminated from political discourse altogether." *The Principles of Politics* (London: Clarendon Press, 1966), pp. 243-50.
51. Hayek: *Law, Legislation and Liberty* (Chicago: Chicago University Press, 1976), Vol. 2, p. 69.
52. *Ibid.*, p. 85.
53. *Ibid*, p. 96.
54. *Ibid.*, p. 99.
55. Hayek: *The Road to Serfdom* (London: Routledge and Kegan Paul, 1970).
56. Hayek: *The Constitution of Liberty* (London: Routledge and Kegan Paul, I960) and *Law, Legislation and Liberty: The Mirage of Social Justice* (London: Routlege and Kegan Paul, 1976), VoL 3.

Pound's Illustration of Social Justice

Social Justice

Social Interest	**Jural Postulates**
1. in General Security, e.g., peace, public health, security of acquisitions, etc.	1. that no wanton aggression is made by other, institutions, etc.
2. in Security and Social Institutions, e.g., marriage, religious institutions, etc.	2. that parties with whom transactions are entered into will act in good faith;
3. in General Morals, e.g., gambling, drinking, immoral traffic, etc.	3. that there will be no hindrance in the enjoyment of one's acquisitions and creations ;
4. in Conservation of Social Resources, e.g., food, minerals, etc.	4. that the person will not be exposed to undue risks and that others will act with due care and caution ;
5. in General Progress, e.g., freedom of trade, encouragement of research, etc.	5. that dangerous things kept by others shall be cautiously and carefully kept within its bounds ;
6. in Individual Rights, e.g., wages, conditions of work, etc.	6. that an employee has a right to employment;
	7. that society will share the misfortunes which befall on individual; and
	8. that proper compensation will be paid to workers for necessary human wear and tear in an industrial society.

The same line of argument is contained in the views of Robert Nozick who advances the argument of minimum nightwatchman state'— a state limited to protecting persons against murder, assault, theft, fraud and so forth. Historical principles hold that past circumstances or actions of people can create differential entitlements or different deserts to things. The distribution of rewards should conform to particular standards. As such, no one has a right to a minimum of welfare because to grant it would necessitate unjustified taxation of the deserving for the sake of giving rewards to the undeserving. He claims it as his broader conception of liberty which may be harmonised with the principle of equality and justice (rather social justice) if the principle of desert is properly honoured. It is based on the touchstone of 'enablements' that would certainly lead to different results, for then persons whose taxes are increased to make up for the loss of public revenue resulting from the tax advantage given to farmers would be deprived of their liberty. A stricter version of property rights, according to which all taxation constitutes an invasion of liberty, would lead to the same result.[57]

57. Robert Nozick: *Anarchy, State and Utopia* (New York: Basic Books, 1974), pp. 167-74.

The difficulty about defining the ideal of social justice and its proper realisation by the state is that it lacks a precise connotation on account of varying social and economic theories and, more than that, in view of the conflicting interpretations of thinkers and jurists belonging to the liberal and Marxist schools. It is owing to this formidable difficulty that the ideal "remains such a variable from Robinhood to levellers and those conducting the 'gherao' (i.e., encirclement of a person for coercing him to accept the demands), all declare themselves to be in pursuit of social justice."[58] An eminent writer on this subject thus observes: "We hear much today of 'Social Justice'. I am not sure that those men who use the term most glibly know very clearly what they mean by it. Some mean distribution or redistribution of wealth; some interpret it as 'equality of opportunity'—a misleading term, since opportunity can never be equal among human beings who have unequal capacities to grasp it. Many, I suspect, mean simply that it is "unjust that anybody should be fortunate than themselves and the more intelligent mean that it is just—I would rather say benevolent—that every effort should be made at least to mitigate the asperities of natural human inequality and that no obstacle should be offered, but rather help afforded, to practicable opportunities of self-improvement."[59]

Economic Justice: Elimination of Exploitation and Equitable Distribution of National Wealth

The case of economic justice should be treated as a corollary to what we have said in the above section. As a matter of fact, the two are closely related so much so that a discussion of one covers much what comes within the fold of the discussion of another. It is owing to this that while social justice demands eradication of gigantic social evils, most of them (as exploitation of the workers by the capitalists or concentration of national wealth into fewer hands) find their place, in particular, in the economic sphere. Thus, the whole idea of liberty issuing forth in the form of economic justice crosses the domain of politics and enters into those of economics and sociology. It is said: "Freedom is meaningless if it prevents the achievement of economic justice. To a hungry man or to a man who is denied human dignity, political freedom is an empty word. The problem of today is how to bring about economic and social justice without sacrificing the individual to the ever-increasing power of the State."[60]

Simply stated, the idea of economic justice means non-discrimination between man and man on the basis of economic values. In positive terms, it implies adequate payments for work without any discrimination on some artificial ground. It also enjoins freedom for all in the spheres of production and distribution of goods subject to the conditions of general welfare. It also demands that the state of national economy be reshaped in a way that the benefits are made more and more available to the common man. In this way, the idea of economic justice comes to imply a socialistic pattern of society. What Nehru said about the case of economic justice in a poor and backward country like ours applies to the case of economic justice in general that

58. Bakhshish Singh, *op. cit.*, p. 17.
59. Allen, *op. cit.*, p. 3.
60. M.C. Chagla: *The Individual and the State* (Bombay: Asia Pub. House, 1951), p 8.

it necessarily relates itself with feeding the starving and clothing the naked masses, providing them with shelters, and affording them all opportunities of progress.

In this sense, economic justice is an important concept in the modern age of science and industrialisation. Since planning has become the chief mode of bringing about the state of general welfare, this ideal enjoins upon the state to revise the meaning of the term in a way so as to avoid the areas of conflict between the demands of a developing society and the traditional norms of law and justice. The implementation of social welfare programmes certainly cuts at the roots of most of the traditional economic rights and men of vested interests strain their every nerve to contain the area of state activity in the name of their 'fundamental freedoms' as enshrined in the basic law of the land. These figure among important matters like compulsory acquisition of private property in the public interest and imposition of reasonable restrictions on the growth and role of private sector.

It is, however, possible that a power-drunk government may encroach upon the essential freedoms of the people in the name of its planning programmes for the welfare of the society. If so, the idea of economic justice calls for the imposition of suitable restraints on the authority of the state so that the people are saved from the economic tyranny of the planners. The modern concept of jurisprudence has, therefore, to face the challenge of planning whether it is democratic, or socialistic, or communistic. "Law, therefore, will have to accept planning and justice, will have to find some accommodation for that law. One thing is certain that planning cannot be a substitute for law. Law has tamed many tyrants in legal history. Modern jurisprudence and theory of justice will, therefore, have to inspire and guide modern laws to control the tyranny and abuse of planning and make planning a part of legal and social order. To some extent, administrative jurisprudence is the modern answer to make planning a part of and not a substitute for the rule of law."[61]

One may easily take note of the fact that, like social justice, the case of economic justice is also a matter of acute controversy between the Liberal and Marxist thinkers. Not only this, it is a matter of controversy among the proponents of Liberalism too in view of their commitments varying from the canons of classicism to those of socialism. Thus, we find that while the Communists desire to abolish the institution of private property for the sake of bringing about an era of economic justice, the Liberals invoke varying standards ranging from the maintenance of private property system to the imposition of reasonable limitations on its use and enjoyment by the people. As a result, both notions suffer from inherent fallacies. For instance, while one may say that the Marxist formula of 'to each according to his work' in the era of socialism and 'from each according to his ability, to each according to his need' in the final stage of socialism (communism) would be contrary to the just principle of distribution as well as to the humanistic norm of help to the weak and the disabled even when they do not work. Likewise, he may say that the norm of 'regulatory legislation' or 'reasonable restrictions' as laid down by the jurists of free and democratic countries, would make the whole idea of economic justice fluid, perhaps touching the verge of meaninglessness. He may have to come to appreciate

61. Mukharji, *op. cit.*, pp. 12-13.

the view that justice and ideas about it are therefore, seeking a new balance and a new harmony in the present conflicts between large national economic and social interests, on the one hand, and the individuals or group rights and interests on the other.[62]

Political Justice: Commitment to the Values of a Liberal-Democratic Order

Finally, we come to deal with the last important dimension of positive justice. It is political justice that desires a free and fair participation of people in their political life. As such, it involves the guarantee of universal adult franchise and no distinction on some artificial grounds in matters of recruitment to public services. What the policy of the state should be, and how the society should be organised in political and economic directions are matters which should be decided by the people themselves according to prevailing needs and circumstances. Here the idea of the preservation of political rights of the individual dominates the scene so much so that the very notion of justice, by and large, assumes an individualistic tenor in view of the fact that, despite being a social creature, some of his deeper pursuits in the field of knowledge, mind and spirit are individual affairs As a matter of fact, they "are the springs from which civilisation grows."[63]

In other words, the notion of political justice requires that the state must protect and preserve certain valuable rights of the individual so that he may develop his personality as a citizen and thereby contribute his share to the welfare of the political community. We may refer, in this connection, to the view of Justice Brandies of the American Supreme Court who strongly pleaded for the protection and sanctity of individual thoughts, emotions and sensations by legal recognition. Arguing the case of 'right to privacy', he says: "Still, the protection of society must come mainly through a recognition of the rights of the individual. Each man is responsible for his own acts and omissions only. If he condones what he reprobates, with a weapon in hand equal to his defence, he is responsible for the result. If he resists, public opinion will rally to his support. Has he then such a weapon? It is believed that the common law provides him with one forged in the slow fire of the centuries, and today fitly tempered to his hand. The common law has always recognised a man's house as a castle, impregnable, often even to its own officers engaged in the execution of its commands."[64]

It is obvious that the idea of political justice desires a liberal-democratic order in which rights of the individuals, including those of the minorities, are well protected. Viewed in a wider perspective, it naturally covers much of what falls under the categories of social justice. Moreover, it makes itself coterminous with the case of a full-fledged democratic order. As such, it involves not merely recognition to and protection of rights relating to the maintenance of a political creed, it also enjoins the prevalence of right to dissent and duty to tolerate. As Justice Mukharji says: "Loyalty in a free society depends upon the tolerance of disloyalty. If tolerance of diversity involves an admitted element of risk to national security, intolerance involves

62. *Ibid.*, p. 10.
63. *Ibid.*, p. 20.
64. *Ibid.*, p. 22.

a certainty that unity will be destroyed. If unity does not grow out of uniformity, it grows out of resolved conflict."[65]

In the end, it may be commented that while the case of positive justice may be said to involve three broad dimensions—social, economic ard political—we cannot draw a watertight boundary line between them. As a matter of fact, borderlines are fluid and what comes under one category is amenable to fall under another also. The result is that the task of a modern state has become increasingly complex. Available evidence shows that hardly any major decision can be made without a careful evaluation of the conflicting values and interests. Thus, while liberal-democratic systems defend and preserve the values of liberty and equality, correctly speaking the postulates of the rule of law, totalitarian systems eliminate much of the conflict by dictating what should be done strictly in a particular direction as conceived by the men in power, the violation of which would be visited by 'death or mutilation'. Law prevails in both the systems with a substantial point of difference—with justice in one, without it in another. It is well observed: "The law must aspire at certainty, at justice, at progressiveness but these objectives are constantly in conflict with one another."[66]

Norms of Justice: Corrective and Distributive Varieties

After studying various theories on the nature of justice followed by a discussion of the three broad dimensions of 'positive' justice, we pass on to deal with its 'norms' which are of two varieties— corrective and distributive. Joseph Pieper gives three basic norms of justice in this regard, namely, (1) reciprocal or mutually exchanged justice which orders the relations of individuals called 'cumulative justice' or 'justice in exchange', (2) ministering justice which brings order to the relations between the community as such and the individuals composing it with the result that it marks the inseparable association between law and order, and (3) legal or general justice which orders the members' relations to the social whole. One may find this threefold division a little confusing, since justice in practical terms is either 'corrective' or 'distributive' depending on the nature of its administration.

Corrective justice is contained in the verdict of the judicial bodies delivered after hearing the statements of the parties in dispute. The aim of this norm is to correct the erratic behaviour of the party in dispute. Obviously, it emanates from the decisions of the courts in which we find an interpretation of the law of the land, a wise distinction between 'just' and 'unjust situations', award of punishment to the wrongdoer, strictures passed against the delinquent person and the like. It is possible that, in certain cases, the courts may significantly reduce the scope of inequality created by the statutory provisions of the land. For instance, in an area which is not covered by any enactment, courts "have an authority to bridge the gap and prevent the wickedness of many who disrupt the order of the society and the courts can, in the interest of justice, exercise superintendence over the offences *contra bonons mores* (against good manners or morals)."[67]

65. *Ibid.*, p. 24.
66. Friedman, *op. cit.*, p. 67.
67. Bakhshish Singh, *op. cit.*, p. 31.

We have already discussed the notion of corrective justice in the preceding sections while dealing with the matter of 'positive justice'. It shall now be in the natural fitness of things to discuss in detail the concept of 'distributive justice' that has assumed an importance of its own in the present era of 'socialist democracy' or 'revisionist liberalism'. We have already seen that the principle of liberalism has taken a distinctly positive direction in the present age on account of making the case of democracy in consonance with the philosophy of socialism. As a result of this, the idea of distributive justice has become more important which can be visualised in the works of neo-liberals of the United States like J. W. Chapman and John Rawls. As we shall see, abundant literature on this subject has appeared so much so that democracy "is reduced from a humanistic aspiration to a market equilibrium system."[68]

The expression expression of the notion of distributive justice is given by Aristotle. According to him, justice requires that equals should be treated equally and unequals unequally. Injustice arises when the reverse comes to take place. In other words, this idea establishes an organic relationship between the norm of justice and the principle of equality. The modern interpretation of this term, however, is different which establishes an organic relationship of a juristic norm with a particular system of economy. In this sense, distributive justice desires equal distribution of income among the equals only. It is, however, a different matter that a judicial organisation mixes up the two norms of justice in a particular case. For instance, in 1925 the British House of Lords invalidated an expensive welfare scheme that sought to give benefit to a small section at the cost of other sections of the community.

As pointed out above, the idea of distributive justice finds its conspicuous place in the works of some recent political economists who have sought to redefine the premises of liberal political theory so as to meet the challenge of a socialist system. We may, in this direction, refer to the works of J.W. Chapman who seeks to integrate the idea of justice with his principles of 'economic rationality of man' and 'consumer's sovereignty' coupled with individual's claim of 'moral freedom'. To him, the first principle of justice appears to be the distribution of benefits which maximises benefits in accordance with the principle of consumer's sovereignty. The second principle is that a system is unjust if the material well-being of the few is purchased at the expense of the many. It implies that justice requires that no one shall gain at the expense of another.[69]

As Chapman says: "Consider an economy in which returns to capital are taxed from the owner, in part invested, and the remainder distributed in the form of the public-services available to all. Assume further that there is full equality of opportunity, unrestricted competition for the position of 'owner', which is now rather

68. C.B. Macpherson: *Democratic Theory: Essays in Retrieval* (London: Oxford University Press, 1976), pp. 78-79.

69. Chapman: "Justice and Fairness" in Friedrich and Chapman (ed.s): *Justice in Nomos,* VI (New York, 1963), pp. 30-34.

that of 'manager', and that both workers and owners receive their marginal, value productivity and are compensated for disutility. Their incomes would not be equal, and the differential would reflect not only differences in productivity but also the equalising increase in real incomes from the free services. This inequality is now seen as being dictated by the requirements of economic rationality. It would hardly seem appropriate to say that it 'measures' a transfer of 'powers' of both workers and owners that have been mutually enhanced; the income inequality performs an allocative function; it is the result of processes which are both competitive and optimising."[70]

John Rawls sets out two basic moral principles of justice which a constitutional democracy should satisfy: first, each person engaged in institution affected by it has an equal right to the most extensive liberty compatible with a like liberty for all; second, inequalities as defined by the institutional structure or fostered by it are arbitrary unless it is reasonable to expect that they will work out to everyone's advantage and provided that the positions and offices to which they attach or from which they may be gained are open to all.[71] These are offered as principles by which should be judged the basic structure of any society, including the political constitution and the principal economic and social institutions which together define a persons's liberties and rights and affect his life-prospects, what he may expect to be and how well he may expect to be fair. Rawls, thus, comes to lay down a contractarian theory of justice in which participation in the understanding of justice as fairness makes a type of government called 'constitutional democracy'.[72]

The model which Rawls proposes as satisfying has two principles of justice. It is a constitutional democracy in which the government "regulates a free economy in a certain way. More fully, if law and government act effectively to keep markets competitive, resources fully employed, property and wealth widely distributed over time, and to maintain the appropriate social minimum, then if there is equality of opportunity underwritten by education for all, the resulting distribution will be just."[73] It, therefore, appears that, like Chapman, Rawls "is assuming capitalistic economic rationality, and is dealing with justice only within the limits imposed by it. His postulates about the requirements of capitalist rationality are more realistic than Chapman's in two respects: he assumes that any capitalist society will still be a class-divided one; and he assumes that inequality of income will always be necessary in such a society as an incentive to efficient production and that, therefore, welfare state transfer payments must be limited to an amount which will still leave one class better off than another."[74]

70. *Ibid.*, p. 29.
71. Rawls: "Distributive Justice" in Peter Laslett and W.G. Runciman (eds.) *Philosophy, Politics and Society* (III Series) (Oxford: Basil Blackwell, 1962), p. 61.
72. Rawls: "Constitutional Liberty and the Concept of Justice" in Friedirich and Chapman (ed.s), *op. cit.*, p. 125.
73. Rawls: "Distributive Justice", *op. cit.*, p. 71.
74. Macpherson, *op. cit.*, p. 92.

The idea of distributive justice, in simple terms, requires that the courts should take a liberal view of the premises of law and so interpret them as to distribute benefits to the largest number of people so that the 'harsh effects' of the technicalities of law are contained within the 'narrowest limits'.[75] Yet, such an idea has its own weaknesses. It claims to have its basis in the principle of equality. But then the question remains as to what the idea of equality really implies in this context. It is a very controversial subject and we may find that in a given legal order, justice may, and also may not, have to serve the purpose of *laissez faire* economy, or of public ownership of all productive enterprises, or of a parliamentary multiparty democracy, or of a single party political order.'[76] The most important point of attack, however, finds place in the affirmation that the idea of distributive justice, as developed by recent political economists, is just a shrewd way of defending the *status quo*. "It may be termed as another clever device of fighting against the winds of progressivism. Thus, a Marxist may call such elaborations as bourgeois tactics to defraud the people or to distract their attention from the side of socialism. Not only this, even an enlightened liberal may not appreciate the whole case of distributive justice as made out by men like Chapman and Rawls on the ground that it falls short of making the case of pragmatic liberalism in consonance with the system of a liberal-democratic theory as needed today. Thus, any theory whose horizon is, for the most part, bounded by the supposed wants of man as consumer, or which makes this satisfaction of those wants the main ingredient of moral freedom or of maximisation of powers, is not adequate as a liberal-democratic theory, however adequate it might once have been as a liberal theory."[77]

Rawls on Justice: A Redistributionist Plea for Justified Inequalities

A significant study on the subject of justice appeared in a book that, as claimed by his admirers, put its author (John Rawls) in the category of great political and social theorists like Plato, Kant and Mill.[78] It is a developed form of what Rawls wrote earlier in his papers beginning with his 'Justice as Fairness' published in 1958.[79] The publication of this book created a stir in the world of great liberal theorists of the West who took it as an outstanding work on social and political theory in the second half of the twentieth century—a phase in which normative political theory was taken as declined, nay demised. Covering about 600 pages and weighing in over a quarter of a million words contained in 87 sections having many ramifications, it appeared as a mammoth, complex and ambitious contribution that could send the practitioners of moral and political philosophy into a reflective sequestration, as they sought to come to grips with its intricate argumentation. It is said that with

75. See Benjamin Cardozo: *The Nature of Judicial Process* (New Haven: Yale Univ. Press), pp, 149-52.
76. Mukharji, *op. cit.*, p. 4.
77. Macpherson, *op. cit.*, p. 94.
78. John Rawls: *A Theory of Justice* (Harvard: Harvard University Press, 1971).
79. Rawls: "Justice as Fairness" in *The Philosophical Review*, Vol. LXVII, (1958), pp. 164-94 reproduced in Pater Laslett and W.G. Runciman (eds.): *Philosophy, Politics and Society* (Oxford: Basil Blackwell, 1962), III Series pp. 132-57.

the appearance of this work the name of Rawls "soared blazingly into prominence throughout intellectual world."[80]

The outstanding feature of the theory of justice, as contained in the book of Rawls, is that here the argument of utilitarianism as given by Bentham is apparently rejected but really modified so as to be in harmony with the idealism of Kant. However, what really attracts the community of the lovers of normative political theory is the way Rawls has been able to revive, rather revitalise, the trend of normativism that was so relentlessly overshadowed by 'the champions of empirical, neo-empirical and trans-empirical theories. One may, therefore, prefer to establish a line of similarity between Rawls' *A Theory of Justice* and Sidgwick's *The Methods of Ethics* (1874) in view of the systematic and comprehensive statements of a thoroughgoing liberal position. Among recent writers, Blondel takes the contribution of Rawls as a bold proof of the existence of value-laden theory[81], and another writer observes that it "appears at a time when liberalism is becoming unfashionable, dismissed in smart circles as shallow compared with the deep (not to say unfathomable) truths of Hegel or a Hegelianised Marx."[82].

As said above, the first striking feature of the contribution of Rawls is the rejection of the utilitarian philosophy and its substitution by an alternative moral perspective. In his view, the argument of utilitarianism as given by Hume and Bentham is inconsistent to the extent that it may be made compatible with unjust social institutions like slavery. But justice, in a correct sense, should be regarded as the first virtue of social institutions and the primary domain over which it operates is the 'distribution of goods'.[83] The utilitarian principle is not compatible with stability also as maximising average utility may conceivably require that some be made wretched in order to make others very happy indeed.[84] The criterion of potential ability, therefore, sets limits on the range of principles that can be chosen by the

80. Samuel Gorovitz: "John Rawls: A Theory of Justice" in Anthony de Crespigny and Kenneth Minnogue (eds): *Contemporary Political Philosophers* (New York: Dodd Mead & Co., 1975), p. 272. This book is full of maxims and considerations that combine the elements of Benthamite and Kantian philosophy in order to argue for a largely egalitarian distribution of society's goods and services. H.A.L. Hart says that no book on political philosophy, since he read the great classics of the subject, had stirred his thoughts as deeply as this. See his paper titled "Rawls on Liberty and Its Priority" in Norman Daniels (ed.): *Reading Rawls* (New York: Basic Books, 1975), p. 230.
81. Jean Blondel: *The Discipline of Politics* (London: Butterworths, 1981), Ch. 6 titled 'Whither Political Theory.'
82. Brian Barry: *The Liberal Theory of Justice: A Critical Examination of the Principal Doctrines in A Theory of Justice by Rawls* (Oxford: Clarendon Press, 1973), p. 4.
83. Compare it with the statement of John Stuart Mill that "there must be some standard to determine the goodness or badness, absolute and comparative, of ends or subjects of desires. And whatever the standard is, there can be but one – the general principle by which all rules of practice ought to conform and the test by which they should be tried is that of conduciveness to the happiness of mankind." *A System of Logic,* Book II, Chapter 12, Sec 7.
84. Rawls: *A Theory of Justice;* pp. 157-58.

parties in the 'original position'.[85] "They cannot enter into agreements that may have consequences they cannot accept. They will avoid those that they can adhere to only with great difficulty."[86]

The question of justice arises only where there is conflict of interest. If there were perfect coincidence of interest, there would be no disputes requiring adjudication and therefore no call to have the principles of justice. In their real life, people disagree on moral principles, because they have conflicting interests; if we put them into a situation where these conflicting interests cannot influence them, they can reach agreement. When it "is supposed that parties are severally disinterested and are not willing to have their interests sacrificed to the others, the intention is to express men's conduct and motives in cases where questions of justice arise."[87] The parties in the 'original position' have available to them a body of psychological generalisations and some elements of social and economic theory. Here the idea of 'original position' signifies that man is like an intelligent 'negotiator' or like a rational 'agent' concerned with the advancement of his own interest and, for this reason, he wants to achieve certain goods (like wealth, position, opportunity, skill, liberty, self-respect, etc.) for the advancement of his own interest. But how it all can be done depends upon the system of law and justice of a country.

But this principle of rationality does not apply to all in an equal measure, because there is a constant 'veil of ignorance'. Most of the negotiators are utterly without the knowledge of particular facts about themselves or about others. Thus, although they have an immense amount of knowledge of great truths as those of the laws of physics, the laws of the supply and demand in an unrestrained economy and the efforts—say of social isolation—they know literally nothing about who they are, what their personal characteristics are, or what type of social contexts they are from. But it should be remembered that no biases can occur among rational deliberators that beset the veil of ignorance, since no such negotiator has any such idea whether a biased position will help or hinder him once the veil is lifted and he can discover his position in the real world.[88]

The whole idea of the 'original position' and the 'veil of ignorance', as given by Rawls, may be understood in the light of this interpretation that the people as negotiators have general wisdom but particular ignorance. They strive protect and promote their material interests, but in doing so they are unable to dis..nguish their interests with the interests of others. They are not informed by the canons of altruism as supposed by an idealist like Green. They "have no recourse but to adopt principles that are optimal with respect to the advancement of the interests of whoever is least favoured by the principles. That is, in the original position, "the rational agent will realise that at least as far as he can tell from behind the veil of ignorance, he is as likely to suffer as to benefit from the application of any principle that promotes the interest of some more than that of others. In order to advance his own interests, then,

85. The idea of original or initial position suggests that the people would generally stick to the most favoured or standard interpretation of its principle. *Ibid.*, p. 121.
86. *Ibid.*, p. 176.
87. *Ibid.*, p. 129.
88. Samuel Gorovitz, *op. cit.*, p. 279.

he must favour principles which allow the maximum opportunity for the pursuit of one's life plan to everyone and hence—no matter who may turn out to be—to him. A new constraint thus emerges from the deliberation: the principle adopted to regulate the fashioning of a social order must be such that one could rationally agree to live by them realising that one might be society's least advantaged man."[89]

The basic flaw of the theory of utilitarianism is that it threatens to oppress some members of the society in the interest of the greatest good of the greatest number. What is required is that the whole case of justice should be studied in the light of an individual's liberty to achieve the goods in the midst of their scarcity and by maintaining the standards of self-respect. Each individual as a negotiator needs the guarantee of liberty and each desires to have it in the maximum possible form. The principle of liberty cannot reasonably require the unqualified granting of total liberty to everyone, rather the liberty of each must be constrained by the need to protect the liberty of each. The case of individual liberty must be viewed in the light of the 'thin theory of the good'. Since primary goods are limited, each cannot get in a way that all become equal in respect of the achievement of the goods. But the principle of distribution must be based on the standard of equality so that the deserving may get more than the undeserving. The negotiator may consider a principle that mandates a thoroughly equal distribution of goods, so that no person may worry about the achievement of goods for his purpose than any other person. But they "will soon come to realise that they stand to benefit by the introduction of certain inequalities."[90] In their final form, the two principles of justice are:[91]

First Principle: Each person is to have an equal right to the most extensive total system of equal basic liberties compatible with similar system of liberty for all.

Second Principle: Social and economic inequalities are to be so arranged that they are both: (a) to the greatest benefit of the least advantaged, consistent with the just saving principle, and *(b)* attached to offices and position open to all under the conditions of fair equality of opportunity. At the same time, self-respect of man should be protected. The basis of self-esteem in a just society is the publicly affirmed distribution of fundamental rights and liberties. It is central and a fundamental characteristic of human beings in their desire to express their nature in a free social union with others. In this way, liberty moves closer to inequality and Rawls calls it the 'process of chain connectedness'.

It all leads to the matter of having a 'just constitution'. Given their theoretical knowledge and the appropriate general facts about their society, the negotiators are to choose the most effective 'just constitution' that satisfies the principles of justice and is best calculated to lead to just and effective legislation.[92] Only such a constitution would produce just laws under conditions of ideal legislation. The statutes must satisfy not only the principles of justice but whatever limits are laid down in the constitution. By moving back and forth between the stages of the constitutional convention and the legislature, the best constitution is found."[93]

89. Gorovitz, *op. cit.*, p. 279.
90. *Ibid.*, pp. 280-81.
91. Rawls, *op..cit.*, p. 302.
92. *Ibid.*, pp. 196-97.
93. *Ibid.*, p. 198.

It may, therefore, be noted that Rawls is a typical egalitarian in his own right. He is an advocate of the case of justified inequalities in view of the principle of 'desert' to be recognised in some form.[94] A system of privileges is bad, but it is also good. It is bad, because it is needed to maximise social good at the cost of the individual good. It is essential to improve the plight of the least advantaged. But Rawls is not an egalitarian desiring equal distribution of social and economic advantages, .and yet he is an egalitarian in his insistence on the value and autonomy of each individual. His position is like that of a liberal redistributionist. It is, therefore, observed that he "is closely a redistributionist in that he tests the proper function of government to include not merely the maintenance of a social order but the achievement of distributive justice by placing the highest social value on the needs of the neediest. Since natural abilities and the circumstances of birth are among the advantages the inequitable distribution of which fosters privileges, and since much inequitable distribution is, as a matter of empirical fact, essentially ineliminable, it is a consequence of Rawls' position that the just society will seek to compensate for the resulting privilege by investing its resources including the abilities of the most talented in efforts assigned to improve the plight of the least fortunate. Such a view is plainly at odds with the rugged individualism of the unconstrained free enterprise economy, and it is equally at odds with the highly controlled communist or socialist state that submerges the individual's autonomy in the quest for greater social welfare."[95]

The basic objective of the study of Rawls, it is said, is to provide a coherent theoretical foundation for a conception of justice that can be offered in opposition to the utilitarian point of view that has been a significant feature of liberal political theory since the times of Bentham. But it has been taken differently by its friends

94. Though we have touched the issue of "desert" in the chapter on Equality, it shall be worthwhile to take it up again here in the context of the idea of 'greatest good of the greatest number' as stressed by the utilitarians and of 'social justice' as advanced by the collectivists. Undeniable is the fact that the concept of 'desert' has a wide variety of meanings. One may say, for example, that a person is deserving because of his personal character, or because of the status characteristic of some position that he occupies, or one may say that he is deserving due to the performance of certain specially meritorious acts, or because he has hitherto been a victim of misfortune. We may focus upon his work and say that he is deserving, because the work itself is arduous, or dangerous, or is specially valuable in some way. 'All of these are meaningful statements and can be found in both vernacular and scholarly discussions of justice." Scott Gordon: *Welfare, Justice and Freedom* (Columbia: Columbia University Press, 1980), p. 94. So Aristotle in his *Nicomachean Ethics* says that in a just society each man receives relative to others in accordance with his relative merit. *Ibid.* According to Brian Barry, the concept of desert refers to those properties of a man's actions that are "worthy of special treatment". *Political Argument* (London: Routledge and Kegan Paul, 1965), p. 106. The concept of desert can function in a context where it is a question of awarding blame or punishment and in contexts where it is a question of awarding praise or reward. It can function as a specialised consideration in judgements about justice of an allocation or award." Albert Weale: *Political Theory and Social Policy* (London: Macmillan, 1983). p. 159.

95. Gorovitz, *op. cit.*, p. 286.

and foes.[96] Gorovitz has discovered three points of attack: First, the adequacy of the method of Rawls may be questioned in the 'original position'. It is not intelligible in the real sense of the term, or that the veil of ignorance may be immobilising with the result that the negotiators would be unable to make any decision at all. Second, we may ask about the total list of 'primary goods' and their equitable distribution. Might not an ascetic anticipate that an equitable distribution of material goods and power would impose on him more than what suits his own life plan? Last, one may be uncomfortable about the abuse of sustained consideration of the jurisprudential aspects of justice as are reflected in the belief that punishment is appropriate for the guilty but not for the innocent.[97]

Brian Barry has made a critical study of this subject and found that Rawls'theory of justice "will not work and that many of his individual arguments are unsound."[98] There is a certain amount of redundancy with similar arguments coming round several times at different places. It is crammed with arguments and the reader has to refer backward and forward without knowing where he is going."[99] The whole plan is like a maze and one may differ from this argument of Rawls that man is never altruistic.[100] He hovers between a want-regarding and an ideal-regarding situation.[101] Rawls is also not very clear as to what he includes in the connotation of self-respect.[102] He wishes to specify the condition under which inequalities are justified, so we could make no sense of his discussion if we were to understand by inequality as unjustified difference.[103] Another problem is how to earmark the least advantaged individual or group in a society.[104] He offers an exceptionally fragile theory of constitutional engineering. He occasionally glances at the question as to what happens, if it turns out that people do not behave in an ideal way, and support legislation on the basis of self-interest rather than what they believe to be the requirements of justice.[105]

---

96. Some commentators like Stuart Hampshire, G.J. Warnock and Marshall Cohen described this book as 'magisterial', 'a peerless contribution to political theory', and a permanent refutation of the reproach that analytical philosophy cannot contribute to substantial moral and political thought. Even this much was said that its political implications may change our lives, though Gorovitz is of the view that the book may not be properly understood for years and may well become the sort of a classic over which disputes rage for generations. *Ibid.*, pp. 272-73. Doughlas Rae says that it is "perhaps the bravest work of political theory written in this country (USA) since the times of Madison and Calhoun". Refer to his paper titled "Maximum Justice and an Alternative Principle of General Advantage" in the *American Political Science Review* (June, 1975), p 630. Also see B.R. Barber: "Justifying Justice: Problems of Psychology, Measurement and Politics in Rawls" in *American Political Science Review* (June 1975); R.K Fullinwider: "A Chronological Bibliography of Works in John Rawls', Theory of Justice", in *Political Theory,* (London), November 1977, pp. 561-70.
97. Gorovitz, *op. cit.,* pp. 287-88.
98. Brian Barry: *The Liberal Theory of Justice, op. cit.,* p. ix.
99. *Ibid.,* p. 1.
100. *Ibid.,* p. 2.
101. *Ibid.,* p. 24.
102. *Ibid.,* p. 31.
103. *Ibid.,* p. 44.
104. *Ibid.,* p. 49.
105. *Ibid.,* p. 137.

Rawlsian Theory of Justice

Rawls' life-long project has been to present a theory of justice that works out a reasonable and practical philosophical conception for a just constitutional democratic society, a concept that, at the same time, provides a reasonably systematic alternative to utilitarianism.

—**P.B. Lehning**

John Rawls: An Introduction (Cambridge: Cambridge University Press, 2006), p. 16.

But we cannot make the Rawlsian mode of thinking on justice into an intellectual 'standstill'. We have to benefit from the richness of the idea we have got from Eawls and then move on rather than taking a vacation. We do need justitia, not justitium.

—**A.K. Sen**

The Idea of Justice (London: Allen Lane, 2009), p. 74.

The idea of Rawls is to refine the social contract tradition. Justice is conceived to be what persons would agree to under conditions for choosing principles to regulate the basic structure of society that are ideally fair. The original position argument exemplifies a fair proceduralist standard of justification. What is right is what people following an ideal procedure would accept as right.

—**Richard J. Arneson**

"Justice after Rawls" in R.E. Goodin: (ed.): ***The Oxford Handbook of Political Science*** (Oxford: Oxford University Press, 2009), p. 112.

But the theory of Rawls has also been considered as a contribution to the case of substantive social justice, because he persistently stresses that all departures from the norm of equality have to be rationally justified; there is no presumption in favour of equality which contrasts strongly with various versions of the entitlement theory. Such an affirmation may also be designated as his radical egalitarianism, though some may treat it as a particular elegant restatement of the social principles of liberal capitalism. It may also be questioned that in his system the pleasure of the better off, however great, cannot compensate for the pains of the worst off.[106] The collectivist critics of Rawls are particularly concerned about his commitment to the marginal productivity principle of wages; this permits inequalities which they would exclude by reference to other principles of justice. It is true that by describing the problems of justice in terms of what rules would be chosen in a hypothetical state of ignorance, Rawls is departing significantly from the view of justice as a backward-looking concept and seems therefore to sidestep the traditional problems of justifying inequalities."[107]

The Marxists would say, of course, that the idea that the principles of justice "can be demonstrated in the absence of knowledge of economic and social facts is erroneous. Moral systems can be understood only in the context of class relationships and systems of ownership."[108] Some penetrating criticisms of Rawls' theory of justice have come from economic liberals who "see it as a strongly egalitarian doctrine. Specifically, they maintain that although it is a procedural theory of justice, it does

106. Norman P. Barry, *op. cit.*, p. 134.
107. *Ibid.*, p. 136.
108. *Ibid.*

nevertheless pick out a particular end-state; that is, the distribution is just which maximises the well-being of the least advantaged. They also object to the presumption in favour of equality and the assumption that natural assets should constitute a 'common pool' to be distributed according to the principle of social justice."[109]

It is commented that Rawls formulates no theory of state, rather he conceptualises a type of liberal state where his theory of justice becomes workable.[110] The communitarians like Michael Sandel, Michael Walzer, A. MacIntyre and Charles Taylor comment that Rawls thinks of an utterly selfish person who has no obligations towards the community. It is also argued that the norms of justice differ from community to community. Hence, an empirical theory of justice cannot be formulated. In case an abstract or a purely normative theory of justice is formulated, as done by Rawls, it cannot be put into effect. "The weakness of such a notion is that it abstracts the individual from his or her social context and so ignores the contribution which society has made to cultivating individual skills and talents in the first place."[111]

Amartya Sen finds fault with some of the formulations of Rawls. He objects that the individuals born with diferent physical and psychological propensities will generally be unequally efficient transformers of the resources such as primary social goods into whatever goals they might seek.[112] He criticises Rawls for subscribing to the trend of transcendental institutionalism. All individuals cannot be equally 'rational actors' or 'intelligent negotiators' in the 'original position'. That is, the panorama of hypothetical 'original position' may have many forms. As he asserts: "The advancement of justice and the removal of injustice demand joint engagement with institutional choice (dealing among other things with private income and public goods), behavioural adjustments and procedures for the correction of social arrangements based on public discussion of what is promised, how the institutions actually work out, and how things can be improved. There is no leave to shut off interactive public reasoning, resting on the promised virtue of a once-and-for-all market based institutional choice. The social role of institutions, including imaginary ones, is more complex than that."[113]

What is certain, however, is that Rawls has given us a powerful new instrument for illuminating certain important social problems emanating from the basic issue of 'ideal' relationship between liberty and equality and thereby suggested a picture of justice in the liberal society. He has redirected moral and political philosophy in the tradition of Aristotle, Bentham, Mill and Kant and thereby "demonstrated conclusively that lowering achievements in scholarship are not a thing of the past; and this work—analytic but full of substance, rooted in the tradition that novel in approach, abstract in conception yet profound in its practical consequences—constitutes a stunning affirmation of the essential creativity of the human intellect in its ceaseless quest for the understanding of the moral and political dimensions of

109. *Ibid.*
110. R.P. Wolff: *Understanding Rawls* (Princeton: Princeton University Press, 1977), p. 202.
111. Andrew Heywood: *Political Theory: An Introduction*, p. 300.
112. A.K. Sen: *Inequality Re-Examined* (Cambridge, Mass: Harvard University Press, 1992).
113. A.K. Sen: *The Idea of Justice* (London: Allen Lane, 2009), p. 268.

our lives."[114] Robert Nozick has described the book of Rawls as 'a powerful, deep, subtle wide-ranging systematic work in political and moral philosophy' and has gone to the length of saying that now political philosophers "must either work within Rawls' theory, or explain why not: The considerations and distinctions we have developed are illuminated by and help illuminate Rawls' masterful presentation of an alternative conception. Even those who remain unconvinced after wrestling with Rawls' systematic vision will learn much from closely studying it. It is impossible to read Rawls' book without incorporating much, perhaps, transmuted into one's own deepened view. And it is impossible to finish his book without a new and inspiring vision of what a moral theory may attempt to do and write of how *beautiful* a whole theory can be."[115]

Robert Nozick: Entitlement Theory of Justice

Inspired by the great work of John Rawls, Nozick produced his *Anarchy, State and Utopia* in 1974 that was hailed as another notable contribution to the field of liberal political theory. Like Rawls, he is a normativist in offering a procedural theory of justice. If Kant is the inspirer of Rawls, Nozick takes inspiration from Locke. However, both confine their attention to the case of individual good at the expense of public good and, hence, the communitarians accuse them of pleading the case of 'unencumbered self'. Surprisingly, at the hands of Nozick, state is converted into a utopia. The Marxian motto of 'from each according to his capacity, to each according to his need' in the final stage of social development is replaced by Nozick's motto of 'from each as they choose, to each as they are chosen'.

Like Locke, Nozick subscribes to the dogma of natural rights which individual possesses and which cannot be abrogated by the state in the name of anything like public good or social justice. The case of distributive justice or equitable distribution of wealth and rewards is sheer nonsense. What an individual earns or produces by his hard work and by observing the rules of the state, he is entitled for the 'holdings'. He is entitled to his possessions that cannot be taken away by the society or the state in the fictitious name of public interest on any ground whatsoever. For this sake, he suggests three 'justice preserving' rules:[116]

1. Wealth has to be justly acquired. That is, it should not have been stolen and the rights of others should not have been infringed.
2. Wealth has to be justly transferred from one responsible person to another.
3. If wealth has been acquired or transferred unjustly, this injustice should be rectified by the imposition of some penalty on the wrongdoer.

With such arguments, Nozick minimises the role of the state to an extent that it becomes like a 'nightwatchman'. Not only this, he desires its replacement by a token state what he terms 'dominant protective agency'. That is, he desires a new

114. Gorovitz, *op. cit.*, p. 289. Also see R P. Wolff: *Understanding Rawls: A Reconstruction and Critique of the Theory of Justice* (Princeton: Princeton University Press, 1977) and M.J. Sandel: *Liberalism and the Limits of Justice* (Cambridge: Cambridge University Press, 1982).
115. Robert Nozick, *op. cit.*, p. 283. For a comparison of Rawls with Nozick, see M.F. Planner: "The New Political Theory" in *The Political Interest* (Summer, 1975), p. 127.
116. Andrew Heywood, *op. cit.*, p. 299.

form of authority called 'demoktesis'—the highest form of social life or a system in which each person has an equal say (within some specified limits) in the lives of others to the best and fairest imaginable extent. The conclusion is that there is a minimal state limited to the narrow functions of protection against force, theft, fraud, enforcement of contracts, and so on, is justified; any more extensive state will violate persons' rights not to be forced to do certain things, and is unjustified.[117]

Nozick thus arrives at the point of justifying gross inequalities in the distribution of wealth and rewards. It may enable a critic to say that Nozick's minimal state seems to be more of a profit-making enterprise than a political organisation and that he looks like bringing in the 'difference principle' of Rawls through the back door.[118] It may also be attacked in the name of being a proposal to privatise and hence depoliticise virtually all human life.[119] Like Rawls, Nozick becomes a powerful advocate of the case of 'possessive individualism'. His individual is an utterly selfish creature holding as much property as he can, though by legal means, but not at all susceptible to his social obligations. "Individuals are seen to be the possessors of their own talents and capacities, and on this basis they are thought to be morally entitled to own whatever their talents produce. Some would go on to argue further that to treat individuals in this way is, in effect, to reward them for selfishness and actually to promote egotistical behaviour."[120]

Sen on Justice: Omnipresence of Reason in Everyone's Thinking

In Sen one may find a friend as well as a foe of Rawls. He has his starting point in *A Theory of Justice* of Rawls (1971), but his concluding point has its place in the *Political Liberalism* of Rawls (1993) where the element of public reasoning is given utmost importance. And yet one of the principal differences between Sen on the one hand and a number of dominant contemporary theorists like Rawls and Nozick on the other is that they have been concerned primarily, sometimes wholly, with identifying what perfectly just social arrangements might be, rather than clarifying how different realisations of justice might be compared and evaluated. In the case of Sen, the entire focus is on 'reason'. As he affirms: "The requirements of a theory of justice include bringing reason that plays its part in the diagnosis of justice and injustice."[121]

Obviously, in the Kantian fashion, Sen argues that bringing reason to the world becomes the centrepiece of morality rather than metaphysics, and the work as well as the hope of humanity. His arguments may be thus enumerated:[122]

1. He argues against the plausibility of emotions of psychology, or instincts as independent sources of valuation without reasoned appraisal. Impulses and

117. Robert Nozick: *Anarchy, State and Utopia* (Oxford: Basil Blackwell, 1974), p. 290
118. Will Kymlicka: *Contemporary Political Philosophy* (Oxford: Oxford University Press, 2002), p. 104.
119. Prakash Sarangi: *Liberal Theories of State* (New Delhi: Sterling Publishers, 1996), pp. 165 and 168 Also see. Karen Johnson: "Government by Insurance Company: The Anti-Political Philosophy of Robert Nozick" in *Western Political Quarterly,* Vol. 29, 1976, p. 177.
120. Andrew Heywood, *op. cit.,* p. 300.
121. A.K. Sen: *The Idea of Justice,* p. 5.
122. *Ibid.* pp. xvii-xviii

mental attitudes remain important, however, since we have good reasons to take note of them in our assessment of justice and injustice in the world.

2. The particular scepticism of the reach of reasoning does not yield, nor is it intended to yield, any ground for not using reason to the extent one can in pursuing the idea of justice or any other notion of social relevance such as identity.
3. Reasoned discussion can accommodate conflicting positions that may appear to others to be 'unreasoned' prejudice without this being quite the case.
4. The central point in dealing with this question is that prejudices typically ride on the back of some kind of reasoning-weak and arbitrary though it might be. Unreason is mostly not the practice of doing without reasoning altogether, but relying on very primitive and very defective reasoning. Bad reasoning can be confronted by better reasoning.
5. What matters most is the examination of what reasoning would demand for the pursuit of justice includes the possibility that there may exist several different reasonable positions.
6. Reasoning is a robust source of hope and confidence in a world darkened by murky deeds - past and present. Even when we find something immediately upsetting, we can question that response and ask whether it is an appropriate reaction and whether we should really be guided by it. Reasoning can be concerned with the right way of viewing and treating other people, other cultures and other claims, with examining different grounds for respect and tolerance.
7. While it is certainly true that ideology and dogmatic belief can emerge from sources other than religion and custom and have frequently done so, that does not deny the role of reason in assessing the rationale behind instructive attitudes, any less than in the appraisal of arguments presented to justify deliberate policies.
8. The plurality of reasons that a theory of justice has to accommodate relates not only to the diversity of objects of value that the theory recognises as significant, but also to the type of concerns for which this theory may make room, for example, in the importance of different kinds of equality or liberty.
9. Justice is an immensely important idea that has moved people in the past and will continue to move them in the future. And reasoning and critical scrutiny can indeed offer much to extend the reach and to sharpen the concept. And yet it would be a mistake to expect that every decisional problem for which the idea of justice might conceivably be relevant would, in fact, be resolved through reasoned scrutiny.
10. The distribution of the benefits of global relations depends not only on 'domestic policies', but also on a variety of international social arrangements including trade agreements, patent laws, global health initiatives, international educational provisions, facilities for technological dissemination, ecological and environmental restraint, treatment of accumulated debts (often incurred by irresponsible military rulers of the past) and the restraining of conflicts and local wars.

At the heart of Sen's argument is the insistence on the role of public reason in establishing what can make societies less unjust. But it is in the nature of reasoning about justice that it does not allow all questions to be settled even in theory, there are choices to be faced between alternative assessments of what is reasonable and several different and compelling positions can each be well defended. Far from rejecting such pluralities or trying to reduce them beyond the limits of reasoning, we should make use of them to construct a theory of justice that can absorb different points of view. Concerns about the principles of justice in the modern world must avoid parochialism and further address questions of global injustice.[123]

Justice is really a contested concept. Its precise and universally acceptable definition cannot be formulated. Hence, like Plato, Rawls, and Nozick, Sen's theory of justice may be criticised for having some inadequacies. He lays all stress on 'public reasoning' that may be plural or diverse, but he nowhere spells out its implications. He looks like working out a theory of justice with emphasis on collective consensus and universal human rationality without taking into account the fact that conflict is endemic in every given situation and individual choices are of an infinite plurality. He uses the term 'justice' in a broad sense with the twin purpose of enhancing justice and removing injustice without providing the means to deal with specific problems and issues.[124]

Dworkin: Idea of Equality of Resources and Distributional Justice

While Rawls uses the perspective of resources in his principles of justice through the index of primary or basic social goods, effectively ignoring the conversion variations between resources and capacities, Dworkin's use of the resources perspective "is to make room explicitly for taking note of these variations through artful market-oriented thinking in pacticular by the use of an imagined primordial market for insurance against conversion handicaps.[125]

Equality is a 'sovereign virtue' at the hands of Dworkin having its confluence with the Rawlsian theory of justice in its own right.[126] It may be construed as an elaboration of the Rawlsian 'difference principle' with the view of making its rectification. He asks us to imagine that all resources of the society "are up for sale in an auction, to which everyone is a participant. Everyone starts with an equal amount of purchasing power, 160 clamshells for example - and people use their clamshells to bid for those resources that best suit their plan of life."[127]

Such an arrangement would be like an 'envy test'. "If the auction works out - and it can always be rerun if it does not - everyone will be happy with the result in the sense that they do not prefer anyone else's bundle of goods to their own. If they did prefer a different bundle, they could have bid for it, rather than the goods they did bid for.[128] One may invest his money in developing a colony, the other may do so in making himself a fine player of tennis or cricket with the help of one's resources.

123. *Ibid.*, p. 401

124. Review article of Subroto Mukherjee in *The Statesman* (New Delhi), 9 December, 2009.

125. Amartya Sen: *The Idea of Justice.* p. 264.

126. Ronald Dworkin: *Sovereign Virtue: The Theory and Practice of Equality* (Cambridge, Mass: Harvard University Press, 2000).

127. Will Kymlicka, *op. cit.*, p. 75.

128. *Ibid.*

So no question of mutual envy arises. Each will prefer his own 'bundle of goods' to anyone else. In such a situation all people "are treated with equal consideration, for differences between them simply reflect their different ambitions, their different beliefs about what gives value to life. A successful auction meets the 'envy test' and makes each person pay for the costs of their own choices."[129]

A sort of parallelism may be established between the difference principle of Rawls and the idea of equality of resources of Dworkin. In other words, if the idea of Dworkin is put into effect, it would amount to the fulfilment of three main aims of the Rawlsian theory-"respecting the moral equality of persons, mitigating the arbitrariness of natural or social contingencies, and accepting responsibility for our choices. Such a distribution scheme would be just even though it allows some inequality in income."[130]

Like Rawls, Dworkin subscribes to the case of distributive justice, though with a difference. While the former justifies the case of affirmative action of the state for the minimisation of economic inequality so that everyone has some income as an element of basic or primary social goods, the latter pleads the case of state assistance the naturally disadvantaged or handicapped persons. Compensation should be awarded to persons having 'bad luck' before the auction takes place and then the social imbalance should be corrected by the schemes of insurance, taxation and redistribution of national wealth. Any material assistance before the occurrence of the auction coupled with the devised plans of graduated taxation and social insurance "would harbinge the situation of equality as far as possible. Heavy taxation on the naturally advantaged persons would ensure that everyone is equally able to choose and pursue a valuable life plan; equal division of resources within the auction ensures that their choices are fairly treated. Hence, the distribution would be both endowment-insensitive and ambition-sensitive."[131]

Such assertions constitute the case of, what is now called, 'luck egalitarianism.' It looks like an exercise in the direction of blending the idea of divine or natural justice with that of egalitarianism or social justice as espoused by the positive liberals of the last century like Laski and Tawney. It is certainly haunted by the ghost of liberal socialism and thereby discards the merit of the role of 'invisible hand' as stressed by Adam Smith. A person with a humanitarian viewpoint may argue that the rich (lucky) should be heavily taxed for the sake of the poor (unlucky) people, but a humanist would like to bind such an argument with the tag of hard work and enterprise. As Kymlicka says: "Given this distance between the ideal and the practice, it is inevitable that some people are undeservedly penalised for their unfortunate circumstances, while others are undeservedly subsidised for the costs of their choices."[132] "Likewise, Arneson argues that the idea that we might adjust our distributive justice system based on our estimation of persons' overall deservingness or responsibility seems entirely chimerical. Individuals do not display responsibility scores on their foreheads, and the attempt by institutions or individuals to guess the

129. *Ibid.*
130. *Ibid.*,
131. *Ibid.*, p. 81.
132. *Ibid.*, p. 81

Luck Egalitarianism

The fundamental aim of equality is to compensate people for undeserved bad luck. Luck egalitarianism relies on two moral premises: that people should be compensated for undeserved misfortunes, and that the compensation should come only from the part of others' good fortune that is undeserved.

—P.B. Lehning

John Rawls: An Introduction, p. 63.

Social justice demands a differential response to bad luck, depending on how it arises. A complication here is that each person's initial genetic endowment of propensities to traits along with his or her early socialisation is evidently a matter of unchosen and uncourted luck, good or bad.

—R.J. Arneson

"Justice after Rawls" in R.E. Goodin (ed.):

The Oxford Handbook of Political Science, p. 121.

If our goal is to achieve greater ex-ante equality in endowments, we need to directly attack the entrenched economic hierarchies of modern societies which disadvantage the poor, women or racial minorities.

—Will Kymlicka

Contemporary Political Philosophy, p. 89.

scores of people they are dealing with would surely dissolve in practice into giving vent to one's prejudices and piques."[133]

Justice and Scientific Value Relativism: Empirical Determination of the Ideal of Justice

Justice is widely regarded as one of the celebrated normative concepts. But the question arises as to whether it can be subjected to the doctrine of scientific investigation. In other words, can we establish a logical link between a normative concept like that of justice and the doctrine of scientific value relativism which holds that the question whether something is 'valuable' can be answered scientifically only (1) in relation to some goal or purpose for the pursuit of which it is or is not useful (valuable), or to (2) the ideas held by some person or group of persons regarding what is or is not valuable; and that consequently, it is impossible to establish scientifically what goals or purposes are valuable irrespective of the (a) value they have in the pursuit of other goals or purposes, or (b) of someone's ideas about ulterior or ultimate goals or purposes.[134] In other words, it insists that references to ultimate goals or purposes of human life must be debarred as evidence from scientific discussion except in quite hypothetical terms.[135]

133. Richard Arneson: "Egalitarian Justice versus the Right to Privacy" in *Social Philosophy and Policy,* Vol. 17, No. 2, 2000, p. 97. The idea of 'luck egalitarianism' seeks to integrate equality with responsibility. Hence, it is called 'responsibilitarianism'. As such, luck egalitarianism holds that variations in the levels of advantage held by different persons (that is, inequality) are justified if, and only if, facts about those persons' choices or opportunities have made them responsible for those variations. One of the most important things to notice about such statements is the defining role given to both equality and responsibility. Carl Knight: *Luck Egalitarianism*(Edinburgh: Edinburgh University Press, 2009), p. 169.

134. Brecht, *op. cit.,* pp. 117-18.

135. *Ibid.,* p. 125.

If so, it seems improbable that the ideal of justice can be linked with the doctrine of scientific value relativism. And yet we may discover the possibilities of connection between the two in the following important directions:

1. In spite of the fact that the term'justice'carries different connotations to different persons at different times and in different places (that makes it a matter of confusion), a scientific study of the subject may authentically illustrate their broad dimensions and, more than that, which of them are acceptable to most of the people at a given time and place. For instance, on the basis of a scientific investigation we may say that in modern times the doctrine of positive justice has outplaced the theory of metaphysical justice as it prevailed during the Middle Ages. An empirical study may drive home that different ideas of justice may prevail even within the same category of persons at several levels, at different times, and even, at the same time, according to whether existing constitutions are either accepted or criticised, and if the latter, according to whether criticism follows group opinions or the like, or is original.[136]
2. In particular, we may take up the case of distributive justice and link it up with the presentation of an empirical study of the same. For instance, we may collect data about the state of national economy, i.e., per capita income, gross and net national dividend, distribution of national wealth and the like and then come to formulate schemes for the redistribution of national wealth so as to eliminate the wider economic disparities. It is on this basis that we may distinguish between 'liberal-democratic' and 'socialist' systems of the world. Economic justice is, therefore, less a normative and more an empirical concept whose nature and conclusions can be put to scientific investigations.
3. On the basis of a scientific examination we may prove that most of the people take, or do not take, a particular situation as 'just' and that such and such consequences flow out of a state of injustice. Thus, Aristotle could say that the cause of sedition lay in 'inequality' that was another name for 'injustice'. In this way, scientific method can do much help in clarifying the meaning of the premises of justice and injustice in different situations and the implied consequences of each.

It may, however, be pointed out in this connection that while the application of scientific method can lead to an empirical determination of justice in one or of injustice in a converse situation, it has its own limitations. For instance, an empirical investigation cannot tell us about the ultimate or superior value of one form of justice over another. Thus, a pertinent question arises: if justice can be discussed by science only in relative terms, how then can one any longer call with any certainty of language for more justice beyond the deficient existing institutions, how even oppose, with an appeal to justice, any deterioration? In this way, the application of scientific method in the determination of the value of justice throws people into 'a state of bewilderment, into a feeling of helplessness'.[137] And yet we may say: "Granted that there are many particular ideas of justice among which science cannot

136. *Ibid.*, p. 161.
137. *Ibid.*, p. 157.

make any authentic choice, there may in all such ideas be some universal elements that can be scientifically ascertained."[138]

Critical Appreciation

What we have seen so far leaves an impression that justice is essentially a normative concept having its place in various spheres like religion, ethics and law, though its ramifications cover social, political and economic spheres as well. So great is the diversity of its connotations that it becomes difficult to formulate its precise meaning. It is, however, for the sake of convenience that justice is necessarily related with the function of judicial organisations. In this direction too, the problem has its own ramifications by virtue of different, even conflicting, interests of the people. This is the reason that the task of modern age has become increasingly complex. Hardly any major decision "can be made without a careful evaluation of the conflicting values and interests."[139]

Even if we extract the meaning of justice from metaphysical and hypothetical connotations and stick strictly to its 'positive' dimension, the problem remains a baffling one on account of diametrically opposite notions of the liberals and the totalitarians. We have already seen that justice takes a form and character of its own in a totalitarian state whether under the Fascists or the Communists. It is on account of this that while the meaning of justice remains highly fluid in a liberal-democratic order, it assumes a particular variety of its own on account of being a dictated affair by the men of power in a totalitarian system. Even if we confine our attention to the case of positive justice in a liberal-democratic order, the difficulty remains and it cannot be said with full certainty whether the administration of justice should be bound with adherence to precedence or not. Moreover, to say that adherence to precedence should be determined by the rule of social necessity is once again to commit the error by involving the idea of justice into a debate over the nature and meaning of social urgency. In order to get out of the wriggled situation, a man of normative orientation may hardly do anything else than depend upon the observation of Cardozo that the court "best serves the law which recognises that the rule of law grew up in a remote generation may serve another generation badly and it ought not to tie, in helpless submission, the hands of successors."[140]

In the end, however, instead of delving deep into the debate over the perplexing connotations of justice, it shall be worthwhile to say that it is the connecting bond of all important political values. For instance, there can be no liberty if the norm of equality is violated and there can be no equality if there is no justice. Obviously, justice is integrally connected with the norms of liberty and equality. Likewise, we may say that there can be no liberty if there are no rights and that there can be no protection of the rights if there is no well-organised system of law so as to ensure proper administration of justice. Obviously, once again, the idea of justice is essentially bound up with the concepts of rights and law. The most important

138. *Ibid.*, p. 162.

139. Friedman, *op. cit,*, p. 67.

140. Benjamin Cardozo, *op. cit.*, p. 152.

point to be taken note of at this stage is that not only the ideal of justice is integrally connected with the norms of law, liberty, equality and rights, but it also constitutes the essential link. Justice, in this sense, is the reconciler and synthesiser of political values.[141] Daniel Webster is perfectly right when he says that justice "is the chiefest interest of man."[142]

141. Barker: *Principles of Social and Political Theory*, p. 102.

142. See Mukherjl, *op. cit.*, p. 29.

12

Political Obligation

> We know the morality we have received from our fathers as a collection of dogmas or useful prejudices adopted by the national reason. But for this we owe nothing to the particular reason of any individual. On the contrary, whenever such reason intervenes, it perverts morality. In politics we know we must respect authority, established we know not how nor by whom. When time brings abuse capable of altering the principles of government, we know we must suppress the abuse without touching the principles of government.
>
> **—Joseph de Maistre[1]**

Why do men obey the State? Why should they obey authority? When and under what circumstances should they register their disobedience? These are some of the important questions hinging on the issue of relationship between a legitimate political order and an enlightened citizenship. An answer to such questions has been given by a good number of thinkers and statesmen in different ways with the result that the scope of diversity ranges from the conclusions of rank idealists who have sought its solution in the inherently good nature of man to the emphatic affirmations of the pragmatists who have found the same in the world of actual experiences whereby we may determine the worth and legitimacy of the actions of the men-in-authority roles. In particular, this problem pertains to the realm of liberal political theory where we find that a host of eminent thinkers are in a 'dilemma' of how to reconcile the area of individual liberty with the scope of state authority. The baffling problem before them is either to reject the 'possessive individualist assumptions' in which case the theory of political obligation becomes unrealistic, or to retain them in which case a valid doctrine in this regard becomes unavailable. It follows that we "cannot now expect a valid theory of obligation to a liberal-democratic state in a possessive market society."[2]

Meaning and Nature

The term 'obligation' originates from a Latin word *'obligate'* implying something that binds men to an engagement of performing what is enjoined. If so, it has its various connotations. For instance, in the realm of ethics it informs a man to fulfil or discharge a duty enjoined on him and acceptable to him by his rational understanding. In the field of jurisprudence, it requires a man to obey law by which he is tied to some 'performance'. Since law regulates the social life of men, the principle of legal

1. Cited in Benn and Peters: *Social Principles and the Democratic State* (London: George Allen and Unwin, 1975), p. 308.
2. C.B. Macpherson: *The Political Theory of Possessive Individualism: Hobbes to Locke* (London: Oxford Univ. Press, 1977), p. 275.

obligation takes the form of a bond between 'private persons' tied to one another for the performance of some act as desired by the enforcement of law. Finally, in the world of politics, it takes the form of a bond between man as a citizen and the authority under which he lives "to perform an act, or a number of acts, for the governing authority."[3] In other words, it implies that when man is a political creature, he is bound to live under some authority, it becomes his obligation to obey its commands. Hence, when "the authorising rule is a law, and the association a state, we call this political obligation".[4]

Obviously, the idea of political obligation or acceptance of the commands of the 'men-in-authority roles' is integrally connected with the pattern of man's life in an organised whole. We may say that there can be no life if there is no order; and since order implies obedience, we may also say that there can be no order if there is no acceptance of it. As people cannot play the game of cricket without obeying the rulings of an umpire, so they cannot live without accepting the commands of the persons charged with the job of maintaining peace and order in the society. Obviously, the principle of political obligation is based on the maxim of common prudence. As Benn and Peters observe: "Of course, there are plenty of good reasons for accepting authority in general (though they may not always apply in particular). We are often in situations where it is more important to accept an umpire's judgement than to insist on our own. An army will usually do better even with bad generals than with no generals at all. We accept authority because most social enterprises would be hopeless without it."[5]

It follows that the case of political obligation rests upon issues relating to the nature of authority that involves within its fold the whole word of existing rights, laws and political organisation generally. If so, a wider interpretation of the same covers the opposite situation in which people have a legitimate claim for the disobedience of authority. As a matter of fact, it "is the enterprise that counts ; the authority is conditional on the way it promotes or preserves it."[6] The people not only obey the laws of the state or 'the commands of the sovereign', they also scrutinise those orders in terms of the satisfactions they seek from life and, from time to time, they reject them on the ground that they are a denial of those satisfactions. "Obedience, that is to say, is the normal habit of mankind; but marginal cases continually recur in which the decision to disobey is painfully taken and passionately defended."[7] If so, the idea of political obligation inheres these essential characteristics:

1. Government is a difficult art and any wrong move may entail serious consequences. Therefore, it is the duty of every conscientious person to interest himself seriously in the management of public affairs, i.e. in political questions. It is required that those placed in high offices should direct their thought and action to the general good. Political obligations are not merely of an intellectual character; they also involve obligations of honesty and, what is called, public spirit or social service.

3. E. Barker: *Principles of Social and Political Theory* (London: Oxford Univ. Press. 1967), p. 184.
4. Benn and Peters, *op. cit.*, p. 298.
5. *Ibid.*, p. 329.
6. Laski: *The State in Theory and Practice* (London: George Allen and Unwin, 1960). p. 17.
7. *Ibid.*

Political Obligation

If Swaraj is not meant to civilise us, and to purify and stabilise our civilisation, it would be worth nothing. The very essence of our civilisation is that we give a paramount place to morality in all our affairs, public or private.

—**M.K. Gandhi**
Young India, 23 January, 1930, p. 26.

Political obligation denotes not a duty to obey a particular law but rather the citizen's duty to respect and obey the state itself. When the limits of political obligation are reached, the citizen is not merely released from a duty to obey, but in effect gains an entitlement: the right to rebel.

—**Andrew Heywood**
Political Theory: An Introduction, p. 202.

From the ancient world to the present day, all forms of citizenship have had certain common attributes. Citizenship has meant a certain reciprocity of rights against, and duties towards, the community.

—**David Held**
Political Theory and the Modern State. p. 199.

2. The concept of political obligation automatically involves the case of political legitimacy and effectiveness. While political effectiveness implies actual performance, the extent to which the political system provides for the performance of the basic functions of government as the people and powerful groups in society perceive them, the case of political legitimacy refers to the capacity of the system to engender and maintain the belief that the existing social institutions are the most appropriate for the society.
3. The idea of political obligation not only informs people to obey the authority of those in power, it also desires them to be critical about the way authority is exercised. They should scrutinise the actions of their rulers and resent in the event of an invasion on their liberties. Thus, the idea of political obligation also involves the idea of resistance to authority. As we shall see, even great liberals like Locke, Green and Laski have recognised the circumstances under which people may demonstrate their resistance and go to the extent of changing the political order.

The whole case of political obligation may be thus summed up: "There are good grounds for accepting authority in general, but there may be good grounds too for rejecting it in particular cases; if authority derives from a constitution, there would generally be good grounds for rejecting any exercise of it which is unconstitutional. Again, if its legitimacy depends on the way it is used, an invasion of a sphere where political authority is inappropriate might be grounds for disobedience or, in extreme cases, for resistance."[8]

8. Benn and Peters, *op. cit.,* p. 329.

Divine Theory: Sanction of Political Obligation in the Matters of Faith

Various theories have been enunciated on the subject of political obligation, the oldest of which finds its place in the religious doctrines whereby the source of obedience to the commands of men in authority is traced in the matters of faith. Upon this theory the necessity which "stands above and apart from the citizen and the governing authority is that of the Divine Will and ordinance. I am obliged to obey the governing authority because I am obliged to obey God and because any governing authority is essentially an emanation and delegation of divine authority."[9] The authority of the ruler "stems not simply from inheritance according to custom, or from popular acclamation; these are regarded as the consequences rather than the grounds of authority. The true source is divine, and his authority is, therefore, independent both of human choice and custom."[10]

Such a doctrine had its emphatic affirmation in the teachngs of the Bible. St. Paul said that the authority of the prince 'comes from God' and St. Thomas made a slight improvement upon this rule by adding that a ruler 'who fails to act faithfully, as the office of kingship demands, in the government of a community, deserves to suffer the consequences that his subjects should refuse to keep their pact with him.' It implied that the king as the head of a body politic had a claim to the necessary obedience of each member of that body by virtue of an authority coming from God, but coming in is own course, through the body politic of which he was head.[11] Its powerful defence is contained in the *True Law of Free Monarchies* in which King James I of England claims that the ruler has derived his authority directly from God. Even if he be wicked, the subjects have no right to rebel against him. The people are thus bound by the religious injunction to obey the authority of the king. To quote his forcible words: "Kings are justly called gods; for they exercise a manner of resemblance of divine power on earth. As it is atheism and blasphemy to dispute what God can do, so it is presumption and high contempt in a subject to dispute what the king can do or say that a king cannot do this or that."

The idea of 'divine rights of kings' prevailed throughout the Middle Ages. It, however, took a different direction with the advent of new learning. With the fall of Papacy a new consciousness developed. It signified that if the king had his divine rights, the people had their divine rights too. The new awareness informed that if God had instituted government because men needed it, it also followed that divine authorisation depended on king's governing in the interest of his subjects. The appeal to divine rights as made by the rulers thus became an inconclusive affair. The theory that authority is divinely instituted became modified so as to mean that it did not exclude the possibility that under some conditions God would authorise resistance too. "Obligation may be primarily to oneself, or to another, or to one's country, or to all mankind; but it must ultimately be to God. It was inconceivable that there could be any obligation merely to man. For this reason, and for no other, it may be said that all right is divine."[12] On this understanding it may follow that

9. Barker, *op. cit.,* p. 184.
10. Benn and Peters, *op. cit.,* p. 301.
11. Barker, *op. cit.* p. 185.
12. Benn and Peters, *op. cit.,* pp. 301-02.

even "the right to rebel is a divine right, arising from a breach of obligation unless, indeed, rebellion be conceived as a positive duty . . . . as it was by Knox."[13]

Since the time divine theory of political obligation found its sanction in matters of faith, it has lost its significance in the modern age. It received scathing criticism at the hands of eminent thinkers like Grotius, Hobbes and Locke who rejected its metaphysical premises and traced the source of political obligation in the consent of the people. The growing trend of secularism meant separation of the church from the state and consequently led to the supremacy of the temporal power as distinct from its spiritual counterpart. Moreover, the growth of democracy also entailed the doom of this theory. It was denounced as a convenient tool in the hands of the rulers to justify their absolute authority. Under the new conditions of the modern age, the divine theory of political obligation lost its place of honour. "If men are disposed to doubt, they want reasons related to their situation, rather than dogmatic assertions that everything is as it ought to be. Any approach to political obligation that left no room for discussion in the light of the particular situation might confirm the faith of the faithful; it could not convince the doubter."[14]

Consent Theory: Sanction of Political Obligation in the Will of the People

As pointed out above, the divine theory was replaced by the consent theory which underlined that "in its simpler form, the citizen is tied to the governing authority, first, because he in common with all other citizens, has made a contract with a person or body of persons, under which that person or body receives authority in return for the protection and service of declaring and enforcing a system of legal rules, and, secondly, because he and his fellows are bound by natural law to respect and perform the terms of that contract."[15] This theory is based on the hypothesis of a contract entered into by men living in the 'state of nature' whereby political authority came into being. Thus, the authority of the state is based on the consent of the people. The terms of that contract were morally binding on those who made the compact; now these are equally binding on their successors. Thus, political authority is based on the consent of the people.

The idea of social contract found its emphatic affirmation in the works of Hobbes and Locke of England in the seventeenth century and then in the works of Rousseau of France in the following century. Though the views of the three great social contractualists differ in matters of detail, they adopt the same framework so as to prove the contractual nature of the origin and establishment of political authority. The common point is that political authority is derived from a contract whereby the people are collectively bound to obey it so long as the government works for the general good and keeps itself within limits laid down in the compact. It has its best illustration in these words of Locke: 'No one can be subjected to the political power of another, without his own consent.'[16]

13. J.W. Allen: *A History of Political Thought in the Sixteenth Century,* pp. 122-23.
14. Benn and Peters, *op. cit.,* p. 303.
15. Barker, *op. cit.,* p. 188.
16. John Locke: *Second Treatise of Civil Government,* Sec. 95.

The idea of social contract, however, took a highly philosophical form at the hands of Rousseau who reposed the fact of political obligation in the 'general will'. He says: "The passage from the state of nature to the civil state produces a very remarkable change in man by substituting justice for instinct in his conduct, and giving his actions the morality they had formerly lacked. Then only when the voice of duty takes the place of physical impulses and right of appetite, does man, who so far had considered only himself, finds that he is forced to act on different principles, and to consult his reason before listening to his inclinations."[17] Thus, after entering into the civil society, man is no longer the slave of his mere impulses of appetite; he becomes bound to obey the law of the general good (called general will) which he prescribes to all, including himself, and that constitutes his real liberty.[18] Obviously, the authority is legitimate and it is entitled to commanding the obedience of all so long as it is based on the great moral idea—general will—in obeying which man obeys himself alone and thus remains as free in the civil society as he was in the state of nature.[19]

On the whole, the social contract theory justifies the conception that the ruling authority, if it has to be legitimate, must rest ultimately on the consent of the governed. If the government violates the terms of the contract, the people have a right to resist. If the authorities fail, 'the people have with them the reserved ultimate determination to themselves which belongs to all mankind, where there lies no appeal on earth, by a law antecedent and paramount to all positive laws of men, whether they have just cause to make their appeal to Heaven.'[20] In other words, "all men must reserve the right as moral persons to decide for themselves when all else fails then whether their duty is to accept the command of the sovereign, or challenge them. In this way, this theory admits the legitimacy of authority, then, only when it satisfies certain moral criteria."[21]

Though the consent theory had its field day in the seventeenth and eighteenth centuries and even now has its own significance on account of constituting the moral basis of a democratic order, it suffers from certain grave weaknesses. For instance, it makes state an artificial organisation and thereby puts a heavy premium on the reverence that it is entitled to by virtue of being a natural association. It may also be said that the element of consent as enshrined in some contract made in a hypothetical state of nature is nothing else than a fiction not at all legally binding on the existing generations. Thus, the people may go to the extent of staging a rebellion on the plea that they withdraw their consent inasmuch as the government has committed such an action in violation of the 'general will'. The result is that a theory of political obligation is converted into a theory of rebellion. However, the weight of the influence of this theory, in general, "has been in the direction of safeguarding the rights and liberties of the people and of checking the arbitrariness of rulers. It has also engendered a general irreverence towards the State because of

17. Rousseau: *Social Contract*, Book I, Sec. 8.
18. *Ibid.*
19. *Ibid.*
20. Locke, *op. cit.*
21. Benn and Peters, *op. cit.*, p. 328.

its assumption that the state is an artificial creation and the governmental authority is a restraint upon man's natural freedom."[22]

Prescriptive Theory: Sanction of Political Obligation in Reverence to the Established Conventions

According to this theory, both political authority and reverence to it are based on the principle of 'customary rights'. It is the fact of long possession that ripens into an institution wherein lie the source of its 'legitimacy'. As the authority of the ruler has its source in the fact of prescriptive possession, so the fact of popular obedience has its sanction in reverence to the institutions of the past. On the basis of an analogy between the family and the state, Jean Bodin says that as the authority of the patriarch (head of the family) is based on the fact of historical-prescription, so the authority of the king (head of the state) finds its source in the fact of long possession. An established practice has a significance of its own in view of the fact that it embodies the 'wisdom' of the past. The people obey their rulers because the fact of obedience has become like a well-established convention. It may also be called 'traditionalist theory' inasmuch as, according to it, "all authority is legitimate if it is sanctioned by custom; no further question need be asked."[23]

The conservative theory of political obligation, as it may be called, has its affirmation in the writings of Hegel who ascribed to it a metaphysical dimension. His *Philosophy of Right* has an importance of its own in this direction. Here he says that the idea of morality "evolves concretely in the customs and institutions of nation-states ; the established order is justified as the latest stage in this historical process. The individual as a particular manifestation of the social whole has carried out the whole of his duty when he has done what society expects one in his station. The only valid standards are those conventionally accepted from which, therefore, criticism must necessarily begin, if indeed it can begin at all."[24] Paraphrasing the idea of this great German idealist, Prof. Bradley in England said: "We should consider whether the encouraging oneself in having opinions of one's own, in the sense of thinking differently from the world on moral subjects, be not, in any person other than a heaven-born prophet, sheer self-conceit."[25]

It is, however, Edmund Burke in whom the theory of 'self-concious conservatism' assumes the concrete form of 'cult of the past'. As a matter of fact, his *Reflections on the Revolution in France* are not as much a proof of his attack on the advocates of a new social and political order emulating the case of French Revolution as a powerful defence of every well-established system. According to this view, we revere tradition and every tradition has a 'divine' character on account of being a long-established possession. The fact of political obligation is contained in paying unflinching respect to tradition that is a sacrosanct affair. In simple terms, it seeks to conserve whatever there is in existence by virtue of a very long prescription. Thus, the followers of Burke "may defend this or that institution from time to time; here

22. E. Asirvatham: *Political Theory* (Lucknow: Upper India Publishing House, 1961), p. 48:
23. Benn and Peters, *op. cit.*, p. 307.
24. *Ibid.*, p. 311.
25. F.H. Bradley: *Ethical Studies* (London: Oxford University Press, 1927), p. 200.

monarchy, there property-owning democracy, here an established religion, there an ancient constitution."[26]

Mention, in this direction, may be made of Prof. Michael Oakeshott who traces the source of political obligation in the weight of tradition.[27] We are all creatures of an age and environment in which we live and, for this reason, if we are able to engage ourselves in a political activity at all, we must take for granted at least some of the rules and traditions which delimit it as a specific activity. Political reflection, then, cannot exist in advance of political activity, and a political ideology must be understood 'not as an independently premeditated beginning for political activity but as a knowledge in 'an abstract and generalised form' elsewhere styled by him as "abridgement of a traditional manner of attending to the arrangements of a society'. Thus, politics is'a pursuit of intimations'. If all political action consists in working out the intimations of a tradition, the source of political obligation should be discovered in people's habit of revering their traditions. If so, to this arch-philosopher of conservatism, there "is nothing outside tradition, nothing it seems can ever be lost to it, nor anything really added. Tradition has everything—all its parts and all its details—and everything continues."[28]

Like other theories on this subject, the prescriptive theory has its own weaknesses. We may say that the source of political obligation lies not only in paying reverence to the well-established practices of the realm but also in doing away with them. People desire change and in case there is frustration of their hopes, they take to the path of revolution. However, the peculiar thing about the advocates of this theory, particularly Oakeshott, is that they treat even revolution as an experience connected with the past and thereby make it a purely conservative affair. The exponents of this theory, for instance, would advise the Negroes of the African countries to accept racial segregation laws as 'legitimate', for they are based on the 'well-established traditions of the realm'. In practice, it would never happen. People observe their traditions so long as they have their utility, they resort to break them down when their usefulness is no longer existent. What a critic like Randhir Singh has written about the fallacies of the traditionalism of Oakeshott is applicable to this theory as well that such utterances "not only emphasise the very futility of their argument but, in fact, question the very assumption of human capacity to solve problems of human existence."[29]

Idealistic Theory: Sanction of Political Obligation in Innate Rationality of Man

The idealists trace the source of political obligation in the innate rationality of man. It can be visualised in their tendency to regard man as a 'political and rational creature' and the state as 'a self-sufficing community' identical with the whole society. As such, there can be no antithesis between the individual and the state. Right from Plato and Aristotle to Green and Bosanquet, the same line of argument runs through. The life of the individual isolated from his fellow beings is like a life against nature. In

26. H.M. Drucker: *The Political Uses of Ideology* (London: Macmillan, 1974), p. 117.
27. See Oakeshott: *Rationalism in Politics and Other Essays* (London: Methuen, 1962).
28. See Randhir Singh: *Reason, Revolution and Political Theory* (Delhi: People's Pub., 1976), p. 137.
29. *Ibid.*, p. 134.

consequence, an individual can seek his best possible development in society alone. That is, it is by living in society and by obeying the commands of the state that he can realise all that he has in him to be, only by an intercourse with his fellows. It is by the realisation of social duties and the fulfilment of public obligations that he can develop his full life. "Since the state is regarded as representing and containing within itself all the individual's social aspirations, and at the same time fulfilling all his social needs, whatever claims the state may make upon the individual are held to be based upon absolute authority."[30]

In other words, the source of political obligation is contained in obedience to the state which is not an alien entity. So closely man's life is identified with his state that the two become one. Hence, obedience to one's will and the same to an act of the state become alike. Both Plato and Aristotle affirmed that the state and the individuals composing it "form an organic whole, for the state is as natural to man as the family or the clan; it is as natural as water to a fish, the medium without which human faculties can never come to their full compass." Hence, there may arise no situation of conflict between the individual and the state. Paraphrasing the same idea, Rousseau says that the state is like a form of association which defends and protects the person and property of each member with the whole force of the community and in which each while joining hands with all, still obeys none but himself and thereby remains as free as he was before the creation of the 'community'.[31]

Such an affirmation finds its best manifestation at the hands of Hegel who identifies the 'liberty' of the individual with his perfect obedience to the state. As he says: "Nothing short of the state is the actualisation of freedom. If the individual has a real will and a personality of his own, it is because of his membership of the state. The relations which determine his social life make him an integral part of the society and thereby inform him to render complete obedience to the state. The state represents the totality of the wills of its citizens in the form of its General Will in which the will and personality of each member are made to transcend themselves. Naturally, when the individual receives his rights from the state, he can have no rights which conflict with those of the state. It, therefore, follows that the actions of the State in so far as they proceed from the General Will, must always be irreproachably right in the sense that they represent what is best in individual wills. . . . The state can never act unrepresentatively."[32]

In spite of the fact that Green follows the line of English liberalism, he follows into the footsteps of Hegel when he says that laws and political institutions are the constituent elements of conventional morality, the external embodiment of the moral idea. The idea of political obligation is, for this reason, connected with the case of moral obligation. Green suggests that only those actions should be made obligations which are made to serve a certain moral end. This then is the ground and principle of legal obligations and forms its content.[33] It is, however, a different matter that Green fails to shake off the weight of English liberalism when he comes to recognise

30. Joad, *op.cit.*, p. 10.
31. Rousseau: *Social Contract*, Book I, Chapter VI.
32. Joad, *op. cit.* p. 13.
33. Frank Thakurdas: *The English Utilitarians and the Idealists* (Delhi: Vishal Pub., 1978), p. 254.

the right of resistance to political authority in a certain exceptional situation. The yardstick, however, remains the same. It is the 'General Will' that informs individual to obey the state ; it is the same that sanctions resistance to its authority.

Bernard Bosanquet, however, takes a line close to Hegel's than that of Green. As he says: "Any system of institutions which represent to us on the whole the condition essential to affirming such a will, in objects of action such as to constitute to tolerably complete life, has an imperative claim upon our loyalty and obedience as the embodiment of our liberty."[34] And yet the influence of the liberal tradition has its indelible impact on his mind when he seeks to discover some limitations on the principle of political obligation. The only question is whether a particular system is what it pretends to be, viz. does it adequately guarantee the conditions under which our rational will finds full affirmation. For it is not, our obedience becomes conditional; obligation to political authority may be converted into its opposite ; the moral obligation as Green had shown to resist. Like Green, Bosanquet "places the imperative claim of our real will above the claim to obedience of any particular political system, which fails to give adequate expression to it, or lay down conditions for its affirmation."[35]

The idealistic theory of political obligation, as we may easily visualise, is too abstract. It looks like placing ordinary things in a highly philosophical, even metaphysical, form that cannot be understood by a man of average understanding. Thus, William James comments that it all looks like a rationalistic philosophy that keeps itself out of all definite touch with 'concrete facts and joys and sorrow'. The idea of political obligation is not only concerned with man's obedience to the state, it is also integrally connected with his right to resist the abuse of political authority. The Idealists do not like to accommodate the right to resistance in their doctrine of political obligation and if Green and Bosanquet try to do it, their treatment is all the more vague and uncertain. The essence of this theory lies in imparting the lesson of blind adulation of the state. Let us fall down and worship the state. (Trietschke) The idea of political obligation is thus converted into the injunction of the blind worship of authority.[36]

Marxian Theory: Eventual Conversion of Political Obligation into Social Obligation

Basically different from all the theories on the subject of political obligation, as discussed in the preceding sections, is the Marxian theory. It sanctions the case of political non-obligation in the pre-revolutionary stage, total political obligation in the revolutionary stage and its eventual conversion into social obligation in the post-revolutionary stage of social development. In other words, the case of political obligation is integrally connected with the character of authority. In the Marxian theory of politics, the state is described as a 'bourgeois institution' in the capitalist society; it is described as an instrument of power in the hands of the working class after the successful revolution to consolidate the socialist order in a way preparing its

34. Bosanquet: *Philosophical Theory of State* (London: Macmillan, 1923), p. 140.
35. Frank Thakurdas, *op. cit.*, p. 423.
36. See L.T. Hobhouse: *Metaphysical Theory of State* (London: George Allen andUnwin, 1918).

own 'withering away' to happen in the final stage of socialism. In a technical sense, it may be said that the idea of political obligation, according to Marxism, covers the cases of 'discredited state' in the era of capitalism, 'new state' in the period of the 'dictatorship of the proletariat' and 'state proper' when the 'classless' society finds its culmination in the 'stateless' pattern of social existence.

The starting point of the Marxist theory of politics and with it of political obligation "is its categorical rejection of this view of the state as the trustee, instrument, or agent of society as a whole."[37] If so,the oppressed and the exploited masses have no obligation to the existing bourgeois political order. They must develop class consciousness so as to overthrow the oppressive systems. The case of political obligation arises when the 'new state' comes into being after the revolution. As the leading Italian Marxist Gramsci says: "The dictatorship of the proletariat is the installation of a new state, typically proletarian, into which flow the institutional experiences of the oppressed class, in which the social life of the worker and peasant class becomes a system, universal and strongly organised."[38]

The noticeable point in the Marxian theory of political obligation is that what is forbidden in the capitalist society is ordained in the socialist order. Not merely this, a fundamental change takes place that prohibits any opposition to the state at all. There is no freedom of dissent and the people are virtually commanded to 'worship' the state. The dissenters are dubbed as 'reactionary' and 'counter-revolutionary' elements who would be purged, exterminated, exiled or condemned to severe tortures. The leaders of the working class desire nothing else than a state which is strong enough to impose law and order, to suppress challenge, and to ensure stability. However, as the state is now an institution of the 'whole people', no question of civil disobedience arises, or can arise, no matter it is in the hands of the leaders of the Communist Party who, in Lenin's words, are the 'vanguards of the working class'. In a way, the trend of revolution would continue until all the enemies of the new order are fully liquidated. This is called the idea of 'permanent revolution'. The task of the Marxists is, therefore, to subordinate the idea of political obligation to the dictates of a 'permanent revolution'.[39]

Whereas the idea of political obligation is subordinated to the dictates of permanent revolution in the transitional period, it is eventually converted into the norm of social obligation after the transformation of the 'new state' into the 'state proper'. In other words, the idea of political obligation ceases to exist with the 'withering away' of the state in the last stage of socialism (called Communism) and it finds its final conversion into the injunction of social obligation. Since all public affairs would be managed by the free and voluntary associations of the people in the era of human emancipation, naturally everyone would be obliged to obey unflinchingly the 'authority' of social institutions. There will be no state in this era of 'state proper'. Society will be composed of the associations of free and equal producers consciously acting upon a common and rational plan. Engels has made the point clear by adding that even in this era of social organisation "the free choices of the individuals must

37. Ralph Miliband: *Marxism and Politics* (London: Oxford Univ. Press, 1977), p. 66.
38. *Ibid*, p. 181.
39. Marx-Engels: *Collected Works*, Vol. 7, pp. 246-48.

remain circumscribed by the needs of the community and the technical exigencies of production. Marx envisaged the fully socialised man as one who would see no distinction between private and public interest and whose activity would be attuned to the latter."[40] If so, as Marx says, whether decisions are taken by the delegates or by the majority vote, the will of the individual will always have to subordinate itself.[41]

A critical study of the Marxian theory, in this direction, shows that it treats the question of political obligation in a way far away from the real perspective. What is emphatically advocated in the phase of capitalism is firmly denied in the next stage of social development. People who are exhorted to disobey the 'bourgeois state' in all respects are commanded not to disobey the state at all after the inauguration of the new social system. One may, therefore, accuse the Marxists of building up a theory of political obligation on the basis of expediency alone. Such an ambivalent attitude of the Marxists "reduces the question of political obligation to a question of political expediency, and ignores the independent individual whose experience alone counts in the determination of his obedience to the laws of the state."[42]

But the weakest point of the Marxist theory of political obligation is that it is based on, what Karl Popper says, 'historicism'. To say that history moves according to certain inexorable laws and to integrate the question of political obligation with that is to fall prey to the 'poverty of historicism'. There is not all bad in the capitalist system making it unworthy of political obligation at all, nor is there all good in the socialist system making it worthy of people's allegiance forever. The whole interpretation assumes the character of an ideology, or a dogma defying all canons of a scientific insight. It is, therefore, well observed: "To the extent, therefore, that Communist or other claims to authority are based on the historic mission of a leader, a class, or a party, they receive no support from science. They are of the same religious or metaphysical order as claims to Divine Right."[43]

It follows that in no social order all people can be expected to behave in a strictly uniform manner. All people would not like to revolt against the state in the era of capitalism, nor would all like to acquiesce in the transitional stage, what to say of reaching the stage of total agreement in the hypothetical stage of Communism. As Michael Evans says: "It remains difficult for us to conceive of a society of free opinion in which individual motives do not clash either with each other or with the public interest; or in which there would not be different conceptions of what constitutes the public interest. Marx's analogy is in any case a strained one. Assuming agreement on what to play, there are often considerable disagreements between the coductor and the members of the orchestra about the interpretation of the music. And in no society of any complexity has it ever been the case that everyone has wanted to play the same tune."[44]

---

40 Michael Evans: *Karl Marx* (London: George Allen and Unwin, 1975), p. 162.

41. *Ibid.*

42. Ray and Bhattacharya: *Political Theory: Ideas and Institutions* (Calcutta: World Press, 1968), p. 150.

43. Benn and Peters, *op. cit.*, p. 305.

44. Michael Evans, *op. cit.*, p. 163.

Theories of Political Obligation

Divine Theory	: Political obligation is a matter of faith, hence no resistance to the authority of the state as it has a divine sanction.
Prescriptive Theory	: Political authority and reverence to it are based on the principle of established customary injunctions.
Idealistic Theory	: All obedience to state is enjoined as it is a moralising agency, 'a partnership in virtue,' the highest institution ensuring 'good life' to its people.
Consent Theory	: Political authority is based on the consent of the people; it is an artificial contrivance; people may disobey the state if it forfeits their trust.
Marxian Theory	: No obedience to a bourgeois state as it is based on the exploitation and oppression of the proletariat, but all obedience to a socialist state created after revolution ensuring social and economic democracy.

One may ask as to which theory of political obligation should be treated as the most plausible of all. An answer to such a query should be that while the matter has been studied differently by men of different schools, we may appreciate one that stands the test of experience. In other words, we should look into the case of political obligation from a pragmatic point of view that desires "to contend for truth as tested by reality and its fruits."[45] Keeping this in view, we may admire the approach of Laski who says that men "obey the state not merely for the sake of order, but also on account of what they deem that order to make possible. They are, in fact, judging the state from the angle of satisfactions, they think it should provide. Their judgements, no doubt, vary with time and place. Expectations of what is legitimate are always born of experiences; and the demands of one society at one period will differ from those of another society at another period. But the implication is the clear one that the exercise of political authority in a society is never unconditional."[46]

Limits of Political Obligation: Problem of Right to Resistance

What we have said above informs us to look into the case of contingent political obligation as well. Men are not only obliged to obey the state, they have a right to disobey it as well under certain conditions. Even if we depend upon the criterion of 'satisfaction' or 'experience', we are compelled to look into the conditions under which people have a valid right to withdraw their obedience. Once again we find the situation fluid. While the advocates of 'divine' and 'prescriptive' theories do not allow the right to resist political authority under any condition whatsoever,

45. Charles E. Merriam: *A History of Political Theories: Recent Times* (Allahabad: Central Book Depot, 1969), p. 15.
46. Harold J. Laski: *The State in Theory and Practice* (London: George Allen and Unwin. 1960), p. 17. It is well opined: "After all, disobedience of state rules must be in the interest of the state itself, viz., to make it correspond to the ideal. Disobedience does not serve its purpose, if it ushers in uncontrollable chaos and anarchy." A.H. Doctor: *Issues in Political Theory* (New Delhi: Sterling Publishers, 1985), p. 123.

others subscribing to 'consent' and 'pragmatic' theories discover the case of political disobedience in certain exceptional situations. As we have already seen, the case of those subscribing to the Marxist theory is basically different from all, who advocate the idea of insurrection to overthrow the 'bourgeois state', while paying total obedience to the 'socialist' state that is to be eventually converted into man's full, final and unflinching allegiance to a thoroughly popular authority in the final stage of social development.

The case of contingent political obligation has been well studied by the English liberal thinkers of the early and later modern periods who have justified the case of 'rebellion' as a'cruel necessity'in certain exceptional situations. One is astonished to take note of the fact that though a staunch advocate of the idea of absolute and unlimited legal sovereignty, Hobbes recognises the right to resistance in case the Leviathan endangers the life of the people. First he endorses: "Once a man has transferred his right to another, then is he said to be obliged, or bound not to hinder those to whom such right is granted . . . . from the benefit of it: and that he ought, and it is his duty, not to make void that voluntary act of his own."[47] And then he sanctions that everyone has a right to disobey the sovereign if "he is commanded to kill, wound or maim himself; or not to resist those that assault him; or to abstain from the use of food, air, medicine, or any other thing, without which he cannot live."[48]

However, a clear and powerful justification of the 'right to rebellion'is contained in the political philosophy of John Locke who is described as the greatest English liberal thinker of the early modern period. He has no reservations in arming the people with the 'right to revolt', what he calls making an 'appeal to the Heaven' in case the sovereign violates the terms of the contract and thereby forfeits the trust of the community. While explaining the implications of the term 'violation of the trust', Laski says: "The substitution of arbitrary will for law, the corruption of Parliament by packing it with the prince's instruments, betrayed to a foreign prince, prevention of the due assemblage of Parliament—all these are perversions of the trust imposed and operate to effect the dissolution of the contract. The state of nature again supervenes and a new contract may be made with one more fitted to observe it."[49]

In the nineteenth century, the right to resistance is sanctioned by Thomas Hill Green who, within the framework of his liberalistic idealism, examines the case of political obligation in the context of relationship between the implementation of law, on the one hand, and preservation of the common good on the other. There should be no revolt for protecting the interest of a particular individual or a class, or a section of the society. What is required is that resistance must take place when the cause of 'common good' so ardently desires. The peculiar thing to be noted here, however, is that instead of designating it as a 'right to resist', he calls it as a 'duty to disobey'. The state is based on the 'will of the people'. Naturally, the people have a 'duty' to disobey when they find that any action of the sovereign is detrimental to, what Rousseau calls, the 'general will'. In the event of a 'dilemma' between the interest of a particular individual or a class on the one hand and that of the community as a whole on the other, the citizen "should be guided by the general rule of looking

47. Hobbes: *Leviathan,* Ch. 14.
48. *Ibid.*
49. Laski: *Political Thought in England (Locke to Bentham),* p. 37.

Limits of Political Obligation

And thus the community perpetually retains a supreme power of saving themselves from the attempts and designs of anybody, even if their legislators whenever they shall be so foolish or so wicked as to lay and carry on designs against the liberties and properties of the subjects.

—John Locke,
Second Treatise of Civil Government (1690), Ch. 13.

We hold these truths to be self-evident that all men are created equal, that they are endowed by their Creator with certain unalienable rights; that among these are life, liberty and the pursuit of happiness. That to secure these rights, governments are instituted among men deriving their just powers from the consent of the governed; that whenever any form of government becomes destructive of these ends, it is the right of the people to alter or to abolish it, and to institute a new government, laying its foundations on such principles, and organising its powers in such form, as to them shall seem most likely to affect their safety and happiness.

—Thomas Jefferson
Declaration of American Independence (1776)

We believe that it is the inalienable right of the Indian people, as of any other people, to have freedom and to enjoy the fruits of their toil and have the necessities of life so that they may have full opportunities of growth. We believe also that if any Government deprives the people of these rights and oppresses them, the people have a further right to alter it or to abolish it.

—Jawaharlal Nehru
Pledge of Complete Independence (1930)

to the moral good of mankind to which a necessary means is the organistation of the state, which requires the unity of supreme control in the common interest over the outward actions of men."[50]

In present times, Laski discovers the source of political obligation in the factor of 'moral adequacy' to which the state must ever adhere while exercising its authority. He admits that antagonism to the demands of authority "will always be the exception in history; but these demands will win their way from inert acceptance rather than active consent unless . . . . they offer service to the theoretic purpose of the state. For any social order which fails consistently to recognise the claims of personality is built upon a foundation of sand . . . . For to deny the claims of right is to sacrifice the claim to allegiance. The state can exercise moral authority upon no other basis."[51] Like Green, Laski says that 'right to resistance' should be substituted by 'duty to disobey'. From one angle it "is a claim to a right which a citizen cannot surrender without denying himself the full meaning of his citizenship, and, from the other, it is an obligation arising out of the acceptance of, and loyalty to, the idea of common good. There are then circumstances in which resistance to the state becomes an obligation if claims to rights are to be given validity, though no general rule of either time or situation can be laid down as a guide to such an action."[52]

50. Green: *Lectures on the Principles of Political Obligation,* p. 115.
51. Laski : *A Grammar of Politics,* p. 97.
52. *Ibid.,* p. 96.

Following impressions can be gathered from what we have seen above in regard to the right of resistance to political authority as advocated by leading English liberal thinkers:

1. The people have a right to resist political authority in case they, or a majority of them, for all practical purposes, are satisfied that the action of the sovereign is detrimental to the overall interest of the community. Not the interest of a particular individual or a class but of the society as a whole should be kept in view while looking into the problem of political obligation *vis-a-vis* the necessity of civil disobedience.
2. The case of political disobedience is a conditional affair. It is not something absolute. It is due under certain relevant conditions only. It is, however, for the people by and large to decide when the conditions so warrant. No uniform rule of universal applicability can be laid down in this connection. For instance, while the Roman Catholics may stage a revolt in case the rulers make a historic declaration in favour of the Protestant creed, the Protestants may do the same in case their rulers take to the course of Roman Catholicism in the like manner.
3. The idea of political obligation *vis-a-vis* right to resistance is also integrally connected with the norm of, what Barker calls, 'super-political obligation'. In simple terms, it implies that resistance to political authority should not be given the form of a 'political mischief. People may resist the bad action of their rulers, but they are not justified in taking matters to the extent that the general social order is damaged to an irreparable extent. As he says: "But a new and super-political obligation enters as soon as we take into our view the socially created and socially developed idea of social justice: an obligation which we may call 'social', in the sense that it springs from Society and from the product of thought."[53]
4. There are at least three different positions which might be taken concerning the character of the obligation to obey the law or the rightness of obedience to the law. These are: (1) One has an absolute obligation to obey the law; disobedience is never justified. (2) One has an obligation to obey the law, but this obligation can be overridden by conflicting obligations; disobedience can be justified, but only by the presence of outweighing circumstances. (3) One does not have a special obligation to obey the law, but it is, in fact, usually obligatory on the grounds to do so disobedience to law often does turn out to be unjustified.[54]
5. The notions of promise, consent, or voluntary participation do not, however, exhaust the possible sources of the obligation to obey the laws of a democracy. In particular, there is another set of arguments which remains to be considered. It is that which locates the rightness of obedience in the way in which any act of disobedience improperly distributes certain burdens and benefits among the citizenry. For example, Wechsler sees any act of disobedience to the laws of his country (USA) as the 'ultimate negation of all modern principles' to take the benefits accorded by the constitutional system, including the national market and

53. Barker, *op. cit.*, p 222.
54. R. A. Wasserstrom: "The Obligation to Obey the Law" in A de Crespigny and A Wertheimer (ed.s): *Contemporary Political Theory* (London: Nelson, 1970), p. 272.

common defence, while denying it allegiance when a special burden is imposed. That certainly is the antithesis of law."[55] It implies that to disobey any law after having voluntarily received some benefits would be so unjust that there could never be overriding considerations. This surely is both to claim too much for the benefits of personal and commercial security and to say too little for the character of all types of obedience."[56]

Critical Appreciation

What we have said about the concept of political obligation in the preceding sections leaves an unmistakable impression that it is, indeed, a very delicate affair. The views of eminent authorities on this subject are divergent ranging from those of the advocates of the 'divine' and 'prescriptive' theories who lay emphasis on the duty of political obligation to the extent of derecognising the right to resistance to those of the 'consent' theory who justify popular rebellion in the event the sovereign forfeits the trust of the people by violating the terms of the 'contract'. Basically different from both is the position of the Marxists who make the concept of political obligation subservient to the pattern of the existing social order and thereby suggest the withdrawal of obligation to a 'capitalist' state and total obedience to a 'socialist' one that has to be eventually converted into social obligation in the ideal pattern of human existence.

We may easily understand that the idea of political obligation is not only a delicate affair, it is very difficult to determine its precise nature. None can lay down rules of universal applicability in this regard. In a strict sense, the idea of political obligation is not a political but a moral affair. However, as the norms of morality differ from time to time, from place to place, and from people to people, naturally the dimensions of political obligation or, conversely speaking, the injunctions of popular resistance also vary in the like manner. For instance, while the people of a tradition-ridden country like England would prefer to wait till the next general election to change their rulers who have forfeited their trust, the progressive or radical people of a country like France would prefer the return of Bonapartism rather than wait for the next polls as the only way out to save the country from imminent chaos. It is also possible that while a sizeable section of the people may have reservations about the need for staging a popular revolt, another section may cry for the same and then manage to change the existing state of affairs. In such a situation the propriety of the action of any section of the people may remain a matter of debate. Barker thus rightly holds: "There is no simple rule for the weighing of the mischiefs of obedience against the mischiefs of resistance."[57]

It is generally believed that the existence of a constitutional government secures the case of political obligation. People must obey the order of the state in case it conforms to the provisions of the fundamental law of the land—constitution. In case the government violates the constitution, it should be criticised, even overthrown.

55. Wechsler: "Towards Neutral Principles of Constitutional Law" in *Harvard Law Review,* Vol. 73 (1969), no. 1, p. 35.
56. Wasserstrom, *op. cit.,* p. 286.
57. Barker, *op. cit.* p. 224.

The difficulty, however, continues to persist inasmuch as even the enforcement of a particular law may, or may not, be treated as constitutional according to the divergent interpretations of the people. For instance, in India the invocation of emergency provisions and the subsequent actions of the government of Mrs. Indira Gandhi in 1975-76 were described as purely constitutional affairs by the men in power, while they were denounced as 'fascist measures' by the opponents. The only satisfaction in such a situation is that the people have a yardstick (contained in the provisions of the constitution) to judge the nature and character of political authority and accordingly laud or denounce the measure in question.

In this way, we are bound to agree with the view of Margaret MacDonald that "necessary and sufficient grounds for political obligation are not to be found."[58] Even the most widely accepted 'consent' theory has its own weaknesses. "As rational and responsible citizens we can never hope to know once and for all what our political duties are. And so we can never go to sleep."[59] The sanctity of the celebrated maxim stands out : 'Eternal vigilance is the price of freedom.' It may be suggested that the people should never suspend their judgement by cultivating a blind faith in the purity of their administration or in the sincerity of their great democratic leaders to whom Harold Lasswell would happily describe as 'Master Propagandists'. In other words, as suggested by Benn and Peters, while agreeing with the keynote of the 'consent' theory, which is supposed to be the basis of a democratic order, "we can never put our conscience in the keeping of other men, even of a majority of them. And we can, therefore, never go to sleep."[60]

58. Cited in Benn and Peters, *op. cit.*, p. 331.
59. *Ibid.*
60. *Ibid.* Michael Walzer makes an interesting point when he says: "All this is not to suggest that there is anything unreal about individual responsibility. But there is always responsibility *to someone else* and it is always learned with *someone else*. An individual whose moral experiences never reached beyond 'monologue' would know nothing at all about responsibility and would have none. Such a man might well have rights, including the right to rebel, but his possession of the right to rebel would be purely theoretical; he would never become a rebel. No political theory which does not move beyond rights to duties, beyond monologue to fraternal discussion, debate and resolution, can ever explain what men actually do when they disobey or rebel, or why they do so. Nor can it help us very much to weigh the rightness or wrongness of what they do." Refer to his paper titled "The Obligation to Disobey" in Crespigny and Wertheimer, *op. cit.*, p. 311.

13

Political Legitimacy and Effectiveness

> The political system is composed of two elements, closely integrated in mutual causality—power-relationships and legitimating actions backed the dominant control of coercive force. The two elements may be seen in an input-output relationship. Power-relationships are the input that create the legitimising act. The acts, in turn, as outputs, tend to reinforce existing power-relations or to change them. We may proceed from this to see the political system in action.
>
> **—H.V. Wiseman[1]**

A study of the concept of political obligation, as presented in the preceding chapter, necessarily leads to an investigation of two related themes – political legitimacy and revolution. The curious thing to be noted here, however, is that while the concept of political obligation constitutes an important touchstone of political philosophy, in association with the notions of legitimacy and effectiveness, it finds a very significant place in the realm of political sociology. It stands on the assumption that the concern of a political scientist is not confined to the study of authority as such, it also covers within its fold the problem of power being acceptable to the people over whom it is exercised. As such, a political scientist is expected to be concerned with the question of authority as well as its legitimacy in terms of the decision-making process that characterises the operation of a modern political system. In this chapter an attempt has been made to discuss the concept of political legitimacy and effectiveness keeping in view this salient proposition of political sociology that an authoritative decision-making system is "one whose actions are perceived as legitimate, whereas effectiveness concerns operational efficacy than legitimacy. There are, of course, connections between the two and a stable government is likely to possess both."[2]

Nature and Essential Implications

Ours is an 'age of democracy' as described by H.G. Wells. However, the stability of a popular or democratic political system depends not only upon economic development, as is generally understood, but also upon its legitimacy and effectiveness. While "effectiveness is judged according to how well a system performs the basic functions of government as measured by the reactions of most of the population and such powerful

1. Wiseman: *Political Systems: Some Sociological Approaches* (New York: Fredrick A. Praegar, 1967), pp. 177-78.
2. O.R. Young: *Systems of Political Science* (Englewood Cliffs, New Jersey: Prentice-Hall, 1968), pp. 70-71.

groups as business organisations or military forces, legitimacy includes the capacity to produce and maintain a belief that the existing political institutions, or forms, are the most appropriate for society."[3] Legitimacy is the foundation of political power inasmuch as it "is exercised both with a consciousness on government's part that it has a right to govern and with some recognition by the governed of that right."[4] In order to make the meaning of the term clear, Dolf Sternberger seeks to distinguish it with 'usurpation'. The concept of usurpation as the opposite of legitimacy has accompanied the concept of legitimate government since early medieval times and has helped to clarify it. Usurpers after seizing power have often tried to strengthen their positions by giving their governments a legitimate form and their attempts to clothe a usurping power with legitimacy, whether successful or not, have often revealed what the standards of legitimacy are for a given society or civilisation.[5]

However, a line of fundamental distinction should be drawn between usurpation, on the one hand, and revolution, on the other, when we study the concept of political legitimacy and effectiveness. While usurpation of power is always an illegitimate act, revolution may, and also may not, belong to such a category, though one may find fault with the personal or subjective attitude of the observer. Simply stated, the idea of political legitimacy is integrally associated with a successful revolution that exhibits its appreciation by the masses. If a revolution succeeds, it introduces a new principle of legitimacy that supersedes the rightness of the former system. Under such circumstances, recognition by the people will often be acquired only as the new regime begins governing and the process of becoming legitimate may include violence and terror. Foreign diplomatic recognition, while not essential, may help internal consolidation and therefore speed acceptance of the new pattern of legitimacy.[6]

The idea of political legitimacy and effectiveness is also organically connected with the problem of political change. Governments, whether following traditional principles of legitimacy or establishing revolutionary ones, may lose their legitimacy by violating these principles. The desire for having the stamp of legitimacy is so deeply rooted in human communities that it is hard to discover any form of government that does not either enjoy widespread authentic mark of its existence or try to win such a recognition by any possible means whatsoever. Legitimacy is so universal a phenomenon that it "is continuously endangered by the plurality of its patterns. and sources. Rivals for power often automatically consider themselves legitimate and their opponents illegitimate. It is, therefore, difficult to talk about legitimacy in general terms, the different types must be discussed separately and specific examples given."[7]

3. S.M. Lipset: *Political Man : The Social Bases of Politics* (New York: Doubleday, 1959), abridged edition, p. 29.
4. Dolf Sternberger: "Legitimacy" *in International Encyclopaedia of the Social Sciences* edited by David I. Sills (New York: Macmillan and Free Press, 1968), Volumes 9-10, p. 244.
5. *Ibid.*
6. *Ibid.*
7. *Ibid.*

Political Legitimacy

The strongest is never strong enough to be always the master unless he transforms strength into right and obedience into duty.

—**Jean Jacques Rousseau**
Social Contract (1762)

Legitimacy is usually defined simply as 'rightfulness'. As such, it is crucial to the distinction between power and authority. Legitimacy is the quality that transforms naked power into rightful authority; it confers upon an order or command an authoritative or binding character, ensuring that it is obeyed out of duty rather than because of fear.

—**Andrew Heywood**
Political Theory: An Introduction, p. 141.

Citizens will only identify with the state, and accept the demands as legitimate, when there is a 'common form of life', which is seen as a supremely important good, so that its continuance and flourishing matters to the citizens for its own sake and not just instrumentally to their several individual goods or as the sum total of these individual goods.

—**Charles Taylor**
"Alternative Futures: Legitimacy, Identity and Alienation" in Alan Cairns and Cynthia Williams (eds.): ***Constitutionalism, Citizenship and Society in Canada*** (Toronto: University of Toronto Press, 1985), p. 213.

It may, however, be added that as a crisis of legitimacy is a crisis of change, its genesis should be traced in the character of the transformation that affects the social life of the people. It does not matter whether the status of major social institutions is threatened, or if the political system is not open to all major groups in the society during the phase of transition, or at the time when they have developed critical demands. It is also possible that a new crisis "may develop after a new social structure is established if the new system is unable to sustain the expectations of major groups for a period long enough to develop legitimacy upon the new basis."[8] The basic question stands: How people choose to accept, or not to accept, particular governments? It may be answered with two main theses: "first, that people make political decisions, including even decisions about support for government, *rationally,* or at least act as if they did; and second, that the ethnic and occupational divisions of any society are the principal information on which its members would have to base a rational choice among forms of government."[9]

David E. Apter has provided a particularly interesting notion of what legitimacy is. He maintains that legitimacy "is related to a set of conceptions held by significant members of the polity about the rightness of a political pattern which, in turn, provides the patterns with a set of properties. Legitimacy is thus a behavioural term referring to a set of limits on governmental action. It is with reference to legitimacy that right conduct in office is defined. When legitimacy is withdrawn, government

8. Lipset, *op. cit.,* p. 29.
9. Ronald Rogowski: *Rational Legitimacy: A Theory of Political Support* (Princeton: Princeton University Press, 1974), p. 3.

Different Grounds of Political Legitimacy

1. There is no choice in the matter (*following orders or coercion*).
2. No thought has ever been given to it and we do it as it has always been done (*tradition*).
3. We cannot be bothered one way or another (*apathy*).
4. Although we do not like the situation-it is not satisfactory and far from ideal-we cannot imagine things being really different and so we 'shrug our shoulders' and accept what seems like fate (*pragmatic acquiescence*).
5. We are satisfied with things as they are but nevertheles go along with them in order to secure an end; we acquiesce, because it is in, the long run, to our advantage (*instrumental acceptance or conditional agreement/consent*).
6. In the circumstances before us, and with the information available to us at the moment, we conclude it is 'right', 'correct', 'proper' for us as an individual or member of a collectivity: it is what we generally should or ought to do (*normative agreement*).
7. It is what in ideal circumstances-with, for instance, all the knowledge we would like, all the opportunity to discover the circumstances and requirements of others-we would have agreed to do (*ideal normative agreement*).

David Held: *Political Theory and the Modern State*, p. 101.

is weakened."[10] Within the context of this definition of what constitutes legitimacy, three reasons emerge as explanations of its loss. These are:[11]

1. Some of the significant members of the polity may choose to withdraw support from the government. Such was the case, for example, when the army decision not to support the Diem regime in South Vietnam led to the overthrow of the regime through a coup in 1963, followed by a long series of military regimes. It was immaterial whether the population concurred with it.
2. Another possibility involves the rise of a new, politically aware group which is not recognised by political system as having political relevance. For example, for years, the Social Democrats in Germany were not included in any aspects of the decision-making process, instead the regime carefully adopted some social welfare programmes.
3. The last way for the loss of legitimacy to occur is for the political system to close itself off and to drive away former politically-significant members of polity. For instance, in China the Kuomintang regime forced the Communist Party to go into the countryside from where the communists fought for power and gained it in 1949.

Such a conception of legitimacy raises three important problems. First, the idea of a politically-significant element in the polity seems clear enough. Second, the lack of legitimacy may not lead to a weakening of the government. Last, the whole idea is very difficult to operationalise. It is a conception that, at best, provides us with a tautological series of explanations. If a regime collapses, it is because the politically significant part of the population has withdrawn support.

10. Apter: *The Politics of Modernisation* (Chicago: Chicago University Press, 1965), p. 236.
11. A.S. Cohan: *Theories of Revolution: An Introduction* (London: Nelson, 1975), pp. 134-35.

Obviously, the idea of political legitimacy and effectiveness is integrally bound up with the new interpretation of the concept of 'political power' characterised by its potential effect through governmental roles on, what Easton says, the 'authoritative allocation of values'. It expands the study of political behaviour so as to include all forms of social relationships which 'affect', 'influence', and 'control', 'inhibition', 'support' and the like. The concern of a political scientist is not limited to the problem of franchise, freedom of speech and expression, making laws and securing their due enforcement, preservation of the neutrality of public servants and independence and impartiality of the judges and the like. In other words, the idea of 'power' bound up with the notions of political legitimacy and effectiveness covers within its fold the entire stuff of social psychology with reference to group behaviour and political socialisation implying internationalisation of the values of a free and open governmental system. In this way, the study of politics "is the study of the legitimisation of social power in situations of social interaction."[12]

Certain broad conclusions can be drawn from what we have said above. These are:

1. If the political system is to survive and sustain, it should be acceptable to the people so that they may render their obligation to it. The rulers must either make an attempt to bring the real power-relationships into conformity with existing legitimisation, or to revise the legitimisation in terms of the existing or some of the preferred power-relationships.[13]
2. The political function involves not only an adjustment to the established patterns of legitimisation but also a resourceful exploitation of the complex and diffuse power structures, the prevailing culture-based ideologies, attitudes, social relationships and interests of persons occupying governmental roles (and of other interests capable of influencing the role-incumbents). The pattern of effective legitimisation is dependent on politically functional activity and the relative inflexibility of power-relationships.[14]
3. The concept of political legitimacy and effectiveness is such that it cannot be defined abstractly in terms of an ideal type of government with an absolute value; it can be understood concretely in terms of the historic concepts of the ideal type of government. In this sense, we describe a government as 'legitimate' which, at a given moment and in a given country, corresponds to the idea that the general populace has about a legitimate order, or in other words, we are concerned with the popular beliefs about the legitimacy of a political system.[15]
4. The theories of a legitimate political order reflect, more or less, the social structures and especially the class situations: they tend to justify a form of government that meets the requirements of those for whom it is meant. They transform a temporary and relative social institution into something permanent by giving it an absolute and eternal character. Belief in the legitimacy of a government tends to place the latter in the category of the 'sacred', the equivalent of mythical absolutes.

12. Wiseman, *op. cit.*, p. 172.
13. *Ibid.*, p. 178.
14. *Ibid.*, p. 179.
15. Maurice Duverger: *Political Parties* (London: Methuen, 1958, p. 101.

If the governed believe that their rulers are legitimate, they are inclined to obey them spontaneously; they recognise that obedience is due to them. A legitimate government is one in which people feel an obligation to obey whereas no such obligation is felt towards a government considered as 'illegitimate.[16]

5. While the concept of political legitimacy and effectiveness has its application in every political system whether democratic, dictatorial or monarchical and the like, it has its special significance in a democratic system that is said to rest on the 'general will'. There are instances to prove that even autocratic rulers like Caliph Harun al Rashid used to move in disguise to know the mood and mind of the people. Even in modern times dictators have made serious and concerted attempts to secure legitimacy to their system. It has now become a matter of political axiom that the factors involved in the modernisation or economic development are associated with those which establish legitimacy and tolerance.[17]

Legitimacy and Power-relationship: Functional Dimensions of the Political System

The idea of legitimacy and effectiveness involves within itself the study of political system from a sociological standpoint in view of the fact that the latter is a basic part of the social organisation. As Eisenstadt says, a political system has three essential characteristics. First, it is the organisation of a territorial society having a 'legitimate monopoly' over the authorised use and regulation of force in society. Second, it has defined responsibilities for maintaining the system of which it is a part. Third, its organisation imposes severe secular sanctions in order to implement the main collective goals of society, to maintain its internal order, and to regulate its foreign relations. In brief, all the social roles and groups fulfilling these distinct functions in a society, regardless of what other tasks they perform, constitute the political system of the society.[18]

If political system is a part of the wider social organisation, naturally we should look at its functional dimensions so as to examine the case of'legitimacy' in empirical terms. The people, in general, do not obey authority just for the sake of obedience ; rather they do so for the purposes they believe to be secured by its operations.[19] Thus, the issue of the functions of the government figures in. The administrators are required to see that others do the same. That is, the concern of the government is not merely to perform its own functions in a prescribed manner; it should also see that other groups and associations do their jobs within the areas allotted to them. It necessarily pushes us to look into the sphere of power-relationships. As Wiseman says: "The function of government, then is the legitimisation of power in a political system, and the limits of such a system are set by the effective performance of this function."[20]

---

16. *Ibid.*
17. See A.R. Ball: *Modern Politics and Government* (London: Macmillan, 1978), II Ed., Chapters 4 and 5.
18. See S.N. Eisenstadt: *The Political Systems of Empires* (New York; Free Press of Glencoe, 1963).
19. H.J. Laski: *The State in Theory and Practice* (London: George Allen and Unwin, 1960), p. 17.
20. Wiseman, *op. cit.*, p. 176.

It should also be added at this stage that the structure, personnel and legal procedures of, what are usually known as, political institutions lend permanence to certain patterns of existing relationships in any form of government. It is this 'permanence or institutionalisation' what we call legitimisation.[21] One may use it as a workable ground on which different forms of political systems may be chalked out. "A power-relationship", according to Binder, "which one seeks to make permanent through the action of a government is a political power-relationship, the classification of the actions which may lead to such legitimisation being a classification of the political processes and techniques prevalent in any concrete system."[22]

Since the idea of legitimacy covers the case of every 'political' and 'non-political' organisation, it may be pointed out that the government is not the only legitimising institution. In certain situations we may take note of the fact that some social institution may accord the title of legitimacy to a political order. For instance, the movement led by a religious leader (Khomeini) resulting in the forced abdication and exile of the Shah signified the withdrawal of legitimacy to a discredited monarchical order and the conferment of the same on a new one called the 'Islamic Republic of Iran'. It is, however, a different matter that the side of the government is far heavier in according legitimacy to social groups inasmuch as it is endowed with supreme power to coerce the people, for example, to the extent of making them accept Maoism at the debris of Taoism as we see in the recent political developments of China.

The issue of power-relationship between the government, on the one hand, and social organisations, on the other, thus leads to this conclusion that while the latter (like family, church, tribe, party, firm, union, etc.) may play their role in the legitimisation of power-relationships, the role of the former is much important, even decisive. It should also be taken into account that the legitimisation of certain power-relationships does not exhaust all functions of government. A government is concerned not only with the maintenance of its own existence, it is equally concerned with the existence of the structure of power-relationships which it legitimises. So, governments "may perform political as well as legitimisaton functions. Political scientists may, of course, investigate any kind of power, but for the study of the political system, its relevance to legitimisation is of crucial importance."[23]

Idealist Theory: Sanction of Political Legitimacy in the Establishment of a Perfect Order

The credit for thinking in terms of political legitimacy should go to the idealist thinkers who, in the words of Plato, denounce the existing social and political systems as 'city of the swine' and instead contemplate in terms of a perfect order in which, in the words of Rousseau, man who is born free remains without chains even after being a member of the political community. We may refer to the wisest man of ancient Greece (Socrates) who stressed his doctrine 'virtue is knowledge' so as to imply the excellence of the aristocracy of intellect. The idea, however, took an elaborate form in

21. See Leonard Binder: *Iran: Political Development in a Changing Society* (Berkeley: University of California Press, 1962), pp. 1-58.
22. *Ibid.*
23. Wiseman, *op. cit.*, p. 177.

the political philosophy of Plato who in his *Republic* sketched the model of an ideal state having a three-class polity based on the principle of division of labour and functional specialisation headed by a philosopher-king with the supreme authority of implementing the principle of 'justice'. Only such a political order is legitimate, as it is 'just', *i.e.,* in which each individual performs his duties at the appointed place and in which the ruling class is uncorrupt as well as incorruptible. In other words, the sanction of political legitimacy finds place in the implementation of the principle of 'proper stations'.[24]

Following his teacher, Aristotle discovered the sanction of political legitimacy in a system wherein people may lead 'a life of virtue'. That is, the idea of political legitimacy is necessarily connected with the end of the state which lies in the realisation of 'good life'. The point of distinction between the teacher and the taught, however, may be traced in the fact that while the former is in search of a purely ideal order possible in the heaven, the latter is doing the same for the 'best attainable' system on this earth. It is the 'polity' or a particular form of political order where power is in the hands of the middle class representing a wise synthesis of the democratic and oligarchical elements with a weightier share of the former. Such an order is legitimate, because it subscribes to the principle of'golden mean', i.e., it is susceptible to neither the 'extreme' of affluence nor of poverty, a middle course between oligarchy and democracy, showing residence of power in the hands of the 'middle class'.[25]

Theocracy prevailed throughout the Middle Ages with the result that the idea of political legitimacy was mixed up with the dictates of the Christian religion. In other words, a religious state became a legitimate organisation. It was essential for the ruler to be a believer in the faith. Moreover, it became a matter of the monopoly of the religious heads with Pope at the apex of ecclesiastical hierarchy to determine whether the ruler was a worthy member of the Christendom or not. In case a ruler was 'ex-communicated', his government became illegitimate and the people were commanded to withdraw their obedience to him. St. Augustine ruled that a non-Christian ruler was like a tyrant or a 'usurper' who should be killed. This state of affairs continued till the advent of the modern age when the Papacy declined and the trends of nationalism, secularism and sovereignty replaced the system of theocracy.

The idealist tradition witnessed its resuscitation at the hands of Rousseau in the eighteenth century who sought to find out a form of association which "will defend and protect the person and property of each member with the whole common force of community, and where each, while joining with all the rest, still obeys no one else but himself and remains as free as before"[26] Obviously, the task before this 'prophet of the age of reason' is to create an ideal political order which will make power legitimate with this assumption that if power can be made a servant rather than a master, it will be possible to rediscover much of the freedom which man has in the 'state of nature'. In a word, he "is seeking ways to organise political life so that the

24. See R.L. Nettleship: *Lectures on The Republic of Plato* (London: George Allen and Unwin, 1966), p. 152.
25. Ross: *Aristotle*, p. 261.
26 Rousseau: *Social Contract*, Book I, Ch. VI.

men can rise out of the slough of social and psychological despond and use power as a means to achieve freedom."[27]

The impact of Rousseau's quest for a legitimate political order ensuring moral freedom of man can be seen on the German idealists like Kant and Hegel. In particular, it is Hegel who says that in state man has fully raised his outward self to the level of his inward self of thought: his free will has found the broadest expansion which its positive quality demands, and the highest expression which its objective character requires. The peculiar thing about Hegel, however, is that he glorifies the case of his ideal legitimate political order. He goes to the extent of making it a divine institution by emphasising that the state "sustains personality, and it teaches personality to transcend itself by giving its devotion to something beyond itself."[28] The individual is taught to worship the state as a thoroughly legitimate organisation because it not only mantains him as a person, but also promotes his personality and protects the minor groups of family and social life in which he partially seeks his welfare; and that it carries back the individual whose tendency is to become a centre of his own into, what Hegel says, 'the life of universal substance'.[29]

The crime of Hegel is that he identifies the case of political legitimacy with the belief in the divinity of political authority. An elaboration of the same idea without taking state to 'mystical heights' may be visualised in the political philosophy of T.H. Green who boldly declares that *'will* not *force* is the basis of the state'. In order to understand the ideas of this Oxford neo-Hegelian, we should examine the genesis of political obligation instead of at once looking at the nature of political authority. He argues that behind the conception of the state lies the idea of an eternal self-consciousness, which communicates to human consciousness the idea of the social good, and for whose perfection, in turn, human consciousness is ever seeking to attain, and, in the higher forms, of human society, has already partially attained. Naturally, the state "is a product of this consciousness. Human consciousness postulates liberty: liberty involves rights; rights demand the state."[30] The authority of the state is quite a legitimate affair and, for this reason, it may even go to the extent of 'forcing individual to be free'. If consciousness creates rights, it also creates the sovereignty which is the very *sine qua non* of their existence and maintenance. The basis of the state is, for this reason, not force but will. In other words, it "is rather an assertion that the ultimate moving force which inspires and controls political action is a spiritual force—a common conviction that makes for righteousness, a common conscience that alone can arm the ministers and agents of the community with power."[31]

A critic of the idealist theory may easily denounce it for being too abstract and also for taking the real matter far away from the world of reality. What the

---

27. Andrew Hacker: *Political Theory: Philosophy, Ideology, Science* (New York: Macmillan, 1963), p. 301.
28. E. Barker: *Political Thought in England, 1848-1914,* (London: Oxford Univ. Press, 1951), p. 20.
29. *Ibid.*
30. *Ibid.*, p. 23.
31. *Ibid.*, pp. 28-29.

idealists say is certainly beyond the comprehension of an average man. People, in general, expect tangible rewards from their rulers. Their reactions to the acts of commission and omission of their rulers depend upon what they actually get or fail to get. In practical matters, therefore, the idealistic interpretation of the source of political legitimacy fails to have its comprehension. Not only this, its lesson that authority should be adulated, even adored, for being based on the fact of 'common conviction' and that state may even go to the extent of using force to create freedom leaves the door open for the entry of political absolutism. In this way, the source of political legitimacy is identified with the sanction of obedience in the terror of political despotism. The source of political legitimacy, in other words, finds place in the sanction of state as an end, not a means. The approach of the idealists, for this reason, becomes analogous to that of the Fascists and the Communists who advocate the idea of a 'closed society' and are, for the same reason, the enemies of, what Karl Popper says, 'open society'. Obviously, it has nothing to do with the fervour or dignity of democratic conviction in any given situation. We may appreciate this statement: "To realise the relative validity of one's convictions and yet stand for them unflinchingly is what distinguishes a civilised man from a barbarian."[32]

Prescriptive Theory: Sanction of Political Legitimacy in the Force of Tradition

What we have said in the preceding chapter on the prescriptive theory on political obligation should be reiterated here that authority "is legitimate if it is sanctioned by custom."[33] It follows that the sanction of political legitimacy is contained in the force of tradition. Instead of looking into some 'mystical' element like man's free moral will or human consciousness as suggested by the idealists, we should rely on the force of 'prudential judgement' of policies and programmes. It appears that "here the political leader becomes primarily the advocate of policies which he believes will bring nearer the realisation of the ideals in national tradition."[34] In other words, in the demonstration of the validity of authority one should be guided by the lessons of history coupled with, what Russell Kirk says, the force of 'will and intelligence."[35]

Such an affirmation finds its classic manifestation in the ideas of Edmund Burke who, in the last phase of the eighteenth century, rejected the 'ideology' of the French Revolution by lauding the greatness of the 'prescriptive institutions' of England. "The English constitution seemed to him the best of constitutions, the British parliamentary system the best of governments. The values of the established order were to him a matter of positive faith, not something just taken for granted. This made him peculiarly sensitive and hostile to any threat to the maintenance of

32. J.A. Schumpeter: *Capitalism, Socialism and Democracy* (London: George Allen and Unwin, 1966), p. 243.
33. S.I. Benn and R.S. Peters: *Social Principles and the Democratic State* (London: George Allen and Unwin, 1975), p. 307.
34. F.G.Wilson: "The Anatomy of Conservatives" in J. Stankiewicz (ed.): *Political Thought Since World War II* (New York: The Free Press of Glencoe, 1965), p. 343.
35. See S.P. Huntington: "Conservatism as an Ideology", *Ibid.*, p. 357.

those values."[36] According to this self-conscious conservative of England, whether an institution is legitimate or not, should be decided by the weight of tradition. Political institutions grow and develop over a long period of history and, as such, the source of their acceptability to the people finds place in the well-established traditions of the land. A newly established order having no roots in the past would, therefore, be unworkable and, for this reason, unacceptable to the people. For instance, the fruits of the revolution in France failed to survive and instead of a discredited Bourbon monarchy there came into being a despotism of the Directory under Napoleon Bonaparte after a couple of years. Thus, he emphatically asserts: "The science of constructing a commonwealth, or renovating it or reforming it, is like every other experimental science, not to be taught *a priori*."[37]

Among contemporary thinkers, we may refer to the ideas of Michael Oakeshott who, following Hugh Cecil and Quinton Hogg, traces the source of political legitimacy not merely in the force of tradition like Burke but also in the existence of a 'limited government'. Rejecting the case of positive liberalism, he insists that legitimate government is one that is not 'too big'. The role of a 'proper government' is to rule, to referee, to keep order, but not to undertake substantive economic activity where this can be avoided. Its aim is to inject moderation into the conduct of affairs, "to restrain, to deflate, to pacify, and to reconcile; not to stoke the fires of desire, but to dampen them down."[38] It appears that Oakeshott "seems to think that the rulers should possess the qualities, if not of a philosopher, then of a very good Speaker of the House of Commons."[39]

In this way, the sanction of political legitimacy is identified with the canon of orthodoxy by which the validity of a practice, polity or institution may be judged. Moreover, the orthodoxy by which tradition is judged becomes the conservative acceptance of a moral order, or perhaps one should say it is the tradition itself as a 'deposit of truth', something that is handed on without basic change. To a critic, it may also appear that strict adherence to the weight of tradition takes this theory of prescription very close to the approach of the idealists and both look like according divine character to what constitutes the essential sanction behind the existence of a legitimate political authority. For instance, an advocate of conservatism like Russell Kirk has spoken of the belief that a 'divine intent' rules society.[40] Obviously, such a theory of political legitimacy cannot satisfy the Marxists who want to overthrow the *status quo* and then establish an entirely new social and political system. However, what should be taken note of at this stage is that this theory cannot have the appreciation even of the positive liberals like Harold Laski and Harold Lasswell who advocate transformation in the nature and role of the authority in response to the change in the needs and aspirations of the people.

36. F.M. Watkins: *The Age of Ideology – Political Thought, 1750 to the Present Day* (Englewood Cliffs, New Jersey: Prentice-Hall, 1964), p. 31.
37. Burke: *Reflections on the Revolution in France,* p. 154.
38. Oakeshott: *Rationalism in Politics* (London: Methuen, 1963), pp. 188-89.
39. W.H. Greenleaf: *Oakeshott's Philosophical Politics* (London: Longmans, 1956), p. 86.
40. See F.G. Wilson, *op. cit.,* p. 342.

Liberal Theory: Universal Applicability of the Principle of Legitimacy

Right from the days of the ancient Greeks to the present, political thinkers and social theorists have sought to find out a form of order acceptable to the people. However, it is Max Weber of Germany (1864-1920) who is regarded as the first social theorist to discover the applicability of the notion of legitimacy and therefore the first to use the term for classifying and comparing the socio-political phenomena. He is said to have assumed that in a legitimate dominion of any type, legitimacy "is based on belief and elicits obedience."[41] Simply stated, he insists that the ruling group "must be legitimate."[42]

The noticeable point, in this direction, is that Weber does not discuss the general way of legitimacy; instead he concentrates on its pure types. He holds that legitimacy may be ascribed to an order by those acting subject to it in the following ways:[43]

(a) by virtue of *tradition*, a belief in the legitimacy of what has already existed;
(b) by virtue of *effectual attitudes*, especially emotional, legitimising the validity of what is newly revealed or a model to imitate;
(c) by virtue of a *rational belief* in its absolute value, thus lending the validity of an absolute and final commitment;
(d) because it has been established in a manner which is recognised to be *legal*, this legality may be treated as legitimate in either of the two ways: on the one hand, it may derive from a voluntary agreement of the interested parties on the relevant terms, and on the other hand, it may be imposed on the basis of what is held to be a legitimate authority over the relevant persons and a corresponding claim to their obedience.

Weber emphatically notes that the basis of every system of authority and correspondingly of every kind of willingness to obey "is a belief by virtue of which persons exercising authority are lent prestige."[44] His classification of the types of legitimacy is regarded as the basis of a notable investigation of the nature of authority in contemporary civilisation. He mentions three types of legitimate authority—rational-legal, traditional, and charismatic.

1. Rational-legal authority is said to rest on a belief in the legality patterns of normative rules and the right of those elevated to the authority under such rules to issue commands.
2. Traditional authority is derived from an established belief in the sanctity of immemorial traditions and the legitimacy of the status of those exercising authority under them.
3. Charismatic authority rests on the devotion to the specific and exceptional sanctity, heroism or exemplary character of an individual person and of the normative patterns or order revealed or ordained by him. Charisma literally meaning 'gift of grace' in order that it may become a permanent structure, would have to assimilate itself to modern institutions. All types of authority require an administrative staff characterised by efficiency and continuity.

41. Sternberger, *op. cit.*, p. 246.
42. Ilsa Dronberger: *The Political Thought of Max Weber: In Quest of Statesmanship* (New York: Appleton-Century, 1971), p. 197.
43. *Ibid.*
44. *Ibid.*

As Max Weber in his *Politics as Vocation* says: "There are two typical forms of charismatic provision with means—gifts and booty, that is, resources acquired by coercive methods, whether by force or not. But, once the position of authority becomes established, these must be transformed into regular sources of income which takes the form of acquiring segregated property granting benefices in the traditional form. According to circumstances, the authority structure of the charismatic movement may change either in a traditional or rational-legal direction."[45] To him the 'chief is not meant to change the course of world history alone; his free will depends upon the realm of objective possibilities. In his historical writings, the 'great man' is not granted an absolute or exclusive role in the moulding of social organisation and ideas of modern civilisation'. Observing that charisma may be reinterpreted in an anti-authoritarian direction, he points to the use of the plebiscite as a means of legitimising leadership on a democratic basis. The charismatic leader may be said to reign in a democracy by virtue of the people's vote of confidence. His mandate would last as long as he has their confidence. In this way, he notes that the demagogic party leader who might not allow other leaders to coexist with him, turn dictatorial in which case the plebiscite might be affected. He names both Napoleons (Napoleon Bonaparte and Louis Napoleon III) as classic examples, even though legitimation by plebiscite had been carried out after the seizure of power by force.[46]

It may be pointed out that rational legitimacy, which Weber identifies with legality, "is the only type of legitimacy to survive in the modern world. In it every single bearer of the power of command is legitimated by the system of rational norms and his power is legitimate so far as it corresponds with the norms."[47] A critic may, however, add that the relation between the psychological and the nominalist interpretation of a phenomenon like authority is strikingly illustrated in the approach of Max Weber who, while compromising authority with legitimacy, "misses one of the key aspects of authority by maintaining its rational aspect."[48]

Picking up the threads from Weber's interpretations as borrowed by the recent American social theorists like Robert K. Merton and Talcott Parsons, Seymour Martin Lipset has studied the issue of legitimacy *vis-a-vis* social conflict in the context of political change that takes place particularly in a democratic polity. One may say that the real purpose of this political sociologist is to study the problem with a view to examine the security aspect of a democratic system. For this sake, he examines two situational dimensions—one, in which old order continues to have its ramifications or one that may be described as a phase of transitional and gradual change, and second, in which there occurs a radical change signifying the loss of one form of legitimacy and the gain of another. Let us briefly study both in the following manner.

In case the status of major traditional groups and symbols is not threatened during the period of transition, even though most of their power is lost, democracy seems to be more secure. Thus, we have a strange spectacle that the majority of

45. *Ibid.*, pp. 177-78.
46. *Ibid.*, p. 31.
47. See Alexander Passerin d' Entreves: *The Notion of the State: An Introduction to Political Theory* (Oxford: Clarendon Press, 1967), pp. 153-54.
48. Carl J. Friedrich: *Authority* (Camb. Mass: Harvard Univ. Press, 1958), p. 32.

the stable European and English-speaking democracies are monarchies in which the powers of the sovereign are limited by a constitution. The preservation of the monarchy apparently has retained for these nations the loyalties of the aristocratic and traditionalist sectors of the population, including religious groups—in other words, those resenting increased democratisation and equalitarianism. By accepting the lower classes and not resisting to the point where revolution might be necessary, the conservative system won or retained the loyalty of new 'citizens'. In countries where monarchy was overthrown by a revolution, forces allied with the throne had sometimes continued to refuse legitimacy to republican successors for a long time. One main source of legitimacy, then, is the continuity of important traditional institutions which serve to unify that society.[49]

In the second situation, loss of legitimacy is related to the way in which different societies regulate the crises regarding decisions on increased popular participation in politics. Whenever new groups (as those of workers and peasants) become politically active, their loyalty to the system is gained by permitting easy access to the legitimate political institutions and they, in turn, can permit the old dominating groups to maintain their own status. The workers and peasants in a free country and the subject people in a dependent country not only demand more and more share in the decision-making process, they also go to the length of adopting extremist methods so that legitimacy is accorded to their movement. It is due to this that political systems that "deny access to power except through revolutionary means also hinder the growth of democracy by allowing the introduction of unrealistic hopes into the political scene. Groups required to seek access by force are likely to exaggerate too much the effects of actual political participation. Thus, the resulting democratic regimes may be rejected by those whose hopes are unfulfilled, as well as considered illegitimate by traditional power groups."[50]

It enables Lipset to say that the matter of legitimacy will remain in question in spite of the fact that there is an effective political system in the event the status of major traditional groups is threatened and the emerging groups are denied access to power at the decisive stages of political development. On the other hand, even the stability of a legitimate system will be endangered in case there is a lengthy or repeated collapse of effectiveness. In order to finalise the stability of political institutions facing crises, it is necessary to know the relative degree of their legitimacy.[51] He illustrates it with the help of a paradigm.[52]

Effectiveness

		+	–
Legitimacy	+	A	B
	–	C	D

49. Lipset, *op. cit.*, p. 30.
50. *Ibid.*, p. 31.
51. *Ibid.*
52. *Ibid.*

This illustration shows relationship between the degrees of legitimacy and effectiveness. The possible combinations may be used to symbolise various countries. Countries in Box A rate high in both legitimacy and effectiveness and have stable political systems. The United States and Britain may be included in this category. Ineffective and illegitimate regimes in Box D are unstable by definition, unless they are dictatorships ruled by forces as in Hungary and East Germany. The political experiences of different countries in the early 1930's illustrate the effect of other combinations. Neither the German nor the Austrian republic was considered legitimate by large and powerful groups in the late 1920's. Nevertheless, both remained reasonably effective. They may be included in Box C. When effectiveness collapsed in the 1930's, those countries having a high degree of legitimacy remained democratic, while others such as Germany, Austria and Spain lost their freedom. In terms of the paradigm, countries shifting from A to B remained democratic; those which shifted from C to D did not.[53]

Carrying his point further, Lipset adds that situations like these demonstrate the usefulness of this type of analysis. From a short range point of view, a highly effective but illegitimate government is more unstable than a regime having relatively low effectiveness but ranging high in legitimacy. The social stability of Thailand, for example, is in sharp contrast to neighbouring former colonial nations. On the other hand, lengthy effective government may give legitimacy to a political system. Effectiveness in the modern world means primarily constant economic development. These nations which "have adapted more successfully to the requirements of an industrial system have the fewest internal political stresses and have either preserved their traditional legitimacy or developed strong new symbols of legitimacy."[54]

Marxist Theory: Power, Authority and Legitimation

Marx's theory of political legitimacy and effectiveness is contained in his doctrine of the class war whereby he denounces the ruling bourgeois class as a conspiratorial group of the capitalists and their hired lackeys consciously exploiting and dominating the working class. To him the social authority of the ruling class hinges solely on economic factors. It is given in the *Communist Manifesto* that with the advance of capitalism, the bourgeoisie "conquered for itself in the modern representative State, exclusive political sway. The executive of the modern State is but a committee for managing the common affairs of the whole bourgeoise. . . .Political power is merely the organised power of one class for oppressing another."[55] Marx argues that the fact of class domination "flows directly from the class antagonisms inherent in those modes of production built on economic inequality. A division occurs between those who own and exercise control over the means of production and those whose labour power is purchased and exploited for surplus value."[56] It leads to the issue of domination that, according to Marx, may have three dimensions—economic, political and ideological.

53. *Ibid.*, p. 32.
54. *Ibid.*
55. Marx and Engels: *Selected Works*, Vol. I, p. 36.
56. Alan Swingewood: *Marx and Modern Social Theory* (London: Macmillan, 1975), pp. 139-40.

The idea of *economic domination* signifies that it is through capital that the bourgeoisie exercises its power of command over labour. The position of the working class is exclusively dictated by its complete subordination to an economic system which turns labour into the property of someone else to confront the worker as an independent force—capital.[57] Moreover, extended economic reproduction, while specifically creating affluence, only augments the considerable domination of the capital over the worker and as the personification of capital, the power of the capitalist class. The fact of political legitimacy and effectiveness thus finds place in the economic domination of the capitalist class that flows directly from its legal right and physical ability to exploit the labour power of others.[58]

The fact of *political domination* can be visualised in state's being an instrument of exploitation and oppression by one class over another. In the capitalist society, the state is in the hands of the bourgeoisie that legitimises its actions by means of parliamentary or judicial sanctions. The effectiveness of the bourgeois rule is ensured by the existence and working of the army, police, bureaucracy, courts, press, etc. It is given in the *Communist Manifesto* that the modern State is 'a committee for managing the common affairs of the whole bourgeoisie'.

Finally, we come to the point of *ideological domination*. According to Marx, ideology has a very important place in the determination of political legitimacy and effectiveness. If a socialist system is based on the ideology of the working class, a fascist or a bourgeois regime is based on the opposite ideology. It is a different matter that the bourgeoisie pretends not to follow any particular ideology and class domination is made possible without ideological authority in the sense that the rule is enforced through a dictatorial fiat. As Swingewood says: "Bonapartist, Fascist and totalitarian regimes, however, frequently subsist through the anti-ideological legitimations of naked terror, physical elimination of political opposition, police and army, although even here the dominant class feels obliged to justify its totalitarian politics in the ideologically universal terms by invoking symbolic myths of race, class and nation. But typically, the capitalist society has developed the parliamentary shell for bourgeois rule, institutions which emerged historically in many European societies from the conflict between bourgeois aspirations and feudal absolutism. The result is that class domination is no longer legitimated by traditional authority and blind obedience to the existing political institutions, but rather through the rational authority of an elected parliament and government.[59]

The law of dialectics enjoins that the exploited class must struggle to change the locus of power. The consolidation and growth of the bourgeois system creates conditions that lead to class war in which the bourgeoisie is sure to lose its position of power. The 'pressures' of the bourgeoisie take place within the context of a bourgeois social, political and economic structure in which the 'dominant ideological apparatus' expresses the ideas and values of the ruling class. There are thus definite

57. See W. Wesolowski: "Marx's Theory of Class Domination" in N. Lobkowicz (ed.): *Marx and the Western World* (Moscow, 1967), pp. 68-69.
58. Swingewood, *op. cit.*, pp. 141-42.
59. *Ibid.*, p. 144.

limits to the pressures exerted by a subordinate class; it must obey 'the rules of the game'and thus repudiate a direct challenge to the interests of the dominant class. The central point of Marxist contention is, however, contained in the emphasis on the factor of ideology that remains a matter of paramount importance in the capitalist society as well as in the socialist one in which the locus of power is changed from the side of the hitherto 'haves' to that of the 'have-nots'.

Since Marxism has a peculiar notion about the state, naturally its idea of political legitimacy is basically different from what we have seen in the case of liberal theory in this regard. A ' bourgeois' state is not a legitimate organisation in view of the fact that it is an instrument of exploitation and oppression by the ruling class over the class of the workers and peasants. In such a political order, the worker suffers from 'alienation' whose activity, as Marx says, appears as a torment, his own creation of the social and political system as a force alien to him, his wealth made for the society as the very source of his poverty, the essential bond connecting him with other men as something unessential so that his separation from other men appears as his true existence. A fundamental change, according to Marx, comes with the advent of the socialist order when 'dictatorship of the proletariat' in the form of a 'new state' comes into being "into which flow the institutional experiences of the oppressed class, in which the social life of the workers and peasant class becomes a system, universal and strongly organised."[60]

A socialist state is, therefore, a legitimate order which aims at the elimination of exploitation and oppression by one class over another by establishing a classless society. Not merely this, it has its final aim in its own destruction so that the classless pattern of society is eventually transformed into a stateless pattern of social existence. Thus, the Marxist idea of political legitimacy is eventually transposed into the ideal of social legitimacy. Such an ideal social order will witness total and active participation of the 'emancipated man.' Then all free and voluntary organisations dealing with the management of public affairs will be'legitimate'in respect of their composition and working by virtue of which they will enjoy real acceptability of the people. In a word, nothing but democratisation can be the essential sanction behind the source of political legitimacy. Thus, as Ralph Miliband suggests, the Marxist theory of political legitimacy should be studied in the light of this interpretation that it has "a commitment to a thorough political democratisation and to, what may be called, the disalienation of politics."[61]

Marxist and Anti-Marxist Approaches Distinguished: Acceptance as well as Modification and Rejection of Marx by the Political Elitists

As a matter of fact, the idea of political legitimacy as developed by Max Weber and his 'bourgeois' disciples should be regarded as an attempt in a way to modify, rather contradict, what Marx has said. The real purpose behind this is to repudiate the premises of Marxism or to show that the predictions of Marx have been falsified

60. Cited in Ralph Miliband: *Marxism and Politics* (London: Oxford University Press, 1977), p. 181.
61. *Ibid.,* p. 126.

Divergent Views on Political Legitimation

1. **Marx and Engels:** In a capitalist society the bourgeoisie dominates all spheres of life. The ideas of the ruling class are in every epoch the ruling ideas. ***The German Ideology*** (1846)
2. **Antonio Gramsci:** The capitalist state manages to secure legitimacy by establishing its 'hegemony' over all important sections or segments of the people who appreciate the prevailing system in a way and to an extent that the discredited state of the bourgeois class secures the title of legitimacy. Thus occurs a 'passive revolution' that kills the prospects of a socialist revolution as predicted by Marx and Engels. ***Selections from the Prison Notebooks*** (1971)
3. **Jurgen Habermas:** Liberal democracies are ridden with 'crisis tendencies'. There is always a tension between private economy or capitalist system and democratic political system that procreates the revolution of rising expectations. ***Legitimation Crisis*** (1975)
4. **Ralph Miliband:** Liberal democracy is capitalist democracy based upon unequal class power and hence it always suffers from the 'deficit' of legitimacy. ***The State in Capitalist Society*** (1982)
5. **Noam Chomsky:** The mass media is so powerful that it can sustain or subvert liberal democracy and thereby contribute to its legitimacy or illegitimacy. ***Manufacturing Consent*** (1994)
6. **David Beetham:** Three things are required for making the power legitimate exercise of power according to written rules or established conventions, validity of the rules in terms of the shared beliefs of both the rulers and the ruled, and its demonstration or expression by the free consent of the governed. ***The Legitimation of Power*** (1991)

by the growth of modern social, economic and political institutions. For instance, Weber distinguishes 'power' from 'domination' in terms of his threefold typology of legitimacy. He defines that power is the ability to impose one's will on another against opposition, while domination is 'imperative control'; that is, it flows directly from the belief that authorised commands will be obeyed without the sanction of physical coercion. Domination thus hinges on legitimate authority and constitutes a special case of power. He portrays modern capitalist society as characterised by the legal-rational domination of bureaucracy and emphasises the important role which capitalism has played in its development. Capitalist production hinges on bureaucracy, for capitalism creates 'an urgent need for stable, strict, intensive, and calculable administration'. To him capitalism makes the most rational economic basis for bureaucratic administration, for the superiority of bureaucracy 'lies in the role of technical knowledge which through the development of modern technology and business methods in the production of goods, has become completely indispensable.' His critique of Marxian approach can be seen in his bold affirmation that 'future belongs to bureaucracy'.[62]

62. Swingewood, *op. cit.*, pp. 148-49.

A peculiar case of the acceptance, though muffled into the cloak of modification and thereby amounting to the rejection, of the Marxian premises is contained in the elitist theory of modern democracy. Reference should be made to the contribution of Gaetano Mosca who begins like Marx but ends like Max Weber. In his well-known work *The Ruling Class,* Mosca affirms that "in all societies. . . two classes of people appear—a class that rules and a class that is ruled." This apparent likeness with Marx's doctrine of the class war, however, comes to an end when we find him affirming that the political or 'ruling class' enjoys legal and factual authority as an organised minority dominating an unorganised majority, a situation inherent in all social organisations but one which reaches its highest expression in, what he terms, the 'bureaucratic State'.[63] Mention in this regard should also be made of James Burnham whose economic approach is contained in his doctrine of 'managerial revolution'. According to him, the basis of any elite's power lies in its control over the principal means of production and distribution. It is by virtue of this privileged position that the group in power manages to receive 'preferential treatment' from the society and it is because of this position that it manages to prevent others from gaining power. Thus, the easiest way to discover the ruling group in any society is usually to see what group gets the biggest income.'[64] However, he should not be taken as a Marxist for the reason that his purpose is to justify and defend the present capitalist system. He takes from Marx nothing more than the significance of the control of the means of production by an elite. He desires to reconcile the contradiction between managerial control of the state and the state control of the economy by means of a new elite domination.

As a matter of fact, the elitists have made an attempt to justify the legitimacy and effectiveness of the rule of a very small section of the 'privileged few' in a bid to reject the premises of Marxism in the name of a well-founded empirical investigation. It may be traced in the assertion of Pareto that history 'is the graveyard of aristocracies'; likewise, it may be inferred from Michels' 'iron law of oligarchy'. Developing his theory of elites on the basis of the superficial dogma of the masses, O Y. Gasset affirms that the people revolt when aristocracy becomes corrupt and inefficient, and the motive behind the revolt is not that they have objection to being ruled by an aristocracy but would like to be ruled by a more competent aristocracy.[65] Similarly, in the institutional approach of C. Wright Mills we find that the history-making power of the elites "is sufficient to overturn the *status quo,* call into question the existing social relationship and establish a new structure. The inner core of the elite is able, potentially, to determine the roles both it and others will play in society."[66]

Legitimacy and Conflict: Problem of Stability and Security in a Democratic System

Legitimacy itself is, in the last analysis, a question of belief depending strictly on the ideologies and myths prevalent in a society. Every ideology seeks to depict the image of an ideal government. Governments which resemble this image are considered as

63. *Ibid.,* p. 146.
64. Burnham: *The Managerial Revolution* (London: Putnam, 1942), p. 56.
65. S.P. Varma: *Modern Political Theory* (Delhi: Vikas, 1975), p. 233.
66. Geraint Parry: *Political Elites* (London: George Allen and Unwin, 1969), p. 54.

legitimate and those which do not are regarded as illegitimate.[67] It follows that the canon of legitimacy is applicable to any form of political system whether democratic or not, though it has a particular application in the case of a democratic system where power vested in the people is exercised by their representatives chosen in free and fair periodic elections. Elections "are primarily a means of legitimising the right of the rulers to govern. Only conservative-traditional autocracies can afford to dispense with this form of legitimisation, and usually one of the first acts of the revolutionary regimes is to justify their newly acquired power with the authority of the people's consent."[68]

A constant threat to all democratic systems is the hardening of conflicts that are vital to it to the point where they "threaten to shatter the society. Conditions serving to moderate the intensity of battles between parties and groups are necessary to democratic government. The existence of a moderate state of conflict is, in fact, another way of defining legitimate democracy. Thus, as viewed in terms of continuing symbols and statuses, the factors producing legitimacy are closely related to those determining the moderate state of conflict."[69] Lipset, however, emphasises that the character and content of the major divisive forces affecting the political stability of a society are largely shaped by historical factors which have caused the way in which continuous major issues have been solved or not and that a political stability is aided by solving tensions one at a time, a political atmosphere of bitterness and frustration follows from the accumulation of unresolved conflicts.[70]

If the political stability of a society is shaped by the role of historical factors, we must take into account the fact that the security or preservation of a democratic system is very much affected by the role of the established traditions. For instance, religion may be viewed as an important factor in bringing about a state of stability as well as instability in different political systems of the world that call themselves democratic Not only this, the sects of the same religion may also be viewed as engaged in a grim fight to secure legitimacy for their system in a way interpreted by them. Thus, the people of Ireland struggled for the protection of Roman Catholicism, and, for this sake, remained at loggerheads with the Protestants of England. The result was the intensification of the Home Rule Movement that ultimately meant the formation of the Irish Republic without the upper layer of Ireland inhabited mostly by the Protestants that still forms part of the United Kingdom.

The role of economic factor also needs mention in this regard. In case the people belonging to the oppressed and weaker sections of the society manage to have their share in the distribution of political power by peaceful or constitutional means, they treat the political system as 'legitimate', otherwise they fight even by violent and extremist means. While Britain affords the brilliant case of the former category, France is ranked in the latter. Reference may be made to the extension and reform of franchise in the nineteenth and twentieth centuries whereby democratisation of the

67. Maurice Duverger: *The Study of Politics* (English translation by Robert Wagoner), (London: Nelson, 1972), p. 101.
68. A.R. Ball: *Modern Politics and Government*, pp. 129-30.
69. Lipset, *op. cit.*, p. 32.
70. *Ibid.*, pp. 32-33.

English House of Commons took place and that eventually resulted in the decline of the House of Lords. Different from this in a country like France, the people took to the course of revolution in 1789 and thereafter played fast and loose with their obsession for the tradition of 'republicanism' that witnessed intermittent termination as well as restoration of the system of monarchy until 1870. Not only this, the tradition of republicanism failed to have a precise connotation except the mark of having a non-monarchical system that, as the political developments of last one hundred years or so show, hovered from the existence of an effectual parliamentary government to that of a strong administration under a powerful leader—nicknamed by the critics as 'Bonapartism' and now critically termed as 'Gaullist Fascism'. It is owing to this dominant political fact that the tradition of republicanism has also been labelled as 'ambivalence' having its manifestation in the "antimony between authority and freedom that exists within it".[71]

The fact remains that while different kinds of political systems, whether democratic or not, may acquire legitimacy, it is the democracy that is in need of it more than all the other systems. The reason behind it is that, in the long run, such a system cannot be forced on a group of people against their will; in fact, it is unlikely to survive when a large majority opposes it, for democratic institutions "would encounter rough going if a majority always has to impose its rule on a larger minority."[72] If politics is a struggle for power, such a struggle has its full play in a democratic system. Thus, persons engaged in the war of 'influence' strive to win the acceptability of the people. Authority itself being a highly efficient form of influence "is not only more reliable and durable than naked coercion, but it also enables a ruler to govern with a minimum of political resources if it wins the mark of legitimacy."[73]

Acquisition of Legitimacy: Role of Ideology and Political Leadership

However, different is the case when we study the role of ideology in this direction inasmuch as politics based on a particular set of ideas brings about a state of intolerance. Parties committed to a particular ideology try to create an environment in which a definite set of rules endeavours to determine the lives of the people. A line of basic distinction may thus be drawn between the parties of 'representation' (those trying to represent diverse political beliefs and convictions) and parties of 'unification' (those trying to make all others conform to their own convictions). A democratic system loses its legitimacy if there is coercion or imposition of some particular political discipline on the people. Hence, the parties of unification or integration are the exponents of a pattern that smacks of totalitarianism. Parties hoping to gain majority by democratic methods cannot ultimately be parties of integration or complete unity.[74]

We find that leaders of a political system strive to ensure that the decisions taken by them are widely accepted by the people not only due to the fear of violence

71. Roy C. Macridis: "France" in Ward and Macridis (eds): *Modern Political Systems: Europe,* p. 158.
72. R.A. Dahl: *Modern Political Analysis* (Englewood Cliffs, New Jersey: Prentice Hall', 1977), p. 60.
73. *Ibid.*
74. Lipset, *op. cit.,* p. 35.

and coercion but also from a conviction that the men in authority roles have done things well and in the right manner. Thus, the leadership of the men in power is said to be 'legitimate' if the people, to whom the orders are directed, believe that the structures, procedures, acts, decisions, policies, etc., possess the quality of 'rightness', propriety or moral goodness. As such, the decisions taken by the officials have a binding character. The issue of ideology also figures in, since the leaders "usually espouse a set of more or less persistent, integrated doctrines that purport to explain and justify their leadership in the system."[75]

That is, ideology serves the purpose of a convenient tool to endow leadership with the mark of legitimacy. The leaders realise that by means of some ideology or 'political formula' (as called by Mosca), they would be able to convert their political influence into a valid authority and it is far more economical to rule by means of authority taken as legitimate by the people than by means of coercion that leads to the resurgence of people's resentment in the form of agitational and insurrectionary politics. Not only this, the invocation of, and adherence to, a particular ideology is done so as to accord legitimacy to the political system itself. In this way, different ideologies are espoused by different leaderships which "are like suitable garments which can, and should, be changed according to the exigencies of a situation in order that leaders might retain their leadership and constantly legitimise their power into authority—legal and rational component being supplied by the bureaucracy of the Weberian model."[76]

Obviously, such an approach cannot satisfy those against whom it is really directed. To a Marxist, ideology is like a 'false consciousness of reality' and no political system is legitimate unless it strives for the 'emancipation of man.' Only to the men of bourgeois orientation, different ideologies may persist at one and the same time. Not only this, even different political parties interested in the maintenance of the *status quo* may be seen involved in capturing power and seeking the legitimisation of their authority in the name of their respective ideologies. To say, for instance, that the Conservative Party of England at the time of their governance was espousing a reigning ideology and that the Labour Party in opposition was espousing a rival one "may satisfy a structural-functionalist but not a Marxist. It is not leaders who seek an ideology for perpetuating and legitimising their authority. It is the social relationships at a given time that generate corresponding ideologies which different classes of people avow, and leaders are those who champion the ideologies. Leaders cannot be chameleons changing their ideological colour and yet remain in their positions."[77]

Critical Appreciation

The idea of political legitimacy and effectiveness, thus, constitutes the complementary part of the concept of political obligation that we have seen in the preceding chapter. It may be added that while the idea of political obligation constitutes the first half of an important political concept, the notion of political legitimacy and effectiveness does

75. Dahl, *op. cit.*, p. 60.
76 K. Seshadri: *Marxism and Political Science* (New Delhi: People's Pub., 1977), pp. 187-88.
77. Seshadri, *op. cit.*, p. 188.

the same in the form of its second half. People, in general, obey the state, because they treat it as a legitimate organisation. Not only this, they also pay with their lives for the sake of carrying out, what Laski calls, the 'will of the state'. A cursory look into the pages of history shows that different political systems like feudalism, monarchy, aristocracy, oligarchy, plutocracy and the like survived over quite a long period on account of being regarded as legitimate and now their replacement by the system of democracy should be traced in the change in the political convictions of the people.

Since modern age is the age of democracy and socialism, naturally the concept of political legitimacy and effectiveness should be studied in the context of social tensions and conflicts that emanate from different 'ideologies' or ideas of the people about the proper nature of things in the social, economic and political spheres. The merit of democracy is that it not only allows free play of divergent 'ideas' that eventually result in diverse social tensions and conflicts, it also opens avenues for their proper settlement. It stands on the assumption that while political stability is aided by solving tensions one at a time, a political atmosphere of bitterness and frustration would follow from the accumulation of unresolved conflicts. In case a political system manages to survive in the midst of social tensions and their proper management by means of negotiation or consensus, it comes as a bold sign of 'political development'; it also stands as a bold proof of the authority being legitimate and thereby its commands being effective. Different is the situation in case of 'political decay'.

It would, however, not be wrong to say that the emphasis on the concept of political legitimacy and effectiveness owes its inspiration to the challenge coming from the side of Marxism to liberal political theory. A political system is said to be legitimate by the liberal if it stands on the 'will' of the people and its commands are taken as effective if they win the acceptability of the people. Moreover, every political system not only has its superstructures in the forms of legislature, executive and judicial departments, it has an infrastructure of its own in the form of political parties and interest or pressure groups. While the latter plays the role of 'input' agencies, the former delivers 'outputs'. If so, a study of political system should include both and, as such, the notion of legitimacy and effectiveness takes within its fold not only the position of men in authority roles occupying offices in the political organisation of a country, it also allows only those social organisations to play their role in the political process that have a legitimate character.

In other words, a study of the notion of political legitimacy and effectiveness takes us into the realm of sociology and then inspires us to examine the relationship of political authority with the political culture of the people. It is due to this that people not only oppose their rulers for violating their pledges or commitments made particularly on the eve of polls, they also oppose organisations having no legitimacy at all and yet trying to play their part in the political process of the country. An association of a minister with some secret organisation like the CIA in the United States or with some multinational corporation like Lockheed in Japan thus becomes a matter of wide condemnation. An interdisciplinary focus is thus required to examine the problem relating to the rise or fall, triumph or disaster, development or decay of, what John Stuart Mill termed, 'representative government' and James Bryce lauded as 'the best government invented by man'. Such a system is undoubtedly involved in solving the problem of remaining legitimate as well as effective in the midst of so many social tensions and conflicts. However, we cannot ignore the contribution of Marx who has exhorted us to look into the problem as to "why class societies are structurally unable to satisfy the need for legitimation that they produce."[78]

78. Jurgen Habermas: "Reconstruction of Historical Materialism" in F.D. Dallmayr (ed): *From Contract to Community:Political Theory at the Crossroads* (New York: Marcel Dekker, 1978), p. 63.

14

Revolution

> Revolution and the will of the people are one. At the same time, we cling to the conviction that a state is valid only in so far as it expresses the popular will: state legitimacy virtually resides in popular sovereignty. As the two trends converge, the state does not appear legitimate unless founded upon an initial revolutionary act. Its legitimacy is all the firmer if its major concern is spreading revolution and acting in the name of revolution.
>
> **—Jacques Ellul[1]**

After discussing the concept of political legitimacy and effectiveness we pass on to study the idea of revolution that, as already pointed out, forms a complementary part of the study of the notion of political obligation. We have seen that the people obey the state if the authority, in their view, is legitimate, otherwise they may overthrow it. Thus figures in the issue of revolution that may be a peaceful event like the Glorious Revolution of England of 1688 or a violent outburst like the French Revolution of 1789. Moreover, what the people call revolution may signify anything from a mere change in the long established hold of a particular party like the victory of the Janata party in the elections of 1977 in India to a total overthrow of the existing order as happened in Russia in 1917 and in China in 1949. A study of the idea of revolution, therefore, becomes an important subject in the realm of contemporary political theory in view of the fact that politics is described as 'a study of the struggle for power' or, in a technical sense, an investigation of manipulative persuasions, coercions, threats and the application of physical force which "are commonplace aspects of political life".[2]

Revolution: Nature and Necessary Implications

The idea of revolution covers not only political but also economic, social and cultural dimensions of human life with the result that a precise definition of this term involves different ramifications all hinging on the implications of change, whether peaceful or violent, total or partial, minor or major, slow or sudden and the like. However, in social, economic and political theory, it has come to mean essentially a sudden, fundamental and major transformation. Such an implication is basically different from what we find in the disciplines of astrology and astronomy where the restoration of the configuration system of heavenly bodies is treated as a 'cosmic revolution'. In the

1. Ellul: *Autopsy of Revolution,* Translated from French into English by Patricia Wolf (New York: Alfred A. Knopf, 1971), p. 210.
2. Robert A. Dahl: *Modern Political Analysis* (Englewood Cliffs, New Jersey: Prentice-Hall, 1976), p. 51.

field of political theory, in particular, it has a typical connotation signifying alteration in government along with change in the related associations and structures. In its core meaning, it "constitutes a challenge to the established political order and the eventual establishment of a new order radically different from the preceding one."[3]

What, however, creates the problem of offering a precise definition of the term 'revolution' is that it is used interchangeably with other activities like outburst, upheaval, unrest, agitation, rebellion, revolt, *coup d' etat* and the like which aim at changing the *status quo.* Little tells us that revolt is a rebellion against the established authority, while revolution is a sudden and violent change in the political system or the government of a state.[4] In a more complex way, Robert defines revolt as a collective and an ordinarily violent action by which a group rejects the existing authority as well as the established social standards, and prepares to attack and destroy them.[5] A possible line of difference between a revolt and a revolution may, however, be drawn in the affirmation that while both hint at a sudden, jolting and significant change in the existing system, the former does not imply the idea of 'profound change' as does the latter.[6]

Revolution not only differs from revolt in terms of scope and intensity, the same may be said about its difference with reform. A reform is a very little dose of amelioration, it certainly does not aim at a major transformation. There is hardly any place in a reform for the element of fundamental transformation or the use of violent and extremist methods which, necessarily, happens in the case of a revolution. A Marxist may say that 'reformism' is just a strategy of the capitalists to check or defeat the purpose of a revolution.[7] For instance, the doses of constitutional reforms as given by the British rulers in response to the progress of the freedom movement of the Indian people were nothing but shrewd measures to save their imperialistic hold. Revolution took place in 1947 when a major change occurred in the form of the transfer of power. Obviously, revolution "differs from revolt in its scope and consequences, and from reform in its suddenness and recourse to violence."[8]

Though the keynote of a revolution is said to lie in the fact of 'profound change', it is a tedious job to say what it really implies. One may agree with the description of Martin Luther's movement against the Pope as a 'religious revolution', since it brought about the creed of Protestantism and thereby caused a basic change in the character of the Christian society. Likewise, we may designate a major change in the mode of production as 'industrial revolution' entailing the replacement of the era of feudalism by that of capitalism. These important events of the early modern period, generally described as 'revolutions', certainly effected profound changes in the social and economic spheres, in the patterns of existence, in the customs and

3. Carl J. Friedrich: "Revolution" in *Encyclopaedia Britannica,* Vol. 15, XV Edition, 1974, p. 787.
4. See Ellul, *op. cit.* p. 101.
5. *Ibid.*
6. *Ibid.*
7. See Ralph Miliband: *Marxism and Politics* (London: Oxford University Press, 1977), p. 157.
8. Ellul, *op. cit.,* p. 101.

> **Revolution**
>
> When a political regime is overthrown by force in order to impose a new form of government, or a government which proclaims a new policy on some crucial issue, we call it a revolution. The assassination of a king or a president or a premier would not constitute a revolution if it were inspired by personal motives, or were the mere act of a small group of desperadoes who could not hope to establish an alternative government. A revolution implies a deep schism within the state. It reveals a pathological condition of the political will which shows by contrast the normal nature of authority.
>
> —**R.M.MacIver**
>
> *The Modern State,* p. 212.
>
> Revolutions unlike usurpations or coups d'etat are not necessarily illegitimate. If they succeed, they introduce a new principle of legitimacy that supersedes the legitimacy of the former regime.
>
> —**Dolf Sternberger**
>
> "Legitimacy" in David I. Sills (ed.): ***International Encyclopaedia of the Social Sciences*** (New York: Macmillan and Free Press, 1988), Volumes 9-10, p. 244.
>
> Revolution represents the most dramatic and far-reaching form of change. In its most common sense, revolution refers to the overthrow and replacement of a system of government, quite distinct from reform or evolution where change takes place within an enduring constitutional framework.
>
> —**Andrew Heywood**
>
> ***Political Theory: An Introduction,*** p. 361.

behaviour of the people and which, above all, "left no segment of society untouched or unaltered."[9]

One should, therefore, look at the element of a major or profound change before labelling an event as a revolution. Keeping this essential point in view, a French writer Mounier says: "By revolution, we mean a combination of rather far-reaching changes intended virtually to erase the real illness of a society that has reached an impasse, rapid enough to prevent those terminal illnesses from spreading their poisonous decay throughout the national body, yet slow enough to allow for the growth of whatever requires time to mature. The result is what counts, not how romantic, or how restrained the language is. It is enough to know that the operation is a major and vital one, bound to meet violent resistance, which in turn provokes counter-violence."[10] Such a sociological interpretation of the term, obviously, has two ingredients: that the real illness of the society must be erased, and that the activity must be violent in order to counter the violence displayed by the keepers of the established order.

9. *Ibid,* p. 102. Barbara Salvert says: "Although the basic idea of treating revolutions as events initiating widespread social change is probably quite acceptable, there is obvious problem with this definition: it does not indicate how widespread change has to be for a given set of events to be a revolution. Events such as the Chinese Revolution, that introduced changes in everything from the educational system to the land-tenure patterns clearly qualify as revolutions under this definition. But there are many changes of government that have been accompanied by a degree of social change that, while far surpassing routine reform have nevertheless, fallen short of the degree of change produced by such events as the French or Russian revolutions. The Bolivian Revolution of 1952 is an example of this : there are many others." *Revolutions and Revolutionaries* (New York : Elsevier, 1976), p. 6.
10. Ellul, *op. cit.,* p. 105.

The view of Mounier may, or may not, be acceptable to the students of revolution ranging from those who take a highly conservative view and thereby either shun this action strongly or dub even a minor activity like that of a change in the ministry as a revolution to those who profess radicalism and thereby disdain the idea of including an activity in this category unless it manifests a reaction against, or an opposition to, or an assault upon a superior authority that is no longer acceptable to them. Keeping aside the cases of social and economic revolution, Bertrand de Jouvenel reminds us that "a revolutionary phenomenon is primarily a political event, a fact that has tended to be overlooked in emphasising socio-economic considerations. Neither Marx nor Lenin made that error; they consistently and correctly regarded revolution as a political occurrence."[11]

As a matter of fact, the term 'revolution' has been defined by many writers in different ways. For instance, G.S. Petee says that revolution as 'reconstitution of the state association is coincident with the substitution of one myth for another as the main integrating guide in the culture.'[12] S.P. Huntington considers revolution to be 'a rapid, fundamental, and violent domestic change in the dominant values and myths of a society.'[13] Neumann looks at revolution as 'a sweeping fundamental change in the predominant myth of a social order.'[14] According to T.S. Kuhn, political revolutions occur, because the parties to revolution differ about the institutional matrix within which political change is to be achieved and evaluated.'[15] In the words of Hannah Arendt, the modern concept of revolution "is inextricably bound up with the notion that the course of history suddenly begins anew, that an entirely new story never known or told before is about to unfold.'[16]

Those who take a broad view of the revolution describe it as a passage or a transition from one epoch to another. In the form of the transformation of an entire epoch, the revolution occurs when a class of men see no other way out of the misery than revolution.[17] Wilbert E. Moore is more concerned with the use of methods in bringing about such a change. In his view, a revolution is a type of change which is violent and that 'engages a considerable portion of the population, and results in a change in the structure of government'.[18] But others are much concerned with the fact of elite insurgence and change. To them, a successful revolution "occurs where, as a result of challenge to the governmental elite, the insurgents are eventually able

11. *Ibid.*, p. 108.
12. Petee: *The Process of Revolution* (New York, 1938), p. 22.
13. Huntington: *Political Order in Changing Societies* (New Haven: Yale University Press, 1961), p. 264.
14. Sigmund Neumann: "The International Civil War" in *World Politics,* Vol. 1 (1948-49), pp. 333-34.
15. T.S. Kuhn: *The Structure of Scientific Revolution* (Chicago: Chicago University Press, 1962), p. 93.
16. Arendt: *On Revolution* (New York, 1965), p. 21.
17. Franz Schurmann: "On Revolutionary Conflict" in *Journal of International Affairs,* Vol. 2 3(1969), p. 41.
18. Moore: *Social Change* (Englewood Cliffs, New Jersey: Prentice-Hall, 1963), p. 81.

to occupy principal roles within the structure of political authority,"[19] So Harold Lasswell takes revolution as 'a shift in the class composition of elites'.[20] John Dunn also says that all revolutions "are definitionally failures of political control by an existing ruling elite."[21]

If we closely examine all the definitions given above, we may discover these points of emphasis in the meaning and nature of revolution:[22]

1. Alteration of values or myths of the society,
2. Alteration of social structure,
3. Alteration of institutions,
4. Changes in the leadership formation either in the personnel of the elite or its class composition,
5. Transfer of power by legal or non-legal means, and
6. Presence or dominance of violent behaviour made evident in the events leading to the collapse of the regime.

But the Marxian view is different from all wherein a revolution is taken as an inevitable development according to the definite laws of historical materialism and in which the essential factor is the change in class dominance. So, we may appreciate the definition of A.S. Cohan that a revolution "is that process by which a radical alteration of a particular society occurs over a given time span. Such alteration would include (a) a change in the class composition of the elites, (b) the elimination of previous political institutions and their replacement by others (or by none), or an alteration of the functions of these institutions, and (c) changes in the social structure which would be reflected in the class arrangements and or the redistribution of resources and income. The magnitude of the revolution may be measured by the extent to which changes have occurred in any of the above dimensions or in some combination of them."[23]

Following impressions may be gathered from what we have said above:

1. A revolution is an activity having its ramifications not only in the field of politics but also in those of economics and sociology. We are, however, concerned with its political dimension where it signifies a change in the existing authority. It aims at replacing the 'unjust' authority with a just one that may be acceptable to those over whom it is exercised.

---

19. Raymond Tanter and Manus Midlarsky: "A Theory of Revolution" in *Journal of Conflict Resolution*, Vol. 11, p. 267.
20. H.D. Lasswell: *Politics: Who Gets, What, When, How*? p. 113.
21. Dunn; *Modern Revolutions* (London, 1972), p. 13.
22. A.S. Cohan: *Theories of Revolution: An Introduction* (London: Nelson, 1975), p. 31.
23. *Ibid.* It may be added here that the functionalists reject the Marxian view of revolution and prefer to use the term 'social change' instead. Not only that, they also hold the view that the new term adopted by them cannot be theorised in precise terms owing to its so many degrees and varieties. Only some approaches can be adopted. Talcott Parsons says that while "we do not have a complete theory of the process of change in the social systems, we do have a canon of approach to the problems of constructing such a theory." *The Social System* (New York: Alfred A. Knopf, 1964), pp. 534-35.

2. Revolution causes a profound change. As such, it is different from a minor dose of amelioration called 'reform'. Moreover, the change should be sudden, not gradual. Mere repudiation of authority is not enough. Existing authority on account of being devoid of 'legitimacy' should be replaced by a new one that may validly claim the title of 'rightness'. As such, it is different from any activity of disorder like revolt or rebellion.
3. The means employed to bring about a sudden, major and profound change may vary from purely constitutional or non-violent to those thoroughly violent and extremist. We should look at what is actually achieved. A revolution may be the result of a very long march as happened in 1922 that led to the investiture of power in the hands of Mussolini and thereby the inauguration of Fascism in Italy; it may also be effected by the victory of a party like that of the Nazis led by Hitler in 1933 that entailed the doom of liberal democracy in Germany; it may also be a movement of a religious leader like Ayatollah Khomeini that meant the fall of monarchy and the establishment of an Islamic Republic in Iran in 1979; above all, it may be the fruit of an insurrection staged by the Communist Party as in China in 1949.
4. A revolution may also take place to undo the results of a revolution. In such a situation the revolution of the opponents is described by the men in power as a 'counter-revolution.' It has its particular application in the literature on Marxism-Leninism. The leaders of the Communist Party hail their success as 'revolution' and any activity in opposition to what they desire is decried as 'counter-revolution'. For instance, the Communist Party of China staged a revolution in 1927 and its suppression by the 'Nationalists' under Chiang Kai-shek was dubbed as 'counter-revolution'.
5. The real meaning of the term 'revolution' may be discovered in lying somewhere between a sudden and violent thrust culminating in a *coup d'etat* (as happened in Pakistan in 1958 when Field Marshal Ayub Khan overthrew the regime of Iskander Mirza and set up his military rule) to too broad a concept of change in the social structure as, for instance, happened in Turkey after the First World War when the government of Kemal took to the course of secularisation and modernisation of his country even in contravention of the traditional precepts of Islam.

We are thus irresistibly driven to this conclusion that though revolution as an event of history 'rarely fulfils its total definition',[24] it certainly aims at altering the structure of subordination. It is true that though numerous revolutions have taken place in different parts of the world and at different periods of social development, none has revealed itself completely. Even the well-known revolutions of the world have been denounced by the critics as the 'non-events' of this type. For instance, the Marxists are not prepared to designate the Indonesian Revolution of 1965 and the Bangladesh Revolution of 1971 as an event of 'revolution'. Likewise, their opponents do not agree with the view that any movement in the direction of replacing the 'dictatorship of the proletariat' by a democratic order should be labelled as a 'counter-revolution'. We may, therefore, agree with the observation of Ellul: "It is

24. *Ibid.*, p. 109.

impossible, therefore, to establish an objective and general pattern of revolution or even an adequate definition applicable to all periods."[25]

Varieties, Characteristics, Phases and Stages of Revolution

Instead of delving deep into the debate over the precise meaning of the term 'revolution', we should confine our attention to its general implication. Here it signifies an event that effects a profound change, whether by peaceful or violent means. If so, a revolution may have its own varieties which may be enumerated in the following order:

1. A 'liberal' revolution is one which shows the triumph of 'democracy' over the force of 'despotism'. The revolution of 1776 may be referred to in which the Americans overthrew the colonial hold of the British and then established their United States. In 1945 the Indonesian people did the same by repudiating the hold of the Dutch imperialists.
2. A 'communist' revolution is one in which the leaders of the Communist party manage to seize power and then establish their regime, what is technically described as 'the dictatorship of the proletariat.' It entails the replacement of the 'bourgeois' order by a 'classless society'. What happened in Russia in 1917 and subsequently in China, Vietnam and other 'socialist' countries of the world may be cited as the instances of this type.
3. A 'quasi-revolution' is one in which some important leader imposes changes on the people by his imperious will while himself being a beneficiary and not a maker of the revolution. What happened in France in 1958 may be referred to here. We find that it was the people who invited Charles de Gaulle to hold power. He accepted the offer on his own terms and thereupon established a new constitutional system substituting Parliamentarism with Bonapartism.
4. Revolution is also of 'limited' and 'unlimited' varieties. A 'limited' revolution is one which touches a particular aspect of the political system. For instance, a switch over from the parliamentary to a presidential system (as happened in Pakistan under Bhutto in 1972) may be cited in this connection. An 'unlimited' revolution has its wider manifestations. For instance, the 'total revolution' of Jayaprakash Narayan in India was said to have not only political but also other ramifications like economic, social, cultural and educational. As described by Eugene Rosenstock-Huessey, an unlimited revolution is 'a part of the march of history'.
5. A 'revolution proper' may be distinguished from a 'sub-revolution'. In simple terms, the two may be designated as 'complete' and 'incomplete' events. That is, a 'sub-revolution' is one where the attempt remains unsuccessful even after giving a powerful jolt to the established system but whose effects may be discerned in the short time to come. For instance, the revolution of 1905 in Russia failed. Lenin escaped to Switzerland and the Tsar granted important constitutional reforms. Different from this, 'revolution proper' took place in 1917 when Lenin captured power. It may be said that a 'sub-revolution' constitutes a prelude to a 'revolution proper'.

25. *Ibid., p.* 113.

6. However, the most important variety of revolution should be traced in its 'negative' and 'positive' aspects. A negative revolution is one in which 'political decay' is taken as a sign of 'political development'. That is, a trend in the direction of reaction is opted by the people as a move towards progress. For instance, the inauguration of Fascism in Italy in 1922 and of Nazism in Germany in 1933 were hailed as revolutions, though they entailed the doom of liberal democracy. Curiously, the people opted for a dictatorship without showing enthusiasm for replacing a despotic system by a constitutional government. As a matter of fact, a revolution is a 'positive' or constructive event inasmuch as it invariably aims at a change for the better.

The last point, given above, is really very important, one that informs us to distinguish a 'good' revolution from a 'bad' one. It is because of the constructive aspect that the heroes of a revolution are worshipped as 'prophets'. As such, a revolution, if it has to involve social betterment, must imply a change in the fundamental attitude of man towards individual character and social organisation. The essence of a revolution "is, therefore, a new social order established and developed thereby and only a reactionary can suppose that a revolution can be defined otherwise than by a reference to its purpose."[26]

Viewed thus, we may suggest the following characteristics of a revolution:[27]

1. It is a *process* in which the political direction of a state becomes increasingly discredited in the eyes of either the population as a whole or a certain key section of it. Such a process may culminate in the revolutionary event or a change of government by more peaceful means.
2. It implies a *change* of government at a clearly defined point in time by the use of armed force or the credible threat of its use.
3. It also signifies a more or less *coherent programme* of change in either political or social institutions of a state or both induced by the political leadership after a revolutionary event, when the transition of power has occurred.
4. It also hints at a *myth* that gives to the political leadership resulting from a revolutionary transition, short-term status as the legitimate government of the state.

Hence, while conceding that there is the absence of an agreed definition of revolution shared by both trained observers and the lay public, we may rely on this observation that it signifies "a complete overthrow of the established government in any country or state by those who were previously subject to it; a forcible substitution of a new ruler or a form of government."[28]

Revolution is, moreover, not a mere event; it is a series of events. That is, it is not merely concerned with the overthrow of the established order, it is equally concerned with the establishment of a new one in its place. Thus, it begins with the challenge to the existing system and continues until a new order is installed. What happens in between the two may be said to constitute the stages of a revolution which may be enumerated as under:[29]

26. C.D. Burns: *The Principles of Revolution* (London: George Allen and Unwin, 1920), p. 122.
27. Peter Calvert: *A Study of Revolution* (Oxford : Clarendon Press, 1970), p. 4.
28. See 'OED' cited by Alfred Meisel: "Revolution and Counter-Revolution" *in Encyclopaedia of the Social Sciences* edited by Seligman (New York; Macmillan, 1934).
29. See Friedrich, *op. cit.*, p. 784.

Varieties of Revolution—Non-Marxist Versus Marxist

Reformism: It is a political trend within the working class movement; it denies the need for a class struggle, political revolution and the political power of the working class; professes class collaboration and tries, by a series of reforms effected on the basis of bourgeois legality, to transform capitalism into a society of general welfare. It denies revolutionary methods for influencing social development and usually views socialism as an abstract ethical ideal expressed in the principles of freedom, humanism, justice and equality.

Revisionism: It is an ideological and political trend against Marxism. Its aim is to criticise, review, reconsider and develop Marxism. The privileged section of the working class (labour aristocracy and labour bureaucracy) provides its social basis. It is furthered by liberal methods and the policy of reforms employed by the ruling bourgeois parties. The meaning of revolution is gradual growth of capitalism into socialism. The struggle between bourgeois and communist ideologies plays an important part in its appearance. On the one hand, every success of Marxism-Leninism compels its enemies to adopt the mask of being Marxists and socialists, on the other hand, the participants in the communist movement who vacillate and who are theoretically unprepared and are not strong enough to withstand the pressure of bourgeois ideology, eventually descend into revisionist positions.

Bourgeois Revolution: It is a way of transition from the feudal to the capitalist socio-economic formation, carried out by means of a bitter class struggle for political supremacy between the reactionary ruling clique and the people. It occurs as a result of the radical changes in the modes of production and distribution that terminate the feudal society.

National Liberation Revolution: It is an integral part of the single world revolutionary process, a specific kind of class struggle. It is an important political and social change in the life of the peoples of the dependent countries, colonies or semi-colonies signifying liberation through revolution, and the future liquidation of all forms of social oppression, including capitalist. Its main aim is liberation from colonialism and democratic change.

Socialist Revolution: It is the most radical social revolution in the history of class society, a mode of transition from the capitalist socio-economic formation to the communist formation. It is a gigantic leap in social development that includes a host of decisive, qualitative changes in the socio-economic and political structure of a society—seizure of power by the working class in alliance with other strata of the working people, the breakdown of the old state machinery and the establishment of the state of dictatorship of the proletariat, the introduction of the public ownership of the means of production, creation of a system of social regulation and social and economic processes, abolition of all forms of exploitation and oppression, elimination of class antagonisms, development of social democracy and a cultural revolution.

A Dictionary of Scientific Communism, (Moscow: Progress Publishers, 1984), pp. 195-203.

1. A revolution begins when the expectations of the people are very high and the great leaders are engaged in a much perfectionist rhetoric. The result is the replacement of the 'old' with the 'new'.
2. The second stage begins when power is captured. The revolutionary leaders are confronted with realities when they come to govern. Then, difference of opinion prevails and the categories of the 'moderates' and the 'extremists' are earmarked. Evidence shows the defeat of the former in most of the cases. Victory rests with the radicals who concentrate power in their hands and then go to the extreme of using terror and violence for the suppression of opposition.

3. Desperate efforts are made to realise the revolutionary ideals and goals at all costs. And yet this over-extension of revolutionary fervour engenders a reaction (Thermidorean reaction as called by the French) that entails a period of convalescence.
4. Then follows a state of lull. An era of dissensions and resignations comes to prevail that creates a very fertile ground for the coming up of a dictator still animated by some revolutionary aspirations. We may find its example in the extermination of all great leaders like Mirabeau, Danton and Mara and the establishment of a Directory under Napolean Bonaparte in France after a couple of years of the Great Revolution that broke out in 1789.
5. The last stage is one in which gradually revolutionary symbols lose their hold and dictatorship appears as a naked power. Then occurs a trend towards restoration with reconciliation between what was overthrown and what was brought about.

If so, a revolution is not something that, as Indonesian President Sukarno once said in his fiery zeal, 'rejects yesterday'.

Liberal Theory: Emphasis on Preserving the Status Quo in the Process of Change

What we have said above about the meaning and nature of the revolution looms on a horizon ranging from the 'occurrence of cyclical alterations in the forms of government' as said by Aristotle to 'a mad inspiration of history' as suggested by Leon Trotsky. Hence, different theories have come up to highlight the meaning, nature and causes of a revolution. Liberal theory should be described as the first attempt in this direction. Beginning from the days of the Greeks to the end of the early modern period it has sought to study the case of revolution in a way so that the notion of change is made coincident with the preservation of the existing state of social, economic and political life. In some cases, curiously, a leading thinker has sought to justify a return to the past as an act of revolution with the result that liberal theory of revolution has been accused of being reactionary, anti-change, even counter-revolutionary.

It is owing to this that, in the political philosophy of Plato, by revolution we may mean the establishment of an ideal state or a three-class polity based on the principles of the division of labour and specialisation of functions as the only way to save the 'city' from being 'like a house divided against itself,' or convert a 'city of the swine' into 'a community of human beings'. The purpose of a revolution stops here. No more change is required after the establishment of the 'utopia' or the ideal state with the result that the 'community of the human beings' becomes like a fixed tableau.[30] Likewise, Aristotle takes a conservative view by taking the term 'sedition' for revolution in a very comprehensive sense so much so that even 'destruction of a constitution' amounts to the same thing.[31]

Aristotle is known for being the first great political thinker who under the head'revolution' studies its causes and degrees and also offers preventive devices. To him revolution implies a change in the constitution of the state. As such, the

30. Will Durant: *The Story of Philosophy,* p. 45.
31. Ernest Barker (ed): *The Politics of Aristotle,* p. 237.

replacement of one form of government by another, or even a change in the type of the rulers may amount to a revolution. That is, the substitution of the moderates with the extremists becomes a revolution as the new variety of rulers definitely brings about a change in the nature of political authority. To him, a revolution may occur either owing to *material conditions* (uneven distribution of wealth between rich and poor classes), *ideological factor* (ideas of justice moulding divisions), *efficient role* (of leaders in seeking power) and the *end* (achievement of a radically different order). What, however, the first political scientist has really desired is that revolution should be prevented as its occurrence is a matter of political tragedy.[32] Here he seems to be in agreement with Thucydides who in his *History of the Peloponesian War* says: "And so then fell upon the cities on account of revolution many grievous calamities."

The trend of seeing revolution with a sense of apprehension and thus an attempt at making the idea of change in consonance with the existing order continued. The great Roman lawyer Cicero in his *De Republica* defined the term revolution as "a disagreement among the citizens in terms of breaking up, because the citizens divide themselves into several factions." The Church Fathers gave a religious complexion to the idea of justice and thereby sought to manage things in a way as desired by the precepts of Christianity. An unjust ruler should be killed, so advised St. Augustine. It was obviously the best way to prevent things from drifting towards a revolution. As the first modern thinker, Machiavelli desired a revolution in his beloved country (Italy) in a way so that a strong republican system was established for all times to come.[33]

It is John Milton who in his *Areopagitica* linked up the case of revolution to the maintenance of freedom and went to the extent of choosing a new government in case the existing rulers deprived the people of their liberty.[34] It is, however, John Locke's *Second Treatise of Civil Government* wherein the idea of revolution finds such a conspicuous justification that a critic like C.E. Vaughan has charged him with 'formulating not a theory of government but that of a rebellion.' In case the sovereign violates the terms of the social contract whereby he is committed to protect the natural rights of the individuals, they are obliged to make a revolution or, what he calls, 'an appeal to the Heaven."[35]

One may say that the liberal interpretation of the meaning and nature of revolution takes an important turn at the hands of John Locke. The fact, however, remains that

---

32. Aristotle, *Politics,* Book V.
33. Machiavelli: *Discourses,* I, 21.
34. See H.M. Drucker: *The Political Uses of Ideology* (London: Macmillan, 1974), Ch. 5.
35. See Laski: *Political Thought in England (From Locke to Bentham),* p. 37. An act of revolution should, however, be distinguished from an act of disobedience to authority or violation of law. "To view problem in a setting of disobedience or revolution is surely to misconstrue it. It is to neglect, among other things, something that is obviously true—that most people who disobey the law are not revolutionaries and that most acts of disobedience of the law are not acts of revolution. Many who disobey the law are, of course, ordinary criminals: burglars, kidnappers, embezzlers and the like. But even of those who disobey the law under a claim of justification, most are neither advocates nor practitioners of revolution." Richard a. Wasserstrom: "The Obligation to Obey the Law" in A. de Crespigny and A. Wertheimer (ed.s): *Contemporary Political Theory* (London: Nelson, 1970), p. 269.

the keynote of making change in consonance with the defence of the *status quo* to any possible extent remains altogether undiscarded. Thus, the English Revolution of 1688 and the French Revolution of 1789 have been accused of being reactionary events. What the leaders of these two great events did was that, at bottom, they adopted a way of justifying the transfer of political authority from a landowning aristocracy to a commercial middle-class; and, like all philosophers they sought to justify such a transfer by stating its principles in terms of a logic wider in theory than it was prepared to admit in practice. "The men who made both the English and the French Revolutions announced themselves as the protagonists of the 'rights of man'; but any analysis of the measures by which they gave effect to their principles, or, even more, any analysis of the claims they regarded as inadmissible shows clearly that by the 'rights of man', they meant in actual fact the rights of that limited class of men who own the instruments of production in society. The liberal tradition, in historical fact, was an intellectual revolution primarily made in the interest of property-owners in the new (and newly significant) industrial field."[36]

In recent times, a fine analytical study of the subject of 'revolution' may be seen in the work of Crane Brinton, a historian of the Harvard University, that is an expanded form of his lectures on this subject delivered at the Lowell Institute (Boston) in 1938.[37] Here he has sought to lay down some empirical observations on the basis of a case study of four great revolutions of the world—Glorious Revolution of England of 1688, American Revolution of 1776, French Revolution of 1789, and the Russian Revolution of 1917. In his view, people react differently when they are faced with the situation of a revolution. Some see it with a sense of fear or dislike, to others it is a word of good promise, a beginning of better things, a necessary part of the progress of the human race put through either in the name of 'liberty, equality and fraternity' or 'authority, discipline and power'.[38] But the essential thing is that every event of this kind is marked by a popular uprising for a majority against a privileged minority, that emerges successful in establishing a government of its own. What is really striking in this regard is that it "is impossible for us to be indifferent towards revolutions."[39]

'A revolution is certainly a result of social disequilibrium. And as every society lives in a state of disequilibrium, it may occur anywhere in the world. A state of social disequilibrium smacks of a condition in which the varying and conflicting desires and habits of individuals and groups of individuals are in complex mutual adjustment and it is so complex that no mathematical treatment of it seems a possibility. As new desires arise, or as old desires grow stronger in various groups, or as environmental conditions change and the institutions fail to change, a relative disequilibrium may arise and then, what we call a revolution, may break out. However, a general catalogue of the causes of a revolution may include government deficits, complaints over taxation, government favouring of one set of economic intruders over another, administrative entanglements and confusions, desertion of the intellectuals,

36. Laski: *The State in Theory and Practice* (London: George Allen and Unwin, 1960), p. 51.
37. Brinton: *The Anatomy of Revolution* (London: George Allen and Unwin, 1939).
38. *Ibid*, pp. 11-12.
39. *Ibid.*, p. 13.

loss of confidence among many members of the ruling class, conversion of many members of the class to the belief that their privileges are unjust or harmful to the society, intensification of social antagonisms, stoppage at certain points (usually in the profession, arts, perhaps the white collar jobs generally) of the career open to talents, separation of economic power from political power and social distinction. Brinton further makes it clear that "some, if not most, of these signs may be found in almost any modern society at any time."[40]

The nature of the rise and growth of a revolution may be clarified with the help of certain conditions and stages which are:

1. An abortive revolution is no revolution at all, but an actual revolution always carries with it the element of 'surprise'. Brinton identifies it with the appearance of a ' Figaro' at the stage (a character that suddenly emerges on the scene to disturb the frequency of the plot in a surprising way). On that basis he suggests the 'role of Figaro' as the starting point of the first stage of a revolution. The years just preceding the actual outbreak of a revolution witness a crescendo of protests against the tyranny of the government, a hail of pamphlets, plays, addresses, an outburst of activity on the part of the interested pressure groups. Facing all this, the government certainly does not live upto the reputation its opponents seek to make for it. Its tyrannous attempts at suppressing the rebellious opposition may perhaps fail, because that opposition is too strong, resourceful, and virtuous, or its attempts may fail, because they are carried out half-heartedly and insufficiently by governmental agents more than half won over to the opposition. The facts remain that they so do fail.[41]
2. A revolution may be *spontaneous* or a result of some *planning*. While the school of circumstances regards revolution as a wild and natural growth, its seeds sown among the tyranny and corruption, its development wholly determined by forces outside itself, or at any rate outside human planning. But the school of plot regards revolution as a forced and artificial growth, its seeds carefully planted in soil, worked over and fertilised by the gardener—revolutionists mysteriously brought to maturity by these same gardeners against the forces of nature. Actually, as Brinton advises, we must reject both the extremes, for they are nonsense, and hold that revolutions do grow from seeds sown by men who want change, and that these men do a lot of skilful gardening; but that the gardeners are not working against nature, but rather in a soil and in a climate propitious to their work, and that the final fruits represent a collaboration between men and nature.[42]
3. Force plays a decisive role in the occurrence of a revolution. We may take note of the fact that in each revolution there is a point or there are many points where constituted authority is challenged by the illegal acts of the revolutionists. In such instances the routine response is to have recourse to force, police or military. If the force of the revolutionists is weak as compared to those who are in authority, the uprising is suppressed. But in case the revolutionists win, they come to a

40. *Ibid.*, pp. 79-80.
41. *Ibid.*, p. 83.
42. *Ibid.*, p. 105.

stage of rejoicing. Brinton calls it 'honeymoon stage', because now the leaders, poets, businessmen, professionals, country gentlemen and even those who once feared the uprising and looked at it with a sense of horror, join hands in the celebrations of rejoicing.[43]

4. Every revolution includes a cross section of the people. It has cliches, leaders or carriers of a revolution like the Jacobins in France, the Bolsheviks in Russia, the Reds in China, or leaders like Cromwell in England, Washington in America, Talleyrand and Mirabeau in France. The rank and file also join hands in an uprising, though a few may desert at some stage due to certain lurking doubts and apprehensions, or others may jump in with high hopes of a reward in the new set up. The evidence would seem to show that revolutionists are more or less a cross-section of common humanity. It offers an explanation for the undoubted fact that during certain phases of a revolution they behave in a way we do not expect such people to behave, and it must be sought in changes worked on them by the conditions they live under and by their revolutionary environment.[44]
5. Politically, the most striking point of uniformity is that after a revolution some form of dictatorship is established as that of Cromwell in England, of Napoleon Bonaparte in France, of Lenin in Russia. The ultimate establishment of a 'tyrant' is something like, in the old Greek sense of the word, an unconstitutional ruler brought to power by revolution or *stasis.* But it also leads to a condition smacking of a moral let down, concentration of power in the hands of a 'tyrant' is or a 'dictator', sweeping back of exiles, a revulsion against those who had made a 'terror', a return to old habits in daily life. Its best name is the 'Thermidorean reaction'; it is not by any means something unique that happened in France after the Great Revolution, it may occur in any country of the world.[45]

But the most dominant fact stands out that revolution makes changes in the system of the institutions and the ideas. An old era ends, a new era begins. Politically, it means the end of the worst abuses, the worst inefficiencies of the old regime, fall of one ruling class and accession of another recruited from those who were deprived of the position in the pre-revolutionary period.[46] Keeping all such ramifications of the study of a revolution, Brinton confidently asserts that a scientific study of this subject can be made. Some elements of uniformity may be discovered in the annals of revolutions that have occurred in the past or may occur in the time to come. As he asserts: "Wider uniformities will, to judge by the past of science, some day emerge from complete studies of the sociology of revolutions. . . . So precise is a word 'revolution' to many in that tradition and especially to Marxists that they indignantly refuse to apply it to such movements as the relatively bloodless but certainly violent and illegal assumption of power by Mussolini or Hitler. These movements, we are told, were not revolutions, because they did not take power from one class and gave it to another. Obviously, with a word in some ways as imprecise as 'revolutions', you can play all sorts of tricks like this. But for the scientific study

43. *Ibid.*, p. 112.
44. *Ibid.*, p. 147.
45. *Ibid.*, p 270.
46. *Ibid.*, p. 273.

of social change, it seems wise to apply the word 'revolution' to the overthrow of an established and legal parliamentary government by the Fascists."[47]

Marxian Theory: Emphasis on the Idea of 'Permanent Revolution'

At the hands of Marx, the term revolution came to have a basically new interpretation, who in his *Theses on Feuerbach* said: 'Philosophers have so far interpreted the world, the question is how to change it.' While standing at the grave site of Marx on March 17, 1883, his collaborator Fredrick Engels, paying his sincere tribute to him, said that before all else, Marx was a 'revolutionist' and that 'the real mission of his life was to contribute in one way or another to the overthrow of the capitalist society and of the state institutions which it had brought into being, to contribute to the liberation of the modern proletariat.'[48] It is Marx who, for the first time, argues that a social revolution takes place when the existing relations of production have begun to act as a fetter on the further development of the forces of production. Thus, for Marx, the major political revolutions of the modern age upto this time are to be explained as the result of long term social and economic developments, in which new forms of economic exploitation and property-ownership steadily develop. The result is that "a political revolution is a social revolution when it involves the conflict of social classes."[49]

If so, a major change in the means of production resulting in the corresponding change in the relations of production makes a revolution. The termination of the slave society by the feudal society, for instance, was a revolution. It is due to this that Marx lauds the advent of capitalism over the debris of feudalism as a great event which he calls the 'bourgeois revolution'. The 'bourgeois revolution' involves "the displacement of one minority class rule by that of another, 'feudal rule' by 'bourgeois rule'; the use of state power to remodel political and legal structures to suit the interests of the new ruling class; while the ruled majority either aids the rising class or remains passive but acquiescent."[50]

Thus, Marx hails the 'bourgeois revolution' whereby the 'feudal state' is overthrown by the middle class that has grown up inside it and a new state is created as the instrument of the 'bourgeois rule'.[51] The bourgeois class invents new methods of production and distribution of goods, establishes new means of transport and communications, installs industrial units for the employment of those who have nothing to sell but their labour power, discovers new raw materials for the manufacture of goods and new markets to sell those finished products in its lust for reaping more and more profits. The result of all this is the concentration of more and more labour power in few towns of the country. The workers make use of the means of transport and communications as well as new methods of education and training to make their fellowmen aware of the class consciousness. Ties of integration develop that enthuse the proletariat to organise and then to overthrow the capitalist

47. *Ibid.*, p. 299.
48. Marx-Engels: *Selected Works*, p. 436.
49. Ralph Miliband, *op. cit.*, p. 154
50. Michael Evans: *Karl Marx* (London: George Allen and Unwin, 1975), p. 138.
51. *Ibid.*, pp. 138-39.

system in order to free itself from the application of the law of increasing misery and degradation. It all leads to, what he calls, a 'socialist revolution'.

To Marx socialism is not only an ideal to be striven for but something writ large in the actual development of a capitalist society. Capitalism is transcended through its own development. Capital civilises, as Marx says, its enforcement of surplus labour, not only creates the conditions in which scarcity is no longer a problem, but is said to make general industriousness the property of the human species. The relation between wage labour and capital, the last form of servitude assumed by human activity, is cast off like a skin and the casting off itself is the result of the mode of production corresponding to capital.[52] The methods of a proletarian revolution may, however, vary from purely insurrectionist to a democratic one. Marx hopes that in democratically advanced countries (like England, Holland, France and America), a socialist revolution may take place through battle of the ballot box. In the main, however, the burden of Marxian theory is on the use of violent means.

A socialist revolution is said to take place when the proletariat captures state power and the decisive productive forces are concentrated in the hands of the working class. Not merely this, it is also required that the forces of reaction are forcibly suppressed so that there remains no danger of counter-revolution. It is also needed that the ideas, beliefs, convictions, customs and the ways of life of the people are changed so as to make them in tune with the norms of a socialist system. In this way, a cultural revolution to be launched for the sake of brainwashing the people is an integral part of the socialist revolution. Exploitation and oppression will go with the establishment of a 'classless society'. In his *State and Revolution,* Lenin says that a socialist revolution would, therefore, imply that the state under the fundamentally new conditions "is transformed into something which is no longer the state proper."[53]

The course of revolution does not stop even here. It is a permanent affair which with the establishment of the 'dictatorship of the proletariat' during the transitional stage calls for the march towards the inauguration of the final stage of a 'stateless society'. In his monograph titled *The Class Struggles in France,* Marx identifies the distinctiveness of the revolutionary purpose as "the declaration of the permanence of the revolution, the class dictatorship of the proletariat as a necessary intermediate point on the path towards the abolition of class differences in general, the abolition of all social relations which correspond to these relations of production, and the revolutionising of all ideas which stem from these social relations."[54]

The idea of permanent revolution, it should also be borne in mind, implies the case of the 'export of revolution'. In other words, it implies the case of international socialism. *The Communist Manifesto* ends with these words of exhortation: "Workers of all countries unite. You have nothing to lose but chains. You have a world to win." As Marx and Engels say: "It is in our interest and task to make the revolution permanent, until all more or less possessing classes have been forced out of their position of dominance, until the proletariat has conquered state power, and the association of the proletarians, not only in one country but in all the dominant

52. *Ibid.,* p. 141.
53. Lenin: *Selected Works,* p. 293.
54. See Miliband, *op. cit.,* p. 158.

countries of the world, has advanced so far that competition among the proletarians of these countries has ceased and that at least the decisive productive forces are concentrated in the hands of the proletarians. For us the issue cannot be alteration of private property but only its annihilation, not the smoothening over of class antagonism but the abolition of classes, not the improvement of existing society but the foundation of a new one."[55] In very simple terms, it all involves, what Trotsky so ardently desired after the death of Lenin in 1924, the 'fostering of revolution abroad as an essential part of the process'.[56]

At this stage we may take note of the fact that Lenin followed Marx and he added his own contributions to the theory of revolution whose special features may be thus enumerated:[57]

1. No revolutionary movement can be durable without a stable organisation of the leaders which preserves continuity.
2. The broader the mass which is spontaneously drawn into the struggle, which forms the basis of the movement and participates in it, the more urgent is the necessity of such an organisation, and the more durable this organisation must be (because the broader the mass, the easier it is for any demagogue to attract the backward sections of the mass).
3. Such an organisation must consist mainly of people who are professionally engaged in revolutionary activities.
4. In an autocratic country, the more we *narrow* the membership of such an organisation, restricting those who are professionally engaged in revolutionary activities and have received a professional training in the art, of struggle against the political police, the more difficult it will be to 'catch' such an organisation.
5. The wider will be the category of people, both from the working class and from other classes of society, who will have an opportunity of participating in the movement and actively working in it.

The striking feature of Lenin's theory of revolution is that it takes into account the possibility of creating a revolution in any country of the world, if the leadership of the communist party is capable of doing it. The role of the party as the vanguard of the proletariat is very important. Though a party of the working class, it may include all revolutionary sections of the people who have full faith in or revolutionary devotion to the eventual triumph of socialism. In this way, Lenin "removed Marxian revolution as a possibility only in advanced capitalist societies and placed it within the realm of possibility for virtually any country provided a revolutionary situation existed and a revolutionary party was present that could guide the society on the road to socialism. By particularising Marxian analysis to Russia, Lenin taught that the Marxian model was useful in any society. It was a lesson that other revolutionaries, including the Chinese, were to learn well."[58]

55. *Ibid.*, p. 158.
56. See Deutscher: *The Prophet Armed – Trotsky* (London, 1954), Ch. VI.
57. Cohan, *op. cit.*, p. 89.
58. *Ibid.*,p.93.

Further improvement upon the classical theory of revolution, as given by Marx, can be seen in the ideas and strategies of the Chinese communist leader—Mao, whose special features may be thus enumerated:

1. The whole theory of Marxism-Leninism should be revised in the light of the local conditions existing in the poor and backward countries of the Third World like China. Here, a large peasantry combined with other revolutionary elements fighting against the colonial power may form a united front under the leadership of the Communist Party. Thus, a revolution may occur even in a pre-capitalist society, if it is properly guided by the Communist Party that has the potentiality to lead the society through different stages of social development.
2. It follows that in a country where the working class is not available in sufficient strength, or it is unable to participate in the revolutionary movement, other classes constituting 'semi-proletariat' which may be in similar relationship with the dominant class as the proletariat is with the bougeoisie may have class consciousness and therefore revolutionary potential.
3. Since the undeveloped countries of the Third World are predominantly agricultural, much reliance should be laid on the role of the peasantry, but petty-bourgeoisie may also join hands with the peasant forces. Moreover, the real centres of struggle would be in the rural areas. Thus, a Marxist revolution would primarily be anti-feudal and secondarily, anti-bourgeois in character. The slogan should be: 'from villages to the cities'.
4. All means of violence and extremism, including guerilla warfare, should be adopted by the revolutionaries.
5. The concept of the 'mass line' must also be understood. It suggests that there is a continual movement towards communism. It is based on the principle that one stage gives way to another new stage. But the new stage already exists in the minds of the masses. It is, however, scattered and fragmented; therefore, the party leadership must bring the ideas together and return them to the masses. The method of the mass line includes four progressive stages—perception, summarisation, authorisation and implementation.
6. Revolutionary fervour must be maintained even after the successful results of a socialist revolution. Revolution must go on so that revolutionary era does not become part of a dimmer past.[59]

In short, the Marxian theory of revolution has its keynote in the transference of state power from one class to another and thereupon a perennial movement of society in the direction of converting it into first a classless and then a stateless pattern of life. Not only this, the revolution being a permanent process involves the case of the consolidation of socialism in one country and thereafter its advent in other countries in order to have the 'emancipation of man' all over the world. The real purpose is to see an end of the 'bourgeois system' root and branch not only in a particular country but all over the world. "The concept of 'permanent revolution', at least in Marx's usage, involves the application of continuous pressure for pushing the process further and creating the conditions for a revolutionary break with bourgeois democratic regime itself."[60]

59. *Ibid.*, pp. 107-8.

60. Miliband, *op. cit.*, p. 159.

Though Marxism is said to stand for the idea of 'permanent revolution', facts speak otherwise. A critic may say that the Marxian theory of revolution has its stop after the occurrence of the 'socialist revolution'. Revolution means change, a change for the better. But in a socialist state any change is a taboo. Opposition is suppressed and the people are forced to change themselves in a particular direction which may not necessarily amount to a change for the better. Thus, Marx's vision becomes eschatological. "The process is not conceived as continuing indefinitely, rather the revolution of the class-conscious Communist elite of the proletariat is seen as achieving a final stage which puts an end to all class rule and exploitation. The class struggle has then come to an end, and with it the chance of futher revolutionary upheavals."[61]

Another weakness of this theory of revolution is that the precise relationship between revolutionary political action and Marx's general theory of socio-economic development is optimistically vague. It stands on the elaboration of the doctrine of the class war. In other words, it revolves around the uniquely universalist role of the proletariat, a social grouping which was universal precisely because it had escaped from traditional status whatsoever.[62] The development of the Marxian theory in the present times creates a dilemma when we find a controversy between Trotsky desiring 'export of revolution', while Stalin crying for 'socialism in one country' and then with Khrushchev reiterating the principle of peaceful co-existence with the capitalist states of the world, while Mao denouncing all bourgeois nations as 'paper tigers' and ardently desiring armed confrontation with them.

Functionalist View of Revolution: A Critique of the Marxian View

Now we may take up the functionalist approach to the study of revolution finding its source of inspiration in the works of Talcott Parsons whose sociology is taken as a critique of as well as an alternative to the Marxian theory.[63] To Marx every society is class-ridden and the reason of conflict between the two classes is the dominance of one class to exploit and oppress the other class, but in the view of Parsons, the potentiality of class conflict is due to the general scarcity of valuable or valued goods and a competition going on for the sake of their allocation.[64] Such conflicts may lead to a state of revolution, but the people themselves evolve a kind of value system to deal with such conflictual situations. Thus, he suggests four structural categories—values, norms, collectivities and roles. Values define the limits of permissible cost of impulse satisfaction in accord with the whole array of hierarchical enduring goals of the personality and socio-cultural system for order, the need for respecting the interests of others and of the group as a whole in social

61. Friedrich, *op. cit*, p. 788.
62. John Dunn: *Modern Revolutions: An Introduction to the Analysis of a Political Phenomenon* (London: Cambridge Univ. Press, 1972), p. xii.
63. The study of Parsons is important here, because the fact remains that functionalism is regarded as the only current alternative to Marxism as the basis for some kind of general theory in political science and it is Parsons who may be considered as the primary exponent of this theory. See W.G. Runciman: *Social Science and Political Theory* (Cambridge: Cambridge University Press, 1965).
64. Talcott Parsons and Edward Shils: *Towards a General Theory of Action* (New York, 1965).

living Norms define the specific rules of a community and are generally contained in the legal system. A collectivity is punctuated by solidarity which is characterised by the institutionalisation of shared value orientations. It means the community as a whole in its political form. Finally, roles serve to guide the choices and the actions of their incumbents by specifying rights, duties, obligations, sanctions, facilities etc.[65]

The fundamental difference between the functionalist and the Marxian view of revolution is that, according to it a revolution may take any form of alteration in the social, economic and political spheres ranging from the dominant position of the classes to the change in the structures and institutions of a social and political system. The argument of the functionalist is that the revolution brings about a new environment that requires a new set of values, and once the values are adjusted and the environment is altered, the system would once again return to balance or equilibrium, the situation in which values and environment are synchronised. If so, the revolutions must be studied in the context of the social systems in which they occur. It is required because the values and the environment may be considered peculiar to a particular social system. "Because of the need to understand the situation in which the desynchronisation is occurring, that the sociology of functional societies comes logically before the sociology of revolution."[66]

According to Johnson, there may be six types of revolutions— the jacquerie, the millenarian rebellion, anarchistic rebellion, Jacobin communist rebellion, conspiratorial *coup d'etat,* and militarised mass insurrection. All these may be distinguished on four grounds—targets of revolutionary activity, identity of the revolutionaries (masses and elites), revolutionary goals or ideology, and the nature of the revolution in the direction of being spontaneous or not. He is mainly interested in the militarised mass insurrection that is characterised by (1) the desire on the part of the revolutionaries to replace the existing regime, (2) the fact that there is a mass movement which is led by an elite, (3) the adherence of the revolutionaries to a particular ideology, and (4) the following of a calculated and carefully worked out strategy in order to achieve success. Jacqueries, on the other hand, 'aim at the government, have legitimist goals, are made by the masses (jacquerie leaders are usually peasant figures, local priests, or rural secret societies), and are normally spontaneous.[67]

More interesting part of Johnson's study is the interlocking of the notions of legitimacy and elite intransigence with the concept of a revolution. It always takes two to make a revolution and one of these two is always the *status quo* elite. Thus, if the ruling elite is unresponsive to the pressures that do build up in a community, then a revolution will be likely to occur. Further, if the elite is not intransigent, simple

65. Mitchell: *Sociological Analysis and Politics,* p. 100.
66. Chalmers-Johnson: *Revolutionary Change* (Boston, 1966), p. 3. It appears that Johnson's starting point is the definition of revolution given by Sigmund Neumann which treats revolution as "a sweeping, fundamental change in political organisation, social structure, economic property control and the predominant myth of a social order, thus indicating a major break in the continuity of development." In his view, revolutions are the dynamic elements of world affairs. Refer to his paper "The International Civil War" in *World Politics,* Vol. 1 (1948-49), p. 2.
67. Chalmers-Johnson: *Revolution and the Social System* (Stanford: Stanford Univ. Press, 1964), p. 34.

change will occur, dysfunction will be relieved, and no revolution will take place.[68] Three assumptions seem to flow from this remark. First, the elite is seen to have full control over the means of coercion in the state at least until the army deserts. Second, we must assume that the elite knows what the proper solution ought to be, since 'intransigence' suggests 'pig-headedness' in the light of evidence about what the proper course of action ought to be. Third, and most important also, Johnson seems to be saying that regardless of the social situation, an intelligent thoughtful elite always has the ability to head off a revolution. The implication of this idea is that the maintenance, or loss, of legitimacy is dependent upon the actions of the ruling elite.[69]

The functionalist model of revolution is not satisfactory due to some reasons. The whole thrust of argument is that a revolution is caused by a non-synchronisation of the new environment with the prevailing value system and that a state of equilibrium is restored after some time when the necessary synchronisation takes place. Moreover, it rests wholly on the factor of 'political deflation' finding its manifestation in the intransigence of the ruling elites. One may discover an element of 'bias' in a study in favour of a particular kind of social system having its existence in affluent countries of the West. It is all trivial, because it ignores the role of factors that make revolution a necessity. It simply takes it for granted that a revolution in every case is always avoidable. Such a proposal is both ludicrous and empirically non-tenable. Thus, the functionalist view "errs in the direction of inevitability in much the same way that the Marxian tradition does, although the results of each sequence are quite different."[70]

Psychological View: Emphasis on Suppression of Instincts, Relative Deprivation and Upsurge of Rising Expectations

The impact of the Marxian theory of revolution on the new liberal thinkers should, however, be gauged in their examination of the role of sociological and psychological factors in bringing about a profound change by the forcible seizure of power. The new liberal thinkers of the present times have, in a way, tried to follow Marx in so far as he emphasises the use of force in the capture of power, and also rejected him in so far as he confines his attention to the parameters of class war. The result is that, according to neo-liberal thinkers, the meaning of revolution has a different connotation and so its causes may not be discovered in the sphere of economics alone. Thus, Laski says: "Revolution may be defined as an attempt by the use of force against the government legally in power to compel a change in what are held to be, by those using such force, the actual purposes of the state."[71] Another eminent writer observes: "By revolution I mean a political overturn more far-reaching than a *coup d' etat* or 'palace revolution.' I take revolution to mean a transfer of state power by means of involving the use of threat of organised unauthorised force, and the subsequent consolidation of that transferred power, with a view to bringing about a fundamental change in social, economic and political institutions."[72]

68. *Ibid.* p. 7.
69. Cohan, *op. cit.*, p. 134.
70. *Ibid*, p. 141.
71. Laski: *The State in Theory and Practice*, p. 104.
72. C.B. Macpherson: *Democratic Theory: Essays in Retrieval* (London: Oxford Univ. Press, 1975), p. 158.

Several viewpoints may be referred to, in this direction, all pin-pointing that revolutions "are violent civil disturbances that cause the displacement of one ruling group by another that has a broader popular basis of support."[73] The fact is that there is a limit to people's patience. Historical evidence shows that people having nothing like 'class-consciousness' (as Marx so confidently asserted) rise in revolt to change their destiny. As a leading French writer says: "Nations that have endured patiently and almost unconsciously the most overwhelming oppression often burst into rebellion against the yoke the moment it begins to grow lighter. The regime which is destroyed by a revolution is almost always an improvement on its immediate predecessor. . . . Evils which are patiently endured when they seem inevitable become intolerable when once the idea of escape from them is suggested."[74]

If so, the causes of revolution may be manifold which may be discovered in the world of economics, sociology, psychology and the like. Moreover, such an event may have different phases, degrees, stages or areas of involvement. Keeping all this in view, it may be said that whatever their immediate occasion, a revolution "would seem to be the result of a deep-rooted and slowly evolving political and social malformations rather than the sudden outbreak that they appear to be at the surface."[75] It is a different matter, however, that in their last or culminating phase, they are sudden and violent, and that after the seizure of power, a revolution tends to run through certain phases having diverse involvements ranging from global perspectives to that of a *coup d' etat* which "is just like a stroke at the particular persons wielding power, though it is made merely for the purpose of replacing them by others, without any extended or actual change in the system. It is the violent substitution for what an election normally accomplishes."[76]

Not merely in the spheres of sociology and economics, some recent writers have sought to find out the main cause of revolution in the sphere of psychology. According to them, political stability and instability are ultimately dependent on a state of mind, a mood in society. On the one hand, we may take up the case of the satisfied and apathetic people who are poor in goods, status and power and yet who can remain politically quiet, while their opposites can revolt; just as correlatively and more probably, dissatisfied poor can revolt, while the satisfied rich oppose a revolution. It is the dissatisfied state of mind rather than the tangible provision of adequate or inadequate supplies of food, equality, or liberty which produces the revolution. In actuality, there "must be a joining of the forces between dissatisfied, frustrated people who differ in their degree of objective, tangible welfare and status. Well-fed, well-educated, high status individuals who rebel in the face of apathy among the objectively deprived can accomplish at most a *coup d' etat.*"[77]

---

73. James C. Davies: "Toward a Theory of Revolution" in I.K. Fierabend, R.L. Fierabend and T.R. Gurr (ed.s): *Anger, Violence and Politics: Theories and Research* (Englewood Cliffs, New Jersey; Prentice Hall, 1972), p. 68 n 3.
74. Alexis dc Tocqueville: *Ancient Regime and the French Revolution,* Translated from French into English by Stuart Gilbert (New York: Doubleday, 1955), pp.. 176-77.
75. Friedrich, *op. cit.,* p. 790.
76. *Ibid.*
77. Davies, *op. cit.,* p. 68.

The cause of revolution has been discussed from the standpoint of psychoanalysis by David C. Schwartz who has discovered it in the factor of people's estrangement or apathy, known by the appellation of 'alienation'. To him, political alienation precedes a revolutionary outburst. It springs from a psychological conflict between an individual's own value hierarchy and the contradictory values that he perceives to be operative in the political system. In other words, psychological conflict occurs when the values that guide the behaviour of the regime are perceived by the citizens as violating their own individual values. As he says: "Revolutions begin with the attempted withdrawal from politics of individual's (and especially intellectual's) attention, affection and involvement."[78]

This psycho-dynamic approach of alienation, as taken by Schwartz, enables him to construct a 'plausible' theory, as he claims, which has its beginning in the 'ambivalence', then moves on to 'conflict', thereon to 'cognitive consistency' and finally to 'adjustment'. Withdrawal from politics is a very dangerous symptom inasmuch as it cultivates the feelings of estrangement from the system and its accumulated effect results in the form of an outburst of mass anger. To him, the "behavioural manifestations of withdrawal—or better, of passive political alienation—include : diminished effect, support and sense of legitimacy for the political system, individualisation, privatisation, reduction in the scope of loyalties, a sense of public purposelessness, non-voting, decreased political action and interactions as in membership and meeting of political organisations and the like."[79]

Thus, the notion of a withdrawal phase in the process of alienation helps to explain the "earliest symptom of revolution which is an increase in restlessness."[80] Moreover, if political alienation leads to the outbreak of a revolution, withdrawal of people from active politics after the revolution leads to the running of the zealous persons in different directions that may be described as the 'wandering of attention from one individual, object or line of action to another'.[81] Then, it appears that different people have different degrees of attention, salience and affection and disaffection from different institutions and symbols at different rates of speed. What should be taken note of at this stage is that the "change in attitude, sets and attention foci are posited by the very notions of privatisation and withdrawal."[82]

The names of Pitrin Sorokin, James Davies and Tedd Gurr may also be referred to at this stage who have tried to present a psychological study of the theme of revolution. In the view of Sorokin, a revolution is a comparatively sudden, rapid and violent change of the obsolete official law of the group, or of institutions and systems of values which it represents.[83] Such a process involves breaking of the 'official law' to bring about the change, a more rapid tempo than an ordinary change and an attack on a broad front of most of the rules that govern human behaviour. It involves a wide participation by the people and always includes acts of violence

78. Schwartz: "Political Alienation: The Psychology of Revolution's First Stage" in Fierabend and others, *op. cit.*, p. 59.
79. *Ibid.*
80. Crane Brinton: *The Anatomy of Revolution* (New York; Norton, 1938), p. 160.
81. L.P. Edwards: *The History of Revolution* (Chicago: Univ. of Chicago Press, 1962), p. 60.
82. Schwartz, *op. cit.*, p. 60.
83. Sorokin: *The Sociology of Revolution* (New York, 1925), p. 22.

at any scale. Essentially, the basic cause of a revolution is a system of values that is no longer integrated. Once this happens, a revolutionary situation may develop, but this 'lack of integration' is a necessary cause.

Like Aristotle, Sorokin believes that revolutions are avoidable and unnecessary and they inevitably end in greater oppression than the oppression that might have provoked them. The moods of the people are very important in the cause of a revolution that are moulded by the elements of love, hate, frustration, resentment etc. The development of a man's personality over a long period (called 'cruel historical schooling') helps to balance the various instincts and drives man into 'coordination with the environment'. The social control evolves through a long traditional growth of laws, morals, religious beliefs etc. which effectively restrain the wild beast from behaving as if he were living in the forest. Men find outlets for their aggressive tendencies other than killing the nearest neighbour or stealing what someone else has and so arise the conditions of competitions and conflicts.[84]

A revolution is signified by the emergence of a violent beast smacking of the 'biologisation of the behaviour of the multitude'. All social controls are broken down as a result of which, in the form of religious, moral, legal and other habits, the hereditary reflexes attain full freedom. This condition continues until social brakes resurge and normal conditions are restored. A revolution is like a 'perversion' and during its prevalence many changes occur in the life of man. Animal greed appears in the form of some people's act of stealing other's property. Even moral perversion occurs that may be seen in the violation of the norms of a proper sexual life. The society forgets its ideas, traditions and values about good life and a magical wind overtakes people so much so that they give a new name to their country as the USA for America or the USSR for Russia. It all implies that a revolution is caused by the inability of values to cope with the environment. The increasing stress upon the value-environment relationship is always triggered by the growth of repression of the main instincts of the majority of society, and the impossibility of obtaining for those instincts the necessary minimum of satisfaction."[85]

According to Sorokin, there are six general types of repression of the instincts relating to hunger, property, self-preservation, sex, impulse of freedom, and self-expression. Revolution may be caused due to the repression of a particular instinct or some instincts. But what he really desires to say is that there should be a gradual change, because the 'cost in human life suffering and cultural values is so great that it is evident that orderly, evolutionary processes of change are distinctly preferable from every standpoint'[86] It shows that he is particularly interested in how certain social forces affect the psychology of the individual and how, in turn, the psychology of the individual comes to affect the re-establishment of social restraints upon the community.[87]

Now we may throw some light on the theory of 'rising expectations' that was first highlighted by A. de Tocqueville in his study of the French revolution and then partly subscribed to by Brinton, but recently developed by Davies, Tanter

84. *Ibid.*
85. *Ibid.*, p. 367.
86. Sorokin: *Society, Culture and Personality*, p. 495.
87. Cohan, *op. cit.*, p. 189.

and Midlarsky. The burden of argument here is that a revolution is not necessarily created by a condition of acute misery, suffering, injustice, oppression and the like, it may also be created when the people are quite affluent and happy and go to the extent of harbouring some high expectations. For instance, "those parts of France in which the improvement in the standards of living was most pronounced were the chief centres of the revolutionary movement."[88] The reason behind it is that the people whose hearts are enthused with making more and more advancement in some direction create a revolution when they find that social and political conditions are like an obstacle in their way. As de Tocqueville says: "For it is not always when things are going from bad to worse that revolutions break out. On the contrary, it often happens that when people have put up with oppressive rule over a long period without protest, suddenly find the government relaxing its pressure, it takes up arms against it."[89]

In other words, the idea of the revolution of the rising expectations suggests that as the life situation improves, men expect that it will continue to improve. If they perceive that it could decline, or that it is likely to be hindered by an obstreperous or inefficient government, then they will take action to remove the potential impediment to progress. If that impediment happens to be the government, then the government must go.[90] So argues Davies that when the people are in the poorest state of existence, they are unlikely to revolt. "Far from making people into revolutionaries, enduring poverty makes for concern with one's solitary self or solitary family, at best a resignation or mute despair at worst."[91] As long as people receive at least a considerable part of what they expect to receive, they are unlikely to revolt. But if the actual need satisfaction continues to rise, a wide gap begins to develop between the two. When the gap between what people want and what they get becomes intolerable, they rise up to destroy whatever comes in their way.[92]

However, a line of difference may be drawn between the theories of Tocqueville and Davies in this regard. While the former sticks to the case of the 'rising expectations', the latter sticks to it and then tries to mix it up with the factor of social and economic discontent that is the fundamental premise of the Marxian theory on this subject. As Davies says, revolutions "need both a period of rising expectations and a succeeding period in which they are frustrated qualifies substantially the main Marxian notion that revolutions occur after progressive degradation."[93] In this way, this theory makes a modification of the Marxian theory after taking it as partially correct and partially mistaken.

---

88. A.de Tocqueville: *The Ancient Regime and the French Revolution,* p. 195.
89. *Ibid.,* p. 196. Referring to the English, American, French and Russian revolutions, Brinton says that "they occurred because of a feeling on the part of some of the chief enterprising groups that their opportunities for getting on in this world are unduly limited by political arrangements." *op. cit.,* p. 35.
90. Cohan, *op. cit.,* p. 195.
91. J.C. Davies: "Toward a Theory of Revolution" in *American Sociological Review,* Vol. 27, 1962, p. 7.
92. *Ibid.,* p. 6.
93. *Ibid.,* p. 17.

The theory of 'relative deprivation' as recently propounded by Gurr, Fierabend, Rosalind Fierabend and Nesvold may also be referred to in this context.[94] It is based on the frustation-aggression hypothesis and, therefore, implies that the occurrence of an aggressive behaviour always presupposes the existence of frustration and contrariwise that the existence of frustration always leads to some form of aggression. That is, the greater the degree of frustration, the more aggressive will be the response. Thus, the occurrence of any civil strife or violence "presupposes the likelihood of relative deprivation among substantial numbers of individuals in a society ; concomitantly the more severe is relative deprivation, the greater are the likelihood and intensity of civil violence."[95] The civil strife may involve turmoil, conspiracy and internal war. Turmoil is the most spontaneous of uprisings that includes strikes, riots and demonstrations. Conspiracy refers to organised activities such as coups, assassinations, guerilla wars. Last, internal war refers to organised and violent struggles at small or large scales.[96]

The elements of deprivation may pertain to long and short ranges. The indicators of a long term deprivation include economic discrimination, political discrimination, potential separatism on grounds of religion or ethnicity, dependence upon foreign capital by the country, religious cleavages, and lack of educational opportunities. The short-term indicators are inflation, decline in the growth rate, adverse economic conditions, and new restrictions on political participation by the government.[97] The same line of argument may, more or less, be seen in the paper of Frierabends and Nesvold who prefer to use the term 'systematic frustration' instead of relative deprivation that includes: (1) a frustration interfering with the attainment or maintenance of social goals, aspirations and values, (2) frustration simultaneously experienced by members of social aggregates and hence also complex social systems, and (3) frustration or strain that is produced within the structures and processes of social systems.[98]

---

94. A standard definition of the term 'relative deprivation' is provided by Gurr in these words: ". . . . the necessary precondition for violent civil conflict is relative deprivation, defined as actors, perception of discrepancy between their *value expectations* and their environment's apparent *value capabilities.* Value expectations are the goods and conditions of life to which people believe they are justifiably entitled. The referents of value capabilities are to be found largely in the social and physical environment; they are the conditions that determine people's perceived chances of getting or keeping the values they legitimately expect to attain." Refer to his "Psychological Factors in Civil Violence", *World Politics,* Vol. 20, 1967-68, p. 246.
95. *Ibid.,* p. 246.
96. T.R. Gurr: "A Casual Model of Civil Strife: A Comparative Analysis Using New Indices" in *American Political Science Review,* Vol. 62, 1968, p. 1107.
97. *Ibid.,* p. 111.
98. I.K. Frierabend, Rosalind L. Frierabend and A. Nesvold : "Social Change and Political Violence: Gross-National Patterns" in Graham and Gurr (ed. s): *The History of Violence in America : Historical And Comparative Perspectives,* p. 635. We may refer to two other recent writers who take a different view and hold that there may be many degrees of a revolution ranging from a palace revolution to a mass revolution and the degree of difference may be seen in respect of duration, size of mass participation, level of violence and intentions of insurgents. A revolution generally occurs after a period of instability and its form is dependent on the degree of political instability which exists prior to its occurrence. The most significant part of their statement is that the wider the gap between expected and actual need satisfaction, the more extensive the revolution is likely to be. See Raymond Tanter and Manus Midlarsky: "A Theory of Revolution" in *Journal of Conflict Resolution,* Vol. 11, p. 265.

On the whole, here we find much that may be taken as an extension of the functionalist theories on this subject. The writers have made an attempt to look into the causes and consequences of a revolution and their canvas is so broad that the Marxian theory on the subject looks partially correct and partially mistaken. One may also treat these theories as alternatives to the Marxian concept of revolution. However, their distinctly anti-Marxist stance can be easily deciphered in this affirmation that revolutions "are probably avoidable. If people can be satisfied, then the demands for change will subside. If the 'urge' to rebel stems from a feeling that the government is denying valued goods to the individual, then a perception that the authorities are acting to relieve certain problems or restraints may relieve that urge provided the needs of the individual are actually satisfied or perceived to be satisfied"[99]

In conclusion, we may say that the phenomena of political revolutions and resistance "are endemic in any political order and that they are closely related. To avoid them or reduce their menace has to be organised to make possible recurrent adaptations of the institutions and processes of a political order to evolving values, interests and beliefs, otherwise violence will spread sporadically as resistance at first globally and all-engulfing a revolution afterwards."[100] In brief, a revolution is not at all only an event in which one class dislodges another and captures power, it relates to a particular event of history extending over a considerable phase of time but certainly marked by major 'social and ideological change'.[101]

Idealistic-Liberal Theory: Emphasis on a Moral and Cultural Upheaval to Lay a New Foundation of Human Life

Different from both the liberal and the Marxian theories on this subject is the idealistic-liberal interpretation that lays emphasis on an ethical, spiritual or cultural upheaval through which a group of persons seeks to establish a new basis for existence. If so, a revolution is not merely a political process but a part of the unfolding of human potentiality. A major event of historical significance directed towards a higher moral end is a revolution according to this interpretation. It may be visualised in the statement of Immanuel Kant, the Father of Modern Idealism, who, while referring to the American and French Revolutions of the eighteenth century, said that a revolution was a fact of nature, not morally or legally allowable as such but to be accepted as natural if directed towards a higher ethical goal of life.

Such an orientation finds its impressive manifestation at the hands of Hegel. He justified Reformation by adding that "the ancient and ever preserved inwardness of the German people had to effect this resolution out of the simple modest heart." Likewise, he lauded the French Revolution as an event of 'world historical significance'. As he said: "The French nation, by the bath of its revolution has been freed from many institutions which the spirit of man has left behind like its baby shoes and which therefore weighed upon it, as they still weigh upon others, like lifeless feathers."[102]

What, however, makes Hegel a unique thinker in this regard is the laying down of the law of dialectical progression in which he combines logic and metaphysics

99. Cohan, *op cit.,* p. 206.
100. Friedrich, *op. cit.,* p. 791.
101 Stone Lawrence: "Theories of Revolution" in *World Politics,* Vol. XVIII (Jan, 1966), pp. 159-76.
102. Cited in Will Durant: *The Story of Philosophy,* p. 293.

resulting in the union of thought and being. To him it is the 'reason' that plays a decisive part in evolution. An object is a thesis, an element of contradiction develops within it that may be taken as its 'anti-thesis'. The struggle between the two leads to the emergence of the 'synthesis' which has a mixture of both the thesis and its anti-thesis as well as it represents a higher stage of development. A revolution, therefore, takes place on account of the operation of the law of dialectics in which the decisive role is played by the *geist* (spirit). Revolution, in this way, is something central to the"process in which the ideally rational could become actual."

In this way, Hegel speaks of a reassuringly elegant reason of the necessity of a revolution. He desires to insist on the concentration of those aspects under which the present is aptly seen as 'rational'. A revolution is, therefore, a thing to be lauded, since it is "like a rose in the cross of the present".[103] A revolution implies the advent of a higher stage—a stage which will lead to another higher one and thus the process of change will continue. "And that higher stage too will divide into a productive contradiction, and rise to still loftier levels of organisation, complexity and unity. The movement of thought, then, is the same as the movement of things; in each there is a dialectical progression from unity through diversity to diversity-in-unity. Thought and being follow the same law; and logic and metaphysics are one."[104]

An account of this change makes history. Obviously, such a philosophy of history leads to two revolutionary conclusions. The first is that the dialectical process makes change the cardinal principle of life; no condition is permanent; in every stage of things there is a contradiction which only the 'strife of the opposites' can resolve. "The deepest law of politics, therefore, is freedom—an open avenue to change; history is the growth of freedom, and the state is, or should be, freedom organised. Second, the doctrine that the 'real is rational' and *vice versa* has a conservative colour that takes away the very essence of what we mean by a revolution. To Hegel, every condition though destined to disappear has the divine right that belongs to it as a necessary stage in evolution; in a sense it is brutally true that whatever is, is right. And as unity is the goal of development, order is the first requisite of liberty."[105]

An idealistic-cum-liberal interpretation of the idea of revolution is traceable in the political philosophy of M.N. Roy who so skilfully blends rationalism with romanticism in a way that Marxism is replaced by 'radical humanism'. Freedom is a matter of absolute value. Thus, revolution means awakening the urge of freedom in man. Any theory of revolution that restricts freedom should be rejected. Since man is a rational and a moral creature, a theory of revolution should be based on human nature. As such, in order to bring about a revolution nothing like violence or insurrection or capture of state power is required. Only man's urge to freedom is to be awakened.[106] Therefore, any doctrine, whether Communism or Fascism, should be rejected in case it is the enemy of freedom. One must look beyond and say that a revolution "is a subversion of the *status quo* and reorganisation of society on the basis of freedom and equality remains a necessity."[107]

103. Hegel: *The Philosophy of Right* (Oxford, 1942), 12.
104. Will Durant, *op. cit.*, p. 296.
105. *Ibid.*, pp. 197-98.
106. R.K. Awasthi: *Scientific Humanism* (Delhi: Research, 1973), p. 261.
107. D.C. Grover: *M.N. Roy: Revolution and Reason in Indian Politics* (Calcutta: Minerva, 1974), p. 171.

Roy has placed his reliance on the role of ideas in a revolution. As such, a revolution in the spheres of economics or politics should be preceded by a philosophical revolution. If man is the maker of history, he must be made first. The role of a philosopher-revolutionary naturally precedes the occurrence of a revolution. "The urge for progress and freedom asserts itself with a renewed vigour to break down the obstacle. A new social order conducive to a less hampered unfolding of human potentialities is visualised by men embodying the liberating ideas and cultural values created in the past. A new philosophy is born to herald a reorganisation of society."[108]

By way of criticism it may be said that whether it is the purely idealistic version of Kant and Hegel or a liberal-idealistic elaboration of Roy, the fact remains that such an interpretation of the idea of revolution is too abstract to be understood by a man of average comprehension. It may also be added that purely philosophical versions take the subject of revolution far away from the world of reality. Revolution, as a matter of fact, is an important event that changes the pattern of social, economic and political development. That is, it is purely a practical affair. If so, the subject of revolution makes for an empirical study. "All revolutionary theories, whether favourable or hostile, are major premises in a large range of hugely important practical syllogisms. The value-free study of revolution is a logical impossibility."[109]

Revolution and 'Second Revolution': The Problem of Ideological Orientation

The important thing about a revolution is that it is not a single event, rather it is a series of events that should be described as attempts "to embody a set of values in a new or at least a renovated social order."[110] A study of this type demands that we should look into the role of ideas in a revolution that constitute the ideological dimension of a fiercely and an inevitably contentious topic. Not the people at large but a small number of them called elites articulate in quite a sophisticated way the ideas whereby they struggle to change the shape of things. Not merely this, the role of ideas continues even after the seizure of power that may be designated as the 'first revolution'. A new revolution also known as the 'second revolution' follows the first when the men in power endeavour to implement socio-economic changes according to their own ideological orientations. In this way, the role of a 'set of ideas (called ideology) finds its conspicuous manifestation in the major event (called revolution) as well as in the events that follow. Viewed thus, a revolution should be considered as a continuing affair "so long as ideological zeal is needed (and is forthcoming) to secure a sufficient basis for the new institutions."[111]

From this standpoint, we may look into the cases of the Marxian and liberal ideologies as well as a curious combination of the two particularly in the developing countries of the world. According to Marxian ideology, a revolution happens when a set of revolutionaries with quite complex ideas succeed in arousing vast masses of men already deeply discontented with the prevailing order to a sufficient sense of their own superior political and moral capacity to justify the masses in struggling

108. M.N. Roy: *Reason, Romanticism and Revolution,* Vol. I, p. 14.

109. Dunn, *op. cit.,* p. 2.

110. *Ibid.,* p. 12.

111. Macpherson, *op. cit,* p. 158.

to destroy the prevailing system. Revolution begins when the exploited people take to the course of insurrection and continues until the exploiters are thoroughly suppressed. As Lenin in his *Left Wing Communism—An Infantile Disorder* says: "It is not enough for revolution that the exploited and oppressed masses should understand the impossibility of living in the old way and demand changes, it is essential for revolution that the exploiters should not be able to live and rule in the old way. Only when the 'lower classes' do not want the old way, and when the 'upper classes' cannot carry on in the old way—only then can revolution triumph."[112]

Opposed to it is the ideology of liberalism that sticks to the doctrine of, what Macpherson calls, 'possessive individualism'. Its keynote is 'liberty'—a very precious thing that should be possessed and preserved. Thus, the Glorious Revolution of England of 1688 and the French Revolution of 1789 were great events in which people fought and won the boon of 'liberty' by establishing a constitutional government. As such, the case of the role of liberal ideology in a revolution is prior to that of the Marxian ideology. The noticeable thing in this regard, however, is that the ideology of liberalism in the present times has taken the form of 'capitalist ethos' that has taken away the real value of the ideal of egalitarianism and thus informed the deprived sections of the people to find salvation in the triumph of socialism.

The case of the newly independent countries of the Afro-Asian world is different where revolutions for the achievement of national freedom were conducted for the sake of bringing about a new order after the liquidation of the colonial rule. The leaders of the subject countries took inspiration from the ideals of liberal ideology as prevalent in the master country. They also looked towards the Marxian ideology after the victory of Communism in Russia in 1917. Apart from this, they also drew inspiration from the traditional values and thus a sort of blending of the three (Liberal, Marxian and Traditional) sets of values came to take place. So long as the fight for national liberation continued, the choice of values remained a fluid affair. After the successful revolution, differences cropped up as a result of which some revolutionary figures fell out, while others took to the course of a complex system imbibing essential values of different ideologies, as happened in India, or they continued to fight for alternatives as happened in a country like Pakistan. The case of a country overtaken by a communist revolution is a different affair in this regard.

A look at the role of the ideology in the 'second' revolutions going on in the developing countries of the world shows that most of them have sought to mix up the elements of liberal and Marxian ideologies in a way suiting the traditional values of their people. As a result of this, different sets of ideas have developed like Sukarnoism in Indonesia, Nehruism in India, Nkrumahism in Ghana, Nasserism in Egypt, Aminism in Uganda and the like, though the case of Sekou Toure's Guinea is a little different where, by and large, those elements of Marxism have been accepted which fit in with the pre-Marxian democratic position. It may be said that the leaders of the 'second' revolution have, in a sense, "anchored themselves in the earlier Western ideology of pre-liberal democracy. Just as they have rejected alignment with either Western or Communist power blocs, and have been themselves as outside the capitalism-communism continuum, so in rejecting contemporary Western ideology they have swung not

112. Lenin: *Selected Works,* Vol. II, p. 621.

to the Communist ideology but to a position, historically, of both the dominant contemporary ideologies, a pre-liberal democratic and pre-Marxist position."[113]

It may be asked as to why the leaders of the second revolution are so keen to follow a new ideology. The answer is that in order to achieve the ideals of rapid economic development for converting a hitherto colony into a viable independent nation, pursuance of a set of such ideas is essentially needed. A success in this direction would give credit to the makers of the social and economic revolution. In other words, it would contribute to their political legitimacy and effectiveness. How to imbibe the essential elements of the two ideologies of the West (Liberal and Marxian) and then engraft them into a new soil is a big problem whose solution is the condition precedent for according 'legitimacy' to their political authority. It is a fact that "the legitimacy of revolutionary elites in the process of struggle comes from their claim to be able to solve some of the problems of their societies. It is legitimacy which can only survive their success intact if they do not contrive to solve some of these.[114]

Critical Appreciation

What we have discussed above about the meaning, nature and various theories on the subject of revolution informs us to be clear in our minds on two fronts. First, every activity of some significance should not be designated as a revolution. What is really needed is to emphasise that in a revolution, the old established sense of right, what the Greeks called 'nomos', fades away and a new state of affairs comes that is without 'nomos'. In the popular parlance, a revolution is understood as an affair of the most militant sounding slogans, the most extreme and extravagant ideas and, above all, a question of violence and bloodshed, of barricades in the streets, battles with the police, armed warfare in the hilly or forest areas. There is no doubt that in most of the cases a revolution occurs in the form of street barricades, an armed conflict in the rural or urban areas or both, but these particular forms of struggle do not constitute the essence of a revolution. What really matters is the element of 'change'. "A social and political revolution is a matter of change in the whole basis and structure of society from feudalism to capitalism, from capitalism to socialism. It is a change in which decisive political and economic power passes from the hands of a declining ruling class, which has outlived its day, into the hands of a new advancing class which is destined to take society forward to a new phase of development."[115]

Second, a revolution is both a blessing and a curse. Like the doors of the temple of Janus, it "has two faces. One is elegant, abstract and humanitarian face, an idyllic face, the dream of revolution, its meaning under the calm distancing of eternity. The other is crude, violent and very concrete, rather nightmarish, with the hypnotic power of nightmare and the loss of perspective and breath of understanding which you might expect to go with this."[116] Naturally, it informs us to look into the case for and against the revolution before arriving at a plausible conclusion.

113. Macpherson, *op. cit.*, p. 163.

114. Dunn, *op. cit.*, p. 15.

115. Jack Woddis: *New Theories of Revolution* (London: Lawrence and Wishart, 1972), pp. 16-17.

116. Dunn, *op. cit.*, pp. 11-12.

In favour of revolution, it is urged that the evils in a social system are so deep-rooted that no amount of moderate reform will do. Patchwork is not required to ameliorate the lot of the underdog. Nothing but a major operation is required to dispense with the stock of injustice, corruption, demoralisation and the like. "The very basis for all reform needs transformation. What is wrong is not this or that bad habit, this or that bad government, but all present social habits and the very essence of the existing government. The time has come for a change as great as would be involved taking the Sermon on the Mount seriously. The time has come to look to the very foundations of society, for in them is the flaw which has cracked the building."[117]

If points in favour of revolution abound, others against it are no less numerous. It is argued that a revolution is a curse that unsettles the social, political and economic order. Not a revolution but evolution can do what is needed by the people. All revolutionaries are not clear in their minds. Like the great French Syndicalist leader Sorel, they shun the idea of first drawing a clear picture of the future society before treading the path of fire on the plea that it would do harm to the cause of the revolution. What happens, therefore, after the revolution is that it eats up its own children. The worst part of a revolutionary drama is the shedding of blood and shattering of the prevailing system. As Burns says: "In every actual revolution men have run riot: the violent have seized their opportunity: the ordinary man has been uncertain where to look or what to support. Hence come the bloodshed and destruction which, if this argument holds, are essential and not accidental in revolutions."[118]

In brief, the subject of revolution has its two sides. What should be concluded is that a revolution is neither a blessing nor a curse in each and every situation. Change is the law of nature and, as such, it should be hailed in preference to a static pattern of life. Any theory that shuns the idea of revolution in every case should be denounced for being thoroughly reactionary; likewise, a theory desiring radical change to bring about a particular form of social and economic order and then insisting on its perpetuation should be accused of making the idea of revolution vulgar. It applies to the affirmations of the Marxist writers who reiterate that the state and the revolution "are so completely assimilated that whatever opposes one, opposes the other. Any interaction of the administrative or the police code, ordinarily a misdemeanour, becomes a political threat to the goddess Revolution, embodied thereafter in the Cop and the Party Secretary."[119]

Thus, the process of change should continue unhampered and the patterns of social, economic and political life should be adjusted accordingly. "Political orders resemble forests and families. They contain the potentiality of self-renewal, but this potentiality does not exclude the chance of failure and ultimate death. Revolution, when successful, signalises the passing away of such a political order. It is not in itself as good as contemporary political romantics are inclined to feel, but it is

117. C.D. Burns: *The Principles of Revolution* (London: George Allen and Unwin, 1920), p. 130.
118. *Ibid.*, p. 133.
119. Ellul, *op. cit.*, p. 206.

better than the death of the society that such an order is intended to serve."[120] The significance of the words of Woodrow Wilson cannot be ignored when he says: "There is nothing so conservative of life as growth... But not all change is progress, not all growth is the manifestation of life. Let one part of the body be in haste to outgrow the rest and you have a malignant disease, the threat of death."[121]

120. Friedrich, *op. cit.*, p. 791.

121. See Francis G. Wilson: "The Anatomy of Conservatives" in W.J. Stankiewicz (ed.): *Political Thought Since World War II* (New York: Free Press of Glencoe, 1964), p. 342.

15

Ideology

> The crux of the matter is that, for the foreseeable future, the world will be divided between a minority of prosperous and relatively satisfied peoples, much interested in peace and quiet, and a large majority of impoverished and relatively dissatisfied peoples, much given to revolutionary hopes. If the have-nots, inspired by a revolutionary ideology, were to unite their forces in action against the rest, would not their superiority in numbers and enthusiasm enable them to win out in the long run. From the standpoint of the Western world, this unanswered question is the real nightmare of the twentieth century politics.
>
> **—Fredrick M. Watkins[1]**

After making a study of the idea of revolution, we now pass on to examine the role of deep-seated convictions and widely shared ideas of the people that cause drastic political actions and disturbances. These powerful political ideas in the form of a set of their own constitute, what Antoine Louis Claude Destutt de Tracy calls, an 'ideology'. Liberalism, Nationalism, Fascism, Socialism, Communism and the like are all major sets of ideas whose role in the secular politics of a country can very well be understood. Gone are the days of religious obscurantism when the people looked towards some 'Kingdom of Heaven' or hoped for a vision of bliss in the life hereafter. In contrast to this, now the goal before the secular leaders and thinkers is to attain a perfectible life on earth. This trend can be seen in the historic declaration and great charters adopted, for instance, by the people of England in 1689, of America in 1776, of France in 1789, of Russia in 1917 and the like. Thus, the tenets of a secular faith having their goal in the attainment of a blissful life on this earth have led to the creation of different sets of ideas, known as 'ideologies', and carved for them a place of their own 'as one of the characteristic features of contemporary politics.'[2]

Nature and Necessary Implications

The word 'ideology' was first used on May 23, 1797 by a French theorist Destutt de Tracy, a founding member of the *Institute Nationale,* who introduced this term as a newly conceived science in opposition to the subject of metaphysics. By ideology he meant the 'science of ideas' – a fresh discipline intended to be the basis of an entirely new social and political order. As he said: "It is an appropriate name, because it does not hint of anything doubtful or unknown; it does not bring to my mind any idea of cause. Its meaning is very clear to all, if only that of the French word 'idea' is considered, for everyone knows what he means by an 'idea', though few people

1. Watkins: *The Age of Ideology* (Englewood Cliffs, New Jersey: Prentice-Hall, 1964), p. 106.
2. *Ibid.,* p. 2.

know what it really is. This is appropriate, for 'ideology' is the literal translation of the science of ideas."[3] Thus, de Tracy took ideology, according to H.M. Drucker, 'as the modern answer to the unscientific past'.[4]

This French theorist belonged to the community of the *Ideologues* who were of the view that once language had been purged of old mistaken concepts, correct reasoning could prevail. Condillac associated evil with error, and error with the faulty reasoning engendered by the linguistic inadequacies, but he was hopeful enough to say that when the source of error had been discovered, the errors themselves could be readily eliminated. Thus, a key to the salvation of man was reached in the re-education of man and all that remained for the construction of a just or 'perfect' society was the establishment of a proper school system. Cabanis followed what Condillac said, but de Tracy made a little departure. He made a change in the epistemological doctrine of the *Ideologues* by suggesting that the external world is known because of the resistance it offers to our will and action.[5]

The epistemological doctrines of the *Ideologues* assumed a political significance when they, having discovered a method of establishing a good government, gave a proof of their impatient preoccupation with the social application of their theory. They looked towards the formulation of a theory of government and the programme of political action. Thus, ideology could not remain content to stay aloof from politics, until Napoleon Bonaparte placed his strong hand on this band of intellectuals, or 'tiresome theorists' as he called them. However, it "is during the collapse that the word 'ideology' acquired the opprobium which it has never wholly escaped."[6]

Since then, the term 'ideology' has come to have a significance of its own which, however, has become a very important concept of political theory ever since Karl Marx denounced it as 'false consciousness', Karl Mannheim called it a 'utopia' and a recent non-Marxist writer like Daniel Bell has spoken of the 'end of ideology'. As now understood, ideology "is a type of political theory which upholds a certain political system (in its broadest sense) and the values and ideals that sustain it, as the final proximation of the human mind to an ideal arrangement and, therefore, claiming this finality seeks to realise it."[7]

In its broadest sense, the term ideology signifies a set of ideas ranging from one desiring no change in the prevailing order to another crying for a total transformation

3. See Drucker: *The Political Uses of Ideology* (London: Macmillan, 1974), p. 3.
4. *Ibid.*
5. *Ibid.*, pp. 5-6.
6. *Ibid.*, p. 11.
7. Frank Thakurdas: "The Expanding Frontiers of Political Science" in *Indian Journal of Political Science*, Vol. XXXIV, No. 4, 1973, p. 415. According to *Webster's New International Dictionary* (1948), ideology "is the science of ideas." It is further given: "The integrated assertions, theories, and aims constituting a politico-social programme, often with an implication of factitious propagandising, as Fascism was altered in Germany to fit the Nazi ideology." During the Napoleonic era, it came to mean virtually any belief of republican or revolutionary sort, that is to say, any belief hostile to Napoleon himself. "But what Marx and Engels call ideology "includes not only the theory of knowledge and politics, but also metaphysics, ethics, religion and, indeed, any form of consciousness which expresses the basic attitudes or commitments of a social class." H.D. Aiken: *The Age of Ideology*, pp. 16-17.

of society. Moreover, it includes the refutation of one and the justification of another set of ideals irrespective of the fact that a critic may call a particular ideology as a 'utopia' or a 'false consciousness'. The ideas may also be in the form of an explanation of, some fact, or a justification of some claim or a quest for some truth, or a manifestation of some conviction and the like. Keeping all these dimensions in view, an eminent writer says: "I take ideology to be any more or less systematic set of ideas about man's place in nature, in society, and in history, *i.e.*, in relation to particular societies, which can elicit the commitment of significant numbers of people to (or against) political change. This does not exclude a set of ideas essentially concerned with merely a class or a nation, if it relates the place and needs of that section of humanity to the place of man in general. Thus liberalism, conservatism, democracy (in various senses), Marxism, Populism, Nkrumahism, pan-Africanism and various nationalisms are all ideologies. Ideologies contain in varying proportions, elements of explanation (of fact and history), justification (of demands), and faith or belief (in the ultimate truth or rightness of their case). They are informed by, but are less precise and systematic than, political theories or political philosophies. They are necessary to any effective political movement, hence to any revolution, for they perform the triple function of simplifying, demanding and justifying."[8]

However, the most important thing about ideology is its action-oriented character. The test of a political ideology "lies in its applications."[9] Thus, Preston King says that an ideology "will either involve the actual application of a coherent system of political ideas to a political system in such a way as to direct its activities, or it involves the serious distinction of making these applications."[10] In other words, ideology refers to an 'action-related system' of political ideas in the sense that these are sets of ideas concerning the change or defence of the existing political structures and relationship.[11] Ideology involves commitment and action as a part of the political process.[12] It "may, or may not, possess a logical or philosophical character at all; but it must possess a political character, *i.e.*, a content without which it cannot be described an ideology—a guide to direct political action."[13]

If so, the real meaning of ideology differs from the implications of certain other terms that are mistakenly regarded as interchangeable with it. For instance, ideology and mentality cannot be taken as analogous terms. While an ideology "is a system of thought which has been intellectually worked out and organised usually in written form by scholars and intellectuals or with their help, mentality denotes a way of thinking and feeling which is more emotional than rationalised—something like a cast of mind."[14] Ideology also differs from philosophy. As such, political

8. C.B. Macpherson: *Democratic Theory: Essays in Retrieval* (Oxford: Clarendon Press, 1975), pp. 157-58.
9. Frank Thakurdas, *op. cit.*, p. 419.
10. *Ibid.*
11. See Carl J. Friedrich and Z.K. Brzezinski: *Totalitarian Dictatorship and Autocracy* (New York, 1965), p. 88.
12. Preston King cited in Frank Thakurdas, *op. cit.*, p. 416.
13. *Ibid.*
14. S.E. Finer: *Comparative Government* (London: Allen Lane, The Penguin Press, 1970), p. 43.

ideology and political philosophy cannot be regarded as synonymous terms. Political philosophy "evokes reflection and understanding, while ideology is more likely to imply commitment and action."[15]

Following implications may be gathered from what we mean by ideology as understood in the realm of political theory:

1. Ideology is not the same as values and attitudes of the political culture. It is both a programme for action and an instrument of evaluation. It is a response to and a means of defending or changing existing political system; it provides a language to conduct an examination of the political process.[16]
2. It is not the content of the ideologies alone that distinguishes one from another, it is the function of the ideology within the political system that creates differentiation. Ideological emphasis is a significant characteristic of the totalitarian states, but in liberal democracies the role of the underlying ideologies is often less obtrusive but no less important in different respects.[17]
3. Ideologies do change, but this is not necessarily due to their being 'corrupted' or the 'death' of their role in the political process, nor are the changes simply the result of political opportunism. An ideology is impossible to translate directly into practice; there has to be accommodation to political realities, a translation which may result in ideological splits between former ideological colleagues and a distortion of reality to fit the ideological interpretation. It may be that ideologies need 'enemies' to establish their credibility.[18]
4. Ideologies may be classified according to their role in relation to the political system as rightist or leftist, reactionary or progressive, conservative or revolutionary, reformist or radical and the like. No political system is, however, absolutely free from the bond of ideology. It is a different thing that the adherents to the ideology of liberalism may claim and cry for the 'end of ideology.'[19]
5. It is the ideology that constitutes the keystone of the arch of a political party or a group. It may be found that a scuffle between two leaders (as Stalin and Trotsky in Russia), or between two groups (as Maoists and Liuists in China) is conducted within the framework of ideological arguments.[20]
6. An ideology being a set of ideas cannot sustain itself if it stems from faith. Since it rejects metaphysical and abstract notions, it should be based on proper scientific analysis, and political action should be directed towards the objective requirements of the society. Political action should aim at determining the interests of various social groups and not the subjective opinion of any individual or group of elites.[21]

---

15. See Preston King and B. Parekh (ed.s): *Politics and Experience* (Cambridge, 1969), p. 351.
16. A.R. Ball: *Modern Politics and Government* (London: Macmillan, 1971), p. 256.
17. *Ibid*, p. 255.
18. *Ibid.*, p. 254.
19. See Daniel Bell: *End of Ideology: On the Exhaustion of Political Ideas in the Fifties* (New York, 1968), pp. 393-404.
20. Ball, *op, cit.*, p. 254.
21. K. Seshadri: *Studies in Marxism and Political Science* (New Delhi: People's Pub., 1977), p. 193.

Ideology

* The ideas of the ruling class are in every epoch the ruling ideas, i.e., the class which is the material force of society, is at the same time its ruling intellectual force. The class which has the means of material production at its disposal, has control at the same time over the means of mental production, so that thereby, generally speaking, the ideas of those who lack the means of mental production are subject to it.

—Marx and Engels
German Ideology (London: Lawrence and Wishart, 1974), p. 64.

* All those who talk about 'overrating the importance of ideology', about exaggerating the role of the conscious element etc. imagine that the labour movement pure and simple can elaborate, and will elaborate, an independent ideology for itself.... But this is a profound mistake.....Since there can be no talk of an independent ideology formulated by the working masses themselves in the process of their movement, the only choice is either bourgeois or socialist ideology.

—V.L. Lenin
What is to be Done? (Moscow: Progress Publishers, 1973), pp. 39-40.

* Over the past half century, the concept of ideology has emerged as one of the most complex and debatable political ideas. It is remarkable for being discussed on levels that seemingly do not intersect, for attempting to organise phenomena that appear unrelated, and for causing confusion among scholars and political commentators. Political theorists, historians, philosophers, linguists, cultural anthropologists, sociologists and psychologists have all grappled with the notion of ideology.

—Michael Freeden
Ideologies and Political Theory: A Conceptual Approach (Oxford: Clarendon Press, 1996), p. 13.

* In everyday usage, 'ideology' tends to be a pejorative term, used especially to characterise ideas which seem biased and/or extreme. Thus, opponents have ideologies, whereas 'we' are characterised by principles, pragmatism or common sense.

—Roger Eatwell
Eatwell and Anthony Wright (eds.): *Contemporary Political Ideologies,* (Delhi: Rawat Publications, 2003), p. 2.

* Ideology is the most elusive concept in the whole of social science.

—David McLellan
Ideology (Buckingham: Open University Press, 1995), p. 10.

7. Ideology has become an instrument whereby the leaders motivate people to take part in political actions, or they accord the character of 'legitimacy' to their political system. Moreover, others beat their opponents with the stick of their own more or less persistent and integrated doctrines a set of which constitutes their own ideology.[22]

22. R.A. Dahl: *Modern Political Analysis* (Englewood Cliffs, New Jersey: Prentice-Hall, 1976), p. 61.

Characteristics of Ideology: The Doctrine of Reigning Ideology

It is said that all powerful political ideas of our time are almost parts of some ideology or other—a fact that makes the modern period an 'age of ideology'. The result is that ideology means different things to different persons. For instance, while the Liberals lay emphasis on the values of liberty, equality, justice and humanism, the Marxists look down upon ideology and desire to expunge it from the society. Men of conservative orientation detest the very idea of change, or radical change, and fear it (particularly the ideology of totalitarianism) as a set of ideas for the defence and justification of genocide, concentration camps, indiscriminate bombardment or mass arrests of the dissidents and the like. Different from this, others take a too optimistic view and hope that only by following a particular set of persistent and integrated doctrines can the people have the 'blissful life' on this earth.

Keeping this in view, Watkins points out three characteristics of modern ideology in the following manner:[23]

1. The goal to which modern ideologies address themselves are typically utopian. They tend to define their goals in unrealistically optimistic terms. The modern concept of free market, or the Marxist concept of a classless society are typical of this utopian trend. In each case the assumption is that once the promised goal has been reached, all the more taxing problems of modern life will promptly disappear.
2. Modern ideologies have developed the habit of thinking in over-simplified terms of we versus they, friend versus enemy, freemen versus tyrants, proletarians versus capitalists, patriots versus imperialists; such clear-cut alternatives are typical of the ideological way of seeing political realities.
3. Modern ideologies draw sustenance from extreme optimism of their views regarding human progress. In competitive situations, the side that believes it is bound to win has a very real advantage. If progress is the law of history, it follows that the wave of the future is on the side of the friends, and against the enemies, of human progress. Since the supporters of modern ideologies regularly believe that they alone are on the side of the angels, the result has been to give them confidence in the ultimate victory as well as in the justice of their cause.

According to Lane, ideology means a body of concepts having these characteristics:[24]

1. They deal with the questions: Who will be the rulers? How will the rulers be selected? By what principles will they govern?
2. They constitute an *argument*; that is, they are intended to persuade and to counter opposing views.
3. They integrally affect some of the major values of life.
4. They embrace a programme for the defence of the reform or abolition of important social institutions.
5. They are, in part, rationalisations of group interests—but not necessarily the interests of all groups espousing them.

---

23. See Watkins, *op. cit.*, pp. 7-8.
24. R.E. Lane: *Political Ideology* (New York: Free Press, 1962), pp. 14-15.

6. They are normative, ethical, moral in tone and content.
7. They are (inevitably) torn from their context in a broader belief system, and share the structural and stylistic properties of that system.

Some Definitional Statements

1. We speak of a *particular* and of a *total* conception of ideology. Under the first, we include all those utterances the 'falsity' of which is due to an intentional or unintentional, conscious, semi-conscious, deluding of one's self or of the other, taking place on a psychological level and structurally resembling lies.... Since suspicion or falsification is not included in the total conception of ideology, the use or the term 'ideology' in the sociology of knowledge has no moral or denunciatory intent. It points rather to a research interest which leads to the raising of the question when and where social structures come to express themselves in the structure of assertions and in what sense the former completely determine the latter.[a]
2. The term ideology is used in the way that is common in current literature, to stand for an organisation of opinions, attitudes, and values—a way of thinking about man and society. We may speak of an individual's total ideology or of his ideology with respect to different areas of social life: politics, economics, religion, minority groups and so forth. Ideologies have an existence independent of any single individual: and those which exist at a particular time are results of both historical processes and of contemporary social events.[b]
3. The ideologies are compounds of projective systems in the interest of which empirical evidence is mobilised, and have therefore the same structure as rationalisations.[c]
4. Ideology is the conversion of ideals into social levers.... For the ideologue, truth arises in action, and meaning is given to experience by the 'transforming moment'.[d]
5. Ideology refers to a more or less institutionalised set of beliefs—'the views someone picks up'. Belief-disbelief systems contain these two but, in addition, they contain highly personalised pre-ideological beliefs.[e]
6. ....articulated set of ideas, ends and purposes, which help members of the system to interpret the past, explain the present, and offer a vision for the future. Thereby they describe the aims for which some members feel political power ought to be used and its limits. They may be deceptive myths about political life; they may be realistic appraisals and sincere aspirations. But they have the potential, because they are articulated as a set of ethically infused ideals, to capture the imagination.[f]
7. The man of conservative disposition understands it to be the business of a government not to inflame passion and give it new objects to feed upon but to inject into the activities of already too passionate men an ingredient of moderation.... not because passion is vice and moderation virtue, but because moderation is indispensable if passionate men are to escape being locked in an encounter of mutual frustration.[g]

a. Karl Mannheim: *Ideology and Utopia*, pp. 238-39.
b. T.W. Adorno and others: *The Authoritarian Personality*, p. 2.
c. A. Kardiner and others: *The Psychological Frontiers of Society*, p. 36.
d. Daniel Bell: *The End of Ideology*, pp. 370-71.
e. Milton Rokeach and others: *The Open and Closed Mind*, p. 36.
f. David Easton: *A Systems Analysis of Political Life* (New York: Wiley, 1965), p. 290.
g. Michael Oakeshott: "On Being Conservative" reprinted in his *Rationalism and Politics and Other Essays* (London: Methuen, 1962), p. 192.

Besides most ideologies have these qualities also:[25]

1. They are group beliefs that individuals borrow; most people acquire an ideology by identifying (or disidentifying) with a social group.
2. They have a body of sacred documents (constitutions, bills of rights, manifestos, declarations), heroes (founding fathers, seers and sages, originators and great interpreters.)

And ideologies like all other beliefs, imply an empirical theory of cause and effect in the world, and a theory of the nature of man.

Another writer Robert A. Dahl of the United States has sought to present the varying interpretations of modern ideologies in the bifold morphological framework of 'reigning' versus 'rival' ideologies. According to him, "Some leaders, including the highest government official, usually espouse an ideology that justifies not only their own leadership but also the political system itself. Their ideology is then the official or reigning ideology. A reigning ideology indicates the moral, religious, factual and other assumptions that are assumed to justify the system. A highly developed reigning ideology usually contains standards for appraising the organisation, policies, and leaders of the system, and also an idealised description of the way in which the system actually works, a version that narrows the gap between reality and goal and the goal prescribed by the ideology."[26]

The peculiar feature of the reigning ideology (democracy) is that it is a highly flexible and adjustable set of ideas. No leader can arbitrarily invent or manipulate it, for once a political ideology is widely accepted in a political system, the leaders too become its prisoners, for they run the risk of undermining their own legitimacy, if they violate its norms. The case of the initiation of impeachment proceeding against President Nixon may be referred to in this direction. Dahl, therefore, cautions that it "would be unrealistic, however, to assume that a reigning ideology is a unified, consistent body of beliefs accepted by everyone in a political system."[27] He enumerates the following important points in this regard:[28]

1. The extent to which a distinguishable ideology is actually developed and articulated varies enormously from one political system to another. Many political systems simply share the reigning ideology that lends legitimacy to the Government and the State.
2. No ideology is ever entirely integrated or internally consistent. For one thing an ideology is not necessarily static; new situations create a need for new explanations and emphasis on new goals, and thus novel and unrelated or even inconsistent elements creep in. Then, too, a certain amount of ambiguity is sometimes a positive advantage precisely because it permits flexibility and change. For instance, the fact that the Soviet ideology was ambiguous about how and when the final condition of full communism was to be reached permitted Soviet leaders more free play than they could have if it prescribed a rigid time table of specific steps.

---

25. *Ibid.*, p. 15.
26. See Dahl, *op. cit.*, p. 61.
27. *Ibid.*, p. 65.
28. *Ibid*, pp. 61-64.

3. A reigning ideology is probably never uniformly accepted by all the members of a system. Many members have only rudimentary knowledge of the prevailing ideology articulated by the leaders, others may actually hold—perhaps unwittingly, a variety of private views that are at odds with the reigning ideology.
4. The reigning ideology may be rejected. Some members of a political system—Communists or Fascists in a democratic country, or democrats in an authoritarian country—may adhere to rival and conflicting ideologies. Because people differ in their aims, incumbent leaders rarely rule without incurring opposition, overt or covert; few systems can count on the ungrudging support from all their members. Opponents of a regime often formulate criticism that denies the existing system its legitimacy. Often, too, the critics depict an alternative that, unlike the existing system, is held to repose on a legitimate foundation.
5. Sometimes, the revolutionary ideology of one period becomes the reigning ideology of another. For instance, the revolutionary ideology of Marxism becomes the reigning ideology of a country after the successful result of a socialist revolution.

What Dahl has said about the doctrine of the reigning ideology may be applicable to any set of ideas, whether liberal or Marxist, but his bias against the latter is very well evident from his assertion that "not all ideologies are equally valid."[29]

Diffusion of Ideologies: Determination of the Tests of Their Survival

If ideologies are the sets of norms and values that dominate each society as well as its each segment, they cover a broad spectrum ranging from a loose and haphazard variety relying largely on an economic freedom and a glcrified pattern of the way of life to a rationalised and intolerant one smacking of a mental inertia or unwillingness to go beyond the established frame of reference. The result is that we are faced with, what Raymond Aron calls, the "diffusion of ideologies".[30] And he advises that we should cover all 'ideas' in this category which "are accepted by the individuals or peoples without regard to their origin and nature." The source of diffusion should be traced in the nature of the ideology itself. It lies in the fact that it is far more common "to regard an ideology as a set of abstract ideas, self-contained having its own rules of change and development."[31]

This matter has been studied by Hume in a different way who says that, in essence, an ideology "is a system of beliefs rationalised by men's total faculties (including what we call reason) but *produced* by the most fundamental causes of what we have come to call cultural determinism."[32] If so, let us also look into the tests of the survival of ideologies. It is also believed that since the times of Marx, ideology has come to mean a collection of rationalised concepts claiming to unlock the meaning of history or alternatively to supply a 'magic formula' for the control of history.[33]

---

29. *Ibid.*, p. 64.
30. Aron: "The Diffusion of Ideologies" in Stankiewicz, *op cit.*, p. 4.
31. G.E. Pettee: "Ideology in America." *Ibid.*, p. 82.
32. W.Y. Elliott: "Ideas and Ideologies", *Ibid.*, p. 25.
33. *Ibid.*, p. 26.

Accepting the fact of the broader definition of ideology as contained in the case of the diffusion of ideologies, it may be be said that all ideologies must meet the test of survival on the following major points.[34]

1. Ideologies must meet the test of creating institutions adequate to ensure their domestic survival in the group of origin. The ideology is the system. It makes the institutions work to fit into it. It is due to this that in a liberal-democratic country ideology is a very flexible affair which always remains subject to challenge and revision. Contrary to this, in a totalitarian country, it becomes ruthless; it creates a single centre, a one-party elite, a terror, an all-pervasive and controlling espionage system, and periodic purges.
2. In turn institutions depend on ideas—rigid for totalitarian myths, revisable for free societies. It is due to this that while the progress of democracy sees more and more reform of the parliament, extension of suffrage, increase in the scope of state activity toward general welfare and the like, all showing change in the premises of liberal ideology by virtue of its ever remaining subject to the course of revision, a totalitarian ideology has a more or less fixed character. There is very little ambivalence in it. Moreover, it all leads first to the cultivation of some 'magic formula' and then its conversion into a 'religion'.
3. Ideologies must meet the test of survival not only in terms of truth, but also in terms of power, *i.e.*, in conflict with other systems. In a sense, the test of survival depends upon the psychological impact that it makes on the people. Instead of pessimism there should be optimism so that the people may be convinced of something good after the defeat or extermination of the evil. Challenge of the opponent should be countered with a sense of hope. In simple terms, it implies that the ideology of liberalism should reshape itself so as to convince the people with the survival of democracy in the world in the face of all devastating challenges of totalitarianism.
4. Ideologies must meet the condition of economic inadequcy. Indeed, this is the test by which Communism condemns its rivals and justifies its own superiority. It poses the supreme test of so perfect an economic system, brought about by the suppression of all classes and class war and the control of the instruments of production in the hands of the dictatorship of the proletariat that the state can wither away and the economic order would be carried on with anarchic freedom. In opposition to this, the ideology of capitalism thrives on the boons of economic liberty leading to the production and distribution of more goods to the consumers who are free to express their wants and join the world of free competition.
5. The final and ultimate test of any ideology is its hold on men's souls. Whereas Communism proposes no other end or goal of human freedom than 'from each according to his ability, to each according to his need', liberalism postulates that 'man lives by liberty alone'. The line of fundamental difference between the two may be discovered in the fact that while the former manages to establish its hold on the minds of the people by means of force, the latter has the same effect by their free acceptance.

34. *Ibid.*, pp. 27-30.

As a matter of fact, it is due to the fact of diffusion of ideologies that while some are considered to be intolerant and, therefore, contemptible, others are decried by their opponents as no ideology at all, or just an indication of 'false consciousness' or 'utopia' and the like. That is, if the liberals are for a tolerant society, their quarrel with ideology is with its intolerance. As Aron says: "If tolerance is born of doubt, let us teach everyone to doubt all the models and Utopias, to challenge all the prophets of redemption and heralds of catastrophe."[35] According to this thinker, the American way of life is a negation of what the European intellectual means by the word 'ideology'. By the same token it must be said that "the non-party state, the state of parties, in order to tolerate the pluralism of parties and of doctrines is not devoid of doctrine, because the renunciation of violence is itself a philosophy."[36]

Liberal Theory: Ideology as a Highly Flexible Set of Norms and Values

From what we have said above, it may easily be gathered that the term 'ideology.' has its varying connotations in different schools of political philosophy. In the first place, we take up the case of liberal theory which takes a very elastic view of the 'set of ideas' and even goes to the extent of hating it when it is placed in the form of a rigid or a rationalised framework. However, the noticeable thing in this regard is that since the theory of Liberalism has been subject to revision from the days of Locke and Burke to those of Laski and Lasswell, it may be pointed out that the premises of liberal theory in regard to ideology have also been subject to corresponding transformation so much so that a thing like 'liberal ideology' has become a source of confusion for some and a matter of non-entity for others.

Liberalism as an ideology may be classified into two forms— classical and modern. While classical liberalism finding its best manifestation in the works of John Locke portrays men as modest characters of moderate passions and feeble reason who can best be accommodated to one another by a government which interferes with their essential freedoms as little as possible, modern liberalism finding its equally bold manifestation in the works of Hobhouse, Laski and Lasswell stands for the free play of various competing groups and associations into the political process of the country and an increase in the area of state activity with the result that modern state becomes a social welfare organisation. Thus, while the former (also known by the name of 'negative liberalism') stands for the maximum possible individual liberty *vis-a-vis* minimum possible state activity, the latter (also known by the appellation of 'positive liberalism') desires a better reconciliation of individual liberty with political authority so much so that an increase in the scope of state activity is justified, rather ardently desired, to make the life of the people free from the demons of ignorance, poverty, disease, starvation, unemployment, squalor and the like.

Basically opposed to the ideology of totalitarianism (whether of a rightist character called 'Fascism' or of a leftist one called 'Communism'), as we shall see, liberalism stands for the inculcation and cultivation of the values of freedom, democracy and humanism. Its basic assumptions lie in the entire paraphernalia of a democratic order having representative government, responsible executive, political checks and

35. Raymond Aron: *The Opium of the Intellectuals* (London, 1957), p. 324.
36. Aron: *Democracy and Totalitarianism* (London, 1956), p. 236.

balances, rule of law, independence of judiciary, free press and socio-economic justice. It is said to have three fundamental postulates—limited government, pluralistic society, and unlimited scope of free choices. The government operates in the midst of autonomous, spontaneously self-creating, voluntary associations. The society has a pluralistic character which implies that it "is made up of a host of autonomous sections and associations, but to believe that each enshrines values or interests dear to its members."[37]

Tolerance is the hallmark of liberal ideology. It believes that decent life for all is best protected in a society in which every interest is allowed free expression and access to power. Thus, the rise of political pluralism is justified whereby community is said to be in the existence of a large number of such groups. Thus, the classical liberal notion of free, equal, and competing individuals is replaced by a notion of free, substantially equal and ferociously competing interest groups with the proviso that the liberty of the individual is not trampled as a matter of deliberate action or policy of any group including the government. It stands on the assumption that truth is a matter of individual conscience where all consciences are held by an act of faith, to be equal either in the eyes of God or of man. Two practical conclusions follow from this, namely, toleration and the qualification of majority rule."[38]

While the premises of liberal ideology may be broadly indicated in the political sphere, it is very difficult to do the same when we examine it in the sphere of economics. While classical liberalism stood for *laissez faire* and thereby justified the play of unrestricted competition in the spheres of production and distribution of goods, positive liberalism seeks to reconcile the case of economic freedom with the norms of 'social justice'. The peculiar thing in this regard is that the points of Marxian attack on the capitalist system have, to a very appreciable extent, been accepted in the light of which leading economists like J.M. Keynes and J.K. Galbraith have revised their ideas of 'economic freedom'. As a result of this, the gap between classical and liberal ideologues has widened to the extent that it has led some critical commentators to speak of the split between the two as a 'scheme'.[39]

It is owing to a stern emphasis on the elements of freedom and tolerance that liberalism decries totalitarianism as 'anti-ideology'. The set of ideas, norms or values should not be converted into a rigid framework with the result that the respect for certain norms becomes a matter of blind faith. That is, ideology should not be converted into a 'religion'. Totalitarianism, thus, may be said to be devoid of any ideology inasmuch as it points to the fact that the ruling group endeavours to spread its fiat by every possible means at its command throughout the country. In a different way, it may be said that the assertion that the ideology is nothing but an intolerant political thinking leads liberals "to write of religion as a kind of ideology. For them the battle against ideology today is but an echo of the battle against religion yesterday. [40]

37. S E. Finer, *op. cit.*, p. 77.
38. *Ibid.*, p. 88.
39. Drucker, *op. cit.*, p. 38.
40. *Ibid*, p. 137. Also see Eric Hoffer: *The True Believer: Thoughts on the Nature of Mass Movements* (New York, 1951).

However, the real difficulty about the ideology of liberalism is that it is too fluid and flexible to be designated as such. One may say that its essentially flexible character takes it from the one pole of liberal-democratic to the other pole of liberal-authoritarian orders. A set of ideas which cannot at all be subjected to very specific and concrete programmes and where even action-orientedness is missing cannot be designated as an ideology. At the most, it may be decried as 'false consciousness' (Marx) or a 'utopia' (Mannheim). The Fascists and the Communists alike denounce the liberals as "deluded idealists or incompetent intellectuals."[41] According to Oswald Spengler, the liberal's concern for individual or minority rights and freedoms leads only to 'blindess, cowardice and spiritual indiscipline; he describes the modern liberal as either 'bourgeois' or 'plebian' and advises that both these words be taken as 'terms of abuse'. He dwells on the comment of Lenin who named a liberal as 'an armchair fool'.[42]

Conservative Theory: Ideology in Defence of the Established Order

The conservative theory on this subject should be regarded as a part of the liberal theory as well as a reaction against it inasmuch as it shows resentment against new developments suggested by the liberals in opposition to what a great 'self-conscious conservative' like Burke said while launching a vehement attack on the 'ideology' of the French Revolution. In this sense, the theory of conservatism is taken as something in opposition to the liberal theory. While liberalism desires change, conservatism stands for the defence of the established order. It is, however, a different matter to say that conservative theory is in agreement with the basic postulates of the liberal theory as developed in the earlier phase. What the conservatives advocate "is the return to an earlier and purer form of the liberal ideology."[43]

Conservatism as an ideology is said to have its start in Hegel's *Philosophy of Right* and then its best reiteration in Burke's *Reflections on the Revolution in France.* Viewed thus, it seems like indissolubly associated with feudalism, status, established order, landed interests, medievalism and nobility. As such, it looks like irreconcilably opposed to the middle class, labour commercialism, industrialism, democracy, liberalism and individualism. As the earlier liberals defended and justified the interests of the affluent class, so the conservatives and the liberals become alike. However, as the next generation of the liberals appreciated the course of revolution and progress towards democratisation entailing betterment of the political and economic lot of the middle class and other weaker sections of the community, the conservatives parted their ways and thus, to a very large extent, their response to liberalism "was not to develop new ideas but to cling to old and long familiar ways of thought. Against the new ideology many conservatives were simply content to assert the values of the old order.... To abide by the old habits of thought and action was the natural response of those who rejected the liberal tradition."[44]

41. F.W. Coker: "Some Present-Day Critics of Liberalism" in Stankiewicz, *op. cit.*, p. 379.
42. Spengler: *The Hour of Decision,* translated from German into English by Charles Francis Atkins (New York, 1934), p. 119.
43. Watkins, *op. cit.*, p. 29.
44. *Ibid.*, p. 30.

Thus, the ideology of conservatism came to assert passionately in favour of the value of the existing institutions. All protagonists of change became the object of attack at the hands of leading archetypes of conservatism like Edmund Burke, Russell Kirk, Hugh Cecil and Michael Oakeshott. The ideology of conservatism thus came to have these essential characteristics: the role of 'divine tactic' in history, prescription and tradition, dislike of abstraction and metaphysics, distrust of individual human reason, organic conception of society, stress on the evil in man, acceptance of social differentiation—all serving the overriding purpose of justifying the excellence of the established order. "The essence of conservatism is the rationalisation of existing institutions in terms of history, God, nature, and man."[45]

Thus viewed, the conservative theory of ideology may be said to have these important postulates:[46]

1. Man is basically a religious animal, and religion is the foundation of civil society. A divine sanction infuses the legitimate, existing social order.
2. Society is the natural, organic product of slow, historical growth. Existing institutions embody the wisdom of previous generations. Right is a function of time. Prescription is the most solid of all titles.
3. Man is a creature of instinct and emotion as well as reason. Prudence, prejudice, experience, and habit are better guides than reason, logic, abstractions, and metaphysics. Truth exists not in universal propositions but in concrete experiences.
4. The community is superior to the individual. The rights of men derive from their duties. Evil is rooted in human nature, not in any particular social institutions.
5. Except in an ultimate moral sense, men are unequal. Social organisation is complex and always includes a variety of classes, orders and groups. Differentiation, hierarchy and leadership are the inevitable characteristics of any civil society.
6. A presumption exists in favour of any settled scheme of government against any untried project. Man's hopes are high, but his vision is short. Efforts to remedy existing evils usually result in even greater ones.

The peculiar thing about the ideology of conservatism is that it treats the above postulates as a matter of emotional disposition and, as such, detests any ideology that stands for a change, particularly a radical one, likely to be described as a revolution. The result is that conservativism assumes the character of an anti-ideology. It frankly holds that any revolutionary theory is necessarily inadequate and mistaken when it opposes the law as a whole. The wisdom of one generation could never be greater than that of all the past generations who have lived with and formed the common law. It may be vividly traced in the political ideas of Oakeshott who has the image of a completely unreflective, self-conscious and traditional polity. What really counts is not a set of abstract ideas but the social activity governed by the well-established norms of collective life. Thus, he advises: "To think of politics in an ideological way is to see political activity and discussion in terms of relatively few and simple rules determined apart from the activity itself."[47]

45. S.P. Huntington: "Conservatism as an Ideology" in Stankiewicz, *op. cit*, p. 359.
46. *Ibid.*, p. 358.
47. W.H. Greenleaf: *Oakeshott's Philosophical Politics* (London: Longmans, 1966), p. 46.

The merit of the conservative theory is that it is not a highly fluid and flexible affair like the liberal theory. Its postulates are very precise and clear. However, the demerit of this theory is that it detests revolutionary ideas and thus condemns people to live in a condition of social injustice having its sanction in the greatness of the established order. Thus, the conservatives may be seen defending this or that institution from time to time, here monarchy, there property-owning democracy, here an established religion, there an ancient constitution. "This conservatism is so purely formal—it argues in favour of conserving whatever there is to conserve—that it is without boundary. In order to avoid the threat of one doctrine and one revolution, we get a defence useful to every established tyranny."[48]

Marxian Theory: Indictment of Bourgeois Ideology as 'False Consciousness' and its Substitution by a 'New Ideology'

The fascinating thing about Marxian theory on this subject is that while it decries every hitherto existing ideology as 'false consciousness' of social reality, it also offers an ideology of its own. One may marvel at the fact that Marx never defined the term 'ideology' in quite explicit terms though, in general, he used to refer to a more or less coherent system of ideas which purported to explain and justify the social position of class. Hence, the important thing to be taken note of here is that the implications of the term ideology are involved in the doctrine of class war and since social class has a place within the society and its standpoint determines the angle from which it sees in society and thereby what it sees, the notion of social position becomes analogous to that of a physical position.[49]

Marx's theory of ideology begins with his criticism of Feuerbach's *Essence of Christianity* wherein he denounces the significance of religious myths in understanding the reality of man's life. Marx carries his point further in his *Economic and Philosophical Manuscripts,* wherein he says that man is the sole object of ultimate value and that the distinctly human quality is reason or consciousness. In his *Theses on Feuerbach* he emphasises the practical nature of thought and denies the importance of unpractical thinking. To him it is the thought or consciousness which can change the world. Moreover, the consciousness is governed by the conditions of objective reality. As he says: "Man's ideas, views and conceptions, in one word, man's consciousness, changes with every change in the conditions of his material existence, in his social relations; and in his social life."[50] Engels relates ideology to a complex division of labour. As he says: "Society gives rise to certain common functions. The persons appointed for this purpose form a new branch of the division of labour within society. This gives them particular interests."[51]

However, it is in *The German Ideology* where Marx frankly abuses bourgeois ideology as 'false consciousness' and also links it up with the fact of 'class domination'. He emphatically asserts that the German thinkers failed to realise the fundamental advance made by the materialist philosophy and still talked of revolutions in thought.

48. Drucker, *op. cit.,* p. 117.
49. See Plamenatz: *Ideology* (London, 1970), pp. 50ff.
50. See Marx-Engels: *Collected Works,* Vol. IV, p. 480.
51. Engels: *Select Correspondence,* p. 421.

Hegel is declared as the source of all error from whom all German thinkers have learnt the art of changing real objective chains that exist outside 'me' into 'mere ideal', 'mere subjective chains' existing 'in me', and thus to change all 'exterior' palpable struggles into pure struggles of thought. Aganist this sort of inversion, so characteristic of all prevailing ideologies, Marx suggests that all ideas and all words are the products of society. That is, we must return to the study of real individuals, since "the basis of the study of man must be man; active, working, breathing, man and nothing else."[52]

Ideology is integrally connected with the interests of the ruling class. As Marx says in *The Holy Family*: "The examination of ideology as a reflection of 'false consciousness' also provides an explanation of how societies are ruled. The 'false consciousness' of a ruling class, its ideology, guides it according to the direction of its own interests. For example, the ideology of the bourgeoisie is the programme of the capitalistic expansion and power. This figures in the subject of the means of production that necessarily determine the relations of production. When the forms of material production are no longer able to meet the demands of an expanding population, the social system is bound to be overthrown. But before this occurs, a new ideology, one setting forth a programme favourable to the interests of a different class, will emerge."[53]

It follows that, on the whole, the system of ideas which tends to justify and further the aims of the ruling class are the predominant ideas of that age. This happens because the ruling class can control all the products of property—whether goods or ideas. Ideological thinking is said to reflect a false consciousness about society in view of the fact that "at the point at which knowledge of the truth about society becomes a danger to the interests of the possessing class, the ideologist stops his investigations. The main function of ideology is justification, not explanation. Ideology supports class interests. The interest of a ruling class is the maintenance of its political and economic power."[54]

Such a version of ideology, however, cannot prevent the application of the law of dialectical materialism. Progress lies in the struggle of the opposite forces. Thesis has its enemy in the antithesis and as a result of the conflict between the two, synthesis takes place. It is possible that a class may be unconscious of its objective interest and, as such, may entertain beliefs inimical to its interests. Whether it happens or not, the enemy of the ruling class is bound to grow up with a different ideology. As Marx says: "The advance of capitalist production develops a working class which by tradition, education, habit, looks upon the conditions of that mode of production as self-evident laws of nature."[55] The dominant class is able to impose its ideas upon the dispossessed class. The important thing about Marx, however, is that he conceived it as his task to develop a theory which would situate the class position of the proletariat and account for its future development.[56]

52. Marx: *The German Ideology*, p. 37.
53. Michael Evans: *Karl Marx* (London: George Allen and Unwin, 1975) p. 83.
54. *Ibid.*
55. Marx: *Capital*, Vol. I, p. 761.
56. Evans, *op. cit.*, p. 83.

As pointed out above, the important thing about Marx is that he not only denounces all ideologies in the name of their being like a false consciousness about social reality, instead he also offers an ideology of his own. He realises that the objective interest of the working class is what it is to become in the future and, as such, a major function of political and social theory is to combat the so-called contributions of the ruling ideologists who 'make the perfecting of the illusions of the class about itself their chief source of livelihood.'[57] What is really needed is the replacement of a false consciousness by a true and scientific knowledge of social reality and also by methods whereby such knowledge can be acquired. It ultimately leads him to offer a new social and political theory having its own 'scientific' laws of development that may be termed as true ideology or whose ultimate purpose is first to overthrow capitalism and then establish socialism having a classless society that is to be replaced by a stateless society entailing 'emancipation of man'.

The function of ideology is thus to understand social and political reality in terms of the doctrine of the class war according to which class conflict between the haves and the have-nots "would inevitably end in the victory of the larger classes, the proletariat, and this triumph would usher in the classless society."[58] Obviously, such an interpretation may not be acceptable to those who believe in the human liberty as the *sine qua non* of their very existence and on that basis strongly adhere to a free and divergent pattern of social life. The men of liberal ideology cannot accept the Marxian contention that whatever they think and offer in the form of a set of ideas is 'false' and that whatever is said by Marx, is true or 'scientific'. The obnoxious part of the Marxian ideology is that it subordinates the personality of man to an all-powerful and ruthless system called the 'dictatorship of the proletariat'. In other words, the value-system of a liberal state is subverted by the iron laws of a state apparatus. Keeping it in mind, Althusser presents his notion of the 'Ideological State Apparatus' whereby he argues that a vast number of institutions involved in one way or another in the dissemination of ideology are not only ideological apparatuses but 'state ideological apparatuses' which must be distinguished from the 'repressive state apparatus."[59]

Neo-Marxian Theory: Ideology as 'Utopia'

An acceptance of the Marxian theory in certain respects as well as its rejection in certain other respects may be seen in the political philosophy of some neo-Marxists among whom the name of Karl Mannheim finds the most conspicuous place. While he is deeply struck by the force of Marx's argument of ideology as 'false consciousness', he declares it as inadequate and, in particular, calls the *Communist Manifesto* a biased work.[60] He seeks to discover an element of inconsistency in the works of Marx by pointing out that while the 'Father of Scientific Socialism' creates the theory of false consciousness in order to discredit his opponents, he fails to apply the same

---

57. Marx-Engels: *Collected Works,* Vol. III, p. 46.
58. A.R. Ball: *Modern Politics and Government* (London: Macmillan, 1971), p. 257.
59. See Althusser: "Ideology and Ideological State Apparatuses" (Notes Towards an Investigation) in *Lenin and Philosophy* (London, 1972), p.37.
60. Mannheim: *Ideology and Utopia* (London, 1936), p. 143.

criteria to his own works. In this way, while Mannheim accepts the main contention of Marx, he "tries to modify it to make it a less partisan instrument."[61]

It is evident in certain important directions. While Mannheim agrees with Marx that all thinking is socially determined, the social milieu of a thinker is of crucial importance in determining what is thought about and what is not, how the doctrines are presented, and what they are intended to do. Taking support from the postulates of psychology, he argues that there can be nothing like a disinterested or an abstract thought, because all ideas are more or less pathological expressions of social discontent. This psychological or 'psychogenic' approach (as he calls it) enables him to say in very strong terms that while some forms of thinking help the thinker to adapt to reality, some only hide it from him. Therefore, he "calls the more incongruous thoughts, the ones which are so incongruous that they prevent the thinker from acting effectively, ideologies. The more effective ones, the ones which enable them to break through the *status quo* and satisfy the needs of the thinker, are called Utopias."[62]

Partly in the Marxian tradition, Mannheim thinks that ideology is a realm of situationally transcendent ideas cherished by dominant classes which are 'only distorted representations of past or potential social order' in opposition to the situationally transcendent Utopian ideas of the rising classes which are realised in the succeeding order.'[63] But what he is really concerned with is lest the present popularity of the concept of false consciousness "make Utopian responses impossible by unmasking them. When this happens, the group which is shorn of its Utopia reacts to. the situation, not by a recognition of its true position, but by taking refuge in a more intractable, pathological response—an ideology. When a class adopts an ideology, it is incapable of expressing its aspirations effectively and it slowly becomes increasingly defensive and reactionary. In effect, a utopia is a progressive prejudice and an ideology is a conservative one."[64]

In this way, ideology becomes a 'political myth' or a 'pattern of basic political symbols' as well as an instrument to combat the onslaught of the opponents. In other words, it becomes a utopia having its purpose in the destruction of the social structure as well as a myth to preserve certain political symbols.[65] Thus, Mannheim claims to have gone beyond Marx by asserting the doctrine of a 'counter-concept'. He argues that when a 'class' is threatened by a concept, it "will counter the advantages secured by its opponents. Thus, the sociology of knowledge reveals the important function of opposition in the formation of an ideology. The ideologist far from being disturbed by the existence of opponents, takes their presence as a reassuring confirmation of the reality of the evil he is fighting."[66]

The new trend may be taken as partly Marxian in the sense that while it takes ideology both as an 'illusion' and an instrument to defend the *status quo*, it also

61. Drucker, *op. cit.*, p. 20.
62. *Ibid.*, p.21.
63 Mannheim, *op. cit.*, p. 184.
64. Drucker, *op. cit.*, p. 21.
65. See Lasswell and Kaplan: *Power and Society* (New Haven: Yale Univ. Press, 1950), Chapters 3 and 6.
66. Drucker, *op cit.*, p. 22.

stresses that in the neological attempts of the sociology of knowledge, the unmasking of the illusion of the ideological appearance should be stressed. Hence, certain other writers following the line of Marx, like Fianz Neumann hold, that ideological elements are implicit even in the bourgeois slogans of mass participation in the public life, independent judiciary (in other to establish the contractual set-up of the capitalist economy) and individual rights to free the bourgeoisie from state intervention.[67]

A critic may easily discover the element of personal bias in such an interpretation as given by the neo-Marxists. Indeed, so set is the bias that the thinker of the 'sociology of knowledge' completely misses the points of significance in both the 'reactionary' and the 'progressive' ideologies. It should not be forgotten that when the Marxists speak of the derivation of the ideas and ideologies from a given social environment of these being conditioned socially or historically, their position is not to be identified with a mere 'sociology of knowledge', or with a certain sort of simple 'historical relativism', which regards all ideas and ideologies as 'merely ideology' or 'pure illusion', as also rationalisation, or as instruments of winning and defending power and advancing particular interests only, and which thus "implies that no question as to the truth or falsity of these ideas and ideologies can or need be entertained."[68] We may refer to the observation of Maurice Dobb who says: "Yet ideologies were not purely illusion (as Mannheim, for example, seems to have held). Certainly there was a large, even predominating element of 'false consciousness', especially in the ideology of an established ruling class which clung to power when already faced with a revolutionary challenge. But, at the same time, an ideology, especially in its revolutionary and formative phase, could contain an important 'scientific' and realistic element, which could be treated according to the objective criterion of human experience as an addition to human knowledge."[69]

Totalitarian Theory: Ideology as a Matter of 'Operational Code'

An extension of as well as a total opposition to the Marxian theory should be traced in the case of totalitarianism as an ideology which takes ideas as weapons either to reconstruct a new society or to save an existing one from total reconstruction. Thus, the ideology of totalitarianism has two diametrically opposite dimensions. While as a 'leftist' doctrine it implies the establishment of a Communist system drawing inspiration from the tenets of Marxism, as a 'rightist' doctrine, it stands for the preservation of the *status quo* and is generally called by the name of Fascism. Communism denounces the present system as a model of exploitation and oppression by the bourgeois class of the class of workers and thus desires its substitution by a new system in which the government by virtue of being the dictatorship of the proletariat uses every possible means to establish a classless society. Opposed to it is the ideology of Fascism that desires to preserve the *status quo* and thus treats Communism as its mortal enemy. However, the common point is that both stand for a ruthless and uniform system which, in the words of Karl Popper, makes them

67. V.P. Varma: *Political Philosophy* (Agra: Lakshmi Narain, 1970), p. 93.
68. Randhir Singh: *Reason, Revolution and Political Theory* (New Delhi: People's Pub. House, 1976), p. xvi.
69. Maurice Dobb: *On Economic Theory and Socialism* (London, 1955), p. 233.

the enemies of a free and open society. In such a situation, both ideologies "are essentially action-related systems of ideas. They typically contain a programme and a strategy for its realisation and their essential purpose is to unite organisations which are built around them."[70]

It is due to this that a very loose definition of the term ideology may not be applicable to the theory of totalitarianism in this direction. One may find fault with the view of an eminent American sociologist who defines it as "a general system of beliefs held in common by the members of a collectivity, *i.e.*, a society, or a sub-collectivity of one—including a movement deviant from the evaluative integration of the collectivity and of the situation in which it is placed, the processes by which it has developed to its given state, the goals towards which its members are collectively oriented, and their relation to the future course of events."[71] In a strict sense, totalitarianism stands for an 'official ideology' consising of an official body of doctrines converting all vital aspects of man's existence to which everyone living in that society is supposed to adhere, at least passively; this ideology is characteristically focused and projected towards a perfect final state of mankind, that is to say, it contains a chiliastic claim, based upon a radical rejection of the existing society and the conquest of the world for the new one.[72]

As pointed out above, totalitarianism of the left implies the case of Communism. In this direction, the function of ideology is to understand social and political reality in terms of the doctrine of the class war according to which the struggle between the exploiters and the exploited would inevitably end in the victory of the larger class, the proletariat, and culminate in the establishment of a classless and stateless society. The peculiar thing that happens to arise at this stage is that ideology which was deprecated by Marx as 'false consciousness' becomes a matter of explicit cultivation and large-scale indoctrination of the masses. The result is that "an intense concern with ideological conformity is the paradoxical consequence of the doctrine that ideas are nothing but weapons."[73]

It is said that the principles of Marxism, as interpreted by Lenin, constitute the foundation of the Communist ideology. However, recent developments show that the contributions of a good number of Communist leaders and theoreticians cannot be ignored. Thus, we find that while Lenin in his *State and Revolution* says that 'the proletariat needs only a state which is withering away, and which cannot but wither away',[74] his successor (Stalin) modifies it so as to mean that it could not be possible until the victory of socialism happens all over the world.'[75] The Father of Communist China (Mao) lays emphasis on the fact of local variations which the

70. Carl J. Friedrich and Z.K. Brzezinski: "Types of Totalitarian Ideology" in Stankiewicz, *op. cit.*, p. 48.
71. Talcott Parsons: *The Social System* (New York: Free Press of Glencoe, 1951), p. 349.
72. Friedrich and Brzezinski: "The General Characteristics of Totalitarian Dictatorship" in Stankiewicz, *op. cit.*, p. 40.
73. Friedrich and Brzezinski: "Types of Totalitarian Ideology", *op. cit.*, p. 46.
74. Lenin: *Selected Works*, Vol. VII, p. 24.
75. Stalin: *Problems of Leninism*, p. 659 ff.

Russian leaders did not appreciate and which had its impact on the development of Sino-Soviet differences. Irrespective of these differences, all Communist writers, however, agree on this basic point that every historical epoch has its own laws of development.[76]

Totalitarianism of the right means Fascism. Its essential characteristics are: an all-powerful state and preservation of the *status quo.* As such, rightist totalitarianism (as Fascism in Italy and Nazism in Germany) demands, what Mussolini said, an absolute state which, for the sake of a complete, internal and revolutionary fulfilment desires (i) a single party by means of which there shall be effectuated political and economic control and which shall be above the competing interests, a bond which shall unite all people in a common faith, (ii) a single totalitarian state which is all-absorbing, and (iii) life in a period of highest ideal tension."[77] Hitler laid emphasis on the interest of the *volk* over that of any member of the community. Thus, the whole ideology of Fascism is dominated by the dogmas of an all-powerful state and irresistible government. "All particularistic interests of individuals must be suppressed by an omnipotent, hierarchical organisation of the nation."[78] Moreover, it is on account of its rightist character that Fascism is seen as a conservative and reactionary ideology.'[79]

Obviously, the meaning of ideology in the case of totalitarianism assumes a significant form of its own. An ideology is said to be a reasonably coherent body of ideas concerning practical means of how to change and reform a society, based upon a more or less elaborate criticism of what is wrong with the existing, or antecedent, society. And a totalitarian ideology would than be one which is concerned with total destruction and total reconstruction, involving typically an ideological acceptance of violence as the only practicable means for such total destruction. It might accordingly be defined as a reasonably coherent body of ideas concerning practical means of how totally to change and reconstruct a society by force, or violence, based upon an all-inclusive, or total criticism of what is wrong with an existing or antecedent society.[80]

The real difficulty about totalitarian ideology is that it. either becomes a 'myth' or a 'utopia'. It becomes a myth when it is imposed on the people by means of force; it

76. Marx: *Capital,* Vol. I, pp. 23-24. W. Delandy has praised Lenin for having improved the Marxian conception and acknowledged it as an ideology. See his paper "Ideology – A Debate" in C.I. Waxman (ed.): *The End of Ideology Debate* (New York, 1968), p. 273. On this basis, Martin Seliger comments that Lenin really upset the original Marxist theory of ideology. He designates it as 'Lenin's *de facto* breakaway from Marx. *The Marxist Conception of Ideology* (London: Cambridge Univ. Press, 1977), pp. 81-82, We may also refer to the observation of E.H. Carr. He says that while with Marx ideology is a 'negative term', with Lenin it becomes 'positive'. *What is History*? (London, 1962), pp. 132-33. It all informs Seliger to say: "Indeed, in speaking of the socialist ideology and bourgeois ideology, Lenin retained the idea that the latter, but not ideology as such, was false. He thus laid the foundation for what has become known as the Marxist-Leninist "dual theory of ideology". *Op. cit.,* p. 83.
77. Finer, *op. cit.,* p. 88.
78. E. Nolte: *Three Faces of Fascism* (London, 1956), pp. 20-21.
79. F.W. Coker: *Recent Political Thought* (New York: Appleton-Century, 1934), pp. 482-83.
80. Martin Seliger: *The Marxist Conception of Ideology* (London: Cambridge Univ. Press, 1977), p. 1.

becomes a utopia when the people are indoctrinated to cultivate faith in the advent of a golden age of human life. Since the term 'ideology' is used in a variety of senses, its particular form may not be described as the only authentic, or legitimate version. Both Fascism and Communism adhere to a particular way of life and thereby stand for the condemnation of human life in that very direction. Naturally, a definition of ideology comes to have its 'exclusive' instead of an'inclusive' connotation. This is all the more important in the case of Communism where the people are taught to look towards the golden era of human emancipation in which the curse of alienation would be replaced by the boon of free and voluntary participation. Instead of confining ourselves to a restrictive interpretation of ideology, we should accept its inclusive connotation whereby it, in the context of social and political theory and science, implies that it "covers a set of factual and moral propositions which serve to posit and explain and justify ends and means of organised social action, especially political action, irrespective of whether such action aims to preserve, amend, destroy or rebuild any given order."[81]

'End of Ideology' Debate: Emergence of a New Ideology

A new theory on this subject has recently developed in which the names of certain American social therorists like Daniel Bell and Robert E. Lane deserve special mention. According to these writers, ideology has come to an end. The contention is that Western societies have developed in such a way and to such an extent that no ideology is relevant anymore. The functions of ideologies or their programmes of action have been taken over by a scientific social technology. The burden of the argument is that Marx died long back and much has happened to the bourgeois thinking since then. As a matter of fact, bourgeois system has acquired several new forms which Marx and his ardent followers could never imagine with the result that the life of the people, including the proletariat has improved considerably. Hence, has happened the 'end of ideology'.[82]

Bell thinks of ideologies as systems of ideas which serve to 'concretise' social values. Following the line of an eminent American sociologist like Talcott Parsons, he believes that all societies need ideologies and that they are all equally successful. The issue of economic development has come to stay in the forefront as the problem of political stability has almost become a well settled phenomenon. The people have developed their firm faith in the free institutions of their political culture and they have nothing to fear in this regard in the era of 'welfare state'. Moreover, the issue of economic development has come to be their main goal that they want to achieve by living within the broad framework of their well-established political system. It is for this important reason that there is hardly any difference of opinion between the Democratic and Republican parties of the United States. It all shows that ideology which was 'once a road to action, has come to a dead end.'[83]

81. See Karl Wittfogel: "The Historical Position of Communist China: Doctrine and Reality" in *Review of Politics,* Vol. 16 (1954), p 463.
82. Daniel Bell: *The End of Ideology: On the Exhaustion of Political Ideas in the Fifties* (New York: Colliers, 1961), pp. 393-404.
83. *Ibid.,* p. 253.

Forms of Ideology

Marxism :	While it deprecates ideology as 'false consciousness of social reality', it presents an ideology of its own. It is more or less a coherent set of ideas which purport to explain and justify social position of the two rival classes. In political terms, it seeks to change the status quo by overthrowing the rule of the dominant class of the exploiters and the oppressors. Revolution alone can usher in the socialist society. The state known as the 'dictatorship of the proletariat' is an all-powerful institution to protect the interest of the class of the workers and the toilers that would wither away in the final stage of social development. Socialism would replace capitalism and eventuate into communism. Marxism-Leninism may be described as totalitarianism of the left.
Fascism :	It seeks to maintain the status quo so as to protect the interests of the affluent and privileged sections of the society. The state is omnipotent, nothing against it and nothing above it. It may be described as totalitarianism of the right.
Liberalism :	It stands for the values of liberty, democracy and humanism. It has a flexible character by virtue of which it cannot be taken as an ideology. And yet its stern commitment to the norms of freedom and tolerance makes it so. 'Give me liberty or give me death', says Thomas Jefferson.

Lane has contributed to this theme from a different standpoint. He has sought to give a peculiar twist to the argument of Lenin by adding that now even the working class is faced with a number of 'socialist' ideologies that automatically strengthens the case of 'bourgeois' ideology. While referring to the case of the working class of any industrial country, it may be said that it is split up among a number of ideologies. Since there can be no talk of an independent ideology formulated by the working class itself in the process of its movement, the only choice is either bourgeois ideology or socialist ideology. There is no middle course, for mankind has not created a 'third' ideology, and, moreover, in a society torn by class antagonisms, there can never be a non-class or above-class ideology. Hence, to belittle the socialist ideology in any way to turn aside from it in the slightest degree, means to strengthen bourgeois ideology.[84]

While elaborating the point of David Easton and Alfred Cobban regarding the 'decline of political theory', Dante Germino has sought to treat it as a result of the pernicious role of ideology. As a matter of fact, he has also regretted the importance of 'positivism' that has been at the back of certain ideologies. In the main, his main attack is on the prevalence of 'political doctrines' culminating in Marxism. However, the noticeable thing in the elaboration of Germino is that instead of simply wailing at the obnoxious role of 'positive ideas', he has hoped for the 'revival of political theory' on account of the declining effect of ideology with the result that while following the line of Easton and Cobban, he has reached very close to Bell and Lane. According to him, the traditional political theory which had been dangerously eclipsed during the

84. R.E. Lane: 'The Decline of Politics and Ideology in a Knowledgeable Society" in *American Sociological Review*, Vol. XXXI, No. 5 (1966), pp. 649-62.

last 150 years by 'inimical intellectual forces' and 'political movements' on the one side and the 'craze for science' on the other, has undergone a noteworthy resurgence in our times.[85]

In September, 1955 in the city of Milan (Italy) was held the World Congress of Intellectuals. It was attended by almost 150 leading figures like Hugh Gaitskell and Richard Crossman from Britain, Sidney Hook, Arthur Schlesinger and F.A. Hayek from the United States, Andre Philip, Raymond Aron and Bertrand de Jouvenel from France. By all means, it was a grand gathering of liberals, socialists, conservatives, radicals and the like belonging to leading democratic countries of the West. Regardless of their political beliefs, these intellectuals came to hold the view that the traditional issues separating the left from the right had declined to comparative insignificance. In effect, they all agreed that the increase in state control, which had taken place in various democratic countries of the world, would not result in a decline of democratic freedom. The new developments should be taken note of. For instance, the socialists no longer advocated socialism with Miltonian fervour; they were as much concerned as the conservatives with the menace of an all-powerful state. The ideological issues dividing the left and the right had been reduced to a little more or little less governmental ownership and economic planning. No one seemed to believe that it really made much difference which political party controlled the domestic policies of individual nations. Richard Crossman, a left-wing British intellectual, had a little earlier stated that now socialism "is consciously viewed by most European socialist leaders as a Utopian myth.... often remote from the realities of day-to-day politics."[86]

It was also emphasised that a good number of socialist parties had lost their faith in the way of outright nationalisation of private property in the name of public interest. Besides, they had come to register their faith in the way of mixed economy and all change by democratic and constitutional means. Such a momentous change in the Western political life "reflected the fact that the fundamental political problems of the industrial revolution have been solved; the workers have achieved industrial political citizenship; the Conservatives have accepted the welfare state; and the democratic left has recognised that an increase in an overall state power carries with it more dangers to freedom than solution for economic problems. This very triumph of the democratic social revolution in the West ends domestic politics for those intellectuals who must have ideologies or Utopias to motivate them to political action."[87]

In short, the whole idea behind the concept of the 'end of ideology' is that the economic class system, as conceived by the Marxists-Leninists, "is disappearing.... the redistribution of wealth and income has ended economic inequality's political significance."[88] Of course, a realisation of this kind has brought about a change in the ideas of many left wingers as well as positive liberals of the Western countries. A marked decline in the source of political controversy has even led some to raise the question as to whether the conflicts that are so necessary to democracy would continue.

85. See Dante Germino: *Beyond Ideology. The Revival of Political Theory* (New York: Harper, 1967).
86. Crossman: "On Political Neurosis" in *Encounter* (May, 1954), p. 66.
87. S.M. Lipset: *The Political Man* (New Delhi: Arnold-Heinemann, 1960), pp, 404-5.
88. S. Bullitt: *To Be a Politician* (New York: Doubleday, 1959), p. 177.

End of Ideology—Ideologisation Versus De-Ideologisation

Theories of De-Ideologisation

When capital was the key to economic success, social conflict was between the rich and the poor. In recent times, education has become the difference that divides. Politics also reflects the new division. In the United States, suspicion and resentment is no longer directed to the capitalists or the merely rich. It is the intellectuals who are eyed with misgiving and alarm.

—J.K. Galbraith

The intellectual historian of the future will be challenged by a strange phenomenon of the later half of the 20th century - the second coming of Karl Marx. In the second coming he appears not as the dusty frock coat of an economist, as the author of 'Capital' nor as a revolutionary sans-caulotts, the inspired pamphleteer of the *Communist Manifesto.* He comes robed as a philosopher and moral prophet with glad tidings about human freedom valid beyond the narrow circles of class, party or faction. In his train flock not the industrial workers of the world but the literary intellectuals.... not the proletariat but elements of the professoriat, not the socially disinherited but the psychologically alienated, and a varied assortment of writers and artists.

—Sidney Hook

The social function of management becomes decisive for the organisation of production. The industrial society is characterised by a technical approach to nature and human activity.

—Daniel Bell

No End of Ideology

(Operation of modern revisionism in socialist clothing)

The only choice is either bourgeois or socialist ideology. There is no middle course, for mankind has not created a third ideology, and, moreover, in a society torn by class antagonisms, there can never be non-class or an above class ideology.

—V.I. Lenin

The struggle of today's revisionism against Leninism is more than an ideological debate. It is a blow to the international workers' movement with the aim of depriving it of the revolutionary theoretical gains of the last sixty years. It is an attempt to throw back international workers' movement to the level of the period preceding the Great October Socialist Revolution.

—Alfred Kosing

However, despite the fact that the theory of de-ideologisation is obviously groundless and tendentious, it like other theories connected with it, has become rather widespread in the West. The reason for its relative popularity is that in the conditions of the profound crisis of bourgeois social thought as a whole, it conforms to the social practice and interests of certain social groups and political trends in contemporary bourgeois society.

—V.Kortunov

As a matter of fact, the aim of the leading American social theorists is to beat the concept of ideology with the stick of sociology in the 'age of democracy'. The burden of their argument is that democracy being a system of consensus allows no room for the politics of conflict (class struggle) It "requires organisations which support conflict and disagreement as well as those which sustain legitimacy and consensus, or general agreement."[89] Barrington Moore, Jr. observes that as we reduce economic inequalities and privileges, we may also eliminate the sources of contrast and conflict that put drive into genuine political alternatives. He concludes that the driving force of discontent disappears, and a society settles down for a time to a dull acceptance of things as they are.[90] Following this line, Lipset, while seeking to offer an answer to the question 'Has Ideology Ended?' says: "The democratic class struggle will continue, but it will be a fight without ideologies, without red flags, without workers' May Day parades."[91]

The critics of this theory, particularly the Marxists, have looked at it with apprehension and come to decry it as the resurgence of a 'new bourgeois ideology'. They are of the view that the acceptance of welfare state, desirability of decentralised power, mixed economy, political pluralism and the like are just 'concrete' evidences so as to cry for the end of ideology. As a matter of fact, the advocates of the end of ideology theory draw inspiration from pragmatism and *status quoism* and then, instead of exposing the hollowness of their intellectual systems, endeavour to distract the attention of the progressive thinkers. The adjustments made among the diverse elites to the exclusion of the masses without breaking the structure of the society and disturbing its hierarchical class nature by peaceful parliamentary methods exclusively is traded off as 'end of ideology'. "In fact, it is an ideology of an end to maintain the base intact by slight codifications in the superstructure. Ideology, according to the Western social scientists, therefore, is something to be shunned by right thinking men. It is not seen as a false image but as a dogma that demands a fantastic adherence from its believer."[92]

Critical Appreciation

A discussion of the concept of ideology in the realm of contemporary political theory, as contained in the preceding sections, leads to the following important impressions:

1. It is a rather tedious job to offer a standard definition of the term ideology owing to divergent standpoints of the intellectuals. Etymologically, it denotes the science of logic of ideas and, as such, it refers to a complex of doctrines, creeds and myths of political or cultural movement. In this sense, it is often identified with a taxonomic system of concepts whose function is to introduce order and classification into a mass of research materials. It, therefore, helps in the functioning of introducing regularity in a confused heap of data. The more abstract and generalised the conceptual structure of ideologies, the more is the amount of data that can be subsumed under their rubric.[93] Different from this, in the realm of political theory, it refers to a belief system that may be action-oriented. The result is that different schools have different belief-systems and try to denounce each other in a way that all commit the act of 'self-contradiction.'[94]

89. S.M. Lipset: *Political Man* (Bombay: Vakil, Feffer and Simons, 1959), p. 197 (Abridged Edition).
90. *Ibid.*, p. 199.
91. *Ibid.*, p. 200.
92. K. Seshadri, *op. cit.*, pp. 190-91.
93. V.P. Varma, *op. cit.*, p. 93.
94. Seliger, *op. cit.* p. 2.

2. The real difficulty about the term ideology does not lie in the varying or divergent interpretations but in the fact of their conversion into myths or religions. Thus ideology and fanaticism go together. Naturally, it retards the progress of free and, what is called, 'scientific' thinking. It is owing to this that "we cannot but notice that deep in the heart of each theory is a central myth about society; each promulgates a myth and urges us to take heed. Liberalism and Conservatism promulgate a myth about totalitarianism; Marxism promulgates one about class struggle and revolution."[95] Thus, while dealing with the problem of how to explain the nature of ideology, Sills says that it makes for 'dogmatic inflexibility and unwillingness to allow new experience to contribute to the growth of truth'.[96] Likewise, Plamenatz thinks of Machiavelli and Stalin while doing the same and Lasswell considers himself as dealing with an ideology while studying the role of Fascist propaganda in the second world war.[97]
3. Finally, the term 'ideology' is often taken in a derogatory or pejorative sense. In spite of the fact that it flourishes in an affectively political rather than in an objectively epistemological reality, it ever since the times of Napoleon Bonaparte, conveys a derogatory reference by indicating visionary or speculative theorising and idea-spinning of an unpractical character.[98] We know that Marx denounced it as 'false consciousness' and Mannheim deprecated it as 'utopia'. It is perhaps to do the same that Bell has coined the phrase 'end of ideology'. It all shows that the term 'ideology' has an obnoxious expression that has become like an anathema to the liberal intellectuals ever since the triumph of Marxism and Fascism. Today it "means different things to different groups. To Conservatives and Liberals, it means Hitler, Stalin, genocide, concentration camps, the bombing of innocent civilians (Guernica); generally, it means totalitarian ideas. While Liberals and Conservatives may agree about the fact, they disagree about why such ideas are ideological and what ought to be done about it."[99]

Despite all this, two things cannot be lost sight of. First, ours is an age of democracy and socialism in which the role of ideology cannot be denied. Whether it is a curse or a blessing, it has to survive in the midst of different belief systems and the patterning of political systems according to them. Thus, ideology has become a "key feature of our political world. The fact is that we do disagree with each other about the central political and moral issues. We do not live in an age, like the Middle Ages of Scholastic mythology, in which men fundamentally agree."[100] Second, both ideology and politics cannot be separated. If politics is a struggle for power, what motivates people to take part in the struggle is a certain belief system. As a matter of fact, it is the war of ideas that contributes to the material of politics.

95. Drucker, *op. cit.,* p. 141.
96. David 1. Sills: "The Concept of Function of Ideology" in *International Encyclopaedia of the Social Sciences* (New York: Macmillan and Free Press, 1969), Vol. VII, p, 74.
97. Plamenatz, *op. cit.,* pp. 137-42.
98. Varma, *op. cit.,* p. 93.
99. Drucker, *op. cit.,* p. 141.
100. *Ibid.,* p. 142.

The function of a political scientist is "to discover the pathway to 'good ends'. And desiring and influencing so that the 'right path' to the 'good end' is taken, far from being in conflict with his duty as a scientist, is the very essence of his responsibility as a scientist and a man."[101]

101. G.A. Almond: "Value Judgements in Political Thought" in Gould and Thursby (ed s): *Contemporary Political Thought* (New York: Holt, Rinehart and Winston, 1969), p. 288.

16

Political Alienation

> If in renaissance thought, it was the myth of reasonable man which predominated; if in the eighteenth century it was natural man; and in the nineteenth century, economic or political man, it is by no means unlikely that for our own age it is alienated or maladjusted man who will appear to later historians as the key figure of the twentieth century thought.
>
> **-Robert Nisbet[1]**

One of the important sources of the 'crisis of modern political theory', a phrase popularised by Prof. Harold J. Laski, should be traced in the social and economic crises and their impact on the political processes of a country. A discussion of the concept of 'alienation' pertains to such an area of investigation in which we make a study of politics while having our intimate concern with the affairs of psychology, sociology, philosophy and economics. Whether it is a highly organised industrial capitalist system of a free society or a centralised state system of a totalitarian country, we come across a fact that the personality of man remains crushed under, what modern sociologists and psychoanalysts call, the 'dead weight of uniformity' The result is that the individual has to remain so terribly caught up in the pursuit of his economic activities that he hardly gets time to look within himself, or to think of the quality, *i e.*, the real meaning of his life which informs a poet like William Wordsworth to wail 'what man has made of man'. Modern social and political theorists have sought to examine the case of this self-alienated man—"a man who is not, in fact, what he is in essence: a man whose actual existence does not correspond to his human existence."[2]

Political Alienation: Nature and Essential Implications

As a matter of fact, the term 'alienation' has its particular application in the disciplines of philosophy, psychology and sociology. However, as modern political theory has sought to borrow much from other sister-disciplines, concepts like those of 'political legitimacy' and 'political alienation' have come to assume an importance of their own in its realm. The result is that in a study of this type we are bound to have our concern with psychologists like Sigmund Freud and Max Weber, philosophers like Hegel and Feuerbach, sociologists like Talcott Parsons, David Riesman. Simmel and Nathan Glazer, socio-economists like Marx and Engels, neo-leftists like Eric Fromm and Herbert Marcuse and existentialists like Sartre, Jaspers, Marcel, Kafka,

---

1. Nisbet: *Quest for Community: A Study in the Ethics of Order and Freedom* (New York: Oxford Univ. Press, 1950), p. 1.
2. G. Petrovic: "Alienation" in Paul Edwards (ed.): *The Encyclopaedia of Philosophy* (New York: Free Press of Glencoe, 1967), pp. 76-81.

Kierkegaard, Heideggar and the like. An understanding of the meaning of 'political alienation', for this reason, presupposes the need for grasping the general implication of this term and then integrating it with the new meaning of politics as developed by the liberal as well as Marxist thinkers.

The word 'alienation' means aloofness, estrangement, apathy, turning or keeping away, indifference, cutting off and the like from something or somebody whether society, religion, administration, even the self. As generally understood in social sciences, it according to Kurt Lang, "denotes an estrangement or separation between parts of the whole personality and significant aspects of the world of experience. Within this general denotation, it may refer to: (a) an objective state of estrangement or separation, (b) the state of feeling of the estranged personality, (c) a motivational state tending towards estrangement. The separation denoted by the term may be between (a) the self and the objective world; (b) the self and the aspects of the self that have become separated and placed over against the self *e.g*, alienated labour; (c) the self and the self."[3]

In a general sense, alienation is viewed as the state or the result of conforming with institutional expectations in segmented roles when the performance of specialised functions determined by the division of labour and the system of dominance of certain groups, deprives the total personality of opportunities to exercise substantively rational judgement and thereby apply its creative powers in influencing the conditions of its own existence. "Conformity without involvement takes the forms of submission to necessity as represented by objective and alien demands rather than subjective personal needs, while the role performance (alienated labour) perpetuates the conditions of the estranged existence."[4] Viewing thus, a 'social rebel' like Eric Fromm says that man "leads an alienated life when he does not experience himself at the centre of his world, as the creator of his own acts—but his acts and their consequences have become his master's; whom he obeys, or whom he may even worship."[5]

From this conception of alienation as an objective state of separation comes the usage of alienation as the *malaise* that results from such a state, sometimes accompanied by a shift of emphasis from structures of domination to the value content of the culture as the primary causal factor. In this usage, "the estrangement of the self from the self is stressed. There is a loss of emotions which are part of normal experience. The withdrawal of emotional interest from external world, because it is threatening, leads to an exaggerated concern with oneself. This may express itself either in extreme sensitivity and altered feelings, or in depersonalisation and isolation of affect when the overcharged feelings are repressed or dissociated from the conscious personality."[6]

As a matter of fact, alienation is a concept of considerable antiquity whose metaphysical origins have been veiled in the course of time by the progressive secularisation of the Western thought. Historians of philosophy trace the concept

3. See Julius Gould and William K. Kolb (ed.s): *A Dictionary of Social Sciences* (New York: Free Press of Glencoe, 1965), p. 19.
4. *Ibid.*, pp. 19-20.
5. Fromm: *The Sane Society* (New York: Holt, Rinehart and Winston, 1965), p. 120.
6. Kurt Lang, *op. cit.*, p. 20.

back to the writings of Plotinus whose doctrine of emanation assumed a procession from an ultimate indefinable source of principle to a multiplicity of finite beings. Mention in this regard may be made of the great German idealist thinker Hegel who sought to examine the case of alienation from a 'religious' or philosophical point of view. However, from the viewpoint of contemporary sociology, it is Karl Marx (specifically the young Marx of 1843-45 who was a sociologist and not an economist at that time) appears as the crucial figure in the process whereby alienation "was transformed from an ontological into a sociological concept."[7]

The idea of alienation thus implies "a denial of man's potentiality for creative intelligence and the building of a humane society."[8] It has its ramifications in different disciplines which may be briefly mentioned as under:

1. In the realm of philosophy, the concept of alienation (as taken by Hegel and Feuerbach) takes an idealistic overtone. Emphasis is laid on man's estrangement from 'religion' and role of the 'spirit'. History possesses an immanent meaning in the sense of embodying a ceaseless activity and drive toward total consciousness. The surprising thing is that as 'spirit' unfolds itself through history, it is confronted by each concrete historical moment as a part of itself, as something its own activity has created; it, therefore, experiences this activity as something external and alien. Spirit, therefore, seeks to recover these alienated moments and it is this movement which partially derives it onwards towards absolute and thus non-alienated consciousness.[9]
2. In the realm of psychology, it (as suggested by Sigmund Freud and Max Weber) signifies a sense of helplessness, powerlessness, hatred of the self and others, a feeling in man that he is 'a mere rump, a lowest common denominator attained by lopping of all those qualities on which is based his claim to recognition as a man.'[10] It may be discerned in the celebrated thesis of Max Weber about the increasing and ineluctable 'rationalisation' of Western society hinging on a one-sided and fatalistic conception of technology.
3. The same idea is carried into the field of sociology by a good number of writers like Simmel and Parsons who have taken inspiration from Marx and yet tried to give his interpretations a peculiar twist. It is due to this that the implications of this term vary from the pole of the 'estrangement' to that of the 'reification'.[11] Thus, Marx regrets the fact that in a 'bourgeois' society man is separated from the very activity of his life, from the material world and even from his fellow-beings inasmuch as the facts of class war make most forms of co-operation impossible.

7. George Lichtheim: "Alienation" in *International Encyclopaedia of Social Sciences,* edited by David I. Sills (New York: Macmillan and Free Press, 1968), Vol. I, pp. 264-65.
8. Alan Swingewood: *Marx and Modern Social Theory* (London: Macmillan, 1975), p. 93.
9. *Ibid.,* p. 89.
10. Bertell Ollman: *Alienation: Marx's Conception of Man in a Capitalist Society* (London: Cambridge Univ. Press, 1971), p. 131.
11. The term 'reification' literally means conversion of a mentality into a material production. In the realm of Marxism, it hints at a peculiar character of the capitalist society in which men comprehend that the very products of their labour as embodied in social relations and institutions are autonomous objective forces unconnected with human activity. See Swingewood, *op. cit.,* p. 101.

In a different way, Blauner says that while alienation signifies meaninglessness, powerlessness, normlessness, isolation and self-estrangement, the categories of contemporary sociological definition stem from "standardised production and a division of labour that reduces the size of the worker's contribution to the final product."[12]

4. Allied to this is the meaning of alienation in the realm of economics. Marx discovers the fundamental source of the evils of a capitalist system in the exploitation of the workers by the capitalists. In such a system not only does the worker alienate his life expression only as a means towards his life, but the capitalist obtains the only use value which can be utilised to create 'surplus value'. As a result the creative power of the worker's labour 'establishes itself as the power of capital, as an alien power confronting him'.[13] Thus, Marx "has found in the categories of political economy the material expression of alienation, the process of economic exploitation."[14]
5. Since contemporary political theory has borrowed much from other sister-disciplines, the idea of alienation has come to occupy a significant place of its own in it. Here we find concern of a political scientist with the relevance of human personality for political analysis. Recent discussions of the importance of alienation and the danger it poses for a democratic system, in particular, show the value which philosophical, psychological and socio-economic concepts have for political theory. Thus, alienation signifies a disaffection with the present political system including feelings of powerlessness and normlessness (that no clear standards exist). Alienation may bring about withdrawal, the former is thought to be more likely."[15]

It is obvious that now the term 'alienation' is used extensively in sociology, psychology, literature, economics, philosophy and politics and has become a blanket word to describe every conceivable aspect of cultural fragmentation, social isolation, economic exploitation, philosophical abstraction, political non-existence and the like. Here is the study of an 'abstract man' who has become such that he has lost touch with all human specificity. The deplorable fact of modern civilised life shows that man "has been reduced to performing undifferentiated work on humanly indistinguishable object among people deprived of their human variety and compassion."[16] The indomitable fact of alienation has caused profound dislocations in the primary associative area of human life whether in its private or public manifesations. While hitting at the character of modern Western civilisation, a sociologist like Nisbet says that the greatest single influence upon social organisation has been the developing concentration of function and power of the sovereign political organisation with the result that now to regard it as simply a legal relationship "is profoundly delusive. The

12. *Ibid.*, p. 104.
13. Cited in Michael Evans: *Karl Marx* (London: George Allen and Unwin, 1975), p. 91.
14. Daniel Bell: "The Debates on Alienation" in L. Lebedez (ed): *Revisionism* (London: George Allen and Unwin, 1963), pp. 200-01.
15. Stephen L. Wasby: *Political Science – The Discipline and Its Dimensions: An Introduction* (Calcutta: Scientific Book Agency, 1970), p. 56.
16. Ollman, *op. cit.*, p. 134.

real significance of the modern state is inescapable from its successive penetrations of man's economic, religious, kinship and local allegiances and its revolutionary dislocations of established centres of function and authority."[17]

Alienation and Polity: Political Alienation Distinguished from Some Related Themes

The long history of intellectual concern with alienation has resulted in the emergence of abundant literature rich in concepts and suggestive of hypotheses which may provide a valuable perspective to develop an empirical theory relating citizen attitudes to the structures and processes of the political system. It is, however, useful to distinguish different ways in which alienation towards the polity may be expressed:[18]

1. 'Political powerlessness' may be defined as an individual's feeling that he cannot affect the actions of government, that the authoritative allocation of values for society which is at the heart of the political process, is not subject to his influence. Political decisions which determine to a great extent the conditions under which the individual lives, may appear to be happening to individuals who feel powerless, independent of or in spite of their own judgement or wishes. This mode of alienation is closely related (inversely) to the concept of 'political efficacy' which has achieved such prominence in the studies of voting behaviour.
2. 'Political meaninglessness' may be said to exist to the extent that the political decisions are perceived as being unpredictable. A perceived random pattern of decision-making would, of course, prevent an understanding of the political system. This mode of alienation is distinguished from the first in that in the case of powerlessness decisions may be clear and unpredictable, but simply are not subject to the influence of the individual; in the case of meaninglessness, however, the individual perceives no discernible pattern. This feeling is illustrated by an individual's inablity to distinguish any meaningful political choices, and the sense that political choices are themselves meaningless, because one cannot predict their probable outcomes, nor consequently use them to change social conditions.
3. Following Durkheim's use of 'anomie' which denotes a decentralisation of social norms regulating individual's behaviour, 'perceived political normlessness' is defined as the individual's perception that the norms of rules intended to govern political relations have broken down, and that departures from prescribed behaviour are common. A belief that officials violate legal procedures in dealing with the public or in arriving at policy decisions exemplify this mode of alienation.

---

17. Nisbet. *op. cit.*, p. 28. K. Horney calls it 'lack of comprehension of the self. He says: "We cannot suppress or eliminate essential parts of ourselves without becoming estranged from ourselves. The person simply becomes oblivious to what he really feels, likes, rejects, believes – in short, to what he really is. Without knowing it he may live the life of his image.... The person loses interest in life, because it is not he who lives it; he cannot make decisions, because he does not know what he really wants; if difficulties mount, he may be pervaded by a sense of unreality – an accentuated expression of his permanent condition of being unreal to himself." *Our Inner Conflicts* (London: Routledge and Kegan Paul, 1946), p. 111.
18. A.W Finifter: "Dimensions of Political Alienation" in *American Political Science Review*, Vol. LXIV, June 1970, No. 2, pp. 390-91.

4. 'Political isolation' refers to a rejection of political norms and goals that are widely held and shared by other members of a society. It differs from perceived normlessness in which there is implicit *acceptance* of some set of norms from which *others* are perceived to be deviating. Political isolation can be illustrated by a belief that voting or other socially defined political obligations are merely conformist formalities; or indeed that particular participation is inappropriate in the formation of public policy. This type of alienation is consistent with Lane's description of alienated individuals feeling that 'the rules of the game are unfair, loaded, illegitimate; the Constitution is, in some sense, fraudulent'. To the extent that social norms are dynamic, however, a state of isolation at one point of time may entail a different set than isolation at another time. Similarly, to the extent that social norms differ from culture to culture, alienation in this mode can only be understood with reference to prevailing normative patterns of particular societies.[19]
5. Finally, we refer to the variant of'political self-estrangement'. The conditions of public life have become so much distorted that a citizen feels self-estranged even when he plays his role in the political process of his country. For instance, a voter normally feels that he has become an object, or a commodity, or a tool in the hands of others. Thus, he feels self-alienated like a salesgirl who realises that her personality has become an instrument of some alien purpose. One way to state such a meaning is to see alienation as the degree of dependence of the given behaviour upon anticipated future rewards, something that lies outside the activity itself. For instance, as the worker who works merely for his salary, or the housewife who cooks simply to get it over with, the political man also plays his part in a way that he finds his labours not 'self-rewarding' or, in Dewey's phrase, 'self-consummatory'.[20]

Thus, a study of politics from this standpoint hits at the deplorable state of the life of *homo politicus* or political man. It informs us about the "sense of the splitting asunder of what was once together, the breaking of the seamless mould in which *values, behaviour,* and *expectations* were once cast into interlocking forms."[21] It has its distinct ramifications not only in the realm of psychological or sociological or philosophical theory, it has a significant place of its own in the realm of political theory also. In other words, the concept of alienation has become a very important item of social sciences. "At the present time, in all the social sciences, the various synonyms of alienation have a foremost place in the studies of humau relations. Investigations of the 'unattached', the 'marginal', the 'obsessive', the 'normless' and the 'isolated' individual all testify to the central place occupied by the hypothesis of alienation in contemporary social science."[22]

19. Robert E. Lane: *Political Ideology* (New York: Free Press of Glencoe, 1962), p. 162.
20. See Melvin Seeman: "On the Meaning of Alienation" in *American Sociological Review*, Vol. XXIV, December 1959, reproduced in Coser and Rosenberg: (eds.) *Sociological Theory* (New York: Macmillan, 1975), p. 535.
21. Nathan Glazer: "The Alienation of Modern Man", *Commentary* (April, 1947), p. 378.
22. Nisbet, *op. cit.*, p. 15.

Metaphysical Theory: Emphasis on Unity Between the 'Essential' and the 'Real'

As already pointed out, the concept of alienation finds its first expression in the realm of metaphysics where a philosopher seeks to establish logical reconciliation between the 'essential' and the 'real'. Plato is considered to be the first great thinker who thought in these terms. According to this version, the inequality of the two parts of self-alienated man is attributed to a split between his real nature (essence) and the factual properties (existence). Thus, Feuerbach in his *Essence of Christianity* argues that religion is simply man's essential nature refracted through idealism. As he says : "Theology is anthropology, i.e., that which reveals itself in the object of religion...is nothing other than the essence of man. In other words, God of man is nothing other than the divinised essence of man."[23] Simply stated, his point is that religion as well as philosophy require 'materialising', that is, inverting.[24]

However, this idea finds its best expression in the philosophy of Hegel who argues that the history of man is, what he calls, the 'Absolute Spirit', a consciousness which progressively unfolds through a series of dialectical contradictions in the direction of increasing self-knowledge; 'unlimited consciousness' is the ultimate state when, 'spirit' is at one with the 'ethical world'. To him, history possesses an immanent meaning in the sense of embodying this ceaseless activity and drive towards total consciousness. 'Spirit', of course, is man and the concrete situations which characterise historical development are analysed by Hegel as the really specific moments which, in their material form, embody the dialectical development of 'Spirit' from an unreflective unity like the Renaissance, the Enlightenment, the French Revolution. However, as 'Spirit' unfolds itself through history, it is confronted by each historical moment as a part of itself, as something its own activity has created; it, therefore, experiences this activity as something external and alien. 'Spirit', therefore, seeks to recover these alienated moments and it is this movement which partially drives it onwards towards 'absolute' and thus 'non-alienated consciousness'.[25]

While accepting Platonic distinction between understanding (that can only analyse things) and reason (that is more creative, synthetic and synonymous with the texture of reality itself and thus remains in the nature of substantive and infinite power), Hegel also says that the all-pervasive unity of the social and political community is provided by the 'spirit' which is a synthesis of the inward individual experience and the external communal experience.[26] He emphasises the concept of the 'inner

23. Cited in Schacht: *Alienation,* p. 68.
24. See Swingewood, *op. cit.,* p. 90.
25. *Ibid,* p. 89. This concept of alienation is a central part of a move by which Hegel begins to shift epistemology, and philosophy generally, on to a new terrain. For alienation involves loss, loss of self, and it thus provides not only an interpretation of knowledge in terms of activity, but also the initial condition and rationale for a historical saga, in which spirit eventually recovers what it has lost, or at least reconciles itself to its loss by recognising reality as its own alienated product." C. Arthur: "Objectification and Alienation in Marx and Hegel" in *Radical Philosophy,* Vol. 30, (Sept., 1982).
26. Hegel: *The Phenomenology of Mind.* Translated from German into English and with an 'Introduction' by R.S. Hartman (London: Liberal Arts Press, 1954), pp. 242-67.

freedom' and 'individual self-consciousness' that were heralded by the philosophical movements of Stoicism and scepticism at the time when the Roman Empire was seized by calamity and despair. To him, the fullness of the 'spirit' is realised through its alienation and self-externalisation in nature and history. The world is spiritual and there is all-pervasive identity between the world and human beings.[27]

Hence, it is the *Phenomenology* of Hegel which we should look into so as to understand his metaphysical concept of alienation what he calls 'unhappy consciousness'. According to him, mind at first comes to regard this objective world as separate and distinct from itself landing in a state of tension with itself what he calls 'objective cynicism'. However, as he evolves the idea of dialectical development, he says that "there ensues a tension between human needs on the one side and social environment (even the whole sensual world) on the other. In such a condition, the mind finds itself 'alienated', for it becomes self-conscious but not conscious of the world as its own extension."[28] The most characteristic example of this unhappy consciousness is to be found in 'monkish asceticism' or in a state in which an intense opposition to this worldliness reduces human beings to mere animal form in which an attempt is made to subdue the things of the flesh.[29]

The importance of Hegel lies in that he not only understands the fact of alienation or unhappy consciousness, but he also discovers a solution of this philosophical problem. He offers a philosophy of spirit which reconciles self and nature, mind and matter. Its conceptual or abstract formal side is revealed in the study of the evolution of logical categories. Reason is the reconciliation and the synthesis of the abstract-formal logical aspect and the externalised physical. and spatial aspect. In other words, slowly but imperceptibly the mind realises with the help of reason that there is no contradiction between itself and the world and then the latter is no longer regarded as external but a part of the life itself. In order to overcome the contradiction of alienation, the mind realises that it as well as the world are two sides of the same all-pervasive, all-unifying 'Absolute Spirit'. Thus, the true freedom of human spirit lies in transcending "the limitations imposed by the material world with which self-consciousness is at first confronted as external to itself, encompassing and encircling all its activities, and then realising the essential unity between the object and the subject."[30]

Obviously, the problem of alienation finds its solution in search for freedom. The conquest of alienation represents triumph over the sorrow of infinitude when

27. See V.P. Varma: *Political Philosophy (Agra*: Lakshmi Narayan, 1970), p. 103.
28. V.R. Mehta: *Hegel and the Modern State* (New Delhi: Associated Pub., 1968), p. 30.
29. Hegel, *op. cit.*, p. 86. For Hegel, the everyday world in which persons live consists at one and the same time.' of objects which are necessary to and express human life, but from which they are alienated; and which, in both cases are the products of people's activity, without which neither object nor persons would be. For Hegel alienation is the inescapable fate of humanity and its object world. Alienation is thus inherent in human life which necessarily and everywhere creates the social world by making and using objects while making and transforming itself in that very process. At some points, however, these objects no longer coincide with the human purposes, the object world and the inner world as having been brought into existence by their own human activity. See Gouldner: *The Two Marxisms: Contradictions and Anomalies in the Development of Theory* (London: Macmillan, 1980).
30. Hegel: *Philosophy of Right* (Translated from German into English by Wallace), p. 165.

the self of the individual and the objective world (having society and state) are identified. We find that Hegel pleads for the identification of the individual with the civil society, because he perhaps rightly perceives that freedom can be realised only within the framework of the society and the state. Following the line of Aristotle, he comes to hold that outside the social and political framework, freedom degenerates into a licence, for society and state alone ensure maximum possible development of human personality. Behind all this affirmation we can take note of the fact that he sharply reacts against the social and economic conditions which do not enable the individuals to realise their personality. His account of civil society looks like "an outpouring of a frustrated heart against a social order in which there is a wide hiatus between the form and the spirit of man, a condition in which we are faced with what he calls unhappy consciousness"[31]

The weakness of this theory may easily be discovered in its highly abstract and metaphysical interpetations which cannot be comprehended by a man of average understanding. Nor can such affirmations be proved empirically. Thus, the real implications of the concept of alienation could be well understandable when Marx, taking inspiration from the great German idealist thinker, gave an economic complexion to a highly metaphysical notion. As he says: "In the social production of their existence, men enter into relations which are determined, necessary, independent of their will." As we shall see in the following section, he dwells on the fact of social conditions that determine the consciousness of the individual. In this way, Hegel's view of alienation, "while shrouded in obscure language and ambiguous concepts, is nonetheless a reflection of alienation in real life, in the economic structure of society. The metaphysical concept can thus be transformed into material categories."[32] We may, in this direction, refer to the observation of Sartre who says: 'For Marx, indeed, Hegel has confused objectification, the simple externalisation of man in the universe, with alienation which turns his externalisation back against man. Taken by itself—Marx emphasises this again and again—objectification would be an opening out, it would allow man, who produces and reproduces his life without ceasing and who transforms himself by changing nature, tc contemplete himself in a world which he has created. No dialectical sleight of hand can make alienation come out of it; this is why what is involved here is not a mere play of concepts but real History."[33]

Marxian Theory: From 'Fragmentation' to the 'Emancipation' of Man

As pointed out above, Marx takes the idea of alienation from Hegel and gives it a socio-economic complexion first in his early writings (known as *Paris Manuscripts* or *Economic and Philosophical Manuscripts*) when he was a young sociologist and then in his monumental critique of the capitalist economy (called *Capital*) when he became a 'mature' political economist. A highly philosophical concept thus came to have both normative and empirical dimensions at the hands of the 'father of scientific socialism'. He argues that the social division of labour creates vast accumulations

31. Mehta, *op. cit.*, p. 115.
32. Swingewood, *op. cit.*, p. 89.
33. Jean Paul Sartre "Marxism and Existentialism" in Gould and Thursby (ed. s): *Contemporary Political Thought* (New York: Holt, Rinehart and Winston, 1969), p. 237.

Political Alienation

In the higher phase of communist society, after the enslaving subordination of the individual to the division of labour.... has vanished; after labour has become not only a means to life but life's prime want; after the productive forces have also increased with the all-round development of the individual, and all the springs of cooperative wealth flow more abundantly, only then can the narrow horizon of bourgeois right be crossed in its entirety and society inscribe on its banner: From each according to his ability, to each according to his needs'.

—Marx and Engels
Selected Works in One Volume, pp. 320-21.

In Marx's view, capitalist workers suffer from alienation in that they are separated from their own genuine or essential natures: they are alienated from the product of their labour; alienated from the process of labour itself; alienated from their fellow beings; and, finally alienated from their true selves. Freedom is, therefore, linked to the personal fulfilment which only unalienated labour can bring about.

—Andrew Heywood
Political Theory: An Introduction, pp. 262-63.

Such theories are 'perfectionist', because they claim that certain ways of life constitute human 'perfection' (or 'excellence'), and that such ways of life should be promoted, while less worthy ways of life should be penalised. This is unlike liberal or libertarian theories, which do not try to encourage any particular way of life, but rather leave individuals free to use their resources in whatever ways they themselves find most valuable.

—Will Kymlicka
Contemporary Political Philosophy, p. 190.

of capital and personal wealth at one pole of society, an increase in the value of things achieved only at the cost of progressive devaluation of man as a human species. The source of this evil should be found in the capitalist system in which organisation of labour "has the effect of directly transforming man's labour into a saleable commodity."[34] Marx, as a rank sociologist, thus says: "This fact implies that the object produced by labour, its product, now stands opposed to it as an *alien* being, as a power *independent* of the producer. The product of labour is labour which has been embodied in an object and turned into a physical thing; this product is an objectification of labour."[35]

34. Swingewood, *op. cit.*, p 90.
35. Marx: *Early Writings*, p. 122. In supporting this concept of alienation, Marx "retains a vital connection with epistemological concerns, but shifts the concept into a materialist and social scientific key, locating its application not only or basically in the production of ideal but in human practices generally and basically in the sphere of material production in the economy, the production of material goods. Alienation is a historically specific process, relation and condition having a general form in which human products, the products of human powers are alienated from, that is separated from, and lost to, their producers, who are consequently subordinated to the power and domination of what they have produced, in a process that involves the illusion that these items are not the products." Roy Edgley: "Philosophy in Marx: The First Hundred Years" edited by David McLellan (London: Francis Printer, 1983), p. 271.

It may be deciphered that while Marx borrows the idea of alienation from Hegel, he takes a different course that goes to find fault with what the latter says. Hegel takes the two terms 'objectification' and 'alienation' as synonymous. Marx, for this reason, criticises him for adding to the stock of confusion in view of the fact that the two are not interchangeable. "Objectification is the process through which man externalises himself in nature and society, for example, by producing things as tools, a process whereby he becomes *necessarily* an object for others, within the structure of social relations built upon the simplest form of economy. Alienation occurs only when man, having externalised himself in nature and society, finds his activity, his 'essence' operating on him as an external, alien and oppressive power."[36]

To Marx, alienation has four distinct dimensions—from nature, from himself, from fellow beings, and from society. It is the system of capitalism that constitutes the total alienation of human labour, for capital dominates completely the worker as a labourer and also as a man. "This system alienates man essentially from his own activity, from the product of his labour, thus turning labour's product into an alien object; the more he works, the more he finds himself dominated by the world of objects his own labour has created. The worker puts his life into the object, and his life then belongs no longer to himself but to the object. The greater his activity.... the less his processes. What is embodied in the product of his labour is no longer his own. The greater this product is....the more he is diminished."[37]

This idea of 'alienation' finds its manifestation in the later works of Marx as well. For instance, in the *Grundrisse* he says that social wealth confronts labour in more powerful position as an alien and dominated power which, created through labour, belongs not to the worker, but to capital. Thus, he notes that the real emphasis is not on the state of being *objectified,* but of being *'alienated'*, dispossessed, sold.[38] Likewise in his masterpiece contribution to the critique of political economy, he says: "We have seen that the growing accumulation of capital implies its growing concentration. Thus grows the power of capital, the alienation of the conditions of social production personified in the capitalist from the real producers. Capital comes more and more to the fore as a social power, whose agent is the capitalist. This social power no longer stands in any possible relation to that which the labour of a single individual can create. It becomes an alienated, independent social power, which is opposed to society as an object, and as an object that is the capitalist's source of power."[39]

36. Swingewood, *op. cit.*, p. 90.
37. Marx: *Early Writings*, pp. 123-24.
38 Marx: *Grundrisse*, pp. 831-32.
39. Marx: *Capital*, Vol. Ill, p. 259. Marx's critique of labour rests and must rest on a set of tacit standards concerning goods - desirable, non-alienated - and creative labour. The theory of labour alienation entails a tacit theory of *the ideal* labour situation. The Swedish social psychologist Joachim Israel has seen this plainly and holds that for Marx a work is creative (1) if man makes his life activity itself an object of his will and consciousness, (2) if man through work can express his capabilities in a comprehensive way, (3) if through this work he can express his social nature, if work is not simply a means for maintaining man's substance, *i.e.*, if it is not purely instrumental. *Alienation: From Marx to Modern Sociology* (Boston: Allyn and Bacon, 1971), p. 39.

In simple words, under capitalism, the work process invariably leads to alienation. In this direction, two main conditions may be referred to:

1. The worker who has sold his labour power to the capitalist is related to the product of his labour as to an alien object; it exists outside him independently as something alien to him. His labour creates the alien and hostile social power of capitalism.
2. Alienation is found in the act of production within the labour process. The worker is unable to work creatively. His work is not the satisfaction of a need; it is merely a means to satisfy needs external to it. On the one hand, the ownership and control of the work process are vested in the capitalist, who decides what is to be produced, how much, and in what way, as well as the disposal of the product. On the other hand, the technical exigencies of the work process, the subordination of the workers to the machine and the division of labour mean that he cannot engage in his life activity.

In both ways, man is alienated from his species being, his essential nature. This itself logically entails that each man is alienated from every other man and this, for Marx, is reflected in the political economist's conception of civil society.[40]

Marx uses the idea of alienation to identify or characterise a certain sort of human ill or dysfunction which is especially prevalent in modern society. Its features are:[41]

1. Marx perceives a complex interconnection between the various ills and irrationalities which beset people in modern society.
2. Marx insists that what is distinctive about modern society, and what fundamentally explains its system of interconnected irrationalities is something about the kind of labour production which goes on in it.
3. Marx regards this peculiar kind of labour as characteristic of a determinate and historically transitory phase in the generally progressive movement of human history. In the mature theory the interconnection does not consist in a 'system of alienation' but in the economic structure of capitalist society. The mature Marx traces this structure to a kind of labour or production because he holds that the social relations of production which make it up are determined by the degree of the 'development of society's productive powers' and hence by the nature of its material labour.
4. For the mature Marx, the 'essence of human development' is not a process predetermined in the womb of the human species - essence, but only the relentless expansion of society's productive powers, which determines the course of development taken by the social relations of production.

Marx not only discovers the essential weakness of the capitalist system that despiritualises and devalues human life, he also offers a solution to this problem: When will alienation come to an end? His answer is that the end of capitalism and its substitution by the socialist system will entail the era of human emancipation implying the advent of the state of 'disalienation'. Obviously, Marxism has a definite goal—a free and whole man instead of a man like a fragmented creature. Like Rousseau, he

40. Michael Evans, *op. cit.*, pp. 92-93.
41. A.W. Wood: *Karl Marx* (London: Routledge and Kegan Paul, 1981), p. 7.

desires that man must be returned to a non-alienated state, reunited with nature, his fellow-beings and his own personality. Obviously, 'disalienation' would come to take place in the final stage of 'Communism' when division of labour would no longer allocate men to specific occupational roles but allow him, if he so wishes, 'to hunt in the morning, fish in the afternoon, rear cattle in the evening, criticise after dinner.... without ever becoming a hunter, a fisherman, a shepherd or a critic."[42] "If alienation is the splintering of human nature into a number of misgotten parts, we would expect communism to be presented as a kind of reunification.... Many of the characteristics ascribed to full communism, such as the end of the division of labour and the erasure of social classes, are clear instances of this unification process at work."[43]

Marx's theory of alienation has been attacked on two grounds. First, the critics have sought to draw a wedge between 'young Marx,' a sociologist, and 'old Marx', an economist, and thereby sought to prove that the 'two Marxes' are different from each other. The burden of their contention is. that while the 'young Marx' is the friend, philosopher and guide of the capitalist class who very sympathetically makes the 'men of capital aware of the essential weakness of their system which they should remove at the earliest practicable moment so as to save it from inevitable collapse, opposed to this is the 'mature Marx' who is the sworn enemy of the capitalist system and desires nothing short of its total destruction. Obviously, the social, economic and political thought of Marx is inherent with basic contradiction. These papers "contain Marx's first recognisable attempt at a systematic theory of capitalism. The attempt fails because the philosophical concept of alienation is simply too vague and metaphorical to perform the explanatory function Marx tries to assign it."[44]

Contrary to this, the protagonists of Marx are of the view that there is nothing like inherent contradiction in the Marxian theory of alienation as propounded in his early writings *(Paris Manuscripts)* or later writings like *The German Ideology, Grundrisse* and *Capital.* Not only is there a logical connection between the two phases of the evolution of Marxian thought, the latter is certainly a clear and more authoritative improvement upon the former. It is strongly affirmed that Marx's theory of alienation becomes more precise and scientific as he moves from the predominantly critical philosophical standpoint of the *Manuscripts* to the mature theory of his *Capital.* While he writes of the 'inhuman power' dominating social life, frustrating man's essential powers and transforming him into mere object, in his later works he shows how the division of labour and factory production can ruin man's physical and intellectual condition, but at the same time create the conditions for working class political practice. "Stunted they may be, but the working class organise themselves into collective bodies and resist the 'inhuman power' of capital. The concept of *praxis*

42. Marx: *The German Ideology,* pp. 44-45.
43. Ollman *op. cit.,* pp. 135-36.
44. A.W. Wood, *op. cit.,* pp. 6-7. Although the first of Marx's critique is clear, the various aspects or forms of alienated labour are not clearly defined and separate but overlap each other, and interconnect causally, and both critics and disciples differ strongly over just how much of his early assumptions and approaches Marx was to accept upto 1844 or 1846 or 1847, or whenever a crucial disjuncture was supposed to occur." Graeme Duncan: *Marx and Mill: Two Views of Social Conflict and Social Harmony* (London: Cambridge University Press, 1973), p. 74.

thus constitutes the link between Marx's early and later writings: *Capital* is as much about man creating the social world as is the *Paris Manuscripts*."[45]

While we may, or may not, accept the above line of criticism along with its contradiction, the second ground of attack is a little plausible when we find critics discovering an element of 'utopia' in the Marxian theory of alienation. We may agree with Marx when he hits at the essential weaknesses of the capitalist system, but we may have our reservations when we find him affirming that alienation would go in the final stage of socialism (communism), when 'glorious human values' shall prevail and in place of a man with a fragmented personality we shall have a really 'emancipated man'. A basically empirical concept of alienation takes a normative turn at the hands of Marx. Moreover, the whole idea of alienation takes a deterministic form that militates against the fundamental law of Marxism—dialectical materialism. Thus, Marx's humanist concept of alienation is one-directional and deterministic, more philosophical and speculative than sociological and concretely historical.[46]

Sociological Theory: Modification as well as Mutilation of the Marxian Thesis

A very interesting feature of the development of Marxian political theory, so far as the concept of alienation is concerned, is that the idea of 'estrangement' saw its eclipse after the death of the Father of Scientific Socialism so much so that it failed to have its reiteration in the works of his ardent friends and followers like Engels, Plekhanov, Lenin, Trotsky, Stalin, and Kautsky. We may, however, refer to the works of some sociologists like Max Weber and George Simmel who studied the case of man's estrangement *vis-a-vis* reification. It is, as a matter of fact, with the publication of Marx's early writings under the title of *Economic and Philosophical Manuscripts* in 1932 that the concept of alienation became a widely known affair. Soon after social rebels like Eric Fromm and self-styled Marxists like Herbert Marcuse came to the forefront. Its most distinct impact fell on the existentialists like Heidegger and Sartre. However, it is Hungarian Marxist Lukacs whose *History of Class Consciousness* published in 1971 created a stir in the circle of the orthodox Marxists who accused him of being a 'revisionist' and a 'philosophical idealist'.

We may, therefore, refer to the contemporary sociological theory in which we find a clear streak of Marxism either taken to the verge of its rejection or subtle modification giving an inkling of the sneaking acceptance of what Marx has said. The great German sociologist Max Weber has sought to study the case of alienation within the broad framework of his 'ideal type bureaucracy'. Contradicting the optimistic affirmation of Marx that alienation would go after the overthrow of the capitalist system, he says that with intensified technical rationalisation occurring in any organisational society, alienation would be certain to continue under the system

45. Swingewood, *op. cit.*, p. 111. The Russian scholars treat these papers as criticism of the bourgeois political economy and the bourgeois economic system. By 'alienation' Marx means the forced labour of the labourers for the capitalists, the appropriation by the capitalist of the product of worker's labour and the separation of the labourer from the means of production which, being in the capitalist possession, confront the labourer as an alien, enslaving power. Here Marx comes close to an exposition." *Economic and Philosophical Manuscripts of 1844* (Moscow: Progress Publishers, 1974), pp. 7-8.

46 Swingewood, *op. cit.*, p. 96.

of socialism.[47] The celebrated thesis of Weber about the increasing and ineluctable rationalisation of the Western society hinges on a onesided and fatalistic conception of technology.

Weber's theory of alienation finds place in his emphasis on the fact of bureaucratic domination that is common to both the bourgeois and socialist systems. Both systems require bureaucratic organisation. Discipline and control are equally important to both and in this sense some form of alienation becomes inevitable. Without bureaucracy capitalism itself would have become an impossibility. Naturally, the development of capitalism hinges on bureaucratic rationality inasmuch as it creates an urgent need for stable, strict, intensive and calculable administration'.[48] The source of alienation should be traced in bureaucratic rationality that funcions as a force external to and independent of human control. Moreover, rationalisation of the bureaucratic system "transcends its specific historical forms to become a form of domination." In Weber's definition, therefore, we may observe that "rationality and technology have become reified; their impact on society may be modified but not brought under human will and subordinated to human purposes."[49]

The 'technological determinism' of Weber is echoed in the writings of Herbert Marcuse. In his attack on the advanced industrial society he says that a rationalised technology "has created a world of artificial needs, mass consumption and irrational goals which men are too eager to accept. The exploitative relation of capital and labour is thoroughly hidden by the 'false consciousness' which flows directly from the one-dimensional awareness of modern man."[50] Drawing inspiration from Weber and trying to reconcile it with the fundamental premises of Marx, he argues that a technocratic and bureaucratic elite effectively controls the mass media and high 'irrational consumption'; social differences become minimised through the levelling of consumption habits, leisure and activities and social aspirations. The rationalisation of culture is complete and Marx's vision of proletarian revolution becomes Utopian.[51]

Marcuse maintains that throughout the world of industrial civilisation, the dominance of man by man is growing in scope and efficiency. For the vast majority of the people, the scope and mode of satisfaction are determined by their own labour, but their labour is mere work for an apparatus which they do not control, which operates as an independent power to which individuals must submit if they want to survive. As he says: "Men do not live their own lives, but perform pre-established functions. While they work, they do not fulfil their own needs and faculties, but work in alienation."[52] Obviously, such a view demonstrates in fact that man does not realise himself in his labour; that his life has become an instrument of labour; and that his work and its products have assumed a form and power independent

47. Ilsa Dronberger: *The Political Thought of Max Weber: In Quest of Statesmanship* (New York: Appleton-Century, 1971). p 300.
48. Weber: *Economy and Society* (New York, 1968), II, p. 223.
49. Swingewood, *op cit.*, p. 107.
50. *Ibid.*
51. Marcuse: *Eros and Civilisation: A Philosophical Enquiry into Freud* (London: Allen Lane, The Penguin Press, 1969), p. 35.
52. Marcuse: *One-Dimensional Man* (London: Routledge and Kegan Paul, 1964). p. 32.

of him as an individual. Unlike Marx, he envisages the "transformation of labour into pleasure as the solution to the problem of alienation. He believes that this can be achieved only by complete change in social institutions, a distribution of social product according to need, the assignment of functions according to talent, and the provision of attracted labour."[53]

Lukacs has made a bid to reiterate what Marx has said on the subject of alienation irrespective of the fact that he has introduced certain elements which may be dubbed as 'anti-Marxian' by the orthodox Marxists. He argues that since the proletariat is an *object,* then its consciousness, developed historically through concentration in large-scale factory organisation which facilitates *class* identification, constitutes the self-consciousness of the object, a consciousness which automatically cuts through the fetishised and reified structures of its thought.[54] He sees the process of'reification' as total, stamping its imprint upon the whole consciousness of man so that his various qualities and capacities cease to be his expression, but that of another, things which he can own, or dispose off like the various objects of the external world.[55]

Lukacs's version, for this reason, appears like a leftwing analogue of Weber's rationalisation with this essential difference that he places too much reliance on the fact of reification. To him, it is the necessary and immediate reality of every person living in a capitalist society which can be overcome only by constant and constantly renewed efforts to disrupt the reified structure of existence by relating to the concretely manifested contradictions of the total development, by becoming conscious of these contradictions of total development. Taking inspiration from the same, George Simmel in his 'tragic vision' of the Western culture argues that the modern affluent bourgeois society transforms the commodity into a 'universal category' and as the labour power of the work is a commodity, then the fate of the workers becomes the fact of the society as a whole. In this way, reification comes to imply that the society "satisfies its needs through commodity exchange; capitalist development thus brings with it a deepening structure of reification which fatefully dominates social consciousness."[56]

Simmel hits at the evil of the system of the division of labour that draws a wedge between a producer and the thing produced by him. The significance attached to the 'over-specialised' functional performance makes man a mere cog in an enormous organisation of things of powers which tear from his hands all progress, spirituality, and value in order to transform them from a subjective form into the form of a purely objective life.[57] He regrets the development technology' that make man like an alienated creature. The objects which belong to man as a part and parcel of his 'cultural development', attain a 'fetishistic' character as objects, independent of man, becoming more and more linked to each other in a self-contained world

53. B.K. Jha: "Marxism and the New Left" in *The Indian Journal of Political Science,* Vol., XXXIX, No. 4, 1978, p. 545.
54. Lukacs: *History of Class Consciousness,* p. 178.
55. *Ibid.,* p.100.
56. Swingewood, *op. cit.,* p. 109.
57. Simmel: "The Metropolis and Mental Life" in K. Wolff (ed.): *The Sociology of George Simmel* (New York, 1950), p. 422.

which has increasingly fewer contacts with the subjective psyche and its desires and sensibilities.'[58]

It may be seen that in the contemporary sociological theory of alienation, as given above, Marx stands accepted, modified, as well as mutilated. As such, it may be described neither as an extension of what Marx has said, nor its modification or mutilation within the broad framework of reification. Marxism stands on the fundamental premise of dialectical materialism which shows that a dialectical relation exists between reification, alienation and class structure. According to an orthodox interpretation of Marx, the worker "continually resists through class organisation and activity the process whereby his activity and he himself become abstract entities. Different from this, the argument of total reification is monolithic not dialectical : it fails to observe the first axiom of Marx's social theory—that the working class exists in specific societies with a consciousness compounded from local and national traditions, ruling class ideology and working class organisation (trade unions, etc.). It is an attempt to grasp the objective movement and contradictory elements inherent in social development. The theories of the reification and rationalisation of culture as uniform and total processes reflect a non-dialectical, ahistorical, theoretical standpoint."[59]

Existential Theory: Indictment of 'Inauthentic Life'

However, a very candid manifestation of the modification amounting to the rejection of Marx, in this direction, should be seen in the theory of existentialism where alienation is identified with 'inauthentic life'. While Marx desires disalienation, the existentialists crave for an 'authentic life'. The two terms *authenticity* and *inauthenticity* were introduced by Martin Heideggar and later adopted by Jean Paul Sartre with certain variations to designate profoundly the contrasting modes of human existence. Others from Kierkegaard to Marcel have also dwelt upon the same fundamental distinction, and their phenomenological descriptions of how the two modes become manifest in a man's daily life offer some of the most brilliant and searching points in the doctrine of existentialism. Whatever names may be given, the concept of an authentic, as opposed to an inauthentic life, "is one of the most original and important contributions of existentialism, precisely because it provides ethical norms generally rooted in human ontology."[60]

According to existentialists, a non-alienated or inauthentic life is one in which man is not truly himself. It appears that they take inspirations from Tolstoy's fiction *The Death of Ivan llych* in which he has given a scathing portrait of a nineteenth century Russian functionary who had lost all sense of his individuality because of conformity to the conventions of officialdom and polite society. Thus, the well-known Danish existentialist Kierkegaard in his *The Sickness Unto Death* regrets that, in spite of being a husband, a father, a worker, a player and what not, a man "does not dare to believe in himself, finds it too venturesome a thing to be himself, far easier

58. See L. Coser: 'Introduction" in his *Georg Simmel* (New Jersey, 1965).
59. Swingewood, *op. cit,* p. 110.
60. Richard Gill and Ernest Sherman (ed.s): *The Fabric of Existentialism* (Englewood Cliffs, New Jersey: Prentice-Hall, 1973), p. 19.

and safer to be like the others, to become an imitation, a number, a cipher in the crowd."[61]

The most important name in this direction is that of Sartre who refers to the problem of alienation when he gives a description of the life of non-authentic man. According to him, man in the non-authentic world is constituted by the way in which others see him, and by which he becomes petrified into a false, abstract essence. As a result of this, he feels alienated. His concern with the living person and with the concrete emotions of anguish, despair, nausea, and the like also hint at the fact of his alienation.[62] However, the important thing about Sartre is that he seeks to follow the line of Marx by presenting a clear and striking picture of the alienated man of the capitalist system. As he says: "The worker exhausts himself in producing a car and in earning enough to buy one ; the acquisition gives him the impression of having satisfied a 'need'. The system which exploits him provides him simultaneously with a goal and with the possibility of reaching it. The consciousness of the intolerable character of the system must, therefore, no longer be sought in the impossibility of satisfying elementary needs but, above all else, in the consciousness of alienation—in other words, in the fact that this life is not worth living and has no meaning, that this mechanism is a deceptive mechanism, that these needs are artificially created, that they are false, that they are exhausting and only serve profit."[63]

In short, individual is the hallmark of existentialism; a crowd is an untruth. Thus, the theory of existentialism not only hits at the loss of individuality, it also desires that man should remain free as he is a freely born entity. If man is free, he is condemned to be free, because that is the very condition of his nature. However, the real difficulty in appreciating this theory is that not all existentialists lay stress on the same point and in the same manner and this want of unanimity confuses the issue as to what they really mean. We may understand as to what they mean by an 'inauthentic life', but how that is to be substituted by an 'authentic life' is not clear. Leaving aside the case of Sartre, all other existentialists look like determined to refute what Marx has said and even in the case of Sartre it remains a matter of controversy as to which is dominant in him - Existentialism or Marxism? It also appears that too much indictment of 'inauthentic life' and an equally too much emphasis on its replacement by an 'authentic life' indicates a sort of commitment on the part of most of the existentialists that smacks of 'irrational extremism' as well.[64]

Critical Appreciation

The concept of political alienation, as discussed in the preceding sections, has been criticised on these grounds:

1. It is said that though the concept of alienation hits at the character of modern 'civilised' social life, it certainly fails to look to the other side of the picture. It

---

61. *Ibid.*,
62. Sartre: *Being and Nothingness,* Translated from French into English by Hazel E. Barnes (New York: Washington Square Press, 1966), p. xix.
63. Sartre: *Between Existentialism and Marxism.* Translated from French into English by John Mathews (New York: Pantheon Books, 1974), pp. 124-25.
64. See Gould and Thursby, *op. cit.*, p. 100.

is true that man is so terribly caught up in the web of modern competitive life that he has lost the real essence of his existence. However, it cannot be said with any amount of authority at our disposal that modern civilisation is nothing else than being a storehouse of this evil. While the motivational tendency towards the rejection of internalised or external expectations of others may be derived from the conflict between the objective order of the world and the inner core of the self, so much stress on the fact of alienation tends to fall not on this conflict which may exist but on the failure to overcome it. In so far as internalisation "occurs without exceptionally great unmastered conflict, ego will develop needed dispositions to conform with expectations, while faulty internalisation (internalisation attended by ineffective defence mechanism or incomplete resolution of conflicts) may produce alienative need dispositions to refute to fulfil expectations. Partial internalisation is thus a prerequisite for alienation to occur, otherwise the attitude would be considered as one of indifference. Many alienative tendencies do, however, remain covert, since they exist only as the negative component of an ambivalent conformity-alienation disposition."[65]

2. Political alienation is mainly a contribution of the Marxian theory. We have already pointed out that it is Marx who drew inspiration from Hegel's metaphysics and then put the same idea in his sociology which ultimately became an integral feature of his political economy. It has informed the critics to say that the alienation of labour as the self-alienation of man from his essence is a concept that presents considerable intellectual difficulties and in any case it fails to satisfy the emotional needs of societies newly launched upon by the adventure of modernisation. Though one may agree with such an observation or not, yet it is true that the way Marx has sought to solve the problem of alienation introduces an element of utopianism in an otherwise empirical political theory. Recent political developments in different 'socialist' countries have belied the hopes of the Father of Scientific Socialism. Ultimately, it "becomes difficult to understand why Marx should see alienation from the conditions of production as a problem at all, unless he entertains some logically normative conception of human personality and its capacities not given in experience."[66]
3. The idea of political alienation has not been fully studied as yet. Hence, a purely empirical political theory on the basis of available evidence can hardly be formulated. It appears that modern social theorists have drawn over-inspiration from Marx as well as from his ardent protagonists and antagonists. The result is that the concept still lacks thorough clarity. It may be found that some writers have failed to distinguish between certain less-related or even unrelated themes and sought to build up theories from half-baked material. For instance, political isolationism and political cynicism have been used like interchangeable terms. Curiously, some leading American sociologists have even looked at the movements of "American Negroes with considerable apprehension and discovered the roots of the consolidation of, what they call, 'Black Power' of the Black

65. Talcott Parsons and Edward Shils: *Towards a General Theory of Action* (Camb., Mass., Harvard Univ. Press, 1951), pp. 156ff.
66. Michael Evans, *op. cit.*, p. 95.

Panther Party (formed in 1966) in the largely isolationist attitude of the men of the black community.[67] Thus, some writers have gone to the extent of saying that political alienation causes a steady, though imperceptible, accumulation of mass anger that has its outbreak in the form of some insurrection.[68]

Certainly, the concept of political alienation should not be elaborated at the expense of this fundamental postulate of social and political theory that man is by nature and necessity a social and political animal. It is a different matter that by means of a subtle observation, one may say that while man is necessarily a social creature, he is not a political being in the same measure. A study of political cynicism, for instance, may drive home this fact that though a man lives in society, he need not concern himself with the politics of his community, nor participate actively in political life, nor cherish the political institutions and values of his society. And yet the fact remains that as human beings are social creatures, they develop their political culture. Evidently they cannot dwell together without entering into relationships of influence. Whenever these relations "become stable and repetitive, political systems exist."[69]

In short, the concept of political alienation has offered a formidable challenge which has to be met not by making an all-round attack on the achievements of modern civilisation but by seeking ways and means so as to do away with the evil by bringing about a better and harmonious relationship between scientific advancement and human life. The problem is, indeed, a gigantic one and people may, or may not endorse the solutions as given by eminent figures like Gandhi in the form of his 'ideal society' (Ram Raj), or by Lasswell in the optimistic affirmation of his 'Freemen's Co-operative Commonwealth', or by Marx in the form of his 'era of human emancipation', or by Lenin in the form of his 'society of the Soviets', or by Mao in his 'system of communes' and the like. What is really needed is that the monstrous evil should go so that politics witnesses a happy and honest participation of all people. A study of the views of all eminent social theorists on the subject of political alienation leaves this important impression on our minds that there "is a long journey for the alienated individual to take in search of a state and a society in which he can live a life of creative happiness within himself, of love and friendship with his fellowmen, and peace and harmony with nature."[70]

67. See George Feaver : "Black Power" in Maurice Cranston (ed.): *The New Left* (London: Bodley Head, 1970), pp. 139-178.

68. See Schwartz: "Political Alienation" in I.K. Fierabend, R.L. Fieraband and T, Gurr: (ed. s): *Anger, Violence and Politics* (Englewood Cliffs, New Jersey: Pentice Hall, 1972), pp. 58ff.

69. R.A. Dahl: *Modern Political Analysis* (Englewood Cliffs, New Jersey: Prentice-Hall, 1976), p. 100.

70. S.P. Varma: *Modern Political Theory* (Delhi; Vikas, 1975), p. 392.

17

Political Power

> I put for a general inclination of all mankind, a perpetual and a restless desire for power that ceases only in death. And the cause of this is not always that a man does for a more intensive delight, than he has already attained to; or that he cannot be content with a moderate power: but because he cannot assure the power and means to live well, which he has present, without the acquisition of more.
>
> **—Thomas Hobbes**[1]

Ever since Hobbes produced his *Leviathan,* the concept of power in the realms of national and international politics has become a momentous subject so much so that now it is regarded as the most significant area of fundamental research. Curiously, it is so in spite of the fact that the real meaning of this term has been a matter of controversy on account of its social, economic, political, psychological, sociological and spiritual ramifications. Recently the idea of power has assumed an importance of its own in the realm of political theory. The reason for this should be traced in the fact that the meaning of politics has changed from one of being a 'study of state and government', to that of being a 'study of power'. As Curtis says: "Politics is organised dispute about power and its use, involving choice among competing values, ideas, persons, interests and demands. The study of politics is concerned with the description and analysis of the manner in which power is obtained, exercised, and controlled, the purpose for which it is used, the manner in which decisions are made, the factors which influence the making of those decisions, and the context in which those decisions take place."[2]

Power: Meaning and Nature of the Concept

The problem of defining the term 'power' in very precise terms arises from the fact that different writers have taken different views with the result that its real meaning seems to hover from Friedrich's description of it as 'a certain kind of human relationship'[3] to Tawney's emphasis on the identification of power with the'capacity of an individual, or a group of individuals, to modify the conduct of others in the manner which one desires'.[4] Not merely this, while a great political thinker like Hobbes identifies power with 'some future apparent good', a modern psychoanalyst like Harold Lasswell likens it with 'influence'. We also find that while a great Marxist like Mao Zedong claims that 'power comes from the barrel of a gun', an apostle of

---

1. Hobbes: *Leviathan,* Ch. 11.
2. Michael Curtis: *Comparative Government and Politics* (New York: Harper and Row, 1968) p. 1.
3. Carl J. Friedrich: *Constitutional Government and Democracy* (New York: Harper, 1937), pp. 12-14.
4. R.H. Tawney: *Equality* (New York: Harcourt Brace, 1931), p. 230.

peace, truth and non-violence like Gandhi substitutes the force of gun and 'bomb with the power of love and truth emanating from the will of the people.'

The source of this difficulty lies in the fact that the word 'power' is used in different senses. Power is ascribed to different things on different grounds. For instance, we speak of horse power, power of ideas, economic power, power of social status, healing power, brain power, purchasing power, executive power, military power and the like. The common thread among all is that the term 'power' behaves in much the same way as the word 'ability' or 'capacity'. In fact, the English word 'power' derives from certain Latin and French words which mean 'to be able'. Thus, instead of involving one's self in the cobweb of different ramifications of the term and its application in different disciplines and situations, one may take a generalised view and say that power "is taken to denote the whole spectrum of those external influences that, by being brought to bear upon an individual, can make him move in a required direction."[5]

If so, the sense of the term 'power' becomes interchangeable with several related themes like control, influence, authority, force, might, persuasion, coercion, domination and the like irrespective of the fact that different writers make use of different terms at different places and in different situations in their peculiar ways with the result that it becomes a highly tedious job to say as to what the word 'power' precisely conveys. Some other writers, however, warn against the insidious tendency of equating power with other kindred themes like influence, force, control and authority in order to have a proper understanding of each term. For instance, Max Weber says that power and authority are different things inasmuch as the latter invariably conveys within its fold the sense of 'legitimacy'. Likewise, force and power are dissimilar things in view of the fact that the former necessarily involves some brutal manifestation which may, or may not, form an integral part of the idea of power no matter we invoke the observation of Bertrand Russell who takes power as 'the capacity to influence the actions of others.'[6]

Keeping it in mind, the important points of distinction between power and other kindred themes may be thus highlighted:[7]

1. **Power:** It is the faculty or capacity to conquer in a contest. Force is an adjunct, not an essence of power. The potency or capacity to manipulate the will and activities of others to make them conform to the power-seeker's will is the central point in power. Power may be based on other elements like fraud, ingenuity, or combination and group tactics. It can also be derived from established constitutional and legal procedures. In general and also in the ultimate analysis, international politics is the manifestation of power. Ideology may only be the mask for hiding the uglier picture of power.
2. **Force:** It is different from power. It is the most brutal manifestation of power. When we talk of force, the invariable connotation is of physical force which is only the glamorous concentration of force. Its techniques are restraint, coercion, physical threat, intimidation, blackmail, terrorisation and military domination. Power is latent force, force is manifest power.

5. S.E. Finer: *Comparative Government* (London: Penguin Press, 1970), p. 13.
6. See Bertrand Russell: *Power: A New Social Analysis* (London: George Allen and Unwin, 1937).
7. V.P. Varma: *Political Philosophy* (Agra: Lakshmi Narayan, 1970), pp. 410-11.

Political Power

Hobbes: Man wants peace, peace enables him to achieve power, power creates pride or vainglory. Being a selfish creature, man has lust for power. It is like a ceaseless and restless desire that goes with the end of life.

Hegel: State is the embodiment of power, nothing above it. Fall down and worship it. It is a divine idea, an ethical substance, march of God on earth.

Marx: Power is always with a social class by which it dominates and exploits the other class. It is a class instrument that would wither away in the communist society.

C.B. Macpherson: Power signifies ability of the individual to develop his personality or to extract advantages from the like ability of others.

R.H. Tawney: Power is the capacity of an individual or a group of individuals to modify the conduct of others in a manner as one desires.

C.J. Friedrich: Power is a certain kind of human relationship.

H.J. Morgenthau: Lust for power is common to all men and thus it is indispensable for social life itself.

Michael Foucault: Power is omnipresent; it has a transformative character; it is aligned with knowledge.

Mao Zedong: Power flows from the barrel of a gun.

Gandhi: Power means soul-force.

3. **Influence:** If force stands on one extreme, then influence on the other; it represents the sublimation of power. It is a category which represents the inchoate or indeterminate exercise of power. It may be due to social prestige, intellectual eminence, moral worth and the like. More or less, it is an amorphous entity. The most important feature of distinction between the two is that while influence is persuasive, power is coercive. We submit voluntarily to influence, while power requires submission.[8]
4. **Authority:** It represents the moralisation of power. It may also include the legitimisation of power through the provision of legal sanctions to it and through becoming rooted in the traditions, historical institutions and value constellations of a community. Legal sanctions, statutes, commands, writs, rules, regulations, byelaws, etc. represent the technique of authority. Authority is essentially the institutional code within which the use of power as a medium is organised and legitimised. It is the aspect of a status in a system of social organisation, namely, its collective aspect, by virtue of which the incumbent is put in a position legitimately to make decisions which are binding, not only on himself but on the collectivity as a whole and hence its other-member units in the sense that so far as their implications impinge on their respective roles and statuses, they are bound to act in accordance with these implications. This includes the right to insist on such action, though because of the general division of labour, the holder of authority very often is not himself in a position to enforce his decisions but must be dependent on specialised agencies for this. If then, authority be conceived as the institutional counterpart of power, the main difference lies in the fact that authority is not a circulating medium.[9]

8. Bierstedt: "An Analysis of Social Power" in *The American Sociological Review,* Vol. XV, No, 6, pp. 738-39.
9. See Talcott Parsons: "On the Concept of Political Power" in Roderick Bell, D.V. Edwards and R.H. Wagner (ed.s) *Political Power* (New York: Free Press, 1969), pp. 263-64.

5. **Control:** It is a more comprehensive category than power. It also represents something less concentrated than power. Control can be legislative, executive, judicial, financial, administrative, popular. It is more or less equivalent to power except that it is less concentrated in the intensity of its manifestation than power.

From what we have said above, the following implications may be gathered:[10]

1. Power is a social phenomenon *par excellence,* and not merely a political or economic phenomenon.
2. It is useful to distinguish power from prestige, influence, dominance, right, force, authority and the like.
3. Power is latent force, force is manifest power, and authority is institutionalised power.
4. Power which has its incidence only in social opposition of some kind, appears in different ways in formal organisation, in informal organisation, and in unorganised community.
5. The source and necessary components of power reside in combination of numbers (especially majorities), social organisation and resources.

In brief, power "is the ability to determine the behaviour of others in accord with one's own wishes."[11] In other words, a man is said to have power to the extent that it "influences the behaviour of others in accordance with his own intentions."[12] Likewise, "we ascribe power to those who can influence the conduct of others even against their will."[13] Again, it "is simply the probability that men will act as another man wishes. This action may rest on fear, rational calculation of advantage, lack of energy to do otherwise, loyal devotion, indifference, or a dozen other individual motives."[14] Certainly, it is because of this wide diversity in the meaning of the term 'power' that its whole study has become like 'a bottomless swamp.'[15]

---

10. Bierstedt, *op. cit.*
11. Coser and Rosenberg: *Sociological Theory* (New York: Macmillan, 1957), p. 123.
12. Goldhamer and Shils: "Types of Power and Status" in *The American Journal of Sociology,* Vol. XLV, No. 2, 1939, pp. 171-82.
13. Gerth and Mills: *Character and Social Structure* (New York: Harcourt Brace, 1953), pp. 193-95.
14. *Ibid.*
15. R. A. Dahl: "The Concept of Power" in Bell, Edwards and Wagner, *op. cit.,* p. 79. As a matter of fact, the word 'power' has been identified with several related themes like 'authority', 'force', 'coercion' and the like and, due to this, its precise meaning has become a fluid affair. Talcott Parsons holds that unfortunately, this concept "is not a settled one in the social, sciences, either in political science or in sociology." Refer to his paper "Distribution of Power in American Society" in *World Politics,* Vol. 10 (October, 1975). E.M. Coulter opines that power "is the capacity to cause a thing to happen that would not happen without that capacity." But authority is the right to use public power deemed to be legitimate. So legitimacy is the popular perception of a justifiable and acceptable use of public power. This legitimacy is achieved by force of religion (as scriptural invocation), wisdom (as Plato's philosopher-king), force (as in the case of Hitler), blood line (as in the case of hereditary rulers), and ideology (as in the case of a communist society). *Principles of Politics and Government* (Boston: Allyn and Bacon, 1981), pp. 4-6. Another writer treats the concept of power as 'amorphous, spiralling, or chameleon like'. See P.H. Partridge: "Some Notes on the Concept of Power" in *Political Studies,* Vol XI (1963), pp. 107-25. Also see Anthony de Crespigny: "Power and Its Forms" in *Political Studies,* Vol. XVI (1968), pp. 192-205.

Power Theory: Study of Power in Physical Terms

The 'power theory' finds its brilliant manifestation in the political philosophy of Thomas Hobbes. The grandest conclusion of the Hobbesian politics is his clearest and most perfect expression of the naturalistic conception of human nature wherein he tells us that man desires power and ever greater power, spontaneously and continuously in one set of appetite, and not by reason of summation of innumerable isolated desires caused by innumerable isolated perceptions.[16] However, while exposing the lineaments of power, he takes care of defining the term in a very comprehensive way. As he says: "Natural power is the eminence of faculties of body and mind: and extraordinary Strength, Form, Prudence, Arts, Eloquence, Liberality, Nobility. Instrumental are these powers, which acquired by these, or by fortune, are means and instruments to acquire more as Riches, Reputation, Friends and the secret working of God, which men call Good Luck."[17] A clear inference from this explanation informs that, according to Hobbes, search for power is the root cause of competition among the individuals. Interests collide in the race to acquire more and more riches, honours and commands and, for this sake, the competitors take to the means of killing, subduing, supplanting and repelling their opponents. Though the struggle for power has its incessant play among the competitors, it is also true that men like to live in peace in order to enjoy the iota of power they possess, which disposes them to live under a common power.

A proper study of the Hobbesian politics, culminating in the construction of commonwealth under a prefect sovereign ordaining all individuals to live in peace in order to avoid the 'violent fear of death', leads to the conclusion that, in a strict sense, his meaning of power 'means specifically or only power over other men."[18] Studied thus, one may partly accept the observation of Bluhm when he says that power, according to Hobbes, "does not mean only domination but, more broadly, the ability to secure a good. Wealth is power, friends are power, good luck is power."[19] The nature of the civil society is, for this reason, such that everyone, whether with moderate or immoderate desires, "is necessarily pulled into a constant competitive struggle for power over others, or at least to resist his powers being commanded by others."[20]

After Hobbes, the power theory has its reiteration in the works of Hegel who absolutised the sovereign authority to the extent of discarding the ethics of international morality. Power and the urge towards it were very much extolled in the nineteenth century by a good number of writers. In this direction, we may, in particular, refer to great German thinkers like Nietzsche, Trietschke and Bernhardi who elaborated what was given by Hegel. This power current of thought witnessed its ardent protagonist in the twentieth century in Eric Kaufmann, a young German

16. Leo Strauss: *The Political Philosophy of Hobbes: Its Basis and Its Genesis* (Translated from German into English by Elsa M. Sinclair), p. 10.
17. See *Leviathan,* Chapter 10.
18. Macpherson: *The Political Theory of Possessive Individualism* (London: Oxford Univ. Press, 1962), p. 35.
19. W.T. Bluhm: *Theories of the Political System,* p. 289.
20. Macpherson: 'Introduction' in *Leviathan,* p. 37.

student of international law, who found the 'essence' of the state in *Machtentfaltung* meaning anything like development, increase and display of power, along with the will to maintain successfully and assert itself.[21]

Among the leading advocates of this theory in the present age we may refer to Prof. Hans J. Morgenthau who in his *Politics Among Nations* says: "International politics, like all politics, is a struggle for power. Whatever the ultimate aims of international politics, power is always the immediate aim."[22] Likewise, in his *Scientific Man versus Power Politics,* he says that the re-examination of the Western tradition "must start with the assumption that power politics, rooted in the lust for power which is common to all men, is, for this reason, inseparable from social life itself. In order to eliminate from the political sphere not power politics—which is beyond the ability of any political philosopher or system—but the destructiveness of power politics, rational faculties are needed which are different from, and superior to, the reason of the scientific age.... Contemptuous of power politics and incapable of statesmanship which alone is liable to master it, the age has tried to make politics a science. By doing so, it has demonstrated its intellectual confusion, moral blindness and political decay."[23]

The power theory found its concrete manifestation in the emergence of Fascism in Italy in 1922 when Mussolini declared 'nothing against the state, nothing above it'. As a reaction against such affirmations, Prof. Charles Merriam—the Father of the Chicago School—sought to examine the premise of power theory in detail. He undertook to show the situation in which power "comes into being; the plurality of competing loyalities; the sham of power and some of the credanda, miranda and agenda of authority; some of the techniques of the power holders who survive; and some of the defence mechanism of those upon whom power is exercised; the poverty of power; the disintegration, decline and overthrow of authority, the emerging trend of power in our time."[24]

Among the recent writers, we may refer to the contribution of Michael Foucault of France who integrates knowledge with power. In his book *Power/Knowledge* (1980), he says that knowledge is deeply enmeshed in power, truth always being a social construct and that power can be productive, prohibitive and transformative. The omnipresence of power is a solid fact. It is with the free man who exploits the slave, it is also with the slave who raises his voice against any torture. It never stands on a particular centre; it is always moving from one situation to another. It has a transformative feature as well in the sense that the behaviour of a criminal is reformed in the prison when he is punished by those who exercise power according to the rules and regulations of the state. The exercise of power by one invites opposition from the other side. As a result of this, social conflicts take place. An understanding of power in this way adds to the stock of our knowledge. Foucault calls it 'discourse of power'.

---

21. Brecht: *Political Theory.,* p. 345.
22. See G.E.G. Catlin: "What is Political Theory? What is it?" in Gould and Thursby (ed s): *Contemporary Political Thought: Issues in Scope, Value and Direction* (New York: Holt, Rinehart and Winston, 1969), p. 35.
23. *Ibid.,* pp. 35-36.
24. See Merriam: *Political Power* (New York, 1934)

Through the idea of 'discourse of power', we may discover the link between power and systems of thought. As Heywood says: "A discourse is a system of social relations and practices that assign meaning and therefore identities to those who live or work within it. Anything from institutionalised psychiatry and the prison service to academic disciplines and political ideologies can be regarded as discourses in this sense. Discourses are a form of power in that they are antagonisms and structure relations between people who are defined as subjects or objects, as 'insiders' or 'outsiders'.[25] In this way, Foucault agrees with as well as differs from Marx and carves out a place for himself in the category of post-modern thinkers. As Heywood continues: "These identities are internalised, meaning that those who are subject to domination, as in the Marxist view, are unaware of the fact or extent of that domination. Whereas Marxists associate power as thought control with the attempt to maintain class inequality, post-modern theorists come close to seeing power as ubiquitous, all systems of knowledge being viewed as manifestations of power."[26]

Following inferences may be drawn from what Foucault says about the all-pervasive effect power.[27]

1. Power should be regarded as multiple, positive, productive and relational. It has no single form. It is pervasive, productive in all social relations and is exercised at innumerable points.
2. Power does not primarily operate through the repressive form of interdiction and law, and of modes of action.
3. Power is conceived as a balance of forces, an overall complex strategic situation between parties in complex relation of contestation and resistance.
4. Power and liberty exist in an inverse and, in a sense, quantitative relationship. The exercise of power, in this view, entails subtraction of liberty. The exercise of power presupposes liberty in the sense that it is possible for the subject of power to act in ways more than one. It is like a strategic game between liberties and a total structure of actions brought to bear upon the actions of others. Power in this regard is an aspect of all social relations and may take the form of open and reversible relationships.
5. Power is synonymous with domination that involves mobile relations, tactics and strategy within the social body.
6. Such an analysis rests on the thesis that in all modern states the exercise of rule entails the articulation of a form of pastoral power or bio-power with one of sovereign power.
7. Biopolitics is thanatopolitics. It is the counterpart of a power that exerts a positive influence on life and could be a formidable source of death. The heart of his provocative thesis about bio-politics is that there is an intimate connection between the exercise of life administering power and the commission of genocide. Bio-political racism establishes positive relationship between the right to kill and the assurance of life.

25. Andrew Heywood: *Political Theory: An Introduction*, 128.
26. *Ibid.*
27. See Michael Foucault: *Power/Knowledge: Selected Interviews and Other Writings, 1972-77*, edited by C. Gordon (Brighton: Harvester, 1980).

Foucault's Paradigms of Power in Societies and States

Our societies have proved to be really demonic, since they happen to combine those two games-the city-citizen game and the shepherd-flock game-in what we call modern states.

Pastoral Power (Passive Citizenship)	Bio-Power (Active Citizenship)
(Shepherd-Flock Game in Demonic Societies)	(City-Citizen Game in modern states having life-administering power)
It has its birth in Hebraic and early Christian communities. Its geneology concerns its transformation into a centralised and largely secular exercise of power over populations concerned with the life and welfare of 'each and all' with the development of the administrative state in Europe in the seventeenth and eighteenth centuries.	It is a strange game whose elements are life, death, truth, obedience, individuals and self-identity. It has its source in Greece-Roman antiquity and notions of the *polis* and *res publica* and concerns the treatment of the individuals and autonomous and responsible political actors within a self-determining exercising and thinking about power that has been transformed by modern liberal and republican doctrines, notions of direct and representative democracy and by the key status of the citizen; population within the territorial state. The city-citizen game, therefore, concerns the panoply of techniques by which the members of a population are formed or form themselves into a political community, and by which they seek to exercise sovereignty.

Source: Michael Foucault: "Politics and Reason" in L.D. Kritzman (ed.): *Politics, Philosophy, Culture: Interviews and Other Writings, 1977-84* (New York: Routledge, 1988), pp. 57-85.

Though the element of truth in power theory cannot be denied, it may still be said that it lays too much reliance on the fact of power in physical terms alone. As a matter of fact, power is a very broad concept that includes within itself much that may not be covered by the compass of physical power. One may also refer to the power of the soul, power of mind, power of ideas and thus justify what great sages from Buddha to Gandhi have uttered. Catlin is of the view that even co-operation "may be a form of power perhaps more subtle and difficult to construct, but also more subtle than domination."[28] Brecht appreciates the view that even people's sense of justice is power as emphasised by Otto Wels who, in opposition to what was said by his leader Hitler, went to the extent of saying: "No enabling act can give you the power to destroy ideas that are eternal and indestructible."[29]

---

28. Catlin, *op. cit*, p. 36.
29. Brecht, *op. cit.*, p. 347.

Psychoanalytical Theory: Power Identified with Influence and the Role of the Influential

The idea of power has been discussed in detail by recent writers of the United States like Harold Lasswell, Abraham Kaplan and Robert A. Dahl who have taken politics as the study of the influence and the influential. Lasswell and Kaplan have made their own contribution in this regard. They discuss the scope of political science in terms of power inasmuch as the subject-matter of this discipline is constituted by 'power as a process'. In particular, Lasswell argues that political processes operate throughout society and that any attempt to limit political analysis to certain specific political institutions is unacceptable. As he says: "The power process is not a distinct and separable part of the social process but only the political aspect of an interactive whole."[30] In this direction, he even suggests that he has consciously attempted "to disseminate a less trammelled conception of political analysis than the one generally current."[31]

According to Lasswell, the unifying frame of reference for a student of politics is the rich and variable meaning of the 'influence and the influential', 'power and powerful'. He makes a definite attempt to distinguish between power and influence. To him, while the former implies participation in the making of decisions, the latter suggests the value position and potential of a person or group. The exercise of influence consists in affecting policies of others than of the self. It is, therefore, understandable that here power "is viewed in instrumental terms in contrast to its importance as a value in its own right."[32]

In other words, the concept of power is perhaps the most important of all in the whole discipline of political science in view of the fact that the political process is the shaping, distribution and exercise of power (in a wider sense of all the defence, values, or of influence in general). Individuals operate the political process of a society within certain arenas in which power is sought and persons are brought within the 'domain of power'. With approval, Lasswell quotes the view of Catlin that politics, as a theoretical study, is concerned with the relations of men in association and competition, submission and control, insofar as they seek, not the production and consumption of some article, but to have their way with their fellows. What men seek in their political negotiations is power.[33]

The notable thing, in this direction, however, is that while at several places Lasswell treats both power and influence in identical terms, he still holds that there are a number of key variables that apply equally to both. For instance, the *scope* of power and influence refers to the range of values over which control is exercised. *Weight* is the degree of control in the making of decisions or the shaping of policies. And the persons over whom control is exercised constitute the *domain* of power or influence. Similarly, it is important to distinguish between *coercive* and *persuasive* exercises of power and influence. Coercion is present in a situation if the alternative

30. Lasswell and Kaplan: *Power and Society* (New Haven: Yale University Press, 1950), p. xvii.
31. Lasswell: *Politics: Who Gets: What, When, How?* (New York: World Pub., 1958), p. 203.
32. O.R. Young: *Systems of Political Science* (Englewood Cliffs, New Jersey: Prentice-Hall, 1967), p. 66.
33. See Catlin: *Science and the Method of Politics*: (New York: Alfred A. Knopf, 1927), pp. 210-11.

courses of action are associated with severe deprivations or indulgences. Coercion may characterise both power and influence, though severe coercion is especially typical of power processes. Finally, it is worth noting that power and influence include both present and potential capabilities. This is so because "all value positions are looked upon as ultimately exchangeable for some amount of power or influence.'[34]

Instead of dwelling on the term 'power' that may be confused with resources, rewards and deprivations, Dahl prefers to elaborate his psychoanalytical study with the help of another term 'influence' which he defines as "a relation among actors such that the wants, desires, preferences, or intentions of one or more actors affect the actions, or predispositions to act, of one or more other actors."[35] Influence may be explicit or manifest and implicit or latent. Dahl also deals with the scope and domain of influence. To him, the domain of an actor's influence "consists of other actors influenced by him. The scope of an actor's influence refers to the matters on which he can influence them. In exercising influence, then, an actor influences the domain of other actors with respect to a certain scope of their actions or predispositions."[36]

However crude or imperfect our observations may be, one of the most commonly reported characteristics of all political systems is that political influence is unequally distributed owing to three factors:[37]

1. **Difference in the distribution of political resources :** A political resource is a means by which one person can influence the behaviour of other persons; political resources, therefore, include money, information, food, the threat of force, jobs, friendship, social standing, the right to make laws, votes, as well as a great variety of other things.
2. **Variations in the skill or efficiency with which individuals use their political resources:** Differences in political skill stem in turn from differences in endowments, opportunities and incentives to learn and practise political skills.
3. **Variations in the extent to which individuals use their resources for political purposes:** Of two equally wealthy people, for example, one may use his wealth to gain influence while another may use it to achieve success in business. These variations are themselves traceable to differences in motivations that arise out of variations in endowments and experiences.

Though Dahl dwells on the word 'influence', he makes an attempt to distinguish it with other related themes before coming to offer a definition of the term 'power'. Influence through communication that consists of a cue or signal might be called *control by training*. However, influence by means of communications that provide information, whether correct or not, about the advantages and disadvantages of alternative courses of action can be called *persuasion*. Then, influence by means

34. Young, *op. cit.*, p. 67.
35. R.A. Dahl: *Modern Political Analysis* (Englewood Cliffs, New Jersey: Prentice-Hall, 1977), III Ed., p. 30. He appreciates the view of J.K. Nagel who says: "A power-relation, actual or potential, is an actual of potential causal relation between the preferences of an actor regarding an outcome and the outcome itself." *The Descriptive Analysis of Power* (New Haven: Yale University Press, 1975), p. 29.
36. Dahl, *op. cit.*, p. 33.
37. *Ibid*, p. 37.

that bring about a change in the nature of the alternatives themselves by adding advantages to an alternative or imposing new disadvantages on an alternative, or both, can be called *inducement.* He also makes out certain sub-categories so as to explain the implications of these key variables. For instance, persuasion may be rational and manipulative. It is *rational* if the transmission of influence is done by moral and honest means as a teacher does to his students; it is *manipulative* when the same is done by deceitful or deceptive means as a lobbyist does to a legislator. Inducement may be either positive or negative. For instance, it is *positive* when an employer asks his employee to do the job and then get such and such reward. It is *negative* when he issues a general warning that such punishment would be given to those who take part in a strike. Likewise, control may be either unilateral or reciprocal. An instance of *unilateral* control may be seen in a demonstration of the people whereby they force their leader to do or not to do a particular thing. However, a case of *reciprocal* control may be visualised in the system of mutual deterrence that has helped to prevent nuclear war. Finally, an influence, the compliance of which is attained by creating the prospect of severe sanctions for non-compliance, becomes *power.*[38]

With this Dahl comes to hold that the forms of influence may be evaluated so as to highlight the role of power in every political system. As he says: "Manipulative persuasion, power, coercion, the threat and application of physical force are commonplace aspects of political life. Every state uses power internally to secure compliance with the policies of the government. Manipulative persuasion, power, coercion, and physical force have been common in the relations among States; in international politics, war or the threat of war has frequently been used as an alternative to stalemate or peaceful adjustment. Civil wars and revolutions also involve power and coercion, each side resorts to physical force to impose its will on others. It is easy for people accustomed to relatively stable political systems like those of Britain and the United States to lose sight of the frequency of revolutions, civil wars and violence. Even today, in large parts of the world, civil strife, guerilla warfare, revolutionary struggles, violence, and suppression of political opponents by physical force are normal and commonplace political practices."[39]

It may be understood without any difficulty that irrespective of the merits which this theory has on account of offering an empirically verifiable analysis, it is not free from certain shortcomings. We may easily take note of the fact that it widens the scope of the term 'power' so much so that it makes the very meaning of the term 'elusive'. Thus, we are certainly confronted with the situation of conceptual diffuseness. It smacks of the tendency to treat power as simply the generalised capacity to attain ends or goals in social relations independently of the media employed or of the status of authorisation to make decisions or impose obligations. The meaning of the term 'power' becomes analogous to that of the German word 'macht' which, as Weber says, indicates the probability that "one actor within a social relationship will be in a position to carry out his own will despite resistance."[40] Viewed thus,

38. *Ibid.*, pp. 43-50.
39. *Ibid.*, p. 51.
40. Max Weber: *The Theory of Social and Economic Organisation* (New York: Oxford University Press, 1947), p. 152.

the essential line of difference between power, on the one hand, and other related themes like influence, control, persuasion, manipulation and the like, on the other, is blurred and a writer like Banfield comes to hold that while 'control refers to the ability to cause another to give or withhold action, power is the ability to establish control over another.'[41]

Sociological Theory: Power as the Authoritative Allocator of Values in a Hierarchical Social Order

As a matter of fact, the term power has its particular appellation in the context of a social process where several organisations and units subsist and they compete for, what Easton says, securing 'the authoritative allocation of values'. Thus, power really meaning social power, indicates 'the capacity to influence or control others.'[42]

Society is a big whole (collectivity) in which several smaller units (sub-collectivities) exist and compete in a way that their modes of action lead to the use of power in varying degrees and forms which are described as control, influence, manipulation, persuasion and the like. Keeping this in view, power is defined as 'the capacity of a social system to mobilise resources to attain collective goods'.[43]

A study of power in this context brings about a transformation in the meaning of politics. Politics no longer remains the study of state or government as such, it becomes a study of the society in its widest sense, including all organisations like families, trade unions, clubs, business houses, political parties and a host of 'unofficial' groups. In other words, politics far from remaining like a study of the 'superstructures', viz., organs of government -- legislature, executive and judiciary - becomes, in addition to that, a study of the 'infrastructure' as well having its manifestation in political parties and interest organisations also known by the name of pressure groups. As all these units exist and play their part in the political process, the concepts of power, control, influence, coercion, persuasion, manipulation and the like become 'central to the study of politics.'[44]

The sociological theory, therefore, takes power as something widely diffused among several sub-collectivities which determines the position of different social units *vis-a-vis* the state, the custodian of the highest power. Thus, we find a very close connection between emphasis on the coercive element in power systems and on the hierarchical aspect of the structure of the systems of authority and power. As a matter of fact, it is an inherent aspect of the internal structure of the collectivities. It is owing to this that organisations like those of the labour and the capitalist classes have some 'power' of their own which is by all means superior to the power of a club but certainly inferior to that of the state. The diffuseness of power is thus necessarily linked to the hierarchical system of the society. Moreover, the patronage of the state

41. E.C. Banfield: *Political Influence* (New York: Free Press of Glencoe, 1962), p. 348.
42. Pennock and Smith: *Political Science* (New York: Macmillan, 1964), p. 56.
43. See Talcott Parsons: "Voting and the Equilibrium of the American Political System" in E. Burdick and A.J. Brodback: *American Voting Behaviour* (New York: Free Press of Glencoe, 1959), p. 81.
44. S.L Wasby: *Political Science—The Discipline and Its Dimensions: An Introduction* (Calcutta: Scientific Book Agency, 1970), p. 9.

brings about a change in the position of power of different social organisations. In this way, "the collectivity aspect of the total social structure may in a particular case be dominant over others, but in principle it always impinges on at least two sorts of boundary-problems, namely, those involved in its 'support' system and those involved in the mobilisation of services as resources of contribution to its functioning."[45]

Besides, this theory not only looks at power as something widely diffused in the social whole and acting as a determinant of the position of various organisations in a hierarchical system, it also connects the phenomenon of power with the element of 'legitimacy'. It implies that the power of any social organisation right from the family to that of the state should be acceptable to the concerned persons. Here power becomes quite analogous to authority. Commands issued by the men in authority roles should be acceptable to the people, otherwise they will not be effective. The idea of power thus involves the case of legitimation. In case the people do not feel obliged to render obedience, they oppose authority and even take matters to the extreme with the result that a scuffle assumes the form of a rebellion, civil war or revolution. Power is, in this way, a social affair involving legitimation. In other words, it "is the generalised capacity to secure the performance of binding obligations by units in a system of collective organisation when the obligations are legitimised with reference to their bearing or collective goals and where in case of recalcitrance there is a presumption of enforcement by negative situational sanctions whatever the actual agency of that enforcement."[46]

Such an interpretation of the idea of power being an essential part of the study of politics has its brilliant manifestation in the writings of David Easton who defines politics as 'authoritative allocation of values within a society'. When we say that something has a certain value to someone, we mean that he desires it to some extent relative to other items available to him. The extent of the desire may be measurable in terms of the amount of money he is willing to pay to obtain it, or the amount of effort he will expend in its pursuit, and an individual's preference can be ranked in these terms as well so that we can talk about a hierarchy of values which citizens have. The source of authoritative allocation of values finds place in the decision-making process and since the highest power of decision-making is vested in the state, the decision of the government carries the highest sanctity whose enforcement is backed by the ultimate use of monopoly of physical force.[47]

The sociological theory of power, as explained above, is applicable to a liberal-democratic order in which society has a pluralistic character. There is freedom for the 'sub-collectivities' to exist and take part in the struggle for power so that 'values' are allocated, de-allocated and re-allocated and this process operates in an unhampered way. Opposed to it is the system of a 'closed' society in which power is concentrated at the top; decisions of the men in power are always treated as legitimate and, for this reason, binding.

---

45. Talcott Parsons: "The Concept of Political Power" in Bell, Edwards and Wagner, *op. cit.*, p. 271.
46. *Ibid.*, p. 237.
47. David Easton: "An Approach to the Study of Political Systems" in *World Politics*, Vol. IX, 1957, pp. 383-400.

Obviously, this theory cannot be appreciated by the Marxists who think in terms of political power as 'class power' and also hope for its banishment with the 'withering away of the state'. That is, power is necessarily connected with the class character of the society. It is the general and pervasive power which a dominant class "exercises in order to maintain and defend its predominance in civil society. This class power is exercised through many institutions and agencies. Some of these are dominant class, interest and pressure groups, etc. Others may not be specifically designed for the purpose, yet may serve it, *e.g.*, churches, schools, family. But whether designed for the purpose or not, they are not institutions and agencies through which the dominant class seeks to assure its hegemony."[48]

Liberal-Democratic Theory: Power Identified with Developmental and Extractive Capacities of Man

One point of attack directed against all theories on the subject of 'political power', as disscussed in.the preceding sections, is that they have a distinctly empirical character. That is, they treat power in strictly physical terms which misses the normative dimension of such an important concept. Power is not merely a fact having its manifestation in the forms of control, influence, coercion, persuasion and manipulation, it is a value also. Essentially speaking, power signifies the *capacity* of an individual which may either refer to his ability to *develop* his personality or to *extract* advantages from the like abilities of others. In this way, power as a capacity has both developmental and extractive capacities and thereby it carries normative dimension in the former and empirical dimension in the latter. It should always be borne in mind that if power refers to the capacities, the capacities of man are more and higher than those of an animal. Moreover, the norms of social life require that the use of such capacities be made for the betterment of the personality of man as well as of his community. Whether the existence of specially human capacities "is attributed to divine creation, or to some evolutionary development of more complex organism, it is a basic postulate. It is an empirical postulate, verifiable in a broad way by observation. It is at the same time a value postulate, in the sense that rights and obligations can be derived from it without any additional value premise, since the very structure of our thought and language puts an evaluative content into our descriptive statements about man."[49]

As pointed out above, power means ability to use and develop human capacities. It has two important aspects—extractive and developmental—which may be labelled as normative or ethical and empirical or applied dimensions respectively. Since a man's ability to use and develop his capacities becomes the 'power', it may be concisely described as man's *developmental power.* Here power has a qualitative character. It has an ethical connotation in the sense that it informs man to seek, what Laski enjoined, the best possible development of his personality. The idea of power thus desires the use and development of the essentially human capacities. Besides, man should use his capacities in a way so that he may extract benefit from others. It leads to the idea *of extractive power.* Obviously, the idea of power has both qualitative and quantitative aspects.

48. Ralph Miliband: *Marxism and Politics* (London: Oxford Univ. Press, 1977), pp. 54-55.
49. C.B. Macpherson: *Democratic Theory: Essays in Retrieval* (London: Oxford Univ. Press, 1975), p. 53.

Though Western political theory studies the case of power in its normative as well as empirical dimensions, most of the literature from Machiavelli and Hobbes to Max Weber and Harold Lasswell concerns itself with the latter dimension.[50] It dwells on man's ability to get what he wants by controlling others. We have already seen that Hobbes identified power with 'domination'. Likewise, James Stuart Mill says: "The grand instrument for attaining what a man likes is the actions of other men. Power, in its most appropriate signification, therefore, means security for the conformity between the will of one man and the acts of other men. This, we presume, is not a proposition which will be disputed."[51] However, as the power of money has become the most important of all in modern 'market' societies, the idea of political power has become essentially connected with the theme of 'economic power'. Keeping this fact in view, Easton refers to a long line of modern writers who "see that the characteristic of political activity, the property that distinguishes the political from the economic or other aspects of a situation, is the attempt to control others."[52]

The liberal-democratic theory of power thus assumes two important proportions at this stage. First, it integrates the idea of political power with the power of money. Political power issuing in the form of franchise, elections, propaganda, persuasion, manipulation, control and the like is certainly governed by the role of money power. It is due to this that the destiny of the millions of countrymen is controlled by a dozen families having monopoly over the purse of the nation. It is said that only nine families rule the United States or 75 houses run the administration of India. In a technical sense, it may be added that if power means the extractive capacity of man, it lies in the hands of those wealthy persons who can extract the benefits from others and thereby remain the rulers of the country. Obviously, "in a full capitalist model, the whole power of everyone is nearly equivalent to his extractive power. Each non-owner's whole power is near zero, and his extractive power is zero."[53]

Obviously, the source of economic inequality should be traced here. In other words, if equality is to be studied as a 'protest ideal',[54] its root lies in the injustice of the capitalist society in which political power, said to be diffused among the masses, is virtually exercised by a very small section that has control over the money power of the nation and thereby enables itself to extract all possible benefits from those who are superficially lauded as the real sovereign of the country. What should be

50. It may, however, be pointed out that though modern Western political theory gives immense weight to the quantitative or empirical dimension of power, it does not ignore the normative or qualitative aspect of the same. Its reflections may be seen in the views of certain liberal intellectuals who have looked at things from an ethical viewpoint. For instance, while appreciating the statement of Humboldt, John Stuart Mill says that the 'end of man is the highest and most harmonious development of his powers to a complete and consistent whole." See *On Liberty,* Chapter III. In a more emphatic vein, T.H. Green says that freedom means "the liberation of the powers of all men equally for contributions to a common good'. *Works,* Vol. Ill, Sec. 372.

51. James Stuart Mill: *An Essay on Government* (edited by E. Barker) (Cambridge, 1937), Sec. IV, p. 17.

52. Macpherson, *op. cit.,* p. 45. Also see J.E. Meade: *Efficiency, Equality and Ownership of Property* (London, 1964), p. 27.

53. Macpherson, *op. cit.,* p. 45.

54. See Giovanni Sartori: *Democratic Theory* (New Delhi: Oxford and IBH, 1965), Chapter XIV.

done? It is the crucial problem before modern liberal political thinkers who have deliberately taken to the course of abandoning the idea of *laissez faire* so as to make the premises of liberalism in tune with the doctrine of socialism. A possible solution has been offered by Prof. Macpherson who has desired the 'maximisation of democracy'. According to him, democracy can be real only when the extractive power of the few is substituted by the similar power of the many. He has regretted over the fact that political power, being power over others, is used in an unequal society to extract benefits from the ruled for the rulers. Focus on the *source* of political power puts out of the field of vision perception of the necessary *purpose* of political power in any unequal society, which is to maintain the extractive power of the class or classes which have extractive power.... Power because it is seen as control over others, is certainly not seen as something whose increase or maximisation is desirable in itself."[55]

Allied to this it is necessary that the normative aspect of power should not be thoroughly discarded. Man is not merely a power-hungry creature as supposed by Hobbes, he is also a value-loving creature. He not only fights for power, but he has a sense of discrimination too. Thus, while extracting benefits from others by virtue of his capacities, he is also expected to see towards his as well as his fellow beings' development. The developmental and the extractive aspects of human capacities should be joined in a way so that the maximisation of democracy takes place without causing loss or destruction of the values of humanism. Impressed with this assumption, Prof. Macpherson counsels: 'We must attend to the developmental concept of power, and the democratic claim to maximise that power, if our political science is to be analytically adequate."[56]

The liberal-democratic theory of power may be criticised on two counts. In the first place, it offers a source of confusion by identifying power with capacities. Macpherson holds: "No fewer than three different qualities are liable to be confused in the one notion of man's capacities: (i) his actual present capacities, *(ii)* the supposed capacities he might have developed upto the present if society had placed no impediments in his way; *(iii)* the supposed greater capacities he could develop during his whole life if society placed no impediments in his way."[57] Second, the assumptions of this theory cannot be appreciated by the Marxists who examine power in terms of the class composition of society; nor can it be accepted by the non-Marxists who consider power in mere physical terms by pursuing the line of Max Weber and to whom power implies "the capacity of an individual, or group of individuals, to modify the conduct of other individuals or groups in the manner which he desires, and to prevent his own conduct being modified in the manner in which he does not."[58]

Marxian Theory: Power as the Instrument of Class Domination

As already pointed out, the Marxian theory of power is basically different from all theories on the subject as discussed in the preceding sections. Here power is

55. Macpherson, *op. cit.*, pp. 47-48.
56. *Ibid.*, p. 50.
57. *Ibid.* p. 56.
58. R.H. Tawney: *Equality* (London: George Allen and Unwin, 1931), p. 229.

treated as an instrument that connects economics with politics. In the Marxian sense, politics signifies a sphere of social activity in which two contending classes engage in a struggle for the control of the state—the organised force of the society. It is the means of production whose ownership involves control over the labour power of those who own little or no means of production and it is this fact that determines the distribution of political power or, what Marx says, the relations of production. In this sense, property ownership involves control over production as well as political control. Only a class whose members are aware of their objective class interest, who have a will to forward that interest and who possess a political organisation, can be said to act politically.[59] Hence, 'political power, properly so called, is merely the organised power of one class oppressing another.'[60]

Political power, or class power as it may be called in the strict Marxian sense, is the general and pervasive power which a dominant class exercises in order to maintain and defend its predominance in the society. This class power is challenged by a counter-power. Thus, class war takes place in which the contending classes as well as their subordinate allies take part. In the present society it may be traced in the conflict between the capitalist and the labour classes having their subordinate allies—the former in the family, school and churches and the latter in the socialist and communist parties and trade unions. Marx also tells us that in the period of acute social crisis and conflict, class power "does tend to be taken over by the state itself, and indeed gladly surrenders to it; and it may well be argued that even in the normal cirumstances of advanced capitalism, the state takes over more and more of the functions hitherto performed by the dominant class, or at least takes a greater share in the performance of these functions than was the case in the previous periods."[61]

For Marx any political situation must be defined and explained in terms of specific socio-economic structure conditioning a particular configuration of social classes. The winning of political power is vital to the ultimate success of the working class. He, therefore, argues that if the working class thinks in political terms alone, then its labours are likely to go in vain. The workers must think politically, so that they can see the causes of all evils in it and all remedies in *force*. and thereby strive for the overthrow of the prevailing system. In this way, he establishes a necessary relationship between economic system and political action. This is the link between class and politics.[62]

The peculiar feature of the Marxian theory of power should be traced not in the integration of the idea of political power with the prevailing socio-economic system as in the disappearance of the 'political power' with the ushering in of a new society having its hallmark in the emergence of a stateless pattern of collective life. Like politics power also becomes a transient phenomenon. In a capitalist society, out of the separate economic movements of the workers, there grows up everywhere a *political* movement, that is to say, a movement of the class, with the object of enforcing its interests.... in a form possessing general, socially coercive force. However, in a full

59. Michael Evans: *Karl Marx* (London: George Allen and Unwin, 1975), p. 109.
60. Marx-Engels: 'Communist Manifesto' in *Selected Works*, Vol. I, p. 36.
61. Ralph Miliband, *op. cit.*, p. 56.
62. Michael Evans, *op. cit.*, p. 109.

communist society private property will be abolished. It will entail the disappearance of classes and hence of class conflict. And when class rule has disappeared, no state shall exist in the current political sense. In this way, the 'public power' will lose its political character.[63]

The Marxian theory of power may be criticised on certain grounds. First, it "is grasped as a *mechanical* theory in which the economy determines absolutely the political structure."[64] One may refer to the various theories on the subject of power, as already discussed, and then assert that the source of power lies not only in the realm of economics but also very much in the forces of psychology and sociology. Lust for power is a psychological fact. Second, Marx wrongly argues that power is an essential instrument of class war and, as such, in the capitalist society state is a class institution that serves and protects the interest of the dominant bourgeois class in an exclusive manner. State is a welfare agency. It has its ethical end also that consists, as Aristotle said, in the realisation of the ideal of 'good life'. Thus, he may be accused of not working out a satisfactory theory of power in a capitalist society.[65] Finally, Marx fondly hopes for the emergence of a stateless pattern of collective life in which there would be no place for state or power. Hence, what Marx claimed as the acme point of his 'scientific socialism' becomes his 'utopia'.[66]

Elite Theory: Power Having its Source in Political and Bureaucratic Organisations Ruled by the Minorities

A clear contradiction of the Marxian theory of power can be seen in the elite theory which insists that power flows not from the ownership of property but from political and bureaucratic organisations. It argues that politics cannot be properly studied without identifying the ruling class, or the governing and non-governing elites, and measuring their respective roles. Politics being the struggle for power functions within social groups. In this way, elite theory and group theory become intimately related in view of the fact that, in the last analysis, both are concerned with power. The central theme of the elite theory of power lies in the affirmation that power configuration "is basically the configuration of competing and struggling interests organised into groups."[67]

The classic expression of this theory is contained in the works of Gaetano Mosca who superficially seems to follow Marx in his argument that "in all societies two classes of people appear—a class that rules and a class that is ruled". His political or ruling class enjoys legal and factual authority as an organised minority, a situation inherent in all social organisations but one which reaches its highest expression in what he terms, the 'bureaucratic state'. Here the state "embodies specialisation and the salaried official forms part of the 'political class.'[68] Democracy, therefore, becomes the rule of an organised minority which in spite of appearances to the

63. Marx-Engels: *Works,* Vol. 4, p. 482.
64. Alan Swingewood: *Marx and Modern Social Theory* (London: Macmillan 1975), p. 138.
65. *Ibid.,* p. 139.
66. Michael Evans, *op. cit.,* p. 162.
67. R C Macridis and B.E Brown: *Comparative Politics: Notes and Readings* (Illinois: The Dorsey Press, 1964), p. 139.
68. Swingewood, *op. cit.,* p. 146.

contrary and for all the legal principles on which government rests.... still retains actual and effective control of the state."[69]

The argument of power invariably residing with a minority is further adumbrated in the 'iron law of oligarchy' as laid down by Robert Michels. He turns on the sociological law of oligarchical inevitability that all organisations, however democratic their ideology, become necessarily oligarchic and bureaucratic. As a result of organisation, every party or professional union becomes divided into a very small minority of directors and a very large majority of the directed. His 'iron law of oligarchy' working through social institutions means the rule of the bureaucratic officials over democratically elected parliamentary representatives and an authority based on position in a hierarchy of salaried officialdom and not, as Marx said, on the ownership of private property. Bureaucratic organisation becomes a kind of natural law determining the structure of both capitalist and socialist societies: within capitalism administrators require an authority at least equal to that possessed by the private owner of capital, while under socialism the idea of classless society would perish in the moment of its adherents' triumph.[70] If so, bureaucratic organisation would determine social life, an ineluctable process giving "birth to the domination of the elected over the electors, of the mandatories over the mandators, of the delegates over the delegators. *Who says organisation, says oligarchy.*"[71]

What is said by Mosca and Michels is, to a very considerable extent, shared by Max Weber who argues that the highly specialised division of labour, which forms the backbone of a modern economy, must inevitably lead to greater bureaucratisation in a society based on state interference and control of the economy and social life. A line of distinction between Michels and Weber may, however, be seen in that while the former identifies power with domination, the latter treats the two differently. This is on account of his search for discovering the trait of 'legitimacy' which is the condition precedent to political effectiveness. Thus, he defines power as the ability to impose one's will on another against opposition, while domination is imperative control which flows directly from the belief that authorised commands will be obeyed without the sanction of physical coercion. Domination, in this way, "hinges on legitimate authority and constitutes a special case of power."[72]

This line of argument may also be seen in the views of C. Wright Mills who argues that the elite is the product of the 'institutional landscape' of society. Power in modern society is institutionalised with the result that certain institutions and the upper-most ranks of the hierarchy in these institutions constitute the 'strategic command posts of the social structure'.[73] Power is then not the attribute of classes or persons but of institutions. The power elite consists of those "in position to make decisions having major consequences.... in command of the major hierarchies and organisations of modern society."[74] The history-making power of the elite "is

69. Mosca: *The Ruling Class* (New York: McGraw Hill, 1939), pp. 50ff.
70. Swingewood, *op. cit.*, p. 147.
71. Michels: *Political Parties* (New York, 1962), pp. 333-56.
72. Swingewood, *op. cit.*, p. 148.
73. Wright Mills: *The Power Elites* (London: Oxford University Press, 1959), p. 4.
74. *Ibid.*

sufficient to overturn the *status quo,* call into question the existing social relationship and establish a new structure. The inner core of the elite is able, potentially, to determine the roles both it and others will play in society."[75]

In fine, the essence of the elite theory lies in this affirmation that if the principal aim of a political theorist is to uncover key factors in the arena of power, then the study of the elites is indispensable. There can be no organisation without power and power always resides in the hands of a very small section of the 'chosen few'. The struggle for power virtually takes place between contending elites with the result that men in authority roles change from time to time. It may also be described as the conflict between the governing and the counter-elites. If it is asked: Who has power? The answer is the elite. Whether it is a capitalist system in which society has a plural character and the interests are varied with the result that there are several political parties and numerous interest groups, or it is a socialist system having a classless society under the 'dictatorship of the proletariat', the fact remains that power is invariably with a very small section of the community. Keeping this fact in view, Lasswell says: "By this time recognition is widespread that the world-inclusive study of power elites is indispensable to all serious inquiry into political processes."[76]

Though the elite theory presents a study of power verifiable by facts, it cannot be denied that it ignores certain other important dimensions. One may make a scientific analysis of the residence of power in a very small section of the people: he may also prove on the basis of authentic evidence that struggle for power virtually takes place between or among the elites. And yet we may not dismiss the value of this phrase of classical democrats that power resides in the people and that the masses make history. The voice of the people is not the voice of the elites in each and every case. Another point of weakness in this theory is that it adheres to a strictly empirical study of the political processes so much so that it leaves no room for normative considerations. People not only compete for power, at least some of them firmly stick to the value-pattern. Not only this, a section of the people may also be found renouncing power instead of making it their most beloved possession. It leads us to say that like other theories on the subject of power, as discussed in the preceding sections, elite theory also is partly correct. Brecht is right in holding that "the ends for the sake of which power is sought may vary all the way from enjoyment for its own sake and use for selfish purposes to the pursuit of the most unselfish aims."[77]

Critical Appreciation

Certain critical impressions may be formed about the concept of power and its role in the political process of a country from what we have said in this direction. These are:

1. Power is one of the key concepts in political theory. At the same time, it is a concept on which there is, on analytical levels, a notable lack of agreement both about its specific definition, and about the many features of the conceptual context in which

75. Geraint Parry: *Political Elites* (London: George Allen and Unwin, 1969), p. 54.
76. Harold Lasswell and Max Lerner: *World Revolutionary Elites: Studies in Coercive Ideological Movements* (Massachusetts: M.I.T., Press, 1965), p. 4.
77. Brecht, *op. cit.*, p. 347.

it should be placed. And yet there is "a core complex of its meaning, having to do with the capacity of persons or collectives 'to get things done' effectively in particular when their goals are obstructed by some kind of human resistance or opposition. The problem of coping with resistance then leads to the question of the role of coercive measures, including the use of physical force, and the relation of coercion to the voluntary and consensual aspects of power systems."[78]

2. The concept of political power has both normative and empirical dimensions. That is, power is not only a fact or something to be achieved and possessed, it is also a value or an ideal that should be pursued and aspired for. It has both qualitative and quantitative aspects. Thus, it not only hints at the capacity of the man whereby he may achieve the development of his personality, it also informs him to extract benefits from others by peaceful means like persuasion, manipulation and negotiation, or violent means like coercion, control, influence, sanctions and the like. Both aspects should be taken into account while making a study of the concept of political power.
3. As such, power is, and also is not, an empirically verifiable phenomenon. While sticking to its empirical dimension, we may say that here the concept of power may be presented in scientific terms. In this direction, science can do three things: (i) It can criticise the lack of clarity in the concept of power; (ii) It can question logical consistency in a theory that tries to isolate power from resources and purposes; (iii) It can point to the consequences which the enhancement of the value of power entails for other ideals, such as peace, harmony, freedom and equality.[79] It may, however, be added that, by and large, the concept of power pertains to the realm of an empirical direction. It is for this reason that the views of the 'realists' like Machiavelli, Hobbes, Marx and Morgenthau and not of the 'idealists' like Kant and Gandhi are in the like manner widely appreciated.[80]
4. Power is a very comprehensive term. Although it is often identified with other related themes like authority, influence, control, domination, persuasion, coercion, manipulation and the like, it may be differentiated from all at least on a theoretical level. We may disagree with a host of recent writers who have identified political power with economic power on the plea that while money is a material possession that may be used for buying any worldly thing, power cannot be used for the same purpose and in the same manner. For instance, the spiritual power having its charisma and thereby playing its part in a process that may be called 'political' may not be likened with money power. It is, therefore, necessary to say that while making a study of the political power, one should not keep one's attention confined to its integration with economic power or class power alone as, for instance, done by social theorists like Marx and Schumpeter.
5. The concept of political power is integrally connected with the case of political legitimacy and effectiveness as discussed in Chapter 13. People obey not because

78. Talcott Parsons, *op., cit.*, p. 251.
79. Brecht, *op. cit.*, p. 348.
80. See H.J. Morgenthau: "Power as a Political Concept" in Ronald Young (ed.): *Approaches to the Study of Politics* (Evanstone: Northwestern Univ. Press, 1958).

they realise the powerful position of their rulers, they also do it because of 'their convictions about the genuineness of the commands of their'superiors'. It is this point that makes democracy basically different from totalitarian systems. In the former, the people struggle for power and obey or challenge the commands of their rulers; in the latter, the people obey meekly without questioning the propriety of the actions of their rulers, or they do it at the expense of their very existence.

In the context of decision-making process, power is identified with the role of active participation. This point, however, needs its reinterpretation in view of the fact that it also involves the situation of non-participation. We find that while power has its definite role in the process of decision-making, some participate for the mere satisfaction of being in it. That is, they may be completely indifferent to the decision itself. Thus, we may feel that there is no need to restrict the notion of power by attaching any sanction to it, since a decision could be affected by arguments and persuasion, threats, strikes, sit-ins, demonstration and violence. Power, so understood, may, and also may not, be identified with influence, authority and other related themes.[81]

It is for these reasons that the concept of power is regarded as 'extraordinarily difficult and elusive in itself'[82] and no satisfactory definition of it has been produced so far, although both philosophers and political scientists have attempted to do so. It appears that there have been several attempts to make the concept of power something of a key concept. Dorothy Emmet has argued that one of the sources of confusion has been the result of attempts to bring different kinds of power under one definition. For, it is not obvious that distinction in the meaning of the word can be precisely correlated with the kinds of power in such a way that these can be presented as species of a common genus. Owing to these multiple meanings of power, it is probably better to break the concept by using words available for its different aspects, by introducing adjectival qualifications, as best serves to bring the particular sense.[83] Thus, a recent writer has described power as a 'disappointing concept' which "gives us surprisingly little purchase in reasonable models of complex systems of social choice."[84]

The problem of contemporary political theory is how to make conditions for the proper use of political power so that 'maximisation of democracy' takes place. Men are naturally unlike and, for this reason, distribution of power is bound to be unequal in any conceivable social system. The Benthamite principle of 'one person, one vote', or his warning that 'no one is to be counted for more than one' cannot help except justifying a well-established norm of democratic theory. As a practical course, what may be desired is that the operation of political system should be such that no man's power to use his natural talents is diminished, rather it is increased to the extent that the elements of 'developmental' and 'extractive' powers become consistent with

81. See S.C. Ghosh: "Decision, Process and Power: A Conceptual Approach" in *Indian Journal of Political Science,* Vol. XXXVI, No. 4, 1975, p. 355.
82. W.C. Runciman: *Social Science and Political Theory* (London, 1969), p. 97.
83. Dorothy Emmet: "The Concept of Power" in *Proceedings of the Aristotelian Society,* Vol. 54, 1854, pp. 1-26.
84. James G. March: "The Concept of Power" in David Easton (ed.): *Varieties of Political Theory* (Englewood Cliffs, New Jersey: Prentice-Hall, 1966), p. 70.

each other.[85] While feeling convinced with the fact of natural inequality, it should also be borne in mind that "the difference of natural talents in different men is, in reality, much less than we are aware of.... The difference between the most dissimilar characters, between a philosopher and a common street porter, for example, seems to arise not so much from nature, as from habit, custom and education."[86]

Man today is confronted with the most fundamental choice, not that between Capitalism

85. See Macpherson, *op. cit.* p. 73.
86. Adam Smith: *Wealth of Nations*, Book I, Chapter 2.

Part III

MAJOR TRENDS

and Communism, but that between *robotism* (of both the Capitalist and Communist variety) or Humanistic Communitarian socialism. Most facts seem to indicate that he is choosing robotism, and that means, in the long run, insanity and destruction. But all these facts are not strong enough to destroy faith in man's reason, good will and sanity.

—Eric Fromm[1]

For the profession, therefore, the emerging post-behavioural phase is encouraging the development of a new form of behaviour. It sees policy engagement as a social responsibility of the intellectual whatever the institutional form through which this may be expressed. Some day it may also require the release of the social scientist from bondage to the unique needs and objects of his own national political system.

—David Easton[2]

Political theory has consciously or not turned away much from political science with the result that no compromise between the two is in sight.

—George Kateb[3]

1. Fromm: *The Sane Society* (London: Routledge and Kegan Paul, 1963), p. 363.

2. Easton's Presidential Address at the American Political Science Association in 1969 reproduced in his *The Political System: An Inquiry into the State of Political Science* (Calcutta : Scientific Book Agency, 1971), p. 347.
3. Kateb: "The Condition of Political Theory" in *American Behavioural Scientist* (Sept-October, 1977), p. 136.

18

Liberalism

> Nothing is blinder than the supposition that we live in a society and world so static that either nothing new will happen, or else it will happen because of the use of violence. Social change is here as a fact, a fact having multifarious forms and marked in intensity.... Flux does not have to be created. But it does have to be directed. It has to be so controlled that it moves to some end in accordance with the principles of life, since life itself is development.
>
> **—John Dewey[1]**

One of the astounding features of modern political theory should be traced in its start from the appreciation of an authoritarian order resting on the foundations of nationalism and sovereignty and, at the same time, a call of protest—religious, political, economic, social, legal and ethical—against the established system of a secular and sovereign nation-state. The keynote of this paradox finds place in liberalism that has been designated as a doctrine, a principle, a philosophy, a school, a movement, an idea, an attitude, even an ideology. The essential reason for this finds place in looking at the 'essence of man' in relation to his social and political life. Thus, we find 'that whereas from the days of the ancient Greeks until the emergence of the modern sovereign nation-state, it was usual to see the essence of man as a purposeful activity, or as an exercise of one's energies in accordance with some rational purpose than as the consumption of satisfactions, it was with the emergence of the modern *market* society after the fifteenth century that the concept of man was narrowed and turned into almost its opposite. Man was still held to be essentially a purposive, rational creature, but the essence of rational behaviour "was increasingly held to lie in unlimited individual appropriation, as a means of satisfying unlimited desire for utilities."[2] As a result, the thinkers of the modern age came to realise that "a newly moralised, liberal-democratic society could claim, as a *market* society, to maximise individuals' chosen utilities, and, as a free society to maximise their powers."[3] It is due to this that liberalism appears both as an ardent advocate and a stern critic, sometimes even like a destructive and revolutionary critic, of the modern state.[4]

1. John Dewey: "Intelligence in Politics" in W.E. Volkhomer (ed.): *The Liberal Tradition in American Thought* (New York: G.P. Putnam's 1969), p. 302.
2. C.B. Macpherson: *Democratic Theory: Essays in Retrieval* (London: Oxford Univ. Press, 1975). p. 5.
3. *Ibid.*, p. 6.
4. See L.T. Hobhouse: *Liberalism* (New York: Oxford Univ. Press, 1964) (with an Introduction by A.P. Grimes), p. 14.

Liberalism: Meaning and Dynamic Implications

Liberalism, whether a philosophy or an ideology, may be precisely defined as "an idea committed to freedom as a method and policy in government, as an organising principle in society, and a way of life for the individual and community."[5] Obviously, it is very closely connected with the idea of 'liberty', since the very essence of this doctrine is to aim at freedom and thereby expressing and fulfilling the human spirit. In other words, liberalism is the voice of a free life—a life in which freedom is maximised to the extent that the individual may think, believe, move, express, discuss, associate and so on. As such, it serves the purpose of numerous thinkers ranging from the economists desiring man's freedom to produce or distribute goods, or import and export commodities, to the men of politics laying emphasis on men's right to choose and remove their rulers, or form and change their government by persuasion if possible and by revolution if necessary. In short, carnal to the whole idea of liberalism is the principle of liberty; moreover, so crucial 'is the idea of liberty that liberalism might be quite summarily defined as the effect to organise liberty socially and to follow its implication."[6]

As generally understood, liberalism stands against coercive interference of any kind in any walk of life whether moral or religious, social or political, and the like. Socrates, the Stoics, the Fathers of Christianity, Milton, Descartes, Spinoza, Voltaire, Locke, Goethe, Jefferson, Rousseau, Kant, Hume, Diderot, Montesquieu, Lessing, Adam Smith, Vico, Condorcet, Benjamin Franklin, T.H. Green, Cole, Laski, Barker and a host of other eminent social theorists, philosophers and statesmen can be referred to as the leading lights who have defended the cause of liberalism in varying degrees and diverse ways. However, the defence of liberalism at the hands of so many thinkers and statesmen belonging to different countries of the world and living in different periods of history has also resulted in complicating the real meaning of this term. It shall be a synthesised version if we say that liberalism is the only philosophy or ideology that has arrayed its forces against anything standing for the concentration of authority detrimental to the most cherished value of human life—liberty.

Viewed differently, liberalism has its narrow as well as broad perspectives. While its narrow perspective is related to the fields of respective disciplines like economics or politics where it stands for freedom in respect of producing and distributing goods, or choosing and removing the rulers, in its broad perspective it becomes like a mental attitude that attempts in the light of its presuppositions to analyse and integrate the varied intellectual, moral, religious, social, economic and political relationships of human beings. As such, it becomes a complex pattern of interrelated

5. *Encyclopaedia Britannica,* Vol. 13, 1967 Ed., p. 1017.
6. *Ibid.,* p. 1018. According to Derek Heater, freedom "is the quintessence of liberalism.... For the liberal, it is the individual who counts, not society at large or segment of it, for only by placing priority on the rights of the individual can freedom be ensured." *Contemporary Political Ideas* (London: Longman, 1974), pp. 22-23. This writer refers to the case of the English Liberal Party whose constitution declares that "in everything it puts freedom first." See Roy Doughlas: *The History of the Liberal Party, 1895-1970* (London: Sidgwick and Jackson, 1971), p. xvi. So says an American writer: "Liberalism is the belief and commitment to a set of methods and policies that have as their common aim greater freedom for individual men." See D G. Smith: "Liberalism" in David I. Sills (ed.): *International Encyclopaedia of the Social Sciences* (New York : Macmillan and Free Press, 1968), Vol. 9, p. 276.

strands belonging to the spheres of social sciences like ethics, economics, sociology and politics. The astonishing feature of liberalism is that the diverse strands are organically connected and, as such, they cannot be disentangled.

In order to have an understanding of liberalism—more as a habit of mind than as a body of doctrine[7]—we may refer to its implications in three important spheres—social, economic and political.

1. In the social sphere, liberalism stands for secularism, i.e., man's freedom from the shackles of religious orthodoxy. It desires that man should change his habits, customs and institutions which have either outlived their usefulness, or which act like a chain on his real freedom. The social aspect of liberalism has its particular concern with man's freedom in relation to religion and morality. As such, it not only repudiates naturalistic or deterministic interpetations of human action but lays stress on the value of a free individual conscious of his capacity for self-expression and an unfettered development of his personality. It follows, therefore, "as an obvious corollary to the grammar of liberalism that any attempt on the part of a constituted authority to exert artificial pressures or regulations on the individual in his inner and outer adjustments is an unjustifiable interference, a stultification of his personality and initiative."[8]
2. No less significant is the meaning of liberalism in the economic sphere. Here it signifies the appreciation of the ideal of free trade coupled with internal freedom of production and external freedom of exportation. It stands for free competition implying no curb on the import and export of goods. For this reason, it stands for the exploitation of natural resources and distribution of economic dividends at the hands of the individuals. Its natural result may be visualised in the rise and growth of the modern bourgeois class owning and controlling the means of production and distribution. This meaning of classical economic liberalism should, however, be revised in the light of new conditions of a market society that have led to the emergence of the doctrine of socialism. We know that as a result of the emergence of the bourgeois class, conditions of inflation developed entailing misery and starvation of the working class. Socialism, therefore, developed as a by-product of liberalism. This change could be discerned in the divergent interpretations of the 'bourgeois' and 'socialist' liberals. While the former propounded and propagated the doctrine of individualism by describing state as a necessary evil and demanding minimum possible area of state interference, the latter desired a different role of the state in order to place more and more curbs on the production and distribution of goods in the general interest. Liberalism thus finds itself hemmed between two opposite trends—both desiring liberty in their respective interests and thereby showing that the political form of liberalism has remained intact despite the fact that the conflict for power between the forces of plutocracy and economic democracy has threatened to distort them beyond recognition. The concept of a free sphere of activities with an impartial police state "gave way to a concept of a state which should be conquered as a vehicle for the attainment of class objectives."[9]

7. H.J. Laski: *The Rise of European Liberalism* (London: George Allen & Unwin, 1936), p. 13.
8. Guide de Ruggerio: "Liberalism" in Seligman (ed.): *Encyclopaedia of the Social Sciences,* Vol. IX (New York: Macmillan, 1967), p. 435.
9. *Ibid., v.* 447.

Elements of Liberalism

1. **Individualism:** It reflects a belief in the supreme importance of the individual as opposed to any social group or collective body. Each individual should pursue the good as he defines it and strive to the best of his abilities.
2. **Freedom:** Individual should have the right to develop his personality by following the rules of behaviour being consistent with a like liberty for all.
3. **Reason:** Man is a rational creature. The world has a rational structure. As all individuals are rational creatures, they are expected to resolve their differences amicably without recourse to violence.
4. **Equality:** All individuals are born equal at least in terms of moral worth. In practical terms it implies equality before law and equality of opportunity in a way that individuals with talents or merits should not be treated at par with those who lack desert.
5. **Toleration:** Society should have plurality or diversity in different walks of life allowing individuals to live and let others live. Dissent should be permitted and differences should be resolved amicably by following the norm of forbearance.
6. **Consent:** Authority should be based on the willingness of the people. Government should be limited and accountable. Hence, democracy is the best form of government.
7. **Constitutionalism:** The constitutional system should be based on the principles of separation of powers and checks and balances. Both the rulers and the ruled should be bound by the rules of the constitution ensuring boons of liberty, equality and justice.

Andrew Heywood: *Politics* (Houndmills, Basingstoke: Palgrave Foundations, 2005), pp. 43-44.

3. However, it is in the sphere of politics where liberalism has come to have a precise connotation. Here it places its primary emphasis on this point that political liberty constitutes a prerequisite to and a necessary guarantee of the liberty as a whole. It certainly arose in the form of a reaction against increased state activity inasmuch as the maximisation of state control amounted to the minimisation of the scope of individual liberty. It is obvious that in the early stages of its development, the forces of liberalism "concentrated on the crucial problem of limiting the interference of state and of transforming state policy into a vehicle of promoting the liberties of the individuals and groups."[10]

   In the process of formulating its libertarian ideals and objectives, political liberalism gradually evolved into an explicit system as it drew more and more in proximity to the arena of parliamentary democracy like separation of powers, checks and balances, parliamentary control over executive, public law, judicial review, protection of the interests of the minorities and a host of other arrangements militating against the trend of concentration and accumulation of powers. The idea behind an emphasis on all such norms was to desire a permanent curb on governmental activity as an embodiment of the continuity

10. *Ibid.*, p. 435.

of the tradition that came to be known by the name of liberalism. Moreover, a stringent emphasis on these values constituted the formulation of a particular ideology desiring functioning of the government in the interest of social justice.

While keeping the dynamic implications of liberalism in view, an eminent writer on this subject thus defines it: "Liberalism is the belief that society can safely be founded on this self-directing power of personality, that it is only on this foundation that a true community can be built, and that so established, its foundations are so deep and so wide that there is no limit that we can place to the extent of the building. Liberty thus becomes not so much a right of the individual as a necessity of society. It rests not on the claim of A to be let alone by B, but on the duty of B to treat A as a rational being. It is not right to let crime alone or to let error alone, but it is imperative to treat the criminal or the mistaken or the ignorant as being capable of right and truth, and to lead them on instead of merely beating them down. The rule of liberty is just the application of rational method. It is the opening of the door to the appeal of imagination, of social feeling; and except through the response to the appeal there is no assured progress of society."[11]

In short, liberalism is the philosophy of the modern age that replaces religion as the controlling factor in giving shape to the thoughts of men, the idea of a golden age in the past with its concomitant idea of original sin that gives way to the doctrine of scientific progress, with its own concomitant idea of perfectibility through reason. It is liberalism in which the notion of social initiative and control is surrendered to the idea of individual initiative and control. That is, it lays emphasis on the point that new material conditions give birth to new social relationships and in terms of these a new philosophy is required to afford a rational justification for the new world which has come into being. In a word, liberalism "came as a new ideology to fit the needs of a new world."[12]

Nature of Liberalism: A Philosophy with a Pragmatic Course

It may be conceded that in the present age liberalism has become more of an epithet than a truly descriptive expression; it cannot be denied that there is certainly more to liberalism than the label.[13] While seeking to explain the component elements of this philosophy, Grimes says: "It represents a system of ideas that aims at the realisation of the pluralistic society, forcing diversity in politics, economics, religion, and our cultural life. It is opposed to uniformity; it is opposed to conformity. It is, in the broadest sense of the word, anti-monopolistic; for it favours the widest possible degree of self-determination. It denotes an attitude towards human problems as well as goals for human endeavour. It seeks, in its simplest sense, to advance the freedom of man. It is essentially anti-authoritarian, and represents the claims of those who are out of power and thus lacking in authority; but who, had they the power, would not impose authoritarian solutions on others. It seeks to increase the individuality of man by increasing his area of choice and decision. It is essentially

---

11. Hobhouse, *op. cit.*, p. 66.
12. Laski: *The Rise of European Liberalism*, p. 16.
13. Alan P. Grimes: "The Pragmatic Course of Liberalism" in *Western Political Quaterly*, Vol. IX, No. 3 (Sept., 1956), pp. 633-40.

humanitarian in its appeal and therefore endorses toleration and is motivated by a sense of compassion for mankind. Finally, it is flexible in the method of its realisation and, while a doctrine, is itself not a doctrinaire."[14]

With a view to explain the components of liberalism, Grimes enumerates the following essential points:[15]

1. If liberalism seeks to advance the freedom of man, it would seem to be implicit that the freedom of man, rather than his restraint, is a desirable end in itself. Power is, of course, reciprocal and not the possession solely of those in command of institutions, or those who are governed, or those who control in some manner those who do the governing. Implicit, therefore, in liberalism is the concept of human worth, of human dignity, of man as the end and also institutions as the means.
2. Liberalism is anti-authoritarian and arises as a protest of those out of power against the users of power to which an authority is subjecting them. Thus, liberalism arises as a protest against traditional forms of authority wherever found. Liberalism is thus, by and large, the creed of the dispossessed, the dissenter of those who are subject to the decisions which others make.
3. Liberalism seeks to increase the individuality of man by increasing his area of choice. It seeks to increase the individual's opportunity for making meaningful decisions. The area of choice can never be constant or static; but moves with social flux, responding to the felt necessities of the times. Thus, liberalism usually follows the path of protest. Implicit, of course, is the assumption of equality positing man as an end in himself carrying with him the belief that to each man choices are important.
4. Another core concept of liberalism is humanitarianism. It seeks to support the weak and curb the strong. It seeks to redirect the flow of society's benefits—to prevent them from becoming the monopoly of the few, into the hands of the many.
5. Finally, liberalism is not a static creed or dogma, for dogmatism provides its own restraints. It is rather a tentative attitude towards social problems which stresses the role of reason and human ingenuity. In its efforts to free mankind, liberalism seeks to free the mind as well as clothe the body. As social institutions change, new formulae for liberation based on the felt necessities of the present must be devised. In a word, it must be pragmatic. It must seek practical answers to patent problems, but answers which work constantly in the direction of those without power, of those who lack the benefits, of those, in other words, who need the most help in order to fulfil the requirements of their individuality. Liberalism thus looks ahead with a flexible approach, seeking to make the future better for more people.

Now drawing together these five components, liberalism may be thus defined: "It denotes an attitude which seeks to make possible those social conditions in which the individuality of all men may be best realised. Because as a general rule

14. *Ibid.*
15. *Ibid.*

those who possess authority enjoy a large measure of freedom; liberals, impelled by humanitarianism, seek to advance the freedom of those without authority, of those without 'special benefits'. Liberalism is, then, the doctrine of the social and economic underdog. It is usually on the side of those who are neglected by the conventions of society and thus it must eternally plead for the unconventional cause."[16]

The astonishing thing about the philosophy of liberalism, however, is that it is both constant and changing: it is constant in the sense that its goal being the 'liberation of man' remains constant and, as such, it follows a pragmatic course to realise its fundamental aim; it is changing in the sense that it denotes a desire for change in response to the new conditions of the age. Two things should, however, be invariably kept in mind. First, without the constant end of liberation of man there would be no continuity, to liberalism, and the term would possess no more meaning beyond that of a temporary and conventional party label. Second, liberalism denotes far more than a desire for change; it denotes purposeful, reasoned change that would elevate the status and increase the liberty of, what we would today call, the common man. Without pragmatism, liberalism would indicate nothing beyond vague aspirations incapable of fulfilment. With constant goals and changing means liberalism seeks today, as in the past, to refashion social institutions to better realise the equal individuality and dignity of man.[17]

Genesis and Growth of the Movement: From a Crusade for Religious Emancipation to a Struggle against Royal Despotism

As already pointed out, liberalism arose as a reaction first against the forces of religious dominance and then against political authoritarianism that had sought to destroy individualist traditions. As such, it first appeared in the movements of Renaissance and Reformation that sought to free man from the shackles of religious obscurantism and infuse in him the inquisitive spirit of classical antiquity. It also appeared in the defence of a sovereign nation-state for the reason that the modern state emerged as a potential challenge to the omnipotent sway of the Papacy that had become the embodiment of tyranny. The notable thing, in this direction, however, is that liberalism took a turn and thereby looked like a stern critic of the modern state when it found that the sovereign power vested in the monarch had once again taken to the course of absolutism. Hence, the philosophy of liberalism can be traced in all movements of the modern age in which people took part for bringing about a new political order based on the principle of 'general will' or 'popular sovereignty'.

The triumph of the Renaissance and the Reformation movements demonstrated the victory of early liberalism over the forces of religious dominance. However, what is important for our purpose is the triumph of this philosophy over the forces of authoritarianism. In this direction, liberalism had to fight against the despotism of the monarchs who had converted themselves into political popes. Its first brilliant instance was afforded in the English constitutional history where the people struggled against the despotism of the Stuart Kings that culminated not so much in the defeat and execution of Charles I in 1649 as in the abdication of the throne by King James II

16. *Ibid.*
17. *Ibid.*

and Parliament's resolution to offer the same to his daughter Mary and her husband William—an event known as the Glorious Revolution of 1688. Reference in this regard may be made to the Bill of Rights adopted by the Parliament and assented to by the King (William) which provided:

1. That the pretended power of suspending of laws or the execution of laws by regal authority without the consent of Parliament is illegal.
2. That levying money for or to the use of the Crown, by pretence of prerogative, without grant of Parliament for a longer time or in a manner other than the same is or shall be granted, is illegal.
3. That the raising or keeping a standing army within the kingdom in the time of peace without the sanction of the Parliament is illegal.
4. That it is the right of the subjects to petition the King and all commitments and prosecutions for such petitioning are illegal.
5. That the election of the members of Parliament ought to be free.
6. That the freedom of speech and debates or proceedings in Parliament ought not to be impeached or questioned in any court or place out of Parliament.
7. That excessive bail ought not to be required, nor excessive fines imposed, nor cruel and unusual punishment inflicted.
8. That jurors ought to be duly empannelled and returned and those who pass upon men in trials for high treason ought to be free-holders.
9. That all grants and promises of fines and forfeitures of particular persons before conviction are illegal and void.
10. And that for the redress of all grievances and for amending, strengthening and preserving of the laws, Parliament ought to be held frequently.

This event finally decided the 'greater question' whether the popular element should be destroyed by the monarchical element, or be suffered to develop itself freely, and to become dominant. The judgement went in favour of popular authority and since then we find 'a continuity of life to liberal institutions.'[18]

The next important event is the Declaration of Independence (adopted by the Second Continental Congress on July 4, 1776) whereby the Founding Fathers of the American Union asserted strong belief of the people in the natural law and inalienable rights of man, in the right to revolt when no alternative to absolute despotism was available and then made a pronouncement of the legal grounds for the transfer of sovereignty. The most important part of this Declaration was that "all men are created equal; that they are endowed by the Creator with certain inalienable rights.... that to secure these rights, governments are instituted among men, deriving their just powers from the consent of the governed; that whenever any form of government becomes destructive of these ends, it is the right of the people to alter or abolish it, and to institute a new government, laying its foundations on such principles, and organising its powers in such form, as to them shall seem most likely to affect their safety and happiness." This important document was hailed as the 'birth certificate of the American nation' and a learned man of law commented that it "has always

18. W.G. Andrews: *Constitution and Constitutionalism* (New York: Von Nostrand, 1961), p. 54.

been treated as an act of paramount and sovereign authority, complete and perfect *per se, ipso facto* working an entire dissolution of all political connection with and allegiance to Great Britain."[19]

Finally, we may refer to the Declaration of the Rights of Man and of Citizen adopted by the National Assembly of France in 1789 which said: "Men are born free and equal in rights.... The aim of every political association is the preservation of the practical and imprescriptible rights of man. These rights are liberty, property, security and resistance to oppression.... Liberty consists in the power to do anything that does not injure others; accordingly the exercise of natural rights of each man has for its only limits those that secure to the other members of society to the enjoyment of these same rights. These limits can be determined by law.... Law is the expression of the general will.... No one ought to be disturbed on account of his opinions.... The free communication of ideas and opinions is one of the most precious rights of man." Obviously, to the King's absolute rule, the Revolution countered the notion of absolute popular sovereignty—supreme, inalienable, pure and always right. The old maxim, 'The King can do no wrong' was replaced by the new one, 'The people are always right.'[20]

Thus, during the seventeenth and eighteenth centuries, liberalism had to deal first with the authoritarianism of the Church and then with the absolutism of the state by vindicating the elements of personal, civil and economic freedoms and in doing so it took its stand on the rights of men and in proportion as it was forced to be constructive on the supposed harmony of the natural order. Government claimed supernatural sanction and divine ordinance. Liberal theory asserted in effect that the rights of men rested on the law of nature, and those of government, on human institutions. The 'oldest' institution in this view was the individual, and the primordial society, the natural grouping of human beings, under the influence of family affection, and for the sake of mutual aid. Political society was a mere artificial arrangement, a convention arrived at for the specific purpose of securing a better order and maintaining common safety. It was, perhaps, as Locke held, founded on a contract between the king and the people, a contract which was brought to an end if either party violated its terms. Or, as in Rousseau's view, it was essentially a contract of the people with one another, "an arrangement by means of which, out of many conflicting individual wills, a common or general will could be formed; a government might be instituted as the organ of this will, but it would, from the nature of the case, be subordinate to the people from where it derived authority. The people were sovereign. The government was their delegate."[21]

Liberalism—Old and New: Negative versus Positive Dimensions

The movement of the theory of liberalism, however, shows that it has undergone a change from its classical or old to modern or new ramifications that have also resulted in the manifestation of its transformation from its negative to positive dimensions.

19. Joseph Story: *Commentaries on the Constitution of the United States,* Vol. 1, pp. 149-50.
20. R.C. Macridis: "France" in Ward and Macridis: *Modern Political Systems: Europe* (Englewood Cliffs, New Jersey: Prentice-Hall, 1968), p. 164.
21. Hobhouse, *op. cit.,* p. 32.

It is mostly visible in the sphere of social and economic control. The reason for this should be traced in the changing notion of 'liberty' from that of classical economists like Adam Smith to a modern sociologist like L.T. Hobhouse that "offers the best key to the understanding of the evolution of political thought during the past century and a half."[22] It has led to the distinction between early liberalism with its negative view of liberty and functions of state, and later enlightened or idealist liberalism which sought to give a positive view of liberty and the action of state in relation to it.[23]

While the early liberalism stood for anti-authoritarianism of the state in the political sphere, it generally advocated the independence of private enterprise in the economic sphere. Thus, it stood for freedom in exercising rights to property. As such, it appeared as a new form of middle-class social philosophy partly replacing and partly revising the philosophy of natural rights.[24] The state was thus regarded as a 'necessary evil', necessary to protect and defend the interests of the rising capitalist class and an evil as its activity interfered with the economic freedom of man. Thus, the traditional liberal theory struggled to retain its concept of man as an 'infinite consumer and an infinite appropriator—a concept of man clearly inextricable from a concept of property.[25]

An eminent writer sums up the assumptions of classical liberalism as 'beliefs' in.[26]

1. the absolute value of human personality and the spiritual equality of all individuals,
2. the autonomy of the will of the individual,
3. the essential rationality and goodness of man,
4. the existence of certain inalienable rights like those relating to life, liberty and property,
5. the creation of the state by mutual consent for the sole purpose of preserving and protecting the natural rights of the individuals,
6. the contractual relationship between the state and the individual and that when the terms of the contract are violated, individuals have not only the right but the responsibility to revolt and establish a new government,
7. the law being superior to command as an instrument of social control,
8. the limit and negative functions of the government which is the best if it governs the least,
9. the affirmation that the individual is, and should be, free in all spheres of life such as political, economic, social, intellectual and religious, and
10. the existence of a supreme truth based on reason which can be achieved by individual thought and conscience that plays an important role in man's choice between order and anarchy.

---

22. Lewis Rockow: *Contemporary Political Thought in England* (London: Leonard Pearson, 1925), p. 211.
23. Frank Thakurdas: *Recent English Political Theory and the Idea of Liberty* (Calcutta: Minerva, 1972), p. 3.
24. G.H. Sabine: *A History of Political Theory* (London: Harrap, 1944), p. 648.
25. Macpherson, *op. cit.* p. 120.
26. J. H. Hallowell: *Main Currents in Modern Political Thought* (New York: Holt, Rinehart and Winston, 1951), pp. 10-11.

Four Features of Liberalism

1. It is *individualist,* in that it asserts moral primacy of the person against any collectivity.
2. It is *egalitarian,* in that it confers on all human beings the same basic moral status.
3. It is *universalist,* in that it affirms the moral unity of the species.
4. It is *ameliorist,* in that it asserts the open-ended improvability by the use of critical reason of human life.

Source: John Gray: *Liberalism* (Delhi: World View, 1998), p. 86.

Classical liberalism thus demonstrated its negative character inasmuch as it based itself on the foundation of *laissez faire* and thereby assumed that the state would simply hold the ring. That is, political authority would do nothing more than suppress force and fraud, keep individual property safe and aid men in the enforcement of contracts. It assumed that the individual should be left alone, he should be given absolute freedom to compete with others, or that his energies should be called forth so that each feels himself responsible for the guidance of his own life and exerts his manhood to the utmost. Thus, the followers and disciples of Cobden, Adam Smith and David Ricardo advocated the doctrine of minimum possible state activity to ensure maximum possible individual liberty. The burden of their argument was that in the economic struggle the individual was animated mainly by the force of self-interest. As such, if he was allowed to use his capital as he pleased, to dispose of his labour to his best advantage, to exchange the products of his toil freely, and to have the prices of goods fixed by the natural laws of demand and supply, better results would be secured not only to himself but to the whole society. It was the unrestricted competition that stimulated economic production, tended to keep wages and prices at a normal level, to prevent usurious rates of interest, to secure efficient service and the production of better goods than could be obtained by state regulations or state management.[27]

However, as the nineteenth century advanced, the relation of the principle of political liberalism with its economic counterpart became more complicated inasmuch as the idea of unrestricted economic freedom entailed that the people were still living in an age of barbarism. Under the changed social and economic conditions, the new generations of liberals showed reluctance in accepting the contention of the traditional doctrine of economic liberalism that political action was artificial; it went counter to moral, economic, or biological laws and thereby interfered with the normal physical development and spiritual improvement of the human race.[28] As the interests of the industrial and commercial class in the freedom of trade diminished owing to England's loss of superiority over other European countries in the field of industrialisation and also because of the organisation of business in larger and larger commercial units coupled with the opposition between capitalists and landowners reaching a vanishing point, it appeared that as time went on, it

27. J.W. Garner: *Political Science and Government* (Calcutta: World Press, 1952), p. 462.
28. Hobhouse, *op. cit.,* p. 49.

"was more and more replaced by that between capitalists and wage-earners with the result that the body of liberal ideas has tended to divide between conservatism on the one side and some form of socialism on the other."[29]

This change became visible in the works of Jeremy Bentham who propounded the doctrine of utilitarianism and thereby connected the idea of individual liberty with the principle of general happiness. Bentham presented the case of enlightened liberalism by trying to relate the principle of individual liberty with his doctrine of the greatest good of the greatest number. Bentham's utilitarianism involved a calculus of pleasures and pains based on the explicit hypothesis that everybody "is to count for one and nobody is to count for more than one" which implied that there must be no system of social or political privileges, yet such a system might conceivably realise the greatest sum of happiness, except for the assumption that men were by nature equally entitled to happiness. However, the best contribution of Bentham in this regard should be seen in his strong advocacy of reforms in the fields of law, education, parliamentary composition, municipal organisations, poor relief and prisons. So strongly did he criticise the contemporary systems and advocated reforms that he looked like entering like a veritable 'bull in a China shop'.[30] Keeping this in view, F.M. Young observed that it "would be hard to find any corner of our public life where the spirit of Bentham is not working today."[31]

A shift in the philosophy of liberalism from a negative to a positive side is very much evident in the ideas of John Stuart Mill. It may be said that Mill (1806-73) who started as a rank individualist in looking at state interference in the liberty of individual with grave apprehension ended like a collectivist agreeing with the maxim of social control over 'unearned increments'. For instance, in his essay *On liberty* (1859) he laid down: "The sole end for which mankind are warranted individually or collectively in interfering with the liberty of action of any of their members is self-protection. The only purpose for which power can be rightfully exercised over any member of a civilised community against his will, is to prevent harm to others.... Over himself, his own body and mind, the individual is sovereign."[32]

However, a definite change in the ideas of Mill became visible when he revised his *Principles of Political Economy* and in its seventh edition of 1871 advanced a theory of special taxation on'socially created values'. He desired the state to overstep its sphere in a direction so as to enforce compulsory education to remove the incompetency of the citizens, release persons from the obligations of the contracts in perpetuity where parties cannot be competent judges of the effects of such obligations, make subject to public control all monopolies, limit working hours and regulate conditions of work, encourage scientific works and deeds of exploration, increase wages, levy tax on economic rent, protect public health, introduce factory legislation and launch insurance against illness, industrial accidents and indigence in old age.[33] Perhaps

29. Sabine, *op. cit.*, p. 649.
30. W.A. Dunning: *A History of Political Theories* (Allahabad: Central Book Depot, 1969), Vol. Ill, p. 212.
31. See Wayper: *Political Thought* (London: Hutchinson, 1963), p. 83.
32. Mill: *Utilitarianism, Liberty and Representative Government* edited by A.D. Lindsay, pp. 72-73.
33. Mill: *Principles of Political Economy*, VII Ed, pp. 573-603.

he moved still farther when he thus wrote in the last work of his life: "The social problem of the future was considered to be how to unite the greatest individual liberty of action with a common ownership in the raw materials of the globe, and an equal participation of all in the benefits of combined labour."[34]

Liberalism took a distinctly positive turn in the ideas of T.H. Green (1836-82) who sought to mix it up with the tenets of idealism. As a follower of Plato, Aristotle, Rousseau, Kant and Hegel, Green adhered to the school of idealism but made it consonant with the tradition of English liberalism and thereby made it immune from the rigours of a purely metaphysical theory culminating in the doctrine of state absolutism. The peculiar thing about the political philosophy of Green is that he remained both a moderate idealist believing in the indirect action of state in bettering the conditions of the people and, at the same time, a positive liberal desiring direct intervention of state in eradicating three gigantic social evils of ignorance, pauperism and drinking liquor.[35] Obviously, according to Green, the state's characteristic function "is that of removing external hindrances to the voluntary performance of good acts. In executing this task it has much more to do than defend the community from foreign attack and check traditional crimes and torts."[36]

It is, therefore, clear that by the end of the nineteenth century, liberalism took a distinct turn from a negative to a positive direction in view of the fact that the advocates of this philosophy gradually lost their faith in looking at state activity with disfavour and instead came to realise the significance of more and more state intervention in the liberty of the individual in the interests of the society. It led to the enunciation of a new theory of state activity that, later on, came to be known as the doctrine of welfare state. As we shall see in due course, this change moved liberalism more and more in the direction of socialism and a great liberal of the nineteenth century like John Stuart Mill earned the distinction of being the father of Fabianism. 'Not Marx but Mill is the starting point of the English Fabians', said Barker.[37] While appreciating the lectures of Green delivered at the Oxford University in 1879-80, Wayper comments that he "gave Englishmen something more satisfying than Benthamism at a price they were prepared to pay, that he left liberalism a faith instead of an interest, that he made individualism moral and social and idealism civilised and safe."[38]

The noticeable thing about liberalism in the period following the First World War is that it has discarded the line of *laissez faire* as insisted by the classical individualists like Adam Smith, J.S. Mill and Herbert Spencer and instead taken to a new line as given. by H.J. Laski, J.M. Keynes and Joseph Chamberlain. Derek Heater calls it 'second branch of liberalism' represented by the trend of radical reformism. It can be seen in the new emphasis of the Liberal Party on equality of opportunity, human treatment of immigrants, and support for national independence movements. The modern liberals have come to defend the case of social welfare state as expounded by

34. Mill: *Autobiography*, p. 232.
35. Green: *Lectures on the Principles of Political Obligation*, p. 208.
36. F.W. Coker: *Recent Political Thought* (New York: D. Appleton Century, 1934), p. 424.
37. Ernest Barker: *Political Thought in England* (London: Oxford Univ. Press, 1951) Ed. II, p. 189.
38. Wayper, *op. cit.*, p. 193.

Lord William Beveridge in 1942, and yet they desire to give a word of caution about over-statification of man's life. So in its election manifesto of 1945, it was stated that the Liberal Party "exists to build a Liberal Commonwealth in which every citizen shall possess liberty, property and security and none shall be enslaved by poverty, ignorance or unemployment."[39]

The main principles of the positive or modern liberalism may be thus enumerated:[40]

1. Freedom is not just freedom from want. The individual must be able to exercise effective political influence through properly constructed constitutional machinery.'
2. Modernise the machinery of government by bringing new life to the neglected sections and dispelling present political apathy.
3. There should be constitutional reforms involving devolution of power to give effective power to regional councils.
4. Decline of parliamentary system is a serious ill. Efforts should be made to revise the constitutional system for producing a parliament reflecting popular will.
5. In the international field, state sovereignty should be restricted by strengthening supranational bodies like the United Nations.

As David Nicholls says: "By a positive liberal I mean a person who holds an empirical conception of liberty, but together with this accepts a view of society which is somewhat different from that of a negative liberal. He believes that liberty is an end—or the end— in politics, and holds that liberty means the ability to do what one chooses but also he holds that as a man cannot wholly escape the influence of the individuals, of groups and of society at large, there may be cases in which the state can intervene with coercive measures which, while reducing the freedom of the person concerned (at the time he is coerced at least) increases the freedom of others who were perhaps in the power of the person legislated against. There is, thinks the positive liberal, a coercion by society which can be quite as restrictive of individual freedom as coercion by the state."[41] He cites the view of William von Humbolt who in his *The Sphere and Duties of Government* insists that the state "is to abstain from all solicitude for the positive welfare of the citizens and not to proceed a step further than is necessary for their mutual security and protection against foreign enemies; for with no other object should it improve restrictions on freedom."[42] In

39. Roy Doughlas, *op. cit.*, p. 297. However, it may be added here that the modern liberalism of the American thinkers looks at the growing area of state activity in the name of 'social reform' with ample apprehension. Although they deprecate the course of *laissez faire,* they extend a word of caution against the dangers of state planning. Their argument is that the state should stick to the negative side of its role contained in the principle of hindering hindrances to good life of man. "Liberals today see man not only as an individual in society but as a person with a continuing need for self-expansion and reintegration. For this reason, the emphasis of modern liberalism is less upon external motion and more upon the individual person's subjective feeling of freedom and those circumstances that give to this feeling an objective reality in the experience of the individual." D.G. Smith, *op. cit.*, p. 281.
40. See Derek Heater, *op. cit.*, pp. 23-24.
41. David Nicholls: "Positive Liberty" in *The American Political Science Review,* Vol. LVI, No. 1 (March, 1962), p. 117.
42. *Ibid.*, p. 118.

this way, Nicholls comes to hold the view that during the period (1880-1914), the positive liberals held a conception of society, not simply as a heap of atoms, but as a community of mutually interacting beings; these beings are continually influencing each other and there is always the possibility of the state intervening to prevent coercion and increase liberty."[43]

Problem of Change: Liberalism in the Twentieth Century: Shift Towards Socialism and Welfare State

We have seen that the philosophy of liberalism has changed from a purely negative to a positive side at the hands of great thinkers. It, however, creates a baffling problem whether liberalism is a conservative or a progressive philosophy. One may say that it is either, or both, in view of the fact that sometimes it seems closer to conservatism when we find liberals in opposition to change; sometimes it looks like a progressive doctrine when its advocates seem like struggling for reforms. As such, liberalism imbibes the essential qualities of both—conservatism aad progressivism—in varying measures, though it is certain that it is clearly distinguishable from radicalism that stands for a sudden and major transformation. We may first look into the points of resemblance and difference between liberalism, conservatism and radicalism before switching over to examine the movement of liberalism towards democratic socialism in the twentieth century that exists as a solid proof of its being both a highly flexible, though not so a progressive philosophy.

Liberalism and conservatism seem to resemble each other, though it would be highly improper for a student of political philosophy to treat them as interchangeable terms despite the fact that both desire the conservation of cherished values. However, the essential difference between the two lies in this affirmation that while the former is dynamic, the latter is distinctly *status quoist;* while the former is concerned with the past as well as with the future, the latter is concerned with the past alone.[44] Likewise, liberalism resembles radicalism as both desire change. However, the difference between the two lies in this respect that while the former stands for a gradual change, the latter desires a quick transformation; while the former wants change in relation to the past, the latter seeks to break with it. It is obvious that liberalism is basically different from both conservatism and radicalism despite having something that constitutes the ingredients of both. Keeping this in mind, a well-known writer on this subject says: "In contradistinction to the extremist trends of conservatism, and radicalism, liberalism represents a flexible equilibrium which while recognising freedom as an expansive force tending towards the future values, the historical continuity of the actions through which the human spirit gradually realises itself. Only through these actions, it is felt, can both the individual and society acquire the self-mastery capable of finding a lasting embodiment in new achievements. Liberty

43. *Ibid.*, p. 122.
44. In very simple terms, conservatism means a tendency to maintain and defend the *status quo* regardless of what that may be. See R. Michels: "Conservatism" in *Encyclopaedia of the Social Sciences,* edited by Seligman (New York: Macmillan, 1967), Vol. VIII, p. 230. As commonly understood in politics, conservatism denotes a preference for the old and tried in the civil social order than the new and untried." *Encyclopaedia Britannica,* Vol. VI, 1967 Ed., p. 371.

as understood by the liberal is attained not by the man who forever starts his life anew but by him who bears upon every action of his life his whole personality."[45]

That liberalism is not opposed to change may well be visualised in the affirmations of the leading liberals of the twentieth century who have sought to make it more and more in tune with the changing needs and aspirations of the society. Great liberals of the present century from Hobhouse to Laski have emphasised that a healthy social life is impossible unless the personal economic responsibility of all those capable of work is assumed. The recognition of individual responsibility is the individual's return to society for the services rendered or offered to him by the society. It implies that there is no individual freedom without social responsibility. Obviously, such affirmations have taken liberalism very close to the world of socialism that has always stood four square for civil liberties. As such, socialism is said to be the 'legitimate heir of liberalism."[46]

The rudiments of such an orientation can be seen in the affirmations of Prof. L.T. Hobhouse who in his monograph titled *Liberalism* (published in 1906) thus visualised: "The ideal society is conceived as a whole which .lives and flourishes by the harmonious growth of its parts, each of which in developing on its own lines and in accordance with its own nature tends on the whole to further the development of others.... The heart of liberalism is the understanding that progress is not a matter of mechanical contrivance, but of the liberation of living spiritual energy. Good mechanism is that which provides the channels wherein such energy can flow unimpeded, unobstruced by its own exuberance of output, vivifying the social structure, expanding and ennobling the life of mind."[47]

We may also witness the changing trend in some other important works that appeared before the First World War. For intance, Norman Angell in his *The Great Illusion* describes state merely as a piece of administrative mechanism. His main contention is that men are united by a community of feeling based on economic interests which not only run counter to, but frequently transcend, national and geographical boundaries. As he puts it: "It pays men better to think and feel as members of the universal, economic society whose attribute is peace than to think and feel as members of limited political societies whose attribute is war."[48] Mention may also be made of the *Great Society* of Graham Wallas wherein he says that "the transference of the means of production from private to social ownership advocated by the socialists is of no value unless the public body that is to administer them is really representative of the society that owns them."[49]

The philosophy of negative liberalism manifested in the doctrine of *laissez faire* came to an end in the period following the First World War and since then liberal writers and thinkers took to the course of justifying more and more state intervention in the interest of the society that resulted in the advocacy of the doctrine of a positive

45. Laski: *The Rise of European Liberalism*, p. 16.
46. Harry W. Laidler: *Social and Economic Movements* (London: Routledge and Kegan Paul, I960), p. 251.
47. Hobhouse, *op. cit.*, pp. 72-73.
48. See C.E.M. Joad: *Modern Political Theory* (London: Oxford Univ. Press, 1946), p. 34.
49. *Ibid.*, p. 35.

state—something that pushed the principle of liberalism more and more towards the school of socialism. An important work in this direction is that of Prof R.M. Maclver of the United States who stressed the point that order within the community "is justified only as it serves the needs of the community. It is not order for the sake of order but for the sake of protection, and conservation, and development."[50] According to him, the essential functions of a 'modern state' include establishment of the areas and frontiers of political authority and control over import and export, transport and communications, setting up of the units of measurement and computation of value, specification of general rights and obligations of citizenship and territorial residence, determination of the rights and obligations of various associations, regulation of marriage, contracts, currency, occupational status relating to population and trades, provisions for security, justice, rights, decent living, wage rates, employment, upbringing of children, prevention of destitution and social wreckage, promotion of physical conditions by maintaining centres of health, recreation and profession, utilization of natural resources, planning, rural and urban development, education and scientific research, establishment of the centres of cultural and historical interest, promotion of agriculture and industry and scientific development for general good, and provisions for the means of inquiry into problems of general significance.[51]

However, the best representation of this trend can be seen in the affirmations of Prof. Harold J. Laski who sought to examine the matter of individual liberty *vis-a-vis* state interference from a Marxian standpoint. While delivering the inaugural lecture on the occasion of occupying the chair in the London School of Economics and Political Science in 1926, he said about the end of the *laissez faire* system and characterised the existing movement as one 'from the authoritarian to a functional state.[52] Said he: "Where earlier states were typified by the policemen, the modern state is typified.by the administrator."[53] A little earlier, in his monumental contribution, he emphasised the state as an institution for securing general welfare on the largest possible scale. In very strong terms, he stressed: "State insurance becomes as obvious as a state police force."[54] Whatever the character of the state, said he, it would need to secure itself against the inevitable costs of life. Sickness, old age, cost of educating children—all these require to be provided in such a way that the cost to the community is brought down to the lowest possible limits. As an advocate of a positive or social welfare state, he goes on to add: "There is no more fascinating theme in contemporary history than to follow the stages through which the *laissez faire* night-watchman state of the nineteenth century has been transformed into the welfare state of today—at one and the same time its logical opposite and its logical corollary."[55] Keeping these affirmations in view, one may say that in Laski, the English liberal tradition has had paradoxically its "most ardent critic as well as its most eloquent champion."[56]

---

50. Maclver: *The Modern Slate* (London: Oxford Univ. Press, 1966), p. 185.
51. *Ibid.*, pp. 185-86.
52. See Preston King (ed.): *The Study of Politics* (London : Frank Cass, 1977), p. 9.
53. *Ibid.*, p. 10.
54. Laski: *A Grammar of Politics* (London: George Allen and Unwin, 1925), p. 523.
55. *Ibid.*
56. Frank Thakurdas, *op. cit.*, p. 283.

Thus, liberalism not only changed its character, it moved closer to the trend of socialism through its advocacy for the cause of a positive or social service state. It may, however, be borne in mind that when we talk of socialism in this connection, it is the evolutionary or democratic socialism (collectivism or state socialism) and not the scientific socialism of Marx inasmuch as it has sought to establish a happy compromise between the liberty of the individual and the activity of the state in the social sphere without justifying the case of an authoritarian political system. The neo-liberals have appreciated the aim of all socialists who have not sacrificed the factor of the development of human personality at the altar of the state working for the consolidation of socialism through the 'dictatorship of the proletariat'. A careful examination of such socialist measures "will indicate that the coercion involved in the application of these measures is far less than the liberty which they make possible."[57]

Contemporary Liberalism: A Defence of the Bourgeois Order

It follows that liberalism in the post-Second World War period has not only changed its character, it has also taken upon itself the challenge of saving mankind from the tyranny of a totalitarian system. As such, contemporary liberalism manifests a disposition to anti-intellectualism directed in general against the state and in particular against the Hegelian and collectivist theories of the state. It also finds place in more and more emphasis on the personality of the individual and his social groups and thereby regards the state as little more than a federation of groups, a union of guilds, or a community of communities, a piece of administrative machinery useful for coordinating activities and adjusting claims between conflicting groups, but not in itself responding to any unique and peculiar need of the human spirit which is capable of being satisfied by no other form of organisation.[58] However, the most outspoken aspect is the emphasis on saving the individual from tyranny whether of a class (as happens under a communist system), or of a mob (as happens in a democracy), or of a party (as happens in a fascist system) and the like. In brief, contemporary liberalism has faith in the value of the free expression of individual personality, men's ability to make that expression valuable to themselves and to the society, and the upholding of those institutions and policies that protect and foster both free expression and confidence in that freedom.[59]

Contemporary liberalism is, however, interpreted as a defence of the bourgeois order on account of its renewed emphasis on the need for distributive justice implying economic freedom to the individual. Mention in this regard may be made to the works of Schumpeter, Dahl, Chapman and Rawls whose revisionist liberalism has virtually gone to the extent of presenting 'an almost obliteration of the democratic content of traditional liberal democratic theory.'[60] This type of liberalism can be traced in both the criticism and the appreciation of representative system that attaches undue

57. Laidler, *op. cit.*, p. 252.
58 Joad, *op. cit.*, p. 38.
59. W.G. Smith: "Liberalism" in *Encyclopaedia of the Social Sciences*, edited by E.R. Seligman (New York: Macmillan and Free Press, 1968), Vol. 9, p. 276.
60. Macpherson, *op. cit.*, p. 77.

significance to every Tom, Dick and Harry and, at the same time, its justification and appreciation as the best possible system on account of its dedication to the cause of human liberty. Thus, Schumpeter describes the 'democratic method' not as something aimed at the realisation of the common good by the representatives of the people carrying out the will of the people—that might appear as fantastic nonsense—but just as an effort on the part of the individuals to acquire the power to decide by means of a competitive struggle for the people's vote.[61] Robert A. Dahl treats democracy as a mechanism, the essential function of which is to maintain the equilibrium so that the principle of distributive justice remains undisturbed.[62]

Such an affirmation finds its eloquent manifestation in the 'Justice and Fairness' of Prof. J.W. Chapman who says that justice not only permits inequality, but also requires it, since the first principle of distributive justice appears to be the distribution of benefits which maximises benefits in accordance with the principle of consumers' sovereignty.[63] Likewise, Prof. John Rawls in his paper 'Distributive Justice' holds that institutionalised inequalities which affect the prospects of a man's life are inevitable in any society. Social distinction on the basis of wealth or income is in order and the principle of distributive justice has to deal with such an inequality. In this way, Rawls proposes and defends his principles of justice as a criteria for judging the moral worth of various distribution of rights and income only within a class-divided society.[64] In this way, the eminent liberals of the bourgeois class have tried to introduce, or reintroduce, a concept of man as essentially a doer, an exerter, and enjoyer of his human attributes.[65]

That the renewed emphasis on the factor of economic freedom in a free market society has taken contemporary liberalism away from the world of socialism is evident from the argument of Prof. Milton Friedman who has made a bold attempt to defend and explain the meaning of contemporary liberalism with a view to prove that socialism is incompatible with political freedom. The burden of his argument is

61. See J.A. Schumpeter: *Capitalism, Socialism and Democracy* (New York: Harper, 1950).
62. See R.A. Dahl: *A Preface to Democratic Theory* (Chicago: Chicago University Press, 1960).
63. Macpherson, *op. cit.*, p. 81.
64. *Ibid.*, p. 89.
65. *Ibid.*, p. 79. According to R.P. Wolff, John Rawls has, in fact, three purposes. In addition to his conception of rational choice and his settled moral convictions about particular matters of social justice, Rawls also has an extremely powerful commitment to an idealist conception of the harmonious and organic society. Thus, Rawls' work is first a sketch of a proof of theorem in the theory of collective rational choice. Second, it is a complicated sort of rational reconstruction of the social and moral convictions of himself and (he hopes) his audience. And, third, it is a vision of a harmoniously integrated, stable, social and political order whose structure is articulated by the two priciples of justice." *Understanding Rawls* (Princeton: Princeton University Press, 1977), pp. 190-91. But Wolff is not in favour of all that Rawls says. In his view, indeed, Rawls paid so little heed to political facts as to fashion no clear concept of the state even though that agency would presumably have to maintain whatsoever standard of social justice he recommended. *Ibid.*, p. 202. Alan Bloom's complaint is that Rawls tendered no advice as how to work out compromises and a middle path where we find on occasion that reason clashes with revelation, love opposes duty to one's country, life is at odds with dedication to the truth, and soon." See his paper titled "Justice: John Rawls Versus the Tradition of Political Philosophy" in *The American Political Science Review* (June, 1975), p. 659.

that competitive capitalism is a necessary condition of political freedom and as such, a socialist society is so constructed that it cannot guarantee political freedom. While defining the scope of state activity, he says: "A government which maintained law and order, defined property rights, served as a means whereby we could modify property rights and other rules of the economic game, adjudicated disputes about the interpretation of the rules, enforced contracts, promoted competition, provided a monetary framework, engaged in activities to counter technical monopolies and to overcome neighbourhood effects widely regarded as sufficiently important to justify government intervention, and which supplemented private charity and the private family in protecting the irresponsible, whether madman or child—such a government would clearly have important functions to perform. The consistent liberal is an anarchist."[66]

However, one important feature of contemporary liberalism that has its peculiar association with the liberals of the United States is its emphasis on the need for a 'free' or 'open' society that virtually implies a frank denunciation of the communist system. Apart from eulogising the presidential system over the parliamentary model and separation of powers over their concentration (as we find in British parliamentary system), American liberals have been very firm in lauding their federal-republican-presidential political system. However, a change in the line of American liberalism can be traced in their growing faith in the increasing authority of the President in the executive, of the Senate in the legislative, and of the Supreme Court in the judicial spheres. What may, however, be described as the peculiarly American tenet in this direction is its emphasis on the idea of an open and plural society as a fundamental aspect of its political creed.[67]

One thing is, however, certain: whether it is old liberalism or its new version, its keynote is individualism. If one scrutinises the progress of liberalism right from the ideas of Locke to those of Laski, one will find that the chief characteristic of this philosophy has been that of individualism, though its keynote has also been a matter of revision from time to time under the guise of different schools. For instance, while the early liberalism of Locke witnessed its revision at the hands of Benthamite utilitarianism, the latter had the same fate at the hands of Mill's empirical collectivism. The progress of liberalism failed to stop even at this stage. What Mill bequeathed to his people found its rectification in the moderate idealism of Green and that, in turn, had its revision in the pluralism of Lindsay and Barker and in the socialism of Cole and Laski. The process is still going on as a result of which the premises of liberalism may be seen adequately revised in the philosophy of 'possessive individualism'—a term coined by Prof. C.B. Macpherson—which has three cardinal characteristics:[68]

1. Man, the individual, is seen as absolute natural proprietor of his own capacities, owing nothing to society for them. Man's essence is freedom to use his capacities in search of satisfactions. This freedom is limited properly only by some principle of utility or utilitarian natural law which forbids harming others. Freedom, therefore, is restricted to, and comes to be identified with, domination over

66. Milton Friedman: *Capitalism and Freedom* (Chicago: University of Chicago Press, 1962), p. 34.
67. Volkomer: *The Liberal Tradition in American Thought*, p. 13.
68. Macpherson, *op. cit.*, p. 199.

things, not domination over men. The clearest form of domination over things is the relation of ownership or possession. Freedom is, therefore, possession. Everyone is free, for everyone possesses at least his own capacities.

2. Society is seen, not (as it has been) as a system of relations of domination and subordination between men and classes held together by reciprocal rights and duties, but as a lot of free equal individuals related to each other through their possessions, that is, related as owners of their own capacities and of what they have produced and accumulated by the use of their capacities. The relation of exchange (the market relation) is seen as the fundamental relation of society.
3. Finally, political society is seen as a rational device for the protection of property, including capacities; even life and liberty are considered as possessions, rather than as social rights with correlative duties.

From what we have said above, it appears that liberalism is a philosophy whose demands have been for the liberation of man from an oppressive political rule or intolerant ecclesiastical authority, or from a status of slavery or serfdom, from restraints embodied in laws and customs that hamper the rise of new productive forces, or from the limitations on equal opportunity resulting from narrow concentrations of private economic power, from limitations on voting rights and from interferences with freedom of religion, speech and association. "The constant concern has been with pleas for deliverance from restraints which, although perhaps widely regarded at a given time as a normal part of life, have come to be regarded, by some in the community, as unnatural and intolerable."[69] In other words, a liberal is one who is concerned with the inviolability of his rights that are possessed by a man not only as a means for the realisation of certain values, but as values in themselves. He also believes that the rights are 'natural' as a man is distinguished from other animals by his faculties of reason, speech, sense of justice, and a capacity for independent thought and action. He believes that order and agreement are goods that may be sought extravagantly, by means that confuse or destroy the sort of consensus upon which the security and strength of a democracy depend."[70]

Neo-Liberalism or New Right

Also known by different names as 'new individualism', 'neo-conservatism' and 'New Right', neo-liberalism, as advocated by President Reagan in the United States and Prime Minister Thatcher in Britain, seeks to replace the 'welfare' state' by a 'strong state'. The model of welfare state, as given by Laski and Keynes, and established in Britain, West Germany and Sweden after the Second World War revealed its inherent fallacies after about three decades. The liberal-democratic state expanded its area of activity in the name of rendering socially useful services. In course of time, such a state became an 'over-loaded state' ridden with corruption and maladministration. In such a situation, the ideas of the negative liberals like Hayek and Nozick justifying the case of a 'minimal state' came up to pave the way for the 'rolling back' of the welfare state.

69. F.W. Coker: "Some Present-Day Critics of Liberalism" in *The American Political Science Review*, Vol. XL VII, No. 1 (March, 1953), p. 1.
70. *Ibid*, p. 27.

Michael Foucault on Bio-Politics and Liberalism

1. Bio-politics is a politics concerning the administration of life, particularly as it appears at the level of population. Liberalism can be understood as a form of critique of excessive government. It should be regarded as a critique of police doctrines or reason of state as well as of existing and potential form of bio-political government. For liberalism, the problem will not be a rejection of bio-political regulation, but a way of managing it. It retains a concern with security and advances a novel conception of the objective of government as setting in place mechanisms of security whose function is to assure the security of the natural phenomena, economic processes and the intrinsic processes of population. It has more of an affinity with the norm than with the law. First; it constantly seeks a norm of good government in the changing balance between governing too much and governing too little and, second, it implies mechanisms that strive to stabilise and normalise subjects in such a way that they exercise freedom in a respectable and disciplined manner.[1]
2. Liberalism participates in and fosters the 'society of normalisation'. It lays emphasis on the formation of the responsible exercise of freedom as necessary to the security of autonomous processes of economy, society and population. Liberalism multiplies and ramifies 'dividing practices', that is, practices in which 'the subject is either divided inside himself or divided from others'.
3. Liberalism can justify authoritarian types of governments for those regions deemed 'unimproved' like Africa or degenerate or static like China, to use John Stuart Mill's judgements. In such countries, despotism is the best form of government. For such nations, their only hope of making any steps in advance depends upon the chances for a good despot.
4. Foucault's account of liberal governmental formations suggests a complex articulation of the issues of bio-politics and sovereignty. It is an articulation of the elements of the shepherd-flock game concerned in its modern form to optimise the life of the population and normalise the identities of the individuals with it, and of the 'city-citizen' game in which the individual appears as an active and responsible citizen within a self-governing political community and within a commercial society.
5. At the hands of Foucault, liberalism has a curious appreciation in his attack on the doctrine of socialism, particularly national socialism as zealously advocated by Hitler in Germany. It has a kind of state-racism inscribed on its premises. As the Nazis brutally suppressed the Jews, the socialists do the same in dealing with their opponents whom they denounce as exploiters and oppressors by virtue of being the owners of the means of production and distribution. In socialism we find a form of government that combines market-based norms and bio-political interventions into the intimate life of the people in a non-liberal manner in order to realise the objective of quantity and quality of the population necessary for the socialist plan. The tortures and injustices of a socialist state may be visualised in the activities of ethnic cleansing, appropriation of private property, or genocide at a vast scale. As he says: "If genocide is, indeed, the dream of modern powers, this is not because of a recent return of the ancient right to kill; it is because power is situated and exercised at the level of life, the species, the race, and the large scale phenomena of population."[2]

1. Mitchell Dean: *Governmentality: Power and Rule in Modern Society*. (London: Sage Publications, 1999), pp. 121-22.
2. Michael Foucault: *The History of Sexuality*, (London: Allen Lane, 1979), Vol, I. p. 137.

The essential features of neo-liberalism may be enumerated as under:

1. Individuals are 'rational creatures' who know their interests. Only they can decide as to what they need or desire, hence lesser the state intervention in their life, the better for them. The neo-liberals desire extension of 'market' to more and more areas of life and the creation of a state stripped of 'excessive involvement' both in the economy and in the provision of opportunities.
2. If so, the state should reduce its burden of rendering useful public services as the individuals may manage these affairs themselves. State and market should be taken as friendly to each other. Hence, private initiative should be given encouragement. The activities of the labour unions and all other bodies supported by the socialsts demanding more and more restrictions on the private sphere should be restrained.
3. It may be inferred that the neo-liberals desire a return to the *laissez faire* model as advocated by Adam Smith and Mill. But such an inference is misfounded. The neo-liberals desire to curtail the welfare state and replace it by a 'strong state' in the light of the requirements of the day. Now the state is required not to eradicate the gigantic evils of poverty, ignorance, disease, starvation, unemployment and squalor as recommended in the Beveridge Report of 1943, rather its essential function is to deal with the new challenges posed by the new gigantic evils as the menace of nuclear proliferation, cross-border terrorism, environmental pollution, serious epidemics and racial and ethnic conflicts. For this purpose, not a weak or a minimal but a strong and hegemonic state is required.

It shows that the neo-liberals, in general, "are committed to the view that political life is or ought to be a realm of individual freedom and initiative."[71] Thatcher appreciated the view of Hayek that a welfare state clears the 'road to serfdom' and it should be taken as 'state-administered socialism'. The role of the state should be minimised in the political and economic spheres of course, but it should be maximised for the sake of defence of the realm and preservation of the civil society. In this way, neo-liberalism "is committed to the classic liberal doctrine that the collective good (or the good of all individuals) can be properly realised in most cases only by private indviduals acting in competitive isolation and pursuing their sectoral aims with minimal state interference. This commitment to the market as the key mechanism of economic and social regulation has a significant other side in the history of liberalism; a commitment to 'strong state' to provide a secure basis upon which, it is thought, business, trade and family life will prosper."[72]

The New Rightists are said to present a 'hegemonic project' that divides them into two categories. "While the neo-liberals attempt to reassert the autonomy of the market by proclaiming, in essence, that the economy works best when left alone by the government. In this way, economic and social life is portrayed as a private sphere over which the state exercises no rightful influence. Neo-conservatives, on the other hand, call for the restoration of authority, order and discipline. In particular, this reflects a desire to strengthen the authority of the government, at least in relation

71. David Held: *Political Theory and the Modern State*, p. 139.
72. *Ibid.*, pp. 139-40.

Essential Features of New Right

1. **Belief in Freedom:** They place tradition at the top of their values and what they mean by this term is the absence of coercion.
2. **Freedom, Democracy and Equality:** They deny that democratic government is a means of extending freedom. All legislation reduces freedom irrespective of whether it is enacted by elected assemblies or dictatorships. Democratic government is often a means by which majorities can impose their will on minorities and from the viewpoint of the minority the fact that the decision has been arrived at 'democratically' offers little consolation for the loss of individual liberties. It follows from all this that freedom and equality are, to some extent, incompatible objectives. To make people equal is to prevent some of them from doing what they want, since it would benefit them more than others.
3. **Personal Responsibility:** Enjoyment of liberty also entails responsibility for the consequences that follow when we exercise these liberties.
4. **Competition and Innovation:** Innovation will not occur in a society where the state owns or controls the means of production or where higher rewards are prohibited in the name of social justice. A state monopoly has no spur to innovate.
5. **Planning versus Market:** Markets are not chaotic or anarchist, for firms plan to meet anticipated demands, workers plan career moves to enhance their prospects and so on. A state planned system puts all eggs into one basket.

Source: Jean Dearlove and Peter Saunders: *Introduction to British Politics* (Cambridge U.K.: Polity Press, 2000), pp. 409-13.

to what the New Rightists regard as its proper role: law and order, public morality and defence."[73]

One may ask as to where do the neo-liberals stand? Their attack on the 'nanny state' (welfare state) is understandable in that it makes the people indolent and helps the undeserving people at the cost of the deserving ones. Such a state promotes wrong ethos of equality. It repudiates the sane view of Herbert Spencer that 'the ultimate result of shielding fools from folly would be to fill the world with fools'. To overcome these failings of the welfare state, the neo-liberals suggest that "we must go 'beyond entitlements', and focus instead on people's responsibility to earn a living. Since the welfare state discourages people from being self-reliant, the safety net should be cut back, and any remaining welfare benefits should have obligations tied to them."[74]

---

73. Andrew Heywood: *Political Theory: An Introduction,* p. 149. According to Fraser King, the "promise of neo-liberalism seems to be that a just society (narrowly defined) is achieved by uncoerced market exchanges. More markets lead to less state both in totality and in its potential to intervene, if there are no goods for social distribution in a market-led society, the role of the state is limited to the protection of property rights and other related tasks, e.g., national security and external defence." Refer to his paper "Neo-Liberalism: Theoretical Problems and Practical Inconsistencies" in Mike Mills and Fraser King (eds): *The Promise of Liberalism: A Comparative Analysis of Consensus Politics* (1995), p. 12.
74. Will Kymlicka: *Contemporary Political Philosophy: An Introduction* (New Delhi: Oxford University Press, 2002), II ed., p. 157.

Such an affirmation makes the neo-liberals faithful disciples of Hayek and Nozick who are regarded as libertarian thinkers. But the difficulty arises when the neo-liberals want to defend the case of a a mini-welfare state that takes them close to the idea of an egalitarian like Rawls. Their aim is to 'roll back' the welfare state, not to roll it out. The advocates of this trend look like hovering between the poles of libertarianism and egalitarianism with a definite slant towards the former which is vitiated by the 'neo-conservatives'. They certainly fail to draw a clear picture of their attempt to reconcile the model of free economy with a strong state. A line of political and ideological tension between neo-liberalism and neo-conservatism may be seen that enables a critic to say that it "does not so much constitute a coherent and systematic philosophy as an attempt to marry two distinct traditions."[75]

Communitarianism

It is a new philosophy that attacks the premises of both liberalism and socialism and, at the same time, seeks to establish a synthesis of the two in its own way. Popularised in the 1980s and 1990s by some theorists like A. McIntyre, Daniel Bell, Charles Taylor, Michael Sandel and Michael Walzer, it has carved for itself a place somewhere between classical or negative liberalism, on the one hand, and modern or positive liberalism touching the verge of socialism, on the other. It criticises old liberalism for making individual 'unencumbered' or unconcerned with the good of the society. At the same time, it criticises modern liberalism for expanding the role of the welfare state to an extent that the autonomy of the individual is circumscribed or attenuated in the superficial name of the 'public good'.

If man's concern with community's good (public good) is the essential feature of communitarianism, the idea is quite old having its place in any variety of socialist thought. It is a different thing that some writers trace its reflection in the utopian socialism of Robert Owen of England and in the anarchist thought of Peter Kropotkin of Russia who dwell on the salient traits of fraternity and cooperation. The founders of scientific socialism like Marx and Engels and the architects of fascism like Mussolini and Gentile place the interest of the individual under the higher interest of the folk or community and, at the same time, they curiously go to the extent of justifying state absolutism. Basically different from this is the view of the communitarians who align themselves with liberalism by laying stress on the autonomy of the individual to the extent that it is conducive to the higher cause of the public good. While they attack the liberals for portraying the 'self' as social and cultural and for failing to provide a moral basis for social order and collective endeavour, they stress the importance of the common and collective interests and hold that there is no such thing as 'unencumbered self', the self is always constituted through the community.

The central claim of the communitarians "is precisely the necessity of attending to community alongside, if not prior to, liberty and equality. The communitarians believe that the value of community is not sufficiently recognised in liberal theories of justice, or in the public culture of liberal societies."[76] The state should not live like a neutral organisation in matters that are good for the community. Michael Sandel

75. Andrew Heywood: *Politics*, p. 49.
76. Will Kymlicka, *op. cit.*, p. 208.

Communitarianism

What they have in common is a rejection of the core principle of liberalism which can be taken to mean that each individual is the sole legitimate decision-maker in what counts as good for himself.

—David Robertson

A Dictionary of Modern Politics, p. 102.

From the communitarian perspective, the central defect of liberalism is its view of the individual as asocial, atomised, 'unencumbered self'. The communitarians emphasise that the self is embedded in the community, in the sense that each individual is a kind of the embodiment of society that has shaped his or her desires, values and purposes.

—Andrew Heywood

Political Theory: An Introduction, p. 35

We all approach our own circumstances as bearers of a particular social good...Hence, what is good for me has to be the good for one who inhabits these roles.

—Alasdair MacIntyre

After Virtue: A Study in Moral Theory, pp. 204-05.

Communitarians and their Arguments

A. MacIntyre: Moral relativism as preached by liberalism is inadequate in providing a moral basis for social order. There can be no universal norms of justice and virtue, for they are the offshoots of specific intellectual traditions.

M. Walzer: Society is ridden with complex equality, so different rules should apply to the distribution of different social goods.

M. Sandel: The principles of ethical life are socially created and so the preferences or identity of the individuals are structured by the 'moral' bonds of the community.

Charles Taylor: Each culture has its unique and authentic essence that has its manifestation or embodiment in the identity of its members.

Will Kymlicka: Liberalism should be harmonised with multicultural citizenship; cultural affiliations constitute the identity of the citizens.

affirms: "A politics of the common good, by expressing these shared constitutive ends, enables us to know a good in common that we cannot know alone."[77] Likewise, Taylor says that "many liberal theories are based on atomism, on an utterly facile moral psychology according to which individuals are sufficient outside of society."[78]

However, the communitarian conception of the public good is quite different from such a conception of the Marxists. While the former take in their view the case of the society as a whole, the latter confine it to a particular 'class'. "A communitarian state is, therefore, a perfectionist state, since it involves public ranking of the virtues of

77. Michael Sandel: *Liberalism and the Limits of Justice* (Cambridge: Cambridge University Press, 1982), p. 183.
78. Charles Taylor: *Philosophy and the Human Sciences* (Cambridge: Cambridge University Press, 1985), Vol. II, pp. 190-91.

different ways of life. But whereas Marxist perfectionism ranks ways of life according to a trans-historical account of the common good, communitarianism ranks them according to the conformity to existing practices."[79]

The main features of communitarianism may be put as under:

1. Do not treat individual as a selfish, asocial, acultural and atomistic creature having an 'unencumbered self' concerned with his own pleasures that, according to Bentham, make 'greatest happiness of the greatest number'. The self of the individual is embedded in the community in that each individual, in the words of Rousseau, is an integral part of the whole community that shapes his desires, values and purposes. Since man is a social creature, he draws much from his social life. His beliefs and experiences originate from the social contract that makes them meaningful. Individual is not the disembodied subject, his self is 'encumbered by his social and public life'.[80]
2. The society of atomised individuals, as conceived by the liberals like Bentham, Mill, Rawls and Nozick, disintegrates, because there occurs a gap between selfish endeavours of the individuals and their obligations to the community. In the absence of, what Habermas calls, 'communicative action', society cannot be differentiated from the communistic society of the former Soviet Union. Thus, the communitarians desire to rectify the imbalance between modern society and political thought; their projects attempt to restore to society its moral voice and to construct the politics of the 'common good'.
3. The communitarians hold that self or person is constituted through the community in the sense that the individuals are shaped by the communities to which they belong and thus they owe them a debt of respect and consideration. Hence, there are no 'unencumbered selves'. But it has three varieties. Left-wing communitarians hold that the community demands unrestricted freedom and social equality. It is the view of the anarchists. The centrist communitarians hold that the society is grounded in our acknowledgement of reciprocal rights and responsibilities. It is the perspective of Tory paternalism and social democracy. The right-wing communitarians hold that community requires respect for authority and established values. This is the view of the New Right.[81]
4. The communitarian tradition has certain layers within itself. It is said to have two forms - high and low. While the former engages primarily in philosophical debate, the latter is concerned with the issues of public policy. It is also said to have two more forms - old and new. While the old communitarians (social democrats) look to Marx and have a desire to re-make the world, the new communitarians look to Hegel and desire to reconcile people to their world.[82] The new communitarians are united by the belief that political philosophy must pay more attention to the shared practices and understandings within each society. They also agree that it requires modification of the traditional liberal principles

79. Kymlicka, *op. cit.,* p. 220.
80. Ibid.
81. Andrew Heywood: *Politics,* p. 173.
82. Kymlicka, *op. cit.,* p. 209.

of justice and rights. However, they differ on how the principles should be modified.[83]

Differences in the views apart, what all communitarians have in common is the rejection of the core principle of classical liberalism which can be taken to mean that each individual is the sole legitimate decision-maker in what counts good for himself. Communitarians, in contrast, "see community through tradition and history socialising people into moral values, and see actors as most content when they live out the value of their community and assist in its development. Communitarians in their own language wish to stress the duties of the citizens as much as their rights."[84]

From a critical standpoint, it may be commented that there is a deep tension between the communitarian concept of the 'self' and the liberal commitment to the priority of civil rights. This much of the communitarians may be accepted that there are shared ends that can serve the basis for politics of the common good which will be legitimate for all groups in society. But the difficulty is that they "give no examples of such ends – and surely part of the reason is that there are none."[85] We may accept that liberalism may not do enough in regard to public good, but if liberalism is the problem, how could communitarianism be the solution.[86] Derek Phillips says that the communitarians are either looking backward or looking forward and their two perspectives generate very difficult political conclusions.[87] Such a criticism may not be accepted on its face value as it does not apply to all the communitarians if we deeply examine the views of the liberal and conservative communitarians. Though an egalitarian, Rawls says that the people can be communitarians in their private life, liberals in their public life. Communitarianism has a conservative disposition in that it amounts to a defence of the existing social structures and moral codes. But it "is certainly difficult to locate communitarians on a simple left-right continuum: one can find elements of conservative reaction and progressive reform in most communitarian authors."[88]

Critical Appreciation

The political philosophy of liberalism has been a subject of criticism at the hands of its advocates as well as its opponents, by the former on account of their polemical interpretations and by the latter on account of their indictment of the premises of individualism. The curious thing about the philosophy of liberalism is that it has been denounced, rejected, revised and defended by the leading lights. We may, at this stage, refer particularly to the observations of Prof. Laski who criticised the

83. A. Gutman: "Communitarian Critics of Liberalism" in *Philosophy and Public Affairs,* Vol. 22, No. 3, pp. 308-22.
84. David Robertson: *A Dictionary of Modern Politics* (London: Europa Publication, 2002), III ed., p. 102.
85. Kymlicka, *op. cit.,* p. 259.
86. Don Herzog: "Some Questions for Republicans" in *Political Theory,* Vol. 14, No. 3, 1986, p. 484.
87. See Derek Phillips: *Looking Backward: A Critical Appraisal of Communitarian Thought* (Princeton: Princeton University Press, 1993).
88. Kymlicka, *op. cit.,* p. 273.

values of the 'bourgeois' class and yet laid emphasis on the virtues of freedom and tolerance. However, he attacked the elements of 'obedience' in the liberal tradition to the extent it 'emphasises the contingent nature of the state's authority."[89] Likewise, his successor Michael Oakeshott commented that 'a philosophy of crude and uncritical individualism is, in fact, inconsistent with social democracy."[90]

1. The weakest point in the principle of liberalism is contained in its being a highly flexible and fluid philosophy that may mean anything from this much to that much of liberty of the individual. Everyone is a liberal from Locke to Oakeshott if he shows his concern with the problem of liberty *vis-a-vis* authority while keeping himself committed to the cause of preserving, defending and valuing the factor of individual liberty. And it is in this direction that the liberal tradition may be said to have its intellectual coherence. Thus, no student of modern political philosophy (especially of England) "would reasonably deny the name of liberal to any of the men represented in this connection, yet each of them Fox and Bentham, Richard Cobden and Lloyd John Russell, Macaulay and Acton, Herbert Spencer and T.H. Green, Gladstone and Lloyd George, Mill and Keynes held views widely different in some respect from those of others. And these differences are differences not only of policies and programmes—those are more easily explained but also of principle, for example of the role of the state, the vexed question of *laissez faire*."[91]
2. Notwithstanding the highly flexible or fluid character, of the principle of liberalism, it cannot be denied that, in the main, it has been the philosophy of the well-to-do class. Most of the liberals have belonged to the bourgeois class and their arguments have subscribed to the reactionary and anti-socialist literature. One may say that even the assimilation of the elements of socialism in the theory of liberalism in the post-Second World War epoch is nothing else than a shrewd way to keep the philosophy of *laissez faire* up-to-date. By all means, liberalism is the philosophy of the rich class that struggles for freedom in the social, political and economic spheres so that the trends of exploitation and injustice remain perpetrated. Even Laski may be accused of hovering between the poles of capitalism and socialism in his critical appreciation of the traditional English philosophy of liberalism and his ultimate abandonment of the Marxist orientation in the 1940s that he so strongly deemed to have in the 1930s. Thus, an authority on his political ideas says that he (Laski) "alternates between the positions that real liberties are confined to the few who own property and the thesis that the present capitalist crises inevitably mean the destruction of the significant political liberties as well as the social and economic gains of the positive state."[92]

---

89. Laski: *The State in Theory and Practice* (London: George Allen & Unwin, 1960), p. 52.
90. See W.H. Greenleaf: *Oakeshott's Philosophical Politics* (London: Longman's, 1966), p. 61.
91. See Allan Bullock and Maurice Shock (ed. s): *The Liberal Traditions from Fox to Keynes* (London: A and C Black, 1956) p. xix.
92. Herbert A. Deane: *The Political Ideas of Harold J. Laski* (New York: Columbia Univ. Press, 1954), p. 180.

3. Apart from being a fluid, indistinct and reactionary philosophy, liberalism is also accused of being a vulgar and 'deceptive' theory. It may by denounced for dealing with appearances only ruminating on the materials provided by scientific economy in search of plausible explanations of the most obstructive phenomena for the daily use of the bourgeois class. It may also be held guilty of replacing the genuine scientific inquiry with either the bad conscience and the evil intent of an apologetic or a shallow syncretism of which Mill is the best representative who gave a new type of 'socialism' that became the foundation of English Fabianism in clear distinction to the political philosophy of scientific socialism given by Karl Marx. In brief, the contributions of the great liberal thinkers are like a hotchpotch in which we find an attack on, and also a powerful defence of, what are known as great liberal values. It may, therefore, be pointed out: "Over the whole span of three hundred years of liberal society and thought, the deceptive task of political theory appears to vary inversely as the limitation of bourgeois vision and directly as the extent of the apprehended threat to liberal values."[93]

It may, however, not be denied that liberalism is the philosophy of humanism—emphasis on the worth and dignity of the individual who is free to make the best of himself. It may be described as the 'timeless quality' of this philosophy. One may also say that liberalism has its negative as well as positive aspects; it also has its critical and constructive dimensions. It not only attacks the institutions and systems that are detrimental to the liberty of the individual, it also suggests the lines of reform and reconstruction. In appreciation of this peculiar philosophy, an eminent writer on the subject says that the business of liberalism "seems to be not so much to build up as to pull down, to remove obstacles which block human progress, rather than to point out the positive goal of endeavour or fashion the fabric of civilisation. It finds humanity oppressed, and would set it free. It finds a people groaning under arbitrary rule, a nation in bondage to a conquering race, industrial enterprise obstructed by social privileges or crippled by taxation, and it offers relief. Everywhere it is removing superincumbent weights, knocking off fetters, clearing away obstructions."[94]

In a word, the present-day criticisms of liberalism are varied, even mutually contradictory, and they issue from various sources. In particular, the Fascists and the Communists are alike in denouncing liberals as 'deluded idealists or incompetent intellectuals.' Others accuse liberalism of becoming essentially negative, neutral, middle-of-the-road stereotyped, mechanical doctrine, or it is a dogmatic, pretentious, aggressive, positively dangerous doctrine. Thus, the liberal theory is dubbed as a

93. Macpherson, *op. cit.*, p. 203. Such a deceptive meaning of liberalism creates confusion in the sphere of state activity. For instance, it may be said that if the test of a liberal government "is that the rule of law should be secured and that the area of private independence be respected, strictly, even an enlightened despot can satisfy that test. Fredrick of Prussia was highly praised by Kant precisely on that score: for having enabled his subjects to use their reason and to speak their mind, thus removing all hindrances to the spread of enlightenment." Alexander Passerin d' Entreves: *The Notion of the State: An Introduction to Political Theory* (Oxford: Clarendon Press, 1967), p. 211.

94. Hobhouse, *op. cit.*, pp. 14-15.

moral, secular, religiously indifferent, anti-religious, and a liberal as too much the perfectionist—self-righteous and 'priggish' in his political policies. Thus, a liberal is variously identified by these critics as distinctively sentimental, idealistic, romantic, Utopian, intellectual, academic and the like. To Spengler it seems that a liberal's concern for individual or minority rights and freedoms leads only to blindness, cowardice and spiritual indiscipline; he describes modern liberal as either bourgeois or plebian—both being terms of abuse.[95] In very harsh terms, Lenin treats every liberal like 'an armchair fool'.[96] In spite of all this, it cannot be denied that "the principal postulates of the liberal movement—individual freedom, human rights, political rights, the rule of law—are today, at least nominally the accepted common ground of all democratic forces."[97] "Undoctrinaire, tolerant, jealous of the rights of the individual, it is precisely this quality that has provided its resilience and flexibility—perhaps the most precious political quality there is, enabling change to be brought about without crisis."[98] These values have pervaded all sections of the society and the British writers endorse this with a sense of pride: "There is not a single institution in the country which has not felt the impact of these ideas while at the deeper level of instinctive feeling they have become a part of the national character, finding expression in the tradition of 'fair play'."[99]

95. Oswald Spengler: *The Hour of Decision,* Translated from German into English by Charles Francis Atkins (New York, 1934), p. 109.
96. *Ibid,* p. 119.
97. Ernst Bieri: "Modern Liberalism" in *Swiss Review of World Affairs,* Vol. IX, No. 12 (March, 1960), pp. 13-16.
98. Derek Heater, *op. cit.,* p. 25.
99. Allan Bullock and Maurice Shock: *The Liberal Traditions,* p. liv. So says D.G.Smith: "The importance of the liberal temper and of liberal principles applied to politics has not diminished: probably it has increased. Liberalism thrives on material prosperity, social peace, and common enlightenment." *Op. cit.* p. 282.

19

Existentialism

> The animal is immediately identifiable with his life-activity. It does not distinguish itself from it. It is its life-activity. Man makes his life-activity itself the object of his will and of his consciousness. He has conscious life-activity. It is not a determination with which he directly merges. Conscious life-activity directly distinguishes man from animal life-activity.
>
> —Karl Marx[1]

Existentialism—the name of a 'trend', a 'tendency', an 'idea', or an 'attitude' rather than a philosophical school[2]—has come to occupy a significant place in the realm of contemporary political theory in view of the fact that most of its exponents take strong political-philosophical positions in sharp contrast to both logical positivists and analytic political philosophers who, according to them, "tend not to assert political philosophies."[3] Though an 'idea' primarily concerned with analytic philosophy, it is undoubtedly the 'best publicised, the most controversial, and yet still the least understood' development in contemporary political theory.[4] In this chapter an attempt has been made to discuss the meaning and nature of this trend, tendency, attitude, idea or philosophy in its diverse manifestations with special reference to the contribution of its best exponent—Jean-Paul Sartre—who has done the unique work of reconciling this 'anti-Marxist philosophy' with his modified version of Marxism and that has led to this important question: What is dominant in him— Marxism or Existentialism?

Existentialism: Nature and Essential Implications

Though a 'philosophy' having its source of inspiration in different schools and thereby making its meaning rather confusing, existentialism, according to the version of its 'Father' (Soren Kierkegaard), finds its original and fundamental meaning in the rejection of all purely abstract thinking. Claiming themselves as the advocates of a purely logical or scientific philosophy, all existentialists reject the force of abstract rationalism and insist that philosophy should be connected with individual's own life and experience, with the historical situation in which he finds himself. Strictly speaking, it should be a philosophy *capable of being lived.* It is the personal that is real. Reason may help, it cannot dictate. As such, philosophy "should start from one's

1. Marx: *Economic and Philosophical Manuscripts,* p. 75.
2. *Encyclopaedia Britannica,* 1967 Ptg., Vol. 8, p. 964.
3. J.A. Gould and V.V. Thursby: *Contemporary Political Thought: Issues in Scope, Value and Direction* (New York: Holt, Rinehart and Winston, 1969), p. 100.
4. Richard Gill and Ernest Sherman: *The Fabric of Existentialism: Philosophical Literary Sources* (Englewood Cliffs, New Jersey: Prentice-Hall, 1973), p. 3.

own experience, one's own inner knowledge, which should be qualified, enlarged and, in this way, enriched."[5]

A better way to understand the meaning of existentialism is suggested by drawing a line of distinction between 'essence' and 'existence'. While the former is said to refer to the true nature of things that may be considered in an abstract way, the latter is concerned with the actual behaviour or experience of man, that is, a *concrete* phenomenon. Thus, while essentialism is concerned with 'the humanness of man, the horseness of horse', existentialism is 'not the humanity of man, but this man John, whom I know, or this particular horse which I possess and love'. The existentialists contend that idealism is concerned with ideas and concepts or with a man of abstract nature and thus it becomes a 'philosophy of essence'. Opposed to this, existentialism, as Sartre asserts, is contained in the maxim: 'existence precedes essence'. The purpose of the existentialists is, therefore, to start with existence and experience it so that the real things are adhered to and that may be verified by the actual experiences of man.[6]

In other words, existentialism is a violent reaction against the Age of Reason—an age in which eminent thinkers like Rousseau and Kant prided themselves upon being reasonable and rational and thus resuscitated the maxim that 'man is a rational creature'. This well-known Aristotelian dictum found its best manifestation in the affirmation of Hegel that 'what is real is rational and *vice versa*'. It was in the 'age of reason' that the leading lights studied reason not only as man's highest faculty that could act as a solvent of all human problems and, what is more, ultimately provide him with a complete and all-embracing knowledge by virtue of being positive and entirely flawless and thus the highest product of creation. So deep became the emphasis of the idealist thinkers on this particular element of human personality (reason) that it looked like an absolute phenomenon—an ultimate part of reality, underived and not determined by anything else, with inherent powers knowing no finitude. The philosophy of existentialism thus arose against this tendency of rational absolutism. Its leading advocates started with this assumption that "man is not purely a rational creature." Experience shows that "reason is part of human nature, that it is influenced by human nature, that its powers are limited, and that reason, therefore, cannot and must not be considered as absolute. It is this violent, unreasonable, fundamentally irrational claim of reason which, in turn, produces the violent and now purely irrational reaction of Existentialism."[7]

It follows that existentialism stands on the foundation of personal experience. Obviously, it rejects the thesis of determinism that is connected with the relationship of cause and effect. The essential sanction is personal *experience* and not an innate belief in anything of a supernatural, absolute or transcendental nature. Not an objective but a subjective, way is required to understand the weight and role of feelings and sentiments whereby we may understand and describe the actual behaviour of man. External things "will not enable us to make value-judgements, or even to grasp values at all, it can deal neither with ultimate truth which is the basis of our convictions,

5. Paul Roubiczek: *Existentialism For and Against* (London: Cambridge Univ. Press, 1964), p. 10.
6. *Ibid.*, p. 11.
7. *Ibid.*, p. 1.

for even the acceptance of the scientific knowledge as the only knowledge requires a personal decision, nor with goodness or beauty."[8]

It may, however, be added by way of an explanation that the advocates of existentialism do not militate against the faculty of reason in the same way as the thinkers of the Age of Reason did while revolting against the premises of theology. The philosophers of the Age of Reason sought to eliminate all theological presuppositions whatsoever and, therefore, to them, external, practical and scientific thinking seemed to be the best way to use 'reason' at whose altar even God could be sacrificed. Contradistinguished from them, the existentialists took to the course of either totally rejecting the role of reason in man's life or making it subservient to the weight of personal experience. Despite the fact that while some existentialists have gone to the extent of laying down that reason should be dropped completely if we really seek to understand and experience the sphere of values, morality and religion, a balanced version of their approach may, however, be epitomised in the phrase: 'reason must not dominate but serve'. As Unamuno puts it: "Man is said to be a reasoning animal. I do not know why he has not been defined as an affective or feeling animal."[9]

Differently stated, existentialism is a stern reaction against classical philosophy that attempts to rationalise and to think 'Being'. Though a philosophy of Being in its own way, it should be described as 'a philosophy of attestation and acceptance and a refusal of the attempt to rationalise and to think Being'.[10] According to it, Being can be understood not by the actual faculty of man, it can be experienced 'in a personal venture to which philosophy is the call.[11] The existentialists contend that we are given a world where pretensions must be broken, a world to be both accepted and refused, a life to be built on the further side of despair. Knowledge being irremediably incomplete and uncertain throws the weight of responsibility upon personal decision; reason alone can limit reason and its present duty is to restore the concrete and thus to eliminate the false theoretical problems which have haunted philosophy and illumined the real problems for which there are no theoretical solutions. As each aspect of the human situation "is lit up, the light is reflected upon the personal isolation and responsibility of the existing individual at the centre."[12]

Emphasis on 'subjectivity' and 'primacy of the individual' constitutes the essential feature of existentialism. The exponents of this philosophy react against the tendency of actualising the ideal or idealising the actual as it occurs in the systems of Plato,

---

8. *Ibid*, p. 5.
9. Cited in Gill and Sherman, *op. cit.*, p. 17.
10. H.J. Blackham: *Six Existentialist Thinkers* (London: Routledge and Kegan Paul, 1961), p. 150.
11. *Ibid.* Existentialism tends to distinguish between being and existence, using being for the world in which men live and which constitutes the object of enquiry and knowledge. Knowledge requires determinateness—in some degree—in the thing known: it thus aims at essences. 'Existence' is then saved for being-a-man, striving, incomplete, indeterminate, not characterizeable as essence. See Nathaniel Lawrence and Daniel O'Connor: *Readings in Existential Phenomenology* (Englewood Cliffs, New Jersey: Prentice-Hall, 1967), p. 4.
12. *Ibid.*

Rousseau and Hegel in which each individual is given an appointed place and he enjoys expansion and self-transcendence by means of active participation in a world of absolute good. A peculiar form of reconciliation between the ideal and the actual is sought to be established. To the existentialists the two—ideal and actual—should be kept apart as their separation is the 'foundation of all foundations' and to abolish it in a total reconciliation is to undermine personal existence itself.[13] As such, the peculiarity of the philosophy of existentialism is that it deals with the separation of man from himself and from the world, which raises the question of philosophy, not by attempting to establish some universal form of justification which will enable man to readjust himself but by permanently enlarging and lining the separation itself as primordial and constitutive of personal existence. The main business of this philosophy, therefore, "is not to answer the questions which are raised but to drive home the questions themselves until they engage the whole man and are made personal, urgent and anguished."[14]

The existentialists contend that if the speculative fantasies of the classical rationalist philosophies were true in principle and the individual could be assigned an appointed place in a system, man as man could not exist. The real purpose is not to seek or establish a perfect order in which individual is assigned an appointed place but to study the fact that it is disorder which founds and refounds the human order of personalities which are temporal and modest but never final. It is this disorder that always keeps man involved in an ocean of continuous responsibility "It is the solitariness of decision that discharges the responsibility responsibly."[15]

In short, existentialism affirms the primacy, or priority, of *existence.* It may, however, be asked: In relation to what is this primacy or priority affirmed? The answer is: in relation to *existence.* An existentialist is not interested in essences, possibilities, and abstract concepts; he is at the farthest pole from the mentality of a mathematician, or a man of logic or metaphysics; his sole concern is directed towards that 'which *exists,* or rather towards the existence of that which exists.'[16] Existence is not an attribute, but the reality of all attributes; it consists in the first place, in 'a return to veritable reality.'[17] As a leading German existentialist Karl Jaspers puts: "Existence is not a concept but an index which points to what is beyond all objectivity."[18] According to Sartre, existentialism stands for the 'primacy of existence over consciousness' as the object of its fundamental affirmation. In one of his writings *Action* he puts: "Man first is—only afterwards he is this or that. Man must create for himself his own essence." Or even more clearly: "Man is not, but what he makes of himself."[19]

---

13. *Ibid.,* p. 151.
14. *Ibid.,* pp. 151-152.
15. *Ibid.,* p. 155.
16. Paul Foulquie: *Existentialism,* Translated from French into English by Kathleen Raine (London: Dennis Dobson, 1963), II, Impression, p. 42.
17. *Ibid.,*
18. *Ibid,* p. 49.
19. See Roubiczek, *op. cit.,* p. 121.

Existentialism

All the great philosophical ideas of the past century had their beginning in Hegel: the philosophies of Marx and Nietzsche, phenomenology, German existentialism, and psycho-analysis; it was he who started the attempt to explore the irrational and integrate it into an expanded reason which remains the task of our century.

—**M.Merleau-Ponty,**
Sense and Non-Sense, p. 63.

Marxism contains within itself, in its very principle, infinite possibilities of development and renewal.... In order to achieve this aim it was essential forcibly to stress--too forcibly, may be, since it necessitated breaking with an ingrained habitual procedure - the aspect of dialectical transcendence, with all the break and discontinuity in relation to the past that it implies.

—**R.Garaudy,**
Marxism in the Twentieth Century, p. 211.

The total man is both the subject and the object of the Becoming. He is the living subject who is opposed to the object and surmounts this opposition. He is the subject who is broken up into partial activities and scattered determinations and surmounts this dispersion. He is the subject of action, as well as its final object, its product even if it does seem to produce external subjects. The total man is the living subject-object, who is first of all torn asunder, dissociated and chained to necessity and abstraction. Through this tearing apart, he moves towards freedom; he becomes Nature, but by bringing it under control. The total man is de-alienated man.

—**H.Lefebvre,**
Dialectical Materialism, pp. 162-63.

Existentialism in Politics: A Philosophy of Freedom, Choice and Commitment

The 'trend', 'tendency', 'idea' or 'attitude' of existentialism pertains to the realm of philosophy. However, what brings it into the realm of political philosophy is its stark emphasis on, what is euphemistically termed, 'choice of freedom' or 'freedom of choice'. Man is man only when he has 'freedom' and a free life is one in which he may choose actions—actions that may give substance to freedom and even enrich it. The existentialists contend that if we merely act as we like, we may succumb to unnoticed compulsions from within or without and thus bury our freedom again. Freedom may perhaps be best defined as acting "entirely by our own free will, but if we are not to be enslaved again, we must also be willing to act in accordance with our true nature, so that it can find its full expression; otherwise, we shall find that we are forced into actions which violate that nature."[20]

It is choice, then, that becomes the door to 'authentic selfhood' and that, at its deepest level, culminates in commitment. It enables man to choose his life-path rather than that of another, or go for one set of values over others. A 'responsible' individual is one who is unsentimentally choosing whatever obligations or consequences follow from his decision.[21] As Soren Kierkgaard in his work *Either/Or* says that the choice itself "is decisive for the content of the personality, through the

20. *Ibid.*, p. 122.
21. Gill and Sherman, *op. cit.*, p. 32.

choice the personality immerses itself in the thing chosen."[22] Or, as Sartre puts it in his writing *'Existentialism is a Humanism'*: "We want freedom for freedom's sake and in every particular circumstance. And in wanting freedom we discover that it depends entirely on the freedom of others, and that the freedom of others depends on ours. Of course, freedom as the definition of man does not depend on others, but as soon as there is involvement, I am obliged to want others to have freedom at the same time that I want my own freedom. I can take freedom as my goal if only I take that of others as a goal as well. Consequently, when in all honesty, I have recognised that man is a being in whom existence precedes essence, that is he is a free being who, in various circumstances, can want only his freedom, I have at the same time recognised that I can want only the freedom of others."[23]

Two special points may be noted here. First, the existentialists do not talk of a limitless, absolute freedom touching the verge of 'license' but of someting limited by external conditions, more by the essence of human existence. The concept of freedom must not be allowed to degenerate into that of arbitrariness, rather it should be made consonant with the whole sphere of morality, responsibility and fundamental values of social system. Second, the idea of freedom should be studied in positive and not in negative terms. That is, choice should be exercised by man in a way that enriches his freedom and not *lessens* it. In other words, choice should be 'right', not 'wrong', inasmuch as while a 'right choice' makes man free, a 'wrong choice' causes his enslavement. Thus, the existentialists contend that we must choose the right kind of freedom and action.

The concept of freedom is inextricably linked with man's commitment - man's action in the context of his social relationships. As Sartre says: "The individual cannot be human by himself. Self-being is only real in communication with other self-being." Marcel who has, in fact, criticised Sartre's view as 'negative', points towards community in his own primary notions of love, fidelity and participation which assume the actuality of genuine rapport between the individual and others. Albert Camus in his novel *The Plague* shows how men can achieve solidarity through suffering together and can experience community even in the face of death. Among other existentialists, Martin Buber, of course, not only makes community the very cornerstone of his own thinking, but through his eloquent elucidation of 'I-Thou relationship' as a truly essential dialogue between the self and an equally authentic, subjective 'other', really opens up the possibility of a new turning for the whole of existentialism.

It is this stark emphasis of the existentialists on 'choice' and 'freedom' that takes this doctrine to the world of extreme, even anarchic, individualism. The 'primacy of the individual' is the fundamental touchstone. Not an abstract but a concrete man is the real object. As Unamuno in his work *The Tragic Sense of Life* affirms: "The man of flesh and bone; the man who is born, suffers and dies...." As such, a proper political order is one in which man does not suffer from his 'depersonalisation' or from the pattern of an 'inauthentic life'. The 'crowd is untruth' as says Kierkegaard, while man, in the words of ancient Greek philosopher Protagoras, is 'the measure of all

22. *Ibid.*
23. *Ibid.*, p. 531.

things'. The key factor is the possibility of 'free choice' that involves the element of 'subjectivity'. The individal is free and he is condemned to be free according to the dictates of the 'truth of subjectivity'.

It is due to this that the leading existentialists have gone to the extent of subscribing to different 'ideologies' while sticking to their emphasis on the 'freedom' of the individual. For instance, Martin Heidegger embraced Nazism, Karl Jaspers adhered to liberalism and, the most curious of all, Sartre sought to reconcile Marxism with existentialism. And it is because of this that different exponents of this philosophy have differently looked at the political values and thereby lauded or denounced different patterns of social and political order in their own ways. For instance, while Kierkegaard and Nietzsche "looked on all politics as a degradation of the individual; socialistic and democratic socio-political institutions were particularly contemptuous. Heidegger bent to Nazi rule in Germany without resistance and his philosophy says little of politics; in his later writings he rejects all political involvement and all ethics as well. In contrast, Sartre, Merleau-Ponty, Camus and de Beauvoir have been continuously engaged and outspoken in both French and international politics since their fight in the resistance against Nazi occupation armies."[24]

Genesis and Growth of Existentialism : Emphasis on a 'New Philosophy of Life' in Denmark and Germany

Modern existentialism, also called 'contemporary irrationalism' by its critics, is said to have come into being in the later half of the nineteenth century when the so-called 'philosophy of life' as represented by Nietzsche, Dilthey and Simmel in Germany and Henry Bergson in France emerged on the scene. The basic idea of this 'philosophy of life' signified that the concept of matter should be replaced by the concept of life inasmuch as rational knowledge operating with petrified abstract concepts and capable of dealing only with rigid bodies could never comprehend the changing, flowing, actual, individual thing what they called 'life'. The irrationalist thinkers suggested that reason killed life, dissected it, arrested its constant movement and, for this reason, in order to know life, or rather to 'grasp' it, there must be *intuition*—direct experience of life which would fundamentally differ from reason. In their interpretation of the social processes, the 'irrationalists' believed that they "were guided not by the development of objective material factors that man could know and ultimately come to control, but by mysterious instincts, the lust for power, the mystical life urge, in short, by the unknowable irrational forces."[25]

The horrors and disasters of the First World War had an impact of their own in transforming the trend of 'bourgeois liberalism'. The 'illusion' that social progress would spread rationally and harmoniously in the course of history was superseded by a sense of the meaninglessness of social existence, the futility of the historical process and a feeling of profound impotence. As a result, the "movement of existentialism gathered momentum at the hands of its exponents like Martin Heidegger and Karl

24. Robert C. Solomon: *From Rationalism to Existentialism: The Existentialists and Their Nineteenth-Century Backgrounds* (New York: Harper & Row, 1972), p. 245.
25. See *The Fundamentals of Marxist-Leninist Philosophy,* Translated from Russian into English by Robert Daglisb, (Moscow: Progress Publishers, 1974), p. 614.

Jaspers in Germany and Gabriel Marcel, Albert Camus and Jean-Paul Sartre in France, while O.Y. Gasset of Spain and Nikolai Berdyaev of Russia may also be described as the leading existentialists of the day.

It may be pointed out that the existentialist understanding of existence springs from three main sources. In the first place, we may refer to the 'religious philosopher of the nineteenth century' Soren Kierkegaard of Denmark, who proposed the actual concept of 'existentia' and the idea of the 'existing thinker' who must consider reality subjectively—as reflected through his individual existence or his emotional life. He affirmed that a subjective thinker 'is substantially interested in his thought: it exists in him.' Though he himself never intended to initiate a movement or found a school and he did not see himself as a professional philosopher at all, he offered a varied and voluminous literature to outflank and undermine what he considered the dangerous and ever-widening assault of the 'objective philosophers' upon orthodox Christian faith. And yet he was not a religious apologist in the correct sense of the term. In his first work evocatively captioned as *Either/Or* he challenged the Hegelian notion of meditation. In his another work *The Sickness Unto Death,* he diagnosed the more typical but no less agonising forms of despair which are experienced by those who live in accordance with the ethical but which the ethical can neither cope with nor cure.

What, however, made Kierkegaard the 'acknowledged father of modern existentialism' is his stark emphasis on man. In his *The Sickness Unto Death* he asserted: "Man is spirit. But what is spirit? Spirit is the self. The self is a relation which relates itself to its own self...."[26] He did not spare even the values of the prevailing bourgeois society that had undermined the worth and dignity of man. In *The Journals* he went to the length of saying: "The bourgeois always jumps over one fact in life which is why they are always a parody of those above them....Morality is to them the highest, far more important than intelligence; but they have never felt an enthusiasm for greatness, for talent even though in its abnormal form. Their ethics are a short summary of police ordinances; for them the most important thing is to be a useful member of the state, and to air their opinions in the club of an evening; they have never felt homesickness for something unknown and far away, nor the depth which consists for being nothing at all...."[27]

The unique and the unexpected thread in the writings of this Danish philosopher should, however, be traced not in his defence of the orthodox Christian faith as in his consistent attack on all abstract and metaphysical philosophy that had its culmination in the works of Hegel. It is this fact that assigns to him the credit of being the 'father of modern existentialism'. Though inspired by the ideas of Pascal, he claimed "to have found a full explanation of everything, of the universe and man, by his reasoning. He insisted that philosophy should not be abstract, but based on personal experience, on the historical situation in which man finds himself, so that he could become the basis, not of speculation but of each man's life. The only evidence to be accepted was that which both could be and had been tested by experience."[28]

26. See Gill and Sherman, *op. cit.,* p. 151.
27. *Ibid.,* p. 149.
28. Roubiczek, *op. cit.,* p. 55.

Another source of inspiration should be discovered in the teachings of a German philosopher Edmund Husserl who suggested the technique of singling out the *a priori* structure of consciousness, that is, a certain ontological basis of human existence. He tried to discover the structure of cognition in the course of a phenomenological investigation concerning only the phenomenon of 'pure consciousness'. With this end in view, he performed an 'operation' (known as 'reduction' or 'putting in parenthesis') that consisted in abstracting ourselves from the existence of the external world, from the content of the natural and social sciences, from immediate mental reactions—emotions, aesthetic and moral feelings, etc. That which remains as 'pure consciousness', which characteristically is directed at a certain object ('intentionality') and has 'matter' and 'form' and also elements of 'meaning in general' and 'objective meaning', is the *a priori* structure of consciousness that determines the structure of all knowledge.

It was this technique of phenomenological description of consciousness, that was taken over by the existentialists to describe the structure not just of the cognitive consciousness but of the active, suffering, feeling consciousness of 'existence', that is to say, of existence which does not simply know the world but colours it with all the shades of its emotional state. The result is that whereas in classical metaphysical philosophy the world is such as represented by the cognition, in existentialism it is such as the people experience it. Moreover, it is not 'life' as such that matters, it is the individual life. As such, existentialism is concerned with two main themes—the inner significance of the individual in contrast to 'others', and the uniqueness of the individuals in opposition to the 'average' representative of the human race. It is in the light of these problems that existentialism tries to discredit scientific knowledge on the one hand and argues the case for irrationalism on the other. This is mainly apparent in the key concept of existentialism—'existence', human existence, which is 'unique being'.[29]

An elaborate manifestation of this tendency should be found in the works of leading twentieth century existentialists like Karl Jaspers, Martin Heidegger, Gabriel Marcel, Albert Camus and Sartre. Though several features of distinction may be earmarked to show divergence of standpoints in their thought, one thing is certain that all militate against the philosophy of idealism. As a result, while in classical subjective idealism the denial of the 'objective existence' of the external world, of its knowability, is combined with faith in the knowability of the subject and the possibility of substantiating scientific knowledge by proceeding from this subject, existentialism asserts that even the subject itself cannot be known by means of rational recognition.

The leading figures of existentialism cited above may be grouped into the prominent categories of German and French existentialists. While Karl Jaspers and Martin Heidegger belong to the former category, Marcel, Camus and Sartre belong to the latter. First, we refer to the ideas of the two German existentialists-Jaspers and Heidegger—of whom the former is said to be 'most faithful to Kierkegaard.' (Berdyaev). Though professionally trained in medicine and clinical psychiatry rather

29. See *Fundamentals of Marxist-Leninist Philosophy*, p. 617.

than in philosophy and theology, he is regarded as 'the one primarily responsible for consolidating existentialism as a leading force in the twentieth century thought'.[30] Curiously, his vast experience with psychiatric patients inspired him to write *General Psychopathology* wherein he expressed his profound awareness of the difficulties to be met within any scientific attempt to do justice to the complexity and richness of the individual human being. More important is, however, his *Psychology of World Views* that sought to rediscover both Kierkegaard and Nietzsche and 'illumine every corner of the human soul'. His best work is *Reason and Existence* in which he reiterated that such an 'illumination' of the individual must involve a freely communicative thought inevitably time-bound relating of one's self to others in 'loving struggle', since "every advance of the individual comes only if other advances too, and every destruction of the other is my own.... to be self and to be true are nothing else than to be in communication unconditionally."[31]

A distinctive contribution of Jaspers is said to lie in his classification of life into real ('authentic') and unreal ('inauthentic') forms—an idea that was elaborated by Heidegger. Jaspers suggested that the 'real depths' of existence were revealed to us only in special conditions or 'frontier situations' that include death, suffering, terror, struggle, guilt, religious ecstasy, mental health, etc. This idea was borrowed by Heidegger who said that 'this man' being something indefinite and at the same time everything, although not the sum total, 'lays down what the mode of everyday existence *(Dasein)* shall be.' The tragedy, however, lies in the fact that 'this man' leads a life of 'inauthenticity'. That is, 'this man' remains like the embodiment of the anonymous public self that ordains his daily actions and, therefore, evades encounter with his 'self-hood'. This is the central theme of his most important work *Sein and Zeit* wherein he dwells upon the significance of 'boundary situation' and places utmost reliance on the 'dread of the death' that gives 'clue to authentic living, the eventual and omnipresent possibility which binds together and stabilises man's existence.'[32]

Existentialism in France: Emphasis on the Philosophy of Humanism

The trend of existentialism has its strong advocates in France where Marcel, Camus and Sartre may be mentioned as the leading lights of the present age. Gabriel Marcel in his *Being and Having* touches several important problems that have their integral connection with existence. In this direction, we may specially refer to his distinction between 'problems' and 'mystery' that shows his existentialist approach. In *Metaphysical Journal* he writes: ".... between a problem and a mystery there is the essential difference that a problem is something which I encounter, which I find in its entirety before me, but which I can consequently take in and bring under my control, whereas a mystery is something in which I myself am involved, and which is, therefore, conceivable only as a sphere in which the distinction of that which is in me and that which is before me loses its significance and initial value. While an authentic problem obeys a certain technique with the help of which it can be

30. See Gill and Sherman, *op. cit.*, p. 456.
31. *Ibid.*, p. 457.
32. See Blackham, *op. cit.*, p. 96.

clearly defined, a mystery by definition transcends all conceivable techniques.[33] It shows that Marcel, like Kierkegaard, is a religious existentialist and, as such, his statement culminates in the curious defence of the supernatural force what he terms *Metaphysical Atlantis.*

The threads of existentialism are well manifest in the novels of Albert Camus. His peculiar contribution is the doctrine of the '*absurd*'. According to him, life is a dull, monotonous and meaningless affair. It is all absurd and there are three ways of dealing with it – suicide, hope, or living with it. The best course, according to him, is to live with it and to encounter it. For instance, in *The Myth of the Sisyphus* he says: 'If I judge that a thing is true, I must preserve it.' In his another work *The Rebel* he affirms that the absurd being the only truth in this world, the essence of the human situation, the only proper alternative is to live with it and accept it what he calls 'the desperate encounter between human enquiry and the silence of the universe'. Likewise, in his *Resistance, Rebellion and Death* we find him exhorting man 'to exalt justice in order to fight against eternal injustice, to create happiness in order to protest against the universe of unhappiness.'[34]

However, the central figure of French existentialism who has given the movement both its definitive expression and its name is Sartre.[35] He has defined the term 'Existentialism' as a doctrine which makes human life possible and, in addition, declares that "every truth and every action implies a human setting and a human subjectivity."[36] The keynote of Sartre's existentialism is contained in his famous aphorism that 'existence precedes essence'. With a view to explain the meaning of this maxim, Sartre says that it, in the first and foremost place, implies that "man exists, turns up, appears on the scene, and only afterwards, defines himself."[37] In other words, man is nothing but what he makes of himself. "Man is at the start a plan which is aware of itself, rather than a patch of moss, a piece of garbage, or a cauliflower; nothing exists prior to this plan; there is nothing in heaven; man will be what he will have planned to be."[38] Thus, the first principle of existentialism or the first move of an exponent of this philosophy "is to make everyman aware of what he is and to make the full responsibility of his existence rest on him."[39]

Then, subjectivity is the main theme of this tendency. It means, on the one hand, that an individual chooses and makes himself and, on the other, it is impossible for man to transcend his inner self. Man always chooses between good and bad and he invariably goes for the former, and nothing can be good for him as well as for all men without being good for all. The doctrine of existentialism thus comes to rest on the foundation of man's free choice, the absence of which puts him in a

33. See *The Fundamentals of Marxist-Leninist Philosophy,* p. 618.
34. For a better study see Germaine Breed (ed): *Camus: A Collection of Critical Essays* (Englewood Cliffs, New Jersey: Prentice-Hall, 1962).
35. See Robert C. Solomon: *From Rationalism to Existentialism: The Existentialists and Their Nineteenth Century Backgrounds* (New York: Harper & Row, 1972), p. 245.
36. See Sartre's "Existentialism is Humanism", Translated from French into English by Bernard Frechtman, reproduced in Gill and Sherman, *op. cit.,* p. 520.
37. *Ibid.,* p. 521.
38. *Ibid.*
39. *Ibid,* p, 522.

state of *anguish.* This word has a special meaning in Sartre's existentialism. By it he means that the man "who involves himself and who realises that he is not only the person he chooses to be, but also a law-maker who is, at the same time, choosing all mankind as well as himself, cannot help escape the feeling of his total and deep responsibility."[40]

What goes together with *anguish* in Sartre's existentialism is *forlornness* that takes him very close to atheists like Heidegger and Dostoevsky and thus pushes him poles apart from the 'Christian Existentialism' of Kierkegaard and Jaspers. The doctrine of *forlornness* implies that man chooses his own being. As such there is no place for determinism whether idealistic or materialistic. *Man thinks and for this reason he exists.* It is by virtue of this capacity that there is no reality except action. As he says: "It means that we shall confine ourselves to reckoning only with what depends upon our will, or on the ensemble of probabilities which make our action possible.... Man is nothing else than his plan; he exists only to the extent that he fulfils himself; he is, therefore, nothing else than the ensemble of his acts, nothing else than his life."[41]

Sartre, on this basis, comes to lay down his doctrine of *despair.* Despair follows in the absence of man's freedom to do as per his choice. Man wants free and complete involvement in social life so that he may realise himself in realising a type of mankind, an involvement always comprehensible in any age whatsoever and by any person whosoever and the relativeness of the cultural ensemble which may result from such a choice.[42]

Sartre's stress on the element of *forlornness* implying his total rejection of any supernatural or divine power and his stern emphasis on man's action and his free and total involvement in the social process reveals his unmistakable faith in 'humanism'. As he emphatically affirms: "The existentialist will never consider man as an end, because he is always in the making... man is constantly outside of himself; in projecting himself, in losing himself outside of himself, he makes for man's existing; and, on the other hand, it is by pursuing transcendent goals that he is able to exist; man, being this state of passing beyond, and seizing upon things only as they bear upon this passing beyond, is at heart at the centre of this passing-beyond. There is no universe other than a human universe, the universe of human subjectivity. This connection between transcendency as a constituent element of man—not in the sense that God is transcendent, but in the sense of passing beyond and subjectivity in the sense that man is not closed in on himself but is always present in a human universe. is, what we call existential humanism. Humanism, because we remind man that there is no law-maker other than himself, and that in his forlornness, he will decide by himself; because we point out that man will fulfil himself as man, not in turning towards himself, but in seeking outside of himself a goal which is just this liberation, just this particular fulfilment."[43]

In short, existentialism, according to this leading French thinker, is nothing else than an attempt to draw all the consequences of a coherent atheistic position, a

40. *Ibid,*
41. *Ibid,* p, 526.
42. *Ibid.,* p. 529.
43. *Ibid.,* pp. 532-33.

philosophical attempt saving man from plunging into the ocean of despair, a doctrine either believing in the non-existence of a divine force or making Him a'non-issue', and, as such, a theory of action by all means standing for the worth and dignity of man.

Jean-Paul Sartre: Integration of Existentialism and Marxism

Sartre, according to Gill and Sherman, is 'the personification of existentialism'.[44] What, however, makes him a very important, rather controversial, figure in the realm of contemporary political philosophy is his curious attempt to reconcile the principles of existentialism with the premises of Marxism. The motivating reason behind it should be traced in his disillusionment with the Soviet-type Marxism that witnessed its horrible mainfestation in 1956 (when Russian troops suppressed the Hungarian freedom movement) as a result of which he severed his connection with the French Communist Party and then sought to remove the dichotomy between the Marxist doctrine that 'man is made by his environment' and his existentialist faith that 'man makes himself. The result is that Sartre supports both Marxism and existentialism and seeks to reconcile the two rather contradictory 'ideologies' in his own way by revising them in the light of 'new experiments' that informs a commentator to designate him as 'perhaps the most curious socialist who ever lived'.[45]

While existentialism emphasises the individual and his free choice and Marxism stresses the unified group and determining forces, a pertinent question arises as to how the two can be reconciled without sacrificing one at the altar of another.[46] The astonishing feature of Sartre's political philosophy should be traced in his confident affirmation that although existentialism is a 'parasitic system', it has the task of curing the *lethargy* of contemporary Marxism.[47] This distinctive contribution of the eminent French existentialist is contained in his famous tract 'Marxism and Existentialism' of 1957 in which he has dwelt on the following arguments:

1. Sartre begins with his own definition of the term 'philosophy'. To him, it is, first of all, a particular way in which the rising class becomes conscious of itself notwithstanding that this consciousness is clear or confused, direct or indirect. Philosophy is like a mirror that must be presented as the 'totalisation

---

44. *Ibid.*, p. 482.
45. E.M. Burns: *Ideas in Conflict* (London: Methuen, 1963), p. 298.
46. A line of fundamental distinction between existentialism and Marxism may be found in this affirmation that while the latter regards the former as an ideological reflection of Capitalism's inability to prevent crises and wars, the reply of the former is that the latter's ideal of controlling nature and society is unrealistic. Moreover, according to the existentialists, there is an element of pride and presumption in claiming to know what future generations of free men will or ought to do. "Whereas the Marxist honours Prometheus for his inventive and hopeful courage, the Existentialist looks upon Sisyphus as the human exemplar because of his disillusioned, hopeless and therefore still more courageous striving. With its emphasis on individuality, Existentialism is undoubtedly a predominating liberal philosophy, but it is a liberalism with no belief in natural social harmony and no hope in man's perfectibility." *Encyclopaedia Britannica*, 1967 Ptg., Vol. 8, p. 965.
47. See Jean-Paul Sartre: "Marxism and Existentialism" in Gould and Thursby (eds.), *op. cit.*, pp. 230-55.

of contemporary knowledge'. The business of the philosopher is to effect the unification of everything that is known, following certain guiding schemata which express the attitudes and techniques of the rising class regarding its own period and world. As he says: "Born from the movement of society, it is itself a movement and acts upon the future. This concrete totalisation is at the same time the abstract project of pursuing the unification upto its final limits. In this sense, philosophy is characterised as a method of investigation and explication. The confidence which it has in itself and in its future development merely reproduces the certitudes of the class which supports it. Every philosophy is practical, even the one which at first appears to be the most contemplative. Its method is a social and political weapon.... Thus, a philosophy remains efficacious so long as the *praxis* which has engendered it, which supports it, and which is clarified by it, is still alive. But it is transformed, it loses its uniqueness, it is stripped of its original, dated content to the extent that it gradually impregnates the masses so as to become in and through them a collective instrument of emancipation."[48] It is obvious that, like Marx, Sartre treats philosophy as a living affair that serves a cultural *milieu* for its contemporaries.

2. Sartre unreservedly supports the materialism of Marx by holding that the mode of production of the material world generally dominates the development of social, political and intellectual life. He places his main reliance on the affirmation of Marx that in the social production of their existence, men enter into relations which are determined, necessary, independent of their will; these relations of production correspond to a given stage of development of their material productive forces. The totality of these relations of production constitutes the real foundation upon which a legal and political superstructure arises and to which definite forms of social consciousness correspond."[49] He, however, moves farther than Marx in adding that in the present phase of our history, productive forces have entered into conflict with relations of production. Creative work is alienated; man does not recognise himself in his own product, and his exhausting labour appears to him as a hostile force. Since alienation comes about as a result of this conflict, it is an historical reality and completely irreducible to an idea. If men are to free themselves from it, and if their work is to become the pure objectification of themselves, it is not enough that 'consciousness thinks itself, there must be *material* work and revolutionary *praxis*.[50]

48. *Ibid.*, p. 232. Conscious of a distinction between his acts and himself as an actor, it is the individual's choice on any given occasion to act or to rest tranquil. Such conscious and willed activity is unique to man among all living creatures. Marx's meaning here is more than what is commonly meant by self-consciousness, taking in what some existentialists and present day psychoanalysts refer to as establishing the independence of the 'I', or creating the feeling of 'ego identity'. In Marx's case, however, man always possesses this quality. Bertell Ollman: *Alienation: Marx's Concept of Man in a Capitalist Society* (Cambridge: Cambridge University Press, 1971), p. 112.
49. Sartre quotes from Marx's Preface to his *Critique of Political Economy, ibid.*, p. 237.
50. The Greek word 'praxis' means deed or action. Sartre identifies it with any purposeful activity.

3. The Marxist orientation in the work of Sartre can be vividly seen in his attack on the ideas of the acknowledged Father of Existentialism (Kierkegaard) coupled with his frank appreciation of the main pursuit of the 'Father of Scientific Socialism' (Marx). According to him, the former committed the mistake of treating existence as the 'work of inner life—resistances overcome and perpetually reborn, efforts perpetually renewed, despairs surmounted, provisional failures and precarious victories'—something directly opposed to intellectual knowing. Opposed to this is the Marxian contention. When Marx said that "just as we do not judge an individual by his own idea of himself, so we cannot judge a period of revolutionary upheaval by its own self-consciousness," he was indicating the priority of action (work and social *praxis)* over knowledge as well as their heterogeneity. According to Sartre, Marx is right in asserting that human life "is irreducible to knowing, that it must be lived and produced; but he is not going to confuse it with the empty subjectivity of a puritanical and mystified *petite bourgeoisie.* Marx makes of it the immediate theme of the philosophical totalisation, and it is the concrete man whom he puts at the centre of his research, that man who is defined simultaneously by his needs, by the material conditions of his existence, and by the nature of his work—that is, by his struggle against things and against men."[51]
4. What takes Sartre very close to the world of Marxism is his quest for situating man in his class and in the conflicts which oppose him to other classes, starting with the mode and the relations of production. However, he integrates the basic Marxian contention with his existential philosophy by adding that the new situation can be approached only in terms of existence or its comprehension. In an attempt to integrate the two, Sartre goes on to add: "There is no doubt, indeed, that Marxism appears today to be the only possible anthropology which is at once historical and structural. It is the only one which at the same time takes man in his totality—that is, in terms of materiality of his condition. Nobody can propose to it another point of departure, for this would be to offer to it *another man* as the object of its study. It is inside the movement of Marxist thought that we discover a flaw of such a sort that, despite itself, Marxism tends to eliminate the questioner from his investigation and to make of the questioned the object of an absolute knowledge. The very notion which Marxist research employs to describe our historical society—exploitation, alienation, fetishizing, reification, etc., are precisely those which most immediately refer to existential structures. The very notion of *praxis* and that of dialectic—inseparably bound together—are contradictory to the intellectualist idea of knowledge. And to come to the most important point, *labour,* as man's reproduction of his life, can hold no meaning if its fundamental structure is to project. In view of this default— which pertains to the historical development and not to the actual principles of the doctrine—existentialism, at the heart of Marxism and taking the same givens, the same knowledge, as its point of departure, must attempt in its turn—at least as an experiment—the dialectical interpretation of history."[52] In this way, Sartre goes

51. *Ibid.,* p. 238.
52. *Ibid.,* p. 238.

to the extent of designating existentialism as an 'ideology' and sounds a note of caution that Marxism "will degenerate into a non-human anthropology, if it does not reintegrate man into itself as its foundation."[53]

5. However, the real purpose of Sartre is not merely to integrate the 'first principle' of existentialism with the fundamental tenets of Marxism, or to develop one more type of existentialism at the margin of Marxism but to revise Marxism in a way it reaches very close to the world of humanism. A real union of existentialism and Marxism, according to him, is possible only in the revision of both. If the expulsion of man or his historical exclusion from the Marxist knowledge resulted in the renascence of existentialist thought outside of the historical totalisation of knowledge, it is also needed that the contradictions of a capitalist, even socialist, society (as once obtaining in the Soviet Union and now in any other Communist country) should be understood or comprehended in terms of human existence.

Thus, Sartre appears both like a critic of the present socialist systems and an advocate of a new order in which human freedom and human social relations go together. The pangs of 'alienation' should be avoided whether they exist in a bourgeois or in a socialist society established at the debris of the 'discredited' system after the successful results of a revolution. What is really needed is to rediscover man in the social world and which will follow him in his *praxis.* Sartre confidently affirms that the existing man cannot be assimilated by a system of ideas. Marxism is neither dead nor outdated, it is still very young, almost in its infancy. It is the philosophy of our time. Our thoughts can be formed only upon this 'humus'; they must be contained within the framework which it furnishes for them, or be lost in the void or retrogress. At the same time, Marxism, in order to make it updated, should be integrated with existentialism that addresses itself to experience with a view to discover the concrete man. A synthesis of the two can be conceived only within a moving dialectical totalisation which is nothing else but history or—from the strictly cultural point of view— 'philosophy-becoming-the-world'.[54]

Critical Appreciation

The political philosophy of existentialism with its stern emphasis on the freedom of the individual as its first and foremost hallmark may be criticised on these grounds:

1. It is a peculiar mixture of different and divergent trends, tendencies and ideas. The fact of perplexing diversity can be traced in the appreciation of different, even contradictory, ideologies ranging from liberalism to those of Nazism and Communism and also from the pole of staunch theism to that of rank atheism.

---

53. *Ibid.,* p. 253.

54. *Ibid.,* p. 248. Leszek Kolakowski comments that Sartre's existential philosophy "was quite irreconcilable with Marxism. His relations with Communist Party (of France) were marked by hesitation and ambiguity. He oscillated, in fact, between identification with Communists and violent hostility towards them. His whole political activity was vitiated by fear of being in the typical situation of an intellectual condemning events that he had no power to influence; in short, his ideology was that of a politician *manaque,* cherishing unfulfilled 'ambitions, to be on the 'inside'." *Main Currents of Marxism: Its Origin, Growth and Dissolution* (Translated from Polish into English by P.S Falla), (Oxford: Clarendon Press, 1978), Vol. Ill (The Breakdown), pp. 178-79.

As such, existentialism can hardly be treated as a particular brand of philosophy, much less political philosophy, notwithstanding the fact that the aim of human inquiry, according to its leading exponents, is not to enter into philosophical discourses but to understand the 'concrete' man in the specific conditions and circumstances in which he happens to find himself. For this reason, a critic has termed it a 'Salvationist' philosophy, a combination of the romanticism, ritualism, skepticism, pragmatism, and even something of the utopianism of the past hundred years.'[55] The problem, of course, is peculiarly difficult, because no one knows what our Existentialist is."[56]

2. The keynote of existentialism lies in the appreciation of structures in a living effort to embrace from within the human condition in its totality—in order to live it. Such a philosophy sets no goals, for nothing can be achieved, once and for all or objectively established for mankind. Human existence is realised in personal being, and personal being is a difficult and precarious individual attainment constantly striven for and never permanently possessed, but upheld, drawn on, and rewarded by the rich responsiveness of an objective world.[57] It is, however, questionable whether the basic notions of the existentialists are not so vague or their methods so objectionable that this movement fails to offer any philosophical contribution despite the fact that several eminent exponents characteristically express themselves in several literary and artistic forms. It is thus pointed out that, according to existentialists, only the riches of the entire consciousness can be adequate to the rich ambiguity of life itself.[58] The result is that notwithstanding accessibility to familiarity with the abundant literature, anyone who attempts to acquire a comprehensive and unified view of this trend discovers that there "is no royal road to follow, only labyrinthine path disconcertingly strewn with paradoxes."[59]
3. It may also be added that existentialism is a philosophy of despair, frustration and tragedy. A critic is struck with the horrifying impression that though avowedly concerned with immediate realities of human existence, it should have such an abstract and highly forbidding label. The result is that in the last resort, existentialism "is neither a system, nor a school, nor a creed. There is no particular set of tenets to be propounded or endorsed and in spite of the prominence of the individuals like Sartre, no single thinker functions as its canonical spokesman in the way, for example, Aquinas, Kant and Hegel do for their adherents."[60]
4. Existentialism is not a complete philosophy in spite of the fact that its advocates stage a serious revolt against idealism which they term as 'a one-sided philosophy for placing main reliance on the element of reason as sole reality. One may say that existentialism suffers from the same weakness no matter its exponents sacrifice

55. E.M. Burns, *op. cit.*, p. 291.
56. T.L. Thorson: "The Political Philosophy of Camus" in Gould and Thursby, *op. cit.*, pp. 256-71.
57. Blackham, *op. cit.*, pp. 161-62.
58. Abraham Kaplan: *The New World of Philosophy* (New York: Random House, 1961), p. 117.
59. Gill and Sherman, *op. cit*, p. 4.
60. *Ibid.*

the role of reason at the altar of experience. As reason is not the sole determinant of human behaviour, so is the case with the element of experience. As a matter of fact, both reason and experience have their part in the manifestation of human behaviour. The existentialists are, therefore, accused of often going too far in their 'exclusive emphasis on existence'. In order to achieve true understanding, obviously we need both—essence and existence. "We shall not understand man without understanding this humanity; but neither shall we understand humanity without paying attention to single man and to our own inner experience."

5. A critical examination of existentialism by the Marxists shows their treatment of this 'irrationalist philosophy as another vain effort of the bourgeois intellectuals to find a 'third way' beyond materialism and bankrupt idealism, an effort to remain in the metaphysical world of ideas and individuals in order to escape having to accept historical socialism as it was claimed to exist in concrete reality in the Soviet Union. A leading Marxist Professor of Hungary (Lukacs) thus ridicules existentialism in the name of its 'abstract humanism' and accuses its advocate of not seeing that the problems they have uncovered are rooted in real social relationships, and the path to their solution is the path of transforming the objective relations between people. The 'pessimism' of this philosophy is further borne out by the fact that its basic categories—death and fear, guilt and anxiety, distress and loneliness, anguish and suffering —are treated as universal attributes of human existence. These categories "are tinged with reflections of the real contradictions of capitalism. But existentialisms' confession of impotence in any attempt to change the world inevitably repels people who hope either to 'perfect' the world within its existing framework or to destroy the old world of oppression and build up a new one."[62]

6. If so, how can one take Sartre as a real Marxist and, at the same time, a real existentialist. Certainly a student of contemporary political philosophy is at a loss to determine the real position of this eminent French existentialist. One may say that Sartre's conception of 'freedom' "turns out, in the long run, to be a meaningless abstraction."[63] His philosophy is loaded with the chorus of atheism that reduces itself into the form of pessimism and it appears that having lost his faith in God, he finds it impossible to acquire any other ideal.[64] Sartre, therefore, cannot be a Marxist because Marx, like Hegel, "missed the permanent meaning of man's separation from himself and from the world and Marxist theory deprives man of his real being."[65]

---

61. Roubiczek, *op. cit.* p. 11.
62. *The Fundamentals of Marxist-Leninist Philosophy*, p. 624.
63. *Ibid.*, p. 623.
64. *Ibid.*
65. Blackham, *op. cit.*, p. 157. According to W.J.M. Mackenzie, it "is hard to judge what the exact point of compromise lies between Existentialism and Marxism, but certainly the work stands synthetically for 'Marxism with a human face' and this entails a move from the nihilist end of the identity scale towards concepts of the individual as conditioned by society. "*Political Identity* (London: Penguin Books, 1978), p. 75. It appears that Sartre's concept of alienated man has, what Erving Goffman calls, 'spoiled identity'. Other existentialists have their own weaknesses. For instance, like Sartre, "Camus ran myth and philosophy in double harness". *Ibid.*, p. 76.

In short, existentialism is neither an ideology, nor even a thought, if the terms are understood in their traditional senses; at the most it is a revolt, or a series of revolts, against the supposed attempts of classical metaphysics to reduce human reality to abstract propositional terms and to embrace the individual in an absolute universal system. As such, it encompasses a variety of philosophical ventures sharing the same starting point, yet in the end often at odds with one another. One may, however, carefully add that the position of the existentialists is acceptable only if they are right in asserting that the human condition is fundamentally the same for all individuals. As this is not so, it may finally be commented that "the insights of the existentialists are nothing more than a set of prejudices reflecting their own temperamental bias or the social conditions of our time."[66]

66. Robert G. Olson: *An Introduction to Existentialism* (New York: Dover Publications, 1962), p. 29.

20

Behaviouralism

Accumulation of historical data, broader observation of political prudence, some advance in the statistical measurement of political phenomena, the beginnings but only the faint beginnings of political psychology, adumbrations of social psychology not yet achieved',—these constitute the advances towards technical knowledge of the political process. These are the signs of dawn, but assuredly they are not the day.

—Charles E. Merriam[1]

In the present century, but more particularly since the period following the First World War, it has been realised by the new generation of political scientists that as their discipline aims at explaining life in relation to the struggle for power, it must work outward from the nucleus of the study of government, it should take into account social, psychological and economic factors viewing the state not as a discrete but a related phenomenon.[2] As a result, more and more emphasis has been laid on the study of the role and functions of 'political behaviour' involving the study of psychology of political parties, or elections and behaviour of voting as well as the study of propaganda, pressure groups and revolutions. For this reason, it appears that the object of contemporary political theory "is to understand politics in the most comprehensive fashion possible, to discover the general pattern and order in political facts, to explain these facts adequately, and to construct rules of political action based on this analysis."[3]

Behavioural Movement in Politics: Rise and Growth of a Sub-Field of Inquiry Within the General Discipline

The origin of the behavioural movement in the field of politics owes its origin to the two, though not unrelated, intellectual developments of the present century—one in philosophy and the other in psychology. Reference, in this direction, should be made to the contributions of Ivan Pavlov of Russia and John Watson and B.F. Skinner of the United States who wrote extensively on the subject of 'behavioural psychology' by emphasising that the development and employment of the stimuli-response model should be used for explaining human behaviour. Thus, behavioural psychology turned away from the clinical problems and practices of Freudian psycho-pathology and stressed the observable stimuli, which human beings experience, as the root cause of behaviour. Another development took place in the realm of

1. Merriam: "Recent Tendencies in Political Thought" in Merriam and Barnes (ed.s): *A History of Political Theories: Recent Times* (Allahabad: Central Book Depot., 1969), p. 45.
2. G.E.G. Catlin: *The Science and Method of Politics* (New York: Alfred A. Knopf, 1927), p. 148.
3. Haridwar Rai: "Political Theory: New Viewpoints in Meaning and Method" in *Indian Journal of Political Scince,* Delhi, Vol. XXX, No. 4, 1969, p. 352.

philosophy. Drawing inspiration from David Hume, the logical positivists insisted on the separation of facts from values. They argued that it was necessary to distinguish factual propositions (which are observable and objectively verifiable) from value propositions which indicate the subjective preferences of the speaker and, therefore, cannot be objectively verified. The basic message of both—behavioural psychology and logical positivism—was, therefore, a brute and hard-nosed empiricism.[4]

The two powerful contemporary intellectual currents, referred to above, converged on political science and their essential messages reinforced each other. Scientific discourse became the only language in which meaningful communication was possible and every symbol in this universe of discourse became meaningful precisely because each was unequivocally grounded in sheer empiricism. It inspired a few enlightened men of political science who now came to realise that if their discipline was to deserve its name, a 'thorough purge' was necessary. "Traditional inquiry into the form and content of, what Aristotle termed, the 'good life' became useless, because the question posed was scientifically unanswerable. One man's social heaven is another's hell. Traditional categories of explanation had to be reformulated or cast aside, because they were based on non-observable constructs. 'Ghosts' was Arthur Bentley's contemptuous summation of the concepts of political science in his day (1908)."[5]

The new trend witnessed its manifestation in the writings and expressions of certain enlightened political scientists who could grasp the essential nature of the movement and thus sought to swim across the current of traditionalism. Mention in this regard should be made of the *Human Nature in Politics* of Graham Wallas published in 1908 and the *Process of Government* written by Arthur Bentley of America that appeared in the same year. It had its strong reiteration in the presidential address of James Bryce (delivered at the American Political Science Convention in 1908) when he insisted: "We must have facts, facts, facts." It well demonstrated that the powerful currents of behavioural psychology and logical positivism that had made a high watermark in their respective fields contributed their share to the culmination of the behavioural movement that was aboard in the Anglo-American universe.

As a matter of fact, the "first sightings in the oily waters of political science of the phenomenon variously called political behaviour approach, or behaviouralist research, evidently occurred in the 1920's."[6] The ground-breaking work was done by Graham Wallas of England and Arthur Bentley of the United States and then a host of eminent writers appeared on the scene. Mention in this direction should be made of the *New Aspects of Politics* (1925) by Merriam, *The Science and Method in Politics* (1927) by George E.G. Catlin, *Quantitative Methods in Politics* (1928) by Stuart Rice, *Political Behaviour: The Heretofore Unwritten Laws, Customs, and Principles of Politics as Practised in the United States* (1928) by Frank Kent, and *Psychopathology and Politics* (1930) by

4. Don R. Bowen: *Political Behaviour of the American Public* (Columbia, Ohio: C.E. Merril Pub., 1968), p. 4.
5. *Ibid.*, p. 6.
6. Robert A. Dahl: "The Behavioural Approach in Political Science: Epitaph for a Monument to a Successful Protest" in *American Political Science Review* (December, 1961), pp. 763-72 and reproduced in Gould and Thursby (ed.s): *Contemporary Political Thought : Issues In Scope, Value and Direction* (New York : Holt, Rinehart and Winston, 1969), pp. 118-36.

Harold Lasswell. These notable works showed that as the behavioural movement emerged, it "carried with it the signs of its intellectual paternity—a thoroughgoing commitment to empirical data as the only verifiable source of objective knowledge and an even more thoroughgoing commitment to a reconstruction of the categories of explanation describing political phenomena."[7]

Strictly speaking, behaviouralism in politics is mainly a contribution of the American political scientists notwithstanding the fact that they drew inspiration from several European thinkers, psychologists, philosophers and social theorists. However, the credit of being the intellectual father of this movement goes to Charles E. Merriam of the Chicago University who not only adopted the new approach but also exhorted his students and faculty members to contribute their share to the stock of empirical political theory. In his presidential address delivered at the American Political Science Association in 1925, he hopefully visualised: "Some day we may take another angle of approach than the formal as other sciences do, and begin to look at political behaviour as one of the essential objects of enquiry."[8]

The pioneering contribution of Merriam was enriched by a galaxy of his students and faculty members like V.O. Key, Jr., David B.Truman, Herbert Simon and Gabriel A. Almond who came to be known as the leading lights of the 'Chicago School'. The trend, however, failed to remain confined to the university of Chicago. George E.G. Catlin did the same at the University of Cornell. Besides, a good number of European scholars shifted to the United States in the 1920's who brought with them the messages of psychologists like Sigmund Freud and sociologists like Max Weber. The result was that political science moved closer and closer to psychology and sociology at the hands of eminent American political scientists like Franz Neumann, Paul Lazarsfeld, Hans Speier, Hans Gerth, Reinhard Bendix, etc. The trend continued in the 1930's and found its notable impression in the appreciation at the hands of many American political scientists of a path-breaking work *Political Behaviour: Studies in Election Statistics* written by Herbert Tingsten of Sweden in 1937.

The trend of political behaviouralism, however, became the order of the day in the period after the Second World War when a host of American political scientists "temporarily vacated their ivory towers and came to grips with day-to-day political and administrative realities in Washington and elsewhere: a whole generation of American political scientists later drew on these experiences."[9] The name of Pendleton Herring deserves special mention at this stage who not only played an instrumental role in the creation of Social Science Research Committee but also indicated in the Annual Report of the Committee for 1944-45 that the Council had reached a decision to explore the feasibility of developing a new approach to the study of political behaviour. Focused upon the behaviour of individuals in political situations, this approach called for the examination of the political relationships of man—as citizens, administrators, and legislators—by disciplines which can throw light on the problems involved, with the object of formulating and testing hypotheses, concerning uniformities of behaviour in different institutional settings."[10]

7. Bowen, *op. cit.*, p. 7.
8. See Dahl, *op. cit.*, p. 120.
9. *Ibid.*, p. 122.
10. *Ibid.*

It may be added here that two scholarly propensities characterised much of the discipline's work in the period following the Second World War:[11]

1. "The zeal for a scientific mode of research persisted beyond expectation in innovative ideas unfamiliar to pre-War political science. The new generation of professional political scientists called upon their colleagues to practise science in a new style. To some of the Young Turks it was as if the discipline had yet to enter the age of science. In reality, however, it was a typical case of the practitioners in a learned discipline having both professional skill and vocational reputation while riding the shifting tides of twentieth century academic life, where terms and techniques keep changing along with intellectual fashion. In this sense, it was only natural that the very commitment to science would undergo redefinition from time to time."
2. "The revised conception of science found strong justification in the mid-century liberal matrix of discourse. After Second World War, the political scientists worked within a climate of conventional opinion embracing highly satisfactory arguments to the effect that, when properly done, scientific research and teaching can make valuable contributions to public welfare. Thus, the structures on how political scholars should practise a new view of science as opposed to unimaginatively persisting with the old business of data collecting, fit comfortably within a wider view of assigning social utility to the whole enterprise."

Huge financial assistance granted by the great philanthropic foundations of Rockefeller, Carnegie and Ford facilitated the task of the new generation of political scientists. As a result, centres of advanced studies were established at Palo Alto and at the University of Michigan. Soon after, several leading American universities reoriented their courses of study in political science at the graduate and postgraduate levels. An important event took place in 1962 when the Inter-University Consortium for Political Research was set up under the leadership of Warren Miller to make available the Survey Research Centre's election data. In a very short course of time, the Consortium became a major depository of data from many research projects in the field of politics as the most important institutional vehicle for the study of political behaviour.

However, one very important factor that influenced contemporary political theory in the direction of behaviouralism, and one which all behaviouralists invariably sought to conceal, was the growth of Communism after the Second World War. It may be said without any exaggeration that the American political scientists tried to beat Marxism with the stick of behaviouralism. Under the political and ideological impact of the then Soviet Union the nature and character of the political systems of several countries of the East European region swifty started changing from landed aristocracy to 'socialist democracy'. The liquidation of European imperialism and the emergence of free countries in the Afro-Asian world created a new political *milieu* that attracted its adequate attention. It was clear that in this new world of change in the very character and objectives of states accelerated by rapid technological advances and of a fast changing international political system, the new generation

11. David M. Ricci: *The Tragedy of Political Science: Politics, Scholarship and Democracy* (New Haven: Yale University Press, 1984), pp. 133-34.

of political scientists, particularly of the United States, "needed new approaches, new techniques of research and new concepts for which they had to borrow from other social sciences."[12]

In short, the 'behavioural revolution' as lauded by the Americans, that had announced its advent in the 1920s with great fanfare, returned to full vitality in the 1950s as a result of which political science moved closer and closer to the world of psychology, sociology, also economics at the hands of eminent figures like David Easton, Harold Lasswell and Garbiel A. Almond. A sort of new jargon came into being that witnessed its expression in the works of Myron Weiner, Joseph la Palombara, Sidney Verba, Karl Deutsch, G.B. Powell, R.A. Dahl, David Apter, Edward Shils and a host of others who sought to study political issues in the context of 'non-political' phenomena in a number of ways. Thus, it appeared that the term behavioural political science "still represented an approach, and a challenge, an orientation and a reform movement."[13]

Political Behaviouralism: Meaning and Essential Nature of the Movement

Contradistinguished from the classical or traditional theory, contemporary political theory is said to focus research on actualities, that is, on the disclosure of facts and their interrelationships, basing its findings on painstaking observation and measurement, especially on a rapidly growing stock of pertinent statistics. As such, it "is tending to focus the development of new language and new concepts in establishing intellectual links among its several sub-fields, and its exponents are largely responsible for the development and use of such concepts as power, political system, political socialisation and the like. These concepts cross traditional sub-field lines and their pursuit is essential to the attainment of what they believe should be the current major goal of political theory: the building of a body of an empirical and enduring theory about political life."[14] Thus, we understand contemporary political theory "to mean a systematic, empirical, causal explanation of certain phenomena, whereas in great contrast, the classical political theory referred to moral or philosophical prescription and was interchangeable with political philosophy."[15]

Since political theory is now being considered as the master discipline whereby the 'science of politics' is to be unified and systematised and empirical investigation oriented and guided,[16] the present generation of political scientists, like all social theorists, is said to be divided into the camps of 'extensionists' and 'anti-extensionists'. While the latter are those who hold the position that the application of the scientific method to the study of social phenomena is neither proper nor possible, the former are those who urge the adoption of the scientific method in the study of the social, economic or political phenomena. Obviously, the behaviouralists belong to the category of the extensionists who have a different approach, technique or method with a view

12. S.P. Varma: *Modern Political Theory* (Delhi: Vikas, 1975), p. 58.
13. E.M. Kirkpatrick: 'The Impact of the Behavioural Approach on Traditional Political Science" in Austin Ranney (ed.): *Essays on the Behavioural Study of Politics* (Urbana: Univ. of Illinois Press, 1962), p. 11.
14. Arnold Brecht: *Political Theory* (Bombay: The Times of India Press, 1965), p. 6.
15. Guild and Palmer: *Introduction to Politics* (New York: John Wiley, 1968), p. 267.
16. David Easton: *A Systems Analysis of Political Life* (New York: John Wiley, 1965), p. 6.

to describe and explain the behaviour of man as it constitutes an observable fact. The behaviouralists, as they are called, accept *a priori* human behaviour to be a fact independent of our knowing it. In other words, they "do not pretend to know the origin and destiny of man, but conclude that the only way to understand him is to observe him and record what he does in the courtroom, in the legislative hall, in the hustings. If enough records are kept, we can predict after a while (on an actuarial basis) what he will do in the presence of recognised stimuli. Thus, we can objectively and inductively discover *what* and *where* and *how* and *when,* although not *why*."[17]

Though not very sure about the essential meaning of the term 'political behaviouralism', an eminent American political scientist (Dahl) defines it as 'a protest movement within political science' associated with a number of political scientists, mainly American, who shared a strong sense of dissatisfaction with the achievements of conventional political science particularly through historical, philosophical and descriptive-institutional approaches.[18] Advocates of this approach shared a belief that additional methods and approaches either existed or could be developed that would help to provide political science with empirical propositions and theories of a systematic sort, tested by closer, more direct, and more rigorously controlled observations of political events. He further describes it as a movement for bringing political studies into closer affiliation with theories, methods, findings, and outlooks in modern psychology, sociology, anthropology and economics and an attempt to make the empirical component of political science more scientific.[19]

With a view to explain the essential nature of political behaviouralism, Dahl goes on to add that it aims at studying all the phenomena of government in terms of observed and observable behaviour of men and calls for closer attention to methodological niceties, to problems of observation and verification, to the task of giving operational meaning to political concepts, to quantification and testing, to eliminating unproductive intervening variables, to sources of data hypothesis and theory in other social sciences in search of explanation of some important aspects of politics that are more thoroughly verified, less open to methodological objections, richer in implications for further explanation, and are more useful in meeting the

17. J.C. Charlesworth: "Identifiable Approaches to the Study of Politics and Government" in Charlesworth (ed): *Contemporary Political Analysis* (New York: Free Press of Glencoe, 1967), p. 3.
18. Robert A. Dahl in Gould and Thursby (ed. s), *op. cit.*, p. 124. While realising the difficulty of adding a precise definition of the terra, Dahl frankly opens his paper with these words: "Perhaps the most striking characteristic of the 'behavioural approaches' in political science is the ambiguity of the term itself and of its synonym 'political behaviour'. The behavioural approach, in fact, is rather like the Loch Ness monster: one can say with considerable confidence what it is not, but it is difficult to say what it is. Judging from newspaper reports that appear from time to time, particularly just before the summer tourist season, I judge that the monster of Loch Ness is not Moby Dick, not my daughter's goldfish that disappeared down the drain some ten years ago, nor even a misplaced American eight heading for the Henley Regatta. In the same spirit, I judge that the behavioural approach is not that of the speculative philosopher, the historian, the legalist, or the moralist. What then, is it? Indeed, does it actually exist? *Ibid.*, p. 119.
19. *Ibid.*, pp. 124-125.

perennial problems of political life than the explanations they are intended to replace.[20]

In this way, according to Dahl, the behavioural approach is an attempt to improve our understanding of politics by seeking to explain the empirical aspects of political life by means of methods, theories and criteria of proof that are acceptable according to the canons, conventions, and assumptions of modern empirical science. In this sense, the behavioural approach is distinguished predominantly by the nature of the purpose it is designed to serve. The purpose is 'scientific'. Thus, the behavioural approach might better be called the 'behavioural mood' or perhaps even 'scientific outlook.'[21]

The impressions of Dahl are largely based on the statement of David B. Truman with whom he expresses his 'wholehearted agreement'. Truman wrote an essay "The Implications of Political Behaviour Research" for a seminar held at the Chicago University in 1951 in which he said: "Roughly defined, the term 'political behaviour' comprehends those actions and interactions of men and groups which are involved in the process of governing.... At the maximum, this conception brings under the rubric of political behavior any human activity which can be said to be a part of governing. Properly speaking, political behaviour is not a field of social science; it is not even a field of political science.... Political behaviour is not and should not be a speciality, for it represents rather an orientation or a point of view which aims at stating all the phenomena of governments in terms of the observed and observable behaviour of men. To treat it as a field co-ordinate with (and presumably isolated from) public law, state and local government, international relations, and so on, would be able to defeat the major aim. The aim includes an eventual reworking and extension of most of the conventional 'fields' of political science."[22]

Truman pointed out that the developments underlying the current interest in political behaviour implied two basic requirements for adequate research. First, research must be systematic. That is, it must grow out of a precise statement of hypotheses and a rigorous ordering of evidence. Second, research in political behaviour must place primary emphasis upon empirical methods. "Crude empiricism unguided by adequate theory is almost certain to be sterile. Equally fruitless is speculation which is not or cannot be put to empirical test. The ultimate goal of the student of political behaviour is the development of a science of the political process."[23]

In addition, Truman called attention to the advantages of drawing from other social sciences and yet he cautioned against indiscriminate borrowings. He argued that political behaviour orientation necessarily aims at being quantitative wherever possible. As a student of political behaviour deals with political institutions, he is obliged to perform his task in quantitative terms, if he can, and in qualitative terms, if he must. He agreed that an inquiry into how men ought to act is not a concern of research in political behaviour, but he insisted on the importance of studying values as "obviously important determinants of men's behaviour". Moreover, in

20. *Ibid.*, p. 124.
21. *Ibid.*, p. 128.
22. *Ibid.*, p. 126.
23. *Ibid.*, p. 127.

political behaviour research, as in natural sciences, the values of the investigator "are important in the selection of the objects and the lines of inquiry.... A major reason for any inquiry into political behaviour is to discover uniformities, and through discovering them to be better able to indicate the consequences of such patterns and of public policy, existing or proposed, for the maintenance or development of a preferred system of political values."[24]

However, Truman denied that the political behaviour orientation implied a rejection of historical knowledge which was likely to be an essential supplement to contemporary observation of political behaviour. Though he agreed with the proposal of reorienting the study of political science at the graduate and post-graduate levels, he frankly opposed the notion that the behavioural approach needed the elimination of traditional training. Said he: "Any new departure in an established discipline must build upon the accomplishments of the past. Although much of the existing literature of politics may be impressionistic, it is extensive and rich in insights. Without a command of the significant portions of that literature, behavioural research is likely to be naive and unproductive. Many attempts made by persons not familiar with the unsystematised facts have been subsequently naive even when they may have been methodologically sound."[25]

Salient Characteristics: Easton's 'Intellectual Foundations of Political Behaviouralism'

A correct description of political behaviouralism is contained not in the formulation of a precise definition of the term as in the enumeration of certain salient characteristics that may be designated as its 'intellectual foundations' according to David Easton. A searching analysis of Easton offers both a rather loose definition of the term and an elaborate representation of its general characteristics. In his well-known study of the *Political System* with it sub-title *An Inquiry into the State of Political Science,* he opens the section on the 'Study of Political Behaviour' thus : "To precisely what kind of research does the concept of political behaviour refer? It is clear that this term indicates that the research worker wishes to look at participants in the political system as individuals who have the emotions, prejudices, and predispositions of human beings as we know in our daily lives.... Behavioural research has, therefore, sought to elevate the actual human being to the centre of attention. Its premise is that the traditionalists have been reifying institutions, virtually looking at them as entities apart from their component individuals.... Research workers often use the terms.... to indicate that they are studying the political process by looking at the relation of it to the motivations, personalities, or feelings of the participants as individual human beings.[26]

The assumptions and objectives of political behaviouralism or its 'intellectual foundations' are contained in one of the papers written by David Easton.[27] According

24. *Ibid.*
25. *Ibid.*
26. David Easton: *The Political System* (New York: Alfred A. Knopf, 1953), pp. 201-05.
27. Easton: "The Current Meaning of Behaviouralism" in James C. Charlesworth (ed.), *op. cit.,* pp. 11-31.

to him, the movement of political behaviouralism has been constructed on the following assumptions:

1. *Regularities*: There are certain discernible uniformities in the political behaviour of human beings that can be expressed in generalisations or theories capable of explaining and predicting social phenomena. True that human behaviour lacks uniformity on account of being informed by a host of diverse factors, yet it must be borne in mind that human beings have been observed to behave in certain respects in a more or less similar manner and on different occasions. As such, political scientists should engage themselves in an unrelenting search for regularities of political behaviour and for the variables associated with them, and should give up purely descriptive studies in favour of a rigorous analytical treatment.
2. *Verifications* : Knowledge, in order to be valid, should consist of propositions that have been subjected to empirical investigations. All evidence must be based on observations. Whatever is offered by a researcher should be supported by facts or be verified by the concrete realities of the situation. He may also study the 'sub-surface dynamics' or the 'ideal' and 'metaphysical' dimensions of a political institution and then offer his investigations to the extent that they are verifiable by the facts.
3. *Techniques:* What really distinguishes the behaviouralists from others, called 'traditionalists', is the emphasis on the adoption of correct techniques for acquiring and interpreting data, the use of research tools, or methods which generate valid, reliable and comparative data. A researcher must make use of sophisticated tools like those of multivariate analysis, sample surveys, simulation, etc., that would enable him to discount his own 'value preferences' in planning and executing his research work. The technique, in other words, should be so refined and validated that rigorous means could be found for observing, recording, analysing or testing the data.
4. *Quantification* : Ample recourse should be taken by a researcher not merely to data but also to measure and quantify the same. It would be impossible to obtain precise and accurate knowledge about the complexities of political data unless imprecise quantitative judgements are replaced by vigorous measurement and data manipulation procedures. As in other social sciences, so in the field of political science, data for research should be quantified so that the conclusions or impressions of the researcher may be verified on the basis of quantified evidence. It is, however, necessary that data should be revalidated from time to time and the hypotheses retested in the light of new evidences available to the researcher so that the findings may be made correct and reliable no matter by the course of trial and error.
5. *Values*: The behaviouralists want to adhere to the course of putting facts and values apart. The two should be distinct in an analytical investigation so that ethical and empirical dimensions are treated differently. Scientific inquiry in order to be valid must be free from ethical or moral aspects. Normative dimensions of the concepts like those of liberty, equality, rights and justice cannot be testified in a scientific manner. The approach should be value-free so that the researcher

may not be in a position to examine a political issue from his own standpoint of valuational judgement. In other words, the researcher is concerned with a scientific study of politics in its functional aspects carried through empirical methods and, as such, he has nothing to do with moral or ethical questions.

6. *Systematisation*: It means that research in the field of political science should be systematic—theory-oriented or theory-directed. Both theory and research should form as clearly interrelated parts of a coherent and orderly body of knowledge, and that research untutored by theory may prove trivial as theory unsupported by data becomes futile. Theory should be of a causal nature that does not consist of speculation and introspection but of analysis, explanation and prediction. It is on the basis of well-organised, logically interrelated structure of concepts and propositions that hypotheses have to be advanced, and the hypotheses, in their own turn, have to be capable of undergoing rigorous testing and then alone should form the basis of new theories. The theory may be of three types— 'low level' consisting of singular generalisations, 'middle level' or synthetic or narrow-gauge, and 'general', or broad-gauge or overarching. The ultimate objective of the researcher, however, is the development of overarching generalisations or to discover laws for describing an interrelated political phenomenon with as great an accuracy as that of laws of a natural science like physics.
7. *Pure Science*: The behaviouralists contend that both theory and its application are parts of a scientific enterprise. The understanding and explanation of political behaviour logically precedes, and it alone provides the basis for efforts to utilise that knowledge in the solution of urgent practical problems of society. Research should be of a pure type, that is, it should be perfectly verifiable by evidence no matter it may, or may not, apply to a specific social problem.
8. *Integration*: Since the behaviouralists subscribe to the interdisciplinary approach, they do not treat political science as a separate or distinct discipline. To them, political science is one of the social sciences and, for this reason, it should be integrated with other social sciences like economics, psychology and sociology. The study of a political phenomenon requires an understanding of how economic, psychological and cultural phenomena are unfolding themselves. Man is not a unidimensional creature. As such, if an effort is made to detach the political man from the economic, social or cultural man, it would not be possible to understand his political behaviour in a correct perspective. Hence, the emphasis on interdisciplinary approach. The notable point, in this direction, is that political behaviouralism does not so much indicate the striving towards 'science' as an effort to become interdisciplinary.

Easton confidently affirms that his list probably includes "all the major tenets of a behavioural credo and represents the major differences between the behavioural and the traditional modes of research."[28]

In brief, in politics the behaviouralist "tries to discover regular and uniform political behaviour which will permit him to establish generalisations of explanatory and predictive value."[29] As political science is a branch of the social sciences and

28. Easton, *op. cit.*
29. Sami G. Hajjar: "Meaning and Scope of Behavioural Rationality in Political Science" in *Indian Journal of Political Science*, Delhi, Vol. XXXIII No. 1, 1972, p. 5.

as all social sciences *qua* sciences are 'behavioural sciences', the phrase 'behavioural sciences' (that includes political sciences also) "refers to those bodies of knowledge.... that aspire to provide 'verified' principles of human behaviour through the use of method similar to those of the natural sciences."[30] A leading American writer E. Kirkpatrick underlines four characteristics of the 'behavioural movement' as (a) a rejection of political institutions as the basic conceptual unit and a substitution of the individual and group behaviour, (b) an emphasis on the unity of the social sciences, hence an increased willingness to cross-disciplinary lines, (3) a greater attention to precision, measurement and quantitative techniques, and (4) the development of systematic empirical theory.[31]

Behavioural Approach in Politics: Important Features and Phases of Development

What has been said above leads to this unmistakable impression that the behavioural approach in political science, as in other social sciences, seeks to emulate the scientific method as it applies to the physical sciences.[32] Keeping it in view, Lasswell opines that the expression 'behavioural' is taken to refer to a strong emphasis on joining systematic theory with disciplined observation.[33] It may, however, be added that rather than being a separate or separable area of investigation, the political behaviour approach is applicable to all the conventional interests in political science and all the areas of power. In so far as this approach differs from the traditional, historical, descriptive or legal methods of inquiry, the difference "is not one of objectives but of orientation. In emphasising the behaviour of persons or groups as the units of inquiry, the political behaviour approach cannot possibly ignore the structural and situational variants in the political process which have been of interest to political scientists.[34]

If one were to enlist the most important characteristics of the political behaviour approach, the following may be emphasised:[35]

1. In the first place, the political behaviour approach specifies the behaviour of persons and social groups rather than events, structures, institutions or ideologies, as the unit or object of both theoretical and empirical analysis. It is, of course, concerned with these latter phenomena, but only as categories of analysis in terms of which social interaction takes place in the typically political situations.

30. See Bernard Crick: *The American Science of Politics* (Berkeley: Univ. of California Press, 1959), p. xiv.
31. *American Political Science Review,* 1963, No. 1, p. 162.
32. Conceptually, it can be argued that the scientific method is composed of three distinct phases which are mutually interdependent. They are : (a) the location or discovery of a fact, (2) the establishment of that which is located as a fact, namely the determination of its truth; and, (3) theorising on the basis of truth, or the consequences of the discovered fact. See Hajjar, *op. cit.,* p. 10.
33. Harold Lasswell: *The Future of Political Science* (New York: Atherton, 1963), p. 235.
34. Heinz Eulau, S.J. Eldersveld and Morris Janowitz: (eds.): *Political Behaviour: A Reader in Theory and Research* (New York : Free Press of Glencoe, 1956), p. 3.
35. *Ibid.,* pp. 3-4.

2. It seeks to place political theory and research in a frame of reference common to that of social psychology, sociology and cultural anthropology. This interdisciplinary focus follows inevitably from a concern with behaviour— overt or symbolic. Even though the particular transactions studied are limited to those carried out in pursuit of political roles and political goals, political behaviour is assumed to be a function of personality, social organisation and society.
3. It stresses the mutual interdependence of theory and research. Theoretical questions need to be studied in operational terms for purposes of empirical research. And, in turn empirical findings should have a bearing on the development of political theory. Its empiricism is, therefore, quite unlike the 'brute facts' approach of an earlier descriptive empiricism. It is self-consciously theory-oriented.
4. In general, the behaviouralists reject the institution as the basic unit of analysis and centre their attention on the behaviour of the individuals or their groups. To them, strictly speaking, some of the most interesting phenomena with which political scientists deal cannot be classified as institutions. For example, interest groups and political parties are not parts of the formal institutions of government. Similar is the case with other areas of inquiry like public opinion, propaganda and other channels of political socialisation. The attention of a political scientist should not remain confined to the formal institutions of state and government. Instead he should start with this assumption that any act which involves the use of power is a political act and, therefore, is properly defined, as a part of the province of political science.
5. The ultimate purpose of a political scientist is the construction of a systematic empirical theory of politics—a theory that constitutes reliable knowledge. On the one hand, it means a critique of the traditional methods of gathering and analysing information. On the other hand, it has been used to ignore 'values' and rely only on 'facts'. Value judgements which go beyond the realm of objectivity cannot be tested by criteria open to all.[36]
6. This approach cultivates a belief in the unity of the social sciences. It is in view of the fact that all social sciences have a common subject-matter—human behaviour. The divisions among the social sciences are matters of analytic and practical convenience. They are not, as it were, an eternal configuration of social reality. The boundary lines between the social sciences are based according

36. It should, however, be noted that the word 'value' has two connotations-economic and ethical. In the economic sense, it refers to the relative worth of something to something else that may be measured in terms of money. In an ethical sense, it refers to the standard of worth according to subjective or moral understanding of man. In our discussion at this stage, we are concerned with the latter sense only. The political behaviouralist seeks to reject the value-loaded statement as it cannot be made subject to an empirical verification. One important point should, however, be noted at this stage. A political behaviouralist does not reject value-loaded statement in entirety. The fact-value dichotomy need not and should not mean that the political scientist will eschew value-judgements in the bootless chase for the value-free science On the contrary, political theorists should gladly seize the opportunity to throw off the encumbrances of having to claim cognitive status for the ethical reflections, a necessity under the old positivist dispensation. See Dante Germino: *Beyond Ideology: The Revival of Political Theory* (New York : Harper & Row, 1967), p. 81.

to the role that an individual plays as a parent, a consumer, a voter and the like. Obviously, like a social scientist, the political scientist is concerned with a particular or specific role of the individual. Such an assumption has led to an immense cross-fertilisation of theories and techniques. In good part, political science has been the beneficiary, not the source of these trends.

7. It tries to develop rigorous research designs and to apply precise methods of analysis to political behaviour problems. It is concerned with the formulation and derivation of testable hypotheses, operational definitions, problems of experimental or post-facto design, reliability of instruments and criteria of validation, and other features of scientific procedure. It is in this respect that the political behaviour approach differs from the more conventional approaches of political science. Yet it does not assume that the procedures of the scientific method can be simplifically and mechanically applied to the analysis of the political processes.

As a matter of fact, it is the last point, given above, that has an unparalleled significance for our purpose. What really distinguishes the behavioural approach from other approaches is the advocacy of the development and utilisation of more precise techniques of observing, classifying and measuring data and the employment of the most sophisticated available means of mathematical analysis. As an eminent writer has pointed out, probably, the most outstanding immediate characteristic of the work of the political behaviouralists is that their writings are studded with charts, tables, formulae and mathematical symbols.[37] And it "is probably safe to say that few things exasperate the critics of the behavioural movement more than their tendency to employ mathematical notation for that which could be more easily and simply described in ordinary language."[38]

Traditionalism Versus Behaviouralism: A Break, Continuity as well as Continuing Differences

What we have said in the preceding sections leaves an impression that behaviouralism indicates a sharp break in the continuation of political theory in view of the fact that while the parameters of traditional or classical political theory include the history of political ideas and political philosophy, the behaviouralists seek to orient political theory towards empirical research. In other words, while traditionalism wants 'philosophising about the government, behaviouralism is concerned with 'the observed and observable' behaviour of persons including non-state institutions. The classical theory is largely of a normative character inasmuch as it adheres to an elemental moral question, *i.e.*, what criteria one should use in the evaluation of a political order. Opposed to this, behavioural political theory is of an empirical character that seeks to deal with what constitutes a reliable knowledge.[39]

37. E. Kirkpatrick: "The Impact of Behavioural Approach on Traditional Political Science" in Austin Ranney (ed.): *Essays on the Behavioural Study of Politics* (Urbana: Univ. of Illinois Press, 1962), pp. 1-31.
38. Bowen, *op. cit.*, p. 13.
39. See Robert A Dahl: *Modern Political Analysis* (Englewood Cliffs, New Jersey: Prentice-Hall, 1963), Ch. 1.

The main lines of objection raised by the traditionalists against the premises of political behaviouralism are as follows:[40]

1. Political phenomena by their very nature cannot be subjected to any rigorous study. Human behaviour, whether individual or social, cannot be studied with the objectivity which is necessary in the acquisition of scientific knowledge.
2. Political phenomena are not amenable to experimental inquiry. There are far too many variables and historical contingencies to permit anything but a very general kind of statement of regularities which would hardly lead to generalisation or the discovery of the laws of human behaviour.
3. Even if such laws could be discovered, human ingenuity was always capable of evading them in which case they would lose their validity.
4. While one may not object to one's starting with a hypothesis at the early stage of research, the very purpose of research could be defeated if an attempt was made to adhere to it very rigidly.
5. A purely descriptive approach was also not without its advantages. Many an analysis of political phenomena, based on minute description and arrangement of its various aspects in a sequence of development has shed valuable light on events in the past and has been an important factor in our understanding of political phenomena through history.

The main point of difference, however, lies in linking the study of facts with values. While the traditionalists move in the direction of giving an ethical or moral orientation to their study, the behaviouralists attempt to present a value-neutral statement. As an eminent advocate of classical political philosophy says: "All political action aims at either preservation or change. When desiring to preserve, we wish to prevent a change to the worse. When desiring to change, we wish to bring about something better. All political action is, then, guided by some thought of better or worse. But thought of better or worse implies thought of the good. All political action has then in itself a directedness towards knowledge of the good: of the good life, of the good society. For the good society is the complete political good."[41]

It would, however, be wrong to describe behavioural movement as a radical or complete break if we scrutinise the fact that not all behaviouralists have been thoroughly opposed to the value-laden theory, or that a definite change has captured their mind in the recent years particularly since the presidential address of David Easton delivered at the annual session of the American Political Science Association in 1969, what he termed a 'new revolution in Political Science'. In this address Easton heralded the advent of post-behavioural revolution by registering his "deep dissatisfaction with political research and teaching especially of the kind that is striving to convert the study of politics into a more rigorously scientific discipline modelled on the mythology of the natural sciences."[42] The astonishing feature of Easton's statement consisted in his renewed emphasis on the significance of value-laden theory. As he stressed: "Hence, to understand the limits of our knowledge,

40. S.P. Varma, *op. cit.*, pp. 84-85.
41. Leo Strauss: "What is Political Philosophy?" in the *Journal of Politics,* Vol. XIX (Aug., 1957), p. 343.
42. David Easton: *The Political System*, p. 324.

we need to be aware of the value premises on which it stands and the alternatives for which this knowledge could be used."[43]

The age of post-behaviouralism, as it is now called, has witnessed that both the traditionalists and the behaviouralists have realised their limitations and weaknesses and thus sought to understand each other in a serious attempt to integrate normative premises of political theory with empirical dimensions of research. As a result, while the traditionalists "have come to believe that the behaviouralist has made the discipline more self-conscious and self-critical, opened it up to vital interdisciplinary influences and considerably refined the research techniques and methodologies, the behaviouralists are more aware of the limitations of their theories and conceptual frames of reference and the restrictiveness of their fields of operationality, with the result that the two have learnt to co-exist in a fair state of harmony and understanding."[44] Commenting on this situation, Haas and Kariel observe: "In our view, traditionalists who refused in the 1950s to adopt the behavioural mood may be considered intellectually no less shabby than behaviouralists who decided in the 1960's to spurn the traditional legacy and who refused to confess "their guilt of, what Morton A. Kaplan calls, 'crudities and errors' which have remained curiously resistant to the so-called self-correction techniques of science."[45]

And yet we may find a host of traditionalists like Leo Strauss, M.Q. Sibley and Christian Bay accusing the behaviouralists of being over-zealous in taking political theory towards a scientific study—a trend that shows the state of continuing differences between the two. The traditionalists centre their point of argument on the significance of normative aspects so that we are able to understand what goals we have to seek as ends in themselves. Examined from this standpoint, the traditionalists find behavioural political theory inadequate and hope that it "will inevitably be used within a framework of value-judgements which cannot be supported through behavioural techniques alone."[46] While regarding the behavioural approach as useful, they regard it so only to a limited extent with this word of caution that though the scientific method can be applied to any problem, the final putting together of the segments of life will always be a highly subjective and individual task that can be scientised.

In other words, what the traditionalists now contend is that the premises of behavioural political theory should be accepted as valid to a certain point and that these should be revised in the direction of being value-laden to eradicate the burden of crude empiricism. With a view to establish a working synthesis between the traditional and the behavioural approaches, Sibley counsels thus: "But if the understanding of politics includes comprehension, not only of conduct as it could be under specified conditions but also of what it is, has been, will be, and ought to be.... we must turn not only to the behaviouralist but also to the historian of political ideas, the moral philosopher, the cultural historian, the speculative political philosopher of the classical tradition, the descriptive politicist, and the man of direct political experience."[47]

43. *Ibid.*, p. 326.
44. S.P. Varma, *op. cit.*, p. 83.
45. Michael Haas and T.L. Becker: "The Behavioural Revolution and After" in Haas and Kariel (eds.): *Approaches to the Study of Political Science* (New York: Chandler, 1970), p. 480.
46. Sibley in Charlesworth, *op. cit.*, p. 54.
47. *Ibid.*, pp. 66-67.

Traditional, Behavioural and Post-Behavioural Political Science

Traditional	*Behavioural*	*Post-Behavioural*
1. Interrelates facts and values	1. Separates facts and values	1. Facts and values tied to action and relevancy
2. Prescriptive and normative	2. Non-prescriptive, objective and empirical	2. Humanistically problem-oriented
3. Qualitative	3. Quantitative	3. Quantitative and qualitative
4. Concerned with irregularities and regularities	4. Concerned with uniformities and regularities	4. Concerned with regularities and irregularities
5. Focus on European countries	5. Focus on Anglo-American countries	5. Focus on Third World countries

Critical Appreciation

A critical study of the development of political theory since the Second World War shows that while there has been widespread advocacy of behaviouralism particularly at the hands of eminent American scholars, it has also been a subject of much criticism ranging from an attack on the adequacy of its fundamental principles of theory construction on the basis of observed and observable behaviour of individuals and their collective entities coupled with their verification procedures to the matters of value and to the question whether or not behavioural (empirical) approach can meet them satisfactorily. Most of the behaviouralists now frankly admit that a theory based on pure empiricism is sterile and that imaginative or speculative and, for that reason, non-empirical hypotheses are also necessary for the presentation of an adequate theory of politics. It shows that behavioural political theory has its own limitations that smack of its points of weakness which may be enumerated as under:

1. A student of behavioural political theory is at a loss to know as to what the advocates of this theory mean by the word 'political' that precedes the word 'behaviour'. If we examine the views of eminent political behaviouralists in this direction, we find that all of them have defined the term 'politics' in their own way ranging from Easton's thesis of 'authoritative allocation of values' to Lasswell's dictum of the 'influence and the influential'. It is at least doubtful whether it is possible to define the term 'political' without reference to the purposes or goals of groups engaged in the struggle for power. For instance, the purposes or goals of the anarchists or the syndicalists are fundamentally different from others like the socialists and the communists in view of the fact that while the former stand for the abolition of the state, government and authority root and

branch, the latter look at them as instruments for achieving the desired goal. Hence, it becomes a problem to understand as to what constitutes 'political' in the individual or group behaviour in the strict sense of the term.[48]

2. The behaviouralists sacrifice values at the altar of facts and thereby present a barren political theory. They can be, for this reason, charged with committing the crime of vulgar reductionism. They exclude the norms of human teleology in so far as it is not concerned with the basic problem of 'political good' that remained a matter of prominent concern with great political thinkers like Plato, Aristotle, Cicero, St. Augustine, St. Thomas, Kant, Rousseau, Green and a host of others who subscribed to the stock of normative political theory. The contributions of the behaviouralists are, therefore, criticised for reducing norms and values into facts, quality into quantity, reason into unreason, and human components of personality into the animal or the sub-human.[49]
3. The behavioural political theory may also be accused of being reactionary or an intellectual exercise in the direction of justifying and preserving the *status quo*. Instead of working in the direction of analysing the forces of social change or offering the principles of a social revolution, the aim of the behaviouralists is to collect data and analyse it in order to defend and protect democracy in the

48. Keeping this in view, a critic like Christian Bay designates behavioural politics as 'pseudo-politics' or 'counterfeit politics'. See his paper "A Critical Evaluation of Behavioural Literature" in *American Political Science Review* (March, 1965), pp. 39-51. The idea behind such an argument is that so long as the alternative conclusions of a host of traditional political theories (Aristotle, St. Augustine. Hobbes, Locke, Rousseau and Marx) remain matters of opinion rather than inter-subjectively transmissible knowledge, no absolute moral beings about a good society can be proved more true than any other.... It was as if acquainting their studies with an array of well-known writings and thinkers from Plato onwards, while endorsing none of their conclusions, constituted the essence of teaching political theory itself. An implicit lesson of such teaching was that there is no persuasive way to choose among the great political ideals of the past and to say that any one of them embodies a true prescription for what men need in a good society. Indeed, in a world fascinated by scientific standards of proof and truth, merely to present ideas as the product of particular historical circumstances is to suggest that as times change, the truth in these ideas diminishes." Ricci, *op. cit.*, p. 145.
49. V.P. Varma: "The Behavioural Research and Political Philosophy: Some Aspects" in *The Indian Journal of Political Studies,* Jodhpur, Vol. 1, No. 1, 1976, p 27. Prof. L.S. Rathore's complaint is that behavioural political theory cannot explain 'change', because it "dehistoricises social phenomena and is unable to establish dialectical relationships among the various epochs of society." See his paper "The Conflict of Modernity and Tradition in Contemporary Political Theory" in J.S. Bains and R.B. Jain (ed.s): *Political Science in Transition* (New Delhi: Gitanjali, 1981), p. 23. In fact, the behavioural political theory suffers from too much precision misplaced on trivial matters, too little respect for grand theories, too much respect for insights that are commonplace, too much indication and too little proof, too little genuine cumulation of generalisations, too little regard for the learning of the past, far too much jargon." Bersleson and Steiner: *Human Behaviour* (New York: Harcourt Brace, 1964), p 12.

world.[50] Thus, Leo Strauss regards them as 'biased' in favour of a particular form of political system. The result is that the contributions of the behaviouralists may be treated as 'methodologies' and not at all like theories. Keeping his attention confined to the systems analysis of a great behaviouralist like Easton (as he then was), a critic says that at best his theories "can be expected to produce reasonably well-organised information of comparative sort, and perhaps to suggest areas in which further research is needed. They are too weak to be considered theories and they perform none of the essential functions of theory."[51]

4. Finally, what may be described as the greatest weakness of the behaviouralists is their mad craze for 'scientism' evident from their placing total reliance on 'facts'. It may, however, be asked that there is "more to seeing than meets the eyeball."[52] The facts take their place and meaning only after they have been selected and organised, not before. Therefore, one man's fact is another's fiction. For example, the Buddhists do not see right angles and western intimations that such angles are part of the warp and woof of reality which may well strike the average Southeast Asian as more than little impious.[53] In emphasising the behavioural approach beyond all other approaches and the exclusive reliance on 'scientific methods', political science has been reduced to "a device invented by university teachers for avoiding that dangerous subject 'politics', without achieving a science."[54] A learned critic observes that behaviouralists are a frustrated group of intellectuals who want to make *science* out of politics, but they cannot. The increase in the literature of quasi-theories is a manifestation of their untiring

---

50. Undoubtedly, the behavioural revolution had an anti-Marxist bias. It is a fact that an extensive anti-communist literature came into existence during the behavioural era. See A.J. Greggor: *A Survey of Marxism: Problems in Philosophy and the Theory of History* (New York: Random House, 1965). It was also an affair that the profession of this discipline "touched upon obliquely, however, in the sense that typical political science outlooks, as expressed in the behavioural persuasion, contradicted the Marxian position even when specific Marxian tenets as science and analysis were not denounced explicitly. In place of the larger place held by political science in American life, and from what we have seen of the midcentury liberal matrix into which behaviouralism fitted so comfortably, this anti-Marxism was perfectly logical, as the discipline maintained its customary support for liberal sentiments shared with Americans beyond the grooves of academy". Ricci, *op. cit.*, p. 169. Same affirmation may be seen in the views of R.A. Dahl that polyarchy or the model of democratic pluralism (as in the United States) "looks very much better when it is placed alongside rival political forms (such as Marxist model) that have been tried in this century – waves of the fortune that swept the country overboard." *After the Revolution! Authority in a Good Society* (New Haven: Yale University Press, 1970), pp. 140-41.
51. Eugene Meehan: *The Theory and Method of Political Analysis* (Homewood, Illinois: The Dorsey Press, 1965), p. 162.
52. N.R. Hansen: *Patterns of Discovery* (Cambridge: Cambridge University Press, 1961), p. 21.
53. See F.S.C. Northrop: *Logic of the Science and Humanities* (New York: Meridian Books, 1959), pp. 40-49.
54. See Alfred Cobban: "Ethics and the Decline of Political Theory" in *Political Science Quarterly* (Sept., 1953), p. 335.

efforts, and lack of deductive theories that are meaningful is a proof of their dilemma.[55]

Notwithstanding these lines of attack, it may be conceded that the behaviouralists have made some contributions by furnishing valuable predictions about the likely and unlikely acts of man or by making us aware of the significant correlations and also by laying different emphases on the bases enabling us to think in terms of new categories. Certain it is that some of the essential weaknesses have been overcome in the phase of post-behaviouralism keeping which in view a learned American writer has hopefully visualised that "the behavioural movement of protest will disappear by slowly decaying as a distinctive mood and outlook and it will become, and in fact already is becoming, incorporated into the main body of the discipline. The astonishing point is that it will disappear not because it has failed, but because it has succeeded and as a separate, somewhat sectarian, slightly factional outlook, it will be the first victim of its own triumph."[56]

55. Meehan, *op. cit.,* p. 161. Behaviouralism was admired as 'scientific revolution in political theory'. D. B. Truman: "Disillusion and Regeneration: The Quest for a Discipline" in *American Political Science Review* (December, 1965), pp. 856-73. But a student of normative political theory contradicts such a claim of the behaviouralists by holding that even scientific method is not absolutely free from its own weaknesses. "Perhaps, that is why, yesterday's scientific mistakes are tomorrow's discoveries." F.M. Frohock: *The Nature of Political Inquiry* (Homewood, Illinois: The Dorsey Press, 1967), p. 4. Again: "An empirical investigation is a model of theory only if the theory and model share the same logical structure." *Ibid.,* p. 6. Again: "If we move from the assumption that all knowledge derives from experience, then definitive judgements are impossible. The future is open-ended, or tenuous, meaning that one can never rule out the possibility that some later experience may alter even the conceptual apparatus within which arguments take place." *Ibid.,* p. 19.
56. Dahl in Gould and Thursby, *op. cit.,* p. 132.

21

Post-Behaviouralism

> New conditions of the modern world, however, force us to reconsider our image of what we want to be. Scientific progress is slow, and however more reliable our limited knowledge about politics has become in the last fifty years, social crises of unforeseen proportions are upon us.... The search for an answer as to how we as political scientists have proved so disappointingly ineffectual in anticipating the world of the 1960s has contributed significantly to the birth of the post-behavioural revolution.
>
> **—David Easton[1]**

The post-behavioural trend in the growth of contemporary political theory is regarded as a 'new revolution' as well as a 'new challenge'. Having its source in the intellectual ferment and socio-political turbulence that marked the American life in the middle and the late 1960s, it has crept into the 1970s and after. It shows that hardly had the 'first revolution' of the behaviouralists been completed than it had been overtaken by the increasing social and political crises of the age. The weight of these crises was felt in the form of a new conflict in the throes of which leading American political scientists like David Easton and G.A. Almond found themselves caught up and who designated it as the 'latest challenge directed against a developing behavioural orthodoxy.'[2] It may also be commented that an element of 'new dissent' was centred in the creation within the galaxy of the prominent figures of the American Political Science Association that "emerged as a new 'caucus' consisting of predominantly, but by no means exclusively, younger political scientists that acted vigorously, sometimes stridently, in an attempt to nullify or reverse dominant patterns of political science. As a result, the term 'post-behavioural' came to designate the mood and programmatic intent of the new dissenters."[3]

1. Presidential address delivered by David Easton at the annual meeting of the American Political Science Association held at New York in Sept., 1969, incorporated in his *The Political System: An Inquiry into the State of Political Science* (Calcutta: Scientific Book Agency, 1971), p. 323.
2. *Ibid.* For a better study see G.T. Graham and J.A. Carey: *The Post-Behavioural Era: Perspectives in Political Science* (New York: Mckay, 1972); Harry S. Kariel: *Saving Appearance: The Re-Establishment of Political Science* (Mass.: Duxbury Press, 1972); Surkin and Wolf: *An End to Political Science: The Caucus Papers* (New York: Basic Books, 1970).
3. Dwight Waldo: "Political Science Tradition, Discipline, Profession, Science, Enterprise" in Fred Greenstein and N.W. Polsby (ed.s): *Political Science: Scope and Theory,* Vol. I (California, Addison-Wesley, 1975), pp. 113-14. As a matter of fact, the ripples of dissent had started arising in the waters of behaviouralism after 1965. It may be seen in the emergence of an enormous quantity of critical writings expounding a great many strands of social, economic and political thought, combined to challenge the post-Second World War liberal matrix. Some of these were advanced by those seeking to overturn the existing order, while others were offered by people dedicated to preserving liberalism but fearful of the trends they believed would cause that civilisation to destroy itself. "In the light of this common opposition to the *status quo,* even where ultimate objectives differed, the term 'counter culture' will serve as well as any to label the arguments expounded, in opposition to conventional liberalism by such men as Herbert Marcuse, Paul Goodman, Eric Fromm, C Wright Mills, Robert Pirsey, Noam Chomsky, Theodore Roszak, Charles Reich and Robert Paul Wolff. See Ricci: *The Tragedy of Political Science,* p. 177.

Meaning and Nature of the Post-Behavioural Revolution: 'Credo of Relevance': Distinguishing Tenets and Traditions

The call of the post-behavioural trend, designated as a 'new revolution', was given by David Easton in his presidential address in 1969 when he identified this movement as hinging on a deep dissatisfaction with the existing political research and teaching, especially of the kind striving to convert the study of politics into a more rigorously scientific discipline modelled on the methodology of natural sciences.[4] While asserting that the essence of the 'new revolution' was not hard to identify and the tenets of its faith had already emerged clearly enough to be identifiable, Easton highlighted seven points of the new movement as its 'Credo of Relevance'.[5]

1. Substance must precede technique. If one must be sacrificed for the other, and this need not always be so, it is more important to be relevant and meaningful for contemporary urgent social problems than to be sophisticated in the tools of investigation. For the aphorism of science that it is better to be wrong than vague, post-behaviouralism would substitute a new dictum that it is better to be vague than to be non-relevantly precise.
2. Behavioural science conceals an ideology of empirical conservatism. To confine oneself exclusively to the description and analysis of facts is to hamper the understanding of the same facts in their broadest context. As a result, empirical political science must lend its support to the maintenance of the very factual conditions it explores. It unwittingly purveys an ideology of social conservatism tempered by modest incremental change.
3. Behavioural research must not lose touch with reality. The heart of behavioural inquiry is abstraction and analysis and this serves to conceal the brute realities of politics. The task of post-behaviouralism is to break the barriers of silence that behavioural language necessarily has created and to help political science reach out to the real needs of mankind in a time of crisis.
4. Research about and constructive development of values are inextinguishable parts of the study of politics. Science cannot be and never has been evaluatively neutral despite protestations to the contrary. Hence, to understand the limits of our knowledge we need to be aware of the value premises on which it stands and the alternatives for which this knowledge could be used.
5. Members of a learned discipline bear the responsibilities of all intellectuals. The intellectuals' historical role has been and must be to protect the human values of civilisation. This is their unique task and obligation. Without this they become mere technicians, mechanics for tinkering with society. They thereby abandon the special privileges they have come to claim for themselves in academia such as freedom of inquiry and a quasi-extra-territorial protection from the onslaughts of society.
6. To know is to bear the responsibility for acting and to act is to engage in reshaping society. The intellectual as a scientist bears the special obligation to put his knowledge to work. Contemplative science was a product of the nine-

4. Easton: *Political System*, p. 324.
5. *Ibid.*, pp. 325-27.

teenth century when a broader moral agreement was shared. Action science of necessity reflects the contemporary conflict in society over ideals and this must permeate and colour the whole research enterprise itself.

7. If the intellectual has the obligation to implement his knowledge, those organisations composed of intellectuals—the professional associations—and the universities themselves cannot stand apart from the struggles of the day. Politicisation of the professions is inescapable as well as desirable.

Thus, Easton exhorted that in the face of a human situation such as obtaining now, the behavioural movement in political science "is presenting us with a new image of our discipline and the obligations of our professions. It pleads for more relevant research. It pleads for an orientation to the work that will encourage political scientists, even in their professional capacity to prescribe and to act so as to improve political life according to human criteria."[6]

The historic address of Easton stirred the community of the American political scientists. A new awareness came to prevail as a result of which most of the conscientious students of this discipline realised that during the phase of the dominance of the behavioural movement, political science had become too narrowly defined, too professional, too much identified with the established order. They felt that the students of this discipline would be more concerned with the values, issues of justice, freedom, equality and political activity. In a period of stress, turmoil and gross inequalities, the study of political science should be treated as responsible for carrying on, as usual, in academic detachment. At minimum, the political scientist should be concerned with the issues of public policy and political reform; perhaps, they should be engaged with the issues of radical socio-political reconstruction.

Driven by the ambition to become a genuine science, political science, as the post-behaviouralists claim, has constructed and crippled itself philosophically and methodologically. The fact-value distinction has encouraged an undesirable foreshadowing of vision and a moral insensitivity. Emphasis on methodology borrowed from natural sciences has resulted in much research that is trivial and inconsequential even for its ostensible purposes of helping to create the science of politics. In other words, the new realisation informs that concentration on scientific philosophy and on scientific methodology has squeezed the vitality from political science. No longer the discipline is concerned with a narrow range of phenomena that lend themselves to treatment by approved methods. In fact, political science is becoming apolitical. Thus, political science "needs to become imaginative, creative (even playful), open to the world. Modern natural science, after all, is but a school of consciousness, one among many. It represents a monopolistic expropriation of

6. *Ibid.*, p. 329. The post-behavioural trend saw the emergence of a 'counter culture' and 'a new caucus of dissenters' who doubted that the scientific community run by the political scholars was quite as open as that envisioned by the Popperian version of behaviouralism and this doubt led them to recommend that if the discipline were actually leaning in any direction, might as well tend to be on the side of beauty and virtue, or in the argot of the age, in favour of relevance and action. "Ricci, *op. cit.*, p. 190. In other words, the caucus members advanced the idea that political scientists should together take a stand with regard to public affairs, that the discipline had a moral responsibility for seeking the kinds of truth that would serve justice and humanity by questioning existing arrangements." Christian Bay: "For an American Political Science Association" in *Political Studies* (Summer, 1968), p. 37.

meaning of science that is knowledge in its original sense. The monopoly must be broken."[7]

As a result, some of the eminent American political scientists took to a new course, generally known as 'post-behavioural revolution', whose principal assumptions may be thus pointed out:[8]

1. The central conceptual distortions in contemporary political theory result from the attempt to divide the discipline into empirical and normative halves. This dichotomy is based on a faulty epistemology and it, therefore, cannot be maintained without generating theoretical inconsistencies, incapacities or evasions.
2. The ultimate source of the insistence upon dichotomising political theory is the legacy of the Western philosophical tradition that originated in the seventeenth century 'scientific revolution'. Other disciplines, therefore, exhibit problems similar to those in political science.
3. The incapacities and confusions of dichotomised theory have clearly manifested themselves in some of the most important recent theoretical efforts of the discipline such as attempts to conceptualise political development, democracy and the nature of politics itself.
4. These problems can be systematically remedied only by a post-behavioural political science that takes its bearings from contemporary achievements in the philosophy of science—achievements which are radically revising the traditional concept of scientific knowledge.

In this way, the post-behavioural revolution is a clear attack on the obsession or craze for a 'scientific research' that it describes as a 'mopping up operation'[9] and desires a return to the side of value-laden normative theory after leaving little doubt that the Baconian model of scientific methods is a 'vulgar view of science'.[10]

End of the Dichotomy of Facts and Values: Reaffirmation of Norms in Empirical Political Theory

The post-behavioural trend takes into account that the bifurcation of political theory into normative and empirical directions and then adherence to the latter at the expense of the former, as done by the advocates of the behavioural tradition, has resulted in the creation of significant anomalies in the conceptual structure of political science. A line of distinction between the two forms of political theory—normative and empirical—is drawn on the ground that while the former is value-laden, the latter is value-free. Normative political theory is regarded as 'a systematic thinking about the purposes of government'.[11] It has an evaluative character. It lays stress on the significant discussions which look to the establishment of moral criterion of

7. Waldo, *op. cit.*, p. 114.
8. Thomas Spragens, Jr.: *The Dilemmas of Contemporary Political Theory: Towards a Post-Behavioural Science of Politics* (New York: Dunellen, 1973), p. 5.
9. See Thomas Kuhn: *The Structure of Scientific Revolutions* (Chicago: Phoenix Books, 1962), p. 24.
10. See D.K Price: *The Scientific Estate* (New York: Oxford University Press, 1968), p. 173.
11. John Plamenatz: "The Use of Political Theory" in Anthony Quinton (ed.): *Political Philosophy* (London: Oxford Univ. Press, 1967), p. 19.

political conduct and which asks questions about the nature and end of the state, the limits of one's obligations to obey its command, the basis and extent of the rights and duties of an individual, above all, the form of good life [12] As such, its task is to pass moral judgement.[13] Contrary to this, empirical political theory is value-free. It lays emphasis on facts. Theory is no knowledge but an important tool for that purpose. An empiricist is, therefore, a 'fact grubber' believing that collection of data, and investigation of scientific methods and techniques constitute a single intellectual enterprise.[14]

Right from the ancient times of Plato and Aristotle to the modern times of Lasswell and Easton, political theory has been both—normative and empirical. However, the distinguishing feature of the behaviouralists is that they adhered to the latter at the expense of the former. It happened owing to their 'mad craze for scientism'. The behaviouralists wished to orient political theory towards empirical research with a view to seek and understand political action in terms of attitudes and interests constituting 'observed and observable behaviour' of human beings. In other words, the behavioural tradition created and cultivated the myth of a 'value-free political science' so that the fate of political philosophy could be separated from that of political science.[15]

The consequences of this 'mad craze for scientism' could be realised by the enlightened students of the behavioural tradition who shifted to the new line. They could realise that driven by the ambition to become a genuine science, political science "has constricted and crippled itself philosophically and methodologically. The fact-value distinction has encouraged an undesirable foreshortening of vision and a moral insensibility."[16] It has made contemporary political theory 'shaky and confused' and the most penetrating minds of the discipline are beginning to suggest that the divorce made by the behaviouralists was 'too hasty'and that some sort of reconciliation may be possible, if necessary.[17] It is becoming more and more clear that the new models of political investigation are no panacea at the level of theory. Based in part upon the relatively naive view of science that was widely popularised in the social sciences as recently as a decade ago, some practitioners of the behavioural approach apparently expected a new theoretical edifice to arise wholly from the welter of data provided by well-trained cadre of researchers.[18]

Such a wild expectation of the behaviouralists has by now been dampened considerably leaving aside the case of the truest of the true believers. As Spragens, Jr. says: "We have been almost swamped with a proliferation of political 'middle range' theories whose relationship and even compatability with each other is far

12. W.H. Greenleaf: "Theory and Study of Politics" in *British Journal of Political Science,* Vol. 2 (October, 1972), p. 471.
13. G.C. Field: *Political Theory* (London: Methuen, 1963), p. xvi.
14. See Heinz Eulau: "Preface" to D. Marvick (ed.): *Political Decision Makers* (New York: The Free Press, 1961), p. 8
15. L.S. Rathore: "In Defence of Political Theory" in *Indian Journal of Political Science,* Vol. XXXVI, No. 4, 1975, p. 333.
16. Waldo, *op. cit.,* p. 114.
17. Spragens, Jr. *op. cit.,* p. 1.
18. *Ibid.,* p. 4.

from clear. The bulk return of the new empirical studies has been great, but the theoretical landscape has become more confused rather than more clarified."[19] If so, the two dimensions of political theory—normative and empirical— should be integrally connected. As he further adds: "I have the feeling that if empirical theory and normative theory have nothing to say to each other, ultimately they will have nothing to say."[20] The motivating idea behind it is the perception or generation of a new awareness that the two forms of political theory are not disparate and separable forms of inquiry but instead have an intrinsic relevance to each other which cannot be denied without resultant confusion. Obviously, it takes inspiration from Kaplan's formula of 'empirical-theoretician continuum'[21] keeping which in view a recent political scientist says: "The principal challenge to political theory at the present time is to pull ourselves out of this conceptual confusion."[22]

In fact, the admonitions of the behavioural tradition hinging on the point of adhering to empiricism at the expense of normativism emphasise the need to move away from the notion of some kind of unbridgeable dichotomy between the logically distinct types of theory towards another understanding of the relationship between empirical and normative theory. It is suggested that such a reintegration of the theoretical enterprise in political science is a necessity, because politics is the intersection of order and power. The latter cannot be wholly abstracted from the former, however diligent the effort, that may be described apart from patterns and standards which are perceptual or interpretative norms.

It may be understood that the trend of post-behaviouralism is not as much a negation of as an improvement upon, the behavioural tradition in view of the fact that instead of repudiating what the latter says, it seeks to give it a correct channel. It does not discard the premises of empiricism, rather it desires their integration with norms and values. The thrust of the argument is that a purely normative theory unsupported by an empirical theory would be inarticulate and fragmentary, and an empirical theory cut off from a philosophical base would be feckless, soon to dodder and evanesce. What is needed is a new creative political theory based on precision and criticism, meaning thereby, flourishing within the genial range of normative and empirical fields, discarding is-ought disjunction, and evaluating the results in the light of the ideals, and ideals in the light of the results."[23]

In short, the main purpose of the believers in the new trend is not to deny the achievements of their predecessors but to refine them so that the behavioural movement is pulled out of the wrong direction. Those subscribing to the post-behavioural trend admit that the achievements of the behavioural revolution in political science have been vast. However, it is rapidly becoming obvious that one thing this revolution has not achieved is the inherently impossible conversion of

19. *Ibid.*
20. *Ibid*, p. 1.
21. As Kaplan says: "The basic point is that no observation is purely empirical—that is, free of every ideational element—as no theory (in science at any rate) is purely ideational." *The Conduct of Enquiry* (San Francisco: Chandler, 1964), p. 58.
22. G.A. Almond: "Political Development" in *Comparative Political Studies*, Vol. 1, 1969, p. 448.
23. L.S. Rathore: "Political Theory: A Quest for Reconciliation" in *Indian Journal of Political Science*, Vol. XXXVIII, No. 1, 1977, p. 7.

the intellectual task of theorising into a purely technical, impersonal function. It is, therefore, altogether likely that we "are on the verge of entering a post-behavioural era in political science, a time when the many advances of the behavioural era will be consolidated and refined and when the theoretical problems suggested by our new data and techniques will be faced squarely."[24]

Abandonment of the 'Mad Craze for Scientism': Emphasis on the Relevance of Research for Social Purpose and Action

Another important feature of the post-behavioural trend should be traced in the abandonment of the 'mad craze for scientism', as said by David Easton. Research should not be loaded with the rigours of a scientific formulation. Rather it should be oriented to social purpose and action. The crime of the behaviouralists was that they developed and cultivated an image of science associated with technical proficiency in research for a strictly reliable knowledge, with the pursuit of basic understanding, with its necessary divorce from practical concerns, and the exclusion of value sophistication as something beyond the competence of science. While the post-behaviouralists do not deny the importance of technical proficiency, they do not agree with the search for basic understanding and reliable knowledge that cuts the scientist from the practical concerns of the society, nor do they believe that values can be kept out of all scientific pursuits. In simple terms, research should be related to urgent social problems and be purposive. As such, it is the duty of the political scientist to find out solutions to contemporary problems.[25]

Philosophers of science have been active in refining and revising some of the more simple-minded notions about science which have become highly problematic not so much because of difficulties in the social sciences as because of the problems in natural sciences. By now the movement towards empirical political theory has advanced to a level of genuine theoretical relevance. The post-behavioural trend signifies that the emphasis on methodology borrowed from the natural sciences has resulted in much research that is trivial and inconsequential even for its ostensible purpose of helping to create a science of politics. A concentration on scientific philosophy (knowledge of which is not necessary to political science) and no scientific methodology (which pertains only to the method of proof, not the more important matters of discovery or creation) has squeezed the vitality from political science. As a result of this, political science is becoming 'apolitical.'[26]

Once again, we take note of the fact that the post-behavioural trend seeks to refine what the behaviouralists have given. Instead of discarding the value of a 'scientific inquiry', it desires to give it a purposeful direction. Mere research is not enough; it should be purpose-oriented. Thus, it is a critique of as well as an improvement upon its former self. The post-behavioural trend breaks with the prevailing professional paradigm about the moral relationship between research and action. "In the behavioural interpretation the possession of knowledge imposes no

24. Thomas Spragens, Jr., *op. cit.*, p. 168.
25. S.P. Varma: *Modern Political Theory* (Delhi: Vikas, 1975), p. 101.
26. Waldo, *op. cit.*, p. 114. Also see Charles A. McCoy and John Playford; *Apolitical Politics: A Critique of Behaviouralism* (New York: T.Y. Crowell, 1967).

special obligation on the political scientist to put his knowledge to use in the service of society. He remains free to choose whether or not he ought to step outside his scientific role for this purpose. This *laissez faire* attitude towards political engagement has been an accepted moral premise of the profession. It has permitted, if not encouraged, the withdrawal from political strife. Knowledge is divorced from action. For post-behaviouralism, however, the line between pure research and service begins to fade. Knowledge brings an awareness of alternatives and their consequences. This opportunity for rational choice imposes special obligations on the knower. The political scientist as a professional is the knower *par excellence.* It is, therefore, immoral for him not to act on his knowledge. In holding that to know is to bear a responsibility for acting, post-behaviouralism joins a venerable tradition inherited from such diverse sources as Greek classical philosophy, Karl Marx, John Dewey, and modern existentialism."[27]

If political science is to remain like a science, post-behaviouralism virtually has to follow the line of behaviouralism in keeping this discipline off from the world of ideology. Political theory should not be dissolved into the ocean of ideology, for the true scientist is one who is always seeking to enlarge his perspective so as to gain greater catholicity and accuracy in his perception of reality. The replacement of the false ideal of a detached impersonal point of view is neither scepticism, nor the prostitution of science to ideology but instead is the ideal of an essentially human point of view which is within the limits of human perspective, constantly striving to enlarge itself."[28] The commitment of a "scientist is intellectual, his enquiry is autonomous, his attitude questioning: the commitment of the ideologue is political, his formulations contingent on his practical goals, his intellectual stance complacent."[29]

In brief, the business of a political scientist is to study a number of urgent social and economic problems like those of hunger, poverty, violence, racialism, communalism, regionalism, wars and the like that have their impact on the political system and then find out solutions for them. This is the meaning of 'basic research' in political theory. Instead of rushing towards science as was done by the behaviouralists, the post-behavioural trend lays emphasis on taking to the course of applied science. It desires that if applied science is to receive serious attention, it is not enough for the social scientist just to apply himself to specific social policies. He ought to connect them to broader conceptions of the political system in which such policies would be more acceptable or with which they could be consistent. This requires him not to accept mechanically the prevailing political and moral premises. He can question them adequately only by engaging in 'creative moral speculation' after the style of great political philosophers. In sum, we engage in fundamental research, we require in depth exploration of our value premises in order to probe the relationship of values to the nature of empirical research. As we engage in applied science, we

27. Easton, *op. cit.*, p. 343.
28. Karl Mannheim: *Ideology and Utopia,* Translated from German into English by Louis Wirth and Edward Shils (New York: Harcourt Brace. 1936), p. 297.
29. Spragens Jr., *op. cit.*, p. 168.

can understand full implications of specific politics only within the context of our general political philosophy.[30] In this way, Easton maintains that adequate science itself requires involvement in 'creative moral enquiry.'[31]

Appreciation of Applied Politics: From Political Science to Policy Science

The last important feature of the post-behavioural trend should be traced in taking political science towards, what is called, 'policy science'. It says that the business of a political scientist is not merely confined to study state and government in their theoretical or practical aspects, it also covers within its fold his interest in understanding the decision-making process. Since a policy is aimed at the realisation of certain goal-values, it is necessary that the researcher has a clear-cut notion of the values he proposes to realise through the decision-making process. That is, instead of living in a world of academic discussions and debates, a political scientist should live like an enlightened citizen as well as an expert so that he may not only understand the burning problems of and challenges to the political system but also suggest solutions for them. A political scientist must also be a policy scientist and on the basis of his expert knowledge, he should advise his rulers to do a particular thing in certain circumstances or refrain from doing so in certain others.[32]

Naturally, it has brought about a change in our notions about politics and public administration. In the field of the latter, the distinction between policy and administration was originally pursued as a hard and fast dichotomy. It was said that policy was made in the legislative branch and carried out in the executive by the administrators. Stress on this distinction was reinforced by belief in the doctrine of the separation of powers between legislative, executive and judicial branches as well as by the jointly held ideas that politics was corrupt and that administration was neutral. This value-laden view led to attempts aimed at taking matters 'out of politics', that is, to place control of public services in the hands of those not directly responsible to elected partisan political officials. Now while many have come to recognise that this distinction was much too simple, it did make executive branch structure the subject of special study. And the distinction was reinforced by the reform-orientation of many of those interested in public administration in the earliest days; their pre-occupation was with developing the best administrative arrangements for carrying out policy. The idea that there was one best way of doing things led to calling public administration a 'science' with principles of proper action. These principles "were prescriptive in nature instead of being the descriptive generalisations we now associate with the word 'science'. They were also divorced from the ends of purposes of the organisations in which they were being used, although they did embody and imply certain values. The idea was generated that, if the ends were supplied, an administrative specialist could tell what should be done."[33]

30. O.P. Bakshi: "Political Theory and the Scientific Study of Politics: Reflections on David Easton's Concept of Political Theory" in *Indian Journal of Political Science*, Vol. XXXVII, No. 4, 1976, pp. 107-8.
31. Easton, *op. cit.*, p. 363.
32. Paul Kecskemati: "The Policy Science" in *World Politics* (July, 1952).
33. Stephen L. Wasby: *Political Science – The Discipline and Its Dimensions: An Introduction* (Calcutta: Scientific Book Agency, 1970); pp. 417-18.

Behaviouralism	Post-Behaviouralism
1. Emphasis on the study of individual or group behaviour as it is. 2. Use of cross-disciplinary or interdisciplinary approach to the study of politics. 3. Greater attention to the techniques of precision, measurement and quantification so as to formulate empirically tenable theories. 4. Separation of facts from values in theory-building. 5. Attempt to scientise the discipline to make systematic political theory.	1. Emphasis on relevance and meaningfulness so as to make theory full of substance and close to social reality. 2. No blind adherence to fact/value dichotomy, hence assignment of some place to norms, goals and values. 3. Abandonment of the obsession for hyperfactualism or scientising the discipline of politics. 4. Impartial borrowings from diverse sources like liberalism, Platonism, existentialism and Marxism. 5. Study to be in the context of present as well as future perspectives.

The post-behavioural trend takes note of this fact. Its genesis may, however, be seen in the contributions of Harold Lasswell who does not like to talk so much of 'particular values' but rather insists that goal-seeking and policy formulation aspects of political science are more important for the positivistic or the scientific part of political science. He goes to the extent of saying that the thinking in his country (United States) about human relations has been unnecessarily one-sided in the amount of emphasis put upon derivation (justification) and upon science. This has meant a relative de-emphasis upon the clarification of goals, the projection of future developments, including specially the invention of future lines of policy.[34] The emphasis of his argument is on treating political science as a 'policy science' in which knowledge is mustered for clear-cut objectives, and is fully related to the most likely contingencies to appear in the unfolding processes of history [35]

Such an interpretation of Lasswell is based on his developmental analysis whereby one of the distinctive functions of policy sciences becomes to facilitate the modification of trends by making explicit what the trends, in fact, have been and whither they lead with respect to social goals. Lasswell also coins the notion of 'projective thinking' which implies that a policy scientist must revise his opinions and views in the light of what may, or is going to, happen under certain circumstances. "Developmental constructs are, therefore, the product of a mutual cross-fertilisation of five types of thinking— goal thinking, trend thinking, scientific thinking, projective thinking, and probability thinking. In this way, a developmental construct with its characterisation of the present as a transition between a selected pattern of events located in the past and a pattern imputed to the future is more than a simple extrapolation of recent trends, it is a critical weighing of future outcomes considered as an interacting whole."[36]

34. Lasswell: *Power and Personality* (New York: W.W. Norton, 1948), p. 204.
35. *Ibid.*
36. Lasswell: "The World Revolutionary Situation" in Carl J. Friedrich (ed.): *Totalitarianism* (Cambridge: Harvard Univ. Press. 1954), p. 360. Also see Lasswell and Daniel Lerner (ed.s): *The Policy Sciences: Recent Developments in Scope and Method* (Stanford: Stanford Univ. Press, 1951), p. 11.

David Easton picks up threads from what Lasswell said a few years ago. It is evident from what he said in his presidential address: "For the profession, therefore, the emerging post-behavioural phase is encouraging the development of a new norm of behaviour. It sees policy engagement as a social responsibility of the intellectual whatever the institutional form through which these may be exercised. Some day it may also require the release of the social scientist from bondage to the unique needs and objectives of his own national political system. It is clear that changing times require radical rethinking of what we are and what we want to be both as a discipline and as a profession. Post-behaviouralism is a pervasive intellectual tendency today that reveals a major effort to do just this."[37]

It may, therefore, be said that the post-behavioural trend desires the politicisation of the political scientists. The idea behind it is that studies and researches in the sphere of political sciences should be of such a kind that they may well be used by the administrators of the country and that, if need be, the services of the political scientists may be utilised for the operation of a political system. Only such a category of political scientists can bring about, what Lasswell calls, 'a free and co-operative commonwealth'. In the era of 'prevention of politics' the role of a political scientist would be, as he further says, of a 'master propagandist'. In a word, the political scientists should bring their philosophical and scientific learning to bear on the problems that confront their society and offer possible and workable solutions for them without bothering about the criticism of the traditionalists that thinkers like Machiavelli and Locke had done in the past and for which they were criticised for being political propagandists or pamphleteers canvassing for political reforms.[38]

Behaviouralism and Post-Behaviouralism: Whether a Continuity or a Break with the Past

A question may be asked: whether post-behavioural trend is a continuation of the behavioural tradition, or it is a break with the recent past. The correct answer is that it is just a continuation of the former. It is a new attempt to save what was done over the last few years by a new generation of the American political scientists in the face of serious criticism directed against their 'revolutionary' findings. Most of the leading figures like David Easton, Almond and Lasswell who made their massive contribution in the early 1950s and 1960s felt differently in the face of criticism directed against the contributions of behavioural political theory. It is not that they were wholly unmindful of the weaknesses of the behavioural tradition, it is because of the fact that after a lapse of about twenty years, they came to realise that the criticism "had become more vigorous, more organised, more vituperative. Some of them also contained new intellectual elements radically different from the criticism of the 1950s and early 1960s."[39]

37. Easton, *op. cit.*, p. 347.
38. See Dante Germino: "The Revival of Political Theory" in *Journal of Politics*, Vol. XXXV, No. 3 (Aug., 1963), pp. 439-40.
39. Kirkptrick: "From Past to Present" in Donald M. Freeman (ed.): *Foundations of Political Science* (New York; Free Press, 1971), p. 35.

As a matter of fact, the post-behavioural tradition is a contribution of a section of the behaviouralists who may be lauded for being enlightened, or denounced for being betrayers of the cause. They may also be labelled as the 'Young Turks' of the community of American political scientists who, as the critics allege, 'complicated the politics of Political Science'.[40] It is said that the interests of Political Science have always been too diverse, the opinions too varied and subtle to permit division into a small number of sharply defined parties. But the controversies concerning behaviouralism did create a certain bipolarity between those holding more traditional interests and opinions and those seeking to advance the cause of science. Probably, by the mid-sixties, there was decreasing tension and controversy. After years of sometimes heated disputation, the situation could perhaps mostly be conceived as a spectrum, with the position of the majority of political scientists on the philosophic-methodological issues represented by the central bands."[41]

Post-behaviouralism should, however, not be identified with traditionalism, no matter both are critical of the behavioural revolution. There is a basic difference between the two. While traditionalism thoroughly discards the behavioural revolution and reiterates its faith in the classical tradition, post-behaviouralism accepts the achievements of the behavioural trend and yet seeks to remove its essential weaknesses. That is, instead of denying the past heritage, it desires to propel it into new directions. As Easton says: "Behaviouralism was viewed as a threat to the *status quo;* classicism and traditionalism were responses calculated to preserve some part of what had been, by denying the very possibility of a science of politics. The post-behaviouralism is, however, future-oriented.... This new development is then a genuine revolution, not a reaction, not a preservation, a reform not a counter-reformation."[42]

Thus, the post-behavioural trend may be designated as the continuation of the behavioural tradition and not a break from it. The spirit of liberalism continues to run through it. As in the case of behaviouralism, so with post-behaviouralism we find an obdurate tendency on the part of the believers to offer new approaches and techniques so as to revalidate liberal political theory implying their bid to refute the premises of Marxian theory. The disillusioned or the enlightened community of the behaviouralists, as one may say, has reposed its conviction in the fact that the demise of the belief in pure and neutral-sense data, the collapse of the search for a perfect language, and the abandonment of the verifiability principle in its original form constitute the faulty premises of a 'quixotic enterprise' that would lead to a debacle because of its unreality. And yet they are sure that even the 'quixotic pursuit' of possible dreams often has some positive results. The post-behaviouralists may, for this reason, be regarded as optimistic behaviouralists who, like their predecessors, desire to reassure themselves with the greatness of liberal political theory. To them the technical tools of inquiry, a broadened intellectual scope and the development of some highly productive conceptual formats are clear indications of the fact that

40. Waldo, *op. cit.*, p. 115.
41. *Ibid.*
42. Easton, *op. cit.*, p. 324.

political science is rapidly reaching a 'turning point, if indeed it has not already reached it."[43]

Critical Appreciation

It is now hardly open to dispute that tendencies collectively known as behaviouralism, that were in an ascendent position in the 1950s, reached a position approaching dominance in the community of American political scientists in the 1960s till "they had a setback in the 1970s. To be sure, however, political science did not witness a thoroughly restructured form in the revised tradition. Quite a large number of political scientists remained unconvinced with, even antagonistic to, the tradition of 'behavioural revolution'. It was noted that many non-behavioural activities continued; many deep-flowing currents continued largely undisturbed. But those known as behaviouralists became prominent, probably dominant, in the affairs of the American Political Science Association and in most of the leading faculties of political science in major advanced study centres in the United States. However, as the 1960s drew towards a close, the behavioural tradition received a new challenge that had its source in the intellectual ferment and socio-political turbulence.[44]

It may be pointed out that while the post-behavioural trend seeks to rectify the wrongs of the behavioural tradition by ending the dichotomy of facts and values, i.e., by laying renewed emphasis on the significance of norms and values in the field of political theory as well as by revolting against the 'mad craze for scientism' and instead desiring linkage of science with social purpose and action, it has not remained thoroughly immune from certain inherent weaknesses which may be thus enumerated:

1. The post-behavioural trend does not attach due significance to traditional political theory in spite of the fact that it seeks to end the dichotomy of facts and values. Obviously, it cannot be acceptable to the men of classical tradition like Leo Strauss and M.Q. Sibley who would swear by the criteria of hierarchy of goals and moral entities and to whom the quantitativism of modern political science would be repelling. Naturally, they would attack the parochialism of new political science as represented by the post-behavioural trend.[45] Like the behavioural tradition, the post-behavioural trend also lacks much of the freshness and sublimity by not giving a significant place to the norms and values which constitute ethical dimension of political theory. It is said that classical political

43. Spragens Jr., *op. cit.*, p. 164. As Ithiel de Sola Pool says: "If we take the term bebaviouralism to be simply the ideological flag of a group of men who were once Young Turks in the profession, then clearly with the passage of time and the progression of generations the old heterodoxy has become the new orthodoxy. With the transition of generations, wounds are being healed. Our discipline is enjoying a new coherence, a pleasant sense of unity, a self-confident identity that has its rapid growth and healthy mien. At least until some new generation of rebels comes along, we are enjoying a period in which sterile debate between camps can be put aside while we explore as serious men the interrelationships of the different periods of our field" *Contemporary Political Science: Towards Empirical Theory* (New York: McGraw-Hill, 1967), pp. vii-viii.
44. Waldo, *op. cit.*, p. 113.
45. See V.P. Varma: "The Political Philosophy of Leo Strauss" in *Indian Journal of Political Science,* Vol. XXXV, No. 4, 1974, p. 299.

theorists may seem to have violated the requirements of clear thinking by moving freely between logically disparate realms of facts and values, but the classical approach gives a richness and depth to value theory which would be missing if it is conceived in isolation.[46] Easton's proposal, however, renders value theory, as also empirical theory, an autonomous enterprise. Based as it is on a misunderstanding of the traditional political theory, it is bound to result in the emasculation or sterilisation of value theory.[47]

2. Even after seeking to refute the 'mad craze for scientism', the post-behavioural trend does not like to return to the point of telling a student that concepts and theories are human artifacts; they are created by compositions of language which may, or may not, help us to perceive, analyse, gather data about and possibly control the realities that we call 'political'. The craze for scientism is still there with this line of difference that while the behavioural revolution desired mere 'scientism', it seeks to integrate it (scientism) with 'social purpose and action'. The position hardly undergoes a basic change. It is all said at the expense of this statement that there are and will continue to be various levels of research in political science ; the more basic abstracting from a greater variety of temporal and spatial peculiarities, but the continuing institutional focus of political science remains at all levels the defining and, in a sense, limiting factor. Prof. David Truman rightly says that if this point is lost sight of and a student of political science rushes to the course of 'pure scientism', he runs the danger, first, of failing to be what he pretends to be, a student of political institutions, second, of becoming ensnared in futile and synoptic preoccupations with techniques, and, third, of misusing the materials of behavioural science.[48]
3. The appreciation of scientific approach, as conceived even by the men of post-behavioural tradition, has another fallacy. It does not take into account, or rather refutes in a sneaking manner, the premises of Marxian theory which desires unity of theory and practice and lays down some definite laws of social change. Thus, the scientific approach of the revised tradition known by the name of post-behaviouralism deliberately misses the significance of this statement that a scientist is not one who, wishing to open a door, must once and for all, choose from among a bunch of keys the one key which alone is good. It should be remembered that a scientific research "is a series of successive approaches to the truth comparable to an exploration in an unknown land. Each explorer checks

---

46. O.P. Bakshi, *op. cit.*, p. 114.
47. See S.S Wolin: "Political Theory: Trends and Goals" in David I. Sills (ed.): *International Encyclopaedia of Social Sciences* (New York: Macmillan, 1969), Vol. XII, pp. 328-29. Among the latest lovers of normative theory, we may refer to the case of John Rawls whose book *A Theory of Justice* shows that he is "directly and entirely in the line of traditional and classical political theory. "He wants to marry facts and history: he wants to link morality with strategy and he hopes to provide a theory which will make moral principles acceptable on grounds of logic." Jean Blondel : *The Discipline of Politics* (London: Butterworths, 1981), p. 155.
48. Cited in E.M. Kirkpatrick: "The Impact of Behavioural Approaches on Traditional Political Science" in Austin Ranney, *op. cit*, p. 27.

and adds to the finding of his predecessors and facilitates for his successors the attainment of the goal they all have in common."[49]

It is, however, hoped that the long-range significance of the post-behavioural trend which, though complicated and problematical, has been hidden from the view. Perhaps from the vantage point of the coming decade of the 1980s, the rise of the'caucus'or the Young Turks and the proclamation of a 'post-behavioural sensibility' "will appear but a temporary aberration, another detour in a march towards a more scientific politics. Perhaps a new balance of forces will emerge, a rearrangement of professional ends and means, motives and techniques, in which science is cultivated less for its own sake and used more in a conscious attempt to realise preferred values."[50] Easton heralded the post-behavioural trend in 1969, he went ahead in heralding the trend of 'neo-post-behaviouralism' in 1997. Now he favoured the revival of interpretative understanding and historical analysis along with a complete rejection of the systematic methodology while simultaneously emphasising the need to introduce formal modelling and rational actor determinism. He laid stress on the necessity of further expanding the frontiers of the discipline by taking up new themes like ecologism, gender equality and justice, political identity and the like which have now come into lime light.[51]

---

49. Gaetano Salvemini: *Historians and Scientists* (Camb., Mass.: Harvard Univ. Press, 1939), pp. 112-13. The 'cry of post-behaviouralism " suggested that the members of the discipline were increasingly unable to choose from among proffered ideas and to certify some of them as authoritatively as possible so as to persuade practitioners to work along common lines. Such vocational incoherence, literally or failure to cohere reflected the inability of political scientists to behave as a scientific community in the Popperian sense of the term, as behaviouralists had long claimed they would behave. Bernard Susser says that in the post-behavioural era, precision and verifiability continue to be valued scholarly traits." See his paper 'The Behavioural Ideology: A Review and a Prospect' in *Political Studies* (September, 1974), p. 288. H.S. Kariel's complaint is that while the descriptive power of behavioural science is imperative, it does not allow us to come to terms with our ideals." *The Promise of Politics* (Englewood Cliffs, New Jersey: Prentice-Hall, 1966), p. 19. It "was, therefore, a sign of the vocational times that in the 1970s, no one succeeded in publishing a comprehensive and widely acceptable work explaining how bits of the pieces of political science research such as the outpouring of political studies, could be brought together by the community of scholars in a comprehensive and scholarly form." Ricci, *op. cit.*, p. 211.
50. Waldo, *op.cit.*, p. 115. "Even post-behaviouralism which is directed against a developing behavioural orthodoxy and whose battle cries are 'relevance and action', is a raving, rumbling structure without any ultimate destiny.... Its attempt to purport 'modest incremental change' in the behavioural ideology of 'social conservatism' and thereafter to mingle the whole carcass of rigorous techniques with values, looks ridiculous and drivel .... With its heterogeneous adherents ranging widely from the conservatism to the active left, it has taken the wind out of its sails and has driven political theory towards a shapeless monomania.... It is at best a negative unity, a passing phenomenon, as a kind of accident of history that will somehow dither and fade away soon. Its attempts to put a little flesh of classical theory on to the otherwise rather dry semantical bones of behaviouralism has gravely faltered." L.S. Rathore: The Conflict of Modernity and Tradition in Contemporary Political Theory" in J.S. Bains and R.B. Jain (ed.s): *Political Science in Transition* (New Delhi: Gitanjali, 1981), pp. 25-26.
51. David Easton: 'The Future of Post-Behavioural Phase in Political Science" in K.R. Monroe (ed.): *Contemporary Empirical Political Theory* (Berkeley: University of California Press, 1997), pp. 16-17.

22
New Leftism

> Of all the political ideas that have gone into shaping our modern world, none has gained wider usage or wielded greater influence than the left-right concept of political relationships. This is the concept that visualises our political world as a spectrum stretching between two polar extremes, the extreme left denoting revolutionary radicalism, and the extreme right denoting revolutionary reactionism. The various political schools of thought are ranged in between like the colours of a spectrum according to the intensity of their perspective tendencies.
>
> **—Kenneth K. Krogh[1]**

If liberalism has numerous varieties which make it incapable of any precise definition, curiously the same is going to happen with Marxism. It may be visualised in the metamorphoses or transmutations in the theory of classical Marxism whose diverse varieties are contained in Leninism, Stalinism, Khruschevism, Titoism, Maoism, Castroism and the like. New Leftism is another variety in this direction which denounces orthodox Marxian tradition in the name of 'slavish adherence to the Party line and tortuous defences of prescribed positions' and thus 'boasts of its autonomy'.[2] The advocates of this new trend, whether true Marxists or not, like Leszek Kolakowski, S. Stojanovic, Herbert Marcuse, Jean-Paul Sartre, Frantz Fanon, J. Garaudy, Theodore Adorno, Ernest Bloch, Jurgen Habermas, Charles Reich, Theodore Roszak and Che Guevara take inspiration from Marx and yet denounce much of what comes within the fold of classical Marxism. As a result, it has become a matter of serious debate whether New Leftism is an offshoot of Marxism or a new version of anti-Marxism; whether it is a 'leftist' or a 'rightist' movement; above all, whether it is a symbol of Marxist protestantism or a mere haphazard movement of destructive ideologists who breathe 'fire and brimstone in the wilderness of an irreligious age'.[3]

New Leftism: Nature and Essential Implications

The first question that engages our attention at this stage is: What does the term 'New Left' signify? In order to solve this predicament we should first understand the implications of the term 'left' and then see what is peculiar about the adjective 'new' prefixed to it. The term 'left' signifies anything like negation, protest, agitation, revolt and the like aiming at the overthrow of the existing order. Being a relative term, its real meaning can be understood if used in opposition to, what is called, 'right'. While the latter stands for the preservation and maintenance of the old or the

1. Krogh: "Needed New Political Labels" in W.J. Stankiewicz (ed): *Political Thought Since World War II* (New York: The Free Press of Glencoe, 1964), p. 445.
2. Maurice Cranston: *The New Left* (London: Bodley Head, 1970), p. 7.

living, the former desires change by negating, destroying or overthrowing the existing by denouncing it as irrational, obscurantist, Utopian, romantic and the like. In other words, the left "is generally understood to include those parties and movements that demand wider popular participation in government, push actively for reform, and draw particular support from the disinherited, dislocated and disgruntled."[4]

Obviously, the 'left' is the opposite of the 'right' which "is generally understood to include those parties and movements that are sceptical of popular government, oppose the bright plans of reformers and do-gooders and draw particular support from men with a sizable stake in the established order."[5] Right, among other things, means what are you doing, celebrating society as it is, a going concern. Left means, or ought to mean, just the opposite. It means: "structural criticism and reportage and theories of society, which at some point or another are focused politically, as demands and programmes. These criticisms, demands, theories, programmes are guided morally by the humanist and secular ideals of Western civilisation—above all, reason and freedom and justice. To be 'Left' means to connect up cultural with political criticism, and both with demands and programmes."[6]

It is, for this reason, that while the 'Left' is lauded for being progressive, dynamic, rational, practical, revolutionary, the 'Right' is denounced for being reactionary, static, irrational, conservative, *status quoist* and the like. It is obvious that the two terms are antithetical. As Prof. Jha says: "The Left negates existing reality, the Right affirms it; the Left is revolutionary, the Right conservative; the Left needs Utopia, the Right trick; the Left strives to change the actual conditions, the Right to idealise them; the Left adopts an attitude of permanent revisionism towards reality, the Right of opportunism; the Left stands for mobility, the Right for inertia; the Left for ideology, the Right for tactics; the Left clamours for adherence to principle, the Right for power; and, finally, the Left is provoked by conditions, the Right by the actions and the threats of the Left."[7]

The peculiar thing about the meaning of New Leftism is not as to what is meant by the term 'Left', it is as to what is 'new' about it. In simple terms, it may be defined as a movement launched by certain self-styled Marxists, described by Prof. Frank Kermode as 'Modern Masters', who not only denounce the affluent social system of a capitalist country but also hit at the regimentated system of a communist society in which there is no freedom for man. In other words, they attack both the 'bourgeois' and the 'socialist' systems and strive to bring about a new order in which man is free from the exploitation of a capitalist as well as from the suppression of a Communist state. In this way, they look like taking inspiration from Marx while hitting at the inherent evils of the capitalist system; at the same time, they have no reservations in repudiating the 'official Marxism' of the Soviet Union for its own essential weaknesses. To them both have debased and dehumanised the life of man. However, it is the 'young Marx' who is their source of inspiration. Thus, the New

3. *Ibid.*, p. 13.
4. Krogh, *op. cit.*, p. 446.
5. *Ibid.*
6. C. Wright Mills: "Letter to the New Left" in *New Left Review*, London, No. 5 (Sept-Oct, 1960), pp. 20-21.
7. B.K. Jha: "Marxism of the New Left" in *Indian Journal of Political Science*, Vol, XXXIX, No. 4, 1978, p. 539.

New Left

Influenced by the humanist writings of 'young' Marx, anarchism and radical forms of phenomenology and existentialism, New Left theories were often diffuse. Common themes nevertheless included a fundamental rejection of conventional society ('the system') as oppressive, a commitment to personal autonomy and self-fulfilment in the form of 'liberation', disillusionment with the role of the working class as the revolutionary agent, and a preference for decentralisation and participatory democracy.

—Andrew Heywood

Politics, p. 284.

The revival of Marxism in the early 1960s took on a very different aspect. This 'New Left' looked back in many ways to the 'Lyrical Left' of the 1900s. The resurgence of radicalism in the 1960s was galvanised by the increasing involvement of the United States in Vietnam.... From the start, the New Left had an ambivalent relationship to Marxism.

—David McLellan

Marxism after Marz, p. 318.

The extent to which individuals are 'free' in contemporary liberal democracies is questioned by the New Left theorists. To enjoy liberty means not only to enjoy equality before the law, important though this unquestionably is, but also to have the capacities (the material and cultural resources) to be able to choose between different courses of action.

—David Held

Political Theory and the Modern State, p. 176.

Left thinkers "go back to the early Marx and, in fact, expose Leninism and Stalinism as deviations from the humanism of the early Marx which links him to the Christians and the Greeks."[8]

One may, therefore, compare the New Leftists with the social 'drop outs' like the 'Hippies' and the 'Beatniks'. It is true that both the New Leftists and the Hipsters have some seemingly insuperable differences inasmuch as both are united by shared antipathies towards the bourgeoisie and affluent society, towards the square and the old, and united also by certain fantasies about the innocence of man and the wickedness of the rulers, the two are at variance in many important respects. While the Hippies "believe in dropping out, in withdrawing from society, the New Left believes in changing society by revolutionary action. The Hippies are pacifists, noisily dedicated to non-violence and love, which the New Left scorns; the Hippies believe in intuitive wisdom aided by drugs, while the New Left believes in dialectical reason."[9]

8. V.R. Mehta: *Beyond Marxism: Towards an Alternative Perspective* (Delhi: Manohar, 1978), p. 27. As Kolakowski says: "The so called New Left is also a complex of phenomena witnessing, on the one hand, the universalisation of the Marxist phraseology and, on the other, the disintegration of the doctrine and its inadequacy to modern social problems. It is hard to define the common ideological features of all groups and sects which claim to belong to the New Left or are considered by others to form part of it.... The New Left condemned Stalinism in general and the invasion of Hungary in particular, but its members differed among themselves as to how far the 'degeneration' of the Soviet system was inevitable and whether there was any prospect of the political, moral and intellectual renewal of the existing Communist parties. At the same time, they emphasised their fidelity to Marxism as the ideology of the working class, and some even professed allegiance to Leninism." Leszek Kolakowski; *Main Currents of Marxism: Its Origin, Growth and Dissolution,* Translated from Polish into English language by P.S. Falla (Oxford: Clarendon Press, 1978), Vol. III (The Breakdown), pp. 487-88.
9. Canston, *op. cit.,* p. 13.

It is this important point that makes a line of distinction between the 'Old' and 'New' Leftism. Leftism is not a new doctrine as such, it is as old as the socialist movement drawing inspiration from the conditions created by the industrial revolution. In this way, leftist and socialist movements become analogous terms. However, the New Left has a peculiar characteristic of its own. It believes in socialism and yet strives to protect humanism that had become a scapegoat under the 'socialist' system of the Soviet Union. That is, while the achievement of socialism is the sheet anchor of traditional leftism, socialism integrated with democracy and humanism is the keynote of, what is generally known as, New Leftism. What keeps the New Left at fundamental variance with the Old Left is its stern emphasis on pursuing positive social and political goals. It believes in freedom and democracy, and is prepared to fight for these ideals. It may also be added that while the 'Old Left' sticks to 'ideology', the 'New Left' cries for the 'end of ideology'. "The New Left took care to distinguish itself from the Old Left of the thirties and forties inasmuch as while the latter was largely associated with communism, with socialism of various kinds, and to some extent with anarchic syndicalism, the New Left was critical of both the bourgeois culture and Marxism."[10]

From what we have said above, it may be gathered that the New Leftism is a movement having following essential features:

1. It takes inspiration from the 'young Marx' who propounded the sociological theory of alienation and not from the 'old Marx' who made a vehement attack on the system of capitalism and desired its substitution by a socialist order under the 'dictatorship of the proletariat' in which the state will so act as to have its own 'withering away' in time to come. In this way, the Marxism of the New Left is based upon a new Marx. "For the Marx these writers follow, is not so much the economist, the later Marx, the author of *Das Kapital*, but rather Marx the sociologist, the author of the early philosophical manuscripts and a source of inspiration to the leading lights of the Frankfurt School."[11] Their Marx "is, like themselves, a 'Hegelian' of sorts, a metaphysician, neither a positivist, nor a scientific determinist. Their Marx is the philosopher of alienation."[12]

---

10. See E.G. Genovese: "American Left–New and Old" in *National Guardian*, Feb. 19, 1966.
11. The Frankfurt School founded in 1923 included a good number of figures like T.W. Adorno, Walter Benjamin, Otto Kirchheimer, Paul Lazarsfeld, Franz Neumann, Karl Witfogel, Eric Fromm, Herbert Marcuse, George Lukacs etc. They were among the early students of Karl Marx – the young Marx of pre-1848 period – who tried to project a mixture of Freud and Marx. They were critical of Stalinism, and lacked enthusiasm for dogmatic Leninism. They could not be good Bolsheviks, because dogmatism and bureaucracy were their enemies and they sought to sustain the tradition of critical philosophy. But in historical terms, the Frankfurt School has a special place in that it introduced critical Marxism to the American academic world. They were visibly cautious in avoiding a head-on clash with American prejudices about Communism. But the notable thing about them is that they "kept the study of Marx honourably alive even in the harshest times; and their tradition had an extraordinary late flowering in the vogue for Herbert Marcuse who became in his later sixties one of the germs of student revolution." W.J.M. Mackenzie: *Political Identity* (London: Penguin Books, 1978), pp. 54-55.
12. Cranston, *op. cit.*, p. 7.

2. Although the New Leftist thinkers claim themselves as true Marxists, they react against the 'official' version of the same as given by Stalin, Khrushchev and others in the 'Fatherland of Socialism'. That is, they repudiate the Soviet version of Marxism having its manifestation in the forms of Stalinism and Khruschevism. In other words, the New Leftists are against 'official Marxism' or that variety of Marxism which, as the Hungarian Marxist Lukacs says, "developed in the Soviet Union after Stalin gained an ideological, political and organisational victory over Trotsky, Bukharin and others."[13]
3. The New Leftists not only hit at the inherent weaknesses of the bourgeois and socialist tendencies alike, they also espouse the doctrine of 'new proletariat'. It signifies a huge class of workers who have 'embourgeoisified' themselves and thus renounced the path of revolution as envisaged by the classical Marxian tradition. If so, the Marxian law of automatic revolution in a capitalist society cannot operate. Present socio-economic conditions warrant that the class war between the capitalists and the workers has ended not only in collusion between the two, but instead there has taken place a reconciliation of the two. The need is, therefore, not of a 'dictatorship of the proletariat' but of 'welfare through the welfare state'.[14]
4. The New Leftist trend stands for humanism. It means that the advocates of this movement adhere to the values of humanism—that is, any system of thought or action which is concerned with human interests. Humanism treats man as an end in himself. Man should live like a free and rational creature. Thus, the existing social, political and economic systems should be so fashioned that they protect the worth and dignity of man. Marx is a humanist who dreams of an 'era of human emancipation' in the final stage of socialism. Different is the conception of the New Leftists. To them a free and co-operative commonwealth of man can be established even before the advent of anything like 'transitional' and 'final' stages of socialism as emphasised by Marx or his dogmatic Russian followers like Lenin and Stalin. Thus, the New Leftists desire to identify themselves with the underdog and the oppressed humanity. Its leading example can be visualised in the affirmations of Sartre who speaks of 'freedom' as 'taking of mankind as an absolute end'.[15]
5. However, the most astounding feature of the New Leftism is its glorification of violence. The New Leftists follow as well differ from Marx. The general tenor of Marxism shows that the Father of Scientific Socialism treats violence as necessary for the liquidation of the capitalist system. 'Force is the midwife of every social revolution', says Marx. However, it is towards the last phase of his life that he agrees with the idea of peaceful change in advanced democratic countries like Britain, Holland, France and the United States. Different from this, the New

13. *New Left Review*, London, No. 60, March-April, 1970, p. 39.
14. See Herbert Marcuse: *One-Dimensional Man* (London: Sphere Books, 1972).
15. W.T. Deninger: *Problems in Social and Political Thought: A Philosophical Introduction* (New York: Macmillan, 1965), p. 448.

Leftists make no reservations in exalting the case of violent and revolutionary struggles. Obviously, the New Leftists abandon the Marxian hope of a classless society that may, or may not, be established by the use of violent methods and in which violence would go with the abolition of the contending classes.[16]

In a word, the New Leftism seeks to reconstruct a new link between rank bourgeois and socialist systems in both of which persons are turned 'into attributes to be recorded and categorised on punch cards', something that resembles the 'technical system of the concentration camps'.[17] It seeks to imbibe the essential virtues and discard the inherent weaknesses of both in a way so that there looks like 'a convergence of two models'.[18]

Origin and Development: Trend Towards the Convergence of Bourgeois and Socialist Models

The New Leftism is a product of the post-Second World War period. What has led to the origin and growth of this movement which looks like Marxian in some and un-Marxian, even anti-Marxian, in some other respects? An answer to such a question is that three factors should be taken into account—stern reaction against the version of official Marxism as given by the great comrades of the then Soviet Union, vehement protest against the social, economic and political make-up of the affluent societies of the advanced Western countries, and a very strong emphasis on the worth and dignity of man. That is, this movement came into being as a result of many-headed protests—protests against Stalinist excesses, against dogmatic and mechanistic version of Marxism as given by the Soviet leaders, against centralised and undemocratic ways of doing things, against anti-humanistic, bureaucratic and technocratic bourgeois society of oppression, against the all-powerful military industrial complexes, against the aggressive foreign policy pursued by the imperialist powers, and against certain consequences of industrial revolution.[19]

---

16. Isaac Deutscher: *Marxism in Our Time* (San Francisco: The Ramparts Press, 1971), p. 83.
17. J. Ellul: *The Technological Society* (London: Jonathan, 1964), p. 251.
18. See A. Meyer: "Theories of Convergence" in Chalmers Johnson (ed.): *Change in Communist Systems* (Stanford, 1970), pp. 313-43. According to Derek Heater, "For the man who harbours with some bitterness his resentment against the injustices of society and the state as they are currently organised, Communism has for the past century, provided an intellectual refuge. However, when the Communist refuge becomes a prison as offensive as the capitalist gaol, the radical must resume his intellectual journeying. Disillusion came to many with the horrors of Stalinist totalitarianism. But no vigorous alternative was forthcoming until the 1960s. Then, at last, a new generation, offered by Soviet action in Hungary and Czechoslovakia and by what they interpreted as the betrayal of the revolutionary tradition by the moderate tactics of many a Communist Party, fumbled its way towards a new Utopian doctrine. In 1968 they seized public attention by a series of dramatic outbursts in both the USA and Europe. This new movement is too amorphous to be called an organisation—indeed, there is considerable ingredient of anarchist individualism in the mixture.' *Contemporary Political Ideas* (London: Longman, 1974), p. 39.
19. B.K. Jha, *op. cit.*, pp. 540-41.

Kolakowski on Characteristic Tendencies of New Leftism

1. The New Leftists maintain that the concept of a society's ripeness for revolution is a bourgeois deceit; a properly organised group can make a revolution in any country and bring about a radical change of social conditions (revolution here and now). There is no reason to wail; existing states and governing elites must be destroyed by force, without arguing about the political and economic organisation of the future—the revolution will decide these in its own good time.
2. The existing order deserves destruction in all its aspects without exception; the revolution must be worldwide, total, absolute, unlimited, all-embracing. As the idea of total revolution began in the universities, its first blows were naturally directed against fraudulent academic institutions, against knowledge and logical skills. Periodicals, pamphlets and leaflets declared that revolutionaries must not get into discussion with teachers who asked them to explain their demands of terminology. There was much talk of liberation from the inhuman oppression that required students to pass examinations or to learn one subject rather than another. it was also a revolutionary duty to oppose all reforms in the universities or in society; the revolution must be universal, and all partial reforms were a conspiracy of the establishment. Either everything or nothing must be changed, for as Lukacs, Marcuse, and the Frankfurt School had taught, capitalist society was an indivisible whole and could only be transformed as such.
3. The working class could not be relied on, as it had been irredeemably defrauded by the bourgeoisie. At the present time, students were the most oppressed members of society; and, therefore, the most revolutionary. All were oppressed, however, the bourgeoisie had introduced the cult of labour and the first duty, was therefore, to stop work—the necessities of life would be forthcoming in some way or another. One disgraceful form of oppression is the prohibition of drugs, and this too, must be fought against. Sexual liberation and restrictions of all kinds are the essence of communism.
4. The patterns of world revolution were to be found in the Third World. The heroes of the New Left were African, Latin-American and Asian political leaders. The United States must be transformed into the likeness of China, Vietnam or Cuba. Apart from the leaders of the Third World and Western ideologists interested in its problems like Frantz Fanon and Regis Debray, the students of New Left especially admired Negro leaders in the United States who advocated violence and black racialism.

Leszek Kolakowski: *Main Currents of Marxism,* Vol. III, pp. 489-90.

In the first place, we take up the case of reaction against Soviet Marxism that has had its manifestation in certain 'communist' countries of the East European region. Mention should be made of the Polish philosopher Leszek Kolakowski who makes an attempt to reinterpret Marxism and thereby charge Stalin with committing an act of 'historical fallacy'.[20] Likewise, the Yugoslavian teacher S. Stojanovic accuses Stalin of 'primitive politocratic statism' and pleads for the separation of Marxism from the Stalinist myth of the state.[21] Though in their own way, both admit that capitalism

20. See Kolakowski: *Marxism and Beyond* (Paladin, 1971).
21. S. Stojanovic: *Between Ideal and Reality: A Critique of Socialism and Its Future,* Translated from Yugoslavian into English by G.S. Sher, (Oxford, 1973), p. 5.

does a spiritual injury to man and also argue that Marxism too has not given a better account of itself in practice either. Kolakowski has discovered that the Kantian principle that every individual should be treated as an end in himself is not just a typical bourgeois idea but applies to all societies and can prevent many wrongs.[22] He argues that communism cannot be established by practices which educate citizens in fear and lies which are evil in themselves and must be combated by every man of socialist disposition. He goes to the extent of declaring that the maintenance of power by criminal means "is contrary to the ends of socialist construction and fetters its achievement."[23]

Different is the case of the rise and arid growth of the New Left Movement in the United States. Here stern reaction against the affluent society and America's involvement in nuclear wars became the immediate sources of inspiration. That is, in the United States, this movement arose as a consequence of an industrial and technological revolution. Writers like Herbert Marcuse made a scathing attack on the evils of the industrial society. He wailed over the fact of 'alienation' and desired a life of freedom and dignity for man. Motivated by a disgust at affluence without dignity, desire for beauty as well as democracy, belief in creativity rather than consensus, wish for community and communal values and vehement rejection of depersonalised bureaucracy, desire to build a 'counter society' with 'parallel institutions' and not simply to be integrated into and to be accepted by the dominant institutions, hostility to what is conceived of as the dehumanisation and alienation of a cash-nexus society, preference for individuated, intensely felt, and self-generated interpersonal style, including fuller sexual expression and experimentation are the elements that provide stimulus to this movement in the United States.[24]

That is, a study of the American way of life from a sociological standpoint informed the New Leftists like Marcuse, in particular, to attack the norms of functionalism and hierarchical organisation involving business management and public relations that were, by and large, regarded in the free, open and plural society as major instruments for resolving social conflicts and tensions. It had its inevitable effect on other industrially advanced countries of the world as well. Thus, in the countries of the West European region quite a good number of New Leftist thinkers came to realise that the need of the moment was not to fight against nobility as in the era of feudalism, or against economic situation under the industrial society, but against every force that undermined the worth and dignity of human life. We are living in a post-industrial society in which neither the laws of an Adam Smith nor that of a Karl Marx would work in view of the fact that now the struggle is neither a purely economic nor a political affair, rather it is concerned with the very preservation of man's life as a man in the face of the invisible, omnipresent dictatorship of forces which tend to integrate and assimilate all elements (including the human one) into the system.[25]

---

22. See Kolakowski: *Philosophy and Everyday Life* (Warsaw, 1957).
23. See V.R. Mehta: "Marxism in the Modern World" in *Indian Journal of Political Science,* Vol. XXXVI, No. 4, 1975, p. 319.
24. A.W. Gouldner: *The Coming Crisis of Western Sociology* (London: Heinemann, 1970), p. 399.
25. Massimo Teodori ; (ed.): *The New Left: A Documentary History* (London: Jonathan Cape, 1969), p. 10.

Leading New Left Theorists

Herbert Marcuse: The capitalist development has altered the structure and function of these two classes in such a way that they no longer appear to be agents of historical transformation. An overriding interest in the preservation and improvement of the institutional status quo unites the former antagonists in the most advanced areas of contemporary society. And the degree to which technical progress assures the growth and cohesion of communist society, the very idea of qualitative change recedes before the realistic notions of a non-explosive evolution.

– *One-Dimensional Man,* p. 11.

Jurgen Habermas: Technological society could only be rational if its policies were subject to public control. The very act of speech involved the supposition of the possibility of an ideal speech situation in which the force of the better argument alone would decide the issue. This was only possible if all members of society had an equal chance to participate in the discussion; and this involved the notion of the transformation of society in a direction that would enable such a communicative competence to characterise all members of society.

– David MacLellan: *Marxism after Marx,* p. 273.

Carole Pateman: The free and equal individual is, in practice, a person found much more rarely than liberal theory suggests. Inequalities of class, sex and race substantially hinder the extent to which it can legitimately be claimed that individuals are free and equal. The state is inescapably located into the maintenance and reproduction of the inequalities of everyday life.

– *The Problem of Political Obligation,* pp. 171-73.

Nicos Poulantzas: Marx's and Lenin's belief that the institutions of representative democracy can be simply swept away by organisation of rank-and-file democracy is erroneous. Without general elections, without unrestricted freedom of press and assembly, without a free struggle of opinion, life dies out in every public institution.

– *State, Power, Socialism,* p. 283.

Henri Lefebvre: Alienation would persist even after a successful proletarian revolution and the post-revolutionary communist society was not immune from many of the problems currently affecting capitalist society. The total man is a dealienated man.

– *Dialectical Materialism,* p. 162.

The names of Frantz Fanon and Jean-Paul Sartre of France should be referred to, in particular, at this stage who insist that the objective of man's struggle today is 'the reconquest of his individual autonomy' which may perhaps best be attained by working among the forgotten, the poor and the outcastes of the society.'[26] Fanon suggested it as the only practicable course for the betterment of the lot of the Negroes and other suppressed people in the colony of Algeria. Sartre looked at the final point of Marxism and thus sought to integrate his existentialism with it so as to highlight the point that the freedom of man was more important than all social and economic structures.

However, the most recent landmark is the dramatic reappearance of the New Left, the romantic radicals on the left flank of conventional Marxism, lurking in the background ever since the rediscovery of the'young Marx', but making its powerful political debut only with the abortive French uprising of 1968. Intellectuals like

26. S.P. Varma: *Modern Political Theory* (Delhi: Vikas, 1975), p. 371.

Marcuse and Sartre as well as revolutionaries like Che Guevara and Regis Debray have taken inspiration from youth and student movements going on in different parts of the world and have laid special reliance on the use of youth power for bringing about, what may be termed, 'new socialism'. The fight of the American Negroes for civil rights, the student revolt in France for the change in education system, the struggle of the workers in Spain for the democratisation of the political system are some of the momentous events that inspire the New Leftist thinkers to say that the youthful elements can bring about the desired state of affairs inasmuch as they "have penetrated into the technical machinery of the capitalist State, the judiciary, even the army and the forces of public order. They are shattering the conformity of the traditional intellectual circles, the established ones."[27]

Keeping all this in view, one may easily form an impression that the New Left is a movement of protest that may, and also may not, be construed as a reïnterpretation of Marxism in the modern world. As a leading light of this new trend says: "The New Left is, with some exceptions, Neo-Marxist rather than Marxist in the orthodox sense; it is strongly influenced by what is called Maoism, and by the revolutionary movements in the Third World. Moreover, the New Left includes neo-anarchist tendencies, and it is characterised by a deep mistrust of the old leftist parties and their ideology. And the New Left is again with exceptions not bound to the old working class as the sole revolutionary agent. The New Left itself cannot be defined in terms of class, consisting as it does of intellectuals of groups from the civil rights movement, and of youth groups, especially the most radical elements of youth, including those who at first glance do not appear political at all.... It is very interesting that this movement has as spokesmen not traditional politicians but rather such suspect figures as poets, writers and intellectuals.... You have here an opposition that obviously has nothing to do with the classical revolutionary force...."[28]

Search for De-alienation: Fundamental Tenet of New Leftism

As already pointed out, the Marxism of the New Left is based on a new Marx—Marx of the *Economic and Philosophical Manuscripts* and not of the critique of political economy, Marx as a sociologist, not a political economist, the 'young Marx' of the early 1840's and not the 'old Marx' of the late 1840's. In his *Paris Manuscripts,* Marx says: "Since human nature is man's true communal nature, men create and develop their communal nature by their natural action; they develop their social being which is no abstract, universal power as opposed to the single individual, but the nature of each individual, his own activity, his own life, his own enjoyment, his own wealth. Therefore, this true communal nature does not originate in reflection, it takes shape through the need and egotism of individuals, i.e., it is produced directly by the effect of their being. It is not dependent on man whether this communal being exists or not, but so long as man has not recognised himself as man and has not organised this world in a human way, the communal nature appears in the form of alienation because its subject, man, is a self-alienated being. Man, not in the abstract but as real, living, particular individuals are this nature."[29]

27. Santiago Carrillo: *Problem of Socialism Today* (London, 1970), pp. 125-26.
28. Herbert Marcuse: *Five Lectures: Psychoanalysis, Politics and Utopia* (Boston, 1970), pp. 83-84.
29. D. McLellan (ed.): *Marx: Early Writings,* p. 193.

It is this sociological research of Marx contained in his *Economic and Philosophical Manuscripts* or *Paris Manuscripts* written in 1844 that becomes the starting point of the New Leftists. They dwell upon the Marxian idea of 'alienation' and, like him, strive for a passage of human life from the 'kingdom of necessity' to the 'kingdom of happiness'. Looking at the inherent evils of the industrial society, Marcuse laments: Men do not live their own lives, but perform pre-established functions. While they work, they do not fulfil their own needs and faculties, but work in alienation."[30] Marcuse, once a leading light of the Frankfurt School, however, refutes what Marx says in his *Capital* on the plea that the working conditions have changed. In appreciation of the early works of Marx, he says that these "could put the discussion about the origins and original meaning of historical materialism, and the entire body of 'scientific socialism' on a new footing."[31] He insists on the understanding of the reality of the present industrial society whose capabilities (intellectual and material) "are immeasurably greater than ever before—which means that the scope of society's domination over the individual is immeasurably greater than ever before."[32]

Looking at the two main antagonists of modern capitalism, as suggested by Marx, the bourgeoisie and the proletariat, Marcuse admits that they are still the 'basic classes'. However, he insists that the capitalist development "has altered the structure and function of these two classes in such a way that they no longer appear to be the agents of historical transformation. On the contrary, an overriding interest in the preservation and improvement of the *status quo* unites the former antagonists in the most advanced areas of contemporary society". As he says: "The one-dimensional man will vacillate throughout between two contradictory hypotheses (i) that advanced industrial society is capable of containing qualitative changes for the foreseeable future; (ii) that forces and tendencies exist which may break this containment and explode the society."[33]

In simple terms, it follows that the evil of alienation being a by-product of the bourgeois society (as suggested by Marx) can be cured in the present industrial society without liquidating it altogether. It may be noted in Eric Fromm's theory of alienation.[34] Likewise, Sartre hits at the curse of alienation in the life of an 'inauthentic man'.[35] His concern with a living person and with his concrete emotions

30. Marcuse: *Eros and Civilisation: A Philosophical Enquiry into Freud* (London: Allen Lane, The Penguin Press, 1969), p. 45
31. Marcuse: *Studies in Critical Philosophy,* Translated from German into English by Joris de Bres, (London: NLB, 1972), p. 3.
32. Marcuse: *One-Dimensional Man,* p. 9.
33. *Ibid., p. 15.* But Marcuse may be called a Marxist, because there is no Marxist pope or council to declare him heretical. Moreover, it is an open question as to what Marx meant by 'dialectical' and by 'materialism'. Young Marx is strongly critical, strongly historical, but surely he is in a philosophical sense idealist and not materialist. Mackenzie, *op. cit.,* p. 65. Paul Thomas says that "Marx himself never combined the phrase 'dialectical materialism'." See his paper "Marx and Science" in *Political Studies,* Vol. 24 (1979), p. 2.
34. The impact of Marx upon Fromm may be noted in the fact that he never moves far from the spirit of young Marx. He says: "Free man is by necessity insecure, thinking man by necessity uncertain." *The Sane Society* (London: Routledge and Kegan Paul, 1963), pp. 196-97.
35. Sartre: *Being and Nothingness,* Translated from French into English by H.E. Barnes (New York: Washington Square Press, 1966) p. xix.

of anguish, despair, *nausea* and the like should be referred to here. As he says: "The worker exhausts himself in producing a car and in earning enough to buy one; the acquisition gives him the impression of having satisfied a need. The system which exploits him provides him simultaneously with the possibility of reaching it. The consciousness of the intolerable character of the system must, therefore, no longer be sought in the impossibility of satisfying elementary needs but above all else in the consciousness of alienation—in other words, in the fact that this life is not worth living and has no meaning, that this mechanism is deceptive mechanism, that these needs are artificially created, that they are false, that they are exhausting and only serve profit."[36]

Sartre desires that Marxism ought to study real men in depth, not dissolve them in a bath of sulphuric acid and avoid the totalising of living human realities into impersonal collectivities such as the bourgeoisie, imperialism, class war. He argues that a reductionist conception of totality eliminates the real, lived relations and the corresponding concrete mediations: the complex levels of economy and culture disappear if assumed under collective terms and the 'fundamental determinations' are lost. That is, he opposes the reduction of individuals to the status of group or class representative. Like the phenomenologists he criticises the mechanical ahistorical conceptions of totality found in functionalist sociology and some branches of social psychology.[37] Like Marcuse, he suggests that the problem in advanced capitalist states is not so much real but rather alienation caused by the creation of artificial consumer needs. The way out is a 'utopia'— "the withering away not only of the state but of the politics altogether through a full exercise of self-government at every level."[38]

We may discover the same trend in the expressions of 'practical revolutionaries' like Ernesto Che Guevara of Cuba and Regis Debray of Bolivia. Che in his *Man and Socialism in Cuba* yearns for the creation of a new man. He wails that man suffers a kind of death during the eight hours of his daily work, and even the artistic creations by which he might express the anguish of his environmentally determined situation have been restricted by an ideological conditioning through which the monopoly capitalists prevent art from becoming a weapon of denunciation and accusation'.[39] Man is exploited, and consequently his moral stature is diminished; but this happens very largely without his awareness. His attention is focused by the agents of the monopoly capitalists upon the success of a Rockefeller, and diverted away from the unsavoury facts which made such a gigantic accumulation of wealth in the hands of one man possible. What should be done? Che answers in these words: "We are seeking something new that will allow a perfect identification between the government and the community as a whole, adapted to the special conditions of the building of socialism and avoiding to the utmost the commonplace of bourgeois democracy translated to the society information..... the ultimate and most important revolutionary aspiration (is) to see man freed from alienation."[40]

36. Sartre: *Between Existentialism and Marxism,* Translated from French into English by John Mathews (New York: Pantheon, 1974), pp. 124-25.
37. A. Swingewood: *Marx and Modern Social Theory* (London: Macmillan, 1975), pp. 56-57.
38. Francois Bondy: "Jean-Paul Sartre" in Cranston (ed.): *The New Left*, p. 81.
39. John Gerassi (ed.); *The Speeches and Writings of Che Guevara* (London, 1968), p. 547.
40. *Ibid.*, p. 544.

The name of Frantz Fanon, however, deserves a special mention at this stage. A Negro psychiatrist who plunged into the Algerian insurrection stretches the Marxian concept of alienation to encompass a colonial world where the relations of production are themselves superstructures rooted in the relations of colonialism.[41] He says: "Colonialism and imperialism have not paid their score when they withdrew their flags and their police forces from our territories. For centuries the capitalists have behaved in the underdeveloped world like nothing more than war criminals. Deportations, massacres, forced labour and slavery have been the main methods used by capitalism to increase its wealth, its gold and diamond reserves, and to establish its power."[42] He condemns the European powers for filling evils 'in the heart of man' like racial hatred, slavery, exploitation and, above all, the bloodless genocide which consisted in the setting aside of fifteen thousand millions of men. The way out is the freedom of the subject peoples and a change in the 'hearts' of those who have hitherto ruled as well as those who have been ruled. Thus, he exhorts: "For Europe, for ourselves, and for humanity, we must turn over a new leaf, we must work out new concepts, and try to set afoot a new man."[43]

It may be inferred that while the New Leftist thinkers draw inspiration from Marx in lamenting at the sociological fact of alienation, what they suggest as the way out is different from him. They do not agree with Marx that alienation will go with the abolition of class war, i.e. with the establishment of a new society having neither classes nor the state. Rather, they are of the view that the curse of alienation can go even in the present 'industrial' society. It is, however, a different matter that the New Leftist thinkers have their different solutions to bring about the state of de-alienation. For instance, while Marcuse hopes that the evil of alienation would go with the creation of a free man, Fanon would say that it would go with the creation of a free community having a 'changed heart'. A synthesised view, however, leads to this conclusion that the state of de-alienation would come with the availability of freedom to man even in a non-Communist society.

It follows that while alienation is a consequence of the loss of freedom, de-alienation is bound up with the coming of freedom. A communist system is thus no solution to this inhuman problem in view of the fact that a regimentated system can neither ensure freedom to the people groaning under its heel, nor can it pave the way for the eventual inauguration of a new society that may be termed as the 'era of human emancipation'. In this way, the New Leftist thinkers "reject the Marxism implicit in the Stalinist version of it and go back to the earlier Marx who was interested not so much in the problem of economic man as in the problem of the human individual. This was the Marx who emphasised the fact of man's alienation in a capitalist society in terms of the idea of freedom as the supreme goal of every

41. B.K. Jha, *op.cit.*, p. 547.
42. Fanon: *The Wretched of the Earth,* Translated from French into English by C Farrington (London: Penguin Books, 1967), pp. 79-81. "This work of Fanon takes a position of extreme radicalism on the colonial question. It is tagged as Marxist by the occasional use of Marxist fetish words such as dialectical contradictions, consciousness, historic mission. But Fanon was neither a Marxian scholar nor a Partyman, and he seems to use these words not for analysis but as insignia, badge or colour." Mackenzie, *op cit.*, p. 81.
43. See Jack Woddis: *New Theories of Revolution* (New York: International Publishers, 1972), p. 34.

society. Most of the New Leftist thinkers react against orthodox Marxist thinking which relegates freedom to the background and believes that an egalitarian society can be erected only with the help of a centralised, undemocratic revolutionary party with iron discipline in which it is not the will of the common man which is dominant but the will of the party itself. The mechanistic picture of Marxism which early scholars identified with Marx, they identify with the Stalinist regime"[44]

Attack on Soviet Marxism: Enunciation of the Doctrine of 'New Socialism'

The New Leftist thinkers claim themselves as the rational and dynamic followers of Marx, and, on this plea, denounce the Soviet leaders like Stalin and Khruschev for being dogmatist. They are critical not only of the industrial or post-industrial society dominated by the super-capitalists, they are equally critical of the 'socialist' system dominated by a certain leader of the Communist Party or his clique. As such, the system of the Soviet Union, as under Stalin and after him, becomes an object of attack at the hands of the New Leftists. They refute the claim of the Russian Marxists that 'true Marxism', understood as a science of society, is 'historical materialism' whose object is the socio-economic transformation and within which Marx's *Capital* provides the theory of the structure and the laws of motion of the capitalist mode of production.[45]

The fact of 'bureaucratisation' is dwelt upon by the 'modern masters' of the New Left movement. To them the continuous concentration of capital and the increasing intervention of the state in the economic and social matters has provided a new managerial class whose fate is no longer bound up with that of the private ownership of the means of production.[46] In this direction, we may refer to the affirmations of Cohn-Bendit, the student leader of the French revolt of May, 1968. He compares the role of the Communist Party of the then Soviet Union with massive bureaucratic set up. Says he: "Communists and also Trotskyites, Maoists and the rest no less than the capitalists, all look upon the proletariat as a mass that needs to be directed from above. As a result, democracy degenerates into the ratification at the bottom of the decisions taken at the top, and the class struggle is forgotten while the leaders jockey for power within the political hierarchy."[47]

Significantly, the New Leftists contend what even the contemporaries of Lenin like Rosa Luxemburg and Leon Trotsky had said in opposition to the thesis of 'ultra-centralisation'. What these mild critics of Bolshevism had once feared has now come true. The 'dictatorship of the proletariat'has become a 'dictatorship over the proletariat'. Cohn-Bendit says that the Communist Party had put the entire working class of the then Soviet Union behind a barbed wire fencing. He refers to the reactions of conscientious men like Alexander Solzhenitsyn and Volin who harboured no illusions in describing the great Russian leaders as 'men believing in centralised and authoritarian leadership' crushing all opposition with an iron fist.

44. Mehta: *Beyond Marxism*, p. 23.
45. David Fernbach in *New Left Review*, No. 56, July-Aug , 1969, p. 62.
46. Varma, *op cit.*, p. 374.
47. Cohn-Bendit: *Obsolete Communism: The Left Wing's Alternative* (New York: McGraw Hill, 1968), pp. 199 ff.

So strong is the reaction of this French revolutionary that he denounces the system of party as the very name of a tyrannical government.[48]

This line of affirmation may be seen in the writings of several other New Leftist thinkers some of whom are also known by the appellation of 'Euro-communists'. Thus, Santiago Carrillo of Spain says: "The present Soviet State has certainly carried out the functions of achieving development in the economic, industrial and cultural fields, and in the field of health, and also in that of national defence. In other words, it has carried out tasks which in other countries of advanced capitalism have been carried out by the capitalist state. Having suppressed capitalist property, it has created the conditions for going over to evolved socialism. The question that now arises is whether the actual structures of that state have not been transformed, at least in part, into an obstacle to evolved socialism: whether that state, as it now exists, is not in itself already a brake on the development of a real working-class democracy and, in addition, whether it has not constituted a brake on the country's material development.[49]

Looking at the developments of the Soviet Union under the rule of the Communist Party as well as within its own ranks with considerable apprehension, Sartre shows his agreement with Merleau-Ponty's *Humanism et terreur* and holds that in a revolutionary party running a revolutionary regime, opposition is objectively synonymous with treason. For this he refers to the Bukharin trial. In 1956 he denounced the totalitarian rule of Khrushchev particularly when the Russian troops suppressed the liberation movement in Hungary. He expressed his frank disapproval of the Khrushchevian interpretation of Marxism and the change in the Soviet political system made in the name of the 'project of a revolution' by which men should determine their future. He held that a state run on revolutionary principles "must be judged on the basis of its 'project' and its essential need to defend itself against a hostile world: that the logic of this state and its interest must always be borne in mind, whereas bourgeois states must be judged only by their errors, shortcomings and crimes, all of which are in fact not accidental and durable but are the product of an original sin and can be removed only by a violent, purifying and total revolution."[50]

In brief, the aim of the New Leftists is to attack the variety of Marxism that had developed in the Soviet Union under the iron hold of the Communist Party. Instead they think in terms of a new variety of socialism based on the practicable propositions of Marxism. A socialism of this type must be in consonance with the premises of a democratic system so that people may have the boons of freedom, development and happiness. Socialism cannot be created without creating a new man, without providing conditions for creating new needs. It does not consist merely in extending "to the masses those forms of comfort, luxury or art once the sole prerogative of the privileged classes, but rather in creating new needs and new means of satisfying them, thus also creating unprecedented forms of happiness, of beauty, and of life itself."[51]

48. *Ibid.*, p. 250.
49. Carrillo:Euro-communism *and the State* (London: Lawrence and Wishart, 1977), p. 161.
50. Francois Bondy in Cranston, *op. cit.*, p. 53.
51. Roger Garaudy: *The Turning Point of Socialism* (London: Fontana, 1969), p. 199.

Refutation of Class War: Reliance on the Role of 'Lumpenproletariat'

One important direction where the New Leftists look like thoroughly abandoning the line of Marx, though slightly drifting towards that of Mao, is their refutation of the theory of class war and enunciation of the doctrine of a huge poor, backward, neglected, unprivileged, exploited and oppressed class what they call by the name of 'lumpenproletariat'. It signifies the working class as a whole whether poor, backward, impoverished,oppressed and exploited (as suggested by Marx) or comparatively better off and developed under the new conditions of an industrial society. Obviously, the term 'lumpenproletariat' covers all what comes within the'proletariat' of Marx and Mao and also much that does not fall within the ambit of a traditional Marxian interpretation. Not only those working in some industry or on the fields and falling prey to the exploitation of the capitalists and landlords but even those living in the American ghettoes, those groaning under the colonial hold in the Third World, or those who have embourgeoisiefied themselves, all should be included in the category of the 'lumpenproletariat'. All social dropouts like the Hippies and the Beatniks as well as others belonging to a middle class intelligentsia should be included herein. In a word, this class consists of all, what Frantz Fanon designates 'the wretched or damned of the earth'. Marcuse includes students, intellectuals and a host of 'outsiders' in this broad category.

It is, therefore, obvious that the New Leftists not only take inspiration from a 'new Marx', but they also discover a 'new proletariat'. Marx had hoped that the working class of advanced industrial countries would become progressively more and more impoverished and that it would enact the role of a revolutionary class by overthrowing the capitalist system and thereby introducing socialism. In contrast to this, the New Leftism does not entertain this hope. It despairs of any revolutionary action from the workers of the Western world.[52]

Thus, the New Leftists talk of a 'new opposition' staged by a huge section of the disgruntled humanity so as to make the system of democracy really meaningful. As Marcuse says: ".... the struggle for the solution has outgrown the traditional forms. The totalitarian tendencies of the one-dimensional society render the traditional ways and means of protest ineffective— perhaps even dangerous because they preserve the illusion of popular sovereignty.... However, underneath the conservative popular base is the substratum of the outcasts and outsiders, the exploited and persecuted of other races and other colours, the unemployed and the unemployable. They exist outside the democratic process; their life is the most immediate and the most real need for ending intolerable conditions and institutions. Their opposition is revolutionary even if their consciousness is not. Their opposition has the system from without and is, therefore, not deflected by the system; it is an elementary force which violates the rules of the game, and, in doing so, reveals it as a rigged game."[53]

What is really very astonishing in this direction is that the New Leftists not only broaden the meaning of the terms 'oppressed and exploited class' by using the appellation of 'lumpenproletariat', they also refute the thesis of 'class war' on which the entire structure of classical Marxism stands. The advocates of the 'New Left'

52. Maurice Cranston, *op. cit.*, p. 8.
53. Marcuse: *One-Dimensional Man*, p. 200.

discard the idea of 'class consciousness', as suggested by Marx, that would lead to the outbreak of a revolution. To them the change or reform, not revolution as believed by Marx, would be brought about by the huge section of the 'lumpenproletariat' without having a bloody war so as to install the 'dictatorship of the proletariat' as a prelude to the establishment of a classless society to be eventually turned into a stateless pattern of collective life. What Marcuse has said on this subject manifests his "bold rejection of the organised working class, of its trade unions and parties, and of its forms of struggle, and his equally bold claims on behalf of the outsiders who owe no allegiance or commitment to existing organisations, and who refuse to play the 'rigged game' of utilising traditional forms of struggle."[54]

Sartre reaffirms the same on the basis of his personal experiences. In him we may find an increasingly noticeable rejection of the idea of 'European proletariat' as the chosen instrument of revolution and the destroyer of the bourgeoisie, because this proletariat has itself fallen victim to bourgeois and apolitical tendencies. He looks towards the oppressed and exploited mankind of a colonial country and prefers to call it 'new proletariat' in the sense that in a war of liberation they have, in the words of the *Communist Manifesto,* 'nothing to lose but their chains'. He expects this total revolution of the new proletariat "to lead to new, nobler forms of socialism, whose creative revolutionary impulses would then affect the European proletariat itself."[55]

However, the peculiar thing about Fanon, in this direction, is that he placed his reliance mainly on the black and persecuted mankind of the African Negroes groaning for liberation from the white colonial domination having its citadels of strength in the urban areas. As he says: "In fact, the rebellion which began in the country districts, will filter into the towns through that fraction of the peasant population which is blocked on the outer fringe of the urban centres, that fraction which has not yet succeeded in finding a bone to gnaw in the colonial system. The men whom the growing population of the country districts and colonial expropriation have brought to desert their family holdings, circle tirelessly around the different towns, hoping that one day or another they will be allowed inside. It is within this mass of humanity, this people of the shanty towns, at the core of the 'lumpenproletariat', that rebellion will find its urban spearhead. For the 'lumpenproletariat', that horde of starving men, uprooted from their tribe and from their clan, constitutes one of the most spontaneous and the most radically revolutionary forces of a colonised people."[56]

We may easily find a clear-cut case of the abandonment of Marxism by the New Leftist thinkers in this direction. They accept and eulogise the case of 'lumpenproletariat' what Marx decried as 'rag bag of assorted elements'.[57] The key tenets of Marxism contained in the division of society into two contending classes, the element of class consciousness developed in the class of the oppressed and the exploited workers, and, above all, the inevitability of a revolution owing to the

54. Jack Woddis, *op., cit.,* p. 294.
55. Francois Bondy, *op. cit.,* p. 54.
56. Fanon: *The Damned of the Earth,* p. 103.
57. Marx-Engels: *Selected Works,* Vol. 4, p. 472.

application of the law of dialectical materialism all stand refuted at the hands of the New Leftists. Keeping this in view, Prof. Maurice Cranston holds: "But if the new proletariat is a myth, it is an important myth to those who want to believe that in turning their backs on the industrial working classes, they are still Marxists, and perhaps even better Marxists than Marx himself."[58]

Youth and Revolution: Profile of 'New Opposition' in a Free Society

We have already hinted that the New Leftists place their main reliance on the role of youth and student organisations in bringing about a new order without any determination to overthrow the existing bourgeois order. What is needed is change: change towards real democracy. This change can be brought about by the youthful sections of the people. It is this section of the society that may understand the inherent evils of an affluent society as well as the pernicious dimensions of a socialist system and then fight for the restoration of a free and dignified life. It is the community of the students that may overthrow the 'discredited' education system and infuse a 'new culture' in the future rulers of the country. In this direction, the New Leftists look like taking inspiration from Lenin who said: "We are a party of the future and the future belongs to the youth. We are a party of the innovators, and it is always the youth that most eagerly follows innovators. We are a party that is waging a self-sacrificing struggle against the old rottenness, and youth is always the first to undertake a self-sacrificing struggle."[59]

Whether intellectuals like Marcuse and Sartre or revolutionaries like Che and Debray, all lay emphasis on the significance of the role of the youth in staging the 'new opposition' and thereby achieving the goal of a 'democratic society'. It is a matter of their conviction that the intellectuals and students, because of their social origin and position, exercise a tremendous influence on the middle strata, who are generally paralysed by deep-rooted conservative prejudice, who are embedded in the social system and constitute the firmest mass support for the ruling policy and ideology. Sticking his mind to the recent developments in Spain, a well-known figure of the Spanish Communist Party, says that the students and the intellectuals, by their struggles, are disturbing the complacent calm, the conformism, the smug satisfaction, of the functionary who thinks he is at the summit of society because he is one of the cogs of the system; they are jolting the tranquillity of the petit and middle bourgeoisie is, making him realise that this society is not immutable."[60]

The workers alone cannot bring about a successful revolution. On this point Marcuse is very specific who desires a close collaboration of the workers with the students, intellectuals, 'outsiders' including the exploited people of the Third World. He says: "The character of the opposition in the centre of the corporate capitalism is concentrated in the two opposite poles of society; in the ghetto population (itself not homogeneous), and in the middle class intelligentsia, especially among the students."[61]

58. Cranston, *op. cit.*, p. 8.
59. V.I. Lenin: *Collected Works*, Vol.2, p. 354.
60. Carrillo: *Problems of Socialism Today*, pp. 125-26.
61. Marcuse: "Re-examination of the Concept of Revolution" in *Diogenes*, Winter, 1968, No. 64, p. 20.

However, like Sartre, he does not rely merely or mainly on the role of the students.The students cannot achieve their goal unless they have the support of the huge working class and oppressed humanity, though they may lead the revolution. Revolutionary in its theory, instincts and goals, the students do not constitute a revolutionary force, perhaps not even an *avant garde* so long as there are no masses capable of and willing to follow.[62] What is noticeably important about the student community is that it can realise the urgent need for the creation of a free society and, for this purpose, may do much what cannot be done by the non-intelligent sections of the oppressed people. We may find that implicit here "is Marcuse's expectation that the students will become the eventual vanguard of the revolutionary struggle."[63]

Thus, to sum up Marcuse's views on the role of class forces in the revolution in the industrial-capitalist countries:

1. The majority of the working class has become an aristocracy of labour, 'integrated' into the system, passive, conservative and even counter-revolutionary. The only sections which may be won over are the young workers, and the new technical cadres.
2. The decisive new opposition in the metropolis is composed of (a) outsiders, the unemployed and the unemployable, the Black People and other persecuted minorities, acting in unison with (b). the students and intellectuals in whom resides the inspiration and accumulated understanding of the nature of the changes to be made. The essential proletarian ally of these forces is the (c) exploited masses in the Third World.

"Linked to the concept is another major element in Marcuse's thinking—the inadequacy, uselessness and even the danger of the traditional forms of struggle and the traditional institutions of the working class."[64]

Likewise, Sartre pinned hopes on the student revolt of May, 1968 in which Cohn-Bendit played the role of a leader. He appreciated the statement of this student leader that a French university was like 'a sausage machine which turns out people without any real culture, and incapable of thinking for themselves, but trained to fit into the economic system of a highly industrialised society.' He expressed his abhorrence at the failure of the movement and warned French students not to accept any plan of educational reform as offered by Minister Faure and unanimously adopted by the National Assembly. In an interview to the press given on March 3, 1969, he said: "There is need to fight violence with violence We have in common with you the revolutionary negation, the rejection of any kind of participation. Parents, learn that your sons have become revolutionaries because your cowardice has determined their fate. They have nothing to say any more, to those defeated and decrying children who call themselves adults, but either less corrupted or more conscious of our corruption."[65]

Among the men of action, we may refer to Regis Debray who says that the irony of history has willed the assignment of precisely this vanguard role to students and

62. Marcuse: *An Essay in Liberation* (London, 1969), p. 60.
63. Jack Woddis, *op. cit.*, p. 307.
64. *Ibid*, p. 309.
65. Cited in Francois Bondy, *op. cit.*, p. 78.

revolutionary intellectuals who have had to unleash or rather initiate the highest forms of class struggle.[66] Referring to the peculiar conditions of the Latin-American region, he continues that the students and the intellectuals who initiate the revolution by taking up arms, thus arousing the illiterate peasants who, incapable of reaching political understanding on their own, are shaken out of their feudal torpor by the example of the guerillas. The total result of Debray's views on the role of the classes in the Cuban revolution (and other Latin-American revolutionary struggles) "is to denigrate the working class, and to elevate the peasantry as the main potential revolutionary force which can be won only by the efforts of the students and the intellectuals."[67]

We are again confronted with the basic question whether this is all in tune with the traditional doctrine of Marxism. The crux of the whole argument lies in substituting the Stalinist and Maoist perversions of the creed to its very flexibility which has grown with its historical successes. A critic may say that nowhere is this more blatant in our day than in Maoism which repels him by its sheer anti-intellectualism. As Kolakowski explains, the substitution of peasantry for the proletariat as the most revolutionary class is flagrantly at variance with the whole Marxist tradition.[68] The cult of manual labour'as the noblest human occupation' "is a grotesque parody of Marx's Utopia and leads to the policy of packing off intellectuals to the paddy fields. But there we are. So many are ready to tap up Maoism on the very acme of Marxist wisdom."[69]

Armed Struggle: Glorification of Violence as a 'Key to Social Truth and Action'

The last important direction in which the New Leftists look like following Marx in one respect and repudiating him in another is the use of violence in a struggle so as to realise the dream of a 'free and happy society'. The essential point of difference between the two, however, is that while Marxism treats violence as a necessary evil, New Leftism takes it as a 'cleaning force'. Marxism justifies the use of violence for achieving the purpose; as the purpose is achieved, use of violence is denounced. In other words, while the use of violence is justified to bring about first a classless and then a stateless society, it is said to have lost its *rasion d'etre* after the abolition of the classes.[70] Different is the case with New Leftism that considers violence as the essential force that weakens the protest against it.'[71]

We find that Marcuse justifies the use of violence on historical and pragmatic grounds that comes from below, from the oppressed, for it pulls down the edifice of injustice and cruelty and prepares the ground for an increase in the scope of freedom and justice.[72] He, however, shrouds his ideas on the subject of violence in

66. Debray: *Revolution in Revolution*? (New York, 1967), p. 21.
67. Jack Woddis, *op. cit.*, p. 199.
68. See Leszek Kolakowski: *Main Currents of Marxism,* Vol. I, pp. 494-522.
69. Review of Kolakowski's 3 volumes on *Main Currents of Marxism* by Sham Lal in *The Times of India* (New Delhi), May 18, 1979.
70. Issac Deutscher: *Marxism in Our Time,* p. 83.
71. Robert P. Wolff, Babbington Moore and Herbert Marcuse: *A Critique of Pure Tolerance* (Boston: Beacon Press, 1966), p. 103.
72. *Ibid.*, p. 107.

his criticism of pure tolerance. Here he argues that the ideal of tolerance belongs to the liberal-democratic tradition which has exhausted itself. "That type of tolerance is no longer needed, since it serves the cause of the domination of the privileged over the unprivileged. Instead, a new kind of tolerance is needed—tolerance of the Left, tolerance of subversion, tolerance of revolutionary violence, but intolerance of the Right, intolerance of existing institutions, intolerance of any opposition to socialism."[73]

Fanon offers several arguments to justify that violence is good. He says: "Violence alone, violence committed by the people, violence educated and organised by its leaders makes it possible for the masses to understand social truths and gives the key to them.... At the level of individuals, violence is a cleansing force.... violence frees the native from his inferiority complex and from despair and inaction; it makes him fearless and restores his self-respect."[74] The peculiar thing about this New Leftist is that by being a psychiatrist by profession, he advocates the use of violence as a therapeutic device in the struggle of the African Negroes against the colonial domination of the white European races. Thus, he looks at the politically advantageous aspects of the use of violence. Says he: "When the people have taken violent part in the national liberation, they allow no one to set themselves up as 'liberators'.... Illumined by violence, the consciousness of the people rebels against any pacification. From now on the demogogues, the opportunists and the magicians have a difficult task."[75]

Sartre is no less a strong champion of the use of violence. The problem before him is "how to overcome the idea that the Left ought not to answer violence with violence."[76] Two of his plays *Les Mains Sales* of 1948 and *Le Diable et le Bon Dieu* of 1951 pertain to this theme. The burden of his argument is that "one cannot do good in politics unless one is willing to soil one's hand with violent deeds such as assassination and terrorism.... Violence permeates all existing institutions and political relationships. Therefore, the only way to make any impact on them, or to introduce better ones, is to use violence"[77] So deep is the conviction of Sartre in this regard that he subscribes to the idea of 'counter-escalation' which means 'let there be a war to face war' even at the risk of another world war. He has, in very clear terms, supported the idea that subject races should fight with all possible violent means to achieve the goal of national liberation. Thus, feeling impressed with the affirmations of Fanon, he in his Foreword to his (Fanon's) *The Damned of the Earth,* adds: "The native cures himself of colonial neurosis by thrusting out the settler through force of arms. When his rage boils over, he rediscovers his lost innocence and he comes to know himself in the act of creating himself... to shoot down a European is to kill two birds with one stone, to destroy an oppressor and the man who oppresses at the same time...."[78]

---

73. Maurice Cranston, *op. cit.,* p. 87.
74. Fanon, *op. cit.,* pp. 73-74.
75. *Ibid.,* p. 74.
76. Maurice Cranston, *op cit.,* p. 10.
77. *Ibid.*
78. *Ibid.*

The justification of violence finds its clear-cut expression in the emphasis on the need for an armed revolution as given by Regis Debray. For him an armed struggle is everything. The socialist revolution is the result of an armed struggle against the armed power of the bourgeois state. He calls it the 'old historic law'.[79] More so, he does see armed struggle as the decisive and the only way forward for the good of his Latin-American people. He believes that it is the determined action by a group of militants that can itself produce the revolutionary situation and that the action required is the armed action of creating the *foco* or nucleus which spreads like 'an oil patch.... through the peasant masses, to the smaller towns, and finally to the capital'. "Taking inspiration from the Cuban revolution, he says that it offers an answer to fraternal American countries, which has still to be studied in its historical details ; by means of the more or less slow building up, through guerilla warfare carried out in suitably chosen rural zones of a mobile strategic force, nucleus of a people's army and of a future socialist state.[80]

It may now be reiterated that elaborations of the New Leftists on the use of violence are incidentally Marxist. An essential line of difference between Marxists and New Leftists may be drawn here. While the latter are outspoken and thoroughly consistent defenders of the use of violence and frankly go to the extent of exalting it in the war of national liberations in dependent countries and for struggle to bring about a new and happy society in independent countries of the world, the former integrate the use of violence with the existence of objective conditions only. The Marxists connect the problem of violence with the economic factor. For instance, Fredrick Engels criticises Eugene Duhring for attempting to present violence as something self-contained. Lenin links historical development not to naked violence but to material force. Though he admits that no major historical issue has ever been decided otherwise than by material force, under certain circumstances violence "is both necessary and useful but there are circumstances under which violence cannot produce results."[81]

Humanism: Creation of a Free and Happy Commonwealth for Man

However, the most important direction in which Marxism as well as New Leftism seem to converge is the search for a Utopia.It pertains to the creation of a new society in which man has a free, happy and dignified life. We find that though a most uncompromising critic of the bourgeois social, economic and political systems, Marx was a man of vision also. He desired a de-alienated life of man and found the solution of his problem in a new society without classes and state. He termed it 'the era of human emancipation'—a new type of social life in which man is free from all sorts of exploitation and oppression. Glorious human values prevail and all public affairs are managed by the free, voluntary and co-operative associations of men. To Marx, such an ideal society will be composed of the "associations of free and equal producers consciously acting upon a common and rational plan."[82]

79. Jack Woddis, *op. cit.*, p. 250.
80. Debray, *op. cit*, p. 24.
81. Lenin: *Collected Works*, Vol. 29, p. 58.
82. See Michael Evans: *Karl Marx* (London: George Allen and Unwin, 1975), p. 162.

This trend can be visualised in the affirmations of leading New Leftists. For instance, Marcuse attacks both the 'affluent' and 'socialist' societies in the name of 'reducing the personality of man' and lays stress on the values of freedom, individuality and progress.[83] Sartre, who regards man as the maker of his own destiny, propounds an exalted concept of freedom which leads to a respect for the autonomy of all other men.[84] Che Guevara pleads for doing away with human pettiness, for paying attention to the human mass that surrounds one, for 'loving living humanity'.[85] Likewise, Fanon advocates a true revolution so that man "may be transformed, one species of man may by replaced by another species of men and humanity may be organised in a new way."[86]

Thus, the 'romantic radicalism' of the New Leftism assumes a normative character. It becomes a goal-oriented affair—something that takes it very close to the world of Marxism, no matter with certain points of difference about realising the same. Moreover, both look like 'leftist' doctrines, since they desire change—something which realistically cannot be brought about by an immediate action. The changes sought for lie beyond the foreseeable future that may even defy planning. The fact remains that the Left, whether Marxist or not, "cannot renounce Utopia, for it is that which imparts meaning to social change."[87]

New Leftism and Marxism: Controversy about a Revised or Distorted Version of Classical Marxism

Having examined all important tenets of New Leftism, we are faced with the crucial question whether it is another current of Marxism or a clear contradiction of the same. The answer to such a question depends upon what we mean by Marxism today. As Prof. Jha says: "If Marxism means that there can be no revolution without the working class, without the iron march of the proletarian battalions, the New Left thinkers are not Marxists. If Marxism means clinging to the conventional tenets of Marxian dogma, then they are not Marxists. If Marxism means acceptance of communism as a historical necessity, they cannot be considered as Marxists. If Marxism is regarded as a concept of institutional rather than intellectual content, they are not Marxists. If Marxism is identified with a specific world view whose content is defined, surely they are not Marxists. If, however, Marxism means a model rather than a theory, then they are Marxists. If standing on the side of the oppressed against the oppressors, on the side of the wretched against the privileged, on the side of the persecuted against the persecutors is Marxism, then they are Marxists. Above all, if radical orientation, secular view of the world, distrust of all closed doctrines and systems, striving for open-mindedness, and vision of a new man and a new world free from hunger, disease, pettiness, and exploitation are signs of Marxism, then they are certainly Marxists."[88]

---

83. Marcuse: *One-Dimensional Man,* p. 40.
84. See W.T. Deninger, *op. cit.,* p. 448.
85. See Kenneth Minnogue: "Che Guevara" in Maurice Cranston, *op. cit.,* p. 33.
86. See A.R. Zolberg: "Frantz Fanon", *Ibid.,* p. 125.
87. *Jha, op. cit.,* p. 538.
88. *Ibid.,* p. 560.

One may, or may not, agree with such a detached observation which certainly fails to carry conviction with the Marxists. The dogmatic followers of Marxism have no reservations in describing New Leftism as 'a model of neo-Hegelianism', (Fernbach), a 'breakdown' of Marxism (Kolakowski) and 'manifestation of mood, of a certain movement of the petty-bourgeois mind at a historical juncture (Mohit Sen). It is said that the neo-Hegelian break with the classical Marxian tradition is the most fundamental way by making the basis of Marxism a philosophical anthropology that denies scientific objectivity and reconstructs the Marxian theory of society for the concepts of *praxis,* alienation, proletariat as universal class and historical subject, class consciousness, etc. Thus, "historical materialism is transposed from objective science to proletarian self-consciousness; it is asserted that the working class understands society by action on it (*praxis*), and the content of the resolution is considered at the ontological level of overcoming of alienation, rather than as a mere specific transformation of economic and political relations."[89]

It is for this reason that those sworn to follow the traditional line of Marxism accuse New Leftism of 'negative radicalism'[90]— something that signifies a subtle change in the movement's relations to the social milieu; that essentially settles down and adjusts itself to the existing situation; which accepts the established system and its institutionalised procedures as the framework to bring about reforms, which by coming to terms with the existing order loses its revolutionary zeal and thereby creates a wide gulf between theoretical pronouncement and practical performance.[91] It is contended that even Marx himself rejected such notions in his own lifetime which have now become important tenets of New Leftism. The Marxists, therefore, accuse the New Leftists of forgetting the outstanding fact that it is the capitalist system which makes both the oppressor and the oppressed a caricature of human beings and by refusing to break sharply with the establishment, the entrenched monopolistic capitalist power, they 'unconsciously act' as a 'safety valve' and as 'the whipping boys of capitalism'.[92]

Critical Appreciation

Instead of delving deep into the controversy of New Leftism as a revised or distorted version of Marxism, we should examine its inherent weaknesses as given below:

1. The first point that strikes at the very outset is that it does not look like a very precise, coherent and consistent doctrine. Though we have a good number of

89. David Fernbach in *New Left Review,* No. 56, July-Aug., 1969, p. 63.
90. Edward Batalov: *The Philosophy of Revolt: Criticism of the Left Radical Ideology,* translated from Russian into English by Katherine Judelson (Moscow: Progress Publishers, 1975), p. 18.
91. See B.K. Jha: "Un-Marxian Development of Marxism" in *Indian Journal of Political Science,* Vol. XXXVII, No. 4, 1976, p. 35.
92. Mohit Sen: *Communism and the New Left* (New Delhi: People's Pub. House, 1969), p. 3. David Fernbach says: "Neo-Hegelian Marxism, like all speculative philosophy, remains a beautiful but a useless toy and was rejected by Marx soon after he adopted communism. It is an idealism that arose again, among a section of the revolutionary intelligentsia, during certain periods of setback for the working class movement, but it can only obscure the science of Marx and Lenin, and its danger is that it can be and is taken up by the ruling class ideologies such as Avineri (*Social and Political Thought of Karl Marx*) in order to mystify and emasculate the practical revolutionary character of Marxism." *Op. cit.,* p. 68

New Leftist thinkers, they do not agree on all essential points. For instance, what Marcuse says is contradicted by Kolakowski. The category of the New Leftists includes many ranging from the neo-Marxists disillusioned with Russian communism like Kolakowski to neo-Hegelians like Marcuse, the leading light of the Frankfurt School whose members were accused of forming 'an academic intelligentsia with a high bourgeois background'.[93] The result is that complete unanimity, considered to be an essential feature of a constructive doctrine cannot be found in the views of all leading New Leftists on crucial social and economic problems and their solutions. It is, therefore, said that most of the New Leftists "are inspired by a genuine concern to protect human person and rights. But they are not clear as to what changes they envisage and how can they achieve them.... They seem to oscillate between their allegiance to Marxism which was a product of the nineteenth century industrial revolution and the new world that is emerging in the wake of industrial and technological crisis of our time.... They are perhaps all transitional thinkers trying to solve the problems of advanced technological society with the help of an apparatus belonging to a former one."[94]

2. It follows that the New Leftists are like a motley crowd of disgruntled ideologues and revolutionary propagandists. They hover around the ingredients of anarchistic individualism, Maoist Marxism, revisionist socialism, fierce fanaticism and visionary romanticism. The element of Maoist revolutionary fervour is the most outspoken that is, however, laced with visionary romanticism of the leaders like Che and the intellectuals like Marcuse who look towards a paradise on this earth after doing away with the curse of alienation. It is, therefore, well commented: "Because the New Left is so diverse in its origins and appeal, it is a little difficult to generalise about the distinguishing features of its ideology.... But they are a motley crew: blue-collared trade unionists, disaffected middle class students, economically depressed American Negroes, rugged Latin-American peasants, and African victims of colonialism and neo-colonialism. They all share the opportunity of becoming conscious of the oppression wrought by modern class-ridden society, of recognising that the claims of social justice are facades."[95]
3. Another line of weakness in the theory of New Leftism is that it seeks to negate what it professes. Claiming itself as rooted in the world of pragmatism, it pretends to subscribe to, what Daniel Bell says, 'the end of ideology'. Ever since French theoretician de Tracy coined the term in 1801, ideology has been used

93. Goran Therborn: "The Frankfurt School" in *New Left Review,* London, No. 60, March-April, 1970, p. 94. As Derek Heater observes: "Clusters of small groups, usually youthful in age, but often led by ex-Communists, sometimes quarelling with each other but sharing a common hatred of modern industrial society, have emerged especially in Western hemisphere. Their alienation from the regimentation of industrial society has led this New Left to recognise its intellectual roots in the early writings of Marx where he emphasised this social problem of alienation—roots which, it so happens, were already being nurtured by scholars like Adorno and Marcuse of the Frankfurt School of Sociology. The theory of alienation holds that capitalism has divorced us all in our work from any meaningful perception of its product, even of man's very place in nature." *Op. cit.,* p. 39.
94. V.R. Mehta: "Marxism in the Modern World" in *Indian Journal of Political Science,* Vol. XXXVI, No. 4, 1975, p. 320.
95. Derek Heater, *op. cit.,* pp. 41-42.

by a very large number of social theorists though in different senses ranging from 'an action-oriented system of ideas', as suggested by Carl J. Friedrich, to 'a system of abstract ideas' as decried by Michael Oakeshott. The difficulty with the New Leftists is that they shun the use of the term 'ideology' and instead claim to have accepted the line of pragmatism that seeks to examine the value or worth of anything on the basis of experience. They forget that by launching attacks on the bourgeois and communist systems and instead desiring a new social order free from the evils of 'bureaucratism', 'consumerism', 'corporatism', 'oppressionism', 'technocratism' and the like, they are, as a matter of fact, replacing their pragmatism with ideology, or it may be said that they are exchanging one ideology for another.[96]

4. Then, the New Leftists may be accused of offering an impracticable theory of revolution. Though we may not disagree with their affirmation of the role of the students, youth and intellectuals in agitations, revolts and struggle to do away with injustice and slavery, we may doubt the feasibility of all such fights under the leadership of students or intellectuals. The intellectuals are often denounced for.being academic recluses or armchair philosophers and the students constitute just a 'floating population'. Obviously, none of them can play a really constructive part in a revolution. As a matter of fact, it is the seasoned leadership of the grown up men of action that is required for bringing about a successful revolution. Moreover, if one has his legs rooted in the world of Marxism, he is all the more required to say that a successful revolution can be launched only by the leadership of the working class in which students and intellectuals may play a subsidiary role. As G. Coginot says: "The liaison between the movement of the intelligentsia and the movement of the working class as such is quite natural and necessary. The student movement has no future unless its action becomes a part of the general strategy of the class struggle led by the working class...."[97]

5. The New Left contributed to the ferment in the Communist parties and to the general revival of ideological discussion, but they do not appear to have worked out any alternative model of socialism, except in very general terms. The designation 'New Left' was claimed by the various dissidents who sought to revive 'true communism' outside the existing parties as well as bigger and smaller Maoist, Trotskyist, and other groups. In France the name *gauchiste* is generally used by groups who emphasise their opposition to all forms of authority, including Leninist 'advance guard' parties. The post-Stalinist years saw a critical revival of Trotskyism, and this led to the formation of numerous splinter groups, separate internationals etc. In the sixties, the term 'New Left' was generally used in Europe and North America as a collective label for student ideologies, while not identifying with Social Communism, and after expressly disavowing it, used the phraseology of worldwide anti-capitalist revolution and looked chiefly to the Third World for models and heroes. So far these ideologies have not produced any intellectual result worth the name."[98]

96. Isaac Deutscher, *op. cit.*, p. 64.
97. Cited in Batalov, *op. cit.*, p. 117.
98. Kolakowski, *op. cit.*, p. 490.

Kymlicka on the Arguments of Left and Right

Points of debate on several essentially empirical questions

(a) to what extent are people poor because of misfortune and unequal opportunities, or because of their own choices? If we redistribute money to the poor, are we helping the victims of unequal circumstances (as the left tends to believe) or subsidizing expensive tastes and irresponsible choices (as the right tends to believe)?

(b) has the welfare state helped the poor overcome their disadvantage and participate in society (as the left tends to believe), or has it created a class of welfare dependants caught in a poverty trap who are marginalized (as the right tends to believe)?

(c) in cases where the condition of the poor is partly due to their own choices and partly due to unequal circumstances, which comes first? Should we insist that the poor prove they are capable of acting responsibly before they are eligible for assistance (as the right tends to believe), or should we equalize their circumstances before we hold them responsible for their choices (as the left tends to believe)?

(d) does the state have the capacity to remedy involuntary disadvantages (as the left tends to believe), or are the sources of social ills like poverty, homelessness, high school drop-out rates, and so on so complex that state attempts to solve them will generally fail, and often worsen the problem (as the right tends to believe)?

Will Kymlicka: *Contemporary Political Philosophy: An Introduction* (New Delhi: Oxford University Press, 2005, p. 158.

Giddens on Obsoleteness of Distinction between Left and Right

What can it mean to be politically radical today? For the spectre which disturbed the slumbers of bourgeois Europe and which for more than seventy years took on solid flesh has been returned to its nether world. The hopes of radicals for a society in which, as Marx said, human beings could be truly free, seem to have turned out to be empty reveries.

Six Principles

1. There must be a concern to repair damaged solidarities which may sometimes imply the selection, preservation, or even perhaps reinvention of tradition. The concept of civil society lying between the individual and the state is a suspect one.
2. It is a period of life-politics. It is a politics not of life-chances but of life-styles. It concerns disputes and struggles about how (as individuals and as collective humanity) we should live in a world where what used to be fixed either by nature or by tradition is now subject to human decisions.
3. It is a period of generative politics. It is a politics which seeks to allow individuals and groups to make things happen rather than have things happen to them, in the context of overall social concerns and goals.
4. Democratisation of the whole system is needed. It presupposes development of personal relationships in which active trust is mobilised and sustained through discussion and the interchange of views rather than by arbitrary power of some sort or another.
5. Rethinking about welfare state in a fundamental way, and in relation to the wider issues of global poverty and scarcity.
6. A programme of radical politics must be prepared to confront the role of violence in human affairs.

Anthony Giddens: *Beyond Left and Right* (London: Polity Press, 1994), pp. 1-18.

6. Above all, the New Leftists may be criticised for exalting the use of violence. Not only their justification of violence is based on certain illogical and irrational grounds, the horror of the magnitude of the same cannot be denied. Less dangerous are the true Marxists who justify the use of violence *vis-a-vis* the existence of objective conditions. Obviously, the glorification of violence, as made by the New Leftists, pricks the conscience of every peace-loving man particularly one who is convinced with the philosophy of Mahatma Gandhi. A critic of the New Leftist doctrine like Batalov, therefore, accuses it of offering a concept of violence as a queer mixture of revolutionary romanticism and utopianism, of revolutionary integrity and reckless venture, of heroic self-sacrifice and political naivety. He fears that revolutionary violence may degenerate into 'political masochism'.[99]

By way of appreciation it may, however, be said that the New Leftist thinkers have done the right thing in denouncing evils that afflict both the 'bourgeois' and the 'communist' systems and, as such, it cannot be designated as just a 'passing political fashion' as remarked by Batalov. The weight of this outstanding fact cannot be ignored that Marxism in the modern world needs revision in the light of the new objective conditions. What is really necessary is the change in the ontological theory of Marxism so that it "takes into account the multidimensional character of man and connects it to the multidimensional character of society. What is needed is a justificatory theory for both so that different individuals as well as groups are able to develop their unique qualities, their own unique way without which the multidimensionality inherent in life will be crushed by the vast bureaucratic apparatuses of the modern state."[100]

While the ideological fantasies of this movement, which reached its climax around 1968-69, were no more than a nonsensical expression of the whims of spoilt middle class children, and while the extremists among them were virtually indistinguishable from Fascist thugs, the movement "did without doubt express a profound crisis of faith and the values that had inspired democratic societies for many decades. In this sense, it was a 'genuine' movement despite its grotesque phraseology; the same of course, could be said of Nazism and Fascism....The situation is one of a kind that is frequently met in history where people feel they have got into a blind alley; they long desperately for a miracle, they believe that a single magic key will open the door to paradise; they include chiliastic and apocalyptic hopes. Apart from this, its ideology really has little in common with Marxism. It consists of 'revolution' without the working class ; hatred of modern technology as such (Marx glorified technical progress and believed that one reason for the impending breakdown of capitalism was its inability to sustain such progress—a prophecy that could not be repeated today with absurdity); the cult of primitive society (in which Marx took scarcely any interest) as the source of progress; hatred of education and specialised knowledge; and the belief in the American lumpenproletariat as a general revolutionary force. Marxism, however, did have an apocalyptic side which has come to the fore in many of its later versions, and a handful of words and phrases from its vocabulary

99. See Batalov, *op. cit.*, p. 183.
100. V.R. Mehta: *Beyond Marxism*, p. 29.

sufficed to convince the New Left that it was possible at a stroke to transform the world into a miraculous paradise, the only obstacle to this consummation being the monopolies and university professors. The chief complaint of the New Left against official Communist parties was and is that they are not revolutionary enough."[101]

101. Kolakowski, *op.cit.*, pp. 490-91. "Orthodox communism and the New Left are uncomfortable bedfellows. For if there is something that a Communist really must have, it is discipline and rules. His Marxism is scientific, rational doctrine. The New Left is often irrational, violent and intolerant, but it is also speculative and imaginative. The new spectre that is haunting the world is perhaps even more gruesome than the old." Derek Heater, *op. cit.*, p. 43.

23

Eurocommunism and Post-Communism

> Astonishingly, within the entire corpus of Western Marxism, there is not one single serious appraisal or sustained critique of the work of one major theorist by another, revealing close textual knowledge or minimal analytical care in the treatment. At most, there are more cursory aspersions or causal commendations, both equally ill-real and superficial... There is no case within Western Marxism of a full theoretical engagement or conflict of one thinker or school with another—let alone any overall command of the international range of the tradition as such.
>
> **—Perry Anderson[1]**

Major developments in the theory of scientific socialism reveal this astounding fact that an authentic history of Marxism since its birth a little over a hundred and fifty years ago has yet to be written in view of its being a highly complex affair.[2] What now creates a baffling problem for a reader of the Marxian political theory is not what the Father of Scientific Socialism (Marx) said, or his great friend and collaborator (Engels) explained and interpreted, it is the fact of mutual slovenliness having its manifestation in Lenin's attack on Kautsky, Stalin's offensive againt Trotsky, Khrushchev's movement of de-Stalinisation, Mao's rejection of Khrushchev, Djilas's virulent invectives directed against Stalin, Sartre's disagreement with Lukacs, Adorno's reflections on Sartre, Colletti's criticism of Marcuse, dismissal of Althusser's Marx by Delia Volpe, and the like. It is owing to this that contemporary Marxism looks like a storehouse of confusion. What it really signifies, or not, is regarded as "one of the most confused and difficult questions confronting a communist today."[3] Eurocommunism is a new variety in this regard. It has emerged as a new phenomenon on the continent as significant as anything created by the Treaty of Rome. Curiously, it has gathered sufficient strength to be denounced by Moscow, to be analysed in depth in Washington, to upset the social democratic establishment in Bonn and the like.[4]

1. Anderson: *Considerations on Western Marxism* (London: N LB, 1976), p. 69.
2. *Ibid.*, p. 1.
3. Santiago Carrillo: *Eurocommunism and the State,* Translated from Spanish into English by Nan Green and A.M. Elliott, (London: Lawrence and Wishart, 1977), p. 7.
4. See Raymond Fletcher: "Eurocommunism: A Lesson for Some So-called Socialists" in *The Times* (London) July 11, 1977.

Eurocommunism: Nature and Essential Implications

The word 'Eurocommunism' popularised by the Western press, though for a long time ignored by the Communist leaders, was uttered for the first time at a political level by the great Italian Communist leader Signor Eurico Berlinguer in the second of the Italo-French meetings at Porte de Pantin in July, 1975. The term looked highly pricking so much so that the great French Communist leader M. Georges Marchais deliberately refrained from using it. Even Santiago Carrillo, the General Secretary of the Communist Party of Spain, while speaking at the East Berlin Conference of European Communist Parties held in June, 1976, threw light on the restricted scope of this term in view of its application exclusively to the communism of European countries. As he said: "Recently there has been talk of Eurocommunism. This is an unfortunate choice of the term. There is no Eurocommunism, because non-European communist parties such as the Japanese cannot be included in this category. It is obvious, however, that the Communist parties of developed or highly developed capitalist countries are faced with a special set of problems."[5]

Obviously, after the East Berlin Conference, Eurocommunism became a vogue word. It caught the attention of a wide number of people on account of certain essential innovations which it sought to make in the classical Marxian tradition. The way leading communist leaders of different countries, particularly Carrillo, Marchais and Berlinguer spoke on the occasion of the East Berlin meet came to have its effect on the formulation of the *communique* having several important features which were hitherto an anathema to the high priests of socialism sitting in Kremlin. It is evident from the new trend signifying:

1. commitment to the construction of socialism in freedom with a multiplicity system and respecting the rights of different parties to take turns in power,
2. rejection of the concept of a leading party and a leading state, i.e. of the general Soviet revolutionary model, and,
3. systematic denunciation of any specific manifestation of illiberality in the Soviet Union and the satellite countries.

The trend continued to develop. At the Madrid Summit of the Italian, French and Spanish leaders held in March 1977, an important agreement took place on the following points:

1. To respect and defend civil liberties;
2. To abandon the dogma of the dictatorship of the proletariat;
3. To abide by the rules of bourgeois parliamentary democracy;
4. To seek alliance with all democratic forces; and
5. To attain power by peaceful means.

In this way, the acceptance of the ideals of nationalism, democratic socialism and constitutionalism became the fundamental tenets of a new variety of contemporary Western Marxism which assumed the appellation of 'Eurocommunism'. It came to have a distinct form of its own as a result of the active role of three great communist leaders like Carrillo of Spain, Marchais of France and Berlinguer of Italy, though

5. *Keesing's Contemporary Archives,* Sept. 24, 1976, pp. 279-82.

the moral support of Milovan Djilas of Yugoslavia and Dr. Janos Berecz of Hungary could also be visualised in this direction.[6] The leaders of the 'Marxist protestantism', as it was called, thus claimed to have evolved a 'common road to socialism' in the light of the new 'political reality' which they were all confronted with.

However, the most important event in the birth of this new variety of Western Marxism is the publication of Carrillo's *Eurocommunism and the State* in 1977 which forced the leaders of the Kremlin to denounce it as an attempt that would split the international communist movement by bringing about the policy goals sought for several decades by the reactionary forces.[7] In retaliation the Central Committee of the Spanish Communist Party expressed its stand in regard to the rejection of the Soviet Union as the ideal model for socialist countries.[8] Carrillo denied that Eurocommunism was just a 'tactical device' and in very unmistakable terms he warned that his party was prepared for a total rupture with the Communist Party of the USSR.[9] What he said, got its moral support from the leaders of the Romanian Communist Party. Even Janos Berecz, the Director of the International Section of the Hungarian Communist Party, while taking a cautious line in this dispute, expressed the view that every communist party was entitled to have its own course.[10] The official Bucharest party newspaper *(Scintea)* made a spirited defence of Carrillo's contribution by affirming that individual communist parties had a basic right and duty to work out their own policies, free from outside criticism."[11]

With a view to bring out the implications of the term 'Eurocommunism' in the context of the prevailing political and economic situations, Carrillo in his great contribution says: "In Western Europe today, United States imperialism and the ruling social groups, exert themselves to give credibility to the idea that *democracy equals capitalism* and, conversely, that *socialism equals Soviet domination.*"

---

6. One may perhaps dispute the inclusion of Djilas in the category of the Eurocommunists in view of the fact that he has no place in the trio of great Spanish, Italian and French leaders. We should, however, study it in the light of the fact that what the Eurocommunists desired had its genesis in the affirmations of Djilas that he made in his *New Class* about two decades back. Moreover, he lent his moral support to the historic decision of the East Berlin Conference of 1976. He described it as an "extremely important event....for its formal legalisation of differences within the Communist movement." He also said: "What is called Eurocommunism these days is nothing more than a general trend towards separation from Moscow and a search for their own road. But it is impossible that the Italians or the Spaniards, for example, could advocate pluralism without this having an effect on parties run by dogmatic, totalitarian-minded leaders. Hence, the current trend will either isolate the Soviet bloc from other Communist parties, or it will encourage moderate forces within East European parties." *Ibid.* On his return to Belgrade, President Tito appreciated the Conference for reaffirming the principles upon which in the present conditions, it was alone possible to promote genuine co-operation and solidarity of all the revolutionary and progressive forces. These principles were—independence, equality, and non-interference. *Ibid.*
7. See Review of Carrillo's book in *New Times* (Moscow), June 23, 1977.
8. *The Times*, June, 27, 1977.
9. *Ibid.*, June 28, 1977.
10. *Ibid.*, July 1,1977.
11. *Ibid.*, July 7, 1977.

"The trend which has been widely called 'Eurocommunism' must overcome this dilemma, and raise the question of democracy and socialism to the appropriate historic level. That is to say, it must demonstrate, on the one hand, that *democracy is not only substantial with capitalism, but that its defence and development require the overthrow of that social system; that in the historical conditions of today, capitalism tends to reduce and in the end to destroy democracy which is why democracy must proceed to a new dimension with a socialist regime."*

"On the other hand, 'Eurocommunism' should demonstrate that the *victory of the socialist forces in the countries of Western Europe will not augment Soviet State power in the slightest, nor will it imply the spread of the Soviet model of a single party, but will be an independent experience, with a more evolved socialism that will have a positive influence on the democratic evolution of the kind of socialism existing today:"*

"It is a question of the ideological and political battle for democracy and socialism which should lead to the disintegration of capitalism's system of political relations, dominant today in Europe, and to a new correlation of forces favourable to social change."

"In this respect, *the independence of the communist parties in relation to the Soviet State and other socialist states is essential, as is the theoretical and practical definition of an unequivocal democratic world."*

"It is also essential to link the destiny of the working class with that of the broadest non-monopolist social classes. *The socialist revolution is no longer a necessity only for the proletariat, but for the immense majority of the population as well.* In these conditions, the idea of the alliance of the forces of labour and culture, of the new historic bloc and, in general the question of anti-monopolist alliances, acquires decisive importance."[12]

While dealing with a precise definition of the term 'Eurocommunism', it should, however, be kept in mind that it is a phenomenon which one can only understand if one realises that it is not a ready-made set of new political principles, but a process affecting different Western communist parties in different ways and in different degrees. It is a process by which the communist parties of West European countries seek to adapt themselves to the political norms of the societies in which they operate and, at the same time, to dissociate themselves from the Soviet model of socialism which clearly has neither appeal nor relevance to the working people of modern western non-Communist countries.

Historical Growth: Rise and Development of a New Variety of Western Marxism

As a matter of fact, Eurocommunism is not a matter of sudden spurt. It has its roots in the period preceding and following the Second World War. One may understand that as Eurocommunism is a challenge to the official Marxian tradition established by the great Russian comrades, so its roots should be traced in all events having their connection with following a different line dubbed as 'deviationism' by the then leaders of the Kremlin. We may refer back to the stand taken by Leon Trotsky in

12. Carrillo, *op. cit.*, pp. 39-40.

Russia that invited the wrath of Stalin. The successor of Lenin (Stalin) adhered to his doctrine of 'socialism in one country' and on that basis showed his determination to stick to the path of socialism in the national and of 'peaceful co-existence' in the international spheres. We know that it was not all as much against Trotsky and other Bolsheviks like Bukharin and Zinoviev as it was used by Stalin like a convenient tool to suppress and liquidate all dissident elements so as to establish his personal hold in the name of the 'dictatorship of the proletariat'. In fact, he knew that Trotsky, Bukharin, Zinoviev and others were not spies and traitors to the 'socialist fatherland'. However, since their disagreement with him obviously delayed the establishment of totalitarian control, he had to destroy them. His wrongs within the party were that he "transformed 'objective unfriendliness'—the ideological differences in the party— into the subjective guilt of group and individuals attributing to them crimes which they did not commit."[13]

Deviation from the 'official' Marxian line found its manifestation in Italy and Spain in particular. In Italy Gramsci raised the question: Can Marxism be in opposition to the non-theoretical commonsense of the masses? His answer was unequivocal: Between the two there is a 'quantitative' difference of degree, not one of 'quality'. On this basis he asserted that "everyone is a philosopher in that it is not a question of introducing science into people's lives from the outside but rather of renovating and making critical an already existing activity."[14] He made certain modifications in the classical Marxian tradition. Another important communist leader Palmiro Togialatti not only rebuilt the Communist Party of Italy but also developed the technique of bending to Moscow without sacrificing his own views and interpretations of Marxism. No less important is the case of Spain where the communists under Carrillo criticised the totalitarian system of Gen. Franco (that signified their opposition to any dictatorial system including that of Stalin in the Soviet Union) and upheld the right of the petty bourgeois and bourgeois parties to take part in the government and, at the very least, in political life with full rights. For this *moderation,* the Spanish leaders were vehemently criticised by their Russian counterparts.[15]

However, the first important event that captured the attention of the whole world was the call for 'national communism' given by Marshall Tito of Yugoslavia in 1948. He repudiated the concept of 'Comintern', renounced the idea of another imperialist war, desired peaceful co-existence in the strict sense of the term, pleaded for a more determined dissociation of the USSR and the Soviet bloc from revolutionary movements in the outside world, frankly acknowledged the stabilisation of Western capitalism in the post-War era, and, above all, stressed the need to transform the Communist parties of the West into something like left-reformist organisations.[16]

The year 1956 witnessed another important landmark in the development of Western Marxism when at the Twentieth Congress of the Communist Party Khrushchev announced a series of doctrinal innovations affecting particularly the communist thought on international relations. Sticking to the spirit of the doctrine

13. Milovan Djilas: *The New Class* (New York: Fredrick A. Praegar, 1957), p. 77.
14. Alan Swingewood: *Marx and Modern Social Theory* (London : Macmillan, 1975), pp. 83-84.
15. See Carrillo, *op. cit.,* p. 126.
16. See Isaac Deutscher: *Ironies of History* (Berkeley: Ramparts Press, 1971). pp. 79-80.

of peaceful co-existence, he declared that wars were no longer inevitable; that the antagonistic socio-economic systems could peacefully co-exist and actively co-operate in the maintenance of peaceful relations; that instead of military competition there should be economic competition between capitalism and communism; that communist countries should strive to show the superiority of their socialist mode of production and thereby make their socio-economic model compellingly attractive to the developing countries; that communism could spread not by force of arms but by the force of example; and that socialism might be established by a parliamentary path.[17]

Though the comrades of the West European non-Communist countries like those of France, Italy and Spain appreciated the change effected by the de-Stalinisation movement of Khrushchev, they harboured fresh reservations about the genuineness of the same when the Russian troops suppressed the freedom movement of the people of Hungary in the following year. In 1960 Moscow's differences with Peking gave an unprecedented setback to the case of Soviet leadership of the communist world. In China Mao Tse-tung adhered to his own line of 'Sinified Marxism' and, for this sake, he repudiated the leadership of Khrushchev. It had its definite impact on the communist movement in Europe. Albania took to the line of Mao and thereby repudiated the supremacy of the Russian comrades. In 1963 Romanian leaders cautiously moved ahead in the direction of following a line neither strictly pro-Moscow nor strictly pro-Peking which by all means amounted to the taking of an independent line.

Naturally, these events had their effect that became evident at the first Pan-European Conference of the Communist Parties held at Prague in Czechoslovakia in April, 1967 in the wake of the shadow of the Sino-Soviet rift in which the leaders of the Italian, French and Spanish parties played a leading role. The *communique,* which was then adopted, showed their commitment to the pluralistic-libertarian ideals implying their support for the plurality of political parties, the right to existence and activity of the opposition parties, democratic alteration between majority and minority; liberty of thought and expression, freedom of press, etc. It demonstrated that what the world knew about what the Eurocommunist leaders were saying in regard to their affection for democratic principles was not significantly different from what the East European communist leaders declared with equal emphasis and eloquence some three decades ago—that is, before they gained the whole control of political power.

In the wake of such developments it was natural for the West European communist leaders to react sternly when the Russian forces suppressed the movement of the people of Czechoslovakia in 1968 that led to the fall of Dubcek. The leaders of the French, Italian and Spanish communist parties took a leading part in giving reorientation to the traditional doctrine of Marxism. Thus, they could evolve a new road to socialism in their Helsinki accord of 1975. It was followed by the East Berlin accord of June, 1976 that gave a clear proof of the emergence of a new variety of Marxism which, though willy nilly, even the then Soviet leaders had to recognise. It is evident from the fact that on the occasion of the first anniversary of the East

17. B.K. Jha: 'Un-Marxian Development of Marxism" in *Indian Journal of Political Science,* Vol. XXXVII, No. 4, 1976, pp. 30-31.

Berlin Conference, the Soviet as well as the Italian communist ideologues issued a message saying that the USSR was keen to avoid a public dispute with West European Communist parties on the issue of Eurocommunism and was ready to acknowledge their desire to pursue independent policies provided the search for a programme answering national interests should not merge with the rightwing opportunism and submission to pressure from the class enemy.[18]

It may, however, be pointed out that the three leading communist parties of the West European region had reached this stage in their evolution by independent roads on the basis of different experiences. For instance, the Communist Party of Italy had gained its strength from a political and cultural tradition that went back to Gramsci (who emphasised revolution by the slow conquest of leadership achieved with agreement) a tradition that survived the long dark days of Stalinism. The Communist Party of Spain, destroyed by the Civil War of 1938-39, reformulated its strategy and ideology when it was refounded. The Communist Party of France which had remained orthodox and even Stalinist, while the other two had ceased for some time to be either, aligned itself with them with a sensational change, of course, as controlled and firm as its orthodox line had been previously. "But in different ways and at different times all three parties have come to terms with two objective realities: the crisis of the Soviet myth from the Twentieth Congress of the CPSU onwards and the complexity of the Western society which makes the classic type of revolution almost impossible."[19]

National Socialism: Repudiation of Proletarian Internationalism under the Leadership of the then Soviet Union

What we have said above makes it very clear that the first and most important tenet of Eurocommunism is the declaration of national communism in the place of 'communist internationalism'. Marx proclaimed the end of the nation-state system and envisaged the possibility of the emergence of a new international society that would break down the constricting barriers and national frontiers. For Marx all group entities, including the state and nation, stood between man and species. Patriotism, therefore, of any kind, became nothing but alienation. This was the message of internationalism that Marx delivered at the First International Workingmen's Association founded in 1864 and Engels repeated it at his Second International of 1885. Lenin drew inspiration from, what Marx and Engels said and yet, while understanding the political reality of the age, he insisted that the Marxists should support nationalist movements going on in the colonial parts of the world. However, he made it perfectly clear that anything like glorification of the nation-state system was a very archaic and reactionary step essentially tied to the past and not a move towards the future.[20]

A subtle change in this regard, however, took place after the establishment of socialism in Russia in 1917. After the October Revolution, Lenin, Trotsky, Bukharin and Zinoviev set themselves to the task of rescuing European socialism from its patriotic

18. *The Times, (Moscow)*, July 4, 1977.
19. Aldo Rizzo: "West's Communists in Step", *Ibid.*, March 1, 1977.
20. See Isaac Deutscher: *Marxism in Our Time* (San Francisco: The Ramparts Press, 1971), pp. 93-112.

morass and of raising the level of international revolutionary consciousness. Thus, in 1919 the Third International came into being not only to reiterate the principle of proletarian internationalism for realising the message of the *Communist Manifesto* ('Workers of all countries unite') but also to work as a political general staff in the coming European revolution. What caused a fundamental change in this direction was the new meaning of proletarian internationalism. It signified internationalisation of the communist movement under the 'leading and guiding role' of the Russian Communist Party. It "started stifling the independent rhythm and development of the Communist movement outside the USSR because of the dominance of the victorious Russian party. Stalin's doctrine of 'socialism in one country'smacked of a new post-capitalist and post-revolutionary nationalism which sounded the death-knell of the Third International."[21]

In this way, communist internationalism signified two important developments. First, Russian communism itself became more nationalist under the leadership of Lenin and Stalin and, curiously, Stalinism developed itself alongside classical Marxism to the extent that it became distinct from Marxism-Leninism. Second, Russia became the 'Communist Fatherland', a source of inspiration to all poor, backward and oppressed people of the world.[22] More astounding than this was the development of another factor. It found its manifestation in the brutal suppression of other 'communist' countries at the hands of the Russian troops.

Eurocommunism repudiates the case of proletarian internationalism under the dominance of the Soviet leaders. We have already seen that most of the West European communist leaders had appreciated the stand of President Tito of Yugoslavia when he had broken away from the Comintern. After some time, Djilas desired that the 'subordinate'communist governments in East Europe "can, in fact must, declare their independence from the Soviet government."[23] The new trend developed very quickly keeping which in view, he continued: "Today national Communism is a general phenomenon in Communism. To varying degrees all Communist movements—except that of the USSR against which it is directed—are gripped by national Communism. In its time, in the period of Stalin's ascendancy, Soviet Communism also was national Communism. At that time Russian Communism abandoned internationalism, except as an instrument of its foreign policy. Today Soviet Communism is compelled, even if indefinitely, to acknowledge a new reality in Communism."[24]

It had its most conspicuous affirmation at the East Berlin Conference of 1976 when Santiago Carrillo said: "We have built a new kind of church with our own martyrs

---

21. Jha, *op. cit.*, p. 28.
22. William C. Carleton: "The New Nationalism" in W.J. Stankiewicz (ed.): *Political Thought Since World War II* (New York: Free Press of Glencoe, 1964), pp 423-25. As Klaus Mehnert says: "Moscow would like to see only the Soviet Communist ideology in the world, but this wish has not been fulfilled. All other ideologies, religion included, are anathema to the Soviet leadership, even though the technical reasons may compel Moscow temporarily to pretend friendship with some of them, the Mohammedans, the Buddhists, or certain Christian groups." *Moscow and the New Left,* Translated from German into English by Helmut Fischer (Berkeley: University of California Press, 1975), p. 113.
23. Milovan Djilas. *op. cit.*, p. 176.
24. *Ibid.*, p. 181.

and prophets. Moscow, where our dreams first began to come true, was for a long time, a kind of Rome for us. We spoke of the Great October Socialist Revolution as if it were our Christmas. This was our childhood. Today we have grown up.... We are beginning to lose the characteristics of a church. The scientific aspect of our theories is taking over firm faith and the mysticism of predestination.... If we communists, therefore, want to capitalise on our past sacrifices and continue to be the bearers of this hope for emancipation, we must increasingly come to embody the aspirations of the peoples of our nations and states, so as to ensure that the forces of labour and culture assume the hegemonic role assigned to them. It is these new problems which create differences, even divergences, among us, and they can only be overcome by discussion, open criticism, and self-criticism, and a recognition of the diversity of national roads and forms of socialism and socialist policy.... We communists today have no leading centre, and are not tied to any international discipline. We are united by the bonds created by joint activity based on theories of scientific socialism and our refusal to accept any return to the past structures and conceptions of internationalism."[25]

Reiterating the same point, Carrillo in his authoritative work on Eurocommunism says: "We have already indicated that our aim is a Europe independent of the USSR and the United States, a Europe of the peoples, oriented towards socialism, in which our country will preserve its own individuality."[26]

Carrillo justifies his contention on these grounds:[27]

1. The economic environment is more complicated. It is to be expected that imperialism will try to destabilise a democratic power whose leadership is in the hands of the forces of labour and culture. In the face of this pressure it would be necessary to rely on the solidarity of the European left in the broadest sense not only due to the pressure of public opinion but also because of the government policy of those countries where the left is in power. This solidarity would have to be reciprocal, integrated in a varied and many-sided process, but cohesive as regards the transformation of the social and economic structures.
2. It would have to rely on the co-operation of the Third World, especially those countries which pursue anti-imperialist and national policies and are committed to a democratisation of international relations which will assist their development.
3. It would be necessary to strengthen economic relations with the socialist countries of Europe and Asia.
4. A socialist democracy would have to maintain a policy of remaining open to foreign investments and to the multinationals which suit our economic development.
5. A European defensive organisation should be set up to serve as a guarantee for both the United States and the USSR which because of their immense nuclear power do not need bases or the occupation of foreign territories to ensure their defence.

25. *Keesing's Contemporary Archives*, Sept. 24, 1976, p. 27951.
26. Carrillo, *op. cit.*, p. 105.
27. *Ibid.*, pp. 105-07.

It is, therefore, clear that the concept of 'national communism' as evolved by the doctrine of Eurocommunism, is a clear negation of the case of proletarian internationalism as formulated by Marx and Engels and as peculiarly twisted by the great Russian leaders like Lenin and Stalin so as to keep all communist countries of the world under the dominance of the Soviet Union. It re-examines the case of world community in the light of new and developed conditions of science and technology and thereby comes to hold that each country should not only be free to choose its own course of socialism but also have international relations for the sake of mutual benefit.

Ideological Autonomy: Refutation of the 'Dictatorship of the Proletariat' and the 'Withering Away of the State'

The next important tenet of Eurocommunism should be traced in its refutation of the principles of the 'dictatorship of the proletariat' and the 'withering away of the state' which are treated as the fundamental propositions of Marxism-Leninism. Influenced by the. creation and fall of the Paris Commune of 1871, both Marx and Engels formulated the case of the state in a transitional form after the successful revolution. They visualised that a new type of state would come into being after the overthrow of the bourgeois order to establish a classless society by all forcible means as a transitional measure and that would have its own termination in the final stage of socialism. Marx said that, "in order to break down the resistance of the bourgeoisie, the workers give to the state a revolutionary and transitory form". So says Engels: "A revolution is certainly the most authoritarian thing there is: it is the act whereby one part of the population imposes its will upon the other part by means of rifles, bayonets and cannons—authoritative means, if such there be at all; and if the victorious party does not want to have fought in vain, it must maintain this rule by means of the terror which its arms inspire in the reactionaries."[28]

Lenin not only takes the 'little word' of the 'dictatorship of the proletariat' from Marx and Engels, he also refines it so as to bring about a line of basic distinction between discredited state of the pre-revolutionary and the 'state proper' of the post-revolutionary stages. He says that the state after the successful overthrow of the bourgeois order is transformed into something which is no longer the 'State proper'.[29]

28. Marx-Engels: *Selected Works,* Vol. 1, p. 578. With his conversion to communism in 1844, Marx "came to the conclusion that the state was essentially the negation of man." David McLellan: "Marx, Engels and Lenin on Party and State" in Leslie Holmes (ed.) *The Withering Away of the State: Party and State Under Communism* (London: Sage Pub., 1981), p. 18. In his *Economic and Philosophical Manuscripts* of 1844, Marx declared the state to be an expression of human alienation similar to law, religion and morality, and equally based on a particular mode of production. Then, in his *German Ideology* of 1845 he visualised that state was in contradiction to the real interests of the community that served as a screen for real struggles waged by classes against each other. Then, in his *Eighteenth Brumaire of Louis Bonaparte* of 1851 he condemned the state as a bureaucratic institution and desired its destruction so as to transform all governmental functions into simple administrative functions. So, in his *Critique of the Gotha Programme* of 1872 he desired subordination of the state to the society for the real freedom of man. Engels and Lenin repeated the phrase 'withering away of the state' in the final stage of socialism.

29 Lenin: *Selected Works,* p. 293.

For this, we should see his *State and Revolution (1917)* in which he frankly endorses the necessity of suppressing the bourgeoisie and crushing its resistance. What should be noted here is that the majority of the population has to play its part, not the minority as was always the case under slavery and serfdom.[30] More important than this is his affirmation that the state will wither away in time to come. As he says: "Since the majority of the people itself suppresses its oppressors, a 'special force' for suppression is no longer necessary. In this sense, the state begins to wither away. Instead of the special institutions of a privileged minority (privileged officialdom, the chiefs of the standing army), the majority itself can directly fulfil all these functions, and the more the functions of state power are performed by the people as a whole, the less need there is for the existence of this power."[31]

Eurocommunism rejects the case of the 'dictatorship of the proletariat' on the ground that it smacks of the total negation of democracy. By all means it is another name of a totalitarian system that crushes individuality and suppresses civil liberties. It is against what Marx and Engels really desired if we compare it with what Lenin and Stalin did in their country. Keeping this in view, Djilas says: "But a dictatorship of the proletariat which would be directly operated by the proletariat is a pure Utopia, since no government can operate without political organisations. Lenin delegated the dictatorship of the proletariat to the authority of one party, his own, Stalin delegated the dictatorship of the proletariat to his own personal authority—to his personal dictatorship in the party and in the state. Since the death of the Communist emperor, his descendents have been fortunate in that through 'collective leadership' they could distribute authority among themselves. In any case the communist dictatorship of the proletariat is either a Utopian ideal or a function reserved for an elite group of the party leaders."[32]

Likewise, Carrillo says that with the October Revolution of 1917, one type of state was destroyed, but in its place, there has arisen a state which is much improved, much more powerful, much more organised, with mighty instruments of control—a state which, speaking in the name of the society, also finds itself situated above society.[33] The Soviet State is neither evidently a bourgeois state nor a proletarian organised as the working class, or a genuine workers' democracy. Within it there grew up and operated the Stalin phenomenon with a series of formal characteristics similar to those of the fascist dictatorship.[34] Again: "It is clear that the Stalin phenomenon which has been a form of totalitarianism extensively exploited by capitalist propaganda, has weakened the democratic credibility of the communist parties in our countries."[35]

It is also said by the disillusioned community of West European communist leaders that a socialist state as established in the Soviet Union or in any satellite country is the model of a bureaucratic class in which a very small section of the Communist Party has the monopoly of power. Djilas calls it a 'new class'. What should

30. *Ibid.*
31. *Ibid.*
32. Milovan Djilas, *op. cit.*, p. 80.
33. Carrillo, *op. cit.*, p. 156.
34. *Ibid.*, p. 157.
35. *Ibid.*, p. 158.

therefore, happen is that democracy should continue even after the establishment of the socialist society. As Carrillo says: "In reality, democracy, in various forms, antedates the existence of the bourgeoisie as such and will survive beyond class society, the State, socialism.... Even under communism, democracy understood as meaning the active participation of all in the administration of society, will continue to be an indispensable treasure, or rather will achieve its fullest and most complete realisation...."[36]

Eurocommunism is not only critical of the concept of the 'dictatorship of the proletariat' as in actual operation in the then USSR, it is equally critical of the allied idea of the 'withering away of the state'. Djilas says that with increasingly complex forces of social life, it would be naive to try to prove that the need for the state would disappear in the near future. Lenin, in support of Marx, agreed with the anarchists about this, and contemplated and tried to establish precisely such a stateless society. To the great dismay of all revolutionary Marxists, the power of the state has immensely increased. It stands as a clear indication of the non-withering away of political authority in any time to come. Thus, Djilas confidently adds that neither Lenin nor Stalin "are able to bridge the ever-increasing chasm between the Communist theories of the state, with the 'disappearance' of the classes and the 'withering away of the state' in their 'socialism' on the one hand, and the realities of the totalitarian authority of the party bureaucracy on the other."[37] So says Carrillo: "In practice, however, things have turned out to be much more complicated. What is serious is that we are continuing to apply to practice which is more complex, the same theoretical schemes, as a result of which ideological reflection is moving further away from reality and is coming into contradiction with it. This moving apart of ideology and reality give to the former an alienating, mystifying character typical of the relations between ideology and practice in bourgeois society."[38]

Thus, once again we take note of the fact that Eurocommunism repudiates the official version of the Marxian tradition and instead, thinks in terms of a new variety of socialism in which democracy remains far from being finished. The doctrine of 'different roads to socialism' informs it to subscribe to the norms of ideological autonomy or, what is termed, ideological pluralism. As Carrillo said at the East Berlin Conference of 1976: "The specific demands of the development of class struggle in our area lead us into paths and forms of socialism which will not exactly be the same as in other countries. This is an objective fact which we must take into account. The hegemony of the forces of labour and culture, which is today in the front rank of the struggle for socialism in our countries, will not be achieved with dictatorial measures but rather with respect for political and ideological pluralism, not through one-party system but by accepting at all times the results of universal suffrage. We want this process to develop through peaceful channels with intense and constant participation of the popular masses."[39]

36. *Ibid.*, p. 146.
37. Djilas, *op. cit.,p.* 87.
38. Carrillo, *op. cit.*, pp. 160-61.
39. *Keesing's Contemporary Archives*, Sept. 24, 1976, p. 27952.

Democratic Socialism: Transformation of the Capitalist Society with the Will of the People

However, what looks like a startling deviation from the path of classical Marxian tradition is the model of democratic socialism as conceived by the advocates of Eurocommunism. It is asserted that in Russia what the Bolsheviks under Lenin and after him could establish was not a 'democracy' but a 'communist dictatorship' with government ownership. To the advocates of Eurocommunism, the Russian model of state after the revolution of 1917 was a far cry from socialism. Socialism is impossible without democracy. It involves both collective ownership of industry and democratic control of the economic, political and cultural life of the people. In this direction, as we shall see, the advocates of Eurocommunism paid a superficial respect to Lenin and rather emulated Karl Kautsky who maintained: "We understand by modern socialism not merely social organisation of production, but democratic organisation of society as well."[40]

The advocates of Eurocommunism, in a way, claim to follow Lenin who on the eve of October Revolution said: "All nations will arrive at socialism—this is inevitable, but not all will do so in exactly the same way, each will contribute something of its own in one or another form of democracy, one or another variety of the dictatorship of the proletariat, one or another rate at which socialist transformations will be effected in the various aspects of social life."[41] Reiterating the same point, Khrushchev said on the occasion of the Twentieth Congress of the Communist Party of the Soviet Union in 1956: "It is probable that more forms of transition to socialism will appear. Moreover, the implementation of these forms need not be associated with civil war under all circumstances.... In the present circumstances, the working class, by rallying around itself the working peasantry, the intelligentsia, all patriotic forces resolutely repulsing the opportunist elements who are incapable of giving up the policy of compromises with the capitalists and the landlords, is in a position to defeat the reactionary forces opposed to the interests of the people, to capture a stable majority in parliament, and transfer the latter from an organ of bourgeois democracy into a genuine instrument of the people's will."[42]

Eurocommunism desires to bring about a socialism of its own variety. For instance, Palmiro Togialatti of Italy links the idea of democracy with socialism and goes forward to explore new contributions to the enrichment of democracy. In his doctrine of the 'Italian road to socialism', he says that "our democratic drive has been effective, and continues and will continue to be effective precisely because we do not feel satisfied with mere changes of form but are striving to shorten the road towards socialism. This struggle of ours adds a new content to the same democratic liberties, gives a reappraisal of the right to freedom, because these rights bring us nearer to the demands relating to well-being and economic progress; it puts parliamentarianism itself on quite a high plane; calls for profound democratic changes in the political system (development of local powers, of regionalism etc.) and poses the problem of

40. Kautsky: *Dictatorship of the Proletariat*, p. 24.

41. *Report of the Central Committee of the 20th Congress of the Communist Party of the Soviet Union* (London, 1956), p. 29.

42. *Ibid.*, p. 30.

the adoption and development of new forms of democracy, in the factories and in the countryside, with the aim of ensuring that the changes and economic advances serve to satisfy the vital demands of the masses of the working people. Our actions directed towards ensuring that society advances to socialism, our actions which give content and effectiveness to our struggle for democracy and to the entire democratic life of the country."[43]

The peculiar thing about the doctrine of Eurocommunism, in this direction, is that it discards the notion of total abolition of the private property system. It refutes the logic behind wholesale nationalisation of private property. Instead, it desires a mixed economic system in which private as well as public forms of property should co-exist as a long-term measure. One may say that it is not yet socialism, it is also no longer the domination of the state by monopoly capital. The paramount question is of preserving to the greatest possible extent the productive forces and social services already created, recognising the role which private enterprise has in this phase. The slogan that 'land for those who till' does not necessarily mean the individual parcelling out of land; it can also be realised with collective farms or with mixed farms, individual and co-operative, so that social justice and economic yield are in harmony.

Carrillo elaborates this point thus: "The coexistence of forms of public and private ownership means acceptance of unearned increment and the private appropriation of this part, i.e., the existence of a mixed system. Society has the means of taxation, and unearned increment is not exorbitant, by means of taxation, and that it is nevertheless sufficient to encourage private enterprise. Moreover, by controlling credit, it has the opportunity to channel savings towards the purposes best suited to the country as a whole. This system, which will be economically mixed, will translate itself into a political regime in which the owners will be able to organise themselves not only economically but also in a political party or parties representative of their interests; this will be one of the component parts of political and ideological pluralism All this also means that the class struggle is going to manifest itself openly, although the social consensus will logically be greater than that which exists in present day society in which hegemony is exercised by monopoly capital. "This overcoming of social differences will follow a natural process and will not be the result of coercive measures but of the development of the productive forces and of the social services, so that through a gradual process, encouraged by education, all sections of the population will be integrating themselves in the social collective."[44]

The model of democratic socialism, as envisaged by Eurocummunism, not only stands for a mixed economic system, it also desires maintenance and protection of civil liberties so that people enjoy the blessings of life in a free and plural society. Marchais of France made this point very clear in his speech at the East Berlin Conference of June, 1976: "We call upon the working class of our country to struggle for the democratisation of economic, social and political life, democratisation carried to its logical conclusion, socialism. The socialism for which we are struggling will be profoundly democratic.... not only because by eliminating exploitation it will ensure

43. Cited in Carrillo, *op. cit,,* pp. 90-91.

44. *Ibid.,* p. 80.

for the working people the essential condition for their freedom, but also because it will guarantee, develop and extend all the liberties which our people have won by struggle. Whether it is a question of freedom of thought and expression, creation and publication, freedom of demonstration, assembly and association, freedom of movement inside or outside the country, religious freedom or the right to strike; whether it is a question of respect for universal suffrage, with the possibility of alternating in office, the right of political parties including opposition parties, to existence and activity, the independence and freedom of activity of trade unions, the independence of judiciary or the refusal of any official policy, whether finally it is a question of extending worker's right at their places of employment or of the autonomy of religious and local authorities in the exercise of these powers. Such is the socialism inseparable from liberty which we desire for our country and which we believe we can build. It is because the concept of the dictatorship of the proletariat does not correspond to the realities of political power in the socialist France for which we are struggling that the 22nd Congress of our Party in Feb., 1976 decided to drop it."[45]

Moreover, the peculiarity of democratic socialism, as conceived by the Eurocommunists, lies not only in the advocacy of a mixed economic system and emphasis on the maintenance of civil liberties, it also attaches utmost importance to the use of democratic methods for bringing about the desired state of affairs. In this respect Eurocommunism advocates what the English Fabians did about a hundred years back[46] and Marx also emphasised towards the end of his life. Not revolution by means of violence but change by parliamentary means is required. It hopes that socialist forces can enter government and come to power through universal suffrage and they may maintain themselves in a leading position in society if they are able to keep the confidence of the people through periodic elections. However, what makes Eurocommunism basically different from Marxism-Leninism, in this direction, is their affirmation of pluralism in the sphere of party system. Socialism is basically different from Communism in that while the latter stands for political singularism, the former believes in multiformity. That is, while Communism desires the leading and guiding role of a single political party—the vanguard of the working class—Eurocommunism takes it for granted that there may be several parties, even of the socialists, and all should have the freedom to take part in the struggle for power for the sake of realising the goal of achieving social and economic justice.

It may be seen in the affirmation of the great Italian Communist leader Berlinguer who said at the East Berlin Conference of June, 1976: "Some of our opponents claim that Socialism and Communism are and will be the same everywhere. This is not true, nor was it true for the bourgeois revolutions, or for the societies they gave rise

45. *Keesing's Contemporary Archives*, Sept. 24, 1976, p. 27953.
46. As Pease in "The History of the Fabian Society" says that for "the attainment of its ends, Fabianism "looks to the spread of socialist opinions, and the social and political changes consequent thereon, including the establishment of equal citizenship for men and women. It seeks to achieve these ends by the general dissemination of knowledge as to the relation between the individual and society in its economic, ethical and political aspects." *The Fabian Essays in Socialism*, p. 269.

to. There already exist in the world of today a variety of experiences in the building of new societies which are no longer capitalist. And it is logical that other varieties can and must develop, among them the new varieties which will be built in the countries where capitalism has reached the highest point of its development and where deeply rooted democratic traditions and particular forms of organisation and political expression by the working people exist. In Italy where the working class and our party have been and are protagonists in the fight to restore, defend and develop democracy, we are fighting for a socialist society which has at its foundation the value of individual and collective liberties and their guarantee, the principles of the secular, non-ideological nature of the state and its democratic organisation, the plurality of political parties and the possibility of alternation of government majorities, the autonomy of the trade, unions, religious freedom, freedom of expression, culture, arts and sciences...."[47]

The last striking feature in this connection is the role of foreign money in national economy which Eurocommunism fully recognises. It insists on the understanding of economic reality of modern times. The investment of foreign capital and the functioning of multinational corporations should not be hindered. Carrillo asserts that from the standpoint of the principles and the historical experience of socialism, this would be no more than a repetition of what has been and is being done in countries where socialism has been established for many years—countries where for a certain time economic relations with capitalist countries were actually suspended. If things are, as they are, he continues, it is obvious that a socialist democracy "would have to maintain a policy of remaining open to foreign investments and to the multinationals which suit our economic development."[48]

The whole meaning of Eurocommunism is thus explained by Carrillo: "What is commonly called 'Eurocommunism' proposes to transform capitalist society, not to administer it, to work out a socialist alternative to the system of state monopoly capitalism, not to integrate in it and become one of its governmental variants. That is to say, it proposes to develop the world revolutionary process, which today is an objective social necessity, in order to escape from the blind alley into which mankind has been led by the model of capitalist development. At the same time, the Eurocommunist strategy aims to bring about a convergence with the socialist and social democratic parties, with the progressive Christian forces with all the democratic groups that are not the henchmen of monopoly-type property. These aims are not contradictory, if social development is seen as a fluid and changing process and not something static."[49]

Non-Coercive State: Emphasis on the End of a Destructive Ideology

Finally, Eurocommunism stands for a new form of political organisation in which police and military have a 'democratic' character and which allows no room for a 'destructive' ideology in national and international spheres. Thus, like New Leftism, Eurocommunism may be said to be in favour of the 'end of destructive ideology'. In

47. *Keesing's Contemporary Archives,* Sept. 24, 1976, p. 27953.
48. Carrillo, *op. cit.,* p. 107.
49. *Ibid.,* p. 104.

simple terms, it implies no place for the doctrine of 'class war' that desires a particular form of 'ideological apparatus' for the state, as suggested by Louis Althusser. Once again, a line of subtle distinction between Communism and Eurocommunism may be drawn in that while the former desires a 'repressive' state, the latter advocates the case of a non-coercive political organisation. In this way, the advocates of Eurocommunism seem to be in agreement with the view of a 'New Leftist' thinker who says that "unless Marxism detaches itself from Stalinist interpretation, it cannot function as the critical consciousness of our time."[50]

The advocates of Eurocommunism, for this reason, disagree with the 'ideological state apparatus' theory of Althusser who said that a vast number of institutions involved, in one way or another, in the dissemination of knowledge are 'ideological apparatuses' which must be distinguished from the 'repressive state apparatuses'.[51] He lists these 'ideological state apparatuses' (ISA) as the religious ISA (the system of different churches), the educational ISA (the system of the different public and private schools), the family ISA, the legal ISA, the political ISA (the political system including different parties), the trade union ISA, the communications ISA (press, radio and television, etc.), the cultural ISA (literature, arts, sports, etc.).[52] Thus, he tries to make a subtle line of distinction between the 'ideological' and 'repressive' state apparatuses so as to justify what Marx had said after distinguishing it from what the Russian dictators have done in their country.[53]

Eurocommunism asserts that certainly one of the great historical tasks of the present time for the conquest of state power by the socialist forces is the determined, resolute, intelligent struggle to turn the weapon of ideology, the ideological apparatuses, against the classes which are in power. It has become possible to propose this road because 'material upheavals' have taken place in the conditions of economic production with truly extraordinary changes in the structures and social relations in recent decades, all of which have ripened the conditions for socialism. Different from this, the reformists have given the name of socialism to a whole collection of social policy which has been carried out in the developed capitalist countries. Obviously, a new type of socialism is needed which saves it from all forms of falsification having their source of existence in the continuance of the capitalist system.

What is, therefore, desired is that instead of a party state turned into an 'apparatus state' there should be a new conception of public order, a more civilised one, based

50. Kolakowski: *Marxism and Beyond* (Paladin, 1969). See "Althusser's Marx: A Note" in the form of a Review Article by V.R. Mehta in *Indian Journal of Political Science,* Vol. XXXV, No. 4, 1974, pp. 374-79.
51. Ralph Miliband: *Marxism and Politics* (London: Oxford Univ. Press, 1977), p. 54.
52. Louis Althusser: "Ideology and Ideological State Apparatuses (Notes towards an Investigation)" in *Lenin and Philosophy and Other Essays* (London, 1972), p. 143.
53. As Althusser says: "The class (or class alliance) in power cannot lay down the law in the ISAs as easily as it can in the (repressive) State apparatus, not only because the former ruling classes are able to retain strong positions there for a long time, but also because the resistance of the exploited classes is able to find means and occasions to express itself there, either by the utilisation of their contradictions, or by conquering combat positions in them in struggle.... But the class struggle extends beyond these forms, and it is because it extends beyond them that the struggle of the exploited classes may also be exercised in the forms of the ISAs and thus turn the weapon of ideology against the classes in power." *Ibid.*, p. 140.

on the idea of defence of the entire population and not just the interest of a privileged minority, a new conception of a more democratic public order and of instilling this conception into the minds of those who make up the forces of order. These forces, to a great extent, feel increasingly uneasy with the tasks imposed on them by the present system. The conception of such a new 'democratic order' involves the transformation of the character and role of the police and military organisations and the denunciation of military pacts and wars so as to achieve the aim of the 'democratisation of the state apparatus'.[54]

The profile of the non-coercive state, therefore, becomes another name for a new democratic order in which mass action "is combined with action by the representative democratic institutions."[55] It may be visualised in these directions:

1. Eurocommunists take up the matter of internal security and, for this purpose, study the case of police organisation. According to them, the forces of public order should be there but not for the sake of oppressing and harassing the people. The area of police activity should be to maintain law and order, to control traffic, to prevent anti-social activities but certainly not to suppress labour agitations. For instance, popular demonstrations and strikes are not conflicts of public order except when governments launch the police against them. Strikes are a matter of negotiation between the representatives of the employers and the workers. The preservation of order at demonstrations should be carried out by the organisers of demonstrations.[56]
2. Then comes the matter of defence. Military is undoubtedly the most important coercive instrument of the state. Various examples among them that of Chile of 1973 and many others prove that in some conditions the army can become the political party of the oligarchy; a political party with aircraft, tanks, artillery, machine-guns and rifles, which the oligarchy throws on to the scales, when universal suffrage threatens its privileges. Military mentality should be changed in a way that the men of defence learn the values of social interest and prestige. The military academies should devote themselves to the teaching of the doctrines, strategies, tactics and the specifically military application of technology, but the cadet should attend the university for courses in science and technology, humanities and sociology, together with the rest of the students. Those officers and commanders who are already trained should be able to take university courses to compete and develop their qualifications. The officers of a modern army ought to be a highly educated group whose social prestige is based on their intellectual qualifications and not on the fact that they bear arms and wear uniforms which distinguishes them from others. According to this conception, a military man is not a member of a kind of closed order, isolated from and above society but a participant in a teaching body devoted to imparting certain specific information to the citizens so that they may defend the country's territorial integrity in times of crisis.[57]

---

54. Carrillo, *op. cit.*, p. 56.
55. *Ibid.*, p. 51.
56. *Ibid*, p. 64.
57. *Ibid.*, p. 70.

3. Eurocommunism denounces the atmosphere of cold war. Creation of nuclear and thermonuclear weapons and formation of military blocs are decried for being standing challenges and portents to the maintenance of world peace. Moreover, a military defence pact under the supreme leadership of a superpower smacks of its imperialistic domination. Carrillo cites the cases of NATO and Warsaw Pact in this regard. Such organisations, like any military or civil bureacracy, generate a tendency to self-perpetuation, to grow parasitically fat. It also generates the tendency to convert itself into a power in its own right, an autonomous power over which its member-states lose all real control except that which is exercised by the Pentagon and, behind it, the entire military-industrial complex of the United States and its European ramifications.[58]
4. Above all, there is the question of world peace. Once again, the role of military figures in. The military cadre should occupy in the country the role of a technician, an intellectual educator of men skilled in protecting territory from outside attack. In the event of war, the professional military man is not the only saviour of the nation, since in such circumstances an infinite number of civilian professionals also become military personnel who defend their country's integrity just as they do and as do the NCOs and soldiers under their command. A new military policy should be formulated so that the minds of the defenders of the realm are changed. Such a concept of the national, popular war of defence is in total opposition to the imperialist conception of conquest, and, of course, to the ideas of anti-subversive war waged against one's own people. At bottom the idea of an anti-subversive war corresponds to a counter-revolutionary army, trained not to defend the nation but to prepare a *coup d' etat,* not to preserve territorial integrity but to protect the privileges of an oligarchic minority.[59]

In short, Eurocommunism is concerned with the question of creating a 'living democracy' at all levels throughout the country— a democracy in which effective power will reside in the organs of popular power so that the vitality of that power may wipe it out at a blow. It is a question of creating a state apparatus which at every moment faithfully obeys the people's elected representatives and which cannot be maintained against the will of the people. Obviously, such a conception of the state and of the struggle to democratise it presupposes the renunciation of the idea, in its traditional form of a workers' and peasants' state, of a state, that is, built from a scratch, bringing into its offices workers from the factories and peasants from the land and sending the functionaries who had hitherto worked in the offices to occupy their places.[60]

Eurocommunism and Marxism: Whether a New Orientation in the Western Marxian Tradition

What we have seen above shows that the parties included in the trend of 'Eurocommunism' (as those of Italy, Spain and France) are agreed on certain important points like need to advance socialism with democracy, a multiparty system,

58. *Ibid.,* p. 60.
59. *Ibid.,* p.73.
60. *Ibid.,* p. 76.

parliaments and representative institutions, sovereignty of the people regularly exercised through universal suffrage, trade unions independent of the state and of the parties, freedom for the opposition, human rights, religious freedom, freedom for cultural, scientific and artistic creation, and the development of the broadest form of popular participation at all levels and in all branches of social activity. Side by side with this, in one form or another, the parties claim their total independence in relation to any possible international leading centre and to the socialist states, without ceasing on that account to be internationalist. They devote great attention to solidarity with the countries of the Third World which are fighting against colonialism and neo-colonialism and for the increasing democratisation of international relations.[61]

The trend of Eurocommunism in this direction stands on the following important assumptions.[62]

1. The extraordinary development of the productive forces, the fact that education is more integrated to production, with the raising of the quality of the work-force, the development of energy, with the conquest of nuclear power and the discovery of new sources of energy, and the development of technology in general—a fundamental factor in all the changes of the period, in accordance with historical materialism. In reality, the enormous military expenditures, totally unproductive, are in themselves an obstacle to all this progress, and a squandering of wealth which may perhaps have affected the cycle of economic crises—displacing their destructive effects and, above all, reducing their intensity, until recently when the crisis of the system, acquiring new characteristics, has broken all bounds.
2. The inability of the system of private enterprise to administer and channel the torrent of productive forces, even with its new multinational dimension. Today the multinational enterprise relies on the credits and various loans provided for it by the states of those countries where it is installed, which extract them from public funds and savings. Consequently, the essential role of the state and of the society is all the more visible in the creation and maintenance of these enterprises, which continue to be, in defence of all logic, private property. Hence, the conditions for a socialist economy have matured.
3. The assumption by the state of social functions which are a poor imitation of collective solutions, some public services, some enterprises, social security, health, education, compensation for social groups at risk (such as support for farm prices within the Common Market)—all measures which the Capitalist State finds itself obliged to take in order to avoid the imbalance and the serious social conflicts which could be engendered by their neglect, and which enable the Capitalist State to maintain the predominance of the monopolist oligarchy under the appearance of a 'welfare state', but which, at the same time, sharpen the contradiction between state and society.
4. The sharpening of the differences between the oligarchic minority and the rest of the society add—to use a classical, though perhaps in the 'consumer society', a confusing term—the proletarianisation of professional people, in the sense of

61. *Ibid.*, p. 110.
62. *Ibid*, p. 46-48.

the unification of their social position (although in many, but not all, cases the earnings are greater) with that of the wage workers. In addition, the introduction of forms of co-operation, though minimal, in the countryside, in order to resist the capitalist concentration of ownership, and the ever-increasing difference between oligopolist interest and those of small and medium enterprises. To sum up, the development of conditions for a new correlation of forces favourable to socialism, creating the possibility of winning and consolidating it democratically, without recourse to forms of dictatorship.

5. The greater independence in the policy of the former colonies...has had a decisive influence in the present world economic crisis and it operates objectively, though amid tensions, in favour of greater democratisation of international relations. Just as bourgeois society was formed in the womb of the feudal regime, so socialist society has matured in the womb of developed capitalist society. This is what gives us today a material base for setting ourselves the task of turning the ideological apparatuses on which the state relies against the present class society.

Having seen this, a pertinent question arises: Whether Eurocommunism is a faithful variety of Marxism? Carrillo boldly affirms that the advocates of the new trend are dynamic Marxists in spite of the fact that they are dubbed by the fellow-communists as 'opportunists' who have abandoned internationalism for nationalism and who are accused of demonstrating 'anti-Sovietism', of committing desertion of a class position, in a word, of doing something which has a connotation as confusing as revisionism. Claiming his interpretations as a Marxist, he adds: "We shall not, however, abandon the revolutionary ideas of Marxism, the ideas of the class struggle, historical materialism and dialectical materialism, the conception of a worldwide revolutionary process which is putting an end to imperialism— a process understood as the defeat of this or that country, but as the defeat of a social system increasingly harmful to all countries, including those enabled by history to use that instrument to obtain a higher standard of living and lord it over the rest. Such a victory over an unjust system has to be supported by all countries, with their own struggle."[63]

Contrary to this, the Russian comrades minced no words in designating Eurocommunism as 'Eurofanaticism' and a new brand of distorted Marxism as offered by the Western reactionary minds. Prof. Vadim Zagladin, a senior theoretician in the Kremlin, said that the term Eurocommunism was invented by Zbigniew Brzezinski, national security adviser to President Carter, so that Communism could be pluralised as much as possible. He continued that after the Communist parties of Europe met in East Berlin in June, 1976 to agree on a common programme, imperialist propaganda strengthened its subversive activities in socialist countries (Soviet bloc) and the Communist parties in the European capitalist countries initiating the campaign with so-called Eurocommunism, a term which had been systematically exploited since 1975 in the bourgeois countries and was later also accepted by the leftist groups and even by certain Communist party organs."[64]

63. *Ibid*, p. 133.

64. Raymond Fletcher, *op. cit.*

What is the correct position? The answer is that as we have seen in the case of New Leftism (in the preceding chapter) so here, it is all a matter of controversy. While the leading lights of the new trend claim that Marxism has, or may have, different currents and theirs is one of them, the adherents to the 'official' line reject it in the name of being a distorted version of the same. Carrillo, Berlinguer and Marchais all draw inspiration from Lenin's phrase that not one but many are the roads to socialism. Thus, the New Leftists and the Eurocommunists alike reiterated their firm conviction in repudiating the official line laid down by the then Russian leaders and instead adhere to what Che Guevara, for instance, said: "There are truths so evident, so much a part of people's knowledge, that it is now useless to discuss them. One ought to be 'Marxist' with the same naturalness with which one is 'Newtonian' in physics or 'Pasteurian' in biology, considering that if facts determine new concepts, these new concepts will never divest themselves of that portion of truth possessed by the older concepts they have outdated."[65]

Critical Appreciation

It is clear that the real nature of Eurocommunism—a curious variety of Marxist protestantism—is a matter of controversy. Both the'liberal' thinkers of the West and the 'Marxists'subscribing to the 'official' line harbour serious misgivings which lead to the emergence of several conflicting interpretations. Sometimes, it appears that Eurocommunism is a clever subterfuge by hardline Soviet-oriented European Communist parties to broaden their social base and win over all those unwilling to endorse capitalism but unable to support Communist totalitarianism, or it is an ideological Trojan horse planted in the Western camp from which would emerge, when the time is ripe, all those formidable warriors who would take the citadel of liberty from within. It is also asked whether it, in fact, represents the triumph of libertarianism, for it is espoused by certain Communist parties in countries with the right social conditions in which Marx had expected the true socialist revolution to occur spurning the very idea of the dictatorship of the proletariat and conceding that civil rights, freedom of expression, separation of powers and other aspects of an open system were not just bourgeois but universal values.

Let us now look into certain inconsistencies in the doctrine of Eurocommunism.

1. It lacks a clear-cut affirmation on several important points. What we have seen in the case of New Leftism applies to Eurocommunism as well. We may take note of the fact that while its advocates look like being in agreement on some important points, it is not the same with regard to all possible areas of social and economic affairs. Still some crucial problems are awaiting a proper solution. What about the relationship of the Eurocommunists with the past, that is, lack of serious self-criticism or, in other words, the preference by the three parties that they always acted in the only way that was possible under the circumstances of the times—a fact which inevitably casts some doubt if not on the sincerity then on the depth of the present change? All adhere to the persistence of a political

65. See Kenneth Minnogue: "Che Guevara" in Maurice Cranston (ed.): *The New Left* (London: The Bodley Head, 1970), p. 26.

system that suppresses opposition, evades the difficulty in taking or even refusing to take the step from the criticism of individual cases of illiberality in the regimes of the East to open dissociation from them. The three parties have dual ambition: on the one hand, to cause a substantial change in the direction of socialism in their respective countries in West Europe; on the other hand, to represent an increasingly important beacon towards which those political and cultural sectors in the Eastern countries, that do not accept the rule of bureaucratic Communism, can turn their sights. And that, naturally, and for different reasons, arouses hopes and anxieties in both Washington and Moscow. The strategy of Eurocommunism is, therefore, complex with big international implications : and its scale is a fairly extended one with inevitable pauses and contradictions.[66]

2. To carry the point further, it may be said that even in those directions where leading Eurocommunists seem to be in agreement, their elaborations are not immune from inherent contradictions. The role of different motivating forces can also be seen in this regard. While all attacked Soviet dominance and espoused a peculiar strategy to bring about a model of democratic socialism, basic differences could be discovered. For instance, all did not criticise the hold of the'Big Brother' (Soviet Union) in equally strong terms. Marchais and Berlinguer had often held that open and strong condemnation of the Soviet Government for suppressing dissidence would not serve the desired purpose; that the mistake of openly decrying China should not be repeated and that nothing should be done to upset East-West *detente.* While Italian and Spanish Communist parties strongly desire political integration of Western Europe, French Communist party is openly opposed to it. Then, while the Spanish and Italian Communist parties do not equate nationalisation of industry with socialism, their French counterpart does. If the three great parties may be seen well in agreement on any significant point, it is that of 'democratic centralism'—a Leninist tenet which is largely a euphemism for the right of the party bosses to take decisions and pass them down for implementation to those at the lower rungs of the organisation.[67]
3. It is a fact that the Soviet leaders had not been able to digest their serious reactions despite their occasional appreciation of 'independence' of the certain European Communist parties.[68] The Kremlinologists remarked that Eurocommunism was an idea created by the imperialistic propagandists to first divide and then conquer world communism. *Pravda,* the official daily paper of the Soviet Communist Party had, on several occasions, reiterated that it was impossible to build socialism within the framework of a bourgeois democratic state. It decried the resolve of

66. Aldo Rizzo: "West's Communists in Step" in *The Times,* March 1, 1977. An element of basic contradiction can also be traced in this fact that Eurocommunism advocates the case of 'national communism' which is against the whole concept of Marxism. Keeping this in view, Djilas says: "National Communism *per se* is contradictory. Its nature is the same as that of Soviet Communism, but it aspires to detach itself into something of its own, nationally. In reality, national Communism is Communism in decline." *Op. cit.*, p. 190.
67. Raymond Fletcher, *op. cit.*
68. For instance, the *Pravda* claimed that ths East Berlin Conference had produced 'greater cohesion and closer co-operation than ever in the European Communist movement." *Keesing's Contemporary Archives,* Sept. 24, 1976, p. 27955.

the Madrid Meet of March 1977 of the Eurocommunist leaders as a 'charade'. The argument was that Eurocommunism was a far cry from orthodox Marxism-Leninism. We may take note of the fact that while the Soviet leaders had agreed to the formulation of the text of the *communique* adopted at the East Berlin Conference of June 1976, they made their stand clear six months later at the Sophia Conference of 15-17 Dec, 1976 which registered the faith of all satellite countries (Bulgaria, Romania, Czechoslovakia, Hungary, Mongolia, Poland, East Germany and Cuba) in the principles of dictatorship of the proletariat and proletarian internationalism. At this stage the Soviet delegate Alexander Lilov specifically hit at the theoretically inconsistent position of Eurocommunism.[69]

4. It would not be incorrect to say that Eurocommunism seeks to steer through the divergent poles of Fabianism and Leninism in a bid to offer a new variety of Marxism. It looks like an attempt to marry the irreconcilables, to combine communism with liberal democracy. It accepts Marxian premises without relishing what they lead to in practice. It goes along with class conflict but not with the dictatorship of the proletariat; it believes in revolution but wants this to be achieved by constitutional means. Inevitably it falls between two stools. It earns the contumely of both left and right without ensuring the centre. Even as an attempt to the independence of West European Communists from the Soviet domination, it failed, because it could not mobilise European leftist nationalist sentiments. Nor could it remain like a creature with a recognisable identity like the Social Democrats whose commitment to constitutional democracy and new system is unswerving. In a word, Eurocommunism, like the unicorn, is a mythical beast.[70]
5. It is also pointed out that the practical side of the movement of Eurocommunism has been quite dismal. The French Eurocommunists suffered severe disasters in the elections of 1978 and it was because of their mistakes that the Socialists made unexpected gains. The Italian Communists could have an equally chastening experience. In their obsession for a 'historic compromise', they chose to support a Christian Democrat government at a time when they had unparalleled popular support from a wide cross-section of the Italian society. In the event, far from the compromise bringing them nearer to power, it eroded their social base. Though they were not in the government, they had to share the blame for its failures. It naturally annoyed labour circles with the result that the Communists suffered heavy losses in local and regional polls. Only in Spain the Eurocommunists could make some success which is evident from the fact that in the municipal poll of March, 1979 they got 15% of votes as compared to 10% of the preceding national election. It shows that now Eurocommunism has become a moribund affair. It also "reflects the desperate straits to which European Communists have been reduced."[71]

---

69. *Keesing's Contemporary Archives,* April 1, 1977, p. 28276.
70. A.S. Abraham: "End of Eurocommunism" in *The Times of India* (New Delhi), May 28, 1979.
71. *Ibid.*

What Eurocommunism really signifies and what has been its achievement is now a matter of academic dabate. Raymond Fletcher says that "watching a group of people discussing Eurocommunism is like watching the legendary group of blind men trying to describe an elephant by feeling different parts of it."[72] The Western powers may fear Eurocommunism as a danger to NATO and European Economic Community (now European Union) for sharing military secrets or making a hole in the principle that the membership of the European Common Market could be given only to parliamentary democracies. The adherents to the official Marxian line may accuse Eurocommunists of creating contradictions in the Communist camp and thereby doing harm to the cause of proletarian internationalism. Different from both, Carrillo hopefully visualises that differences among Communist leaders of Europe are "a sign of maturity and strength and that they confirm the political and theoretical enrichment our movement has undergone."[73]

Post-Communism

Post-communism is a new term that came into prominence as a result of the disintegration of the communist system in the Soviet Union and in the East European countries. It signifies replacement of a system based on the ideology of Marxism-Leninism by the system of parliamentary democracy and market economy. Its emergence came into limelight when President Gorbachev of the then USSR adopted the course of *glasnost* (open and free society) and *perestroika* (reconstruction of economy) in March, 1985. In Poland it had already appeared as a result of the successful solidarity movement under the leadership of Lech Valesa. Hence, a perceptive analyst of world politics like Zbigniew Brzezinski could take note of it in 1989 when he remarked: "A new phenomenon (post-communism) is now appearing.... Such a system will be one in which the withering away of communism has advanced to the point that neither Marxist theory nor post-communist practice dictate much-if any-on-going public policy. Post-communism, very simply, will be a system in which self-declared communists just do not treat communist doctrine seriously as the guide to social policy."[74]

By definition, post-communism "is a negative concept, defining the present in terms of its past."[75] It is largely because this phenomenon is still crystallising. In seeking to understand as to what it might mean and what it does not mean, it is necessary to study the goals, policies, structures and behaviours that have emerged in the formerly communist world in the period since 1989.[76] In the main, it "is better understood as the rejection of the communist power system than a clear-cut adoption of an alternative system."[77] The most obvious, if also unenlightening, definition of post-communism is that it is whatever follows a communist system. Hence, some of its essential features may be noted as under:

72. *The Times*, London, July 11, 1977.
73. *Keesing's Contemporary Archives*, Sept. 24, 1976, p. 27951.
74. Brzezinski: *The Grand Failure* (New York: Scribners, 1989), p. 252.
75. Richard Sakwa: *Post-Communism* (New Delhi: Viva Books, 2002), p. 3.
76. Leslie Holmes: *Post-Communism: An Introduction* (Cambridge: Polity Press, 1997), p. 3
77. *Ibid.*, p. 13.

Some Important Statements

Broadly speaking, if industrial society is based on machine technology, post-industrial society is shaped by an intellectual technology. And if capital and labour are the major structural features of industrial society, information and knowledge are those of the post-industrial society.

—Daniel Bell,
The Coming of Post-Industrial Society, p. xiii.

If the West, along with all the other democratic forces in the world, is incapable of rapidly engaging in the common creation of a new border in Europe and Euro-Asian affairs—a better order than the old bi-polar one then someone else might well begin to do the job....

—Vaclav Havel,
"A Call for Sacrifice: The Co-Responsibility of the West" in ***Foreign Affairs,*** Vol. 73, No 2, 1994, pp. 2-3.

The end of history, that is, the end point of mankind's ideological revolution. Yet its power relative to other civilisations is declining....A central axis of post-cold war politics is the interaction of Western power and culture with the power and culture of non-western civilisations.

—Samuel P. Huntington,
"The West and the Rest" ***Prospect*** (February, 1997), p. 37.

As an ideal, post-communism had not only a negative, rejective logic namely, overcoming the legacy of communism—but also a more positive, inclusive agenda. This agenda necessarily remains vague in that there is no single post-communist manifesto broadcasting its aims, but it remains central to our age as an opportunity to achieve certain normative goals: the strengthening of international civil society including those aspects concerned with universal justice, the drive to ensure minimum standards of good governance and human rights; and, perhaps, above all, to deepen democracy everywhere while extending the rights associated with the ideal of social citizenship balanced by an acknowledgement of the duties associated with membership in a political community.

—Richard Sakwa
Post-Communism (Delhi: Viva Books, 2002), pp. 126-27.

1. Assertion of independence from the official ideology of Marxism-Leninism and instead appreciation of the principles of modern liberalism.
2. Rise of nationalism and thus rejection of subordination to the dictates of the Communist Party talking about proletarian socialism all over the world.
3. Cynicism towards or mistrust of the political institutions established in the country by the leaders of the Communist Party.
4. Emergence of a multi-party system and a pluralist society demanding free and fair elections in a full-fledged liberal democratic set up.
5. Creation of a civil society with the freedom of the press and independent judiciary alongwith a limited and accountable government under a new constitution.
6. Inauguration of market economy allowing scope for private initiative as well as entry of foreign capital and corporations in the age of globalisation.

Salient Features of Communism and Post-Communism

*Communism**	*Post-Communism***
1. Marxism-Leninism is the official ideology. 2. A communist party organised on the principles of democratic centralism enjoys monopoly of political power. 3. The communist party 'rules' in the sense that it dominates the state machine, creating a fused state-party apparatus. 4. The communist party plays 'a leading and guiding role' in society, controlling all institutions, including the economic, educational, cultural and recreational institutions. 5. Economic life is based on state collectivisation, and it is organised through a central planning system.	1. End of communist party's monopoly over politics, economics and society. 2. Emergence of pluralistic societies but ones where interests are weakly defined and polyarchical system is poorly institutionalised. 3. Uneven introduction of the elements of market into a heavily bureaucratised economy. 4. Rapid change in class structure with the emergence of a thoroughly monetised 'new class' of communist officialdom enjoying the privileges derived from the management of state property. 5. Rapid orientation of foreign and typically security policy.
* Heywood: *Politics*, p. 35.	** Richard Sakwa: *Post-Communism*, p. 5.

It is obvious that post-communism rejects all norms and institutions of the communist system established in Russia by Lenin and consolidated by his successors. The trend had its start in Poland, but it encompassed all the countries of Eastern Europe, including the former Soviet Union. But the problem is that it has not yet taken a concrete form. Its contours are loose and untidy. While its negative aspect may be easily understood that lies in the frank repudiation of the communist system, its positive side is entangled in the web of confusion. Civil society is emerging of course, but the problems "are related to unrealistic expectations and a poor understanding of the ramifications of concepts such as market economy."[78] But the bright feature of post-communism is that it has replaced totalitarian and authoritarian forces of the left by the institutions of liberal democracy. The progress of the erstwhile communist countries may be seen from a dictatorial to a semi-democratic or to a new democratic system.[79]

78. *Ibid.*, p. 15.
79. Andrew Heywood: *Politics*, p. 35.

24
Fascism

> The State as conceived and realised by Fascism is a spiritual and ethical entity for securing the political, juridical and economic organisation of the nation, an organisation which in its origin and growth is a manifestation of the Spirit.... Far from crushing the individual, the Fascist State multiplies his energies just as in a regiment a soldier is not diminished but multiplied by the number of his fellow soldiers.
>
> **—Benito Mussolini[1]**

The English historian H.G. Wells happily described the present age as the 'age of democracy'; but the great Fascist leader of Italy (Mussolini) in a power-drunken state nicknamed the twentieth century as the 'century of fascism'. Fascism, obviously, is the anti-thesis of liberalism; it is another name for totalitarianism of the right.[2] It is not an alternative but a challenge to and a negation of all that is lauded in the name of a liberal democratic system in national and international spheres. Though basically a creation of Italy under the leadership of Mussolini, it saw its repetition in Germany under Hitler and also in other countries as in Spain under Gen. Franco, and in Japan under Prince Fumimaro Konoe in the pre-Second World War period. It has had its inglorious manifestation in the period following the Second World War in various degrees as Salazarism in Portugal, Peronism in Argentina, Gaullism in France and also in the form of military rule in many countries of the Third World. The most striking feature of the study of Fascism is that it has assumed the shape of an ideology negating the principles of liberalism, socialism and internationalism and thereby posing a very serious challenge to those who desire to make the world 'safe for democracy'.

1. Mussolini: *Fascism: Political and Social Doctrines* (Rome: Ardita, 1935), pp. 27-29.
2. Totalitarian ideologies "provide the justificatory arguments in support of a type of Society minimally characterised by (1) an official and highly specific official ideology based upon a radical rejection of some aspects of the past and chiliastic claims for the future, (2) a unitary mass movement of solidarity, hierarchically organised as a single party under the authoritarian leadership of a charismatic (or pseudo-charismatic) leader and a directive and tutelary elite, (3) a technologically conditioned near monopoly of the means of communication and coercion, and (4) centralised direction under bureaucratised control, of the entire economy." A. James Gregor: *The Ideology of Fascism: The Rationale of Totalitarianism* (New York: The Free Press, 1969), p. 7. According to William Kornhauser, totalitarian dictatorship 'involves total domination limited neither by received laws or codes (as in traditional authoritarianism) nor even by the boundaries of governmental functions (as in classical tyranny), since they obliterate the distinction between state and society." *The Politics of Mass Society,* p. 23. Carl J. Friedrich and Z.K. Brzezinski mention six main characteristics of totalitarianism—an official ideology, a single mass party led typically by one man—the dictator, a system of terroristic phase, a technologically conditioned near monopoly of control, centralisation of administration, and a central control and direction of entire economy through bureaucratic coordination of its formerly independent corporate entities. *Totalitarian Dictatorship and Autocracy,* p. 22.

Fascism: Meaning and Essential Features

'Fascism' is primarily used to identify the social, economic and political system that was established in Italy in 1922 under the leadership of Benito Mussolini and his Fascist Party. It is also used to identify a prototype of totalitarianism that had its equally vigorous manifestation in Germany after 1933 under the leadership of Adolph Hitler and his Nazi Party. Though Nazism is the German version of Fascism, the common point is that both stand for the ideology of the totalitarianism of the right.[3] Thus, it is defined as "a political attitude which puts the nation-state or race, its power and growth, in the centre of life and history. It disregards the individual and his rights, as well as humanity, in the exclusive interest of the nation. As a political technique, it follows the lead of the totalitarian bolshevism as a single-party state with a strict regimentation of all aspects of national life."[4]

The word 'Fascism' is derived from an Italian word 'fascio' or 'fasci' literally meaning a 'well-tied bundle of rods'.[5] As the legend goes, in ancient times the Roman army moved with a lictor's fasces in which an axe was inserted into a bundle of well-tied sticks. This emblem signified unity, strength and solidarity of the Italian army. Mussolini invoked this emblem and made it the symbol of his regime. The word 'fascism' appears to have been invented by Mussolini; it became the name of his movement after March, 1919 and of his government after October, 1922. What Mussolini did in Italy was followed in other countries also as in Germany, though the German Fascists had their party called National Socialists and they used the symobl of 'swastika'. A French Fascist group led by Col. de la Rocque called their group as *Croix de Feu* (Cross of Fire); a Belgian movement was known as the Rexists and the followers of William Dudley were known as the 'Silver Shirts'. The Fascist leaders prescribed a particular uniform as 'black shirts' for the followers of Mussolini in Italy, and 'brown shirts' for the followers of Hitler in Germany. Despite these variations, the notable point is that all these organisations and groups should be included in the category of the 'fascists' in view of their standing for a government "with strong centralised power, permitting no opposition or criticism, controlling

3. Totalitarianism of the right is pro-capitalism and anti-communism; totalitarianism of the left is pro-communism and anti-capitalism. But the element of totalitarianism is common whereby both stand for the negation of the values of democracy in national and of pacifism in international spheres. See H.R. Kedward: *Fascism in Western Europe, 1900-45* (London: Ulackie, 1973), p. 240.
4. *Encyclopaedia Britannica,* 1967 Ptg., Vol. 9, p. 103.
5. Keeping it in view, Erwin von Beckerath says: "Fascism is only when viewed as a peculiarly Italian phenomenon that its essence becomes clearly delineated. In its philosophy, its origin and development, its political structure and cultural aspirations, it is an integral part of the Italian matrix. The ideology of Fascism viewed historico-genetically is a peculiar fusion of syndicalist theory and the doctrines of Italian nationalism. While the former has gradually receded into the background, the latter has supplied the movement with its central intellectual pillar, the idea of the national state. The nation becomes transfigured into a *corpus mysticum,* an unbroken chain of generations, armed with a mission which is realised in the course of the historical process. The duty of the individual is to elevate himself to the heights of national consciousness and to lose completely his own identity in it. He has individual's rights only in so far as they do not conflict with the needs of the sovereign state." See his paper "Fascism" in E.R. Seligman (ed.): *Encyclopaedia of the Social Sciences* (New York: Macmillan, 1967), Vol. V, p. 134.

all affairs of the nation (industrial, commercial etc.), emphasising an aggressive nationalism, and often anti-communist."[6]

The main principles of Fascism, as stressed by the leaders of Italy in particular, may be enumerated as under:

1. It stands for an omnipotent state. The authority of the state is absolute, unlimited and indivisible. 'Nothing outside the state, nothing against it, nothing above it', says Mussolini. The interest of the individual is secondary to the interest of the state. Thus, individual interest can be subordinated to the interest of the state. To the Fascists the myth is the state, the nation, an independent entity with a real will that is different from the fictitious popular will assumed in the dogma of liberalism. The national will is distinct from the will of all citizens and even of all governing officials that may be interpreted and formulated in the degrees of self-perpetuating 'party heads', and councils and it is finally expressed in an assent accorded by officially approved delegates of the people or the chosen representatives of the ruling party. Obviously, the state becomes a deity at whose altar all interests of an individual can be sacrificed. The individual is commanded to have full faith in the dictum of state absolutism and for that sake, in Trietschke's words, 'he should fall down and worship the state'. Fascism may thus be defined positively 'as the unlimited sovereignty of the state over all phases of national activity'.[7] While justifying, rather lauding, the hold of his party over the Italian state, Mussolini said that such an event "is a new departure in history. There are no points of reference, nor of comparison."[8]
2. If state is an omnipotent institution in the hands of the ruling party, there is no place for opposition of any kind to it. Freedom of thought and expression is banned; opposition is outlawed. Press and other mass media have to work under strict censorship of the state. The slogans of 'liberty, equality, and fraternity', as raised by the revolutionaries of France, are substituted by the new slogan of 'responsibility, discipline and hierarchy' of the Italian Fascists and the German Nazis. Democracy is condemned as a luxury meant for the rich nations of the world; parliamentary institutions, in the fashion of Thomas Carlyle, are treated as 'talking shops'. But the whole concept of liberty is given a Hegelianised complexion. It is identified with complete obedience to the will of the state. If liberty is understood not as a right but as a duty, then there is no opposition between authority and liberty. Just as the 'private self-realisation' of an individual comes about only under the restraint and direction exercised by his rational and spiritual faculties over his physical instincts, so the development of the finer types of individuals in society is made possible by the supremacy of public law and order over all degenerative activities of its average citizens.[9] It all implies that, as Gentile declares, "always the maximum of liberty coincides with the maximum of State force."[10]

6. *The American College Dictionary* (New York: Random House, 1947), p. 438.
7. E. von Beckerath, *op. cit.*, p. 134.
8. See Mario Einaudi: "Fascism" in "David I. Sills (ed.): *International Encyclopaedia of the Social Sciences* (New York: Macmillan and Free Press, 1968), Vol. 5, p. 337.
9. F.W. Coker: *Recent Political Thought* (New York: Appleton-Century, 1934), p. 476.
10. *Ibid.*

Main Tenets of Fascism

1. ***Irrationalism:*** Fascism rejects objective science and reason. Life is so complex and unpredictable that it cannot be understood by ordinary people. Objective truth is either a hoax or unimportant, because the really important truths defy rational understanding, being random facts with no logical relationship to one another. Those who believe in reason, therefore, delude themselves and grasp at a false reality. Reason is barren intellectualism lacking true meaning. The ordinary mind is not fertile: it is a wasteland full of mirages that give only an illusion of reality.
2. ***Totalitarianism:*** Mussolini created a totalitarian state. (Indeed, it was he who coined the word.) Not content with the political power alone, he believed that the government, and ultimately the government's leader should completely control every aspect of human existence. He tried to build up the state's power extending it into the most private aspects of citizen's lives. Only nominally successful in dominating the Church, he exercised much more power over trade unions, fraternal associations, education, business, arts, media and so forth. Making use of the organic theory of state, he argued that although the state was made up of individuals, it took on an importance that was much greater than the total of the individual parts. As the cells of the body each contribute to a life far greater than their own, so too the state becomes a living being with an importance far beyond that of its individual members.
3. ***Elitism:*** All human beings are not equal and that leaders in every society are the heroes above all moral restraints. People are different in ability and intelligence. Some are stronger than others, some are smarter than their neighbours. Although the people vary greatly, they all have the same function: to serve the state. Being unequal they make unequal contributions. Therefore, those who give the greatest service to the state should receive the greatest benefit. Rejecting democracy as a sham that weakens the society by encouraging incompetence to govern, Mussolini believed that there were only few people in any society who could govern well. Therefore, each society should be ruled by a select elite.
4. ***Corporativism:*** The corporate state was based on the foundation of worker and owner syndicates. Strikes and boycotts being illegal, the syndicates were supposed to settle disputes between management and labour. By the same token, prices, profit margins, production standards, and all the like were set by the state, leaving very few important decisions to the masses. But to be assured of absolute obedience at every level, the state appointed the heads of all the corporations, regional federations and syndicates.
5. ***Nationalist Militarism:*** The higher purpose of the state is imperialism. As every nation must be ruled by an elite, so the world as a whole must be ruled by an elite. National wills are not equal. Superior nations must strive to dominate the poor, weak and backward peoples of the world. To shirk this responsibility is to deny the destiny of the nation, its rightful heritage, and thus warp the natural order of things. War itself is the primary goal of a society. Rather than something to be used only as a last resort, war is a spiritually creative and positive feature of life.

Source: L.P. Baradat: *Political Ideologies: Their Origin and Impact*, pp. 249-57.

3. Fascist state is not the state of the people; it is not even dictatorship of any particular social class. Though sovereignty is said to be vested in the nation, its exercise is in the hands of a small section of the ruling party or *junta* that may be defined as its elite formed around the personality of a charismatic leader. That elite is always right. The leader and his trusted followers are invariably competent to speak for the nation. Charisma, whether in the positive (attractive) or in the negative (repulsive) form, is attached to the personality of the great leader. His life and achievements are included in school and college text-books and his 'golden principles' are displayed in all public places. 'Hero worship' becomes the order of the day. The portraits of the leader decorate every official and non-official place and many significant achievements are credited to his great name. He is addressed in a most celebrated way as 'll Duce' (Mussolini) or 'Fuhrer' (Hitler). The principle of hierarchy is strictly followed that commands every lower unit to obey the dictates of the higher one with the result that all authority is centralised at the top and that too in the hands of a particular leader around whom a series of institutional privileges are built up that intend to make his position, by all means, unchallengeable. As a result, the leader becomes the chief of the state who may even overshadow the authority of the formal head of the state as of King Victor Emmanuel III in Italy and of President von Hindenburg in Germany. "The Party becomes a capillary instrument of power going from its highest body, the Great Council of Fascism, which meets from time to time to decide major policy matters through the secretary of the party and provincial or regional federations to the thousands of party units which convert themselves into the daily instruments of propaganda and contact with the country."[11]
4. Fascism has no doctrinal basis, it is essentially empirical and practical. As Mussolini often declared: "My programme is action, not talk." It may also be described as its irrationalism or anti-intellectualism drawing inspiration from the pragmatism of Sorel. As a movement based on a pragmatic appraisal of the conditions necessarv to retain power, it is never preoccupied with the task of a consistent theoretical interpretation in respect of its origin and growth. Says Rocco: "It is true that Fascism is, above all, action and sentiment and as such

11. Mario Einaudi, *op. cit.*, p. 336. In 1936 M. Palmieri published his book *The Philosophy of Fascism* in which, at one place, he says: "A hero is one who can pierce with the mystic light of the inner vision to the very heart of things; he who can rediscover the greatest and most profound of all truths, viz ., that beyond his realm of fugitive appearances there lies, immutable and eternal, what Fichte called, the 'Divine Idea of the World' and, finally, he, who living already in spirit in this realm of timeless and absolute Reality, is able to translate his vision into deeds and to act according to the dictates of an inner voice telling him that "....they wrong man greatly who say he is to be seduced by ease. Difficulty, abnegation, martyrdom, death are the allurements that act on the heart of man." As a god or a prophet, as a saint or a warrior, as a poet or a king; under whatever aspect they might have appeared on this earth, all heroes have always delivered and, for that matter, will ever deliver the same message to mankind ; viz., that a man lives true human life only when his life is devoted to and, if necessary, sacrificed for the triumph of an ideal and that only by living such a life can he ever find happiness on this earth." See Carl Cohen (ed.): *Communism, Fascism and Democracy: Theoretical Foundations* (New York: Random House, 1972), p. 358.

it must continue to be. Were it otherwise, it could not keep up that immense driving force, that renovating power which it now possesses, and would merely be the solitary meditation of a chosen few."[12] Here Mussolini could discover an important line of difference between his Fascism and Lenin's Bolshevism when he said: "Fascism is based on reality, Bolshevism is based on theory.... We want to be definite and real. We want to come out of the cloud of discussion and theory."[13] It is owing to its highly practical nature that the Fascists may combine the elements of any social and political theory with their own ideology at any stage of its development. Mussolini diluted many important socialistic principles of his Charter of Labour (1927) so as to win over the sympathy of the native bourgeois class; Hitler adopted many anti-labour measures in spite of the fact that his was the National Socialist Party by name. The main aim is to get power and then to consolidate it. The official theoretician of the Fascist Party, Giovanni Gentile, sought to link some of his principles with the idealism of Hegel ; another official interpreter Alfredo Rocco attempted to develop a heavy-handed theory of the state; and the arch-priest of this ideology (Mussolini) himself sought to provide the ideology of totalitarianism.[14]

5. It, however, does not imply that the Fascists have no definite maxims of their political religion. They have their own principles which are of a pragmatic nature and, moreover, which are implemented through the process of political socialisation. The whole educational system of the country is recast in the name of 'building of character' so as to effect the 'inculcation of national tradition'. That is, concerted attempt is made to create more and more Fascists by the instrument of social and political indoctrination. The teachers are exhorted to infuse the new ideology into the minds of their students. Even fine arts are used for the same purpose. Here the movement of the Fascists bears close resemblance to the idea of a 'cultural revolution' of the Marxists in view of the fact that both regard it as an essential function of their government to see that the people of the coming generations are indelibly inspired by and impressed with the principles of their new culture. This may be regarded as the use of education for political purposes that is not confined to the schools alone, nor to the youth organisations of the Fascist party; like Bolshevism in Russia, it determines everything printed in the books and periodicals, heard over the radio, or seen on the screen or stage, so that it "ultimately colours every thought and every sentiment of the people. This kind of indoctrination works especially well, because no other information or critical attitude or independent inquiry is ever allowed to reach the people. Fascism leads also to a complete destruction of all free cultural and intellectual intercourse with other nations."[15]

6. On the economic front, Fascism is certainly a pro-capitalist ideology. One may say that the economic principles of Fascism look like a mixture of liberalism and socialism, but the fact stands out that the pro-capitalism side is too heavy

12. See Coker, *op. cit.*, p. 473.
13. *Ibid.*
14. Mario Einaudi, *op. cit.*, p. 336.
15. *Encyclopaedia Britannica*, 1967 Ptg., Vol. 9, p. 105.

in the economic programme of the Fascists. It is evident from these four points of the Fascist economic philosophy: (i) The community alone is to have the right to determine what the national interest requires, (ii) therefore, the conflicting interests of owners, workers, technicians and the state are to be brought together in a single unit, the corporations operating under public control, (iii) strikes and lock-outs are to be forbidden, and (iv) the doctrine of the primacy of the politician over the expert is to be abandoned ; the divisiveness of politics is to be eliminated by the unity of expertise.[16] The two most important features of Fascist economy are the establishment of a 'corporative state' and the realisation of the goal of 'autarchy'or economic self-sufficiency of the nation. The doctrine of class war is discarded for being absurd. The nation must be economically as well as politically consolidated. It requires that every individual and every group must be made an instrument in the advancement of the nation. Right to private property must be recognised, because it affords the most powerful incentive to productive activity. The workers cannot be given rights to strike so as to weaken or paralyse the process of national production and thereby harm the economy of the nation. Moreover, the amount of production must be according to the requirements of the nation so that the country has nothing to import from other countries of the world. It all can be achieved by a new kind of state—a corporative state—that is like a unified organisation of all productive forces, the capitalists and the workers. "If this aim is accomplished, the resulting economic system would constitute an economic autonomy under state leadership, a type of plan-capitalism, with flexible state intervention always in the background—a system which is far different from the unwieldy state socialism on the German pattern."[17]

7. However, the anti-socialist character of Fascism is more outspoken in its anti-communist postures. The Fascists have no reservations in declaring communists as their arch-enemy. Soon after coming to power, the Fascists assassinated the socialist leader Matteoti in June, 1924. Subsequently, the great Marxist theoretician Gramsci was put behind the bars and he had his tragic end in the jail. Likewise, Hitler in Germany declared his firm resolve to finish the communist system of the USSR. It is for the patently anti-communist postures of the Fascists of Italy and of the Nazis of Germany that the statesmen of Britain, France and the United States had followed the course of appeasement after 1935. Moreover, the way these dictators suppressed the working class in their countries and thereby strengthened the position of the capitalist class informed some leading social and political theorists like Laski to dub this movement as the last remedy to save a tottering capitalist system.[18] Keeping this important feature of Fascism in mind,

16. Mario Einaudi, *op. cit.*, pp. 335-36.
17. E. von. Beckerath, *op. cit.*, p. 137.
18. According to the Marxian theory, Fascism was the last bulwark of capitalism, a conspiracy of capitalists bent upon the preservation of capitalistic property and the system of profits. J.H Hallowell: *Main Currents in Modern Political Thought* (New York : Holt, Rinehart and Winston, 1951), p. 592. So, it is said: "The Marxists follow orthodox lines. Fascism was the defender of capitalist society, threatened by the steady widening power of the Russian Revolution and of the influence of Marxism in Italy. Fascism was a repressive movement developing along the lines Marx had anticipated for the final phase of the bourgeois society." Mario Einaudi, *op. cit*, p. 339.

the communist lexicons define it as "a bloodthirsty, terrorist dictatorship of the most reactionary, chauvinistic and aggressive factions of the exploiting classes, engendered by the general crisis of capitalism. Fascism differs from other forms of reactionary dictatorship in its vast contacts with a rather numerous part of the population, not identified with the ruling classes, by its ability to mobilise these segments of the population and arouse their political activity in the interest of the exploiting class. It depends upon the support of such social groups as the urban and rural petty bourgeoisie, whose material foundations are undermined by growing capitalism. It also finds support among the declassed strata of the population. Riding on the social dissatisfaction of these population brackets, it employs them to tighten the grip of state monopoly capitalism."[19]

8. Racialism may be described as another important feature of the Fascist social and political philosophy, though its place is more powerful in the affirmations of the German Nazis who had no reservations in lauding the Nordics as the best race of the world and denouncing the Jews in the most contemptible words. Alfred Rosenberg thus spoke on the myth of the Nordic blood. "We stand today before a definitive decision. Either through a new experience and cultivation of the old blood, coupled with an enhanced fighting will, we will rise to purificatory action, or the last Germanic-western values of morality and state-culture shall sink away in the filthy human masses of the big cities, become stunted on the sterile burning asphalt of a bestialised inhumanity, or trickle away as a moribund agent in the form of emigrants, bastardising themselves in South America, China, Dutch East Indies, Africa.... A new faith is arising today: the myth of the blood, the divine essence of man. The faith, embodied in clearest knowledge, that the Nordic people represent the *Mysterium* which has replaced and overcome the old sacraments."[20] So says Hitler: "If one were to divide mankind into three groups: culture-founders, culture-bearers, and culture-destroyers, then, as representative of the first kind, only the Aryan would come in question. It is from him that the foundation and the walls of all human creations originate, and only the external form and colour depend on the characteristic of the various peoples involved. He furnishes the gigantic building stones and also the plans for all human progress.... The blood mixing, however, with the lowering of the racial level caused by it, is the sole cause of the dying off of old cultures for the people do not perish by lost wars, but by the loss of that force of resistance which is obtained only in the pure blood."[21]

9. However, the most dangerous feature of the political philosophy of Fascism finds place in its faith in blind and aggressive nationalism. Nationalism is a constructive force and it has played a very significant part in the making

19. *A. Dictionary of Scientific Communism* (Moscow: Progress Publishers, 1980), p. 90.
20. See Carl Cohen, *op. cit.*, p. 367.
21. *Ibid.*, pp. 376-77. Hitler not only eulogised the German race, in very harsh terms he denounced the Jews as a community of usurers, liars and cultureless. He compared them with parasites that destroy an organism. "For the sham culture which the Jew possesses today is the property of other peoples, and is mostly spoiled in his hands." *Ibid.* p. 382.

of nation-state system. But it assumes an extremist form at the hands of the Fascists who exhort the people to be united, disciplined and strong to create a mighty state capable of restoring the grandeur of the past. The glorious past of the community is invoked to sharpen the forces of patriotism. Thus, Mussolini invoked the name of the great Roman empire of the ancient period and inspired his people to re-establish the grandeur of the Roman empire in the present century. Hitler did the same in the name of his pan-Germanism. Obviously, the blind and aggressive nationalism of the Fascists finds its confluence with the dictates of imperialism. It may be seen in the Italian rape of Ethiopia in 1935-36 and the German conquest of Austria and Czechoslovakia in 1938-39. 'Expand or perish' is the motto of the state and to achieve it the Fascist rulers play with the independence of poor and weak states of the world. Fascism, therefore, paves the way for the occurrence of wars on the international plane.

10. For the sake of achieving its goal of irredentism the philosophy of Fascism frankly appreciates the course of violence in both national and international spheres. In this direction, it owes to the ideas of Sorel who advocated the use of violence and to Hegel who in very clear terms justified the way of war among nations. The course of pacifism is frankly discarded and the Fascists declare peace 'as the dream of the cowards'. In Mussolini's words, the leader desires to get everything with his claws like a lion so as to make his mark on the pages of history. The nation must avoid the way of pacific settlement of international disputes and the dictates of any international organisation must be flouted. The state being a sovereign entity knows no master and it can settle its disputes with another state by means of force. War keeps the people alert; the life of peace-loving people may be compared to the stagnant water of a pool. In Hitler's words, a nation must always follow the 'policy of blood and iron'. Mussolini says: "War alone brings up to their highest tension all human energies and puts the stamp of nobility upon the peoples who have the courage to meet it. Fascism carries this anti-pacifist spirit over into the life of the individuals. It is education for combat. War is to man what maternity is to woman. I do not believe in perpetual peace; not only do I not believe in it, but I find it depressing and a negation of all the fundamental virtues of man. The whole nation must be militarised. I consider the Italian nation as a permanent state of war."[22]

It all demonstrates that the ideology of Fascism "is dominated by the dogmas of sovereign state and irresistible government. All particularistic interests of individuals

22. "The fascist style can be characterised – too simply, perhaps but not, I think, wrongly – as the introduction into politics of the ethos of combat. In 'this respect too, the impact of World War I and of the Bolshevik Revolution was very great, perhaps decisive. Fascists exalted military virtues and the experience of a nation at total war: unity setting aside class and regional conflicts; unquestioned acceptance of directorial leadership; and collective commitment to a single, all-important collective goal. The stance of the warrior, the language of combat, and the trappings of populist militarism were adapted to political life. Uniforms and parades abounded. So did paramilitary organisations. Every social, political and economic task was portrayed as a struggle, a battle, a fight. Words such as 'heroism', 'honour' 'loyalty', 'obedience' and 'leadership' were constantly bandied about." Heinz Lubasz: *Fascism: Three Major Regimes* (New York: Wiley & Sons, 1973), p. 3.

Totalitarianism

Implications*

Totalitarian ideologies provide the justificatory arguments in support of a type of society nominally characterised by:

1. an official or highly specific official ideology based upon a radical rejection of some aspects of the past and chiliastic claims for the future.
2. a unitary mass movement of solidarity, hierarchically organised as a single party under the authoritarian leadership of a charismatic (or pseudo-charismatic) leader and a directive and tutelary elite.
3. a technologically conditioned near monopoly of the means of communication and coercion, and.
4. a centralised direction under bureaucratised control of the entire economy.

Features of Totalitarian State**

1. It is a repudiation of reason and glorification of instincts and impulses. It is anti-intellectual. Instinct and will are given priority over reason.
2. It is dictatorial in character. It is opposed to liberalism and parliamentary government. It vests supreme power in the hands of one individual or one party. Parliamentary democracy is criticised as being stupid, corrupt, and slow-moving. Parliaments are looked down upon as mere talking shops, incapable of accomplishing results.
3. It combines the aristocratic principle of government by a privileged elite with a democratic width on the basis of election.
4. It crushes individual liberty. It does not tolerate political opposition.
5. It glorifies the nation and emphasises the idea of state as a power system. It adulates war and condemns peace.

* A James Gregor: *The Ideology of Fascism: The Rationale of Totalitarianism,* p. 7.

** E. Asirvatham: *Political Theory,* 1988 Ed., pp. 690-93.

must be suppressed by an omnipotent, hierarchical organization of the nation. A citizen's political obligations are more important than his rights. This is the Fascist 'totalitarianism', which recognises no sphere of individual life as immune from political authority. The true Fascist, declares Gentile, is Fascist in his home, school and workshop as well as in his politics. The supreme task of a state is to guarantee the interests of the nation, by sacrifice of any conflicting individual or class interests and, in defiance, if necessary, of the interests and opinions of the whole generations of citizens. The state recognises the will and welfare of the majority of its citizens only in so far as it can harmonise them with the higher interests of the nation. Infidelity to the state—in deed, word or attitude—is rebellion, which is the most baleful of all human evils."[23]

23. Coker, *op. cit.,* pp. 482-83.

Intellectual Roots of Fascism: Trends of Absolutism, Irrationalism and Violence in European Political Philosophy

The theory that absolute political power in the hands of the sovereign is a necessary condition for a well-ordered state is very old. Plato afforded a philosophical justification to the absolute and unlimited authority of a philosopher-king in the ideal state of the *Republic* and, for that reason, got the discredit of being the 'first Fascist thinker'. So is the case with Thomas Hobbes of England who in his *Leviathan* justified the existence of an all-powerful head to keep the commonwealth intact. Others like Machiavelli of Italy and Hegel of Germany employed their own arguments to justify the absolute authority of the state from which the Fascists of the twentieth century derived logical reasoning so as to justify the tenets of their totalitarian ideology. It may also be noted at this stage that some thinkers sought to identify the case of an absolute state with the personality of a particular leader and his elite and appreciated the course of violence and war for the sake of maintaining national unity and establishing a powerful empire. However, the noticeable point is that although the arguments of all these thinkers (as Fichte, Nietzsche, Schopenhauer, Wagner, Chamberlain and Sorel) are loaded with different implications, each looks like "presenting the case of national unity and the placement of absolute power in the hands of the sovereign."[24]

Since the affirmations of the great Italian and German fascists take inspiration from the social and political ideas of the thinkers of early modern period, it shall be worthwhile to have a passing reference to some of them. In the first place, we may refer to Niccolo Machiavelli (1469-1527) who in his *Prince* put some important guidelines by following which a ruler could establish a strong and powerful state. As a patriot he wished, above all, for the unity and glory of the Italian state. Discarding all theological and metaphysical assumptions prevailing in those times as a legacy of the middle ages, he asserted that the unity of his beloved country could be achieved and maintained only through the vigorous and ruthless rule of a strong leader. Apart from thoroughly secularising politics, he enunciated the doctrine of double morality signifying that "cruelty, bad faith, deception and other modes of conduct that are clearly vicious when practised by private citizens may be essential for the security of Prince's rule. If their use does result in the stability and prosperity of his reign and the greater well-being of his subjects, then the Prince is deeply justified in resorting to such practices."[25]

However, more important is the case of Hegel of Germany (1770-1831) whose formula of dialectical evolution of society was borrowed by the Marxists, but whose idealisation of the nation-state came handy to the Fascists. The way Hegel exalts the nation-state to mystical heights and goes to appreciate the course of war in the international sphere finds a very sharp resemblance with the utterances of the Fascists and the Nazis during the inter-war period. It may be seen in his *Philosophy*

24. Carl Cohen, *op. cit*,, p. 259.
25. *Ibid*., p. 260. J.W. Allen rightly says that the *Prince* "is an endeavour to show what a Prince must understand, what he must do and what he must be, and what he must not be in order to consolidate and extend his dominion. It has reference throughout to Italian conditions of the moment." *A History of Political Thought in the Sixteenth Century*, p. 466.

of History and *Philosophy of Right.* It may also be noted that Hegel's organicism and the justification of all social ethics on that basis provides a very convenient framework for the organismic nature and character of the Fascist state. Hegel's affirmations that 'nothing short of the state is the actualisation of freedom', or 'state is an ethical substance', or 'state is the march of God on earth' are accepted by the Fascists as canons of gospel truth. What Mussolini and Hitler affirm about the nature of state and sovereign authority, as we shall see in the next section, draws sustenance from the Hegelian theory of state paraphrasing which Joad puts: "Since the State is regarded as representing and containing within itself all the individual's social aspirations and, at the same time, fulfilling all his social needs, whatever the claims the State may make upon the individual are held to be based upon an absolute authority."[26]

What Machiavelli desired for the unification and power of his Italy, J.G Fichte (1762-1814) did the same for Germany. In his *Addresses to the German Nation* he gave an impassioned and effective plea for the unity of the German state based upon the internal and eternal reality of the German nation. He argued that the German people were destined for greatness and, led by a small elite, they could eventually dominate the globe for the reason of being the best race in the world. He hoped that the Germans would establish a new and more perfect order in which they would rule the lesser and inferior races, while the ruling elite stand above ordinary morality and tolerate no opposition to its leadership. His ideas helped to inspire the patriotic zeal and willingness to sacrifice in the interest of the nation that remain strong to the present. His exhortation was: "Love of fatherland must itself govern the State and be the supreme, final and absolute authority."[27]

So is the case with Heinrich von Trietschke (1834-1896)—a Prussian historian and philosopher and a vigorous advocate of German national unity. His work *Politics* (Vol. I) embodies the philosophic culmination of the Hegelian theory that the "state is a real personality; it is identified with power; it is the necessary outward form which the inner life of a people bestows upon itself."[28] Following Fichte's theme, he claimed that the Germans were a superior race. The leaders supplied the thoughts and the 'lesser people' were commanded to obey them meekly and faithfully. He glorified war and lauded it as a worthy institution in human relations. He argued that permanent peace would be a crime and peace-desiring societies would decay. He went to the length of saying: "That war should ever be banished from the world, is not only absurd, but profoundly immoral."[29]

Reference may be made to the political philosophy of Arthur Schöpenhauer (1788-1860) who subscribed to the line of irrationalism. Discarding the idealism or rationalism of Hegel, he suggested that life was irrational and incomprehensible, because it was the product of an uncontrollable impulse. Calling this mysterious energy as *will,* he argued that it was a blind, erratic, unpredictable force that manifested itself in the physical world but could not be analysed rationally. Beyond

26. C.E.M. Joad: *Introduction to Modern Political Theory* (Oxford: Clarendon Press, 1946), p. 10.
27. See Carl Cohen, *op. cit.,* p. 285.
28. *Ibid,* p. 289.
29. L.P. Baradat: *Political Ideologies: Their Origins and Impact* (Englewood Cliffs, New Jersey: Prentice-Hall, 1979), p. 267.

the reach of human reason, the will that produced all physical and intellectual reality made life meaningless. Finding no meaning or rational pattern of life, people were fools to try to resist the will. Any rational explanation of life is artificial, since the will is a senseless fury, a force with no justification. Since their source cannot be understood, the conditions of life cannot be improved by human effort. Life is only a meaningless struggle and resistance is pointless. Faced with such uncontrollable and incomprehensible power people have no alternative but to submit and let the will have its way."[30]

But the most important philosopher of the Third Reich was Friedrich Nietzsche (1844-1900) whose theories were adopted by the Nazis with a lot of disortions in their favour. What came handy to the Germans was his idea of supermen ('over-men') who would some day rule this earth. It smacked of a community of people whose members were stronger and more righteous than the human beings of his generation. Differing from Schopenhauer, he in his work *Beyond Good and Evil* insisted that life was a struggle. Conflict purified humanity as it strengthened the survivor and finished the undeserving or parasitic members of the society. Man has a *will to power,* a force that stimulates people to fight and win and dominate. Thus, any attempt to protect the weak against the strong is both unnatural and immoral. So he rejected Christian values of peace and non-violence and proposed the 'trans-valuation' of societal norms. "In the places of the Christian values of peace, humility, charity, and pity, Nietzsche demanded eternal struggle, arrogance, selfishness, and ruthlessness. Instead of the democratic virtues of equality, fairness and happiness, he demanded an oligarchy of strength, deceit, and pain."[31]

The line of the superiority of the German race and on that basis the title of the Nordic people to dominate the whole world finds its reiteration at the hands of Richard W. Wagner (1813-83). Basically a dramatist and a musician, he disseminated his social and cultural ideas based on the myth of the greatness of the Teutonic race. His main argument was that the universality in the spirit of German literature and music cried out to be reborn in the sphere of politics through the victory of the German power.[32] H.S. Chamberlain (1855-1927) was an Anglo-German writer on music and literature in the Wagnerian tradition. His chief work *Foundations of the Nineteenth Century* (Vol. I) was ostensibly the historical scholarly justification of the myth of the superiority of the German people. The final exhortation of this work was that "the Aryans are by right the lords of the world."[33]

Last, we may refer to the French socialist-syndicalist leader Georges Sorel (1847-1922) whose work *Reflections on Violence* is an attempt to justify violent and extremist means for the achievement of the goal. For some time, he was a great admirer of Lenin, but his attachment to syndicalist philosophy prevented him from being a Marxist. His name is associated with the school of irrationalism, because he preferred the course of doing things for the cause without first getting getting involved into the web of theoretical considerations. He showed his deep scorn for intellectualism

30. *Ibid,,* pp. 267-68.
31. *Ibid,* p 268.
32. Carl Cohen, *op. cit.,* p. 302.
33. *Ibid,* p. 305.

and always revealed his passion for revolutionary activity in place of academic or theoretical discussions. He developed the theory of 'myth' (that accepted ideas can neither be proved nor disproved) and advocated that "it can be used with great political effect. It can unite and motivate the masses, turning millions of individuals into a single entity by giving them a belief to cling and a goal to work toward."[34]

Fascism in Italy: Doctrinal Expositions of Rocco, Gentile and Mussolini

Fascism as an ideology of the twentieth century was originally and significantly an Italian movement led by Mussolini. The very word, fasciare' means to bind or to envelop and, for this reason, the movement was intended by its founder and his ardent followers as a doctrine that would bind, once and for all, the entire Italian nation into an organic entity so as to restore the great traditions of the ancient Roman empire. The notable thing about Fascism is that it emerged as a movement and its social, economic and political philosophy appeared after about a couple of years at the hands of great theoreticians of this movement who occupied important positions in the government of Prime Minister Mussolini. Its core was laid down by Alfredo Rocco (Mussolini's Minister for Justice) who in 1925 produced his thesis on the 'Political Doctrines of Fascism' in which he proved himself as a vigorous admirer of Machiavelli and a supporter of the idea of the supreme power of the organic nation-state in the tradition of Hegel. The great leader (Duce) of Italy was so much impressed with Rocco's thesis that he endorsed everything said by his intimate adviser and friend and regarded the work as a 'presentation of the theme in a masterful way'.[35]

The main points of the thesis of Rocco have an importance of their own for being the first authentic exposition of the doctrine of Fascism and may be enumerated as under:[36]

1. Let us ask ourselves if there is a political doctrine of Fascism, if there is any ideal content in the Fascist State. For in order to link Fascism, both as concept and system, with the history of Italian thought and find therein a place for it, we must first show that it is thought; that it is a doctrine. It is true that Fascism is, above all, action and sentiment and that as such it must continue to be. Were it otherwise, it could not keep up that immense driving force, that renovating power which it now possesses and would merely be the solitary meditation of a chosen few. But Fascism is a thought as well as a theory, which is an essential part of this historical phenomenon, and which is responsible in a great measure for the success that has been achieved. The originality of Fascism is due in great part to the autonomy of its theoretical principles. For even when in its external behaviour and in its conclusions, it seems identical with other political creeds, in reality it possesses an inner originality due to the new spirit which animates it and to an entirely different theoretical approach.

---

34. Baradat, *op. cit.*, p. 250.
35. Carl Cohen: *Communism,Fascism and Democracy: The Theoretical Foundations* (New York: Random House, 1972), II Ed:, p. 315.
36. *Ibid.*, pp. 315-28.

The First Programme of the Fascist Movement (23 March, 1919)

1. A national Constituent Assembly, Italian section of the international Constituent Assembly of nations, which will proceed to a radical transformation of the political and economic foundations of collective life.
2. Proclamation of the Italian republic. Decentralisation of executive power; autonomous administration of regions and municipalities by their own legislative bodies. Sovereignty of the people exercised by means of universal, equal and direct suffrage, by all citizens of both sexes, the people keeping the right of initiative for referendum and veto.
3. Abolition of the senate. Suppression of political police. Election of magistrates independently of the executive power.
4. Suppression of all titles of nobility and orders of knighthood.
5. Suppression of compulsory military service.
6. Freedom of opinion, of conscience and of belief, freedom of association and of the press.
7. An educational system, general and professional, open to all.
8. A maximum of public health measures.
9. Suppression of limited liability companies and share-holding companies, suppression of all forms of speculation; separation of Banks and Stock Exchanges.
10. Census and taxation of private wealth. Confiscation of unproductive revenues.
11. Prohibition of child labour under the age of 16. Eight-hour day.
12. Reorganisation of production according to the cooperative principle, including the workers' direct share of profit.
13. Abolition of secret diplomacy.
14. Foreign policy inspired by international solidarity and national independence within a Confederation of States.

Charter of Labour (1927)

1. The Italian nation is an organic whole having life, purpose and means of action superior in power and duration to those of the individuals, single or associated, of which it is composed. It is a moral, political and economic unity, which is realised integrally in the Fascist States.
2. Work in all its forms—intellectual, technical or manual—whether organisation or execution—is a social duty. And for this reason only it is regulated by the State. The process of production, from the national point of view, is a single whole, its aims are united and identified with the well-being of the producers and the promotion of national power.
3. Occupational or syndical organisation is free; but only the juridically organised syndicate which submits to the control of the State has the right to represent legally the entire category of employers or workers for which it is constituted, in safeguarding its interests *vis-a-vis* the State and other occupational association, in making collective contracts of work binding on all the members of the category, in levying contributions and exercising over its members functions delegated to it in the public interest.
4. In the collective contract work the solidarity of the various factors of production finds its concrete expression in the reconciliation of the conflicting interests of employers and employees and in their subordination to the superior interests of production.

The Fascist Decalogue (1934)

1. Know that the Fascist, and in particular the soldier, must not believe in perpetual peace.
2. Days of imprisonment are always deserved.
3. The nation serves even as a sentinel over a can of petrol.
4. A companion must be a brother, first, because he lives with you, and, secondly, because he thinks like you.
5. The rifle and the cartridge belt, and the rest are confided to you not to rust in leisure, but to be preserved in war.
6. Do not ever say "The Government will pay....," because it is *you* who pay; and the Government is that which you willed to have, and for which you put on a uniform.
7. Discipline is the soul of armies; without it there are no soldiers, only confusion and defeat.
8. Mussolini is always right.
9. For a volunteer there are no extenuating circumstances when he is disobedient.
10. One thing must be dear to you above all: the life of the Duce.

Fascist Decalogue (1938)

1. Remember that those who fell for the revolution and for the empire march at the head of your columns.
2. Your comrade is your brother. He lives with you, thinks with you, and is at your side in the battle.
3. Service to Italy can be rendered at all times, in all places, and by every means. It can be paid with toil and also with blood.
4. The enemy of Fascism is your enemy. Give him no quarter.
5. Discipline is the sunshine of armies. It prepares and illuminates the victory.
6. He who advances to the attack with decision has victory already in his grasp.
7. Conspicuous and complete obedience is the virtue of the Legionary.
8. There do not exist things important and things unimportant. There is only one duty.
9. The Fascist revolution has depended in the past and still depends on the bayonets of its Legionaries.
10. Mussolini is always right.

2. All political doctrines of the modern age arising out of the events of the Protestant Reformation and having their roots in the doctrine of natural law have a mechanical or atomistic character. The great political thinkers of Europe and America from Languet, Buchanan and Althusen to Marx, Lenin and Wilson regard society as a sum total of individuals or a plurality which breaks up into its single components. Thus, in their view, the ends of society are nothing more than the ends of the individuals who compose it and for whose sake it exists. Such a view is also necessarily anti-historical inasmuch as it considers society in its spatial attributes and not in its temporal ones; and because it reduces social life to the existence of a single generation. In its endeavour to isolate the present from the past and the future, it rejects the spiritual inheritance of ideas and sentiments which each generation receives from those preceding and hands down to the following generations thus destroying the unity and the spiritual life itself of the human society.

3. Liberalism confines itself to the demands of certain guarantees which are to keep the state off from overstepping its functions as general coordinator of liberties and from sacrificing the freedom of the individuals more than is absolutely necessary for the accomplishment of its purpose. But, according to Fascism, the state cannot limit itself to merely a negative function of the defence of liberty. It must become active, on behalf of everybody, for the welfare of the people. It must intervene, when necessary, in order to improve the material, intellectual and moral conditions of the masses ; it must find work for the unemployed, instruct and educate the people, and care for health and hygiene.
4. The argument of Socialism is that if the state is created for the welfare of its citizens, how can it tolerate an economic system that divides the population into a small minority of the capitalists or the exploiters on one side and the poor and working people on the other. Moreover, it, in its turn, generates the still more extreme doctrine of Bolshevism (Communism) that demands violent suppression of the holders of capital, dictatorship of proletariat as the means for a fairer economic organisation of society and the rescue of the labouring classes from capitalist exploitation.
5. If man is a social and a political animal, then we must come to hold that humanity exists solely as a biological concept. Therefore, Fascism replaces the old atomistic and mechanical state theory that was at the basis of liberal and democratic doctrines with an organic and historic concept. The important thing is to ascertain that this organic concept of the state gives to society a continuous life over and beyond the existence of several individuals. Instead of the liberal-democratic formula of 'society for the individuals', we have the formula of 'individuals for society'.
6. Liberalism, Democracy and Socialism look upon social groups as aggregates of living individuals; for Fascism they are the recapitulating unity of the infinite series of generations. For Fascism, society is the end, individuals are the means, and its whole life consists in using the individuals as instruments for its social ends. The state, therefore, guards and protects the welfare and development of individuals not for their exclusive interest, but because of the identification of the needs of individuals with those of society as a whole.
7. We do not, however, accept a bill of rights which tends to make the individual superior to the state and to empower him to act in opposition to society. Freedom is, therefore, due to the citizen and to the classes on condition that they exercise it in the interest of society as a whole and within the limits set by social exigencies, liberty being, like any other individual rights, a concession of the State.
8. Fascism not only rejects the dogma of popular sovereignty and substitutes for it that of State sovereignty, it also proclaims that the great mass of citizens is not a suitable advocate of social interests for the reason that the capacity to ignore individual private interests in favour of the higher demands of society and history is a very rare gift and the privilege of the chosen few. Natural intelligence and cultural preparation are of great service in such tasks. Still more valuable perhaps is the intuitiveness of great minds, their traditionalism and their inherited qualities.

Elements of Fascism

1. **Distrust of Reason:** It rejects the Greek (rational) root of western civilisation and is frankly anti-rationalist, distrusting in human affairs and stressing the irrational, sentimental, uncontrollable elements of man. Psychologically fascism is *fanatical* rather than *reflective, dogmatic rather than open-minded;* as a result each fascist regime has its 'taboo' issues that must be accepted on faith and cannot be critically discussed.
2. **Denial of Human Equality:** True enough that democratic doctrines always live up to the ideal of human equality, but they are subject to attacks of conscience if they fail and if they at least accept equality on the long-term goal of policy. By contrast, fascist societies not only accept the fact of human inequality, but go further and affirm inequality as an ideal. Thus, in the fascist code men are superior to women, soldiers to civilians, party members to non-party members, one's own nation to others, the strong to the weak and (perhaps most important in the first outlook), the victors in the war to the vanquished. The chief criteria of inequality in the western tradition are men's mind and soul, whereas the fascist affirmation of inequality is based ultimately on *strength*.
3. **Code of Behaviour Based on Lies and Violence:** The fascist code of behaviour stresses *violence and lies* in all human relations within and between nations. From the democratic viewpoint, politics is the mechanism through which social conflicts of interest are perpetually adjusted. By contrast, the fascist view is that politics is characterised by the friend-enemy relations. Politics begins and ends in this fascist way of thinking with the personality of an enemy and his *total annihilation*. The fascist knows only enemies, not opponents and since enemies represent evil incarnate, total annihilation is the only solution. This happy doctrine applies to domestic as well as to foreign enemies; thus Nazis first set up concentration camps and gas chambers for German citizens and later used the same facilities on non-Germans. It is in the concentration and slave labour camps that totalitarian regimes can completely destroy the legal and moral person in man, can deprive him of the last residue of individuality by reducing him to the automatic reflexes of Pavlov's days. The technique of brainwashing seeks to break men's mind to the point where he will publicly confess to crimes he did not commit and perhaps could not have been committed. After a period of brainwashing, the victim no longer has a mind of his own; he merely plays back like a record of what is expected of him. By institutionalising organised mass murder in concentrated and slave labour camps, totalitarian regimes demonstrate to the entire population what is in store for anyone in disfavour with the men in power, and at the same time they provide the shock troops of the regime with a peace-time outlet for savagery and fanaticism. Immediate death is often considered too humane a penalty by such regimes; moreover, the slow death of concentration or slave labour camps has a great demonstrative value than the clean, old-fashioned method of the executive squad on the gallows.
4. **Government by Elites:** It stands for a government by a self-appreciated elite. Its leadership principle expresses the extreme form of the elite concept. It fully reflects the traditional nature of fascist politics; the leader is considered infallible, endowed with mystical gifts and insights. In a conflict between popular opinion and the fascist leader, the will of the latter prevails; the leader represents the public interest the way all people express only individual whims and desires not necessarily in harmony with the public good.

5. **Totalitarianism:** It employs authority and violence in all kinds of social relations. It will use any form of coercion from verbal threats to mass murder in obtaining its ends. It seeks to control all phases of human life from the cradle to the grave. It begins control even before the cradle by pushing definite population policies, and has been known to reach into the grave, so to speak, to decide whether a dead person should have a burial at all, and if so in what form.
6. **Racialism and Imperialism:** Within the nation fascist doctrine holds that elite is superior to the rest and may impose its will upon them by force. Similarly, between nations the *elite nation* is superior to others and entitled to rule them. German fascism went furthest in its racialist and imperialist policies. A straight line led from the theories of the superiority of the German-Nordic race to the mass murder of the millions of the non-German people.
7. **Opposition to International Law and Order:** Whereas non-fascists accept war as a tragic fact which should be abolished, fascists raise war to the level of an *ideal,* because, as Mussolini said, war alone brings up to their highest tension all human energies and puts the stamp of nobility upon the people who have the courage to meet it. Any type of international organisation assumes some form of *government by consent,* which is directly contradictory to the fascist principle of *government by force*.... Diplomatically, fascist states shy away from general multilateral agreements, they prefer *bilateral agreements* particularly with states they plan to over-run.

Source: William Ebenstein: *Today's Isms,* pp. 65-72.

From this we may draw the conclusion that the doctrine of Fascism rejects liberalism and socialism (including communism) and instead desires an all-powerful state in which power is concentrated in the hands of a very small privileged section of the people under a charismatic leader.

The second important event in this direction took place in 1928 when Giovanni Gentile (Mussolini's Education Minister) presented his thesis on the 'Philosophic Basis of Fascism'. In the style of a neo-Hegelian, he emphasises these basic principles of Fascism:[37]

1. Fascism is not a philosophy, much less a religion. It is not even a political theory which may be stated in a series of formulae. It appreciates Mazzinian anti-intellectualism contained in the dictum of divorce of thought from action, of knowledge from life, of brain from heart, of theory from practice. Fascism is hostile to all Utopian systems which are destined never to face the test of reality. It is hostile to all science and all philosophy which remain matters of mere fancy or intelligence. It rejects the case of a man who plays with knowledge and with thought without any sense of responsibility for the practical world. Therefore, Fascism prefers not to waste time on constructing abstract theories about itself.
2. The Fascist system is not a political system, but it has the centre of gravity in politics. Fascism came into being to meet serious problems of politics in post-war Italy. And it presents itself as a political method. The politics of Fascism revolves wholly around the concept of nation-state; and accordingly it has points of contact with nationalist doctrines, along with distinctions from the latter which

37. *Ibid.,* pp. 340-44.

is important to bear in mind. Both Fascism and nationalism regard the State as the foundation of all rights and the source of all values in the individuals composing it. In the case of Fascism, state and individual are one and the same thing, or rather they are inseparable terms of a necessary synthesis. For the nationalist, the nation exists not by virtue of citizen's will, but as datum., fact of nature.

3. On the popular character of the Fascist State depends its greatest social and constitutional reform—the foundation of the Corporations of Syndicates. In this reform Fascism took over from syndicalism the notion of the moral and educational function of the syndicate. But the Corporations of Syndicates were necessary in order to reduce the syndicates to state discipline and make them an expression of the state's organism from within.
4. The Fascist conception of liberty reconciles the elements of force and consent. The two are inseparable. The authority of the state and the freedom of the citizens constitute a continuous circle wherein authority presupposes liberty and liberty authority. Liberalism breaks this circle by setting the individual against the state and liberty against authority. Fascism has its own solution of this paradox. The authority of the State is absolute. It does not compromise, it does not bargain, it does not surrender any portion of its field to other moral or religious principles which may interfere with the individual conscience. But, on the other hand, the State becomes a reality only on the consciousness of its individuals.
5. The Fascist Corporative State supplies a speculative system more sincere and more in touch with realities than any other previously devised and is, therefore, freer than the old liberal state.

These points throw light on the anti-intellectual and totalitarian character of the Fascist philosophy.

However, the most authoritative version of the social, economic and political philosophy of Fascism can be seen in the statement of its arch-priest (Mussolini) that he contributed in 1932 to the *Encyclopaedia Italiana* and was soon known as the most famous statement of this doctrine. According to him, the 'fundamental ideas' of Fascism are:[38]

1. Like every sound political conception, Fascism is both practice and thought; action in which a doctrine is immanent, and a doctrine which arising out of a given system of historical forces, remains embedded in them and works there from within. In order to know men, it is necessary to know man, and in order to know man, it is necessary to know reality and its laws. There is no concept of the State which is not fundamentally a concept of life; philosophy or intuition, a system of ideas which develops logically, or is gathered up into a vision or into a faith, but which is always, at least virtually, an organic conception of the world.
2. The world seen through Fascism is not this material world which appears on the surface, in which man is an individual separated from all others and standing by himself, and in which he is governed by a natural law that makes

38. *Ibid.*, pp. 328-39.

him instinctively live a life of selfish and momentary pleasures. The man of Fascism is an individual who is nation and fatherland, which is a moral law, binding together individuals and the generations into a tradition and a mission, suppressing the instinct for a life enclosed within the brief round of pleasure in order to restore within duty a higher life free from the limits of time and space : a life in which the individual, through the denial of himself, through the sacrifice of his own private interests, through death itself, realises completely that spiritual existence in which his value as a man lies.

3. Fascism desires an active man, one engaged in activity with all his energies; it desires a man very much conscious of the difficulties that exist in action and ready to face them. It conceives of life as a struggle, considering that it behooves man to conquer for himself that life truly worthy of him, creating first of all in himself the instrument (physical, moral, intellectual) in order to construct it.
4. The positive conception of life is clearly an ethical conception. It covers the whole of reality, not merely the human activity which controls it. Life, therefore, as conceived by the Fascist, is serious, austere, religious: the whole of it is poised in a world supported by the moral and responsible forces of the spirit. The Fascist disdains the 'comfortable' life.
5. Fascism is a religious conception in which man is seen in his immanent relationship with a superior law and with an objective will that transcends the particular individual and raises him to conscious membership in a particular society.
6. Fascism is a historical conception, in which man is what he only is in so far as he works with the spiritual process in which he finds himself in the family or social group, in the nation and in the history in which all nations collaborate. This implies putting oneself outside history and life, which is a continual change and coming to be. Politically, Fascism wishes to be a realistic doctrine; practically, it aspires to solve only the problems which arise historically of themselves and that of themselves find or suggest their own solution.
7. Against individualism, the Fascist conception is for the state ; and it is for the individual in so far as he coincides with the State, which is the conscience and universal will of man in his historical existence. Liberalism denies the State in the interests of particular individuals. Fascism reaffirms the State as true reality of the individual. And if liberty is to be the attribute of the real man, and not of that abstract puppet envisaged by individualistic liberalism, Fascism is for liberty. And for the only liberty which can be a real thing—the liberty of the State and of the individual within the State. Therefore, for the Fascist, everything is in the State, and nothing human or spiritual exists, much less has value, outside the State. In this sense, Fascism is totalitarian and the Fascist State, the synthesis and unity of all values, interprets, develops and gives strength to the whole life of the people.
8. Outside the State there can be neither individuals nor groups (political parties, associations, syndicates, classes). Therefore, Fascism is opposed to Socialism which confines the movement of history within the class struggle, and ignores the unity of classes established in one economic and moral reality in the State; and analogously it is opposed to class syndicalism.

9. Individuals form classes according to similarity of their interests; they form syndicates according to differentiated economic activities within these interests; but they form, first and above all, the State which is not to be thought of numerically as the sum-total of the individuals forming the majority of a nation. And consequently, Fascism is opposed to democracy which equates the notion to the majority, lowering it to the level of that majority.
10. It is not the nation that generates the State, rather the nation is created by the State that gives to the people, conscious of their own moral unity, a will and therefore an effective existence. The State, in fact, as the universal ethical will, is the creator of right.
11. The nation as the State is an ethical reality which exists and lives in so far as it develops. To arrest its development is to kill it. The State is organisation and expansion. It can be likened to the human will that knows no limits to its development and realises itself in testing its own limitations.
12. The Fascist State, the highest and most powerful form of personality, is a force, but a spiritual force. It is the form, the inner standard, and the discipline of the whole person; it saturates the will as well as intelligence.
13. Fascism is not only the giver of laws and the founder of institutions, but the educator and promoter of spiritual life. It wants to remake not the forms of human life, but its content, man, character, faith. And to this end it requires discipline and authority that can enter into the spirits of men and there govern unopposed. Its sign, therefore, is the Lictor's rods, the symbol of unity, of strength and justice.

Besides, Mussolini offers a catalogue of the following political and social doctrines of Fascism:

1. The present method of political representation cannot be sufficient for the Italians, we wish for a direct representation of individual interests.
2. Fascism is not a regime but a doctrine that is self-critical as well as critical of other movements; it has an unequivocal point of view of its own, a criterion, and hence an aim, in the face of all the material and intellectual problems which oppress the people of the world.
3. Fascism believes neither in the possibility nor in the utility of perpetual peace. It considers renunciation of the struggle as an act of cowardice. War alone brings up to their highest tension all human energies and puts the stamp of nobility upon the peoples who have the courage to meet it. Fascism carries over this anti-pacifist spirit even into the lives of the individuals. Thus, the Fascist accepts and loves life, he knows nothing of suicide and despises it; he looks on life as duty, ascent, conquest; life which must be noble and full; lived for onself, but above all for the others near and far away, present and future.
4. Fascism rejects universal accord and since it lives in the community of the civilised peoples, it keeps them vigilantly and suspiciously before its eyes, it follows their states of minds and the changes in their interests and does not let itself be deceived by temporary and fallacious appearances.

5. Fascism believes, now and always, in holiness and in heroism, that is, in acts in which no economic motive—remote or immediate—plays a part. Fascism denies the possibility of materialistic conception of history as given by Marx.
6. After Socialism, Fascism attacks the whole complex of democratic ideologies and rejects them both in their theoretical premises and in their applications or practical manifestations.
7. Fascism rejects in democracy the absurd conventional lie of political equalitarianism clothed in the dress of collective irresponsibility and the myth of happiness and infinite progress. But if democracy can be understood in other ways, that is, if democracy means not to relegate the people to the periphery of the State, then Fascism could be defined as an 'organised, centralised, authoritarian democracy'.
8. In the face of the Liberal doctrines, Fascism takes up an attitude of absolute opposition both in the field of politics and in that of economics. It desires Activism—Nationalism, Futurism, Fascism.
9. Political doctrines pass, peoples remain. It is to be expected that this century may be that of authority, a century of the 'Right', a Fascist century. No doctrine is born quite new, shining, never before seen. No doctrine can boast of an absolute originality.
10. For Fascism the State is an absolute before which individuals and groups are relative. The Fascist State has a consciousness of its own, a will of its own, on this account it is called an Ethical State.
11. It is the State alone that grows in size, in power. It is the State alone that can solve the dramatic contradictions of capitalism. What is called the crisis cannot be overcome except by the State, within the State.
12. The State has no theology, but it has an ethic. In the Fascist State, religion is looked upon as one of the deepest manifestations of the spirit; it is, therefore, not only respected, but defended and protected.
13. The Fascist State is a will to power and government. Fascism is the doctrine that is most fitted to represent the aims, the states of mind, of a people, like the Italian people rising again after many centuries of abandonment or slavery to foreigners. But the Empire calls for discipline, coordination of forces, duty and sacrifice.

Fascist Philosophy in Germany: Doctrinal Expositions of Goring, Rosenberg and Hitler

The culmination of the Fascist philosophy occurred in Germany with the rise of the National Socialist (Nazi) Party under the leadership of Hitler. Here we may refer to the ideas of three great Nazi theoreticians like Goring, Rosenberg and, above all, Hitler. The noticeable thing in this direction is that philosophically, the Nazis added little to the principles of this ideology which was already laid down in Italy before the rise of Hitler to power in 1933. But what is really striking in this direction is that the German Fascists "did succeed in carrying out these principles more effectively and developing more fully a deliberately irrational totalitarianism.... particular characteristic of the German development of fascist philosophy was its intensely irrational character, largely responsible for its intolerant racism, its inhuman persecution of minorities, and armed aggression leading to the most catastrophic war in history."[39]

Among the leading Nazi theoreticians of the interwar period, we may, first of all, refer to Hermann Goring (1893-1946) who was one of the very close associates of Hitler and who had acted as the Prime Minister of Prussia and commander of the German air forces during the Second World War. His book *Germany Reborn* (1934) is representative of the fascist hero-worship and also of the Nazi claim that they were the last bulwark of Europe against Russian Communism. As he says: "May the other peoples realise that the Leader in Germany is the first guarantor of European peace. For the task which Hitler has taken over, and the fight which he is waging at home, does not only concern Germany. Hitler's mission is of importance for the history of the world, because he took up the war to the death against Communism and therewith raised a bulwark for the other European nations. Many times before in world history have mighty spiritual struggles been decided on German territory. It is our solemn belief that, if in the mighty struggle between National Socialism and Communism, the latter had won, then the deadly bacillus would have spread from Communist Germany to the other European countries. The day will come when the other countries will begin to realise this and on that day France, England and other peoples will be thankful that at the critical moment there was Adolf Hitler in Germany"[40]

Alfred Rosenberg (1893-1946) was the leading apologist of German racialism and he elaborated at length the myth of German blood and Aryan superiority in his *The Myth of the Twentieth Century* (1930). In this book he underlined these important points:[41]

1. Racial history is natural history and soul mystique. The history of the religion of blood is, conversely, the great world-narrative of the rise and decline of peoples, their heroes and thinkers, their inventors and artists.
2. The meaning of world history has radiated out from the north over the whole world, borne by a blue-eyed blond race which in several great waves determined the spiritual face of the world.
3. The new real struggle today is concerned not so much with external changes in power, along with an internal compromise as hitherto, but conversely with the new rebuilding of the soul-cells of the Nordic peoples, for the sake of the reinstitution in their sovereign rights of those ideals and values from which originates everything which signifies culture to us, and for the sake of the preservation of the racial substance itself.
4. The idea of honour, national honour, is for us the beginning and the end of our entire thinking and doing.
5. The state is now-a-days no longer an independent idol before which every thing must bow down; the state is not even an end but is only a means for the preservation of the folk.
6. The foundation for the arising of a *new aristocracy* lies in those who have stood—in a spiritual, military and political sense—in the foremost positions in the struggle for the coming Reich.

39. See Carl Cohen, *op. cit.*, p. 365.
40. *Ibid.*, p. 366.
41. *Ibid.*

7. Nordic Europe is the fated future, with German central Europe, Germany as racial and national state, as central power of the Continent safeguarding the South and the Southeast; the Scandinavian state with Finland as the second group, safeguarding the northeast; and Great Britain safeguarding the west and overseas at those places where required in the interests of the Nordic man.

But the **the** most important name is that of Adolph Hitler (1889-1945) whose *Mein Kampf* (1925) became the gospel of German Fascism. The main points of Hitler's 'Political Testament' as outlined in his great work may be thus enumerated: [42]

1. What we have seen of human culture today, the results of art, science and techniques, is almost exclusively the creative product of the Aryans. Therefore, it is no accident that the first cultures originated in those places where the Aryans, by meeting lower peoples, subdued them and made them subject to their will. They, then, were the first technical instrument in the service of a growing culture.
2. The state represents the *volk* (folk). Its highest purpose is the care for the preservation of those racial primal elements which supplying culture, create the beauty and dignity of a higher humanity. We, as Aryans, are, therefore, able to imagine a State only to be the living organism of a nationality which not only safeguards the preservation of that nationality, but which by a further training of its spiritual and ideal abilities, leads it to the highest freedom.
3. The folkish state divides its inhabitants into three classes—citizens, subjects, and aliens. Only the citizen class is privileged and only a citizen is the master of the Reich.
4. A view of life which by rejecting the democratic mass idea, endeavours to give this world to the best people, that means to the most superior men, has logically to obey the same aristocratic principle also within this people and has to guarantee leadership and highest influence within the respective people to the best heads. With this it does not build up on the idea of the majority, but on that of the personality.
5. To employ the citizen profitably for the community is the first and the highest task of the organisation of the national community. Organisation in itself has to be the incorporation of the endeavour of putting the heads above the masses and of subjecting the masses to the heads.
6. The army is the mightiest school of the German nation. What the German people owe to it is 'everything'.
7. The Jews offer the strongest contrast to the Aryan race. In them the will to sacrifice onself does not go beyond the bare instinct of self-preservation.
8. The stronger has the right before God and the world to enforce his will. If one does not have the power to enforce his right, that right alone will profit him absolutely nothing. The stronger have always been victorious. The whole of nature is a continuous struggle between strength and weakness, an eternal victory of the strong over the weak. All the states which do not wish to recognise this law will decay.

42. *Ibid.*, pp. 374-91.

9. The force and the power are determining factors. Force is the first law. Only through struggle have states and the world become great. World history proves that in the struggle between nations, that race has always been won where drive for self-preservation was the more pronounced.
10. There is nothing like humanitarianism but only an eternal struggle which is pre-requisite for the development of all humanity. If men wish to kill, then they are forced to kill others.
11. We know only two Gods; A God in the Heaven and a God on earth; the latter is our fatherland.
12. We do not talk, we act. We will harden ourselves to such an extent that any storm will find us strong. We will never forget that the sum-total of all virtues and all strength can be effective only when it is subservient to one will and to one command. We must train our people so that whenever someone has been appointed to command, the others will recognise as their duty to obey him.

From a comparative standpoint, we may say that in the points of German Fascists, the elements of racialism and irrationalism are on the higher side, but the common points in Italian and German Fascisms are related to the establishment of an all-powerful state under the iron hold of a leader and his organisation. A Nazi spokesman (W. Stapel) was, therefore, right in holding: "According to the National Socialist principle, what guarantees the maximum formation of state power is Right. The feeling of Right is brought in relation to the State, not to the individual. Therefore, nothing is 'safe' from interference.... Right is not a matter of agreement; it is determined by the Fuhrer. It is based not on contract but on command.... We have no longer any competition between ideas; only ideas that are made good, and the ideas that are expunged."[43]

Fascism in Action: Italian and German Experiments

The movement of Fascism in Italy took an organised form at Milan on 23 March, 1919 in a small meeting summoned by Mussolini. This meeting formed a 'fighting band' *(Fascio di Combat-timento)* of the Fascists as bearers of a Napoleonic will to power and dedicated to a nationalist-syndicalist program which contained, in addition, heterogenous elements. They adopted a programme of vigorous action designed to secure for the country the fruits of her victory in the First World War and to effect some important changes in the domestic policy of the nation. This programme had many liberal as well as socialist items. But under the stress of the prevailing conditions, Mussolini preferred to play the role of an opportunist. In November, 1921 the Fascists organised themselves as a political party and soon a fusion of the Fascists and the Nationalists was achieved in the Chamber of Deputies. Now the Fascists were bold enough to declare that they intended to replace the state, if it showed itself unable to suppress disorder and prevent national disintegration. Through his paper *Popolo d'Italia* as well as in public utterances, Mussolini made it clear in August, 1922 that the Fascists would march to Rome if the Parliament was not dissolved and the cabinet of Premier Facta did not resign; moreover, they would take possession of the city halls, post offices, and railway stations.

43. See Auriel Kolnai: *The War Against the West* (London: Gollancz, 1938), p. 299.

Important Points of First Programme of Nazi Party (24 February, 1920)

1. We demand on the basis of the right of national self-determination, the union of all Germans to form one Great Germany. We demand juridical equality for the German people in its dealings with other nations, and the abolition of the Peace Treaties of Versailles and St. Germain. We demand territories and soil (colonies) for the establishment of our people and for settling our surplus population.
2. None but the members of the nation may be citizens of the State. None but those of German blood, whatever their creed, may be members of the nation. No Jew, therefore, may be considered a member of the nation. Anyone who is not a citizen of the State may live in Germany only as a guest and must be regarded as subject to the laws governing aliens.
3. The right to determine leadership and laws of the State is to be enjoyed by the citizens of the State alone. We oppose the corrupt Parliamentary custom of filling public offices merely with a view to party considerations and without reference to character or capacity.
4. We demand that the State shall make it one of its chief duties to provide work and the means of livelihood for the citizens of the State. All further non-German immigrants must be prevented. We demand that all non-Germans who have entered Germany subsequently to 2 August, 1914 must be required forthwith to depart from the Reich.
5. It must be the duty of every citizen of the State to work with his mind or with his body. The activities of the individual must not clash with the interests of the whole, but must be pursued within the framework of the national activity and must be for the general good.
6. Because of the enormous sacrifice of life and property demanded of a nation by every war, personal profit through war must be regarded as a crime against the nation. We demand, therefore, the complete confiscation of all war profits. We demand the nationalisation of all business combines (trusts). We demand the great industries shall be organised on a profi-sharing basis.
7. We demand the creation and maintenance of a healthy middle class; the immediate communalisation of the big department stores and the lease of various departments at a low rate to small traders, and that the greatest consideration shall be shown to all small traders supplying goods to the State, the federal states or the municipalities.
8. We demand a programme of land reform suitable to our national requirements, the enactment of law for confiscation without compensation of land for communal purposes, the abolition of ground rents, and the prohibition of all speculation in land. We demand a ruthless campaign against all whose activities are injurious to the common interest. Oppressors of the nation, usurers, profiteers, etc., must be punished with death, whatever their creed or race.
9. The State must undertake a thorough reconstruction of our national system of education, with the aim of giving to every capable and industrious German the benefits of a higher education and therewith the capacity to take his place in the leadership of the nation. The curricula of all educational establishments must be brought into line with the necessities of practical life.
10. The state must concern itself with raising the standards of health in the nation by exercising its guardianship over mothers and infants, by prohibiting child labour, and by increasing bodily efficiency by legally obligatory gymnastics and sports, and by the extensive support of clubs engaged in the physical training of the young.

11. We demand the abolition of a paid army and the foundation of national army.
12. We demand legal measures against intentional political lies and their dissemination in the Press. We demand: (i) that all editors and newspapers and all contributors employing the German language shall be members of the nation, (ii) that special permission from the State shall be necessary before non-German newspapers may appear. These must not be printed in the German language, and (iii) that non-German people shall be prohibited by law from participating financially in, or from influencing German newspapers.
13. We demand liberty for all religious denominations in the State, in so far as they are not a danger to it and do not militate against the moral sense of the German race. It is strenuously opposed to Jewish materialist spirit.
14. That all the foregoing demands must be realised, we do demand the creation of a strong central power of the Reich; the unconditional authority of the Central Parliament over the entire Reich and its organisation; the formation of Diets and vocational Chambers for the purpose of administering in the various federal States the general laws promulgated by the Reich. The leaders of the Party swear to proceed regardless of consequences—if necessary to sarcifice their lives—in securing the fulfilment of these points.

Thus, **on 27** October, 1922 about 25,000 Fascists in black shirts moved from Milan to Rome in vehicles supplied and fuelled from the northern army garrisons commanded by the generals whom Mussolini had by now won over to his side. Within hours, conditions were so out of gear that the Prime Minister advised the King (Victor Emmanuel III) to proclaim a state of emergency and arrest all Fascists. But the King declined to accept the advice of his Prime Minister and instead he summoned Mussolini to form the government on 29 October. The great Fascists leader (who had directed the procession from Milan with a railway ticket to Switzerland in his pocket in the event of the suppression of this movement) immediately took up the coveted chance with the promise to "clarify the situation within 48 hours."[44] As a result, the militia was soon mobilised, over a hundred members of the opposition were arrested, hundreds of homes were searched by the police and all 'subversive' groups were dissolved. Orders were given to all prefects to deal drastically with any expression of anti-Fascism and to tighten their control over the press. It all occurred according to the authority given to Mussolini by the King on 25 November so as to exercise dictatorial power till 31 December 1923 in the name of establishing order and instituting reforms in the country. As later developments confirmed, the King fell under a 'colossal bluff' in appointing Mussolini as the Prime Minister in collaboration with the Nationalists and the Socialists. It was a coalition government in which the Fascists were in a very dominant position. But the whole episode was like a Latin *coup d' etat* made possible by the aid of a disloyal section of the army officers class.

44. C.C. Rodee, T.J. Anderson and C. Q. Christol: *Introduction to Political Science* (New York: McGraw-Hill, 1957), p. 320.

In not much time, Mussolini showed himself in true colours when he made it public: "We wish to make the nation Fascist so that tomorrow the Italian and the Fascist would be the same thing." The anti-socialist character of the Fascists became evident when the great socialist leader (Matteoti) was assassinated in June 1924 and, shortly after, Mussolini himself assumed responsibility for it. In February, 1925 an extremist Farinacci was appointed as secretary of the Fascist party. Mussolini's interior minister (Federzoni) did not prevent periodic outbursts of the Fascists (squadrismo) so much so that in the month of October Florence was subjected to a night of systematic violence, arson, looting and terror. The independence of judiciary went to the winds as a result of Fascists' 'free for all'.

When the *squadristi,* that had purged Molinella of socialism, were acquitted on charges of murder and assault, Farinacci congratulated the judges on understanding the difference between a crime and 'an episode of the revolution'. De Bono was acquitted by the High Court for lack of evidence and a week after he was appointed as Governor of Tripolitania. On 31 July an amnesty was declared for all political crimes except murder and genocide and the penalties for such crimes were also reduced. In December, 1925 the public prosecutor released all but five of the persons implicated in the murder of Matteoti on the ground that it was a case of political abduction, not premeditated murder. Mussolini himself commented on it: 'a practical joke which degenerated into a horrible tragedy'. The five accused in this case were tried, two were acquitted and three (who were sentenced to six years imprisonment) were released two months later under the terms of amnesty.

The dictatorial activities of the Fascist government continued. In November, 1925, 123 opposition deputies (including the communists) were formally deprived of their seats in the House. On 2 October, 1925, representatives of the Confindustria and the General Confederations met under the chairmanship of Farinacci at the Lazzo Vidoni (headquarters of the Fascist Party in Rome) where an agreement was hammered out in which a Fascist syndicalist leader (Rossoni) played a very crucial part. Vide this agreement factory councils were abolished, chambers of labour were occupied by the police, strikes and lock-outs were made illegal, wage contracts were given the force of law, and a machinery was set up for compulsory arbitration. Obviously, it all entailed the doom of labour autonomy as espoused by the philosophy of syndicalism.

Moreover, in the name of taking reprisals against attempts on the life of Mussolini during 1925-26, the Fascists adopted many repressive measures for dealing with their opponents and improving the machinery of their dictatorship. Due to this the Unitary Socialist Party was dissolved. Censorship was imposed on the press and Albertini was forced out of the editorship of a leading paper. The servile Parliament passed a series of 'Fascist laws' for the defence of the regime which left the constitutional facade threadbare. The role of the Parliament was further reduced by the grant to the government of power to legislate by decrees. A thorough reorganisation of the police was carried out by its new chief (Arturo Bocchini) and the death penalty, abolished by the Zanardelli's penal code, was reintroduced. In January, 1927, another law for the defence of the state made anti-Fascist propaganda a treasonable offence and created a special tribunal for judging crimes against the state in secret. The machinery of the police state was complete."[45]

By this time Italy had by all means come under the sway of a dictatorial system in the hands of the Fascist party. However, what appeared as a new development at this stage was the idea of a 'corporative state' standing on these significant principles:[46]

1. The economic life of man cannot be abstracted and separated from the whole of his spiritual life.
2. The economic life of man is influenced, if not actually determined, by idealistic factors.
3. True economic progress can derive only from the concerted effort of individuals who know how to sacrifice their personal egotism and ambitions for the good of the whole.
4. Economic initiatives cannot be left to the arbitrary decisions of private individual interests.
5. Open competition, if not wisely directed and restricted, actually destroys wealth instead of creating it.
6. The wealth of a community is something intangible which cannot be identified with the sum of riches of single individuals.
7. The proper function of the State in the Fascist system is that of supervising, regulating and arbitrating the relationships of capital and labour, employers and employees, individuals and associations, private interests and national interests.
8. Class war is avoidable and must be avoided. Class war is deleterious to the orderly and fruitful life of the nation, therefore it has no place in the Fascist State.
9. More important than the production of wealth is its right distribution which must benefit in the best possible way all the classes of nation, hence, the nation itself.
10. Private wealth belongs not only to the individuals but in a symbolic sense to the State as well.

The Fascist idea of 'corporation' was that of a segment of the economy completely organised on a national scale to include the representatives of the employers, employees and the general public, and to possess extensive powers over labour relations, production, wage, other production costs and prices. Such powers could, however, be exercised by a corporation with the approval of Mussolini and, of course, all corporation's officials were really selected by the Fascist party.

45. Edward R. Tannenbaum: *"The Fascist Experience: Italian Society and Culture, 1922-1945.* (New York: Basic Books, 1972). After 1930 two principal institutions were set up for the sake of consolidating the dictatorial position of the regime, The Institution for Industrial Reconstruction (IRI) set up in 1931 as an anti-depression drive was converted into an agency to pursue military goals that after 1935 became the heart of the dictatorship. By controlling all major financial institutions and nearly all heavy industries through the IRI, the regime transformed it into an expanding industrial complex on which fascist war production plans were based. The second was the National Fascist Corporation that imposed controls over all forms of economic activity.

46. See Mario Palmieri: *The Philosophy of Fascism* (1936), excerpts in Carl Cohen, *op. cit.*, p. 353.

The representatives of the consumers were invariably party members assigned to this function. Twenty-two such corporations were created in 1934 and the National Council of Corporations became the supreme arbiter of country's economic life. In 1939 the governing councils of corporations, in effect, replaced the Chamber of Deputies with the Chamber of Fasces and Corporations. As a matter of fact, Fascism in the economic sphere signfied neither state socialism nor state capitalism; it meant the reorganisation of big business in a way, as Rocco said, that "would avoid useless internal competition in order to face, under conditions of maximum economic efficiency, the battles of international competition."[47]

It all shows that Mussolini, who was once a revolutionary syndicalist and who in early 1921 had allied himself and his party with the propertied class of the landowners and the industrialists, managed to get and do what he wanted with the force of his fierce nationalism and spirit of adventure. Working on the ground prepared by the capture of Fieume by a group of revolutionary Italians, under a poet and aviator D' Annunzio in September, 1919, followed by the fascist expeditions in 1921, he could give a peculiar twist to his ideas in a way that he could win over the middle class, the capitalists and military officers to his side. The party of the Fascists became a state within a state after the coup of 1922 and then a state after a couple of years enjoying all exclusive powers and privileges. Developments took place in a way that he could establish a totalitarian order in which the state was completely identified with his party and that, in turn, was identified with the leader himself.

Various social, economic and political factors played their part in the rise of Fascism in Italy. These were: chaotic conditions in the country after the war, economic and social disorganisation, gross profiteering, monetary inflation, strikes for higher wages and allowances, serious deficits in the national budget, dissatisfaction among the soldiers who had returned from the war fronts, national humiliation at the Paris peace settlements, criticism of the inept attitude of the government in dealing with the critical problems of the country, failure of parliamentary institutions, weak position of the socialists and the communists in the country and, above all, the capability of Mussolini as a leader. Every branch of the state (executive, police, magistracy, bureaucracy) gave its support to the Fascists in ways ranging from tolerance and acquiescence to direct complicity. Even the middle class fell easily to the charm of the Fascist commitments displayed by the great leader.[48] By 1922 it was evident that

---

47. Tannenbaum, *op. cit.*

48. According to S.M. Lipset, Fascism "is basically a middle class movement represented by a protest against both capitalism and socialism, big business and big unions. As the relative position of the middle class declined and resentments against ongoing social and economic trends continued its liberal ideology, the support of individual rights against large scale power, changed from one of a revolutionary class to that of a reactionary class." *The Political Man* (New Delhi: Arnold Heinemann, I960), pp. 134-36. The observation of Rudolf Herberk is that such extremist movements "are supported by those who for some reason or other had failed to make a success in their business of occupation, and those who lost their social status or were in danger of losing it. The masses of the organised (Nazi) party members consisted therefore before 1933 largely of people who were outsiders in their own class, black sheep in their family, thwarted in their ambitions." *From Democracy to Nazism* (Baton Rouge: Louisiana State University Press, 1945), p. 10.

the people in general "relied on Fascism as a temporary ally which could easily be disposed of later."[49]

Fascism in Germany came through the ballot box in 1933 owing to the similar conditions that had played their part in the rise of this pernicious tendency in Italy in 1922. The Nazis got many parliamentary seats in the elections of 1933 and the President von Hindenberg appointed Hitler as the Chancellor of the Reich. But the zealous Nazis set fire to the Reichstag building and blamed it on the communists. The President declared a state of emergency and fresh elections to the Parliament were held in 1934. Since the communists and other anti-Nazi elements were suppressed, it became very easy for the Nazis to win elections. As a result, Hitler now became the Chancellor with a heavy majority behind him. The way for the entry of totalitarianism was paved. The Reichstag passed the Enabling Act whereby all powers of the Parliament were transferred to the cabinet for 4 years. Thus, Hitler could adopt many severe measures like outlawing all political parties and purging public services of the non-Aryan and anti-Nazi persons. After the death of von Hindenberg on 2 August, 1934, Hitler assumed the powers of the President. A new law came into force that gave life tenure to Hitler. The judiciary was deprived of its independence and law system was revised in a way to provide one law for the Aryans and the Nazis and another for the non-Aryans and the anti-Nazis.

Thus, Hitler established strong and powerful government of the Nazi party under his leadership. The propaganda machine was handled by Joseph Goebbels who utilised every possible method of disseminating false information to the people in appreciation of the doings of the Nazi regime. The debasement of the people reached barbaric depths in the concentration camps in which more than a million anti-Nazi and non-Aryan people (mostly Jews) were herded by the secret police (Gestapo). Anti-Jewish propaganda became one of the important functions of the state. Even the families, schools and the church were made to serve the Nazi state according to Hitler's political testament of 1925 followed by his propositions of the *Mein Kampf*. Hardly within a year of Hitler's coming to power, it was evident that he was the supreme and final authority in all matters and his principle of leadership *(fuhrerprinzipo)* was calculated to emphasise the unity of purpose of the whole nation."[50]

We may say that the Italian and the German variants of Fascism have many common points. "Unswering obedience to an inclad autocracy was the ideal of the Nazi-Fascist state. In Italy and Germany under the regime of Mussolini and Hitler, the dictatorship of the party over the people was as intense as the pre-eminence within the party of the Duce or Fuhrer. 'Believe, obey, fight' was the motto prescribed by

---

49 A. Rossi: *The Rise of Italian Fascism. 1918-22* (London: Methuen, 1938) (reprinted by New York: Howard Fertig, 1966), pp. 323-37. But such calculations of the people were misfounded. At the time of elections in 1921 Giolitti got the Fascists included in the list of national bloc. When Count Sforaza warned him of the danger of such a combination, he replied: "The fascist candidates are nothing but fireworks, they will make a great deal of noise, but nothing will come out of it. As late as December, 1924, the King shared this illusion that fascism would not last." *Ibid.*

50. W.C Langsam: *The World since 1919* (Delhi: Surjeet Pub., 1981), p. 143.

Mussolini for his countrymen. *Mein Kampf,* the Bible of the Nazi movement, enunciated with grotesque clarity the contempt that Hitler felt for the mass of humanity and his determination to subject them to a disciplined inferiority. Potential organisation, therefore, requires 'putting the head above the masses' and 'subjecting the masses to the heads'. Mankind's interest is not satisfied and is not served by the rule of the masses who are either unable to think or are inefficient, in any case not inspired."[51]

However, three lines of distinction between Italian Fascism and German Nazism may be thus drawn: First, Germany's philosophical and intellectual traditions prepared her people for a much more complete acceptance of reactionary irrationalism compared to the case in Italy. Second, again because of traditional German philosophy and also because Germany was a much more powerful state than Italy, Hitler established a far more complete totalitarian regime than Mussolini did. Mussolini talked about popular commitment to the will of the state; Hitler achieved it. The warrior state became a reality in Germany, while it remained an illusive dream for Mussolini. Last, and perhaps most important, Hitler focused on the concept of race. Though in 1938 Mussolini hurriedly tried to incorporate racism into fascist dogmas, it never really gained much importance among the Italians.[52]

Neo-Fascism or Post-Fascism

Fascism as established by Mussolini in Italy and by Hitler in Germany in the pre-1945 period went into the pages of history with a bad name. Its remnants, however, appeared in the period following Second World War that could be seen particularly in the dictatorial rule of Peron in Argentina, Pinochet in Chile and Saddam Hussain in Iraq. Military dictatorships came into being in many countries of the world like Sudan, Pakistan, Indonesia, Thailand, Burma and Bangladesh which could be taken as the new versions of fascism. The leaders of some political parties made unsuccessful efforts to establish such a rule in their countries the examples of which may be seen in the activities of German Socialist Reich Party (SRP), National Democratic Party (NDP) and German People's Union (DVU) and Socialist Movement of Italy (MSI). In Germany the faithful followers of the Nazi line strongly criticised American hold over their country and they denounced the provisions of the Basic Law (Constitution)

51. Leslie Lipson: *The Great Issues of Politics: An Introduction to Political Science* (Englewood Cliffs, New Jersey: Prentice-Hall, 1960), pp. 231-32. The common character of the two movements may be seen in this fine interpretation: "Fascism in its beginnings was not a doctrine and had clearly no elaborate programme. It was a technique for gaining and retaining power by violence and with an astonishing flexibility it subordinated all questions of programme to this one aim. But it was dominated from the beginning by a definite attitude of mind which exalted the fighting spirit, military discipline, ruthlessness in action and rejected contemptuously all ethical motives as weakening the resoluteness of will. Fascism is power politics and Realpolitik in their most naked form; all theoretical considerations are subordinated to what is regarded as the 'inexorable dynamics' of the factual situation. Ultimately everything depends upon the ever-changing decisions of the *leader,* decisions which cannot be discussed but are blindly obeyed and immediately executed. Thus, Fascism could present itself in a given situation a bulwark of the social order against social revolution, against Marxism and the proletariat, and could in a different situation become the propagandist and spearhead of a proletarian world revolution." *Encyclopaedia Britannica,* 1967 Ptg., Vol. 9, p 104.
52. L.P. Baradat, *op. cit.,* pp. 264-65.

putting a ban on the creation of the fascist party in their country. More particularly, Giorgia Almirante of Italy called for the restoration of the Mussolini-type rule in his country and for this sake he coined the slogan 'Back to the Future'. A French writer Maurice Berdeche appreciated the call of Almirante for the restoration of the Salo Republic of Mussolini.

Neo-Fascism is, however, different from its old or classical form in some important respects. First, it advocates the case of a very hard rule allowing some room for the imbecile role of the opposition parties. Multi-party system is allowed and thereby it is a little short of totalitarianism. A superficial form is granted to a liberal-democratic order. Thus, a kind of 'quasi-democracy' or 'facade democracy' comes into being. Second, it exploits the bogey of socialism so as to attract the support of the poor, backward and alienated segments of the society. Since Otto Strasser of Germany, though living in exile, laid stress on this strategy, it came to be known as 'Stasserism', while others subscribing to this line like Ernest Junger preferred to call it the 'third way'.[53] But the anti-communist stance continued to have its place in its contentions. Degrelle insisted on 'saving Europe from communism' and he invoked ideological concerns to strengthen the Nazi slogan of 'blood and soil'. Third, the most striking feature of neo-fascism appeared in the form of its frank defence of the terroristic methods. For this reason, the neo-fascists of Germany were given the nickname of 'Nazi Maoists'.

If critically studied, it may be commented that neo-fascism is not a clear-cut doctrine. Its adherents look like desperately trying to restore the dictatorial order established by Mussolini and Hitler and, at the same time, seeking to refine their strategies with the tools of liberalism, socialism and ecologism. The neo-fascists are not unanimous in appreciating the factor of racialism. While Le Pen of the French National Front (FN) often defended the case of racism, his successor Bruno Megret carefully sought to keep down the cruder type of racist approach.

Fascism is an ideology as well as a system that desires an all-powerful state at the altar of which individual is sacrificed. It is the arch-enemy of liberalism, socialism and internationalism. But the prefix 'neo' is added to it in the post-1945 period so as to highlight some significant modifications in its basic premises. It is done to mark out a break from or to distinguish between its old and new forms. Though the new form patently rejects the notions of totalitarianism and racialism, it still stands for an authoritarian system that destroys the civil society and converts the people into deaf and dumb-driven cattle. It raises its ugly head and may establish itself in a country where liberal-democratic traditions are very weak the instances of which may be seen in many countries of the Third World. Hence, it is aptly commented: "It is, therefore, a serious mistake to write off the salience of fascism, especially when adapted by shrewd leaders to fit the context of the turn of the twenty-first century."[54]

---

53. 'Third Way' is a slogan that encapsulates the idea of an alternative to both capitalism and socialism. Mussolini used it to define his model of a corporatist state. Andrew Heywood: *Key Concepts in Politics* (New York: Palgrave-Macmillan, 2005), p. 78.
54. Roger Eatwell: "Fascism" in Eatwell and Anthony Wright (eds.): *Contemporary Political Ideologies* (New Delhi: Rawat Publications, 2003), p. 201.

Critical Appreciation

After the First World War, Facism witnessed its expression in Italy and then in Germany; it saw its doom in the defeat of these countries in World War II in 1945. But the trend of Fascism has survived and now it may be seen in the form of 'neo-fascism' in many countries of the world under the rule of a military *junta,* though its soft forms may be noted in the countries having a weak democratic system. By all means, it is a curse and although it condemns democracy and socialism in its own way, it may not at all be taken as an alternative to a system based on the celebrated principles of positive and dynamic liberalism. Surprisingly, it has its admirers who contend that it gives to the people what they really need in times of crisis. It provides roads, bridges and drains, safety and security in homes and workshops, punctuality in the running of trains and public transport, orderly industry, and pride in the destiny of the nation. It creates a new awareness in the minds of the people towards their public duties and replaces the evils of inefficiency, corruption and treason with the virtues of efficiency, integrity and patriotism. The progress made by a country in a very short span of time and the elevation of national status in the comity of nations are also cited as strong points in defence of Fascism.[55]

However, the evils of Fascism are many that may be thus enumerated:

1. Fascism is not a coherent ideology. It is another name for the course of opportunism in which any principle can be accommodated if it goes to serve the interest of a power-drunk leader and his loyal organisation. The Fascists thus subscribe to the law of 'transgression' as laid down by Robert Michels. They want to 'catch all' for their purpose, though the Nazis would exclude the Jews.[56] We may take note of the fact that the first programme of 1919 of the Italian Fascists presented to the public was progressive, republican, democratic, libertarian, peace-loving and anti-capitalist. But very quickly it showed itself to be unprogressive, willing to compromise with monarchy, dictatorial, anti-libertarian, imperialistic and not remotely anti-capitalist. The socialist professions of the Fascists became a fraud not so much when they killed a communist leader in 1919 (Lavaguini), but when they finished Matteoti in 1924 and the ruling party owed publicly responsibility for the same. Mussolini used his ardent supporters as a tool.[57] It is, therefore, well commented that Fascism is revolution of nihilism'.[58] It is a revolution without a doctrine, 'dynamics in vacuo', action for the sake of action alone, power sought for its own sake. It uses ideas, of course, but the ideas

55. See Coker, *op. cit.,* p. 489.
56. Martin Seliger: *Ideology and Politics* (London: George Allen and Unwin, 1976), pp. 200-201.
57. For instance, Gentile was requisitioned for writing a thesis on the philosophy of Fascism that is mistakenly regarded as Mussolini's own official writing. Rocco was forced to leave the ministry of Justice in 1932 and the same happened with other collaborators like Giuseppe Volpi (Finance Minister), Dino Grandi (Foreign Minister), Guiseppe Bottai (Corporations Minister) and Balbino (Education Minister). Thus every possible attempt was made by the great leader to suit his political purpose.
58. Hermann Rauschning: *The Revolution of Nihilism* (London: William Heinemann, 1939), p. 24.

are means, not the guiding principles and whatever doctrines are espoused are deliberately and carefully manufactured."[59]

2. Nationalism is a very constructive force, but the Fascists make misuse of it for their nefarious ends. It becomes an instrument in their hands to suppress all kinds of opposition at home and to enter into war abroad just for imperialistic ends. All national exhortations are like instruments of 'window dressing'. Hitler made use of German nationalism for extending the frontiers of the Reich and thereby destroying the existence of Austria and Czechoslovakia in violation of the peace settlements of 1919. Similarly, Mussolini exploited national sentiments for restoring the glory of the ancient Roman empire and in its name played with the freedom of Abyssinia. Likewise, by identifying German nationalism with Aryan racialism, Hitler could do every possible torture to the non-Germans, particularly the Jews. Although Mussolini was not an advocate of the myth of racial superiority, he also succumbed to it after 1936 in the interest of his own power game. In not much time, it became clear that Hitler had no intention of being confined to his nationalistic aspirations and that his regime "was totally despotic and totally destructive even of nationalistic concentrations and achievements."[60]
3. So is the case with the Fascist argument in defence of war. Man loves peace and all progress of mankind is possible only in the conditions of peace. By any standard of civilisation recourse to war cannot be appreciated. It is a fad with the barbarians. The way the Fascists of Italy and the Nazis of Germany eulogised war and threw their country into the conditions of a great war entailed untold suffering to mankind. Naturally, this part of the Fascist ideology deserves condemnation in the strongest possible terms. It is well remarked: "That war, however, is not the father but the destroyer of all things, the destroyer of all order and all the things of mind. There is nothing that this destruction would spare. And nothing will be taken over from the old order into the new, neither army nor church, neither the institutions of property, nor the elements of culture.... Whatever it cannot dominate it must destroy, whatever it cannot absorb and master must go. Such is the truly barbaric maxim of National Socialism. It is the process, an enemy occupation of all the vital elements in the nation, ending in their destruction."[61]
4. It is obvious that Fascism is the enemy of internationalism. Instead of advocating the case of friendship and cooperation among the nations and pacific settlement of international disputes, it prefers the course of confrontation and war by

---

59. *Ibid.* Same thing may be noted in the case of Nazi Socialists who did so many things in violation of the principle of nationalism as well as socialism. So says a critic: "If political philosophy is a coherent system of thought intent upon justifying before ethics and reason a certain political program and certain political institutions, Nazism has not developed a political philosophy. What passes as the political philosophy of Nazism is a conglomeration of fragments of ideas, often inconsistent with each other, always vague and capable of contradictory interpretations, and hence adaptable to the exigencies of changing political conditions. H.J. Morgenthau: "Nazism" in J.C. Roucek (ed.) : *Twentieth Century Political Thought* (New York, 1946), p. 132.
60. Rauschning, *op. cit.*, p. 55.
61. *Ibid.*, pp. 87-88.

sticking to 'the policy of blood and iron'. So, in the economic sphere, its policy of 'autarchy' is very pernicious. Every state desires self-sufficiency, but it should not be converted into the way of economic isolationism. The meaning of economic self-sufficiency, as given by the Fascists, rejects the case of international collaboration in the economic sphere for the sake of mutual benefit so that all states of the world may be benefited. On the whole, the entire economic philosophy of Fascism goes to the benefit of the native capitalist class. We have taken note of the fact how Mussolini abandoned his syndicalist postures by taking away the authority of the trade unions and giving all powers to the 22 corporations that were controlled by the Fascists and thereby the workers were deprived of all trade union rights. Hence, Fascism can be criticised for being an ideology of conservatism.[62]

5. Another dangerous feature of the philosophy or Fascism is the cult of 'hero worship'. What Nietzsche and Schopenhauer said about the role of a 'superman' is evident in the affirmations of Mussolini and Hitler.[63] The leader uses all demagogic methods to impress the people with his indispensability and the people, in general, take it all for granted. They accept the title of the leader for life-long tenure in office. Their power of reasoning is atrophied to any extent.[64] It has its disastrous consequences which can be seen in the fates of Italy and Germany. As Schapiro says: "And it is, indeed, the mass that the Leader's main effort is directed at: he woos, cajoles, bewitches, befuddles, and blinds the mass with all the instruments which his skill, his imagination, his resources, above all, his style make possible. Mussolini, in this sense, was a showman: he acted out his part in front of a people whom in his heart he despised for the credence which they bestowed on his histrionics. The more hysterical Hitler used the methods of necromancy to mobilise mass hysteria and to induce crowd hypnosis on a scale hitherto unkown in the modern history of mankind, and, be it said, with a degree of success among civilised people comparable only to the manifestations of religious dementia in the Middle Ages."[65]

---

62. See R.A. Brady: *The Spirit and Structure of German Fascism* (New York, 1937). As Mihaly Vajda says: "The definitive character of fascist dictatorship is that it sprang from a *mass movement* as a capitalist form of rule, depended on this movement for support." *Fascism* (London: Allison and Busby, 1976), p. 13.
63. Hitler said: "Let it be written on our epitaph: "We have been hard; we have been ruthless; but we have been good Germans." The cult of superman enabled another hero of Hitlerism to cry cynically: 'The State must have the courage to break its own laws.' (Goebbels). The moral sanction for such arbitrary, absolutely unrestricted power on earth can be derived only from the pseudo-philosophical conception of a supernatural spiritual force, of an absolute divine will, which is not bound by the laws of nature, yet it is the sovereign principle or power governing the destiny of man. That is the philosophy of Fascism, quintessence of which is the cult of superman." M.N Roy: *Fascism: Its Philosophy, Profession and Practice* (Calcutta: Renaissance Publishers, 1938), p. 43.
64. Leonard Schapiro says that "had Hitler been born, say, in a Buckinghamshire village, he would have no doubt, ended on the gallows or in a madhouse." *Totalitarianism* (London: Macmillan, 1972), p. 21.

6. Above all, Fascism is the ideology of totalitarianism. As such, it is the enemy of the values of a democratic system. It stands for the idealisation of a particular leader and his official line of thought and action and thereby negates the way of a free and decent life. The people are converted into deaf and dumb-driven cattle led by a shepherd who plays the role of a butcher as per his personal choice. In this respect, every kind of totalitarianism deserves all condemnation. Democracy is the best form of government just for this reason that it ensures the boons of liberty and equality to all; it treats the individual as an end and the state as a means for his welfare. But Fascism reverses the whole course by making the state an end at whose altar the individual may be sacrificed. As such, it is a curse and that too of the worst kind. "If liberalism is a combination of two principles of democracy and individualism.... the Fascist tradition is an expression of the two opposing principles of autocracy and authoritarianism and of state worship or etatism."[66]

On the whole, Fascism is a pernicious tendency. The essential fact stands out that it is a curse. The ideology is based on, what Talcott Parsons says, 'the irrationalisation of the society'. By imbibing all the essential traits of the philosophy of irrationalism or anti-intellectualism, economic conservatism, and political totalitarianism, it offers a formidable challenge to the universally acclaimed excellence of a democratic system. The people should know that Fascism "has striven somewhat paradoxically, to unite philosophy with a bias towards conservatism and one that glorified revolutionary violence, an ethics that regarded conformity as a chief virtue and one that saw 'sacred egoism' as the highest form of character."[67] The very word 'Fascism' "should be banned from our political vocabulary."[68]

---

65. *Ibid.*, pp. 52-53.
66. William McGovern: *From Luther to Hitler*, p. 14.
67. G.H. Sabine: *A History of Political Theory*, p. 757.
68. R.P. Woolf: "Introduction" in his (ed.): *Fascism in Europe* (London; Methuen, 1981), p. l.

25

Post-Modernism

> Marx and Freud are the two great heroes of the radicalised Enlightenment. Both discovered the dark underside of the philosophes' empire of reason. Marx uncovered the exploitation and oppression without which the progress of bourgeois society would have been impossible. Freud discovered the transparency of reason itself, exposing the conscious self as the the product of a history of desire and repression whose effects are still stored in the unconscious. After their intervention, theory could no longer be conceived as simply the disinterested contemplation of eternal truths, as it had been since Plato.
>
> **—Alex Callinicos**[1]

In the later part of the twentieth century, or in the phase of 'post-industrial society', as labelled by the French sociologist Alain Touraine, a number of new issues engaged the attention of the social and political theorists who ascribed to them different names as post-liberalism, post-positivism, post-structuralism, post-industrialism, post-colonialism, post-communism, post-developmentalism and the like. Post-modernism belongs to the same trend. What is interesting as well as perplexing about it is that now this term has become a shibboleth for new trends in film, drama, theatre, dance, music, art, architecture, literature, philosophy, theology, psychoanalysis, historiography, cybernetic technologies and all hues of social and cultural life. Like other social sciences, political science has not remained unaffected by this ultra-modern trend popularised by Jean-Francois Lyotard of France by the name of 'post-modern tradition'.

Nature and Essential Implications

Post-modernism appeared as a new trend first in the spheres of culture, fine arts and aesthetics and then entered into the domains of social and political philosophy in the last phase of the twentieth century. Originally a contribution of the French social theorists like Jean-Francois Lyotard, Jacques Derrida, Jean Baudrillard and Michael Foucault, it had its followers in other countries like Richard Rorty in the United States. Its advocates sharply reacted against the trinity of Enlightement-reason, nature, and progress.[2] They insisted that there "is nothing like certainty;

1. Callinicos: *Against Post-Modernism: A Post-Marxist Critique* (Cambridge: Polity Press, 1994), p. 172.
2. Gary Woller: "Public Administration and Post-Modernism", Special Issue of *American Behavioural Scientist,* Vol. 41, No. 1, 1997, p. 9. The creed of 'enlightenment' "stressed the possibility of man's own intellect planning a society on rational grounds and denied, therefore, the traditional authority of kings and the Church. Freedom, especially of thought and cooperative human behaviour were the high points of the philosophy, which was on the whole, optimistic about human nature, while the prevailing religiously-derived notion of man was pessimistic, accepting the Christian doctrine of the Original Sin. In many ways, enlightenment social thought was developed as an analogy with physical science, seeking almost mathematically perfect designs for society." David Robertson: *A Dictionary of Modern Politics* (London and New York: Europa Publications, 2002), III ed., p. 165.

the idea of absolute or universal truth must be discarded as an arrogant pretence. Interchangeable with post-structuralism, it emphasises that all ideas and concepts are expressed in language which itself is enmeshed in complex relations of power."[3]

It shows that post-modernism rejects the consensus in Western thought that sees the Enlightenment as its break with medieval thought and its celebration of rationality as heralding an unstoppable progress in human life, understanding and experience. "The universalistic claims of rationality of the hubris of thinking society on the way to real truth rather than local belief, are the objects of post-modern scorn. A central concept of post-modern thinking, the idea of meta-narrative can best display what it is all about. The modern age, the post-modernists claim, thinks in terms of a great valid truth. Post-modernists argue that we are all prisoners of our conditions, our characteristics, our communities, and that only local narratives, no longer presented as meta, can tell us our own partial truths."[4]

A subtle line of distinction between modernism and post-modernism may be drawn in that while the former denotes the mode of thought rooted in the 'enlightenment' and based on faith in rationalism, the latter rejects any 'meta-narrative' of this kind. That is, while the former implies that truth, beauty and morality exist as objective realities that can be comprehended through rational or scientific means, the latter argues that truth, beauty and morality do not have an objective existence beyond how we think and talk about them. So Lyotard affirms: "Simplifying to the extreme, I define post-modernism as incredulity towards meta-narratives."[5]

Modernism is informed by the faith in progress and the hope that increased control over human condition would pave the way for the increased freedom of the individual. Post-modernism is also informed by the norm of the freedom of the individual. It rejects the case of authoritarianism of every kind and argues that no particular version of truth or morality can be absolutely correct. In the ultimate analysis, no version can be regarded to be the most superior or final. Thus, Stephen Eric Bronner highlights its three features:[6]

1. Disgust with totalitarian ideologies of recent memories having profound impact on the post-modern imagination;
2. Incredulity towards metanarratives implying skepticism towards all general claims, universal theories of history, and attempts to view society as a coherent whole with fixed and stable subject.
3. Truth to be always seen as a specific contrast of specific circumstances.

3. Andrew Heywood: *Key Concepts in Politics* (New York: Palgrave-Macmillan, 2005), pp. 101-102. Stephen Eric Bronner holds a different view. As he comments: "Post-modernism and post-structuralism are often used interchangeably. But there is a difference between them. The former usually refers to the complex of social and political trends expressive of a new historical phase in which the structure and the assumptions of modernity are no longer valid. The latter, by contrast, deals with the philosophical methods through which these structures and assumptions are exposed as arbitrary and as serving particular forms of domination. Neither post-modernism nor post-structuralism should be understood as a unified or coherent doctrine." *Twentieth Century Political Theory: A Reader* (New York: Routledge, 2006), p. 397.
4. Robertson, *op. cit.*, pp. 398-99.
5. Lyotard: *The Post-Modern Tradition*, (1997), p. xxiv.
6. Bronner, *op. cit.*, p. 397.

Some Important Statements

The bourgeoisie cannot exist without constantly revolutionising the instruments of production, and with them the relations of society....Constant revolutionising of production, uninterrupted disturbance of social relations, ever-lasting uncertainty and agitation, distinguish the bourgeois epoch form all earlier ones.

—Karl Marx and Fredrick Engels
'Communist Manifesto' in *Selected Works* (Moscow Progress Publishers, 1977), Vol. 1, p. 111.

The best argument we partisans of solidarity have against the realistic partisans of objectivity is Nietzsche's argument that the traditional Western metaphysical-epistemological way of firming up our habits is simply not working any more.

—Richard Rorty
Objectivity, Relativism and Truth (Cambridge: Cambridge University Press, 1991), p. 33.

Modern societies were seen to be structured by industrialisation and class solidarity, social identity being largely determined by one's position within the productive system. Post-modern societies, on the other hand, are increasingly fragmented and pluralistic 'information' societies in which individuals are transformed from producers to consumers, and individualism replaces class, religious and ethnic loyalties. Post-modernity is thus linked to post-industrialism, the development of a society no longer dependent upon manufacturing industry, but more reliant upon knowledge and communication.

—Andrew Heywood
Political Theory: An Introduction (New York: Palgrave-Macmillan, 2004,), p. 7.

Prior to the emergence of the trend of post-modernism, the currents of Liberalism and Marxism dominated the Western social and political thought. Both were informed by the 'spirit' of the enlightenment in view of the fact that both defined truth and reality in an absolute sense and thus produced their metanarratives on this count. Both desired emancipation of man from the shackles of slavery or domination in their own ways. A fierce debate between the two resulted in the emergence of many varieties of liberalism and socialism, each boasting of its superiority over the other. Post-modernism shattered the foundations of both. As Heywood observes: "As a tool of social and political analysis, post-modernism highlights the shift away from societies structured by industrialisation and class solidarity to increasingly fragmented and pluralistic information societies (that is, to post-modernity) in which individuals are transformed from producers to consumers, and individualism replaces class, religious and ethnic loyalties. From this perspective, conventional political ideologies, such as Marxism and Liberalism, tend to be rejected as irrelevant 'metanarratives' that developed out of the progress of modernisation. Post-modernists argue that there is no such thing as certainty; the idea of absolute and universal truth must be discarded as an arrogant pretence. In this sense, post-modernism is an example of anti-foundationalism. Emphasis is thus placed on the importance of discussion, debate and democracy."[7]

7. Andrew Heywood: *Politics* (Houndmills, Basingstroke: Palgrave, 2005), p. 65.

One of the most basic themes of post-modern debate revolves around reality, or lack of reality, or multiplicity of realities. When the restless doubting attitude of modern reason turns on reason itself, nihilism results. Nihilism is the Nietzschean concept corresponding most closely to this fluid and anchorless sense of reality. "If the post-modern mood exhibits nihilistic tendencies, then this means that reality is blurred and that establishing truth is not as straightforward as it once seemed. It does not necessarily mean that people believe in nothing, or that they are paralysed by the senselessness of existence."[8]

The salient features of the post-modern perspective may be enumerated as under:

1. It rejects the view that there may be absolute or final versions of beauty, truth and morality. Discourses on the theme of 'reality' must go on endlessly.
2. Modernity went beyond Providence of the Middle Ages and appreciated the course of humanism so as to pave the way of human progress on rational or scientific grounds. Post-modernity moves from progressivism to nihilism.
3. It signifies 'deconstruction' which implies the task of raising questions about the 'texts' which constitute cultural life exposing its complications and contradictions.
4. It is anti-Marxism. It refutes the laws of Marx which are lauded by the Marxists as objective and scientific. Post-modernists denounce the Marxian propositions as 'fallen metanarratives in the present phase of hyper-reality.'
5. It is a reaction against modernity of course, but it imbibes within itself the traits of modernity. Thus, it may be treated as the extension and exhaustion but not the demise of modernity. It certainly inflates certain features of modernity and, by contrast, shrinks others into insignificance so as to create new social configurations.
6. It mixes social and economic with the cultural. Initially its queries covered the realms of art and architecture, but in course of time, they covered all the dimensions of human life and activity. Post-modern queries embrace ideals, values, symbols, tastes and styles of the people.
7. Post-modernity is linked to post-industrialism. The development of society no longer is dependent upon manufacturing industry, it is more reliant upon knowledge, information and communication.

By its nature anti-foundationalist, post-modernism "suggests that there is a plurality of legitimate ethical and political positions, and that our language and political concepts are valid only in terms of the context in which they are generated and employed."[9]

Precursors and Luminaries

The post-modern perspective, whose bold manifestation found place in the works of some recent French thinkers, may be said to have its rudiments in the ideas of German thinkers like Nietzsche (1844-1908) and Heidegger (1889-1976). Thus, post-modern perspective takes inspiration from the nihilist thought of Germany. In the view of Nietzsche, truth is only the 'solidification of old metaphors'. The so-called

8. David Lyon: *Post-Modernity* (Delhi: Viva Books, 2002), p. 9.
9. Andrew Heywood: *Political Theory: An Introduction*, p. 13.

systems of reason are actually systems of persuasion. His slogan 'the death of God' means that 'we should no longer be sure of anything'. Morality is a lie, truth is a fiction. By discarding anything like a larger reality (God), he advocates the case of a 'life without illusions.[10]

Martin Heidegger follows the same line with a difference in his work *Being and Time* (1927). Humanism replaces God and so man becomes the maker of his own destiny. Secularism and humanism join hands by rejecting the premises of mysticism and metaphysics and thus create a twilight in the Western thought. Instead of committing the mistake of starting from a conception of human nature as done by social and political philosophers earlier, he laid stress on the recognition of human essence as 'a realm of disclosure'.[11] In this way, he contributed to the existentialist thought that later crept into the thought of post-modernism. Georg Simmel, 'widely recognised as one of the founding fathers of sociology' and also as 'the sole post-modern thinker' talked about the 'crisis of culture' that had its place in the widening of the gap between the 'objective culture' visible in the technological developments and the 'increasingly alienated individual frustrated in the quest for genuine individuality.'[12]

Lyotard, Baudrillard, Derrida and Foucault of France may be taken as the leading lights of this trend. Lyotard deserves the credit for coining and popularising the term 'post-modernism' or 'post-modernity' in 1979. He offers a succinct definition of this term by calling it 'an incredulity towards metanarratives.' It implies rejection of all theories based on the assumption of universally valid norms viewing society as a coherent reality. He argues that the claims of the scientific socialism of Marx have been refuted and replaced by liberal capitalism. Science, once taken to be the touchstone of legitimate knowledge, has lost its assumed unity. The growth of knowledge is a social and cultural process as well. The collapse of communism as an ideology clears the way for the 'atomisation of the social', or into a consumer cluster of tastes and fashions. Implicit in the whole analysis is a kind of obsession that the new knowledge in the age of information and technology has made the whole case of the inevitability of a socialist revolution irrelevant. Hence, Lyotard "treats the rejection of revolution as an instance of a more general phenomenon constitutive of the post-modern, namely, the collapse of the grand narratives."[13]

The influence of Nietzsche on Lyotard is obvious. But Derrida looks like taking inspiration from Heidegger. He adheres to the task of 'deconstruction' and thereby raises pertinent questions about our own texts and those of others with the aim of denying that any text is settled or stable. Boundaries between knowledge and the world, or text and interpretation no longer exist; the mind is always renewing and re-defining the texts it tries to contain. It implies that science can no longer presume

10. David Lyon: *Post-Modernity* p. 11.
11. *Ibid.*, p. 12.
12. Lyon is of the view that similar line may be noticed in the affirmation of Marx who, like Prospero of Shakespeare's *Tempest*, says that 'all that is solid melts into air'. However, the line of distinction between Marx and Nietzsche may be seen in his stress on the capitalist system, as all solid realities dissolve in the bath of bourgeois acids decomposing meaning and reality themselves. *Ibid.*
13. Callinicos, *op. cit.*, p. 9.

logical coherence, or the discoverability of truth. It includes social sciences of course, long riven by disputes over positivist and hermeneutic-interpretive-approaches."[14]

If 'textuality' is the keynote of Derrida's thought, Foucault presents a blending of knowledge and power. In his scheme, two main *epistemes* may be discerned in the Western thought—neo-classical and modern. While the former prevailed in the seventeenth and eighteenth centuries according no special place to man, the latter prevailing in the nineteenth and twentieth centuries took man as both the object and the subject. Thus, he rambles into the history of ideas what he calls 'geneology' and seeks to integrate knowledge with power in his two works *Knowledge/Power* and *Discipline and Punish.* As a matter of fact, he is concerned with knowledge and the construction of the human subject. His writings analyse different branches of knowledge what he calls 'archaeologies' leading to an emphasis upon discourse or 'discourse formation'. Central to this is his belief that knowledge "is deeply enmeshed in power, truth always being a social construct, and that power can be productive as well as prohibitive."[15]

Jean Baudrillard is a post-modern philosopher, but he refutes the arguments of Foucault in his work *Forget Foucault* (1987). He subscribes to a different line. Though an anarchist like Joseph Proudhon, he dismisses the propositions of Marx as 'fallen metanarratives' in the present phase of hyperreality. In his view, while the earlier eras depended either on face-to-face symbolic exchanges, the contemporary world is dominated by images from the new means of print and electronic media. In the consumer society the process is different because our understanding of reality is radically revised. The perplexing feature of his political philosophy is that while he advises us to forget Foucault and dabbles in the 'debate with the ghost of Marx', he in his *America* chastises the Americans for their nostalgic tendencies. It provokes Bryan Turner to call him not 'post-modern' but 'anti-modern' and advises to 'forget Baudrillard'.[16]

A reference should be made to the ideas of Richard Rorty of the United States who denounces the philosophers of Enlightenment as 'superficial dreamers' and, at the same time, scoffs at the attempt of Habermas to 'rehabilitate the radicalised Enlightenment'. He dismisses the argument that there is an objective or transcendental standpoint from which beliefs can be evaluated. For this reason, philosophy cannot have eternally and universally valid theories. Known as the analyst of language and mind, he argues that philosophy itself should be understood as nothing more than a conversation. But he is a skeptic. He has reservations about some of the relativist trends in post-modernism and, unlike other post-modernists, defends the case of pragmatic brand of liberalism that overlaps at times with social democracy. The reason for including him in the category of post-modernists is that he has tried to claim the philosophy of language for pragmatism understood as the doctrine that there "are no constraints on inquiry save conversational ones-no wholesale restraints derived from the nature of the objects, or of the mind, or of language, but only those whose retail constraints are provided by the remarks of our fellow-inquirers."[17]

---

14. Lyon, *op. cit.*, p. 19.
15. Andrew Heywood: *Political Theory : An Introduction*, p. 8.
16. See Bryan Turner: (ed.): *Theories of Modernity and Post-Modernity* (London: Sage Publications, 1990).
17. Richard Rorty: *The Consequences of Pragmatism* (Brighton, 1982), p. 165.

A cursory look at the ideas of the leading lights of the trend of post-modernism makes it evident that they are running in diverse directions. In the heap of wide variations, one may trace the common thread of rejection of the legacy of Enlightement and, by hook or by crook, acceptance of the profile of a liberal and pluralistic order. One cannot say whether it has its place in the end of ideology debate, or it has come forward in the shape of a new ideology of its own in view of their stern assertion that the current world "is characterised by a crisis of 'metanarratives', a loss of faith in the grand sweep of ideology. Instead, it celebrates pluralism; it rejects monocausalism and stresses different possibilities. It supports the politics of personal identity over those of class, nation, and so on."[18]

Analysis of Power and Resistance

Machiavelli and Hobbes are regarded as power theorists who studied politics in terms of 'struggle for power' and identified power with a repressive force. The post-modernists take a different view in this regard. They argue that power has its manifestation in many other forms such as social privileges or disciplinary norms and in any form of resistance. As such, power by nature has productive, prohibitive and reformative aspects. The place of power may be traced both in the privileged position of some social institutions and in the role of other institutions that resist it. Such an analysis may be seen in Derrida's *Of Grammatology* (1976) wherein he propounds the thesis of 'deconstruction'[19] and in Foucault's *Power/Knowledge* (1980) wherein he integrates power with knowledge.

The post-modernists like Derrida and Foucault argue that the structure of 'privilege' and 'power' pervades the entire social system and thus finds its place in the acquisition of knowledge. The paradigm of power creates stuff for 'discourse' and that contributes to the stock of political theory. Power, in the traditional sense, signifies relationship between the ruler and the ruled, between the master and the slave, between the command and its obedience. In the view of the post-modernists, particularly Foucault, power has its place in the rules and norms of discipline which regulate the behaviour and role of social institutions and have prohibitive as well as productive effects.

Power may, therefore, be seen in the relationship between those who prescribe the rules of behaviour and those who are allowed to do something and not to do something else. In feudal times, the lords had the power to lay down such disciplinary rules, but the vassals could display their power by means of resistance. In present times, hitherto neglected segments of the society have come forward to fight against discrimination and injustice like women, negroes, *dalits* (depressed castes), minorities etc. and they have carved out a place of their own in the category of 'new social movements'. The new concept of power operates through the disciplinary norms

18. Roger Eatwell: "Introduction" in Eatwell and Anthony Wright (ed.s): *Contemporary Political Ideologies* (Delhi: Rawat Publications, 2003), p. 11.
19. Derrida is known for giving the idea of 'deconstruction'. It implies that the meaning of a term can be understood by contrasting it with its antonymn as masculine can be understood by contrasting it with feminine, or metaphysical by contrasting it with empirical. Thus, it is an approach to understand the meaning of words not as representing some concrete reality or truth, but by contrasting them with their opposite concepts which they want to suppress.

rather than through command-and-obedience relationship. In the modern regime, the rulers and their agents do not reach out from a centre to control unruly subjects through fear. Instead, people are now ruled through social institutions which rise up from the ground and reach out to people through various social channels. These institutions lay down disciplinary norms and make people conform to the prevailing standards of reason and order. "Power is not exercised through several institutions that organise and manage the people in a complex division of labour. These institutions include not only schools, offices, police departments and prisons, but also hospitals, clinics and many welfare organisations."[20]

However, Foucault has his distinctive place in the study of power from this viewpoint. His main arguments may be thus enumerated:

1. There is no power-relation without the correlative constitution of a field of knowledge, nor at the same time any knowledge that does not presuppose and constitute at the same time power-relations.[21]
2. Power is productive; it does not operate by repressing individuals, circumscribing their activity, but rather by *constituting* them. His main example is the 'disciplinary institutions' such as the prison which punishes and thereby reforms the erratic behaviour of the criminal.[22]
3. The exercise of power has its contrast in resistance. Resistance is both an element of the functioning of power and a source of its perpetual disorder.
4. Power is omnipresent. It may be traced in the relationship between the contending parties. Its comprehension creates knowledge. Marx committed the mistake of comprehending it merely in economic terms. Only then one can rethink and redefine reality.
5. There is an integral link between power and systems of thought through the idea of a 'discourse' of power. A discourse is a system of social relations and practices that assign meaning and thus identities to those who live or work within it.[23]

Obviously, the post-modern analysis of power contradicts what Marx so powerfully asserted and it inspires the new leftists and the neo-Marxists to redefine the term 'power' in a way that it supports as well as cuts across the argument of Foucault. "Whereas Marxists associate power as thought control with the attempt to maintain class inequality, post-modern theorists come close to seeing power as ubiquitous, all systems of knowledge being viewed as manifestations of power."[24]

Such an analysis of power, as done by Foucault particularly, makes the issue very wide and, for this reason, vague and unmanageable. In the face of an attack from many sides, he himself said in an interview: "I am far from being a theoretician of power. At the limit, I would say that power, as an autonomous question, does not interest me." The fact is that his analysis of power in relationship with knowledge

20. O.P. Gauba: *Political Ideas and Ideologies* (Delhi: Macmillan, 2010), p. 110.
21. Michael Foucault: *Discipline and Punish* (London: Tavistick, 1977), p. 27.
22. Cited in Callinicos, *op. cit.*, p. 82
23. Foucault: *Power/Knowledge* (London: Harvester Wheatsheaf, 1980), pp. 85 and 141.
24. Heywood, *Political Theory: An Introduction*, p. 128.

has been praised for its originality as well as criticised for its vagueness. Habermas charges him with generating 'a metaphysics of power' and others like Deluze and Guattari comment that his model of power "rests on the undue generalisation of observations that are more limited in scope and time. However, even from his own perspective, there was a heavy theoretical price to pay for his claims; the circularity of the relationships between power and knowledge was such that it made the identification of a specific level for the conditions of possibility for discourse impossible."[25]

Repositioning of the Modernity

The process of socio-cultural transformation goes on uninterruptedly having its indelible impact on the patterns of human life. The feudal society was replaced by the capitalist society. The capitalist society became industrial society and now some sociologists prefer to call it post-industrial society. The basic question arises whether past has its creep into the future to maintain the trend of continuity, or whether the present has its own distinctive features in which the past is repositioned, or the present allows no room for reclaiming the pre-modern. So is the case with pre-modernism, modernism and post-modernism. A French writer Wolfgang Welsh has coined the term 'post-modern modernity'. The fact is that shifts in the social, economic, cultural and political spheres inform the philosopher to invent such terms loaded with concrete as well as contradictory implications.

The renaissance and reformation movements heralded the advent of the modern age. People discarded their mythical assumptions. Secularism and humanism replaced scholasticism. Industrial revolution brought about a fundamental change in the economic, social, political and ethical systems. The thinkers appreciated the ways of science. Reason replaced faith and progress became the goal. It was given the name of Enlightenment in which modernity witnessed its triumph. A fundamental change could be noticed in the working of the market system, in the operation of public administration, and in the manifestation of the art and culture of the people. It also appeared in the prevalence of a new value system in defence of free competition in the economic and of free individual in the political spheres.

In the last phase of the last century, post-modernism emerged as a phenomenon on the 'ruins' of Enlightenment as a consequence of the marvellous developments in the spheres of technology and informatics. The cybernetic revolution put a new layer on modernity without replacing it in toto. Thus, the question arises whether the present trend is a break from the past, or it is a repositioning of the past into its premises. Crises occur from time to time and, as a result of their solution or management, new value system emerges. The heartless and the bloodless modernity informed by the Enlightenment led to a search for antidotes in the 'irrationalities' of Emile Durkheim, or the 'illusions' of Sigmund Freud, or the 'search for man's total emancipation' of Marx.[26] The new thinkers may hold a negative or pessimistic view by taking inspiration from the nihilism of Nietzsche, or they may have a

25. Beatrice Han: "Michael Foucault" in Christopher John Murray (ed.): *The Encyclopaedia of Modern French Thought* (London: Fitzroy Dearborn, 2004), pp. 227-28.
26. Lyon, *op. cit.*, p. 93.

positive and optimistic view by taking inspiration from the techno-science of Donna Haraway.

Post-modernism does not entail the exhaustion of modernity, it retains much of what comes under the rubric of modernity and thereby it may be treated as a double-faced phenomenon. As a 'modernist' Marx studied capitalism, as a neo-Marxist Marcuse took note of the conversion of the capitalist society into an industrial society and Touraine called it post-industrial society. All looked at contemporary crises in their own way and thereby offered their courses to resolve them as a result of which new ideas emerged in consonance with the new ways of people's lives. "Today's post-modern challenge returns the spotlight to the ideals, values and symbols of economic life, as they appear in the life of consumers and in consumerism. Taste and style, far from being marginal reflexes of production, are now viewed as centrally significant."[27]

Modernity has its mark in the quest for 'reality' that may be possible by adopting a rational and scientific outlook. So is the case with post-modernity. However, the point of distinction to be noted is that where modernity stops, post-modernity moves ahead by discarding the notion of the finality of truth. What is truth to modernity is rejected as 'fiction' if search for reality leads to such a conclusion. The discourse should continue and widen itself so as to cover new themes like ecologism, feminism, multiculturalism, racialism, terrorism, globalism and the like. Thus, post-modernism is not a break from but a continuity with the past with wider and broader ramifications. As Harvey remarks, it "swims, even wallows, in the fragmentary and chaotic currents of change as if that is all there is."[28] Instead of adhering to some utopia as Marx's vision of a communist society, Foucault advocates the case of 'heterotopia' where apparently incongruous worlds exist. Lyotard advises to open the databanks to all.[29]

If so, post-modernism rejects Marxism as a scientific creed that sticks to a unilinear development of society and state through the closed and autocratic system of the dictatorship of the proletariat. It defends the case of a pluralist order in the classical liberal framework in all spheres of life—social, cultural, economic and political. A new ideal of emancipation emerges based on oscillation, plurality and ultimately on the erosion of the very principle of reality. Babel is valued; disorientation becomes a virtue. Such an experience of oscillation is an opportunity of a new way of being (finally perhaps) human. A defender of Marxism or neo-Marxism may say that such reflections may be traced in the critical theory of the Frankfurt School, but the fact speaks otherwise. As Lyotard says: "The challenge of (post) modern conditions is to seek new forms of critical theory that both avoid moralism and provide adequate protections for those - such as the poor - whose vulnerability to exploitation and domination is greatest."[30]

The chain of break as well as continuity remains at work. Crises occur and are resolved; new crises occur and are resolved in a new way. So new issues come up and the process of resolution also remains in operation. The link between pre-modern

27. *Ibid.*, p. 95.
28. *Ibid.*, p. 97.
29. *Ibid.*, p. 98.
30. *Ibid.*, p. 100.

Lyon's Conclusions on Post-Modernity

1. The concept of post-modernity is a valuable 'problematic' that alerts us to key questions concerning contemporary social changes.
2. The ways that debates over post-modernity are inextricably intertwined with those concerning post-modernism act as a vital reminder that the social and the cultural belong together.
3. The debate over post-modernity stimulates a reappraisal of modernity as a socio-cultural phenomenon.
4. The post-modern debate forces us to form judgements, both analytical and philosophical, on modernity itself.
5. The study of post-modernism in a broader frame reminds us that even post-modernity can be contextualised and relativised.

David Lyon: *Post-Modernity*, pp. 109-10.

and modern and then between modern and post-modern should never be lost sight of. This link has its place in a set of complex interaction, interpenetration and interdependence. As Lyon says: "My own sympathies lie in a complex interaction between the pre-modern, modern and post-modern."[31]

Critical Appreciation

Post-modernism is a debate about 'reality' in the present age of cybernetic revolution. By rejecting the message of Enlightenment, it holds that modernity has come to an end. But it is not clear whether post-modernity is an idea, a cultural experience, a social condition, or a form of critique in the minds of the intellectuals who have converted it into a 'figment of over-heated academic imagination.'[32] As a matter of fact, it is a trend or a perspective that may be criticised on these grounds:

1. It is a controversial and confusing trend on account of lacking the character of a coherent doctrine. Its advocates look like wandering in diverse directions. Their starting point is the same – rejection of the message of Enlightenment, but their arguments and conclusions are conflicting. As such, it looks like a bundle of contradictions. While Baudrillard advises 'to forget Foucault', Turner advises to 'forget Baudrillard'. Lyon is correct in remarking: "Modernity itself is a pretty fragile and incomplete invention, to which at one level the post-modern adds little more than illusion and irony."[33]
2. It is the philosophy of negation on account of having its foundations in the nihilism of Nietzsche. Its advocates know how to demolish an existing system without constructing a new one instead. Its anti-foundationalism cannot be appreciated as progressivism, rather it may be identified with conservatism that provides no perspective for evaluating an existing system in the light of new developments, or for constructing an alternative social order.[34]

31. *Ibid.*, p. 109.
32. *Ibid.*, p. 6.
33. *Ibid.*, pp. xi-xii.
34. Andrew Heywood, *Political Theory: An Introduction*, p. 7.

Some Critical Comments

The question of post-modernism is surely a question, for is there, after all, something called post-modernism? It is an historical characterisation, a certain kind of theoretical position, and what does it mean for a term that has described a certain aesthetic practice now to apply to social theory and to feminist social and political theory in particular? Who are these post-modernists? Is this the name one takes on for oneself, or is it more often a name that one is called if and when one offers a critique of the subject, a discursive analysis, or questions the integrity or coherence of totalising social descriptions.

—Judith Butler

"Contingent Foundations: Feminism and the Question of Post-Modernism" in J. Butler and J.W. Scott (eds): *Feminists Theorise the Political* (New York: Routledge, 1992), p. 3.

Post-modernism is a controversial and confusing term that was first used to describe experimental movements in western arts, architecture and cultural development in general. As a tool of social and political analysis, post-modernism highlights the shift away from societies structured by industrialisation and class solidarity to increasingly fragmented and pluralistic information societies (that is, to post-modernity) in which individuals are transformed from producers to consumers, and individualism replaces class, religion and ethnic loyalties.

—Andrew Heywood

Politics (Houndmills: Palgrave Foundations, 2005), p. 65.

Post-modernism is itself a term that is notoriously difficult to define, as it encompasses a wide range of theories and positions.

—Jane Freedman

Feminism (Delhi: Viva Books, 2002), p. 88.

3. It may be accused of relativism in that it holds that different modes of knowing can be equally valid. It rejects Marxism that claims to lay down inexorable laws of social development. It also finds fault with liberalism for being inadequate in understanding and resolving social conflicts. Thus, post-modernism invites attack from the side of both. Despite advocating the case of communicative action in the public sphere, Habermas charges Foucault with committing 'performative contradictions by surreptitously using the tools of reason'. Likewise, Lyotard, whose notion of post-modernity seems to be supported by another meta-narrative (a residual Marxism?); Kellner suggests that there can be no theory without one.[35]

The trend of post-modernism may be appreciated for touching new issues of social life ridden with tensions, tortures and injustice of many kinds, but it has not been able to offer remedial measures or alternatives for bringing about a better social and cultural order. Its fiery advocates look like "fiddling while the Rome burns."[36]

35. Douglas Kellner: "Post-Modernism as Social Theory: Some Challenges and Problems" in *Theory, Culture and Society*, Vol. 5, 1988, pp. 2-3.
36. Callinicos, *op. cit.*, p. 174.

26

Feminism

> A thought, or dim raw material of a thought, was fermenting all night, universally in the female head, and might explode. In squalid garret, on Monday morning, Maternity awakes, to hear children weeping for bread. Maternity must forth to the streets....In one of the guard-houses of the Quartier Saint-Eustache, a 'young Woman' seizes a drum-for how shall National Guards give fire on women, on a young woman? The young woman seizes the drum; sets forth beating it, 'uttering cries relative to the dearth of grains'.... All women gather and go: crowds storm all stairs, force out all women.
>
> **—Thomas Carlyle[1]**

Feminism is a form of 'identity politics' in a general sense and an examination of the concept of woman in an effort "to understand, reveal, or subvert the sexist practices."[2] The feminists react against the trend or tendency of treating women as 'exchange objects' and in very clear terms, ranging from soft and modest to harsh and immodest, they desire to eliminate the evil of gender inequality and injustice coming down since ancient times. "A common point for all feminist ideas is the belief that women are disadvantaged in comparison with men, and this advantage is not a natural and inevitable result of biological differences but something that can and should be challenged and changed. Unlike traditional political theories and ideologies, feminism provides a way of looking at the world that sees women's situations and inequalities between men and women as central political issues; as such, it provides a fundamental challenge to dominant assumptions about the scope and nature of politics."[3]

Nature and Ramifications of the Movement

Among the 'new social movements', feminism has an importance of its own. We may take note of the divergence of views of the leading feminists with regard to the nature and categories of this movement, but all "concern themselves with women's inferior position in society and with discrimination encountered by women because of their sex."[4] Furthermore, all feminists "call for changes in the social, economic, political and cultural order to reduce and eventually overcome the discrimination against women."[5] The protagonists of this movement reject the contention that "whereas

1. Thomas Carlyle: *The French Revolution* (London, 1900), Part I, p.238.
2. Carol Mastrangalo: "Feminism" in Christopher John Murray (ed.): *Encyclopaedia of Modern French Thought* (London: Fitzroy Dearborn, 2004), p. 217.
3. Valerie Bryson: "Feminism" in Roger Eatwell and Anthony Wright (eds.): *Contemporary Political Ideologies* (Delhi: Rawat Publications, 2003), p. 206.
4. Jane Freedman: *Feminism* (New Delhi: Viva Books, 2002), p. 1.
5. *Ibid.,*

women have been seen as closer to 'nature', men have been perceived as closer to 'culture', more suited to public role and political association. This is the reason that women have been relegated to a secondary status in society, often confined to the role in homes rather than able to accede to powerful public positions."[6]

Feminism as a movement has both empirical and normative aspects. It is a critique as well as an ideal and, surprisingly, it assumes the form of an ideology in its own right in view of its stress as a programme of action aimed at the eradication of all forms of injustice and oppression so that the women enjoy a life of security, equality and dignity. As Robert Leach says: "Like other ideologies, feminism involves a critique, an ideal and a programme. The critique contains an analysis of the discrimination and injustices suffered by women in existing society; the ideal is justice for women, generally but not exclusively interpreted to mean sexual equality. The practical programme has included action to achieve political and legal rights, equality in the economic sphere, the elimination of sexual discrimination in education, the workplace and the home, and protection against physical and sexual violence. All political ideologies contain implications for political action, but feminism is markedly action-oriented."[7]

The feminists charge that all social sciences have been designed by men so as to establish and exalt the place of 'man' to the exclusion of 'woman'. In theology God is celebrated as the Father or the Lord. Aristotle's view of natural inequality of mankind confines the life of woman to her household. Weber's theories do not take cognisance of the existence of women. Durkheim's figures for suicide rates do not exclude women, but they are incorporated without any distinct recognition of gender as a meaningful category in their search for variation, proof or validity of his theory of suicide. Surprisingly, Marx's conceptualisation of labour value and work insufficiently recognise women's contribution to the process of social life, to production and social re-production. So, in economic theories concepts and techniques of analysis are generally premised on the insignificance and, indeed, the absence of women. Comte's is only a romanticised exaltation of women's role in the historical process. Malinowski says that 'anthropology is the science of man embracing woman'. In short, in all theories of social sciences, it may be taken note of that man in the sense of 'male' overshadows man in the sense of 'human being' inasmuch as all theories are characterised by their forms of female invisibility – exclusion, pseudo-exclusion and alienation.

Examined from a juristic-cum-sociological standpoint, the same fact stands out. The feminists endorse the view that while inequality between man and woman in many matters has been abolished, the domestic factor has been logically left untouched. So C. Mackinnon complains: "In spite of legal equality injustice remains, because all important roles and positions in the society are gender-based. Every quality that distinguishes man from woman goes in favour of man. For example, men's psychology defines most sports, their needs define auto and health insurance coverage, their socially designed biographies define workplace expectations and successful career patterns, their perspectives and concerns define quality in scholarship, their

6. *Ibid.*, p. 10.
7. Robert Leach: *Political Ideology in Britain* (New York: Palgrave, 2003), p. 143.

Some Important Statements

The modern individual family is based on the open or disguised mass composed solely of individual families as its molecules. Today, in the great majority of cases, the man has to be the earner, the bread-winner of the family, at least among the propertied classes, and this gives him a dominating position which requires no special privileges. In the family he is the bourgeois; the wife represents the proletariat.

—Fredrick Engels

"Origin of the Family, Private Property and State" in Marx and Engels: *Selected Works* (Moscow: Progress Publishers, 1977), Vol. III, p. 247.

One is not born, but rather becomes, a woman. No biological, psychological or economic fate determines the figure that the human female presents in society; it is civilisation as a whole that produces this creature, intermediate between male and eunuch, which is described as feminine.

—Simone de Beauvior

The Second Sex (Penguin, Harmondsworth, 1972), p. 295.

Women constitute half the world's population, perform nearly two-thirds of the work hours, receive one-tenth of the world's income, and own less than one hundredth of the world's property.

—United Nations Report, 1980.

experiences and obsessions define merit, their objectification of life defines art, their military service defines citizenship, their role in wars and rulership defines history, their image defines God."[8]

As we shall see, the feminist movement is more than two centuries old and its appearance may be noticed in the Western countries like France, Britain and the United States. It covered other countries of the world as well in the twentieth century. However, it may be noted that the ramifications of this movement in the West somewhat differ from their counterparts in the East. In the East, the movement has put particular emphasis on crimes against women, surprisingly and shockingly, having their sanction in nasty social traditions such as female infanticide, bride-burning, dowry-demanding and a housewife's suicide owing to family tortures. In such countries, discrimination against women starts in the foetus, proceeds through systematic under-nourishment in childhood and thereafter, deprivation of education in adolescence, and it ends in all sorts of domestic violence done shockingly by the 'femi-nazists' and 'femi-terrorists'. Unfortunately, the degree of discrimination bears no relationship with economic prosperity of the people. Some crimes as those of sexual harassment, assault or molestation may be common to the West and the East. However, the common point in both may be noted in their gender struggle against gender-powerplay or gender politics going to the detriment of the basic interests of women.

We may also take note of this significant fact that the feminist cry for justice forms part of the modern, even post-modern, social and political theory. It takes the movement of women from their 'emancipation' to their 'empowerment'. It hinges

8. Mackinnon: *Feminism Unmodified: Discourses on Life and Law* (Cambridge, Mass.: Harvard University Press, 1987).

on the maxim that their liberation means empowerment and the means to a 'power for' not 'power over'. It signifies honour not domination and, as such, it transcends the phenomenon of leadership. It desires to bring about a new pattern of social order governed by a different set of values and ethos in which equality means no discrimination on the basis of sex in all spheres of public life. The focus is shifted from mere liberation of women to their social, cultural and political empowerment so as to blend their distinct identity with their distinct place in a civilised society. This is the only way to align the ideal of 'good life' with the reality of the 'goodness of life'.

The views of the liberal, socialist (Marxist) and radical feminists followed by those of the black and conservative feminists may not be alike on certain women-related issues, but their common concern with the following points may be noted:

1. Gender-based discrimination should be eliminated. Thus, women should have equality in all spheres which are open to men. It will dispense with their inferior or subordinate position in the society.
2. Women should be liberated from servitude, exploitation and injustice of all kinds. They should be able to lead a life of security and dignity.For this education is very important as it creates such a consciousness in them.
3. Male dominance in the family, in the community and in the state is responsible for the weak position of women. Hence, it should be terminated as far as possible.
4. Women alone can understand and appreciate their problems. They may represent and safeguard their interests themselves.
5. Crimes against women as those of molestation, rape, sexual assault or harassment, dowry-demanding, bride-burning, pornographic displays etc. can be checked and the grievances of women can be redressed if the women have power. So the women should have proper representation in the national legislature and in all important decision-making bodies.

A woman is a woman and so everywhere the problems of women are the same. Their solution can be sought in the recognition of their identity, in the security of their dignity, and in the elimination of all kinds of discrimination and torture. It is gender bias that "views woman as basically different from man - psychologically, physiologically and often intellectually."[9] This is the way to universalise the feminist movement. It constitutes the case of the 'essentialism' of this movement, but the cracks and contradictions in this movement negate it. It is particularly noticeable in the role of the black feminists who deprecate 'essentialism' as false universalism.

Origin and Development

The history of the feminist movement begins from 1791 when a French lady Olympe de Gouges brought out her monograph (A Declaration of the Rights of Woman and Citizen) in retaliation to the Declaration of the Rights of Man and Citizen adopted by the French National Assembly in 1789. The revolutionaries had raised the slogan of 'Liberty, Equality, Fraternity', but the women leaders raised a cry that the benefits

9. See K. Claire Fullenwider: *Feminism in American Politics: A Study of Ideological Influence* (New York: Praeger, 1980).

of equality could not be shared by the women. Olympe de Gouges argued that the women were naturally men's equals, that they were individuals just as men were, and that they should, therefore, have all the rights that formed the 'Declaration' adopted by the National Assembly. Women were excluded from active political citizenship. Her famous statement that 'woman has the right to mount to the scaffold; she ought equally have the right to mount to the tribune' was taken up as a rallying cry for the feminists after she herself had been guillotined.[10]

Mary Wollstonecraft brought out her monograph (*A Vindication of the Rights of Women*) in 1792 that was widely hailed as the first key feminist text.[11] In it she argued that women were as capable of reason as men and should be educated in the same way as men, they should be free to exercise their reason and choose their role in life. An equality of work between men and women implied an equality of rights, including political rights. She pleaded: "Let us consider women in the grand light of human creatures, who in common with men are placed on the earth to unfold their faculties."[12] No doubt, as de Reincourt says, her work "was the first clarion call for the forthcoming battle of the sexes, the first appearance and explicit statement of a problem that had not existed previously in Western consciousness since the distant days of Graeco-Roman antiquity."[13]

The United States could not remain immune from the impact of the feminist movement that broke out in France after the revolution and that gathered more weight after the promulgation of the Code Napoleon in 1797.[14] Its first brilliant instance should be traced in the Seneca Falls Convention which adopted the Declaration of the Sentiments and Resolutions in 1848. It claimed for women the principle of liberty and equality expounded in the American Declaration of Independence written by Thomas Jefferson and adopted on 4 July 1776. Denial of suffrage was one of the grouses of course, but other items included in this Declaration were the status of civil death and wardship for wives, the limited economic and educational opportunities

10. Freedman, *op. cit.*, p. 31. The Declaration adopted by the French National Assembly on 16 August, 1789 had 17 Articles. Its Art. 1 reads: "Men are born and always continue, free and equal in respect of their rights." At the same time appeared Tom Paine's *Rights of Man* which stressed that "all men are born equal and with equal natural rights."
11. In 1787 Wollstonecraft had published a monograph (*Thoughts on the Education of Daughters*) in which she stoutly defended that nature had made the two sexes equal and that education should strive for the development of that equality. Biological facts were unimportant and that education had made all the differences. She thus raved against Rousseau's statement according to which woman was subordinate to man.
12. Cited in Amaury de Reincourt: *Woman and Power in History* (NewDelhi: Sterling Publishers, 1997), p. 293.
13. *Ibid.*
14. It was the most advanced and comprehensive legal monument of that time, but quite regressive as far as women's rights were concerned. It enjoined wife's subordination to her husband (Art. 213); she was compelled to live in the domicile of his choice and follow him wherever he chose to reside. (Art. 214); she could not dispose of her personal estate without his permission. (Art. 217); in the case of divorce the husband kept the children (Art. 267); in the case of adultery the wife could be sentenced for an imprisonment upto two years (Art. 298).

for their sex, unfair divorce laws, exclusion of women from Church business, and the prevailing double moral standards.

The opening sentence of the Declaration was symptomatic of the new mythology that was springing up: "The history of mankind is the history of the repeated injuries and usurpations on the part of man towards woman having in direct object the establishment of an absolute tyranny over her."[15] This important event prepared a fertile ground for the development of feminist movement in the United States. Elizabeth Cady Stanton and Susan B. Anthony founded National Women Suffrage Association. The pioneers of this movement could win, bit by bit, from their grudging legislators all the legal and political rights in the form of the Nineteenth Constitution Amendment that granted suffrage to women in 1920.

The development of feminist movement in Britain has a glorious record. Here Mrs. Harriet Taylor, regarded as the 'first political feminist and Mary Wollstonecraft's intellectual heiress', played the leading role whose hands were strengthened by her new husband John Stuart Mill. Mill's *Essay on the Subjection of Women* (written in 1861 but published in 1869) came as the most reasoned document in favour of active citizenship of women arguing that it would enrich the contemporary civilisation. In the words of Fitzjames Stephen, this work "goes to prove that of the two sexes which between them constitute the human race, one has all the vices of a tyrant and the other, all the vices of a slave."[16] At one place in this work, Mill says: "Without seeing any reason to believe that women are, on the average, so strong physically, intellectually, or morally, as men, I cannot shut my eyes to the fact that many women are much better endowed in all these respects than many men, and I am at a loss to understand on what grounds of justice or public policy a career which is opened to the weakest and most foolish of the male sex should be forcibly closed to women of vigour and capacity."[17]

Around this time Lydia Becker made her name by founding the Manchester Women's Suffrage Committee and launched *Women Suffrage Journal.* Owing to her leading role, the matter of female suffrage was debated in the English Parliament, but nothing could be done in the face of its opposition not only by the leading politicians but by Queen Victoria herself. When Lady Amberley demanded suffrage for women, the Queen remaked that the "Lady ought to get a good whipping". And yet the movement for female suffrage went on and the saying grew that in England there were three sexes - male, female, and Lydia Becker. Labours were rewarded in 1918 when the women got the right to vote by a law made by the Parliament. It culminated in what was once demanded by the Troy Female Seminary (founded by Emma Willard) in 1821.

The cases of the three countries of the West provide ample material for the history of the feminist movement in the West. Much can be said about similar movement in other countries of the world like New Zealand where women got the right to vote in 1894 and in Australia where it occurred in 1902. The fact stands out that from 1791 to 1920 feminine self-consciousness had amply manifested itself.

15. Cited in A. de Reincourt, *op. cit.*, p. 314.
16. See C. L. Wayper: *Political Thought* (London: English Universities Press, 1964), p. 121.
17. Cited in A. de Reincourt, *op. cit.*, p. 323.

Two Waves of Feminism

First Wave: After the French revolution of 1789, the feminists fought for suffrage that would enable them to enter the legislative bodies and other popular institutions. Olympe de Gouges of France, Mary Wollstonecraft, Harriet Taylor and Lydia Becker of Britain, Elizabeth Cady Stanton and Susan B. Anthony of the United States etc. played a leading role. As a result of this, the women got the right to vote in New Zealand, Australia, Britain, America and other countries. The argument of the advocates of the movement was that women were equal as regards their emotional and intellectual capacities and requirements. After the Second World War, some zealous figures of this movement like Simone de Beauvoir of France and Kate Millett of the United States raised more demands, particularly the demolition of all systems and practices of patriarchal hegemony. The struggle assumed the name of women's liberation movement.

Second Wave: After 1960, the movement took a radicalised form. The leaders identified the liberation of women with their empowerment in all walks of social, cultural and political life. The revolutionary demands included elimination of violence of all sorts against women and also termination of the practices of enforced domestically. They insisted on the establishment of female solidarity and sisterhood. Mies and Shiva bracketed this movement with ecologism and thus it assumed the name of 'eco-feminism'. Some intellectuals like J.Flax, C. Weedon and Patricia Waugh went to the length of dismantling all anti-woman traditions and systems of belief and thus assigned to it the name of 'post-feminism'. The burden of their insistence was that the women should regard themselves not as victims of the prevailing social system, but as agents of social and political change. Notably, the movement covered the countries of the Third World as well.

It was designated as 'sexualisation of the objectified world' and now the writers on feminism regard it as the 'first wave', the 'second wave' having its start in the period after 1960. The feminist movement in the first phase was concerned (although not exclusively) with gaining equal rights for women with regard to franchise in particular, the second wave refers to the resurgence of feminist activity in the 1960s when protest centred around notions of equality, family, sexuality, work and empowerment. As we shall see, the movement took a jump from demand for equality to emancipation and then to empowerment in all spheres of public life - social, cultural and political.

Categorisation of Feminism – Liberal, Socialist (Marxist) and Radical

Feminist movements, as we shall see in due course, transcend national boundaries and touch sensitive issues like those of gender inequality, sexual harassment, exploitation and oppression of women and the like. The question is as to how the problems of women should be solved? For this, feminists have come forward with their demands which range from their enfranchisement to their empowerment. It is in the sphere of their action programme that their agitations are characterised as liberal, socialist (Marxist) and radical. There are sharp differences among the feminists on the nature and ramification of the issues and their proper solution, though all are unanimous on achieving the goal of gender equality and justice.

First of all, we take the case of 'liberal' feminism. It includes all those feminists who campaign for equal rights for women within the framework of a liberal political order. The leaders of this movement argue that the theoretical basis of the state is sound, but the rights and privileges it confers must be extended to women in the same manner as they are available to men. As a matter of fact, in its initial stages, the movement was launched by the leaders of liberal disposition like Olympe de Gouges in France and Mary Wollstonecraft, Harriet Taylor and Lydia Becker in England. They sought equality for both the sexes in matters of civil rights and economic opportunities and considered education as the best means to achieve their objective. Mill's work on the subjection of women was one of the landmarks of British feminist movement in which he provocatively claimed that 'no slave is a slave to the same length and in so full a sense of the word as a wife is'. He demanded women's admissibility to all the functions and occupations hitherto retained as a monopoly of the stronger sex.

The second wave of liberal feminism includes figures like Betty Friedan, Janet Radcliffe Richards and Susan Moller Okin. Friedan advocated the cause of women having a career in the public share without abandoning the traditional values of motherhood and family.[18] In her work *The Skeptical Feminist* (1982) Richards reaffirmed traditional liberal feminist support to reason, equality and social justice. Moller Okin in her work The *Subjection of Women* (1988) sought to extend the Rawlsian theory of justice to the family.[19] Since such demands raised by the earlier leaders of the movement (as equality before law and right to vote) were conceded by the liberal-democratic state of many countries of the West, the modern leaders now came forward with new demands for the empowerment of women in social, cultural and political spheres as the panacea for the elimination of all kinds of discrimination and injustice on the basis of sex. Success could be achieved to a certain extent. For example, in Britain, Equal Pay Act came into being in 1970 and in order to implement it Equal Opportunities Commission was set up.

Liberals are generally criticised by the radicals and the extremists of any hue for being soft and slow-movers. Hence, their achievements are not much appreciated. It is contended that neither rational persuasion nor legal compulsion may be adequate to secure justice for women. Their approach is taken as flawed and inappropriate for the purpose of bringing about radical changes in the desired direction. The distinction between civil society and state, as made by the liberals, is also criticised in the name of narrowing the scope of the movement. Thus, modern feminists "criticise liberals for concentrating on discrimination and injustice in the public sphere of law, politics, school and work, and neglecting women's role in the private world of home and family, to many feminists the very centre of women's exploitation and subordination."[20]

Then, 'socialist' (Marxist) feminism links gender inequality and women's oppression to the capitalist system of production and the division of labour consistent with this system. The division between the male and the female is merely a product of social power-relations with no basis in nature of human biology. Taking the Marxist line, Wittig argues: "There is no sex. There is but a sex that is the oppressor sex and that oppresses. It is oppression that creates sex and not the contrary."[21] Thus,

18. Robert Leach, *op. cit.*, pp. 145-46.
19. *Ibid.*, p. 146.
20. *Ibid.*, pp. 147-48.
21. Monique Wittig: "The Category of Sex" in D. Leonard and L. Adkins (eds.): *Sex in Question: French Materialist Feminism* (London: Taylor and Francis, 1996), p. 25.

women are nothing but an oppressed social class. The disappearance of oppression and, therefore, of the dominant and the dominated, will see the elimination of women and of men as distinct groups of human beings. In this world of nature, sex and classes will no longer exist, freedom for all human beings will be attained beyond the categories of sex and both the concept and the real existence of men and women will give way to the advent of individual subjects.[22]

Since Marxism studies politics in terms of class war, these feminists regard women as belonging to the exploited and oppressed class of the society. They refute the argument of an anarchist like Joseph Proudhon that women should not work outside their homes for the obvious reason that it prevents them from securing public employments and working there in a secure and dignified manner. A German socialist Clara Zetkin who had once argued that the women needed no special protection other than one given to the workers in general, changed her view and demanded protectionist legislation in favour of women.[23] The grouse of such feminists is that the women are either denied jobs in public concerns, or they are not paid adequately. Moreover, they suffer from sexual harassment in places of work. They work in very humiliating conditions which open the way for the occurrence of bad events like molestation, torture and rape.

Among other socialist feminists, we may refer to Alison Jaggar who integrates plight of women with the Marxian concept of 'alienation'.[24] Dalla Costa and James give a new twist to the Marxian theory of value by pointing out that the males working in an industry really work for their capitalists and it is possible only due to the fact that the women do much work at home which remains unpaid and unrecognised. The males have abundant time for work, but their work goes to the benefit of the capitalists. It is for this reason that the feminists desire to bring about significant changes in the household and the relationships between men and women in the family.[25]

Not only this, in the poor and backward countries of the world, the women of the lower castes or classes go out for work and the capitalists engage them at a very low payment. The result is that manpower is not fully utilised, while women labour is engaged at a very cheap rate. It certainly goes to the benefit of the capitalist class whether native or foreign. Mies and Shiva call it 'externalisation of costs'.[26] In their view, women in the industrialised world are exploited through 'housewifisation' —a historical process necessary for the growth of industry through which women were and are mobilised as the primary consumers of the products of this industry. These two processes of colonisation and housewifisation are closely and causally interlinked.[27]

22. *Ibid.*, p. 20.
23. S. Rowbotham: *Women in Movement: Feminism and Social Action* (New York: Routledge, 1992), p. 146.
24. Alison Jaggar: *Feminist Politics and Human Nature* (Totowa, N. J.: Rowman and Allanheld, 1983).
25. Dalla Costa and Selma James: *The Power of Women and the Subordination of the Community* (Boston: Falling Wall Press, 1972).
26. Maria Mies and Vandana Shiva: *Eco-feminism* (London: Zed Books, 1993), p. 98.
27. *Ibid.*, p. 110.

Firestone coins a term 'cybernetic communism'. In her view, women's liberation is at the very heart of a communist revolution and so cybernetic communism would be achieved only by the abolition of sex class which, in her view, goes deeper than the economic class of traditional Marxist analysis.[28]

The socialist and the Marxist feminists have played a leading role in women's liberation movement by raising the consciousness of women and stimulating their fight in this regard. The demands of the founding conference at Ruskin in 1970, in large part, reflected such an agenda by including such themes as equality in respect of education, opportunities and payments, 24-hour nurseries, and free contraception and abortion demand. But both the liberal and the radical feminists "contend that socialism and feminism do not invariably go together."[29] Sargent highlights it in his work *The Unhappy Marriage of Marxism and Feminism* (1981).[30] By picking up some threads from this work, Mackinnon argues that while Marxism focuses on work, feminism focuses on sexuality. That is, it lays more emphasis on class exploitation and less on gender discrimination as a result of which the issue of class becomes primary and the issue of gender secondary.[31]

In the end, we take up the case of 'radical' feminism. It may be taken as an extension of liberal feminism with its special stress on the destruction of male dominance in every sphere of social and cultural life whether it is family, or the community, or the state. Since patriarchal family system is the base of male dominance, it should go. Simone de Beauvoir argues that 'one is not born as a woman, but becomes so'. It implies that woman's inferior position in the society is a social construct and not a natural fact. The liberation of woman thus depends on freeing women from their social construct of the eternal feminine which has reduced them to a position of social and economic inferiority'.[32]

Similar line of thought may be seen in the work of Oakley who explains: "Many classics of feminist writing during this period are hard-hitting elaborations on the basic themes of social construction, society, psychology, sociology, literature, medicine, science, all construct woman differently, slipping cultural rhetoric under the heading of biological fact."[33] In the view of the radical feminists, the problem is neither an adequate legal or political framework as argued by the liberals, nor is it the capitalist system as explained by the socialist and the Marxist feminists but just male domination. Kate Millett gives the slogan: 'Personal is political'. All others cry out: "Everywhere man exploits woman. It is the sex war, not the class war, what is fundamental."[34] Its another characteristic may be seen in its style as its advocates freely use the language of revolution rather than reform; they challenge and set out to shock. The prevailing time is anger and outrage, and there is a clear difference

28. S. Firestone: *The Dialectic of Sex* (London: Women's Press, 1997), p. 12.
29. Leach, *op. cit.*, pp. 150.
30. *Ibid.*, p. 151.
31. C. Mackinnon: "Feminism, Marxism, Method and the State: An Agenda for Theory" in *Signs*, 1982, Vol. 7, No. 3, pp. 530-45.
32. Simone de Beauvoir: *The Second Sex* (1949), p. 13.
33. A. Oakley: *Sex, Gender and Society* (London: Temple Smith, 1972), p. 33.
34. Leach, *op. cit.*, p. 152.

in approach from that of the liberals. The enemy is male power, embodied in the universal institution of patriarchy.[35]

So the radical feminists widen the implications of the term 'dignity of woman'. They attack pornography which stimulates men to rape woman, or it excites them to do sexual violence againt women. In Britain the leaders of an association named Women Against Violence Against Women (WAVAW) attacked cinema halls and shops selling porn literature. Their argument is that 'pornography is theory, rape is its practice'. Such feminists desire to put woman in the form of a 'new man' that entails the positive exclusion of men. They revolutionise thinking on gender relations and thus convert their commitments into a distinctive political ideology. But the radical forms of this movement have done much harm to it by alienating the support of both the liberal and the socialist (Marxist) feminists. So Friedan claims that their shock tactic has made sexual politics a red herring. Radical feminists forget the unforgettable fact that male domination, though ridden with some evils, cannot be dispensed with totally. The truth of the old saying cannot be thoroughly dismissed that 'families need fathers'.[36]

Sub-categorisation: Black Feminism, Conservative Feminism, Eco-Feminism and Post-Feminism

Apart from the three categories of feminism, as discussed above, we may also have a brief look at its allied varieties which are regarded as its 'subsets' and cover the spheres of colour of the skin, attachment with the past, environmental protection, and post-structuralism. It should be taken as an extension of what we have said in the preceding section in view of the fact that here we come across a situation comparable with that of wheels within wheels, though connected with each other in some respect like concentric circles. A critic may say that such a categorisation followed by a sub-categorisation of the feminist movement does no justice to the complexity of this momentous subject in spite of the fact that, in the words of A. Nye, it is like 'a tangled and forbidden web'.[37] However, a broad view of this movement shows that it is ridden with multiplicity and so it would not be wrong to use the appellation of feminisms.

First of all, we take up the case of 'black feminism.' The champions of this movement not only fight for the rights of women and their liberation from social injustice like the feminists in general, but they also challenge the superiority of white

35. *Ibid.*

36. The radical feminists do injustice to Marx by placing him in an anti-feminist category like Rousseau and Proudhon. Marx says that the modern family "contains in germ not only slavery but it also contains in miniature all the contradictions which later extend throughout society and its state." One may argue that the treatment of Marx is casual, but Engels in his monograph (*The Origin of Family, Private Property and State*) says something for the purpose of the radical feminists. The idea does not seem to have struck Marx very forcibly, but Engels looks into the problem of women and develops a comprehensive theory on this subject. In the *Communist Manifesto* (1848), Marx and Engels say: "The bourgeois sees in his wife a mere instrument of production. He hears that instrument of production are to be exploited in common, and naturally he cannot imagine, but that the women will share the same fate." A. de Reincourt, *op. cit.*, pp. 365-66.

37. A. Nye: *Feminist Theory and the Philosophies of Man* (New York: Routledge, 1989), p. 1.

women and their competence as well as their right to speak for the black women. Its glimpse may be seen in the cry of the American negro women who criticised the role of white women, who even after the abolition of slavery by President Lincoln in 1863 and the sanction of civil rights to them by President Kennedy a century later, still maintained the old psyche in treating black women as 'fallen women, whores and prostitutes'.[38] The state of the devaluation of black womanhood persists and so the feminism of the white and black women cannot be theorised in the same manner.

It follows that the black feminists attack the superiority complex of their white counterparts and desire to fight for their demands after rejecting the claim of 'universal sisterhood' as made by the white women. Audre Lorde, a black lesbian feminist, says: "By and large within the women's movement today, white women focus upon the oppression as women and ignore differences of race, sexual preference, class and age. There is a pretence to a homogeneity of experience covered by the word 'sisterhood' that does not, in fact, exist.[39] Not only are white feminists accused of a false universalisation which hides women's different experiences and situations under the blanket concept of sisterhood, but perhaps even more importantly, they are charged with failure to acknowledge their part in the racist structure of society. Similarly, Herzel Carby argues: "Black feminists have been and are still demanding that the existence of racism must be acknowledged as a structuring feature of our relationships with white women. Both white feminist theory and practice have to recognise that white women stand in a power-relation as oppressors of black women. This compromises any feminist theory and practice founded on the notion of simple equality.[40]

In the light of what we have said above, it may be argued that black feminism has demonstrated the impossibility of untangling race and gender and shown that although dominant discourses may have tried to separate them, the two are inextricably intertwined. So Valerie Smith argues: "Within dominant discourse race and gender are treated as if they are mutually exclusive categories of experience. In contrast, black feminism presumes the 'inter-sectionality' of race and gender in the lives of black women, thereby rendering inapplicable to the lives of black women any single axis theory about racism or sex."[41]

The black feminists repudiate the contention that the movement for women's liberation was invented in the West, or it has been imposed by the Westerners on the people of the East. Feminist movements have had their own history in the countries of the East like China and India, though it must be admitted that they had an impact on their Western counterparts in the twentieth century particularly during the days of anti-colonial resistances. Kumari Jayawardena of Sri Lanka claims that the struggles for women's emancipation were an essential and integral part of the national movements.[42] Likewise, Uma Narayan of India says: "I am arguing that Third World feminism is not a mindless mimicking of Western agendas in one

38. Jane Freedman, *op. cit.*, p. 77.
39. Audre Lorde: *Sister Outside* (Trumansberg, N.Y.: Crossing Press, 1948), p. 116.
40. H.V. Carby: "White Women Listen: Black Feminism and the Boundaries of Sisterhood" in H.S. Mirza (ed.): *Black British Feminism* (London: Routledge, 1997), p. 46.
41. Valerie Smith: "Split Affinities: The Case of Inter-racial Rape" in M. Hirsch and E. Fox Keller (eds): *Conflicts in Feminism* (New York: Routledge, 1990), p. 272.
42. Jayawardena (ed.): *Feminism and Nationalism in the Third World* (London: Zed Press, 1986), p. 8.

clear and simple sense that, for instance, Indian feminism is clearly a response to issues specifically confronting many Indian women like dowry-related harassment, rape of women in police custody, poverty etc.[43] But Cynthia Enloe takes a different view and holds the system of colonialism for being the arch-culprit in this regard. She says: "Colonised women have served as sex objects for foreign men."[44]

One thing is, however, certain that black feminism rejects the case of 'essentialism' of this movement. Essentialism is, of course, a precondition of any kind of normative social and political theory or, indeed to any theory that intends to mobilise people in order to effect social change.[45] A woman is a woman whether white or black, rich or poor, Western or Eastern and the like and only on this basis feminist movement can be universalised. But to create conflicting layers within this movement, as done by the radical and socialist (Marxist) feminists, is to contradict the feature of its essentialism. The black feminists militate against white feminists who, in their view, are not concerned with the similar oppression of all women. If the case of all women is the same, there can be no essential differences between them, but as the white and the black feminists have divergent views, the factor of 'difference' supervenes to negate the feature of similarity. For instance, in Britain black and Asian women have pointed out their distinctive problems and injustices they suffer, leading to claims that the women's liberation movement as a whole is irrelevant to the needs and demands of most black women.[46]

Now we take up the case of conservative or new right feminism. Feminist movement all over the world has been both progressive and reactionary, both leftist and rightist. Mary Wollstonecraft mixed herself with French revolutionaries and yet she married William Godwin, a British anarchist and an anti-feminist. Many nineteenth century women feminists of America were closely associated with the anti-slavery movement. The British Tories always deprecated the moves of the liberal feminists and Margaret Thatcher could agree to assign some subordinate places to women in her Conservative Party. And yet the English feminists appreciate the new right approach of economic liberalisation as it would open avenues of employment for women in the labour market, particularly in the new meritocratic competition for career advancement. As a result of the market-friendly attitude of the state, "the economic position of the women in general has been transformed; their purchasing power in the economy is increasingly evident not only in the advertising of traditional female products but in the promotion of cars, banks and insurance policies."[47]

The new right feminists deplore disintegration of traditional family life and

43. Uma Narayan: *Dislocating Cultures: Identities, Traditions and Third World Feminisms* (New York: Routledge, 1997), p. 13.

44. C. Enloe: *Bananas, Beaches and Bases: Making Feminist Sense of International Politics* (Berkeley, CA: University of California Press, 1990), p. 44.

45. This type of essentialism is necessary for social mobilisation and can be a strategic tool to create group identity. And for those who find themselves in dominated or marginalised positions in society, the adoption of fixed or 'essentialised' identities can and does serve as an important strategic tool in their struggle against oppressions". See D. Fuss: *Essentially Speaking Feminism, Nature and Difference* (London: Routledge, 1989).

46. Leach, *op. cit.*, p. 156.

47. *Ibid.*, p. 159.

condemn recourse to easy divorce or sexual permissiveness. Family life as coming down from the ages is really a source of comfort, support and fulfilment for women and, as such, family values must be endorsed. Their slogan is 'families need fathers'. At the same time, they join hands with radical feminists in attacking pornography that stimulates activities of molestation and rape of women. A critic may, however, say that neo-conservative feminism dwindles between the poles of liberal and radical feminisms and stands in the danger of falling between the two stools. Their affirmations on certain points look problematic. So Nietzsche Walter strenuously argues that the feminists "can be conservative" and concedes that "individual women, who are both conservative and feminist, feel isolated and misrepresented by a culture that denies the compatibility of the two creeds."[48]

Some feminists like M. Mies and Vandana Shiva have integrated the issue of environmental pollution with the case of women suffering from social injustice. In their view, ecology is specifically feminist issue. Nature and women are the procreators and sustainers of human beings. Natural forces should be regarded as feminist in view of the fact that they have powers of fertility and birth. If woman gives birth to a child, nature sustains and helps in his healthy development. Exploitation of women and ecological destruction are thus twins evils; woman's knowledge is vital to the maintenance of biodiversity. The feminists argue that 'return to nature' is the only panacea for the ills created by gender discrimination and ecological destruction. "If the world's eco-system and biodiversity are to be conserved, it is, therefore, vital to start listening to women and taking their knowledge seriously.[49] As Mary Mellor points out: "The case made by both eco-centrists and eco-feminists is that the Western model of modernity based on this 'human' is achieved at the expense of both women and nature."[50]

If so, it is clear that women are prominently involved in the Green movement for the simple reason that there is a clear link between their feminist values and their Green commitments. "There is a strong female presence likewise in the associated animal rights and vegetarian movements. It may be that experience of pregnancy, giving birth and child nurture do give women a closer sense of kinship with the natural and animal world. Concern for the health of their children entails perhaps a greater awareness of the possible dangers in the environment and in the food chain. Women's nurturing role also gives them a greater felt stake in the future."[51]

Finally, we take up the case of 'post-feminism'. It is said that the feminist movement is ridden with certain conflicts and contradictions on account of the divergence of views and emphases of the liberal, socialist (Marxist), radical and conservative or new right feminists. At the same time, it is argued by some recent writers that this dilemma may be resolved if we study the case of feminism in the light of post-structuralism or post-modernism. That is, the tenets of the feminist

48. *Ibid.*, p. 160.
49. M. Mies and Vandana Shiva: *Eco-feminism* (London: Zed Books, 1993), p. 167. These two writers regretfully note that the "invisibility of women's work and knowledge arises from the gender bias which has a blind spot for realistic assessment of women's contribution." *Ibid.*
50. Cited in Freedman, *op. cit.*, p. 57.
51. Leach, *op. cit.*, p. 157.

Heywood's Taxonomic Analysis of Feminism

Liberal Feminism	**Radical Feminism**
1. female emancipation	1. women's liberation
2. gender inequality	2. attack on patriarchy
3. individualism	3. universal sisterhood
4. conventional politics	4. personal is political
5. public/private divide	5. transform private realm
6. access to public realm	6. gender equality
7. equal rights/opportunities	7. sexual politics
8. reform/gradualism	8. revolutionary change
9. political activism	9. consciousness raising

Egalitarian Feminism	**Difference Feminism**
1. androgyny	1. essentialism
2. personhood	2. sisterhood
3. human rights	3. women's rights
4. gender equality	4. sexual liberation
5. reduction of difference	5. celebrate difference
6. sex/gender divide	6. sex equals gender
7. transcend biology	7. embrace biology
8. pro-human	8. pro-woman
9. men are redeemable	9. men are the problems
10. engagement with men	10. feminist separation

Andrew Heywood: *Political Ideologies: An Introduction* (New York: Palgrave Macmillan, 2005), pp. 251 and 261.

movement should be reconciled with the features of post-modernism and that would lead to the emergence of post-feminism. The post-structuralists segregate what cannot be otherwise segregated; they negate what is universally or generally accepted. They disagree with the finality of any accepted creed or doctrine and so they may find out 'differences' within a woman.[52] They reject the notion of a fixed female identity and, in this way, believe that they overcome the problems of 'essentialism' which other feminists have had to face. For some feminists this move away from fixed knowable identities is a way forward that can overcome the seemingly never-ending debate over equality and difference. Jane Flax argues that feminist theory is necessarily post-modern in that it challenges the natural, fixed and universal definition of gender relations.[53]

Though the number of such feminists is very small, their contention is quite significant. To Patricia Waugh, feminism reacts against ideas emanating from the Enlightenment.[54] The notion of a universal rational subject is inherently masculine. But the difficulty with post-structuralism or post-modernism is that while they negate

52. J. Evans: *Feminist Theory Today* (London: Sage Pub., 1995).
53. J. Flax: "Post-Modernism and Gender in Feminist Theory" in L. Nicholson (ed.): *Feminism/Post-modernism* (New York: Routledge, 1990).
54. Patricia Waugh: "Post-Modernism and Feminism" in S. Jackson and J. Jones (eds): *Contemporary Feminist Theories* (New York: New York University Press, 1998), p. 177.

Varieties of Feminism

1. ***Liberal Feminism:*** Struggle for suffrage and for equality of rights with men in all spheres so as to terminate discrimination and injustice on the basis of gender; cry for 'universal sisterhood'.
2. ***Radical Feminism:*** Struggle for complete equality and justice on the basis of sex by dismantling all spheres of male dominance like patriarchal family system; no distinction between personal (private) and public (political) spheres in the life of women – 'personal is political'; demand for stringent laws to prevent crimes against women.
3. ***Socialist (Marxist) Feminism:*** Identification of 'sex war' with 'class war'; denunciation of the capitalist system for exploitation, oppression and alienation of women that would go only in a socialist system.
4. ***Conservative (New Right) Feminism:*** Stress on the retention of traditional values; appreciation of family life as a source of comfort, support and fulfilment for both men and women; 'all families need fathers'; demand for ban on pornography and making of laws or promulgation of orders to protect the person and the dignity of women.
5. ***Black Feminism:*** Attack on colonialism as well as on the superiority of the white women who look at the black women with contempt; rejection of the motto of 'universal sisterhood' based on the feature of 'essentialism'; demand for the prevention of crimes against women such as rape, molestation, sexual harassment, dowry-demanding, bride-burning etc.
6. ***Eco-Feminism:*** Integration of feminism with environmental protection or ecologism; struggle for saving both nature and woman from exploitation and damage, for both are essential for the preservation of human life and bio-diversity.

what is generally accepted, they do not give another meaning that would have finality in its implications. So Chris Weedon, a post-structuralist feminist, committed as it is to the principle of difference and deferral, never fixes meaning once and for all.[55] Niral Yuval-Davis coins the term 'transversal politics' in which perceived unity and homogeneity are replaced by dialogues which give recognition to the specific functionings of those who participate in them as well as to the unfinished knowledge that each such situated positioning can offer.[56]

The success of the feminist movement has certainly raised the status of woman in society and converted her into a 'new man' irrespective of the fact that much still remains to be achieved. The 'new feminism', as it may also be called, desires to see women as self-reliant in securing their aims with this impression in their minds that all men are irredeemably bad as sloganised by the Leeds Revolutionary Group in Britain. More and more success in this direction would certainly transform the state of affairs and create a wishful condition in which men, rather than women, have the problem. Some feminists have seen rationalisation as 'male logic', antipathetic to feminine feeling and intuition. Post-modernist literary criticism has provided feminists with a powerful conceptual framework to reveal the gender-bias in the use

55. C. Weedon: *Feminist Practice and Post-Structuralist Theory* (Oxford: Blackwell, 1987), p. 99.
56. N. Yuval-Davis and F. Anthias: *Women-Nation State* (London: Macmillan, 1989), p. 131.

of language, to uncover new messages in and behind texts, and to attack traditional male-oriented canons of literary excellence.[57] Liberal feminism thus stands defeated whose champions ever insist that women's liberation would benefit men too.

Women Empowerment

Feminism is one of the highly political movements in terms of its attempt to effect social change for the sake of elimination of all kinds of injustice done to the women in the name of gender discrimination. The contention of the feminists is that their desired goals cannot be achieved until the women share power. After much struggle, the feminists could get the right to vote, but their repeated grouse is that they are under-represented in the legislative chambers and almost unrepresented in crucial decision-making bodies. So Brown argues: "More than any other kind of human activity, politics has historically been an explicitly human activity."[58] Carole Pateman attacks patriarchal system that is male-dominated and links it to the denial of citizenship for women.[59] Patriarchy is then seen as a private familial problem that can be overcome if public laws and policies treat women as if they are explicitly the same as men. Like Olympe de Gouges and Mary Wollstonecraft, Fraisse complains that although women took part in the bloody French revolution, the post-revolutionary regime excluded them from full political citizenship. She refuted Rousseau's argument that 'although women were precious half of the Republic, they made the customs while men made the laws'. Thus, she cried out that personal problems could be solved only through political means and political action.[60]

The feminists reject the notion coming down from the centuries that the personal and public affairs of life can be distinguished in the case of women. In 1792 Wollstonecraft argued: "I really think that the women ought to have representations, instead of being arbitrarily governed without having any direct share allowed to them and the deliberations of the government."[61] Kate Millett asserts that the issue of relationship between the two sexes should be studied in the light of politics what she calls 'informal' or 'institutional' politics.[62] Power-relations operate within primary and social relations as well as within more impersonal secondary social relations of the civil and political domain. In forceful words, Stacey and Price hold: "If women wish to make changes in the society they live in, they must seek and achieve power positions."[63]

The crux of all such arguments is that women must have a say in all social, cultural and political spheres like men, as only then the face of this informal or institutional politics can be changed. Phillips complains that it is patently and grotesquely unfair for men to monopolise representation.[64] If Rousseau argues that the will of a person cannot be represented by another person, so Phillips contends

57. Leach, *op. cit.*, p. 161.
58. W. Brown: *Manhood and Politics* (Totowa, N. J.: Rowman and Littlefield, 1988), p. 4.
59. Carole Pateman: *The Sexual Contract* (Cambridge: Polity Press, 1988), p. 17.
60. Cited in Freedman, *op. cit.*, p. 27.
61. *Ibid.*, p. 28.
62. Kate Millett: *Sexual Politics* (New York: Doubleday, 1970), p. 34.
63. M. Stacey and M. Price: *Women, Power and Politics* (London: Tavistock, 1931), 189.
64. A. Phillips: *Feminism and Politics* (London: Oxford University Press, 1998), p. 229.

that the interests of the women can be represented only by them. If Mill says that the participation of women in politics would help in the creation of a civilised political culture, Hedlund argues that the women could bring their experience of informal politics into the formal political arena and thus create a more open political culture.[65] Likewise, Anna Jonasdottir maintains: "Women must be visible politically as men, and be empowered to act in that capacity, because there is the continual possibility (not necessity) that they may have needs and attitudes on vital issues which differ from those of men."[66]

Politics is an activity centred on the theme of power. It is power and struggle for its sake. Hence, feminist movement has a patently political character. Since it aims at the presence of women in the legislative chambers and also in the decision-making bodies, it is also known as the 'politics of presence'. The empowerment of women would replace the 'politics of ideas' or mere debates on the social status or issues of women. A male-dominated family is patriarchal; a male-dominated state constitutes the case of public patriarchy. Even in the welfare state, hierarchies of power are male-dominated. "So women have moved out of their position of private dependency as men in the house into a postion of public dependency on the male-controlled state."[67]

Empowerment is envisaged "as an aid to help women to achieve equality with men, or at least to reduce gender gap considerably."[68] It would enable women to perform certain roles which they cannot perform without it. It is indicative of a shift in perspective or emphasis from welfare development to one of development of authoritative decision-making skills. "Empowerment strategies are varied and refer to those ones which enable women to realise their full potential. They consist of greater access to knowledge and resources, greater autonomy in decision-making, greater ability to plan their lives, greater control over the circumstances that influence their lives and, finally, factors which would free them from the shackles of customs, beliefs and practices."[69] New social movements are, by and large, of a defensive character, but they become of a marginally offensive character as well. As is the case with ecological and human rights movements, so is the case with the women's movements which "seek to improve women's position in the society itself, albeit at a time when the economic crisis is undermining women's economic opportunities."[70]

Critical Appreciation

The contributions of women in various walks of life cannot be lost sight of. A long list of eminent figures may be prepared to show the great role played by the women in the making of civilisation and culture of the people. A historian may refer to the

65. Cited in Freedman, *op. cit.*, p. 38.
66. K.B. Jones and A.G. Jonasdottir (eds): *The Political Interest of Gender* (London: Sage Pub., 1988), p. 53.
67. Freedman, *op. cit.*, p. 44.
68. P.K.B. Nayar: "Empowerment of Women: Its Overall Perspectives" in K. Shanthi (ed.): *Empowerment of Women* (New Delhi: Anmol Publications, 1998), p. 24.
69. Rajkumari Chandrasekharan: "Education Empowers Women", *ibid.*, , p. 77.
70. A.G. Frank and Marta Fuentes: "Nine Theses on Social Movements" in Ghanshyam Shah (ed.): *Social Movements and the State: Readings in Indian Government and Politics* 4 (Delhi: Sage Publications, 2002), p. 41.

names of great queens like Elizabeth I, Victoria and Elizabeth II of England, Christina of Sweden, Maria Theresa of Austria, and Catherine the Great of Russia. He may also refer to the names of great heads of governments like Golda Meir of Israel, Srimavo Bandarnaike of Sri Lanka, Indira Gandhi of India, Margaret Thatcher of Britain, Angela Merkel of Germany, Benazir Bhutto of Pakistan, Sheikh Hasina and Begum Khaleda of Bangladesh and I. Shinwatra of Thailand. He may also refer to the names of the Presidents or the heads of the states like Chandrika Kumaratunga of Sri Lanka, Meghawati Sukarnoputri of Indonesia, Pratibha Patil of India and E. J. Sirleaf of Liberia: A political theorist may admire the ideas of Rosa Luxemburg of Germany, Miss M.P. Follet of America and Hannah Arendt of England.

If the French revolution witnessed the assassination of men like King Louis XVI, Robespierre, Mirabeau, Danton and Mara, it also witnessed the same fate of women like Queen Mary Antoinette, Madame du Barry, Olympe de Gouges and Lucile Desmoulins. A. de Reincourt says: "Yet women did acquire equal respects in one respect-the right to have their heads chopped off like those of their male counterparts."[71] Joan of Arc of France and Laxmibai of India paid with their life for the sake of love for their country. Martin Luther shut the doors of Protestant church for women, but Mary Paker Eddy founded a church for her followers and thereby she solved the problem of women's place in the Christian religion. She undid Luther and Calvin and got the nickname of 'God-like man' and 'God-like women', 'God anointed'. Germaine de Stail played a crucial part in the downfall of Napoleon Bonaparte and commented that the 'genius has no sex'. Like Socrates, Rosa Luxemburg paid the price with her life for the freedom of thought and expression. Many more brilliant names may be added to this catalogue to demonstrate the great services and sacrifices of women in the construction and reconstruction of human civilisation and culture. Memorable are the words of Rabindranath Tagore: "Deprived of *Shakti,* the creative process in society languishes and man, losing his vitality, becomes mechanical."

And yet the feminist movement may be said to suffer from certain weaknesses which may be enumerated as under:

1. All categories of the feminists have sharp differences among themselves on many crucial issues. While the liberals feel satisfied if the women are enfranchised and they have their representation in the national legislature and in some important decision-making bodies, the socialists (Marxists) identify 'sex war' with 'class war' and so clamour for their abolition, while the radicals want to destroy male-dominance in every sphere. Family cannot be identified with a class and to think in terms of its abolition defies commonsense. Patriarchy is an age-old institution that cannot be terminated as desired by the radical feminists.
2. The feminists forget that, biologically or naturally, the women are weak and so they should stop at a point in demanding equality with men. The rash statement of Nietzsche should not be mercilessly discarded, rather it should be taken with a cool mind that "men are trained for war, and women for the procreation of the warriors." They should realise that hard and hazardous tasks are not meant for women. They may operate a computer, but they cannot defend the Siachen

71. A. de. Reincourt, *op. cit.,* p. 360.

glacier. Only men can provide security to women. The feminists forget that in the name of equality, they want much more than that. They want to share all rights which are available to men and, at the same time, they claim for themselves all other privileges available to them since the dawn of civilisation. They would like to have administrative and police offices, but would shirk in leaving their homes after sunset. Chantal Mouffe calls it 'Wollstonecraft's dilemma'. As A. de Reincourt says: "In a nutshell, many contemporary women would like to have their cake and eat it too—share with the men the status, power and privileges that they apparently enjoy in social and professional life, while keeping all the special privileges that were allotted to women as compensation for having been virtually idled by the machine. This, of course, will never come to pass."[72]

3. The feminists should also keep in their mind the psychological fact that by nature women harbour feelings of grudge towards other women. This point may well be taken note of in the movement of the black feminists who have their grievances against white women. Schopenhauer is not wrong in his assessment: "The natural feeling between men is mere indifference, but between women it is actual enemity.... Even when they meet women in the street, women look at one another like Guelphs and Ghibbelines."[73] It is also a fact that the women lack in some other respects. For instance, their contribution is negligible in the field of scientific research. Marie Curie, who could win a Nobel prize by virtue of being a partner of her husband, said that 'women of genius are rare'. Such an impression was in the mind of Queen Victoria when she deprecated the movement for female franchise.[74]
4. The feminists take a wrong view of the patterns of social and political life of human beings. They ignore the reality of religious and cultural norms which determine the composition and operation of family life. The two sexes constitute a family, the family grows into a community for whose security and protection state ushers in. Division of labour becomes a natural development. Men and women put together manage all private and public spheres in their respective domains. The evil of male-dominance cannot be ignored, but to do away with it in entirety would be like jumping from a fry pan into the fire. The relationship between the two sexes should be of a positive not negative, or a cooperative not conflicting nature. It should be inspired by the bonds of reciprocity, tolerance, communion, concord and harmony between the two sexes.
5. Above all, the feminists, like the idealists and the anarchists, go to the extent of rambling in utopia. They look for a social and political order in which women have full equality with men and that they enjoy power after dismantling all bastions of male dominance. As Rousseau's natural born man would see the end of his chains in a community in which each citizen is a ruler and the ruled, or in Gandhi's Ram Raj there 'would be no distinction between a prince and a

72. *Ibid.*, p. 415.
73. Cited in A.de Reincourt, *op. cit.*, p. 316.
74. "The Queen is most anxious to enlist everyone who can speak or write or join in checking that mad, wicked folly of 'Women's Rights' with all its attendant horrors, on which her poor feble sex is bent, forgetting every sense of womanly feeling and propriety. Lady Anderlay ought to get a *good whipping*." *Ibid.*, p. 315.

pauper and that justice would be done even to the dog', so the feminists have a dream of their own. For every action-oriented programme sky is the limit, but the feminists in their fit of zeal desire to go beyond it.

Since nature has made the woman weak and also 'incomplete', the feminists should struggle for the achievement of equality for the women with a sense of caution. The Hindi word 'stree' (woman) is such in which no letter is full. It is a collection of half letters which signifies that woman is just half and her fullness comes with her association with man. The English word 'femina' comes from Fe and Minus. Thus, the etymology of this word indicates that the element of 'minus' very much exists in the word 'femina' itself. What is needed, however, is that the liberation of women should not be done at the cost of dehumanisation of the existing society. In 1872 the Gordian brothers, the anarchists, established an association in Spain to realise the goal of 'gynatropism' which implied emancipation and humanisation of women.[75]

75. *Ibid*, p. 336.

27

State in Different Perspectives

> For the laws of nature, (such) as justice, equity, modesty, mercy... without the terror of some power, to cause them to be observed, are contrary to our natural passions.... And covenants without the sword are but words, and of no strength to secure a man at all.
>
> —**Thomas Hobbes**[1]

A significant development in the sphere of contemporary social and political theory should be seen in the 'return' to the conception of the 'state' in which social sciences had lost their interest in the latter half of the last century due to the dominance of the behavioural trend launched by the leading lights of the Chicago School. David Easton committed the wrong by replacing the 'state' with 'political system' in 1953;[2] G.A. Almond happily recognised the call for 'return to the state' in 1988.[3] The Committee on States and Social Structure set up by the American Social Science Research Council in 1985 produced its *magnum opus* with the title of *Bringing the State Back In*[4], loaded with state-centric perspective that sharpened the course of its rejection by the society-centric focus. The debate on the meaning and nature of the state involving the contributions of the liberals, the Marxists, the Neo-Marxists and now the Neo-Liberals may go on, but the fact stands out that with the 'return to the state' in the 1980s, "happily, we are now better placed."[5]

Meaning, Nature and End of State

Ever since Bluntschli defined political science in 1895 as the 'theory of state'[6] and Garner regarded state as the point 'wherefrom the study of politics starts and where it ends',[7] the term 'state' has been the central theme of political theory irrespective of the fact that keeping its numerous implications in his view in 1927, John Dewey compared them with 'a score of intellectual ghosts rising to obscure our vision',[8] and David Easton opined in 1981 that any attempt in the direction of precisely

1. Hobbes: *Leviathan,* Chapter 14.
2. David Easton: *Political System : An Enquiry into the State of Political Science* (New York: Alfred A. Knopf, 1953).
3. G.A. Almond: "The Return to the State" in *American Political Science Review,* Vol. 82, No. 3, 1988.
4. P. Evans, D. Reuschemeyer and T. Skocpol: *Bringing the State Back In* (Cambridge: Cambridge University Press, 1985).
5. J.A. Hall and G.J.Ikenberry: *The State* (Delhi: World View/Bookland, 1997), p. 1.
6. J.K. Bluntschli: *The Theory of the State* (English translation published by the Oxford University Press.)
7. J.W. Garner: *Political Science and Government* (Calcutta: World Press, 1952), p. 9.
8. John Dewey: *The Public and Its Problems* (London: George Allen and Unwin, 1927), p. 89.

defining it would lead to 'vapid debates and conceptual morass'.[9] This diversity is stupendous if we prepare a catalogue of several terms used by the social and political theorists in this regard. To Plato and Aristotle, it is *polis* (city-state), but to Roman thinkers like Cicero and Seneca, it is *respublica* (republic). With the advent of Christianity, it becomes *respublica Christiana* (Christian republic) to the Church fathers like St. Augustine and St. Ambrose, but to Machiavelli it is *stato* or *stati* from which the English word 'state' originates. To Bodin it is republique (republic), but to Hobbes it is *commonwealth* embracing society, state and government. To carry the point further, it is *community* to Locke with an atomistic character, to Rousseau it is *body politik* (community) having an organic form. Among the leading theorists of the twentieth century, we may refer to those who like to retain it in other forms that may be *guild cooperative commonwealth* to G.D. H. Cole,[10] or *dominant protective agency* to Robert Nozick.[11] Regardless of such perplexing as well as interesting descriptions, the fact remains that the state "stands out at the centre of any theory of politics."[12]

Such a bewildering variety finds its essential component in the diversity of views about the precise meaning, nature and end of the state. To the Greeks like Plato and Aristotle it is a natural and thus a moral organisation like a 'partnership in virtue', but to the social contractualists like Hobbes and Locke it is an artificial contrivance designed by the self-seeking individuals for the protection of their 'natural rights'. To the individualists or classical liberals like J.S. Mill and Herbert Spencer it is a 'necessary evil' having minimum possible sphere of activity, it is an instrument of public welfare to the positive or revisionist liberals like Hobhouse and Laski that may expand its area of intervention in the general interest. To the anarchists like Proudhon and Bakunin as well as to the scientific socialists like Marx and Engels, it is an instrument of class exploitation and oppression and, as such, it has no place in the future or ideal society. But it is an ethical institution to the idealists like Rousseau and Hegel who idealise and take it to mystical heights. Keeping it all in his view, an English writer says: "The state - an apparatus of government - appears to be everywhere; regulating the conditions of our lives from birth registration to death certification. Yet the nature of the state is hard to grasp. This may seem peculiar to something so pervasive in public and private life, but it is precisely this pervasiveness which makes it difficult to understand. There is nothing more central to political and social theory than the nature of the state, and nothing more contested."[13]

State, being the first condition of a civilised life, terminates the condition of 'statelessness' (lawlessness or anarchy) and instead establishes what is now empirically called 'stateness', a term coined by J.P. Nettle. Viewed historically, we may think of an age when there was no state; conceived philosophically, as by the Marxists and the Anarchists, in future there may be an age without state. However, after discarding both these extremes, we may safely assert that the state being a product

9. David Easton: "The Political System Besieged by the State" in *Political Theory*, No. 3, 1981, pp. 303-25.
10. G.D.H. Cole: *Guild Socialism Restated* (London: George Allen and Unwin, 1920).
11. Robert Nozick: *Anarchy, State and Utopia* (Oxford: Basil Blackwell, 1974).
12. John Hoffmann: *State, Power and Democracy* (Sussex: Wheatsheaf, 1988).
13. David Held: *Political Theory and the Modern State: Essays on State, Power and Democracy* (Cambridge: Polity Press, 1984), p. 11.

of human association is the protector of the organised and peaceful life of the people. It is an association of the people who live in a particular territory of the world, but in respect of its power it is unique. It has 'legitimate power of coercion' as Weber says,[14] which no other social association has, or may have, though its relation to the society has been viewed differently by the social and political theorists as a result of which we come across state-centric and society-centric perspectives.

In a traditional sense, state is an association of people having four essential elements – population, territory, government or political organisation, and sovereignty. While the first two are described as its 'physical' or 'material' elements, the last two are its 'spiritual' or 'metaphysical' elements. So Garner defines it as "a community of persons, more or less numerous, permanently occupying a definite portion of territory, independent or nearly so of external control, and possessing an organised government to which the great body of inhabitants render habitual obedience."[15] But new writers have thrown much light on its capacity to exercise 'coercive' authority so as to ensure obedience of its members to its commands. For instance, Roberts defines it in terms of "the presence of a supreme authority, ruling over a defined territory, who is recognised as having power to make decisions in matters of government (and) is able to enforce such decisions and generally maintain order within the state. Thus, the capacity to exercise coercive authority is an essential ingredient: the ultimate test of a ruler's authority is whether he possesses the power of life and death over his subjects."[16]

If there is a lot of disagreement among some social and political theorists as to how the term 'state' should be defined, there is an equal lot of agreement among others on this point. Taking it in their view, two English writers hold: "A composite definition would include three elements. First, the state is a set of institutions; these are manned by the state's own personnel. The state's most important institution is that of the means of violence and coercion. Second, these institutions are at the centre of a geographically bounded territory, usually referred to as a society. Critically, the state looks inwards to its national society and outwards for higher societies in which it must make its way; its behaviour in one area can often only be explained by its activities in the other. Third, the state monopolises rule-making within its territory. This tends towards the creation of a common political culture shared by all citizens."[17]

Historical Development: From Polis to the Nation-State

The story of the origin and development of the modern state has its place in the pages of history. Its earliest traces can be seen in the primitive communities where power in an organised form came into being. The Greeks called it *polis* having its existence in a small city and its power was in the hands of a small section of the rulers. It was a kind of monarchical system. Pericles became a great figure by

14. Max Weber: "Politics as Vocation" in H.H. Gerth and C.W.Mills (ed.s); *From Max Weber* (New York: Oxford University Press, 1972), p. 78.
15. Garner, *op. cit.*, p. 52.
16. K. Roberts: *Order and Dispute* (Harmondsworth: Pelican, 1979), p. 32.
17. Hall and Ikenberry, *op. cit.*, pp. 1-2.

establishing direct democracy in Athens that offered a counterweight to the military rule of the neighbouring city-state of Sparta as well as to other smaller city-states ruled by the kings. But Alexander, the ruler of the city-state of Macedonia, finished the city-state system by establishing the Greek empire that after his death was replaced by the empire of the Romans who introduced the legal system. Things changed after the fall of this great empire in the fifth century A.D. The destruction of the Roman empire at the hands of the Teutonic tribes entailed a new system that came to be known as feudalism marking decentralisation of power and existence of a hierarchical system of authority with serf at the base, then a petty lord, then nobles or big lords, then a king who came under an emperor after some time. Moreover, with the establishment of Christianity as the official religion, the highest place was assumed by the Pope of Rome who managed to have both the spiritual and the temporal powers (swords) in his hands.

Such a profound change brought about a new situation in which the meaning of the state changed and, more than that, with the supremacy of the Church, state came to be despised as a temporal institution requiring the touch of the Church for the sake of its legitimation. As Barker says: "The world empire of Alexander, succeeded by centuries of universal domination by Rome, made the world the one actual unit of politics; and the teaching of the Christian Church, which recognised one body of all the faithful, strengthened by a spiritual sanction the trend of secular affairs. Political philosophy became the philosophy of universal empire; in 1300 the *De Monarchia* of Dante showed this width of view. But, at the same time, the unit of political thought gained in extension, it lost its intensity of meaning. Membership of a universal empire in any case means but little; but membership of the secular organisation, however, great or small, could mean little indeed to minds imbued with Christianity, and counting things spiritual the only things of price. The State came to be despised. By its side there arose, overshadowing its dignity and claims, the spiritual organisation of the Church."[18]

The feudal state was constantly rent by internal tensions between adverse and overlapping centres or levels of power. The monarchy tried to distinguish itself as a separate authority. The lords, however, used their lands and local military power to check the trend towards the centralisation of royal power. The feudal monarch was, therefore, never 'sovereign', only a *suzerain*: a particularly limited type of secular authority.... The papacy's claim to be a unique and sovereign spiritual power provoked, on the other side, the claim by the monarchy to a supreme, independent, secular authority."[19]

The medieval feudal state saw its wreckage with the rise of the nation-state in the sixteenth century. It was a new form of state in which the monarch overthrew the hold of the Pope and managed to establish a strong order by tightening law and

18. E. Barker: *The Political Thought of Plato and Aristotle* (New York: Dover Publications, 1959), pp. 499-500.
19. Stuart Hall in Greggor McLellan, David Held and Stuart Hall: *The Idea of the Modern State* (Buckingham: Open University Press, 1993), pp. 6-7. Medieval towns were 'islands in the sea of feudalism' with a large and wealthy merchant class, skilled craftsmen, artisans and wage-earning labourers. The larger among them evolved an autonomous system of rule – like the Italian *commune* – based on an oath of loyalty in a 'community' of equal citizens. H.Pirenne: *Medieval Cities* (New Jersey: Princeton University Press, 1969).

order in his realm. He could suppress all rebellious forces sustaining themselves on the support of the petty lords or the bishops. "The all-powerful king expanded his kingdom and replaced his dependence on mercenary forces by his regular militia. This involved the strengthening of a unified territorial rule, the absorption of weaker and smaller territories into stronger and larger ones, the tightening of law and order and security throughout the kingdom; the application of a more 'unitary continuous, calculable and effective' rule with its power gathered under a single sovereign head."[20]

After the termination of the feudal state came the modern state that, in course of time, got the proud name of the 'nation-state'. It had to cope with the transformation of its governmental apparatus according to the demand of the enlightened people. It had its natural impact upon the character of the state itself. If the monarchs managed to be the sovereigns after overthrowing the yoke of the Pope, they had to face the challenge of their opponents in their own country who stood up against royal despotism that led to the execution of King Charles I in 1649 and abdication of James II in 1688 in England and the assassination of King Louis XVI in France in 1791. The leaders of 13 American colonies fought under the leadership of George Washington and they overthrew British rule in 1776. As a result of great popular movements, the absolutist state of the early modern period saw its replacement by a contractual state that assumed the popular appellation of a constitutional state and in the twentieth century became the liberal-democratic state. It was a *contractual* state where power was shared and the rights of the upper and middle ranks of society to participate in power along with the ruler were guaranteed by law and formalised in a constitutional system. Its essential features were sharing of power, rights to participate in government as are legally or constitutionally defined; representation is wide, state power is fully secular and the boundaries of national sovereignty are clearly defined."[21]

After the First World War, things changed and the *laissez faire* state committed to the course of least possible intervention in the life of the people had to become an interventionist state. The ideas of Keynes, Laski and Beveridge had their definite impact and so the case of increasing state activity for the sake of public welfare became the new creed of positive liberalism. The concept of citizenship was widened so as to include a new set of social and economic rights. Surprisingly, the conservative ideologues drew closer to the case of a welfare state that created a new model having the name of 'Butskellism' on account of being a happy synthesis of the ideas of Butler (a Conservative) and Gaitskell (a Labourite). However, after a decade or so, the case of welfare state lost its relevance. "When growth became harder to achieve in the 1970s, many came to believe that organised groups, notably the working class, freed by citizenship rights from all kinds of deferential behaviour, had become so aggressive that an 'overloaded' state faced a 'rationality crisis', because it had no room 'to steer the system'. The radical right reacted by turning from Keynes to Darwin: it sought to dismantle many citizenship rights and to reintroduce social discipline, largely and probably consciously through extending unemployment. What are we

20. G. Poggi: *The Development of the Modern State* (London: Hutchinson, 1978), p. 61.
21. Stuart Hall, *op. cit.*, pp. 9-10.

to make of this attempt to dismantle the powers that had accrued to the modern state."[22]

Obviously, the inherent pitfalls of this state came into light in the 1970s. It became identifiable with a 'bureaucratic state', an 'inefficient, wasteful and a spendthrift state', an 'ungovernable state', an 'overworked state', an 'overloaded state' and the like. A call for 'rolling back of state' gathered more and more weight. At the same time, a strong state was desired to deal with the new menaces and challenges posed by the terrorists, the environmentalists, the feminists, the unprivileged sections etc. The case of a welfare state revealed the symptoms of 'creeping totalitarianism'. "Hence the proposals to curb state intervention, cut state bureaucracy and public expenditure, reduce welfare, restore state-run enterprise to the private economy ('privatisation'), break the trend of collectivism, restrict the power of the unions, and restore competitive individualism and the doctrines of free-market liberalism which constitute the programme of the 'New Right'. This became the *dominant* trend in the British state in the 1980s. It represented a move to restore the ideal of the classical liberal state, but under advanced twentieth-century capitalist conditions: therefore, the *neo-liberal* state."[23]

Nation-State Under Transformation in the Era of Globalisation

Modern state is a nation-state and its three essential attributes are nationalism, secularism, and sovereignty. It is a state of the French, the English, the Romans, the Germans, the Russians, the Poles, etc., who, though Christians, do not subscribe to the cult of the Christendom. The red leviathan may create a big empire of different nationalities but its disintegration would occur sooner or later when the people of different racial or ethnic stocks would have their own states after the dismemberment of a multinational totalitarian state. It stands on the principle of national self-determination which caused the disintegration of the Austro-Hungarian and Turkish empires after the First World War. It also enjoins that if its sanctity is violated by means of any *ad hoc* or haphazard arrangement, essential consequences must follow. If the Poles are a nation, they should have their Poland; if the Czechs and the Slovaks belong to different stocks, they should have their own states after the destruction of Czechoslovakia.

The triumph of renaissance and reformation movements brought about the nation-state. The miraculous achievements of science in the spheres of transport and communication contributed to the transformation of such a state. Civic state-building was helped by the expanding reach of government by railways, telegraphs, spread of suffrage, national flags and national anthems, nuclear and thermo-nuclear weapons produced by advanced technology, etc. The state thus expanded itself and became an empire. The advanced nations of Europe established their empires in Africa, Asia and Latin America. But this system of empire-building created the force of 'nationalism' in the subject countries which fought for their freedom and emerged as nation-states after the Second World War. The empire-state thus shrank itself. And yet powerful nations devised certain new or dexterous arrangements to perpetrate

22. Hall and Ikenberry, *op. cit.*,p. 79.
23. Stuart Hall, *op. cit.*, p. 13.

their hold over the backward peoples of the world and this phenomenon got the name of 'neo-colonialism', also known as 'new imperialism' or 'late capitalism'.

The nation-state became a celebrated term and while the French boasted of creating a 'state-nation', the Americans created the 'ultimate idea-based nation'. However, present developments show the rise of a supra-national or transnational state - a state in which other states happily accept the system of shared or pooled sovereignty, the brilliant example of which may be seen in the European Union of some European countries. The trend of globalisation has its own effect. The international market is controlling national economy and state sovereignty is facing the onslaught of extraterritorial forces. The technological advances that made nation-states and empires governable now whisk capital and information ungovernably across their frontiers. These advances have created enterprises that can no longer act as national champions if they are to survive against international competition. Educated elites no longer advance only within their nations; they move in galaxies of films, finance and fashion that bestride nations. It may be called 'virtual state'.

The character of modern state has been considerably modified by such developments, particularly by the strategy of international trade. It has realised its limitations and put a stop on its functions then and there. Britain prefers to import grapes from Portugal rather than to take to the expensive course of creating hot houses for this sake in Scotland. It is well said: "Like the headquarters of a virtual corporation, the virtual state determines overall strategy and invests in its people rather than amassing expansive productive capacity. It contracts out other functions to the states that specialise or need them. Imperial Great Britain may have been the model for the nineteenth century, but Hong Kong will be the model for the 21st."[24]

Such a transformation may be noted in the sphere of new meaning given to three essential elements of state - territory, government, and sovereignty. Territory, hitherto regarded as one of the essential elements of state in political theory, though not in international law, has now become a *passe* or a faded element. It may be visualised in two important directions:[25]

1. In the age of computers, labour, capital and information have become so mobile that they have their existence inside as well as outside the boundaries of a state. Land is fixed of course, but its resources can be shifted to foreign countries like quick silver in case they are endangered by the aggression of a foreign power. Saddam Hussain of Iraq ransacked computers in downtown Kuwait in August, 1990 only to find out that the cash in bank accounts had already been transferred by electronic means. The result was that though the Kuwaiti government had abandoned its territory, it could continue to spend billions of dollars to resist foreign aggression - a mission in which it succeeded.
2. Developed countries have abandoned the lust for territorial aggrandisements, they would rather plumb the world market than strive for annexing the territory of another state. The virtual state that has downsized its territorially based productive capacity is the logical consequence of this emancipation from the

24. Richard Rosecrance: "The Virtual State" in *Foreign Affairs,* New York, Vol. 75, No. 4, July-August, 1996, p. 47.
25. *Ibid.,* pp. 48-59.

land. Like a virtual corporation, it is spreading its wings where economically profitable. It looks like a developed form of its predecessor – trading state. As more production by domestic industries takes place abroad and land becomes less valuable than technology, knowledge and direct investment, the function of state is being further redefined. The state no longer commands resources as it did in the mercantile past; it negotiates with foreign and domestic capital and labour to lure them into its own economic sphere and stimulate its growth. A nation's economic strategy is now at least as important as its military strategy; its ambassadors have become foreign trade and investment representatives. Major foreign trade and investment deals command executive action as political and military issues did two decades ago.

The virtual state is like a country whose economy is reliant on mobile factors of production, hence, it becomes like a virtual corporation and pervades our foreign direct investment by its enterprises. But more than this, it encourages, stimulates and to a degree even coordinates such activities. "In formulating economic strategy, the virtual state recognises that its own production does not have to take place at home, equally it may play host to the capital and labour of other nations. Virtual nations hold the competitive key to greater wealth in the twenty-first century."[26]

The fact of transformation may also be discerned in the role of the government which is regarded as the soul of the state. It acts autonomously of course, but the pressures and constraints should also be taken into account which affect its working. These may be intra-societal as well as extra-societal, but they are so powerful that, in the words of Jurgen Habermas, they 'create a crisis of rational administration'.[27] A conservative government cannot drastically reduce its costs and spending for fear of the power of the unions to cause large-scale disruption. Similarly, the labour government cannot efficiently pursue strong socialist policies, because business confidence would be undermined and the economy might be drastically weakened. "Hence governments of different persuasions come and go, and policy chops and changes."[28]

Finally, we may look into the element of sovereignty. The nation-state is no more sovereign as was once conceived by Hobbes and Austin. International, multinational or extra-societal forces have their own impact which have put a powerful check on the absolute power of the state. The existence and working of the European Union shows that the nation-state "today survives even though some of its powers have to be pooled with others, and even though many apparently sovereign decisions are seriously constrained, or made ineffective, by the decisions of others as well as by economic trends uncontrolled by anyone."[29] However, this point should be taken very cautiously. It does not mean the end of sovereignty as such, it smacks of resilience in the attitude of the state as to how it should deal with supra-national forces so as to protect and promote its national interest without sacrificing its supreme power.

26. *Ibid.*, p. 47.
27. See David Held, *op. cit.*, p. 133.
28. *Ibid.*, p. 124.
29. Stanley Hoffmann: "Reflections on the Nation-State in Western Europe Today", *Journal of Common Market Studies*, XXI (1 and 2, 1982), pp. 34-25.

Hoffmann rightly affirms that it "has strengthened the nation-state's capacity to act at home and abroad."[30]

The case of modern nation-state requires to be revisited in the present age of globalisation when the new phenomenon of 'states without borders' has become so vivid. Clusters of nation-states provide the stratification order of globalism.[31] The idea of a 'civil society' is finding its dim counterpart in the creation of a 'global civil society'. It may be visualised in many spheres like growing integration of national economies, increasing awareness of ecological interdependence, proliferation of multinational companies, social movements and intergovernmental agencies having their network in many countries of the world, global consciousness generated by communications revolution etc. Surprisingly, what adds up to the 'global' is the mix of the local, the national and the international. It has given birth to the new trend of 'transnationalism'. A number of new writers have paid due attention to such developments and come to hold the view about the 'undermining', 'undercutting', 'outflanking' and 'marginalisation' of the nation-states.[32] A deep examination of the situation, as it prevails now, shows that the nation-states "actually possess rather limited control over their territories and boundaries, while their claims to represent the nation are often spurious. For much of the world a true nation-state remains more an aspiration for the future than a present reality. The nation-state's rise has been global, but modest and very uneven. The modest 'nation-state' that came to dominate the 'North' has been part of its expansion, and represents a desired future for the bulk of the world's people."[33]

The nation-state perhaps offers the most conspicuous example of disjunctions that are sure to be replaced by institutional and actual transformation.[34] Despite this, the fact remains that the nation-state system has not seen its substitute so far, nor does it seem to be possible in the near future.[35] The nation-state is still much

---

30. *Ibid.*, p. 35.
31. Globalisation "is the name given to the process whereby social transactions of all kinds increasingly take place without account for national or state boundaries with the result that the world has become 'one relatively borderless social sphere'. Steve Hobden and Richard Wyn Jones: "World-System Theory" in John Baylis and Steve Smith (ed.s): *The Globalisation of World Politics: An Introduction to International Relations* (New York: Oxford University Press, 1997), p. 143.
32. Some writers have thrown light on the point of weakening of the modern nation-states in the light of new developments. Scott Lash and John Urry: *Economies of Signs and Space* (London: Sage, 1994); Anthony Giddens: *The Consequences of Modernity* (Cambridge: Polity Press, 1990); Martin Carnoy: "Whither the Nation-State?" in his (ed.): *The Global Economy in the Information Age* (College Park, Penn.: Pennsylvania University Press, 1993), pp. 44-96.
33. Michael Mann: "Has Globalisation Ended the Rise of the Nation-State?" in T.V. Paul and John A. Hall (eds.) *International Order and the Future World Politics* (Cambridge: Cambridge University Press, 1999), p. 243.
34. David Beetham: "The Future of the Nation-State" in George McLellan, David Held and Stuart Hall, *op. cit.*, p. 221.
35. Beetham says that though many supra-national and international agencies are at work and they provide the framework and some of the potential elements for the developments leading to a system of world government that might entail the end of the nation-state system, yet as things stand at present, they act "merely as an extension of the interests of individual nation-states." *Ibid.*, pp. 219-20.

desired despite the fact that it is being undressed both from above and from below. The poor and backward states may fall prey to the hold and influence of the big and advanced nations, but the advanced nations are not prepared to sacrifice their sovereign identity or national sensitivity. The tentative upshot of all these thoughts is that the nation-state "is far from dead. It is still the main repository of loyalty and legitimacy. Asian nation-states are moving into the phase of high self-confidence that pioneers of the nation-state knew in the nineteenth century. The birth rate of nations is particularly high as the Russian empire dissolves and the newcomers experience the normal post-colonial agony of poorly matched states and peoples."[36]

Marxist Perspective: State as a Class Organisation

In Western political thought, the idea of state "is often linked to the notion of an impersonal and privileged legal or constitutional order with the capability of administering and controlling a given territory."[37] But to Marx and Engels, it is a class institution; it is not an independent structure, or a set of institutions above society, *i.e.*, public power. On the contrary, it is deeply embodied in socio-economic relations and linked to particular interests.[38] Rejecting the view of Hegel, Marx says that bureaucracy is 'state's consciousness' and being a corps of state officials, it is a particularly closed society within the state which extends its power or capacity through secrecy and mystery.[39] Again: "The bureaucracy asserts itself to be the final end of the state.... The aims of the state are transformed into aims of bureaus, or the aims of the bureaus into the aims of the state."[40]

This line of thought has a powerful reflection in the *Communist Manifesto.* The state is a superstructure which develops on the foundations of social and economic relations. The state in its formulation serves directly the interests of the economically dominant class. "The executive of the modern state is but a committee for managing the common affairs of the whole bourgeoisie." Nevertheless, the state is characterised as essentially dependent upon civil society and upon those who dominate the economy. The state maintains the overall interests of the bourgeoisie in the name of public or general interest. However, a marked shift in the view of Marx is visible when he looked at the rise of Louis Napoleon Bonaparte in France in 1848 as accumulation of power in the hands of the executive at the expense of both, the civil society and the political responsibilities of the capitalist class – the bourgeoisie.[41] This work highlights Marx's distance from any view of the state as an 'instrument of universal insight' or

36. Nicholas Colchester: "The Nation-State is Fast Becoming a Relic" in *The Times of India,* Delhi, 8 Aug., 1994, p. 11.
37. Quinton Skinner: *The Foundations of Modern Political Thought* (Cambridge: Cambridge University Press, 1978).
38. David Held, *op. cit.,* p. 33.
39. Marx: *The Critique of Hegel's Philosophy of Right,* p. 46.
40. *Ibid.,* pp. 46-47.
41. The changed position of Marx in his *Eighteenth Brumaire of Louis Napoleon Bonaparte* highlighting relative autonomy of the state by being able to balance between competing fragments of the ruling class "allows it to force through welfare measures which are of long-term interest of capital, both so as to ensure stability and as to create a skilled and productive work force." Hall and Ikenberry, *op. cit.,* p. 7.

'ethical community', for he emphasises that the state apparatus is simultaneously a 'parasitic body' on civil society and an autonomous source of political action. "The state is portrayed as an immense set of institutions with the capacity to shape civil society and even to curtail the bourgeoisie's capacity to control the state. Marx granted the state a certain autonomy from society: political outcomes are the result of the interlock between complex coalitions and constitutional arrangements."[42]

The Marxian view of state is thus full of variations having patent and latent dimensions which may be condensed into three points:

1. In the *German Ideology* (1845), state is the representative of the dominant forces of society. It is the practical idealist expression of the rule of the propertied classes. So in the *Communist Manifesto* (1848), state is taken as the 'executive committee of the bourgeoisie'.
2. In the *Eighteenth Brumaire* (1852), state is a semi-independent structure of power which seeks to mould civil society from above. As such, in specific historical situations, it becomes relatively autonomous of any class and it may impose its own dominance upon society. That is, state might gain relative autonomy by being able to balance between competing fragments of the ruling class.
3. In *Capital* (Vol. I) (1867) state is a social force imbricated in social contradictions of civil society. As such, it must confine itself to formal or negative activities, since the scope of its own power comes to an end at the very point where civil life and work begin.

But the above strands are interconnected which impinge on two salient points: "The first conceives the state with a degree of power independent of class forces; the second upholds the view that the state is merely a 'superstructure' serving the interests of the dominant class."[43]

Lenin claims himself as a staunch Marxist and lists his first task as the resuscitation of the real teachings of Marx on the state.[44] He regards state as a class institution and condemns modern representative state as an instrument for the exploitation of wage labour by capital. Like Marx, he denounces the role of bureaucracy. However, the noticeable point here is that what Marx leaves unfinished, Lenin seeks to complete. His monograph *State and Revolution* (1917) offers a detailed account of the 'quasi-state' established after the successful socialist revolution what Marx designated as the 'dictatorship of the proletariat'. But, like Marx, he evades any account of the final stage of social development in which state 'will wither away'. His remark 'where there is state, there is no freedom; where there is freedom, there is no state', signifies that the existence of a stateless society would ensure the era of complete emancipation of man. But both Marx and Lenin can be accused of taking a one-sided view of the state. Several important questions remain unanswered relating to the real basis of power, the method of the functioning of bureaucracy, the real relationship between state and society, etc. Like Marx, Lenin fails to examine the degree to which state organisations "are influenced by diverse interests, political compromises and

42. Held, *op. cit.*, p. 35.
43. *Ibid.*, p. 36.
44. Lenin: *State and Revolution*, p. 7.

complex circumstances which do not merely reflect class antagonisms which must be restricted from above."[45]

Gramsci's concept of 'integral state' presents the paradox of being Marxian in one respect and un-Marxian in another. It is Marxian in accepting the dominance of the capitalist class. It encompasses the entire complex of activities with which the ruling class maintains itself in a dominant position and, at the same time, endeavours to legitimise itself. Thus, the political sphere includes much what falls in the private sphere. The capitalist system engages itself in the production of the *consent* of the people through devious means such as symbols, mythologies, institutions, customs and practices in which the pedagogic role of the intellectuals has its own significance. All these things help to sustain hegemony of the ruling class.[46] In the multiplicity of private institutions, one or the other predominates relatively or absolutely – constituting the hegemonic apparatus of the social group over the rest of the population. Such an analysis by Gramsci takes him closer to Hegel's view of civil society and looks like creating a paradox that "while his conception is Hegelian, the solution is Marxian."[47]

What Marx said about the 'relative autonomy of state' in his *Eighteenth Brumaire* became a handy tool for some theorists at whose hands the state-centric and society-centric formulations witnessed a peculiar fusion as well as diffusion. Ralph Miliband says that Marx's statement about state as 'the executive committee of the bourgeoisie' does not imply that the state is dominated by the bourgeoisie as a whole, it may even be independent of certain sections of the bourgeois class.[48] Subscribing to a kind of pluralist view, he takes state as a neutral arbiter among social interests. His assumption is based on three points: (a) in contemporary Western societies, there is a dominant or ruling class which owns and controls the means of production; (b) the dominant class has close links with powerful institutions, political parties, military, universities, media, etc., and (c) it has disproportionate representation at all levels of the state apparatus especially in the command positions.[49] The capitalist class is highly cohesive in constituting a formidable constraint on Western governments and state institutions ensuring that they remain like instruments for the dominance of society.[50]

Poulantzas dismisses such an approach of Miliband by calling it 'subjectivist' on account of being based on his personal impressions about the interrelationship of social classes and state officials that have their definite impact on its 'concrete functioning'.[51] More important are the structural components of a capitalist state which sustain and endure the system itself. The state is the only agency which prevents fragmentations among the capitalist class and the political disorganisation of the

45. Held, *op. cit.*, p. 38.
46. Hare and Smith (ed.): *Selections from Prison Note-Books of A. Gramsci* (New York: International Publishers, 1971), pp. 264-65.
47. Neera Chandhoke: *State and Civil Society: Explorations in Political Theory* (New Delhi: Sage Pub., 1995), p. 153.
48. Ralph Miliband: "Marx and the State" in *Socialist Register* (London: Merlin Press, 1965).
49. Ralph Miliband: *The State in Capitalist Society* (London: Weidenfeld and Nicolson, 1968).
50. Nicos Poulantzas: *Political Power and Social Classes* (London: New Left Books, 1973), pp. 331-40.
51. Held: "Central Perspectives on the Modern State" in McLellan and others (ed.): *The Idea of the Modern State*, p. 59.

workers. This is called by him the 'condensation of class forces'. If so, state is bound to maintain itself as independent of both the dominant and the dominated classes.

It appears that both Miliband and Poulantzas look at the negative perspective of the state. They are concerned only with how a state stabilises the capitalist system and, for this sake, prevents revolutionary influences which pose a challenge to it. Hence, the state requires autonomy from determinate sections of the bourgeoisie so that it could function in the interest of the capitalist system as a whole. What he says in the first edition of his *State, Power, Socialism* (1975) makes a change in it after three years when he holds that social struggles in society set limits to the state. Moreover, state policy looks phenomenally incoherent or chaotic. It is the class struggle which not only modifies the state apparatus but goes beyond the apparatus, generally escapes their control and, in fact, assigns them their limits. The state apparatus materialises and endures class relations and the state is constituted by and reflects the struggle.[52]

Claus Offe lays all stress on the element of legitimacy or 'legitimation crisis'. The state has to deal with two extremes, or antagonistic situations, namely, demands of the capitalist system and response to wider social forces in order to ensure its legitimacy. That is, while state acts as the 'flanking sub-system of the economy', it also produces a non-commodified sector outside the ambit of exchange requirements. State takes upon itself the onus of dealing with the economic crisis created by the capitalists and, at the same time, takes steps to meet the expectations of the people so as to keep its legitimacy intact.[53] The task becomes very challenging as the revolution of rising expectations goes on and it is possible that by falling short in this mission the state is faced with 'legitimation deficit' that might destroy its own stability.[54]

It may be said that both Poulantzas and Offe constitute the bridge between classical Marxism and post-Marxism inasmuch as they subscribe to structural determinism. Both take their start from the basic tenet of Marxism that state is a class institution in the hands of the capitalists, but they take a turn when they discuss the role of the state in dealing with economic and social crises which set limits to the autonomy of the state itself.[55] Jurgen Habermas may also be dragged into this category who holds that bourgeois public sphere exists in a field of conflictual social relations. And as its discourse is couched in universal terms, it has to respond and modify itself. However, from all this, one point is easily discernible that contemporary Marxism "is in a state of flux. There are now as many differences between Marxists as between liberals or liberal democrats. Moreover, the reconsideration of the classical Marxist account of the state - in part stimulated by the state's growth in Western and Eastern Europe during recent decades - has led to a reappraisal by some Marxists of the liberal democratic tradition with its emphasis on the importance of individual liberties and rights, *i.e.*, citizenship."[56]

52. Nicos Poulantzas: *State, Power, Socialism* (London: New Left Books, 1978), p. 135.
53. See Offe: *Contradictions of the Welfare State* (London: Hutchinson, 1984).
54. See Offe: *Disorganised Capitalism* (Cambridge: Polity Press, 1985).
55. Wood regards Poulantzas as the 'precursor of post-Marxism'. *Retreat from Class* (London: Verso, 1986). But Pierson regards Offe as 'a post-Marxist theorist'. *Marxist Theory and Democratic Politics* (Berkeley: University of California Press, 1986). An Indian writer takes both as 'transitional theorists'. Neera Chandhoke, *op. cit.*, p. 23.
56. Held in McLellan, *op. cit.*, pp. 60-61. Also see Anthony Giddens: *Profiles and Critiques in Social Theory* (London: Macmillan, 1981).

Marxist Perspective of State

Since the State is only a temporary institution which is to be made use of in the revolution in order forcibly to suppress the opponents, it is perfectly absurd to talk about a free and popular State; so long as the proletariat needs the State, it needs not in the interests of freedom, but in order to suppress its opponents; and when it becomes possible to speak of freedom, the State as such ceases to exist.

—Fredrick Engels

Cited in C.E.M. Joad: *Modern Political Theory* (London: Oxford University Press, 1946), p. 93.

The State will be able to wither away completely when society adopts the rule 'From each according to his ability, to each according to his needs'. When there is state, there is no freedom; when there will be freedom, there will be no state.

—V.I.Lenin

'State and Revolution' in *Collected Works,* Vol. 25, p. 474.

To begin with, there must be political compulsion, but as the State withers away, the functions will gradually lose their political character and become matters of pure administration. Orders will no longer be given from the top; necessary central planning will be combined with broad territorial autonomy.

—L. Kolakowski

Main Currents of Marxism (Oxford: Clarendon Press, 1978), Vol. II, pp. 499-500.

Although Marxism has developed as one of the most radical anti-statist conceptions with suitable modifications, it was transformed into a statist ideology.

—S. Stojanovic

Between Ideal and Reality: A Critique of Socialism and the Future (Oxford: Oxford University Press, 1973), p. 8.

Liberal Perspective: State as an Instrument of Protection and Public Welfare

The liberal perspective of state is older than its Marxian counterpart as seen in the preceding section. But what engages our attention now is its reinterpretation with a view to find fault with the Marxist notion as well as to offer a plausible alternative so as to meet its challenge. The views of such writers are perplexingly divergent ranging from Weber's affirmation of state as a 'bureaucratic institution' to Dahl's stress on the role of numerous interest groups making it a 'polyarchical entity' and its modification by the neo-pluralists like Lindblom denying state's being constrained by such social groups to their desired extent. In the case of Third World or post-colonial countries, state enlarges its interventionist role in the name of social welfare to an extent that it assumes the title of a 'developmentalist state', or an 'overextended state', or an 'overloaded state'. State once regarded as the instrument of 'protection' and then of 'promotion', is now evaluated in terms of what it delivers to its people to meet the tide of their rising expectations. And since state fails on this front in many countries of the Third World, it is deprecated as the 'lame leviathan.'[57]

57. See T. Callaghy: "The State as Lame Leviathan: The Patrimonial Administrative State in Africa" in Z. Ergas (ed.): *The African States in Transition* (London: Macmillan, 1987).

Max Weber is a great liberal theoretician who deeply scrutinises and then dismisses the Marxist view of taking state as a rank bureaucratic organisation sustaining the bourgeois system. In his view, both public and private organisations are managed by bureaucracies and so centralised administration has become inescapable. The modern state has its identity in professional administrative, specialised officialdom and law based on the concept of citizenship. The modern state is not an effect of capitalism, rather it preceded and helped promote capitalist development.[58] Force is not the normal or the only means of the state, it is a means specific to the state; it is a relation supported by means of legitimate coercion or violence. Considerable power accrues to bureaucrats through their *expertise* and, as such, this power may become 'over-towering'.[59] Attacking the socialist system, as visualised by Marx and established by Lenin in Russia in 1917, Weber confidently asserts: "The decisive reason for the advance of bureaucratic organisation has always been its purely *technical* superiority over any other form of organisation."[60]

Weber contributes to the case of empirical democratic theory which rejects the Marxian notion of class as the central structural determinant of the state and of all political outcomes and instead lays stress on the role of institutional arrangements in the form of social groups which interact and constrain the role of the 'classes' as well as of the 'state'. Not all power is concentrated in the classes or in their struggle as Marx says. Social inequality is a fact due to which all social groups do not have equal access to resources. The democratic system permits 'endless process of bargaining' as a result of which, as Lasswell says, counter-elites become elites and *vice versa.* It is due to this that the government does not pay equal regard to all social groups. "In this process the state becomes indistinguishable from the web and flow of bargaining, the competitive pressures of interests. Indeed, individual government departments are sometimes conceived as just another kinds of interest groups."[61]

Such an interpretation constitutes the case of 'pluralism' in its own right and has its re-examination at the hands of its critical advocates. Known as 'neo-pluralism', it retains its stress on the role of numerous interest groups which prevent the development of a monolithic unresponsive state. However, by aligning it with the nuances of Marxism, it holds that as all social groups do not have equal access to power, the state manages to be in a position of 'discriminating' among them and obliging some at the expense of others amounting to constraining the liberty of some groups at the expense of others. If it is so, the groups of the businessmen have an edge over the groups of the workers. The market controls the state, not *vice versa.* So Lindblom says that "depression, inflation and other economic disasters can bring down a government. A major function of the government is, therefore, to see to it that businessmen perform their task."[62]

---

58. Max Weber: *Economy and Society* (Berkeley: University of California Press, 1978), Vol. II, pp. 1381ff.
59. Weber: "Politics as Vocation" in H.H. Gerth and C.W. Mills (ed.): *From Max Weber* (New York: Oxford University Press, 1972), p. 78.
60. Weber: *Economy and Society* , Vol. II, p. 973.
61. Held in Stuart Hall, *op. cit.*,p. 67.
62. Charles E. Lindblom: *Politics and Markets,* pp. 122-23.

Liberal Perspective of State

But if we can speak of the state at all, we must define it in terms of what is common to all states, while perhaps laying stress on those aspects which become more prominent in the process of historical development. In no attitude of worship, as did Hegel, and in no attitude of belittlement, as did Spencer, but in the spirit of scientific exactitude, must we seek the criterion of the state.

—R.M. MacIver

The Modern State (New York: Oxford University Press, 1962), p. 4.

Political group (state) refuses the swaddling clothes of finality and becomes a shifting conception. It cannot be Hegelianised into a permanent compromise. It asks for the validation of men and actions in terms of historical experience.

—H.J. Laski

Authority in the Modern State (London: George Allen and Unwin, 1960), p. 166.

So powerful and extensive is the modern state that its nature has become the centrepiece of political argument and ideological debate. This is reflected, in the first place, in disagreement about the nature of state power and the interests it represents, that is, competing theories of state. Second, there are profound differences about the proper functions or role of the state; what should be done by the state and what should be left to private individuals.

—Andrew Heywood

Political Theory: An Introduction (Houndmills, Basingstroke: Palgrave Macmillan, 2005), p. 75.

However, the shining feature of this liberal perspective should be seen in bracketing the role of the state with the currents of international politics. State is not an isolated institution, it lives in the 'community of states'. The multidimensionality of power of the state should be understood in the context of global constraints. It leads to the geopolitical conception of politics. Theda Skocpol takes a correct view of it when she regards state as a 'Janus-faced' or two-sided organisation. No doubt, the state is a set of administrative, policing and military organisations headed by an executive authority which fundamentally extracts resources from the society and deploys them to create and support coercive and administrative organisations.[63] However, the struggle among social classes at home and conflict among nations abroad have a definite impact on the organisation and power of states. "The state has an intrinsically due anchorage in class-divided socio-economic structures and an international system of states."[64]

A critic may point out that what has been stressed by the liberal theorists, excluding Weber, has hardly anything strikingly new. The pressure group theory of politics had already carved a place of its own when the Marxist perspective of state was in its heyday. The reaffirmations of social theorists like Dahl, Lasswell and Lindblom are just like reiterations or amplifications to emphasise what remained to be covered by A. Bentley, D.B. Truman, V.O. Key, Jr. and James Burnham in the first half of the twentieth century. However, Lindblom deserves the credit for saying something different that displays his cryptic acceptance of the Marxist or

63. Theda Skocpol: *States and Revolutions,* p. 29.
64. Cited by Held in McLellan and others (ed.), *op. cit.,*p. 69.

neo-Marxist argument to a certain extent. His formulation that business groups have a dominant position and they have the potentiality to bring down the government is proto-Marxian. But Skocpol recapitulates what Laski had said in 1925 about the constraints of the international system which restrict the role of the sovereign state.[65] Keeping all such formulations in view, David Held says that they "constitute less a theory and more a framework for the analysis of the state."[66]

State and Society

The relationship between state and society has been viewed differently by a number of contemporary social and political theorists who may be labelled as state-centric and society-centric. The former, also known as statists, regard state as independent of society by virtue of having its power of coercion, or 'legitimate coercion' as called by Weber. According to the affirmations of such theorists, state should not, and cannot, be plunged into the ocean of society to the extent that it loses its autonomous position. State has its distinct place and presence and so the affirmation of Marx in respect of taking it as a relatively autonomous entity in his *Eighteenth Brumaire* should be appreciated. The officials of the state may act on behalf of private organisations, but their perspectives are quite different from those of the social groups. The state plays the role of an autonomous actor rather than as a recorder of social forces. According to Skocpol, any state, first and fundamentally, extracts resources from society and deploys them to create and support coercive and administrative organisations. But in her later writings, she becomes more aggressive when she holds that the states "may be viewed more microscopically as a configuration of organisations and actions that influence the meanings and methods of politics for all groups and classes in society."[67]

Nordlinger subscribes to this view and he delineates the core of the statist perspective thus:[68]

1. Public officials form their own policy preferences and as they may differ among themselves, their position is distinctive.
2. The state may have its own preferences which may, or may not, be in agreement with social preferences.
3. The activities of the state have their definite impact upon the activities of the society, including upon those who try to limit or sustain the role of the state.
4. The autonomy determinants of the state need not be questioned.

However, this view may be criticised for laying too much emphasis on the role of the state officials (or the regime) who by no means constitute the state as a whole. Their view of the detachment of the state from the society is not justified and the society, though ruled by the state, should not be regarded as a non-resistant entity.

65. As Harold J. Laski says: "In such an aspect the notion of an independent sovereign State is, on the international side, fatal to the well-being of humanity. The way in which a State should live its life in relation to other States is clearly not a matter in which the State is entitled to be the sole judge." *A Grammar of Politics*, p. 65.
66. David Held in McLellan, *op. cit.*, p. 69.
67. Skocpol: *Bringing the State Back In*, p. 28.
68. E. Nordlinger: "The Return to the State: Critique", *American Political Science Review*, September, 1998, p. 881.

Collapsing of the political into the social, or *vice versa,* negates the fact of the real relationship between state and society. The statists may, therefore, be criticised for "giving us states without societies, without either origins, or conditions of reception. Their state exists in a condition of social vacuum."[69] Again, such a perspective "tells us a great deal about the kind of society a state needs, it does not tell us anything about he kind of state a society needs."[70] It may also be pointed out that by blurring the distinction between the rulers and the ruled such a view violates certain principles of democracy.[71]

The trend of society-centric study of state having its start from Gramsci has its elaborate manifestation in the works of Michael Foucault. The 'integral state' theory of Gramsci seeks to establish 'hegemony' in society through coercive, moral and pedagogic means. Even the patently looking private spheres become a part of the state in their own right which suggests specificity of the state as an autonomous institution. Foucault frankly demolishes the statist perspective by covering all sorts of social interactions in his analysis of power equations. Struggle for power is a fact and it is going on at every level or in every corner of social life. Even such a struggle at the base has its impact in the ascending order and the pattern of social contestations whether peaceful or violent, whether persuasive or aggressive, at the local or national or international level, determines the power equations which place the state in a unique position.

Hence, not all importance should be given to the state. It is better to 'cut off the king's head' so as to reveal the role of numerous subaltern social entities. In this way, Foucault takes the discourse away to the micro-sites of power and denies to the state any specificity as a matter in this regard. He affirms: "The state for all the omnipotence of its apparatuses, is far from being able to occupy the whole field of actual power-relations and, further, the state can only operate on the basis of other already existing power-relations."[72] Again, the state "can only hold and secure its footing where it is rooted in a whole series of multiple and indefinite power-relations that supply the necessary basis for the negative forces of power."[73]

However, such a view has its limitations beyond which it cannot be stretched. All social groups may have some power after 'cutting sovereign's head', but the power of the state remains paramount. The constitution of the state, the entire legal system, administrative decrees and judicial pronouncements all go to strengthen the power of the state. They circumscribe the role of social groups in spite of the fact that the latter have their own share in constraining the fragile leviathan. The fact stands out that the state "organises and arranges other forms of power whose specific means in force helps to explain why it is always looked upon as the ultimate power, the power whose possession indicates the dominant group in society."[74]

The real merit of state-centric theories cannot be easily dismissed, as the case of society-centric theories cannot be easily taken for granted. Both have their strong and

69. Neera Chandhoke, *op. cit.*, p. 56.
70. *Ibid.*, p. 57.
71. *Ibid.*,
72. Michael Foucault: *Power/Knowledge* (Brighton: Harvester Press, 1980), p. 122.
73. *Ibid.*
74. N. Bobbio: *Democracy and Dictatorship* (Cambridge: Polity Press, 1989), p. 77.

weak sides. The state-centric view cripples the social sphere to an extent that the way for the emergence of a 'leviathan' is opened. So the society-centric view cripples the political sphere to an extent that it becomes incapable of arresting anarchic forces raising their head after invoking the plea of 'new Medievalism'. A correct appraisal of the situation is that the states do not just maintain order. "They maintain *public forums of social order:* a particular set of institutions, a particular configuration of power-relationships, a particular social structure and economy. "The 'empty state' – without social content – does not exist."[75]

Social change is natural and inevitable. If so, the relationship of state with society changes automatically in response to new conditions and constraints of collective life. What could be possible in the feudal society cannot be so in the present industrial, even post-industrial, society. It is well commented: "The State, then, is not autonomous of society. It does not mean that it is *wholly* determined in form and functions by society. There are complex interrelationships and interdependencies between the forms of the state and the type of society. But the state has been vested by society with the ultimate power of supreme rule, and authorised to stand above society and govern it. It cannot be *wholly* reducible to society. Something is added, when power in society is organised into separate and distinct instance of rule. From this perspective it seems clear that the state *constitutes* society as well as being constituted by it. States, then, are not autonomous of society. They are only 'relatively autonomous'."[76]

Third World Perspective: Case of Developing Countries

What we have said in the preceding sections pertains to the domain of the Western or developed countries. Let us now examine the case of the post-colonial world or the countries of the Asian, African and Latin American regions misnamed as the Third World. The pattern of state in a very large number of such countries is so varied and perplexing that it can be given the name of anything ranging from a 'behemoth' to a 'lame' or 'fragile leviathan'. A study of the works of certain writers like Hamza Alavi, John Saul and Rajni Kothari shows that the epithets of the vocabulary of the Western social and political theory as 'state capitalism', 'bureaucratic bourgeoisie', 'administrative state', 'political-administrative classes', 'developmental state', 'over-loaded state', 'soft state' and the like may have limited applicability in the case of any state of the Third World.

Since most of the countries of the post-colonial world were under the imperial control of some foreign power, their founding fathers or state-builders appreciated the model of the political system of the master-country and so they endeavoured to 'import' or plant it in their soil after gaining independence. In a fit of zeal, they demolished much of what was done by the alien masters. As a result of this, the 'colonial state' went out of existence as it was superficially 'rootless'. But its roots had gone so deep that the new masters had to build up a new state on the same foundations. The superstructures could not stand on such a base. The 'imported' system could not synchronise with the norms of the political culture of the country with the result that it collapsed after a couple of years or decades. The 'democratic'

75. Stuart Hall in McLellan, *op. cit.*, p. 22.
76. *Ibid.*, p. 23.

system of the alien soil saw its replacement by some kind of 'authoritarian' system. In the words of David Apter, it afforded the case of 'institutional indigestion'.

The emergence of these states coincided with the rising popularity of the model of a social welfare state that had its birth in Britain after the installation of Labour Government in 1945. That is, they adopted the model of 'developmentalist state'. The messages of Keynes, Laski and Beveridge became the source of inspiration'. In not much time, the social welfare state became anything like an 'overworked' or 'overloaded state' and so it had to face the music created by it. It failed to fulfil its tall promises and assurances matching the rising expectations of the people. A retreat from the proclaimed goal thus became natural, rather essential. Facts demonstrate that while the Western countries could manage their position by taking to the strategy of damage-control, the Third World countries had to bear with the utter failure of the welfare state model. The demise of the 'development model' marked the demise of confidence in the state."[77]

In these countries state-centric model prevailed owing to the non-existence of 'civil society'. The widespread ignorance, illiteracy, poverty and backwardness played its own part in this direction. Their old or primitive loyalties prevented them from understanding the requirements of the new times. The rulers became arrogant and power-drunk; they threw all norms of accountability to the wind. Corruption and maladministration grew more and more that led to the emergence of, what Gunnar Myrdal said, a 'soft state' or a system in which legal arrangements and illegal transactions exist side by side. In the absence of a civil society, state became unresponsive and irresponsible and so the disgruntled elements had to take to the course of violence as a result of which many so-called popular leaders were assassinated or their regimes were overthrown.

In the Marxian terminology, state is a class institution and, as such, it is in the hands of a dominant class which oppresses and exploits the dominated class. But in the post-colonial countries the situation is just the reverse. Surprisingly, the state creates classes or in some sensitive cases we find that the state arouses or sharpens class consciousness. The clever and crafty leaders inspire unprivileged or depressed groups to come forward with the call for social justice for the sake of strengthening their hold over the vote-bank. Schemes of welfare of such castes, classes and tribes are launched with the sole purpose of widening the democratic base of such leaders, their implementation is full of inherent defects as a result of which public money is squandered and the lot of the *dalits* remains unimproved.

As pointed out above, since there is no civil society in such countries, the rulers hardly bother for what they ought or ought not to do. Their invocation of the 'mandate' of the people secured by them in a general election is an instrument to cheat the innocent people. When the really oppressed sections raise their voice, they are suppressed to an extent that their cry is stifled by the use of police, paramilitary and armed forces. Former heads of state or government are taken to the jails for their serious acts of commission or omission by the masters of the new regime and this process is repeated when the new incumbents are out of office. The so-called modern state of such countries becomes the prototype of its feudal model. It is well commented:

77. Neera Chandhoke: "Of States and Civil Societies" in Neera Chandhoke (ed.): *Understanding the Post-Colonial World: Theory and Method* (New Delhi: Sterling Publishers, 1994), p. 193.

Key Features of State in Developed and Developing Countries

Case of Developed Countries

1. Modern states are the key political institutions of rule which are in principle differentiated and distinct from both the rulers and the ruled.
2. The modern state emerged, evolved, consolidated and was borrowed as the centralised and organised institution of rule whose central function was to manage, protect and promote national transitions from agrarian to industrial society, and to sustain economic growth.
3. Historically, the modern state has been characterised in ideal typical terms by its public institutions, its sovereignty and hegemony, its formal monopoly over legitimate coercion (violence) and its theoretically important bureaucracy.
4. Though different states adopt different strategies, successful economic growth and successful states have without exception been inextricably linked.
5. In promoting economic growth and development, modern states have had to provide defence and ensure law and order, respond to the demands of a wider set of civic rights - notably greater democratic participation in policy-making and resources through tax and welfare arrangements.
6. The broad strategy adopted in the pursuit of economic growth has depended crucially on the character of the public forces and coalitions underpinning state power which in turn has influenced the achievement of development goals.

Case of Developing (Third World) Countries

1. Unlike the development of the modern states in Europe, most contemporary states in the developing world have had their borders and main institutions imposed from without.
2. With few exceptions, the original purpose and point of colonial rule and hence colonial institutions of state were extractive rather than developmental.
3. The institutions of the rule of the colonial state reflected these purposes being characterised by generally authoritarian patterns, designed to promote attraction and the control of labour.
4. Yet more colonial states were marked by the paradox of having strong despotic (coercive) power and weak infrastructural and transformative capacities.
5. So many countries in the developing world achieved independence in circumstances where powerful economic and political forces in society exerted considerable regional and local influences and hence constrained dramatically the emergence of centralised, autonomous and effective modern states.
6. Colonial rule was commonly built on extended and institutionalised patron-client relations from top to bottom.
7. In the post-colonial era, these institutions of patronage emerged with the formal institutions of the modern state, commonly transforming it so that it has been unable to perform the central functions of the modern state, namely, encouragement, promotion and maintenance of economic growth.
8. Many of the characteristics of pre-modern politics and patrimonial polities were entrenched within the institutions of the modern state leading to their characterisation as neo-patrimonial states.

Source: Adrian Leftwich: "Theories of the State" in Peter Burnell and Vicky Randall (eds.): *Politics in the Developing World* (London: Oxford University Press, 2005), pp. 142-49.

"The increasing role of the coercive apparatus and marginalisation of the developmental wing suggests that the state is getting back to its primitive fold."[78]

In the case of some countries, the post-colonial state may be identified with a neo-colonial state - a state having all the trappings of a sovereign entity, but whose politics and economics are under the superintendence, direction and control of a foreign country. To A.G. Frank such a state falls within the rank of a 'dependency',[79] to Wallerstein it belongs to the domain of a 'periphery'.[80] The leaders of such states are not willing to realise that their obsession for 'development' would create more and more avenues for corruption and that forced development might entail a system of dictatorship. Nor are they prepared to understand that the loss of economic independence would ultimately amount to the loss of their sovereign status. With a determination to solve their gigantic social and economic problems they run from one post to another, but the world capitalist system controlled by the small group of 'core countries' (like USA, Britain, France, Germany and Japan) does not permit them to move from a peripheral to a semi-peripheral status.[81]

In short, state in the Third World countries is in search for its identity. Progress is going on through the process of trial and error. While some countries like India, Malaysia, Indonesia and Egypt have been able to maintain their position as sovereign and independent nations, others like Tanzania, Kenya and Ghana are midway through. However, the common point is that the colonial hold of the bureaucracy stands on a firm foundation that has built up the case of an 'administrative state'. It is hampering the advent of civil society and, more than that, it has become a party to the growing trend of criminalisation of politics. "In fact, in the Third World, context, the administrative apparatus is not only the concrete form of state power, but it occupies considerable political space."[82]

Critical Appreciation

Following impressions may be formed on the basis of what has been mentioned in the preceding sections:

1. The term 'state' has astonishingly divergent implications and interpretations. It is often interchanged with the country, the government, the community, the nation and the like. To a student of political theory, it becomes a matter of confusion which can be eliminated if this point is driven home that the state has its distinct identity by virtue of having the legitimate power of coercion. Sovereignty is its attribute and government is the institution that implements its will. Laski rightly counsels that, for all practical purposes, state should be

78. G. Hargopal and C. Chandrasekhar: "The State Apparatus in the Third World: The Theoretical and Methodological Dimension" in Neera Chandhoke, *op. cit.*, p. 183.
79. A.G. Frank: *The Sociology of Development and the Underdevelopment of Sociology* (London: Pluto Press, 1971).
80. Immanuel Wallerstein: *The World Capitalist Economy* (Cambridge: Cambridge University Press, 1979).
81. Samir Amin: "Crisis, Nationalism and Socialism" in Amin and others (ed.): *Dynamics of Global Crisis* (New York: Monthly Review Press, 1982), pp. 193-94.
82. Hargopal and Chandrasekhar, *op. cit.*, p. 172.

identified with the government. As Heywood says: "The term 'state' can be used to refer to a bewildering range of things: a collection of institutions, a territorial unit, a historical entity, a philosophical idea and so on. In everyday language, the state is often confused with the government, the two terms being used interchangeably."[83]

2. Widely divergent are the views of social and political theorists about the nature and end of the state. To the negative liberals, it is a 'necessary evil'. It is required for the sake of protection despite the fact that its authority in inimical to individual liberty. To the positive liberals, it is essential for the protection as well as welfare of the people. To the Marxists, it is an instrument of exploitation and oppression of one class by another. It has its origin in the outbreak of the class war and so it shall have its eventual withering away in a classless society. The holders of such a view called by various names such as the Anarchists, the Marxists, and the Anarcho-Syndicalists ramble in the world of dreamland or utopia. The idealists go to the length of glorifying the state as 'march of God on earth' and thereby regarding it as a natural and moral organisation ensuring 'good life' to its members. A critic may find fault with all theories relating to the nature and end of the state, but he cannot offer a universally plausible view in this regard.
3. The profile of a modern state may be seen in the developed countries of the West. The case of the developing countries of the Third World is quite different where state is generally identified with the society, community, government, nation, some political party, even with the powerful elements that convert it into some form of a leviathan. The result is that it is known by various nick-names such as 'overdeveloped state', 'overloaded state', 'bureaucratic state', 'soft state' 'garrison state', 'rogue state', 'failed state', 'flailing state' and the like. All such epithets are used to reveal the fact that the state as an institution of public protection and welfare based on the consent of the people no longer exists in such countries. The whole system is badly ridden with the evils of corruption, maladministration, bureaucratisation, indiscipline and disorder of all kinds. People live in a state of nature under a leviathan chosen by them or not. In a nutshell, the state exists in such countries without its specific identity. The increasing role of the coercive apparatus and marginalisation of the developmental wings suggests that in such countries the state is getting back to its primitive role. The state "is caught up in a peculiar mix of force and right that constrains and shapes the lives of generations."[84]
4. Diverse are the perspectives of nation-state, but they all point at its normative character. The state is a peculiar blending of force and right. On the one hand, we take for granted state's ability to work through other centres of power. Its capacity to act rationally is furthered and not curtailed when it coordinates with other autonomous power sources. Moreover, this power is the greatest when it is able to maximise its options at subsequent moments of decision. Latest developments in the form of globalisation and liberalisation hit at the absolutist

83. Andrew Heywood: *Political Theory: An Introduction* p. 75.
84. David Held in McLellan and others, *op. cit.*, p. 73.

character of the state's power and force the students of political theory to re-evaluate the case of modern state as a sovereign entity in sheer positivistic terms. Sovereignty stands compromised to a certain extent by the growing significance of international law and international obligations coupled with fast developing trends of interconnectedness and interdependence among nation-states of the world.

5. However, these developments call for a reinterpretation of the 'corporate identity' of the state in the light of the formulations of world-system theorists. Normatively considered, the concept of the state as an impersonal and anonymous structure of power still stands, but stress on the new obligations and duties of the active and critical members of a civil society necessitate search for a better reconciliation of its authority vis-a-vis the liberty of the people. "The ability to act flexibly to intervene, withdraw, reform or abstain is at the heart of state's capacity."[85]

The relevance of the nation-state is still unquestioned and will remain unquestionable in the foreseeable future. "As long as politics is organised on a territorial basis, states will likely dominate politics, and sub-state nationalists will prefer territorial states of their own."[86]

85. Hall and Ikenberry, *op. cit.,*p. 97.
86. Hudson Meadwell: "Stateless Nations and the Emerging International Order" in T.V. Paul and J.A. Hall, *op. cit.,*p. 262.

28

Terrorism

> For the manner in which men live is so different from the way in which they ought to live, that he who leaves the common course for that which he ought to follow will find that it leads him to ruin rather than to safety.... For, all things considered, it will be found that same things that seem like virtue will lead you to ruin if you follow them; whilst others, that apparently are vices, will, if followed, result in your safety and well-being.
>
> **—Niccolo Machiavelli**[1]

The word 'terrorism' originates from a Latin word 'terrere' having its synonym in a French word 'terrorisme' implying 'to frighten'. It is particularly associated with the 'reign of terror' unleashed by the French revolutionaries like Robespierre, Danton and Mara who during 1793-94 guillotined more than 20,000 people. It was included in the English dictionary in 1798 signifying 'systematic use of terror as a policy'. In course of time, it assumed several forms as 'unofficial terrorism', 'state-sponsored terrorism' and 'state terrorism' so much so that it has now led to the birth of 'counter-terrorism'. The astonishing development in this regard is that now both have come to exist together each accusing the other of being terrorist. If the conspirators murdered Julius Caesar in Rome in B.C. 44, the American navy seals caught and killed Osama bin Laden in Pakistan in 2011. So the saying goes that 'one's terrorist is another's freedom fighter'.[2]

Meaning, Nature and Manifestations

Terrorism is not a new phenomenon. Its horrifying instances are available in the ancient, medieval and modern history of the world. What is notable is that now it has assumed the form of a dangerous trend, a pernicious tendency, an insidious form of religious fanaticism, and a menacing ideology that may be visualised in the operation of numerous such organisations like Irish Republican Army in Northern Ireland, Hamas in Palestine, Basques in Spain, Quebecords in Canada, Revolutionary Armed Forces of Colombia, Croatians in Yugoslavia, Armenians in Turkey, Maros in the Philippines, Islamic Brotherhood in Egypt, Jemmiah Islamia in Indonesia, Tamil Liberation Tigers in Sri Lanka, Islamic Movement in Uzbekistan, Hezbollah in Lebanon, Al-Qaida, Jaish-e-Muhammed, Lashkar-e-Taiba and Haqqani in Pakistan, Jammu-Kashmir Liberation Front in India and the like. The objects of such organisations may be different, but all subscribe to the use of violence with a

1. Niccolo Machiavelli: *The Prince,* Chapter 15.
2. J.M.Lutz: *Global Terrorism* (London: Routledge, 2004).

view to intimidate, cause fear, or punish its targeted victims so as to achieve their political goals.[3]

The word 'terrorism' was officially used, for the first time, at the Third Conference for the Unification of Penal Law held at Brussels under the auspices of the League of Nations in 1931. Here it ('terrorism') was defined as "the deliberate use of means capable of producing a common danger to commit an act of imperilling life, physical integrity of human health, or threatening to destroy substantial property by such acts as arson, explosion, flooding or subversion, ignition of asphyxiating or noxious substances; interruption of the normal operation of the means of transport and communications, damage to or destruction of government property and public utilities; pollution, fouling or deliberate poisoning of drinking water or staple foods; causing, propagating contagious or epidemic diseases, any wilful act which endangers human lives and the community."

A resolution (No. 49/60) adopted by the United Nations General Assembly on 9 December, 1994 takes a very comprehensive view of terrorism. It includes all activities, methods and practices of the terrorists in all manifestations as under:

1. Crimes like drug-trafficking, illicit arms trade, money laundering, smuggling of nuclear and other potentially deadly materials constituting grave violation of law relating to peace, security, human rights, fundamental freedoms, territorial integrity and friendly relations among the states;
2. Organising, instigating, assisting, facilitating, financing, encouraging, participating or tolerating terrorist activites, including acquiescence in such activities by the official as well as unofficial agencies;
3. Obstructing the process of extradition of such criminals or granting political asylum to them, or suppressing or distorting information in this regard;
4. Allowing use of territory or space for terrorist installations or training camps, or for the perpetration and organisation of terrorist acts intended to be committed against other citizens or states; and
5. Any such act committed by anybody whatsoever and whenever even by the state, directly or indirectly, calculable to provoke a state of terror in the general public for political purposes.

Taking into account the fact that a precise definition of terrorism cannot be formulated, its working definition may highlight "the use of violence by sub-state

3. Terrorism assumed a very serious form in the later part of the twentieth century. For example, in December, 1973, the Arab terrorists killed 32 people at Rome airport during an attack on an American aircraft. Hostages were taken in support of the hijackers' demand for the release of the imprisoned Palestinians. In 1976 a French plane with mostly Israeli passengers was hijacked by a Middle Eastern organisation and flown to Uganda, where the hijackers threatened to kill the hostages unless Arab prisoners in Israel were released. From there we may proceed to note the attack of the terrorists on two cities of America on 11 September, 2001 and the attack of such terrorists on the city of Mumbai in India on 26 November, 2008. It shows that international terrorism, sponsored both by states and by an ever-increasing number of non-state actors, "has evolved as an insidious form of warfare, often intended to selectively hurt civilian populations." Karen Mingst: *Essentials of International Relations* (New York: W.W. Norton and Company, 1999), p. 191.

Terrorism

In the spectre of political violence, terrorism is unique. Terrorists seek to influence a wide audience by generating fear. Other forms of political violence include attacks against infrastructures (sabotages), assassination of political leaders, guerilla warfare and ethnic cleansing.

—**Martin Griffiths**
Encyclopaedia of International Relations and Global Politics
(London: Routledge, 2005), p. 800.

It includes any use of violence towards political, moral and religious ends which is not carried out by the official military institutions of a state.

—**David Robertson**
A Dictionary of Modern Politics (London: Europa Publications, 2002), p. 472.

Terrorism, in its broadest sense, refers to the use of terror for furthering of political ends; it seeks to create a climate of fear, apprehension and uncertainty. The most common forms of terrorist action are assassinations, bombings, seizures and plane hijacks, although the advent of terrorism with a global reach, as demonstrated by the September 11, 2001 attacks on the United States, threatened to redefine the phenomenon.

—**Andrew Heywood,**
Politics (Houndmills, Basingstoke: Palgrave, 2005), p. 382.

groups to inspire fear, by attacking civilians and/or symbolic targets, for purposes such as drawing widespread attention to a grievance, provoking a severe response, or wearing down their opponent's moral resolve, to effect political change."[4]

It is said that no word in contemporary national and international political lexicons is more frequently involved and more emotionally charged than the word 'terrorist'.[5] One may hold that there is no unanimity of views on it. However, social science literature and the mass media have rarely found this line of thinking taken to its logical conclusion. The present position is that this heinous crime is being committed openly or clandestinely, by private individuals and organisations as well as by some states. It may also be noted that some states are indirectly involved in it. As such, it is an official, or semi-official, or non-official activity having its manifestations in underground operations, surprising attacks and use of extreme violence to achieve the goal. "Usually used by the powerless against the powerful, terrorism operates through surprise. Violence designed to instill fear in a population, a state, and the international community is the means that terrorists use to make a political statement."[6]

Viewed thus, the essential features of terrorism may be enumerated as under:[7]

4. James D. Kiras: "Terrorism and Globalisation" in John Baylis and Steve Smith (eds.): *Globalisation and World Politics: An Introduction* (New York: Oxford University Press, 2005), p. 482.
5. Lon Troyer: "The Calling of Counter-Terrorism" in *Theory and Event*, Vol. 5, No. 4, 2001.
6. Karen Mingst, *op. cit.*, p. 191.
7. Mark Seldon and A.Y. So: "Introduction" in their (ed.): *War and State Terrorism* (The US, Japan and the Asia Pacific in the Long Run) (New York: Rournan and Littlefield, 2004), p. 4.

1. The unlawful use of force or violence against persons or property to intimidate or coerce a government, civilian population or any segment thereof in furtherance of social and political objectives.
2. The calculated use of violence to inculcate fear intended to coerce or intimidate governments or societies so as to pursue goals that are generally political, religious and ideological.
3. The use of threat for the purpose of advancing political, religious or an ideological cause of action which involves a serious violence against any person or property.
4. The threat or use of violence for political purposes when (a) such action is intended to influence the attitude and behaviour of the target group wider than its immediate victim, (b) its ramifications transcend national boundaries.

Thus viewed, terrorism "appears to be fundamentally and inherently political—the pursuit of power and the use of power to achieve political goals."[8]

As a matter of fact, 'terrorism' is a very pejorative as well as a controversial term whose contours cannot be precisely marked out. It may, and also may not, be identified with a war, a guerilla war, a proxy war, asymmetric warfare or a war of attrition in which the direct or indirect role of the official, semi-official and non-official elements may be discerned. The points of distinction are there, but often the lines of distinction are blurred that dissuades an investigator to determine its definitional boundaries. The investigator may study the case subjectively or objectively and thus confuse the line of demarcation between terrorism and counter-terrorism. Nevertheless, each of the following activity forms part of the definition of this term:

1. In a war, a state directs its means of violence against one or more of the states targeting military objectives.
2. In state terrorism, a state systematically directs violence against the civilian population of its own or of another state.
3. In oppositional terrorism, non-state actors direct violence against a state, including its military, its officials and its functions.
4. In a violent crime, one segment of a civilian population acts against groups, individuals or society.

As the phenomenon is studied differently by different investigators, its ramifications remain uncovered in any definitional statement. Benjamin Netanyahu, Israeli ambassador to the United Nations, defined it as "deliberate and systematic murder, maiming and menacing of the innocent to inspire fear for political ends." No doubt, terrorism is pre-planned and politically motivated violence perpetrated against non-combatant targets by sub-national or anti-national groups or clandestine agents of the state. According to Stephen Segaller, it is 'a war of attrition fought by an invisible but vocal army.' Its special marks may be enumerated as under:

8. Mohammed Yasin and P.K. Sengupta: "Indian Politics: Promises, Issues and Trends" in B. Morrison (ed.): *Transnational Democracy in Critical and Contemporary Perspectives* (Burlington: Ashgate, 2003), p. 184.

Essential Features of Terrorism

1. Terrorism refers to political violence that targets civilians deliberately and indiscriminately.
2. More than guerilla war, terrorism is a shadowy world of faceless enemies and irregular tactics marked by extreme brutality.
3. Generally, the purpose of terrorism is to demoralise a civilian population in order to use its discontent as leverage on national governments or other parties in a conflict.
4. Terrorism is seldom mindless; it is usually a calculated use of violence as leverage. However, motives and means of terrorism vary widely, having in common only that some actor is using violence to influence other actors.
5. The primary effect of terrorism is psychological. In part the effectiveness of terrorism in capturing attention is due to the dramatic nature of the incidents, especially as shown on television news. Terrorism also gains attention because of the randomness of victims.
6. Terrorism amplifies a small amount of power by its psychological effect on large populations; this is why it is usually a tool of the powerless.
7. Terrorists are more willing than states are to violate the norms of international system, because, unlike states, they do not have a stake in the system. Conversely, when a political group gains some power of legitimacy, its use of terrorism usually diminishes.
8. States themselves carry out acts designed to terrorise their own populations or those of other states, for scholars tend to avoid the label of 'terrorism' for such acts, preferring to call it repression or war. In fact, no violent act committed during a civil or international war - by or towards a warring party - can necessarily fit neatly into the category of terrorism.
9. State-sponsored terrorism refers to the use of terrorist groups by states - usually under the control of a state's intelligence agency - to achieve political aims.

J.S. Goldstein and J.C. Pevenhouse: *International Relations* (New Delhi: Pearson, 2011), pp. 200-201.

1. It involves a criminal act.
2. There may be killings, random or selective.
3. The proximate target may be an individual, but the ultimate targets are the people. Kill one man to threaten a thousand.
4. There is an element of suspicion in terrorist actions.
5. Responsibility to war is acknowledged. This is to give publicity to the terrorist groups and also to create public scare.
6. Terrorist actions are accompanied by demand for some action by way of redress or relief.
7. It thrives on outside support which may be in terms of money, armament and sanctions.[9]

All terrorists firmly believe in the cult of the pistol and the bomb. "It is not mere violence but coercion by terror compelling the people to do that which they would not otherwise do, by dread or death, injury or pain, either for themselves or for

9. Giriraj Shah: *Terrorism: Tenets and Tactics* (Delhi: Anmol Publications, 2000), p. xi.

others."[10] One may say that here the psychological aspect is more important than the political one. Hence, it is described as "a political action, involving the use or threat of extraordinary violence performed for psychological rather than material effect, and the victims of which are symbolic rather than instrumental."[11] However, for our purpose, its political aspect is very important keeping which in view, Wardlaw says that it "is the use, or threat of use, of violence by an individual or a group, whether acting for or in opposition to established authority, when such action is designed to create extreme anxiety and/or fear-inducing effects in a target group larger than the immediate victims with the purpose of coercing that group into acceding to the political demands of the perpetrators."[12]

Distinctive Characteristics

Terrorism, as its name signifies, involves the creation of an atmosphere of extreme fear to put pressure on the targeted party so as to concede demands that would not be usually conceded except by the force of arms or the use of extreme violence. The group or faction that feels aggrieved is, more often than not, militarily weaker than the state. Since such elements cannot resort to conventional warfare, they turn to the low cost warfare that requires a few committed, highly trained and brain-washed individuals who are willing to sacrifice themselves for the cause. Instead of delving into the definitional labyrinth, we may pinpoint its following distinctive characteristics:

1. Simply stated, terrorism may be defined as a method whereby a well-knit or organised faction or group seeks to achieve its avowed objectives mainly through the systematic use of violence. It is a symbolic act intended to influence political behaviour of the targeted people by extra-legal, extra-constitutional and extra-moral means entailing the unabashed use of violence or its severe threat. The component of propagandist technique is also implicit in it inasmuch as such acts are invariably designed to convey some message, demand or warning to those who are the philes or the phobes of the terrorist movement.
2. Many acts of violence such as wounding, arson, assassination of the top leaders, destruction of property, etc. are committed by the groups of the terrorists, but all cannot be identified with the misdeeds of terrorism. Such activities are defined as 'crimes' in the law of the state and so persons involved in such wrongs are prosecuted and punished by the machinery of the state. However, such activities fall in the category of the acts of terrorism if the persons involved in them remain underground and, while launching their surprise attacks, do not discriminate between their opponents and the innocent people. Not only the organised gangs of the individuals, but the rulers of the state may also indulge in such heinous activities directly for suppressing or finishing their rivals.
3. In spite of the fact that the term 'terrorism' has been comprehensively explained, differences among the scholars and investigators still persist about its contents or components. For this reason, no standard definition of this term has been coined so far. The fact stands out that the acts of terrorism may be done by

10. H.V. Hodson (ed.): *The Annual Register: A Record of World Events, 1977*, Vol, 219, pp. 3-4.
11. Chalmers-Johnson: "Terror" in A.A. Said (ed.): *Human Rights and World Order*, p. 48.
12. Grant Wardlaw: *Political Terrorism: Theory, Tactics and Counter-Measures*, p. 16.

unofficial, semi-official and official elements. The objects of such persons may be to terminate or to restructure the existing order or to overthrow the men in power by violent means. Thus, terrorism breeds counter-terrorism and sometimes it becomes difficult to distinguish between the two in a situation of a grim civil war.

4. Terrorism may be differentiated from sectarian strife. Traditionally, sectarian violence implies asymmetrical confrontation between two or more non-state actors representing different or rival groups of a country's population. It may be intra-sectarian or extra-sectarian. That is, the fight may be between persons of the same sect or between different sects of the people. The state is expected to play the role of an impartial referee, but in some exceptional cases, it may be a party to such a strife. In matters of sectarian strifes, state cannot be a silent spectator. But the problem becomes very serious or complicated when the state takes sides and thus plays its part in fomenting the conditions of civil war. The close association of some sectarian groups with the state may reach a point as in Yugoslavia under Slobodan Milosevic or in Iraq under Saddam Hussain that the state itself becomes a semi-sectarian entity.[13]
5. Terrorism is an evil; state-sponsored terrorism is a bigger evil; state terrorism (also called proxy terrorism) is the biggest evil. State is lauded as 'the first condition of a civilised life'. It is a moral organisation, because, as Aristotle says, its aim is to ensure 'good life' to its people. If some individuals or their groups go astray, it is the task of the state to put them on the right track. Hence, suppression of terrorism is an essential function of the state. If a state patronises or renders assistance to the groups of terrorists openly or clandestinely, it plays the role of a criminal. The worst situation occurs when the state itself commits acts of terrorism and thereby demonises itself. Such a state is known as a 'rogue' entity. In view of the increasing number of such states, particularly in the Third World, it may be commented that now such a role may be played by the 'pillars' of international community, including democratic states. In fact, states are uniquely imbued with the capacity to commit not only acts of war but also acts of terrorism as they go about seeking to monopolise violence for their own purposes. Known by the name of 'state terrorism', it may be defined as "a systematic state violence against the civilians in violation of international agreements, state edicts and precedents established by international courts designed to protect the rights of the civilians."[14]

It shows that the direct or indirect role of the state as a semi-criminal or a full-fledged criminal has converted terrorism, generally understood as an activity of the underground unofficial elements, into a lesser evil. "The dark side of state terrorism needs to be comprehended, theorised and challenged, including its moralising war myth that was coupled with the dehumanisation of the enemy, an emphasis on the atrocities of only the other side, and a propagandistic insistence that respectability for terror tactics should be attributed to the enemy."[15]

13. Ekaterina Stephanova: "Trends in Armed Conflict" in *SIPRI Year-Book, 2008, Armaments, Disarmament and International Security* (Oxford: Oxford University Press, 2008), p. 45.
14. Seldon and So, *op. cit.*, p. 6.
15. *Ibid.*, The Geneva Convention of 1949 prohibits violence to life and person, in particular murder of all kinds, mutilation, cruel treatment and torture to all innocent people or non-combatants including non-fighting armed personnel.

Terrorism and Insurgency

A line of distinction may be drawn between terrorism and insurgency. While both look alike, the latter has a different overtone. Insurgency may be defined as efforts "to obtain political goals by an organised group (or groups) using protracted, irregular warfare and allied potential techniques."[16] It is "a multifaceted activity in which conflict takes place on different planes, very often simultaneously."[17] It is also defined as "an attempt by militarily inferior factions (insurgents), operating within a geo-political system, by the use of guerilla warfare and population control measures to usurp the control of that system from military factions (the de facto government)."[18]

Thus, while it is difficult to mark out precisely the difference between insurgency and terrorism, a line of subtle distinction between the two may be seen in that the insurgents are the nationals who rise in revolt against the constitutional government of their country and desire to overthrow it by violent or revolutionary means. The terrorists may, or may not be, the nationals of a country in which they operate. Moreover, while the insurgents have the support of a sizable section of the people of their country, the terrorists may, or may not, have it. The content of nationalism is implicit in the activities of the insurgents which may, or may not, be in the case of the terrorists. Thus, the insurgents may be described as the nationalist terrorists of a country who never think in terms of creating a separate and sovereign state of their own, though the line of distinction cannot be drawn in respect of the violent activities of both which look like an irregular warfare mixed with politics. So Scott observes: "The term 'irregular warfare' applies only to military activities. Insurgency, on the other hand, has both military and political opponents. Insurgency is irregular warfare plus politics, irregular warfare is insurgency minus politics."[19]

Terrorism is not always linked to insurgency, but insurgency cannot exist without terror. The goals of the terrorists in an insurgency situation are:[20]

1. To weaken or finish the government's control of the population;
2. To convince the people that the insurgents are the stronger party;
3. To make them realise that collaboration with government agencies is not only futile but dangerous;
4. To force the people not to reveal any secrets of the insurgents;
5. To make it unsafe to serve the government and to terrify public servants by systematic assassinations; and
6. To lead to a stage ultimately where the government itself finds that it is too expensive in terms of manpower and financial resources to suppress the insurgents and thus it loses its will to govern.

---

16. A.M. Scott and others: *Insurgency*, p. 5.
17. John Baylis: "Revolutionary Warfare" in Baylis and others (eds.): Contemporary Strategy, p. 134.
18. A.T. Rambo: "The Concept of Revolutionary Warfare" in J.M. Tinker (ed.): *Strategies of Revolutionary Warfare*, p. 6.
19. Scott, *op. cit.*, p. 10.
20. N.S. Saksena: *Terrorism: History and Facets in the World and in India* (Delhi: Abhinav Publications, 1985), pp. 128-29.

In recent times, terrorism has taken a new form. The acts of the terrorists, including the insurgents transcend the boundaries of one state. They have their shelter in different countries and operate therefrom with the open or concealed help of some other state or states. Their network is widespread and so they become capable of saving themselves from the clutches of the law of a country. They have new targets which include large aircrafts, super-tankers, international power grids and pipelines, transportation bombs, commercial and communications centres, motorcades, offshore oil rings, liquid natural gas facilities, nuclear power plants and computerised information and management systems. They adopt advanced technology in their operational activities with the help of new, rather latest, weapons whereby they engage global attention. As a result, a kind of 'new toleration' has developed in the form of direct or indirect support to the terrorist organisations by the states and also by other law-abiding sections of the people due to the fear of retaliation.

Causes of Occurrence

Many are the causes which incite or compel some people or their groups, even the sovereign states, to resort to the means of extreme violence. A list of such causes may include several points as their unredressed grievances, denial of legitimate political and economic rights, social injustice, increasing poverty and backwardness, ethnic and racial persecution, spreading the influence of a particular faith or ideology, termination of the alien rule, desire for accumulation of wealth by illegal means, and the like. Some of the important causes may be thus enumerated:

1. **Colonial System:** The colonial powers of Europe enslaved many countries of Asia and Africa and placed them under their political subjugation and economic exploitation. As they were guided by the interests of their empire, they resorted to brutal methods of suppression, physical torture and cultural dehumanisation.[21] As a result of this, some zealous nationalists or freedom fighters took to the ways of terrorism by secretly attacking the citadels of the imperial power. In retaliation, the colonial masters took to the ways of 'teaching a lesson to their subjects' in the name of their 'civilianisation'. Gen. Nathenial Dyer was honoured in England as the 'hero of the Amritsar Massacre', Bhagat Singh is remembered as a great martyr by the Indian people.
2. **Ideological Hegemony:** During the Cold War era (1946-91) the USSR was a superpower. It included a large number of East European states into its military bloc and thereby established 'socialist commonwealth'. If the people of any satellite country raised their voice to demand some dose of 'liberalisation', they were forcibly suppressed by the great communist power as happened in

21. For instance, an Algerian revolutionary leader (Frantz Fanon) observes: "In the colonies it is the soldier and policeman who are the officials instituted to go between the spokesman of settler and his rule of oppression. On the other hand, in colonial countries, the policeman and the soldier by their immediate presence and their frequent and direct action maintain contact with natives and advise them by means of rifle and napalm not to budge. It is quite obvious that the agents of the government use pure force only. The intermediary does not lighten the oppression, nor seek to hide the domination, he shows them up and puts them into practice with the clear conscience of an upholder of peace, yet he is the bringer of violence into the home and mind of the native." *The Wretched of the Earth* (Harmondsworth: Penguin, 1990), p. 74.

East Germany, Hungary, Czechoslovakia and Poland. Surprisingly, the great communist leaders justified such actions of 'state terrorism' in the name of the 'unity of the socialist world'. The American leaders followed suit in the name of 'saving the free world'. The cases of American intervention in countries like Panama, Haiti, Nicaragua, Chile and Argentina may be referred to in this regard. Nothing but the factor of ideological hegemony may be seen at work in such instances of intervention by violent means of a superpower in the domestic affairs of the satellite states.

3. **Role of Failed and Flailing States:** After the Second World War, many dependent countries of Asia and Africa emerged as sovereign nation-states. But in some countries the rulers failed to establish a strong and stable political system. Hence, many power-hungry groups came forward to capture power by means of violence. They created serious problems of law and order. Such states came to be known as 'failed states' in view of the fact that they could not protect the life and property of their people.[22] Some countries established and developed the entire paraphernalia of a modern democratic political system and yet their rulers failed to maintain law and order effectively. Such a state is called a 'flailing state'. While a failed state is an ungoverned state (like Somalia and Rwanda in Africa), a flailing state (like Afghanistan and Pakistan in Asia) moves vigorously as well as erratically in thrashing out the law-breaking elements and, at the same time, shows its helplessness or limitations in thoroughly eliminating such elements owing to the compulsions of a backward economy or a fragile democratic system.[23]
4. **Role of Rogue States:** An ungoverned or an ungovernable state lives in the midst of serious tensions. At the same time, it creates problems for other states by exporting its nasty elements and, directly or indirectly, extending all kinds of assistance to them.[24] During the Cold War era, the Communist powers did so in the name of 'exporting their revolution', the states under the sway of the Islamic

22. A 'failed state' is one that has collapsed and cannot provide protection to its citizens without substantial external support and where the government of the state has ceased to exist inside its territorial borders. John Baylis and Steve Smith: *Globalisation of World Politics: An Introduction* (Delhi: Oxford University Press, 2005), p. 772). According to Rand, a member of the US Think Tank, a failed or an ungoverned state has four attributes: (a) lack of state penetration evidenced by corruption, prevalence of informal economy, and absence of effective state institutions, (b) lack of monopoly of force indicated by illegal armed groups, criminal networks and population with access to arms, (c) lack of border controls, and (d) external interference.
23. According to Lant Pritchett of the Harvard University, a flailing state is a nation-state in which the head, that is the elite institutions at the national level and also in some of the states remain sound and functional, but this head is no longer reliably connected via nerves and sinews to its own limbs. In many parts of the country and also in many sectors of the everyday actions of the field level agents of the state: policemen, engineers, teachers, health workers, are increasingly beyond the control of the administration at the national and state levels.
24. A rogue state is one that remains ridden with its problems and, at the same time, it seeks to export its problems so that other states remain in a state of insecurity. The Bush administration named some countries like North Korea, Iraq, Iran and Libya. Such states may threaten regional peace and security, but are not in a position to threaten the global balance of power. Robert Jackson and Georg Sorensen: *Introduction to International Relations* (Oxford: Oxford University Press, 2003), p. 102.

fundamentalists are doing the same now. It is well known that the organisations of the Islamic fundamentalists have their bases in Pakistan, Afghanistan, and the Gulf countries, they have widened their network so as to cover the countries of Europe like Britain, France and the Russian Federation. Their object seems to be the Islamisation of non-Islamic states.

5. **Trend of Globalisation:** Terrorism has now become an economic activity. If the industrialists accumulate wealth by following the laws and rules of the state, the terrorists have a similar aim and seek to realise it by indulging in the activities of illicit arms trade, smuggling of goods, drug-trafficking, money laundering, etc., As the trend of globalisation has broken the territorial barriers and circumvented the sovereignty of the state, it has in its own way paved the way for the increasing role of the terrorist organisations. Cybernetic revolution has provided new tools with the help of which the terrorist organisations become successful in creating an atmosphere of fear and instability in which they can carry on their trade by illegal means. They invest their money in the prosecution of illegal activities and thereby manage to earn more money as a result of which such a movement goes on unchecked. The invocation of an ideological or religious precept is just a trick to hoodwink the innocent people; it is like putting a cover on their black deeds. Obviously, terrorism which was once a local or regional or national issue, has assumed a universal form in the present age of globalisation and liberalisation. It may, however, be added that globalisation "has changed the scope of terrorism but not its nature."[25]

Different may the causes of the rise of terrorism be, but the fact stands out that, in present times distortion of Islamic injunctions has its place at the top. Also known as 'post-modern terrorism', or 'new terrorism', or 'sacred terrorism', it "is motivated by promises of rewards in the afterlife, that some terrorists are driven by religious reasons to kill as many of the non-believers and unfaithful as possible."[26]

Varieties of Terrorism

A deeper study of terrorism shows that it has certain varieties which may be briefly mentioned as under the following:

1. **Ideological Terrorism:** The terrorists may invoke a particular ideology to achieve their sinister goals. Ideology signifies a set of ideas or convictions in which its subscribers have blind faith and they may go to the extent of paying with their life for the sake of achieving what is aimed at. It may be noticed in the terrorist activities of the Nazis, the Fascists and the Communists. The leaders may also twist the precepts of a particular ideology or a religion for their nefarious purposes. For instance, the Prophet delivered the message of peace and love, but the fanatics have twisted the precepts of Islam to use terrorist methods for converting, what they call, the 'land of the infidels' (Darul Harb) into the 'land of Faith' (Darul Islam). Herein lies the root of Islamic fundamentalism preached and practised by a number of organisations of the Islamic terrorists.
2. **Revolutionary Terrorism:** It has its manifestation where some political party or junta uses extremely violent means to overthrow the existing political order with

25. J.D. Kiras, *op. cit.*, p. 495.
26. W. Laqueur: "Post-Modern Terrorism" in *Foreign Affairs,* No. 75 (5), 1996, pp. 32-33.

the object of establishing an entirely new one in its place. In such an activity the head of the state or government and his trusted lieutenants are butchered and a concerted attempt is made to brutally finish all 'enemies' of the revolution. It was done by the French revolutionary leaders during 1793-94. So happened in Russia in 1917 when Lenin staged a successful socialist revolution. After his death in 1924, his successor (Stalin) followed the course of ruthlessly suppressing all opponents by calling them 'deviationists'. It may occur after a gap of some years as well. In China, Mao finished his opponents and critics in 1966-68 by means of force and called it the 'great proletarian cultural revolution'.

3. **Sub-Revolutionary Terrorism:** It may be described as the softer variety of revolutionary terrorism. The revolutionary leaders use tactics of terrorism with the aim of restructuring their social, economic and political system without overthrowing the existing system as a whole. It may be noticed in the activities of the Irish Republican Army whose leaders use such methods to compel the British Government to have Protestant-dominated Northern Ireland merged with the Catholic-dominated Irish Republic. The Maoist leaders managed to capture power in 2008 by such tactics and then they converted Nepal into a secular republic.
4. **Bio-Terrorism:** Terrorism is an inhuman act involving violence of all sorts to kill or threaten the opponents and thereby create fear or panic for the sake of some definite purpose. It may also be done by releasing disease-causing germs with the intent of killing large number of people and panicking many more. The targeted people suffer from serious diseases like small pox, plague and cholera. The use of anthrax may also be done for this purpose. So bio-terrorism (also known as microbial terrorism), like nuclear terrorism, has its sinister aim of crippling the enemy.
5. **Eco-Terrorism:** It may be taken as an extension of bio-terrorism in that the terrorists may adopt the tactics of polluting the atmosphere by releasing asphyxiating or toxic gases or by poisoning drinking water and thereby do a lot of damage to the life of the people, including their livestock. In order to survive man needs pure air and pure water. Killing human beings and other creatures by poisoning the air and water is certainly an act of terrorism. It is called ecocide.

Islamic Fundamentalism

In recent times, Islamic fundamentalism has emerged as a very volatile form of terrorism as a result of the deliberate distortions and misinterpretations of the Koranic precepts. In the nineteenth century Maulana Wahab of Medina launched a movement for reforming the Islamic society. He sought to invigorate Islam by sweeping away centuries-old evils of corruption, distortion and sinful practices. In the twentieth century Mustafa Kemal Ataturk established a national and secular republic in Turkey – a Western-type state in the heart of the former seat of the Sultanate and the Caliphate. Thus, the Western notions of nationalism, secularism and democracy inspired many leaders like Col. Nasser of Egypt and Shah Raza of Iran to modernise their political systems.

Islamic fundamentalism arose as a stern reaction against such developments. In 1979 Ayatollah Ruhollah Khomeini, a religious fundamentalist, captured power and subverted the political system established by the Shah of Iran. The number of fundamentalists grew in time to come who argued that "modernity in its cultural, political and economic dimensions had caused gradual decline of Islam or its virtual disappearance as an active force in international and state affairs. The institutions and concepts of secularism, liberalism, nationalism and Marxism are blamed for eroding the religion of the Muslims, leading them to forsake its way of life for other ideologies and Western models."[27]

The notable point is that the Islamic fundamentalists have given the shape of an ideology to the notorious trend of terrorism by reinterpreting, rather distorting, the essential tenets of Islam for their nefarious purposes. Marxism exhorts the workers of all countries to unite and win the whole world, Islamic fundamentalism does the same by instigating its adherents to convert the whole world into Darul Islam (Land of Islam) by taking recourse to *jehad* (holy war). For this reason, the followers of this political faith reject the notions of nationalism, secularism and liberalism and they desire to place the whole world under the sway of Islam by taking to the ways of crusades. So Choueiri says: "Islamic fundamentalism is an ideology that works to re-establish the religion of Islam as a political system in the modern world. It does so either by reinterpreting key elements in Islam, or by inventing new categories that are deemed to be self-evident and unique in their configuration."[28]

Ideology is like a political religion. As such, its adherents do not question its precepts or injunctions. The word of the supreme leader or the ideologue is like a command of God which must be blindly obeyed or carried out. Hence, a deviationist must be purged or eliminated by any possible means. A critical investigator may ask as to how acts of money laundering, illicit drug-trafficking and smuggling of goods and dangerous arms can be fitted into the precepts of Islam. Which principles of the Koran sanction killing of the innocent people or indulging in extremely violent activities like explosion of bombs, showering of bullets, damaging public property and the like? Obviously, Islamic terrorism is inspired not by theological or metaphysical but certainly by political and economic considerations.

Taking such a view of things, Mrs. Margaret Thatcher, former British Prime Minister, went to the length of calling upon the Western (Christian) powers to deal with militant Islam in the same manner as they had dealt with Communism. She identified Islamic terrorism of the present with Bolshevism of the past. Designating it as an armed doctrine or an aggressive ideology promoted by a band of fanatical and armed devotees, she insisted that it required an all-embracing long-term strategy to defeat the enemy of Western values. Drawing the attention of the United States, she observed: "For too long we have not been vigilant. We harboured those who hated us, tolerated those who threatened us, and integrated those who weakened us. As a result, for example, we remain all but defenceless against ballistic missiles that could be launched against our cities."[29]

27. Youssef Choueiri: "Islam and Fundamentalism" in Roger Eatwell and Anthony Wright (eds.): *Contemporary Political Ideologies* (Delhi: Rawat Publications, 2003), p. 267.
28. *Ibid.*, p. 255.
29. Rafiq Zakaria: "Anti-Islam Crusade: Liberal Islam is Best Defence" in *The Times of India* (New Delhi) March 15, 2002, p. 12.

Declaration of Jehad Against Country's Tyrants

These young men (returning to Allah) realised that an Islamic government would never be established except by the bomb and rifle. Islam does not coincide or make truce with unbelief, but rather confronts it. The confrontation that Islam calls for with these godless and apostate regimes, does not know Socratic debates, Platonic ideals, nor Aristotelian diplomacy. But it knows the dialogue of bullets, the ideals of assassination, bombing and destruction, and the diplomacy of the canon and machine gun.

I present this humble effort to these young Muslim men who are pure, believing, and fighting for the cause of Allah. It is my contribution toward paving the roads to majestic Allah and establish a caliphate according to the prophecy.

Cited by Kiras in Baylis and Smith, *op. cit.*, p. 488.

Propaganda for *jehad* has assumed a pedagogic form. Schools (called madarsas) are opened to infuse the appeal or message into the minds of the trainees. "Radical mullahs and imams twist the tenets of the religion into a doctrine of action and hatred, where spiritual achievement occurs through destruction, rather than personal enlightenment. In other words, suicide attacks offer the promise of immediate spiritual accomplishment and relieve the individual of the burden of lifetime piety and positive contributions to the community."[30]

Critical Appreciation

Following impressions may be drawn from what we have said in the preceding sections:

1. Terrorism has two faces - black and white. Generally, it is condemned by its phobes for being associated with illegal as well as immoral activities and so it is insisted that its perpetrators must be caught, prosecuted and suitably punished. At the same time, it is lauded by the philes in the name of great service to the cause of the nation at the cost of life and hence its eminent practitioners are honoured like great martyrs. Each situation is differently evaluated or interpreted and, for this reason, 'one's villain is another's national hero'.
2. Terrorism is typically the work of the fighters who are neither properly uniformed nor well organised in an elaborate hierarchical command structures. They are trained in the art of handling explosives and light weaponry within urban or semi-urban areas. Their object may be to capture enemy's territory or not, but they very carefully adhere to the tactics of lightning attacks and swift retreats. These terrorists "have neither the numerical strength nor military capacity nor the will to physically defeat their opponents. Like rats in a sewer, they operate in small and practically autonomous units within the more or less invisible channels of the local civil society, in order to wear down and demoralise their governmental enemy, whom they suppose - ultimately, despite everything - to be capable of negotiations, concessions and retreat."[31]
3. The terrorists take to the ways of extreme violence when they know that their enemy is unworthy of negotiations or incapable of any compromise. Such

30. Kiras, *op. cit.*, p. 495.
31. John Keane: *Global Civil Society?* (Cambridge: Cambridge University Press, 2003), p. 151.

activities are reinforced by the doses of frustrations and miscalculations of the practitioners. This is the reason that when, for example, five terrorists are killed by the forces of the state, revenge is taken by them by killing ten or twenty persons as a measure of retaliation. Curiously, such actions are justified by them in pragmatic terms by invoking the motto of 'tit for tat'. As Keane observes: "The enemy is seen both as morally null and void and worthy of annihilation. Hence, unlimited violence, bloodcurdling in its technical simplicity and witnessed by millions, is justified."[32]

4. The problem becomes all the more critical when some states involve themselves in this heinous act, directly or indirectly. The position of the terrorists is much strengthened when they receive assistance from some state or states in the shape of money, arms and shelter. The press and the media expose such activities and thereby they create an atmosphere of fear in which terrorism has oxygen for its growth. It is well pointed out: "In practice, the real danger lies not in the actual danger from anonymous handfuls of fanatics but from the unreasonable fear their activities provoke, and which today both media and unwise governments encourage. This is one of the major dangers of our time, certainly a greater one than small terrorist groups."[33]
5. Like corruption, terrorism in all its forms and manifestations cannot be totally eliminated from the face of the earth, though its intensity or recurrence may be checked. The use of military and paramilitary forces must be made to deal with this formidable enemy of humankind, but the object cannot be achieved without winning the heads and the hearts of the community from which such elements emerge. Violence begets violence, hence the course of non-violence should also be resorted to. Sooner or later, reason may prevail and the persons involved in this zero-sum game of terrorism may realise the implication of this sound maxim that 'crime never pays'.

Terrorism cannot at all be defended either by the leftists or the rightists as a method or strategy to establish a legitimate political order. It cannot have a normative or value-laden orientation in view of its pejorative forms and manifestations which repudiate all norms of liberalism and humanism.[34]

32. *Ibid.*, p. 152.
33. Eric J. Hobsbawm: *Globalisation, Democracy and Terrorism* (London: Little Brown, 2007), pp. 152-53.
34. M Crenshaw (ed.): *Terrorism, Legitimacy and Power* (Middletown, Conn.: Wesleyan University Press, 1983), pp. 2-4.

29

Globalisation

> The peoples of the earth have thus entered in varying degrees into a universal community, and it has developed to a point where a violation of rights in one part of the world is felt everywhere. The idea of a cosmopolitan right is, therefore, not fantastic and overstrained; it is a necessary complement to the unwritten code of political and international right, transforming it into a universal right of humanity.
>
> **—Immanuel Kant**[1]

Globalisation—now a buzzword—is a trend, a process, a policy, a strategy, a predicament, a philosophy, a doctrine, even an ideology. It has its many philes (as Anthony Giddens, J.N. Bhagwati, Kenichi Ohamae and Francis Fukuyama) who regard it as an irresistible movement for the good of all people of the world; it has its phobes also (as Immanuel Wallerstein, Noam Chomsky and Eric Hobsbawm) who take it as a slippery and an elusive idea, a mind-boggling phenomenon, a new variant of colonialism or neo-colonialism, a bundle of contradictory forces. For the sake of convenience, one may take it as an omnibus expression covering everything from this to that with the aim of establishing interconnectedness and interdependence of the people and their associations all over the world. So, according to Robertson, it is "a catch-all phrase".[2]

Comprehensive Implications and Nature

Globalisation, a term popularised by Theodore Levit in 1985, has comprehensive connotations involving economic, socio-cultural and political aspects. More or less interchangeable with terms like internationalisation, liberalisation, universalisation, westernisation, marketisation, privatisation, deterritorialisation, etc., its salient features may be traced in rapid expansion of capitalism, technological sophistication, economic integration and ideological universalisation. Surprisingly, it may be dramatised as a mixed array of issues like environmental protection, gender quality and justice, racial and ethnic conflicts, cross-border terrorism and the like.[3]

The problem which a student of this subject is faced with at the very outset is: what does globalisation precisely mean? It means different things to different scholars of different countries of the world. To Giddens, it "is the intensification of worldwide relations which link distant localities in a way that local happenings are

1. Kant: *Political Writings,* edited by Hans Reiss (Cambridge: Cambridge University Press, 1991), p. 108.
2. See R. Robertson: *Globalisation: Social Theory and Global Culture* (London: Sage Publications, 1992).
3. See Jan Aart: *Globalisation: A Critical Introduction* (London: Macmillan, 2000).

shaped by events occurring many miles away and *vice versa*."[4] Hence, it signifies elimination of distances in integrating the peoples and their associations in a way that none remains like an island in itself in this vast world which, in the words of Marshall McLuhan, has now become a 'global village'. Obviously, globalisation is a system in which human beings are no longer like a part of the isolated communities that are themselves linked through narrow channels of diplomatic relations and trade. Entire societies are now directly 'plugged in' to global affairs.[5]

Obviously, the term 'globalisation' has different implications in different contexts.

1. Many people equate the term 'globalisation' with 'internationalisation'. From this perspective, a global situation is marked by intense interaction and interdependence between country units.
2. Many commentators take the word 'globalisation' to mean 'liberalisation'. In this usage, globality refers to an open world where resources can move away anywhere, unencumbered by state imposed restrictions like trade barriers, capital controls and travel visas.
3. Many analysts understand globalisation to entail 'universalisation'. In this case, a global phenomenon is one that is found in all corners of the earth.
4. Some observers invoke the term 'globalisation' as the synonym for 'Westernisation' or 'Americanisation'. In this context, globality involves the imposition of modern structures especially of an American consumerist variant.
5. Some researchers identify 'globalisation' with 'deterritorialisation'. Here global relations are seen as occupying a special space that transcends territorial geography.

In view of different ideas about 'globalisation' and the role of official and non-official or non-governmental organisations, this term has its synonyms in 'transnational advocacy networks' and 'worldwide multilateralism'.[6]

A look at the meaning and nature of the term 'globalisation' may enable us to derive its following implications:

1. The term 'globalisation' has its synonyms in many words like internationalisation, universalisation, de-territorialisation, Westernisation, Americanisation, worldwide multilateralisation, etc. It, however, does not liquidate entirely what comes within the range of 'localisation'. Rather it seeks to integrate each other in a way that the difference between the local and the global loses its place or relevance. So Giddens regards its as a phenomenon where local and global happenings affect each other. R. Robertson has coined the term 'glocal' to signify it.[7] It implies that "the local and the global are commingling in new glocal modes of production across and outside of national boundaries.[8]"

---

4. Anthony Giddens: *The Consequences of Modernity* (Stanford: Stanford University Press, 1990), p. 64.
5. R.O. Keohane and Joseph Nye, Jr., "Introduction" in J.D. Donahue and Nye, Jr. (eds.): *Governance in a Globalizing World* (Washington, D. C.: Brookings Institution Press, 2000), pp. 1-41.
6. J.A. Scholte: 'Global Civil Society" in Richard Little and Michael Smith (eds.): *Perspectives in World Politics* (New York: Routledge, 2006), p. 213.
7. R. Robertson: "Glocalisation" in M. Featherstone, S. Lash and R. Robertson (eds.): *Global Modernisation* (London: Sage Publications, 1995).
8. T.W. Luke: "New World Order or Neo-World Orders", *Ibid.*, p. 10.

Globalisation

Globalisation is a social process to which the constraints of geography and social and cultural arrangements recede and in which people become increasingly aware that they are receding.

—M. Waters

Globalisation (London: Routledge, 1995), p. 3.

Global relations are social connections in which territorial location, territorial distances and territorial borders do not have a determining influence. In global space, 'place' is not territorially fixed, territorial distance is covered in effectively no time and territorial frontiers present no particular impediments. Thus, global relations have what could be called 'supra-territorial border or trans-world character.'

—J.A. Scholte

"Global Civil Society" in Richard Little and Michael Smith (eds.): *Perspectives on World Politics* (New York: Routledge, 2006), p. 214.

It (globalisation) can be described, simply as the expression of economic activities across national boundaries..... It refers to the expansion of economic transactions and the organisation of economic activities across political boundaries of nation-states. More precisely, it can be defined as a process associated with increasing economic openness, growing economic interdependence, and deepening economic integration in the world economy.

—Deepak Nayyar

Trade and Globalisation (New Delhi: Oxford University Press, 2008), pp. 347-48.

2. A minute study of the trend of 'globalisation' enables its student to differentiate between globality, globalisation and globalism. Globality refers to the fact that we are increasingly living in a world society in the sense that the notion of closed spaces has become illusory, for now nothing, which happens on our planet, is a limited local event. Globalisation is the view that the world market is now powerful enough to support local and national action. Globalisation is the blank term to describe the processes through which sovereign nation-states are criss-crossed and undermined by transnational actors in the varying prospects of power, orientations, identities and networks.[9]
3. In globalisation, markets are embedded in the webs of government. Capitalism assumes a colossal form and thus becomes 'turbo-capitalism'. That is, it becomes a species of private enterprise driven by the desire for emancipation from social custom, territorial state interference, taxation restrictions, trade union intransigence and all other external restrictions upon the free movement of capital in search of profit. Turbo-capitalism kicks against the so-called 'law' (formulated by the nineteenth-century economist Adolph Wagner) of the expanding public sector. Its advocates push for a new global regulatory regime for deregulation, or lighter and more flexible regulation, on a global scale."[10]

Globalisation covers many spheres—political, economic and socio-cultural. But, the economic aspect is like the pivot around which other aspects revolve. Hence,

9. U. Beck: *What is Globalisation* (Cambridge: Polity Press, 2000), pp. 10-11.
10. John Keane: *Global Civil Society?* (Cambridge: Cambridge University Press, 2003), pp. 67-68.

it is generally studied in terms of economic integration of national economies that has its definite impact on the operation of political systems and cultural patterns of different peoples or countries of the world. While keeping its attention confined to its economic aspect, the Organisation of Economic Cooperation and Development (OECD) in its report of 1995 defined it as "a shift from a world of distinct national economies to a global economy in which production is internationalised and financial capital flows freely and instantly between countries of the world".[11] So, the Second National Commission on Labour, while quoting Human Development Report of South Asia (2001), defined globalisation in its report of 2002 as follows: "The free movement of goods, services, people and information across national boundaries. It creates and, in turn, is driven by integrated global economy, which influences both economic and social relations within and across countries. The opening up of an economy increases competition internally as well as externally, leads to structural global economy, which influences both economic and social relations within and across countries and alters consumer preferences, lifestyles and demands of citizens."

As comprehensively understood, the salient features of globalisation may be enumerated as under:

1. Many things happen in contemporary world largely irrespective of territorial distances and borders.
2. It involves a complex mix of concurrent tendencies towards cultural convergence on the one hand, and an increase in differentiation of groups on the other.
3. It has not brought about the end of geography; it has created a new super-territorial sphere alongside and interrelated with old territorial geography.
4. Within globalisation social relations acquire a host of non-territorial qualities.
5. Crucial conditions for effective sovereignty are removed, system is dissolved in a deluge of electronic and other flows.
6. It is not dissolving the state, but it has not left the state untouched either.New role of the state in the super-territorial sphere should be examined.
7. It highlights interdependence of states in the international sphere.

In short, globalisation refers to processes whereby social and economic relations require relatively distanceless and borderless qualities, so that human lives are increasingly played out in the world as a single place. Social relations, that is, the countless and complex ways the people interact with the effect upon each other are more and more being conducted and organised on the basis of a planetary unit. By the same token, country locations and, in particular, boundaries between territorial states are, in some important senses, becoming less central to our lives, although they do remain significant. Globalisation is thus an ongoing trend whereby the world has, in many respects, and at a gradually accelerated rate, become one relatively boundless social and economic sphere.

Dimensions of Globalisation

As pointed out earlier, globalisation has its different dimensions - economic, socio-cultural and political - each having its strong and weak points.

11. Andrew Heywood: *Politics* (Basingstroke: Palgrave Foundation, 2005), 2nd ed., p. 139.

Economic Dimension: Mainly as an economic affair, globalisation refers to a process of deepening economic integration; increasing economic openness and growing economic interdependence between countries in the world economy.[12] It is shaping a new system of international economic relations—be it in the field of investment, production, trade, finance or technology. It reveals the fact that now no country can live in a state of isolation; autarchy or economic self-sufficiency cannot be practised by any state of the world. The growing trend of interlocking of national economies into a global economic system cannot be reversed. The fact is that we are now living in the age of 'technological determinism' which makes the rise and growth of new economic patterns inevitable. It has the potential to enrich everyone in the world, specifically the poor and the backward, and may be a force of the 'common good.'[13]

However, it has its positive and negative effects. On the positive side, it has caused a shift in the pace and patterns of both the developed and the developing countries of the world. It may be noticed in the removal of qualitative restrictions and subsidies, reduction of tariffs, changes in patent regimes and in the patterns of investments, new rules of dumping and anti-dumping measures, adoption of safeguards, etc. If so, the rise and development of globalisation must be analysed in terms of the underlying economic factors, the political conjectures which enable it to gather momentum and the intellectual rationale that is almost prescriptive. The rapid integration of financial markets has its impact on the international monetary system which underwent three revolutions all at once—regulation, internationalisation and innovation.[14]

On the negative side, it is contended that such a development has been to the advantage of the rich and advanced countries of the world alone. It has done a lot of harm to the poor, backward and undeveloped countries which are devoid of resources and technology. In the international market the poor countries cannot compete with the rich and highly industrialised countries. While the developed countries with their saturated markets are seeking access for their surplus products or goods to the poor and backward countries, the developing countries remain technologically excluded and they cannot export their surplus labour even to the developed countries due to restrictions of visa or unfavourable immigration rules. Globalisation and development coincide with each other along the lines of ensuring markets for western goods, retaining cheap labour and raw materials and in this process sovereignty of the state is undermined.

Financial liberalisation might help increase in access to global financial resources, but it is mostly of a speculative nature as but far as the case of the developing countries is concerned. It follows that the developing countries would provide access to their markets without capital mobility and without a corresponding provision for labour mobility. Thus, asymmetry in the form of free movement of capital and the unfree movement of labour across national boundaries lies at the heart of inequality

12. P.D. Shenoy: *Globalisation: Its Impact on Industrial Relations in India* (New Delhi: New Dawn Press, 2006), p. 6.
13. See J.N. Bhagwati: *In Defense of Globalisation* (New Delhi: Penguin, 2002).
14. See Deepak Nayyar: "Challenges of Globalisation" in Bibek Debroy (ed.): Globalisation: What Does It Mean for Development (Delhi: Konark Publishers, 1998).

in the rules of game for liberalisation. Globalisation has the power to do enormous good to the rich countries; it has similar power to do enormous harm to the poor and developing countries of the world. So, a critic comments that "in much of the world, it has not brought about comparable benefits, for many it seems closer to an unmitigated disaster.[15]

Globalisation is a game between the gainers and the losers. It is a good game for the rich countries alone. The poor and backward countries cannot get their expected rewards, for they cannot compete with them on account of the want of resources and technology. So, another critic comments: "The currently fashionable free market globalisation has brought about a dramatic growth in economic and social inequalities both within states and internationally; there is no sign that this polarisation is not continuing within countries, in spite of a general diminution of external powers."[16]

Socio-cultural Dimension: Socio-cultural globalisation is the process whereby information, communications and images, that have been produced in one part of the world, enter into a global flow that tends to 'flatten out' cultural differences between nations, regions and individuals.[17] Driven to impart by the growth of transnational companies and the emergence of global commodities, cultural globalisation is also fuelled by the so-called 'information revolution'—spread of satellite communication, telecommunication networks, information technology, internet and global media corporations. It may be visualised in the changing patterns of social norms and etiquettes. People's preferences for sipping Coca Cola, or taking food in the McDonald restaurants, or wearing European garments, etc., leave an impression that they are moving towards cultural homogenisation.

However, its adverse effects may be seen in two directions—rise of religious fundamentalism and the emergence of multiculturalism. The fundamentalists exhort their co-religionists to maintain purity of their faith and traditional ways of life and also try to export their ideology, while the multiculturalists clamour for maintaining their separate and distinct identity for the sake of recognition in their country. Both vehemently oppose the 'imposition' of an alien culture or the value system of the foreigners and may go to the extent of using violent and unconstitutional means for this sake. The communitarians like Michael Sandel, Michael Walzer, Charles Taylor and A. MacIntyre assert that there can never be unanimity on the conception of 'good life' even at the local and regional levels in spite of the fact that the majority is said to have the right to promote or popularise its conception of the 'public good' or 'good life'.

While the wave of globalisation is blowing with vigour, the trend of multiculturalism is also gathering weight. It may be taken note of in, what is known by various names, as 'politics of identity', 'politics of recognition', or 'politics of difference'. While each term has slightly different connotations, the underlying idea is the same. It covers the case of the people who have been victims of marginalisation, tranquillisation, exclusion, segregation and dehumanisation for

15. Joseph Stiglitz: *Globalisation and Its Discontents* (New Delhi: Penguin Books, 2002), p. 20.
16. Eric Hobsbawm: *Globalisation: Democracy and Terrorism* (London: Little Brown, 2007), p. 3.
17. Heywood, *op. cit.*, p. 139.

centuries. While globalisation desires cultural homogenisation of the people of the world, multiculturalism lays stress on the trait of indigenisation. Such groups struggle for maintaining their distinct identity in terms of race, culture, religion, ways of life and the like. The politics of this kind throws light on cultural injustices rooted in the social patterns of representation, interpenetration and communication, including cultural domination, non-recognition and disrespect, so as to dispense with the condition of 'differentiated citizenship'.[18]

The problem is that certain minorities (as the Kurds in Iraq, the French in Canada, the Roman Catholics in Northern Ireland, the Tamils in Sri Lanka, etc.) are not willing to assimilate themselves with what is called the 'national culture'. Then, how can they be willing to assimilate themselves with the 'global culture'. Not only this, the excluded, neglected and exploited people have developed political awareness. They have formed their groups in their countries and have taken to the way of strengthening their position by joining hands with similar groups operating in other countries of the world. Its examples may be seen in their meets at Durban, London and Bhopal. At the national level, this struggle may be seen between liberal 'civic nationalism' and illiberal 'ethnic nationalism'.[19] The leaders of the liberal-democratic systems have come to realise that the best way to ensure the loyalty of the national minorities is to accept, not to attack, their sense of distinct nationality.[20]

Apprehensively, the trend of multiculturalism may be seen to have a remote connection with the rising trend of cross-border terrorism. Hitler raised the slogan of 'Pan-Germanism' that enthused the German minorities of Austria and Czechoslovakia to rebel. In not much time Nazi Germany could destroy the independence of these two states. So now some Muslim terrorist organisations have developed international links operating from any place like Karachi, Dubai or Sharjah to provoke their co-religionists in the U.S.A, Britain, France and Russia to rise in revolt. Their mission is to establish purity of faith and rule of Islam over as many parts of the world as possible. Its sinister instances may be seen in their attacks on the cities of America, Britain, France, Russia and India. Globalisation requires a progressive outlook so that the nations of the world take to the course of integration in different directions, multiculturalism, if blended with secessionism, foments a reactionary or regressive outlook that hampers such a process. This type of multiculturalism is certainly different from its liberal counterpart which "is the enemy of cultural conservatism and both reflects and embraces the openness, pluralism, and autonomy that modernisation and globalisation entail."[21]

Political Dimension: Political globalisation is evident in the growing significance of many international organisation as the United Nations, International Labour Organisation, International Monetary Fund, International Bank for Reconstruction

18. I.M. Young: "Polity and Groups Differences: A Critique of the Ideal of Universal Citizenship" in *Ethics*, Vol. 99, No. 2, pp. 250-74.
19. William Pfaff, *The Wrath of Nations: Civilization and the Furies of Nationalism* (New York: Simon and Schuster, 1993), p. 162.
20. Will Kymlicka: *Contemporary Political Philosophy: An Introduction* (New Delhi: Oxford University, Press, 2005), Indian Edition, p. 352.
21. *Ibid.*, p. 369.

and Development (World Bank), World Trade Organisation, etc., as well as in many regional organisations like Organisation of European Cooperation and Development and the European Union. These bodies exercise their jurisdiction over a defined area and the member-states honour their control, even intervention, without sacrificing their national sovereignty, though the fact of its erosion cannot be lost sight of. Laudable has been the role of such organisations in improving the lot of the poor and backward countries of the world that may not be acceptable to the men of Marxist disposition.[22]

The report of the World Commission on Development (also known as the Brandt Commission) titled North-South: A Programme for Survival (1980) and its second report titled Common Crisis: North-South Cooperation for World Recovery (1983) had their aims in eradicating structural inequalities between the high wage, low investment, predominantly rural and agricultural countries of the South. At the same time, these reports highlight the interdependence of the North and the South in that the long-term prosperity of the advanced countries of the North is dependent on the development of the poor and developing countries of the South. It clearly refutes the view of neo-Marxists like A.G. Frank, Samir Amin and Immanuel Wallerstein that the development of the few is dependent on the underdevelopment of the many.[23]

Globalisation postulates universalisation of the democratic system. Undeniable is the fact that such a system alone may ensure proper integration of national economies and polities into a sound global order. Heywood is right in observing that "the most significant political debate associated with globalisation concerns its impact on democracy. The complex and diverse pressures unleashed by the market to the economies can be contained only within open and democratic societies."[24] It has its corroboration in the prophetic affirmation of Fukuyama: "The triumph of the West, of the Western idea, is evident first of all in the real exhaustion of viable systematic alternative to Western liberalism."[25]

The new means of communications like cellular phones, cable television and internet system revealing astounding achievements of a democratic system have produced a new kind of 'enlightenment' whose abiding impact may be seen in the banishment of the unpopular communist and fascist systems.[26] The success of the Solidarity Movement in Poland under the leadership of Lech Walesa in the 1980s was hailed as the 'rebirth of civil society' there. It made the first dent into the fort of the socialist commonwealth created by Stalin and retained by his successors like

22. Such writers subscribe to the view of Lenin that 'imperialism is the last stage of capitalism', of Kwame Nkrumah that 'neo-colonialism is the final stage of imperialism' and of Noam Chomsky that 'globalisation is the latest form of colonialism and neo-colonialism.'
23. Samir Amin, Giovanni Arrighi, A.G. Frank and Immanuel Wallerstein: *Dynamics of Global Crisis* (New York: Monthly Review Press, 1982), pp. 9-10.
24. Heywood, *op. cit.*, pp. 142-43.
25. Francis Fukuyama: "End of History" in *National Interest* (Summer, 1989), p. 3.
26. The creed of enlightenment stressed the possibility of man's own intellect in planning a society on rational grounds. Therefore, it denied the traditional authority of the monarchs and the church. Freedoms especially of thought and cooperative human behaviour, were the high points of this philosophy. David Robertson: *A Dictionary of Modern Politics* (London and New York: Europa Publications, 2002), 3rd ed., p. 165.

Khrushchev and Brezhnev. The enlightened people of East Germany broke down the Berlin Wall in 1990 so as to merge with the democratic part of West Germany. The countries of Eastern Europe adopted the liberal-democratic system. Russia became a member of the G-8 and other countries like Poland and Hungary joined the European Union.

However, such developments have created the problem of 'democratic deficit'. The hold of the developed countries of the world supported by the role of the transnational and multinational companies and corporations has created numerous problems for the developing countries of the world. Globalisation in the form of 'market fundamentalism' threatens the existence of a sovereign nation-state. In effect, it denies democratic rights to the smaller and less developed states and to the people at large to determine their national economic and social future. "The irony of globalisation is that while it advocates political ideals like freedom, democracy, human rights, good governance, etc., the very nature and essence of this process is inherently undemocratic. The unfair system of voting rights in the decision-making process of global financial institutions like the IMF, and the World Bank, the rise of monopoly and oligopolistic practices in trade, investment and technology, unfair competition, bypassing of the democratic and parliamentary institutions in the making of key decisions at the national and international levels, and the rising social costs are some of the indicators that reflect the undemocratic nature of the globalisation process.[27]

Globalisation, as a process of free and unbridled flow of trade, investment, technology, information and culture across territorial borders, has enabled the industrialised countries to control the destinies of the poor and backward countries of the world. Surprisingly, the visible or invisible links of the great industrialists with the petty bureaucratic elites reveal that the nation-state is no longer an association of the native people. State is an instrument in the hands of such influential groups which frame constitutional provisions, make legislative enactments, promulgate administrative orders, secure judicial pronouncements and, in short, take all important decisions regarding integration of the national economies and polities into the process of globalisation.

Globalisation has affected the nation-state system by demolishing the sanctity of territorial borders and its sovereign status. In the words of Ralph Braibanti, it has resolved the dilemma of 'ceaseless dialectic' between maintaining national boundaries and transcending them. It may be taken note of that the nation-state is retreating in the face of the superior power of globalisation. The states were once the masters of the markets, now it is the markets which have their lordship over the states on many crucial issues.[28] However, this point should not be overstretched. The model of the nation-state is in decline, of course, but it has not demised. It may take time. As its evolution took about two hundred years after the Westphalia treaties of 1648, it may take an equally long time in being replaced by another workable model.

27. SRTP Sugunakararaju, "Globalisation and Changing Role of the Nation-State" in Rumki Basu (ed.): *Globalisation and the Changing Role of the State: Issues and Impacts* (New Delhi: New Dawn Press, 2008), p. 42.
28. Stiglitz, *op. cit.*, p. 248.

The developments of the day are understandable. In time to come, people "may experience the end of the nation-state, not as a gradual erosion of its power, but as a final convulsion which would engulf its citizens."[29]

Multiculturalism, in its negative or illiberal form, like blind or aggressive nationalism, creates impediments in the way of globalisation, but its positive or liberal manifestation may have its consonance with the growing process of globalisation. Basically different is the case of cross-border terrorism, also known as Islamic fundamentalism, that is posing a very serious threat to the nation-state system. The core idea of enlightenment that development process resulting from the impact of science and technology would certainly lead to secularisation of human relations seems to have been belied by the heinous activities of the Islamic fundamentalists.

It is a pity that the trend of 'enlightenment' failed to secularise and humanise the people of Islamic countries in whose view the roots of new learning lie in skepticism, iconoclasm and eclecticism in sharp contrast to their faith in traditions which constitute the bedrock of their religion. The precepts and the message of the holy Quran have their eternal relevance, but their misinterpretations by the fundamentalists create a tragic state of affairs. The cry for '*jehad*' (holy war) may be taken as a case in point whose real meaning has been perverted by the fanatic elements associated with a number of terrorist organisations having their bases in Pakistan, Iran, Iraq, Lebanon, Libya, Afghanistan, Bangladesh, etc. These fundamentalist elements may invoke the argument of 'jehad' for any purpose of their choice ranging from the liberation of Palestine from the yoke of the Jews to the termination of the American military intervention in Afghanistan and Iraq.[30]

The sinister manifestations of cross-border terrorism stand as a great impediment in the way of globalisation. It is evident from its following features:[31]

- International terrorism counterpoises the problem of the nation-state being confronted by non-state actors that threaten it with violence in order to attain and extract political benefits.
- International terrorism is a problem that has attained menacing proportions in the wake of the growth of globalisation.
- Terrorism is a global problem and by way of a solution it calls for the establishment of an architecture of international jurisprudence or a genuinely cosmopolitan and global rule of law.

Nation-states have brought to light their own absolutist foundations in that they have often tended to use extremely coercive methods that have come down too

29. Roger Dale: "the Future of the Nation-State" in Gregor McLellan, David Held and Stuart Hall (eds.): *The Idea of the Modern State* (Buckingham: Oxford University Press, 1993), p. 219.
30. 'Jehad' literally means a crusade or a religious war for the cause of Islam. It may be a fight for a cause like liberation of the land from the hold of the 'infidels' or forcing the co-religionists to lead a life of 'purity'. According to R.L. Canfield, it may be regarded as the most honourable quest of the Muslims for a pure inner life as well as for maintaining upright relations to one's social affairs and a just society in the world at large in strictly Islamic terms. See M. Hauner and Canfield, (eds.): *Afghanistan and the Soviet Union: Collision and Transformation* (San Francisco: Westview Press, 1989), p. 23.
31. Amir Ali: "Globalisation and the State: A Contested Terrain" in Rumki Basu, (ed.): *Globalisation*, pp. 27-28.

heavily, often not on terrorists' outfits but on ordinary citizens whose freedoms have been subject to blatant violations. The establishment of an international architecture of jurisprudence grounded in a global rule of law as a response to terrorism has to be comprehensive, all-inclusive and cosmopolitan. It must, therefore, be all to transcend the narrow confines of the nation-state. It is deplorable that "in the era of globalisation the response of the nation-states to international terrorism has been retrogressive patriotism that easily descends into jingoism."[32]

The masterminds of global terrorism may coin any typical argument to justify their actions which cannot be acceptable to a man of liberal disposition. For instance, one of their arguments is that globalisation has created vast disparities of wealth between the developed and the developing countries and so they make the United States and other rich countries like Britain and France their targets of attack.[33] But the problem of dealing with this latest menace involves the issue of the protection of human rights. The states may deal with this problem individually or in a collective manner, but the delicate issue remains that it should be done without violation of the human rights.[34] The attack of the terrorists on the two cities of the United States on 11th September 2001 was an astounding event which forced the Security Council of the United Nations to pass a resolution so as to deal with this menace at the international level. It whetted the appetite of the *jehadis* as some of their leaders had started dreaming of world domination or a grand Muslim Caliphate from the Mediterranean through Middle East to the South China Sea.

Violence has no place in the process of globalisation. But, the Islamic fundamentalists have full faith in it that imparts to their affirmations the character of an ideology. They may be taken as the committed disciples of Frantz Fanon in whose words "violence is a cleansing force. It frees the native of his inferiority complex and from his despair and inaction. It makes him fearless and restores his self-respect." Thus, according to Vinod Saighal, fight against global terrorism "has been turning out to be, disclaimers notwithstanding, fight against Islamic fundamentalism."[35]

32. *Ibid.*, Also see Danielle Archibugi and I.M. Young: "Ensuring a Global Rule of Law" in J.P. Sterba (ed.). *Terrorism and International Justice* (Oxford: Oxford University Press, 2003).
33. Klaus Schwab, the President of the World Economic Forum, likened the event of 9/11 (2001) to the fall of the Berlin Wall in its impact on world economy and politics. The President of the World Bank (James Wolfensohn) gave a statement the following day that this tragedy "broke the illusion that rich countries could ignore desperation and poverty in other parts of the globe. The issue of poverty is really the issue of peace."
34. The then Secretary-General of the United Nations (Kofi Annan) cautioned: "Terrorism is one of the threats against which states have to protect their citizens. They have not only the right but also the duty to do so. But the states must also take the greatest care to ensure that counter-terrorism does not, any more than sovereignty, become an all-embracing concept that is used to cloak or justify violation of human rights". Cited in Vinod Saighal: *Dealing with Global Terrorism: The Way Forward* (New Delhi: New Dawn Press, 2004), p. 175.
35. *Ibid.*, p. 141. Politics has outstripped the religious rhetoric that still "represents a distorted reflection of a blocked system that is unable to respond to the democratic aspirations of the citizenry." Youssef Choueiri, "Islam and Fundamentalism" in Roger Eatwell and Anthony Wright (eds.): *Contemporary Political Ideologies* (Delhi: Rawat Publications, 1999), p. 278.

Issue of Global Governance

If globalisation is the process of interconnectedness and interdependence of the states, the issue of global governance may be described as its logical outcome. If the process remains at work in a humane way, the dream of global governance may be realised in a long time to come. As Fukuyama hopefully visualised: "What we are witnessing is not just the end of the Cold War, or the passing away of a particular period of post-war history, but the end of the history as such; that is the end point of mankind's ideological revolution and the universalisation of western liberal democracy as the final form of human government."[36] It may be in spite of the fact that there is, and can be, no fixed form of global governance, nor is there a single structure for this purpose. It is a broad, dynamic and complex process of interactive decision-making, that is constantly evolving and responding to changing circumstances.[37]

It was Chancellor Willy Brandt of Germany who took the lead in the establishment of the Commission on Global Governance in 1992 in the belief that international developments had created a unique opportunity for strengthening global cooperation so as to meet the challenge of securing for all and achieving sustainable development and universalising democracy. With the blessings of the then Secretary-General of the United Nations (Dr B.B. Ghali), the Commission (having 28 members from different countries of the world) came into being as an informal private group. It aimed to contribute to the improvement of global governance, to analyse the main forces of global change, to examine the major issues facing the world community, to assess the adequacy of global institutional arrangements and to suggest how they should be reformed or restrengthened.[38]

The theme of global governance may be like a distant dream at the moment, but it should not be taken as a figment of imagination. The growing trend of liberalisation may soften the passage. The goal may be realised by the sincere cooperation and concerted efforts of the people of the world. As an Indian scholar says: "Global governance must take an integrated approach to questions of human survival and prosperity. Effective global decision-making needs to build up and influence decision-makers. It must build partnerships—networks of institutions and processes—that enable global actors to pool information, knowledge and cooperation and to develop just policies and practices on issues of common concern. There must be an agreed global framework for actions and policies to be carried out at appropriate levels. A multifaceted strategy for global governance is required. This will involve reforming and strengthening the existing system of intergovernmental institutions, and improving the means of collaboration. The international system that the U.N. Charter put in place thus needs to be renewed."[39]

36. Francis Fukuyama: *The End of History and the Last Man* (London: Penguin Books, 1992), pp. 1xxii and 418.
37. Ingvar Carlson and Sridath Ramphal: *Our Global Neighbourhood: The Report of the Commission on Global Governance* (Oxford University Press, 1995), p. 4.
38. In April, 1991, 36 eminent persons had a meeting at Stockholm in Sweden to discuss the needs of the 1990s under the auspices of the Stockholm Initiatives on Global Security and Governance. On this occasion, it was proposed that an international commission be set up to explore the opportunities created by the end of the Cold War so as to build a more effective system of international security and global governance.
39. B.N. Mehrish: *The United Nations in a New Millennium: A Changing Scenario* (Delhi: Academic Excellence Publishers, 2007), p. 14.

Hallmarks and Foundational Factors of Globalisation

Hallmarks

1. More inter-state connections and the decreasing effect of state policy,
2. Development of increasingly transnational communications and activities,
3. Decline in the importance of the nation-state,
4. Emergence of global political, economic and cultural organisations and bureaucracies.
5. Emergence of global cities such as London, New York, Paris, Tokyo as local sites of global interaction,
6. Huge increase in the flows of commodities and cultural products, and
7. Worldwide spread of Western style consumerism.

Foundational Factors

1. Expansion of trading relationships and the use of symbolic tokens of which money is an obvious example,
2. Copernicusean conception of the world as a globe,
3. Invention of the mechanical clock, time, measurement and global time zones,
4. Invention of the navigational aids and the steady advance of travel technologies,
5. Outward expansion of European institutions and culture,
6. Capitalism's insatiable drive to maximise profit leading it to go global in its post-modern phase and to open up and exploit new markets with new products.

S.Lash and J. Urry: *The End of Organised Capitalism* (Cambridge: Polity Press, 1987) cited in John Beynoon and David Dunkerley (eds.): *Globalisation: The Reader* (London: The Athlone Press, 2000), pp. 5-7.

Significant Features of Globalisation

1. The pace of economic transformation is so great that it has created a new world politics. States are no longer closed units and they cannot control their economies. The world economy is more interdependent than ever, with trade and finances ever expanding.
2. Communications have fundamentally revolutionised the way we deal with the rest of the world. We now live in a world where events in one location can be immediately observed on the other side of the world. Electronic communications alter the notions of the social groups we work with and live in.
3. There is now, more than ever before, a global culture, so that most urban areas resemble one another, the world shares a common culture, much of it emanating from Hollywood.
4. The world is becoming more homogeneous. Differences between peoples are diminishing.
5. Time and space seem to be collapsing. Our old ideas of geographical space and of chronological time are undermined by the speed of modern communications and media.
6. There is emerging a global polity, with transnational social and political movements and the beginnings of a transfer of allegiance from the state to sub-state, transnational, and international bodies.
7. A cosmopolitan culture is developing. People are beginning 'to think globally and act locally'.
8. A risk culture is emerging with people realising both that the main risks that face them are global (pollution and AIDS) and that states are unable to deal with the problem.

John Baylis and Steve Smith: *The Globalisation of World Politics: An Introduction* (New York: Oxford University Press, 2005), p. 11.

Globalisation and Development

Globalisation and development appear to be interrelated, but, in fact, it is not so. The former signifies the trend of increasing interaction and interdependence of the states particularly in the economic sphere, while the latter has its aim in bringing about an improvement in the living conditions of the people. No state can remain immune from the impact of globalisation and so no people should be excluded from the effects of development. Progress should be made in both directions, but it cannot be simultaneous in view of the fact that, unlike markets, the governments are accountable to their people. And yet the two may be brought to an irreducible minimum. Development must bring about an improvement in the living conditions of the people. It should, therefore, ensure that the basic needs of all are satisfied. Globalisation must serve the purpose of development which after all "is to create a milieu that enables people, ordinary people, to lead a good life."[40]

The real difficulty is that while the process of globalisation is fast, the pace of development is retarded by increasing disparities at the level of economic development on account of being governed by the politics of hegemony or dominance. Increasing progress in the direction of globalisation requires the role of some dominant economic power with a strong and stable currency so as to maintain international monetary system. It may result in international economic welfare of course, but it puts the poor and backward countries in a state of disadvantage. Market becomes more important than the state and as it is dominated by the barons of industry, the welfare of the weaker sections of the society is not properly looked after. The quality of life of the affluent sections is improved without having similar impact on the lot of the unprivileged sections of the people. "As a result of privatisation and deregulation, capital has gained at the expense of labour almost everywhere, for profit shares have arisen while wage shares have fallen."[41]

The 'hegemonic stability theory' as propounded by Charles Kindleberger and further developed by Robert Gilpin is based on the hypothesis that a dominant economic and military power is necessary for the creation and full development of a liberal world market economy, because in the absence of such a power, liberal rules cannot be enforced around the world. However, different from the contention of the mercantilists, it contains a liberal element in that the dominant power "does not merely manipulate international economic relations for its own sake; it creates an open world economy based on free trade which is to the benefit of all participating states and not only the hegemon."[42]

A critic may comment that the altruistic aspect of the hegemonic stability theory is quite superficial and misleading. The hegemonic state becomes 'predatory' inasmuch as it establishes its sway over many other economically weaker states and puts a mask on it by obliging them with certain tangible benefits. Some of such states become 'free riders' by making use of the goods without paying for them. More

40. Deepak Nayyar: *Trade and Development* (Delhi: Oxford University Press, 2008), p. 344.
41. *Ibid.*, p. 352.
42. Robert Jackson and Georg Sorensen: *Introduction to International Relations: Theories and Approaches* (Oxford: Oxford University Press, 2003), p. 196.

deplorable is the fact that the services and contributions of the weaker states for the development of liberal world economy are ignored. So Jackson and Sorensen comment: "Hegemonic stability theory tends to view smaller powers as egoistic free riders. In fact, they have contributed greatly to the setting up of a liberal world economy by assisting in the establishment of liberal international regimes. Furthermore, US hegemony was always less altruistic than the theory leads us to believe."[43]

It may be noticed in the game of inclusion and exclusion. While the developed countries have found their place in the club of the multimillionaires, the developing and the undeveloped countries have seen their exclusion from development. It is simply about their inability to satisfy basic human needs. Three reasons may be assigned for it:[44]

1. There are different rules in different spheres. The rules of the game for the international trading system, being progressively set in the World Trade Organisation, provide the most obvious example. This implies more openness in some spheres but less openness in other spheres.
2. There are rules for some, but not for others. In the WTO, for instance, major trading countries resort to a unilateral exercise of power, ignoring the rules, because small countries do not have the economic strength even if they have the legal right to retaliate.
3. The agenda for new rules is partisan, but the unsaid is just as important as the said. The Brettonwoods institutions (International Monetary Fund and World Bank) seek to harmonise policies and institutions across countries which is in consonance with the needs of globalisation.

"The politics of globalisation combined with these rules, is bound to significantly reduce the autonomy of developing countries in the formulation of economic policies in their pursuit of development. This is attributable, in part, to the asymmetric rules and, in part, to the economic implications of globalisation."[45]

Cosmocracy: Emerging World Polity in the Age of Globalisation

Philosophers and poets have thought in terms of a world state, world government, world law, world citizenship and the like and they have drawn a faint picture of an ideal order beyond, what is now called, the Westphalian model of state. Such ideas were criticised for being the figments of imagination by the realists who took nation-state, in the vein of Hegel, as the highest stage of social development. However, progress in the direction of globalisation has made the case optimistic so much so that new writers like Georg Sorensen and Robert Cooper talk about 'post-modern' and 'post-colonial states' and distinguish between 'pre-modern' and 'post-modern' states. John Keane has taken up the case of 'global governance in the making' of what he calls 'cosmocracy' or a new form of governmental power, a type of institutionalised power defying all previous accounts of different forms of government ranging from the illustrations of Aristotle and Polybius in the ancient to

43. *Ibid.*, p 201.
44. Deepak Nayyar, *op. cit.*, pp. 357-58.
45. *Ibid.*, p. 358.

that of Leacock and Marriott in the modern times.[46] It looks like struggling to carve out a place of its own in the globalised order with these salient features:

1. It is the first-ever polity. Despite the fact that it does not appear as such on the maps of the world, it is a system of worldwide webs of interdependence of actions and reactions at a distance, a complex melange of networks of legal, governmental, police and military interdependence at worldwide distances.[47]
2. It stands on the spectrum between the so-called Westphalian model of competing sovereign states and a single, unitary system of world government. It functions as something more and other than an international community of otherwise sovereign governments. It is a conglomeration of interlocking and overlapping sub-state, state and supra-state institutions and multidimensional and social effects on a global scale.[48]
3. It becomes understandable as a modularised system of government in which decision-making power, especially in its core, is distributed among three different but linked form of governmental spaces. For the sake of convenience, these can be described as micro-government, meso-government and macro-government. Micro-government refers to sub-territorial state institutions, like local and regional governing institutions, whose decision-making powers either on an *ad hoc* or more permanent basis, have felt effects elsewhere in some or other corners of the globe. The strengthening tendency of local courts to examine and prosecute symbolically 'foreign' acts of wrongdoing is an example. Meso-governments include territorially defined states and actual or proto-regional institutions like the European Union and the ASEAN pact. Despite being the Supreme Court of a country, it may refer a case for final adjudication to a higher judicial authority like the European Court of Human Rights. Finally, cosmocracy is structured by macro-governments or supra-national institutions like the United Nations Security Council or the International Criminal Court.[49]
4. It is a dynamic polity. It is a conglomeration of institutions shaped by several structuring principles, whose resultant reminds its subjects and observers alike, or at least gives them the impression, that these institutions have one thing in common: their particular power to shape and reshape people's lives has global effects. It comprises recombinant structures, which are themselves the products of a constantly changing, permanently unfolding hybridisation of existing processes and decisions. That is, it is a polity shaped by multi-level governance and, hence, it may be described as a polymerous form of rule.[50]
5. It is a conglomeration of political power cemented together with laws and legal procedures. There has been a definite trend towards not only the legalisation of governmental structures, but also the development of new forms of multilateral legal networks that highlight the passing away of the fiction of legal sovereignty of territorial states. In the Pinochet case, the European Court of Human Rights

46. John Keane: *Global Civil Society?* (Cambridge: Cambridge University Press, 2003), p. 97.
47. *Ibid.*, pp. 97-98.
48. *Ibid.*, p. 98.
49. *Ibid.*, pp. 101-02.
50. *Ibid.*, p. 103.

invoked the doctrine of *jus cogens,* according to which there are definable norms like a common interest of humanity from which no dissent or derogation by governmental or non-governmental parties is justified.[51]

6. It has not yet been established; it is on the move. And yet it is a compound form of government wrapped in law and having a definite durability. It might be described as a dynamic system of clumsy institutions. In the form of a complex, multilayered, dynamic and open-ended totality, it has zones of tensions created by law-breaking forces (like terrorists) that enables a critic to hit at the inappropriateness of identifying it with the system of trans-governmentalism.[52]
7. Quite a few institutions which comprise the system of cosmocracy are publicly accountable. It is not quite a species of absolutism, since its core contains rich networks of democratic procedures designed to expose and oppose hubris. Yet when considered overall, as an integrated polity, it definitely has an affinity with authoritarian, rather than representative democratic procedures.[53]
8. For its existence, it cannot tolerate the hegemony of a single state. It repudiates the case of anything like Pax-Romana, Pax-Britannica, or Pax-Americana. The role of a single dominant power destabilises it. So the problem of the day is as to how the single dominant power can be tamed or compounded by the pressing need to develop a more effective and legitimate form of democracy. However, its solution may he found in the system of geo-governance or going beyond what Held and Archibugi call 'cosmopolitan democracy.[54]
9. It is a much more complex and self-contradictory polity than revised cosmopolitanism supposes. It is an intricate system of power that cannot be understood by means of empty moralising or metaphors like 'levels' or emergent cosmopolitan covenants and the like. It resembles a thoroughly modern version of the political world pondered by Johannes Althusius (1557-1638), a strangely neo-medieval melange of overlapping legal structures and political bodies that come in all shapes and sizes—a many-sided world of overlapping and potentially conflicting political structures, primordial groups, differently sized political institutions, and federalist strivings for both particularism and universalism, ecumene and community.[55]

In the age of globalisation, global civil society is emerging as its natural concomitant. With it is gradually coming up the system of global governance. It contradicts the view that there can be no global civil society without a world government. Things are in the melting pot and may take a shape of their own in time to come. Marsiglio of Padua gave the ideas of democratisation of the church and independence of the state from the hold of the ecclesiastical power. It became a reality in the modern world. Hence, what was once dreamt by philosophers like Dante, Althusius, Rousseau, Grotius, Bentham, Kant and Green may take the form of a reality in the age of globalisation. One should take it into view that many

51. *Ibid.,* pp. 104-05.
52. *Ibid.,* p. 107.
53. *Ibid.,* p. 116.
54. *Ibid.,* p. 118.
55. *Ibid.,* pp. 125-26.

developments take place as a result of the exercise of the rational power of man. It is well observed: "Global governance, then is not so much about world government, as it is about institutions and practices combined with rules that facilitate cooperation among sovereign nation-states."[56]

Critical Appreciation

To sum up, globalisation is an omnibus or a catch-all phrase that includes an array of processes such as time and space compression, cultural and commercial homogenisation, technological sophistication, and a general intensification of the consciousness of the world as a whole. It is a process by which the world is becoming more and more like a single unit. So, it is like a set of related processes which "interconnect individuals, groups, communities, states, markets, corporations, international governmental and non-governmental organisations in a complex web of social relations."[57]

Like any other process or system, globalisation has its merits and demerits, but in this case the former outweigh the latter. To say that globalisation creates 'economic dominance' and 'democratic deficit' may be correct on a theoretical plane; in fact, it is a reality which cannot be effaced by any means. Equality exists in the midst of inequality. It implies equal rights and opportunities for all, but all cannot be equalised. Natural equality is an ideal that cannot be put into practice. Complete equality may be possible in a hypothetical condition of communist society as conceived by Marx or in the 'Ram Raj' of Mahatma Gandhi. The 'superiors' shall ever rule the 'inferiors'. However, the merit of globalisation should be traced in the fact that it aims at the equalisation of opportunities whereby the disadvantaged countries may reap its benefits, the examples of which may be seen in the miraculous development of Germany, Japan and China. Even small entities like South Korea, Malaysia, Singapore, Indonesia and Vietnam are now labelled as 'economic tigers'. Critical allegations are levelled by those who, instead of taking to the path of hard work and sacrifices, clamour for bringing about a new and equitable international economic order by showering abuses on the industrious and industrialised countries of the world.

It is commented that globalisation is creating a 'risk society'—one that is characterised by rising individualism with associated weakening of established traditions and institutions.[58] It is the same thing what C.B. Macpherson calls 'possessive individualism' and on that count he hits at the pitfalls of a liberal-democratic system. Another critic holds that globalisation creates crises which pose threats to an 'open society' and which can be prevented only by greater control.[59] The ecologists comment that globalisation creates environmental pollution and they lay blame on the unsympathetic and indifferent attitude of the industrialised

56. Deepak Nayyar, *op. cit.*, p. 365.
57. Alberto Martinelli: "Markets, Governments, Communities and Global Governance" in *International Sociology,* Vol. 18, No. 2, (2003).
58. See U. Beck: *Risk Society: Towards New Modernity* (London: Sage Publication, 1992).
59. See G. Soros: *The Crisis of Global Capitalism: Open Society Endangered* (New York: BBS/Public Affairs, 1998).

countries which deliberately ignore their calls, the example of which may be seen in the non-implementation of the Kyoto Protocol on Climate Change adopted in the summer of 1997.

From what we have said above, following critical inferences may be drawn:

1. Contemporary globalisation is not reducible to a single causal process, but it involves a complex configuration of causal logics - whether political, military, economic, migratory, ecological or cultural. They raise two important issues. First, while the process of globalisation may be uniting the globe physically, it is not necessarily inculcating a sense of global community and citizenship, a prerequisite for any democratic global government.
2. Globalisation means different things to different people. The term is used in two ways which create a source of confusion. It is used in a positive sense to describe the process of increasing integration of the world economy. It is also used in a normative sense to describe a strategy of development based on rapid integration with world economy. Even its characterisation, however, is by no means uniform. It can be described in simple terms as the expansion of economic activities.
3. Since globalisation has created a universe of unequal partners, it is not surprising that the rules of the game are asymmetrical in terms of construct and inequitable in terms of outcome. The strong have the power to make the rules and the authority to implement them. In contrast, the weak can neither make such rules nor invoke them in their defence. The reaction of the people who express such exclusion or frustration has its forms in new social movements involving issues of ethnic identities, cultural chauvinism and religious fundamentalism. Obviously, globalisation leads to the erosion of social stability and harmony. In this way, economic integration with the world outside may accentuate social tensions or provoke social fragmentations in the developed as well as undeveloped or developing countries of the world.

These critical points are not without weight. But the question arises as to what should be done. Should we go back to the days of the mid-20th century, or should we look forward to find out new solutions for new problems and new challenges? Since the theme of globalisation is aligned with the goal of universalisation of liberal-democratic system, all problems can be solved within the framework of a 're-invented democracy.'[60] At the root of globalisation lies the fact of the emerging civil society in many parts of the world. Its expansion is providing strength to the process of globalisation. The simultaneous development of both is now an irreversible phenomenon. "Civil society based on the activities of transnational corporations, non-governmental agencies and international pressure groups has become very much a reality."[61]

---

60. David Held calls it 'cosmopolitan democracy' that "is concerned with disclosing the cultural, legal and ethical bases of political order in a world where political communities and stages matter, but not only and exclusively". *Taming Globalisation: Frontiers of Governance* (London: Polity Press, 2003), p. 2.

61. Heywood, *op. cit.*, p. 139.

Hence, it is required that "instead of ensuring that the state provides equal rights to all citizens, its retreat from the public arena is presented as being a condition necessary for re-strengthening and re-inventing democracy".[62] How can freedom and equality be reconciled all over the world? The answer is that political globalisation "may bring about a more peaceful world order constraining the tendencies which constrain the capacity and autonomy of states".[63] The slogan of the day should be: 'There is no alternative (TINA) to globalisation and we must learn to live with it.'

62. Gurpreet Mahajan: "Civil Society and Its Avtars: What Happened to Freedom and Democracy?" in C.M. Eliot (ed.): *Civil Society and Democracy: A Reader* (Delhi: Oxford University Press, 2003), p. 168.
63. Patrick O' Neil: *Essentials of Comparative Politics* (New York: W.W. Norton and Company, 2004), p. 286.

30

Multiculturalism

> In structural terms, we are all, of course, both Insiders and Outsiders, members of some groups and sometimes derivatively, not of others; occupants of certain statuses which thereby exclude us form occupying other cognate statuses..... The greater the number and the variety of group affiliations and statuses distributed among individuals in society, the smaller on the average, the number of individuals having precisely the same configuration.
>
> **—Robert K. Merton[1]**

Liberalism has seen its astonishing triumph in the age of globalisation and yet its critics have hit at its inadequacies by throwing light on certain new themes related to the 'politics of identity or recognition'. Multiculturalism is one of them and, though a reference has been made to it in the preceding chapter, its detailed treatment is given here. Its ardent advocates like Charles Taylor, Will Kymlicka and Bhiku Parekh lay stress on the fact that cultures have their unique and authentic essences. As such, liberal social and political orders should be based upon guaranteed basic freedoms having their source in the cultural contexts. Hence, multiculturalism having its core implication in the case of active citizenship or civic republicanism looks like hovering between the poles of liberalism and communitarianism.

Nature and Essential Implications

The phenomenon of cultural pluralism may be noticed in almost all countries of the world. It may be owing to many factors such as migration of the people whether as fleeing refugees or as inspiring visitors in search of work or some gainful engagement. The influx of such people and their contact or assimilation with the culture of the natives may be compared with the 'melting pot' or 'salad models'. That is, either such elements happily or willy-nilly merge themselves with the people of that country and thereby lose their distinct identity as may be noticed in the United States or it is also possible that such elements desire to maintain their distinct identity like the ingredients of a 'salad bowl' (Ashish Nandy) or a 'sandwitch' (Yogesh Atal) and thereby create the scenario of 'insider/outsider duality' (R.K. Merton). In fact, the present concern for multiculturalism in academic circles is attributed to this new and emerging phenomenon.

The 'insider/outsider duality' creates a situation of resistance as well as of resilience depending upon the attitude of such numerically smaller and diverse groups. Certain elements may adhere to their distinct identity of course, but with

1. Robert K. Merton: "Insiders and Outsiders: A Chapter in the Sociology of Knowledge" in *The American Journal of Sociology*, Vol. 78, No. 1, 1972, pp. 22 and 24.

the change of time, such resistance becomes weak. The line of distinction between the 'insider' and the 'outsider' is gradually blurred. The element of innovation imperceptibly creeps into the core of the culture and thus the process of resilience remains at work. It denotes the capacity of a culture to withstand shock so as not to allow any kind of breakdown, rupture or deformation of the cultural system of a country as a whole. "Resilience may be equated with the pliancy of a bamboo – 'bending with the storm but not breaking'. It is a synonym of 'homeostasis' or 'Gaia', springing back to former position: recidivism."[2]

A liberal-democratic order requires active participation of the people in the political process of the country. As such, active citizenship involves the stance of multiculturalism that provides ample material for the study of the politics of 'identity', or 'recognition', or 'difference'. It emerged as a theoretical stance through the activities of the 'Black Panthers' in the United States in the 1960s, but it, in a short course of time, covered all agitations of the excluded, marginalised or stigmatised sections of the society in other countries of the world. It hinted at the communal diversity usually arising from racial, ethnic, linguistic and sexual differences that created a typical consciousness among the people belonging to such groups. The movements of the Negroes, minorities, depressed classes, women, etc. appeared in the form of political assertiveness that sometimes became violent to the extent of breaking the bonds of national identity. The notable point is that such groups demonstrate their pride in their 'exclusive identity' which they like to preserve and then demand a proper place for themselves the social and political set-up of the country.

Multiculturalism, therefore, attaches importance to the separate and distinct identity of certain neglected and stigmatised sections of the society. Its advocates proudly claim and desire to preserve their distinct recognition and, at the same time, struggle for having a respected place in the political community so that they are not treated as 'second-rate citizens'. The main features of this trend may be enumerated as the following:[3]

1. Distinctive cultures deserve to be protected or strengthened particularly when they belong to minority or vulnerable groups.
2. Such a position is based upon a belief in value pluralism, the idea that there is no single or overriding conception of good life, rather there are many competing conceptions.
3. Such groups are entitled for 'social justice' and so the state should adopt the policy of affirmative action for the benefit of the unprivileged sections of the society.
4. Such groups are no longer willing to be silenced or marginalised, or to be defined as 'deviant' simply because they differ in race, culture, gender, ability or sexual orientation from the so-called 'normal'citizens. They demand a more inclusive conception of citizenship which recognises (rather than stigmatises) their identities and which accommodates (rather than excludes) their differences.
5. It desires a pluralistic order ensuring differentiated citizenship.

---

2. Yogesh Atal: "Culture and Human Development" in *Madhya Pradesh Journal of Social Sciences*, Ujjain, Vol. 11, No. 1, 2006, p. 35.
3. Andrew Heywood: *Political Theory: An Introduction*, pp. 215-16.

Some Important Statements

Identity is revealed to us only as something to be invented rather than discovered, as a target of an effort, an objective, as something one still needs to be built from scratch or to choose from alternative offers and then to struggle for and then to protect through yet more struggle, though for struggle to be victorious, the truth of the precarious and forever incomplete status of identity needs to be, and tends to be, suppressed and laboriously covered up.

—**Zygmunt Bauman**

Identity (Cambridge: Polity Press, 2004), p. 16.

Group-differentiated self-government rights compensate for unequal circumstances which put the members of minority cultures at a systematic disadvantage in the cultural marketplace, regardless of their personal choices in life. This is one of the many areas in which true equality requires not identical treatment but rather differential treatment in order to accommodate differential needs.

—**Will Kymlicka**

"Multicultural Citizenship" in Gurpreet Mahajan (ed.): *Democracy, Differences and Social Justice* (New Delhi: Oxford University Press, 1998), p. 109.

Multiculturalism reflects, most basically, a positive endorsement of communal diversity, usually arising from racial, ethnic and language differences. As such, multiculturalism is more a distinctive political stance than a coherent and programmic political doctrine.

—**Andrew Heywood**

Political Theory: An Introduction (Houndmills, Basingstroke: Palgrave Macmillan, 2004), p. 215.

It is obvious that multiculturalism is a new variety of liberalism that attaches particular significance to the rights and freedoms of the hitherto neglected, excluded and humiliated people and, at the same time, desires to maintain their distinct place in a pluralistic society and a democratic state. It rejects the case of a fascist system which imposes a particular kind of culture on all sections of the people; it also reacts against the tendency of forced assimilation of different stocks of people in a particular pattern of *vox* (community) by a dictatorial state. A system of equality of rights with the equality of worth and dignity of all the members of a political community should be maintained to realise the ideal of unity in diversity.

Multiculturalism, therefore, attacks the present order based on social and political injustice, it also offers remedial measures for its eradication. It focuses on cultural injustices rooted in social patterns of representation, interpretation and communication, including cultural domination (being subject to patterns of interpenetration associated with another culture); non-recognition (being rendered invisible in the authoritative communicative practices of one's culture) and disrespect (being disparaged in stereotypical public cultural representations or in everyday life interactions. Its targets are status groups, defined by relations of recognition in which they enjoy lesser esteem, honour, and prestige than the other groups. It aims to affirm group differences. The remedy is cultural or symbolic change to upwardly revalue disrespected identities and cultural products of maligned groups, or positively value cultural diversity.[4]

4. Kymlicka: *Contemporary Political Philosophy: An Introduction* (Delhi: Oxford University Press, 2005), pp. 332-33.

Liberalism and Its Inadequacy

Multiculturalism may exist and prosper only in a liberal-democratic order where essential freedoms of the people are legally recognised and the state has no power to suppress or virtually blot out the minorities. People belonging to multicultural groups have the right to preserve their distinct identity so much so that they enjoy the status of 'nationalities' in a nation-state. The state may recognise four languages as in Switzerland (French, German, Roman and Swiss), or two languages (English and French) as in Canada. It is also possible that in a pluralistic social order, the state may have only one national language as we may see in the United States and the United Kingdom. It is also possible that the state may put a ban on the wearing of a particular dress by a community (as the wearing of veil by the Muslim women in France) for the reasons of security. But the state should not dispense with the separate or distinct identity of multicultural groups. Only in a fascist system it may happen like the torture of the Jews in Germany, of the Kurds in Iraq, and of the Christians in Sudan and Lebanon.

A liberal-democratic state adopts a soft attitude towards various multicultural groups. At the same time, it is desired that distinct identities should have their volitional assimilation with the national mainstream. Still, there remains a possibility of some kind of discrimination against some groups or communities and the state is accused of 'benign neglect' towards them. For this reason, the communitarians (as Michael Walzer and A. MacIntyre) attack the liberal democratic order for ignoring the case of the 'public good'. They redefine the premises of liberalism in a way that the interest of the individual is dominated by the consideration of the public good. Liberal majorities and communitarian minorities should enjoy equality in terms of rights, opportunities and positions of honour in the midst of a common national language and some common social institutions.

Obviously, multiculturalism desires a modified or revised liberal-democratic order that ensures 'civic nationalism' or 'societal culture'. That is, it calls for a territorially concentrated culture, centred on a shared language which is used in a wide variety of societal institutions in both public and private life (schools, media, law, economy, government, etc.). In other words, it "involves a common language and social institutions rather than common religious beliefs, family customs or personal life styles. Societal cultures within a modern liberal democracy are inevitably pluralistic, containing Christians as well as Muslims, Jews, and atheists; heterosexuals as well as gays; urban professionals as well as rural farmers; conservatives as well as socialists. Such diversity is the inevitable result of the rights and freedoms guaranteed to liberal citizens, particularly when combined with an ethnically diverse population. The diversity, however, is balanced and constrained by linguistic and institutional cohesion; cohesion that has not emerged on its own, but rather is the result of deliberate state policies."[5]

Multiculturalism may survive and develop only in a liberal social and political order. However, Bhiku Parekh (who worked as the Chairperson of the Commission for Racial Equality set up by the British Government) hits at its inadequacy.[6] He is of

5. *Ibid.*, p. 346.
6. Bhiku Parekh: *Rethinking Multiculturalism: Cultural Diversity and Political Theory* (Basingstroke: Palgrave Macmillan, 2000).

the view that all societies are multicultural and that this phenomenon shall survive in the times to come. It should not be studied with a sense of scorn or fear, because it is the way to properly understand human society. This multicultural perspective is a consequence of mutually constructive effects of mutually complementary visions. It may be noted in three directions:

1. Each community is rooted in a cultural context and its members are born and brought up in the same. They organise themselves in the same cultural structure, they attach value to it, and thereby they maintain their distinct identity. It is, however, possible that sometimes they are critical of their own cultural contexts, or they go to the extent of emulating the cultural contexts of others. And yet they evaluate other cultural systems with the help of their own ethical standards.
2. Different cultures represent some patterns of 'good life' along with varying dimensions of its philosophy. It is, therefore, required that one should mix with the people of other cultures to expand his ethical horizon. He may have a view of 'good life' of his own, but he may expand or develop it after realising that no culture is either significant or insignificant in an absolute sense. Hence, he has no right to impose his value-judgement on others.
3. Putting aside the case of very primitive communities, Parekh argues that each developed culture is inherently plural and a constant interaction goes on between its varying traditions and currents of thought. It absorbs the traits of other cultures, albeit in an autonomous manner, and then gives a new shape or definition to its norms. Each culture affects other cultures and, at the same time, is affected by them. All epithets like Euro-centrism, Afro-centrism, West-centrism, etc., are baseless, because they falsify the total history of cultures.

No particular ideology can serve the purpose of multiculturalism in view of the fact that it lacks a holistic framework. Whether liberalism claiming itself to be based on the high ideals of liberty, equality, justice and humanism, or any variety of socialism (Fabianism or Communism) having its aim in the establishment of a society free from the evils of exploitation, oppression and injustice, take a partial view of the cultural reality, or present before us a partisan picture of 'good life'. Liberalism may, of course, be admired for advocating the values of human dignity, autonomy and egalitarianism, but it forbids their interpretation in a different way. As such, it becomes an ideology in its own right that makes its believers insensitive to the cultural norms and traditions of the marginalised sections of the society.

In this way, Parekh argues that liberalism draws a maginot line between the culture of the majority and that of the minority. It informs the members of the majority culture to be obstinate and egotist in their behaviour towards the people subscribing to other ways of life. What is, therefore, required is that multiculturalism should not be treated as a nightmare, rather attempts should be made to reshape social, political and economic institutions so as to preserve and nurture ethical traits of all cultures existing in the state. It is clear that he advances a defence of pluralistic perspective on cultural diversity and highlights the inadequacy of liberal multiculturalism. His view "is based upon a dialectical interplay between human nature and culture, in which human beings are culturally constituted in the sense that their attitudes, behaviour and ways of life are shaped by the groups to which

Parekh on MultiCulturalism

Multiculturalism is not about difference and identity per se but about those that are embedded in and sustained by culture; that is, a body of beliefs and practices in terms of which a group of people understand themselves and the world and organise their individual and collective lives.....Neither naturalism nor culturalism gives a coherent account of human life and helps us theorise multicultural varieties. One stresses the undeniable fact of shared humanity, but ignores the equally obvious fact that human nature is culturally mediated and reconstituted and cannot by itself provide a transcendental basis for a cross-culturally valid vision of the good life; the other makes the opposite mistake. Neither grasps the two in their relationship and appreciates that human beings are at once both natural and cultural, both alike and unlike, and like in unlike ways.

Bhiku Parekh: *Rethinking Multiculturalism: Cultural Diversity and Political Theory*, pp. 2-3 and 11.

they belong. The complexity of human nature is thus reflected in the diversity of cultures."[7]

Varieties of Multiculturalism

Multiculturalism may be seen in the existence of the 'minorities' of various hues in many states of the world. There may be 'national minorities' (as the Tamils in Sri Lanka, the Hindus in Pakistan, and the Muslims in France), or 'immigrant groups' (as the Bangladeshis in India, the Muhajirs in Pakistan and the Chinese in Indonesia), or 'isolationist ethnic and religious groups' (as the Mexicans in the United States and the Jews in the Russian Federation), 'metics' or 'resident aliens' (as the Turks in Germany and the North Africans in Italy) and the 'African-Americans' or negroes in the States of USA. Examples may be multiplied and the points of difference in their status in different countries may also be noted. For instance, in some countries these people have rights equal to those of the citizens, or they may be victims of some kind of discrimination. They may have the status of 'stateless people' or 'partial citizens' as well.[8]

Such groups may feel like 'sub-state nations' or citizens deprived of former power, glory and status. Such people form their unions or organisations to fight for their specific interests. The question is as to what they should do to redress their grievances or to immunise themselves from the onslaught of injustice. Such groups may choose the course of leaving their country and taking shelter in some friendly country as was done by the Germans of Kazakhistan who, after the disintegration of the USSR in 1991, moved to Germany. It is also possible that they fight for 'autonomy' and may feel satisfied by having their institutions of governance at the local and regional levels like the Roman Catholics in Northern Ireland. Then, it is also possible that such groups have their integration with the majority culture on some better or fairer terms as we may see in the case of the French people in the English-dominated provinces of Canada. The last option is that such groups accept permanent marginalisation without murmur as the Tibetans in China.

7. Heywood, *op. cit.*, p. 217.
8. Jeff Spinner: *The Boundaries of Citizenship, Race, Ethnicity and Nationality in the Liberal State* (Baltimore: John Hopkins University Press, 1994).

Nancy Fraser on the Features of the Politics of Recognition

1. Focus on cultural injustices, rooted in social patterns of representation, interpretation and communication, including cultural domination (being subject to patterns of interpretations associated with another culture), non-recognition (being rendered invisible in the authoritative communicative practices of one's culture); and disrespect (being disparaged in stereotypical public cultural representations or in everyday life interactions).
2. Remedy cultural or symbolic change to upwardly revalue disrespected identities and cultural products of maligned groups, or positively value cultural diversity.
3. Targets status groups, defined by relations of recognition in which they enjoy lesser esteem, honour and prestige than other groups.
4. Aims to affirm group differences.

Fraser: "Social Justice in the Age of Identity Politics: Redistribution, Recognition and Participation" in Grethe Peterson (ed.): *The Tanner Lecture on Human Values* (University of Utah Press, Salt Lake City, 1998), Vol. 6, pp. 1-67 cited in Kymlicka, *Contemporary Political Philosophy*, pp. 332-33.

This fact cannot be refuted that such 'minorities' have to suffer injustices of different kinds, for example, in the form of separate classes of the Turkish children in some states of Germany, or ban on wearing head scarf for the Sikh males in France, or non-availability of citizenship of the United States to a foreigner on the ground of his ignorance of the English language and the like. The result is that the deprived and segregated sections of the people agitate and their struggle may assume the form of a civil war as happened in Serbia, Croatia and Kosovo of former Yugoslavia. The best way to deal with such sensitive problems is to create conditions so that such people join the national mainstream. At the same time, this point should be repeated that no association or group claiming its separate and distinct identity should be allowed to subvert the constitutional framework of the liberal-democratic nation-state. In the advanced democracies of the West it has been possible by making "a complex package of robust forms of nation-building combined and constrained by robust forms of minority rights."[9]

Multiculturalism and the Case of Human Development and Human Rights

The theme of multiculturalism has carved its place in the study of development in its revisited form. The idea of development, which was once confined to the economic domain, has now assumed a human face. In the case of the Third World countries, development became a sort of ideology for rapid, planned and directed cultural change. The newly independent nation-states sought to move in a pre-determined direction with defined goals and targets as well as with preconceived strategies. It created a revolution of rising expectations. But the results were frustrating. The process of development, in fact, created wider disparities, broadened the divide between the rich and the poor sections of the people, and even falsified many tenets of modernisation. The institutions or the mechanisms imported from the advanced countries of the West failed to yield positive dividends.

9. Kymlicka, *op. cit.*, p. 365.

This realisation led to the reconsideration of development strategies. That is why, the United Nations started talking in terms of human development. The World Summit on Social Development held at Copenhagen (1995) voted for a central role of culture. It was taken into recognition that the roots of social breakdown or disintegration were embedded in the cultural contexts. The result is that the word 'development' assumed a new meaning - enhancement of the effective freedom of the people involved to pursue whatever they have reasons to value. Good life is be an ideal, but it may have numerous forms or norms. As the Report of the World Commission on Development says: "This view of human development (in contrast to narrow economic development) is a culturally conditioned view of economic and social progress. Poverty of life, in this view, implies not only lack of essential goods and services, but also lack of opportunities to choose a fuller, more satisfying, more valuable and valued existence. The choice can also be for a different style of development, a different path, based on different values from those of the highest income countries now. The recent spread of democratic institutions, of marked choices, of participatory management of firms, has enabled individuals and groups and different cultures to choose for themselves."[10]

Like development, the issue of human rights constitutes an intergral part of the comprehensive study of multiculturalism. Laski says that a state is known by the system of rights it maintains and that such a system creates the conditions in which a person may have the best possible development of his personality. The Protection of Human Rights Act (1993) of India defines "human rights as those relating to life, liberty, equality and dignity of the individual guaranteed by the Constitution or embodied in the International Covenants." Thus, a positive approach to the subject of human rights "necessitates constructive reconciliation between individual and community, universality and specificity, and non-discrimination principle of equality and social justice."[11]

Obviously, such an interpretation contradicts the Benthamite principle of the 'greatest good of the greatest number' and instead endorses the view of John Stuart Mill that in a democratic system minorities must not be blotted out. The fact of social plurality or multiculturalism cannot be lost sight of in any political system whether democratic or not. The laws of the state must protect the interests of all whether those in majority or in minority. A situation should not be allowed to exist in which discrimination or protective discrimination of any kind creates inequality upon inequality. The commands of the state affect different communities in different ways of course, but the salient fact should be borne in mind that the principles of liberal democracy and the universal agenda of human rights do not address the disadvantages to which minority groups are subjected.[12] Group-differentiated rights can only help rectify the disadvantage by alleviating the vulnerability of minority

10. *Our Creative Diversity-Report of the World Commission on Culture and Development,* UNESCO, Paris, 1995, p. 22.
11. V.K. Tyagi: "Dynamics of Human Rights in a Federal Polity: The Indian Experience" in *Madhya Pradesh Journal of Social Sciences,* Ujjain, Vol. 13, No.1, 2008, p. 2.
12. Gurpreet Mahajan: *Identities and Rights: Aspects of Liberal Democracy in India* (New Delhi: Oxford University Press, 1998), p. 2.

> **Iris Young on Four Virtues of Pluralist Homogeneity**
>
> 1. It encourages and enables interactive and intersecting multiplicities in social and subject positions. It thus gives voice to, and works to clear an institutional space for, that which might otherwise be eclipsed or effaced.
> 2. It makes possible the living out of variety, imparting contextualised nuance and specificity to the general and the various.
> 3. It is committed critically to satisfying the excitement and desirability of the new or multiple and diffused possibilities.
> 4. Political heterogeneity must not only exist (silently), it must be seen to exist (publicly).
>
> Iris M. Young in David Theo Goldberg (ed.): *Multiculturalism: A Critical Reader* (Oxford: Basil Blackwell, 1994), pp. 30-31.

cultures to majority decisions. These external protections ensure that the members of the minority have the same opportunity to live and work in their own cultures as members of the majority. The principle of pluralism, therefore, renders the presumption of homogeneity and uniformity of cultural mode in a multicultural, multi-religious, multiethnic, multi-caste and multiregional society theoretically, empirically and operationally invalid."[13]

Multiculturalism has its blending with anti-colonialism and post-colonialism when its theorists stretch their canvas to compare the case of human rights with a sort of cultural or ethnic dominance. They question the relevance and value of human rights in modern, open and pluralistic societies. "In particular, they reflect a form of ethnocentrism, in which the norms and values of dominant cultural groups take precedence over those of minority cultural groups. Anti-colonial and post-colonial theories have at times portrayed the doctrine of human rights as an example of cultural imperialism."[14] They discover its panacea in the existence of active citizenship that may allow room for weightage in favour of certain minority groups. The traditional conception of citizenship "is based on the idea of universality, and derives its emancipatory character from the notion that disadvantaged groups may aspire to fulfil citizenship rights. Multiculturalists, however, argue that in view of the deeper cultural and moral diversity of modern societies, citizenship should be 'differentiated' to take account of the special rights of particular cultural groups."[15]

Critical Appreciation

The idea of multiculturalism has its positive and negative aspects. In its defence, it may be said that it enables the 'minorities' of any hue to preserve their distinct identity by living in a liberal-democratic state and also seek their development like other people in majority. It embodies the ideal of 'unity in diversity'. There may be many models of 'good life', but their operation is possible only in a multicultural order.

---

13. Tyagi, *op. cit.*, p. 4.
14. Heywood, op. cit., p. 191. Elsewhere, he says: "To define certain values as 'established', 'traditional' or 'majority values' may simply be an attempt to impose a particular moral system upon the rest of the society." *Ibid.*, p. 271.
15. *Ibid.*, p. 219.

The merit of everyone should be recognised regardless of the fact that he belongs to a 'minority' community. Such groups play a significant part in the nation-building process as well as in the operation of a pluralistic system. The communitarians are justified in dismissing the idea of the 'unencumbered self' and in arguing that the 'politics of the rights' should be replaced by the 'politics of the common good'.

On the other side, multiculturalism foments anti-national tendencies. It is a great obstacle in the way of the realisation of the goal of national integration. The groups of the German people living in the states of Austria and Czechoslovakia supported Hitler's call for pan-Germanism and thereby Germany could swallow the whole of Austria and Sudetenland of Czechoslovakia. The groups of the Chinese people living in the countries of South-East Asia obdurately stick to their distinct identity and often create problems for the governments of Indonesia and Vietnam. Such groups may join hands with other secessionist and terrorist elements living abroad and then may create problems in a country like India and the Russian Federation.

To sum up, the phenomenon of multiculturalism has negative and positive aspects. As Atal says: "Increasing geographical mobility and resettlement of migrant groups in different lands has made most cultures plural societies. The migrant groups evolve their own mechanisms to preserve their cultural identity and yet develop interfaces with the culture of the host society. The emerging culture of the immigrants is the result of sandwiching between the forces of the host culture and the parent culture. Since host cultures vary, the sandwich cultures of peoples originating from the same country but settled in different countries also differ. The existence of sandwich cultures will make cultures more diverse and heterogeneous."[16]

We may safely conclude that the spectre of multiculturalism elicits starkly different political responses. Its supporters highlight its personal and social advantages in stressing the extent to which human beings are culturally embedded. Hence, cultural diversity "promotes the vigour and health of society, each culture reflecting a particular range of human capacities and attributes. By contrast, its critics portray multicultural societies as inherently fractured and conflict-ridden, arguing that successful societies must be based upon shared values and a common culture."[17]

16. Yogesh Atal : "Asian Cultures: What Destination?" in E.B. Masini and Yogesh Atal (eds.): *The Future of Asian Cultures,* Bangkok, UNESCO, 1993, p. 17.
17. Heywood, *op. cit.,* p. 49.

Bibliography

Aart, John : *Globalisation: A Critical Introduction* (London: Macmillan, 2000).

Afanasyev, V.G. : *Marxist Philosophy* (Moscow: Progress Publishers, 1980).

Allen, C.K. : *Aspects of Social Justice* (London: Stevens, 1955).

Amin, Samir and others : *Dynamics of Global Crisis* (New York: Monthly Review Press, 1982).

Anderson, P. : *Considerations on Western Marxism* (London: NLB, 1976).

Apter, David : *Introduction to Political Analysis* (New Delhi: Prentice-Hall of India, 1977).

Avineri, S. : *Social and Political Thought of Karl Marx* (New Delhi: S. Chand & Co., 1979).

Bains, J.S. and Jain, R.B. (eds.) : *Political Science in Transition* (New Delhi Gitanjali Publications, 1981).

Ball, A.R. : *Modern Politics and Government* (London: Macmillan, 1976).

Banfield, E.C. : *Political Influence* (New York: Free Press of Glencoe, 1962).

Bannerji, B.N. : *Natural and Social Justice* (Calcutta: Eastern Law House, 1960).

Baradat, L P. : *Political Ideologies: Their Origins and Impact* (Englewood Cliffs, New Jersey: Prentice-Hall, 1979).

Bardhan, Pranab and Roemer, J. : *Market Socialism: The Current Debate* (Oxford: Oxford University Press, 1993).

Barker, E. : *Principles of Social and Political Theory* (London: Oxford Univ. Press, 1951).

________ *Political Thought in England (1848-1914)*: (London: Oxford Univ. Press, 1951).

Barry, Brian : *The Liberal Theory of Justice* (Oxford: Clarendon Press, 1973).

________ : *Political Argument* (London: Routledge and Kegan Paul, 1965).

Barry, Norman P. : *An Introduction to Modern Political Theory* (London : Macmillan, 1981).

Batalov, E.N. : *The Philosophy of Revolt: Criticism of Left Radical Ideology*, (Moscow: Progress Pub., 1975).

Beck, U. : *What is Globalisation?* (Cambridge: Polity Press, 2000).

________ : *Risk Society: Towards New Modernity* (London: Sage Publications, 1992).

Beetham, David : *Max Weber and the Theory of Modern Politics* (London: George Allen and Unwin, 1974).

Bell, Daniel : *The End of Ideology* (New York: Colliers, 1961).

Benn, S.I. and *Peters, R.S.* : *Social Principles and the Democratic State* (London: George Allen and Unwin, 1975).

Berlin, Isaiah : *Four Essays on Liberty* (London: Oxford University Press, 1973).

Bernstein, R.J. : *The Restructuring of Social and Political Theory* (Oxford : Basil Blackwell, 1976).

Beynoon, J. and Dunkerley (eds.) : *Globalisation: The Reader* (London: The Athlone Press, 2000).

Bhagwati, J.N. : *In Defense of Globalisation* (New Delhi: Penguin Books, 2002).

Blondel, J. : *The Discipline of Politics* (London: Butterworths, 1981).

Bluhm, W.T. : *The Theories of the Political System* (New Delhi: Prentice-Hall of India, 1981).

Bosanquet, B. : *The Philosophical Theory of State* (London: Macmillan, 1920).

Bottomore, T. (ed.) : *A Dictionary of Marxist Thought* (Worldview Maya Blackwell, 1991).

Brady, R.A. : *The Spirit and Structure of German Fascism* (New York, 1937).

Brandt, Richard (ed.) : *Social Justice* (New York: Prentice Hall, 1965).

Brecht, Arnold : *Political Theory* (Princeton: Princeton Univ. Press, 1959).

Brinton, Crane : *The Anatomy of Revolution* (New York: Norton, 1938).

Bronner, S.E. : *Twentieth Century Political Theory: A Reader* (New York: Routledge, 2006).

Brown, W. : *Womanhood and Politics* (Totowa, N.J.: Rowman and Littlefield, 1988).

Brzezinski, Z.K. : *The Grand Failure* (New York: Scribners, 1989).

Bullock, A. and Shock, M. (eds.) : *The Liberal Tradition from Fox to Keynes* (London : A & C Black, 1956).

Burnell, P. and Randall, V. : (eds.) : *Politics in the Developing World* (London: Oxford University Press, 2005).

Burns, C.D. : *Principles of Revolution* (London: George Allen and Unwin, 1920).

Butler, J.D. and Scott, J.W. : *Feminists Theorise the Political* (New York: Routledge, 1992).

Callinicos, A. : *Against Post-Modernism: A Marxist Critique* (Cambridge: Polity Press, 1994).

Calvert, P. : *A Study of Revolution* (Oxford: Clarendon Press, 1971).

Catlin, G.E.G. : *The Science and Methods of Politics* (London: Kegan Paul, 1927).

________	:	*A Study of the Principles of Politics* (New York: Macmillan, 1930).
________	:	*Systematic Politics* (Toronto: University of Toronto Press, 1962).
Carrillo, Santiago	:	*Eurocommunism and the State* (London: Lawrence and Wishart, 1977).
Chalmers, J. (ed.)	:	*Change in Communist Systems* (Stanford: Stanford University Press, 1970).
Chandhoke, Neera	:	*State and Civil Society: Explorations in Political Theory* (New Delhi: Sage, 1995).
________ (ed.)	:	*Understanding the Post-Colonial World: Theory and Method* (New Delhi: Sterling Publishers, 1994).
Charlesworth, J.C. (ed.)	:	*Contemporary Political Analysis* (New York: Free Press of Glencoe, 1967).
Chilcote, R.H.	:	*Theories of Comparative Politics* (Boulder, Colarado: Westview Press, 1981).
Cohn-Bendit	:	*Obsolete Communism: The Left Wing Alternative* (New York: McGraw Hill, 1968).
Cohan, A.S.	:	*Theories of Revolution: An Introduction* (London: Nelson, 1975).
Cohen, Carl (ed.)	:	*Communism, Fascism and Democracy: Theoretical Foundations* (New York: Random House, 1972).
Coker, F.W.	:	*Recent Political Thought* (New York: D. Appleton-Century, 1934).
Coser and Rosenberger (eds.)	:	*Sociological Theory* (New York : Macmillan, 1975)
Costa, Dalla and James, S.	:	*The Power of Women and the Subordination of the Community* (Boston: Falling Wall Press, 1972).
Cranston, M. (ed.)	:	*The New Left* (London: Bodley Head, 1970).
Cranston, M.	:	*Freedom: A New Analysis* (London: Longmans, 1953).
Crick, Bernard	:	*The American Science of Politics* (Berkeley: Univ. of California Press, 1959).
	:	*In Defence of Politics* (London: Weidenfeld and Nicolson, 1962).
Dahl, R.A.	:	*Modern Political Analysis* (Englewood Cliffs, New Jersey: Prentice-Hall, 1976).
Daniels, N.	:	*Reading Rawls* (New York: Basic Books, 1975).
Dallmyr, F.D. (ed.)	:	*From Contract to Community: Political Theory at the Crossroads* (New York: Marcel Dukker, 1978).
Debroy, Bibek: (ed.)	:	*Globalisation: What Does It Mean for Development?* (Delhi: Konark Publishers, 1998).
de Beauvoir, Simone	:	*The Second Sex* (Harmondsworth: Penguin, 1972).
de Crespigny, A and Minnogue, K. (eds.)	:	*Contemporary Political Philosophers* (New York: Dodd Mead and Co., 1975).

de Crespigny, A. and Wertheimer (eds.) : *Contemporary Political Theory* (London: Nelson, 1970).

de Reincourt, A. : *Women and Power in History* (New Delhi: Sterling Publishers, 1997).

de Tocqueville, A. : *Ancient Regime and the French Revolution* (New York: Doubleday, 1955).

de Jouvenel, B. : *Sovereignty: An Inquiry into the Political Good* (Chicago: Chicago University Press, 1957).

Deane, H.A. : *The Political Ideas of Harold J. Laski* (Columbia: Columbia Univ. Press, 1954).

De Caute (ed.) : *The Essential Writings of Karl Marx* (London: Panther, 1967).

Deutscher, I. : *Marxism in Our Time* (San Francisco: The Ramparts Press, 1971).

Djilas, M. : *The New Class* (New York: Alfred A. Knopf, 1957).

Doctor, A.H. : *Issues in Political Theory* (New Delhi: Sterling, 1985).

Dronberger, Ilsa : *The Political Thought of Max Weber* (New York : Appleton-Century, 1971).

Drucker, H.M. : *The Political Uses of Ideology* (London: Macmillan, 1974).

Duncan, Greame : *Marx and Mill: Two Views of Social Conflict and Social Harmony* (London: Cambridge University Press, 1973).

Dunn, John : *Modern Revolutions: An Introduction to the Analysis of Political Phenomenon* (London: Cambridge Univ. Press, 1972).

Duverger, M. : *The Study of Politics* (London: Nelson, 1972).

Dworkin, R. : *Sovereign Virtue: The Theory and Practice of Equality* (Cambridge, Mass.: Harvard University Press, 2000).

Dyke, V.V. : *Political Science: A Philosophical Analysis* (Stanford: Stanford Univ. Press, 1962).

Easton, D. : *A Systems Analysis of Political Life* (New York : Wiley, 1965).

________ : *The Political System*: (New York: Alfred A. Knopf, 1953).

________ : *A Framework for Political Analysis* (Englewood Cliffs, New Jersey: Prentice-Hall, 1965).

Eatwell, R. and Wright,A. (eds.) : *Contemporary Political Ideologies* (Delhi: Rawat Publications, 2003).

Edwards, L.P. : *The Natural History of Revolution* (London: Lawrence and Wishart, 1962).

Ellul, J. : *Autopsy of Revolution* (New York: Alfred A. Knopf, 1971).

Eulau, H., Eldersveld, *S.J. and Janowitz,* M. (eds.) : *Political Behaviour: A Reader in Theory and Research* (New York : Free Press of Glencoe, 1956).

Enloe, Cynthia : *Bananas, Beaches and Bases : Making Feminist Sense of International Politics* (Berkeley: University of California Press, 1990).

Evans, J. : *Feminist Theory Today* (London: Sage Publications, 1995).

Evans, M. : *Karl Marx* (London: George Allen and Unwin, 1975).

Evans, P., Reuschmeyer, D. and Skocpol, T. : *Bringing the State Back In* (Cambridge; Cambridge University Press, 1985).

Falco, M.J. : *Truth and Meaning in Political Science* (Columbus, Ohio: Charles Merril Pub., 1973).

Fanon, F. : *The Wretched of the Earth* (London: NLB, 1972).

Featherstone, M., Lash, S. And Robertson, R. (eds.) : *Global Modernisation* (London: Sage Publications, 1995).

Feuer, L.S. (ed.) : *Marx and Engels* (London: Fontana, 1969).

Firestone, S. : *The Dialectic of Sex* (London: Women's Press, 1979).

Field, G.C. : *Political Theory* (London: Methuen, 1963).

Fierabend, I.K., *Fierabend, R.L. and* Gurr, T. : *Anger, Violence and Politics: Theories and Research* (Englewood Cliffs, New Jersey: Prentice-Hall, 1972).

Foucault, M. : *Discipline and Punish* (London: Tavistock, 1977).

_______ : *Power/Knowledge: Selected Interviews and Other Essays 1972-77, edited by C. Gordon* (London: Harvester Wheatsheaf, 1980).

_______ : *The History of Sexuality* (London: Allen Lane, 1979), Vol. I.

Frank, A.G. : *The Sociology of Development and the Under-Development of Sociology* (London: Pluto Press, 1971).

Freedman, J. : *Feminism* (Delhi: Viva Books, 2002).

Freeden, M. : *Ideologies and Political Theory: A Conceptual Approach* (Oxford: Clarendon Press, 1996).

Friedman, D.M. : *Foundations of Political Science* (New York: Free Press of Glencoe, 1971).

Friedman, M. : *Capitalism and Freedom* (Chicago: Chicago Univ. Press, 1962).

Friedman, W. : *Law in a Changing Society* (Middlesex: Penguin Books, 1964).

Friedrich, C.J. : *Authority* (Camb., Mass.: Harvard Univ. Press, 1958).

Friedrich, C.J. and Brzezinski, Z.K. : *Dictatorship and Autocracy* (New York, 1965).

Frohock, F.M. : *The Nature of Political Inquiry* (Homewood, Illinois: The Dorsey Press, 1967).

Fromm, Eric : *The Sane Society* (New York: Holt, Rinehart and Winston. 1965).

Fullenwinder, K.C. : *Feminism in American Politics: A Study of the Ideological Influence* (New York: Praegar, 1980).

Fukuyama, F. : *The End of History and the Last Man* (London: Penguin Books, 1992).

Fuss, D. : *Essentially Speaking: Feminism, Nature and Difference* (London: Routledge, 1989).

Garaudy, R. : *The Turning Points of Socialism* (London: Fontana, 1969).

Garner, J. W. : *Political Science and Government* (Calcutta: World Press, 1952).

Gary, Dorsey (ed.) : *Equality and Freedom: International and Cooperative Jurisprudence* (New York: Dobbs Ferry, 1966) (3 Volumes).

Germino, Dante : *Beyond Ideology: The Revival of Political Theory* (New York: Harper, 1967).

——— : *Modern Western Political Thought: Machiavelli to Marx* (Chicago: Rand McNally, 1972).

Ghosh. B.N. : *Scientific Method and Social Research* (New Delhi : Sterling, 2011).

Gill, R. and Sherman, S. (eds.) : *The Fabric of Existentialism,* (Englewood Cliffs, New Jersey: Prentice-Hall, 1973).

Giddens, A. : *Beyond Left and Right* (London: Polity Press, 1994).

——— : *Profiles and Critiques in Social Theory* (London: Macmillan, 1981).

——— : *Consequences of Modernity* (Cambridge: Polity Press, 1990).

Goldberg, D.T. (ed.) : *Multiculturalism: A Critical Reader* (Oxford: Basil Blackwell, 1994).

Goode, G.G. and Hatt, P.K. : *Methods in Social Research* (New York: McGraw-Hill, 1952)

Goodin, R. (ed.) : *The Oxford Handbook of Political Science* (Oxford: Oxford University Press, 2009).

Goodin, R.E. and Hans Dieter, K.: (eds.) : *A New Handbook of Political Science* (Oxford: Oxford University Press, 1996).

Gould, J.A. and Thursby, V.V. (eds.) : *Contemporary Political Thought: Issues in Scope, Value and Direction* (New York: Holt, Rinehart and Winston. 1969).

Gouldner, A.W. : *The Coming Crisis of Western Sociology* (London: Heinemann, 1970).

Graham, G.T. and Carey, J.A. (eds.) : *The Post-Behavioural Era: Perspectives in Political Science* (New York: McKay, 1972).

Graham, Keith (ed.) : *Contemporary Political Philosophy* (London: Cambridge University Press, 1982).

Gray, Alexander : *The Socialist Tradition* (New York: Longmans, 1946).

Greenleaf, W.A. : *Oakeshott's Philosophical Politics* (London: Longmans, 1966)

Greenstein, F. and *Polsby, N.* : *Political Science: Scope and Theory, Vol. I,* (California: Addison Wesley, 1975).

Gross, L. (ed.) : *Symposium on Sociological Theory* (New York: Harper and Row, 1959).

Greggor, A.J. : *An Introduction to Metapolitics* (New York: Free Press, 1971).

Guild and Palmer : *Introduction to Politics* (New York: Wiley, 1968).

Gunnell, J.S. : *Philosophy and Politics* (Morristown, New Jersey, General Learning Press, 1975).

Hacker, A. : *Political Theory: Philosophy, Ideology, Science* (New York: Macmillan, 1963).

Hall, J.A. and Ikenberry, G.T. : *The State* (Delhi: Worldview/Bookland, 1997).

Hall, S., Gregor McLellan, G. and Held, D. (eds.) : *The Idea of the Modern State* (Buckingham: Oxford University Press, 1993).

Hallowell, J.H. : *Main Currents in Modern Political Thought* (New York: Holt, Rinehart and Winston, 1950).

Han, Beatrice (ed.) : *The Encyclopaedia of Modern French Thought* (London: Fitzroy Dearborn, 2004).

Harsh, D. and Stoker, R. : *Theory and Method in Political Science* (London: Macmillan, 1995).

Hart, H.A.L. : *The Concept of Law* (Oxford: Clarendon Press, 1961).

Hart, H.A.L. (ed.) : *Austin's Province of Jurisprudence Determined* (London, 1964).

Hass and Kariel (eds.) : *Approaches to the Study of Behavioural Science* (New York: Chandler, 1970).

Hayek, F.A. : *Law, Legislation and Liberty* (Chicago: Chicago University Press, 1976), (2 Volumes).

________ : *The Constitution of Liberty* (London: Routledge and Kegan Paul, 1960).

________ : *The Road to Serfdom* (London: Routledge and Kegan Paul, 1960).

________ : *The Mirage of Social Justice* (London: Routledge and Kegan Paul, 1976).

Heater, Derek : *Contemporary Political Ideas* (London: Longman, 1974).

Held, David : *Taming Globalisation: Frontiers of Governance* (London: Polity Press, 2003).

________ : *Political Theory and the Modern State* (Cambridge: Polity Press, 1995).

________ : *Political Theory Today* (Cambridge: Polity Press, 1986).

Hempel, Carl J. : *Fundamentals of Concept Formation in Empirical Science* (Chicago: Chicago University Press, 1952).

Herberk, R. : *From Democracy to Nazism* (Baton Rouge: Louisiana State University Press, 1945).

Heywood, Andrew : *Political Theory: An Introduction* (New York: Palgrave Macmillan, 2005).

________ : *Politics* (Houndmills, Basingstroke: Palgrave Foundations, 2005).

________ : *Key Concepts in Politics* (New York: Palgrave Macmillan, 2005).

________ : *Political Ideologies: An Introduction* (New York: Palgrave Macmillan, 2005).

Hirsch, M. and Keller, E.F. : *Conflicts in Feminism* (New York: Routledge, 1990).

Hobhouse, L.T. : *Liberalism* (New York: Oxford Univ. Press, 1964).

Hobsbawm, E.J. : *Globalisation, Democracy and Terrorism* (London: Little Brown, 2007).

Hoffman, John : *State, Power and Democracy* (Sussex: Wheatsheaf, 1988).

Holmes, L. : *Post-Communism: An Introduction* (Cambridge: Polity Press, 1997).

Howard, W.C. : *The Recovery of Political Theory: Limits and Possibilities* (Baton Rouge: Louisiana State University, 1984).

Hyneman, C.S. : *The Study of Politics: The Present State of American Political Science* (Urbana: University of Illinois Press, 1971).

Isaak, A.C. : *Scope and Methods of Political Science* (Homewood, Illinois: The Dorsey Press, 1969).

Irish, M.D. (ed.) : *Political Science: Advance of the Discipline* (Englewood Cliffs, New Jersey: Prentice-Hall, 1968).

Jackson, S. and Jones, J. (eds.) : *Contemporary Feminist Theories* (New York: New York University Press, 1998).

Jaggar, A. : *Feminist Politics and Human Nature* (Totowa, N.J.: Rowman and Allenheld, 1983).

James, Elizabeth : *Political Theory* (Chicago: Rand McNally, 1976).

Jayawardene, K. : *Feminism and Nationalism in the Third World* (London: Zed Books, 1986).

Jenkin, T.P. : *The Study of Political Theory* (Garden City: Doubleday, 1956).

Joad, C.E.M. : *Modern Political Theory* (London: Oxford Univ. Press, 1946).

Johnson, Chalmers : *Revolution and Social System* (Stanford: Stanford University Press, 1964).

Jones, K.B. and Jonasdottir (eds.) : *The Political Interest of Gender* (London: Sage Publications, 1988).

Joseph. K. and Sumption, J. : *Equality* (London: John Murray, 1979).

Kariel, H.S. : *Saving Appearances: The Re-Establishment of Political Sciences* (Mass: Duxbury Press, 1972).

________ : *The Promise of Politics* (Englewood Cliffs, New Jersey : Prentice-Hall, 1966).

Kaviraj, S. and others : *The State of Political Theory: Some Marxist Essays* (Calcutta: Research India Pub., 1971).

Keane, John : *Global Civil Society?* (Cambridge: Cambridge University Press, 2005).

Kedward, H.S. : *Fascism in Western Europe* (London: Blackie, 1973).

King, Preston (ed.) : *The Study of Politics* (London: Frank Cass, 1977).

Kolakowski, L. : *Main Currents in Marxism* (Oxford: Clarendon Press, 1978). (3 Volumes)

——— : *Marxism and Beyond* (London: Paladin, 1971).

Kuhn, Thomas : *The Structure of Scientific Revolution* (Chicago: Chicago University Press, 1962).

Kymlicka, W. : *Contemporary Political Philosophy: An Introduction* (Oxford: Oxford University Press, 2005).

Laidler, H.W. : *Social and Economic Movements* (London: Routledge and Kegan Paul, 1960).

Lash, S. and Urry, J. : *The End of Organised Capitalism* (Cambridge: Polity Press, 1987).

Lane, R.E. : *Political Ideology* (New York: Free Press of Glencoe, 1962).

Laski, H. J. : *Liberty in the Modern State* (London: George Allen and Unwin, 1930).

——— : *Authority in the Modern State* (New Haven: Yale Univ. Press, 1919).

——— : *The Rise of European Liberalism* (London: George Allen and Unwin, 1936).

——— : *The Foundations of Sovereignty and Other Essays* (London: George Allen and Unwin, 1922).

——— : *A Grammar of Politics* (London: George Allen and Unwin, 1951).

——— : *The State in Theory and Practice* (London: George Allen and Unwin, 1960).

Laslett, P. and Runciman, G. (eds.) : *Introduction to Philosophy, Politics and Society* (New York: Macmillan, 1956) (I and II Series).

Lasswell, H.D. : *The Future of Political Science* (New York: Atherton, 1963).

——— : *The Policy Science: Recent Developments in Scope and Method* (Stanford: Stanford Univ. Press, 1951).

——— : *Politics: Who Gets What? When? How?* (New York: World Pub., 1958).

Lasswell, H. and Kaplan, M. : *Power and Society* (New Haven: Yale Univ. Press, 1950).

Leach, R. : *Political Ideology in Britain* (New York: Palgrave, 2003).

Lehning, P.B. : *John Rawls: An Introduction* (Cambridge: Cambridge University Press, 2006).

Leonard, D. and Adkins, L. (eds.) : *Sex in Question: French Materialist Feminism* (London: Taylor and Francis, 1996).

Lipset, S.M. : *The Political Man* (Bombay: Vakil, Feffer, Simons, 1959) (Abridged Edition).

Lipson, Leslie : *The Great Issues of Politics: An Introduction to Political Science* (Englewood Cliffs, New Jersey: Prentice-Hall, 1960).

Lobkowicz, N. (ed.) : *Marx and Western World* (Moscow, 1967).

Lorde, Audre : *Sister-Outsider* (Trumanaberg: New York Crossing Press, 1984).

Lubasz, H. : *Fascism: Three Major Regimes* (New York: Wiley and Sons, 1973).

Lutz, J.M. : *Global Terrorism* (London: Routledge, 2004).

Lucas, J.L. : *The Principles of Politics* (Oxford: Clarendon Press, 1966).

Lyon, D. : *Post-Modernity* (Delhi: Viva Books, 2002).

Lyotard, T.F. : *The Post-Modern Condition (1979).*

Mabbot, J.D. : *The State and the Citizen* (London: Hutchinson Univ. Press, 1948).

Maclver, R.M. : *The Modern State* (London: Oxford Univ. Press, 1962).

Mackinnon, C. : *Feminism Unmodified: Discourse on Life and Law* (Cambridge, Mass.: Harvard University Press, 1987).

MacIntyre, A. : *After Virtue: A Study in Moral Theory* (London: Duckworth, 1981).

Macpherson, C.B. : *Democratic Theory: Essays in Retrieval* (London: Oxford Univ. Press, 1976).

Mahajan, Gurpreet : *Identities and Rights: Aspects of Liberal Democracy in India* (New Delhi: Oxford University Press, 1998).

Mahajan, Gurpreet (ed.) : *Democracy, Differences and Social Justice* (New Delhi: Oxford University Press, 1998).

Mannheim, Karl : *Ideology and Utopia,* (New York: Harcourt Brace, 1906).

Marcuse, H. : *Studies in Critical Philosophy,* (London: NLB, 1972).

________ : *One-Dimensional Man* (London: Routledge and Kegan Paul, 1964).

________ : *Eros and Civilisation: A Philosophical Enquiry into Freud* (London: The Penguin Press, 1969).

Marshall, T.H. : *Sociology at the Crossroads* (London: Heinemann, 1963).

Marx-Engels : *Selected Works* (Moscow: Progress Publishers, 1976) (3 Volumes)

McCoy and Playford (eds.) : *Apolitical Politics: A Critique of Behaviouralism* (New York: T.Y. Crowell, 1967).

McLellan, David : *Ideology* (Buckingham: Open University Press, 1995).

________ : *Marxism after Marx* (London: Macmillan, 1979).

Meehan, E. : *The Theory and Method of Political Analysis* (Homewood, Illinois: The Dorsey Press, 1965).

Mehta, V.R. : *Beyond Marxism: Towards an Alternative Perspective* (Delhi: Manohar, 1978).

Mies, M. and Shiva, V. : *Eco-Feminism* (London: Zed Books, 1993).

Miliband, R. : *The State in Capitalist Society* (London: Weidenfeld and Nicolson, 1968).

Miller, David : *Social Justice*: (Oxford: Oxford University Press, 1976).

Mill, J.S. : *Essay on Liberty*: (London: Everyman, 1984).

——— : *Utilitarianism, On Liberty, and Essay on Bentham* (London: Fontana and Collins, 1972).

Millett, Kate : *Sexual Politics* (New York: Doubleday, 1970).

Mirza, H.S. (ed.) : *Black British Feminism* (London: Routledge, 1997).

Morgenthau, H.J. : *The Decline of Democratic Politics* (Chicago: Chicago University Press, 1962)

Monroe, R.K. (ed.) : *Contemporary Empirical Political Theory* (Berkeley: University of California Press, 1997).

Mussolini, B. : *Fascism: Political and Social Doctrines* (Rome: Ardrita, 1935).

Myrdal, Gunnar : *Values in Social Theory* (London: Routledge and Kegan Paul, 1958).

Nagel, Ernest : *The Structure of Science* (New York: Harcourt, Brace and World, 1961).

Narayan, Uma : *Dislocating Cultures: Identities, Traditions and Third World Feminism* (New York: Routledge, 1997).

Nayyar, Deepak : *Trade and Globalisation* (New Delhi: Oxford University Press, 2008).

Nicholoson, L. : *Feminism: Post-Modernism* (New York: Routledge, 1990).

Nozick, Robert : *Anarchy, State and Utopia* (New York: Basic Books, 1970).

Nye, A. : *Feminist Theory and the Philosophies of Man* (New York: Routledge, 1989).

Oakley, A. : *Sex, Gender and Society* (London: Temple Smith, 1982).

Oakeshott, M. : *Rationalism in Politics and Other Essays* (London : Methuen, 1962).

Oakeshott, M. (ed.) : *Leviathan of Hobbes* (Oxford: Basil Blackwell, 1946).

Offe, Claus : *Contradictions of the Welfare State* (London: Hutchinson, 1984).

——— : *Disorganised Capitalism* (Cambridge: Polity Press, 1985).

Ollman, B. : *Alienation: Marx's Conception of Man in Capitalist Society* (London: Cambridge Univ. Press, 1971).

Olson, R.G. : *An Introduction to Existentialism* (New York: Dover Publications, 1980).

Parekh, Bhiku : *Rethinking Multiculturalism: Cultural Diversity and Political Theory* (Basingstroke: Palgrave Macmillan, 2000).

Parry, G. : *Political Elites* (London: George Allen and Unwin, 1969).

Parsons, T. : *The Social System* (New York: Free Press of Glencoe, 1951).

Parsons and Shils (eds.) : *Towards a General Theory of Alienation* (Camb., Mass.: Harvard Univ. Press, 1951).

Pateman, Carole : *The Sexual Contract* (Cambridge: Polity Press, 1988).

Paul, T.V and Hall, A.J. : *International Order and the Future World Politics* (Cambridge: Cambridge University Press, 1999).

Pennock, J.R. : *Democratic Political Theory* (Princeton: Princeton University Press, 1979).

Pennock and Smith : *Political Science* (New York: Macmillan, 1964).

Phillips, A. : *Feminism in Politics* (London: Oxford University Press, 1998).

Phillips, Derek : *Looking Backward: A Critical Appraisal of Communitarian Thought* (Princeton: Princeton University Press, 1993).

Plamenatz, J. : *Ideology* (London, 1970).

Poggi, G. : *The Development of the Modern State* (London: Hutchinson, 1978).

Pollock, Sir F. : *An Introduction to the History of the Science of Politics* (London: Macmillan, 1923).

Popper, Karl : *Unended Quest* (London: Fontana and Collins, 1976).

________ : *The Poverty of Historicism* (New York: Harper and Row, 1961).

Ponton, G. and Gill, P. : *Introduction to Politics* (Oxford: Martin Robertson, 1982).

Poulantzas, N. : *Power and Social Classes* (London: New Left Books, 1973).

________ : *State, Power, Socialism* (London: New Left Books, 1978).

Quinton, Anthony : *Political Philosophy* (London: Oxford University Press, 1967).

Ranney, A. (ed.) : *Essays on the Behavioural Studies of Politics* (Urbana: University of Illinois Press, 1962).

Raphael, D.D. : *Political Theory and the Rights of Men* (London: Macmillan, 1967).

________ : *Problems of Political Philosophy* (London: Macmillan, 1976).

Rausching, Herman : *The Revolution of Nihilism* (London: William Heinemann, 1939).

Rawls, J. : *A Theory of Justice* (Camb., Mass.: Harvard University Press, 1971).

Ricci, David M. : *The Tragedy of Political Science* (New Haven: Yale University Press, 1984).

Riemer, Neil : *The Revival of Democratic Theory* (New York: Appleton-Century-Crofts, 1961).

Riker, W.H. and Ordeshook, P.C. : *An Introduction to Positive Political Theory* (Englewood Cliffs, New Jersey: Prentice-Hall, 1973).

Robertson, D. : *A Dictionary of Modern Politics* (London: Europa, 2002).

Robertson, R.L. : *Globalisation: Social Theory and Political Culture* (London: Sage Publications, 1992).

Rorty, Richard : *Objectivity, Relativism and Truth* (Cambridge: Cambridge University Press, 1991).

________ : *The Consequences of Pragmatism* (London: Brighton, 1982).

Rossi, A. : *The Rise of Italian Fascism* (London: Methuen, 1938).

Rockow, L. : *Contemporary Political Thought in England* (London: Leonard Pearson, 1925).

Roucek, J.C. (ed.) : *Twentieth Century Political Thought* (New York, 1946).

Rowbotham, S. : *Women in Movement: Feminism and Social Action* (New York: Routledge, 1992).

Roy, M.N. : *Fascism* (Calcutta: Renaissance Publishers, 1938).

Runciman, W.C. : *Social Science and Political Theory* (London: Macmillan, 1969).

Russell, B. : *Roads to Freedom* (London: George Allen and Unwin, 1919).

________ : *Power: A New Social Analysis* (London: George Allen and Unwin, 1937).

Sabine, G.H. : *A History of Political Theory* (New York: Harrap, 1948).

Saighal, V. : *Dealing with Global Terrorism: The Way Forward* (New Delhi: New Dawn Press, 2004).

Saksena, N.S. : *Terrorism: History and Facets in the World and in India* (Delhi: Abhinav Publications, 1985).

Sakwa, Richard : *Post-Communism* (Delhi: Viva Books, 2002).

Salvert, B. : *Revolution and Revolutionaries* (New York: Elsvier, 1976).

Sandel, Michael : *Liberalism and the Limits of Justice* (Cambridge: Cambridge University Press, 1981).

Sarangi, P. : *Liberal Theories of the State* (New Delhi: Sterling Publishers, 1996).

Sartori, G. : *Democratic Theory* (New Delhi: Oxford and IBH, 1965).

Sartre, J.P. : *Being and Nothingness,* (New York: Washington Square Press, 1966).

________ : *Between Existentialism and Marxism* (New York: Pantheon Books, 1974).

Schumpeter, J. : *Capitalism, Socialism and Democracy* (London: George Allen and Unwin, 1966).

Seliger, M. : *The Marxist Conception of Ideology* (London: Cambridge Univ. Press, 1977).

________ : *Ideology and Politics* (London: George Allen and Unwin, 1976).

Sen, A.K. : *The Idea of Justice* (London: Allen Lane, 2009).

________ : *Inequality Re-examined* (Cambridge, Mass.: Harvard University Press, 1992).

Sen, Mohit : *Communism and the New Left* (New Delhi: People's Pub. House, 1969).

Seshadri, K. : *Marxism and Political Science* (New Delhi: People's Pub. House, 1977).

Shah, A.B. : *Scientific Method* (Bombay: Allied, 1964).

Shah, Giriraj : *Terrorism: Tenets and Tactics* (Delhi: Anmol Publications, 2000).

Singh, Randhir : *Reason, Revolution and Political Theory* (New Delhi: People's Pub. House, 1976).

Shanthi, K. (ed.) : *Empowerment of Women* (New Delhi: Anmol Publications, 1998).

Shah, Ghanshyam (ed.) : *Social Movements and the State: Readings in Indian Government and Politics, Vol. 4* (Delhi: Sage Publications, 2002).

Sola Pool, I. de (ed.) : *Contemporary Political Science : Towards Empirical Political Theory* (New York: McGraw Hill, 1967).

Sorauf, F.J. : *Perspectives on Political Science* (Columbus, Ohio: Charles Merril Pub., 1965).

Somit, A. and Tanenhaus, J. : *The Development of American Political Science* (Boston: Allyn and Beacon, 1967).

Spinner, Jeff : *The Boundaries of Citizenship, Race, Ethnicity and Nationalism in the Liberal State* (Baltimore: John Hopkins University, 1994).

Spragens, T. Jr. : *The Dilemma of Contemporary Political Theory: Towards a Post-Behavioural Science of Politics* (New York: Dunellen, 1973).

Stacey, M. and Price, M. : *Women, Power and Politics* (London: Tavistock, 1981).

Stiglitz, J. : *Globalisation and Its Discontents* (New Delhi: Penguin Books, 2002).

Stankiewicz, J. (ed.) : *Political Thought since World War II* (New York: Free Press of Glencoe, 1965).

Stojanowic, S. : *Between Ideal and Reality: A Critique of Socialism and Its Future* (Oxford, 1973).

Swingewood, A. : *Marx and Modern Social Theory* (London: Macmillan, 1975).

Surkin and Wolfe : *An End to Political Science: The Caucus Papers* (New York: Basic Books, 1970).

Skinner, Quinton : *The Foundations of Modern Political Thought* (Cambridge: Cambridge University Press, 1978).

Tannenbaum, E.R. : *The Fascist Experience: Italian Society and Culture, 1922-45* (New York: Basic Books, 1972).

Taylor, Charles : *Philosophy and Human Sciences: Philosophical Papers* (Cambridge: Cambridge University Press, 2005).

Tawney, R.H. : *Equality* (New York: Harcourt Brace, 1931).

Teodori, M. (ed.) : *The New Left: A Documentary History* (London: Jonathan Cape, 1969).

Thakurdas, F. : *Recent English Political Theory and the Idea of Liberty* (Calcutta: Minerva, 1972).

———— : *The English Utilitarians and the Idealists* (Delhi: Vishal Pub., 1977),

———— : *Essays in Political Theory* (New Delhi: Gitanjali, 1982).

Thorson, T.L. : *Biopolitics* (New York: Holt, Rinehart and Winston, 1970).

Turner, B.S. : *Theories of Modernity and Post-Modernity* (London: Sage Publications, 1990).

———— : *Equality* (London: Tavistock Publications, 1986).

Vajda, Mihaly : *Fascism* (London: Allison and Busby, 1976).

Varma, S.P. : *Modern Political Theory* (Delhi: Vikas, 1975).

Varma, V.P. : *Political Philosophy* (Agra: Lakshmi Narain, 1970).

Vogelin, Eric : *The Science of Politics* (Chicago: Chicago University Press, 1952).

Volkhomer, W.E. : *The Liberal Tradition in American Thought* (New York: G.P. Putnam's, 1969).

Vyshinsky, A. : *The Law of the Soviet State* (New York: Macmillan, 1948).

Wasby, S.L. : *Political Science: The Discipline and Its Dimensions* (Calcutta: Scientific Book Agency, 1970).

Wallerstein, I. : *The World Capitalist Economy* (Cambridge: Cambridge University Press, 1979).

Waters, M. : *Globalisation* (London: Routledge, 1995).

Watkins, F.M. : *The Age of Ideology*: (Englewood Cliffs, New Jersey: Prentice-Hall, 1964).

Wayper, C.L. : *Political Thought* (London: Hutchinson, 1965).

Weale, Albert : *Political Theory and Social Policy* (London: Macmillan, 1983).

Weedon, C. : *Feminist Practice and Post-Structural Theory* (Oxford: Blackwell, 1987)

Weinstein, M. : *Systematic Political Theory* (Columbus, Ohio: Charles Merril Pub., 1971).

Weldon, T.D. : *The Vocabulary of Politics* (Middlesex: Penguin Books, 1955).

Whitehead, A.N. : *Science and Modern World* (New York: Macmillan, 1925).

Wilson, F.G. : *The Elements of Modern Politics* (New York: McGraw-Hill, 1956).

Wilson, J. : *Equality* (London: Hutchinson, 1966).

Wiserman, H.V. : *Politics: The Master Science* (London: Routledge and Kegan Paul, 1969).

———— : *Political Systems: Some Sociological Approaches* (New York: Fredrick A. Praegar, 1967).

Woddis, Jack : *New Theories of Revolution* (London: Lawrence and Wishart, 1972).

Wolff, R.P. : *Understanding Rawls* (Princeton: Princeton University Press, 1977).

Wood, A.W. : *Karl Marx* (London: Routledge and Kegan Paul, 1981).

Wolf, A. : *Essentials of Scientific Method* (London: George Allen and Unwin, n.y).

Woolf, S.J. (ed.) : *Fascism in Europe* (London: Methuen, 1981).

Wolff, Moore and Marcuse (eds.) : *A Critique of Pure Tolerance* (Boston: Beacon Press, 1966).

Wolin, S.S. : *Politics and Vision* (Boston, 1960).

Wright Mills, C. : *The Power Elites* (London: Oxford Univ.: Press, 1959).

Young, O.R. : *Systems of Political Science* (Englewood Cliffs, New Jersey: Prentice-Hall, 1968).

Yuval-Davis and Anthias, F. : *Women Nation-State* (London: Macmillan, 1989).

Young, R. (ed.) : *Approaches to the Study of Politics* (Evanstone: Northwestern Univ. Press, 1958).

Wollstonocraft, M. : *A Vindication of the Rights of Women*, edited by C. W. Hagelman (New York: W.W. Norton and Company, **1967**).

Young, I.M. : *Justice and the Politics of Difference* (Princeton: Princeton University Press, 1990)

Zubaida, Sami : *Islam, the People and the State* (London: Routledge and Kegan Paul, 1989)

Index